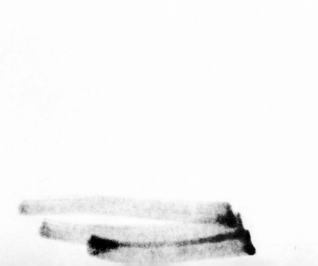

THE CAMBRIDGE HISTORY OF
ENGLISH LITERATURE

VOLUME XV

GENERAL INDEX

THE
CAMBRIDGE HISTORY OF
ENGLISH LITERATURE

VOLUME XV

GENERAL INDEX

CAMBRIDGE

AT THE UNIVERSITY PRESS

1968

47015

Published by the Syndics of the Cambridge University Press
Bentley House, P.O. Box 92, 200 Euston Road, London, N.W. 1
American Branch: 32 East 57th Street, New York, N.Y. 10022

Standard Book Number: 521 04529 0

First edition 1927
Cheap edition 1932
Reprinted 1934 1953
1962 1965 1968

Printed in Great Britain
at the University Printing House, Cambridge
(Brooke Crutchley, University Printer)

PREFATORY NOTE

The Cambridge History of English Literature was first published between the years 1907 and 1916. The General Index Volume was issued in 1927.

In the preface to Volume I the general editors explained their intentions. They proposed to give a connected account of the successive movements of English literature, to describe the work of writers both of primary and of secondary importance, and to discuss the interaction between English and foreign literatures. They included certain allied subjects such as oratory, scholarship, journalism and typography, and they did not neglect the literature of America and the British Dominions. The History was to unfold itself, "unfettered by any preconceived notions of artificial eras or controlling dates," and its judgments were not to be regarded as final.

This reprint of the text and general index of the *History* is issued in the hope that its low price may make it easily available to a wider circle of students and other readers who wish to have on their shelves the full story of English literature.

Entries in the General Index to pages beyond the following are references to the Bibliographies of the original edition, which are not included in the present reprint of the text:

Volume	I	*page* 418
"	II	429
"	III	465
"	IV	434
"	V	380
"	VI	409
"	VII	397
"	VIII	390
"	IX	414
"	X	410
"	XI	387
"	XII	371
"	XIII	463
"	XIV	463

CAMBRIDGE
1932

CONTENTS

A LIST OF CONTENTS

OF THE

CAMBRIDGE HISTORY OF ENGLISH LITERATURE

VOLUME I

Chap. 1	The Beginnings	A. R. WALLER
2	Runes and MSS.	Miss A. C. PAUES
3	Early National Poetry	H. M. CHADWICK
4	Old English Christian Poetry	Miss M. BENTINCK SMITH
5	Latin Writings in England to the Time of Alfred	M. R. JAMES
6	Alfred and the Old English Prose of his Reign	P. G. THOMAS
7	From Alfred to the Conquest	J. S. WESTLAKE
8	The Norman Conquest	A. R. WALLER
9	Latin Chroniclers from the Eleventh to the Thirteenth Centuries	W. LEWIS JONES
10	English Scholars of Paris and Franciscans of Oxford	Sir J. E. SANDYS
11	Early Transition English	J. W. H. ATKINS
12	The Arthurian Legend	W. LEWIS JONES
13	Metrical Romances, 1200–1500. I	W. P. KER
14	Metrical Romances, 1200–1500. II	J. W. H. ATKINS
15	Pearl, Cleanness, Patience and Sir Gawayne	Sir I. GOLLANCZ
16	Later Transition English: I. Legendaries and Chroniclers	Miss C. L. THOMSON
17	Later Transition English: II. Secular Lyrics. Tales. Social Satire	A. R. WALLER
18	The Prosody of Old and Middle English	G. SAINTSBURY
19	Changes in the Language to the Days of Chaucer	HENRY BRADLEY
20	The Anglo-French Law Language	F. W. MAITLAND

VOLUME II

Chap. 1	Piers the Plowman and its Sequence	J. M. MANLY
2	Religious Movements in the Fourteenth Century	J. P. WHITNEY
3	The Beginnings of English Prose	Miss A. D. GREENWOOD
4	The Scottish Language	G. GREGORY SMITH
5	The Earliest Scottish Literature	P. GILES
6	John Gower	G. C. MACAULAY
7	Chaucer	G. SAINTSBURY
8	The English Chaucerians	G. SAINTSBURY
9	Stephen Hawes	W. MURISON

ix

10 The Scottish Chaucerians — G. Gregory Smith

11 The Middle Scots Anthologies: Anonymous Verse and Early Prose — G. Gregory Smith

12 English Prose in the Fifteenth Century: I. Pecock. Fortescue. The Paston Letters — Miss A. D. Greenwood

13 The Introduction of Printing into England and the Early Work of the Press — E. Gordon Duff

14 English Prose in the Fifteenth Century: II. Caxton. Malory. Berners — Miss A. D. Greenwood

15 English and Scottish Education. Universities and Public Schools to the Time of Colet — T. A. Walker

16 Transition English Song Collections — F. M. Padelford

17 Ballads — F. B. Gummere

18 Political and Religious Verse to the Close of the Fifteenth Century—Final Words — A. R. Waller

VOLUME III

Chap. 1 Englishmen and the Classical Renascence — T. M. Lindsay

2 Reformation Literature in England — J. P. Whitney

3 The Dissolution of the Religious Houses — R. H. Benson

4 Barclay and Skelton — A. Koelbing

5 Progress of Social Literature in Tudor Times — H. V. Routh

6 Sir David Lyndsay and the Later Scottish 'Makaris' — T F. Henderson

7 Reformation and Renascence in Scotland — P. Hume Brown

8 The New English Poetry — H. H. Child

9 A Mirror for Magistrates — J. W. Cunliffe

10 George Gascoigne — J. W. Cunliffe

11 The Poetry of Spenser — W. J. Courthope

12 The Elizabethan Sonnet — Sir Sidney Lee

13 Prosody from Chaucer to Spenser — G. Saintsbury

14 Elizabethan Criticism — G. Saintsbury

15 Chroniclers and Antiquaries — C. Whibley

16 Elizabethan Prose Fiction — J. W. H. Atkins

17 The Marprelate Controversy — J. Dover Wilson

18 Of the Laws of Ecclesiastical Polity — F. J. Foakes-Jackson

19 English Universities, Schools and Scholarship in the Sixteenth Century — W. H. Woodward

20 The Language from Chaucer to Shakespeare — J. W. H. Atkins

VOLUME IV

Chap. 1 Translators — C. Whibley

2 The Authorised Version and its Influence — A. S. Cook

3 Sir Walter Ralegh — Mrs L. Creighton

4 The Literature of the Sea — C. N. Robinson

5	Seafaring and Travel	C. N. ROBINSON
6	The Song-Books and Miscellanies	H. H. CHILD
7	Robert Southwell. Samuel Daniel	H. H. CHILD
8	Thomas Campion	S. P. VIVIAN
9	The Successors of Spenser	H. DE SÉLINCOURT
10	Michael Drayton	H. H. CHILD
11	John Donne	H. J. C. GRIERSON
12	The English Pulpit from Fisher to Donne	F. E. HUTCHINSON
13	Robert Burton, John Barclay and John Owen	E. BENSLY
14	The Beginnings of English Philosophy	W. R. SORLEY
15	Early Writings on Politics and Economics	W. CUNNINGHAM
16	London and the Development of Popular Literature	H. V. ROUTH
17	Writers on Country Pursuits and Pastimes	H. G. ALDIS
18	The Book-Trade, 1557–1625	H. G. ALDIS
19	The Foundation of Libraries	J. B. MULLINGER

VOLUME V

Chap.		
1	The Origins of English Drama	Sir A. W. WARD
2	Secular Influences on the Early English Drama	H. H. CHILD
3	The Early Religious Drama	W. CREIZENACH
4	Early English Tragedy	J. W. CUNLIFFE
5	Early English Comedy	F. S. BOAS
6	The Plays of the University Wits	G. P. BAKER
7	Marlowe and Kyd	G. GREGORY SMITH
8	Shakespeare: Life and Plays	G. SAINTSBURY
9	Shakespeare: Poems	G. SAINTSBURY
10	Plays of Uncertain Authorship attributed to Shakespeare	F. W. MOORMAN
11	The Text of Shakespeare	E. WALDER
12	Shakespeare on the Continent	J. G. ROBERTSON
13	Lesser Elizabethan Dramatists	RONALD BAYNE
14	Some Political and Social Aspects of the Later Elizabethan and Earlier Stewart Period	Sir A. W. WARD

VOLUME VI

Chap.		
1	Ben Jonson	A. H. THORNDIKE
2	Chapman. Marston. Dekker	W. MACNEILE DIXON
3	Middleton and Rowley	ARTHUR SYMONS
4	Thomas Heywood	Sir A. W. WARD
5	Beaumont and Fletcher	G. C. MACAULAY
6	Philip Massinger	EMIL KOEPPEL
7	Tourneur and Webster	C. E. VAUGHAN
8	Ford and Shirley	W. A. NEILSON
9	Lesser Jacobean and Caroline Dramatists	RONALD BAYNE

10 The Elizabethan Theatre   H. H. Child

11 The Children of the Chapel Royal and their Masters   J. M. Manly

12 University Plays   F. S. Boas

13 Masque and Pastoral   Ronald Bayne

14 The Puritan Attack upon the Stage   J. Dover Wilson

VOLUME VII

Chap. 1 Cavalier Lyrists   F. W. Moorman

2 The Sacred Poets   F. E. Hutchinson

3 Writers of the Couplet   A. H. Thompson

4 Lesser Caroline Poets   G. Saintsbury

5 Milton   G. Saintsbury

6 Caroline Divines   W. H. Hutton

7 John Bunyan. Andrew Marvell   John Brown

8 Historical and Political Writings: I. State Papers and Letters   Sir A. W. Ward

9 Historical and Political Writings: II. Histories and Memoirs   Sir A. W. Ward

10 Antiquaries   G. Saintsbury

11 Jacobean and Caroline Criticism   J. E. Spingarn

12 Hobbes and Contemporary Philosophy   W. R. Sorley

13 Scholars and Scholarship, 1600–1660   Foster Watson

14 English Grammar Schools   J. B. Mullinger

15 Beginnings of English Journalism   J. B. Williams

16 The Advent of Modern Thought in Popular Literature   H. V. Routh

VOLUME VIII

Chap. 1 Dryden   Sir A. W. Ward

2 Samuel Butler   W. F. Smith

3 Political and Ecclesiastical Satire   C. W. Previté-Orton

4 The Early Quakers   Edward Grubb

5 The Restoration Drama. I   F. E. Schelling

6 The Restoration Drama. II   C. Whibley

7 The Restoration Drama. III   A. T. Bartholomew

8 The Court Poets   C. Whibley

9 The Prosody of the Seventeenth Century   G. Saintsbury

10 Memoir and Letter Writers. I and II a   H. B. Wheatley

Memoir and Letter Writers. II b   Sir A. W. Ward

11 Platonists and Latitudinarians   J. B. Mullinger

12 Divines of the Church of England, 1600–1700   W. H. Hutton

13 Legal Literature. I   F. J. C. Hearnshaw

Legal Literature. II   Sir A. W. Ward

14 John Locke   W. R. Sorley

15 The Progress of Science   Sir A. E. Shipley

16 The Essay and the Beginning of Modern English Prose   A. A. Tilley

LIST OF CONTENTS

VOLUME IX

Chap. 1 Defoe—The Newspaper and the Novel — W. P. Trent
2 Steele and Addison — H. V. Routh
3 Pope — E. Bensly
4 Swift — G. A. Aitken
5 Arbuthnot and Lesser Prose Writers — G. A. Aitken
6 Lesser Verse-Writers. I — T. Seccombe
   Lesser Verse-Writers. II — G. Saintsbury
7 Historical and Political Writers: I. Burnet — Sir A. W. Ward
8 Historical and Political Writers: II. Bolingbroke — Sir A. W. Ward
9 Memoir-Writers, 1715–1760 — T. Seccombe
10 Writers of Burlesque and Translators — C. Whibley
11 Berkeley and Contemporary Philosophy — W. R. Sorley
12 William Law and the Mystics — Miss C. F. E. Spurgeon
13 Scholars and Antiquaries. I. Bentley, etc. — J. D. Duff
   Scholars and Antiquaries. II. Antiquaries — H. G. Aldis
14 Scottish Popular Poetry before Burns — T. F. Henderson
15 Education — J. W. Adamson

VOLUME X

Chap. 1 Richardson — L. Cazamian
2 Fielding and Smollett — H. H. Child
3 Sterne, and the Novel of his Times — C. E. Vaughan
4 The Drama and the Stage — G. H. Nettleton
5 Thomson and Natural Description in Poetry — A. H. Thompson
6 Gray — D. C. Tovey
7 Young, Collins and Lesser Poets of the Age of Johnson — G. Saintsbury
8 Johnson and Boswell — D. N. Smith
9 Oliver Goldsmith — H. A. Dobson
10 The Literary Influence of the Middle Ages — W. P. Ker
11 Letter-Writers. I — H. B. Wheatley
   Letter-Writers. II. Warwickshire Coterie — W. H. Hutton
12 Historians. I. Hume and Modern Historians — W. Hunt
13 Historians. II. Gibbon — Sir A. W. Ward
14 Philosophers: I. David Hume. II. Adam Smith. III. Other Philosophical Writers — W. R. Sorley
15 Divines — W. H. Hutton
16 The Literature of Dissent, 1660–1760 — W. A. Shaw
17 Political Literature, 1755–1775 — C. W. Previté-Orton

VOLUME XI

Chap. 1 Edmund Burke — H. J. C. Grierson
2 Political Writers and Speakers — C. W. Previté-Orton
3 Bentham and the Early Utilitarians — W. R. Sorley

4 William Cowper — H. H. CHILD
5 William Wordsworth — EMILE LEGOUIS
6 Coleridge — C. E. VAUGHAN
7 George Crabbe — H. H. CHILD
8 Southey. Lesser Poets of the Later Eighteenth Century — G. SAINTSBURY
9 Blake — J. P. R. WALLIS
10 Burns. Lesser Scottish Verse — T. F. HENDERSON
11 The Prosody of the Eighteenth Century — G. SAINTSBURY
12 The Georgian Drama — H. V. ROUTH
13 The Growth of the Later Novel — G. SAINTSBURY
14 Book Production and Distribution, 1625–1800 — H. G. ALDIS
15 The Bluestockings — Mrs H. G. ALDIS
16 Children's Books — F. J. H. DARTON

VOLUME XII

Chap. 1 Sir Walter Scott — T. F. HENDERSON
2 Byron — F. W. MOORMAN
3 Shelley — C. H. HERFORD
4 Keats — C. H. HERFORD
5 Lesser Poets, 1790–1837 — G. SAINTSBURY
6 Reviews and Magazines in the Early Years of the Nineteenth Century — Hon. A. R. D. ELLIOT
7 Hazlitt — W. D. HOWE
8 Lamb — A. H. THOMPSON
9 The Landors. Leigh Hunt. De Quincey — G. SAINTSBURY
10 Jane Austen — H. H. CHILD
11 Lesser Novelists — H. H. CHILD
12 The Oxford Movement — W. H. HUTTON
13 The Growth of Liberal Theology — F. E. HUTCHINSON
14 Historians — Sir A. W. WARD
15 Scholars, Antiquaries and Bibliographers — Sir J. E. SANDYS

VOLUME XIII

Chap. 1 Carlyle — J. G. ROBERTSON
2 The Tennysons — H. J. C. GRIERSON
3 Robert Browning and Elizabeth Barrett Browning — Sir HENRY JONES
4 Matthew Arnold. Arthur Hugh Clough. James Thomson — W. LEWIS JONES
5 The Rossettis. William Morris. Swinburne and others — A. H. THOMPSON
6 Lesser Poets of the Middle and Later Nineteenth Century — G. SAINTSBURY
7 The Prosody of the Nineteenth Century — G. SAINTSBURY
8 Nineteenth-Century Drama — H. H. CHILD
9 Thackeray — A. H. THOMPSON
10 Dickens — G. SAINTSBURY

11 The Political and Social Novel .... Sir A. W. Ward
12 The Brontës .... A. A. Jack
13 Lesser Novelists .... W. T. Young
14 George Meredith. Samuel Butler. George
        Gissing .... W. T. Young

VOLUME XIV

Chap. 1 Philosophers .... W. R. Sorley
     2 Historians, Biographers and Political
            Orators .... Sir A. W. Ward
     3 Critical and Miscellaneous Prose .... Hugh Walker
     4 The Growth of Journalism .... J. S. R. Phillips
     5 University Journalism .... V. H. Rendall
     6 Caricature and the Literature of Sport .... H. H. Child
     7 The Literature of Travel, 1700–1900 .... F. A. Kirkpatrick
     8 The Literature of Science:
            (a) Physics and Mathematics .... W. W. Rouse Ball
            (b) Chemistry .... M. M. P. Muir
            (c) Biology .... Sir A. E. Shipley
     9 Anglo-Irish Literature .... A. P. Graves
    10 Anglo-Indian Literature .... E. F. Oaten
    11 English-Canadian Literature .... Pelham Edgar
    12 The Literature of Australia and New
            Zealand .... H. H. Child
    13 South African Poetry .... Sir T. H. Warren
    14 Education .... J. W. Adamson
    15 Changes in the Language since Shake-
            speare's Time .... W. Murison

'A,' v. 480

'A. B.' iv. 117

A., *The Passionate Morrice*, v. 480

'A. W.' iv. 117, 124, 125; 'Thine eyes so bright,' iv. 125; *The Tomb of the Dead*, iv. 125

A Apple Pie, xi. 386, 487

A' the Blue Bonnets are over the Border, xiv. 377

'A was an Apple-pie,' xi. 368

A was an Archer, xi. 370

Aachen, ii. 74

Aaron, in *Titus Andronicus*, v. 147, 179

Abacuk, in *The Palice of Honour*, ii. 261

Abbey and Overton, *English Church in the 18th century*, ix. 326; xiv. 101, 496

Abbey, Charles John, ix. 326; xiv. 101, 496

Abbey Mill farm, in Jane Austen's *Emma*, xii. 240

Abbey of the Holy Ghost, ii. 308, 438

Abbo of Fleury, i. 120, 121, 131

Abbot, Charles, 1st lord Colchester (1757–1829), xiv. 501, 502

Abbot, George (1562–1633), archbishop of Canterbury, iv. 63, 265, 424; vii. 187, 316

Abbot, John (*fl.* 1623), vii. 406

Abbotsford, ii. 284; xii. 6, 20, 28, 154, 372, 378 ff., 430; xiv. 278, 375

Abbotsford club, xii. 358, 377

Abbott, Edwin Abbott, xiii. 511; *Philomythus*, xii. 460; *A Shakespearian Grammar*, xiii. 248; xiv. 445

Abbott, Evelyn (1843–1901), xii. 479, 482, 486; xiv. 503

Abbott, Jacob (1803–1879), xi. 492

Abbreochy, diocese of Moray, ii. 115

Abdalrahman, caliph, x. 298

Abdullah, the peasant, xiv. 248

À Beckett, Arthur William, xiv. 238, 548

À Beckett, Gilbert Abbott (1811–1856), xiv. 235 ff., 541, 548; *Comic Blackstone, The*, xiv. 237; *Comic History of England, The*, xiv. 237; *Comic History of Rome, The*, xiv. 237

À Beckett, Gilbert Arthur (1837–1891), xiv. 238

Abeken, Caspar, *Life and letters of Cicero*, xii. 306

Abel, i. 30, 74

Abel, in *The Cytezen and Uplondyshman* iii. 63

Abel, Niels Henrik, xiv. 258

Abelard, Peter, i. 183, 184, 191, 216; v. 38; vii. 312; ix. 71, 477, 538

Abercorn, earl of. *See* Hamilton, James

Abercrombie, H. R., xiv. Add. 9

Abercrombie, John (1780–1844), xiv. 467

Abercromby, Patrick (1656–1716?), ix. 552

Aberdare, baron. *See* Bruce, Henry Austin

Aberdeen, ii. 88, 102, 127, 128, 369, 371; iii. 122, 137, 155; ix. 372, 374, 542 ff.; x. 355; xii. 31, 359, 394, 513; xiv. 23, 209, 428

King's college, ii. 369; vii. 254; x. 347

Marischal college, ix. 129; x. 38, 347

Aberdeen, earl of. *See* Gordon, George Hamilton

Aberdeen Breviary, iv. 412

Aberdeen Intelligencer, The, ix. 563

Aberdeen printers, iv. 547; xi. 469

Aberdeen university, x. 230; xii. 296, 333, 342

Aberdeenshire, ii. 99, 100, 103, 259; iv. 253; ix. 372, 373; xiii. 431

Aberdonensis, Musa Latina, ix. 554, 555

Aberfoil, xii. 17

Abergavenny, x. 386, 387

Aberigh-Mackay, George Robert (1848–1881), xiv. 341, 574; *Twenty-one Days in India*, xiv. 340

Aberystwyth, University college, xiv. 433

Abgarus, legend of, i. 120

Abingdon, i. 113, 114; iv. 409; v. 330; vii. 454

Abingdon, Thomas. *See* Habington

Abingdon, William, viii. 412

Abingdon Chronicle, i. 109–112

Abington, Frances (1737–1815), x. 264; xi. 257

Abishag, iv. 231

Ablancourt, Nicolas Perrot d', vii. 263; ix. 267

Ablett, J., *Literary Hours*, xii. 440

Ablewhite, Godfrey, in *The Moonstone*, xiii. 437

Abou ben Adhem, Leigh Hunt's, xiii. 308

Abra, in *Jacob and Esau*, v. 112

Abraham, i. 46; ii. 424; vii. 377; xii. 321

Abraham, in Cowley's *Davideis*, vii. 66

Abraham (or Faith), in *Piers the Plowman*, II. 27
Abraham and Isaac, V. 17, 46, 390
Abraham man, the, in *The Fraternitye of vacabones*, III. 102
Abram, père, *Histoire de l'université et du Collège de Pont-à-Mousson*, IV. 256, 499
Abrey Hatch, IV. 240
Abry, Louis, II. 81
Absalom, in *Absalom and Achitophel*, VIII. 36, 38, 39
Absalom's Conspiracy, VIII. 37
'Absence, hear thou my protestation,' IV. 209
Absence, Song of, II. 283
Absolute, Sir Anthony, in Sheridan's *Rivals*, XI. 266, 267; XIII. 64; XIV. 387
Absolute, captain, in Sheridan's *Rivals*, XI. 266, 269
Abury, IX. 540
Abyndon, or Abingdon, Henry, VI. 281
Abyssinia, X. 179, 460, 461; XIV. 241, 246, 247
Abyssinians, the, X. 160
Academia Secretorum Naturae of Naples, VIII. 364
Academic, The, IX. 414
Academico, in *The Returne from Pernassus*, VI. 313
Académie des Inscriptions, X. 282
Académie Française, IX. 397; XIV. 397, 460
Academy, The, XII. 347; XIV. 200, 533
Acapulco, IV. 100
Acca, Bede's letters to, I. 80
Accent and Rhythm. See Blake, J. W.
Accoram boni, Vittoria, story of, VI. 174
Account of the sickness and death of Dr Woodward, IX. 132
Account of the state of learning in the Empire of Lilliput, IX. 132
Accursius, II. 350, 363
Aceronia, in Gray's *Agrippina*, X. 119
Achaians, IV. 33
Acheron, II. 265
Acheson, lady, in Swift's *Grand Question debated*, IX. 119
Achilles, III. 231; IV. 21; VI. 106; VIII. 25, 76
Achilles, in *The Birth of Merlin*, V. 249
Achilles, in *Confessio Amantis*, II. 148
Achilles Tatius, *Clitophon and Leucippe*, III. 351; IV. 435; VII. 489
Achitophel, in *Absalom and Achitophel*, VIII. 37, 38, 41, 75; XIV. 113
Achitophel, in *The Palice of Honour*, II. 260, 261
Acignius, in *Euphormio*, IV. 255, 258, 259
Acircius, Aldhelm's letter to, I. 76
Acis and Galatea, in *Confessio Amantis*, II. 147, 151
Ackermann, Rudolph (1764–1834), XIV. 216, 217, 221, 222
Ackermann Rudolph, the younger, XIV. 233

Acland, Sir Thos. Dyke (1809–1898), XIV. 136, 596
Acolastus. See under Gnaphaeus
Acres, Bob, in Sheridan's *Rivals*, XI. 266, 267; XIII. 64
Act for the Encouragement of Learning, XI. 314
Act of Settlement, IX. 200; XIV. 57
Act of Succession, IX. 197
Act of Supremacy, IX. 197
Act of Uniformity, IX. 573
Acta Regia, X. 280
Acta Sanctorum, X. 282
Actaeon, IV. 196
Actaeon's hounds, in Sandys's *Ovid*, VII. 51
Actium, battle of, V. 171
Activa Vita, in *Piers the Plowman*, II. 26, 27; V. 4
Acton, John Emerich Edward Dalberg-Acton, lord (1834–1902), X. 299; XII. 272, 430; XIII. 383; XIV. 100, 101, 116 ff., 484
  'Conflicts with Rome,' XIV. 118
  'Döllinger's Historical Work,' XIV. 118
  'German Schools of History,' XIV. 118
  Lectures on Modern History, XIV. 117
  Letters of Quirinus, XIV. 118
  'Mill *On Liberty*,' XIV. 118
  On the Study of History, XII. 303
  Open Letter to a German Bishop, XIV. 118
Acton common, X. 395
Actors Remonstrance, The, VI. 407, 492
Acts of the Apostles, MS. Laud. Gr. 35 at Oxford, I. 72
Adah, in Byron's *Cain*, XII. 48
Adam, I. 134, 353; V. 56; VII. 301; VIII. 341; IX. 28, 60, 327
Adam, in *As You Like It*, V. 374; VI. 248
Adam, in *Paradise Lost*, VII. 101, 119; XII. 85
Adam, in *The Cytezen and Uplondyshman*, III. 63
Adam, in *The Golden Legend*, II. 335
Adam (play), V. 11, 39, 390
Adam, Book of, I. 133
Adam, James (1860–1907), *The Religious Teachers of Greece*, XII. 333, 479; *The Vitality of Platonism*, XII. 333
Adam, Thomas (1701–1784), IX. 313; XII. 471
Adam and Eve, III. 130
Adam Bell, Clim of the Clough, and William of Cloudesley, I. 300; II. 408, 416, 501
Adam du Petit Pont, I. 185
Adam house, an, XI. 377
Adam of Domerham (d. after 1291), IX. 535
Adam of Usk (*fl.* 1400), II. 496
Adam Spencer, in *Gamelyn*, I. 298
'Adam Unparadized,' VII. 117
Adamites, the, VII. 387
Adamnan, St (625?–704), I. 82, 96, 433; II. 131; *Life of St Columba*, XII. 361, 518
Adams, Clement (1519?–1587), IV. 72
Adams, Clement (? *fl.* 1516), VI. 282

Adams, Francis, printer (*fl.* 1585), IV. 386
Adams, Francis (1796–1861), XII. 479
Adams, Francis, of Birmingham, XIV. 590
Adams, Francis William Lauderdale(1862
  –1893), XIII. 560; XIV. 369, 584
Adams, George (d. 1773), X. 470
Adams, Jean, IX. 374
Adams, John, XIV. 590
Adams, John Couch (1819–1892), XIV. 262,
  264, 555
Adams, John Quincy, XI. 266
Adams, parson, in Fielding's *Joseph An-
  drews*, IX. 408; X. 24 ff., 28, 206; XI.
  143; XIV. 218
Adams, Sarah Flower (1805–1848), XII.
  413; XIII. 498; *Nearer, my God, to Thee*,
  XIII. 53, 176; *Vivia Perpetua*, XIII. 176
Adams, Thomas (*fl.* 1612–1653), VII. 423
Adams, William (d. 1620), IV. 99 ff.
Adams, William (1814–1848), XII. 447
Adams, William Davenport (1851–1904),
  XIII. 513
Adams, W. E., XIV. 533
Adams, William Henry Davenport (1828–
  1891), XIV. 515
Adamson, Henry (d. 1639), IX. 554
Adamson, John (d. 1653), IX. 542, 554
Adamson, John Ernest, XIV. Add. 4
Adamson, John William, XIV. Add. 11
Adamson, Robert (1852–1902), XIV. 467,
  475
  Development of Modern Philosophy, The,
    XIV. 49
  Fichte, XIV. 48
  On the Philosophy of Kant, XIV. 48
  Short History of Logic, A, XIV. 48
Adderley, William, VII. 316
Addington, Henry, viscount Sidmouth
  (1757–1844), XIV. 506
Addison, Joseph (1672–1719), II. 163, 192,
  415; III. 304, 373; IV. 30, 213, 335, 525;
  VII. 30, 72, 108, 109, 176, 244, 266, 388,
  390; VIII. 174, 194, 220, 292, 293, 296,
  303, 428, 430; IX. 5, 26, 27, 41, 43 ff.
  (main entry), 67, 75, 78, 86, 94, 125,
  142, 151, 165, 166, 170 ff., 180 ff., 220,
  237, 434 ff., 440, 442, 444, 445, 448, 483,
  485, *also see* Add.; X. 1, 2, 20, 26, 27, 56,
  80, 110, 119, 139, 140, 143, 172, 173,
  193, 199, 205, 215, 219, 220, 226, 241,
  279, 352, 353, 458, 484, *also see* Add.;
  XI. 2, 206, 280, 320, 330; XII. 177, 218,
  221; XIII. 170, 312, 429, 445; XIV. 62,
  169, 197, 209, 211, 396, 441, 442, 444,
  461, 550
  Campaign, The, IX. 44
  Cato, IX. 63, 64, 77, 171, 184, 474; X. 69,
    81, 83; XI. 273
  Coverly papers, X. 178
  Dialogues upon...Ancient Medals, IX. 43
  Dissertatio de Romanorum poetis, IX. 43
  Drummer, The, IX. 172
  Essay on Travel, IX. 44
  First Vision of Mirza, IX. 63
  Musae Anglicanae, IX. 43

Addison, Joseph
  'On the Pleasures of the Imagination,'
    IX. 61
  Oratio de nova philosophia, IX. 43
  Remarks on Italy, IX. 44
  Travels in Italy, IX. 94
  See, also, *Spectator, The*, and *Tatler, The*
Addison, Lancelot (1632–1703), IX. 38, 438
Adeane, Jane, *The Girlhood of Maria Jo-
  sepha Holroyd*, X. 299
Adela of Louvain, II. 419
Adelaide, XIV. 365
Adelard or Aethelard of Bath (12th cen-
  tury), IV. 68; *De Eodem et Diverso*, etc.,
  I. 153
Adelbright, in *Albion's England*, IV. 136
Adeline, in *La Cousine Bette*, XIII. 290
Adeline, in Mrs Radcliffe's *Romance of the
  Forest*, XI. 302
Adeline, Tennyson's, XIII. 29
Adis, Henry, VII. 515
Adlard, H., engraver, XII. 323
Adlington, William, *The Golden Ass*, IV. 3,
  9, 435
Admetus, in *The Court of Love*, II. 220
Admirable Crichton, VII. 250, 255; VIII.
  195
Admiral's company, the, V. 136, 316, 333;
  VI. 83, 89, 90, 93, 245, 247, 249, 250,
  255, 259, 269, 274
Admonition to the Parliament, An, IV. 411
Ado of Vienne, I. 81
Adolphus, John Leycester (1795–1862),
  XII. 377
Adonais, in Shelley's poem, XII. 74
Adonis, XIII. 183
Adonis, in *Venus and Adonis*, V. 226
Adoptionist controversy, I. 84
Adorni, in *The Maid of Honour*, VI. 158,
  164
Adraien van Berghen, printer, of Antwerp,
  II. 320
Adria, in the tale of *Colkelbie's sow*, II. 126
Adrian VI, pope, XIV. 100
Adrian, in *Confessio Amantis*, II. 151
Adriana, in *The Comedy of Errors*, V. 169,
  178
Adrianus and Ritheus, I. 218
Adriatic sea, X. 119; XII. 33, 63
Adso, *Libellus de Antichristo*, I. 343
Adson, John, IV. 463
Adullam, in *Davideis*, VII. 67
Adurni, in *The Ladies Triall*, VI. 194
Adventurer, The, X. 171, 175, 466; XII. 363
Adventures of Dr Comicus, The, XIV. 219
Adversyte, in *Magnyfycence*, III. 77
Advertisement of a Sale of Choice Goods,
  VIII. 99
Advice to a Young Nobleman, XI. 371
Advices to a Painter, VIII. 91; Second and
  Third (1667), VII. 409; New Advice
  (1679), VII. 91
Ady, Thomas, VII. 396; *A Candle in the
  Dark*, VII. 395, 507
Æ., XIV. 573

Aeacus, in *Locrine*, v. 240

Aecius, in *Valentinian*, vi. 122, 129, 130

Aeditio (Colet's), vii. 332

Aegeon of Syracuse, in *The Comedy of Errors*, iv. 79

Aegisthus, in *Agamemnon*, v. 79

Aeglamour, in *The Sad Shepherd*, vi. 11, 369, 370

Aelfhēah (St Alphege) (954–1012), i. 109, 127, 139, 153

Aelfhere, i. 138

Aelfnoth, i. 144

Aelfric (*fl.* 1006), i. 86, 96, 107, 113 ff., 116–129 (main entry), 131, 133, 136, 142, 143, 148, 150, 218, 221, 224, 369; ix. 536, 539; xi. 366

  Advice to a Spiritual Son, trans. from St Basil, i. 124

  Colloquy, i. 118, 119; xi. 367

  De Veteri et de Novo Testamento, i. 126

  Deuteronomy, i. 119

  Grammar, i. 118, 119

  Hexameron, trans. from St Basil, i. 122, 124

  Homilies, i. 86, 96, 115, 116 ff., 120, 127 ff., 133; iv. 37, 397; ix. 402

  Letter to the Monks of Eynsham, i. 114

  Lives (Passions) of the Saints, The, i. 120, 121, 122, 128; iv. 424

  Pastoral letter, i. 127

  Version of Bede's *De Temporibus*, i. 122

  Vita Aethelwoldi, i. 125

  Vocabulary, i. 118, 119

Aelfric society, xii. 355

Aelfwine (Alboin), in *Widsith*, i. 35

Aelfwine, in *The Battle of Maldon*, i. 144

Aelian, iv. 435

Aeneas, viii. 67; ix. 45, 60, 256, 257; xiii. 123

Aeneas, in *Dido*, v. 146

Aeneas, James I described as, in *The Hue and Cry after Cupid*, vi. 347

'Aeolian lyre,' x. 128

Aeolus, vii. 370

Aeschere, in *The Battle of Maldon*, i. 145

Aeschere, in *Beowulf*, i. 23

Aeschines, vii. 147; ix. 528; xii. 493

Aeschylus, iv. 4, 248; v. 30; vii. 83; ix. 477; xii. 93, 99, 265, 324, 328, 331, 333, 480 ff., 485, 487 ff., 491, 494, 495; xiii. 191, 497; xiv. 211, 515

  Agamemnon, xii. 318, 329, 334; xiii. 145

  Choëphoroe, xii. 329, 334

  Persae, vi. 92; xii. 329

  Prometheus Bound, xii. 64, 65, 329; xiii. 70

  Seven against Thebes, xii. 329

Aesculapius, in *The Faerie Queene*, iii. 234

Aeson, vi. 163

Aesop, ix. 102, 275, 391, 418, 473, 524, 525, 561; x. 196; xi. 366, 425, 479, 490, 491; *Fables*, i. 106, 355; ii. 245, 314, 334, 484; iii. 22; iv. 427, 435; v. 157; vi. 250; viii. 59

Aethelard. *See* Adelard

Aethelbriht, laws of, i. 98

Aethelflaed, the Lady of Mercia (d. 918?), i. 110, 141, 143

Aethelmaer, i. 125, 143

Aethelney, i. 89

Aethelred II, king (979?–1016), i. 112, 127, 129, 130, 145; v. 31

Aethelred, king of Mercia, i. 11

Aethelred, ealdorman of Mercia, i. 104

Aethelstan (Athelstan), king (925–940), i. 62, 108, 123, 137, 305; viii. 310

Aethelstan, abbot of Abingdon, i. 110

Aethelstan of Kent, prince, xiv. 83

Aethelweard, the ealdorman, i. 120, 122, 123

Aethelweard the chronicler (d. 998?), i. 443

Aethelwold, in *Havelok*, i. 303, 351

Aethelwold or Ethelwold, St (908?–984), bishop of Winchester, abbot of Abingdon, i. 16, 113, 114, 117, 118, 121, 125, 127, 148

Aethelwulf, i. 104

Aethilwald or Ethelbald, i. 78, 87

Aethiopians, in *The Masque of Blacknesse*, vi. 342, 343

Æþred's ring, i. 11

Aetion, v. 171

Aetna, xii. 335, 337

Affections, the, in *Pathomachia*, vi. 324

Affections, the four, in *Hymenaei*, vi. 346

Affery, in *Little Dorrit*, xiii. 331

Affirmation bill, the, xiv. 135

Affonso, Pedro, iv. 70

Afghanistan, xii. 352

Africa, ix. 19; xi. 112; xiii. 362; xiv. 192, 247, 252 ff., 434

African church, the, iii. 411

African languages, xiv. 459

Africander's War Song, The, xiv. 377

Africans, the, xi. 159

Agamemnon, in *Confessio Amantis*, ii. 148

Agape, St, i. 74

Agar, Anne (born Milton), vii. 108

Agar, Ralph (1540?–1621), vi. 462

Agatha, St, i. 74

Agathocles, xi. 316

Agathon (Plato's), iii. 216

Age, in *Nature*, v. 54

Age, in *Piers the Plowman*, ii. 25

Age, in *The Parlement of the Thre Ages*, ii. 37

Age, in *The Passetyme of Pleasure*, ii. 226

Ager, captain, in *A Faire Quarrell*, vi. 73, 74

Aggas, Edward (*fl.* 1564–1601), iv. 445, 447

Agincourt, battle of, ii. 423; iii. 314, 325; iv. 298; vii. 343; poems on, ii. 499, 501

Agincourt song, the, iv. 462

Agnellus, friar, i. 203

Agnes, in *David Copperfield*, xiii. 327

Agnes, St, i. 74

Agnes, St, Tennyson's, xiii. 29

Agnoli, G., xii. 377

Agra, iv. 90, 99

4

'Agra,' ship, XIII. 428
Agricola, XIV. 95
Agricola, Rodolphus, III. 50, 424
Agrigentum, IX. 332
Agrippa, Henricus Cornelius, of Nettesheim, III. 11, 112, 363, 365; VII. 370, 509 ff., 514, 517; VIII. 64; IX. 315; *De incertitudine et vanitate scientiarum*, VI. 377, 492; VII. 394; *De Occulta Philosophia*, III. 112; VIII. 67, 407
Aguecheek, Sir Andrew, in *Twelfth Night*, V. 194; XI. 266
Ahania, Blake's, XI. 194
Ahlwardt, Christian Wilhelm, X. 488
Ahmed, the cobbler, XIV. 248
Aholibamah, in Byron's *Heaven and Earth*, XII. 48
Aidan (d. 651), I. 42, 82, 121, 148
Aikin, Anna Laetitia. *See* Barbauld
Aikin, John (1747–1822), X. 385, 446, 449, 452, 455; XI. 382, 384, 477; XIV. 603
Aikin, J. and A. L., *Miscellaneous Pieces in Prose*, X. 188
Aikin, Lucy (1781–1864), XI. 477
Ailesbury, Susanna, countess of (d. 1783), XI. 282
Ailred or Ethelred of Rievaulx (1109?–1166), I. 161, 230, 337. 450
Aimonius of Fleury, II. 366
Aimwell, in Farquhar's *Beaux Stratagem*, VIII. 172
Ainderby, near Northallerton, II. 45
Ainger, Alfred (1837–1904), XI. 403, 410, 416, 419, 438; XII. 377, 418, 435, 473; XIII. 476, 542, *also see* Add. 2; XIV. 515; *Crabbe*, XI. 146, 475
Ainger, Arthur Campbell, XIV. 597
Ainsworth, Henry (1571–1623?), VII. 481, 490
Ainsworth, Robert (1660–1743), IX. 526, 568
Ainsworth, William Francis (1807–1896), XII. 429
Ainsworth, William Harrison (1805–1882), XII. 429 ff., 447, 448; XIII. 279, 307, 418
Guy Fawkes, XII. 250
Jack Sheppard, XII. 250
Lancashire Witches, The, XII. 250
Old St Paul's, XII. 250
Rookwood, XII. 250
South Sea Bubble, The, XII. 250
Tower of London, The, XII. 250
Aird, Thomas (1802–1876), XIII. 498
Airedale, XII. 421
Airy, Sir George Biddell (1801–1892), XIV. 258, 555
Airy, Osmund, IX. 203, 209
Aitken, Edward Hamilton (1851–1909), XIV. 574; *Behind the Bungalow*, XIV. 341
Aitken, George A., IX. 12, *also see* Add.; XI. 438
Aitken, J. C., XIII. 467
Aix-la-Chapelle, IX. 162; XIII. 61
Aix-la-Chapelle, treaty of, X. 40
Aix-les-Bains, II. 74

Ajax, VIII. 68
Ajax, in *Troilus and Cressida*, VI. 44
Ajax, An Anatomie of the Metamorpho-sed, IV. 533
Ajax Flagellifer, VI. 298, 317
Ajmere, IV. 90
Akenside, Mark (1721–1770), IX. 190, 220, 475; X. 39, 125, 138, 147, 152–153 (main entry), 156, 452; XI. 324; XII. 97
Epistle to Curio, X. 152, 153
Hymn to the Naiads, IX. 191; X. 152, 153
Inscriptions, X. 153
Odes, X. 153
Pleasures of Imagination, IX. 62; X. 122, 152, 153; XI. 323
Akerman, John Yonge (1806–1873), XII. 507
Akinetos, in Horne's *Orion*, XII. 118
Alabaster, William (1567–1640), *Roxana*, VI. 266, 268, 302, 463, 469, 470
Alain de Lille (1114–1203), I. 452; *Anti-Claudianus* and *De Planctu Naturae*, I. 193, 256
Alamanni, Luigi, III. 173
'Alamode Castle,' X. 250
Alane (Alesius), Alexander (1500–1565), III. 140, 141, 500
Cohortatio ad Concordiam, III. 141
Description of Edinburgh, III. 141
Epistola contra Decretum quoddam Episcoporum in Scotia, III. 141
Responsio ad Cochlaei Calumnias, III. 141
Alanius (Yong's), IV. 122
Alans, the, XIV. 302
Alarcon y Mendoza, Juan Ruiz de, VIII. 130
Alasco, Albertus, Polish prince palatine, V. 128
Alasi, prince, in Beckford's *Episodes*, XI. 291
Alba, VI. 317
Alban, Scottish settlers in, II. 89
Alban, St, Passion of, I. 81
Albanact, III. 192
Albania, X. 77; XII. 32, 42, 43; XIV. 252
Albany, duke of. *See* Stewart, John
Albemarle, earls of. *See* Keppel, Arnold; Keppel, George
Albemarle Papers, the, IX. 563
Alberic, master, I. 184
Albert, prince consort (1819–1861), XII. 311; XIV. 189, 415
Albert of Aix, II. 80
Albert of York, I. 84
Alberti, George William (1723–1758), VIII. 402
Alberti, L. B., IV. 441
Albertini di Prato, Niccolò, cardinal, V. 61
Albertino (Mussatus), *Eccerinis*, V. 62
Albertus Magnus (1193–1280), I. 200, 210, 211; II. 350; III. 494; VII. 503; *Philosophia*, II. 363
Albery, James (1838–1889), XIII. 273, 516
Albigenses, the, XIV. 79, 110
Albin, St, in Layamon, I. 234

Albina, in Racine's *Britannicus*, x. 119
Albinus of Canterbury, I. 82
Albion, in Blake's *Jerusalem*, XI. 198, 199
Albion, in *The Masque of Blacknesse*, VI. 342
Albion, The, XII. 187, 188
Albion Knight, v. 58, 124, 393
Alboin, in *Confessio Amantis*, II. 151
Alboin, in *Widsith*, I. 35
Albumazar, Galbrion, VII. 509
Alcaeus, VII. 65; XII. 329
Alcalà, IV. 69
Alcazar, battle of, VIII. 31
Alceone, in *Confessio Amantis*, II. 151
Alceste (Molière's), v. 194
Alcester, x. 112, 271
Alcester academy, x. 385
Alcestis, I. 321; VII. 105, 227; x. 108
Alcestis, in *The Court of Love*, II. 220
Alcestis, in *The Legend of Good Women*, II. 176
Alchemists, in *Mercury Vindicated*, VI. 357, 358
Alchfrith, I. 12
Alciati, Andrea, III. 423; VII. 47
Alcides, VI. 163
Alcilia, IV. 469
Alcimus Avitus, I. 76
Alcina, in *Orlando Furioso*, III. 231
Alcinous, XII. 198
Alcluyd, II. 74
Alcmaeon, v. 123
Alcmaeon, XII. Add.
Alcmena, in *Amphitruo*, v. 107
Alcmena, in *The Silver Age*, VI. 93
Alcock, John (1430–1500), bishop of Ely, II. 323, 355, 358; III. 66; IV. 494
Alcofribas, Messer, IV. 9
Alcon, in *A Looking Glasse for London and England*, v. 354
Alcon, in *The Queenes Arcadia*, VI. 318
Alcott, Louisa May, XI. 492
Alcuin or Ealhwine (735–804), I. 5, 59, 79, 84 ff., 89, 117, 121, 145, 153, 433; IV. 269; XI. 366
Alcuine's Bible, XII. 517
Aldeburgh, XI. 140, 141, 143, 144, 146, 147, 419
Alden, Raymond Macdonald, XIII. 511
Alderton, Suffolk, IV. 164, 165
Aldfrith (d. 705), king of Northumbria, I. 76, 77
Aldhelm (640?–709), bishop of Sherborne, I. 15, 17, 60, 61, 72 ff., 82, 83, 86, 87, 91, 102, 230, 433; XI. 366
Aldingar, Sir, II. 412
Aldis, Harry Gidney (d. 1919), IV. 547; XI. 469; XII. 519
Aldred, the glossator (10th century), I. 132, 460
Aldrich, Henry (1647–1710), IX. 528; XIV. 476; *Artis logicæ rudimenta*, XIV. 13
Aldus Manutius, Romanus, III. 5, 427
Aldwinkle, Northants, VII. 244; VIII. 2
Alec-Tweedie, Mrs Ethel Brilliana, XIV. 533

Aleman, M., *The Rogue, or the Life of Guzman de Alfarache*, IV. 395, 441; VI. 139
Alembert, Jean B. le Rond d', XI. 354
Alembic Club Reprints, XIV. 557, 558
Aleppo, IV. 84, 90; VII. 308; x. 466
Aleppo, basha of, in *The Renegado*, VI. 156
Alesius, Aless. *See* Alane, Alexander
Alessio, IV. 441
Alethea, in Butler's *The Way of all Flesh*, XIII. 454
Alexander I, emperor of Russia, XII. 39
Alexander III, king of Scots, I. 283; II. 100, 101, 109; XIV. 95
Alexander, in Lee's *Rival Queens*, VIII. 186
Alexander, Mrs Cecil Frances, born Humphreys (1818–1895), XIII. 498; XIV. 567; *Burial of Moses, The*, XIV. 321; *Irish Mother's Lament, The*, XIV. 321; *Siege of Derry, The*, XIV. 321
Alexander, John (d. 1743), x. 385
Alexander, Patrick Proctor, XIII. 470; XIV. 525
Alexander, The Buik of, II. 104, 448
Alexander, The Wars of, I. 291, 333, 334, 466
Alexander, W. F., XIV. 584
Alexander, Sir William, earl of Stirling (1567?–1640), II. 95; III. 266; IV. 152, 311, 413, 509; v. 473; VI. 19; VII. 273; VIII. 133; IX. 554; *Anacrisis*, VII. 263; *Aurora*, III. 257, 267, 522; *Monarchick Tragedies*, v. 335
Alexander, William (1826–1894), XIII. 560
Alexander, William (1824–1911), archbishop of Armagh, XIV. 321, 567
Alexander de Villa Dei, II. 359, 366; *Doctrinale Puerorum*, II. 363
Alexander Hieronymus, IV. 259
Alexander of Blois, I. 166, 167
Alexander of Hales (d. 1245), I. 199 ff., 205, 207, 452; IV. 269, 271; VII. 504
Alexander of Lincoln, I. 156, 169, 258
Alexander the Great, x. 27; XII. 309, 313, 315, 331; XIV. 579
Alexander the Great, in romance, I. 135, 148, 169, 279, 285, 291, 307, 308, 333, 334, 342, 466; II. 112, 301; III. 24, 61; IV. 196
See, also, *Alisaunder, Secreta Secretorum*
Alexander to Aristotle, The Letter of, I. 35; II. 80
Alexandri, Historia, II. 151
Alexandria, II. 13, 131; XIII. 362; XIV. 247
Alexandrian poets, VII. 9
Alexandrines, XI. 246; XII. 88, 229; XIII. 35, 151, 238, 251
Alexis (Virgil's), III. 264
Alexis, or the young Adventurer (1746), IX. 563
Alexius, St, I. 293, 356
Alfieri, Vittorio, count, XII. 33, 40, 47, 49, 397, 438
Alford, Henry (1810–1871), XII. 340, 500; XIII. 24, 476

Alfoxden, XI. 99, 102, 405

Alfred, king of West-Saxons (849–901?),
I. 19, 84, 87 ff., 109, 113, 115, 123, 128,
136, 144, 150, 198, 219, 239, 363, 380 ff.,
436 ff.; II. 341; III. 160; IV. 74; V. 2; VIII.
310; IX. 534
  Falconry attributed to, I. 106
  Handbook, I. 91
  Translations: of Augustine, I. 102, 103;
  of Bede, I. 96; of Boethius, I. 99 ff.;
  II.186; of Gregory, I. 91 ff.; of Orosius,
  I.93 ff.

Alfred, Proverbs of, I. 218, 438, 459, 460

Alfred aetheling, I. 139, 374

Alfred of Beverley (*fl.* 1143), I. 262; II. 76;
IX. 534

Algarotti, Francesco, *Newtonianismo per
le Dame*, XI. 356

Algeria, XII. 480

Algiers, VII. 364

Ali, I. 26, 27

Ali pasha, XII. 32

Alicante, XIV. 73

Alice, in Lamb's *Essays of Elia*, XII. 182,
186

Alice, in Mrs Gaskell's *Mary Barton*, XIII.
375

Alinda, in *Rosalynde*, III. 358

Alinda, in *The Pilgrim*, VI. 123

Alington, Syr Giles, knight, III. 57

Alipur, near Calcutta, XIII. 276

Alisaunder, King, I. 288, 306, 308, 309,
317, 356, 399

Alison, Archibald (1757–1839), XIV. 467;
XIV. 57, 94, 485; *Autobiography*, XIV. 66;
History of Europe, XIV. 66; *History of
Scottish Criminal Law*, XIV. 66

Alison, Richard (*fl.* 1606), IV. 113, 463

Alison, in *Misogonus*, V. 111

Alithia (Philosophy), in Wyclif's *Trialogus*
II. 65

Alken, Henry (*fl.* 1816–1831), XIV. 225,
232 ff., 542; *National Sports of Great
Britain*, XIV. 232; *Specimens of Riding*,
XIV. 232; *Symptoms of being amazed*,
XIV. 232

Alken, in *The Sad Shepherd*, VI. 370

Alkington academy, X. 387

Alkmaar, IV. 246

All Fools, game of, V. 179

All is True, VI. 256

All the Year Round, XIII. 178, 315, 323,
326, 332, 335, 376, 437

All wyckednes doth beginne to amende, etc.,
III. 491

Allam, Andrew (1655–1685), IX. 351

Allan, David (1744–1796), IX. 567

Allan-a-Maut, II. 279

Allardyce, Alexander (1846–1896), XIV.
574; *The City of Sunshine*, XIV. 339

Allbut, Robert, XIII. 542

Allde, Edward (*fl.* 1583–1634), IV. 384,
390; V. 158

Allde, John (*fl.* 1555–1592), V. 92, 312

Allen, Giles, VI. 252, 253

Allen, Grant (*pseud.* Cecil Power, 1848–
1899), XIII. 560; XIV. 343, 467, 535

Allen, Henry Ellis, XII. 337, 479

Allen, John (1771–1843), XII. 144, 426;
XIV. 54, 485, 492

Allen, John (1810–1886), archdeacon of
Salop, XIII. 142

Allen, Joseph, *Punch* artist, XIV. 236

Allen, Joshua, viscount (1685–1758), IX.
121

Allen, Ralph (1694–1764), IX. 443; X. 29,
33, 276

Allen, Thomas (1803–1833), XII. 507

Allen, William (1532–1594), cardinal, III.
422; *Modest Answer to the English Per-
secutors*, VII. 432

Allen, William (1770–1843), XIV. 603

Alley, William (1510?–1570), *The Poore
Man's Librarie*, VI. 378, 492

Alleyn, Edward (1566–1626), IV. 407;
V. 144; VI. 41, 51, 87, 247, 249, 250,
255, 258, 278, 292

Alleyn, Ellen, *pseud. See* Rossetti, Christina Georgina

Alleyn's college, Dulwich, VII. 339

Allibone, S. Austin, XII. 519

Allingham, Helen, XIII. 498

Allingham, William (1824–1889), XII. 409;
XIII. 189, 498; XIV. 567; *Lovely Mary
Donnelly*, XIII. 190; *Up the Fairy Moun-
tain*, XIII. 190

Allington, Kent, III. 167

Allison, Thomas (*fl.* 1697), IV. 453

Allison Gross, II. 414

Alliterative revival, I. 291

All-Night, countess of, in Goldsmith's
Citizen of the World, X. 206

Allot, Robert (*fl.* 1600), *England's Parnassus*, IV. 394, 467; V. 134, 162

Alloway, XI. 219, 435

Allsop, Thomas (1795–1880), XI. 415, 416;
XII. 199, 200

Allworthy, in Fielding's *Tom Jones*, X. 28,
29, 31

Alma, battle of the, XIII. 173; XIV. 94

Alma, house of, in *The Faerie Queene*,
III. 233

Alma Mater (Aberdeen), XIV. 209

Alma redemptoris mater, in Chaucer's *The
Prioress's Tale*, II. 359

Almaigne, Song against the King of, I. 368

Almanacs, III. 19

Almanzor, in Dryden's *Conquest of Granada*, VIII. 25, 27

Almerine, in *Brennoralt*, VI. 238

Almira, in *A Very Woman*, VI. 156

Almon, John (1737–1805), X. 522, 524 ff.;
Anecdotes of Eminent Persons, X. 400

Almond, Hely Hutchinson (1832–1903),
XIV. 590, 601

Almond for a Parrat, An, VI. 393

Alms, in *The Exeter Book*, I. 428

Alne, Robert, fellow of Peterhouse, II. 366

Alnwick, IX. 566; XI. 469; XIV. 227

Alonso, in *The Tempest*, V. 206

Alonzo, in *The Bashful Lover*, VI. 158

Aloỹse, in Rossetti's *Bride's Prelude*, XIII 114

Alpers, O. T. J., XIV. 584

Alphabet, Irish and Roman, I. 13

Alphege, St. *See* Aelfhēah

Alphere, in *Waltharius*, I. 32

Alphonso, in *The Mourning Bride*, VIII.152

Alphonso I, king of Aragon and Navarre, v. 137

Alphonso V, king of Aragon, Sicily and Naples, v. 137

Alphus (Mantuan's), III. 223

Alpine Journal, The, XIV. 255

Alps, the, II. 119; IV. 6; v. 101; VIII. 245; x. 119, 202, 510; XI. 96; XII. 44, 47, 61, 63, 64; XIII. 443; XIV. 254, 255, 292, 294

Alresford, VII. 207, 454

Alscrip, in Burgoyne's *Heiress*, XI. 275,276

Alscrip, Miss, in Burgoyne's *Heiress*, XI. 275; XIV. 387

Alsop, Vincent (d. 1703), IX. 503

Alspice, in Morton's *Way to get Married*, XI. 281

Altamont, in Rowe's *Fair Penitent*, VIII. 196

Altamont, colonel, in *Pendennis*, XIII. 291

Altdorf, v. 285

Althaus, Friedrich, XIII. 70

Althorp, VI. 4, 339

Althorp, viscount. *See* Spencer, John Charles

Althorp library, XII. 365, 366

Alton, Miss, in Burgoyne's *Heiress*, XI. 275

Alton, Hampshire, XIII. 381

Altrive farm, in Yarrow, XI. 239

Altus prosator, I. 69

Alucius, History of, VI. 286

Alva, duke of, v. 344; VII. 306; VIII. 160

Alvan, Sigismund, in Meredith's *The Tragic Comedians*, XIII. 444

Alvanley, baron. *See* Arden, Richard Pepper

Alvar, in Coleridge's *Remorse*, XI. 414

Alvarez Espriella, Don Manuel, in Southey's *Letters from Spain*, XI. 163

Alys Esry, in *Cocke Lorell's bote*, III. 84

Amada, Philip, IV. 85

Amadas and Ydoine, I. 286

Amadas, Sir, I. 293, 294, 470

Amadeus, in *The Bugbears*, v. 115

Amadine, in *Mucedorus*, v. 253

Amadis, IV. 9; VII. 75, 235

Amadis and Palmerin cycles, III. 359

Amadis of Gaul, VII. 74; x. 220; XII. 422; XIII. 35

Amalekites, II. 10; VIII. 78

Amalteo, Geronimo, IV. 264

Amanda, in Sheridan's *Trip to Scarborough*, XI. 268

Amanda, in Thomson's *Seasons*, x. 95, 99, 102

Amanda, in Vanbrugh's *Relapse*, VIII. 161; XI. 268

Amaranta, in *The Spanish Curate*, VI. 134

Amarillis (Herrick's), VII. 12, 13

Amaryllis, in *The Shepheards Calender*, III. 222, 226

Amatus Lusitanus, in Burton's *Anatomy*, IV. 246

Amaziah, in Cowley's *Davideis*, VII. 67

Amazon, river, XIV. 250

'Amazon,' ship, XIV. 251

Amazonian maids in *Ralph Roister Doister*, v. 106

Amazons, the, IV. 57, 61; x. 464

Ambassadorial despatches and newsletters, VII. 436 ff.

Ambodexter, in *A Dialogue...against the fever Pestilence*, III. 109

Amboyna (Amboina), outrage at, IV. 99; VI. 183; VIII. Add.

Amboyna, A true relation of the unjust, cruel and barbarous proceeding against the English at, VII. 433

Ambroise, *Histoire de la Guerre Sainte*, II. 420, 507

Ambrosden, parish of, IX. 536; x. 517

Ambrose, St, I. 59, 74, 75; II. 365; VII. 483; XII. 266

Ambrose, in *The Example of Virtue*, II. 227

Ambrose's tavern, XII. 159

Ambrosius Aurelianus, Aurelius Ambrosius (G. of M.), Embreis Guletic (Nennius), Emrys Wledig in Welsh literature, I. 66, 247, 268

'Ambusheer,' the, x. 198

Amelia, x. 33, 34

Amelia, in George Eliot's *Amos Barton*, XIII. 388

Amelia, in Fielding's novel, x. 23, 28, 33, 34

Amelia, in Thomson's *Seasons*, x. 103

Amelotte, in Rossetti's *Bride's Prelude*, XIII. 114

America, IV. 73, 74, 86, 95, 96, 101, 311; VII. 176, 305, 308; VIII. 101, 243, 257, 314, 341, 342; IX. 19, 212; x. 43, 199, 200, 364, 504; XI. 3, 7, 10 ff., 15, 20, 75, 119, 189, 190, 235, 236, 275, 380, 383; XII. 89, 165, 316; XIII. 10, 58, 88, 107, 150, 152, 294, 321, 322, 334, 455; XIV. 86, 98, 166, 207, 255, 263, 267, 293, 318, 397, 457. *See, also,* United States

America, Central, XIV. 297

America, South, IX. 23; XI. 60; XIV. 249, 250, 252

America, discovery of, III. 97; IV. 68, 69, 75

America, first English books on, II. 330; IV. 69, 70

America, study of Shakespeare in, v. 308

American Celt, The, XIV. 318

American character, XIV. 346

American church, x. 356

American civil war, XIV. 91, 143, 182,326

American colonies, x. 306; XI. 5, 22; XIV. 361

American congress, x. 182

American constitution, XI. 71

American declaration of independence, XI. 71

American languages, XIV. 459

American philosophy, IX. 281

American politics, XIV. 346

American scholars, XII. 340

American slang, XIV. 211

American war of independence, X 251, 393; XI. 5, 6, 16, 24; XIV. 89

Americans, the, XI, 11, 15, 19, 52

Amersham, VII. 53, 54

Ames, Joseph (1689–1759), Typographical Antiquities, IX. 356, 530; XII. 362, 366, 520

Ames, William (1576–1633), VII. 308; De Conscientia et ejus jure vel casibus, VII. 280, 469

Amesbury, IX. 163

Amhurst, Nicholas (1697–1742), IX. 220. 411, 433, 491, 574; XI. 172

Amie, in The Sad Shepherd, VI. 370

Amiel, Henri Frédéric, XIII. 99

Amiens, X. 118; XII. 341

Amiens, in As You Like It, VII. 3; VIII. 225

Amiens, peace of, XIV. 120, 184

Aminta, in Meredith's Lord Ormont and his Aminta, XIII. 444

Amintor, in The Maides Tragedy, VI. 120, 126 ff.

Amis and Amiloun, I. 314, 315, 467

Amitiez de Ami et Amile, Li, IX. 39

Amlet, Mrs, in The Confederacy, VIII. 162

Amlethus (Hamlet) in Saxo Grammaticus, I. 9. See, also, under Hamlet

Ammianus Marcellinus, I. 35

Ammonius, Andreas, III. 14

Amner, John (d. 1641), IV. 463

Amoret (Spenser's), III. 236

Amoret (Vaughan's), VII. 38, 40

Amoret (Waller's), VII. 55

Amoretta, in The Ladies Triall, VI. 194

Amoretto, in The Pilgrimage to Parnassus, VI. 310

Amoretto, in The Returne from Parnassus, VI. 313

Amorgen, incantation of, XIV. 303

Amorous La-Foole, Sir, in The Silent Woman, VI. 22, 152

Amorphus, in Cynthia's Revels, VI. 41, 44

Amory, Blanche, in Pendennis, XIII. 290 ff.

Amory, J., in Pendennis, XIII. 291

Amory, Thomas (1691?–1788), X. 386, 423; XI. 285 ff. (main entry), 307; Life of John Buncle, X. 56; XI. 285 ff., 328, 329; Memoirs of Several Ladies, XI. 285, 287

Amos, Andrew, XIV. 594

Amos, hermit, I. 74

Amours, Francis Joseph, II. 113, 115, 121, 126, 450

Amphitryon, VII. 125

Amphitryon, in Confessio Amantis, II. 148

Amsarey, in Disraeli's Tancred, XIII. 351

Amsterdam, IV. 402, 403; V. 286; VI. 22, 324; VII. 286, 289, 308, 344; IX. 197, 199, 306, 515, 519; X. 296

Amsterdam, Letter from, to a Friend in England, VIII. 100

Amurath, VI. 481

Amwell, Hertfordshire, XII. 191

Amyas, in Westward Ho!, XIII. 364

Amyntas, in The Cytezen and Uplondysh-man, III. 63

Amyntas, in The Queenes Arcadia, VI. 317

Amyot, Jacques, IV. 3, 10, 11

Anacreon, IV. 123 ff., 186; VII. 1, 2, 4, 9, 18, 83, 489; VIII. 444; IX. 526; X. 454; XI. 426; XII. 223, 410

Anacreon, the pseudo-, VII. 83

Anaides, in Cynthia's Revels, VI. 18, 41

Analysis of the Hunting Field, The, XIV. 232, 234

Analytical Review, The, XI. 402

Ananias, in The Alchemist, VI. 22

Anastasius, emperor, X. 314

Anatolia, XIV. 251

Anatolia, St, I. 74, 75

Anatomy of Wit, VI. 394

An Bispel, I. 227, 228, 458, 459

Ancient Buildings, society for the pro tection of, XIII. 128

Ancient Pistol, in Henry IV. See Pistol, Ancient

Ancor, river, IV. 169, 173 ff., 190

Ancren Riwle, I. 222, 230, 234, 398, 400, 458, 459; II. 300; III. 440

Anderdon, J., IX. 518

Andersen, Hans Christian, XI. 387, 491

Anderson, Alexander (1845–1909), XIII. 498

Anderson, George (1676?–1756), IX. 547

Anderson, James (1662–1728), IX. 552; X. 498

Anderson, James (1739–1808), IX. 560; XIV. 467; Enquiry into the Nature of Corn-Laws, XIV. 3

Anderson, John P., X. 421, 483; XI. 456; XII. 382, 397, 404, 407, 447; XIII. 464, 480, 531, 554

Anderson, Joseph (b. 1832), XII. 507

Anderson, Robert (1750–1830), IX. 187, 479; X. 138, 469, 473; XII. 413; XIII. 224; The Works of the British Poets, X. 452

André (Bernard Andreas) of Toulouse, VII. 203; Les Douze Triomphes de Henry VII, II. 223, 471

Andrea, ghost of, in Jeronimo, V. 160

Andrea, Joannes, II. 364

Andreae, Antonius, commentary on Aris-totle's Metaphysics, II. 318

Andreae, Johann Valentin (? fl. 1619), Menippus, IV. 248; VII. Add.

Andreas, I. 51 ff., 58, 143, 430

Andreini, Giovanni Battista, Adamo, VII. 118; XI. 403

Andreos, in The Purple Island, IV. 166

'Ανδρέου καὶ Ματθαίου, Πράξεις, I. 54

Andrew, merchant in Lyme Regis, x. 21

Andrew, St, I. 54, 115. See, also, *Andreas Andrew Lammie*, II. 412

Andrew of Wyntoun. *See* Wyntoun

Andrewe, Laurence (*fl.* 1510–1537), printer, II. 330; IV. 542

Andrewes, George, XIV. 539; *Dictionary of the Slang and Cant Languages*, XIV. 224

Andrewes, Lancelot (1555–1626), bishop of Winchester, IV. 228, 237 ff., 491, 494, 509; VII. 28, 139, 157 ff., 309, 310, 317, 333; VIII. 293, 294, 301; x. 359, 360; *Private Devotions*, IV. 238; VII. 43

Andrews, Alexander, XIV. 531; *The History of British Journalism*, XIV. 178, 184, 204

Andrews, Apology for the Life of Mrs Shamela, x. 6

Andrews, John (*fl.* 1615), IV. 473

Andrews, Joseph, in Fielding's novel, x. 24 ff.

Andrews, Thomas (1813–1885), XIV. 595

'Andrian, Solomon,' IX. 471

Andromache, in the *Iliad*, VIII. 50

Andromache, in Dryden's *Troilus and Cressida*, VIII. 29

Andromana, or The Merchant's Wife, VI. 451

Andromeda (a giant), II. 79

Andronicus, Livius, IX. 270

Andronicus Commenus, VI. 481

Androphilus, in *The Purple Island*, IV. 166

Androse, Richard (*fl.* 1569), IV. 441

Andrugio, in *Promos and Cassandra*, v. 120

Aneirin (Aneurin) (*fl.* 603?), *Gododin*, I. 248, 249, 461

Angantyr, x. 223, 224

Angel of Death, XI. 31

Angela, sister (St Beatrix), XIII. 178

Angelica, in Congreve's *Love for Love*, VIII. 151, 156

Angelica, in Farquhar's *Sir Harry Wildair*, VIII. 169

Angell, John (*fl.* 1758), x. 469

Angellier, Auguste, XI. 115, 438

Angelo, in *Measure for Measure*, v. 190

Angelo, in *The Virgin Martir*, VI. 54

Angelo, Michael, IV. 222, 223; VII. 176

Angels, The treatise of the Song of, II. 327

Anger, in *Confessio Amantis*, II. 147

Angevin reigns, the, XIV. 72

Angevins, the, VIII. 311

Angharad, in *The Misfortunes of Arthur*, v. 78

Angier of St Frideswide, II. 508

Angiolieri, Cecco, XIII. 118

Anglia, IX. 106

Anglican church, the, XII. 134, 275, 291, 299; XIII. 138

Anglican clergy, XI. 309

Anglicans, IX. 100

Angling, writers on, IV. 541

Anglo-Canadians, XIV. 345

Anglo-catholic movement, the, XIII. 435

Anglo-French law language, the, I. 407 ff.; VIII. 319

Anglo-French literature, XIV. 307

Anglo-Indian literature, XIV. 331 ff.

Anglo-Irish, the, XIV. 308

Anglomanie, the, x. 16

Anglo-Norman *chanson*, XIV. 67

Anglo-Norman works, II. 419 ff., 503 507 ff.; v. 38

Anglo-Normans, the, in Ireland, XIV. 306, 308

Anglo-Roman hierarchy, XII. 274

Anglo-Saxon chair, at Cambridge, XII. 344; at Oxford, IX. 413; XII. 344; XIV. 385

Anglo-Saxon Chronicle, XII. 344; XIV. 69

Anglo-Saxon language, I. 379 ff.; VII. 319

Angus, Archibald, 5th earl of (1449?–1514), 'Bell the Cat,' II. 259

Anian, strait of, IV. 78

Anicetus, in Gray's *Agrippina*, x. 119

Anima, in *Piers the Plowman* (also called Will, Reason, Love, Conscience), II. 19, 21, 22, 27, 28

Anima, in *Mind, Will and Understanding*, v. 52

Animalibus, De, II. 363

Anjou, Francis, duke of (formerly duke of Alençon), v. 341; VII. 191

Anlaf, I. 109, 144, 305

Anlaf Cuaran, I. 287

'Anna Matilda.' *See* Cowley, Hannah

Annalia Dubrensia, IV. 487

Annals and Magazines of Natural History, The, XIV. 288, 565

Annals of Agriculture, XI. 72

Annals of England, IV. 424

Annals of the Fine Arts, XIV. 539

Annals of the Four Masters, XII. 360, 518 XIV. 309

Annan, Dumfriesshire, XIII. 2, 3

Annand, James (1843–1906), XIV. 533

Annand, William (1633–1689), IX. 545

Annas, in the York plays, v. 46

Anne, in *The Misfortunes of Arthur*, v. 78

Anne, mastres, friend of John Skelton, III. 71

Anne, queen of Great Britain, IV. 251, 433; VIII. 96, 113, 220, 261, 373; IX. 30, 44, 72, 78, 96, 97, 103, 113, 124, 130, 131, 139, 150 ff., 155, 160, 161, 169, 175, 177, 180, 200, 202, 205, 208, 216, 217, 219, 222, 228, 231, 232, 309, 394, 395, 407, 408; x. 67 ff., 73, 139, 196, 352, 374, 502; XI. 370, 372; XII. 488; XIII. 300, 453; XIV. 212, 383, 463

Anne, queen, in *Richard III*, VI. 129; VIII. 123

Anne Boleyn, 2nd queen of Henry VIII III. 16, 26, 167, 168, 175, 332, 336, 337; v. 103; VI. 335; x. 27; XII. 477; XIII. 261

Anne of Bohemia, II. 62, 170

Anne of Cleves, III. 175

Anne of Denmark, queen consort of James I, IV. 134, 143; VI. 83, 337

339 ff., 348, 350, 361, 366; VII. 79, 205; XIV. 93; companies of, VI. 104, 254, 258
Annesley, Arthur, earl of Anglesea (1614–1686), VII. 229
Annesley claimant, the, XIII. 426
Annet, Peter (1693–1769), IX. 288, 504; *Resurrection of Jesus examined*, IX. 294
Annibal, in George Eliot's *The Spanish Gypsy*, XIII. 398
Annie of Lochryan, I. 300
Annual Register, X. 357, 474, 482, 483; XI. 145, 324; XII. 138; XIV. 228
Annual Review, The, XIV. 98
Annus Mirabilis primus et secundus, VIII. 10
'Ἄνοδος, *pseud.* of Mary E. Coleridge, XIII. 183
Anselm, St (1033–1109), archbishop of Canterbury, I. 16, 128, 149, 151, 154, 162, 163, 186, 217, 222, 224, 228, 231, 234, 355, 446; II. 365; XII. 455; XIV. 113
Anson, George, baron Anson (1697–1762), XIV. 243, 550
Anson, Sir William Reynell (1843–1914), XIV. 485, 487
Anster, John (1793–1867), XIV. Add. 3
Anstey, Christopher (1724–1805), IX. 481; XI. 158, 160, 172, 424; XII. 7, 120; *New Bath Guide*, XI. 173
Anstey, John (d. 1819), XI. 424
Anstis, John (1669–1744), IX. 355, 531
Anstruther, Fife, XI. 243
Anstruther, lady Margaret, IX. 369
Answerall, lady, in Swift's *Complete Collection of...Conversation*, IX. 106
Antarctic exploration, XIV. 245
Ante Crucem Virgo Stabat, II. 383
Antenorius, in *Argenis*, IV. 259
Anthea (Herrick's), VII. 6, 9
Anthony, Now-Now, in *The Gentle Craft*, III. 370
Anthropological society, the, XII. 350
Anti-christ, VI. 374
Antichrist, in Dunbar's *Vision*, II. 256
Antichrist, in *Piers the Plowman*, II. 28
Antidote against Melancholy, IV. 536; VII. 512
Antigone, XII. 68
Antigone, in *Phoenissae*, V. 71, 72
Antigonus, in *The Humorous Lieutenant*, VI. 122
Antigonus, in *The Winter's Tale*, V. 206
Anti-Jacobin, The, XI. 39 ff., 157, 392; XII. 150; XIII. 260; XIV. 194, 214
Anti-Jacobin Review, The, XI. 392; XII. 526
Antioch, XII. 107
Antiochus, Asiatic king, in *Believe as you List*, VI. 147 ff.
Antiochus, in *The Tatler*, IX. 38
Antipodes, the, XIV. 255
Anti-projector, The, IV. 308, 509
Antiquaries, in Stuart times, VII. 232–258, 460 ff.
Antiquaries, in Tudor times, III. 313–338, 527 ff.
Antiquaries, Scottish society of, IX. 372; XII. 349

Antiquaries, society of (founded 1572), IV. 55; VII. 305
Antiquaries of London, society of (founded 1717–18), IX. 352, 357, 358, 531; XII. 506, 510
Anti-Romish propaganda in stage plays, VI. 150
'Anti-Sejanus,' X. 401
Anton, Robert (*fl.* 1616), IV. 516, 520, 533; *Moriomachia*, IV. 359
Antoninus, in *The Virgin Martir*, VI. 154
Antoninus Bassianus Caracalla, VI. 481
Antonio, in *Albumazar*, VI. 323
Antonio, in Otway's *Venice Preserv'd*, VIII. 94, 184
Antonio, in *The Case is Altered*, V. 321
Antonio, in *The Coxcombe*, VI. 133
Antonio, in *The Dutchesse of Malfy*, VI. 181, 182
Antonio, in *The Merchant of Venice*, V. 183, 355
Antonio, in *The Tempest*, V. 206
Antonio de Eslava, *Noches de Invierno*, VIII. 126
Antonius, in *A Dialogue...against the fever Pestilence*, III. 108
Antonius, in *Ignoramus*, VI. 322
Antony, in *Antony and Cleopatra*, V. 199
Antony, in *Julius Caesar*, V. 197
Antony, in *Romeo and Juliet*, V. 182
Antony, Life of, Athanasius's, I. 75
Antrobus, Dorothy, mother of Thomas Gray, X. 116
Antrobus, Mary, X. 116, 121, 127
Antrobus, Robert, X. 116, 117
Antrobus, William, X. 116
Antwerp, II. 319, 320, 329, 330; III. 18, 43, 208; IV. 69, 266, 274, 316, 324, 396, 402, 403; V. 90, 113, 114; VII. 460; VIII. 141; XII. 365; XIII. 433
Antwerp, Plantin Museum at, I. 72
Antwerpe, Tragical Historie of the citie of, IV. 324
Apelles, IV. 14
Apennines, the, XII. 63
Apicius Caelius, IX. 478
Apius and Virginia. See R. B.
Apocrypha, the. See under Bible
Apollinaris (Laodicean bishop), V. 5
Apollo, II. 78; IV. 196; VI. 368; VII. 370; VIII. 204; IX. 257; XIII. 59, 191, 213
Apollo, in Keats's *The Fall of Hyperion*, XII. 80, 86
Apollo, in Suckling's *Session of the Poets*, VII. 274
Apollo press, XI. 325
Apollodorus, III. 86
Apollonius, hermit, I. 74
Apollonius Rhodius, XI. 426
Apollonius of Tyre, in *Confessio Amantis*, II. 149, 152
Apollonius of Tyre, I. 135, 151
Apostolic Fathers, the, X. 353; XII. 501
Apostolical Constitutions, IX. 221
Apothecaries' company, the, XIV. 286

Apperley, Charles James (*pseud.* Nimrod, 1779–1843), XIV. 216, 232, 542, 598; *Life of a Sportsman, The,* XIV. 233; *Memoirs of...John Mytton,* XIV. 233

Appian, IV. 435

Applebee, John, IX. 16, 22. 433

Appleton, Charles Edward Cutts Birch (1841–1879), XIV. 533

Appletree, Thomas, in Farquhar's *Recruiting Officer,* VIII. 171

Appolyn of Thyre, King, II. 324, 325, 484

Aprile, in Browning's *Paracelsus,* XIII. 57, 59

Apsley, Lucy, VIII. 270

Apthorpe, East (1753–1816), X. 507; *Letters on the Prevalence of Christianity,* X. 308

Apuleius, I. 135; IV. 9, 242, 414, 435; VI. 82; VII. 77, 370, 503

Apuleius, in *Loves Maistresse,* VI. 103

Apuleius, *The Golden Ass,* XIV. 311

Aquila, IX. 330

Aquilegiensis, Laurence, *Practica sive Usus Dictaminis* ('Complete Letter Writer'), II. 363

Aquinas, St Thomas, I. 200, 210 ff.; II. 350, 363; III. 4, 9, 19, 416; VII. 277, 279, 312, 504, 510; XII. 201; *Summa,* II. 365; IV. 272

Aquitania, in *The Masque of Blacknesse,* VI. 342

Ara Fortunae, VI. 319, 474

Arabella, in *The Pickwick Papers,* XIII. 314

Arabi pasha, XII. 342

Arabia, VI. 35; XII. 342; XIV. 252

Arabian learning, I. 153

Arabian Nights, The, I. 286; III. 485; IX. 106; XI. 161, 291, 477; XII. 342, 499; XIII. 124, 305; XIV. 338

Arabian tales, XI. 290, 374

Arabians, II. 362, 365

Arabic chair, at Cambridge, IX. 413

Arabic language, VII. 317 ff., 491

Arabic language and literature, IX. 291; XI. 290, 291, 355; XII. 341, 342, 362; XIV. 416, 457, 458

Arabin, dean, Trollope's, XIII. 422

Arabs, the, XIV. 238, 252, 253

Arachne, in Ovid's *Metamorphoses,* IX. 160

Arachne and Pallas, IX. 115

Aragon, V. 183

Aram, Eugene (1704–1759), IX. 574; XII. 418

Aram, Eugene, lord Lytton's, XIII. 418

Arator, I. 76

Arbaces, in *A King and no King,* VI. 120, 127

Arber, Edward (1836–1912), IV. 69, 70, 110, 388; VIII. 182, 422; XI. 311, 339, 466, 467, 470, 471; XII. 357, 515

Arblay, Alexandre G. P. d', X. 63, 261

Arblay, Frances Burney, Madame d' (1752–1840), X. 46, 63 ff. (main entry), **135**, 150, 254, 259 ff. (main entry), 267,

424, 473, 493, *also see* Add.; XI. 289, 296, 344, 349, 354, 458, 473; XII. 133, 447

Camilla, X. 64, 66, 261; XII. 231

Cecilia, X. 63, 64, 66

Diary and Letters, X. 63, 65, 260, 261

Early Diary, X. 260

Evelina, X. 15, 64 ff., 259; XI. 365; XII. 233

Wanderer, The, X. 63, 64, 66

Arbury, Warwickshire, X. 113

Arbuthnet, Alexander (d. 1585), printer, IV. 412

Arbuthnot, Alexander (1538–1583), III. 137, 498

Arbuthnot, Archibald (*fl.* 1746), IX. 563

Arbuthnot, Charles, IX. 469

Arbuthnot, George, IX. 133

Arbuthnot, John (1667–1735), IX. 72, 78, 96, 98, 124, 127, 129 ff. (main entry), 152, 161, 163, 171, 220, 249, 445 ff., 452, 466 ff., 481, 498; XII. 168

Account of the...death of Dr Woodward, IX. 132

Art of Political Lying, IX. 131, 136

Brief account of Mr John Ginglicutt's Treatise, IX. 133, 138, 464

Essay concerning the effects of Air..., IX. 133, 138

Essay concerning the nature of Ailments, IX. 133, 138

Examination of Dr Woodward's Account of the Deluge, IX. 129

History of John Bull, IX. 131, 133, 137

Humble Petition of the Colliers, IX. 132

John Bull in his Senses, IX. 131

John Bull still in his Senses (and *Appendix*), IX. 131

Know Yourself, IX. 133, 138

Law is a Bottomless Pit, IX. 130; XIV. 212

Lewis Baboon turned Honest, IX. 131

Miscellaneous Works, IX. 133

On the Usefulness of Mathematical Learning, IX. 130, 138

Reasons humbly offered by the Company ...of Upholders, IX. 132

Sermon...at the Mercat Cross, IX. 130, 138

Tables of...Measures, Weights and Coins, IX. 130, 132

Arbuthnott, Robert, 2nd viscount (d. 1682), IX. 129

Arcadia, VI. 11, 317, 318, 341, 364, 368; X. 179; XI. 142, 287

Arcadia and Arcadianism, III. 265, 340, 348, 352, 353, 356, 357 ff., 367, 370

Arcadian shepherds, in *Piers Plainnes seaven yeres Prentiship,* III. 367

Arcana Aulica; or Walsingham's Manual, VII. 518

Archaeologia, IX. 358, 530, 531; XII. 506

Archaeologia Cambrensis, XII. 506

Archaeological association, XII. 349

Archaeological association, British, Journal, XII. 506

Archaeological Journal, XII. 506

Archangel, IX. 240

Archas, in *The Loyal Subject*, VI. 122, 130

Archdall, Mervyn (1723–1791), XII. 349

Archdeacon, Daniel (*fl.* 1588), IV. 453

Archer, in Farquhar's *Beaux' Stratagem*, VIII. 172

Archer or Frizer, or Ingram, murderer of Marlowe. *See* Frizer

Archer, Thomas (1554–1630?), VII. 344

Archer, Thomas (1894), XIII. 532

Archer, William (1856–1924), VI. 266, 269; XI. 447, 453; XIII. 513

Archer-Hind, Richard Dacre (1849–1910), XII. 333, 479

Archibald, Raymond Clare, XIII. 470

Archie o' Cawfield, II. 415

Archimago, in *The Faerie Queene*, III. 231

Architectural Magazine, The, XIV. 149

Architecture, Anglo-Norman, I. 155, 222, 223

Architecture, Elizabethan and Jacobean, V. 372

Architrenius, or Arch-Mourner, of Jean de Hauteville, I. 193

Archombrotus, in *Argenis*, IV. 258, 259

Archon, lord, in *Oceana*, VII. 299, 300

Archytas, I. 279

Arcite, in *Palamon and Arcyte*, VI. 299

Arcite, in *The Knightes Tale*, XIII. 123

Arcite, in *The Two Noble Kinsmen*, V. 256

Arctic regions, XIV. 241, 245, 248, 358

Arctic voyages, IV. 76

Ardagh, VII. 318; X. 197

Ardelia, in *The Dukes Mistris*, VI. 200

'Ardelia' (Winchilsea, Anne, countess of), IX. 169

Arden, forest of, III. 355; V. 192; VI. 27; XIII. 382

Arden, Mary, V. 167; XIV. 307

Arden, Mrs, VII. 55

Arden, Richard Pepper, baron Alvanley (1745–1804), XIV. 115, 127

Arden of Feversham, V. 162, 237, 240 ff., 324, 441, 443; VI. 95; X. 73, 436; XII. 186

Ardens, Radulphus, I. 221

Areopagus, the, VII. 140

Arethusa, in Keats's *Endymion*, XII. 82

Aretine, in Jonson's *Volpone*, VII. 274

Aretino, Leonardo, II. 325; IV. 441; *Poliscene*, V. 101

Aretino, Pietro, IV. 322

Aretino, in *The Unfortunate Traveller*, III. 366

Arfeville, Nicolas d', III. 156

Argalia, in Chamberlayne's *Pharonnida*, VII. 75

Argall, Anne, IV. 141

Argall, Thomas, IV. 141

Argante, in Layamon's *Brut*, I. 235, 236, 265, 266

Argemone, in Kingsley's *Yeast*, XIII. 360; XIV. 84

Argensola, Bartolomeo de, VI. 139

Argensola, Bartolomeo de (the younger), VIII. 129

Argentile, in *Albion's England*, III. 357; IV. 136

Argentine, Richarde (d. 1568), IV. 447, 448

Argogastis, XIV. 303

Argonauts, the, IV. 62

Argus, Arabella, XI. 477; *Adventures of a Donkey*, XI. 383; *Juvenile Spectator*, XI. 383

Argyll, Elizabeth, duchess of. *See* Gunning, Elizabeth

Argyll, dukes of. *See* Campbell, George Douglas; Campbell, John

Argyll, marquis of. *See* Campbell, Archibald

Argyll commission (Scottish schools), XIV. 421

Argyllshire, XIII. 431

Ariadne, X. 199

Ariadne, Titian's, XIV. 171

Ariana, mistress (Etherege's), VIII. 138

Arianism, IX. 295, 297; X. 360, 362, 371, 372, 377 ff., 384 ff.

Ariel, in *The Tempest*, V. 207, 317; VII. 3; VIII. 28, 225; XII. 196, 220; XIII. 62

Arimanes, spirits of, in Byron's *Manfred*, XII. 47

Ariodante and Genevora, V. 102, 116

Arion, XIII. 50

Ariosto, Ludovico, III. 23, 176, 204, 210 229 ff., 236, 244, 262, 305; IV. 23, 24, 196, 441, 540; V. 116, 132, 191, 220; VII. 74, 78, 271; VIII. 22; IX. 338, 481; X. 221, 234, 241, 435; XI. 157; XII. 3, 80; *Orlando Furioso*, III. 230 ff., 236; V. 102, 137; IX. 61; *Gli Suppositi*, V. 71, 114

Ariosto (trans.), XII. Add.

'Aristarch,' an, IX. 191

Aristarchus, XII. 332

Aristides, X. 154; XIII. 182

Aristippus, in *Damon and Pithias*, V. 118

Aristophanes, III. 20; IV. 526; V. 22; VI. 18, 24, 79, 315, 322, 327, 352, 362, 363; VIII. 38, 58, 164; IX. 336; X. 25, 34, 53, 415; XI. 392; XII. 309, 324, 325, 329 ff., 480, 483 ff., 488 ff., 494, *also see* Add.; XIII. 81, 82, 175, 445

Birds, XII. 329

Εἰρήνη or *Pax*, VI. 294

Plutus, VI. 25, 294

Wasps, The, VI. 25

Aristophanes, in D'Avenant's *First Day's Entertainment*, VIII. 117

Aristophanic comedy, XIV. 13

Aristotle, I. 153, 185, 187, 204, 205, 210, 212, 213; II. 21, 129, 186, 201, 207, 231, 301, 350, 354, 360 ff., 370, 371; III. 6, 20, 23, 50, 109, 233, 291, 305, 416, 420, 425, 430; IV. 3, 24, 269, 271, 273 ff., 286, 287, 291, 298, 430, 521; V. 65, 167, 172, 204, 206, 214, 295 ff.; VI. 6, 225, 232, 296; VII. 182, 228, 261, 265, 267, 277, 278, 282, 288, 302 ff., 323, 376, 377; VIII. 8, 29, 170, 203, 221, 277, 278, 287, 289, 291, 329, 350; IX. 51, 59, 60, 64, 383, 386, 562; X. 137, 514; XI. 17,

Aristotle
  134; XII. 211, 230, 311, 476, 480 ff.,
  484 ff., 488, 489, 492, 494, *also see* Add.;
  XIII. 152, 167, 169, 172, 312; XIV. 9, 16,
  23, 140, 398, 473, 475
  Constitution of Athens, XII. 340
  Ethics, I. 204, 213; III. 430; IV. 5, 335,
  414, 428, 435; VI. 233; XII. 334
  History of Animals, I. 199
  Metaphysics, I. 201; II. 318
  Nichomachean Ethics, XII. 520
  Organon, I. 187, 207; IV. 276
  Physics, I. 201, 204, 211, 212
  Poetics, V. 70; VI. 8; VII. 265; VIII. 375,
  376; XII. 334
  Politics, I. 213; IV. 5, 435; XII. 333, 334
  Rhetoric, IV. 335, 347; XI. 16; XII. 328,
  331
Aristotle, Aldine edition, III. 5; IV. 422
Aristotle, in *The Palice of Honour*, II. 260
Aristotle, The Letter of Alexander to, II. 80
Aristotelian society, XIV. 39
Arithmetic, in *The Passetyme of Pleasure*,
  II. 225
Arius, IV. 214
Arkinholm, II. 113
'Arley,' Della Cruscan poet, XI. 177
Arley Regis, Worcester, I. 234
Arlington, 1st earl (1618–1685). *See* Ben-
  net, Henry
Armada, the, III. 188, 211, 244; IV. 136,
  142; V. 77, 81, 136, 309, 345, 361; VI.
  27, 53, 92, 174; VII. 157; XIII. 135, 136
Armado, don, in *Love's Labour's Lost*, V.
  178, 239
Armageddon, XIII. 153
Armagh, VII. 139, 301, 318; XIV. 309, 321
Armenia, II. 13, 79
Armida, in *Orlando Furioso*, III. 230
Armin, Robert (1564?–1612?), VI. 273,
  452
  Foole upon Foole, VI. 218
  Italian Taylor and his Boy, The, VI. 218
  Nest of Ninnies, A, IV. 532; VI. 218
  Two Maids of More-clacke, The, VI. 217
Arminianism, VII. 437; X. 367, 377, 381
Arminius, I. 20; VIII. 291, 292
Armorican Bretons, I. 256
Armour, Jean, XI. 222
Armstrong, Cecil Ferard, XIII. 513;
  Shakespeare to Shaw, XI. 269
Armstrong, Edmund John (1841–1865),
  XIV. 567
Armstrong, G. F. Savage- (1845–1906),
  XIV. 567
Armstrong, John (1709–1779), X. 138, 147,
  148, 452; *Art of Preserving Health, The*,
  X. 148; XIII. 200; *Economy of Love*, X.
  148; *Epistle to Wilkes*, X. 148
Armstrong, Johnny, in *Pendennis*, XIII.
  291
*Armys, The Buke of the Law of, or Buke
  of Bataillis*, II. 284
Armytage, Mrs, Mrs Gore's, XII. 246
Arnall, William (1715?–1741?), IX. 433

Arne, Thomas Augustine (1710–1778),
  VIII. 426; X. 109, 199, 425, 426, 429,
  433, 447
Arngosk, The Lady of, II. 411
Arno river, XIII. 136, 149
Arnold, A. S., XIII. 470
Arnold, Sir Edwin (1832–1904), XIII. 194,
  203, 498; XIV. 191, 192, 574, 575; *He
  and She*, XIII. 201; *The Light of Asia*,
  XIII. 200; XIV. 340
Arnold, Fanny, XIII. 103
Arnold, Frances Lucy, born Wightman,
  XIII. 87
Arnold, Frank Bishop, XIII. 513
Arnold, Rev. Frederick, XIV. 493
Arnold, Frederick Octavius, XIV. 536
Arnold, Matthew (1822–1888), I. 249, 251,
  254, 274, 275; II. 107, 180; IV. 132, 135,
  139; VI. 57; IX. 31, 169; X. 361; XI. 136,
  161, 388, 406, 408, 411, 438; XII. 77,
  108, 154, 177, 178, 207, 208, 297, 384,
  392, 402, 406, 527; XIII. 85 ff. (main
  entry), 147 ff., 155, 159, 160, 174, 183,
  188 ff., 221, 223, 486 ff. (main entry),
  557, *also see* Add. 2; XIV. 141, 144, 147,
  159, 172, 180, 191, 304, 306, 307, 350,
  351, 420, 422 ff., 432, 433, 453, 601, 603
  Balder Dead, XIII. 89, 94
  Cromwell, XIII. 87
  Culture and Anarchy, XIII. 88, 101; XIV.
  425
  Democracy, XIII. 88
  Discourses in America, XIII. 87, 88, 99
  Dover Beach, XIII. 89, 96
  Empedocles on Etna, XIII. 89, 91, 95
  Essays in Criticism, XIII. 98, 100, 101
  Forsaken Merman, The, XIII. 91, 251
  Fragment of an 'Antigone,' The, XIII.
  90
  French Eton, A, XIII. 88
  Friendship's Garland, XIII. 101, 451
  Geist's Grave, XIII. 89
  God and the Bible, XIII. 101
  Heine's Grave, XIII. 89
  'Joubert,' XIII. 100
  Last Essays on Church and Religion,
  XIII. 101
  Last words on Translating Homer, XIII.
  103
  Letters, XIII. 85, 94, 99, 103
  Literature and Dogma, XIII. 101
  Memorial Verses, XIII. 94
  Merope, a Tragedy, VII. 122; XIII. 89,
  91, 95
  Mixed Essays, XIII. 88, 99
  Mycerinus, XIII. 90
  New Poems, XIII. 89, 95
  New Sirens, The, XIII. 90
  'Numbers,' XIII. 99
  Obermann, XIII. 98
  Obermann Once More, XIII. 89, 94
  On Translating Homer, XI. 90; XIII.
  88, 98
  Poems (1853), XIV. 139
  Poems (1854), XIII. 98

Arnold, Matthew
Poems, Second Series, XIII. 89
Popular Education of France, XIII. 88;
XIV. 422
Reports on Elementary Schools, XIII. 88
Requiescat, XIII. 96
Resignation, XII. 220; XIII. 90
Rugby Chapel, XIII. 89, 96
St Paul and Protestantism, XIII. 101
Scholar-Gipsy, The, XIII. 89, 92, 93, 96,
251
Schools and Universities on the Continent,
XIII. 88; XIV. 422
Self-Dependence, XIII. 94, 97
Separation, XIII. 89
Sick King in Bokhara, The, XIII. 90,
91
Sohrab and Rustum, XIII. 89, 92, 94, 95,
251
Southern Night, A, XIII. 89, 96, 251
'Speech at Eton, A,' XIII. 99
Stanzas from the Grande Chartreuse, XIII.
95
Stanzas in Memory of the Author of
'Obermann,' XIII. 93, 94
Strayed Reveller, The, XIII. 89, 90, 252
Study of Celtic Literature, The, XIII. 88,
98, 100
Summer Night, A, XIII. 94, 251
Thyrsis, VII. 114; XIII. 89, 92, 96, 102
To a Gipsy Child, XIII. 90
Tristram and Iseult, XIII. 93, 251
Westminster Abbey, XIII. 89, 96
Arnold, Richard (d. 1521), Chronicle, II.
320, 329, 484; III. 532
Arnold, Samuel (1740–1802), X. 425, 428,
429
Arnold, Samuel James (1774–1852), XIII.
517
Arnold, Thomas (1795–1842), I. 167; VII.
152; X. 355; XII. 153, 259, 287–288, 292,
294, 302 ff. (main entry), 309, 318, 321,
338, 464, 474; XIII. 86, 103 ff., 109, 370,
433; XIV. 70, 409, 411, 413, 414, 594,
601, 603; History of Rome, XII. 303, 304,
339; History of the later Roman Com-
monwealth, XII. 303; Life and Corre-
spondence, XII. 303, 304, 320
Arnold, Thomas (junior) (1823–1900), XII.
504
Arnold, William Delafield (1828–1859),
XIV. 575; Oakfield, XIV. 338, 339
Arnold, William Thomas (1852–1904), XII.
405, 474; XIV. 533; Roman System of
Provincial Administration, XII. 304
Arnold's Magazine, XIV. 539
Arqua, IV. 429
Arran, isles of, XIV. 312
Arrêts d'Amour, Les, VIII. 59
Arrivall, The History of the (1471), II. 302
Arrogance, in Mirour de l'Omme, II. 140
Arrowsmith, Reformation (1673), VIII. 26
Ars Moriendi, V. 53
Arsilius (Yong's), IV. 122
Art, in Cowley's The Muse, VII. 65

Art and Poetry, XIII. 111
Art de bien vivre et de bien mourir, L', II.
329
Art of good living and dying, The, II. 324,
328, 329
Artaban, in La Calprenède's Cléopâtre,
VIII. 25
Artegall, in The Faerie Queene, II. 234;
III. 231, 234, 236; VII. 209
Arthour and Merlin, I. 269, 317, 399, 467
Arthur, Death of, I. 190. See, also, under
Morte
Arthur, king, X. 231; XII. 13, 354
Arthur, Kyng (Southey's), XI. 422
Arthur, prince, in The Faerie Queene, III.
230, 232 ff., 237
Arthur, prince, in King John, V. 185
Arthur, prince (1486–1502), son of Henry
VII, III. 6, 8; VI. 332, 333
Arthur, Tennyson's, XIII. 37, 38
Arthur, The Dethe of, begynyng at Cassa-
belaun, II. 308
Arthur, The Misfortunes of, V. 78, 79
Arthur and the Arthurian legend, I. 70,
133, 148, 158, 169, 170, 177, 198, 223,
235 ff., 243–276 (main entry), 279, 284,
286, 296, 309, 311 ff., 326, 336, 342,
350, 351, 461 ff., 467, also see Add.;
II. 112, 115, 116, 118 ff., 181, 184, 228,
230, 234, 307, 337 ff., 428; III. 359; IV
67; V. 10, 108, 250; X. 228; XIII. 36;
XIV. 304, 306
See, also, under the separate title of the
Arthurian romances, Wace, Layamon,
etc.
Arthur and King Cornwall, King, II. 414
Arthur of Little Britain, II. 322, 339
Arthure, Gret Gest of, II. 116
Arthurian ballads, I. 464
Articles, Ten, III. 13
Articles, the XXXIX, XII. 260, 296
Articles of Grievance and Oppression,VI.275
Articuli ad Novas Narrationes (1561), VIII.
465, 466
Artotrogos, in Miles Gloriosus, V. 106
Arundel, earls of. See Howard, Philip;
Howard, Thomas
Arundel, Thomas, archbishop(1353–1414),
II. 59, 62, 67, 68, 154, 348; III. 42
Arundel, William, earl of (1417–1487),
Caxton's patron, II. 314
Arundel, the horse in Sir Beves, I. 292
Arviragus, in Layamon's Brut, I. 237
Arviragus, in The Franklin's Tale, II. 184
Arwaker, Edmund (d. 1730), VII. 405;
VIII. 411
Aryan origin of ballads, II. 417
As I came in by Edinburgh town, IX. 363
Asbies mortgage, V. 219
Asbjörnsen, Peter Christen, XI. 491
Ascanius, VIII. 70
Ascapart the giant, in Sir Beves, I. 293, 343
Ascensio, V. 12
Ascension island, XIV. 242
Ascham, Anthony (fl. 1553), IV. 542

Ascham, Roger (1515–1568), III. 290 ff., 308, 310, 311, 317, 318, 327, 341, 348, 419, 421, 425, 431 ff., 438, 444, 446, 447, 454, 526, 549; IV. 6, 7, 276, 320, 345, 390; V. 350, 394; VI. 378, 480, 492; VII. 315, 329, 335; X. 177, 184, 469
  De Imitatione, III. 433
  Report and Discourse of the affairs of Germany, III. 432
  Scholemaster, The, II. 213; III. 311, 341, 433 ff.; IV. 344, 397; VI. 295; IX. 55; XII. 488; XIII. 104
  Toxophilus, III. 308, 433, 445; IV. 16
Aschillus, in *The Misfortunes of Arthur*, V. 78
Ascolot, maid of, I. 313
Ascue, Sir G., VIII. 218
Ascyltus, IX. 266
Asgill, John (1659–1738), IX. 11
Ashantee, XIV. 254
Ashburnham, John (1603–1671), VII. 449
Ashburnham, lady, IX. 125
Ashburton, Devonshire, XI. 39
Ashby, George (d. 1475), II. 209, 469; *Active Policy of a Prince*, II. 210
Ashby-de-la-Zouch, VII. 335; XI. 340
Ashe, St George (1658?–1718), IX. 166
Ashe, Simeon (d. 1662), *Intelligence*, VII. 351
Ashe, Thomas, *Carolina* (1682), IV. 453
Ashe, Thomas (1836–1889), XI. 412, 415, 416; XIII. 194, 498; *The Sorrows of Hypsipyle*, XIII. 206
Ashfield, dame, in Morton's *Speed the Plough*, XI. 281
Ashford, Kent, III. 395; VII. 341
Ashley, Sir Anthony (1551–1627), IV. 453
Ashley, A. Evelyn M., XIV. 505
Ashley, Sir John, IV. 383
Ashley, William James, XIV. 477
Ashley-Cooper, Frederick Samuel, XIV. 545
Ashmole, Elias (1617–1692), VII. 369; VIII. 247; IX. 355, 413, 531; XIV. 285, 558; *Antiquities of Berkshire*, IX. 353; *Theatrum Chemicum*, II. 211, 212
Ashton, John, XI. 475; XII. 418; XIV. 540
Ashton, Lucy, in Scott's *Bride of Lammermoor*, XII. 22
Ashton, Thomas (d. 1578), III. 428, 429; V. 103; VII. 337
Ashton, Thomas (1716–1775), X. 117, 119, 123, 243, 251
Ashton, Sir William, in Scott's *Bride of Lammermoor*, XII. 22
Ashworth, Caleb (1722–1775), X. 384
Ashworth, John (1813–1875), XIII. 560
Asia, XI. 16, 190; XII. 66; XIV. 246, 247, 252, 457, 458
Asia Minor, V. 37
Asiatic society, Greek, XII. 506
Asiatic society of Bengal, XII. 352; XIV. 334, 337
Aske, Christopher, Kingsley's, XIII. 366
Aske, Robert, Kingsley's, XIII. 366

Askesian society, XIV. 287
Aslackton, Nottinghamshire, III. **32**
Asloan MS., II. 478
Asolo, XIII. 61, 62, 84
'Aspasia' (Lady Elizabeth Hastings (1682–1739), IX. 38
Aspatia, in *The Maides Tragedy*, VI. 120, 123, 126
Asper, in *Every Man out of his Humour*, VI. 17, 39
Aspland, Robert (1782–1845), XII. 428, 465
Aspley, William (*fl.* 1588–1637), IV. 393 ff.
Assaye, battle of, XII. 98
Asser (d. 909?), bishop of Sherborne, I. 89 ff., 101, 105; *Aelfredi regis res gestae*, IV. 397
Asses, feast of, V. 8
Assisi, I. 200, 210, 364
Assmann, I. 124
Association for the protection of the queen's person, V. 345
Assoucy, Charles Coypeau d', IX. 256
Assumptio Mariae, I. 232, 458, 459
Assurbanipal, Annals of, XII. 499
Assyria, II. 296; XII. 342, 477
Assyrian host, in *Ezechias*, VI. 298
Assyrians, IV. 31
Astarte, in Byron's *Manfred*, XII. 47, 393, 395, 396
Astell, Mary (1668–1731), IX. 244, 498; *Serious proposal to the Ladies*, IX. 404, 569
'Asteria' (lady Luxborough). See Knight, Henrietta
Asthall, I. 126
Astley, John (d. 1595), IV. 444, 540
Astley, Sir John Dugdale (1828–1894), XIV. 540
Astley, Philip (1742–1814), XIII. 264, 265
Aston, colonel, VIII. 211
Aston, Edward, IV. 442
Aston, John (*fl.* 1382), II. 61
Aston, lady Gertrude, IV. 194
Aston, R., *Placita Latine Rediviva* (1661), VIII. 467
Aston, Walter, baron Aston (1584–1639), IV. 173, 176, 179, 184, 188, 216
Astragon, in D'Avenant's *Gondibert*, VII. 71
Astrology and occultism, VII. 508 ff.
Astronomia, in *Technogamia*, VI. 323
Astronomy, in *The Passetyme of Pleasure*, II. 225
Astrophel (Waller's), VII. 54
Astrophell (*i.e.* Sidney), IV. 116
Astrophil, VIII. 61
Astrophill, V. 349
Atalantis Major, IX. 13
Até, in *Locrine*, V. 84
Ateukin, in *James IV*, V. 138
Athanase, in Shelley's *Prince Athanase*, XII. 61
Athanasian controversy, X. 362
Athanasian creed, VIII. 42; X. 360

Athanasius, I. 74, 75; II. 79, 86; XI. 287;
 Festal Letters, XII. 341
Atheist's Tragedie, The (ballad), V. 143
Athelstan. *See* Aethelstan
Athelston, I. 287, 467
Athenaeum, The, IX. 106; XII. 349, 359,
 365, 437; XIII. 54, 69; XIV. 144, 145,
 171, 174, 193, 200, 364, 530, 531, 533,
 534
Athenaeus, VII. 311; XII. 325; *Deipno-
 sophia*, VI. 102
Athenais, in *The Emperour of the East*, VI.
 158, 163
Athenian democracy, XII. 311, 312
Athenian Gazette (Dunton's), IX. 5
Athenian Letters, XI. 475
Athenian Mercury (Dunton's), IX. 5, 34,
 41, 92
Athenians, the, IX. 223; XIV. 120
Athens, IV. 1, 270, 335; V. 64; VI. 308;
 XII. 32, 72, 312, 313; XIII. 129, 133, 135,
 136, 256; XIV. 122, 205, 211
 Parthenon, XII. 340
 Temple of Theseus, XII. 39
Athens, in *The Anatomy of Wit*, III. 345
Atherstone, Edwin (1788–1872), XII. 129,
 413; *The Fall of Nineveh*, XII. 128
Aðils, king of the Svear, I. 25 ff.
Athlone, X. 196, 197
Atholl, 3rd duke of. *See* Murray, John
Athos, mount, XIV. 252
Atkins, John Black, XIV. 535
Atkins, Samuel, VIII. 257
Atkinson, Henry George, XIV. 476
Atkinson, Joseph, *The Mutual Deception*,
 X. 429
Atkinson, Robert, XII. 361, 362, 515
Atkinson, Thomas (1600–1639), VI. 470
Atkyns, Sir Robert (1647–1711), *Gloces-
 tershire*, IX. 353, 531
Atkynson, William (d. 1509), translator of
 Imitatio Christi, II. 321
Atlámal, in the *Edda*, I. 21
Atlante, in *Orlando Furioso*, III. 231
Atlantic, the, IV. 68; XI. 190
Atlantic ocean, XIII. 88
Atlantis, XI. 190
Atlantis (of Plato), IV. 73
Atlas, in *Pleasure Reconciled*, VI. 359 ff.
Atlas, sign of, on the Globe theatre, VI.
 256
Atlas, The, XII. 444
Atlay, James Beresford (1860–1913), XIV.
 500, 507, 508, 511
Atli, the hall of, XIII. 126
Atossa, in Pope's *Characters of Women*,
 IX. 82, 89
Atreus, in *Thyestes*, VI. 301
Atropos, in *Filostrato e Panfila*, V. 62
Attendant spirit, the, in *Comus*, VII. 113
Atterbury, Francis (1662–1732), VII. 410,
 444; VIII. 394; IX. 131, 147, 153, 176,
 196, 234, 333, 334, 337, 340, 425, 525;
 X. 351 ff., 515, 517; XIV. 61; *Discourse
 on the death of the Lady Cutts*, X. 352

Attercliffe, IX. 393
Attercliffe academy, X. 386
Attey, John (c. 1622), IV. 463
Attic democracy, the, XIV. 134
Attic drama, V. 1, 5; VI. 232. *See, also,*
 Greek drama
Attic dramatists, IX. 330
Attic eloquence, XI. 13
Attic idiom, XII. 328
Attic law, XII. 327
Attic orators, XII. 329
Attic prose, XIII. 99
Attic tragedy, XIII. 90
Atticus, T. Pomponius, IX. 198
'Atticus,' in Dibdin's *Bibliomania*, XII. 365
Atticus, in Graves's *Columella*, X. 277
Attila, I. 20, 32, 34
Attilia, in *Fedele and Fortunio*, V. 315
Atwit, colonel, in Swift's *Complete Col-
 lection of...Conversation*, IX. 106
Atwood, William (d. 1705?), X. 498
Auban, Vie de Seint, XII. 362
Auberon, in *Huon of Bordeaux*, II. 339
Aubignac, abbé d', *Pratique du théâtre*,
 VIII. 375
Aubrey, Augusta, in Cumberland's *Fash-
 ionable Lover*, XI. 265
Aubrey, John (1626–1697), III. 323; IV.
 509; V. 167; VII. 22, 38, 42, 56, 58, 59,
 61, 70, 107, 118, 153, 282 ff., 290, 329,
 362, 507, *also see* Add.; VIII. 295, 322,
 361; IX. 267, 351 (main entry), 531, 536,
 574; XI. 393
 Brief Lives, IX. 308, 351
 Miscellanies, IX. 351
 Monumenta Britannica, IX. 354
 Perambulation of Surrey, IX. 351, 353
 Surrey, IV. 308
 Wilts, IV. 308
Aubrey, Mary (K. Philips's 'Rosania'),
 VII. 88
Auburn, in Goldsmith's *Deserted Village*,
 X. 212
Aubusson regiment, the, X. 203
Aucassin et Nicolette, IX. 39
Auchinleck, X. 190, 191, 193; XI. 235, 236,
 442
Auchinleck MS., I. 370, 465; XII. 376
Auchinleck press, XII. 357
Audax, grammarian, I. 76
Audax, in *The Floating Island*, VI. 325
Audelay, John (fl. 1426), II. 496, 504
Auditor, The, X. 390, 392, 522
Auditus, in *Lingua*, VI. 315
Audlem, Cheshire, VII. 341
Audley, in *Edward III*, V. 246
Audley, George, lord, IV. 161
Audley, James de (1316?–1369), II. 336
Audley, Thomas, baron Audley of Walden
 (1488–1544), II. 358
Audley, Thomas (fl. 1643), VII. 494; *Mer-
 curius Britannicus*, VII. 350; *Mercurius
 Diutinus*, VII. 351
Audoin, in *Widsith*, I. 35
Audry, St, IX. 343

Aue. *See* Hartmann von

Aufidius, in *Coriolanus*, v. 198

Augsberg Interim, III. 34

Augusel, in Arthurian legend, I. 259

Augusta, princess of Wales, x. 108, xiv. 287

Augustalis, Threnodia. *See* Cornelys, Mrs Theresa

Augustan age, IV. 330

Augustan school of poetry, XII. 36, 40, 41, 43, 77

Augustine, St, of Hippo, I. 93, 94, 102, 103, 117, 120, 124, 126, 127, 213, 224, 231, 234, 355, 436, 438, 440; II. 20, 52, 53, 182, 199, 230, 308, 324, 355, 365; III. 9, 19, 400, 416; IV. 220, 241, 395, 441; VII. 312, 370, 372, 376, 504, 510; VIII. 348; XII. 260; *Confessions*, VII. 170; VIII. 103; *De Civitate Dei*, III. 15, 16; IV. 395; IX. 318; *Meditations*, II. 383

Augustine, St (d. 604), archbishop of Canterbury, I. 1, 5, 13, 41, 42, 71, 72, 351

Augustinian monastery in London, v. 104

Augustinianism, III. 12

Augustinians (Austin Friars), II. 287, 349, 367

Augustus, emperor of Rome, IV. 416; XII. 304, 493

Augustus Frederick, duke of Sussex (1773–1843), XII. 367; XIV. 411

Aulay, I. 287

Auld Guidman, The, IX. 360

'Auld Hornie,' XI. 212

'Auld Licht' clergy, XI. 212, 213, 216

Auld Maitland, II. 408, 493

Auld Nick, in Burns's *Tam o' Shanter*, XI. 219

Auld Reekie, IX. 379

Auld Rob Morris, IX. 360

Auld Wife ayont the Fire, IX. 360

Aulnoy, Mary Catherine, countess de, XI. 375, 485, 491

Aulus, in Owen's *Epigrammata*, IV. 265

Aulus Gellius, III. 20

Aungerville, Sir Richard (1281–1345), I. 213

Aurelia, duchess of Siena, in *The Maid of Honour*, VI. 152, 155

Aurelia, in *The Prophetesse*, VI. 152

Aurelian, emperor of Rome, XII. 304

Aurelian, in Congreve's *Incognita*, VIII. 146

Aurelio, in *The Ladies Triall*, VI. 194

Aurelius, Caninus, I. 67

Aurelius, Marcus, IX. 300; X. 275; XII. 307; XIII. 98; *Meditations*, XII. 335

Aurelius, in *The Franklin's Tale*, II. 184

Auria, a Genoese, in *The Ladies Triall*, VI. 194

Aurifaber, John (*fl.* 1566), VIII. 321

Aurora, in *The Penates*, VI. 341

Aurora, The, XIV. 177

Aurungzebe the Great, X. 110; XIV. 333

Ausonius, III. 173, 187; IV. 250, 267, 435; VII. 83, 489; *Collige, virgo, rosas*, VII. 2

Aust, prebend of, II. 49

Austen, Cassandra, XII. 232, 237

Austen, Charles, XII. 239

Austen, Jane, II. 192; IX. 338; XI. 285, 286; XII. 24, 231 ff. (main entry), 246, 247, 252, 379, 446, *also see* Add.; XIII. 307, 313, 377, 430, 431; XIV. 208
   Elinor and Marianne, XII. 233, 236
   Emma, XII. 151, 234, 239
   First Impressions (*Pride and Prejudice*), XII. 233, 234
   Kitty, or the Bower, XII. 233
   Lady Susan, XII. 233
   Mansfield Park, X. 66; XII. 234, 238, 241
   Northanger Abbey, XI. 299; XII. 233 ff., 247
   Persuasion, XII. 234, 235, 237, 238, 240, 241
   Pride and Prejudice, XII. 233 ff., 237, 238, 241, 243
   Sense and Sensibility, X. 15; XII. 233 ff., 241
   Susan, XII. 234
   Watsons, The, XII. 234

Austen, lady Anne, XI. 83, 87, 88

Austen-Leigh, J. E., *Memoir of Jane Austen*, XII. 233, 234, 446

Austen-Leigh, R. A., XIV. 597

Austen-Leigh, W. and R. A., *Jane Austen*, XII. 232, 234, 239

Austerlitz, battle of, XII. 166

Austin, Alfred (1835–1913), XIII. 194, 498, 499; XIV. 189; *Human Tragedy, The*, XIII. 203; *Prince Lucifer*, XIII. 203

Austin, John (1613–1669), VII. 406

Austin, John (1790–1859), VIII. 321; XIV. 468

Austin, lieutenant, XIII. 427

Austin, Mrs, *Shakespeare in Paris*, XII. 153

Austin, Sarah (1793–1867), XI. 491; XIII. 560

Austin, St, in Layamon, I. 234

Austin, William (1587–1634), VII. 423, 512

Austin, William (*fl.* 1662), IX. 429

Australasia, XIV. 289

Australasian, The, XIV. 367

Australasian languages, XIV. 459

Australia, IV. 100; XI. 119; XIV. 86, 137, 241, 289, 319, 331, 361 ff., 434, 457

Australian Journal, The, XIV. 370

Australian journalism, XIV. 371

Australian literature, XIV. 361 ff

Australian tales, XIII. 432, 433

Austria, IX. 232; XII. 50; XIV. 383

Austria-Hungary, II. 310

Authority, in *Respublica*, v. 60

Autolycus, in *The Winter's Tale*, III. 356; v. 95, 206; XIII. 64

Auvergne, XIV. 293, 294

Auvergne (La Chaise Dieu), III. 100

Avalon, isle of, I. 243, 264, 266, 272, 311; II. 120

Avantance, in *Mirour de l'Omme*, II. 140

Avarice, in *Confessio Amantis*, II. 147, 149

Avarice, in *Nature*, v. 54

Avarice, in *Negromansir*, III. 77

Avarice, in *The Passetyme of Pleasure*, II. 226

Avarice, in *Piers the Plowman*, II. 23, 28

Avarice, in *Two Lamentable Tragedies*, V. 326

Avaritia, in *The Castle of Perseverance*, V. 52

Avaritia, in *Psychomachia*, V. 60

Avarus, in *A Dialogue...against the fever Pestilence*, III. 109

Ave Maria, II. 359

Ave maris Stella, IV. 129

Avebury, Sir John Lubbock, lord (1834–1913), XII. 511; XIV. 476, 562; *Prehistoric Times*, XII. 348; *The Origin of Civilization*, XII. 348

Averroes, II. 363

Averroists, the, I. 213

Avianus, XII. 337

Avicenna, I. 205

Avignon, I. 212, 213, 216; II. 53, 57; V. 61; IX. 245, 483; XIV. 22

Avila y Zuniga, Luis de, IV. 441

Avison, Charles (1710?–1770), musician, XIII. 84

Avitus of Vienne, I. 47

Avogadro, count Amadeo, XIV. 277, 557

Avon, river, IV. 190; X. 112

Avondale, lord, in Morton's *School of Reform*, XI. 281

Avowing of Arthur, I. 313

Awa Whigs Awa, IX. 377

Awdeley or Awdelay, John (*fl.*1559–1577), IV. 317, 318, 320, 390; *The Fraternitye of vacabones*, III. 87, 102, 103, 104, 343, 360, 448, 484, 492; IV. 509, 521; V. 480

Awntyrs [Adventures] *of Arthure at the Terne Wathelyne*, I. 291, 312; II. 112, 116, 121 ff., 450; III. 278

Axon, William Edward Armytage, VII. 247, 462; XI. 467; XIII. 542, 549, 553

Axtell, col. Daniel (d. 1600), VIII. 470

Ayenbite of Inwyt, I. 353 ff., 388, 396, 397, 475

Aylesbury, VII. 440; X. 391

Aylesford, earl of. *See* Finch, Heneage

Aylett, Robert (1583–1655?), IV. 521; VII. 406

Ayliffe, John (1676–1732), IX. 570

Aylmer, Brabazon, XI. 319, 332

Aylmer, John (1521–1594), bishop of London, III. 145, 376, 385, 386, 397, 593; IV. 382, 410, 509; V. 482; VII. 316; IX. 496

Aylmer, Rose, XII. 441

Ayloffe, John (d. 1685), VIII. 408, 410; IX. 266, 499

Aylott and Jones, publishers, XIII. 415

Aylward, Alfred, XIV. Add. 5

Aymon, The Four Sons of, I. 292. *See, also, under* Caxton

Aynard, Joseph, XI. 416

Ayre, William (*fl.* 1744), IX. 447

Ayrer, Jacob, V. 284, 457; *Comedia von der schönen Sidea*, V. 220, 285; *Schöne Phoenicia*, V. 285

Ayres, Philip (1638–1712), VII. 88, 405, 412

Ayrshire, III. 45; X. 191; XI. 220, 235, 440 ff., 445; XIII. 432

Ayscough, George Edward (d. 1779), *Semiramis*, X. 86, 439

Aytoun or Ayton, Sir Robert (1570–1638), II. 95; VII. 412

Aytoun, William Edmonstoune (1813–1865), XII. 421; XIII. 147, 187, 189, 499; XIV. 504

    Bon Gaultier Ballads, The (with Sir Th. Martin), XIII. 161

    Firmilian, XIII. 160, 161

    Island of the Scots, The, XIII. 160

    Lays of the Scottish Cavaliers, XIII. 160

Azalais, in Morris's *Love is Enough*, XIII. 125

Azarias, I. 48, 428

Azo of Bologna, I. 181; II. 364; VIII. 312, 465; *Brocardica*, II. 364; *Summa*, II. 364

Azores, IV. 200; VI. 101; IX. 175

Azov, sea of, XIV. 294

B., Mr, in Richardson's *Pamela*, X. 5, 7

B. B. *See* Nairne, Caroline Oliphant

B. R. (*fl.* 1584), IV. 4, 436

B[oreman], R[obert] (d. 1675), VII. 342

Bab, lady, in Burgoyne's *Maid of the Oaks*, XI. 265

Babbage, Charles (1792–1871), XIV. 258, 288, 555

Babees' Boke, The, etc., II. 499; III. 341; XI. 368

Babel, tower of, in Alfred's *Boethius*, I. 101

Babes in the Wood, The, IV. 393; XI. 385

Babes in Wood, Italian version, V. 325; VI. 96

Babilon, Saudan of, in Fortescue's *Monarchia*, II. 298

Babington, Churchill (1821–1889), XII. 331, 480

Babington, Gervase (1550?–1610), IV. 495; *Very Fruitful Exposition of the Commandments*, VI. 396, 492

Babington, William (1756–1833), XIV. 287, 558

Bab-lock-hithe, XIII. 93

Baboon, Lewis, in Arbuthnot's *History of John Bull*, IX. 134, 135; IX. 134

Babrius, XI. 479; XII. 339

Babson, J. E., XII. 435

Baby-Cake, in *The Masque of Christmas*, VI. 358

Babylas, martyr, I. 74

Babylon, II. 13, 71; IV. 84; V. 49; VIII. 122; X. 117, 228; XIII. 214

Babylon, in Blake's poems, XI. 197, 199

Babylon, paynim porter of, in *Huon of Bordeaux*, II. 339

Babylon, sultan of, I. 302. *See, also*, Babilon

Babylon, II. 403, 410 ff.
Babylonia, XII. 342, 477
Babyngton, Anthony, V. 345, 371
Baby's Début, I. 289
Bacchus, III. 317; VII. 370; VIII. 203; XIII. 247
Bacchus, in Keats's *Endymion*, XII. 82
Bacchus, in *Lingua*, VI. 315
Bacchus, in *The Penates*, VI. 341
Bacchylides, XII. 332, 485; *Odes*, XII. 340
Bacha, in *Cupid's Revenge*, VI. 128
Back, John, XI. 335
Backbite, Sir Benjamin, in *The School for Scandal*, IV. 114
Backstead, IV. 360
Bacon, in Lamb's *Mr H—*, XII. 189
Bacon, lady Ann (1528–1610), IV. 278; VII. 193
Bacon, Anthony (1558–1601), IV. 123, 278, 279; VII. 343, 436; X. 295, 498
Bacon, Francis, 1st baron Verulam and viscount St Albans (1561–1626), III. 308, 324, 325, 337, 392, 417, 425, 438, 445, 459, *also see* Add.; IV. 31, 77, 237, 269, 273, 275, 277, 278–292 (main entry), 298, 318, 325, 343 ff., 348, 375, 434, 504 ff., 521, 524, 525, 542; V. 77, 167, 222, 357, 367, 477; VI. 2, 112, 356; VII. 95, 163, 193, 221, 238, 259, 264 ff., 269, 270, 272, 277, 283, 289, 290, 298, 303, 306, 319, 323, 339, 366, 379, 433, 438, 440 ff., 453, 465, 469; VIII. 8, 273, 275, 278, 317, 321, 332, 351, 367, 368, 377, 467; IX. 47, 351, 381, 385, 386, 388, 396, 508, 529, 573; XI. 11, 57, 432; XII. 363, 427, 455, 505; XIII. 169, 212; XIV. 29, 63, 82, 169, 460, 472, 506
  A Reading on the Statute of Uses, VIII. 316
  Advancement of Learning, IV. 268, 279, 282, 283, 285, 290, 291, 349; VII. 314; IX. 388
  Augmentis Scientiarum, De, IV. 279, 280, 283, 290, 291; VII. 190, 374; VIII. 316; IX. 388
  Considerations Touching the War with Spain, IV. 87
  'Coulers of good and evill, The,' IV. 343
  Essays, IV. 279, 290, 343, 347, 524; V. 338, 357; VI. 8, 189; VIII. 376; IX. 44; X. 206
  History of Henry VII, IV. 279, 408; VI. 193; VII. 201 ff.; IX. 227
  History of Henry VIII, VII. 442
  Instauratio Magna, IV. 401; VII. 194
  Letter to the King, VII. 194
  Maxims of the Law, VIII. 316
  New Atlantis, IV. 280, 281; VII. 299, 303, 470; IX. 388
  Novum Organum, IV. 279, 284, 285, 287, 289; VII. 276, 314
  Sapientia Veterum, De, IV. 279; VII. 260
  Sylva Sylvarum, IV. 280, 283
  Witty Apophthegms, VII. 392
Bacon, friar, XI. 373

Bacon, Nathaniel (1593–1660), VII. Add.; VIII. 142, 467
Bacon, Sir Nicholas, IV. 278
Bacon, Robert, I. 202
Bacon, Roger (1214?–1294), I. 199 ff., 204 ff., 452, *also see* Add.; II. 50, 350, 366; IV. 269, 271, 273; VII. 367, 372, 504, 510; XIV. 82, 467, 469; *De Grammatica*, II. 363; *De multiplicatione specierum cum perspectiva ejusdem*, II. 362
Baconian philosophy, XIV. 418
Baconthorpe, John (d. 1346), the "Resolute Doctor," I. 213, 452
Bactria, VI. 302
Baden, treaty of, IX. 228
Badenoch, X. 230, 232
Badger, squire, in Fielding's *Don Quixote in England*, X. 22
Badham, Charles (1813–1884), XII. 330, 480
Badius, Jodocus, III. 59, 485
Badmington Library of Sports, The, XIV. 539
Badon, mount, I. 66, 246 ff.
Baffin, William (d. 1622), IV. 99, 107
Bagdad. *See* Baghdad
Bage, Robert (1728–1801), X. 423; XI. 295 ff., 459
  Barham Downs, XI. 295, 296
  Fair Syrian, XI. 295
  Hermsprong, or Man as he is not, X. 59; XI. 292, 295
  James Wallace, XI. 295
  Man as he is, XI. 295, 296
  Mount Henneth, XI. 295, 296
Bagehot, Walter (1826–1877), X. 509, 512; XI. 408; XII. 179, 377, 402, 431; XIII 104, 155, 476, 483, 489, 542; XIV. 141 ff., 164, 199, 493, 515
  Biographical Studies, XIV. 142
  Economic Studies, XIV. 36
  English Constitution, The, XIV. 36, 58, 142, 143
  Literary Studies, XII. 152; XIV. 142
  Lombard Street, XIV. 36, 142, 143
  Physics and Politics, XIV. 36, 142
Bagford, John (1650–1716), III. 97
Bagford Ballads, VIII. 411
Baggily hall, Cheshire, II. 40
Baghdad, I. 153
Baghdad, caliph of, XII. 55
Bagley wood, XIII. 93
Bagnet, Mrs, XII. 125
Bagstock, major, in *Dombey and Son*, XIII. 325
Bagwell, William (*fl.* 1655), VII. 515
Bailey, J. C., *The Poems of William Cowper*, XI. 83
Bailey, J. E., VII. 247
Bailey, Nathan (d. 1742), *Universal Etymological Dictionary*, X. 173 ff., 236
Bailey, Philip James (1816–1902), XIII 147, 148, 157, 161, 187, 223, 499
  Angel World, The, XIII. 154
  Festus, XII. 114; XIII. 152 ff., 159

Bailey, Philip James
  Mystic, The, XIII. 154
  Spiritual Legend, The, XIII. 154
  Universal Hymn, XIII. 154
Bailey, Samuel (1791–1870), XIV. 468
Baillie, lady Grizel (1665–1746), XI. 231;
  The Ewe-buchtin's bonnie, IX. 364; *Were
  na my Heart licht*, IX. 364
Baillie, Joanna (1762–1851), XI. 149, 231
  (main entry), 442, 456; XII. 12, 373, 413;
  XIII. 467
  Chough and the Crow, The, XII. 125
  De Montfort, XI. 274
  Fugitive Pieces, XI. 231
  Good night, XII. 125
  It was on a morn, XI. 231
  Metrical Legends, XI. 231
  'My Bride he is winsome and bonnie,'
  XI. 231
  On the passions, XII. 124
  Poverty parts Good Company, XI. 231
  Saw Ye Johnie Comin, XI. 231
  Tam o' the Lin, XI. 231
Baillie, Robert (1599–1662), VII. 455; XII.
  517
Baillie, Sir William, of Lamington (*fl.*
  1648), VII. 455
Baily, in *Gammer Gurton's Nedle*, VI. 297
Baily, or Bayly, Lewes (d. 1631), *The
  Practice of Piety*, VII. 147, 423
Bain, Alexander (1818–1903), XII. 476;
  XIV. 5, 48, 97, 98, 468, 473, 477 ff., 495,
  594, 601, 604
  Education as a Science, XIV. 428
  Emotions and the Will, The, XIV. 23
  On teaching English, XIV. 429
  Senses and the Intellect, The, XIV. 23
  The British Settler's Song, XIV. 377
Bain, James, XIV. 358, 583
Bain, Joseph, XII. 515
Bainbridge, John (1582–1643), IX. 530
Baines, Edward (1774–1848), XII. 507;
  XIV. 533
Baines, Sir Edward (1800–1890), XIV.
  604
Bajazet (Louis XIV), in Rowe's *Tamerlane*,
  VIII. 195
Baker, Arthur E., XIII. 476, 567
Baker, David (Augustin) (1575–1641), VII.
  143, 144, 423
Baker, David Erskine (1730–1767), VIII.
  423; X. 442; *Biographia Dramatica*,
  XIV. 334; *Companion to the playhouses*,
  XI. 453
Baker, E. A., IX. 327
Baker, Geoffrey (*fl.* 1350), II. 496
Baker, George (1540–1600), IV. 444
Baker, George (1781–1851), XII. 507: *His-
  tory and Antiquities of Northampton-
  shire*, XII. 346
Baker, George Pierce, VI. 266; XIII. 542
Baker, Henry (1698–1774), IX. 24, 25,
  433; X. 452
Baker, James, XIV. 601
Baker, Sir Richard (1568–1645), IV. 525;

VII. Add.; *Theatrum Redivivum*, VI.
  406, 460, 496
Baker, Samuel (d. 1788), XI. 336, 467
Baker, Sir Samuel White (1821–1893),
  XIV. 550
Baker, Thomas (1656–1740), IX. 354, 477,
  531, 541, 568; XII. 481; *Reflections on
  Learning*, IX. 354, 531; *History of St
  John's College*, XII. 326, 488
Baker, Thomas, dramatist (*fl.* 1703), *The
  Yeoman of Kent*, XI. 321
Baker, W. T., XIII. 513
Baker, 'collonel,' *The Blazing-Star*, VII.
  383
Baker, Jesuit father, X. 301
Bakewell, C. M., XIV. 472
Bala, Merionethshire, X. 115
Bala rocks, XIV. 292
Balaam, VII. 370; XIII. 170
Balaam, in Cowley's *Davideis*, VII. 66
Balaam, Sir, in Pope's *Epistles*, IX. 81
'Balaam,' newspaper, XIII. 308
Balaustion, Browning's, XIII. 80, 81
Balboa, Vasco Nuñez de, IV. 68
Balcanqual, or Balcanquhall, W. (1586?–
  1645), VII. 435; IX. 542
Balcarres, Fife, XI. 231
Balcarres, house of, XII. 377. *See, also*,
  Lindsays
Balclutha, I. 275
Baldassare, in *Romola*, XIII. 395
Balderstone, Caleb, in Scott's *Bride of
  Lammermoor*, XII. 23
Baldi, Octavio (*i.e.* Sir Henry Wotton),
  IV. 163
Baldock, Herts, VIII. 243
Baldwin (d. 1190), archbishop of Canter-
  bury, I. 194, 195
Baldwin, Edwin, newspaper owner, XIV.
  188
Baldwin, Edwin (*pseud.* of William God-
  win), XI. 394
Baldwin, Prudence, VII. 6
Baldwin, Sir, I. 313
Baldwin, William (*fl.* 1547), editor of
  A Mirror for Magistrates, which also see,
  III. 192 ff., 198, 200, 494; *A Brief
  Memorial*, III. 194; *The Canticles*, III.
  194; *A Treatise of Moral Philosophy*,
  III. 194; IV. 436, 507
Baldwin, William (*fl.* 1824–1826), XIV. 228
Bale, John (1495–1563), bishop of Ossory,
  II. 36, 39, 40, 152, 225, 441; III. 55, 123,
  124, 531; V. 103, 104, 391, 392, 395, 399,
  401; VI. 374, 482; XIV. 485; *Catalogus*,
  V. 58; *King John*, III. 123, 280; V. 65,
  66, 152, 153; *The Three Laws*, V. 58
Bale, Robert (*fl.* 1461), III. 48, 57, 77, 81
Balfour, Alexander (1767–1829), XII. 448
Balfour, Sir Andrew (1630–1694), IX. 552,
  558
Balfour, Arthur James, earl of, XIV. 509
Balfour, Francis Maitland (1851–1882),
  XIV. 558; *Text-book of Embryology*, XIV.
  300

Balfour, lady F., xiv. 507
Balfour, Graham, xiv. 526, 590
Balfour, John, xi. 342
Balfour, Robert, 2nd baron Burleigh (d. 1663), iv. 265
Balguy, John (1686–1748), ix. 504; *Foundation of Moral Goodness*, ix. 299
Balibari, the chevalier de, in Thackeray's *Barry Lyndon*, xiii. 282
Balin and Balan, i. 269
Baliol, Edward, i. 357
Baliol, John de (1249–1315), ii. 104
Balkan peninsula, xii. 32, 42
Ball, Edward. *See* Fitzball
Ball, John (d. 1381), i. 369, 477; ii. 63
Ball, John (1818–1889), xiv. 553
Ball, John, in Morris's *Dream of John Ball*, xiii. 128
Ball, John, of Honiton, x. 387
Ball, Sir Robert Stawell (1840–1913), xiv. 263, 265, 500, 555
Ball, W. V., xiv. 536
Ballad in Imitation of Martial, xi. 174
Ballad society, ii. 493; xii. 355, 504
Ballada, in *Fucus Histriomastix*, vi. 324
Ballade of Ballades, iv. 249
Balladino, in *The Case is Altered*, v. 314, 321
Ballads, ii. 492 ff., 395–418
Ballads (street), iii. 19, 491; iv. 535
Ballantine, A., xii. 377
Ballantyne, James (1772–1833), xi. 342, 469; xii. 5, 12, 372
Ballantyne, John (1774–1821), xii. 2, 366, 375
Ballantyne, Robert Michael (1825–1894), xi. 387
Ballantyne, Thomas (1806–1871), xiii. 464, 466
Ballantyne Humbug handled, The, xii. 377, 380
Ballantyne novels (the Novelist's Library), xi. 295; xii. 2, 366, 375
Ballantyne press, xi. 342, 469; xii. 377
Ballantyne's *Annual Register*, xi. 162
Ballard, Edward (d. 1796), xi. 332
Ballard, George (1706–1755), xi. 426, xiv. 599
Ballards, the, xi. 336, 337
Ballengeich, the Gudeman of (= James V of Scotland), ii. 244, 270
Baller, Joseph, ix. 164
Ballincollig, county Cork, xiii. 107; xiv. 326
Balliol. *See* Baliol
Ballitore, Ireland, xi. 1
Ballymahon, x. 195, 196, 199
Ballymote, Book of, xii. 362, 515
'Balmquhapple,' Fife, xi. 242
'Balnaves,' *O Gallandis All I cry and call*, iii. 131
Balochistan, xii. 352
Balormy, John, in *Lives of the Saints*, ii. 128
Balsara, iv. 84

Balsham, Hugo de, i. 205
Baltic, the, iv. 67, 310
Baltimore, xiv. 263
Baltinglas, viscount, vii. 245
Balzac, Honoré de, ix. 20; xi. 290, 305; xii. 20; xiii. 286, 301, 339, 422, 456
 Béatrix, xiii. 283
 Chef d'Œuvre inconnu, ix. 39
 Comédie Humaine, La, xii. 54; xiii. 292
 Cousine Bette, La, xiii. 290
 Curé de Tours, Le, xiii. 283
 Eugénie Grandet, xiii. 283
 Père Goriot, Le, xiii. 283
Balzac, Jean Louis Guez de, iv. 221, 525; vii. 263, 391; *Letters*, viii. 371 ff.
Bamberg, iv. 429
Bamford, Rev., xiv. 604
Bamford, Samuel, *Passages in the Life of a Radical*, xii. 397; xiv. 202
Bampfield, Joseph (*fl.* 1639–1685), vii. 450
Bampfylde, Coplestone Warre (d. 1791), xi. 424; xiv. 214
Bampfylde, John Codrington (1754–1796), x. 453; xi. 178; xii. 132, 413
 Country enjoyment, xii. 133
 Evening, xii. 133
 Morning, xii. 133
 The Sea, xii. 133
 To the River Teign, xii. 133
Bampton lectures, x. 309; xii. 273, 286, 294; xiv. 13
Banaster, Gilbert, vi. 281, 283
Banbury, xi. 373
Banbury, Roman amphitheatre at, vi. 252
Bancks, J., publisher of Prior's *Miscellaneous Works*, ix. 482; *also see* Add.
Bancroft, John (d. 1696), viii. 400
Bancroft, Richard (1544–1610), archbishop of Canterbury, iii. 391, 392, 394, 544; iv. 382, 422, 424, 425, 491, 519, 545; vii. 327, 332; *Sermon preached at Paules crosse*, iii. 392, 543
Bancroft, Thomas (*fl.* 1633–1658), vii. 412
Bancrofts, the, xiii. 513
Band, Cuffe and Ruffe, vi. 481
Bandello, Matteo, iii. 343; iv. 3, 6, 7, 377, 441, 442; v. 191, 220, 221, 244, 245, 247; vi. 49, 99, 100, 123, 180; viii 126
Bandon, county Cork, xii. 165
Banff, ii. 100; xii. 513
Bang, W., vi. 102
Bangor, ix. 309, 310, 541; x. 354, 362
Bangor, antiphonary hymns of, i. 65
Bangor college, xiv. 433
Bangorian controversy, ix. 17, 19, 309, 477, 510, 511
Banim, John (1798–1842), xiv. 312, 314, 567
 Aileen, xiv. 316
 Damon and Pythias, xiii. 259; xiv. 316
 Nowlans, The, xiv. 316
 Revelations of the Dead, xiv. 316
 Soggarth Aroon, xiv. 316
 Tales by the O'Hara Family, xiv. 316

Banim, Michael (1796–1874), XIV. 312, 314, 567; *Father Connell*, XIV. 316, 317; *Tales by the O'Hara Family*, XIV. 316; *Town of the Cascades, The*, XIV. 317
Banishment of Poverty, The, IX. 366
'Banjo Byron' (Alfred Austin), XIII. 203
Bank of England, XI. 39
Bankes, G. N., XIV. 597
'Bankes his Curtall,' IV. 366
Banks (a Scotsman), IV. 366, 367, 531, 540
Banks, John (*fl.* 1696), VIII. 21, 195, 401, 434; *The Unhappy Favourite, or the Earl of Essex*, V. 346; VIII. 194; X. 86; *Vertue Betray'd or Anna Bullen*, VIII. 194
Banks, Sir Joseph (1743–1820), VIII. 361; XIV. 245, 289, 290, 550, 558
Bannatyne, George (1545–1608?), II. 282, 478; III. 132; XII. 358, 377
Bannatyne, Richard, *The Memorials of the Transactions of Scotland*, III. 148, 149, 500
Bannatyne club, XI. 231; XII. 358, 359, 361, 370, 377, 378; XIV. 94
Bannatyne MS., II. 478; III. 122, 131, 132, 499; IX. 361, 365, 367, 369, 553, 567
Bannatyne Miscellany, IV. 414
Bannister, John (1760–1836), XII. 171; XIV. 217
Bannockburn, battle of, I. 357, 370; II. 101, 102, 109; X. 224; XII. 1; XIV. 95
Banquet of Daintie Conceits, A, IV. 467
Banquo, in an Interlude, VI. 318
Banquo, in *Macbeth*, II. 104; V. 255; VI. 318
Bansley, Charles (*fl.* 1548), IV. 317; V. 477; *The Pryde and Abuse of Women*, III. 97, 491; IV. 328
Banville, Théodore de, XIII. 162, 211
Baptist education society, X. 387
Baptist general assembly, X. 378
Baptist general association, X. 378, 387
Baptist historical society, X. 519
Baptist histories, X. 519
Baptist Rawdon college, X. 387
Baptists, X. 522
Barabas, in *The Jew of Malta*, V. 145, 326, 366; VI. 250
Barabas, in the Passion play, V. 18
Barabbas, in Marlowe's *Jew of Malta*, XII. 68
Baradoun, Henry (*fl.* 1483), II. 502
Barak, IV. 170
Barante, Pierre A. P. B., baron de, XII. 322; *Histoire des Ducs de Bourgogne*, XIV. 107
Barbadoes, XI. 279, 280
Barbarisme, in *The Tears of the Muses*, III. 241
Barbarus, Hermolas, III. 5
Barbary, IV. 4, 99; XIV. 246
Barbauld, Anna Laetitia, born Aikin (1743–1825), X. 11, 412, 452, 454; XI. 132, 343, 382, 477; XII. 4, 124, 133, 447; XIII. 324; XIV. 393, 603
Easy Lessons, XI. 384
Evenings at Home, XI. 384

Barbauld, Anna Laetitia
  Hymns in Prose, XI. 384
  'On Romances,' X. 188
'Barber, Francis,' X. 472
Barber, Margaret Fairless (*pseud.* Michael Fairless, 1869–1901), XIV. 515
Barber, Mary (1690?–1757), IX. 106, 460, 484; XI. 426
Barberini, cardinal, IV. 259
Barbès, Armand, XIII. 283
Barbeyrac, Jean, X. 308
Barbones parliament, IX. 386
Barbour, John (*c.* 1320–1395), II. 100 ff., 114, 117, 127, 129, 130, 447 ff.; IV. 413; X. 224
  The Bruce, I. 359; II. 88, 91, 101, 104–108 (main entry), 239, 280, 447; XII. 13, 344
  Other works attributed to Barbour:
  The Brut, II. 103; *Lives* or *Legends of the Saints*, II. 103, 127, 128, 239; *Siege of Troy*, II. 104; *The Stewartis Oryginalle*, II. 103
Barckley, Sir Richard, *A Discourse of the felicitie of man: or his Summum bonum*, IV. 268, 507, 531
Barclay, Alexander (1475?–1552), II. 210; III. 56 ff., 75, 85, 95, 185, 478 ff.; IV. 4, 322, 439, 476
  Bellum Jugurthinum, translation of, III. 56
  Chasteau de labour, Le, translation of Gringore's, II. 329; III. 56
  Codrus and Minalcus, III. 64
  Contra Skeltonum, III. 66
  Cytezen and Uplondyshman, III. 63, 64
  Eclogues, III. 56, 57, 62 ff.
  Introductory to write and to pronounce Frenche, III. 56, 57
  Myrrour of Good Maners, The, translation of, III. 57, 341
  St George, Life of, III. 57
  St Thomas of Canterbury, Life of, III. 57
  Sallust, III. 57
  Ship of Fools, The (trans. *Narrenschiff*), II. 321; III. 56, 57, 60 ff., 64 ff., 71, 74, 79, 485, 489; IV. 320, 400, 521, 531, 532
Barclay, David (1610–1686), VIII. 111
Barclay, James, X. 474
Barclay, John (1582–1621), IV. 242, 243, 253 ff., 499 ff.
  Apologia Euphormionis pro se, IV. 255 ff.
  Argenis, IV. 245, 254, 255, 257, 260; VII. 315
  Euphormionis Satyricon, IV. 254 ff.; VII. 315
  Icon Animorum, IV. 254, 257, 260
  Paraenesis ad sectarios, IV. 254
  Pietas, sive publicae pro regibus ac principibus et privatae, pro G. Barclaio contra Bellarminum Vindiciae, IV. 254
  Thebais, commentary on, IV. 253
Barclay, John (1734–1798), *Dialogue betwixt William Lickladle and Thomas Cleancogue*, IX. 373

Barclay, Robert (1648–1690), VIII. 415; IX. 520, 546; *An Apology for the True Christian Divinity*, VIII. 111, 112

Barclay, Robert (1779–1854), XIV. 230; *Religious Societies of the Commonwealth*, IX. 307

Barclay, William (1570?–1630?), IV. 253, 254; *De Potestate Papae*, IV. 254; *Nepenthes*, IV. 531

'Bard, The,' Della Cruscan poet, XI. 177

Bardell, Mrs, in *The Pickwick Papers*, XIII. 313

Bardolph, Shakespeare's, V. 187, 367; XI. 289; XIV. 125

Bardsey, near Leeds, VIII. 146

Bardus, in *Confessio Amantis*, II. 151

Bareacres, house of, in Thackeray's *Vanity Fair*, XIII. 287

Barebone's parliament, VII. 190; XIV. 452

Barents, IV. 460

Baret, John (*fl.* 1441–1446), II. 198

Baret, John (d. 1580?), III. 555

Baret, M., IV. 540

Baretti, Giuseppe, V. 293; X. 159, 468 ff.

Bargrave, John (1610–1680), VII. 35

Barham, Richard Harris (1788–1845), X. 154; XI. 160; XII. 111, 122–123 (main entry), 138, 413; XIV. 200; *As I lay a thynkynge*, XII. 122; *Ingoldsby Legends, The*, VIII. 96; XI. 38; XII. 122, 123; XIII. 161

Bari, V. 37

Barillon, Paul, marquis de Branges, X. 290

Baring, Evelyn, earl of Cromer, XIII. 546

Baring, Mrs H., XIV. 507

Baring-Gould, S., XII. 417

Barker, Christopher (1529?–1599), queen's printer, IV. 384, 386, 387, 389, 395, 398, 400

Barker, Edmund Henry (1788–1839), XII. 327, 490, 491

Barker, John (*fl.* 1464), III. 99

Barker, Matthew (1619–1698), VII. 316

Barker, Robert (d. 1645), IV. 398, 400, 406

Barker, T. (*fl.* 1651), *The Art of Angling*, VII. 463

Barker, William (*fl.* 1572), IV. 444

Barkham, John (1572?–1642), III. 324

Barkiarokh, in Beckford's *Episodes*, XI. 291

Barking, II. 157; IV. 141

Barkstead, John, 'goldsmith in the Strand' (d. 1662), VII. 512

Barkstead, William (*fl.* 1611), *Hiren, or the Faire Greeke*, VI. 49; *Mirrha, the Mother of Adonis*, VI. 49

Barlaam and Josaphat, I. 286, 467; II. 150, 507; V. 53

Barley, William (*fl.* 1596), IV. 113, 463

Barleycorn, John (*alias* 'Allan-a-Maut'), II. 279

Barlow, Arthur, IV. 85

Barlow, George, XIII. 542

Barlow, Jerome (*fl.* 1528–1533), III. 80; *upon the origin of the protestant*

fashions, III. 80; *Proper Dyalogue betwene a Gentillman and a Husbandman*, III. 80; *Rede me and be not wrothe*, III. 80, 105

Barlow, Mr, in *Sandford and Merton*, XI. 381, 382

Barlow, William (d. 1613), IV. 382; VII. 316

Barn Elms, on the Thames, VIII. 377

Barnabas, Gospel of, IX. 291

Barnabas, St, VII. 318

Barnabees Journal, VII. 390

Barnaby, in *The New Inn*, IV. 361

Barnaby Bunch the botcher, in *The weak est goeth to the Wall*, V. 316

Barnacle, in *The Gamester*, VI. 202

Barnakill, in Kingsley's *Yeast*, XIII. 360

Barnard, lady Anne (lady Anne Lindsay, 1750–1825), XI. 442; XII. 377; XIV. Add. 5; *Auld Robin Gray*, XI. 231; *Why Tarries My Love*, XI. 232

Barnard, Edward, XI. 346

Barnard, Frederick, XIII. 540, 541

Barnard, Sir John, X. 84

Barnard Castle, XIII. 317

Barnes, Barnabe (1569?–1609), III. 256, 264, 265, 271, 522; IV. 115, 468; *The Devil's Charter*, VI. 150, 452; *Parthenophil and Parthenope*, III. 265

Barnes, Joseph, III. 427; IV. 410, 411

Barnes or Berners, Juliana. *See* Berners

Barnes, J. H., XIII. 513

Barnes, Robert (1495–1540), III. 27, 37, 43, 53, 474

Barnes, Thomas (? 1624), IV. 437

Barnes, Thomas (1747–1810), XIV. 386, 599, 604

Barnes, Thomas (1785–1841), XIV. 179 ff., 198

Barnes, William (1801–1886), I. 240; XII. 134, 413; XIV. 459

Barnet, VIII. 351; XIII. 276

Barnett, Percy Arthur, XIV. Add. 5

Barnfield, Richard (1574–1627), IV. 117, 121, 468; V. 224

Affectionate Shepherd, The, IV. 120, 126

Another of the same shepherd's, IV. 120

'As it fell upon a day,' IV. 119

Complainte of Poetrie for the Death of Liberalitie, The, IV. 120

Cynthia, with certaine Sonnets, III. 256, 264, 522; IV. 120

Encomion of Lady Pecunia, The, IV. 119, 120, 519

Hellens Rape, or a light Lanthorne for light Ladies, IV. 120

'If Musique and sweet Poetrie agree,' IV. 113, 119

Poems in divers Humors, IV. 119, 120

Barnham, Alice, IV. 280

Barnstaple, IX. 160

Barnwell, George, in Lillo's *London Merchant*, X. 75 ff., 79

Barnwell priory, Cambridge, II. 343, 347, 352, 500; XII. 348, 508

Barocci, Giacomo, IV. 431
Baron, George (*fl.* 1652), VII. 512
Baron, Robert (1593?–1639), IX. 542
Baron, Robert (*fl.* 1645), VII. 88, 137, 412; VIII. 434
Baron hill, X. 115
Baron o' Brackley, The, II. 412
Baron-Wilson, Margaret, XI. 462
Baroni, Leonora, VII. 99
Baronius, Caesar, cardinal, VII. 311; *Annales Ecclesiastici*, VII. 310
Baronius, Justus, IV. 249
Barontus, St, of Pistoja, I. 86
Barot, O., XIII. 465
Barratt, Alfred (1844–1881), XIV. 468
Barrels, near Henley-in-Arden, X. 271, 273, 278
Barret, Robert (*fl.* 1600), IV. 473
Barret, William (*fl.* 1609), IV. 395
Barretier, Johann Philipp, X. 164, 460, 464, 465
Barrett, Charlotte, X. 260
Barrett, E., XIII. 464
Barrett, Eaton Stannard (1786–1820), XI. 299, 459
Barrett, Edward Moulton, XIII. 70
Barrett, Elizabeth. *See* Browning, Elizabeth Barrett
Barrett, J. A. S., XIII. 465
Barrie, Sir J. M., XIII. 569; *Auld Licht Idylls*, XIV. 436; *When a Man's Single*, XIV. 447
Barrington, Daines, X. 269
Barrington, Emilie I., XIV. 515
Barrington, John Shute, 1st viscount Barrington (1678–1734), X. 380
Barrington, Sir Jonah (1760–1834), XIV. 567; *Personal Sketches*, XIV. 322
Barrington, Rutland, XIII. 513
Barrington, William Wildman, 2nd viscount Barrington (1717–1793), X. 405, 408, 410
Barrosa, X. 230
Barrow or Barrowe, Henry (d. 1593), III. 389, 390
Barrow, Isaac (1630–1677), VII. 487; VIII. 295 ff., 301, 308, 389, 458, 476; *Exposition of the Creed, Decalogue and Sacraments*, VIII. 297; *On the Pope's Supremacy*, VIII. 296; *Works*, VIII. 296
Barrow, Sir John (1764–1848), XII. 154, 426; XIV. 550; *Autobiographical Memoir*, XIV. 248; *Travels in China*, XIV. 248; *Voyage to Cochin-China, A*, XIV. 248
Barrow, John, XIV. 596
Barrow, William (1754–1836), XIV. 604
Barrowists, the, III. 408
Barry, Mrs Elizabeth (1658–1713), VIII. 136, 179, 182, 184, 191, 439
Barry, Henry Boothby, XIV. 596
Barry, Lodowick, *Ram-Alley or Merrie-Trickes*, V. 367; VI. 218, 219, 452
Barry, M. J., XIV. 572
Barry, Redmond, in Thackeray's *Barry Lyndon*, XIII. 281 ff.

Barry, Spranger (1719–1777), XI. 257, 260, 450, 454
Bartello, IV. 441
Bartello, in *Dan Bartholmew of Bathe*, III. 205, 206
Barter, Charles, XIV. Add. 5
Barth, Caspar, IV. 253; *Amphitheatrum Seriorum Jocorum*, IV. 266; *Scioppius excellens*, IV. 266
Barthélémon, François H., XI. 258
Barthélemy, E., XIII. 465, 466, 470
Bartholinus, Thomas, X. 225
Bartholomaeus Anglicus (*fl.* 1230–1250), I. 184, 452; IV. 521; *De Proprietatibus Rerum*, II. 71, 72, 74, 76, 80, 86, 311, 323, 443; IV. 320
Bartholomew, A. T., XIII. 572, *also see* Add. 1; XIV. 539
Bartholomew de Cotton (d. 1298?), I. 449
Bartholomew fair, VIII. 115, 193
Bartholus, II. 363
Bartlet, John (*fl.* 1662), IV. 113, 463
Bartolozzi, Francesco, XIV. 216
Barton, Amos, George Eliot's, XIII. 387, 388
Barton, Bernard (1784–1849), VIII. 113; XI. 483; XII. 135, 198 ff., 413, 438; XIII. 142, 143
Barton, John, Mrs Gaskell's, XIII. 373
Barton, Mary, Mrs Gaskell's, XIII. 372
Barton, in Jane Austen's *Sense and Sensibility*, XII. 241
Barton, Sir Andrew, II. 408, 414
Barty, lord Charles, in Henry Kingsley's *Austin Eliot*, XIII. 433
Basedow, Johann Bernhard (1724–1790), IX. 401; XIV. 382, 402
Basel, III. 41, 58, 100, 333, 532; IV. 374, 389, 403; V. 71, 101
Basil, St, I. 74, 75, 77, 122, 124; XII. 266
Basilisco, in *Solimon and Perseda*, V. 161, 162
Basilissa, martyr, I. 74
Basilius, in *The Ile of Guls*, VI. 212
Basilius, St, bishop of Caesarea, VII. 503
Basing, VI. 246, 454
Basire, Isaac (1607–1676), VIII. 459
Basire, James (1730–1802), XI. 181
Baskerville, John (1706–1775), XI. 341, 469
Basoche, Confrérie de la, V. 22, 25
Bassandyne, Thomas (d. 1577), IV. 412. 547
Bassanes, in *The Broken Heart*, VI. 191
Basse or Bas, William (d. 1653?), IV. 150, 479
Basset, Thomas, VIII. 464
Bassett, lady, in Reade's *A Terrible Temptation*, XIII. 426
Bassingbourne, V. 34
Bastard, Thomas (1566–1618), IV. 334, 335, 519
Bastiat, Frederick, IV. 299; XIV. 509
Baston, Robert (*fl.* 1300), II. 496
Bastwick, John (1593–1654), VII. 145, 423, 433, 456, 498

Basyn, The T le of the, II. 501
Bat Burst, in *The New Inne*, VI. 25
Bateman, Christopher, XI. 331, 332, 336
Bateman, Thomas (1821–1861), XII. 507
Bateman, William (1298?–1355), bishop of Norwich, II. 354
Bates, Cadwallader John, XII. 507; *Border Holds of Northumberland*, XII. 349, 507
Bates, Charley, in *Oliver Twist*, XIII. 316
Bates, Henry Walter (1825–1892), XIV. 550
Bates, Miss, in Jane Austen's *Emma*, XII. 240
Bates, William, *Harmony of the divine attributes*, XI. 316
Bateson, Mary (1865–1906), XIV. 485
  Borough Customs, XIV. 81
  Charters of the Borough of Cambridge, The, XIV. 81
  Laws of Breteuil, The, XIV. 81
  Medieval England, I. 446
  Origin and Early History of Double Monasteries, The, XIV. 81
  Records of the Borough of Leicester, XIV. 81
Bateson, Thomas (1580?–1620?), IV. 113, 463; *First Set of English Madrigals*, VII. 8
Bath, I. 40; VIII. 159, 363; IX. 34, 163, 167, 172, 538; X. 22, 28, 29, 35, 39, 42, 206, 207, 261, 276, 277, 409, 427; XI. 149, 173, 175, 283, 344, 347, *also see* Add.; XII. 232, 236, 513; XIV. 220, 225, 324
Bath, colonel, in Fielding's *Amelia*, X. 34; XI. 265
Bath, earl of. *See* Pulteney, William
Bath, knights of the, XI. 282
Bath, marquis of. *See* Thynne, Thomas
Bath, marquis of, *Papers*, IX. 96, 99, 141, 443, 483. See, also, *Longleat Papers*
Bath Easton, X. 277, 456
Bath school, VII. 330
Bathurst, Allen, 1st earl Bathurst (1684–1775), IX. 79, 152, 228, 443, 445
Bathurst, Ralph, M.D. (1620–1704), X. 492
Batrachomyomachia, VIII. 64
Batt, in *Dan Bartholmew of Bathe*, III. 205
Battie, J., IV. 509
Battle of Falkirk Muir, IX. 378
Battle Royal, The, VIII. 92
Baucida, XII. 201
Baucis, XII. 201
Baucis and Philemon, VII. 252
Baucis and Philemon, in Sandys's *Ovid*, VII. 51
Baudelaire, Charles Pierre, IV. 218; XII. 525; XIII. 129, 133, 490
Baudissin, count, v. 303; VI. 165
Bauermeister, actor, V. 306
Bauhusius of Antwerp, IV. 266
Baumgarten, O., XIII. 470
Baur, Frederick Christian, IX. 291
Bavand or Bavande, William (*fl.* 1559), VI. 377, 409; *A Woorke of Joannes Ferrarius Montanus touchynge the good orderynge of a Common Weale*, VI. 377, 493

Bavaria, VII. 200
Baxter, Andrew (1686–1750), IX. 504
Baxter, Lucy W., XIII. 530
Baxter, Nathaniel (*fl.* 1606), IV. 473
Baxter, Richard (1615–1691), IV. 433; VII. 145, 146, 207, 424, 427, 433; IX. 574; X. 373, 377, 499, 519; XI. 334; XII. 523
  Call to the Unconverted, XI. 369
  Holy Commonwealth, VII. 433
  Life and Times, VIII. 297
  Quaker's Catechism, VIII. 110
  Reliquiae Baxterianae, VII. 145; VIII. 462, 463; IX. 307, 383; XI. 316
  Saints' Everlasting Rest, The, VII. 146; IX. 269; X. 383; XI. 316
Baxter, William (1650–1723), IX. 526
Baxter's Dead, A Winding Sheet for Mr, IX. 514
Bayard, in *Four Sons of Aymon*, I. 292
Bayes, in *The Rehearsal*, VII. 184; VIII. 26; IX. 147. *See, also*, IX. 476
Bayham, Frederick, in *The Newcomes*, XIII. 297
Bayle, Pierre, V. 286, 292; IX. 211, 477, 529; X. 177; *Dictionary*, XI. 320
Bayley, John [Whitcomb] (d. 1869), XII. 507
Bayly, Lewis, bishop of Bangor (d. 1631), IV. 495; *The Practice of Piety*, XI. 369
Bayly, Thomas Haynes (1797–1839), VII. 84; XII. 130, 414; XIII. 154; XIV. 200
Bayne, Alicia, XIV. 602
Bayne, Peter (1830–1896), XIII. 470, 483; XIV. 515, 522
Baynes, A. H., XIV. Add. 5
Baynes, Mrs, in Thackeray's *Adventures of Philip*, XIII. 299
Baynes, Thomas Spencer (1823–1887), XII. 402; XIV. 468, 474; *Essay on the New Analytic*, XIV. 9
Baynham, W., XIII. 513
Bayreuth, V. 305
Bazalgette, Mrs, in Reade's *Love me Little, Love me Long*, XIII. 426
Be Domes Daege, I. 129, 145 ff., 220, 227, 444
Be Merry and Wise, VII. 393
Beach, Joseph Warren, XIII. 570
Beach, Michael Hicks, XII. 143
Beaconsfield, Burke's residence, XI. 142
Beaconsfield, earl of. *See* Disraeli, Benjamin
Beadnell, Maria, XIII. 542
Beaduhild, in *Deor*, I. 36
Beagle, Sir Harry, in Colman's *Jealous Wife*, X. 89, 90
'Beagle,' ship, XIV. 250, 296, 298
Beagnoþ, owner of the Thames runic sword, I. 11
Beale, Catherine Hutton, XIV. 520
Beale, Dorothea (1831–1905), XIV. 429, 599
Bear, the, in *Mum, Sothsegger*, II. 36
Beard, Thomas (d. 1632), III. 552; VI. 492
Beardsley, Aubrey, XIII. 502
Beare, John Isaac (1857–1918), XII. Add. 3

Beare, Philip O'Sullivan (1590?–1660), XIV. 308

Beaton, David (1494–1546), archbishop of St Andrews, II. 369

Beaton or Bethune, James (d. 1539), archbishop of St Andrews, II. 369; III. 160

Beatrice (Dante's), III. 234; IV. 210, 217; XII. 85, 86

Beatrice, in Middleton's *Changeling*, VI. 76, 77; XII. 222

Beatrice, in *The Dutch Courtezan*, VI. 48

Beatrice, in *Much Ado about Nothing*, V. 191, 193, 214, 379; VI. 46, 100, 123; VIII. 120, 154

Beatrix, in *Esmond*, XIII. 292, 293, 296, 298

Beatrix, St (sister Angela), XIII. 178

Beattie, James (1735–1803), X. 138, 154, 155, 347, 453, 480, 512, 514; XI. 206, 342, 350; XII. 100, 132; XIII. 235; XIV. 601, 604

   Essay on Truth, X. 155, 348; XI. 351

   Judgment of Paris, X. 155

   Minstrel, The, IX. 374; X. 132, 154; XI. 247, 351; XIII. 149

   Pastorals, X. 155

   Retirement, X. 155

   To Mr Alexander Ross, IX. 374

Beattie, William (1793–1875), XII. 410; XIV. 56, 595

Beatty-Kingston, William, XIV. 192

Beau Bunter, in *Sir Harry Wildair*, VIII. 169

Beau Clincher, in Farquhar's *The Constant Couple*, VIII. 175

Beauchamp, George Meredith's, XIII. 446

Beauchamp, Philip (*see* Bentham, Jeremy), XI. 398

Beauchamp, Richard de, earl of Warwick (1382–1439), II. 76, 335

Beauchamp court, Warwickshire, IV. 159

Beauclerk, Charles, 1st duke of St Albans (1670–1726), VIII. 376

Beauclerk, Topham, X. 207

Beaudesert, Warwickshire, X. 112

Beauford, in D'Urfey's *The Virtuous Wife*, VIII. 175

Beaufort, cardinal, bishop of Winchester, in *Henry VI*, V. 186

Beaufort, duke of. *See* Somerset, Henry Charles

Beaufort, Henry (d. 1447), II. 352, 355

Beaufort, Joan, II. 244

Beaufort, Margaret (1443–1509), countess of Richmond and Derby, II. 300, 309, 316, 321, 324, 325, 358; III. 8, 13, 67; IV. 224, 226, 227, 426; XII. 488, 515

Beaumarchais, Pierre A. C. de, *Figaro*, XI. 262

Beaumaris, X. 115

Beaumont, Charles, VIII. 284

Beaumont, Francis (1584–1616), IV. 55, 115, 194; V. 347; VI. 2, 5, 27, 107–140 (main entry); 145, 177, 195, 205, 208, 248, 272, 329, 435 ff., 488, *and see* Add.;

VII. 7, 82, 272; VIII. 13, 127, 132, 226, 425; IX. 140, 145; X. 91; XII. 89, 186, 444, 504; XIII. 144, 289. *See, also, under* Fletcher, John

Beaumont, Sir George Howland, of Coleorton (1753–1827), XI. 130, 416; XII. 376

Beaumont, Jeanne Marie, le prince de (*c*. 1775), XI. 491

Beaumont, lady, of Coleorton, IX. 328; XI. 408, 416; XII. 376

Beaumont and Fletcher, plays and poems attributed to, whether singly, jointly, or in collaboration with others, VI. 435 ff.; XI. 319; XIII. Add. 2

   'All ye woods and trees and bowers,' VI. 125

   'Arm, arm,' VI. 125

   'Away, delights,' VI. 128

   Barnavelt, Sir John van Olden, VI. 116, 123, 130, 138

   'Beauty clear and fair,' VI. 125

   Beggars Bush, The, V. 376; VI. 121, 125, 131, 139; VIII. 121

   Bloody Brother, The, VI. 26, 125, 129, 138

   Bonduca, VI. 123, 128, 138; X. 429

   Captaine, The, VI. 125, 128, 137

   Cardenio, The History of, VI. 140; VIII. 127

   'Care-charming Sleep,' VI. 125

   'Cast our caps and cares away,' VI. 125

   Chances, The, VI. 135, 136, 140; VIII. 128; X. 433

   Coronation, The. See under Shirley

   Coxcombe, The, V. 362; VI. 119, 120, 133, 137; VIII. 128

   Cupid's Revenge, III. 355; VI. 114, 119, 127, 137

   Custome of the Countrey, The, V. 366; VI. 122, 130, 138; VIII. 128

   Demetrius and Enanthe, VI. 138

   Devil of Dowgate, The, VI. 140

   Double Marriage, The, VI. 131, 139; VIII. 128

   Elder Brother, The, VI. 121, 125, 136, 140

   Elegy on lady Penelope Clifton (daughter of Sidney's Stella), VI. 113

   Elegy on lady Markham, VI. 113

   Elegy on the countess of Rutland (Sidney's daughter), VI. 113

   Faire Maide of the Inne, The, VI. 132, 140, 183; VIII. 128

   Faithfull Shepherdesse, The, VI. 31, 112, 114, 117, 125, 126, 137, 340, 353, 363, 366, 367, 369, 490; VIII. 18, 271

   False One, The, VI. 111, 121, 123, 131, 139

   Four Plays in One, VI. 119, 128, 137

   'God Lyaeus, ever young,' VI. 125

   'Hence, all you vain delights,' VI. 124, 134

   Honest man's Fortune, The, VI. 128, 137

   Humorous Lieutenant, The, VI. 134, 138

   Island Princesse, The, VI. 123, 131, 139; VIII. 120, 129, 443

Beaumont and Fletcher
 Jeweller of Amsterdam, The, VI. 140
 King and no King, A, VI. 114, 119, 120, 126, 127, 129, 137
 Knight of Malta, The, VI. 130, 138
 Knight of the Burning Pestle, The, I. 292; IV. 359; 363; V. 130; VI. 89, 114, 119, 133, 137, 234; VIII. 121, 128, 425; X. 220
 Lawes of Candy, The, VI. 131, 139
 'Let the bells ring,' VI. 125
 Little French Lawyer, The, VI. 119, 134, 138, 152, 184
 Lovers' Progress, The, VI. 131, 139
 Loves Cure, VI. 119, 124, 136, 140; VIII. 128
 Loves Pilgrimage, VI. 132, 140; VIII. 31, 128
 Loyal Subject, The, VI. 100, 130, 138
 Mad Lover, The, VI. 130, 138, 152
 Mador, King of Great Britain, VI. 140
 Maid in the Mill, The, VI. 69, 70, 132, 139; VIII. 128, 129
 Maides Tragedy, The, VI. 111, 114, 119, 120, 124, 126, 127, 129, 137, 199; VIII. 120, 215
 Masque of Grayes Inne and the Inner-Temple, The, VI. 137, 353, 356, 488
 Monsieur Thomas, VI. 123, 135, 138
 Nice Valour, The, IV. 251; VI. 119, 134, 140
 Night-Walker, The, VI. 134, 135, 140
 Noble Gentleman, The, VI. 136, 140
 'O how my lungs do tickle,' VI. 125
 Ovid's Salmacis and Hermaphroditus, IV. 20; VI. 112
 Philaster, VI. 111, 113, 114, 119 ff., 126, 128, 129, 137, 190; VIII. 441; X. 429
 Pilgrim, The, VI. 122, 131, 139; VIII. 31, 52, 54, 120, 396, 401, 431
 Prophetesse, The, VI. 123, 131, 139, 152; VIII. 120, 128, 135, 401
 Queene of Corinth, The, V. 350; VI. 130, 138; VIII. 128
 Right Woman, A, VI. 140
 Rule a Wife and have a Wife, V. 356; VI. 135, 139; VIII. 128
 Scorneful Ladie, The, VI. 114, 119, 133, 137
 Sea Voyage, The, V. 347; VI. 131, 139; VIII. 120
 'Sit, soldiers, sit and sing,' VI. 125
 Spanish Curate, The, VI. 125, 134, 139, 183; VIII. 20, 128
 Tamer Tamed, VIII. 121
 'Tell me, dearest, what is love,' VI. 125, 128
 Thierry and Theodoret, VI. 114, 123, 129, 138
 'Three merry boys,' VI. 125
 ''Tis late and cold,' VI. 125
 Triumph of Death, The, VI. 128, 137
 Triumph of Honour, The, VI. 128, 137
 Triumph of Love, The, VI. 120, 128, 137
 Triumph of Time, The, VI. 128, 137

Beaumont and Fletcher
 Two Noble Kinsmen, The, VI. 132, 139, 299. See, also, under *Two Noble Kinsmen*
 Valentinian, VI. 122, 123, 125, 129, 138
 Wandering Lovers, The, VI. 139
 Wife for a Month, The, VI. 122, 132, 139
 Wild-Goose Chase, The, VI. 135, 139; VIII. 120
 Wit At severall Weapons, VI. 119, 134, 138
 Wit Without Money, VI. 134, 138
 Woman Hater, The, VI. 27, 112, 114, 119, 124, 132, 137
 Woman's Plot, A, VI. 140
 Womans Prize, The, VI. 134, 135, 138
 Women pleas'd, VI. 130, 138; VIII. 128
 See, also, under Middleton and Shirley
Beaumont, Sir Francis (d. 1598), VI. 111
Beaumont, Sir John (1583–1627), IV. 194, 435, 436, 487; VII. 56, 57, 75, 90, 406; VIII. 228, 447; *Bosworth Field*, VI. 111; *To His Late Majesty, concerning the True Forme of English Poetry*, VII. 49
Beaumont, Joseph (1616–1699), VII. 34, 406, *also see* Add.; VIII. 283 ff., 453; *Psyche*, VIII. 283, 284
Beaupré, in *The Parliament of Love*, VI. 155
Beaupuy, Michel, XI. 98
Beauty, in *The Golden Targe*, II. 253
Beauty of the World, I. 294
Beaw or Beo, son of Scyld (Sceldwea), I. 28
Bec, monastic school at, I. 153; "Geoffrey Arthur's" book at, I. 170
Beccaria, Cesare Bonesana, marquis di, XI. 66, 70; *Crimes and Punishments*, XI. 64; *Dei Delitti e delle Pene*, IX. 302
Beche, Sir Henry Thomas de la (1796–1855), XIV. 294, 560; *A Geological Manual*, XIV. 292; *Report on the Geology of Cornwall, etc.*, XIV. 292
Becher, Anne. *See* Thackeray, Anne
Becher, Miss, XIII. 276
Becke, Edmund (*fl.* 1550), IV. 443
Becke, George Louis (1848–1913), XIV. 584
Becker, Wilhelm Adolph, *Charicles*, XII. 230; *Gallus*, XII. 230
Becket, St Thomas à, archbishop of Canterbury, I. 173, 185, 186, 191, 202, 339, 341, 448; II. 84, 87, 342; III. 12, 332; IV. 417, 418; V. 38, 56, 58; XI. 315; XII. 258, 321, 416
Becket, St Thomas à, in Caxton's *Golden Legend*, II. 334
Becket and Dehorde, booksellers, X. 191
Beckford, Peter (1740–1811), XIV. 542; *Essays on Hunting*, XIV. 232; *Thoughts upon Hare and Fox Hunting*, XIV. 232
Beckford, Richard, X. 388
Beckford, William (1709–1770), X. 485
Beckford, William (1759–1844), X. 423, *also see* Add.; XI. 289 ff., 306, 307, 459
 Azemia, XI. 289
 Dreams, Waking Thoughts and Incidents, XI. 289
 Episodes, XI. 290 ff.

Beckford, William
  History of Extraordinary Painters, **XI.**
  289
  Letters from Portugal, XI. 289
  Modern Novel Writing, XI. 289
  Vathek, XI. 161, 289 ff., 304
Bockington, Somerset, IV. 133
Becon, Thomas (1512–1567), III. 27; IV.
  380, 397, 491, 495
Bedam, Historia post, I. 174
Beddoe, John (1826–1911), XII. 507; *An-*
  thropological History of Europe, XII. 351;
  Contributions to Scottish Ethnology, XII.
  350; *The Races of Britain*, XII. 350
Beddoes, Thomas Lovell (1803–1849), XII.
  107, 115 ff. (main entry), 126, 139, 414;
  XIII. 141, 149, 198, 230, 238, 517
  Bride's Tragedy, The, XII. 115
  Death's Jest Book or *The Fool's Revenge*,
  XII. 115, 116; XIII. 239
  Dirge for Wolfram, XII. 116
  Dream-Pedlary, XII. 116
  Improvisatore, The, XII. 115
  Letter from Oxford, XII. 116
  Old Adam, the carrion crow, XII. 116
  Pygmalion, XII. 116
  Song of the Stygian Naiades, XII. 116
Bede, in *The Example of Virtue*, II. 227
Bede or Baeda, the Venerable (673–735),
  I. 5, 10, 14, 19, 20, 43 ff., 53, 55, 57, 59,
  66, 68, 70, 71, 79–84 (main entry), 89,
  96, 117, 119 ff., 131, 145, 148, 159 ff.,
  163 ff., 167 ff., 172, 198, 224, 257, 342,
  347, 350, 351, 380, 433, 434, 436, 437,
  439; IV. 67; VII. 510; XIV. 69, 302
  Death Song, I. 61
  De Natura Rerum, I. 80.
  De Temporibus, I. 81
  Historia Ecclesiastica, I. 81 ff., 93, 96,
  101, 106, 110, 112, 234, 434, 436, 437,
  439; IV. 37; VIII. 309; IX. 539; XII. 487
  Martyrology, I. 80
  Retractationes, I. 80
  Other works, I. 80–81, 224
Bede, Adam, George Eliot's, XIII. 382,
  389 ff.
Bede, Cuthbert, *pseud. See* Bradley, Ed-
  ward
Bede, Seth, George Eliot's, XIII. 389, 391
Bedell, William (1571–1642), VII. 308, 318,
  442; IX. 489; XII. 488
Bedford, II. 336; III. 202; VII. 167 ff., 172;
  IX. 169
Bedford, Arthur (1668–1745), VIII. 432;
  IX. 528
Bedford, countess of (d. 1627). *See*
  Russell, Lucy
Bedford, dukes of. *See* Lancaster, John
  of; Russell, Francis; Russell, John;
  Russell, Wriothesley
Bedford, Grosvenor, the elder, XI. 154
Bedford, Grosvenor, the younger, XI. 154,
  169, 172
Bedford, H., XIII. 570
Bedford gaol, VII. 170, 172
Bedford level, IX. 343

Bedford missal, XII. 510
Bedford school, VII. 330
Bedfordshire, II. 206; VIII. 60; IX. 145;
  XII. 345; XIII. 145
Bedingfield, lady, XIV. 503
Bedingfield, Thomas (d. 1613), IV. 7, 398,
  442, 443, 540
Bedivere. *See* Bedwyr
Bedlam, X. 56
Bedwell, William (d. 1632), IV. 453; VII. 470
Bedworth academy, X. 385
Bedwyr or Bedivere, Arthurian knight, I.
  250, 254, 255, 260; II. 119
Bee, The (Anderson's), IX. 560; XI. 236
Bee, The (Budgell's), IX. 492
Bee and the Spider, The, in Swift's *Battle*
  of the Books, IX. 102
Beech, Robert (d. 1594), V. 325
Beeching, Henry Charles (1859–1919), XI.
  434; XII. 257, 453, 455; XIV. 515;
  Francis Atterbury, X. 352
Beedome, Thomas (d. 1641?), VII. 88, 412
Beef-steak club, IX. 139
Beelzebub, V. 33
Beer-Hofmann, *Der Graf von Charolais*,
  VI. 165
Bees, writers on, IV. 542
Beesly, Edward Spencer (1831–1915), XIV
  468
Beeston, Christopher, VI. 103
Beethoven, Ludwig van, XII. 64, 268
Beets, Heinrich, IX. 515
Beghard communities, II. 47
Begum, the, in *Pendennis*, XIII. 291
Beha-ed-din Zoheir, XII. 499
Behaim, Martin, of Nürnberg, IV. 82
Behmen, Jacob. *See* Boehme
Behmenists, IX. 306
Behn, Mrs Aphra or Aphara (1640–1689),
  VIII. 140, 168, 416, 422, 424, 425; IX. 18,
  174; X. 72; XII. 246
  City Heiress, The, VIII. 142
  Debauchee, The, VIII. 141
  Dutch Lover, The, VIII. 131, 141
  False Count, The, VIII. 131, 142
  Forced Marriage, The, VIII. 141, 181
  Maximes, trans. of La Rochefoucauld's,
  VIII. 373
  Moor's Revenge, The, VIII. 141, 195
  Nun, The, or The Perjur'd Beauty, VIII.
  191
  Oronooko, or the Royal Slave, VIII. 141,
  191
  Roundheads, The, VIII. 122, 142
  Rover, The, or the Banished Cavaliers,
  VIII. 131, 141
  Town Fop, The, VIII. 142
  Widow Ranter, The, VIII. 142, 401
  Young King, The, VIII. 141
Beid, IV. 363
Bek, Thomas, of Castleford, I. 335, 338
Bekinsau, John (1496?–1559), VIII. 466
Bekynton, or Beckington, T. (1390?–1465 ,
  II. 303, 482
Bel-Anna, in *The Masque of Queens*, VI. 349
Belarius, in *Cymbeline*, V. 205

Belcarre, lord, XIV. 284

Belch, Sir Toby, in *Twelfth Night*, v. 194

Belcour, in Cumberland's *West Indian*, XI. 264, 265, 275

Belfast, XI. 283; XIV. 311, 317, 327

Belfast, books printed in, XI. 470

Belfast, Queen's college, XIV. 417, *also see* Add. 3

'Belfast man, the,' Francis Davis, XIV. 326

Belfastman's Journal, The, XIV. 327

Belfield, in Cumberland's *Brothers*, XI. 264

Belgarde, in *The Unnaturall Combat*, VI. 160 ff.

Belgian writers, IX. 314

Belgic Kymrys, XIV. 68

Belgioioso, duchess of, XII. 440

Belgium, II. 310; XIII. 88, 112

Belgrade, IX. 244; XIV. 251

Belial, XII. 36

Belial, in *Paradise Lost*, VII. 121; x. 310

Belianis, don, in *The Tatler*, XI. 373

Belinda, in Congreve's *Old Bachelor*, VIII. 148

Belinda, Miss Edgeworth's, XI. 297

Belinda, in Vanbrugh's *Provok'd Wife*, VIII. 161

Belisante, in *Amis and Amiloun*, I. 314

Beljame, Alexandre, X. 444; XI. 466; XII. 400, 524

Bell, Alfred Henry Haynes, XIV. Add. 4; *Knight of Avelon*, XIV. 378; *Last Stand, The*, XIV. 378; *To a Sea Conch*, XIV. 378

Bell, Andrew (1753–1832), XI. 422; XIV. 395, 403, 404, 590, 601, 604; *Experiments in Education*, XIV. 401

Bell, Sir Charles (1774–1842), x. 513; XIV. 559

Bell, Charles Dent (d. 1898), XIII. 499

Bell, Henry (1767–1830), XIV. 258

Bell, Henry Glassford (1803–1874), XII. 414

Bell, Henry Thomas Mackenzie, XIII. 496

Bell, James (*fl.* 1551–1596), IV. 446

Bell, John (1691–1780), IX. 560; XI. 325, 342, 453, 456; *Poets of Great Britain from Chaucer to Churchill*, IX. 479; x. 451

Bell, Paul, *pseud. See* Chorley, Henry Fothergill

Bell, Peter, in Wordsworth's poem, XII. 70

Bell, Robert (1800–1867), XI. 422; XIV. 533

Bell, Thomas (*fl.* 1573–1610), IV. 509

Bell, Thomas (*fl.* 1672), IX. 545

Bell, Thomas (1792–1880), x. 269, 270

Bell's Life in London, XIV. 231, 232, 234, 235, 239

Bell's Life in Victoria, XIV. 366, 367

Bell's Weekly Messenger, XI. 325

Bellafront, in *The Honest Whore*, v. 251; VI. 53, 172

Bellafront, in *A Woman is a Weathercocke*, VI. 221

Bellair, in Etherege's *The Man of Mode*, VIII. 138

Bellamia, in *The Example*, VI. 202

Bellamont, in *North-Ward Hoe*, VI. 172

Bellamy, Daniel, the elder (b. 1687), XI. 172, 424

Bellamy, David, the younger (d. 1788), XI. 424

Bellamy, Miss George Anne (1731?–1788), XI. 260, 453

Bellamy, Henry (*fl.* 1630), VI. 470

Bellamy, Thomas (1745–1800), XI. 448

'Bellamy's' in Dickens's 'Parliamentary Sketch,' XIII. 309

Bellario, in *Philaster*, VI. 126

Bellarmine, cardinal, III. 414; IV. 500; VII. 301, 309; VIII. 462; *Disputationes*, IV. 199

Bellasis, Edward (1800–1873), XII. 454

Bellaston, lady, in Fielding's *Tom Jones*, x. 31, 32, 89

Belleforest, F. de, IV. 3; v. 159, 221; *Histoires Tragiques*, VI. 180

Bellenden, Edith, in Scott's *Old Mortality*, XII. 22

Bellenden, John (*fl.* 1533–1587), III. 131, 156, 319, 500; *The Banner of Pietie*, III. 131; Scottish translation of Livy, II. 285; III. 156; translation of Boece's *History of Scotland*, II. 285; IV. 412

Bellenden, Mary, IX. 250

Bellenden, William (*fl.* 1616), XII. 326

Bellers, John (1654–1725), *Proposals for Raising a Colledge of Industry*, IX. 406, 570

'Belleville,' Badenoch, x. 232

Bellimperia, in *The Spanish Tragedie*, v. 161 ff.

Bellingham, Northumberland, XIII. 129

Bellings, Richard (d. 1677), *History of the Irish Confederation*, VII. 212, 448

Bellisant, in *The Parliament of Love*, VI. 155

Bellmour, in Congreve's *Old Bachelor*, VIII. 148

Belloc, L. Sw., XIII. 551

Bellot, J., IV. 541

Belloy, Pierre L. B. de, *Le Siège de Calais*, XI. 274

Bellum grammaticale, VI. 482; IX. 551

Belman's Brother, The, IV. 354

Beloe, William (1756–1817), x. 473; XII. 491, 520; *Anecdotes of Literature*, XII. 363; *The Sexagenarian*, XII. 363

Belphegor, in *The Devil and his Dame*, v. 329

Belphoebe, in *The Faerie Queene*, III. 233, 237

Belsham, Thomas (1750–1829), XII. 465

Belshazzar, XII. 229, 477

Belshazzar, in *Cleanness*, I. 323

Belson, Mrs. *See* Elliott, Mary

Beltayne, At, II. 244

Beltrees, Renfrewshire, IX. 364, 556

Belvedere Or The Garden Of The Muses, IV. 467

Belvidera, in Otway's *Venice Preserv'd*, VIII. 183, 184

Belvoir, Leicestershire, XI. 143, 144

Belzoni, Giovanni Battista (1778–1823), XIV. 248, 550

Bembo, Pietro, cardinal, III. 262; IV. 428

Bemerton, Wilts, VII. 29; VIII. 348

Ben, in Congreve's *Love for Love*, VIII. 150 ff.

Ben, sailor, in Congreve's *Love for Love*, X. 90

Benares, rajah of, XI. 14

Benatzi, in *The Ladies Triall*, VI. 194

Bendall, Cecil (1856–1906), XII. 502

Bendo, Alexander, *i.e.* Rochester, earl of, VIII. 208

Bendz, E., XIII. 488

Benedetti, Anna, XIII. 570

Benedick, in *Much Ado about Nothing*, V. 191; VIII. 120, 155

Benedict of Peterborough (d. 1193), I. 160, 173, 174, 449; IV. 417; IX. 349; *Gesta Regis Henrici*, XIV. 74

Benedict Biscop (628?–690), abbot of Wearmouth, I. 5, 71, 84, 89, 151

Benedict, St, I. 74, 105; VII. 391

Benedict XII, pope, II. 349

Benedict XIII, pope, II. 368

'Benedict,' Della Cruscan poet, XI. 177

Benedictbeuern, monastery in Bavaria, I. 190

Benedictines, the, II. 2, 245, 349, 350, 354, 362; III. 48, 51, 57; IV. 416 ff.; VII. 143; X. 282; XIV. 53

Benedix, Roderich, *Aschenbrödel*, XIII. 272

Benet, St, Rule of, I. 15, 230, 458, 459

Bengal, XI. 242; XIV. 338

Bengal army, the, XIV. 337

Bengali literature, XIV. 341

Benger, Elizabeth Ogilvy (1778–1827), XI. 460

Benham, Allen Rogers, I. Add.

Benion, Samuel (*fl.* 1706), X. 386

Benkhausen, chevalier George de, XIII. 55

Benlow (or Bruce), Mrs Marinda, in Amory's *Memoirs of Several Ladies*, XI. 287

Benlowes, Edward (1603?–1676), VII. 73, 88 ff., 94, 137, 412; XIII. 218; *Theophila or Love's Sacrifice*, VII. 90

Benn, Alfred William, XIV. 467

Bennet, Benjamin (1674–1726), IX. 476; X. 521

Bennet, Elizabeth, in Jane Austen's *Pride and Prejudice*, XII. 237 ff., 243

Bennet, Henry, 1st earl of Arlington (1618–1685), VII. 363; VIII. 92, 198, 376, 379, 380, 384, 480, 482

Bennet, James (*fl.* 1761), X. 177, 469

Bennet, Jane, in Jane Austen's *Pride and Prejudice*, XII. 238

Bennet, John (*fl.* 1600), IV. 463

Bennet, Mr, in Jane Austen's *Pride and Prejudice*, XII. 238

Bennet, Mrs, in Jane Austen's *Pride and Prejudice*, XII. 238

Bennet, Mrs, in Fielding's *Amelia*, X. 33

Bennett, Edward Turner, X. 270

Bennett, James (1774–1862) and Bogue' D., *History of Dissenters*, X. 518

Bennett, Joseph, XIV. 192

Bennett, Samuel (1815–1878), XIV. 584; *History of Australian Discovery*, XIV. 371

Bennett, William Cox (1820–1895), XIII. 499

Benoit, historiographer, II. 419, 507

Benoît de Ste More, I. 280, 306, 467; II. 150; *Roman de Troie*, II. 172

Bensley, Robert (1738?–1817?), XI. 257

Bensly, Robert Lubbock (1831–1893), XII. 341, 503

Benson, Arthur Christopher (1862–1925), XIII. 476, 486, 490, 497, 503, 555, 557; XIV. 523, 524

Benson, George (1699–1762), X. 386, 521

Benson, Thurston, in Mrs Gaskell's *Ruth*, XIII. 372

Benson, William (1682–1754), IX. 562

Bent, James Theodore (1852–1897), XII. 496

Bent, William (*fl.* 1770), XI. 339

Bentham, Edward (*fl.* 1748), XIV. 595

Bentham, George (1800–1884), XIV. 468

Bentham, James (1708–1794), XII. 507; *History of Ely Cathedral*, IX. 354, 532

Bentham, Jeremy (1748–1832), III. 425; VII. 104; VIII. 321; IX. 299, 301, 409; X. 335, 346; XI. 57 ff. (main entry), 136, 397; XII. 152, 309, 430; XIV. 2, 4, 8, 14 ff., 20, 59, 98, 127, 187, 194, 198, 290, 336, 407, 559, 604

 Anarchical Fallacies, XI. 71

 Book of Fallacies, XI. 71

 Chrestomathia, XI. 72; XIV. 404

 Codification Proposals, XI. 72

 Constitutional Code, XI. 71

 Defence of Usury, XI. 58

 Deontology, XI. 61

 Fragment on Government, XI. 58, 61 ff., 71

 Influence of Time and Place in Matters of Legislation, XI. 72

 Introduction to the Principles of Morals and Legislation, XI. 58, 59, 64, 65, 69

 Introductory view of the Rationale of Evidence, XI. 61

 Poor Laws and Pauper Management, XI. 72

 Rationale of Evidence, XI. 61

 Table of the Springs of Action, XI. 61, 65

 Theory of Legislation, XI. 68

 Works, XI. 60, 61

Bentham, Samuel (brother of Jeremy Bentham), XI. 58

Benthamism, XIII. 22

Bentinck, countess, VIII. 272

Bentinck, lord George (1802–1848), XIII. 353, 546; XIV. 115, 129, 130, 336, 508

Bentinck, William, 1st earl of Portland (1649–1709), IX. 149, 150, 206

Bentinck, William, 2nd duke of Portland (1709–1762), X. 262; XI. 347, 389

Bentinck, William Henry Cavendish, 3rd duke of Portland (1738–1809), X. 403

Bentivoglio, cardinal, X. 291

Bentley, Richard (1662–1742), IV. 250;
v. 273; VII. 109; VIII. 230, 385; IX. 80,
86, 88, 103, 132, 138, 139, 297, 329 ff.
(main entry), 381, 382, 411, 412, 449,
478, 504, 524 ff., 561, 572, 574; x. 309;
XI. 341, 380; XII. 324, 325, 332, 485,
488; XIV. 283
'Confutation of Atheism,' IX. 331
Dissertation on the Epistles of Phalaris,
IX. 329, 330, 333, 338, 391
Epistola ad Millium, IX. 330, 331
Horace, IX. 336, 337
Manilius, IX. 338
Milton, IX. 338, 339
*Remarks upon a late Discourse of Free-
thinking,* IX. 292, 293, 337
Terence, IX. 338
Bentley, Richard (1708–1782), x. 245, 248;
XI. 456; *Designs for six Poems by Mr
T. Gray,* x. 126, 450; *Philodamus,* XI.
274
Bentley and Newton correspondence, x.
466
Bentley's Miscellany, XII. 413, 447; XIII.
315, 316; XIV. 316
Bentworth, near Alton, Hampshire, IV.
154
Beowa, I. 27, 28
Beowanham, I. 27
Beowulf, I. 1 ff., 11, 12, 20, 21, 22–30 (main
entry), 34, 35, 41, 43, 54, 58, 63, 99,
115, 124, 137, 143, 277, 306, 421, *also see*
Add. to third impression; II. 1, 398;
IV. 517; v. 26; XII. 344; XIII. 127; XIV.
453
Beppo, in Byron's poem, XII. 53
Berachyah Nakden, I. 478
Beranger, Gabriel (d. 1817), XII. 514
Berdoe, Edward, XIII. 483
Berdok, King, II. 276
Bere, Richard (d. 1524), III. 49
Bereblock or Bearblock, John (*fl.* 1566),
v. 400; VI. 299
Bereker, W., IV. 441
Berengarius, I. 154
Berenger, Richard (d. 1782), XI. 362
Bergen, VIII. 202
Bergenroth, Gustav Adolph (1813–1869),
XIV. 485
Bergerac, Cyrano de. *See* Cyrano
Bergers, Calendrier des, II. 328
Bergetto, in *Tis Pitty Shees a Whore,* VI.
192
Berghen. *See* Adraien van
Berinthia, in Sheridan's *Trip to Scar-
borough,* XI. 268
Berinthia, in Vanbrugh's *Relapse,* VIII.
161; XI. 268
Berkeley, Charles, 2nd earl of Berkeley
(1693?–1746), IX. 93
Berkeley, Elizabeth, countess of, IX. 93
Berkeley, George, 1st earl of (1628–1698),
II. 77
Berkeley, George (1685–1753), bishop of
Cloyne, III. 416; VII. 278, 289, 290; VIII.
428; IX. 171, 279 ff., 502, *also see* Add.;

x. 35, 328 ff., 342, 343, 348, 381; XI.
57, 100; XII. 60; XIV. 8, 19, 41, 43, 47,
468, 473
Alciphron, IX. 282, 283, 286, 301, 302
Analyst, The, IX. 282
Common-place Book, IX. 280, 283, 287
De Motu, IX. 280
Essay towards a new theory of vision,
IX. 61, 280, 283, 284
*Essay towards preventing the ruin of Great
Britain,* IX. 280
Miscellany, IX. 282
Principles of human knowledge, IX. 280,
284, 286, 287
Querist, The, IX. 282
Siris, IX. 282, 287
Theory of Vision, IX. 282, 284
*Three Dialogues between Hylas and Philo-
nous,* IX. 131, 280, 286
*Verses on the prospect of planting arts...
in America,* IX. 281
Works, XIV. 48
Berkeley, Hon. George (1712–1767), IX.
498
Berkeley, George Monck (1763–1793),
VIII. 428; IX. 453, 470
Berkeley, Jane Martha, dowager lady,
afterwards countess of Portland (1672–
1751), VIII. 380
Berkeley, Sir John (d. 1678), VII. 449
Berkeley, Miles Joseph (1803–1889), XIV.
559; *Phytophthora infestans,* XIV. 290
Berkeley, Thomas, 5th lord (1353–1417),
II. 74, 76, 77
Berkeley, Sir William (d. 1677), VIII. 434;
The Lost Lady, VI. 452
Berkeley, Gloucestershire, II. 74, 77
Berkeley castle, IV. 181
Berkenhead or Birkenhead, Sir John
(1616–1679), VI. 136; VII. 494; *Mer-
curius Aulicus,* VII. 348; *Mercurius
Bellicus,* VII. 349
Berkshire, III. 368; IV. 431; IX. 531; x. 356;
XIII. 367
Berkshire, 3rd earl of, father of Sir Robert
Howard, VIII. 8
Berlin, VII. 309; VIII. 330; XIII. 385; XIV. 382
Berlioz, Hector, v. 302
Bermuda, IX. 281; XII. 103
Bermudas, the, IV. 78; v. 220, 347
Bernard, Charles de, XIII. 283
Bernard, Edward (1638–1696), IX. 356, 552
Bernard, John (1756–1828), XI. 447
Bernard, Little, St, XII. 496, 497
Bernard, Mountague (1820–1882), XII. 454
Bernard, Richard (1568–1641), IV. 440;
VII. 374; *Guide to Grand Jury Men,* VII.
375, 507
Bernard, Sir Thomas (1750–1818), XIV.
601, 604
Bernard, St, I. 185, 221, 231, 355; II. 230,
365; III. 189; IV. 235; XIV. 504; *Tractat,*
II. 383; *Sayings of,* II. 425
Bernard, William Bayle (1807–1875), XIII.
517; XIV. 569
Doge of Venice, The, XIII. 266

Bernard, William Bayle
  Marie Ducange, XIII. 266
  Passing Cloud, The, XIII. 266
  Round of Wrong, The, XIII. 266
Bernard, in *Specula Stultorum*, I. 193
Bernard of Chartres, I. 184, 188
Bernard of Clugny or Morlaix, *De Contemptu Mundi*, XIII. 172, 173
Bernardo, in Shelley's *The Cenci*, XII. 69
Bernays, Jacob, *Life of Scaliger*, XIV. 109
Berners, Isopel, Borrow's, XIII. 442
Berners, Juliana (b. 1388?), IV. 538; *The Book of St Albans*, II. 318, 323, 420, 485, 496.
Berners, Lord (1467–1533). See Bourchier, John
Berni, Francesco, XII. 33, 52, 56
Bernier, François, XIV. 333; *Voyage*, X. 110
Bernlak de Hautdesert, *the Green Knight*. See *Sir Gawayne*
Bernstein, baroness, in *The Virginians*, XIII. 298
Bernysdale, II. 309
Beroaldus, Philippus (d. 1505), IV. 249, 429
Béroul (*c.* 1150), I. 273, 310
Berquin, Arnaud, XI. 491; *L'Ami des Enfans*, XI. 378, 382; *Le Petit Grandisson*, XI. 382
Berrow's Worcester Journal, XIV. 169
Berry, Arthur, XIV. 555
Berry, Mary (1763–1852), X. 249 ff., 494 ff.
Berry, Mrs, George Meredith's, XIII. 447
Berryer, Pierre Antoine, XIV. 127
Berrys, the (Robert, Mary and Agnes), X. 495
Bert, Edmund, IV. 541
Bertha, in Keats's *Eve of St Mark's*, XII. 87
Bertha, mother of Charles the Great, V. 40
Berthe aux grands pieds, I. 468
Berthelet, Thomas, printer to Henry VIII, III. 315, 486; IV. 400, 405, 546
Bertholdi, in *The Imposture*, VI. 205
Bertoldo, in *The Maid of Honour*, VI. 155, 156, 162
Bertram, Charles (1723–1765), IX. 540; XII. 336
Bertram, Edmund, in Jane Austen's *Mansfield Park*, XII. 238, 239
Bertram, Godfrey, laird of Ellangowan, in Scott's *Guy Mannering*, XII. 29, 151
Bertram, in Scott's *Rokeby*, XII. 12
Bertram, lady, in Jane Austen's *Mansfield Park*, XII. 239
Bertram, Lucy, in Scott's *Guy Mannering*, XII. 22
Bertram, Sir Stephen, in Cumberland's *Jew*, XI. 282
Bertram, Sir Thomas, in Jane Austen's *Mansfield Park*, XII. 239, 241
Bertram, the misses, in Jane Austen's *Mansfield Park*, XII. 238, 243
Berwick Advertiser, The, XIV. 203
Berwick, siege of, II. 101
Berwick-upon-Tweed, XI. 469; XIII. 372

Berwickshire, X. 323
Berwyn mountains, X. 115
Beryn, The Tale of, or *The Second Merchant's Tale*, I. 298, 299, 467; II. 162, 164, 215, 216, 469
Besançon, Etienne de, III. 489
Besant, Sir Walter (1836–1901), XII. 507; XIII. 438, 560; *A Survey of London*, XII. 349; *All Sorts and Conditions of Men*, XIII. 458
Besler of Nürnberg, IV. 247
Bess the Gawkie, IX. 374
Besse, Joseph (1683?–1757), VIII. 413, 414
Besselaar, G., XIV. Add. 4
Bessus, in *A King and no King*, VI. 127
Bessy, the, in folk plays, V. 31 ff.
Bessy Bell and Marie Gray, IX. 368
Best, Charles (*fl.* 1602), IV. 124
Best, captain George (d. 1584), *A True discourse of the late voyages . . . to Cathaya*, IV. 74, 453
Best, Paul (1590?–1657), X. 377
Best, William Draper, 1st baron Wynford (1767–1845), VIII. 317
Bestiaries, Old English, I. 59; Middle English, I. 226, 227, 239, 292, 458 ff.
Beta (queen Elizabeth), in Drayton's *Idea*, IV. 172, 173, 184
Betham, Mary Matilda (1776–1852), XI. 423
Bethell, Richard, 1st baron Westbury (1800–1873), XIV. 124, 507
Bethlehem, II. 13; V. 37
Bethulia, I. 142, 143
Bethune, Alexander (1804–1843), XII. 414
Betokis bour, in *Gyre Carling*, II. 275, 277
Betraying of Christ, The, V. 17
Betsey, Miss, in *David Copperfield*, XIII. 327
Betteridge, Wilkie Collins's, XIII. 438
Betterton, Thomas (1635?–1710), VI. 47, 248, 271; VIII. 29, 31, 121, 146, 150, 166, 177, 179, 182, 184, 186, 191, 192, 194, 195, 422, 423, 439; IX. 144, 476; X. 442; XI. 257, 447, 454; *Henry IV*, version of, VIII. 120; *The Prophetesse*, VIII. 120, 401
Betty, in Phillips's *Don Quixote*, IX. 269
Betty, William Henry West (1791–1874), XI. 283, 452
Betuleius, Xystus, V. 101
Beuchame, Lewes, IV. 446
Beulah, daughters of, in Blake's *Four Zoas*, XI. 196
Beulah, land of, XII. 175, 253
Beulan, teacher of Nennius, I. 70
Beveridge, William (1637–1708), VII. 490; VIII. 298, 301, 302, 457; IX. 528
Beverley, V. 41, 45, 103
Beverley. See Alfred of; St John of
Beverley, in Sheridan's *Rivals*, XI. 266
Beverley, Mrs, in Moore's *Gamester*, X. 80
Beverley, Yorks., IX. 470
Beversham, James (*fl.* 1618), IV. 93

Beves or *Bevis of Hamtoun*, I. 218, 282, 287, 291 ff., 303, 305, 306, 470; II. 320, 323; V. 108; VII. 167

Bevil junior, in Steele's *Conscious Lovers*, IX. 64

Beville, William (*fl.* 1782), X. 475

Bevis, in *The Tatler*, XI. 373

Bew, M., III. 189

Beware the Cat, III. 112, 494

Bewcastle column, Cumberland, I. 12, 426

Bewick, Thomas (1753–1828), IX. 481; XI. 377, 436, 485, 487, 489, 490, 492; XIV. 201, 227, 235, 236, 540, 542

Bewick and Graham, II. 411

Bexley, 1st lord. *See* Vansittart, Nicholas

Bexley heath, XIII. 119

Beyle, Henri (De Stendhal), XII. 381, 392, 397; *Racine et Shakespeare*, X. 181

Beyrout, XIV. 251

Beza, Theodore, III. 45, 46, 174; IV. 429; VIII. 277, 363; *Abraham's Sacrifice*, V. 394; *Praefatio Poetica*, III. 174

Bhagalpur, XIV. 334

Bhagavadgītā, the, XII. 343, 503

Biagi, Guido, XIII. 552

Bianca, in *Loves Sacrifice*, VI. 192

Bianca, in *The Taming of the Shrew*, V. 181

Bianca, in *Women beware Women*, VI. 78, 176

Biberach, V. 298

Bible, the, I. 72, 89; II. 150, 151, 230, 289, 291, 314, 366, 367; III. 10, 11, 13, 25, 27, 28, 29, 31, 40 ff., 44, 45, 47, 53, 58, 86, 110, 130, 133, 140, 141, 145, 157, 163, 214, 339, 363, 400, 407, 410 ff., 416, 423, 445, 455, 462, 463; IV. 26 ff., 81, 230, 241, 248, 270, 303, 347, 389, 396, 412, 421, *also see* Add.; V. 17, 40, 44, 101, 111, 342; VI. 91, 375, 378, 401, 402, 405; VII. 6, 151, 157, 164, 169, 171, 177, 236, 253, 269, 296, 297, 303 ff., 315 ff., 321 ff., 371, 375, 382, 396; VIII. 42, 78, 86, 91, 92, 101, 103, 105, 110 ff., 164, 274 ff., 278, 294, 298, 302, 326, 346, 364; IX. 42, 118, 393, 402; X. 154, 229, 236; XI. 48, 89, 181, 188, 189, 237, 326, 363, 369; XII. 156, 177, 280, 282 ff., 293, 295, 318, 331, 488, 501, 502, 520, 521; XIII. 102; XIV. 148, 329, 405

See, also, *Old and New Testament*

New Testament, IX. 294, 330; XII. 286, 290, 293, 297, 298, 340 (revised version), 501; the first printed English, XII. 515; in Scots, XIV. 101

Old Testament, IX. 296; XII. 501; XIV. 132

Bible, Versions of the:

Authorised Version, the, III. 45, 423, 465; IV. 26–50, 185, 238, 398, 449; XIV. 435, 441, 446 ff.

Bassandyne, the, II. 94, 285

Bishops', the, III. 45, 423; IV. 400, 401

Challoner's Roman Catholic, IV. 49

Chinese, XII. 342, 500

Coverdale's, III. 45; IV. 41, 402

Cranmer's, III. 44

Bible, Versions of the:

Douay, IV. 41, 49; X. Add.

Early translations, IV. 37, 39; VII. 127

English, III. 474, IV. 26 ff. (main entry)

Genevan, II. 94; III. 45, 46; IV. 41, 403

Great, the, III. 44, 45

Greek Testament, IX. 336; XII. 340, 500

Hebrew, IX. 330; XII. 341

Matthew's, III. 45

Polyglot, IV. 427

Rheims translation of, III. 446; IV. 38, 41, 42, 49; X. Add.

Sanskrit, XII. 343

Septuagint, I. 77; VII. 316; IV. 46

Syriac (*Gospels*), XII. 341

Tindale's, III. 41 ff.; IV. 38 ff.

Trevisa's, II. 77

Vulgate, the, I. 46, 84, 85, 91, 97, 208, 400; II. 59, 60, 62, 94, 431; III. 41, 45, 463, 464; IV. 36, 46

Wyclifite, II. 300, 430, 431, 440; IV 38, 39, 42, 428

Bible, single vols. or MSS. of:

Codex Amiatinus at Florence, I. 72

Codex Argenteus at Upsala, I. 16

King Philip's, IV. 427

Metz, I. 89

Rushworth Gospels, the, I. 132

St Denis, I. 89

Sir Walter Ralegh's, IV. 65

Thomas Cromwell's, IV. 426

Bible, books and parts of:

Acts of the Apostles, IV. 32; IX. 534; XIV. 449

Apocalypse. See *Revelation*

Apocrypha, the, II. 120, 230, 430; III. 43 ff.; VII. 316, 317; XII. 502

Baruch, II. 61

Canticles. See, post, *Song of Songs*

Chronicles, III. 44; IV. 43

Colossians, XII. 501

Corinthians, IV. 38; VII. 140, 322; XI. 355

Corinthians I, XII. 483, 501

Corinthians II, XII. 501

Daniel, XII. 501, 503

Deuteronomy, IV. 170; VII. 140, 395; XII. 501

Ecclesiastes, III. 271; VII. 317; XII. 341, 501; XIII. 138

Ephesians, II. 234, 431; IX. 560

Esther, XII. 316

Exodus, IV. 30, 36, 37, 39; XII. 499, 501

Exodus (Old English), I. 46 ff., 58, 63, 428

Exodus (Wyclifite), II. 430

Ezekiel, VII. 322; XII. 501

Four Gospels, IX. 561

Galatians, XII. 486, 501

Genesis, II. 14; IV. 31; VII. 140; VIII. 352; XII. 48, 499, 501, 503; XIV. 149

Genesis, A and B, Old English, I. 46 ff., 63, 428

Genesis and Exodus, Middle English, I. 225, 376, 387, 399, 458, 459

Gospels, the, IV. 39, 424

Bible, books and parts of:
  Gospels, X. 365; XII. 280, 503, 505
  Habakkuk, XII. 501
  Hebrews, IV. 43; XII. 340, 503
  Hosea, VII. 322
  Isaiah, II. 430; III. 101; IV. 77, 170; XII. 501
  Jeremiah, XII. 501
  Job, IV. 30, 33, 47, 48; VII. 317, 322; X. 458; XI. 434; XII. 341, 416, 501, 502
  Joel and Amos, XII. 501
  John, epistles of St, XII. 340
  John, First Epistle of St, X. 309
  John, Gospel of St, II. 365; IV. 37, 38; V. 37, 42; VII. 322; X. 463; XII. 340, 481, 489, 490
  Jonah, III. 44; VII. 46
  Judges, IV. 43, 170
  2 *Kings*, IV. 33
  Leviticus, XII. 501
  Luke, Gospel of St, IV. 41; XII. 503
  Maccabees iv, XII. 503
  Mark, Gospel of St, I. 132; III. 42; V. 42; XII. 505
  Matthew, Gospel of St, I. 132; III. 42; VII. 140
  Nahum, XII. 501
  Paul, Epistles of St, IV. 27, 30; XII. 340, 506
  Paul, speech of St, IV. 29
  Pentateuch, III. 44; IV. 39, 238; XII. 296
  Philemon, XII. 501
  Philippians, XII. 501
  Proverbs, II. 14; IV. 34; VII. 317
  Psalm cxix, XIV. 74
  Psalms, III. 46, 101, 174; IV. 30, 33, 34, 44, 81, 131, 407; V. 21; VII. 31, 109, 215, 322; IX. 63, 78, 556, 559, 562; X. 456, 457; XI. 206, 237; XII. 419
  Psalms, Buchanan's version, III. 162, 164
  Psalms in metre, III. 476; IV. 384, 395, 397
  Psalms, versions of Sternhold and Hopkins, III. 46
  Psalter, IV. 28, 31, 384
  Psalter, Gallican, IV. 422
  Psalter, the Genevan, III. 46
  Psalter, Irish, IV. 426
  Psalter, Prayer Book version, IV. 41
  Psalter, the Scots (1564), III. 46
  Revelation of St John (*Apocalypse*), II. 60; IV. 28, 30, 47; VII. 170; VIII. 286; XI. 197; XII. 501; XIII. 139; XIV. 149
  Romans, III. 45; IV. 38, 42; XII. 484, 486, 492
  Samuel, IV. 33
  Song of Songs, The (*Canticles, Song of Solomon*), II. 48; IV. 170, 249; VII. 109, 317; X. 489, 522; XII. 341, 501
  Thessalonians, XII. 486
  Zephaniah, XII. 501
Bible societies in Scotland, XI. 469
Bible society, the, IX. 247; XI. 259; XIV. 146
Bibles, prices of, II. 308

Biblical parodies, IX. 563
Biblical studies, VII. 311, 318, 321, 481
Bibliographical society, XII. 355, 369, 519
Bibliothèque universelle, VIII. 331
Bickerstaff, Isaac (d. 1812?), IX. 35, 39, 40, 46 ff., 50, 51, 54; X. 71, 425; XI. 451; XIV. 461
  Lionel and Clarissa, X. 89
  Love in a Village, X. 89
  Maid of the Mill, X. 89
  Padlock, The, X. 89; XI. 262
  Schools for Fathers, X. 89
Bickerstaff, Isaac, of *The Tatler*, XI. 373
Bickersteth, Edward (1786–1850), XII. 471
Bickersteth, Henry, lord Langdale (1783–1851), XII. 355, 356, 516
Bickham, George (d. 1758), XIV. 212, 214
Bickley, Francis, IX. Add.
Bickley, Francis L., XIII. 488
Bicknell, Alexander (d. 1796), XI. 453
Bidding prayer, III. 31
Biddle, John (1615–1662), X. 359, 377, 378
Bideford, Devon, XIV. 84
Bidpai, fables of, XI. 479; XII. 499
Biffen, in Gissing's *New Grub Street*, XIII. 460
Big Endians, IX. 229
Bigg, Charles, IX. 321, 324
Bigg, John Stanyan (1828–1865), XIII. 499
Bigg, Mrs, X. 119
Biggs, Noah, VII. 511
Bigland, Ralph (1711–1784), XII. 510
Bigmore, E. C., XIV. 535
Bignell, Mrs, in D'Urfey's *The Modern Prophets*, VIII. 175
Bignold, Thomas Francis (d. 1888), XIV. 575; *Leviora*, XIV. 340
Bigod, Ralph, in Lamb's *Essays of Elia*, XII. 188
Bijapur army, the, XIV. 338
Bilberg, John, IV. 453
Bilboe, in Wilson's *The Cheats*, VIII. 122
Biliotti, Édouard, XII. 339
Bill, John, *Books printed in English*, IV. 403, 404
Bill, William (d. 1561), III. 421
Billings, Robert William (1813–1874), XII. 507
Billingsgate, in Trevisa, II. 78
Billingsley, Sir Henry (d. 1606), III. 551; IV. 436, 453
Billy, Jacques de, IV. 24
'Billy, perfidious,' XIV. 116
Bilney, Thomas (d. 1531), III. 27, 36; IV. 231
Bilson, Thomas (1547–1616), IV. 265, 491; VII. 318, 484; *Christian subjection*, IV. 411
Bindley, Charles (*pseud.* Harry Hieover, 1795–1859), XIV. 542
Binfield, IX. 67, 68, 161, 167
Bing, Thomas (*fl.* 1603), *Sorrowe's Joy*, IV. 351
Bingham, Joseph (1668–1723), X. 515; *Origines Ecclesiasticae*, X. 357
Bingham, Peregrine (1788–1864), XI. 398

Bingley, in Jane Austen's *Pride and Prejudice*, XII. 238
'Bingo,' Japan, IV. 99
Binney, E., XIV. 492
Binney, Edward William (1812–1881), XIV. 290, 559
Binning, Hugh (1627–1653), IX. 542
Binning, Thomas, IV. 453
Binns, Henry Bryan, XIV. 590, 592
Binyon, Laurence, XII. 406
Biographia Britannica, IX. 472, 530; X. 184
Biographia Dramatica, VIII. 188, 423; XI. 453
Biographical Dictionary (society for the Diffusion of Useful Knowledge), XII. 307; XIV. 409
Biographisches Jahrbuch, XII. 332
Bion, III. 218, 221, 222, 223; VII. 83, 489; IX. 526; X. 454; XI. 426; XII. 495
Bion, Greek pastoral translated by Oldham, VIII. 86
Birch, John (1616–1691), *Negotiations*, VII. 190
Birch, Samuel (1813–1885), XII. 500; *Book of the Dead*, XII. 342; *Hieroglyphical Grammar and Dictionary*, XII. 342; *History of Ancient Pottery*, XII. 342
Birch, Thomas (1705–1766), VIII. 453, 461, 462, 477, 479; IX. 529; X. 294, 498, *also see* Add.; XI. 356, 475
  The Court and Times of James I, VII. 193, 433, 436
  Court and Times of James I and Charles I, X. 295
  History of the Royal Society, X. 466
  Inquiry into Transactions of Glamorgan, X. 294
  Life of Dr John Tillotson, X. 295
  Life of Henry, Prince of Wales, X. 295
  Memoirs of the Reign of Elizabeth, X. 295
  Negotiations, X. 295
  Thurloe papers, X. 294
Birch, Walter, XII. 440
Birch, Walter de Gray, I. 451; XIV. 491
Birchenough, Charles, XIV. 590
Birchington, near Margate, XIII. 112
Birckbek, Simon (1584–1656), VII. 484
Birckman, Arnold (*fl.* 1568), IV. 403
Birckmans, the, IV. 402
Bird, John, XIV. Add. 5
Bird, William (*fl.* 1780), XII. 181
Bird, in *The Muses Looking-Glasse*, VI. 234
Birde, W. (*fl.* 1602), V. 333
Birel, Robert, The Diary of, III. 149, 501
Biringaccio, Vannuccio, *Pyrotechnica*, IV. 70
Birkabeyn, in *Havelok*, I. 303
Birkbeck, George (1776–1841), XIV. 407 ff., 601
Birkenhead or Berkenhead, Sir John (1616–1679), VI. 136
Birks, Thomas Rawson (1810–1883), XII. 471
Birmingham, III. 427; X. 159, 160, 163, 176, 187, 476; XI. 338, 340, 341, 469, 484; XII. 174, 184, 279, 511; XIII. 119, 427

Birmingham, Mason's college, XIV. 432
Birmingham Journal, X. 159
Birmingham school, VII. 330
Birnam wood, in Wyntoun's *Cronykil*, II. 132
Birnie, Pat, IX. 366
Biron, in *Love's Labour's Lost*, V. 178, 315
Biron, in Southerne's *Fatal Marriage*, VIII. 191, 192
Birrell, Augustine, XI. 466; XII. 437, 445; XIII. 470, 479, 484, 488, 505, 557
Birrenswark, in Dumfriesshire, XII. 350
Birth of Merlin, The, V. 236, 238, 249 ff., 441, 443; VI. 69, 70
Birtha, in D'Avenant's *Gondibert*, VII. 71; VIII. 9
Bishop, George (*fl.* 1590), IV. 82, 389, 398
Bishop, Sir Henry Rowley (1786–1855), XIII. 264
Bishop, Isabella L., born Bird (1831–1904), XIV. 550
Bishop, Richard (*fl.* 1645), VII. 361
Bishops' Book, The, III. 13, 36
Bishop's court, Kirk Michael, X. 359
Bishop's wood, in Pecock, II. 291
Bishopsbourne, III. 406
Bisland, Elizabeth, XIV. 519
Bismarck, prince von, XIII. 20; XIV. 183, 192, 194
Bisset, James (1762?–1832), XI. 452, 484
Bisset, Robert (1759–1805), IX. 441; XI. 390
Bisset, William (d. 1747), IX. 478
Bithynia, queen of, in *Believe as you List*, VI. 148, 149
Björkman, E., XIII. 573
Blachford, lord. *See* Rogers, Frederic
Black, A. and C., publishers, XII. 372
Black, John (1783–1855), XIV. 187
Black, John Sutherland, XII. 470
Black, Joseph (1728–1799), XIV. 272 ff., 406, 557; *Magnesia alba, Quicklime, and other alcaline substances*, XIV. 274
Black, Stephen, XIV. Add. 5
Black, William (1841–1898), XIII. 431, 560; XIV. 199; *Daughter of Heth, A*, XIII. 432; *Macleod of Dare*, XIII. 432; *Strange Adventures of a Phaeton, The*, XIII. 432
Black Almaine, the (a tune), III. 190
Black Bateman of the North, V. 325
Black Book of Carmarthen, I. 243, 249, 250, 251, 461
Black Death, the, I. 371; II. 41, 42, 45, 70, 71, 354
Blacke Dogge of Newgate, The, III. 99
Black Friars. *See* Dominicans
Black hole of Calcutta, the, XIV. 334
Black Knight, the, in *A Game at Chesse*, VI. 79
Black Knight, the, in Scott's *Ivanhoe*, XII. 18
Black Magic, VII. 368
'Black Mill,' VIII. 212, 219

Black Prince, the, II. 22; IV. 182; VI. 330; XI. 131

Black Prince, the, in *Edward III*, V. 246

Blackall, Offspring, IX. 41; X. 354

Blackbird, The, XI. 234

Blackbourne, Richard (b. 1652), VII. Add.

Blackburn, Douglas, XIV. Add. 5

Blackburn, Henry, XIV. 536

Blackfriars, children of, VI. 292

'Blackfriars preachers,' VI. 257

'Black-Fryers, Sanctified Fraternity of,' the, VI. 234

Blackie, John Stuart (1809–1895), XI. 439; XII. 335, 480; XIV. 515, 516

Blacklock, Thomas (1721–1791), IX. 556; X. 477; XI. 233, 234, 442

Blackman, John, XIV. 601

Blackmantle, Bernard, *pseud. See* Westmacott, Charles Molloy

Blackmore, Sir Richard (d. 1729), VIII. 32, 54, 168, 428, 432; IX. 29, 78, 177, 178, 180–181 (main entry), 477, 484; X. 72, 148, 183; XII. 128

Alfred, IX. 180

Arthur, IX. 180

Creation, IX. 180, 181, 184

Eliza, IX. 180

King Arthur, VIII. 52

Prince Arthur, VIII. 163

Satyr on Wit, VIII. 52

Blackmore, Richard Doddridge (1825–1900), XIII. 560; *Lorna Doone*, XIII. 434, 435; *Springhaven*, XIII. 435

Blackstone, Sir William (1723–1780), VIII. 321; X. 275, 499; XIV. 80; *Commentaries*, VIII. 315; XI. 61, 62, 66; *Law Tracts*, XI. 61

Blackwater, river, XIV. 308

Blackwater river (*Battle of Maldon*), I. 144

Blackwell, B. H., XIV. 528

Blackwell, Thomas (1660?–1728), IX. 547

Blackwell, Thomas (1701–1757), IX. 552; *Memoirs of the Court of Augustus*, X. 466

Blackwood, Frederick Temple Hamilton-Temple, marquis of Dufferin (1826–1902), XIV. 98, 552, 568; *Letters from High Latitudes*, XIV. 240

Blackwood, Helen Selina, born Sheridan, countess of Dufferin (1807–1867), XIII. 177, 499; XIV. 309, 508; *Bay of Dublin, The*, XIV. 310; *I'm sitting on the stile, Mary*, XIV. 310

Blackwood, John (1818–1879), XII. 425

Blackwood, William (1776–1834), XII. 156, 157, 159, 161, 425; *Annals of a Publishing House*, XII. 159

Blackwood, Tales from, XII. 425

Blackwood's Edinburgh Magazine ('Maga'), XII. 36, 141, 153, 154, 155 ff. (main entry), 221, 409 ff., 425; XI. 148; XIII. 5, 160, 187, 372, 386, 396, 425; XIV. 66, 150, 161, 188, 232, 313, 319, 327, 373

Bladen, William (*fl.* 1640), IV. 414

Blades, William (1824–1890), XII. 520

Blagrave, John (d. 1611), *The Mathematical Jewel*, III. 549; IV. 453

Blague, in *The Merry Devill*, V. 252

Blague, mistress, in *Edward IV*, VI. 91

Blaiman, Irish tale, I. 293

Blair, Hugh (1718–1800), IX. 560; X. 227 ff., 324, 488; XII. 426; XIV. 604; *Lectures on Rhetoric*, XIV. 398, 399; *Sermons*, XI. 327

Blair, John (*fl.* 1300), II. 110

Blair, Robert (1593–1666), VII. 455

Blair, Robert (1699–1746), IX. 167; X. 138, 144, 147 (main entry), 453; *The Grave*, X. 147; XI. 244

Blake, J. W., *Accent and Rhythm explained by the law of Monopressures*, XIII. 249, 511

Blake, Robert (1599–1657), X. 164, 464

Blake, William (1757–1827), VI. 71; VIII. 230; X. 147, 236, 458; XI. 176, 181 ff. (main entry), 245, 250, 395, 431, *also see* Add.; XIII. 43, 108, 151, 195, 197, 198, 225, 406, 489, 495; XIV. 363, 525

Africa, XI. 194

America, XI. 189, 190, 193

Auguries of Innocence, XI. 200

Birds, The, XI. 200

Blossom, The, XI. 185

Book of Ahania, XI. 193, 194

Book of Los, XI. 193, 194

Book of Thel, XI. 186, 187

Book of Urizen, XI. 193 ff.

Chimney Sweeper, The, XI. 185, 186

Clod and the Pebble, XI. 191

Cradle Song, XI. 186, 193

Crystal Cabinet, The, XI. 199

Descriptive Catalogue, XI. 200

Divine Image, The, XI. 184

Dream, A, XI. 185

Earth's Answer, XI. 192

Echoing Green, The, XI. 185

Europe, XI. 193, 194, 197

Everlasting Gospel, The, XI. 200

Fair Elenor, XI. 182

Four Zoas, The, XI. 196, 197

French Revolution, XI. 189, 190

Ghost of Abel, XI. 199

Golden Net, The, XI. 199

Grey Monk, The, XI. 199

Holy Thursday, XI. 185, 191

'How sweet I roam'd from field to field, XI. 182

'I laid me down upon a bank,' XI. 192

I love the jocund dance, XI. 185

I told my love, XI. 193

Infant Joy, XI. 186

Infant Sorrow, XI. 192

Introduction, XI. 192

Island in the Moon, XI. 183

Jerusalem, XI. 197 ff.

King Edward the Third, XI. 183

Lamb, The, XI. 186

Land of Dreams, XI. 199

Laocoon, XI. 199, 201

Laughing Song, XI. 185

Little Black Boy, XI. 186

Little Boy Lost, XI. 192

Mad Song, XI. 170, 183

Blake, William
  Marriage of Heaven and Hell, XI. 187 ff.,
  192, 200
  Mary, XI. 200
  Memorable Fancies, XI. 188
  Mental Traveller, The, XI. 200
  Milton, XI. 188, 197
  Morning, XI. 199
  My silks and fine array, XI. 183
  My Spectre around me, XI. 200
  Night, XI. 185
  No Natural Religion, XI. 187
  Note on *The Canterbury Tales*, XI. 200
  On Homer's Poetry, XI. 201
  On Virgil, XI. 201
  Passions, The, XI. 182
  Poetical Sketches, XI. 181, 182, 184, 185
  Prophetic Books, XIII. 226
  Public Address, XI. 201
  Schoolboy, The, XI. 192
  Smile, The, XI. 199
  Song of Liberty, XI. 189
  Song of Los, XI. 193, 194
  Song of Phebe, XI. 184
  Songs of Experience, XI. 190 ff.
  Songs of Innocence, XI. 184 ff., 191, 192,
  196, 197, 384
  Spring, XI. 185
  Sunflower, The, XI. 192
  Tiger, The, XI. 191, 192
  Tiriel, XI. 187
  To My Myrtle, XI. 193
  To the Christians, XI. 200
  To the Deists, XI. 200
  To the Muses, XI. 182
  Vala, XI. 195, 196
  Vision of the Last Judgment, XI. 197
  Visions of the Daughters of Albion, XI.
  190, 192
  War Song to Englishmen, XI. 183
  When old corruption first begun, XI. 184
  Wild Flower's Song, The, XI. 193
  William Bond, XI. 200
  Lambeth books, XI. 189, 193, 195 ff.
  199
  Pickering MS., XI. 199, 432
  Rossetti MS., XI. 191, 197, 199, 200, 431
Blakeney, colonel, X. 65
Blakesley, Joseph Williams (1808–1885),
  XII. 330, 480; XIV. 593
Blakesley, Northants., VIII. 2
Blakesware, in Widford, XII. 182, 186,
  189, 191
Blamire, Susanna (1747–1794), X. 453;
  And ye shall walk in Silk Attire, XI. 232;
  Nabob, XI. 232; *What ails this heart of
  Mine*, XI. 232
Blamsdon, Yorkshire, III. 314
Blanchard, Edward Litt Laman (1820–
  1889), XIII. 517
Blanchard, Samuel Laman (1804–1845),
  XII. 131, 414, 419, 428, 450; XIV. 188,
  192, 196
Blanche blab-it-out, in *The Disobedient
  Child*, V. 109
Blanche of Lancaster, II. 170

Blanchefleur, I. 308
Blanco, E. González, XIII. 465
Bland, Tobias (*fl.* 1563?–1604), III. Add.
Blandish, Mr and Mrs, in Burgoyne's
  Heiress, XI. 276
Blandford, X. 94
Blandy, William (*fl.* 1580), IV. 444
Blane, William, XIV. Add. 4
Blaneford, Henry (*fl.* 1330), II. 496
Blaquiere, captain, XII. 38
Blasour, in *Gyre Carling*, II. 275
Blastist, XIII. 214
Blaydes, Frederick H. M. (1818–1908),
  XII. 480
Bleek, Wilhelm Heinrich Immanuel, XIV.
  Add. 5
Bleheris of Wales, II. 451
Bleking, in Ohthere's voyage, I. 94
Bleloch, William Edwin, XIV. Add. 5
Blencowe, John, VI. Add. 2
Blenerhasset, Thomas (1550?–1625?), III.
  197
Blenheim, IX. 44, 150, 151, 155, 182
Blenheim palace, VIII. 163; XII. 173, 192
Blerblowan, in *Colkelbie's sow*, II. 127
Blessednes of Brytaine, The, V. 340
Blessington, Charles John Gardiner, 1st
  earl of, XII. 37
Blessington, Marguerite, countess of (1789
  –1849), XIV. 567
  Conversations, XII. 37, 384, 392, 441
  Idler in France, The, XIV. 322
  Idler in Italy, The, XIV. 322
  *Journal of Conversations with Lord
  Byron*, XIV. 322
Bletchingley, Surrey, VI. 282
Blickling Homilies, I. 114, 129, 442
Blifil, in Fielding's *Tom Jones*, VIII. 148;
  X. 26, 31, 89
Bligh, William (1754–1817), XIV. 550
Blimber, Dr, in *Dombey and Son*, XIII. 325
Blind, Mathilde (1841–1896), XIII. 181,
  499, 553
Blind Devotion, in *A True Inventory*, VII.
  382
Bliss, Philip (1787–1857), IX. 342, 535
Bliss, bower of, in *The Faerie Queene*, III.
  233, 237
Blith, Walter (*fl.* 1649), IV. 509
Bloet, Robert, bishop of Lincoln (d. 1123),
  I. 166
Blois, VIII. 245; XI. 97
Blois. *See* Alexander, and Peter, of
Blome, Richard (d. 1705), *The Gentle-
  man's Recreation*, XIV. 232
Blomefield, Francis (1705–1752), IX. 532;
  History of Norfolk, IX. 353
Blomfield, Alfred, XII. 481
Blomfield, Charles James (1786–1857), XII.
  291, 325, 327, 328, 329 (main entry),
  454, 481, 483, 488, 491
Blomfield, Edward Valentine (1788–1816),
  XII. 481
'Bloomerism,' XIV. 239
Bloomfield, Robert (1766–1823), XI. 484
  XII. 131, 132, 139, 414, 508

Blou northerne wynd, II. 393

Bloudy Newes, IV. 389

Blougram, bishop, Browning's, XIII. 63, 72

Blount, Charles, earl of Devonshire (1563–1606), IV. 132, 133; V. 347; VI. 196; VII. 211

Blount, Charles (1654–1693), VIII. 403, *also see* Add.; IX. 288, 289, 475, 504
  Anima Mundi, IX. 288
  Great is Diana of the Ephesians, IX. 288
  Miscellaneous Works, IX. 289
  Oracles of Reason, IX. 289
  Sale of Esau's Birthright, VIII. 97
  Two first books of Philostratus, IX. 288

Blount or Blunt, Edward (*fl.* 1588–1632), IV. 341, 395, 443, 526, 546; V. 122, 125, 148

Blount, Sir Henry (1602–1682), IV. 453

Blount, Martha (1690–1762), IX. 71, 72, 82, 443, 444

Blount, Teresa, IX. 71, 443, 444

Blount, Thomas (1618–1679), VII. 517; VIII. 468; IX. 528

Blount, William, 4th lord Mountjoy (d. 1534), III. 3, 4, 7, 8, 14

Blow, John (1648–1708), VIII. 395

Blowbol. See *Colin Blowbol*

Blowitz, Henri G. S. A. O. de (1832–1903), XIV. 183, 533

Bloxam, John Rouse (1807–1891), XII. 459, 460

Bloxam MSS., Magd. Coll. Oxford, XII. 460

Bluebeard, XI. 375; XIII. 415

Bluebeard, a female, III. 88

Blue Stockings, the, X. 261, 268; XI. 343 ff., 473

Bluffe, captain, in Congreve's *Old Bachelor*, VIII. 147, 152

Bluhm, G. R., XIII. 542

'Blumine,' in Carlyle's *Sartor Resartus*, XIII. 3

Blundell, James (1780–1877), XIII. 53

Blundell, James, prosodist, XIII. 241

Blunden, Humphrey (*fl.* 1648), IX. 515, 517, 518

Blunderbore, giant, XI. 374

Blunderhead family, in Anstey's *New Bath Guide*, XI. 173

Blundeston, friend of Barnabe Googe, III. 185

Blundeville, M., His exercises...in Cosmographie..., III. 425, 549; IV. 453

Blundeville, Thomas (*fl.* 1561), IV. 443, 444, 540

Blunt, Henry (1794–1843), XII. 471

Blunt, John James (1794–1855), XII. 490

Blunt, Reginald, XIII. 470

Blurt, in *Blurt Master-Constable*, V. 362

Blyth, Edmund Kell, XIV. 601

'Blyth, John,' II. 279

Blyth (near Rotherham), XII. 512

Blythesome Bridal, The, IX. 363 ff.

Boaden, James (1762–1839), X. 263, 264; XI. 428, 452 ff., 461

Boadicea, VI. 128; VII. 443

Boadicea, in Milton's *England*, VII. 129

Boake, Barcroft Henry (1866–1892), XIV. 369, 584

Board of Works, XIV. 285

Boas, Frederick Samuel, IV. 164; V 414, 424; VI. Add. 2

Boas, Henrietta O'Brien, Mrs F. S., XIII. 490

Boase, George Clement (1829–1897), XII. 521; XIV. 512

Boaz, X. 104

Bobadil, captain, in *Solimon and Perseda*, V. 161

Bobadill, in Jonson's *Every Man in His Humour*, IV. 15; V. 33, 315, 361, 367; VI. 16, 26, 28, 127, 249, 272; VIII. 127, 147, 171; XI. 283

Bobbin, Tim. *See* Collier, John

Boccaccio, Giovanni, I. 199, 214, 360; II. 134, 145, 168, 174, 176, 182, 184, 199, 204, 262, 264, 321, 325; III. 65, 130, 181, 192, 198, 337, 339, 343, 375; IV. 6, 441, 442; VIII. 4, 51, 52, 183, 433; XII. 58, 168, 217, 365
  Admeto, VI. 364
  Decameron, I. 286; II. 177; III. 356; IV. 7, 361; V. 62, 72, 73, 75, 103, 116, 220, 221; VI. 48, 137, 138, 205, 304, 364, 484; XII. 53, 82; XIII. 400, 401
  De Casibus Virorum Illustrium, III. 130, 192, 198
  Fiammetta, IV. 7
  Filocopo, I. 286; IV. 7
  Filostrato, Il, II. 172
  Olympia, I. 323
  Teseide, II. 180

Boccalini, T., *Ragguagli di Parnaso*, VII. 274

Bocking, VIII. 269

Böddeker, K., I. 477; XIII. 564

Bodel, Jean, *Chanson de Saisnes*, I. 279, 302

Bodenham, John (*fl.* 1600), III. 522; IV. 117, 526; *Belvedere*, VI. 312

Bodenstedt, F. von, V. 303

Bodin, Jean, III. 145; IV. 296, 298, 509; VI. 377, 492; VII. 394, 405; *Démonomie des Sorciers*, III. 112

Bodley, John, father of Sir Thomas Bodley, IV. 429

Bodley, Sir Thomas (1545–1613), III. 425; IV. 56, 403, 406, 415, 429 ff., 433; VII. 153; IX. 342, 349, 534

Bodli, in Morris's *The Lovers of Gudrun*, XIII. 125

Bodmer, Johann Jakob, V. 290

Body and Soul. See *Soul and Body*

Boece or Boethius, Hector (1465?–1536), II. 114, 251, 370, 371; III. 131, 148, 154, 155, 156, 319, 501; *Historia Gentis Scotorum*, II. 104; III. 148, 155, 156; IV. 412; *Vitae Episcoporum Murthlacensium et Aberdonensium*, III. 155

Boeckh, Philipp August, *The Public Economy of Athens*, XII. 301, 339

Boehme, Jacob, VII. 303, 351; IX. 307, 308, 314 ff., 327, 328, 511 ff., 521 ff.; XIII. 431
Forty Questions, IX. 307
Mysterium Magnum, IX. 317
Signatura Rerum, IX. 307, 316
Three Principles, IX. 307
Threefold Life of Man, IX. 316
Boehme, Johann, IV. 442
Boeotia, IV. 10
Boeotia (*i.e.* Germany), in *Euphormio*, IV. 256
Boer war (1898), XIV. 193, 456
Boer zijn Zaterdag Aand, Die, XIV. 377
Boerhaave, Hermann, X. 164, 464
Boers, the, XIV. 173, 254
Boethius, I. 213, 355; II. 241, 247, 355, 360, 363, 456; IV. 417, 442; *Arithmetica*, II. 362; *De Consolatione Philosophiae*, III. 290; IV. 409, (Alfred's version, I. 91, 99 ff., 107, 436, 437, 439)
Boffin, Mr, in *Our Mutual Friend*, XIII. 336
Bogue, David and Bennett, J. (1750–1825), *History of Dissenters*, X. 518
Bohemia, II. 69, 292, 298; III. 355, 357, 359; V. 167, 205, 206; VII. 344
Bohemian, the, in *The Fyrste Boke of the Introduction of Knowledge*, III. 105
Bohemian scholars in England in Wyclif's day, II. 67
Bohemianism, XIII. 162, 163, 290; XIV. 176
Bohemund, in *Orlando Furioso*, III. 230
Bohn, Henry George (1796–1884), X. 410; XII. 520; XIV. 612; *Antiquarian Library*, XII. 368; *Guinea Catalogue*, XII. 368
Boiardo, Matteo Maria, XII. 3; *Orlando Innamorato*, IV. 442; XII. 422
Boiastuan, III. 109
Boice, Sir, in *Morte Arthure*, II. 119
Boileau, Abbé, X. 501
Boileau-Despréaux, Nicolas, V. 176; VIII. 133, 203, 214, 219, 220, 373 ff., 385; IX. 140, 150, 155, 257, 473; X. 115; XII. 104
L'Art Poétique, VIII. 373, 375; X. 169
Lutrin, VIII. 197, 373, 436, 440; IX. 70, 179
Ode sur la Prise de Namur, IX. 148
Satire (second), VIII. 63
Satire touching Nobility, VIII. 88
Bois, John (1561–1644), VII. 316, 318, 482
Boisil, I. 148
Bokenam, Osbern (1393–1447?), II. 469; *Lives* or *Legends of Saints*, II. 198, 214
Bokyngham, John (d. 1398), *Super Sententias*, II. 366
Bolas, Thomas, XIV. 535
Bold, Henry (1627–1683), VII. 88, 412
Bold, Samuel (1649–1737), VIII. 347, 472
Boldon Buke, XII. 510
Boldrewood, Rolf, *pseud.* *See* Browne, Thomas Alexander
Boleyn, Anne. *See* Anne
Boleyn, Sir Thomas, earl of Wiltshire (1477–1539), III. 32, 167

Bolingbroke, viscount. *See* St John, Henry
Bolingbroke, in *King Richard II*, V. 271
Bolmer, in Yorkshire, V. 90
Bologna, II. 350, 364; III. 5, 7, 49, 167, 423; VIII. 5, 312
Bologna, schools of, I. 187, 192, 199, 200
Bolomyer, Henry, canon of Lausanne, II. 315
Bolton, Edmund ('Philanactophil') (1575?–1633?), III. 199, 201, 306; IV. 117, 118, 436, 482, 543; VII. 205, 443; *Corpus Rerum Anglicarum*, VII. 205; *Florus's Epitome of Roman History* (trans.), VII. 205; *Hypercritica*, III. 201, 528; VII. 262, 265, 273, 465
Bolton, M. P. W., XIV. 474
Bolton, Lancashire, XIV. 195
Bolton-le-Moors, Lancashire, VII. 342
Bolts, William (1740?–1808), XIV. 334, 575
Bombay, XIV. 59, 336
Bon Gaultier Ballads, The, XIII. 150, 161
Bona, Jaonnes, *Guide to Eternity*, IX. 274, 418
Bonarelli, *Filli di Sciro*, VI. 321
Bonar, Horatius (1808–1889), XII. 471
Bonaventura, St, I. 110, 154, 206; *Meditations*, V. 42
Bond, Sir Edward Augustus (1815–1898), XI. 396; XIV. 356, 515
Bond, Henry, IV. 453
Bond, John (1550–1612), VII. 486
Bond, R. Warwick, V. 123, 125, 401, 402, 415
Bond, Thomas (1765–1837), XII. 508
Bond, William (*fl.* 1726), IX. 21
Bonducci, Andrea, X. 447
Bone Aventure, in *The Bowge of Courte*, III. 73
Bonet, Honoré, II. 284
Bongrace, in *Jacke Jugeler*, V. 107
Bonheur de ce Monde, IX. 170
Bonhill, X. 36
Boniface, in Farquhar's *Beaux' Stratagem*, VIII. 171
Boniface VIII, pope, II. 148; *Liber Sextus*, II. 364
Boniface IX, pope, II. 348
Boniface, St, I. 73, 78, 86, 435, *also see* Add. to third impression
Boniface, Sir, in *The Wise-woman Of Hogsdon*, VI. 83
Bonn, XII. 302
Bonn university, XIV. 410
Bonner or Boner, Edmund (1500?–1569), bishop of London, III. 167, 186, 337
Bonner, Hypatia Bradlaugh (1833–1891), XIV. 501
Bonner, W. S., XIV. 513
Bonnie Annie, II. 413
Bonnie Charlie, IX. 378
Bonnie Dundee, III. 184
Bonnie James Campbell, II. 413
Bonnie Scotch Lad, The, IX. 363
Bonnivard, in Byron's *Prisoner of Chillon*, XII. 46

Bonny Baby Livingstone, II. 411
Bonny Earl of Murray, The, II. 413
Bonoeil, John, IV. 453
Bononcini, IX. 326
Bonstetten, Charles-Victor de, X. 134
Bonwick, James (1817–1906), XIV. 531, 584, 585; *Daily Life and Origin of the Tasmanians*, XIV. 371; *Last of the Tasmanians, The*, XIV. 371
Bonwicke, Ambrose (1652–1722), XII. 488; *A Pattern for Young Students*, X. 356
Bonwicke, Ambrose (1692–1714), IX. 412, 574
Booby, lady, in Fielding's *Joseph Andrews*, X. 24
Booby, squire, in Fielding's *Joseph Andrews*, X. 24
'Boojum,' Lewis Carroll's, XIII. 167
Book of Anzac, The, XIV. 367
Book of Common Prayer, IV. 384, 396, 407, 414; VII. 149, 455, 488; XIV. 402, 444, 450, 451; Irish version of, IV. 414
Book of Kells, The, XIV. 309
Book of the Universal Kirk of Scotland, The, VII. 208, 448
Book production and distribution, II. 331 ff., 483 ff.; IV. 378 ff., 544 ff.; XI. 466 ff.
Bookbinding, 1557–1625, IV. 548–549
Booke of Honor and Armes, The, IV. 525, 543
Booker, John (1603–1667), VII. 501; *The bloudy Almanac*, VII. 352, 499, 509; *Several Speeches at a Conference*, VII. 352
Bookwit, in Steele's *Lying Lover*, IX. 30
Boole, George (1815–1864), XIV. 263, 469, 555; *The Laws of Thought*, XIV. 10
Boon, Martin James, XIV. Add. 5
Boor, John (*fl.* 1389), VI. 280
Boorde, Andrew (1490?–1549), III. 105 ff., 488, 493; IV. 343, 523; V. 359; *A Compendyous Regyment or a Dyetary of Helth*, III. 91, 106; *The Fyrst boke of the Introduction of Knowledge*, III. 105, 106; IV. 320
Booth, Barton (1681–1733), X. 21, 444; XI. 257
Booth, Edwin, V. 308
Booth, James (1806–1878), XIV. 556, 604
Booth, Junius Brutus (1796–1852), V. 308; XII. 171
Booth, William, *In darkest England and the way out*, VII. 292
Booth, in Fielding's *Amelia*, X. 23, 33
Boothby, Guy Newell (1867–1905), XIV. 370, 585
Boothby, Miss Hill (1708–1756), X. 463
Boothby, Richard, *Briefe Discovery…of Madagascar*, IV. 102, 454
Boots, in *Our Mutual Friend*, XIII. 337
Boquet, Monsieur, XI. 258
Borachia, in *A Very Woman*, VI. 157
Borachio, in *The Atheist's Tragedie*, VI. 168
Boraskie, in *The Loyal Subject*, VI. 130
Borbonius, Matthew, IV. 264
Borbonius, Nicholas, *Nugae*, IV. 264

Borck, C. W. von, V. 294, 300, 462; *Julius Caesar*, V. 290, 296
Bord-à-Plouffe, Canada, XIV. 355
Bordeaux, III. 161; VI. 295, 322; VII. 309
Bordeaux, Collège de Guyenne, III. 160, 161, 426
Border, Daniel, anabaptist (*fl.* 1643–1650), VII. 351
    England's Moderate Messenger, VII. 351
    Impartial Scout, The, VII. 351
    Kingdoms Faithfull Scout, The, VII. 351
    Kingdoms Weekly Post, The, VII. 351
    Perfect Weekly Account, The, VII. 351
    Weekly Accompt, A, VII. 351
    Weekly Account, The, VII. 351
Border, the, II. 128, 251; VII. 26; IX. 361, 568; XII. 255; XIV. 96
Border ballads, XII. 3
Borderers, the, II. 415
Boreman, Robert (d. 1675), IX. 570
Borgias, the, XIV. 99
Borkowsky, T., IX. 106
Borlase, William (1695–1772), IX. 532; X. 466
Borough muir, the, in Scott's *Marmion*, XII. 10
Boroughbridge, battle of, II. 81
Borowlaski, count, XII. 22
Borromeo, cardinal, IV. 429
Borron, Robert de, I. 268, 271
Borrow, George (1803–1881), I. 275; VI. 230; IX. 247; XIII. 442; XIV. 138, 180, 251, 516; *also see* Add. 2
    Bible in Spain, The, XIV. 145, 240, 241, 250
    Lavengro, XIV. 145
    Romany Rye, The, XIV. 145
    Wild Wales, XIV. 146
Borrowdale, XI. 110
Borsa, Mario, XIV. 531
Borthwick, Sir Algernon, lord Glenesk, XIV. 185, 533
Borthwick, Peter (1804–1852), XIV. 185
Bos, C., XIII. 466
Bosanquet, Bernard, XIV. 469
Boscan-Almogaver, Juan, VII. 83
Boscawen, Mrs F., wife of admiral Boscawen, XI. 348, 354, 361 ff.
Boscombe, near Salisbury, rectory of, III. 406
Bosham. *See* Herbert of Bosham
Bosman, H. S., XIV. 380
Bosman, John, XIV. 244
Bosman, Walter, XIV. Add. 5
Bosola, in *The Dutchesse of Malfy*, VI. 180 ff.
Bossewell, John (*fl.* 1572), IV. 376, 543
Bossuet, Jacques-Bénigne, bishop of Meaux, VIII. 303, 305, 456
    Conférence avec M. Claude, VIII. 373
    Discours sur l'Histoire Universelle, VIII. 373
    Exposition de la Doctrine de l'Église Catholique, VIII. 373
    Histoire des Variations, IX. 198
Boston, Thomas (1676–1732), IX. 548

Boston, U.S.A., xiv. 318, 322
Boston Pilot, The, xiv. 318, 322
Boswell, Sir Alexander (1775–1822), x.
  192, 478; xi. 442; xii. 357, 515; xiv.
  188
  Ah! Mary, sweetest maid, Farewell, xi.
  235
  East Neuk of Fife, xi. 236
  Jenny Dang the Weaver, xi. 236
  Jenny's Bawbee, xi. 236
  New Whig Song, xi. 236
  Paddy O'Rafferty, xi. 236
  Sir Albyn, xi. 236
  Skeldon Haughs or the Sow flitted, xi.
  236
  Songs Chiefly in the Scottish Dialect, xi.
  236
  Taste Life's Glad Moments, xi. 236
Boswell, G. (*fl.* 1657), vii. 390
Boswell, James (1740–1795), iii. 336; iv.
  247; ix. 325, 330; x. 157, 158, 161, 164,
  167, 168, 172, 174, 176, 181 ff., 187,
  189 ff. (main entry), 200, 207, 213, 215,
  216, 259, 263, 312, 459 ff., 477 ff., 482,
  also see Add.; xi. 38, 235, 326, 333,
  344 ff., 364; xiv. 188, 503, 550
  Account of Corsica, x. 192
  Boswelliana, x. 193
  *British Essays in favour of the Brave
  Corsicans,* x. 192
  Critical Strictures on Malloch's Elvira
  (by Boswell, Erskine, and Dempster),
  x. 477
  Cub at Newmarket, The, x. 191
  Dorando, x. 191
  *Elegy on the death of an amiable young
  lady,* x. 191
  Essence of the Douglas Cause, x. 191
  Hypochrondriack, The, x. 192
  Journal of a Tour to the Hebrides, x. 194
  Life of Johnson, viii. 322; ix. 313, 340;
  x. 181, 184, 186, 189, 190, 193, 194,
  260, 267, 289, 291; xi. 13, 253, 325,
  344; xii. 363; xiv. 63
  'Memoirs' (in *The European Magazine*),
  x. 193
  No Abolition of Slavery, x. 193
  Ode to Tragedy, x. 191, 193
  *On the Alarming Attempt to infringe the
  Articles of the Union,* x. 193
  On the present state of the Nation, x. 193
  Songs in the Justiciary Opera, x. 192
Boswell, James, the younger (1778–1822),
  v. 276; x. 192
Boswell, John (1698–1756), x. 498
Bosworth, Joseph (1789–1876), i. 91;
  xii. 344, 504
Bosworth, or Boxworth, William (1607–
  1650?), vii. 412; *Chaste and Lost Lovers,
  The,* or *Arcadius and Sepha,* vii. 79, 80;
  Hinc Lachrimae, vii. 80; *To Aurora,* vii.
  80
Bosworth, battle of, ii. 41; vi. 301
Bosworth, battlefield of, v. 171
Botanical Magazine, The, xiv. 288, 565
Botany bay, xi. 58; xii. 195

Boteler, Nathaniel (*fl.* 1625–1627), iv. 107;
  Six Dialogues about Sea Services, iv.
  108, 454
Botener, John (*fl.* 1376), iv. 423
Botero, Giovanni, iv. 442, 454
Botes, iii. 482
Botfield, Beriah (1807–1863), xii. 355,
  365, 515
Botha, Louis, xiv. Add. 5
Böðvarr Biarki, i. 27
Bothwell, 1st earl of. *See* Hepburn, Patrick
Bothwell Bridge, ii. 415
Botolph, St, v. 49
Böttger, C., xiii. 546
Bottom, in *A Midsummer-Night's Dream,*
  v. 74, 317; vi. 207, 285; xiii. 64
Bouchain, ix. 455, 461
Boucicault, Dion (1820?–1890), xiii. 264,
  266 ff., 517, 522; xiv. 567
  Arrah-na-Pogue, xiii. 267
  Colleen Bawn, The, xiii. 267
  Corsican Brothers, The, xiii. 267
  London Assurance, xiii. 269
  Louis XI, xiii. 267
  Shaughraun, The, xiii. 267
Boudoin, J., *L'Artisan de la Fortune* (trans.
  of Bacon's *Essays*), iv. 347
Boufflers, Louis-François, duc de, ix. 256
Bough, Samuel (1822–1878), xi. 437
Boughton hall, Boughton Malherbe, Kent,
  iv. 163
Boughton-under-Blee, ii. 184
Bouhours, Dominique, viii. 402; *Manière
  de penser sur les ouvrages de l'esprit,*
  viii. 376
Boulainvilliers, count de, x. 283
Boulge, near Woodbridge, xiii. 142
Boulogne, iii. 175; x. 193, 395
Boulter, Hugh (1672–1742), archbishop
  of Armagh, ix. 407; x. 468
Boulton, Matthew (1728–1809), xiv. 381
Bouncer, Mrs, in *Verdant Green,* xiv. 225
Bounderby, Josiah, in Dickens's *Hard
  Times,* xiii. 330
Bounteous Progress, Sir, in *A Mad World,
  My Masters,* vi. 64
Bourbon, the constable de, iii. 167
Bourbon, house of, ix. 215; xiii. 258
Bourchier family, the, ii. 208
Bourchier, John, 2nd lord Berners (1467–
  1533), ii. 332, 337 ff., 484; iv. 435, 445;
  v. 123
  Castle of Love, The, ii. 322
  Froissart's Chronicle, ii. 322, 340; iii.
  348
  Golden Book of Marcus Aurelius, The,
  ii. 340
  History of Arthur of Little Britain, ii.
  322, 339
  Huon of Bordeaux, ii. 322, 339, 340
Bourchier, Thomas (1404?–1486), arch-
  bishop of Canterbury, ii. 289
Bourdaloue, Louis, viii. 303
Bourgeois, Maurice, xiv. 571
Bourget, Louis, xiv. 484
Bourget, Paul, xi. 408

Bourgh, lady Catherine de, in Jane Austen's *Pride and Prejudice*, XII. 238

Bourignon, Antoinette (1616–1680), IX. 307, 314, 519, 523

Bourinot, Sir John George (1837–1902), XIV. 581, 582; *The Story of Canada*, XIV. 359

Bourn, Samuel (1689–1754), *Address to Protestant Dissenters*, X. 380

Bourne, Henry (1696–1733), IX. 532; *Antiquities of the Common People, The*, IX. 355; XII. 346, 508

Bourne, Henry Richard Fox, *Life of John Locke*, IX. 406; *English Newspapers*, XIV. 179, 190, 531

Bourne, Nicholas (*fl.* 1622). IV. 398; VII. 344, 345

Bourne, Vincent (1695–1747), IX. 173, 526; XI. 83

Bourne, William (d. 1583), IV. 82, 104, 454

Bournemouth, XII. 331

Boursault, Edme, VIII. 162

Boutell, Charles (1812–1877), XII. 508

Bouterwek, K. W., I. 147

Bovaldo, in *Loves Crueltie*, VI. 199

Bove, Jean de, *Des trois larrons*, IX. 39

Bow Bells, XII. 448

Bowden, John Edward, XII. 456; XIII. 502

Bowden, John William (1798–1844), XII. 258, 454, 455, 459; XIII. 507

Bowdler, Thomas (1754–1825), XI. 260

Bowdler, in *The Fayre Mayde of the Exchange*, VI. 86

Bowdlerising, V. 187

Bowen, Edward Ernest (1836–1901), XIV. 597, 601, 606

Bowen, Herbert Courthope, XIV. 590

Bower, Alexander (*fl.* 1804–1830), X. 453

Bower, Archibald (1686–1766), X. 115, 499; *History of the Popes*, X. 292, 293

Bower, George Spencer, XIV. 477

Bower, Richard (d. 1561?), VI. 282, 286, *and see* Bowyer, Richard

Bower or Bowmaker, Walter (d. 1449), II. 128, 129, 451

Bower of Bliss, in *The Faerie Queene*, VI. 335; VII. 2

Bowes, Sir Hierome, III. 315

Bowes, Sir Jerome, in Milton's *Moscovia*, VII. 128

Bowes, Robert, XI. 468

Bowes, Thomas (*fl.* 1586), III. 356, 437; *The French Academy*, III. 437, 552

Bowes's academy, IX. 393

Bowker, Richard Rogers, XIV. 536

Bowles, Caroline. *See* Southey, Mrs Caroline Anne

Bowles, John (*fl.* 1807), *Letter to Whitbread*, XIV. 403, 590

Bowles, William Lisle (1762–1850), IX. 69, 451; XI. 118, 148, 177, 413, 424; XII. 100, 133, 183, 384, 392; XIII. 46
Bamborough Castle, XI. 178
Fourteen Sonnets, XI. 178
Hope, XI. 178
Influence of Time on Grief, XI. 178

Bowles, William Lisle
Sonnets, XI. 172
Tynemouth, XI. 178
Vindiciae Wykehamicae, XIV. 406, 598

Bowley, Sir Joseph, in Dickens's *The Chimes*, XIII. 324

Bowling, Tom, in Smollett's *Roderick Random*, X. 37, 50

Bowring, Sir John (1792–1872), XI. 61, 397, 398; XII. 38, 310, 430; XIV. 512, 550, 604

Bows, Mr, in *Pendennis*, XIII. 292

Bowyer, Richard, *alias* Styrley or Strylly or Strelley, VI. 282

Bowyer, W. (*fl.* 1710), VIII. 461

Bowyer, William, *The Valiant Scot* (1637), VI. 453

Bowyer, William, the younger (1699–1777), XI. 327, 471; *Literary Anecdotes of the Eighteenth Century*, XII. 345

Box hill, XIII. 440

Boxley, VII. 53

Boy, the, in *The Play of the wether*, V. 94

Boy and the Mantle, The, I. 464; II. 414

Boy bishop, V. 8; VI. 294

Boy of Battlesdon, VII. 375

Boy of Bilson, the, IV. 535; VII. 375

Boyce, Samuel (d. 1775), X. 453

Boyce, William B., XIV. Add. 5

Boycotting system, XIV. 320

Boyd, Andrew Kennedy Hutchinson (1825–1899), XIV. 516; *Last Years of St Andrews, The*, XIV. 161; *Recreations of a Country Parson*, XIV. 161

Boyd, Hugh (1746–1794), XIV. 335, 575

Boyd, Robert (1578–1627), IX. 542

Boyd, William, 4th earl of Kilmarnock (1704–1746), IX. 564

Boyd, Zachary (1585?–1653), IX. 542

Boydell, John (1719–1804), XIV. 215, 216, 221

Boyer, Abel (1667–1729), VIII. 261, 451; IX. 17, 236, 237, 433, 491
Achilles, or Iphigenia in Aulis (Racine's), VIII. 181
History of Queen Anne, IX. 236
History of the Reign of Queen Anne..., IX. 236
History of William III, IX. 236

Boyer, Clarence Valentine, VI. Add.

Boyle, Charles, 4th earl of Orrery and 1st baron Marston (1676–1731), VIII. 385; IX. 103, 139, 216, 332, 333, 391, 443, 492, 525, 572; XI. 316

Boyle, Dorothy, countess of Burlington XIV. 213

Boyle, Frederick, XIV. Add. 5

Boyle, George David (1828–1901), XIV 501

Boyle, John, 5th earl of Orrery (1707–1762), IX. 460, 467

Boyle, Miss, XII. 440

Boyle, Richard, 1st earl of Cork (1566–1643), VIII. 268

Boyle, Richard, 3rd earl of Burlington (1695–1753), IX. 79, 162, 445

Boyle, Robert (1627–1691), vii. 266, 288, 396, 470; viii. 247, 363 ff., 476; ix. 199, 331, 332, 389, 412, 489; x. 498; xii. 363; xiv. 281, 283; *Origine of Formes...and Qualities*, viii. 338; *Seraphic Love*, viii. 268; *Tracts*, viii. 338

Boyle, Robert, v. 257, 444

Boyle, Roger, lord Broghill and 1st earl of Orrery (1621–1679), vii. 23; viii. 21, 121, 124, 133, 190, 218, 268, 420, 424, 444

Black Prince, The, viii. 18, 22

English Adventures. By a Person of Honour (1676) (attributed to Roger Boyle), viii. 182

Guzman, viii. 124, 131

History of Henry the Fifth, The, viii. 18, 22

Mr Anthony (attributed to Roger Boyle), viii. 123

Mustapha, viii. 18, 22

Parthenissa, iv. 260; vii. 391; viii. 22, 185, 371

Boyle lectures, ix. 297, 298, 331, 412, 524, 529; xii. 306

Boyne, William, *The Yorkshire Library*, xii. 519

Boyne, battle of, x. 358

Boynton, P. Holmes, xiii. 567; xiv. 528

Boys, John (1571–1625), iv. 415

Boys' Own Book, The, viii. 359

Boyse, Samuel (1708–1749), ix. 563; xi. 172, 331, 425

Boythorn, in Dickens's *Bleak House*, xii. 205, 208; xiii. 323

Bozon, Nicole, ii. 420, 507

Brabant, xiii. 436

Brabant, in *Jacke Drums Entertainment*, vi. 41

Brabine, Thomas, v. 121

Brabourne, ii. 134

Bracebridge, in Kingsley's *Yeast*, xiii. 360

Bracegirdle, Anne (1663?–1748), viii. 146, 159, 166, 177

Brachiano, in *The White Divel*, vi. 176

Bracken, Thomas (1843–1898), xiv. 368, 585; *Not Understood*, xiv. 368

Brackley, iii. 430

Brackyn, Francis, vi. 313, 314, 322

Bracton or Bratton, Henry de (d. 1268), i. 181, 449; viii. 313, 465; *De Legibus et Consuetudinibus Angliae*, viii. 312; xiv. 80

Bradamante, in *Orlando Furioso*, iii. 231, 236

Bradbury, Thomas (1677–1759), x. 380

Braddon, Laurence (d. 1724), ix. 490

Braddon, Mary Elizabeth (Mrs John Maxwell, 1837–1915), xiii. 438, 560

Bradfield school, xiv. 414

Bradford, x. 385

Bradford school, vii. 330, 342

Bradford, John (1510?–1555), iv. 232 ff., 446, 448, 491, 495; *Meditations*, iv. 414

Bradlaugh, Charles (1833–1891), xiii. 107; xiv. 501

Bradley, Andrew Cecil, xi. 408; xii. 77, 402, 406, 447; xiii. 476; *A Commentary on Tennyson's* 'In Memoriam,' xiii. 33

Bradley, Arthur Granville, xiv. 598

Bradley, Edward (*pseud.* Cuthbert Bede, 1827–1889), xiii. 560; *Verdant Green*, xiv. 225, 238

Bradley, Francis Herbert (1846–1924), xiv. 469, 480

Appearance and Reality, xiv. 46

Essays on Truth and Reality, xiv. 47

Ethical Studies, xiv. 46

Principles of Logic, xiv. 46

Bradley, George Granville, xii. 470, 478

Bradley, Henry (1845–1924), i. 87, 419; ii. 35, 36, 39

Bradley, James (1693–1762), xiv. 258, 556

Bradley, Katharine Harris. See Field, Michael

Bradley, Richard (d. 1732), xiv. 286, 559

Bradshaw, in *Arden of Feversham*, v. 241

Bradshaw, Henry (d. 1513), ii. 210, 469; *Life of Saynt Werburghe*, iii. 66

Bradshaw, Henry (1831–1886), ii. 45, 62, 103, 167, 448; iv. 423, 425, 432; xii. 520; *Collected Papers*, xii. 369; 'Memoranda,' xii. 369

Bradshaw, John (1602–1659), vii. 219; viii. 312; ix. 258

Bradshaw, Mrs, Gissing's, xiii. 460

Bradshaw, Richard (*fl.* 1650), vii. 438

Bradshaw, William (*fl.* 1700), xi. 329; *Parable of the Magpye*, viii. 99; xi. 330

Bradshaw's *Guide*, xiii. 330

Bradsheet, Anne (1612–1672), vii. 412

Bradwardine, baron of, in *Waverley*, vii. 231

Bradwardine, Thomas, *Doctor profundus* (1290?–1349), i. 213, 452; ii. 18, 31, 355; iv. 269

Brady, Nicholas (1659–1726), viii. 91, 92, 411, 431; *Psalms*, version of, by Nahum Tate and Nicholas Brady, viii. 41, 443

Brady, Thomas John Bellingham, xii. 494

Braes o' Yarrow, The, ii. 412

Brahma, xi. 194

Brahmanical religion, xi. 18

Brâhmî alphabet, the, xii. 352

Brailsford, Henry Noel, *Shelley, Godwin and their Circle*, xi. 276

Braintree, v. 104

Brainworm, in D'Urfey's *Virtuous Wife*, viii. 175

Bramber, Sussex, vii. 22

Bramble, Matthew, in Smollett's *Humphrey Clinker*, x. 38, 43, 206

Bramble, Mrs Tabitha, in Smollett's *Humphrey Clinker*, x. 43; xi. 266

Bramdean, vii. 454

Bramhall, John (1594–1663), vii. 285, 288, 289, 470; viii. 369; *Castigations of Mr Hobbes*, viii. 301; *A Defence of the True Liberty of Human Actions*, viii. 301

Brampton, Thomas (*fl.* 1414), ii. 496

Bramston, James (1694?-1744), IX. 189, 484

Bramston, Sir John (1611-1700), VII. 335

Brand, Hannah (d. 1821), XI. 456

Brand, John (1744-1806), IX. 532; XII. 346, 508

Brand, Robert Henry, XIV. Add. 6

Brandan, St, XIII. 199

Brandenburg, Frederick William, elector of, VIII. 329

Brandes, Georg, I. ix; v. 308; XI. 409, 416; XII. 524; XIII. 21, 546

Brandl, Alois, I. ix, 421; XI. 409, 416

Brandon, Charles, duke of Suffolk (d. 1545), IV. 182; VIII. 182

Brandon, colonel, in Jane Austen's *Sense and Sensibility*, XII. 327

Brandon, George, in Thackeray's *A Shabby Genteel Story*, XII. 299

Brandon, Richard (d. 1649), VII. 513

Branghtons, the, in Burney's *Evelina*, x. 64

Brankston (Branxton) hill or moor, II. 371; III. 70; *and see* Flodden

Brant, Sebastian, *Das Narrenschiff*, III. 57, 58, 59, 60, 61, 74, 82, 83, 85, 480; IV. 528; VIII. 59. *See, also, under* Barclay, Alexander

Brantham, Suffolk, III. 183

Brantôme, III. 94

Brantwood, XII. 372

Branwell, Elizabeth (d. 1822), XIII. 404, 405

Branwell, Maria. *See* Brontë, Maria

Branwen, daughter of Llŷr, I. 252

Brash and Reid's *Poetry Ancient and Select*, XI. 243

Brasidas, IV. 43

Brass, in Vanbrugh's *Confederacy*, VIII. 162

Brasses, the, in *The Old Curiosity Shop*, XIII. 319

Brassey, Anna, lady (1839-1887), XIV. 550

Brathwaite, Richard (1588?-1673), III. 114; IV. 520, 521, 522, 524, 525, 531, 533, 534; V. 477
  Barnabae Itinerarium or Barnabee's Journal, IV. 361, 533
  The Prodigals Teares: or His fare-well to Vanity, IV. 323
  The Smoking Age, or the Man in the Mist, IV. 349, 531
  Whimzies, IV. 102

Brattle, Carry, in Trollope's *The Vicar of Bullhampton*, XIII. 423

Braun, Mrs C., XIII. 515

Braune, Wilhelm, I. ix

Braunschweig, H., IV. 442

Brawne, Fanny, XII. 92, 406

Brawny Bishop's Complaint, The, VIII. 97

Braxfield, Robert Macqueen, lord (1722-1799), X. 478

Bray, Charles (1811-1884), XII. 465; XIII. 384, 553; *The Philosophy of Necessity*, XIII. 383

Bray, William (1736-1832), VIII. 242; XII. 508, 511

Bray, vicar of, in Prior's *Dialogues*, IX. 16

Braybrook, near Leicester, II. 67

Braybrooke, lord. *See* Neville, R. G.

Brayley, Edward Wedlake (1773-1854), XII. 345, 508

Brayne, father-in-law of J. Burbage, VI. 252

Brayne, John, VII. 509

Brazil, IV. 72; XIV. 250

Breach, mistress, XI. 332

Breca, in *Beowulf*, I. 22

Breca, in *Widsith*, I. 34

Crecon, VII. 37

Bredfield, Suffolk, XIII. 142, 143

Bredt, P., XIII. 466, 467

Brehons, XIV. 302

Breisach on the Rhine, II. 74

Brek, Simon, in Wyntoun's *Cronykil*, II. 130

Bremen, IX. 231

Bremner, Christina S., XIV. 599

Bremner, Robert, XIV. 550

Brémond, abbé, XII. 299

Brendan, St, I. 339, 474; II. 419, 507; XIV. 306

Brende, John, IV. 2; *Quintus Curtius*, IV. 4, 436

Brent, Charlotte (d. 1802), XI. 260

Brent, Sir Nathaniel (1573?-1652), IV. 448

Brent hall, Essex, VII. 89

Brentford, VI. 171; X. 385

Brentford, battle of, VIII. 245

Brentwood school, VII. 331

Brenz, J., IV. 442

Brer Rabbit, XIV. 314

Brereton, Austin, XIII. 513

Brerewood, Edward (1565?-1613), VII. 479

Brescia, IX. 245

Brest, III. 64

Bretherne and systars, The rule of the living of the, II. 325

Bretherton, print-seller, XIV. 216

Breton, Nicholas (1545?-1626?), III. 114, 203, 249, 359, 367, 487, 522, 536; IV. 114, 116 ff., 345, 360, 411, 468, 469, 473, 519, 522, 525, 526, 534; V. 478; VII. 7, 16, 390
  Characters upon Essays, IV. 346
  Chesse Play, The, IV. 116
  Countesse of Pembrook's love, The, IV. 118
  Excellent dreame of ladies, and their riddles, An, IV. 116
  Miseries of Mavillia, III. 367
  Passionate Shepherd, The, III. 249; IV. 118
  Pilgrimage to Paradise, The, IV. 118
  Poste with a Packet of Mad Letters, A, VII. 391
  Soules immortall Crowne, The, IV. 118
  Strange description of a rare garden plot, A, IV. 116
  Strange Fortunes of two excellent princes, III. 359
  Wit's Trenchmour, VII. 463

Breton, cape, IV. 66

Breton language, XIV. 458

Breton lays, I. 294

Breton saints, I. 68
Bretons, Geste des, I. 337
Brett, Thomas (1667–1744), X. 356, 515
Bretts (or 'Welsh'), II. 89
Breval, John Durant (1680?–1738), IX.
472; *Remarks on several parts of Europe,*
XI. 322
Breviaries, III. 19; Roman, III. 31; Sarum,
III. 30, 31
Brewer, George (b. 1766), XI. 485
Brewer, John Sherren (1810–1879), I.
202 ff., 207, 210; XII. 356; XIV. 485, 489;
English Studies, XIV. 82; *Reign of
Henry VIII, The,* XIV. 82
Brewer, Robert Frederick, *A Manual of
English Prosody,* XIII. 247, 511
Brewer, Thomas (*fl.* 1624), *The Merry
Devill of Edmonton,* V. 253
Brewster, Sir David (1781–1868), XIII. 4;
XIV. 259, 288, 555, 556
Brewster, Thomas (*fl.* 1656), VII. 359
Briareus, legend of, IV. 347
Brice, Andrew (1690–1773), XI. 471
Bricot, III. 50
Bricriu's Feast, I. 296, 327; XIV. 307
Bridall, John (b. 1635?), VIII. 468
Bride, in *The Golden Legend,* II. 335
Bridegroom Greets when the Sun gae's doon,
XI. 231
Bridekirk, IX. 170
Bridell-Fox, E. F., XIII. 498
Bridges, Besse, in *The Fair Maid Of The
West,* VI. 101, 102
Bridges, G., VII. 518
Bridges, John (d. 1618), dean of Sarum,
bishop of Oxford, III. 383, 384, 385, 386,
392; VI. 296; *A Defence of the Govern-
ment established in the Church of England
for ecclesiastical matters,* III. 383, 539
Bridges, John (1666–1724), IX. 532; X. 505
Bridges, John Henry (1832–1906), XIV. 469
Comte's General View of Positivism, XIV.
24
Comte's System of Positive Polity (trans.),
XIV. 24
Essays and Addresses, XIV. 25
Five Discourses on Positive Religion,
XIV. 25
The Unity of Comte's Life and Doctrine,
XIV. 25
Bridges, Robert, poet laureate, XII. 406,
456; XIII. 197, 211, 246, 501, 511;
Prosody of Milton, XIII. 249
Bridges, Thomas (*fl.* 1759–1775), IV. 18
Bridgewater, earl of. *See* Egerton, John
Bridgewater, Mrs. *See* Hazlitt, Mrs
Bridgewater treatises, XIV. 290
Bridgman, or Bridgeman, Sir Orlando
(1606?–1674), VII. 42; VIII. 380, 468
Bridgman, Richard Whalley (1761?–
1820), XII. 520
Bridgnorth, VII. 145; XIV. 117
Bridgnorth academy, X. 385, 387
Bridgwater, IX. 237
Bridlington, II. 211
Bridlington, Augustinian priory, I. 344

'Briefless, Mr,' *pseud.* of À Beckett, Gil-
bert Abbott, XIV. 237
'Briefless, Junior, A.,' *pseud.* of À Beckett,
Arthur William, XIV. 238
Brierley, Benjamin (1825–1896), XIII. 560
Brigden, Mrs. *See* Richardson, Mary
Briggs, Arabella, in Thackeray's *Vanity
Fair,* XIII. 287
Briggs, Henry (1561–1630), III. 426; IX.
530
Briggs, John (1785–1875), XIV. 337, 575
Briggs, William, XIV. 536
Briggs, Mr, in Burney's *Cecilia,* X. 64
Briggs, Mr, Leech's, XIV. 239
Brigham, Nicholas (d. 1558), I. 332; II.
36
Bright, Edward Brailsford, XIV. 613
Bright, John (1811–1889), XI. 31; XIV.
129, 131 ff., 179, 181, 190, 508, 509
Bright, William (1824–1901), XII. 454,
474, *also see* Add. 3; *Chapters of Early
English Church History,* XII. 322; *History
of the Church,* XII. 321
Bright, lady, in *Amends for Ladies,* VI. 223
Brightland, John, XI. 250
Brighton, XII. 291, 508; XIII. 287; XIV.
225, 414
Brigittine order, IV. 418
Brihtwold, bishop of Ramsbury (d. 1045),
I. 133
Brill, III. 203
Brimblecombe, John, in Kingsley's *West-
ward Ho!,* XII. 102
Brimley, George (1819–1857), XIII. 148,
365, 367, 466, 476; XIV. 139, 208, 516
Brindley, John, XI. 323, 332
Brine, John (1703–1765), X. 387
Brine, *Punch* artist, XIV. 236
Brink, Melt J., *Grappige Stories,* XIV. 377
Brinkelow, Henry (d. 1546), III. 87, 477;
IV. 317; *The Complaynt of Roderyck
Mors,* III. 99, 105, 491
Brinsley, John, the elder (*fl.* 1663), IX.
387, 405, 568; *Aesop,* XI. 490; *Ludus
Literarius,* VII. 314, 335, 478, 479, 491
Brinton, Sybil G., *Old Friends and New
Fancies,* XII. 244
Brisbane, John, IX. 203
Briscoe, Samuel, IX. 264
Briseida, I. 306
Brisk, Fastidious, in *Every Man out of his
Humour,* X. 50
Brisk, Mr, in Congreve's *Double-Dealer,*
VIII. 149, 156, 375
Bristol, II. 212, 338, 423; III. 40; IV. 68, 87,
94, 106, 409; VI. 110, 281, 301, 319,
386; VII. 245, 350; IX. 163, 407; X. 165,
236, 237, 268, 269, 322, 353, 362; XI. 6,
15, 30, 132, 155, 156, 159, 283, 340,
341, 359, 361, 390, 413, 414, 420, 421,
474; XII. 340
Bristol, Colston's hospital, X. 237
Bristol, earldom of, IX. 251
Bristol, earls of. *See* Digby, George;
Digby, John; Hervey, Augustus John;
Hervey, John

Bristol, St Mary Redcliffe church, x. 236, 486; xii. 345, 508
Bristol academy, x. 387
Bristol Journal, xi. 133, 134, 461
Bristol university, xiv. 432
Bristow, W., ix. 574
Britain, ii. 342, 396; ix. 214
Britain, Benjamin, in Dickens's *Battle of Life*, xiii. 323
Britain, Book of, i. 70 ff.
Britain, early, xiv. 69
Britain, Roman, xii. 347
Britain's Buss, iv. 509
Britannia, ix. 154
Britannia, in Thomson's *Castle of Indolence*, x. 107
Britanniae, De Situ, xii. 336
Britanny, v. 16
Britanny, duchess of, in *Morte Arthure*, ii. 118
Britanny, duke of, in *Froissart*, ii. 338
British academy, viii. 220; xii. 332
British and Foreign school society, xiv. 403 ff., 419
British archaeological association, xii. 347
British association, the, xiv. 259, 288
British constitution, xi. 8, 10, 12, 20, 26
British empire, xi. 13, 18
British kings, line of, in *The Faerie Queene*, iii. 234
British parliament, xi. 20
British school of archaeology at Athens, xii. 340
British school of archaeology at Rome, xii. 340
British school of archaeology in Egypt, xii. 339
'British shell,' x. 143
British Album, xi. 177
British Censor, The, ix. 438
British Critic, The, xii. 259, 273, 453, 455, 460, 461
British Journal, ix. 571
British Magazine, The, x. 41, 205, 421; xi. 260; xii. 257, 453, 454; xiv. 79
British Poets, The, ix. 183; xi. 325, 326
Brito, William (d. 1356), *Quaestiones*, ii. 363; *Summa de expositione verborum Bibliae*, ii. 363
Britomart, in Spenser's *Faerie Queene*, iii. 231, 234, 236; xii. 61, 87
Briton, The, x. 41, 390 ff., 421, 522
Britons, the, xiv. 68
Britons, Caesar on, reproduced in Mandeville, ii. 80
Britton, John (d. 1275), viii. 313, 465
Britton, John (1771–1857), xii. 508
  Architectural Antiquities of Great Britain, xii. 345
  Beauties of England and Wales, xii. 345
  Beauties of Wiltshire, xii. 345
  Cathedral Antiquities, xii. 345
  'Picturesque Antiquities of English Cities,' xii. 345
Brixen, xiv. 247
Broad church, xii. 464

Broadhurst, Frances, xiv. 599
Broadhurst, Thomas, xiv. 599
Broadley, Alexander Mayrick, xiv. 541
Broadley, A. M. and Seccombe, Thomas, *Doctor Johnson and Mrs Thrale*, x. 157
Broadsides and Street Ballads, iii. 490, 494; iv. 530, 535
Broadwindsor, vii. 245, 258
Brobdingnag, ix. 104, 128
Broceliande, fountain of, in *Ywain and Gawain*, i. 312
Brockett, Lawrence (*fl.* 1763), x. 131, 133
Broderip, Mrs Frances Freeling (1830–1878), xii. 418
Brodie, Alexander (1617–1680), ix. 551
Brodmeier, C., vi. 265, 266
Brodrick, George Charles, *Memorials of Merton*, ix. 411; xiv. 383
Broke, Arthur (d. 1563), iv. 441; v. 221
Brokesby, Francis (1637–1714), *Life of Hy. Dodwell*, viii. 307, 459; *Of Education*, ix. 405, 568
Brome, Alexander (1620–1666), vi. 453, 492; vii. 512
Brome, Charles (*fl.* 1687–1700), viii. 405, 412
Brome, Joanna (*fl.* 1681), viii. 412
Brome, Richard (d. 1652?), v. 311, 315; vi. 153, 211, 212, 224–232 (main entry), 234, 236, 431, 453, *and see* Add. 2; vii. 513; viii. 124, 142; xiii. Add. 2
  Antipodes, The, vi. 226, 227, 231
  City Witt, The, vi. 225, 226, 228
  Court Beggar, The, vi. 226
  Covent Garden Weeded, vi. 226
  Damoiselle, The, vi. 226
  English Moor, The, vi. 230
  Fault in Friendship, A, vi. 224
  Joviall Crew, A, vi. 229 ff.
  Love-sick Court, The, vi. 230, 231
  Madd Couple well matcht, The, vi. 226; viii. 141
  New Academy, The, vi. 226
  Northern Lasse, The, vi. 224, 226 ff.
  Novella, The, vi. 230
  Queen and Concubine, The, vi. 230, 231
  Queenes Exchange, The, vi. 230, 231
  Sparagus Garden, The, vi. 226, 227
  'What if a day, or a month, or a year,' vi. 231
  See, also, under Heywood
Brome, Stephen (d. 1652?), vi. 224
Brome play, the (Abraham and Isaac), ii. 426
Bromion, in Blake's *Visions of the Daughters of Albion*, xi. 190
Bromley, Mrs Beatrice, xiv. Add. 4
Bromley, Sir George, vii. 438
Bromley, Thomas (d. 1691), ix. 307, 513, 515
Brommerton, William, vii. 509
Bromsgrove, xi. 340
Bromyarde, John de (*fl.* 1390), *Summa Praedicantium*, i. 367
Brontë, Anne (1820–1849), xiii. 403 ff., 409, 554, 555, 557; *Agnes Grey*, xiii

Brontë, Anne
 408, 414; *Tenant of Wildfell Hall, The,*
 XIII. 408, 414
Brontë, Charlotte (1816–1855), XII. 446;
 XIII. 379, 403 ff. (main entry), 483, 495,
 550, 554 ff., *also see* Add. 3; XIV. 515
 Emma, XIII. 410
 Jane Eyre, XIII. 404, 406 ff., 410 ff., 414,
 415
 Poems (by Currer, Ellis and Acton Bell),
 XIII. 406, 415
 Professor, The, XIII. 406, 409, 414
 Shirley, XIII. 408, 409
 Villette, XIII. 409, 410
Brontë, Elizabeth, 2nd daughter of
 Patrick Brontë, XIII. 404
Brontë, Emily Jane (1818–1848), XIII.
 175, 214, 404, 405, 410 ff. (main entry),
 554 ff.; XIV. 349
 Old Stoic, The, XIII. 412
 Remembrance, XIII. 412
 Stanzas, XIII. 412
 Wuthering Heights, XIII. 408, 410 ff.
Brontë, Maria (born Branwell), XIII. 404
Brontë, Maria, daughter of Patrick Brontë,
 XIII. 404
Brontë, Patrick (1777–1861), XIII. 403,
 557; XIV. 567
Brontë, Patrick Branwell (1817–1848),
 XIII. 404 ff., 508, 557
Brook, Benjamin (1776–1848), X. 520
Brooke, Charles Frederick Tucker, V. 237,
 255
Brooke, Charlotte (d. 1793), XIV. 305, 567,
 572; *Reliques of Irish Poetry,* XIV. 311
Brooke, Christopher (d. 1628), IV. 117,
 121, 157, 158, 200, 201, 479
Brooke, Frances (1724–1789), X. 426;
 XI. 448; *The History of Emily Montague,*
 XIV. 359, 582
Brooke, Henry (1703?–1783), IX. 181,
 184, 185, 513; X. 46, 55, 58 ff. (main
 entry), 423, 437, 460
 Conrade, IX. 185
 Fables, IX. 185
 Farmer's Letters, X. 58
 Fool of Quality, The, IX. 181, 184, 327,
 328; X. 15, 49, 58 ff.
 Gustavus Vasa, X. 175
 History of Henry Earl of Moreland, IX.
 328
 Juliet Grenville, X. 60
 Universal Beauty, IX. 184
Brooke, Henry, of Dublin, IX. 327
Brooke, lord. *See* Greville, Sir Fulke; 2nd
 lord. *See* Greville, Robert
Brooke, Mr, in *Middlemarch,* XIII. 299
Brooke, rajah, XIII. 364
Brooke, Ralph (1553–1625), III. 328, 528
Brooke, Sir Robert, VIII. 466; *Abridge-
 ment of the Year Books,* VIII. 315
Brooke, Rupert Chawner (1887–1915),
 VI. Add.; XIII. 499, 574
Brooke, Samuel (d. 1632), IV. 201; VI.
 470; *Adelphe,* VI. 321, 323; *Melanthe,*
 VI. 323; *Scyros,* VI. 321, 323

Brooke, Stopford Augustus (1832–1916),
 Pref. x; I. 2 ff., 47, 48, 51, 59; XI. 403,
 406, 407, 409, 412, 416, 434, 439; XII. 399,
 400, 402, 406, 469; XIII. 476, 484, 488 ff.;
 XIV. 516, 517, 573, *also see* Add. 2, 3;
 *The Need and Use of getting Irish Litera-
 ture into the English Tongue,* XIV. 305
Brooke, William, 7th lord Cobham (d.
 1597), VI. 385
Brooke, Sir William, III. 321
Brooke family, the, IV. 216
Brookfield, Charles, XIII. 530
Brookfield, Frances, XIII. 530
Brookfield, Jane Octavia, XIII. 530
Brookfield, William Henry (1809–1874),
 XIII. 277
Brooks, Charles William Shirley (1816–
 1874), XIII. 264, 266, 517; XIV. 196, 238,
 548; *The Exposition,* XIII. 271
Brooks, Henry, XIV. Add. 6
Brooks, Van Wyck, XIV. 527
Brooks's club, XI. 52
Broom o' Cowden knowes, The, II. 413
Broome, William (1689–1745), IX. 75, 76,
 181, 183, 184, 443, 484; XI. 246
Broome of Cowden Knowes, IX. 363
Broomfield Hill, The, II. 414
Brosch, Moritz, *Lord Bolingbroke,* IX. 226
Brotanek, R., V. 85
Brother, The Cruel, II. 412
'Brotherhood, the,' XIII. 119, 120
Brothers, Richard (1757–1824), XI. 163
Brothers, The Twa, II. 412
Brothers club, IX. 96, 151
Brough, John, in Thackeray's *Great Hog-
 garty Diamond,* XIII. 281
Brough, Robert Barnabas (1828–1860),
 XIII. 499, 517
Brough, Westmorland, X. 133
Brougham, Henry Peter, 1st lord Brougham
 and Vaux (1778–1868), VIII. 316; X. 513;
 XII. 32, 143 ff., 147, 393, 426, 427;
 XIV. 54, 60, 115, 116, 123 ff., 180, 186,
 197, 403 ff., 418, 485, 508, 512, 555, 601,
 604
 *Letter to Samuel Romilly...upon the
 abuse of charities,* XIV. 405, 408
 Life and Times, XIV. 112
 *Practical Observations upon the education
 of the people,* XIV. 408
 'The Crisis in the Sugar Colonies,' XII.
 145
Brougham, John (1814–1880), *The Duke's
 Motto,* XIII. 525
Broughamiana, XIV. 123
Broughton, Hugh (1549–1612), IV. 491
Broughton, Jack (1705–1789), XIV. 229,
 231
Broughton, John (*fl.* 1703), VIII. 347, 472
Broughton, Richard (d. 1634), IX. 532
Broughton de Gyfford, lord. *See* Hob-
 house, John Cam
Broughton Papers, the, XII. 390
Brouncker, lady, in *Pendennis,* XIV. 440
Brouncker, William, 2nd viscount Brouncker
 (1620?–1684), VIII. 61, 218

Brounsmith, J., x. 443
Brown, Andrew (*fl.* 1700), IX. 558, 560
Brown, Charles Armitage (1786–1842),
    XII. 83 ff., 91, 93
Brown, Ford Madox (1821–1893), XII. 384;
    XIII. 110, 140
Brown, George Douglas (*pseud.* George
    Douglas, 1869–1902), XIII. 561
Brown, Horatio F., XIV. 527
Brown, John (1610?–1679), IX. 545
Brown, John (1715–1766), IX. 508; X. 426;
    XIV. 604; *The Estimate*, X. 133, 136;
    Thoughts on Civil Liberty, XIV. 400
Brown, John (1722–1787), IX. 548
Brown, John, XIV. 590
Brown, John (1810–1882), XI. 476; XIV.
    517, 543, *also see* Add. 2; *Horae Sub-
    secivae*, XIII. 437; *Rab and his Friends*,
    XIV. 160
Brown, John Croumbie, XIV. Add. 6
Brown, lady, X. 126
Brown, Lucky, XII. 3
Brown, M. J., XIV. 574
Brown, Mrs, of Falkland, II. 409
Brown, Oliver Madox (1855–1874), XIII.
    216, 499, 561
Brown, P. Hume, XIV. 491; *History of
    Scotland*, X. 281
Brown, Robert (1773–1858), XIV. 289,
    290, 559
Brown, Robinson, XIII. 557
Brown, Thomas, *Nature's Cabinet Un-
    lock'd*, 1657, VII. 510
Brown, Thomas (1663–1704), VIII. 48,
    168, 404, 405, 432, 445, 480; IX. 256,
    260, 263 ff., 329, 499
    Amusements Serious and Comical, IX.
    262, 263
    Colloquies of Erasmus, IX. 275
    Elegy on Mr Edward Millington, XI.
    336
    Miscellanea Aulica, IX. 496
Brown, Thomas (1778–1820), XIV. 6 ff.,
    10, 12, 469; *Lectures on the Philosophy
    of the Human Mind*, XIV. 6; *Observations
    on the...Doctrine of Mr Hume*, XIV. 6;
    *Observations on the Zoonomia of Erasmus
    Darwin*, XIV. 6
Brown, Thomas Edward (1830–1897),
    XIII. 194 ff., 499; XIV. 145
    Bella Gorry, XIII. 196
    Betsy Lee, XIII. 194
    Dartmoor pieces, XIII. 196
    'Englishwoman on the Pincian,' XIII.
    195
    Fo'c'sle Yarns, XIII. 194
    Mary Quayle, XIII. 196
    Opifex, XIII. 196
    Peel Life Boat, The, XIII. 195
    Prayer, The, XIII. 196
    Risus Dei, XIII. 196
    Roman Women, XIII. 195
    Schooner, The, XIII. 196
    Sermon at Church on Good Friday, A,
    XIII. 185
    Sinking of the Victoria, The, XIII. 196

Brown, Thomas Edward
    White Foxglove, XIII. 196
Brown, Vanbeest, in Scott's *Guy Man-
    nering*, XII. 17, 18
Brown, William (*fl.* 1671), VIII. 468
Brown, William (*fl.* 1768), XI. 335
Brown, William Harvey, XIV. Add. 6
Brown Dozen of Drunkards..., *A*, IV. 361,
    522
Brown Robin, II. 411
Brown Robyn's Confession, II. 413
Browne, a serving man, VI. 243
Browne, Edgar A., XIII. 540
Browne, Edward (1644–1708), son of Sir
    Thomas Browne, VII. 233, 244
Browne, Edward Granville, XII. 503
Browne, Mrs. *See* Hemans, Felicia
    Dorothea
Browne, mistress Frances, wife of Sir J.
    Reresby, VIII. 266
Browne, Frances (1816–1879), XIV. 567
Browne, George (d. 1556), archbishop of
    Dublin, III. 426
Browne, Hablot Knight (*pseud.* Phiz,
    1815–1882), XII. 447, 452; XIII. 540,
    541; XIV. 234, 238, 545 ff.
Browne, Henry (1804–1875), XII. 454
Browne, Henry, *pseud. See* Erskine
    Francis Robert St Claire
Browne, Isaac Hawkins (1705–1760), IX.
    484; *Pipe of Tobacco*, IX. 188, 191
Browne, Mary, wife of John Evelyn. *See*
    Evelyn, Mary
Browne, Ned, in *The Blacke Bookes Mes-
    senger*, III. 361
Browne, Patrick (1720?–1790), X. 467
Browne, Peter (d. 1735), IX. 504; *Answer
    (to Toland)*, IX. 282; *Divine Analogy*,
    IX. 283; *Procedure, extent and limits of
    human understanding*, IX. 282
Browne, Sir Richard (d. 1669), VIII. 245,
    246
Browne, Robert (1550?–1633?), III. 389,
    422, 548
Browne, Simon (1680–1732), X. 521, 522
Browne, Thomas (1604?–1673), translator
    of Camden, III. 326, 528, 554
Browne, Sir Thomas (1605–1682), III. 463;
    IV. 216, 221, 252; VI. 187; VII. 99, 130,
    132, 163, 232–244 (main entry), 249,
    250, 253, 256 ff., 366, 460 ff., 511, *also
    see* Add.; VIII. 292, 357, 368, 378, 386;
    XI. 2, 28; XII. 169, 176, 197; XIII. 195;
    XIV. 457, 460
    Christian Morals, VII. 239, 241, 243;
    X. 177, 466, 468
    Dreams, VII. 241
    Garden of Cyrus, The, VII. 237, 241, 242;
    XII. 197
    Hydriotaphia or Urn Burial, VII. 237,
    241, 242
    Hydriotaphia, XII. 197
    Letter to a Friend, A, VII. 241, 243
    Miscellanies, VII. 241
    Pseudodoxia Epidemica (Vulgar Errors),
    VII. 236, 238, 241; XII. 197

Browne, Sir Thomas
  Religio Medici, IV. 246; VII. 44, 233,
    234 ff., 239, 241, 313, 449; VIII. 42;
    XI. 318
  Works, VII. 241
Browne, Tom, son of Sir Thomas Browne,
  VII. 234, 244
Browne, Thomas Alexander (*pseud.* Rolf
  Boldrewood, 1826–1915), XIV. 585
  Colonial Reformer, A, XIV. 370
  Miner's Right, The, XIV. 370
  Robbery under Arms, XIV. 370
  Squatter's Dream, The, XIV. 370
Browne, William (of Tavistock) (1591–
  1643?), III. 311; IV. 117, 124, 150, 154,
  155, 157 ff. (main entry), 194, 479;
  VI. 10, 113, 329; VII. 75, 83, 112, 113;
  VIII. 227; XII. 79, 93; *Britannia's Pas-
  torals*, IV. 157, 158; VI. 215; VII. 38;
  Inner Temple Masque, IV. 159; *Shepherd's
  Pipe*, IV. 121, 158
Browne, W., trans. of Gomberville's
  Polexandre, VII. 391
Browne medal, the, XIII. 45
Brownell, William Crary, XIII. 470, 488,
  570, 574
Browning, Elizabeth Barrett (1806–1861),
  II. 233; X. 141; XII. 106, 118, 124; XIII.
  46, 49 ff., 57, 61 ff., 70 ff. (main entry),
  139, 147, 148, 160, 161, 175, 177, 180,
  181, 480, 481 ff., *also see* Add. 2; XIV.515
  Aurora Leigh, XIII. 70, 72, 74, 75, 179
  Battle of Marathon, The, XIII. 70
  Casa Guidi Windows, XIII. 74
  Child's Grave at Florence, A, XIII. 75
  Cowper's Grave, XIII. 75
  Cry of the Children, The, XIII. 75
  Drama of Exile, XIII. 71
  Essay on Mind and other Poems, An,
    XIII. 70
  *Greek Christian poets and the English
  poets*, XIII. 69, 77
  Lady Geraldine's Courtship, XIII. 69
  Last Poems, XIII. 74
  Lost Bower, The, XIII. 70
  Poems (1844), XIII. 69, 71
  Poems before Congress, XIII. 74
  Rhyme of the Duchess May, XIII. 75
  Seraphim and other Poems, The, XIII.
    70, 71
  Sonnets by E. B. B., XIII. 71
  Sonnets from the Portuguese, XIII. 49, 50,
    70, 71, 75
  Trans. of Aeschylus's *Prometheus Bound*,
    XIII. 70
Browning, Oscar, XIII. Add. 3
Browning, Robert (1812–1889), v. 231;
  VII. 91; X. 236, 457; XI. 409; XII. 106,
  113, 115, 118, 154, 177, 178, 219, 223,
  402; XIII. 10, 43 ff., 47, 49 ff. (main
  entry), 85, 89, 108, 120, 121, 131, 147,
  152, 153, 155, 157 ff., 165, 179, 180, 184,
  186, 187, 190, 194, 195, 202, 219, 221,
  230, 250 ff., 309, 401, 442, 448, 479 ff.,
  494, *also see* Add. 2; XIV. 132, 255, 320,
  354, 365, 368, 445, 453, 456, 517

Browning, Robert
  Agamemnon of Aeschylus, The, XIII. 58,
    81
  Any Wife to Any Husband, XIII. 76
  Aristophanes' Apology, VI. 232; XIII. 81
  Asolando, XIII. 52, 78, 84
  At the 'Mermaid,' XIII. 82
  Balaustion's Adventure, XIII. 80
  Bells and Pomegranates, XII. 101; XIII.
    61, 62, 228
  Bishop Blougram's Apology, XIII. 55
  Bishop orders his Tomb, The, XIII. 69
  Blot in the 'Scutcheon, A, XIII. 62, 68
  Caliban upon Setebos, XIII. 55, 78
  Caponsacchi, XIII. 80
  Christmas Eve and Easter Day, XII. 100;
    XIII. 75, 76
  Cleon, XIII. 76
  Clive, XIII. 84
  Colombe's Birthday, XIII. 62, 69
  Confessional, The, XIII. 63
  'Confidence lit swift the forehead up,'
    XIII. 62
  Cristina, XIII. 76
  Death in the Desert, A, XIII. 78
  Dramatic Idyls, XIII. 83
  Dramatic Lyrics, XIII. 76
  Dramatic Romances and Lyrics, XIII. 62,
    63, 76
  Dramatis Personae, XIII. 63, 77 ff., 81
  Epilogue (in *Asolando*), XIII. 84
  Ferishtah's Fancies, XIII. 55, 84
  Fifine at the Fair, XIII. 50, 77, 81, 82,
    251
  Flight of the Duchess, The, XIII. 69
  Fra Lippo Lippi, XIII. 72
  Garden Fancies, XIII. 65
  Glove, The, XIII. 63
  Gold Hair: a Story of Pornic, XIII. 77
  Guido, XIII. 80
  Hervé Riel, XIII. 80
  Home Thoughts from the Sea, XIII. 61
  'Hope rose a-tiptoe,' XIII. 62
  House, XIII. 82
  How they brought the Good News, XIII. 83
  In a Gondola, XIII. 76
  Incondita, XIII. 53
  Inn Album, The, XIII. 81, 82
  Introduction to *Certain Letters of Percy
  Bysshe Shelley*, XIII. 75
  Iván Ivanovitch, XIII. 83
  Ixion, XIII. 84
  James Lee's Wife, XIII. 55
  Jocoseria, XIII. 84
  Karshish, An Epistle...of, XIII. 76
  King Victor and King Charles, XIII. 61,
    62
  Laboratory, The, XIII. 63
  Last Ride Together, The, XIII. 76
  Lost Mistress, The, XIII. 76
  Luria, XIII. 62
  Martin Relph, XIII. 83
  Men and Women, XIII. 72, 75 ff.
  Mr Sludge, 'The Medium,' XIII. 46, 72,
    78
  Muléykeh, XIII. 84

Browning, Robert
  Ned Bratts, XIII. 83
  Never the Time and the Place, XIII. 84
  Numpholeptos, XIII. 83
  One Way of Love, XIII. 76
  One Word More, XIII. 72
  Pacchiarotto, XIII. 64, 82, 203
  Paracelsus, XIII. 55 ff., 60, 70, 75
  Parleyings with Certain People, XIII. 52, 84
  Pauline, XIII. 52 ff., 58, 75, 116
  Pheidippides, XIII. 83
  Pied Piper of Hamelin, The, XIII. 64
  Pippa Passes, XIII. 61, 62, 75 ff., 84
  Pompilia, XIII. 80
  Pope, The, XIII. 80
  Porphyria's Lover, XIII. 55
  Prince Hohenstiel-Schwangau, XIII. 55, 74, 81
  Prospice, XIII. 78
  Rabbi Ben Ezra, XIII. 78
  'Rapture drooped the eyes,' XIII. 62
  Red Cotton Night-cap Country, XIII. 77, 81, 82
  Return of the Druses, The, XIII. 61, 62
  Ring and the Book, The, IV. 249; XIII. 50, 60, 65, 77 ff.
  St Martin's Summer, XIII. 83
  Saisiaz, La, XIII. 83
  Saul, XIII. 76
  Sibrandus Schafnaburgensis, XIII. 64
  Sordello, XIII. 52, 55, 58 ff., 64, 76, 82
  Soul's Tragedy, A, XIII. 62
  'Still ailing, Wind?' XIII. 55
  Strafford, VII. 17; XIII. 55, 58, 59
  Two Poets of Croisic, The, XIII. 77, 83
  Waring, XIV. 241
  Woman's Last Word, A, XIII. 76
  Youth and Art, XIII. 65
Browning, Robert Wiedemann Barrett, XIII. 71
Browning society, the, XII. 504
Brownists, the, IV. 52
Brownlow, William Robert, XII. 508, 512
Bruce, Alexander (brother of Robert Bruce), I. 344
Bruce, Alexander Balmain (1831–1899), XII. 465; XIV. 469
Bruce, Edward (d. 1318), II. 101; in Barbour's *Bruce*, II. 105, 106
Bruce, Henry Austin, 1st baron Aberdare (1815–1895), XIV. 107, 496, 590
Bruce, James (1730–1794), XIV. 246, 247, 550; *Travels in Abyssinia*, XIV. 241
Bruce, John (1745–1826), XII. 354, 515; XIV. 97, 485
Bruce, John (1802–1869), XIV. 486
Bruce, John Collingwood (1805–1892), XII. 508; *Lapidarium Septentrionale*, XII. 346
Bruce, Michael (1746–1767), IX. 557; X. 484; XI. 442; *Cuckoo, The*, XI. 244; *Elegy on Spring*, XI. 244; *Poems on Several Occasions*, XI. 244
Bruce, Robert (1274–1329), I. 344, 352; II. 100, 101 ff., 109, 114, 130, 280; X. 224; XIV. 95

Bruce, Robert (1559–1631), IX. 543
Bruce's *Anglo-Saxon Version of the Book of Psalms*, I. 106
Bruces, the, in *Robert, Earle of Huntington*, V. 323, 324
Brueys and Palaprat, *Le Grondeur*, VIII. 139
Bruges, II. 54, 311, 312, 338; III. 18
Brugis, Thomas (*fl.* 1640?), IV. 454
Bruliferius, III. 50
Brumoy, father, X. 469
Brumpton, lord, in Steele's *Funeral*, IX. 30
Brunanburh, battle of, I. 137, 141, 150, 167, 287, 443; II. 400
Brunanburh, X. 487
Brunellus, the donkey of Nigel Wireker, I. 192
Brunetière, Ferdinand, IX. 20
Brunetto Latini, *Trésor*, II. 80, 149, 150
Brunhalt, in *Thierry and Theodoret*, VI. 122, 129
Brunnëwake in Kestevene, I. 344
Brunnow, baron, XIV. 129
Brunnus, in *The Scourge of Folly*, IV. 334
Bruno, Giordano, *Il Candelaio*, VI. 22
Brunswick, V. 298
Brunswick-Lüneburg, VII. 438
Brunton, Mary (1778–1818), XI. 459; XIII. 561
Brunton, Thomas (*fl.* 1373–1389), bishop of Rochester, II. 55, 58
Brunty, Patrick. *See* Brontë
Brushfield, Thomas Nadauld, IV. 450
Brussels, I. 57; III. 431; VIII. 267; XII. 365; XIII. 282, 406, 409
Brussels, Rue d'Isabelle, XIII. 405
Brut, Brute, the *Bruts*, the Brutus legend, I. 170, 175, 234 ff., 258, 306, 336, 375; II. 301, 322, 482; III. 315; IV. 136; VII. 117; X. 231
Brut, The Chronicle of the, II. 313, 334, 482
Brut, Layamon's, I. 137, 170, 223, 234 ff., 265, 375, 397, 398
Brut, Tysilio's, I. 235
Brut, Wace's, I. 234, 235, 350
Brute, lady, in Vanbrugh's *Provok'd Wife*, VIII. 161
Brute, Sir John, in Vanbrugh's *Provok'd Wife*, VIII. 161, 162, 168
Bruton, William (*fl.* 1638), XIV. 333, 575
Brutus, IX. 28
Brutus, in *Julius Caesar*, V. 197, 379; VI. 127
Brutus, in Milton's *England*, VII. 129
Brutus legend, the. *See Brut*
Brutus of Troy, IX. 74
Bruyère, la, VIII. 373
Bryan, Sir Francis (d. 1550), II. 340; III. 173, 181; IV. 445
Bryan, John (d. 1676), X. 385
Bryant, Jacob (1715–1804), X. 485, 486
Bryant, Sophie, XIV. 599
Bryce, James Bryce, viscount, XII. 271; XIV. 71, 74, 525; *Studies in Contemporary Biography*, XIV. 118
Bryce, M. A. L., XIV. 483

Bryce commission (1896), XIV. 423, 433
Brydall, John. *See* Bridall
Bryden, H. Anderson, XIV. Add. 6
Brydges, Grey, 5th lord Chandos (1579?–1621), IV. 524
Brydges, James, 1st duke of Chandos (1673–1744), IX. 81
Brydges, Sir Samuel Egerton (1762–1837), IV. 54; VII. 84; XI. 471; XII. 384, 393, 520; XIV. 232, 512; *British Bibliographer, The*, XII. 364; *Censura Literaria*, XII. 363; *Restituta*, XII. 364
Brylinger, N., V. 412
Brynllywarch academy, X. 386, 387
Bryskett, Lodowick or Lewis (*fl.* 1571–1611), III. 229, 521; IV. 444, 525; *The Mourning Muse of Thestylis*, XI. 179
Brysson, George (*c.* 1649–*c.* 1730), XIV. 493, 507
Bubble, in *Greene's Tu Quoque*, VI. 219
Buc *See* Buck
Bucan, earl of. *See* Erskine, David Steuart
Buccleuch, dukes of. *See* Scott, Charles W. H.; Scott, Henry
Buccleugh, in Scott's *Lay of the Last Minstrel*, XII. 8
Bucephalus, I. 307
Bucer, Martin (1491–1551), III. 34, 53, 419, 428, 474; IV. 233; VII. 417; *De honestis ludis*, VI. 374, 492
Buchan, Peter (1790–1854), II. 409; IX. 371, 565; *Gleanings of...Ballads*, IX. 374
Buchan, the harrying of, by Robert Bruce, II. 100
Buchanan, George (1506–1582), II. 96; III. 1, 6, 16, 116, 123, 138, 143, 151, 152, 156, 157–165 (main entry), 301, 424, 466, 501; IV. 253, 254, 261, 304, 509; V. 394; IX. 526, 552, 562; XII. 520, 522
 Ad Carolum V Imperatorem, III. 160
 Admonition to the trew Lordis, The, III. 164
 Adventus in Galliam, III. 162
 Alcestis, translation of, III. 161
 Baptistes, III. 16, 161; V. 82; VI. 295
 Book of Elegies, III. 158
 Chamaeleon, II. 285; III. 164
 Detectis, III. 164
 Epithalamium, an, III. 163
 Franciscanus, III. 159; VIII. 85
 Gencthliacon, a, III. 164
 Jephthes, III. 161; V. 82; VI. 296
 Jure Regni apud Scotos, De, III. 165; IV. 303
 Masque, a (for Mary's marriage with Darnley), III. 164
 Medea, translation of, III. 161
 Odes on the capture of Calais and of Metz, III. 163
 Palinodia, III. 159
 Psalmorum Davidis Paraphrasis Poetica, III. 162
 Psalms, translation of the, III. 162 ff.

Buchanan, George
 Ptolomaeum Luxium Tastaeum et Jacobum Taevium cum articulari morbo laboravit, Ad, III. 161
 Quam misera sit conditio docentium literas humaniores Lutetiae, III. 158
 Rerum Scoticarum Historia, III. 164 IV. 412
 Sphaera, De, III. 163
 Somnium (How Dunbar wes desyrd to be ane freir), III. 159
Buchanan, Robert Williams (1841–1901), XIII. 117, 207 ff., 217, 490, 500, 517, 561; *Ballad of Judas Iscariot, The*, XIII. 209; *Ratcliff Meg*, XIII. 209; *Vision of the Man Accurst, The*, XIII. 209
Buchanan-Hamilton, Francis (1762–1829), XIV. 575; *An account of the Kingdom of Nipal*, XIV. 335
Buchell, Arend von, VI. 260
Buck or Buc, Sir George (d. 1623), IV. 383; VII. 443; X. 291; *History of the Life and Reigne of Richard III*, III 334
Buckbasket Mishap, The, VIII. 116
Buckeridge, John (1562?–1631), IV. 239
Buckhurst, lords. *See* Sackville, Charles; Sackville, Thomas
Buckhurst, Sir Charles, in Disraeli's *Coningsby*, XIII. 350
Buckingham, IX. 541
Buckingham, duke of, in *King Henry VIII*, V. 346
Buckingham, dukes of. *See* Stafford, Edward; Stafford, Henry; Villiers, George
Buckingham, James Silk (1786–1855), XIV. 533
Buckingham and Normanby, duchess of, IX. 82
Buckingham and Normanby, duke of. *See* Sheffield, John
Buckinghamshire, III. 11; VII. 98, 107; X. 351; XII. 511
Buckland, Charles Edward, XIV. 574
Buckland, Francis Trevelyan (1826–1880), XIV. 559
Buckland, William (1784–1856), XIV. 292 ff., 559; *Reliquiae Diluvianae*, XIV. 292
Buckle, George Earle, XIII. 345, 547; XIV. 504
Buckle, Henry Thomas (1821–1862), XIII. 383; XIV. 486; *History of Civilisation in England*, XIV. 102 ff.
Buckley, Michael B., XIV. 570
Buckley, Samuel, *Daily Courant*, IX. 5
Buckman, Sydney S., XIV. 562
Buckstone, John Baldwin (1802–1879), XIII. 265, 270, 518; *Bear-hunters (The); or, The Fatal Ravine*, XIII. 266; *Flower of the Forest, The*, XIII. 266; *Green Bushes (The); or, A Hundred Years Ago*, XIII. 266
Budaeus, VII. 307, 320
Budd, Thomas, IV. 454
Buddeus, Johan Franz, V. 286
Buddha, I. 286; XIII. 400

Buddhism, XIII. 200
Buddhist topes, XII. 353
Budé, Guillaume, III. 1, 18, 20, 325
Budgell, Eustace (1686–1737), IX. 86, 220,
436, 492, 568
Budleigh, Devon, IV. 51
Buelt, Builth or Buallt, I. 247
Buffer, in *Our Mutual Friend*, XIII. 337
Buffle, Sir Raffle, Trollope's, XIII. 422
Buffon, George Louis Leclerc, comte de,
IX. 321; X. 135; XIII. 450
Buffone, Carlo, in *Every Man out of his
Humour*, VI. 17, 40
Bufo, in Pope's *Epistle to Arbuthnot*,
IX. 147
Bugbears, The, V. 115, 117, 413
Bugge, Sophus, II. 417
Bugnot, L. G. (attributed to), *Alitophilus
castigatus*, IV. 257, 500
Buist, G., XIV. 496
Buke of Order of Knighthood, The, XII.
515
Bukton (Chaucer's), II. 161, 187
Bull, George (1634–1710), bishop of St
David's, VIII. 308, 459; X. 359; *Har-
monia Apostolica*, VIII. 305; *Judicia
Ecclesiae Catholicae*, VIII. 305; *Sermon
on the Fall*, VIII. 305
Bull, Henry (d. 1575?), IV. 446, 495
Bull, John (1563?–1628), IV. 464
'Bull, John,' X. 29, 182; XII. 230; XIV.
212, 213
Bull, John, in Arbuthnot's *History of John
Bull*, IX. 134, 135
Bull, Mrs, in Arbuthnot's *History of John
Bull*, IX. 134, 135
Bullein, William (d. 1576), III. 66, 87,
107 ff. (main entry), 493; IV. 317, 343,
523; VII. 366; *Bulwarke of Defence*, III.
107; IV. 326; *Dialogue...against the
fever Pestilence*, III. 66, 107 ff.; IV. 330
Bullen, Arthur Henry (1857–1920), III.
182; IV. 110, 113, 117, 119, 125; V. 221;
VI. 10, 58, 65, 102, 214, 459; VII. 453;
X. 161; XII. 428
Buller, Charles (1806–1848), XIII. 5; XIV.
125, 508, 512
Buller, William Archer, XIV. 469
Bullinger, Heinrich ('Black Bullinger'),
III. 127; IV. 380
Bullock, Henry (d. 1526), III. 27
Bullock, William, *Virginia Impartially
examined*, IV. 96, 454, 510
Bulloign, earl of, in *Godfrey of Bulloigne*,
VI. 89
Bullokar, William (*fl.* 1586), III. 444, 550;
IV. 435
Bulstred, Mrs, Donne's elegy on, IV. 216
Bulstrode, Buckinghamshire, XI. 347
Bulstrode, Sir Richard (1610–1711), VII.
436; VIII. 266, 452; *Life of James II*,
VIII. 267; *Memoirs and Reflections*, VIII.
267; *Original Letters*, VIII. 267
Bulteel, John (*fl.* 1683), VIII. 422
Bulwer, John (*fl.* 1654), *Anthropometa-
morphosis*, VII. 387

Bulwer-Lytton. *See* Lytton, lord
Bulwer, William Henry Lytton Earle (Sir
Henry Bulwer) (1801–1872), XII. 384;
XIV. 505
Bumble, in *Oliver Twist*, XIII. 316
Bunbury, Henry William (1750–1811), X.
215, 482; XIV. 215, 232, 542
*Academy for Grown Horsemen...by
Geoffrey Gambado, Esq.*, XIV. 216
Chop House, A, XIV. 216
Long Minuet, A, XIV. 216
Propagation of a lie, The, XIV. 216
Buncle, John, in Amory's *Life of John
Buncle*, XI. 288, 296
Bungay. *See* Thomas de
Bunion, Miss, in Thackeray's *Mrs Per-
kins's Ball*, XII. 125
Bunn, Alfred, XIII. 513
Bunny, Edmund (1540–1619), IV. 495
Bunsen, Christian Carl Josias, baron, XII.
283, 302, 303, 500; *Biblical Researches*,
XII. 295; *Memoir*, XIII. 363
Bunting, Edward (1773–1843), *Ancient
Irish Music*, XIV. 311
Bunyan, John (1628–1688), I. 58; II. 201;
IV. 45, 50; VII. 154, 155, 166–178 (main
entry), 251, 428 ff., *also see* Add.; VIII.
105, 293; IX. 18, 98; X. 1, 9, 20, 26, 383;
XI. 381, 477; XII. 169; XIII. 388; XIV.
61, 461
Book for Boys and Girls, XI. 372
Confession of my Faith, A, VII. 172
Divine Emblems, XI. 372
Grace Abounding to the Chief of Sinners,
VII. 168, 170, 171, 177; VIII. 104
Holy City or the New Jerusalem, The,
VII. 170, 177
Life and Death of Mr Badman, The,
VII. 177
Pilgrim's Progress, The, II. 200, 229;
III. 221, 230, 234; IV. 47; VII. 172–177
(main entry), 178; VIII. 284; X. 2; XI.
334, 422; XIII. 452; XIV. 444; trans-
lations of, VII. 176
Some Gospel Truths Opened, VII. 169;
VIII. 110
Buonaparte, Louis, XII. 377
Burana, Carmina, I. 190
Buranic verse, II. 385
Burbage, Cuthbert, son of Richard Bur-
bage, VI. 253, 255, 276, 277
Burbage, James (d. 1597), VI. 246, 249,
251 ff., 257, 276, 289
Burbage, Richard (1567?–1619), V. 169;
VI. 170, 220, 247, 248, 253, 255, 256,
258, 272, 274, 276, 277, 289, 358, *and
see* Add. 2
Burbage, Richard, in *The Returne from
Pernassus*, VI. 44, 312
Burbon, in *The Faerie Queene*, II. 234
Burbridge, Thomas, XIII. 104
Burby, Cuthbert (*fl.* 1594–1600), IV. 394
Burch, R. M., XIV. 536
Burchard Wormaciensis, VII. 372, 504
Burchell, Mr, in *Vicar of Wakefield*, X.
209

Burchell, William John (1782–1863), xiv. 550

Burckhardt, John Lewis (1784–1817), xiv. 247, 248, 250, 550

Burden, Jane. *See* Morris, Jane

Burdet, Sir Nicholas (*fl.* 1541), iii. 197

Burdett, Sir Francis (1770–1844), xiv. 121, 408, 508

Burdy, Samuel (1760?–1820), xiv. 486, 567

Burel or Burrel, John (*fl.* 1590), *The Description of the Queenis Majesties most honourable entry in the Town of Edinburgh,* iii. 137; *The Passage of the Pilgrim,* iii. 137, 498

Burford, Oxfordshire, viii. 206

Bürger, Gottfried August, xi. 303; xii. 6, 7, 373, 422, 526; *Der wilde Jäger,* xii. 4; *Leonore,* xii. 4

Burgersdijk, Leendert, v. 307

Burgersdyck, Francis, x. 198

Burges, George (1786?–1864), xii. 327

Burges, Sir James Bland (Sir James Lamb) (1752–1824), xi. 177, 425

Burgess, Anthony (*fl.* 1652), vii. 322

Burgess, Cornelius (1589?–1665), vii. 314

Burgess, Thomas (1756–1837), xii. 481

Burgh, Benet or Benedict (d. 1483), ii. 199, 208, 469; iii. 277, 290
    A Christmas Game, ii. 209
    Aristotle's ABC, ii. 209
    Cato, ii. 209, 312, 427
    Poem to Lydgate, ii. 209
    Secrets of Philosophers, ii. 208

Burgh, Elizabeth de, duchess of Clarence, ii. 156

Burgh, James (1714–1775), xiv. 604

Burgh, John de, *Pupilla Oculi,* ii. 498

Burgh, Thomas (*fl.* 1447), ii. 214

Burgh, Thomas (*fl.* 1790), xi. 6

Burgh, William (1741–1808), *Enquiry,* x. 308, 507; *Political Disquisitions,* x. 308

Burgher, the, and wife, in *A Dialogue... against the fever Pestilence,* iii. 109

Burghley, lord. *See* Cecil, William

Burgon, John William (1813–1888), iv. 263; xii. 274, 455

Burgonians Tragedy, The, iv. 362

Burgos, v. 99

Burgoyne, John (1722–1792), xi. 31, 456; *Heiress, The,* xi. 275, 276; xiv. 387; *Maid of the Oaks,* xi. 265, 275

Burgundian court, ii. 312

Burgundy, Margaret, duchess of (1446–1503), ii. 307, 309

Burgundy, Philip III, duke of, ii. 311

Burhill or Burghill, Robert (1572–1641), iv. 59

Burke, Edmund (1729–1797), iii. 235, 236; viii. 56; iv. 233; x. 63, 64, 207, 215, 262, 264 ff., 306, 316, 317, 405 ff., 503, 522; xi. 1 ff. (main entry), 34, 42, 47, 48, 52, 58, 93, 139, 142, 143, 145, 146, 262, 324, 360, 388 ff., 395, 396, 399; xii. 168, 179, 175; xiii. 487; xiv. 58, 105, 110, 119, 120, 122, 143, 323, 462

Burke, Edmund
    Address to the British Colonists, xi. 5
    Address to the King, xi. 5, 21
    Appeal from the New to the Old Whigs, xi. 7, 21 ff.
    Letter...to a Member of the National Assembly, xi. 7
    Letter...to a Noble Lord, xi. 7, 29; xii. 166
    Letter...to...Sheriffs of...Bristol, xi. 5, 13
    Letter to William Smith, xi. 25
    Letters on a Regicide Peace, xi. 25, 31, 138
    Letters...on the proposals for peace, xi. 7
    Observations on...'The Present State of the Nation,' xi. 5, 7
    On American Taxation, xi. 5, 12, 21
    On moving his Resolutions for Conciliation, xi. 5, 11, 12, 20, 26
    On Mr Fox's East-India Bill, xi. 16, 18, 19
    On the Sublime, x. 202
    Philosophical Enquiry into...the Sublime and Beautiful, xi. 2, 3
    Reflections, x. 251, 344
    Reflections on the Revolution in France, xi. 4, 7, 20, 22, 138, 413
    Remarks on the Policy of the Allies, xi. 7
    Short Account of a Short Administration, x. 399
    Speech at the Guildhall in Bristol, xi. 6,15
    Speech on the...Nabob of Arcot's Private Debts, xi. 6, 16, 18, 31
    Thoughts on French Affairs, xi. 7
    Thoughts on the...Present Discontents, x. 503; xi. 5, 8, 9; xiv. 438, 439
    To a peer of Ireland on the Penal Laws, xi. 15
    To Sir Hercules Langrishe, xi. 15
    Tracts relative to the Laws against Popery, xi. 14, 24
    Two Letters...to Gentlemen...of Bristol, xi. 6, 15
    Vindication of Natural Society, ix. 232; xi. 2 ff.

Burke, Richard, brother of Edmund Burke, xi. 6, 361

Burke, Richard, son of Edmund Burke xi. 6

Burke, Robert O'Hara (1820–1881), xiv 364

Burke, Thomas Henry (1829–1882), xiv. 320

Burke, William (d. 1798), xi. 2, 6, 388

Burke, William (1792–1829), xiv. 453

Burke, W. T., viii. 54

Burleigh, Bennet (d. 1914), xiv. 192

Burleigh, lord. *See* Balfour, Robert

Burleigh or Burley, Walter (1275–1345?) i. 213, 452; ii. 363

Burleigh house, ix. 148

Burlesques, iv. 516, 533

Burleus, iii. 50

Burley, in Scott's *Old Mortality,* xii. 22

Burlington, countess of. *See* Boyle, Dorothy

Burlington, earl of. *See* Boyle, Richard

Burman, Francis, IX. 574; XII. 488

Burmann, Peter (1668–1741), IX. 336; X. 164, 465

Burn, Robert (1829–1904), XII. 496

Burnaby, Frederick Gustavus (1842–1885), XIV. 550

Burnaby, J., IX. 266, 499

Burnand, Sir Francis Cowley (1836–1917), XIV. 548

Burne, Nicol (*fl.* 1581), II. 285

Burne-Jones, Sir Edward Coley (1833–1898), XIII. 118, 119, 137, 139, 297, 493

Burnell, Arthur Coke (1840–1882), XII. 502

Burnet, Gilbert (1643–1715), bishop of Salisbury, VII. 185, 214, 476; VIII. 23, 46, 97, 202, 206, 207, 209, 213, 214, 216, 272, 298, 299, 300 ff., 360, 459; IX. 94, 112, 132, 192 ff. (main entry), 211, 213, 214, 217, 221, 234, 247, 335, 402, 488 ff., 541; X. 115, 117, 354, 373, 379; XIV. 604
Censure of M. de Meaux' History, IX. 198
Discourse of the Pastoral Care, IX. 201
Discourse on...Sir Robert Fletcher, IX. 192
Eighteen papers, IX. 199
Enquiry into the measures of submission, IX. 199
Essay on...the late Queen Mary, IX. 200
Exposition of the Thirty-nine Articles, VIII. 300; IX. 200
History of My Own Time, VIII. 48, 273, 278, 445, 463; IX. 199, 202 ff., 212
History of the Reformation, IV. 228, 239; VIII. 250; IX. 110, 195, 197, 198, 200, 210, 212
Letter...on the two papers writ by King Charles II, IX. 199
Life and Death of Sir Matthew Hale, VIII. 10; IX. 198
Memoires of the...Dukes of Hamilton and Castleherald, VII. 435; IX. 193, 194, 196
Memoirs or *Secret History,* IX. 199, 200, 202 ff.
Memorial...of the Constitution and Policy of England, IX. 201
Modest and Free Conference, IX. 192
Pastoral Care, The, VIII. 300
Reasons against Repealing the Test, VIII. 48
Reflections on the Declaration for Liberty of Conscience, IX. 199
Reflections on the pamphlet *Parliamentum Pacificum,* IX. 199
Review of the Reflections on the Prince's Declaration, IX. 200
Second Collection of Several Tracts, IX. 200
Some letters, IX. 199
Some passages in the Life and Death of the right honorable John Earl of Rochester, VIII. 300, 445
Thoughts on Education, IX. 192; XIV. 604
Utopia, trans. of, IX. 198

Burnet, Gilbert
Vindication from the two *Letters* containing some *Reflections on His Majesty's Proclamation,* IX. 199
Vindication of the...Church of Scotland, IX. 194

Burnet, Thomas (1635?–1715), VIII. 292, 472, 473, 474; IX. 434, 474, 572; *Sacra telluris theoria,* VIII. 347; *The Theory of the Earth,* IX. 390

Burnet, Thomas, of Kemnay, VIII. 347

Burnet, Sir Thomas (1694–1753), IX. 204

Burnet, Thomas (Sir Iliad Doggrel) (*fl.* 1715), IX. 258, 448

Burnett, James, lord Monboddo (1714–1799), IX. 562; X. 513; XI. 250

Burney, Charles (1726–1814), X. 63, 260, 263, 473

Burney, Charles (1757–1817), XII. 325

Burney, Frances. *See* Arblay, Madame d'

Burney, J., XIV. 550

Burney, Martin Charles, XII. 188, 192, 434

Burnham, baron. *See* Lawson, Edward Levy

Burnham, Cant's hall at, X. 117

Burnham Thorpe, II. 301

Burnouf, Jean Louis, XII. 343

Burns, Gilbert, XI. 436, 437

Burns, Robert (1759–1796), I. 290; II. 247, 267, 274, 278, 413; III. 129, 136, 188; IV. 112, 212; VII. 13; IX. 360, 363, 367 ff., 372 ff., 376 ff., 567; X. 224, 226; XI. 182, 183, 203 ff. (main entry), 233 ff., 237 ff., 242, 243, 408, 419, 435, 441, 469, 472, *also see* Add.; XII. 1, 19, 30, 125, 132, 134, 382, 429, 480, 505; XIII. 9, 13, 16, 178, 226, 233, 242, 465, 468; XIV. 357, 375
Address to Edinburgh, XI. 217
Address to the Deil, II. 255; XI. 212, 213
Address to the Unco Guid, XI. 218
Auld Farmer's New Year Salutation, XI. 212, 214
Auld Lang Syne, XI. 225, 228, 232
Author's Earnest Cry and Prayer, XI. 212
Banks o' Doon, XI. 230
Bard's Epitaph, XI. 208
Birthday Ode, XI. 208
Blue-eyed Lassie, XI. 230
Brigs of Ayr, IX. 380; XI. 218
Captain Matthew Henderson, XI. 211, 219
Centenary Burns, The, XIV. 148
Charlie he's my Darling, XI. 229
Chevalier's Lament, IX. 377
Comin Thro' the Rye, XI. 230
Corn Rigs, XI. 205
Cotter's Saturday Night, The, XI. 144, 206; XIV. 377
Death and Doctor Hornbook, XI. 212
Death and Dying Words of Poor Mailie, II. 255; IX. 366, 372; XI. 214
Despondency, XI. 206, 217
Dream, A, XI. 215
Duncan Davison, XI. 229
Duncan Gray, XIV. 377
Epistle to a Young Friend, XI. 218

Burns, Robert
Epistle to Davie, XI. 207, 217
Epistle to Lord Daer, XI. 218
Epistles, XI. 234
Epistles to Graham of Fintry, XI. 208
Farewell, The, XI. 217
Fintry My Stay, XI. 218
From Esopus to Maria, XI. 208
Gloomy Night, XI. 205
Green grow the Rashes o', XI. 205
Guildford Good, XI. 218
Halloween, XI. 215, 216, 235
Handsome Nell, XI. 206
'Hear, land o' Cakes,' XII. 349
Here's to the Health, XI. 206
Holy Fair, XI. 213, 215
Holy Willie's Prayer, XI. 212, 213
How Lang and Drearie is the Night, XI. 229
In Lamington Kirk, XI. 208
Inscribed on a Work of Hannah More's, XI. 217
Inscribed to the Hon. C. J. Fox, XI. 208
Is there for Honest Poverty, XI. 229
It was a' for our Richtfu' King, XI. 225, 229; XII. 14
James Smith, XI. 211
John Anderson My Jo, XI. 229
John Barleycorn, II. 279
John Lapraik, XI. 211
Jolly Beggars, III. 131, 136, 188; XI. 206, 215, 217 ff., 224
'Ken ye ought o' Captain Grose,' XII. 349
Kirk's Alarm, XI. 213
Lament, The, XI. 206, 217
Lass of Cessnock Banks, XI. 206
Lines on the Fall of Fyers, XI. 208
Logan Water, XI. 235
MacPherson's Farewell, XI. 228
Man was made to Mourn, XI. 206, 217
Mary Morison, XI. 230
Mauchline Wedding, XI. 215
My Father was a Farmer, XI. 206
No Churchman am I, XI. 205
O Leeze me on my Spinnin Wheel, XI. 230
O Merry Hae I been, XI. 229
O Tibbie I hae seen the Day, XI. 206
O Wert thou in the Cauld blast, XI. 230
Ode Sacred to the Memory of Mrs Oswald, XI. 208
Ode to General Washington's Birthday, XI. 208
Ode to the Departed Regency Bill, XI. 208
Ode to the Departed Year, XI. 208
Of a' the Airts, XI. 230
On a Wag in Mauchline, XI. 208
On Captain Grose, XI. 208
On Grizzel Grimme, XI. 208
On Holy Willie, XI. 208
On John Dove, Innkeeper, XI. 208
On Tam the Chapman, XI. 208
On the Death of Lord President Dundas, XI. 208
On the Death of Robert Ruisseaux, XI. 208
On the Death of Sir James Hunter Blair, XI. 208

Burns, Robert
On the Late Miss Burnet of Monboddo, XI. 208
On Willie Nicol's Mare, XI. 208
Ordination, The, XI. 213, 215
Poems (Kilmarnock, 1786), XI. 204 ff., 220, 221, 342
Poems (Edinburgh, 1787), XI. 205
Poet's Welcome to his Love-Begotten Daughter, XI. 212
Poor Mailie, XI. 211, 214
Prayer in the prospect of Death, XI. 206
Rantin Dog the Daddie O't, XI. 230
Red, Red Rose, XI. 225, 229
Remorse, XI. 206
Reply to a Trimming Epistle, XI. 211
Ruined Farmer, XI. 206
Scotch Drink, II. 278; XI. 212
Scots Wha hae, XI. 229
Strathallan's Lament, IX. 377
Tam o' Shanter, XI. 215, 217 ff., 224, 238; XIV. 377
Tam Samson, XI. 211
To a Louse, XI. 214
To a Mountain Daisy, XI. 214
To a Mouse, XI. 214
To John Rankine, XI. 211
To Ruin, XI. 206, 217
To the Guidwife of Wauchope House, XI. 217
Tragic Fragment, XI. 206
Twa Dogs, XI. 214, 217
Twa Herds, XI. 213
Up in the Morning Early, XI. 229
Vision, The, XI. 207, 214
What can a Young Lassie, XI. 229
Who is that at My Bower Door, XI. 229
Willie Brew'd a Peck o' Maut, XI. 230
Willie Simpson, XI. 211
Works (1834–5), XI. 237
Written with a Pencil at Taymouth, XI. 208
Ye Banks and Braes, XI. 230
Yestreen I had a pint o' Wine, XI. 230
Burnt Njal, XIII. 125
Burrhus, in Racine's *Britannicus*, X. 119
Burrough or Borough, Christopher (*fl.* 1579–1587), IV. 69
Burrough, Edward (1634–1662), VII. 169, 428; VIII. 110
Burrough, Sir John (d. 1643), IV. 454
Burrough, Stephen (1525–1584), IV. 84
Burroughs, Jeremiah (1599–1646), VII. 322
Burroughs, John, XIII. 470
Burroughs, Ronald Montague (1867–1920), XII. Add. 2
Burrowes, Robert (*fl.* 1787), X. 475
Burstall, Sara A., XIV. 599
Burthogge, Richard (1638?–1694?), VIII. 472; *An Essay upon Reason and the Nature of Spirits*, VIII. 347; *Organum vetus et novum*, VIII. 347
Burton, Alfred, *pseud. See* Mitford, John
Burton, Alfred Richard Edward, XIV. Add. 6

Burton, Henry (1578–1648), VII. 145, 424, 433, 441, 456, 498

Burton, Hezekiah (d. 1681), VIII. 292

Burton, Isabel, lady (1831–1896), XIV. 550

Burton, John (1710–1771), IX. 563

Burton, John Hill (1809–1881), XI. 397; XII. 445, 520; XIV. 486
  Book-Hunter, The, XII. 359, 360, 371; XIV. 95
  History of Scotland, XII. 371; XIV. 95
  History of the Reign of Queen Anne, XIV. 95
  Life of David Hume, X. 283, 284, 289, 293, 321, 323, 511; XIV. 95
  Scot Abroad, The, XIV. 95

Burton, Richard, *pseud. See* Crouch, Nathaniel

Burton, Sir Richard Francis (1821–1890), XIV. 246, 252, 337, 551; *The Lake Regions of Central Africa*, XIV. 253

Burton, Robert (1577–1640), III. 532; IV. 242–253 (main entry), 257, 260, 261, 267, 496 ff., 519, *also see* Add.; VII. 163, 253, 366; X. 50; XIV. 460; *Anatomy of Melancholy*, IV. 244 ff. (main entry), 411, 432; VI. 187, 190, 191; VII. 313; VIII. 357, 378; XII. 86, 88, 187, 188, 434, 436; *Philosophaster*, IV. 244; VI. 470

Burton, Thomas (*fl.* 1656–9), VII. 440

Burton, William (d. 1461), IV. 496

Burton, William (1575–1645), III. 532; *Description of Leicester Shire*, IX. 352, 532

Burton, William (1609–1657), VII. 482, 487; *Commentary on Antoninus, his Itinerary*, IX. 355, 532

Burton, Annals of, I. 178

Burton Hall, VIII. 96

Burton-on-Trent, V. 97

Bury. *See* Richard of

Bury, Arthur (1624–1713), *The Naked Gospel*, X. 378

Bury, lady Charlotte Susan Maria (1775–1861), XI. 434; XII. 458

Bury, John Bagnell, X. 313 ff., 318, 506; XII. 475; XIV. 538

Bury, Richard de (1281–1345), bishop of Durham. *See* Richard of Bury

Bury St Edmunds, or St Edmundsbury, Benedictine abbey of, I. 162, 176, 182, 213; II. 197, 198, 307; IV. 418; V. 9; VI. 282; VII. 61, 234; VIII. 357; X. 464; XI. 140; XII. 192, 201, 331; XIII. 15

Bury St Edmunds, King Edward VI's school, VII. 330; XIII. 142

Busby, John (*fl.* 1600), IV. 393

Busby, Richard (1606–1695), VII. 317, 341, 486, 487; IX. 146, 272; Dryden's transl. of *Fifth Satire of Persius* ascribed to, VIII. 2

Busher, Leonard (*fl.* 1614), VII. 456; X. 520

Bushnell, Edmund, IV. 454

Busino (chaplain to Venetian embassy), VI. 181

Busirane, castle of, I. 295

Busiris, in Alfred's *Boethius*, I. 100

Busleiden (Buslidianus), Jerome, III. 7

Buss, Frances Mary, XIV. 429, 599

Bussey, H. Findlater, XIV. 533

Bussy-Rabutin, *Histoire Amoureuse de Gaule*, VIII. 385

Busteed, Henry Elmsley (1833–1912), XIV. 575; *Echoes from Old Calcutta*, XIV. 338

Bustus, Matthaeus, VII. 482

Busy Body, The, X. 205

But, John, II. 21, 22, 35

Butcher, Samuel Henry (1850–1910), IX. 64; XII. 332, 333, 481; XIV. 521

Bute, 3rd earl of. *See* Stuart, John

Bute, Mary, countess of (d. 1794), IX. 245, 246, 248, 403

Butler, Alban (1711–1773), X. Add.

Butler, Arthur Gray (1831–1909), XIII. 500

Butler, Arthur John (1844–1910), XII. 137; XIV. 501; *Dante, his Times and his Work*, XIV. 113

Butler, Charles (d. 1647), IV. 542

Butler, Charles (1750–1832), XI. 422; XIV. 55, 115, 492, 512; *The Book of the Roman Catholic Church*, XIV. 53

Butler, George (1819–1889), XIV. 598

Butler, James, 4th earl of Ormonde and earl of Wiltshire (1420–1461), II. 302

Butler, James, 1st duke of Ormonde (1610–1688), VII. 212, 224, 356, 436

Butler, John (*fl.* 1680), VII. 510; VIII. 455

Butler, Joseph (1692–1752), bishop of Durham, VIII. 296; IX. 289, 296, 303, 304, 326, 393, 394, 502, 504; X. 351, 358, 360 ff., 381, 386; XII. 269; *Analogy of Religion, The*, IX. 303, 304; X. 361, 362; XII. 270; *Sermons*, IX. 303; X. 361, 362

Butler, Josephine E. (1828–1906), XIV. 501, 598

Butler, Nathaniel (d. 1664), IV. 394; VII. 344

Butler, Pierce, II. 335

Butler, Samuel (1612–1680), III. 95; IV. 342, 522; VII. 72, 92, 167, 238, 345; VIII. 17, 26, 43, 58–79 (main entry), 88, 215, 232, 372, 373, 402, 406 ff.; IX. 119, 260; XI. 247; XIII. 218
  Characters, VIII. 60, 62 ff., 75
  Contradictions, VIII. 61
  Critics who judge of modern plays by the rules of the Ancients, Upon, VIII. 375
  Cynarctomachy, or Battle between Bear and Dogs, VIII. 65, 68
  Elephant in the Moon, The, VIII. 61, 62, 366
  Genuine Remains in Verse and Prose of Mr Samuel Butler, The, VIII. 60, 62, 63
  Hudibras, IV. 359; VII. 167; VIII. 19, 37, 49, 59 ff., 64–67 (main entry), 90, 92, 93; IX. 145, 154, 158, 201, 259, 272, 308, 418, 476, 477 (*cf.* 499, 502, 567); X. 396; XI. 318; XIII. 233, 451; XIV. 206
  Miscellaneous Thoughts, VIII. 63
  Observations and Reflexions, VIII. 60
  Occasional thoughts, VIII. 62

Butler, Samuel
  On Philip Nye's Thanksgiving Beard,
    VIII. 63
  Posthumous Works, VIII. 62
  Reflections, VIII. 61
  *Repartees between Cat and Puss at a
    Caterwauling*, VIII. 17
  Small Poet, A, VII. 89
  Thoughts on Learning and Knowledge,
    VIII. 61
Butler, Samuel (1774–1839), bishop of
    Lichfield, VII. 336; XII. 327 ff., 481; XIII.
    449, 572; XIV. 413, 594, 598, 601; *Atlas
    of Ancient Geography*, XII. 328
Butler, Samuel (1835–1902), XI. 426; XIII.
    449 ff., 570 ff., *also see* Add. 1
  Alps and Sanctuaries, XIII. 450, 451, 454
  Authoress of the Odyssey, The, XIII. 450
  Darwin among the Machines, XIII. 449
  Darwin on the Origin of Species, XIII. 449
  Deadlock in Darwinism, The, XIII. 449
  Erewhon, VII. 378; X. 42; XIII. 420, 449,
    451 ff.
  Erewhon Revisited, XIII. 450 ff.
  *Evidence for the Resurrection of Jesus
    Christ*, XIII. 449
  Evolution Old and New, XIII. 449
  Ex Voto, XIII. 450
  Fair Haven, The, XIII. 449, 453
  *First Year in a Canterbury Settlement,
    A*, XIII. 449
  God the Known and God the Unknown,
    XIII. 449, 453
  Life and Habit, XIII. 449
  Life and Letters of Dr Samuel Butler,
    XIII. 450, 453
  Luck or Cunning, XIII. 449
  Note-Books, XIII. 450, 451
  On the Trapanese origin of the Odyssey,
    XIII. 450
  Psalm of Montreal, A, XIII. 449, 451, 452
  Quis Desiderio...? XIII. 455
  Shakespeare's Sonnets reconsidered, XIII.
    450
  Unconscious Memory, XIII. 449
  Way of all Flesh, The, XIII. 449, 451, 453
Butler, Thomas, earl of Ossory (1634–
    1680), VIII. 202
Butler, Thomas (1806–1886), XIII. 449
Butler, William Archer (1814?–1848), XIV.
    37, 312, 469, 567
Butler, Sir William Francis (1838–1910),
    XIV. 551, 567
Butler, William John (1818–1894), XII. 454
Buttes, Henry (*fl.* 1599), *Dyets Dry Dinner*,
    IV. 349, 530, 543
Button, Ralph (d. 1680), X. 385
Button, Sir Thomas (d. 1634), IV. 99
Button's coffee-house, IX. 165, 171
Butts, captain Thomas, XI. 196
Buzzard, the, in Dryden's *Fables*, VIII. 48
Byblis, The Passion of, IX. 473
By-Ends, Mr, in Bunyan's *Pilgrim's Pro-
    gress*, VII. 173
Byerley, Thomas (d. 1826), XI. 472
Byfield, Nicholas (1579–1622), IV. 495

Byng, John, admiral (1663–1733), IX. 185,
    254; X. 244, 467
Bynneman, Henry (d. 1583), IV. 384, 398,
    546
Byrd, William (1538?–1623), IV. 110,
    112 ff., 121, 126, 384, 463, 464
Byrhtferth (*fl.* 1000), I. 131
Byrhtnoth, in *The Battle of Malden*, I. 41,
    109, 137, 143, 144, 306
Byrhtwold, I. 137
Byrne, Desmond, XIV. 584
Byrne, Thomas (*fl.* 1730), X. 196, 197
Byrom, John (1692–1763), IX. 191, 309,
    314, 325 ff. (main entry), 513, 515, 518,
    520, 523; XI. 248; XIII. 239; XIV. 230
  Enthusiasm, IX. 326; X. 350
  Epistle to a Gentleman of the Temple,
    IX. 326
  Journal, IX. 307, 313, 318, 325
  Poems, IX. 322, 327
  Redemption, IX. 327
  Universal Beauty, IX. 327
Byron, Augusta, XII. 382
Byron, George Gordon, 6th lord (1788–
    1824), I. 275; IV. 89, 252; VI. 239; X. 152,
    154, 155, 236, 242, 253, 254; XI. 83, 91,
    102, 108, 109, 117, 124, 144, 150, 158,
    166, 167, 171, 178, 179, 300, 302 ff.,
    306, 308, 410, 414, 420, 423; XII. 15,
    30, 31 ff. (main entry), 57, 60 ff., 67,
    74, 76, 81, 92, 96, 98, 100, 102, 106,
    111, 120, 122, 126, 131, 135, 136, 162,
    174, 179, 180, 199, 205, 219, 228, 247,
    314, 318, 382 ff., 402 ff., 407, 412, 426,
    441, 443, 450, 485, 505, *also see* Add.;
    XIII. 7, 10, 23 ff., 52, 94, 101, 109, 135,
    136, 157, 161, 184, 203, 230, 239, 258,
    259, 307, 346, 352, 417, 418, 421, 436,
    495, 503, 512, 514; XIV. 56, 126, 187,
    198, 206, 230, 322, 327, 373, 399
  'Adieu, adieu, my native land,' XIV. 374
  Age of Bronze, The, XII. 37
  Assyrian came down, The, XIII. 235
  Beppo, XII. 33, 34, 52, 53, 63; XIII. 236;
    XIV. 438
  Blues, The, XII. 37
  Bride of Abydos, The, XII. 32, 45
  British Bards, XII. 382
  Cain, XI. 106, 199; XII. 35, 47, 48
  Childe Harold, II. 413; III. 246; X. 301;
    XI. 131; XII. 32, 34, 38, 42 ff., 60, 145,
    158, 382; XIII. 236, 253; XIV. 249, 374,
    436
  Childish Recollections, XII. 41
  Corsair, The, XII. 32, 44, 45
  Darkness, XII. 51
  Death of Calmar and Orla, The, XII. 40
  Deformed Transformed, The, XII. 37, 50
  Don Juan, VII. 79; XII. 32 ff., 37, 40,
    46, 51, 52, 54 ff., 71, 95, 383; XIII. 236;
    XIV. 244
  Dorset, To the Duke of, XII. 41
  Dream, The, XII. 51
  Elegy on Newstead Abbey, XII. 41
  English Bards and Scotch Reviewers,
    XII. 32, 41, 49, 52, 147

Byron, George Gordon
  Epistle to Augusta, XII. 52
  Epitaph on a Friend, XII. 41
  Francesca of Rimini, XII. 33, 35
  Fugitive Pieces, XII. 31
  Giaour, The, XII. 32, 45
  Heaven and Earth, XII. 35, 37, 47, 48
  Hints from Horace, XII. 382
  Hours of Idleness, XII. 31, 33, 40, 147
  I would I were a careless child, XII. 40, 41
  Island, The, XII. 38, 45, 46, 52
  'Isles of Greece,' XII. 54
  Lachin y Gair, XII. 40
  Lament of Tasso, The, XII. 33, 50
  Lara, XII. 45, 408
  *Letter to John Murray Esq. on...
  Bowles's Strictures on the Life...of Pope*,
  XII. 35
  Letters, XII. 382
  Letters and Journals, XIV. 107
  Maid of Athens, XIV. 377
  Manfred, XII. 34, 35, 41, 47, 48, 60
  Marino Faliero, XII. 35, 47, 49
  Mazeppa, XII. 34, 45, 46
  Memoirs, XII. 34, 103
  Ode to the Framers of the Frame Bill,
  XII. 390
  Oscar of Alva, XII. 40
  Parisina, XII. 45, 46
  Prisoner of Chillon, The, XII. 34, 45, 46
  Prophecy of Dante, The, XII. 33, 35,
  50, 56
  Romance, To, XII. 41
  Sardanapalus, XII. 33 ff., 47 ff.
  Siege of Corinth, XI. 127; XII. 32, 45
  Some Observations, XII. 36
  Sonnet on Chillon, XII. 46
  Speech on Frame-work bill, XII. 382
  Stanzas to Jessy, XII. 382
  Trans. of Pulci's *Morgante Maggiore*,
  XII. 35, 37
  Two Foscari, The, XII. 35, 47, 49
  Venetian tragedies, XII. 48, 49
  Vision of Judgment, The, V. 96; XII. 36,
  37, 53
  Werner, XII. 37, 47, 50
  When I roved a young Highlander, XII. 40
  When we two parted, XII. 51
  Conversations of (Medwin's), XII. 37
  Life and Works of (ed. Moore), XII. 53
  See, also, Astarte
Byron, George Gordon (natural son of the
  poet), XII. 382
Byron, Harriet, in Richardson's *Sir
  Charles Grandison*, X. 10, 62
Byron, Henry James (1834–1884), XIII.
  271, 518; *Cyril's Success*, XIII. 273;
  Our Boys, XIII. 273; *Uncle Dick's
  Darling*, XIII. 273
Byron, John, 1st baron (d. 1652), VII. 436
Byron, John (1723–1786), XIV. 244, 551
Byron, lady (Anne Isabella Milbanke),
  XII. 32
Byron, lady, XII. 392, 393, 396, 398
Byron, 'Mad Jack' (1756–1791), XII. 31
Byron, William, 5th lord (d. 1798), XII. 31

Byse, Mrs, Fanny, VII. 98
Bysset, Abacuck, II. 93, 479; *Rolment
  of Courtis*, II. 285
Bysshe, Sir Edward (1615?–1679), IV. 376
Bysshe, Edward (*fl.* 1712), VIII. 230, 231,
  240; IX. 529; XIII. 228, 229, 240, 249;
  Art of Poetry, XI. 249, 250, 256; *Art of
  English Poetry, The*, XIII. 228, 512
'Bysshe Vanolis', *pseud. See* Thomson,
  James B. V.
Bythner, Victorinus (1605?–1670?), VII.
  490
Bywater, Ingram (1840–1914), XII. 334,
  481, 482, *also see* Add. 3
Bywater, Mrs Henry Wood's, XIII. 430
Byzantine empire, X. 314; XII. 315

C., C. S. *See* Calverley, Charles Stuart
C Mery Talys, A, IX. 39
Cabal ministry, VII. 42
Cabal the hound, in Nennius, I. 247
Cabala, sive Scrinia Sacra (1654), VII. 191,
  433; VIII. 281
Cabala (1663), VIII. 99
Cabala, The Prince's, VII. 188, 191, 458
Cabbala, the Jewish, IX. 315
Cabbalistica, Conjectura, VIII. 455
Cabillavus, IV. 266
Cabot, John, IV. 66, 68, 69, 85
Cabot, Sebastian (1474–1557), IV. 69 ff.,
  75, 85
Cacurgus, in *Misogonus*, V. 111
Cade, Jack, in *Henry VI*, V. 186, 248
Cade's rebellion, II. 302, 424; IV. 137, 300,
  529
Caddell, W. Waithman, XIV. Add. 5
Cadell, Jessie Ellen (1844–1884), XIV. 575;
  Ida Craven, XIV. 339
Cadell, Thomas (1742–1802), X. 213; XI.
  326, 327, 361
Cadell, Thomas, the younger (1773–1836),
  XI. 327; XII. 234
Cadesia, battle of, X. 281
Cadiou, Andrew, II. 284
Cadiz, IV. 85, 103, 200, 221; V. 361; VII. 454
Cadmus, in *Dialogues of the Dead*, XI. 351
Cadoc, St (d. 570?), I. 262
Cadogan, William Bromley, XII. 473
Cador, in Layamon, I. 266
Cador, in *Emarè*, I. 311
Cador, in *The Misfortunes of Arthur*, V.
  78, 79
Cadwalader, in Layamon, I. 234
Cadwalader, in Mannyng, I. 351
Cadwallader, X. 154
Cadwallader, Mrs, in *Middlemarch*, XIII.
  399
Caedmon (*fl.* 670), I. 14, 30, 41 ff., 56,
  57, 61, 63, 82, 89, 96, 119, 142, 382, 383,
  428; XII. 344; XIII. 241; *Genesis*, VII. 118
Caelia, in Whitehead's *School for Lovers*,
  X. 86
Caelius Rhodiginus, Ludovicus, VIII. 407
Caelo et Olympo, VI. 93
Caen, VIII. 220
Caer Rigor, I. 251

Caer Sidi, I. 251
Caerleon, or Caerlleon, or Carleon, upon
Usk, I. 197, 246, 260; II. 303; XII. 346,
511
Caesar, in *The False One*, VI. 131
Caesar, in *The Poetaster*, VI. 42
Caesar, Julius, I. 13, 71, 81, 93, 187, 197,
342; II. 80, 111, 339; III. 24, 164, 329,
429; VII. 159, 164, 443; VIII. 67, 76;
IX. 63, 204; X. 27, 119, 284, 319; XIII.
221; *Commentaries*, IX. 297
Caesar, Julius, in Byron's *The Deformed
Transformed*, XII. 50
Caesar, P., IV. 510
Caesar and Pompey, VI. 483
Caesar's Ghost, VIII. 93
Caesars, the, V. 4; XII. 182, 487
Caffyn, Matthew (1628–1714), X. 378
Cagliostro, Alessandro, count, XI. 293;
XIII. 468
Cahergillagh court, in Le Fanu's story,
XIII. 415
Caiaphas, V. 46, 47
Caigniez, Louis Charles, XIII. 264
Caim, II. 443
Cain, I. 30; II. 20; IV. 214; X. 376
Cain, Byron's, XI. 106, 199; XII. 45, 48
Cain, Grendel's ancestor, in *Beowulf*, I. 22
Cain, in the *Towneley Mysteries*, V. 47
Cain and Abel, V. 45, 388
Caine, Sir T. H. Hall, XIII. 491
Caird, Edward (1835–1908), XIV. 45 ff.,
469; *Critical Account of the Philosophy
of Kant*, XIV. 45; *Critical Philosophy of
Immanuel Kant, The*, XIV. 45; *Evolution
of Religion, The*, XIV. 45
Caird, John (1820–1898), XII. 465; XIV.
469; *An Introduction to the Philosophy
of Religion*, XIV. 45
Cairnes, John Elliot (1823–1875), XIV. 470
Cairns, Hugh McCalmont, 1st earl (1819–
1885), XIV. 124, 508
Cairo, II. 80, 82, 298; XIV. 192, 251
Caithness, bishop of, III. 194
Caius, Dr, in *The Merry Wives of Windsor*,
V. 268
Caius, John (1510–1573), III. 419 ff., 466;
IV. 442, 541
Caius, Thomas (d. 1572), IX. 535
Caius Cestius, VI. 37
Caius Martius, in *Coriolanus*, V. 198
Caladbolg, XIV. 307
Calahorra, Diego Ortuñez de, IV. 442
Calais, II. 338, 423, 424; III. 3, 163, 167,
328; IV. 200; VI. 185; VII. 232; VIII. 271;
XI. 97; XIV. 233
Calais, siege of, Minot's poem on, I. 357,
358
Calais, Chronicle of, III. 532
Calamy, Edmund (1600–1666), VII. 145,
312, 416, 424
Calamy, Edmund (1671–1732), IX. 574;
X. 373, 386, 387, 499, 519, 521; *Abridge-
ment of the Life of Baxter*, X. 374;
Defence of Moderate Conformity, X. 374;
Historical Account of my own Life, X. 377

Calandrino, in *The Great Duke of Florence*,
VI. 161
Calantha, in Ford's *The Broken Heart*,
VI. 191, 195; XII. 190
Calcraft, John (1726–1772), X. 409, 410
Calcutta, XII. 138; XIII. 276; XIV. 334 ff.
Hindu college, XIV. 336, 337
Sanskrit college, XII. 343
University, XIV. 341
Calcutta Review, The, XIV. 337, 339, 574
Caldecott, Randolph (1846–1886), XI. 478,
491
Calder, Robert (1658–1723), IX. 548, 549
Calderon de La Barca, Pedro, IV. 353;
V. 207, 303; VI. 140; XIII. 143, 144, 497;
XIV. 318
Dama Duende, VIII. 120, 130
El Maestro de Danzar, VIII. 131, 144
El Magico Prodigioso, XIII. 146
La Vida es Sueño, XIII. 145
No Siempre lo Peor es Cierto, VIII. 130
Calderwood, David (1575–1650), III. 122,
141; VII. 448; *Historie of the Kirk of
Scotland*, VII. 209; *Recantation* (so-
called), VII. 209
Calderwood, Henry (1830–1897), XIV. 470
Calderwood, Margaret (1715–1774), X. 493
Calderwood, W., XIV. 470
Caldoro, in *The Guardian*, VI. 158
Caldwell, Mrs Anne, afterwards Marsh
(1791–1874), XIII. 561; *Chronicles of
Dartmoor*, XIII. 430
Caledonia, X. 231
Caledonian Musical Museum, XI. 436, 442
Caledonian Musical Repository, XI. 442
Caledonian verse, X. 232
*Calendar of Letters and Papers of the Reign
of Henry VIII*, II. 393; XIV. 82
Calendars of State Papers, XIV. 111
Caletfwlch (Excalibur), XIV. 307
Calfhill or Calfield, James (1530?–1570),
VI. 320; *Progne*, VI. 299
Caliban, Browning's, XIII. 63
Caliban, in *The Tempest*, V. 207; VIII. 28,
72; XII. 128
Caliburn, Arthur's sword, I. 266
Caliburnus (Excalibur), XIV. 307
California, XIV. 241, 245, 325
Caligula, in Orosius, I. 95
Calipso, in *The Guardian*, VI. 157
Calis, princess, in *The Mad Lover*, VI. 152
Calista, in Rowe's *Fair Penitent*, VIII. 196;
X. 74
Calisto and Melebea, V. 99, 100, 409; VIII.
125
Call, Wathen Mark Wilks, XIII. 167, 500;
Bird and the Bower, The, XIII. 174;
Manoli, XIII. 174
Callaghan, Sir, in Macklin's *Love à-la-
mode*, XI. 257
Callaman, Jeremiah John (1795–1829),
XIV. 305, 567
Callander, John (d. 1789), IX. 560; X. 475,
490
Callaway, Henry, XIV. Add. 6
Calle, Richard, II. 305

Callet, Auguste, x. 485

Callianax, in *The Maides Tragedy*, vi. 127

Callidamus et Callanthia, vi. 483

Callières, François de, *Le Combat des Livres*, ix. 102

Callimachus, ix. 331; xii. 329

Callington, Cornwall, x. 244

Callio, in *Euphormio*, iv. 255

Calliope, in *The Palice of Honour*, ii. 260

Callis, Robert (*fl.* 1634), viii. 468

Calman, A. L., xiii. 560

Calne, Wiltshire, xii. 191

Calpurnia, in *Julius Caesar*, v. 197

Calton in Craven, x. 386

Calvary, hill of, v. 44

Calverley, Charles Stuart (1831–1884), iv. 249; viii. 9; xi. 379; xiii. 162, 165 ff., 246, 500, 543; xiv. 205, 537; *Fly Leaves*, xiii. 165; *Remains*, xiii. 166; *Wanderers*, xiii. 36

Calverley hall, in *A Yorkshire Tragedy*, v. 242, 243

Calvert, Adelaide H., xiii. 513

Calvert, *Judy*, artist, xiv. 239

Calvert, W., xiii. 513

Calvin, John (1509–1564), iii. 10, 46, 144, 145, 383, 399, 400, 402, 403, 407, 411, 431; iv. 21, 214, 220, 303, 380, 429, 433, 442, 510; v. 114, 365; vi. 374; vii. 152, 159, 160, 208, 308, 309, 321, 477; viii. 108, 111, 277, 279, 291, 295, 299, 306, 407; x. 370; xiv. 102; *Institutes of the Christian Religion*, iii. 145, 400; vii. 306

Calvinism, vii. 143, 148, 152, 153, 157, 279, 280; x. 364, 367, 368, 376, 381, 383; xi. 43, 213; xii. 279, 284; xiii. 431; xiv. 428

Calvinistic methodists, x. 364, 365

Calvinists, the, iv. 276, 296; xi. 19; attacked in *Loiola*, vi. 324

Cam, river, vi. 93, 327; vii. 327

Cambert, Robert, viii. 135; *Pomone*, viii. 134

Cambert and Perrin, P., *Ariane, ou le Mariage de Bacchus*, viii. 134

Cambray, congress of, ix. 221

Cambrensis, Giraldus. *See* Giraldus

Cambriae Annales, i. 246, 248, 461

Cambrian rocks, xiv. 292

Cambridge, i. 184, 382; ii. 67, 103, 104, 130, 199, 221, 305, 307, 341 ff., 367, 368, 487, 488; iii. 8, 13, 14, 26, 27, 28, 34, 36, 37, 39, 43, 50, 51, 53, 56, 67, 151, 175, 179, 183, 185, 213, 214, 290, 292, 293, 301, 318, 321, 337, 355, 362, 366, 418 ff., 427, 429 ff., 436; iv. 70, 131, 190, 198, 200, 224, 228, 229, 274 ff., 374, 381, 398, 403, 406, 409 ff., 416, 418, 419, 422 ff., 433; v. 104, 109, 121, 132 ff., 343, 363 ff., 368, 369; vi. 86, 105, 218, 220, 232, 293 ff., 300, 303, 311 ff., 316, 374; vii. 5, 9, 28, 32, 42, 46, 78, 85, 98, 143, 148, 155, 180, 189, 223, 228, 245, 305, 312, 316, 317 ff.,

Cambridge

327, 336, 364, 437, 441, 476 ff.; viii. 60, 108, 122, 273, 286, 317, 361, 472; ix. 130, 142, 150, 165, 184, 188, 195, 235, 294, 295, 308, 309, 313, 321, 325, 326, 330, 335, 336, 340, 341, 354, 355, 382, 383, 386, 387, 390, 395, 406, 410 ff., 485, 526, 532, 571, 573, 574; x. 47, 117, 118, 121, 122, 128, 130, 131, 133, 262, 300, 310, 357, 359, 360, 397, 450, 457; xi. 57, 118, 150, 173, 335, 338 340, 347, 355, 407; xii. 132, 198, 200, 256, 273, 294, 296, 298, 305, 306, 325 327 ff., 338 ff., 342, 354, 357, 369, 370 467, 488, 508, 515, 522; xiii. 23, 25, 40, 46, 143, 165, 172, 174, 203, 206, 209, 240, 277, 278, 346, 361, 362, 368, 369, 414, 449; xiv. 25, 26, 37, 64, 79, 90 ff., 100, 109, 110, 117, 119, 168, 205 ff. 215, 247, 257 ff., 262 ff., 268, 269, 284, 300, 362, 383 ff., 395, 403, 409, 414, 416, 417, 429 ff.

Cambridge, Dominicans and Franciscans at, i. 200; ii. 349, 350

Cambridge, Richard Owen (1717–1802), xi. 350, 365, 425

Cambridge, South Africa, xiv. 377

Cambridge, University of (Ackermann's), xiv. 222

Cambridge books and printers:
Books, xi. 468
Printers, iv. 546 ff.; xi. 468

Cambridge buildings and churches:
Augustinian priory, iii. 37
Benedictine school, ii. 349
Botanic garden, xiv. 286
Cavendish laboratory, xiv. 270
Churches, xii. 489
Fitzwilliam museum, xii. 498
Gaol, x. 280
St Bene't's church, vii. 244
St Edward's Church, iii. 37
St John, hospital of, ii. 353
St Mary's church, iii. 389; vii. 34; viii. 290
St Radegund, priory of, ii. 358
Sedgwick museum, xiv. 291
Senate house, xiv. 384, 412
Sturbridge fair, iv. 409; xi. 340
Trinity church, vii. 274
University library, iv. 424, 426, 432; ix. 532; xii. 323, 341, 342, 369, 480, 502, 503, 518; xiv. 484
University press, iv. 277, 409 ff.; viii. 278; xi. 341; xii. 324, 328, 329
White Horse, the (Little Germany), iii. 34, 37

Cambridge college magazines, xiv. 538–539

Cambridge colleges:
Bene't, or Corpus Christi college, ii. 346, 354. *See* Corpus Christi college
Buckingham college. *See* Magdalene college
Caius college. *See* Gonville and Caius college

Cambridge colleges:
Catherine hall, VI. 196, VII. 301, *and see* St Catharine's college
Christ's college, II. 354; III. 14, 328; V. 111; VI. 295, 296; VII. 91, 92, 97, 114, 279, 342; VIII. 278 ff., 287, 290, 292, 360; XII. 344, 490, 516
Clare hall or college, II. 354; III. 36; V. 132; VI. 307, 308, 322; VIII. 281, 292; IX. 250, 516
Corpus Christi college, II. 354; IV. 4, 18, 423, 426; V. 142, 143; VI. 111; X. 131; XII. 344, 363, 498, 517; XIV. 283; Parker MSS., IV. 424
Emmanuel college, III. 432; IV. 159, 329, 424 ff.; VI. 317; VII. 224, 279, 317, 339, 340, 354; VIII. 274, 276, 277, 281, 288, 290, 359, 461, 482; IX. 308; XII. 187, 326, 333, 493, 516
Girton college, XIV. 430
God's house, II. 358
Gonville and Caius college, III. 420, 422; VI. 216, 301, 306; VII. 188, 320, 321, 345; VIII. 4, 363; IX. 386; XII. 187, 333, 341, 517; XIII. 241
Jesus college, II. 358; III. 20, 32; IV. 159, 424; VI. 307; VII. 310; VIII. 282; IX. 240; X. 342; XII. 326; XIV. 298
King's college, II. 288, 357, 358, 489; III. 183, 265, 315, 431; IV. 165, 275, 407, 410; V. 70; VI. 285, 294, 298, 317, 321; VII. 53, 326, 328, 329; VIII. 274, 275, 279, 292; X. 117, 243; XII. 333
King's college chapel, III. 320
King's hall, II. 352, 354, 358; IV. 426
Magdalene college, II. 358; III. 32; IV. 427; VIII. 242, 253, 292, 355; X. 359; XII. 517; XIII. 355
Magdalene college, Pepysian library, II. 224, 316, 423; III. 133; IV. 427; VIII. 242, 250, 260
Michael house, II. 354, 358, 366; III. 13; IV. 426; VI. 294
Newnham college, XIV. 430
Pembroke college, IV. 427; VI. 296; VII. 32, 33, 83; IX. 257; X. 117, 123, 124, 128, 131, 132, 281, 450; XII. 327, 516
Pembroke hall or college, II. 355; III. 213, 422; IV. 238
Peterhouse, I. 205; II. 302, 308, 347, 352, 353 ff., 362 ff., 371; III. 67; IV. 141, 142, 422, 423, 432; VI. 83, 99, 307; VII. 33 ff., 326, 406, 449; VIII. 284, 295; IX. 341; X. 116, 117, 133; XII. 330, 516; XIII. 241; XIV. 109, 121, 385
Peterhouse, chained library at, II. 362, 364 ff.
Queens' college, II. 358; III. 27; IV. 426; V. 103, 108; VI. 305, 324; VII. 244; VIII. 288; IX. 169, 340; XII. 516, 522
St Catharine's college, II. 358; IV. 426; VIII. 290
St John's college, II. 358; III. 292, 293, 420, 422, 425, 430, 432; IV. 31, 91, 232, 274, 277, 426; V. 81, 132, 140; VI. 3, 294, 296, 301, 304, 306 ff., 312, 321,

Cambridge colleges:
397; VII. 4, 84, 89, 91, 329, 330, 337, 362; VIII. 243; IX. 147, 152, 153, 165, 182, 330, 341, 354, 381, 411, 412, 483, 531, 573; X. 393, 525; XI. 96; XII. 280, 326, 328, 329, 331, 335 ff., 341, 345, 481, 488, 517; XIII. 45, 404
St John's college magazine, *The Eagle*, IV. 275; XII. 487
Sidney Sussex college, III. 422; VII. 244; VIII. 360
Trinity college, II. 354, 358; III. 202, 418, 420, 422, 424; IV. 12, 164, 274, 278, 427, 431; V. 103; VI. 232, 294, 295, 302, 305, 306, 314, 321, 322, 324 ff., 397; VIII. 3, 4, 21, 185, 277, 278, 295, 297, 366; IX. 240, 241, 335, 340, 411, 412, 525; XI. 417; XII. 31, 288, 302, 308, 323, 328 ff., 335, 344, 347, 353, 369, 491, 499, 516, 523; XIII. 45, 142, 189, 276; XIV. 60, 251, 282, 283, 295; *and see* Michael house; King's hall
Trinity college library, XIII. 473
Trinity hall, II. 354; III. 183, 424, 426; VII. 4, 21, 27, 62, 117, 179, 317, 333, 342, 361; VIII. 253; XII. 517
University hall. *See* Clare college
Cambridge English Classics, XI. 150
Cambridge Essays, XII. 324; XIV. 139
Cambridge Modern History, The, XIV. 81, 101, 119
Cambridge Observer, The, XIV. 208, 537
Cambridge Platonists, the, VII. 278, 279, 302, 316; VIII. 110, 273 ff., 301, 330; IX. 209, 300, 306
Cambridge Review, The, XIV. 207, 208, 537
Cambridge Review, The Book of the, XIV. 207
Cambridge Shakespeare, The, V. 271, 275, 280
Cambridge societies:
Antiquarian, XII. 506
'Apostles,' the, XIII. 24
Philosophical, XIV. 288, 289
Cambridge University:
Clark lectures, XII. 331
'Local' Examinations, XIV. 429
Moral Sciences tripos, XIV. 416
Natural Sciences tripos, XIV. 416
Rede lecture, XIV. 81
Cambridge University Magazine, The, XIV. 208
Cambridge University Prize, Townshend's, XIV. 385
Cambridge University professors:
Anglo-Saxon (Elrington and Bosworth), XII. 344
Arabic (Lord Almoner's), IX. 413
Archaeology (Disney), XII. 331
Astronomy (Plumian), VII. 342; IX. 412, 413
Astronomy and Geometry (Lowndean), IX. 413
Chinese, XII. 343
Divinity (Lady Margaret's), III. 13, 14
Experimental Physics (Cavendish), XIV. 269

Cambridge University professors:
Geology (Woodwardian), XIV. 291
Greek (Regius), XII. 323, 328 ff., 332
Latin (Kennedy), XII. 335
Mathematics (Lucasian), XIV. 266
Natural Philosophy (Jacksonian), XIV. 385
Sanskrit, XII. 343
Cambridgeshire, II. 197; X. 280; XI. 347; XIII. 216; XIV. 221, 282
Cambuscan, II. 184
Cambyses, IV. 232
Camden, earl of. *See* Pratt, Charles
Camden, William (1551–1623), I. 89, 381; III. 157, 237, 313, 315, 318, 321, 324 ff., 330, 331, 334, 428, 438, 451, 527; IV. 59, 159, 325, 327; V. 477; VI. 3, 6, 9; VII. 337, 338, 442, 487; VIII. 318; IX. 350 ff., 551; X. 293
Britannia, III. 327, 328, 331, 438; IV. 190, 401, 442; IX. 353, 534; XII. 345, 353
Greek Grammar, IV. 407
Remains, IV. 266
Rerum Anglicarum et Hibernicarum Annales, III. 325, 326, 550; IV. 262, 299, 510
Camden society, II. 500; IX. 212; XII. 353, 354, 368, 369; XIII. 15; XIV. 87, 88
Cameiros, necropolis of, XII. 339
Camel, river, I. 261
Camelford (Camlan), battle of, I. 248, 250, 266
Camelford, lord. *See* Pitt, Thomas
Camelot, I. 326
Camerarius, Joachim, IV. 249
Cameron, Archibald (1707–1753), IX. 563
Cameron, George Frederick (1854–1885), XIV. 357, 582
Cameron, Jenny, IX. 563
Cameron, Lucy Lyttleton (1781–1858), XI. 485
Cameron, Richard (d. 1680), IX. 549
Cameronians, the, XII. 18, 25
Camfield, B., VII. 507
Camilla, in Owen's *Epigrammata*, IV. 265
Camilla Lacey, Mme d'Arblay's house, X. 261
Camilla (Lyly's), III. 346
Camillo, in *The White Divel*, VI. 177
Camiola, in *The Maid of Honour*, VI. 150, 156, 163, 164
Camlan. *See* Camelford
Cammelli, Antonio, *Filostrato e Panfila*, V. 62, 69
Camoëns, Luis de, VIII. 271; X. 456; XII. 422
Campagna, the, XII. 69
Campan, Mme de, XIII. 343
Campanella, Tommaso, VII. 298, 470
Campania, VI. 299
Campbell, Alexander (1764–1824), XII. 373; *Albyn's Anthology*, XI. 236, 442
Campbell, Archibald, marquis of Argyll and 8th earl (1598–1661), XII. 21, 29
Campbell, Archibald, bishop of Aberdeen (d. 1744), X. 355
Campbell, Archibald (1691–1756), IX. 548

Campbell, Archibald (1726?–1780), **X.** 131, 474
Campbell, Colin Turing, XIV. Add. 6
Campbell, Duncan, IX. 21, 428; *Secret Memoirs*, IX. 22
Campbell, Frank B. F., *The Battle of Bibliography*, XII. 519
Campbell, George (1719–1796), IX. 561; X. 347, 512; *Dissertation on Miracles*, X. 348; *Philosophy of Rhetoric, The*, X. 348; XIV. 399, 605
Campbell, George Douglas, 8th duke of Argyll (1823–1900), XIV. 468
Campbell, James Dykes, XI. 412, 416
Campbell, John, 2nd duke of Argyll (1678–1743), XII. 19
Campbell, John, 1st lord (1779–1861), XIV. 124, 186, 501, 508; *Lives of Lord Lyndhurst and Lord Brougham*, XIV. 112; *Lives of the Lord Chancellors*, XIV. 112; *Lives of the Lord Chief Justices*, XIV. 112
Campbell, John Francis (1822–1885), *Popular Tales of the West Highlands*, I. 294; XIII. 561
Campbell, John McLeod (1800–1872), XII. 283, 289, 465; *The Nature of the Atonement*, XII. 284
Campbell, Lawrence Dundas, XIV. 575
Campbell, Lewis (1830–1908), XII. 220, 409, 468, 479, 480, 482, 486; XIII. 310; XIV. 503, 594
Campbell, major, in Kingsley's *Two Years Ago*, XIII. 365
Campbell, Thomas (1733–1795), X. 473
Campbell, Thomas (1777–1844), VII. 73; IX. 451, *also see* Add.; XI. 148, 150, 178; XII. 95, 96, 98 ff. (main entry), 102, 126, 138, 139, 148, 384, 385, 409, 429; XIII. 186, 230; XIV. 186, 410 ff., 595
Argyllshire, Lines on Revisiting a Scene in, XII. 99
Battle of the Baltic, The, VIII. 11; XII. 99
Gertrude of Wyoming, XII. 100
Hohenlinden, XII. 99, 101; XIV. 437
How delicious is the winning, XII. 99
Last Man, The, XII. 99, 161
Lectures on Poetry, XII. 161
Life and Letters, XIV. 56
Lochiel's Warning, XII. 98, 99
Lord Ullin's Daughter, XII. 98, 99
Pilgrim of Glencoe, The, XII. 100
Pleasures of Hope, The, XII. 41, 100
Soldier's Dream, The, XII. 99
Song of Hybrias the Cretan, The, XII. 99
Specimens, XII. 99, 100
Theodoric, XII. 100
Withdraw not yet those lips and fingers, XII. 99
Ye Mariners of England, XII. 99
Campbell, William Wilfred, XIV. 582
Campion, Edmund (1540–1581), IV. 127, 237, 411, 536; XIV. 118, 308; *Description of Ireland*, III. 319
Campion, John (d. 1576), IV. 141
Campion, Lucy, afterwards Steward (d. 1580), IV. 141

Campion, M., *A true reporte of the death...*
  of, VI. 387, 498
Campion, Rose, IV. 141
Campion, Thomas (d. 1619), III. 178, 295,
  306, 307, 526; IV. 112, 113, 124 ff.,
  141 ff. (main entry), 266, 463, 478; VI.
  231, 329, 354; VIII. 229, 231, 237, 239;
  XI. 160, 161, 179; XIII. 245
  *Ayres that were sung and played at
    Brougham Castle*, IV. 143
  Book of Ayres, IV. 142, 143, 146
  'Follow your Saint,' IV. 148
  'Harke, al you ladies,' IV. 145, 148
  Lords' Maske, III. 353; IV. 143, 145, 146
  Man of Life upright, The, IV. 126
  Masques, VI. 488
  'My sweetest Lesbia,' VII. 2
  *New Way of Making Fowre Parts in
    Counter-point, A*, IV. 143, 144
  'Now hath Flora,' IV. 145
  Observations in the Art of English Poesie,
    III. 306; IV. 133, 142, 144
  Poemata, IV. 142
  'So be it ever,' IV. 145
  *Songs of Divers Noblemen and Gentle-
    men*, IV. 145
  Songs of Mourning, IV. 143
  'There is a garden in her face,' IV. 145;
    VII. 8
  'Young and simple though I am,' IV.
    145
Campion, in *Westward Ho!* XIII. 364
Canaanites, in *The Silver Age*, VI. 93
Canace, in *Confessio Amantis*, II. 151, 152
Canada, XIII. 449; XIV. 125, 293, 318, 323,
  331, 343 ff., 434
Canada balsam, XIV. 445
Canadian Fiction, Bibliography of, XIV.
  359
Canadian house of commons, XIV. 359
Canadian literature, XIV. 343 ff.
Canaries, the, III. 358; V. 139; XIV. 293
Canby, Henry Seidel, XIII. 567
Cancer: Comoedia, VI. 483
Cancioneros, Spanish, II. 268
Cancrone, in *Sicelides*, VI. 323
Candido, in *The Honest Whore*, VI. 172
Candidus (Mantuan's), III. 223 ff.
Candish, Richard. *See* Cavendish
Candlemas, II. 378
Candlish, Robert Smith (1806–1873), XII.
  471
'Candor,' X. 399, 400, 405, 523
Candy, Pennyloaf, in Gissing's *The Nether
  World*, XIII. 458
Canmore, Malcolm, II. 130
Cannae, VIII. 11
Cannan, Gilbert, XIII. 572
Canne, John (d. 1667), VII. 360, 361
Cannes, X. 42
Canning, Hon. Albert S. G., XIII. 542
Canning, Elizabeth (1734–1773), X. 34
Canning, George (1770–1827), VIII. 38;
  XI. 39, 40, 42, 52, 174, 175, 392; XII.
  120, 136, 150, 155; XIII. 24, 161, 166,
  238; XIV. 123, 126, 128, 134, 188, 214,

Canning, George
  506, 508, 597; 'On unlawful Societies in
  Ireland,' XIV. 122; *Speeches*, XIV. 122;
  The New Morality, XI. 42
Canning, Stratford, 1st viscount Stratford
  de Redcliffe (1786–1880), XIV. 179, 182
Canon or Canonicus, John (*fl.* 1329), I.
  211, 452
Canonbury tower, X. 212
Canons, IV. 424
Canons, IX. 81
Canons-Ashby, Northants, VIII. 2
Cantalupo, in *The Bugbears*, V. 115
Canterbury, I. 50, 71, 127, 139, 202; III.
  30, 49, 375, 407; IV. 381, 382, 409;
  V. 21, 56, 103, 371; VII. 157, 301, 309;
  VIII. 3, 302, 303, 305; IX. 151, 210, 532,
  539; X. 362; XI. 354; XII. 320, 340, 364,
  478; XIV. 390
  Christ church priory, III. 5; IV. 417, 424
  King's school, V. 102, 142
  Lee Priory, XII. 520
  St Augustine's abbey, IV. 417, 424
  Shrine of Thomas à Beckett, III. 12
Canterbury, convocation of, X. 360
Canterbury, early school and culture of,
  I. 13, 79, 87
Canterbury, Franciscans at, I. 202; III. 57
Canterbury, in *Euphues and his England*,
  III. 345
Canterbury, in Shakespeare's *King Henry
  V*, II. 77
Canterbury, monk-chronicler of, II. 301
Canterbury Chronicle at Christ church, I. 109
Canters' college, the, in *The Staple of
  Newes*, VI. 25
Cantilenae, V. 26, 29 ff., 34
Cant's hall, Burnham, X. 117
Canute, king of the English (994?–1035),
  I. 111, 127, 150, 337; VIII. 310
Canute Song, The, I. 219, 458; II. 397 ff.
Canutus, Benedict, *Regimen contra pesti-
  lentiam*, II. 319
Canynge's coffer, X. 236
Canynges, the, X. 485, 486
Canzonets to foure voyces, VII. 2
Cape Argus, The, XIV. 588
Cape Colony, XIV. 372, 374, 377
Cape Monthly Magazine, The, XIV. 588
Cape of Good Hope, XIV. 192, 241
Cape Town, XIV. 373
Cape-Dutch language and literature, XIV.
  373, 374, 377, 458
Capel, of Hoxton square academy, X. 385
Capel family, XIV. 286
Capell, Edward (1713–1781), V. 267, 274,
  275; X. 433; XII. 369; *Prolusiones*, V.
  243; *Shakespeare*, XI. 320
Caper Sauce, XIV. 377
Caperwit, in *Changes*, VI. 202
Capgrave, John (1393–1464), II. 287, 295,
  479; III. 440
  Annals, II. 287
  Chronicle, II. 287
  Famous Henries, II. 287
  Guide to Rome, II. 287

Capgrave, John
  Life of Humphrey, duke of Gloucester,
    II. 287
  Life of St Augustine, II. 480
  Life of St Gilbert of Sempringham, II. 287
  Life of St Katherine, II. 287
  Life of St Norbert, II. 480
Capheaton, Northumberland, XIII. 129
Capodistrias, Joannes Antonios, count,
    XII. 314
Capon's Tale, in *The Miscellany,* IX. 85
Caponsacchi, in *The Ring and the Book,*
    XIII. 64, 66, 80
Caporali, VII. 274
Capriccio, in *The Masque of the Middle
    Temple,* VI. 355
Capro, in Marston's *Scourge of Villanie,*
    IV. 332
Captain Car, II. 406, 408, 412
Captain Stukeley, VIII. 125
Captain Wedderburn's Courtship, II. 409
Capuchin friars, X. 499
Capulet, in *Romeo and Juliet,* V. 172, 182
Capystranus, metrical romance, II. 326
Carabas, in Disraeli's *Vivian Grey,* XIII. 349
Caracalla, baths of, XII. 67
Caracona, in Casti's *Il Poema Tartaro,*
    XII. 55
Caractacus, VI. 128
Caradoc or Caradog of Llancarvan (d.
    1147?), I. 65, 262
Carados, in *Conte del Graal,* I. 328
Carannog, St (*fl.* 450), I. 262
Carathis, in Beckford's *Vathek,* XI. 290, 291
Carbery, lady, VIII. 456
Carbery, earl of. *See* Vaughan, Richard
Carbonari movement, XII. 33, 36, 38, 51
Carcani, Giulio, V. 306
*Card or rutter of the Sea lyenge betwene
    Holland and Ffryseland,* IV. 399
Cardan, Jerome, III. 113, 420; IV. 249
Cardano, Girolamo, IV. 442
Cardenio, in *Don Quixote,* IX. 269
Carder, Peter (*fl.* 1577–1586), IV. 93
Cardiff, IV. 192
Cardiff castle, IV. 421
Cardiff, University college, XIV. 433
Cardross, X. 36
'Cards, Monopolies of,' VII. 440
Care, Henry (1646–1688), VIII. 403, 412;
    Pacquet of Advice from Rome, IX. 4;
    Weekly Pacquet, IX. 4
Carew, Sir George (d. 1612), VIII. 468
Carew, Sir George, afterwards lord Carew
    of Clopton and earl of Totnes (1555–
    1629), VII. 211, 437, 438, 448; *Relation
    of the State of France,* VII. 190
Carew, John (d. 1660), VIII. 470
Carew, lady, IV. 211
Carew, Sir Matthew (d. 1618), VII. 16
Carew, Peter (*fl.* 1566), VI. 287
Carew, Richard (1555–1620), IV. 18, 23,
    445, 448, 510; VI. 89; IX. 352; *The Ex-
    cellency of the English Tongue,* III. 305,
    330, 446, 526; *A Survey of Cornwall,*
    III. 330, 528; V. 15

Carew, Thomas (1598?–1639?), IV. 139,
    168, 197, 213, 214; VI. 11, 363; VII. 4,
    7, 13, 15 ff. (main entry), 22, 23, 25,
    57, 81, 87, 398; VIII. 141
  'Ask me no more where Jove bestows,'
    VII. 19
  Boldness in Love, VII. 18
  Coelum Britannicum, VI. 363; VII. 16,
    19
  Elegy upon the Death of Dr Donne,
    VII. 17, 18
  'Fair copy of my Celia's face,' VII. 19
  'He that loves a rosy lip,' VII. 19
  'I'll gaze no more on her bewitching
    face,' VII. 17
  'Mark how the bashful morn, in vain,'
    VII. 18
  Murdering Beauty, VII. 18
  Rapture, The, IV. 210; VII. 19
  Spring, The, VII. 20
  'Sweetly breathing vernal air,' VII. 19
  Upon the Death of the King of Sweden,
    VII. 20
Carew papers, VII. 436
Carey, David, XIV. 225, 542
Carey, George, 2nd lord Hunsdon (1547–
    1603), VI. 247, 385
Carey, George Saville (1743–1807), XI.
    451
Carey, Henry (d. 1743), II. 272; IX. 484;
    X. 71, 426; *Chrononhotonthologos,* IX.
    190; X. 83; *Dragon of Wantley,* X. 83;
    Sally in our Alley, IX. 165, 190
Carey, Henry, 1st lord Hunsdon (1524?–
    1596), VI. 247
Carey, James, XIV. 320
Carey, John, 3rd lord Hunsdon (d. 1617),
    IV. 19, 161; VI. 161
Carey, Patrick (*fl.* 1651), VII. 412; XII. 376;
    XIII. 211; *Trivial Poems and Triolets,*
    VII. 88
Carey, Robert, earl of Monmouth (1560?–
    1639), VII. 449; *Memoirs,* VII. 221, 449
Carey, William (1761–1834), XII. 343, 502
Cargill, Daniel or Donald (1619?–1681),
    IX. 549
Carinthia, George Meredith's, XIII. 444 ff.
Carisbrooke, VII. 39
Carisophus, in *Damon and Pithias,* V. 118
Carker, James, in *Dombey and Son,* XIII.
    317, 325, 331
Carle an' the King come, IX. 377
Carlell, Lodowick (*fl.* 1629–1664), VI. 239,
    240; VIII. 119, 400; Corneille's *Héraclius*
    translated by, VIII. 133, 180
Carleton, Sir Dudley, viscount Dor-
    chester (1573–1632), VI. 3, 291; VII. 16,
    152, 193, 343, 394, 437; X. 502
Carleton, George (1559–1628), ΑΣΤΡΟΛΟ-
    ΓΟΜΑΝΙΑ: *the madness of astrologers,*
    VII. 377, 508
Carleton, captain George (*fl.* 1728), IX.
    23; XII. 376; *Military Memoirs,* XII. 16
Carleton, William (1794–1869), XIV. 312,
    314 ff., 567

Carleton, William
  Anne Cosgrave, XIV. 315
  Black Prophet, The, XIV. 315
  Fardorougha the Miser, XIV. 315
  Tales of Ireland, XIV. 315
  Traits and Stories of the Irish Peasantry, XIV. 315
  Valentine McClutchy, XIV. 315
Carlia, in Whitehead's *School for Lovers*, x. 86
Carlile, Richard (1790–1843), XI. 395; XIV. 187, 470
Carlisle, II. 116, 122, 411; x. 193, 352; XI. 240; XII. 511; XIII. 196; XIV. 100
Carlisle, in Arthurian romance, I. 312, 313
Carlisle, bishop of, in *Richard II*, V. 249
Carlisle, lady, in Browning's *Strafford*, XIII. 59
Carlisle, Lucy Hay, countess of (1599–1660), VII. 17, 55
Carlisle, Nicholas (1771–1847), VII. 333; IX. 408; XII. 419; *Endowed Grammar Schools*, VII. 333; XIV. 389
Carlo Alberto, king, XII. 440
Carlton or Carleton, Richard (1560?–1638?), IV. 113, 463
Carlton house, XII. 232
Carlyle, Alexander ('Jupiter' Carlyle) (1722–1805), IX. 561; XI. 220; XII. 472; XIII. 467, 470
Carlyle, John Aitken (1801–1879), XII. 137, 522
Carlyle, J. E., XIV. Add. 6
Carlyle, Jane Welsh (1801–1866), XIII. 5, 6, 467, 470
Carlyle, Thomas (1795–1881), III. 147; IV. 45; VI. 239; VII. 91, 189, 191, 194, 225, 356, 440, 501; x. 42, 66, 288, 315, 316, 476, 480; XI. 28, 137, 209, 218, 228 ff., 409, 417, 439, 491; XII. 23 ff., 97, 159, 162, 177, 178, 219, 253, 273, 283, 378, 430, 431, 445, 505; XIII. 1 ff. (main entry), 57, 58, 71, 77, 81, 86, 128, 143, 158, 185, 320, 343, 355, 361, 362, 364 ff., 420, 422, 425, 436, 442, 447, 451, 458, 464 ff. (main entry), 483, 552; XIV. 1, 14, 42, 63, 83, 84, 86, 112, 113, 138, 144, 153, 180, 318a, 462, 470, 486, 515, 518
  Characteristics, XIII. 8
  Chartism, XIII. 14
  Critical and Miscellaneous Essays, XIII. 5
  Early Kings of Norway, The, XIII. 20
  Essay on Goethe's *Faust*, XIII. 4
  Frederick the Great, XIII. 17 ff.
  German Romance, XIII. 4, 5
  History of the French Revolution, XIII. 11 ff., 17, 19, 278, 332, 333, 384; XIV. 15
  Latter Day Pamphlets, XIII. 15
  Lectures on Heroes, XIII. 3
  Letters and Speeches of Oliver Cromwell, XIII. 17, 19
  Life of John Sterling, XI. 136; XIII. 18
  Life of Schiller, XIII. 1, 4
  On Heroes, Hero-Worship and the Heroic in History, XIII. 12 ff.

Carlyle, Thomas
  On the Choice of Books, XIII. 19
  Past and Present, I. 176; XIII. 14
  Reminiscences, XIII. 2
  Sartor Resartus, IX. 100; XII. 163, 431; XIII. 2, 3, 5 ff., 9 ff., 60; XIV. 416
  Trans. of Goethe's *Wilhelm Meister's Apprenticeship*, XIII. 4, 5
  Trans. of Goethe's *Wilhelm Meister's Travels*, XIII. 5
  Trans. of Legendre's *Elements of Geometry and Trigonometry*, XIII. 4
  Wotton Reinfred, XIII. 9
Carmarthen, x. 386
Carmarthen, Presbyterian college, x. 387
Carmarthen, Roman walls at, I. 197
Carmarthen. See *Black Book of*
Carmelites, the, I. 213; II. 349, 350; IV. 419
Carmen Heroicum, III. 293
Carmichael, Grace Jennings (1867?–1904), XIV. 369, 585
Carmichael-Smyth, major, XIII. 276
Carnan, Thomas, XI. 377
Carnarvon castle, XI. 131
Carnarvon, earls of. See Dormer, Robert; Herbert, H. H. M.
Carnarvonshire, IV. 262; x. 115
Carnatic, the, XI. 19
Caro (Flesh), in *Piers the Plowman*, II. 19
Carol, in *The Masque of Christmas*, VI. 358
Carolina, South, IX. 12
Caroline, in Thackeray's *A Shabby Genteel Story*, XIII. 280, 299
Caroline (1683–1737), queen of George II, IX. 132, 175, 187, 222, 249 ff., 281, 338; x. 274, 353; XII. 19
Caroline (1768–1821), queen of George IV, XIV. 121, 201
Caroline divines, XII. 253, 255, 261, 262, 265, 277
Caroline dramatists, x. 108
Caroline essayists, IX. 36
Caroline literature, VIII. 222, 227, 389
Caroline poetry, XIII. 192, 218, 237
Caroline poets, VII. 1, 2, 10, 17; x. 151; XII. 127, 221
Carolingian empire, VIII. 310
Carolingian romances, I. 302, 309. See, also, under Charlemagne
Carolings, the, V. 4
Carolles, Christmasse (Wynkyn de Worde's), II. 393
Carolostadius, III. 363
Carols, II. 373 ff.
Carols, Christmas, III. 19
Carols sung at Queen's College, Oxford, II. 326
Carové, Friedrich Wilhelm, XI. 491
Carow, black nuns at, V. 8
Carow, in *Phyllyp Sparowe*, III. 71
Carpenter, Agricola, *Pseuchographia Anthropomagica* (1652), VII. 509
Carpenter, J. Estlin, XII. 468; XIV. 470, 477
Carpenter, Nathaniel (1589–1628?), *Philosophia libera*, IV. 278, 507
Carpenter, Richard (d. 1670?), VII. 509

Carpenter, William Benjamin (1813–1885), xiv. 296, 470, 559

Carpenter's Tools, Debate of the, ii. 501

Carr, Henry, iv. 390

Carr, James Anderson, xiv. 572

Carr, J. Comyns, xiii. 522

Carr, Robert, earl of Somerset (d. 1645), iv. 202; vi. 31, 37, 344; vii. 441

Carré, H., *Histoire de France*, x. 283

'Carré, Jérôme,' v. 292

Carre, Thomas, *pseud. See* Pinkney, Miles

Carric, i. 236

Carroll. *See under* Centlivre, Susannah

Carroll, Lewis, *pseud. See* Dodgson, Charles Lutwidge

Carroll, William, viii. 473

Carrow. *See* Carow

Carruthers, R. (1799–1878), xi. 439; xiv. 517, 574

Carsons, the, in Mrs Gaskell's *Mary Barton*, xiii. 374

Carstares, William (1649–1715), ix. 492; x. 295; xiv. 507

Cartagena, x. 36, 37, 41

Carte, Thomas (1686–1754), x. 291, 293, 355, 498 ff.; *History of England*, x. 280; *Life of James, Duke of Ormond*, x. 280, 294, 295

Carte mss., the, xiv. 96

Carter, Elizabeth (1717–1806), x. 171, 464, 473; xi. 343, 350 ff., 354 ff. (main entry), 361, 363, 365, 473
  Epictetus, xi. 356 ff.
  Examination of Mr Pope's Essay on Man, xi. 356
  Memoirs, xi. 356
  Ode to Wisdom, xi. 356
  Sir Isaac Newton's Philosophy Explained, xi. 356

Carter, Huntley, xiii. 513

Carter, Matthew (*fl.* 1660), ix. 532

Carter, Nicholas (*fl.* 1717), xi. 354

Carter, Thos. Fortescue, xiv. Add. 6

Carter, William (d. 1584), iv. 381

Carteret, John, 1st earl Granville (1690–1763), ix. 88, 172, 458, 459, 465

Carteret, lady, ix. 457, 459, 463

Carteret, Philip (d. 1796), xiv. 244

Cartesian philosophy, xi. 57

Cartesianism, vii. 303. *See, also*, Descartes

Carthage, ii. 74; viii. 65; ix. 258; xii. 301, 316, 475, 478, 480

Carthage, in Alfred's *Orosius*, i. 95

Carthusian order, i. 189; ii. 61; vii. 338; xiii. 95

Cartier, J., iv. 442

Cartmell, Lancashire, xii. 514

Carton, Sydney, in *A Tale of Two Cities*, xiii. 333

Cartwright, Christopher (1602–1658), vii. 424

Cartwright, Mrs, xiv. 599

Cartwright, Thomas (1535–1603), iii. 213, 214, 389, 405, 413, 422, 426, 548; iv. 411, 433; ix. 235; xi. 32

Cartwright, Thomas (1634–1689), xii. 516

Cartwright, William (1611–1643), v. 371; vi. 11, 28, 109, 240; vii. 4, 39, 272
  Lady Errant, The, vi. 237
  Ordinary, The, vi. 237
  Royall Slave, The, vi. 237, 326; viii. 118
  Siedge or Love's Convert, The, vi. 237

Cartwright, William (d. 1687), vi. 83, 480

Cartwright, William Cornwallis, xiv. 485

Carve, Thomas (1590–1672?), vii 453

Carver, Jonathan (1732–1780), xiv. 551

Carving, book on, iii. 19

Cary, Elizabeth L., xiii. 476, 491, 493, 496, 574

Cary, Sir George, vi. 257

Cary, Sir Henry, 1st viscount Falkland (d. 1633), *The Marriage Night*, viii. 130, 418

Cary, Henry Francis (1772–1844), xi. 402; xii. 137, 415; *Dante*, xii. 85, 202; xiii. 174

Cary, Lettice, wife of 2nd viscount Falkland, vii. 151, 155

Cary, Sir Lucius, 2nd viscount Falkland (1610?–1643), vi. 6; vii. 21, 52, 88, 143, 150 ff., 218, 305, 424, 441, 484; viii. 63, 298; *Discourse of Infallibility*, vii. 150, 151

Cary, Sir Robert, *Memoirs*, xii. 16

Caryl, Joseph (1602–1673), vii. 316, 322

Caryll, John (1666?–1736), ix. 70, 73, 82, 84, 85, 443

Casa, G. della, *Il Galateo*, iii. 341

Casa Guidi, Florence, xiii. 70, 73, 79

Casa Magni, vii. 76

Casas, Bartolomé de las, ix. 500

Casaubon, Isaac (1559–1614), iii. 424; iv. 161, 238, 353, 500, 521; vii. 109, 250, 307 ff., 311, 312, 314, 319, 320, 324, 477, 485 ff.; viii. 63; ix. 331; xiv. 109; *De rebus sacris et ecclesiasticis exercitationes XVI ad Baronii annales*, vii. 310, 484

Casaubon, Meric (1599–1671), vii. 109, 322, 477, 486, 487, 488, 510, 517
  Commentary on the Hebrew and (Anglo-Saxon language, vii. 319
  Epictetus, vii. 319
  Marcus Antoninus, vii. 319
  Of Credulity and Incredulity, vii. 395, 484, 507
  Treatise concerning Enthusiasm, A, vii. 393

Casaubon, Mr, in *Middlemarch*, xiii. 399

Casby, Flora, in *Little Dorrit*, xiii. 331

Casby, Mr, in *Little Dorrit*, xiii. 331

Casca, in *Julius Caesar*, v. 197

Case, John (d. 1600), iv. 507; vi. 398; *Speculum moralium questionum in universam ethicen Aristotelis*, iv. 274; vi. 398

Casere, in *Widsith*, i. 35

Casey, Elizabeth Owens Blackburne (1845?–1894), xiv. 567; *A bunch of Shamrocks*, xiv. 327

Casey, John (1820–1891), XIV. 555
Casimir, VII. 87
Casimir, in Coleridge's *Zapolya*, XI. 414
Casket, The, a Miscellany (1829), XI. 419
Casket letters, VII. 161
Caspian sea, IV. 84
Cassandra, IV. 120
Cassandra, in *Promos and Cassandra*, V. 119
Cassano library, XII. 366
Cassell, John (1817–1865), XIV. 533, 612
Cassels, Walter Richard (1826–1907), XII. 465
Cassilis, Catherine, in Black's *A Daughter of Heth*, XIII. 432
Cassillis, earls of. *See* Kennedy, Gilbert
Cassio, in *Othello*, V. 202
Cassiodorien, in *Richard Coeur de Lion*, I. 307
Cassiodorus, I. 20, 213; II. 363, 366; XII. 272, 322, 476; XIII. 461
Cassius, in *Julius Caesar*, V. 197; VI. 127; XIII. 221
Cassius Longinus, Gaius, IX. 28
Cassius Severus, IV. 349; VII. 272
Castabala, XIV. 53
Castalio, in Otway's *Orphan*, VIII. 183
Castalio, Sebastian, III. 145
Castamela, in *The Fancies*, VI. 193, 194
Castanheda, Hernan Lopes de, IV. 442
Castelain, Maurice, VI. 5, 9, 10, 362, 370
Castell, Edmund (1606–1685), VII. 490, 491
Castelvetro, Lodovico, VII. 265
Casti, Giambattista, XII. 33, 51, 52, 56; *Il Poema Tartaro*, XII. 55
Castiglione, Balthazar or Baldasarre, III. 174, 344; IV. 135, 159, 342, V. 132; *Il Cortegiano*, III. 171, 235, 341, 434, 437, 438, 505, 550; IV. 7, 397, 443; V. 124, 349; IX. 396
Castillo, John (1792–1845), XII. 415
Castle, Egerton, XIV. 503
Castle Howard, VIII. 162
Castle inn, in *The Fair Maid Of The West*, VI. 101
Castle of Perseverance, The, V. 52, 391, 392
Castle of Pleasure, The, II. 327
Castlemaine, countess of. *See* Villiers, Barbara
Castlemaine, earl of. *See* Palmer, Roger
Castlereagh, viscount. *See* Stewart, Robert
Castlewood, lady, in *Esmond*, XIII. 293, 296, 407
Castlewood family, in *The Virginians*, XIII. 298
Castro, Guillen de, VI. 124, 136, 140; VIII. 128
Caswall, Edward (1814–1878), XII. 455
'Cataline, Colonel,' X. 393
Catalogi Librorum Manuscriptorum, IX. 356
Catalogue, complete, of modern books, XI. 339
Catalogue of all the Books...since the Dreadful Fire, XI. 339

Catalogue of Books (term catalogue), XI. 339
Catalogue of the most vendible Books, XI. 338
Catalogues, XI. 470
Catalogus Bibliothecae Harleianae, X. 166
Cataneo, Girolamo, IV. 443, 454
Catch, Nehemiah, VIII. 122
Catchpole, in Rabelais, VIII. 67
Catesby, Monsignore, in Disraeli's *Lothair*, XIII. 350
Catharine II, empress of Russia, V. 308; X. 246, 266, 288; XI. 358, 430; XII. 52, 55
Catharine, St, in *Tyrannick Love*, VIII. 22
Catharine of Alexandria, St, V. 7, 37, 38
Catharine of Braganza, queen, IX. 278
Cathay, IV. 66, 71 ff., 76, 86
Cathcart, lord, in Glover's *Boadicea*, XI. 258
Catherine, in Emily Brontë's *Wuthering Heights*, XIII. 411
Catherine, in Thackeray's novel, XIII. 280
Catherine de' Medici, IV. 429
Catherine of Aragon (1485–1536), 1st queen of Henry VIII, III. 15, 16; V. 201; VI. 332, 333; IX. 197
Catherine of Aragon, queen, in *Henry VIII*, V. 195; VI. 231
Catherine of Aragon, queen, song in praise of, II. 394
Catherine of Valois, queen of Henry V, IV. 182
Catherine Parr (1512–1548), 6th queen of Henry VIII, IV. 231, 495
Catherlough, Robert Knight, earl of (lord Luxborough), X. 272, 273
Catholic emancipation, XIII. 24
Catholic reaction, the, V. 337
Catholic Standard, The, XII. 463
Catholicon Anglicum, II. 483; III. 555
Catiline, in *The Palice of Honour*, II. 261
Catley, Ann (1745–1789), XI. 450, 453
Catling, Thomas, XIV. 533
Catnach, James (1792–1841), XI. 373, 469; XIV. 226 ff., 540, 542
Cato, IX. 28, 63, 64
Cato, in *Caesar and Pompey*, VI. 35
Cato, Distichs of, I. 119
Cato street conspiracy, XIV. 201, 228
Cats, Vader, *Maechden-Pflicht*, VI. 87
Cattaro, Dalmatia, III. 262
Cattraeth, I. 249
Cattuna, empress, in Casti's *Il Poema Tartaro*, XII. 55
Catullus, I. 362; IV. 197, 334, 516; VI. 346; VII. 1, 12, 13, 36; XII. 337, 483, 488, 490; XIII. 42, 45, 175; *Attis*, XIII. 449; *Vivamus, mea Lesbia, et amemus*, VII. 2; *Luctus in morte passeris*, VII. 9
Caucasus, the, XII. 65, 70
Caulah, in Ockley's *History of the Saracens*, X. 281
Causidicade, The, X. 28
Caussin, N., VI. 140
Caustic, in Morton's *Way to get Married*, XI. 281
Cavalcanti, Guido, IV. 197; XIII. 118

Cavalier songs and jests, VII. 512
Cavaliers Catechisme and confession of his faith, The, VII. 383
Cavaliers' Catechisme, or the Reformed Protestant catechising the anti-christian Papist, VII. 382
Cavaliers' Diurnall, The, VII. 388
Cavaliers Letanie, The, VII. 383
Cavall, the hound. See Cabal
Cavallilly Man, The, VIII. 96
Cave, Edward (1691–1754), X. 162 ff., 175, 465, 466; XI. 323, 355, 467; XII. 428; XIV. 169
Cave, Henry, Narration of the Fall of Paris Garden, VI. 393
Cave, R., XII. 428
'Cave of Adullam,' the, XIV. 133
Cave of Envy, in Sandys's Ovid, VII. 51
Cave of Harmony, the, in The Newcomes, XIII. 296
Cave of Mammon, in The Faerie Queene, VI. 335
Cavenagh, F. A., XIV. 525
Cavendish family, VII. 282, 289. See, also, under Devonshire and Newcastle
Cavendish, lord Frederick Charles (1836–1882), XIV. 320
Cavendish, George (1500–1561?), III. 198, 325, 334 ff., 528; IV. 428; VII. 514; Life and Death of Thomas Woolsey, III. 325, 335; Metrical Visions, III. 198
Cavendish, Georgiana, duchess of Devonshire (1757–1806), XI. 456
Cavendish, Gilbert, IV. 524
Cavendish, Henry (1731–1810), XIV. 258, 272, 274, 275, 556, 557
Cavendish, Margaret, duchess of Newcastle (1624?–1674), IV. 193; VII. 229, 452; VIII. 124, 149, 419, 424; The ccxi Sociable Letters, VII. 228; The Life of William Cavendish, duke of Newcastle, VII. 227; True Relation of the Birth, Breeding and Life of Margaret, duchess of Newcastle, VII. 228
Cavendish, Richard (d. 1601), IV. 436
Cavendish, Spencer Compton, 8th duke of Devonshire, marquis of Hartington (1833–1908), XIV. 131, 509
Cavendish, Thomas (1560–1592), III. 358, 359; IV. 78, 92; V. 139
Cavendish, William, 1st duke of Devonshire (1640–1707), VIII. 411
Cavendish, William George Spencer, 6th duke of Devonshire (1790–1858), XII. 368
Cavendish, Sir William, 7th duke of Devonshire (1808–1891), XIV. 270
Cavendish, William, marquis and 1st duke of Newcastle (1592–1676), VI. 6, 197; VII. 226, 227, 229, 285; VIII. 17, 149, 398, 420, 424; The Humorous Lovers, VIII. 124; The Triumphant Widow, VIII. 124
Cavendish, Sir William (d. 1557), III. 335
Cavendish, William, 1st earl of Devonshire (d. 1626), VII. 282
Cavendish, William, 2nd earl of Devonshire (1591?–1628), VII. 287

Cavendish, William, 3rd earl of Devonshire (1617–1684), VII. 284
Cavour, Camillo, count di, XIII. 73
Caw, G., Poetical Museum, IX. 565
Cawarden, Sir Thomas (d. 1559), VI. 257
Cawline, Sir, II. 414
Cawood, John (1514–1572), III. 59; IV. 397, 400
Caxton, William (1421-8-1491), I. 245, 285; II. 73, 77, 97, 160, 161, 198, 209, 228, 245, 264, 310 ff., 316, 332 ff., 421, 429, 483 ff.; III. 19, 67, 289, 290, 308, 339, 439 ff., 443 ff., 459, 460, 526; IV. 343, 353, 427, 428, 523; V. 53; IX. 536; XII. 520; XIV. 491
  Aesop's Fables, II. 314, 334
  Art of good living and good dying, II. 324
  Aymon, The History of the Four Sons of, II. 316, 332, 484; IV. 397
  Blanchardyn and Eglantine, The History of, 316
  Bonne meurs, Le livre des, II. 315
  Cato, II. 209, 314
  Charles the Great, The Life of, II. 314, 315
  Chesse, Game and playe of the, II. 309, 312, 313; IV. 300, 510
  Chivalry, The Order of, II. 228, 314
  Chronicle of Brute, II. 313, 334
  Curtesye, Book of, II. 313, 427
  Dictes and Sayings of the Philosophers, II. 313, 427, 485
  Eneydos, II. 316; III. 19, 67; IV. 39
  Fayttes of Arms, The, II. 316
  Godfrey of Bologne, The History of, II. 313
  Golden Legend, The, II. 314; IV. 39
  Good Manners, The Book of, II. 314, 333, 420
  Knight of the Tower, The Book of, II. 314, 333, 420
  Mirror of the World, The, II. 313
  Paris and Vienne, The History of, II. 314, 315, 319, 332
  Recuyell of the Histories of Troy, II. 230, 311 ff.; III. 289; IV. 397
  Reynard the Fox, II. 245, 313, 314, 332
  Royal Book, The, II. 315
  Trevisa's Higden's Polychronicon, Caxton's revision of, II. 313
  Vitae Sanctorum Patrum, II. 323
Caxton society, XII. 355
Cayet, Pierre Victor Palma, VI. 148, 149
Cayley, Arthur (1821–1895), XIV. 262, 264, 556
Cayley, Charles Bagot, XIII. 246, 247
Cayley, George John (1826–1878), XIV. 551
Cazamian, L., XIII. 470, 545, 546, 548, 551; Le Roman Social en Angleterre, XIII. 344, 348
Ceadda (Chad), IV. 421. See, also, Chad
Cearbhall (d. 888), Irish king, I. 287
Cebes, X. 468
Cebes his Table, VII. 489
Cecil, Edward, Aemilia, VI. 321
Cecil, in Kelly's False Delicacy, X. 91; XI. 263

Cecil, Richard (1748–1810), XII. 471
Cecil, Sir Robert, 1st earl of Salisbury (1563?–1612), IV. 82, 83, 94, 225; V. 345; VII. 331, 435, 438, 440; X. 501
Cecil, William, lord Burghley (1520–1598), III. 185, 241, 242, 319, 326, 380, 419, 421; IV. 1, 8, 10, 225, 275, 277 ff., 281, 300 ff., 307, 308, 312, 382, 386, 401, 405, 410, 510; V. 64, 89, 90, 341, 343, 345, 362; VI. 47, 305, 381, 382, 384; VII. 191, 325, 328, 331; VIII. 8; X. 500; XIV. 86; *Precepts*, IV. 343, 344, 523
Cecilia, St, I. 74
Cecilia, St, The Life of, II. 503
Cecilia de Chaumpaigne, II. 159
Cecils, the, IV. 278, 279; VI. 6
Cedd, St (d. 664), I. 82
Ceix, in *Confessio Amantis*, II. 151
Celadon, in Dryden's *Secret Love*, VIII. 20
Celadon, in Thomson's *Seasons*, X. 103
Celand, in *Britannia's Pastorals*, IV. 157
Celesia, Dorothea (Mallet, 1738–1790), XI. 263; *Almida*, X. 86, 439; XI. 456
Celestial Hierarchy, The, III. 6, 214
Celestina, in *Calisto and Melebea*, V. 99, 100
Celestina, in *The Lady of Pleasure*, VI. 202
Celestine, pope, II. 148
Celia, in *As You Like It*, I. 298
Celia, in *The Humorous Lieutenant*, VI. 123
Celia (Carew's), VII. 17, 20
Celia (Waller's), VII. 55
Célimène, in *The Spectator*, IX. 57
Cellier, François A., XIII. 519
Celling. *See* Tilly, William
Cellini, Benvenuto, *Memoirs*, XIV. 108
Celsus, XII. 521
Celtic ancestry, XIII. 122, 440
Celtic influence on English literature, I 274 ff.
Celtic language and literature, XII. 327, 343, 344, 361, 362; XIII. 100, 101, 196; XIV. 303, 307, 434, 457
Celtic legend, XIII. 36, 42
Celtic minstrels, V. 27
Celtic mysticism, VII. 15, 42
Celtic scholars, XIV. 307
Celtic society, XII. 361
Celtic tales, II. 407
Celticism, X. 230, 296
Celts, XIV. 68, 69
Cenci, Beatrice, in Shelley's *The Cenci*, XII. 67 ff., 113
Cenci, count, in Shelley's *The Cenci*, XII. 68
Cenci, Francesco, VI. 159
Cenci family, the, VI. 153
Cenci palace, XII. 70
Cenis, Mont, XII. 496
'Censor of Great Britain,' IX. 41
Censure of the Rota on Mr Dryden's Conquest of Granada, The, VIII. 4
Centlivre, Susannah (1667?–1723), VIII. 132, 168, 176, 426; X. 71 ff., 427; XI. 322 *Artifice, The*, X. 72
Bold Stroke for a Wife, X. 72

Centlivre, Susannah
  Busy-Body, The, X. 72
  Marplot in Lisbon, X. 72
  Perjur'd Husband, The, X. 72
  Perplexed Lover, The, VIII. 131
  Wonder, The, X. 72
Ceolfrid, saint (642–716), I. 55, 82
Ceolwulf, saint (d. 764), king of Northumbria, I. 82
Cephalonia, island of, XII. 38
Cephalus, in *Confessio Amantis*, II. 152
'Cerbera' (Mrs Schwellenberg), X. 260
Cerberon, in Drayton's *Eglogs*, IV. 173 176
Cerberus, in *Hudibras*, VIII. 73
Cerdic, I. 236
Cerdogni, Camillo, VII. 100
Cerdon, the cobbler, in *Hudibras*, VIII. 68, 69
Ceres, VII. 370
Ceres, in *Lingua*, VI. 315
Ceriol, Federico Furió, IV. 443
Cerne, abbey of, in Dorsetshire, and *Book of*, I. 86, 116, 120, 125, 150, 434
Cervantes-Saavedra, Miguel de, VI. 132, 135, 136, 138, 140, 154; VIII. 67, 425; X. 26, 44, 50 ff., 414; XII. 168
  Curioso Impertinente, VI. 133, 137, 223, 236
  Don Quixote, IV. 360, 395, 443; VI. 133, 137, 223, 236; VIII. 65, 68, 70, 126 ff., 189, 191; IX. 268, 269, 272, 275, 278, 500 ff., 529; X. 25, 40, 51, 52, 417; XI. 280, *also see* Add.; XIII. 305; XIV. 249, 251
  El Viejo celoso, VIII. 129
  La Fuerza de la Sangre, VIII. 129
  La Gitanilla, VIII. 129
  Los Baños de Argel, VIII. 129
  Novelas Exemplares, IV. 9; VI. 123, 139, 140; VIII. 128, 129
  Persiles y Sigismunda, VI. 123, 130, 138; VIII. 128
  Voyage to Parnassus, VII. 274
Cesario, in *The Faire Maide of the Innc*, VI. 140
'Cesario,' Della Cruscan poet, XI. 177
Cesarotti, X. 488
Cespedes, Gonzalo de, VIII. 128, 129; *Gerardo*, VI. 123, 139, 183
Cestre, C., XI. 417
Ceylon, II. 80
Chabot, Madame, X. 248
Chad, St (d. 672), I. 82; IV. 421
Chad, St, in *The Golden Legend*, II. 335
Chadderton, William (1540?–1608), XII. 493
Chaderton, Laurence (1536?–1640), VII. 317, 340
Chadwick, Esther E., XIII. 557
Chadwick, Hector Munro, I. 419, 425
Chaeronea, IV. 10
Chaffanbrass, Trollope's, XIII. 422
Chagford, VII. 86
Chalcedon, XII. 262
Chalcondylas, Demetrius, III. 5, 6
Chaldea, XII. 477
Chaldee language, IX. 393

Chaldee learning, VII. 318, 319; VIII. 364

'Chaldee MS., the,' XII. 156, 157, 160, 163

Chaldee Targums, VII. 319

Chalfont St Giles, Bucks., VII. 107, 120

Chaliz, VII. 173

Chalk farm, XII. 161

Chalkhill, John (*fl.* 1600), VII. 77 ff., 81, 113, 252; VIII. 227; XIII. 237; *Thealma and Clearchus*, II. 218; VII. 76, 78, 250, 412

'Challenger,' H.M.S., XIV. 297

Challoner, Luke (*fl.* 1603), IV. 433

Challoner, Richard (1691–1781), IV. 49; x. Add.

Chalmers, Alexander (1759–1834), VI. 1; IX. 187, 190, 480; X. 138, 153, 154, 172, 452, 462, 476, 478; XI. 467; XIII. 224

Chalmers, George (1742–1825), IX. 562; X. 459, 463; XI. 395, 470; XII. 508

Caledonia, XII. 350

'Political Annals of the Colonies,' XII. 350

'Treaties,' XII. 350

Chalmers, James (1841–1901), XIV. 551

Chalmers, J. A., XIV. Add. 7

Chalmers, Thomas (1780–1847), XII. 472; XIV. 119, 470

Chalmers, William, XIV. 517

Chalmers's *Poets*, II. 199

Chalon-sur-Saône, I. 34

Chaloner, Sir Thomas (1521–1565), IV. 443; *De Re Publica Anglorum instauranda*, IV. 261

Chaloner, Sir Thomas (1561–1615), IV. 84

Cham, the Great, II. 79, 86

Chamber, John (1546–1604), IV. 535; VII. 394; *A Confutation of Astrological Demonology*, VII. 377; *A Treatise against Judicial Astrologie*, VII. 376, 508

Chambéri, IX. 245

Chamberlain or Chamberlayne, Edward (1616–1703), VII. 514

Chamberlain, John (1553–1627), VI. 291, 324; VII. 193, 343, 345, 437

Chamberlain, Joseph, XIV. 134, 186

Chamberlain, Robert, XIII. 244

Chamberlaine, Frances. *See* Sheridan, Frances

Chamberlain's company, the lord, V. 309; VI. 3, 4, 40, 182, 245, 247, 250, 253, 255, 256, 258, 274, 275, 312

Chamberlayne, Dr, IX. 464

Chamberlayne, Edward (1616–1703), *Angliae Notitia*, IX. 352, 532

Chamberlayne, John (1666–1723), *Magnae Britanniae Notitia*, IX. 353, 532

Chamberlayne, William (1619–1689), VII. 73, 81, 94, 113, 412; VIII. 227, 435; XIII. 237

England's Jubile, VII. 74; VIII. 229

Love's Victory, VII. 74

Pharonnidia, VII. 49, 74, 76 ff., 80; VIII. 229; XIII. 238, 244

Wits led by the Nose, VII. 74

Chamberlen, P., *The Poore Man's Advocate*, IV. 510

Chambers, Edmund Kerchever, VI. 267; *Mediaeval Stage, The*, II. 380

Chambers, Raymond Wilson, I. Add.

Chambers, Robert (1802–1871), IX. 566; XI. 437, 440, 442; XII. 378, 425, 465; XIII. 500; XIV. 159, 517, 533, 559, 612; *Vestiges of Creation*, XIV. 298

Chambers, Sir William, X. 199

Chambers, William (1800–1883), XII. 425; XIV. 159, 533, 612

Chambers's Cyclopaedia of English Literature, I. ix; XIV. 145, 527, 528, 574

Chambers's Journal, XII. 425; XIV. 159, 326

Chambray, Roland Fréart, Sieur de, VIII. 449

Chamfort, Nicolas, XI. 175

Chamier, Anthony (1725–1780), X. 405

Chamier, Frederick (1796–1870), XII. 251, 448; XIV. 490

Chamisso de Boncourt, L. C. A. von, XIII. 192

Chamont, in Otway's *Orphan*, VIII. 184

Champfleury (*pseud.*), XIV. 540

Champion, The, X. 23, 24, 27, 417; XII. 171, 434

Champneys, Arthur Charles, XIV. 598

Champneys, Basil, XIII. 507, 508

Chance, J. F., X. 295

Chancellor, Richard (d. 1556), IV. 68, 71, 72, 84, 88

Chancery, court of, XI. 315

Chandler, Edward (1668?–1750), VIII. 282, 453

Chandler, Frank Wadleigh, IV. 530; XIII. 513; XIV. 540; *The Literature of Roguery*, XIII. 437

Chandler, Henry William (1828–1889), XII. 520

Chandler, Richard (1738–1810), XII. 496; *Antiquities of Ionia*, XII. 338

Chandler, Samuel (1693–1766), IX. 476, 570; X. 386, 499, 521; *Case of Subscription*, X. 374; *History of Persecution*, X. 374

Chandler, or Chaundler, T. (1418?–1490), VII. 326

Chandos, duke of. *See* Brydges, James

Chandos, lord. *See* Brydges, Grey

Chandra Sen, Keshab, XIV. 341

Channel islands, IV. 190; XIV. 434

Channing, William Ellery, XII. 378

Chansons de geste, I. 279, 291, 447; V. 3, and see 34

Chanteloup, IX. 226

Chantrey, Sir Francis Legatt (1781–1842), XI. 242; XII. 323

Chantries act (1547), III. 418; VII. 326

Chapbook editions of children's books, XI. 477

Chapbooks, XI. 475, 476

Chapel Royal, the, VI. 279. *See, also, under* Children of the Chapel Royal

Chapel Royal, The Old Cheque Book of the, VI. 280, 282

Chapelain, Jean, VII. 268; VIII. 374; X. 220; *La Pucelle*, VII. 268

Chapman, George (1559?–1634), III. 191,
199, 271, 292, 305, 449, 452, 526, 550;
IV. 22, 266, 393 ff.; V. 148, 224, 311, 312,
344, 371, 422; VI. 2, 16, 19, 28–57 (main
entry), 147, 202, 225, 250, 329, 353 ff.,
420 ff., 451, 488, *also see* Add.; VII. 51,
465; IX. 75; XII. 191; XIII. 448, 495, *also
see* Add. 2
Achilles Shield, VI. 37
Al Fooles, VI. 15, 32, 290
Alphonsus Emperour of Germany, VI. 35
Amorous Zodiac, The, VI. 30, 31
Andromache Literata, VI. 31
Batrachomyomachia, VI. 37
Blinde begger of Alexandria, The, VI. 15,
31
*Byron, The Conspiracie, And Tragedie
of Charles Duke of*, VI. 30, 33 ff., 175, 258
Caesar, trans. of, IV. 435
Caesar and Pompey, VI. 35, 172
Chabot, Admirall of France, VI. 35, 207
Comodey of Umers, The, VI. 32
Coronet for his Mistress Philosophy, A,
VI. 31
De Guiana Carmen, IV. 88
Eastward Hoe, III. 191; V. 255; VI. 4, 20,
30, 32, 43, 47, 48, 171, 173, 258, 355;
VII. 433
Euthymiae Raptus, VI. 29
Fatal Love, a French tragedy, VI. 36
Gentleman Usher, The, VI. 32, 290
Gyles Goosecappe, Sir, VI. 35, 290, 459
Hesiod's *Works and Days*, Chapman's
trans. of, IV. 436; VI. 37
Homer, III. 305; IV. 2, 19, 21, 394, 437,
516, 526; VI. 29, 30, 32, 37; XI. 90;
XII. 79, 190
Homeric *Epigrams*, VI. 37
Homeric *Hymns*, VI. 37
Humerous Dayes Myrth, An, V. 331;
VI. 15, 31
Marlowe's *Hero and Leander*, Chap-
man's continuation of, VI. 31
*Masque...of the Middle Temple and
Lyncolnes Inn*, VI. 36, 353
May-Day, III. 199; V. 34; VI. 32, 290
Monsieur D'Olive, The, VI. 32
Musaeus, translation of, VI. 30
Ovid's Banquet of Sence, IV. 19, 439;
VI. 31
Revenge for Honour, VI. 35
Revenge of Bussy D'Ambois, The, VI.
33 ff., 178, 223
Shadow of Night, The, VI. 31
Tears of Peace, The, VI. 31
Widdowes Teares, The, VI 32
World runs on Wheels, The (Al Fooles),
VI. 32
*Yorkshire Gentlewoman and her Son,
The*, VI. 36
See, *also, under* Marston and Shirley
Chapman, George (1723–1806), XIV. 605
Chapman, John (1822–1894), XII. 430;
XIII. 383, 385
Chapman, Maria Weston, XIII. 343, 554
Chapman and Hall, publishers, XIII. 440

Chapone, Mrs Hester, born Mulso (1727–
1801), X. 171, 270; XI. 356, 473; XIV.
599; *Letters*, XI. 365, 379
Chappell, Jennie, XIV. 517
Chappell, William (1582–1649), VII. 97, 98
Chappell, William, X. 233
Chappell, W., *Popular Music of the Olden
Time*, IX. 361 ff., 568
Chapter books, XI. 325
Character of a Coffee-house, The, VII. 389
Character of Italy, The, VII. 392
Character of Spain, The, VII. 392
Character of Warre, The, VII. 386
Character sketches, VII. 517
Character writers, IV. 521, 522
Charissa, in *The Faerie Queene*, VI. 335
Chariton, *Chereas and Callirrhoe*, III. 351
Charity, in *Confessio Amantis*, II. 148
Charity, in *The Example of Virtue*, II. 227,
228
Charity, in *The Passetyme of Pleasure*, II.
228
Charity, the tree of, in *Piers the Plowman*,
II. 24, 27
Charity commission, XIV. 422, 433
Charity schools, IX. 570, 571
Charivari, XIV. 235, 326
Charlemagne in romance, I. 169, 281, 283,
284, 302, 342, 467
Charlemont, in *The Atheist's Tragedie*, VI.
168
Charles I, IV. 92, 107, 195, 238 ff., 265,
301, 302, 312, 366, 381, 411, 426; V. 222,
348, 360; VI. 6, 7, 83, 147 ff., 201, 203,
208, 232, 237, 238, 240, 243, 245, 246,
271, 278, 321, 324 ff., 336, 359, 360,
363, 403; VII. 1, 6, 16, 17, 24, 29, 35,
39, 50, 52 ff., 59, 61, 63, 79, 80, 106,
140, 142, 144, 146 ff., 154, 159, 161 ff.,
165, 179, 188, 191, 192, 194, 195, 198,
205, 212, 214, 215, 218, 219, 221 ff.,
229, 254, 280, 300, 306, 335, 340, 352,
353, 361, 382, 383, 392, 433, 435, 436,
438 ff., 447, 449, 450, 455; VIII. 2, 67,
101, 119, 130, 134, 245, 246, 267, 277,
294, 295, 297, 312, 318, 319, 323, 358,
361, 371, 383, *also see* Add.; IX. 27,
201, 222, 233, 235, 240, 250, 307, 309,
403; X. 279, 283, 286, 287, 290, 295,
318, 355, 498 ff.; XI. 280, 311; XII. 253,
260, 521; XIV. 93, 396
Charles I, in Shelley's drama, XII. 75
*Charles I, Just Defence of the Royal Martyr
King*, VII. 225
Charles I, pamphlets on, VII. 513
Charles II, I. 282; IV. 204; V. 237, 375;
VI. 250, 271; VII. 61, 62, 150, 161, 179,
180, 183, 188, 196, 197, 206, 213 ff.,
219, 234, 250, 254, 285, 314, 360, 365,
434, 436, 441, 455; VIII. 6, 7, 9, 18, 20,
21, 30, 34, 35, 37, 39, 43 ff., 61, 62, 64,
77, 80, 82, 88, 92 ff., 97 ff., 118, 122,
123, 131, 132, 155, 158, 174, 185, 198,
199, 206, 207, 213, 247, 248, 254, 256,
261, 262, 264 ff., 269, 272, 291, 293,
295, 297, 302, 304, 358, 370, 372, 382,

Charles II
  387, 481, 482; IX. 2, 194, 199, 201, 203,
  205, 206, 208, 213, 225, 233, 234, 239,
  307, 362, 363; X. 287, 290, 351, 373;
  XIII. 434
Charles II, king of Spain, IX. 8, 133; XIV.
  212
Charles V, emperor, X. 504
Charles V, king of Spain, II. 83, 338, 340;
  III. 32, 160
Charles VIII, king, in Romola, XIII. 394
Charles VIII, king of France, X. 303
Charles IX, king of France, VIII. 87
Charles XII, king of Sweden, IX. 19; X. 169
Charles, archduke of Austria, IX. 134
Charles Edward, prince (the Young Pre-
  tender), IX. 371, 373, 563 ff.; XII. 26;
  XIV. 360
Charles, Edwin, XIII. 537
Charles, Émile, I. 208 ff.
Charles Frederick, king of Prussia, X. 463
Charles Lewis (Karl Ludwig), elector Pala-
  tine, V. 284; VII. 231
Charles the Bald, I. 88, 89; IV. 270
Charles the Bold, II. 307
Charles the Great (Charlemagne), I. 5, 84,
  88 ff.; II. 112, 181, 339, 416; III. 211,
  245, 437; IV. 24, 269; V. 40; X. 314;
  XII. 322, 476
    For Romances, see under Charlemagne
    and Carolingian
Charles the Great, in Rauf Coilzear, II.
  125, 126
Charles the Great, Life of, II. 314, 315, 485
Charles's men, prince, VI. 232
Charleton, Walter (1619–1707), VIII. 362,
  395, 476; Chorea Gigantum, IX. 354, 532
Charlett, Arthur (1655–1722), IX. 57, 470
Charley, in Mrs Gaskell's Mary Barton,
  XIII. 376
Charlie is my Darling, IX. 376
Charlotte, in Cumberland's West Indian,
  XI. 264
Charlotte, in Goethe's Werther, X. 227
Charlotte, in Oliver Twist, XIII. 317
Charlotte, in Thackeray's Adventures of
  Philip, XIII. 299
Charlotte, Augusta, princess (1796–1817),
  XI. 166; XII. 401; XIII. 276; XIV. 227
Charlotte, Sophia (1744–1818), queen of
  George III, X. 63, 65, 260
'Charlotte Elizabeth.' See Tonna, Char-
  lotte Elizabeth
Charlton, Sir Job (1614–1697), IX. 392
Charlton, Stephen, VII. 438
Charlton, Wilts., VIII. 9
Charlwood, John (d. 1592), IV. 394
Charm for Barren Land, I. 64
Charmer, The, IX. 371, 566
Charms, Old English, I. 40, 422, 423
Charnock, Richard, prior, III. 3, 4, 11, 49
Charolais, in The Fatall Dowry, VI. 158
Charon, VII. 381
Charon, in Dialogues of the Dead, XI. 351
Charon, in Friar Rush, VI. 53
Chart, near Leeds in Kent, I. 353

Charter. Elizabeth (fl. 1815–1825), XI. 419
Charter Rolls, the, XII. 516
Charterhouse, XII 288, 329, 332; XIII. 276;
  XIV. 404, 422
Charteris, Francis (1675–1732), IX. 469, 470
Charteris, Henry (d. 1599), III. 123; IV. 413
Chartier, Alain, II. 164, 216, 485; III. 489,
  502; IV. 443; VIII 59; Le Quadrilogue
  Invectif, III. 152, 153
Chartley, in The Wise woman of Hogsdon,
  VI. 99
Chartres, school of, I. 183 ff., 216
Chase, John Centlivres, XIV. Add. 6, 11
Chase side, Enfield, XII. 201
Chasles, Ph., XII. 524
Chastitie, in Ane Pleasant Satyre, III. 125,
  126
Chastity, tower of, in The Passetyme of
  Pleasure, II. 231
Chateaubriand, François René, vicomte
  de, IV. 43; V. 301; XII. 396, 524; XIV.
  107; Génie du Christianisme, XI. 108;
  XII. 254
Chatham, VIII. 249, 381
Chatham, earl of. See Pitt, William
Chatteris, Cambridgeshire, XIII. 216
Chatteris, in Thackeray's Pendennis, XIII.
  276
Chatterji, Bankim Chandra, XIV. 341
Chatterton, Thomas (1752–1770), X.
  234 ff. (main entry), 239, 485, 486, 525,
  also see Add.; XI. 181, 245, 250, 390,
  422; XII. 81, 86; XIII. 225, 226; XIV. 504
  Bristowe Tragedie, X. 234
  Consuliad, X. 399
  Elinoure and Juga, X. 235, 238
  Excelente Balade of Charitie, X. 235
  Revenge, The, X. 237
  Ryse of Peyncteyning in Englande, X. 237
  Saxon Atchievements, X. 237
  Songe to Ælla, X. 235
  Unknown Knight, The, X. 236
  Works, XII. 146
  See, also, Rowley, Thomas, and the
  Rowley Poems
Chattuarii, the, I. 26
Chaucer, Agnes, wife of John Chaucer,
  II. 156
Chaucer, Elizabeth, II. 157
Chaucer, Geoffrey (1340?–1400), I. 16, 99,
  155, 170, 177, 193, 213, 270, 275 ff.,
  280, 282, 283, 288, 289, 292, 298, 299,
  309, 316, 319, 332, 335, 348 ff., 355,
  366, 367, 380, 382, 386 ff., 394 ff.; II. 18,
  39, 41, 72, 92 ff., 103, 110, 134, 135,
  142, 143, 145, 146, 150 ff., 156–196
  (main entry), 197, 198, 200, 204, 205,
  207, 208, 210, 211, 213 ff., 222, 225,
  227 ff., 236, 239, 240, 243 ff., 247, 248,
  250, 252 ff., 257, 258, 261, 263 ff., 272,
  295, 308, 314, 317, 323, 332, 334, 337,
  340, 351, 352, 355, 364, 391, 403, 412,
  416, 422, 429, 455 ff., 488; III. 24, 68,
  70, 73, 79, 98, 108, 116, 117, 119, 120,
  130, 138, 149, 168, 169, 173, 174, 177,
  178, 188, 192, 200, 212, 227, 239, 244,

Chaucer, Geoffrey
246, 273 ff., 280 ff., 286, 287, 289, 290 ff.,
296 ff., 301, 303, 308, 324, 325, 327,
435, 439, 441 ff., 448, 449, 555; IV. 22,
194, 207, 246, 248, 421, 432; V. 22, 96,
98, 103, 196, 220, 221, 226, 227, 234,
327; VI. 52, 113, 137, 299, 311; VII. 75,
132, 135, 156, 173, 235; VIII. 20, 48,
51, 52, 55, 222, 227, 228, 230, 232, 233,
433; IX. 68, 151, 158, 362, 369, 446;
X. 183, 218, 219, 221, 223, 227, 236,
239, 241, 491; XI. 161, 251, 255, 368,
394, 431; XII. 54, 98, 120, 168, 177, 344,
354, 443; XIII. 104, 119, 128, 211, 238,
242, 423
Chaucer, Geoffrey, works by, or attributed
to:
    A.B.C., II. 161, 162, 164, 167, 170
    Anelida and Arcite, II. 161, 162, 164,
    167, 171, 217, 312; III. 116
    Assembly of Fowls, The. See Parliament
    Assembly of Ladies, The, II. 162, 164,
    215, 217, 223
    Astrolabe, II. 157, 161, 162, 185
    Ballade in Commendation of our Lady,
    A, II. 162
    Boethius, II. 160 ff., 185, 186, 317; IV. 422
    Bukton, The Envoy to, II. 162, 187
    Canon's Yeoman's Tale, The, II. 211
    Canterbury Tales, I. 16, 193, 213, 286,
    298, 352; II. 135, 143, 145, 160 ff., 167,
    168, 174, 177, 180, 185, 187, 194, 215,
    216, 218, 313, 314, 320, 323; III. 235,
    241, 285, 290, 298; IV. 330; XI. 200
    Circumstance, II. 162
    Clerk's Tale, The, II. 183, 188, 192, 350,
    413; V. 117
    Complaint of Mars, The, II. 161, 162,
    164, 167, 170
    Complaint of Venus, The, II. 161, 162,
    164, 187
    Complaint to his Lady, The, II. 167, 170
    Complaint unto Pity, The, II. 161, 164,
    167, 170
    Cook's Tale, The, II. 181
    Death of Pity, The, II. 162
    Dream, The. See Duchess, The book of
    Duchess, The book of the [Death of
    Blanche], II. 160 ff., 164, 167, 168, 170;
    XIII. 124
    Empty Purse, Complaint of Chaucer to
    his, II. 161, 162, 187
    Flower of Courtesy, The, II. 162
    Former Age, The, II. 161, 186
    Fortune, II. 161, 162, 186
    Franklin's Tale, The, II. 184
    Gentilesse, II. 161, 186
    Good Counsel, Ballad of. See Truth
    Goodly Ballade of Chaucer, A, II. 162
    House of Fame, I. 170; II. 160 ff., 167,
    174, 175, 187, 188, 261, 314, 412; III.
    70, 117; XIII. 124
    Knight's Tale, The, II. 168, 171, 174,
    176, 178, 180, 188, 191, 193, 243; V.
    256; VI. 139, 299, 300; X. 230; XIII.
    122, 123

Chaucer, Geoffrey, works by, or attributed
to:
    Lack of Steadfastness, II. 161, 162, 186
    Legend of Good Women, The, II. 145,
    150, 160 ff., 164, 167 ff., 174, 175, 217,
    219; (prologue), III. 71
    Lion, The book of the, II. 160, 161
    Man of Law's Prologue and Tale, The,
    I. 181, 292; II. 161, 181
    Man of Law's Tale, IX. 185
    Manciple's Tale, The, II. 184
    Melibeus, The tale of, II. 180, 182, 185;
    III. 178
    Merchant's Prologue and Tale, The, II.
    184, 215
    Merciles Beaute, II. 187
    Miller's Tale, The, II. 216; V. 19
    Monk's Tale, The, II. 216; III. 192
    Nun's Priest's Tale, The, I. 193, 290;
    II. 183, 187; III. 241
    Palamon and Arcite, II. 161
    Pardoner's Tale, The, II. 183, 215
    Parliament of Fowls, The, II. 160 ff.,
    164, 167, 170, 172, 312; III. 98; IV. 184
    Parson's Prologue and Tale, The, I. 355;
    II. 160, 185, 194, 216
    Phyllis and Demophoon (Legend of
    Good Women), II. 217
    Physician's Tale of Virginia, II. 182, 183
    Praise of Women, A, II. 162
    Prioress's Tale, The, II. 169, 180 ff.,
    190 ff., 359
    Prologue, The, II. 168, 178 ff., 182, 185,
    191, 193; III. 441
    Reeve's Tale, The, II. 216
    Romaunt of the Rose, II. 161, 162, 164
    167 ff., 170, 240, 244
    Rosemounde ballade, The, II. 161, 186
    St Cecily. See Second Nun's Tale, The
    Sapience, II. 162
    Scogan, The Envoy to, II. 187
    Second Nun's Tale, The, II. 174, 178
    184; IV. 38
    Shipman's Tale, The, II. 181
    Sir Thopas, I. 277, 281, 282, 289, 291,
    292, 295, 299, 319, 365 ff.; II. 167, 180,
    181, 188, 189, 195, 196; III. 289; IV.
    173; V. 3; X. 154; XI. 218
    Squire's Tale, The, I. 3, 9; II. 174; III. 130
    Temple of Brass, II. 312
    Troilus and Criseyde, I. 332; II. 135,
    145, 160 ff., 167, 168, 170 ff., 176, 185,
    188, 193, 230, 308, 314, 391, 474; VII.
    78, 314, 487; XIII. 124
    Truth, II. 161, 162, 186
    Wife of Bath's Prologue and Tale, The,
    I. 177, 295; II. 169, 179, 180, 183, 192,
    218, 254, 413; III. 88, 486; IV. 340;
    VI. 138
    Yeoman's Tale, The, I. 298
Chaucer, John (d. 1366), II. 156, 159
Chaucer, Philippa, wife of Geoffrey
    Chaucer, II. 157
Chaucer, Robert le, II. 156
Chaucer, Thomas (1367?–1434), II. 157
Chaucer society, II. 166, 216; XII. 355, 504

Chaucer's 'little Lewis,' II. 157, 185

Chaucerian school, I. 321, 334

Chaucerians, II. 215 ff., 469, 470

Chaucerians, the English, II. 197 ff., 467 ff.

Chaucerians, the Scottish, II. 239 ff., 471 ff.

Chauncy, Sir Henry (1632–1719), *Antiquities of Hertfordshire*, IX. 353, 532

Chauncy, Isaac (1632–1712), X. 384; *Neo-Nomianism Unmasked*, X. 377

Chaundler, Thomas (1418?–1490), dean of Hereford, III. 5

Chaunteclere, in *Phyllyp Sparowe*, III. 71

Chaworth, Mary Ann, XII. 31, 51

Chawton, Hampshire, XII. 236

Cheadle, Walter Butler, XIV. 553

Cheats of London, The, IX. 264

Cheddar Hole, III. 322

Chedreux, VIII. 375

Cheem, Aliph, *pseud. See* Yeldham, Walter

Cheerybles, the, in *Nicholas Nickleby*, XIII. 318

Cheke, Sir Hatton, VII. 232

Cheke, Henry (1548?–1586?), IV. 441

Cheke, Sir John (1514–1557), III. 290, 291, 293, 348, 418, 419, 424, 425, 430 ff., 446 ff., 550, 555; IX. 496

Cheldrich, in *The Misfortunes of Arthur*, v. 78

Chelmsford school, VII. 330

Chelsea, VIII. 269; XIII. 107

Chelsum, James (1740?–1801), *Remarks on... Mr Gibbon's History*, X. 307, 507

Cheltenham, X. 277; XIII. 46, 287; XIV. 225, 414

Chelwood, Knightly (1650–1720), VIII. 446

Chenery, Thomas (1826–1884), XIV. 182, 183

Chenevix, Richard (1698–1779), bishop of Waterford, X. 256, 257

Cheney, Sir Thomas, III. 167

Chénier, Marie-Joseph, V. 294

Chapman, Walter (1473?–1538?). *See* Chapman and Myllar

Chapman and Myllar, II. 92, 123, 284, 478, 479; IV. 412; IX. 359

Cherbuliez, Victor, XIII. 470

Cherokee, X. 57

Cherry, in Farquhar's *Beaux' Stratagem*, VIII. 172

Cherry, Andrew (1762–1812), XIV. 567

Cherry, Francis (1665?–1713), X. 356

Cherry, J. L., *Life of John Clare*, XII. 132, 415

Chertsey, Andrew (*fl.* 1508–1532), II. 324, 329

    Craft to live well and to die well, II. 324

    The Flower of commandments of God, II. 324

    The Lucydarye, II. 324

    The Ordinary of Christian Men, II. 324

    The Treatise of the Passion of Christ, II. 324

Chertsey, Cowley at, VII. 63; VIII. 378

Chertsey abbey, Denham on, VII. 59

Cherwell, vale of the, X. 112

Cheshire, III. 319; VII. 214, 232, 341; IX. 166, 536; XI. 469; XII. 355, 509, 511, 512, 514; XIII. 372, 377

Cheshire (and Lancashire) Record society, XII. 506

Chesney, Sir George Tomkyns (1830–1895), XIV. 575; *Battle of Dorking, The*, XIV. 339; *Dilemma, The*, XIV. 339

Chess, in *Reason and Sensuality*, II. 202

Chess, The Book of the, XII. 515

Chesse, A Game at (1624), VII. 433

Chesse, The Game of (1643), VII. 385

Chessington hall, X. 260

Chester, II. 71, 210; III. 429; IV. 190, 408; VII. 319; VIII. 297, 313, 369; IX. 167; X. 309; XI. 12, 469; XII. 329, 509; XIII. 103, 369; XIV. 74

Chester, Charles, VI. 40

Chester, St Werburgh's, II. 71, 210

Chester, Sir John, in *Barnaby Rudge*, X. 255; XIII. 321, 333

Chester, Philippa, in Reade's *The Wandering Heir*, XIII. 426

Chester, Robert (1566?–1640?), *Loves Martyr*, IV. 473; V. 224; VI. 423

Chester Plays (or Mysteries), II. 426; III. 91; V. 12 ff., 17, 19, 20, 46 ff., 124, 389

Chester Rolls, XII. 355

Chesterfield, earl of. *See* Stanhope, Philip Dormer, and Stanhope, Philip

Chesterfield free school, IX. 393

Chesterton, near Harbury, X. 112

Chesterton, Gilbert Keith, XII. 476, 484, 532, 539, 543

Chesterton, George Luval, XIV. 551

Chestre, Thomas (*fl.* 1430), *Launfal Miles*, I. 295

Chetham, Humphrey (1580–1653), IV. 432, 433

Chetham society, IX. 322; XII. 355

Chettam, Sir James, in *Middlemarch*, XIII. 399

Chettle, Henry (d. 1607?), III. 114, 367, 536; IV. 514; V. 117, 138, 166, 171, 219, 221, 310 ff., 319, 321 ff., 330 ff., 361, 473, 475; VI. 12, 13, 51, 54, 97, 218, 424, 459; VII. 395

    Black Bateman of the North, VI. 96

    Englandes Mourning Garment, IV. 184, 351; v. 328

    Hoffman, The Tragedy of, V. 310, 323, 324, 326, 327; VI. 178, 217

    Italian Tragedy, The, VI. 96

    Kind Hart's Dream, III. 545; IV. 363, 530; V. 323; VI. 397, 492

    Matilda's Tragedy, V. 327

    Patient Grissill, V. 117, 323

    Piers Plainnes seaven yeres Prentiship, III. 367

    Shore, VI. 90

    See, also, under Day

Chettle and Dekker, *Kinge Sebastiane of Portingalle*, VIII. 126

Chetwood, William Rufus (d. 1766) VIII. 190; X. 442; XI. 317, 448

Chevalerie, L'Ordre de, II. 284

Chevalier de Coucy, I. 300

Chevallier (of Geneva), IV. 429

Chevelere Assigne (Swan-Knight), I. 291, 467

Cheveril, in Holcroft's *Deserted Daughter*, XI. 277

Cheviot, II. 398, 408, 415

Chevrillon, André, XII. 427

Chevy Chase, II. 395, 415; III. 280, 300; VIII. 96; IX. 59, 370; X. 219, 220, 226, 484

Chew, Samuel C., XIII. 514

Cheyne, Elspeth, in Scott's *Antiquary*, XIII. 234

Cheyne, George (1671–1743), IX. 307, 325, 513, 519

Cheyne, Thomas Kelly (1841–1915), XII. 465, *also see* Add. 4

Cheynell, Francis (1608–1665), VII. 495; X. 175, 466

Chicheley, or Chichele, Henry (1362?–1443), II. 358; VII. 326

Chichester, II. 288; IV. 422; VII. 377, 459; VIII. 301; IX. 530; XI. 403, 427; XII. 86, 274, 327; XIV. 112

Chicksands, VIII. 15

Chiffinch, William (1602?–1688), IX. 240

Child, Francis James, X. 233; *Ballads*, I. 295; II. 395, 399 ff., 408, 409, 413 ff.

Child, Sir Josiah (1630–1699), VIII. 342, 473

Child Christ, the, II. 380 ff., 392, 427

Child Maurice, II. 410, 412

Child of Ell, II. 410

Child Waters, II. 413

Childe, L., IV. 454

Childe Harold, in Byron's poem, XII. 43, 45

Childe of Bristowe, The, II. 500

Childers, Robert Caesar (1838–1876), XII. 502

Childhood of Jesus, I. 368

Children in the Wood, The, II. 408; IX. 59, 166; X. 226

Children of the Chapel Royal and other children's companies, V. 64, 118, 122 ff., 161; VI. 4, 41, 212, 220, 221, 246, 258, 262, 279–292 (main entry), 402, 467

Children of the Chapel Stript and Whipt, The, VI. 280

Children's books, XI. 475 ff.

Children's books, magazine articles on, XI. 476

Childrey, Joshua (1623–1670), VII. 509

Childric, in Layamon, I. 237

Chile, XIV. 243

Chillingworth, William (1602–1644), IV. 433; VII. 150, 153, 157, 163, 218, 424, 427; IX. 401; *The Religion of Protestants*, VII. 151, 304, 484; XIV. 102

Chillip, Mr, in *David Copperfield*, XIII. 327

Chilmead, Edmund (1610–1654), VII. 488

Chimenti, F. è G., XIII. Add. 2

China, II. 79; IV. 92, 98; IX. 391; X. 465; XII. 188; XIV. 169

China goods, IX. 263, 271

Chinaman, Goldsmith's, XIII. 445

Chinese imperial yellow dye, XIV. 286

Chinese language and literature, XI. 381; XII. 342, 343, 362; XIV. 421

Chinese Letters, X. 205, 206

Chinese poetry, X. 489

Chinese room, Mrs Montagu's, XI. 348

Chionia, St, I. 74

Chippenham, III. 430

Chipping Campden, X. 113

Chipping Wycombe, VII. 54

Chisholm, John, XII. Add. 1

Chiswell, Richard (1639–1711), XI. 323

Chiswick, VII. 333; IX. 566

Chit-Chat, IX. 442

'Chits,' VIII. 94

Chivalry, tower of, in *The Passetyme of Pleasure*, II. 225

Chloe, XII. 133

Chloe, in Pope's *Characters of Women*, IX. 82

Chloris (Waller's), VII. 55

Chohilaicus (Chlochilaicus) or Huiglaucus, I. 26

Choice Drollery (1656), VII. 512

Choice Song-Books, XI. 218

Chorley, Henry Fothergill (*pseud.* Paul Bell, 1808–1872), XII. 417; XIII. 483; XIV. 517

Chorlton, John (1666–1705), X. 385, 386

Chrestomathic day school, XIV. 404

Chretien de Troyes, I. 263, 268, 269, 271, 273, 279 ff., 285, 299, 462

　Chevalier de la Charrette, I. 270

　Cligès, I. 286

　Conte del Graal, I. 253, 269, 271, 284, 294, 328

　Erec, I. 250, 253, 274

　Le Chevalier au Lion (*Yvain*), I. 253, 274, 279, 280, 284

　Perceval le Gallois, II. 124, 450

　Tristan (ascribed to C. de T.), I. 273

Chrisoganus, 'Master Pedant,' in *Histriomastix*, VI. 40

Christ, in religious plays, V. 15, 37, 41, 42, 44 ff., 49

Christ, Bull on, VIII. 305

Christ, Bunyan on, VII. 169

Christ, hymns of, II. 426. *See, also, under* Child Christ *and* Jesus

Christ, life of (Cornish play), V. 15

Christ (Milton's), VII. 119, 121, 136

Christ, On Serving I. 227, 458

Christ, on the lowering of, from the cross (play), V. 43

Christ, R. Barclay on, VIII. 112

Christ, The Passion of (various works), II. 266, 284, 324, 328, 329

Christ, The Suffering (Χριστὸς πάσχων), V. 5

Christabel, I. 148, 376

Christchurch, Hampshire, VI. 38

Christchurch, New Zealand, XIII. 449

Christendome, The present estate of, VII. 385

Christian, in Bunyan's *Pilgrim's Progress*, I. 58; VII. 173, 177

Christian IV, of Denmark, IV. 151; VI 189; VII. 231

Christian Brethren, association of, III. 40
Christian commonwealth of Hobbes, VII. 296 ff.
Christian doctrine, XII. 259, 264, 275, 278 ff., 292, 295 ff.
Christian drama, V. 36, 37
Christian mysticism, VIII. 108, 110
Christian scholarship, XII. 280, 298
Christian science, VIII. 359
Christian socialism, XIII. 359
Christian socialist, XII. 290
Christian Examiner, The, XIV. 315
Christian Instructor, XII. 472
Christian Observer, The, XI. 404; XII. 281
Christian Paradoxes, VIII. 276
Christian Remembrancer, The, XII. 454 ff., 459
Christian Socialist The, XIII. 358
Christiana, in Bunyan's *Pilgrim's Progress,* VII. 177
Christianity, V. 21, 29; VI. 373; VII. 305, 367; VIII. 42, 100, 102, 276, 346, 389; IX. 28, 83, 100, 101, 108, 112, 290 ff., 300, 305, 331; X. 7, 114, 308, 309, 313, 317, 363; XI. 18, 48, 194, 196, 198, 199, 286, 287, 380; XII. 254, 269, 270, 276 ff., 282, 283, 290 ff., 297 ff., 322; XIII. 24, 40, 75, 76, 113, 138, 174, 366, 436; XIV. 13, 46, 110, 253, 302, 303, 401, 402, 409, 411, 414
Christianorum Tractatus de decem nationibus, II. 330
Christians, in *Tyrannick Love,* VIII. 22
Christians, Duty of, I. 228
'Christianus Presbyteromastix' = Sir Thomas Urquhart, VII. 253
Christie, Albany, XII. 460
Christie, Jonathan, XII. 161, 163
Christie, Richard Copley (1830–1901), XII. 333, 369, 515, 520; XIV. 501; *Étienne Dolet,* XII. 334; XIV. 109
Christie, Robert (1788–1856), XIV. 358, 582
Christie, William Dougal (1816–1874), VIII. 3, 4; IX. 212; XIV. 501; *Life of the First Earl of Shaftesbury,* XIV. 113
Christie's sale room, X. 471
Christina, queen, in Milton's *Defensio,* VII. 130
Christina, queen of Sweden, VII. 230; VIII. 20
Christina, St, I. 74, 75; V. 49
Christine de Pisan, II. 208, 316; III. 90; *City of Ladies,* II. 327; *Moral Proverbs of,* II. 313, 485
Christis Kirk on the Grene, II. 244, 250, 270, 271, 273, 274, 471, 473; III. 130, 135; IX. 366, 367, 379, 560; X. 223, 226; XI. 215, 218
Christmas, in *The Masque of Christmas,* VI. 355, 358
Christmas, tracts against, VII. 514
'Christmas Abbess,' V. 8
Christmas carols, XIII. 125, 140
Christmas eve, XIII. 111
'Christmas lord,' V. 8

Christmas numbers, XIII. 376
Christmas plays, V. 15, 32, 37 ff., 44, 47, 48, 68
Christmas stories, XIII. 323, 326, 334, 335
Christmas Prince, The, VI. 319, 474
Christopher, in Dickens's *Somebody's Luggage,* XIII. 335
Christopher, The, English warship, I. 357
Christopherson, John (d. 1558), *Jephtha,* VI. 295
Christ's college, Attercliffe, X. 386
Christ's Descent into Hell, I. 428
Christus Patiens, V. 6
Chronica Monasterii de Melsa, XII. 356
Chronicle, the Old English, I. 5, 62, 89, 90, 104, 107 ff., 137 ff., 145, 150, 161, 167, 219, 236, 245, 317, 352, 369, 374, 443; II. 400, 420; III. 458; VIII. 313 *See, also, under* Peterborough, Winchester, etc.
Chronicle, English (1377–1461), II. 301, 482
Chronicle, The, XIV. 118
Chronicle of the Brute, The, II. 313, 334, 482
Chronicle plays, IX. 136; V. 35, 142, 151 ff., 199, 425
Chronicle to Edwarde the iii, II. 308
Chroniclers, transition, I. 335 ff.
Chroniclers, 14th and 15th century, II. 496 ff.
Chroniclers in Tudor times, III. 313 ff., 527 ff.
Chronicles and Memorials of Great Britain and Ireland, XII. 356
Chronicles of England, The, II. 301, 318, 319
Chronicon Boguphali Episcopi, I. 32
Chrysanthus, martyr, I. 74
Chrysoloras, Manuel, grammar of, III. 14
Chrysostom, St John, I. 154; II. 365; III. 4, 431; IV. 235, 265, 325, 411; VII. 304; VIII. 449; XII. 266, 501; Eton edition of his works, VII. 312
Chrystal, George, XII. 470
Chubb, Thomas (1679–1747), IX. 288, 294, 504; X. 521
Chudleigh, Devon, IV. 418
Chudleigh, James (d. 1643), VII. 348
Chudleigh, John (*fl.* 1650), VII. 31
Church, Frederick John (1854–1888), XII. 455
Church, Mary C., XII. 455
Church, Nathanael, *Cheap Riches,* 1654, VII. 517
Church, Richard William (1815–1890), XII. 255, 261, 271 ff. (main entry), 319, 453 ff., 459, 460; XIV. 113, 486, 501; on Anselm, I. 164; VII. 210; *The Oxford Movement,* XII. 256, 265, 272
Church, Holy, in *Piers the Plowman,* II. 2, 6 ff., 11, 17, 32
Church, The Last Age of the, II. 49
Church Missionary society, the, XII. 471
Church of England Quarterly Review, The, XII. 491
Church of Evil Men and Women, The, II. 324

Churchill, Awnsham, XI. 323
Churchill, Charles (1731–1764), X. 40,
  207, 393 ff., 522, 524; XI. 34, 42, 78, 82,
  246, 450
    Apology, The, X. 395
    Author, The, X. 397
    Bard, The, X. 394
    Candidate, The, X. 397
    Conclave, The, X. 394
    Conference, The, X. 397
    Duellist, The, X. 396, 397
    Epistle to William Hogarth, X. 396, 398
    Farewell, The, X. 397
    Ghost, The, V. 273; X. 179, 397
    Gotham, X. 397
    Independence, X. 397, 398
    Journey, The, X. 397
    Night, X. 395
    Prophecy of Famine, The, X. 394, 396,
      398
    Rosciad, The, X. 394, 395, 398
    Times, The, X. 397
Churchill, G. B., V. 82
Churchill, Henrietta, duchess of Marl-
  borough, wife of Francis Godolphin,
  VIII. 159; IX. 82
Churchill, J., collection of voyages, IV. 103
Churchill, John (publisher), XI. 323
Churchill, John, 1st duke of Marlborough
  (1650–1722), VIII. 220; IX. 44, 94, 96,
  124, 130, 134, 139, 174, 200, 206, 217,
  218, 261, 336, 435, 494; X. 502; XIV. 65
Churchill, lord Randolph (1849–1894),
  XIV. 509
Churchill, Sarah (born Jennings), duchess
  of Marlborough (1660–1744), VIII. 208;
  IX. 82, 98, 130, 185, 217, 218, 220; X. 465
Churchill, Winston Spencer, XIV. 509
Churchyard, Thomas (1520?–1604), III.
  114, 182, 183, 189, 197, 198, 201, 506;
  IV. 114, 322, 411, 434, 456
    Churchyardes Chippes, III. 182
    Myrrour of man, The, III. 182; XII. 357,
      515
    Ovid's De Tristibus, IV. 20, 439
    Praise of Poetrie, The, III. 183
    Shore's Wife, in *A Mirror for Magis-
      trates,* III. 182, 198; IV. 134; VI. 90
    Sieges of Leith and Edinburgh, de-
      scriptions of, III. 182
    *Warres, A Generall Rehearsall of (Church-
      yard's Choise),* III. 182
    Wofull Warres in Flaunders, The, III.
      182
    Worthines of Wales, The, III. 183
Churne, William, XI. 374
Churton, Edward, *Life of Joshua Watson,*
  XII. 256
Chusi, in *Absalom,* VI. 296
Chuzzlewit, Jonas, Dickens's, XIII. 317,
  322
Chuzzlewit, Martin, Dickens's, XIII. 322
Cibber, Colley (1671–1757), VIII. 146, 151,
  152, 159, 166, 189, 426, 431; IX. 86,
  88, 89, 449; X. 21, 39, 67, 68, 81, 92,
  216, 425, 428, 442

Cibber, Colley
  An Apology for his Life, VIII. 177, 179;
    IX. 143
  Apology, X. 24, 70, 71
  Careless Husband, VIII. 168; X. 72
  Hamlet, XI. 258
  Love's Last Shift, VIII. 160, 176; XI. 321
  Non-Juror, X. 89
  Richard III, V. 298
  She Would and She Would Not, VIII. 132
Cibber, Susannah Maria, VIII. 191; X. 264;
  XI. 260
Cibber, Theophilus (1703–1758), VIII. 422;
  IX. 480; X. 24, 85, 444, 445; *Lives of the
    Poets,* X. 77, 184
Ciccotti-D'Errico, Ernestina, XIII. Add. 2
Cicero, M. Tullius (Tully), I. 76, 100, 185,
  187; II. 359, 360, 363; III. 20, 23, 24,
  90, 92, 157, 180, 187, 345, 416, 424, 429;
  IV. 255, 260, 322, 342, 435, 436, 470,
  525; V. 123; VI. 406; VII. 131, 261, 313,
  390, 392; VIII. 273, 278, 282; IX. 28,
  54, 55, 204, 218, 229, 334, 337, 340,
  418, 527, 528; X. 159, 197, 319, 509,
  510; XI. 2, 30, 31; XII. 230, 326, 338,
  476, 479, 483, 485, 487, 492 ff., *also see*
  Add.; XIV. 303
    De Amicitia, II. 308; III. 345; IV. 5, 264
    De Natura Deorum, III. 345
    De Officiis, III. 180; IV. 5, 6, 24; IX. 274,
      525, 526; XII. 332
    De Oratore, XI. 13; XII. 335, 337
    De Senectute, IV. 5; VII. 61
    In Verrem, XI. 16, 17, 274
    Letters, III. 67, 429; VII. 315
    Life and Letters, XII. 306
    Pro Milone, II. 331
    Second Philippic, XII. 336
    Speeches against Catiline, XII. 337
    Tusculan Questions, IV. 5
Cicero, Don, in *The Pilgrimage to Parnassus,*
  VI. 310
Cicero, in *Catiline,* VI. 19, 20
Cicero, translators of, IV. 5
Ciceronian manner, the, XIV. 121
Cid, The, II. 412; XI. 422
Cieza, Peter de, IX. 501
Cigarette, in *Under Two Flags,* XIII. 436
Cincinnati, XIV. 165
Cinderella, XI. 380
Cino da Pistoia, XIII. 118
Cinqbars, lord, Thackeray's, XIII. 280
Cinque ports, IV. 84; IX. 536
Cinque ports, barons of the, XI. 282
Cinric, I. 236
Cinthio, Giambattista Giraldi, IV. 443;
  V. 63, 65, 220, 221, 409; VI. 139, 199;
  Hecatommithi, V. 119, 137, 138; *Orecche,*
  V. 62
Cintra convention, the, XIV. 187
Cinus of Pistoja (d. 1336), II. 363
Cipriano, in Calderon's *El Magico Pro-
  digioso,* XIII. 144
Circe, VII. 370
Circle of the Sciences, XI. 367, 376
Circumcision, feast of, V. 8

Circumlocution office, the, in *Little Dorrit*, XIII. 331

Cirencester, VI. 237; VIII. 106

Cirencester, Richard of (d. 1401?), XII. 366

Cis, the shoemaker's wife, in *Piers the Plowman*, II. 16

Cistercian nuns, II. 45

Cistercians, I. 189; II. 351; III. 51

Citherea, palace of, in *The Court of Love*, II. 220

Citizen of the World, Letters from a, X. 53, 171, 199, 206, 207, 209, 229

City Dames Petition, The, VII. 382

City of Prague, The. See Prowse, W. J.

Civil (Civil Law), in *Piers the Plowman*, II. 7

Civil war, the, III. 87, 114; IV. 55, 156, 342, 363; XIV. 57, 59, 87

Civil war pamphlets and broadsides, VII. 512, 514, 515; XI. 470

Civis, in *A Dialogue...against the fever Pestilence*, III. 109

Civyle and uncivyle life, On, V. 349

Clack, Miss, Wilkie Collins's, XIII. 438

Clack the miller, in *The Devil and his Dame*, V. 329

Claire, in Rousseau's *La Nouvelle Héloïse*, X. 17

Clairmont, Allegra, XII. 37

Clairmont, Clara Mary Jane (1798–1879), XII. 37, 401

Clairmont, Mary Jane. *See* Godwin, Mrs

Clairon, Mlle, X. 264

Clanvowe, Sir Thomas, *The Cuckoo and the Nightingale*, II. 162, 164, 166, 215 ff.

Clapham, VIII. 258

Clapham, John Harold, XIII. 545

'Clapham sect,' the, XII. 281; XIV. 110

Clapp, H. A., XIII. 514

Clapperton, *In Bowdin on Blak Monanday*, III. 132

Clara, in Bailey's *Festus*, XIII. 153

Clara, in *The Scowrers*, IX. 362

Clara, in Scott's *Marmion*, XII. 11

Clara, Sta., XII. 260

Clarange, in *The Lovers Progress*, VI. 131

Clare. *See* Osbert de

Clare, Allan, in Lamb's *Rosamund Gray*, XII. 185, 186

Clare, Elinor, in Lamb's *Rosamund Gray*, XII. 186

Clare, Elizabeth de (1291?–1360), II. 354

Clare, in Mrs Gaskell's *Wives and Daughters*, XIII. 381

Clare, John (1793–1864), XII. 131, 134, 415; *The Last of March*, XII. 132

Clare, Robert Nugent. *See* Nugent, Robert, earl Nugent

Clarence, George, duke of (1444–1478), III. 334

Clarence, George, duke of, in *Richard III*, V. 186

Clarence, Reginald, XIII. 516

Clarendon, Constitutions of, I. 337

Clarendon, earls of. *See* Hyde, Edward; Villiers, George W. F.

Clarendon commission (Public Schools), XIV. 413, 421, 422

Clarges, Sir Thomas (d. 1695), VII. 362, 363

Clarice, in *Piers the Plowman*, II. 16

Clarinda. *See* Maclehose, Mrs Agnes (1759–1841)

Clariodus, I. 291, 467

Clarissa, in *Loves Crueltie*, VI. 199

Clarissa, in Richardson's novel, X. 2, 7 ff., 17; XIII. 288

Clarissa, in *The Tatler*, IX. 50

Clark, Andrew, IX. 346; *Life of Anthony Wood*, IX. 341, 382, 383, 413, 541

Clark, George Thomas (1809–1898), XII. 508; *Mediaeval Military Architecture in England*, XII. 349

Clark, Mrs Godfrey, XI. 348

Clark, James (d. 1724), IX. 546

Clark, John (*fl.* 1759), VIII. 62

Clark, John (d. 1807), X. 471

Clark, John, XIV. Add. 4

Clark, J. S., *Life of James the Second*, IX. 213

Clark, John Willis (1833–1910), XII. 508; XIV. 539, 563; *The Care of Books*, XII. 348

Clark, William (*fl.* 1685), IX. 556

Clark, William George (1821–1878), V. 280; XIV. 516; *Peloponnesus*, XII. 331

Clarke, Abraham, VII. 107

Clarke, Adam (1762?–1832), XII. 491, 520; XIV. 567

Clarke, Charles (1787–1877) and Mary Cowden (1809–1898), XI. 437; XII. 79, 406, 437, 444; *and see* Clarke, Mary Cowden

Clarke, Sir Edward, XIII. 543

Clarke, Edward Daniel (1769–1822), XII. 484, 491; XIV. 241, 551; *Travels*, XIV. 247

Clarke, Sir Ernest, VIII. 28; X. Add.

Clarke, Sir G. S., XIV. 491

Clarke, Helen A., XIII. 479

Clarke, Henry Butler (1863–1904), XIV. 486

Clarke, Herbert Edwin, XIII. 500
  By the Washes, XIII. 216
  Chant d'Amour, XIII. 216
  Failure, XIII. 216
  Nocturn at Twilight, A, XIII. 216
  Poems and Sonnets, XIII. 215
  Poems in Exile, XIII. 215
  Storm-Drift, XIII. 215
  Tannhäuser and other Poems, XIII. 215
  Voluntary, A, XIII. 216

Clarke, Hyde (b. 1815), XII. 508

Clarke, John, *Paroemiologia* (1639), VII. 479

Clarke, John (1682–1757), IX. 505

Clarke, John (1687–1734), IX. 568

Clarke, John (d. 1730), IX. 505

Clarke, John, XIV. 604

Clarke, Joseph (d. 1749), IX. 505

Clarke, J. S., X. 295, 454; XII. 232

Clarke, Marcus Andrew Hislop (1846–1881), XIV. 367, 585; *His Natural Life*, XIV. 370; *Long Odds* (*Heavy Odds*), XIV. 370

Clarke, Mary Cowden (1809–1898), XI. 485

Clarke, Matthew (1664–1726), X. 386

Clarke, Samuel (1599–1683), VII. 479, 484

Clarke, Samuel (1625–1669), VII. 319

Clarke, Samuel (1675–1729), VIII. 473; IX. 279, 281, 289, 293, 294, 296, 297 ff. (main entry), 394, 505, 507; X. 345; XI. 481; XIV. 37

　Being and Attributes of God, IX. 292, 297

　Boyle Lectures, IX. 297, 298

　Discourse concerning...Natural Religion, IX. 297

　Lives, VIII. 278

　Scripture Doctrine of the Trinity, IX. 297; X. 359, 379

Clarke, T. E. S., *Life of Gilbert Burnet*, IX. 202

Clarke papers at Worcester college, Oxford, VII. 347, 435, 438

Clarkson, Laurence (1615–1667), VII. 509

Clarkson, Mrs, XI. 121

Clarkson, Thomas (1760–1846), XIV. 373, 486

Classus, in *The Scourge of Folly*, IV. 334

Claude, in Kingsley's *Two Years Ago*, XIII. 365

Claude de Pontoux, III. 258, 263; *L'Idée*, III. 263

Claude Lorraine, XII. 172, 173

Claudia, in *Gismond of Salerne*, V. 75

Claudian, I. 68; IV. 250, 417, 436

Claudio, in *Measure for Measure*, I. 1

Claudio, in *Much Ado about Nothing*, XIII. 262

Claudius, in *Hamlet*, V. 200 ff., 211

Claus, P., XIV. 524

Clavell, John (1603–1642), IV. 530

Clavell, Robert (d. 1711), XI. 339, 471

Claverhouse, John Graham of. *See* Graham, John, viscount Dundee

Clavering, in *Pendennis*, XIII. 276, 291

Clavering, Mary. *See* Cowper, countess

Claverton, X. 276

Clavis Apocalyptica, VIII. 286

Clavius, C., VII. 320

Clay, James (1805–1873), V. 173

Clay, Mrs, in Jane Austen's *Persuasion*, XII. 240

Clay, William F., XIV. 557

Claypole, Noah, in *Oliver Twist*, XIII. 317

Clayton, J., VIII. 468

'Clean contrary way, The,' VIII. 96

Cleanness, I. 320 ff., 343, 472

Cleanness, lady, in *The Example of Virtue*, II. 227, 234

Cleges, Sir, I. 315, 470

Cleland, J.. *The Institution of a Nobleman*, III. 437

Cleland, William (1661?–1689), VIII. 408; IX. 556

Clem, in *The Fair Maid Of The West*, VI. 102

Clemens, S. L. *See* Twain, **Mark**

Clement IV, pope, I. 206

Clement VI, pope, V. 13

Clement VII, pope, II. 56

Clement VIII, pope, III. 415

Clement, Gregory (d. 1660), VIII. 470

Clement, Justice, in *Every Man in His Humour*, V. 350

Clément, Nicolas, V. 285

Clement, saint, XII. 266, 340

Clement, William Innell (d. 1852), XIV. 228, 235

Clement of Alexandria, III. 409, 416

Clement of Llanthony (d. 1190?), *Harmony of the Gospels*, II. 60

Clement of Rome, I. 74, 118; XII. 501; *Recognitions of*, I. 75

Clementina, in Richardson's *Sir Charles Grandison*, X. 10

Clementines, II. 364

Clenard, Nicholas, III. 429

Clene Maidenhod, II. 503

Clennan family, in *Little Dorrit*, XIII. 331

Clennell, Luke (1781–1840), XIV. 227

Cleobulus, in *Argenis*, IV. 259

Cleobury Mortimer, II. 2

Cléomadès, French romance, II. 184

Cleopatra, I. 95; II. 177; VIII. 216

Cleopatra, in *Antony and Cleopatra*, V. 180, 183, 199, 213, 214; VI. 72, 273

Cleora, in *The Bond-man*, VI. 154, 155, 157, 158

Clephane, Dr John (d. 1758), X. 284

Clergy (Learning), in *Piers the Plowman*, II. 20, 21, 27

Clerical subscription act, XII. 296

Clericus and Puella, dialogue between, I. 365; V. 25, 55, 91

Clerimont, in Steele's *Tender Husband*, IX. 30

Clerk, John, II. 274

Clerk, Sir John, of Penicuik (1684–1755), IX. 553; XII. 350; *Merry may the Maid*, IX. 371

Clerk Colvill, II. 413

Clerk Saunders, II. 413

Clerk of Tranent, II. 122

Clerke, Agnes Mary, XIV. 265, 555

Clerke, Gilbert (1626–1697?), X. 359, 377

Clerke, Henry (d. 1687), VIII. 358

Clerkenwell News, The, XIV. 193

Clerk-Maxwell, James (1831–1879), XIV. 261, 265, 266, 268 ff., 556

Clerselius, VIII. 455

Cléry, Jean Baptiste, XIV. 66

Cleveland, Yorkshire, XI. 174

Cleveland, or Cleiveland, John (1613–1658), IV. 342, 522; VII. 73, 85, 88, 91 ff., 111, 356, 412, 495, 496, 502, 513, 516 ff.; VIII. 80, 88, 91

　Character of a London Diurnall, VII. 348, 384

　Mark Antony, VII. 93; VIII. 231

　Mercurius Politicus, Character of, VII. 358

Cleveland, or Cleiveland, John
 Mercurius Politicus, The Second Cha-
  racter of, VII. 353
 Mixed Assembly, The, VII. 92
 Rebel Scot, The, VII. 92
 Square-Cap, VIII. 231
Cleveland, duchess of. *See* Villiers, Bar-
 bara
Clèves, la princesse de, XII. 381
Cliefdon. *See* Cliveden
Clifford, lady Anne (1590–1676), IV. 132,
 133, 138
Clifford, Arthur (1778–1830), XII. 376
Clifford, Christopher, IV. 368; *The Schoole
 of Horsemanship*, IV 369, 540
Clifford, George, 3rd earl of Cumberland
 (1558–1605), IV. 455
Clifford, Margaret, countess of Cumber-
 land, IV. 132, 133
Clifford, Martin (d. 1677), VIII. 23, 25,
 26, 48, 402, 404
Clifford, Paul, lord Lytton's, XIII. 418
Clifford, Thos. (1630–1673), VIII. 380
Clifford, William Kingdon (1845–1879),
 XIV. 34, 470, 556
Clifford, in Burgoyne's *Heiress*, XI. 275,
 276
Clifford, in *Henry VI*, v. 186
Clifford Chambers, near Evesham, IV.
 174
Clifton, Henry (*fl.* 1587–1600), VI. 290,
 291
Clifton, Thomas (b. 1587), VI. 290, 291
Climenson, Emily J., *Elizabeth Montagu*,
 XI. 328
Clincher, in Farquhar's *The Constant
 Couple*, VIII. 169, 170
Clinker, Humphrey, in Smollett's novel,
 X. 43
Clinton, Henry Fiennes, 9th earl of Lin-
 coln (1720–1794), X. 244
Clinton, Henry Fynes (1781–1852), XII.
 496; *Fasti Hellenici*, XII. 310, 339; *Fasti
 Romani*, XII. 310, 339
Clinton, H. P. F. Pelham, 5th duke of
 Newcastle (1811–1864), XIV. 510
Clinton, Mr, in Brooke's *Fool of Quality*,
 IX. 327, 328
Clinton (pirate), in *Fortune by Land and
 Sea*, VI. 104
Clio, XII. 136
Clisthenes, XII. 313
Clithero, Yorks., XII. 514
Clive, Caroline Archer, 'V' (1801–1873),
 XII. 448; XIII. 180, 500, 561
 Death, XIII. 176
 Heart's Ease, XIII. 176
 I watched the Heavens, XIII. 176
 Paul Ferroll, XIII. 175, 437
 Valley of the Morlas, The, XIII. 176
 Venice, XIII. 176
 Why Paul Ferroll killed his Wife, XIII.
 176
 IX Poems by V, XIII. 176
Clive, Catherine (1711–1785), X. 22, 254,
 264, 439; XI. 257

Clive, Robert Clive, lord (1725–1774), XIV.
 63, 578
Cliveden, X. 108, 109
Clodd, Edward, XIII. 569
Cloe, in *The Faithfull Shepherdesse*, VI. 368
Cloete, Henry, XIV. Add. 6
Clogher, IX. 166
Clogy, or Clogie, Alexander (1614–1698),
 VII. 442
Clokyd Colusyon, in *Magnyfycence*, III. 77
Cloncurry, lord, XIV. 324
Clongowes college, XIV. 316
Clonmacnoise, XIV. 312
'Clootie,' II. 409; XI. 212
Clorin, in *The Faithfull Shepheardesse*,
 VI. 368
Clorinda, in *Orlando Furioso*, III. 230
Cloris, in *The Queenes Arcadia*, VI. 317, 318
Close, Francis (1797–1882), XII. 472; XIV.
 590, 598
Close, John (1816–1891), XIII. 500
Close Rolls, XII. 355, 516
Closet, A, for ladies and gentlewomen,
 IV. 543
Cloten, in Layamon, I. 237
Cloth-Breeches, in *A Quip for an Upstart
 Courtier*, III. 361
Clough, Arthur Hugh (1819–1861), XI.
 409; XII. 255, 293; XIII. 87, 91, 102 ff.
 (main entry), 174, 245 ff., 488, 489
 (main entry)
 Ambarvalia, XIII. 104
 Amours de Voyage, XIII. 104
 Bothie of Tober-na-Vuolich, The, XIII
 103 ff.
 Dipsychus, XIII. 104, 105
 Duty, XIII. 104
 Higher Courage, The, XIII. 104
 Mari Magno, XIII. 104, 105
 New Sinai, The, XIII. 104
 Prose Remains, XIII. 91
 Qua Cursum Ventus, XIII. 104
 Questioning Spirit, The, XIII. 104
 Qui Laborat Orat, XIII. 104
 Say not the struggle nought availeth, XIII.
 106
 Sic Itur, XIII. 104
 Songs in Absence, XIII. 104, 106
Clough, Blanche Athena, XIII. 103; XIV.
 599
Clouston, W. A., II. 216
Clove, in *Every Man out of His Humour*,
 VI. 225
Clovesho, synod of, I. 50
Clovis, I. 20, 21; XIV. 68
Clowes, Alice A., XIV. 613
Clowes, John, VII. 352
Clowes, Sir William Laird (1856–1905),
 XIV. 486
Clown, the, in a broadside, III. 87
Cloyne, IX. 166
'Club, The,' X. 181, 187, 192, 207, 212,
 214, 260, 261, 264
Club-Law, VI. 307, 308, 313, 315, 327, 483
Clubs, Varlet of, in *Terminus et non Ter-
 minus*, VI. 307

Clumsey, Sir Tunbelly, in Vanbrugh's *The Relapse*, VIII. 161, 162
Cluniac order, the, IV. 419
Clust, son of Clustveinad, I. 255
Clustveinad, I. 255
Clutterbuck, Robert (1772–1831), XII. 509
Clutton-Brock, Arthur, XIII. 493, 572
Cluverius, Philippus, VII. 307; X. 305
Clwyd, vale of, 115
Clyde, the, II. 89
Clytemnestra, in *Agamemnon*, V. 79
Clytemnestra, in Thomson's *Agamemnon*, X. 108
Clytemnestra, in *Horestes*, V. 64, 65
Clytophon, VI. 483
Cnidos, XII. 339
Cnitthon. *See* Knighton
Cnossos, palace of, XII. 339
Cobalt, Canada, XIV. 356
Cobb, James (1756–1818), XI. 281, 456
Cobbe, Frances Power (1822–1904), XIV. 470, 517, 599
Cobbes Prophecies, IV. 534
Cobbett, William (1762–1835), I. 370; XI. 49 ff., 393; XII. 170, 179; XIV. 125, 137, 197, 202, 461; *Political Register*, XI. 49; XIV. 197; *Rural Rides*, XI. 51; *State Trials*, XI. 49
Cobbold, Thomas Spencer (1828–1886), XIV. 301
Cobden, Richard (1804–1865), XIV. 78, 131–132 (main entry), 137, 173, 179, 181, 190, 509, 512
Cobet, Carel Gabriel, XII. 330
Cobham, Eleanor, duchess of Gloucester (d. 1446?), IV. 182
Cobham, lady, X. 126
Cobham, lord. *See* Brooke, William
Cobham, lord. *See* Oldcastle, Sir John
Cobham, Thomas de (d. 1327), IV. 430
Cobham, viscount. *See* Temple, Sir Richard
Cobler of Canterburie, The, IV. 362, 521, 523, 531
Coburg, house of, IX. 338; XII. 232
Cocai, Merlin (Teofilo Folengo), *Baldus*, VIII. 59
Cochrane, John George (1781–1852), XII. 378
Cochrane, Thomas, 10th earl of Dundonald (1775–1860), XIV. 502, 552
Cock and the Jewel, in Henryson's *Fables*, II. 246
Cock lane ghost, X. 179, 206, 465, 481
Cock Lawrel (tune), VIII. 96
Cock up your Bonnet, IX. 377
Cockayne, Oswald, I. 105, 135, 136
Cockayne, or Cokayne, Thomas (1587–1638), VII. 316
Cockburn, Sir Alexander J. E. Cockburn, lord (1802–1880), XIV. 124, 509, 513
Cockburn, Alison (1712?–1794), XI. 231, 232; 'I have seen the Smiling,' IX. 373
Cockburn, Mrs Catherine (born Trotter) (1679–1749), VIII. 347, 435, 473

Cockburn, Henry Thomas Cockburn, lord (1779–1854), XII. 426; XIV. 501
    Journal, X. 324
    Life of Jeffrey, X. 188
    Memorials of His Time, XIV. 112
    'Scottish Criminal Jurisprudence,' XII. 153, 378
Cockburn, John (1652–1729), IX. 520, 551
Cocke, J., IV. 339, 518
Cocke Lorell's bote, III. 61, 83 ff., 482; IV. 362, 521, 529
Cocker, Edmund (*fl.* 1664), VIII. 256
Cockeram, Henry (*fl.* 1650), IX. 529
Cockeram, Richard (*fl.* 1468–1482), IV. 432
Cockerell, Sydney Carlyle, XIII. 491, 493
Cockerell, Thomas, XI. 332
Cockermouth, XI. 94
Cockledemoy, in *The Dutch Courtezan*, VI. 46
Cocklorrel's song, in *The Masque of the Metamorphos'd Gypsies*, VI. 362
Cockney school of poetry, XII. 157, 160
Cockshutt of the Inner Temple, friend of Henry More, VIII. 456
Cockton, Henry (1807–1853), XII. 448
Cockwood, lady (Etherege's), VIII. 138
Codex Alexandrinus, XII. 501
Codex Augiensis, the, XII. 501
Codex Bezae, the, XII. 501
Codex Galeanus, XII. 325, 491
Codlin and Short, in *The Old Curiosity Shop*, XIII. 319
Codlo, Antonio, *Los Empeños de Seis Horas*, VIII. 130
Codronchus, IV. 247
Codrus, in Juvenal's *Third Satire*, VIII. 89
Codrus, in *Misogonus*, V. 111
Coelia, in *The Faerie Queene*, VI. 335
Coelum, in *Lingua*, VI. 315
Coffee (1727), IX. 434
Coffee, A Brief Description of the Excellent Virtues o' that sober and wholesome drink called, VII. 389, 390
Coffee, A Cup of, VII. 389
Coffee pamphlets, VII. 516
Coffee-House Dialogue, A, VII. 390; IX. 32
Coffee-house, News from the, VII. 389
Coffee-house, Rules and Orders of the, VII. 390
Coffee-houses, VII. 389
Coffee-houses Vindicated, The, VII. 389
Coffee-Scuffle, The, VII. 390; IX. 32
Coffey, Charles (d. 1745), X. 439; XIV. 567; *The Beggar's Wedding*, XI. 218
Coffin, Robert Aston (1819–1885), XII. 460
Coffin for King Charles, A, VII. 381
Cogan, Thomas (1545?–1607), VII. 486, 488
Coggeshall. *See* Ralph of
Coghill, Mrs Harry, XIII. 565
Coghlan, C. H., *A Quiet Rubber*, XIII. 525
Cohen, Francis. *See* Palgrave, Sir Francis
Cohen, H. T., XIV. 509
Coignet, Matthieu, IV. 443
Coillard, François, XIV. Add. 6
Coimbra, III. 162
Cokaygne. See Land of

Cokayne or Cokain, Sir Aston (1608–1684), VI. 114, 142, 144, 145; VIII. 417

Cokayne, Sir Thomas (1519?–1592), IV. 541

Coke, Sir Edward, lord Coke or Cooke (1552–1634), III. 424; IV. 265; V. 367; VIII. 309, 312 ff., 321, 465, 466, 468; *Institutes*, VIII. 317, 320; *Law Reports*, VIII. 316, 317; *The Lord Coke his Speech & charge*, VI. 400, 492

Coke, Thomas (1747–1814), X. 518

Cokes, a booby, in *Bartholomew Fayre*, VI. 23

Coketown, in Dickens's *Hard Times*, XIII. 330

Cokwold's Daunce, The, I. 464; II. 501

Colax, in *The Queenes Arcadia*, VI. 317

Colbrand, in *Guy of Warwick*, I. 304 ff., 343

Colburn, Henry (d. 1855), XII. 161, 200

Colburne, V. 108

Colby and Mrs Colby, in *Club Law*, VI. 308

Colchester, II. 208; III. 428; VII. 82; VIII. 101, 363; IX. 537

Colchester, lord. *See* Abbot, Charles

Coldicott, H. R. S., 'How Cowper got his pension,' XI. 90

Cole, Alfred Whaley, XIV. Add. 6

Cole, Charles Nelson (1723–1804), IX. 533

Cole, Sir Henry ('Felix Summerly,' 1808–1882), XI. 462, 478; *The Home Treasury*, XI. 386

Cole, John (1792–1848), XI. 474

Cole, John William, XIII. 514

Cole, Thomas (d. 1571), IV. 491

Cole, Thomas (1627?–1697), X. 385

Cole, William, *A Rod for the Lawyers* (1659), VII. 515

Cole, William (1714–1782), IX. 354, 532; X. 249, 255, 495

Colebrooke, E., XIV. 576

Colebrooke, Henry Thomas (1765–1837), XII. 502; XIV. 335; *Essays on Sanskrit literature*, XII. 343

Coleman, Edward (d. 1669), VIII. 117

Coleman, John, XIII. 514, 566

Coleman, Mrs (*fl.* 1656), VIII. 118

Coleman, Thomas (1598–1647), IX. 544

Colenso, Durnford E., XIV. Add. 6

Colenso, Frances, Ellen (1849–1887), XIV. Add. 6

Colenso, John William (1814–1883), bishop of Natal, XII. 296, 297, 314, 465, 474; XIV. Add. 6

Coleorton, XI. 410, 416, 423; XII. 376

Colepeper, John, 1st baron (d. 1660), VII. 218

Coleridge, Derwent (1800–1883), XI. 412, 415, 417; XII. 415, 421; XIII. 355

Coleridge, Ernest Hartley, XI. 412, 416; XII. 385, 388; *also see* Add. 1

Coleridge, Hartley (1796–1849), XI. 127, 162, 417; *also see* Add.; XII. 104, 107–108 (main entry), 124, 127, 415; XIII. 183
  Homer, XII. 108
  Medley, A, XII. 108

Coleridge, Hartley
  Poietes Apoietes, XII. 108
  Prayer, XII. 108
  Prometheus, XII. 107
  Shakespeare, XII. 108
  Youth, XII. 108

Coleridge, Henry Nelson (1798–1843), XI. 405, 415, 417

Coleridge, Sir John Duke, 1st lord (1820–1894), XIV. 596

Coleridge, Sir John Taylor (1790–1876), XII. 153, 429, 457; XIII. 504

Coleridge, Mary Elizabeth (1861–1907), XIII. 182 ff., 197, 198, 500, 501
  Day-dream, A, XIII. 184
  Difference, A, XIII. 184
  He came unto His Own, XIII. 184
  On the Arrival of a Visitor, XIII. 184
  Other Side of a Mirror, The, XIII. 184
  Unwelcome, XIII. 183
  Witch, The, XIII. 184

Coleridge, Samuel Taylor (1772–1834), I. 148, 376; II. 186, 190, 205; III. 465; IV. 43, 46, 50, 236, 241, 259, 260; V. 209, 222, 270, 304; VI. 23, 129, 131; VII. 163, 236, 247; VIII. 298; IX. 106, 277, 328; X. 137, 186, 316, 526; XI. 28, 71, 99 ff., 104, 112, 113, 117 ff. (main entry), 150, 154 ff., 162, 163, 168, 171, 172, 178, 201, 202, 250, 294, 305, 308, 309, 341, 405, 407, 409, 411, 412, 421, 423, 468; XII. 39, 48, 57 ff., 77, 78, 93, 95, 101, 107, 120, 147, 158, 159, 166, 169, 170, 175, 176, 178, 180 ff., 187, 188, 191, 196, 197, 201, 203, 205, 211, 218, 219, 223, 255, 280, 282–283, 289, 399, 402, 405, 434, 436, 445, 465, 471, 527, *and see* Add. 1; XIII. 7 ff., 18, 23 ff., 40, 46, 52, 57, 86, 148, 183, 196, 198, 225, 230 ff., 241, 243 ff., 258 ff., 276, 312, 318, 420, 442; XIV. 1, 8, 15, 16, 40, 138, 144, 146, 170, 177, 180, 275, 373, 374, 471, 518, 560
  Aids to Reflexion, IX. 328; XI. 138; XII. 283
  Ancient Mariner, X. 217, 234; XI. 101, 120, 123 ff., 130, 132, 160, 169, 170, 201; XII. 71, 108, 110, 113, 124, 133; XIII. 231, 233, 244, 324; XIV. 255
  Anima Poetæ, XI. 129, 130
  Biographia Literaria, IX. 328; XI. 122, 123, 126, 133, 135 ff., 176, 304; XII. 157; XIV. 184, 403
  Christabel, III. 286; X. 236; XI. 120, 126 ff., 131, 132, 169, 170, 200, 201; XII. 7, 8, 46, 62, 71, 87, 108; XIII. 184, 228, 231, 233, 244
  Collection of Political Tracts, IX. 223
  Conciones ad populum, XI. 138
  Confessions of an Enquiring Spirit, XII. 282, 283, 288
  Constitution of Church and State, XI. 138
  Dejection, XI. 104, 120, 123, 129, 130
  Devil's Thoughts, The, XIV. 184
  Eolian Harp, XI. 119
  Essays on his own Times, XI. 139; XIV. 184

Coleridge, Samuel Taylor
 Fall of Robespierre, XI. 161
 Fears in Solitude, XI. 115
 Friend, The, XI. 122, 138, 139
 Kubla Khan, X. 153; XI. 120, 124, 125,
  169; XII. 59, 108
 Lay Sermons, XI. 139
 Letters, XI. 122, 131, 139
 Lyrical Ballads, X. 217; XI. 86, 101, 123,
  150, 151; XII. 40, 42
 Nightingale, The, XI. 129
 Ode to France, XI. 115
 Ode to the Departing Year, XI. 124
 Poems (Oct. 1797), XII. 184
 Poems on Various Subjects, XII. 183
 Preliminary Treatise on Method, XI. 133
 Religious Musings, XI. 124; XII. 183
 Sibylline Leaves, XI. 119
 Spiritual Philosophy, XI. 121
 Statesman's Manual, XI. 139
 Table Talk, IV. 139; XI. 131
 This lime-tree bower, my prison, XI. 129
 Three Graves, The, XI. 132
 Wallenstein (trans.), XIII. 260
 Watchman, The, XI. 138
Coleridge, Mrs Sara (1802–1852), born
  Fricker, XI. 119, 412, 415, 417; *also see*
  Add.; XII. 124, 128, 415; XIII. 183
 Envoy, XII. 127
 False Love, too long thou hast delayed,
  XII. 127
 One face alone, XII. 127
 Phantasmion, XII. 127
Coles, Francis (*fl.* 1626–1681), VII. 347
Coleshill, VII. 53
Colet, John (1467?–1519), II. 48, 61, 341,
  367, 489; III. 1, 3, 4, 6, 8–13 (main
  entry), 15, 17, 18, 26, 66, 428, 466;
  IV. 224, 225, 227, 228, 491; VII. 332 ff.;
  IX. 529; *An Exposition of St Paul's
  First Epistle to the Corinthians*, III. 11;
  *An Exposition of St Paul's Epistle to
  the Romans*, III. 11; lectures on the
  Epistle to the Romans, III. 10
Colet, John (d. 1637), XIV. 79
Colgan, John (d. 1657?), XIV. 308, *also
  see* Add. 3
Colgrim, in Layamon, I. 237
Colin, in *The Shepheards Calender*, III. 222,
  224, 226, 228. *See, also, under* Spenser
Colin (or *Colyn*) *Blowbol's Testament*, II.
  501; III. 84, 86, 483
Colkelbeis Feist, II. 277
Colkelbie, Stewarton, Ayrshire, in *Col-
  kelbie's sow*, II. 126, 127
Colkelbie's sow, II. 126, 127
Collatinus, in *The Rape of Lucrece*, VI. 101
Collbrande (Excalibur), in *Morte Arthure*,
  II. 119
*Collection of Fundamental Liberties and
  Laws*, VIII. 319
*Collection of Original Poems, by the Rev.
  Mr Blacklock and other Scottish Gentle-
  men*, X. 191
College, Stephen (1635?–1681), VIII. 36,
  97, 188

College of Arms, IX. 344, 355
Colles, H. Cresswell, IV. 111
Collet, Collet Dobson, XIV. 590
Collet, Mary, IV. 406; VII. 154
Collett, John (1725?–1780), XIV. 214
Collier, Arthur (1680–1732), IX. 287, 288,
  505; *Clavis Universalis*, IX. 287
Collier, James, XIV. 481
Collier, Jeremy (1650–1726), VI. 408, 492;
  VIII. 33, 52, 54, 145, 146, 157, 164 ff.,
  194, 427, 432 ff.; IX. 29, 141, 142, 210 ff.
  (main entry), 492; X. 70, 72; XI. 282
 Dissuasive from the Playhouse, VIII. 167
 Duelling, IX. 211
 Ecclesiastical History, VIII. 32; IX. 211,
  212
 Essays, IX. 211
 Historical Dictionary, IX. 211, 212
 Of Lying, IX. 211
 Office of a Chaplain, IX. 211
 Short view of the...English Stage, VIII.
  32, 163, 197; IX. 211; X. 67
Collier, John ['Tim Bobbin'] (1708–1786),
  X. 453
Collier, John Payne (1789–1883), V. 10,
  13, 54, 143, 146, 277 ff., 286, 314, 315;
  VI. 33, 50, 89, 249, 281, 398; XI. 133;
  XII. 353, 520
 *Extracts from the Registers of the Sta-
  tioners' Company*, XII. 368
 Notes on Rare English Books, XII. 368
 Roxburghe Ballads, The, XII. 368
 Shakespeare's Library, XII. 368
Collier, Thomas (*fl.* 1691), X. 377
Collier, The Historie of the, V. 329
Collin (i.e. Spenser), IV. 180
Collings, Samuel (*fl.* 1780–1790?), X. 479
Collingtree, X. 365
Collingwood, Ralph, dean of Lichfield, IV.
  225
Collingwood, Stuart Dodgson, XIII. 501
Collingwood, William Gershom, XIV.
  Add. 3
Collins, Anthony (1676–1729), VIII. 332,
  471; IX. 111, 288, 292, 293, 505, 512
 Discourse of Free-thinking, IX. 292, 293,
  337, 456
 Discourse of the...Christian Religion,
  IX. 293
 Essay concerning the use of Reason, IX.
  293
 *Philosophical Inquiry concerning Human
  Liberty*, IX. 293
 Priestcraft in perfection, IX. 293
Collins, Arthur (1690?–1760), VIII. 267;
  IX. 496; X. 500; *Peerage*, XI. 327
Collins, Benjamin (*fl.* 1762), X. 207, 209,
  210, 482
Collins, Charles Allston (1828–1873), XIII.
  326, 332, 561
Collins, Charles MacCarthy, XIV. 573
Collins, F. H., XIV. 481
Collins, John Churton (1848–1908), IV.
  43; V. 133 ff.; VI. 166; IX. 230; X. Add.;
  XII. 504; XIII. 476, 486, 488; XIV. 517,
  518, 594; *Bolingbroke*, IX. 218, 224

Collins, Mortimer (1827–1876), XIII. 500;
  British Birds, The, XIII. 163; *To F. C.*,
  XIII. 163
Collins, Mr, in Jane Austen's *Pride and
  Prejudice*, XII. 234, 238, 240, 243, 245
Collins, Thomas (*fl.* 1615), VII. 406
Collins, William (1721–1759), V. 205; IX.
  167, 169, 179, 191, 481; X. 60, 87, 93, 132,
  138, 142 ff. (main entry), 147, 149, 153,
  156, 164, 183, 186, 230, 447, 453, 454,
  469, *also see* Add.; XI. 77, 86, 124, 158,
  160, 161, 248, 250, 255; XII. 101, 177
  Dirge in Cymbeline, X. 126, 144
  Eclogues, X. 143
  Evening, XII. 124
  'How sleep the brave,' X. 143, 144
  Ode...death of Mr Thomson, X. 109
  Ode to Evening, X. 125, 143, 144, 218;
    XI. 85, 179
  Ode to Liberty, X. 144
  Ode to Simplicity, X. 128
  Odes, X. 142 ff.
  Superstitions of the Highlands, X. 144
Collins, William Edward (1867–1911),
  XIV. 101, 486
Collins, William Lucas, XIV. 597
Collins, William Wilkie (1824–1889), XIII.
  326, 335, 336, 420, 423, 425, 437–438
  (main entry), 538, 541, 542, 561
  Antonina, XIII. 434
  Moonstone, The, XIII. 437
  No Name, XIII. 437
  Woman in White, The, XIII. 437
Collinson, James (1825?–1881), XIII. 110
Collinson, John (1757?–1793), XII. 509
Collis, Ramsay, XIV. 533
Collison-Morley, L., *Giuseppe Baretti*, X.
  159
Collop, John (*fl.* 1660), VII. 88, 412, 465
Collyer, N., XIV. 591
Colman, Francis (d. 1733), X. 430
Colman, George, the elder (1732–1794),
  X. 77, 89 ff., 211, 214, 428 ff., 432, 436,
  441, 474; XI. 78, 270; XIII. 269; XIV.
  590, 594
  Clandestine Marriage, X. 91 ff.
  Connoisseur, The, XI. 448, 451; XIV.
    590, 594
  Deuce is in Him, X. 90
  English Merchant, X. 86
  Jealous Wife, X. 89 ff.
  Man of Business, XI. 265
  Musical Lady, X. 90
  New Brooms, XI. 282
  Philaster, X. 90
  Polly Honeycombe, X. 89
  Ut Pictura Poesis, XI. 282
Colman, George, the younger (1762–1836),
  XI. 276, 278 ff., 453, 455, 457
  Battle of Hexham, XI. 280
  Heir at Law, XI. 280
  Inkle and Yarico, XI. 279
  Iron Chest, The, XI. 280, 393
  John Bull, XI. 280
  Mountaineers, The, XI. 280
  Siege of Paris, XI. 257

Coleman, George, the younger
  Surrender of Calais, XI. 280
  Turk and no Turk, XI. 279
  Two to One, XI. 279
Colne river, VII. 98
Cologne, II. 311, 312, 321; III. 42; IV. 402,
  403; VI. 295; VII. 212; VIII. 261, 262
Cologne, Three Kings of, II. 323, 335, 486,
  503
Colombe, Browning's, XIII. 64
Colomies or Colomesius, Paul (1638–
  1692), VII. 484
Colon, the ostler, in *Hudibras*, VIII. 68
Colonial and Indian Exhibition, XIV. 369
Colonial Monthly, The, XIV. 367
Colonna palace, XII. 67
Colour, in *Lingua*, VI. 315
Colquhoun, Archibald Ross, XIV. Add. 6
Colquhoun, John (1805–1885), XIV. 542
Colquhoun, John Campbell (1803–1870),
  XIV. 605
Colquhoun, Patrick (1745–1820), XIV. 605
Colson, Nathaniel, IV. 454
'Colson, Tom,' in *The Tatler*, IX. 34
Colt, the, in *Mum, Sothsegger*, II. 36
Colton, John (d. 1404), XII. 518
Columba, St (521–597), I. 42, 69, 435;
  XII. 518
Columban, St (543–615), I. 65, 435
Columbus, Christopher, I. 209; IV. 68,
  70–82, 86, 92, 101; VII. 305; X. 289
Columbus, in *Perfidus Hetruscus*, VI. 302
Columella, II. 363; IV. 371
Columne, Jacob, IV. 454
Coluthus, VII. 87
Coluthus, in *The Rape of Helen*, V. 143
Colvile, George (*fl.* 1556), IV. 442
Colvill, Robert (d. 1788), IX. 557
Colvill, Samuel (*fl.* 1681), IX. 499, 556
Colvin, Ian D., XIV. Add. 6
Colvin, Sir Sidney, XII. 219, 405 ff., 439,
  441, 499, *also see* Add. 2; XIII. 484; XIV.
  526
Colwell, Thomas, IV. 390; V. 116; VI. 296
Colyton academy, X. 385
Combe, George (1788–1858), XIV. 414,
  471, 542, 543, 605
Combe, William (1741–1823), XIV. 217 ff.,
  542, 543
  Anti-Diabo-lady, The, XIV. 217
  Dance of Life, The, XIV. 219
  Diabo-lady, The, XIV. 217
  Diaboliad, The, XIV. 217
  English Dance of Death, The, XIV. 219
  Johnny Quae Genus, XIV. 220
  Letters of the late Lord Lyttelton, XIV. 217
  Letters of Sterne to Eliza, XIV. 217
  Life of Napoleon, XIV. 223
  Second Tour of Dr Syntax, The, XIV. 220
  Third Tour of Dr Syntax, The, XIV. 220
  Tour of Dr Syntax, The, XIV. 218, 219,
    221
Combe abbey, IV. 175
Comber, Thomas (1645–1699), VII. 342
Comedies of Italian or Romantic origin,
  Anonymous, V. 413

Comedus, in *Lingua*, VI. 315
Comedy, early English, v. 401 ff.
Comedy, in *Mucedorus*, v. 254
Comedy, in *The Muses Looking-Glasse*, VI. 233
Comedy, in *A Warning for Faire Women*, v. 326
Comenius, John Amos, IX. 381, 403, 569; *Didactica Magna*, IX. 388; *Opera Didactica Omnia*, IX. 388, 568, 573
Comestor, Peter, *Magister Historiarum, Historia Scholastica* of, II. 365; IV. 39, 60
Comet, The, XIV. 318a
Comic dialogues, VII. 516
Comic Magazine, The, XIV. 235
Comines, Philippe de, *Mémoires*, XII. 26
Coming of Antichrist, The, v. 15
Comment, Cuthbert. *See* Tucker, Abraham
Commines or Comines, Philippe de, III. 315; IV. 3, 443
Commodus, I. 95
Common Conditions, v. 117, 130, 138, 413; VI. 284
Common Thift, in *Ane Pleasant Satyre*, III. 128
Commons, house of, III. 402; IV. 162, 279, 305, 306; IX. 64, 194, 195, 216, 219, 225, 232, 240, 281; x. 3, 84, 94, 163, 244, 283, 284, 296, 306, 320, 399, 401, 404; XI. 2, 5, 8, 9, 12, 13, 21, 29, 34, 50, 52; XII. 307; XIII. 305
Commons Journals, The, VIII. 255
Commonwealth, the, IV. 396, 433; XI. 394
Commonwealth acts, VIII. 468
Commonwealth pamphlets, etc., XI. 470
Communis Sensus, in *Lingua*, VI. 314, 315
Comnenus, Andronicus, VII. 248
Comoedia, in *Fucus Histriomastix*, VI. 324
Compassio Mariae and *Assumptio Mariae*, I. 232, 458
Compendious Booke of Godly and Spirituall Songs, IX. 361, 362
Complaint, in Davison's *Rapsody*, IV. 124
Complaint of a lover's life, The, II. 485
Complaynt of Scotlande, The, II. 93, 94, 97, 98, 251, 268, 279, 280, 285; III. 131, 152, 153, 502
Complaynte of the Heart, The, II. 326
Compleat Devotions, x. 356
Compleat History of England, IX. 233, 234
Complete Courtier, IV. 344
Compters Common Wealth, III. 99
Compton, Charles, 7th earl of Northampton (d. 1763), x. 113
Compton, Henry (1632–1713), bishop of London, IX. 170; *Episcopalia*, VIII. 305, 459
Compton, Spencer, earl of Wilmington (1673?–1743), IX. 252; x. 94
Compton Wynyates, x. 113
Comput. See Thaun, P. de
Comte, Auguste, XIII. 22, 385, 457; XIV. 22, 24, 32, 33, 102 ff., 468, 469, 471, 475 ff.; *Cours de philosophie positive*, XIV. 17; *Système de Politique Positive*, XIII. 397

Comus, in Milton's *Comus*, VII. 113
Comus, in *Pleasure Reconciled*, VI. 359 ff.
Comyns, the, II. 100
Conan, in *The Misfortunes of Arthur*, v. 78, 79
Conant, John (1608–1694), VII. 317
Concanen, Matthew (1701–1749), IX. 434; XIV. 568
Conceits, in Cowley's *The Muse*, VII. 65
Concini, marshal d'Ancre, IV. 259, VI. 181
Concordia Regularis, v. 36, 37
Concupiscencia-carnis, in *Piers the Plowman*, II. 25
Condé, Louis II de Bourbon, prince de, VIII. 246
Conde Lucanor, VIII. 126
Condell, Henry (d. 1627), v. 169; VI. 248, 249, 276 ff.
Conder, Claude Reignier (1848–1910), XIV. 551
Conder, Eustace R., XIV. 533
Conder, Josiah (1789–1855), XII. 415
Condillac, Etienne Bonnot de Marly de, VIII. 335, 336
Condorcet, marquis de, XI. 399, 414; *Esquisse d'un tableau historique*, XI. 73, 276
Conestaggio, G., IV. 443
Coney-Catching pamphlets, IV. 515
Confessio, in *The Castle of Perseverance*, v. 52
Confession, in *Every-man*, v. 54
Confucian canon, the, XII. 343
Confucius, XII. 500
Conger, the, XI. 325
Congleton, IX. 166
Congleton, lord. *See* Parnell, Henry Brooke
Congo, the, XIV. 192
Congregational Historical society, x. 519
Congregational histories, x. 519
Congreve, Richard (1818–1899), XII. 334; XIV. 471; *The Catechism of Positive Religion translated*, XIV. 24
Congreve, William (1670–1729), IV. 185; v. 127, 189; VI. 492; VIII. 57, 137, 139, 146 ff. (main entry), 161, 163, 165 ff., 171, 172, 176, 189, 191, 423, 427, 428, 430, 432, 433, 442; IX. 38, 69, 75, 91, 124, 131, 163, 228, 270, 436, 439, 440, 473, 475; x. 21, 22, 67, 185, 446; XI. 248; XII. 168, 443; XIII. 269
Amendments, VIII. 168
Double Dealer, The, VIII. 55, 148, 149, 375, 396
Incognita, or Love and Duty Reconciled, VIII. 146
Love for Love, VIII. 150, 152, 157, 158, 168; x. 90
Mourning Bride, The, VIII. 152, 166, 168; x. 218
Ode to the Queen, x. 127
Old Bachelor, The, VIII. 146, 147
Way of the World, The, VIII. 150, 153, 155 ff., 168

Congreve, Vanbrugh and Walsh, *Squire Trelooby*, VIII. 157
Coningham, James (1670–1716), X. 385
Coningsby, Disraeli's, XIII. 350
Coningsby, Sir Thomas (d. 1625), VII. 449
Conington, John (1825–1869), IX. 74; X. 124; XII. 334, 337, 482; XIII. 175, 500
Conjecture, Essays of, IV. 524
Connoisseur, The, X. 171, 202, 429; XI. 402
Connolly, Daniel, XIV. 573
Connor, Ireland, XII. 361
Connycatching, The Groundworke of, V. 480
Conquest, the Norman, III. 193, 196, 197, 440; IV. 60, 137
Conrad, in Byron's *Corsair,* XII. 46
Conscience, in an *estrif* by Barnfield, IV. 120
Conscience, in *Mirour de l'Omme,* II. 140 ff.
Conscience, in *Piers the Plowman,* II. 8 ff., 16, 19, 20, 26 ff.
Conscience, in *Robin Conscience,* III. 97
Conscience, in *The Palice of Honour,* II. 261
Consolation, The Rote or mirror of, II. 323
Constable, Archibald (1774–1827), XI. 342, 459, 469; XII. 142, 144, 155, 156, 378, 427, 450; XIV. 612
Constable, George, XII. 350
Constable, Henry (1562–1613), III. 522; IV. 117, 124; *Diana,* III. 247, 256, 260, 261, 271
Constable, Thomas (1812–1881), XI. 477; XII. 378, 427, 450; XIV. 612
Constable country, XII. 305
Constance, Browning's, XIII. 64
Constance, council of, II. 69
Constance, in *Confessio Amantis,* II. 147
Constance, in *King John,* V. 185
Constance, in Scott's *Marmion,* XII. 10
Constance, in *The Man of Law's Tale,* I. 311; II. 181, 182
Constance, in *The Northern Lasse,* VI. 226
Constancy, legend of, in *The Faerie Queene,* III. 238
Constantina, St, I. 74
Constantine, *Breviary (Viaticus)* of, II. 365
Constantine, in *Confessio Amantis,* II. 148, 151, 152
Constantine, in Layamon, I. 266
Constantine, in *Morte Arthure,* II. 120
Constantine, *Lexicon graeco-latinum,* IV. 429
Constantine, the donation of, III. 179
Constantine of Devon and Cornwall, I. 67
Constantine the Great, I. 55; II. 58, 293; V. 16; X. 317; XII. 305, 321
Constantinople, II. 131; IV. 90; VII. 437; VIII. 291, 295; IX. 240, 244, 246, 391; X. 391; XII. 273; XIV. 251
'Constantinus Afer,' X. 204
Constantius, *Life of St Germanus of Auxerre,* I. 81
Constantius Chlorus, I. 34
Constanza, in *The Spanish Gipsie,* VI. 77
Constitutional, The, XIII. 278; XIV. 196
Consultation, The, of Hermann of Wied, III. 31

Contarine, Jane (Mrs Lawder) (*fl.* 1750), X. 199, 481
Contarine, Thomas (uncle of Goldsmith, Oliver), X. 198, 200, 209
Contarini, Gaspar, IV. 443
Contemplacio, in Coventry plays, V. 12, 49
Contemporary Review, The, XIV. 523, 534
Contention, The First Part of the, IV. 393
Contention, The, betwixt the two famous Houses of Yorke and Lancaster, V. 135, 147, 153, 184, 220, 237, 238, 260, 397, 433
Contention between Liberalitie and Prodigalitie, V. 394
Contes de ma mère l'Oie, XI. 374, 375
Con-Test, The, X. 389, 390, 522
Conti, Antonio, *Il Cesare,* V. 288, 289
Contrition, in *Piers the Plowman,* II. 28
Contrition, in *The Passetyme of Pleasure* and *The Example of Virtue,* II. 228
Conventicle Act of 1593, VII. 170, 172
Conversion of St Paul, The, V. 19
Conway, Anne, viscountess (d. 1679), VIII. 110, 280
Conway, Edward, 1st viscount (d. 1631), VII. 434; VIII. 280
Conway, George, X. 199
Conway, Gilbert, *Treatise of Versification,* XIII. 248, 512
Conway, Henry Seymour (1721–1795), X. 245, 249, 251, 399, 495, 523; XI. 12
Conway, Hugh, *pseud.* See Fargus, Frederick John
Conway, lord. See Seymour-Conway
Conway, Moncure Daniel, XI. 395; XIII. 470
Conybeare, William John (1815–1857), XII. 293, 464, 472
Conyngton. See Richard de
Cook, Albert Stanburrough, I. 50, 57, 59, 419, Add.; X. Add.; XIII. 507
Cook, Dutton, XIII. 514
Cook, Eliza (1818–1889), XIII. 177, 189, 500
Cook, Ernest Thomas, XIV. 153, 524, 533, 534
Cook, George (1772–1845), XIV. 487
Cook, captain James (1728–1779), IV. 102
Cook, James, XIII. 531; XIV. 244, 289, 459, 551; *Narrative,* XIV. 241; *To the Pacific Ocean,* XIV. 245; *Towards the South Pole,* XIV. 245
Cook, John (d. 1660), VIII. 470
Cook, John Douglas (1808?–1868), XIV. 533
Cook, William (*fl.* 1632–1641), VII. 347
Cook, William (d. 1824), XI. 448
Cooke, Sir Anthony (1504–1576), IV. 175, 177, 278
Cooke, George Frederick (1756–1811), XI. 453
Cooke, George Wingrove (1814–1865), XII. 426; XIII. 553
Cooke, J. (*fl.* 1614), *Greene's Tu Quoque or The Cittie Gallant,* VI. 219, 454
Cooke, Sir J., *Unum necessarium* (1648), IV. 510
Cooke, John (1731–1810), XI. 326; XIV. 573

Cooke, Thomas (1703–1756), VII. 430; IX. 78, 220, 526

Cooke, Thomas Potter (1786–1864), XIII. 264, 265

Cooke, W. (d. 1814), X. 195, 445, 470, 471, 483

Cookery books, II. 483, 500; III. 19

Cookery, Boke of, IV. 543

Cookesley, William, XI. 40

Cookson, Anne. *See* Wordsworth, Anne

Coolidge, William Augustus Brevoort, XIV. 552

Coolin district, Skye, XIII. 209

Cooling Carde for all Fond Lovers, A, in *The Anatomy of Wit*, III. 345, 346

Coolney, XIV. 304

Cooper, Anthony Ashley, 1st earl of Shaftesbury (1621–1683), VII. 451; VIII. 17, 30, 36 ff., 40, 75, 90, 92 ff., 97, 100, 184, 188, 190, 329, 330, 440; IX. 3, 234

Cooper, Anthony Ashley, 3rd earl of Shaftesbury (1671–1713), VIII. 457, 471; IX. 204, 288, 295, 299 ff. (main entry), 302, 303, 506, 508, *also see* Add.; X. 122, 337, 426, 469
  Characteristics, VIII. 329; IX. 300
  Inquiry concerning Virtue, IX. 300
  Letter concerning Enthusiasm, IX. 204, 300
  Miscellaneous Reflections, IX. 300
  Moralists, The, IX. 300
  Notion of the Historical Draught...of the Judgment of Hercules, IX. 300
  Sensus Communis, IX. 300
  Soliloquy: or Advice to an Author, IX. 300

Cooper, Charles A. (1829–1916), XIV. 533; *Fifty Years of Newspaper Work*, XIV. 176

Cooper, Charles Henry (1808–1866), XII. 488, 515
  Annals of Cambridge, XII. 357
  Athenae Cantabrigienses, XII. 357
  Memoir of Margaret Countess of Richmond and Derby, XII. 357
  Memorials of Cambridge, XII. 357

Cooper, Charles Purton (1793–1873), XII. 515; *An Account of the Public Records*, XII. 354

Cooper, Edith Emma. *See* Field, Michael

Cooper, Edward Herbert (1867–1910), XIII. 561

Cooper, Elizabeth (*fl.* 1737), *The Muses' Library*, VII. 193, 199

Cooper, John Gilbert (1723–1769), X. 452

Cooper, Lane, XI. 409

Cooper or Couper, Thomas (1517?–1594), III. 385 ff., 391, 392, 537; *An Admonition to the People of England*, III. 386, 387, 391, 392, 537; *Advertisement touching the Controversies of the Church of England*, III. 392

Cooper, Thomas (*fl.* 1626), IV. 535; VII. 506

Cooper, Thomas (*fl.* 1744), XI. 323, 375

Cooper, Thomas (1805–1892), XIII. 500; XIV. 471, 601

Cooper, Thompson, XIII. 564

Cooper, William (d. 1689), XI. 335, 336

Cooper, William Durrant (1812–1875), XI. 429, 485; XII. 511

'Cooper,' earl, *A Letter to Isaac Bickerstaffe, Esq.*, IX. 217

Cooper's hill, VII. 59

Coorson, Margery, in *The foure P. P.*, V. 96

Coote, Edmund (*fl.* 1597), *The English Schoolmaster...*, III. 556

Coote, Henry Charles (1815–1885), XII. 515

Cope, Sir Antony (d. 1551), IV. 4, 438

Cope, Edward Meredith (1818–1873), XII. 331, 475, 482

Cope's Tobacco Plant, XIII. 108, 489

Copeland, C. T., XIII. 470

Copeland, William John (1804–1885), XII. 454, 459

Copenhagen, V. 283, 307; IX. 165; XII. 336, 344

Coperario or Coprario, Giovanni, or John Cooper (d. 1626), IV. 463

Copernicus, Nicholas, III. 163, 425; IV. 66, 278, 290; VII. 238, 314; VIII. 283, 350, 352; IX. 391; XIV. 27

Copinger, Walter Arthur (1847–1910), XII. 427, 520; XIV. 536; *Incunabula Biblica*, XII. 369

Copland, Robert (*fl.* 1508–1547), II. 312, 324, 325, 329; III. 62, 82, 94, 101, 102, 105, 360; IV. 317, 397, 521, 546
  Art of good living and dying, II. 329
  Helias Knight of the Swan, II. 325
  Hye Way to the Spyttell House, The, II. 324, 485, 501; III. 62, 101, 360, 492
  Jyl of Braintford's Testament, II. 324, 485
  Kalendar of Shepherds, II. 324
  Kynge Appolyn of Thyre, II. 324
  Mirror of the Church, The, II. 324

Copland, William (*fl.* 1556–1569), IV. 397, 448, 518, 542; V. 92

Cople Hoo, near Bedford, VIII. 60

Cople Woodend, VII. 167

Copleston, Edward (1776–1849), XII. 284, 427; XIV. 596, 601; *Replies* (to the *Edinburgh Review*), XIV. 410

Copleston, Reginald Stephen, XIV. 209

Copley, Anthony (1567–1607?), IV. 119, 469

Copley, John Singleton, lord Lyndhurst (1772–1863), XIII. 347; XIV. 112, 124, 510

Copperfield, David, Dickens's, XIII. 305, 307, 326, 339

Coppin, Richard (*fl.* 1646–1659), X. 377

Coptic language, XII. 362

Copyright act, the, XI. 313 ff., 317, 342; XIV. 89

Coquerel, J. G., XI. 430

Corah (Titus Oates), in Dryden's *Absalom*, VIII. 39

Coran. *See* Koran

Corantos, IV. 389; VII. 345, 346, 385; IX. 1, 5

Corbet, John (1603–1641), IX. 543

Corbet, Richard (1582–1635), IV. 362; VII. 412; XI. 374; *The Fairies Farewell*, X. 233

Corbie. *See* John of

Corbould, E. H., XII. 448

Corbulo, in *Appius and Virginia*, VI. 182

Cordelia, in *King Lear*, V. 203, 204

Cordella, in *King Leir*, V. 83, 84

Corder, William (1804–1828), XIV. 228

Cordier, Mathurin, III. 429; *Pueriles Confabulatiunculae*, XI. 367

Cordifiamma, in Kingsley's *Two Years Ago*, XIII. 365

Cordova, in Alfred's *Orosius*, I. 95

Cordus, Euricius, IV. 264

Cordyale, II. 313

Corfe castle, XII. 508

Corfesgeat, I. 138

Coridon, in Barclay's *Epilogues*, III. 65

Corineus, in Layamon, I. 237

Corineus, in *Locrine*, V. 240

Corineus of Cornwall, IV. 190

Corinna (Herrick's), II. 393; VII. 6

Corinth, VI. 163, 317

Corinthian pillars, X. 110

Coriolanus, III. 24; IV. 11

Coriolanus (Shakespeare's), IV. 11

Corippus, I. 76

Cork, III. 244; IX. 282; XII. 159; XIII. 107; XIV. 263, 311, 316

Cork, countess of. *See* Monckton, Mary

Cork, county, XII. 165; XIV. 326

Cork, earl of. *See* Boyle, Richard

Cork, Queen's college, XIV. 417

Corkine, William, IV. 113, 463

Cormac, Irish scholar (831–903), I. 246

Corn law, the, XIV. 132

Corn law agitation, XIII. 14

'Corn Law Rhymer,' XII. 136, 416

Cornaro, Luigi (1475–1566), VII. 402

Cornbury, viscount. *See* Hyde, Henry

Corneille, Pierre, V. 292, 293, 295; VI. 49; VII. 275; VIII. 14, 18, 24, 30, 31, 33, 56, 131, 134, 165, 376, 422, 424, 483; IX. 256; X. 83, 444; XI. 353

   Cid, Le, VIII. 13, 180, 371; X. 69

   Cinna, X. 69

   Discours, VIII. 23, 374

   Examens, VIII. 23, 374

   Héraclius, VIII. 133, 180

   Horace, VII. 88; VIII. 180; IX. 276, 499; X. 86

   Lyer, The, VIII. 373

   Médée, VIII. 13

   Menteur, Le, VIII. 13, 373; IX. 30; see also, *The Lyer* and *The Mistaken Beauty*

   Mistaken Beauty, The, VIII. 373

   Nicomède, VIII. 180

   Polyeucte, VIII. 180

   Pompée, VII. 88; VIII. 133, 180

Corneille, Thomas, X. 86

Cornelia, in *The White Divel*, VI. 177, 187

Cornelius, in *Memoirs of Martinus Scriblerus*, IX. 136

Cornelius Agrippa, IV. 249

Cornelius Nepos, I. 195

Cornelius Tacitus, in *The City Witt*, VI. 225

Cornelys, Mrs Theresa (Threnodia Augustalis) (1723–1797), X. 482

Cornford, L. C., XIII. 503; XIV. 526

Cornhill Magazine, The, X. 204, XI. 90; XII. 426, 431; XIII. 299, 300, 380, 425; XIV. 143, 152, 194, 316

Corniche road, X. 42

Cornish, bishop, III. 56

Cornish, Francis Warre, XII. 447, 464; XIII. 503

Cornish, Joseph (1750–1823), XIV. 605

Cornish dialect, XIV. 434

Cornish drama, XII. 512

Cornish giant, a, XIII. 278

Cornish miracle plays, V. 15, 16, 391

Cornish 'rounds,' VI. 252

Cornishman, the, in *The Fyrste Boke of the Introduction of Knowledge*, III. 105

Cornix, in Barclay's *Eclogues*, III. 65

Cornix, in Barnabe Googe's *Eclogues*, III. 186

Cornwall, IV. 190, 200; VI. 242; VII. 16, 86; VIII. 119; IX. 532; X. 77, 193, 244, 365, 490; XI. 37; XII. 346, 417, 521; XIV. 434

Cornwall. *See* John of

Cornwall, Barry, *pseud. See* Procter, Bryan Waller

Cornwallis, Caroline Frances (1786–1858), XIV. 471

Cornwallis, Frederick (1713–1783), archbishop of Canterbury, X. 308

Cornwallis, Sir William (d. 1631), IV. 343 ff., 362, 517, 524, 525; VI. 341; VII. 389

Cornyshe, or Cornish, William (d. 1524?), VI. 281 ff., 287; *Triumphe of Love and Bewte, The*, VI. 284, 287

Coromandel, X. 204

Coronation stone, the, II. 130

Corporation act, X. 374

Corpus Christi, feast of, III. 81; and plays, V. 9, 12, 13, 44, 45, 48, 52, 56, 389

Corpus Historicum, XII. 355

Corpus juris, II. 350, 363; VIII. 312

Corpus Poetarum Infantilium, XI. 375

Correggio, Antonio, VII. 176

Correspondence between Frances Countess of Hertford and Henrietta Louisa Countess of Pomfret, X. 274

Correspondent, The, IX. 460

Corrupt Doctrine, in *A True Inventory*, VII. 382

Corry, Isaac (1755–1813), XI. 156

Corsica, X. 190, 192, 477, 479

Corsica, the Syracusan, in *The Bond-man*, VI. 157

Corstopitum, Corbridge, Northumberland, XII. 509

Corstorphine, George Stewart, XIV. Add. 7

Corte, Claudio, IV. 443

Cortes, Martin, *Breve compendio de la Sphera y de la arte de navigar*, IV. 71, 104, 443, 455

Coruisk district, Skye, XIII. 209

89

Coruns, raisins of, II. 305

Cory, G. E., XIV. Add. 6

Cory, William Johnson (1823–1892), XIII. 189, 503; XIV. 597, 606; *Invocation, An*, XIII. 193; *Ionica*, XIII. 193; *Mimnermus in Church*, XIII. 193

Coryate, George (father of Thomas), IV. 89

Coryate, Thomas (1577?–1617), IV. 89 ff., 392, 454; V. 350; VI. 138, 219; XIV. 333

  Coryats Cramb, IV. 90

  Coryats Crudities, IV. 89, 203; VII. 201; X. 200

  Odcombian Banquet, The, IV. 90

  Thomas Coriate Traveller for the English Wits: Greeting, IV. 90

Coryate, T., in *Love Restored*, VI. 351

Corydon (Vergil's), III. 264

Cosimo II, grand duke of Tuscany, VIII. 358

Cosin, John (1594–1672), IV. 421; VII. 34, 424, 482; VIII. 294 ff., 459; IX. 530; X. 360; *A Collection of Private Devotions*, VII. 147; VIII. 294; *Correspondence*, VIII. 296; *Historia Transubstantionis Papalis*, VIII. 296

Cosin Cutpurse, VI. 285

Cosma, in *Sicelides*, VI. 323

Cosmas, martyr, I. 74

Cosmo, in *The Traytor*, VI. 199

'Cosmopolis,' IX. 292

Cosroe, in *Tamburlaine*, V. 151

Cossacks, XII. 46

Cossé, Charles du, comte de Brissac, III. 163

Cossé, Timoleon du, III. 163

Costar Pearmain, in Farquhar's *Recruiting Officer*, VIII. 171

Costard, in *Love's Labour's Lost*, V. 178

Coste, Pierre (1668–1747), VIII. 472; IX. 400

Costeker, John Littleton, *The Fine Gentleman*, IX. 397, 569

Costigan, captain, Thackeray's, XIII. 283, 292, 296

Costlie Whore, The, III. 81

Costume, poems on, II. 502

Cotentin, the, II. 118

Cotes, Roger (1682–1716), IX. 335, 412

Cotgrave, John (*fl.* 1655), VII. 512; *Le Mercure Anglois*, VII. 360

Cotgrave, Randle (d. 1634?), *Dictionary*, IX. 255, 271, 529

Cotswolds, the, IV. 190; VIII. 83; X. 113; XII. 256, 257, 265

Cotta, in Owen's *Epigrammata*, IV. 265

Cotta, John (1575?–1650?), IV. 535; VII. 375, 394, 506, 511; *Discovery of... Ignorant Practicers of Physice*, VII. 374; *The Triall of Witchcraft*, VII. 374

Cottenham, manor of, II. 343

Cottin, Sophie, *Elisabeth*, XIII. 522

Cottington, Francis, lord (1578?–1652), VII. 215

Cottle, Amos Simon (1768?–1800), X. 487

Cottle, Joseph (1770–1853), X. 485, 486; XI. 341, 409, 417, 422, 423, 468; *Early Recollections*, XI. 133

Cotton. *See* Bartholomew de

Cotton, Charles (1630–1687), IV. 16, 18; VI. 115; VII. 251, 463; IX. 257, 272, 276, 277, 499

  Burlesque upon Burlesque, IX. 257

  Compleat Gamester, IX. 277

  Horace, Corneille's, translation of, VIII. 180

  Montaigne, VIII. 387

  Planter's Manual, IX. 277

  Scarronides, or Virgil Travestie, VIII. 372; IX. 257

  Transactions, IX. 276

Cotton, Geo. Edw. Lynch (1813–1866), XIV. 598

Cotton, Sir Henry, VII. 442

Cotton, Henry (1789–1879), XI. 468; XII. 520

Cotton, John (1584–1652), III. 422

Cotton, Sir John (1621–1701), IX. 196, 197

Cotton, Nathaniel (1705–1788), XI. 186

Cotton, Sir Robert Bruce (1571–1631), III. 55, 324, 326; IV. 55, 59, 60, 429; VII. 203; VIII. 318, 323; IX. 357; XIV. 285, 566; *Henry III*, VII. 433, 514

Cotton, Sophia Anne, XIV. 598

Cottoni Posthuma (1651), VIII. 470

Cottonian library, IX. 349, 357; XIV. 52, 560

Cottrell, Sir Charles (1615–1687), translation of La Calprenède's *Cléopâtre*, VIII. 371

Coucy, Raoul de, XI. 274

Coues, Elliott, XIV. 583

Coulson, Walter (1794?–1860), XIV. 533

Council, the King's, II. 286

Counsel, in *The Passetyme of Pleasure*, II. 225

Countenance, in *The Assembly of Ladies*, II. 217

Counterfesaunce, in *The Tears of the Muses*, III. 241

Counterfet Countenaunce, in *Magnyfycence*, III. 77

Country Gentleman, The, IX. 220

Country pursuits and pastimes, writers on, IV. 364 ff., 537 ff.

Couper, A. S., XIV. 557

Courage, in *The Example of Virtue*, II. 227

Courier, The, XIII. 259; XIV. 172, 184, 187, 188, 194

'Court of Good Company,' II. 208

Court of High Commission, V. 371, 372

Court of Love, The, II. 162, 164, 166, 167, 215, 217, 218, 220, 221, 223, 240, 243, 261

Court Poems, IX. 78, 247; XI. 328

Courtall, in *She Would if She Could*, VIII. 138

Courtenay, Edward, earl of Devonshire (1526?–1556), IV. 447

Courtenay, John (1741–1816), X. 472, 480

Courtenay, Thomas Peregrine (1782–1841), XIV. 513

Courtenay, William (1342?–1396), II. 55, 56

Courtes, The Booke of the Diversities of (1561), VIII. 465, 466

Courtesy, in *The Pastyme of Pleasure*, II. 229, 234

Courtesy, in *The Faerie Queene*, II. 234

Courtesy books, IX. 569

Courthope, William John (1842–1917), I. 419; IX. 76; XII. 524; *History of English Poetry*, I. 240; II. 139; III. 180, 181; IV. 146; VIII. 423; IX. 153

Courtier's Calling, The, IX. 396, 570

Courtly Abusyon, in *Magnyfycence*, III. 77

Courtly Nice, Sir (Crowne's), VIII. 188 ff.

Courtney, William Leonard, XIII. 514; XIV. 478

Courtney, William Prideaux (1845–1913), IX. 191; XII. 521; XIV. 508, 512, 531; *A Register of National Bibliography*, XII. 369

Courts of Justice Corrected and Amended, The, VII. 388

Cousin, Victor, XIV. 11; *History of Modern Philosophy*, XII. 371

Coutances, André de, *Roman des Franceis*, I. 236

Coutts, Jas., XIV. 595

Covenant, the, VII. 455

Covent Garden Drolery (1672), VIII. 395

Covent-Garden Journal, X. 33, 34, 39, 417

Coventry, II. 61; III. 381, 382, 386; IV. 190, 409; VI. 37; IX. 196; XIII. 276, 383, 384

Coventry, Francis (d. 1759?), XI. 459; *Pompey the Little*, IX. 245, 391, 409, 574

Coventry, Mick Parke, IV. 174

Coventry, Thomas, 1st baron (1578–1640), VII. 219

Coventry, Sir William (1628?–1686), VIII. 255, 256, 259, 387, 481

Coventry academy, X. 385

Coventry family, VII. 87

Coventry grammar school, IV. 12

Coventry Plays, II. 425; V. 10, 12, 13, 16, 17, 19 ff., 30, 31, 44, 46, 48, 49, 56, 69, 389, *and see* Add. 1

Coveras, don Francisco de las (imaginary author), VIII. 141

Coverdale, Miles (1488–1568), III. 27, 43, 44, 79, 96, 473, 486; IV. 41, 380, 402, 421, 442; *Goostly Psalmes and Spiritual Songes*, III. 79

Coverdale's Bible, XII. 521

Coverley, Sir Roger de, IV. 342; IX. 50 ff.; X. 56; XI. 146

Coverly hall, XIV. 231

Coverly papers, X. 56

Coverte, Robert, IV. 455

Covetousness, in an *estrif* by Barnfield, IV. 120

Covetousness, in *Ane Pleasant Satyre*, III. 127, 128

Covetousness, in *Piers the Plowman*, II. 12

Covetousness, Ballet agaynst, III. 491

Covetyse-of-eyes, **in** *Piers the Plowman*, II. 25

Covilla, in Landor's *Count Julian*, XII. 211

Coward, William (1657?–1725), VIII. 394

Coward, William (*fl.* 1729–1751), X. 384

Coward trustees, X. 384

Cowden Knowes, X. 233

Cowell, Edward Byles (1826–1903), XII. 343, 489, 502; XIII. 143, 145; XIV. 487

Cowell, John (1554–1611), III. 424; IV. 510; VIII. 468; *Institutiones Juris Anglicani*, VIII. 317; *Interpreter, The*, law dictionary, VI. 322, 477; VII. 433; VIII. 317

Cowen, Joseph (1831–1900), XIV. 533

Cowes, XIV. 225

Cowes castle, VII. 70

Cowley, Abraham (1618–1667), IV. 163, 187, 223, 261; VI. 471; VII. 61–70 (main entry), 89, 91, 109, 268, 275, 315, 407, 411, 465, 467; VIII. 4, 5, 43, 51, 56, 84, 228, 233, 234, 239, 292, 366, 369, 371, 376 ff., 381, 386, 389, 390, 417, 480, *also see* Add.; IX. 47, 119, 158, 168, 264, 406, 570; X. 96, 127, 183, 219, 225; XII. 182; XIII. 429; XIV. 281, 448

Anacreontiques, VII. 63

Battle of Newbury, VII. 63

Change, The, VII. 64

Chronicle, The, VII. 63

Complaint, The, VII. 69

Constantia and Philetus, VII. 62

Cutter of Coleman-Street, VI. 326; VII. 62, 63; VIII. 122, 377

Danger of Procrastination, The, VIII. 378

Dangers of an Honest Man in Such Company, The, VIII. 378

Davideis, VII. 63, 66, 67, 269; VIII. 229

Discourse by way of Vision concerning the Government of Oliver Cromwell, VII. 63, 68; VIII. 377

Extasie, The, VII. 66

Garden, The, VIII. 378

Guardian, The, VI. 326; VII. 62; VIII. 122

Hymn to Light, IX. 176

Inconstant, The, VII. 64

Love and Life, VII. 64

'Love in her Sunny Eyes does basking play,' VII. 64

Love's Riddle, VII. 62

Miscellanies, VII. 63

Mistress, The, VII. 25, 63, 64

Muse, The, VII. 65, 66

Naufragium Joculare, VI. 102, 326; VII. 62

Ode Sitting and Drinking in the Chair, made out of the Reliques of Sir Francis Drake's Ship, VII. 68

Ode upon His Majesties Restoration and Return, VII. 68

Odes, VII. 70

Of Agriculture, VIII. 378

Of Greatness, VIII. 378

Of My Self, VII. 61; VIII. **378**

Of Obscurity, VIII. 378

Of Solitude, VIII. 378

Cowley, Abraham
  On the Death of Mr Crashaw, VII. 35, 63
  On the Death of Mr William Hervey,
    VII. 63; VIII. 362
  Parting, The, VII. 64
  Passions, The, VII. 64
  Pindarique Odes, VII. 63, 64, 264
  Poeticall Blossomes, VII. 35, 62
  Poeticall Revenge, A, VII. 62
  Prophet, The, VII. 64
  *Proposition for the Advancement of Ex-
    perimental Philosophy*, VII. 68; VIII. 365;
    IX. 389, 390
  Puritan and the Papist, The, VII. 68
  Pyramus and Thisbe, VII. 62
  Resurrection, The, VII. 65
  *Several Discourses by way of Essays in
    Verse and Prose*, VII. 68, 69; VIII. 379
  *Shortness of Life and uncertainty of
    Riches, The*, VIII. 378
  Spring, The, VII. 64
  Sylva, VII. 62
  To Dr Scarborough, VII. 65
  To Mr Hobs, VII. 65
  To the Royal Society, VII. 68
  Verses on Several Occasions, VII. 68
  Vote, The, VII. 62
  Written in Juice of Lemmon, VII. 64
Cowley, Hannah, 'Anna Matilda' (1743–
  1809), XI. 273, 425; *Belle's Stratagem*,
  XI. 177, 275; *Bold Stroke for a Husband*,
  XI. 275; *Runaway, The*, XI. 274
Cowper, Ashley, XI. 78
Cowper, Harriet. *See* Hesketh, lady
Cowper, John, XI. 79
Cowper, John, Ramsay's elegy on, IX. 367,
  370
Cowper, Mary, countess (1685–1724), IX.
  249, 497
Cowper, Spencer, IX. 249, 497
Cowper, Theodora, XI. 78
Cowper, major William, XI. 79
Cowper, William, 1st earl Cowper (d.
  1723), IX. 249
Cowper, William (1731–1800), III. 184;
  IV. 260, 267; VII. 176; VIII. 230; IX. 154,
  162, 169, 410; X. 60, 242, 300, 397, 521;
  XI. 77 ff. (main entry), 145, 150, 152,
  167, 175, 176, 179, 246, 247, 251, 252,
  254, 259, 327, 362, 401, 427; XII. 132,
  177, 231, 473; XIII. 239, 244; XIV. 435,
  498, 590
  Absence and Bereavement, XI. 78
  Anti-Thelyphthora, XI. 81
  Boadicea, XI. 83
  Castaway, The, XI. 90
  Charity, XI. 81
  Colubriad, The, XI. 88
  Conversation, XI. 81
  Dog and the Water-lily, XI. 87
  Expostulation, XI. 81
  Garden, The, XI. 86
  God moves in a mysterious way, XI. 80
  Hark, my soul! it is the Lord, XI. 80
  Homer, XI. 88 ff.
  Hope, XI. 81

Cowper, William
  Invitation into the Country, XI. 83
  Jesus! where'er thy people meet, XI. 80
  John Gilpin, XI. 79, 87; XIV. 438
  Letters, XI. 85
  Oh for a closer walk with God, XI. 80
  'Old Tiney, surliest of his kind,' XI.
    88
  Olney Hymns, XI. 80
  *On her endeavouring to conceal her Grief
    at Parting*, XI. 78
  On receipt of my Mother's Picture, XI.
    78, 87
  On the Loss of the Royal George, XI. 88
  Poems (1782), XI. 83
  Poplar Field, The, XI. 88
  Progress of Error, XI. 81, 82
  Retirement, XI. 81 ff.
  Rose, The, XI. 87
  Shrubbery, The, XI. 79, 83
  Sofa, The, XI. 84 ff.
  Table Talk, XI. 81
  Task, The, XI. 81, 83 ff.
  There is a fountain filled with blood,
    XI. 80
  Time-piece, The, XI. 86, 87
  Tirocinium, XI. 78, 87; XIV. 386
  To Mary, XI. 80, 88
  To Mrs Unwin, XI. 80, 88
  Truth, XI. 81
  *Verses supposed to be written by Alex-
    ander Selkirk*, XI. 83
  Winter Evening, XI. 86
  Winter Morning Walk, XI. 86
  Winter Walk at Noon, XI. 86
  Yardley Oak, XI. 248
Cowper manuscripts, IX. 249
Cowslip green, XI. 363
Cox, captain (*fl.* 1575), III. 489, 496
Cox, E. G., II. 407
Cox, Geo. Valentine (1786–1875), XIV.
  596
Cox, Sir George William (1827–1902),
  XII. 465, 474; XIV. 70, 488; *History of
  Greece*, XII. 313, 314; *Poems Legendary
  and Historical*, XII. 314
Cox, Harold, XII. 426
Cox, Richard (1500–1581), VII. 327, 328,
  516
Cox, Sir Richard (1650–1733), IX. 476;
  X. 293
Cox, Robert, VIII. 417; *Humours of
  Simpleton the Smith*, VIII. 116; *John
  Swabber*, VIII. 116
Cox, Samuel (1826–1893), XII. 465
Cox, Thomas (d. 1734), *Magna Britannia
  et Hibernia*, IX. 353, 537
Cox of Collumpton, V. 325
Coxe, Leonard, of Reading, III. 290, 550
Coxe, William (1747–1828), IX. 481; XI.
  430; XIV. 501; *House of Austria, The*,
  XIV. 89; *Memoirs of the Duke of Marl-
  borough*, XIV. 89; *Memoirs of Sir Robert
  Walpole*, XIV. 88
Coxeter, Thomas (1689–1747), X. 429
Coxhoe hall, Durham, XIII. 70

Coy, dame, in *Jacke Jugeler*, v. 107

Coyne, Joseph Stirling (1803-1868), XIII. 266, 270, 518; XIV. 236

Coysevox, Antoine, IX. 153

Crabbe, George (1754-1832), IX. 154, 161; X. 277; XI. 86, 111, 140 ff. (main entry), 418, *also see* Add.; XII. 36, 42, 95, 136, 231, 232, 268; XIII. 40, 186, 191, 230, 373, 497; XIV. 200, 515

  Amusements, XI. 151

  Ancient Mansion, The, XI. 150

  Birth of Flattery, The, XI. 147

  Borough, The, XI. 140, 146 ff., 151

  Confidant, The, XI. 148

  Delay has Danger, The, XI. 149, 151

  Ellen Orford, XI. 140

  Epistle from the Devil, XI. 141

  Epistle to Mira, XI. 142

  Equal Marriage, The, XI. 150

  Farewell and Return, The, XI. 150

  Foes of Mankind, XI. 141

  Frank Courtship, The, XI. 148

  Gentleman Farmer, The, XI. 148

  Hall of Justice, The, XI. 147

  His Mother's Wedding-Ring, XI. 150

  Inebriety, XI. 140, 141

  Library, The, XI. 143, 145

  Lover's Journey, XI. 141

  Midnight, XI. 141

  Natural Death of Love, XI. 149

  Newspaper, The, XI. 145

  Parham Revisited, XI. 150

  Parish Register, The, XI. 140, 145 ff.

  Parting Hour, The, XI. 148; XIII. 38

  Patron, The, XI. 143, 148, 151

  Readings from Crabbe, XIII. 143

  Silford Hall, XI. 150

  Sir Eustace Grey, XI. 147

  Smugglers and Poachers, XI. 149

  Tales, XI. 141, 148, 149, 151

  Tales of the Hall, XI. 149, 151; XIII. 377, 380

  'To the Authors of the *Monthly Review*,' XI. 142

  Village, The, X. 186; XI. 143 ff., 150

  Widow, The, XI. 149

  Wish, The, XI. 140

  Works, XI. 143

  World of Dreams, The, XI. 147

Crabbe, George (1785-1857), XI. 150

Crabbe, George, grandson of the poet, XIII. 143

Crabbe, Maria, XI. 383

Crabbe, Mrs Sarah, born Elmy (d. 1813), XI. 140 ff., 145, 148

Crabs, earl of, Thackeray's, XIII. 279

Crabshaw, Timothy, in Smollett's *Sir Launcelot Greaves*, X. 41

Crackanthorpe, Hubert (d. 1897), XIII. 500; XIV. 518, *also see* Add. 2

Crackstone, captain, in *Fedele and Fortunio*, v. 314, 315; VI. 304

Cradle of Security, The, v. 57, 394

Cradock, Catherine, X. 23

Cradock, Charlotte. *See* Fielding, Charlotte

Cradock, Mrs Harriet, *Hulse House*, XII. 247

Cradock, Joseph (1742-1826), X. 473; *Zobeide*, X. 86, 439; XI. 265

Cradock, Samuel (1621-1706), X. 387

Cradok, Sir, in *Morte Arthure*, II. 120

Craft of Deyng, II. 284, 479

Craftsman, The, IX. 98, 132, 219 ff., 252, 433, 491, 492, 497; X. 389. *See, also*, Amhurst, Nicholas

Crafty Conveyaunce, in *Magnyfycence*, III. 77

Craig, Alexander, of Rosecraig (1567?-1627), IX. 555

Craig, Isa. *See* Knox, Isa

Craig, John (1512?-1600), III. 502

Craig, R. S., XIII. 470

Craig, Sir Thomas (1538-1608), IX. 549

Craig-Ereri, in *Pleasure Reconciled*, VI. 361

Craigenputtock, XIII. 5, 10

Craigie, Pearl Mary Teresa (*pseud.* John Oliver Hobbes, 1867-1906), XIII. 561

Craigie, William Alexander, XI. 438, 439; XIV. 611

Craik, Dinah Maria. *See* Mulock, Dinah Maria

Craik, George Lillie (1798-1866), I. viii; XII. 504; XIV. 487, 612

Craik, Sir Henry, VII. 241; XIV. 502, 590

Crakanthorp, Richard (1567-1624), VII. 470, 484 *bis*; *Logicae libri quinque de Praedicabilibus*, VII. 276

Crake, Augustine David (1836-1890), XI. 485

Crambe, in *Memoirs of Martinus Scriblerus*, IX. 137

Cramer, John Anthony (1793-1848), XII. 496

Cramond, cocks of, II. 276

Cranborne Chase, XII. 512

Crane, mistress, III. 379, 380

Crane, Ralph (*fl.* 1625), VII. 406

Crane, Walter (1845-1915), XI. 476, 491

Crane, William (*fl.* 1530), VI. 282, 284

Cranfield, Lionel, earl of Middlesex (1575-1645), VII. 440

Cranford, VII. 246

Cranford, Mrs Gaskell's, XIII. 372

Cranley, Thomas (*fl.* 1635), VII. 412

Cranmer, George (1563-1600), III. 406

Cranmer, Thomas (1489-1556), II. 62; III. 13, 26, 30 ff., 38, 44, 471; IV. 41, 298, 301, 380; v. 58; VII. 250; IX. 235, 496

  Answer, III. 33

  Appeal to a Council, III. 35

  Defence of the true and Catholic Doctrine of the Sacrement of the Body and Blood of Christ, III. 33

  Homilies, III. 35

  Institution of a Christian Man, The, III. 35

  Reply to the Three Articles, III. 33

Cranmer's Bible, XII. 521

Crape, Sir, in Oldham, *Satyr address'd to a Friend*, VIII. 88

Crashaw, Richard (1613?–1649), I. 232;
IV. 218, 260; VII. 15, 26, 32 ff. (main
entry), 42, 47, 63, 91, 142, 317, 400,
467, 489, *also see* Add.; X. 369; XI. 81,
318; XIII. 431; XIV. 460
 An Apologie, VII. 34
 Carmen Deo Nostro, VII. 34, 35
 Come and let us live my dear, VII. 36
 Death, what dost? o hold thy Blow, VII. 33
 Delights of the Muses, The, VII. 36
 Dies Irae, VII. 36
 Epigrammatum Sacrorum Liber, VII. 33
 Flaming Heart, The, VII. 37; XIII. 113
 Hymne to St Teresa, VII. 33, 36; XIII.
113, 218
 'Know you faire on what you look,'
VII. 32
 Loves Horoscope, VII. 36
 Musicks Duell, VII. 36
 Odes to John Tournay, VII. 33
 On a Treatise of Charity, VII. 33, 153
 Sospetto d'Herode, VII. 36
 Steps to the Temple, VII. 29, 32, 34, 35
 To the Countess of Denbigh, VII. 37
 To thy Lover, Deere, discover, VII. 36
 Translations of Latin hymns, VII. 36
 Vexilla Regis, VII. 36
 Weeper, The, VII. 31, 33, 37
 Wishes. To his (supposed) Mistresse,
VII. 36
Crashawe or Crashaw, William (1572–
1626), VI. 375, 492; VII. 32, 33; VIII. 324;
 The Honour of Vertue, VII. 32; *The
Jesuittes Gospel*, VII. 33; *A Manuall for
true Catholickes*, VII. 33
Crassus,' in *The Examiner*, IX. 218
Crasy, Mr, in *The City Witt*, VI. 228, 229
Cratander, Ephesian captive, in *The Royall
Slave*, VI. 326
Cratchits, the, in *A Christmas Carol*, XIII.
324
Crathie, IX. 373
Crauford, in Lytton's *The Disowned*, XIII.
418
Craven, Henry Thornton (1818–1905),
XIII. 518
Craven, James Brown, X. 357
Craven, Pauline M. A. A., XIII. 562
Craven scholar, XII. 323
Craven, Yorks., XII. 514
Crawfoot, J. R., VIII. 461
Crawford, Charles, V. 85, 87, 238; VI. 180,
see also Add.
Crawford, David (1665–1726), IX. 559
Crawford, earl of. *See* Lindsay, J. L.
Crawford, Mrs Emily, XIV. 190
Crawford, Francis Marion (1854–1909),
XIII. 562
Crawford, Henry, in Jane Austen's *Mans-
field Park*, XII. 239
Crawford, Isabella Valancy (1850–1886),
XIV. 348 ff., 582
 Helot, The, XIV. 349
 Love's Forget Me Not, XIV. 349
 Malcolm's Katie, XIV. 349
 Old Spookses' Pass, XIV. 349

Crawford, Miss, in Jane Austen's *Mans-
field Park*, XII. 238
Crawford, Robert (d. 1733), IX. 370, 566
 Allan Water, IX. 371
 Bush aboon Traquair, IX. 371
 Down the Burn Davie, IX. 371
 Tweedside, IX. 371
Crawfurd, George (d. 1748), X. 500
Crawfurd, Thomas (d. 1662), IX. 550
Crawley, Josiah, Trollope's, XIII. 424
Crawley, lady Jane, in *Vanity Fair*, XIII.
289
Crawley, Sir Pitt, in *Vanity Fair*, VIII.
162; XIII. 287, 289
Crawley, Rawdon, in *Vanity Fair*, XIII.
287 ff.
Crawleys, the, in *Vanity Fair*, XIII. 286 ff.
Crawleys, the, Trollope's, XIII. 422
Crayke, near York, monastery at, I. 86
Crayon, Geoffrey. *See* Irving, Washington
'Crazy Castle,' XI. 174
Creakle, Mr, in *David Copperfield*, XIII.
325
Creation, the, IV. 59 ff.
Crecy, battle of, I. 357, 359; II. 120
Credenhill, Herefordshire, VII. 42
Crediton, X. 375
Crediton school, VII. 330
Credo à l'userier, La, III. 90, 487
Creech, Thomas (1659–1701), VIII. 408;
IX. 526
Creech, William (1745–1815), XI. 220, 221,
342, 469
Creed, a play on the, V. 52
Creede, Thomas (d. 1616?), IV. 377
Creevey, Thomas, XIV. 116, 501; *The
Creevey Papers*, XIV. 115
Creichton, captain John, IX. 459
Creighton, Charles, VI. 284
Creighton, Louise, XII. Add.; XIV. 487;
 Life and Letters of Mandell Creighton,
XIV. 101, 487
Creighton, Mandell (1843–1901), bishop
of London, VII. 208; XII. 271; XIV.
81, 99 ff., 487, 500, 605; *History of the
Papacy*, XIV. 99, 100
Creizenach, Wilhelm, V. 284, 341, 344,
345, 365, 367
Creole, in Miss Edgeworth's *Belinda*, XI.
297
Creon, V. 72
Creon, in *The Bond-man*, VI. 157
Cresseid, in Henryson's *Testament of
Cresseid*, II. 247, 248
Cressy, father Hugh Paulinus (1605–
1674), VII. 143, 424; *Sancta Sophia, or
Holy Wisdom*, VII. 142, 143
Crete, V. 64; XII. 339
Crèvecœur, J. Hector St John (1731–
1813), XI. 399
Crewe hall, XI. 390
Crewe, marquess of, X. 193
Creweltie of a Stepmother, The, V. 117,
325
Crib, Tom (1781–1848), XII. 411; XIV.
231

Crichton, Admirable, VII. 254, 255; VIII. 195
Crichton, Andrew, XIV. 493
Crichton castle, in Scott's *Marmion*, XII. 10
Crichton-Browne, Sir J., XIII. 467, 471
Cricket, in *Club Law*, VI. 308
Crimean war, the, XII. 154, 227; XIII. 103, 156, 363 ff., 433; XIV. 165, 173, 176, 181, 182, 187, 190, 196, 239, 251
Crimsworth, in Charlotte Brontë's *The Professor*, XIII. 414
Cripple, the, in *The Fayre Mayd of the Exchange*, VI. 86, 100
Cripps, Arthur Shearley, XIV. Add. 4
Crisp, Samuel (miscalled Henry, d. 1783), X. 260, 430
Crisp, Tobias (1600–1643), X. 376, 377
Crispinella, in *The Dutch Courtezan*, VI. 48
Crispinus, in *The Poetaster*, VI. 18, 42, 43
Crist. See Cynewulf
Crist and Satan, I. 48, 49, 428
Crites, in *Cynthia's Revels*, VI. 39, 41
Crites (Sir Robert Howard), in Dryden's *An Essay of Dramatick Poesie*, VIII. 21, 24
Critical Remarks on Capt. Gulliver's Travels, by Doctor Bantley, IX. 132
Critical Review, The, X. 40, 201, 395, 421, 467, 474; XI. 339, 353
Critici Sacri, VII. 322, 481
Criticisms of the Rolliad, XI. 34
Crito Cantabrigienses, *A Vindication of the Literary Character of Prof. Porson*, XII. 325
Croaker, in *The Good-Natur'd Man*, X. 211, 212
Crochallan club, XI. 221
Crocker, Thomas, VII. 513
Crockett, Samuel Rutherford (1860–1914), XIII. 467
Croese, G., *The General History of Quakers* (1696), VIII. 413
Croft, Sir Herbert (1751–1816), X. 183, 476, 486; *Love and Madness*, XI. 231
Crofts, H. H. S., III. 302
Crofts, John (*fl.* 1629), VII. 17
Croisic, XIII. 77
Croisnel, Renée de, in Meredith's *Beauchamp's Career*, XIII. 446
Croke, Richard (1489?–1558), III. 27, 467
Croker, John Wilson (1780–1857), IX. 250, 252; X. 158, 473, 476, 478; XI. 346; XII. 150, 154, 155, 162, 163, 363, 380, 412, 429; XIII. 240, 350; XIV. 63, 129, 322, 323, 501; *The Croker Papers*, XIV. 115
Croker, Thomas Crofton (1798–1854), XII. 353, 412, 516; XIV. 312, 315, 568, 572
Fairy Legends and Traditions, XII. 360
Fairy Legends and Traditions of Ireland, XIV. 314
Legends of the Lakes, XII. 360
Popular Songs, XII. 360
Researches in the South of Ireland, XII. 360
Crole, Robert. *See* Crowley

Croly, George (1780–1860), XII. 416, 448; *also see* Add.; *Marston*, XII. 249; *Salathiel*, XII. 249
Cromarty, VII. 253, 254, 258
Cromarty, earl of. *See* Mackenzie, George
Crome, the shrine of Our Lady at, V. 97
Cromek, Robert Hartley (1770–1812), IX. 566; X. 456; XI. 436, 437, 441, 443, *Remains of Nithsdale and Galloway Songs*, IX. 374, 377; XI. 234, 242
Cromer, earl of. *See* Baring, Evelyn
Crompton, Richard (*fl.*1573–1599), VIII.466
Crompton, proprietor of *The Morning Post*, XIV. 185
Cromwell, Henry (1628–1674), VII. 436; VIII. 343; IX. 34, 68, 73, 83 ff., 447
Cromwell, Oliver (1599–1658), IV. 64, 141, 156, 310, 421, 426, 432, 434; VI. 316; VII. 54, 56, 68, 85, 91, 105, 148, 178, 187, 189, 190, 191, 194, 197, 218, 225, 227, 231, 254, 299, 306, 344, 349, 350 ff., 365, 383, 434, 449, 450, 451, 455, 458, 460, 513, *also see* Add.; VIII. 2, 3, 5, 7, 21, 60, 68, 73, 74, 116, 119, 198, 265, 267, 360; IX. 2, 160, 203, 212, 234, 258, 267, 269, 387, 392, 443; X. 279, 372, 373, 464; XI. 312; XIII. 13, 17, 19, 268, 469; XIV. 88, 91, 96, 113, 114, 242, 507; *Proclamation*, VIII. 274
Cromwell, Richard (1626–1712), IV. 64; VII. 190; VIII. 3, 118, 119
Cromwell, Thomas (1485?–1540), earl of Essex, I. 211; III. 42, 43, 160, 167, 244, 332, 336, 337, 490; IV. 8, 297; V. 58, 59, 102, 104; X. 233
Cromwell, Milton's, in *Defensio*, VII. 130
Cromwell, Vindication of Oliver, VII. 225
Cromwell's Nose, A Case for Nol, VII. 383
Cromwell's widow, VIII. 121
Cronica duo Anglica, I. 110
Cronke, Dickory (the 'Dumb Philosopher'), IX. 21
Crooke, Andrew, VII. 235; XI. 318
Crooke, William (*fl.* 1682), IX. 385
Crooke, W., XIV. 576
Crosfeild, Robert (*fl.* 1693), IV. 102, 455
Cross, John Walter, XIII. 402, 553; *George Eliot's Life*, XIII. 373, 381 ff., 388, 389, 391 ff.
Cross, Lancelot, *pseud.* Carr, F., XII. 442
Cross, Mary Ann, born Evans. *See* Eliot, George
Cross, Thomas, *The Autobiography of a Stage Coachman*, XIV. 233, 540
Cross, Wilbur L., X. Add.; XIII. 567
Cross, festivals and legends of the, I. 55, 56, 134; Aelfric's homily, I. 118. See, also, *Dream of the Rood*
Crosse, Mrs Andrew, XII. 441
Crossen, siege of, VII. 22
Crossley, James (1800–1883), IV. 252; VI. 105; IX. 15
Crossman, Samuel (1624?–1684), VII. 406; XI. 370, 478
Crosthwaite, X. 386
Crotch, W. Walter, XIII. 543

Crouch, Edward Heath, XIV. 377, 588, *also see* Add. 4

Crouch, John (*fl.* 1660–1681)
Fumigosus, VII. 357
Man in the Moon, VII. 357
Mercurius Democritus, VII. 357
Mercurius Melancholicus, counterfeit of, VII. 357
Pragmaticus, counterfeit of, VII. 357

Crouch, Nathaniel ('Richard Burton') (1632?–1725?), IX. 18; XI. 330, 478; *Winter Evening Entertainments*, XI. 370

Croucher, John (*fl.* 1408–1453?), IV. 432; VI. 280

Crousaz, Jean-Pierre de, IX. 83, 449; X. 465; XI. 356

Crow, William (*fl.* 1663), VII. 479

Crow and Pie, II. 414

Crowdero, in *Hudibras*, VIII. 68, 70

Crowdy, Wallace Lowe, XIII. 540

Crowe, captain, in Smollett's *Sir Launcelot Greaves*, X. 41

Crowe, Catherine (1800?–1876), XII. 448; XIII. 430; *Adventures of Susan Hopley*, XII. 249; *Night Side of Nature, The*, XII. 248; *Story of Lilly Dawson, The*, XII. 249

Crowe, Sir Joseph Archer (1825–1896), XIV. 533

Crowe, William (1745–1829), X. 454; XII. 416; XIII. Add. 2; *Treatise on English Versification*, XIII. 240, 512

Crowland, XIII. 366

Crowley (Crole or Croleus), Robert (1518?–1588), III. 87, 100, 101, 492; IV. 324, 328, 334, 382; IX. 51
Epigrams, The one and thirty, III. 100; IV. 328, 334
Information and Peticion agaynst the oppressours of the pore commons of the realme, III. 101
Pleasure and pain, heaven and hell, III. 101
Voice of the Last Trumpet, The, III. 100
Way to Wealth, The, III. 100

Crowne, Dryden and Shadwell, *Notes and Observations*, VIII. 193, 441

Crowne, John (d. 1703?), VIII. 21, 133, 213, 214, 400, 401, 435, 441
Ambitious Statesman, The, VIII. 188
Andromache, VIII. 181, 187
Caligula, VIII. 189
Calisto, or the Chast Nymph, VIII. 187
City Politiques, VIII. 122, 188
Country Wit, The, VIII. 134, 188
Darius, VIII. 189
Destruction of Jerusalem, The, VIII. 188, 190
English Frier, The, VIII. 134, 188, 189
Henry the Sixth, the First Part With the Murder of Humphrey, Duke of Glocester, VIII. 188
History of Charles the Eighth of France, The, VIII. 187
Juliana, or the Princess of Poland, VIII. 187

Crowne, John
Justice Busy, VIII. 189
Married Beau, The, VIII. 189
Misery of Civil-War, The, VIII. 188
Pandion and Amphigenia, VII. 391; VIII. 187
Regulus, VIII. 189
Sir Courtly Nice, or It cannot be, VIII. 131, 179, 188, 189
Thyestes, VIII. 188

Crowne, William, father of Crowne, John, VIII. 187

Crowned King, The, II. 40, 432, 435

Crowquill, Alfred, *pseud.* See Forrester, Alfred Henry

Crowther, Joseph, VI. Add. 2

Croxall, Samuel (d. 1752), XI. 172, 425, 490; *Fables*, XIII. 52

Croxton play, the, V. 391

Croydon, III. 57; V. 119, 141; VI. 287; XIV. 406

Croydon, Whitgift's school, VIII. 83

Croyland, abbey of, I. 89; II. 343; IV. 417; forged chronicle of, II. 399, 497

Croyland. *See* Felix of

Crozier, John Beattie, XIII. 470

Cruden, Alexander (1701–1770), *Concordance*, XI. 327, 467

Cruelty, in Chronicle plays, V. 151

Cruikshank, George (1792–1878), X. 416, 418, 421; XI. 386, 402, 478, 491; XII. 447; XIII. 526, 540, 542; XIV. 188, 221 ff., 232, 234, 237, 520, 539, 541, 543 ff.; *Comic Almanac*, XIV. 235; *George Cruikshank's Magazine*, XIV. 234; *Table Book*, XIII. 284

Cruikshank, George and Robert, IX. 567

Cruikshank, Isaac Robert or Robert (1789–1856), XIV. 222, 223, 225, 226, 235, 236, 543

Crummleses, the, in *Nicholas Nickleby*, XIII. 317, 318

Crump, Charles G., XII. 439, 440

Crump, James, XI. 334

Crump, Mrs Lucy, XIV. 503

Crump, Mrs and Miss, in Thackeray's *The Ravenswing*, XIII. 281

Cruncher, Jerry, in *A Tale of Two Cities*, XIII. 332

Crusade, first, in Wm. of Malmesbury, I. 165

Crusades, the, II. 337

Cruso, Aquila, VI. 471

Crusoe, Robinson, X. 66; XIII. 438

Crux de te Volo Conqueri, II. 383

Cuchulinn, in *Fled Bricrend* (*Bricriu's Feast*), I. 296, 327

Cuchullain, X. 231; XIII. 188; XIV. 307

Cuculo, in *A Very Woman*, VI. 161

Cuddie, in *The Shepheards Calender*, III. 225

Cuddy, in Davison's *Rapsody*, IV. 125

Cudworth, Ralph (1617–1688), VII. 279, 302; VIII. 273, 274, 279 ff., 286, 290 ff. 330, 453 ff.; IX. 299, 401; X. 345; XI. 57

Cudworth, Ralph
  Moral Good or Evil, or Natural Ethics,
  VIII. 281; *Treatise concerning Eternal
  and Immutable Morality*, VIII. 282;
  *The true Intellectual System of the Uni-
  verse*, VIII. 287
Cuffe or Cuff, Henry (1563–1601), IV. 114;
  VII. 329, 343
Cuirass. See *Lorica*
Cujas, Jacques de, III. 423
Cujus contrarium verum est, VII. 381
Cul de Jatte, in *The Cloister and the
  Hearth*, XIII. 429
Culdees at St Andrews, II. 367
Cullercoats, XIV. 297
Cullinan, Maxwell Cormac, XII. 494
Culloden, IX. 563 ff.
Culpeper, Nicholas (1616–1654), VII. 509
Culpeper, Sir Thomas, the elder (1578–
  1662), IV. 510
Culpeper, Sir Thomas (1626–1697), *Morall
  Discourses and Essayes*, VII. 517
Culross, II. 131
Culross, lady (Elizabeth Melville) (*fl.*
  1603), IX. 555
Culverwel, Nathaniel (d. 1651), VII. 280;
  VIII. 287, 292, 454; *Commonplaces*, VIII.
  290; *Light of Nature*, VII. 279, 470;
  VIII. 288, 289
Cumberland, IX. 170; XI. 232, 410; XII.
  17, 511; XIII. 426; XIV. 221
Cumberland, ship, X. 36
Cumberland, countess of. See Clifford,
  Margaret
Cumberland, duke of. See William Augus-
  tus (1721–1765)
Cumberland, earl of. See Clifford, George
Cumberland, Richard (1631–1718), bishop
  of Peterborough, VI. 9; IX. 506, 525;
  X. 351; *De Legibus Naturae*, VII. 303,
  470; VIII. 292, 468
Cumberland, Richard (1732–1811), IX.
  574; X. 90, 473, 483; XI. 263 ff., 270,
  272, 448, 457, *also see* Add.; XIV. 592
  Brothers, The, XI. 263, 264, 277, 279, 414
  Choleric Man, The, XI. 265
  Fashionable Lover, The, XI. 265
  Jew, The, XI. 282
  Timon of Athens, XI. 265
  West Indian,The, X. 92, 214; XI. 257, 264
Cumbrian dialect, XII. 413
Cumming, fiddler, X. 196
Cumming, Joseph George (1812–1868),
  XII. 509
Cumner hills, XIII. 93
Cundall, Joseph, XI. 386
Cuneburga, abbess, I. 79
Cuneglasus, king, I. 67
Cuningham or Cunningham, William (*fl.*
  1586), *The Cosmographical Glasse*, III.
  550; IV. 400
Cunliffe, John William, V. Add. 2; XIII.
  572, *also see* Add. 1
Cunningham, Alexander, 5th earl of Glen-
  cairn (d. 1574), *Epistle direct from the
  Holy hermit of Allarit*, III. 132

Cunningham, Alexander (1655?–1730), IX.
  561
Cunningham, Sir Alexander (1814–1893),
  XII. 352, 509
  Ancient Geography of India, XII. 353
  Architecture of the Temples of Kashmir,
  XII. 353
  Bhilsa Topes, The, XII. 353
  Corpus Inscriptionum Indicarum, XII.
  353
Cunningham, Allan (1784–1842), IX. 566;
  XI. 234, 434, 437, 439, 443; XIII. 54
  *Biographical and Critical History of
  British Literature*, XII. 365, 378, 437
  Bonnie Lady Anne, XI. 243
  Hame Hame, Hame, XI. 243
  John Grumlie, XI. 243
  Maid of Elvar, XI. 242
  My Nannie O, XI. 243
  She's Gane to dwell in Heaven, XI. 243
  Sir Marmaduke, XI. 242
  Songs of Scotland, XI. 242
  Wee, Wee German Lairdie, IX. 377; XI.
  243
  Wet Sheet and a Flowing Sea, XI. 243
  Young Maxwell, XI. 242
Cunningham, lady Elizabeth, XI. 223
Cunningham, Francis (1820–1875), V. 143
Cunningham, James, 14th earl of Glen-
  cairn (1749–1791), XI. 220, 223
Cunningham, John William (1780–1861),
  XI. 401
Cunningham, Mary (d. 1615), IV. 152
Cunningham, Peter (1816–1869), X. 247,
  249; XII. 409
Cunningham, Thomas Mounsey (1776–
  1834), *Hairst Kirn*, XI. 243; *Hills o'
  Gallowa*, XI. 243
Cunningham, William, 9th earl of Glen-
  cairn (1610?–1664), XII. 377
Cupar-Fife, III. 123; XII. 513
Cupid, III. 17; IV. 196, 330; XII. 90; XIV.
  311
Cupid (lap-dog), IX. 46
Cupid, god of love, in *Confessio Amantis*,
  II. 146
Cupid, in *Gismond of Salerne*, V. 73 ff.
Cupid, in *The Hue and Cry after Cupid*,
  VI. 346, 347
Cupid, in *Love Restored*, VI. 351, 352
Cupid, in *Loves Maistresse*, VI. 103
Cupid, in *The Masque of Christmas*, VI.
  358, 359
Cupid, in *The Palice of Honour*, II. 260
Cupid, in *The Testament of Cresseid*, II. 248
Cupid God of Love, The book of, II. 216
Cupid's Court of Salutations, XI. 334
Cupids, in *The Masque of Beauty*, VI. 347
Cur, Sir John, in Barnabe Googe's
  Eclogues, III. 186
Curan, in *Albion's England*, III. 357; IV.
  136
Curchod, Suzanne. See Necker
Cures for the Itch, III. 487
Cureton, William (1808–1864), XII. 341,
  503

'Curious Impertinent, The,' in *Don Quixote*, VI. 133, 137, 223, 236; VIII. 189, 191

Curle, James, XII. 509

Curle, Richard H. P., XIII. 570

Curlicism, XI. 328

Curll, Edmund (1675–1747), IX. 78, 83, 84, 86, 123, 165, 247, 446, 447, 452, 462, 469, 475, 535; XI. 288, 327 ff., 467

Curran, John Philpot (1750–1817), XIV. 311; *Cushla ma Chree*, XIV. 319; *Deserter's Meditation*, XIV. 319

Curran, William Henry, *Sketches of the Irish Bar*, XIV. 319

Currawn, county Leitrim, XIV. 355

Currie, A. E., XIV. 584

Currie, James (1756–1805), XI. 408, 436, 437

Currie, Mary Montgomerie, lady, born Lamb (*pseud*. Violet Fane, 1843–1905), XIII. 180, 504

Curson of Kedleston, cardinal (d. 1218), I. 199, 453

Cursor Mundi, I. 134, 341 ff., 348, 399, 474; II. 189; III. 289; V. 15, 389

Curtasy, The Boke of, II. 502

Curteis, T., IX. 463

Curtin, *Hero Tales of Ireland*, I. 293

Curtis, William (1746–1799), XIV. 288, 559

Curtius, Ernst, XII. 322, 476

Curtius, George, *Principles of Greek Etymology*, XII. 337; *The Greek Verb*, XII. 337

Curtius, Quintus, IV. 2, 4, 436

Curwen, Henry (1845–1892), XI. 466; XIV. 339, 575

Curzon, lord, of Kedleston, XIV. 597

Curzon, Robert, lord Zouche (1810–1873), XIV. 551; *The Monasteries of the Levant*, XIV. 252

Cusack, Mary Frances, XIV. 510

Cusanus, C., VII. 517

Cussans, John Edwin (1837–1899), XII. 509

Cust, Lionel, XII. 499

Custance, dame, in *Ralph Roister Doister*, V. 105, 106

Cut pursses, A ballett..., III. 492

Cutchery court, XI. 12

Cute, alderman, in Dickens's *The Chimes*, XIII. 324

Cuthbert, abbot of Wearmouth and Jarrow, I. 61, 79

Cuthbert Cutpurse, II. 232

Cuthbert, St, of Lindisfarne (d. 687), I. 64, 80, 82, 83, 85, 117, 118 148, 435; IV. 421; XII. 10

Cuthbertson, James Lister (1851–1910), XIV. 369, 585

Cuthwin, I. 61, 71, 79

Cutter, in Cowley's *Cutter of Coleman Street*, VIII. 122

Cutting Capers, XIV. 377

Cuttle, captain, in *Dombey and Son*, XIII. 325

Cutts, John, lord (1661–1707), VIII. 410

Cutwode, Thomas, *Caltha Poetarum*, IV. 469

Cuvelier de Trye, Jean G. A., XIII. 264

Cuvier, Georges L. C. F. D., XIV. 295

Cybele, in Keats's *Endymion*, XII. 82

Cyclope, in *Mercury Vindicated*, VI. 357

Cyclopes, in *The Hue and Cry after Cupid*, VI. 347, 348

Cymbeline, in Geoffrey of Monmouth, I. 171

Cymmodorion, Honourable society of, XII. 506

Cymric language and literature, I. 464

Cynara, Dowson's, XIII. 220

Cynewulf (*fl.* 1750), I. 38, 41, 49 ff., 133, 134, 143, 325, 428, 430; XI. 366; *also see* XIII. Add. 2

Crist, I. 49, 52, 53, 56, 58, 59, 63, 64; runes in, I. 12; Cook's edn., I. 59; IV. 37

Elene, I. 50 ff., 55, 57, 62, 63, 134, 143; runes in, I. 12

Fata Apostolorum, I. 52 ff.; runes in, I. 12

Juliana, I. 52, 53; runes in, I. 12

Cynewulf, bishop of Lindisfarne, I. 49, 430

Cynewulf, king, in O.E. *Chronicle*, I. 107 443

Cynthia, IV. 196

Cynthia, in Congreve's *Double-Dealer*, VIII. 148, 150

Cynthia, in *Endimion*, V. 341

Cynthia, in *The Faerie Queene*, III. 233, 238

Cynthia, in Mrs Gaskell's *Wives and Daughters*, XIII. 381

Cynthio, IX. 50, 57

Cynulf of Clovesho, I. 50

Cynus super Codicem, II. 364

Cyprian, bishop of Toulon, XII. 487

Cyprian, St, II. 365; III. 411; VI. 375; IX. 527; XII. 266

'Cyprians,' XIV. 227

Cyprianus (Juvencus), I. 76

Cyprus, IX. 251, 253

Cyrano de Bergerac, S., *Histoire comique*, IX. 106

Cyrene, XII. 339

Cyril, XII. 503

Cyril, in Tennyson's *The Princess*, XIII. 31

Cyrus, III. 437

Cyrus, Le Grand, I. 280

Cytherea: or poems upon Love and Intrigue, IX. 78

Cythna, in Shelley's *Revolt of Islam*, XII. 61

Daantjie Gouws, XIV. 377

Daborne, Robert (d. 1628), VI. 116, 146, 454; *A Christian turned Turke*, V. 366

Dacia, in Geoffrey of Monmouth, I. 259

Dacier, André, IX. 75; Aristotle's *Poetics*, trans. of, VIII. 375; *Essai sur la Satire*, VIII. 374

Dacier, Madame, X. 27

Dacier, in Meredith's *Diana of the Crossways*, XIII. 445

Dacre, lord, friend of Gavin Douglas, II. 260

Dacre, Mary, in Disraeli's *The Young Duke*, XIII. 348
Dacres, Edward, IV. 8, 446
Daedalus, III. 86
Daeghrefn, in *Beowulf*, I. 24, 27
Daffy's Elixir Salutis, XI. 335
Dagon's Fall, VIII. 97
Dahlia, in Meredith's *Rhoda Fleming*, XIII. 447
Dahra, XIV. 238
Daillé, John, *Traité de l'employ des saincts pères*, VII. 313, 484
Daily Advertiser, The, XI. 391
Daily Chronicle, The, XIV. 192, 193
Daily Courant, The, IX. 5; XI. 333
Daily Express, The, XIV. 193
Daily Gazetteer, The, X. 467
Daily Graphic, The, XIV. 201
Daily Mail, The, XIV. 193
Daily News, The, XIII. 324; XIV. 90, 173, 188 ff., 316, 530, 535
Daily Post, The, IX. 21, 433; XIV. 201
Daily Telegraph, The, XIV. 180, 183, 188, 190 ff., 196, 328, 530, 534
Daily Universal Register, The, XIV. 177
Dakins, William (d. 1607), VII. 316
Dalbeattie, XI. 444, 445
Dale, Alfred William Winterslow, XII. 465
Dale, David (1739–1806), XIV. 404
Dale, Edmund, I. Add.
Dale, Robert William (1829–1895), XII. 465, 471
D'Alembert, J. le Rond, V. 293
Dales, the, in Trollope's novels, XIII. 422
Daley, Victor James (1858–1905), XIV. 369, 585
Dalgairns, John Dobree (1818–1876), XII. 275, 456, 460
Dalgetty, Dugald, in Scott's *Legend of Montrose*, X. 43; XII. 21, 25, 29
Dalhousie, marquis J. *See* Ramsay, J. A. B.
Dalila, in *Samson Agonistes*, VII. 122, 137; VIII. 154
Dalkeith, XI. 469
Dalkeith, countess of, XII. 7
Dallas, Rev. Alexander Robert Charles (1791–1869), XII. 386
Dallas, Eneas Sweetland (1828–1879), XII. 398; XIII. 245, 512; XIV. 142, 147, 518; *Gay Science, The*, XIV. 140; *Kettner's Book of the Table*, XIV. 140; *Poetics, an Essay on Poetry*, XIV. 139
Dallas, Robert Charles (1754–1824), XII. 384, 386
Dallas, William Sweetland, XIV. 559
Dallaway, James (1763–1834), IX. 246
Dalquhurn, Cardross, X. 36
Dalrymple, Sir David, lord Hailes (1726–1792), VIII. 262; IX. 553; X. 192, 245, 294, 501, 507; XI. 273, 341
  Ancient Scottish Poems, XI. 204
  Annals of Scotland, X. 290
  Inquiry, X. 310
  Memorials and Letters, X. 290

Dalrymple, James (*fl.* 1596), II. 398; III. 155
Dalrymple, James, viscount Stair (1619–1695), VIII. 468; IX. 560
Dalrymple, Sir James (*fl.* 1714), IX. 551
Dalrymple, Sir John, 1st earl of Stair (1648–1707), IX. 495
Dalrymple, John, 2nd earl of Stair (1693–1747), IX. 152, 495
Dalrymple, Sir John, 4th baronet of Cranstoun (1726–1810), IX. 553; X. 294, 500; *Memoirs of Great Britain and Ireland*, X. 290, 291
Dalrymple of Orangefield, XI. 220
Dalton, in Norton's *Ordinall*, II. 213
Dalton, tutor to lady Hertford's son, X. 272
Dalton family, the, patrons of Rolle, II. 44
Dalton, Sir Cornelius Neale, IX. Add.
Dalton, John (1766–1844), XIV. 259, 261, 271, 272, 275 ff. (main entry), 556, 557, 605; *A new system of Chemical Philosophy*, XIV. 275
D'Alton, John (1792–1867), XIV. 312, 568; *Annals of Boyle, The*, XIV. 325; *Dermid*, XIV. 325; *History of County Dublin, The*, XIV. 325
Dalton, Michael (d. 1648?), VIII. 468
Dalyell, Sir John Graham (1775–1851), XII. 516; *The Darker Superstitions of Scotland*, XII. 350
Dalyell, in *Perkin Warbeck*, VI. 193
Dalziel, Edward George, XIV. 239
Damascus, XIV. 251
Damasus, pseudo-, II. 293
D'Ambois, Clermont, in *The Revenge of Bussy D'Ambois*, VI. 34
D'Ambra, *Cofanaria*, V. 69
Dame and her Donkey's Five, XI. 386
Dame Siriz, I. 365, 366, 479
Dame Wiggins of Lee, XI. 386
Damerval, IV. 527
Dametas, in Sidney's *Arcadia*, III. 353
Dametas, in *The Ile of Guls*, VI. 213
Damian, martyr, I. 74
Dammee Cavaliers Warning piece (1643), VII. 382
Damocles, in *The Usurper*, VIII. 21
Damoetas, in Barnabe Googe's *Eclogues*, III. 186
Damon, in Thomson's *Summer*, X. 104
Dampier, H., X. 485
Dampier, William (1652–1715), IX. 106, 492, *also see* Add.; XIV. 242, 551; *Journals*, XIV. 241
Dampit, in *A Trick to catch the Old-one*, VI. 65
D'Amville, in *The Atheist's Tragedie*, VI. 167
Dan Michel of Northgate, Kent, I. 353 ff., 400, 475
Dan Robert of Malton, I. 350
Danaë, in *The Bird in a Cage*, VI. 204
Danaides, in *Phoenissae*, V. 71
Dance of Death, The, III. 87, 100, 484; XIV. 219

Dancer, John (*fl.* 1675), VI. 490; *Nico-mède* (Corneille's), translated by, VIII. 180

D'Ancourt, Florent Carton, *Les Bour-geoises à la Mode*, VIII. 162, 431

D'Ancre, marshal, VI. 138

Dane Hew Monk of Leicestre, A Mery Jest of, II. 501

Danelaw, the, VIII. 311

Danes, the, IV. 417, 418; V. 31; IX. 354; laws and customs of, VIII. 311, 318

Danes, the, in *Morte Arthure*, II. 120

Danett, Thomas (*fl.* 1566–1601), IV. 3, 443, 445; *Commines*, IV. 8

'Dangerus Fortrees,' VI. 283

Dangle, in Sheridan's *Critic*, XI. 272

Daniel I. 74; V. 48; X. 222

Daniel, bishop of Winchester (d. 745), I. 82

Daniel, Charles Henry Olive (b. 1836–1919), XII. Add. 5

Daniel, George of Berwick (1616–1657), VII. Add.

Daniel, George (1789–1864), XIII. 516; XIV. 518

Daniel, John (*fl.* 1625), *Songs for the Lute, Viol and Voice*, IV. 113, 133, 134, 463

Daniel, Mary, X. 28

Daniel (Donellan), Nehemias (d. 1609?), archbishop of Tuam, IV. 414

Daniel, Old English poem, I. 46, 48, 428; runes in, I. 11

Daniel, Peter Augustin, V. 85

Daniel, Samuel (1562–1619), III. 198, 247, 256, 260, 261, 264 ff., 270, 295, 304, 306, 307, 312; IV. 24, 25, 88, 115, 118, 127, 132–140 (main entry), 158, 159, 179 ff., 191, 248, 265, 266, 398, 434, 444, 474; V. 63, 226, 338, 371, 473; VI. 4, 23, 37, 39, 40, 44, 317, 337, 339, 343, 345, 350, 366, 471, 489, 490; VII. 444; VIII. 237, 239

Certaine Small Poems, IV. 134

Civil Wars, The, III. 198; IV. 132 ff., 136 ff., 140

Cleopatra, IV. 133, 139; V. 334

Complaynt of Rosamund, The, III. 198; IV. 133, 134, 140, 176

Defence of Ryme, III. 304, 306, 307, 526; IV. 132, 133, 135

Delia, III. 256, 260, 522; IV. 133, 177

England, history of, IV. 134

Epistle to the Lady Margaret, IV. 126, 137, 138

Epistles, IV. 138

Hymen's Triumph, IV. 134, 138, 140; VI. 190, 366

Musophilus, or a General Defence of Learning, III. 446; IV. 88, 133, 135, 140

Octavia to Marcus Antoninus, Epistle of, IV. 133, 138, 140

Panegyrike Congratulatorie, IV. 132, 134, 135, 140

Philotas, IV. 132, 134, 135; V. 334, 346, 371; VI. 339; VII. 122

Poeticall Essayes, IV. 133

Daniel, Samuel
Queenes Arcadia, The, IV. 134; VI. 317, 318, 327, 366

Senecan tragedies, IV. 134

Sonnets to Delia, IV. 139

Tethys Festival, IV. 134; VI. 350

Ulisses and the Syren, IV. 134, 138, 140; XIII. 141

Vision of Twelve Goddesses, The, IV. 134; VI. 337, 345, 350

Daniel, Story of, by Hilarius, I. 191

Daniel of Morley, I. 153

Daniell, John Frederick, XIV. 557

Daniell, John Jeremiah, VII. 28, 403

Daniello, III. 290

Danish fleet, the, XIV. 120, 122

Danish Tragedy, The, V. 327

Danse Macabre, II. 199, 256; III. 87

Dante, Alighieri, I. 43, 99, 199, 200, 227, 232, 270, 363; II. 80, 133, 134, 161, 175, 179, 180, 188, 231, 258, 435; III. 200, 234, 245, 300, 305, *also see* Add.; IV. 23, 45, 196, 197, 210, 217, 527; V. 213, 214, 324; VII. 95, 101, 122, 136 ff., 240; VIII. 67, 78, 351; X. 9, 220, *also see* Add.; XII. 50, 58, 137, 221, 222, 229, 272, 394, 396, 398, 403, 415, 525; XIII. 13, 42, 195, 312; XIV. 113, 306

Commedia, XII. 51, 85

De Monarchia, XII. 455

De vulgari eloquentia, XIII. 186

Inferno, X. 240; XII. 202

La Divina Commedia, XIII. 30

La Vita Nuova, XII. 73; XIII. 112, 118

Paradiso, I. 99, 154; V. 233, 339; XII. 76

Purgatorio, XIII. 32

Danter, John, IV. 393; V. 322, 323

Danton, Georges Jacques, XIII. 12

'D'Anvers, Caleb' (N. Amhurst), IX. 220, 225, 491

Danvers, Jane (wife of George Herbert), VII. 29

Danvers, lady (mother of George Herbert), IV. 240; VII. 28

Danzig, V. 283

Dapper, in *The Alchemist*, VI. 22

Dapper, Tim, in *The Tatler*, IX. 41

Darbishire, Arthur Duckinfield, XIII. 572

D'Arblay, Frances Burney, Mme. *See* Arblay, Madame d'

Darbyshire, Thomas (1518–1604), IV. 127

Darch, Robert, X. 386

Darcie, Abraham (*fl.* 1625), III. 326, 528

Darcy, in Jane Austen's *Pride and Preju-dice*, XII. 237, 238, 243, 247

D'Arcy, Robert, 4th earl of Holdernesse (1718–1778), X. 118

Dares Phrygius, I. 170, 467, 469; II. 172

Daria, martyr, I. 74

Darien expedition, IX. 214, 215, 542

Darius, I. 307

Dark Blue, The, XIV. 206

Darley, George (1795–1846), XII. 107 114–115 (main entry), 139, 201, 416 XIII. 230, 238; XIV. 214

Beckett, XII. 114

Darley, George
  Enchanted Lyre, The, XII. 115
  Errors of Ecstacie, XII. 114
  Ethelstan, XII. 114
  It is not Beauty I demand, XII. 115
  I've been roaming, XII. 115
  Labours of Idleness, XII. 114
  Maiden's Grave, The, XII. 115
  Nepenthe, XII. 114, 119; XIII. 204
  Sylvia, XII. 114, 115; XIII. 239
Darling, James (1797–1862), XII. 521
Darlington, XIV. 193
Darlow, Thomas Hult, XIV. 516
Darmesteter, James, XI. 409
Darnal, Sheffield, VII. 353
Darnaway (Moray), II. 112, 115
Darnley, earl of. *See* Stewart, Henry
Darrell, John (*fl.* 1562–1602), IV. 535
Dart, John (d. 1730), IX. 532
Darter, Adrian, XIV. Add. 6
Dartle, Rosa, in *David Copperfield*, XIII. 327
Dartmoor, VII. 5; X. 115
Dartmouth, X. 387
Dartmouth, earl of. *See* Legge, William
Darton, F. J. Harvey, XI. 482; XIV. 590
Darton, William, XI. 377, 485
Darton and Clarke, publishers, XI. 481
Darwin, Charles Robert (1809–1882), IV. 290; XI. 75, 426; XIII. 470, 571, 572, *also see* Add. 1; XIV. 28, 29, 34, 35, 296, 298 ff. (main entry), 479, 501, 551, 559
  Descent of Man, The, XIV. 32
  Expression of the Emotions, The, XIV. 32
  Life and Letters, XIV. 293
  Origin of Species, The, XIV. 27, 293, 298 ff., 381
  Voyage of the Beagle, The, XIV. 241, 250
Darwin, Erasmus (1731–1802), XI. 41, 172, 175 ff., 180, 246, 425; XII. 247; XIII. 450; XIV. 298, 469, 560; *Botanic Garden*, XI. 175; *Loves of the Plants*, XI. 41, 175, 176
Darwin, Sir Francis, XIV. 284, 501, 559
Darwin, Sir George Howard (1845–1912), XIV. 265, 556
Darwinism, XII. 154, 269; XIII. 451
Dasent, Sir George Webbe (1817–1896), XI. 491
Dashall, Dick, in Morton's *Way to get Married*, XI. 281
Dashall, Tom, in *Real Life in London*, XIV. 227
Dashwood, Elinor, in Jane Austen's *Sense and Sensibility*, XII. 237, 241, 243
Dashwood, John, in Jane Austen's *Sense and Sensibility*, XII. 237
Dashwood, Marianne, in Jane Austen's *Sense and Sensibility*, XII. 235, 237, 241
Dashwood, Mrs, in Jane Austen's *Sense and Sensibility*, XII. 237
Dassent, Arthur Irwin, XIV. 533
Dastin or Daustin, John (*fl.* 1320), I. 453
Daubeny, Mr, Trollope's, XIII. 423
D'Aubigny, lord, V. 370; VI. 4, 6
Daudet, Alphonse, XIII. 544

D'Audiguier, VI. 123, 139
Daughters of God, the Four, in *Piers the Plowman*, II. 27
D'Aulnoy, countess, *Travels into Spain*, VIII. 191
Daunce and Song of Death, The, III. 87
Daunger, in *The Bouge of Courte*, III. 73
Daunses, A Treatise of, VI. 391, 498
Dauphine, Sir, in *The Silent Woman*, VI. 22
Daus, John (*fl.* 1561), IV. 448
D'Auvergne, Martial, VI. 154
Davenant, Charles (1656–1714), VIII. 400, 473; IX. 11; *An Essay on the East India Trade*, VIII. 342
Davenant, Judith (mother of Thomas Fuller), VII. 244
D'Avenant, Sir William (1606–1668), IV. 115, 159; VI. 212, 262, 271, 454, 489; VII. 16, 39, 105, 106, 267, 269, 270, 274, 275, 333, 408, 411, 465, 467; VIII. 26, 34, 116 ff., 132 ff., 179, 398, 417, 418, 422, 423, 424; IX. 157; X. 78; XI. 318
  Albovine, VIII. 226
  Britannia Triumphans, VII. 433
  Cruelty of the Spaniards in Peru, The, VIII. 118
  Fair Favourite, The, VI. 240
  First Day's Entertainment at Rutland House, The, VIII. 117, 118
  Gondibert, VII. 70, 71, 73, 263, 266 ff.; VIII. 9, 371, 374
  History of Sir Francis Drake, The, VIII. 118
  Law Against Lovers, The, VIII. 120
  Love and Honour, VI. 240; VIII. 120, 121, 132
  Macbeth, D'Avenant's alteration, VIII. 20
  Platonick Lovers, The, VI. 240; VIII. 120, 132
  Playhouse to be Let, The, VIII. 118, 134
  Preface to Gondibert, VIII. 9
  Rivals, The, VIII. 120
  Romeo and Juliet, VIII. 120
  Salmacida Spolia, VI. 363
  Siege, The, X. 73; XI. 282
  Siege of Rhodes, VIII. 18, 117, 118, 121, 137, 194, 261
  Sir Martin Mar-all, VIII. 134
  Tempest, The, or The Enchanted Island (with Dryden), VIII. 28, 120
  Temple of Love, The, VIII. 132
  Unfortunate Lovers, The, VI. 240
  Wits, The, VIII. 120
Davenport, Elizabeth, VIII. 261
Davenport, J., *The Witches of Huntingdon* (1646), VII. 507
Davenport, Mrs, in Mrs Gaskell's *Mary Barton*, XIII. 375
Davenport, Robert (*fl.* 1623), VI. 235, 236, 454; *The City-Night-Cap*, VI. 236, *also see* XIII. Add. 2; *A New Tricke to Cheat the Divell*, VI. 236
Davenport, William Bromley (1821–1884), XIV. 543
Daventry, X. 384
Davers, lady, in Richardson's *Pamela*, X. 5

Davey, Samuel, XIII. 470
David, I. 74, 93, 134, 147; II. 15, 106;
III. 174; IV. 33, 195, 231; X. 229; XIII.
369
David, in Cowley's *Davideis*, VII. 66, 67
David, in Watson's *Absalom*, VI. 296
David I, king of Scotland, II. 100, 101, 129
David II, king of Scotland, II. 102, 117,
129
David, king, in *Absalom and Achitophel*,
VIII. 37, 39
David, St (d. 601), I. 67
Davids, C. A. F. Rhys, XIV. 479
Davidson, Andrew Bruce (1831–1902),
XII. 341, 501
Davidson, James (d. 1866), XII. 519
Davidson, John (printer, 1541), IV. 412
Davidson, John (1549?–1603), III. 122,
150, 502; *Ane Schort Discurs of the
Estaitis quha hes caus to deploir the
Deith of this excellent Servand of God*,
III. 150
Davidson, John (1857–1909), XII. 113;
XIII. 216 ff., 223, 501
Ballad of Heaven, A, XIII. 217
Bruce, XIII. 216
Fleet Street Eclogues, XIII. 217
For Lovers, XIII. 217
Kinnoull Hill, XIII. 217
London, XIII. 217
Lutanist, The, XIII. 217
Scaramouch in Naxos, XIII. 216
Smith, XIII. 216
Davidson, Samuel (1806–1898), XII. 466
Davidson, Thomas (1838–1870), XIII. 501
Davidson, Thomas (1840–1900), XIV. 472
Davidson, W. L., XIV. 468
Davies, Emily, XIV. 429, 430, 599
Davies, Evan, X. 386
Davies, George, XIV. 591
Davies, Sir John (1569–1626), II. 201,
268; IV. 123, 150, 161 ff., 166, 311, 334,
479, 480, 519; V. 422, 477; VII. 110,
211, 432, 448, 470
*Contention betwixt a Wife, a Widdow and
a Maide, A*, IV. 161, 357
*Dialogue between a Gentleman Usher and
a Poet, A*, IV. 161
*Discoverie of the true causes why Ireland
has never been intirely subdued*, IV. 161,
162; VII. 212
Epigrammes, III. 201; VII. 432
Hymns to Astræa, IV. 161, 163
Lark, To the, IV. 163
Lottery, A, IV. 161
Nosce Teipsum, IV. 131, 161, 162; VII.
277, 278; VIII. 9
Orchestra, IV. 161, 162
Davies, John (1627?–1693), IV. 455; VII.
390, 505
Davies, John (1679–1732), IX. 340, 526,
528
Davies, John, of Hereford (1565?–1618?),
IV. 132, 146, 158, 159, 161, 335, 475,
487, 520, 521, 533; VI. 248; VII. 501
Microcosmos, IV. 131, 411

Davies, John, of Hereford
Mirum in Modum, IV. 131
Scourge of Folly, The, IV. 334, 517; VI.
137
Summa Totalis, IV. 131
Davies, John, of Kidwelly, *Clélie*, trans.
of, VIII. 372; *Cléopâtre*, trans. of, 372
Davies, John Llewelyn, XIV. 591
Davies, Myles (1662–1715?), *The Critical
History of Pamphlets*, X. 166
Davies, Richard (1635–1708), VIII. 106,
415
Davies, Richard (d. 1762), XIV. 592
Davies, Robert (1793–1875), XI. 468; XIV.
531
Davies, Sneyd (1709–1769), X. 454
Davies, Thomas, chaplain at Aleppo (*fl.*
1624–1627), VII. 308
Davies, Thomas (1712?–1785), VIII. 423;
X. 191, 212, 433, 436, 445, 471, 483;
XI. 327, 448, 453; *Dramatic Miscellanies*,
VIII. 159; *Life of Garrick*, XI. 326, 333;
Miscellaneous and Fugitive Pieces, X.
459, 463
Davies, William, XIV. 525
Davila, Enrico Caterino, VIII. 30
Davis, Alexander, XIV. Add. 6
Davis, Francis, XIV. 326, 327, 568
Davis, Henry Edwards (1756–1784), *Ex-
amination of...Mr Gibbon's History*,
X. 308, 507
Davis, James, XIV. 51
Davis, John (d. 1622), III. 327
Davis, Sir John Francis (1795–1890), XII.
500
Davis, Lockyer (1719–1791), XI. 336
Davis, Miss, VII. 103
Davis, Nathan (1812–1882), XII. 316, 475
Davis, Richard, X. 371
Davis, Thomas Osborne (1814–1845), XIV.
317 ff., 568
Boatman of Kinsale, XIV. 317
Lament for Owen Roe O'Neill, XIV. 317
My Grave, XIV. 317
O the Marriage, XIV. 317
Sack of Baltimore, The, XIV. 317
Davis strait, IV. 76
Davison, Francis (*fl.* 1602), III. 523
Davison, Francis and Walter (*fl.* 1602),
In praise of a beggar's life, IV. 124;
A Poetical Rapsody, IV. 109, 117, 118,
123 ff., 138, 196, 357, 467; *Relation of
Saxony*, IV. 123
Davison, John (1777–1834), XII. 466; XIV.
596
Davison, William (1541?–1608), IV. 123,
124
Davisson, John (d. 1721), X. 387
D'Avolos, in *Loves Sacrifice*, VI. 192
Davy, Adam (*fl.* 1308?), I. 335, 353, 355,
474
Davy, Sir Humphry (1778–1829), XIV.
260, 272, 278 ff., 287, 294, 557
Davy Diceplayer, II. 232
Davy Drunken-nole, II. 232
Davyd ap Gwilym, I. 275

Davys, John (1550?–1605), IV. 78, 455; *The Seaman's Secrets*, IV. 76, 82, 104; *The Worlde's Hydrographical Description*, IV. 76

Daw, in *The Silent Woman*, VI. 22

Dawes, Richard (1708–1766), IV. 265; XII. 325; *Miscellanea Critica*, IX. 341, 526

Dawes, Richard (1793–1867), XIV. 414, 601, 605

Dawes, Sir William (1671–1724), archbishop of York, X. 360

Dawks, Ichabod (1661–1730), IX. 5

Dawkyn, in *Turnament of Totenham*, I. 366

Dawley, IX. 81, 226

Dawney, Edmund, XIV. 533

Dawson, Coningsby William, XIV. 501

Dawson, George (1821–1876), XII. 472

Dawson, Phoebe, in Crabbe's *Parish Register*, XI. 146

Dawson, S., XIII. 471

Dawson, T., *The good huswifes jewell*, IV. 543

Dawson, William Harbutt, XIII. 488

Dawson, William James, XIV. 501

Dawsonfield, Westmorland, X. 386

Daxara, in Thomson's *Edward and Eleonora*, X. 109

Day, Angell (*fl.* 1586), IV. 438, 525; *English Secretary*, VII. 391

Day, Isaac, XI. 383, 485

Day, John, printer (1522–1584), III. 80, 333, 494; IV. 384, 386, 389, 397, 399, 400, 546

Day, John (*fl.* 1606), V. 147, 311, 312, 323, 326, 328, 332 ff., 361, 332, 474; VI. 211–217 (main entry), 231, 309, 371, 455
   Blind Beggar of Bednal Green, The, V. 332, 474
   'Characters,' VI. 216
   'Colloquies,' VI. 216
   Cox of Collumpton, VI. 96
   Humour out of Breath, VI. 215
   Ile of Guls, The, III. 355; VI. 212 ff.
   Italian Tragedy, The, V 325
   Law Trickes, VI. 215
   Maiden's Holiday, The, V. 146
   Orphan's Tragedy, The, VI. 96
   Parliament of Bees, The, V. 332, 334; VI. 212, 215 ff., 233
   Peregrinatio Scholastica, VI. 216
   Thomas Merry, VI. 96
   Travailes of The three English Brothers, The, VI. 69
   See, also, under Chettle, Dekker *and* Marlowe

Day, John, Hathway, R. and Haughton, W., *The Conqueste of Spayne by John a Gaunt*, VIII. 126

Day, Lal Behari, XIV. 575, 576; *Folk Tales of Bengal*, XIV. 342; *Govinda Sámanta*, XIV. 342

Day, Thomas (1748–1789), X. 424; XI. 478; XIV. 601; *Sandford and Merton*, XI. 381, 382; XIV. 392, 393; *History of Little Jack*, XI. 382

Day (a lady's name), in *The Lover asketh pardon of his dere*, III. 180

Day and Chettle, *Orphan's Tragedy*, V. 325

Day and Haughton, *Thomas Merry, or Beech's Tragedy*, V. 325, 326

Day and William Rowley, *Travailes of The three English Brothers*, V. 366

Daye or Day, Richard (1552–1607?), IV. 495; V. 394

Dayot, Armand, XIV. 540

Dayrolles, Solomon, X. 257

Deacon, Thomas (1697–1753), X. 355, 356, 516

Dead Man's Song, The, IV. 353

De adventu Normannorum in Angliam et de jure quod habuit Willelmus bastardus ad regnum Angliae, II. 366

Deakin, Mary H., XIII. 553

Deal, XI. 354, 358

Dean Prior, Dartmoor, VII. 5 ff., 11, 13, 17

Deane, Sir Anthony (1638?–1721), VIII. 257

Deans, David, in Scott's *Heart of Midlothian*, XII. 25

Deans, Jeanie, in Scott's *Heart of Midlothian*, XII. 18, 25

Death, I. 227, 458

Death, in a broadside, III. 87

Death, in *Death and Liffe*, II. 40

Death, in *Every-man*, V. 53

Death, in folk plays, V. 31

Death, in *Mirour de l'Omme*, II. 140

Death, in *Piers the Plowman*, II. 22, 27, 28, 38

Death, in *The Example of Virtue*, II. 227

Death, in *The Parlement of the Three Ages*, II. 38

Death, in *The Passetyme of Pleasure*, II. 226

Death, in *The Wonderfull Yeare*, IV. 351

Death, king of, in *The Pride of Life*, V. 3

Death, The Doctrinal of, II. 323

Death and Liffe, II. 40, 41, 432, 435

Death-Song of Ragnar Lodbrok, X. 221, 222, 224; XIV. 51

Debarrys, the, in *Felix Holt*, XIII. 397

Debates, II. 500, 501. See, also, *The Controversy between a lover and a Jay*, II. 224, 326

Debates and speeches in Jacobean times, XII. 439 ff.

Débats, I. 239; V. 2, 31, 92, 94

Debauched Cavalier, The, VII. 382

Deben, river, XIII. 142

Debet, Sir Daniel, in *The Serving Man's Comfort*, V. 374

De Bonnefons, F., VIII. 449

Deborah, IV. 170

Deborah, in *Jacob and Esau*, V. 112

Deceit, in *The World tost at Tennis*, VI. 75

'Declaration of the Rights of Man and the Citizen,' XI. 71

Declaratory act, XI. 10

Decle, Lionel, XIV. 192

Decretals of Gregory IX, VIII. 312

Dedekind, Friedrich, III. 82; *Grobiana's Nuptials*, III. 82; *Grobianus* (trans. as *The School of Slovenrie*), III. 82; IV. 355, 443, 528; *Grobianus et Grobiana*, III. 82
Dedlock, lady, in *Bleak House*, XIII. 329
Dee, John (1527–1608), IV. 73, 436, 453, 455, 534; V. 377, 477; VI. 294; VII. 222, 369, 510, 511; VIII. 350; IX. 530; *British Monarchy*, IV. 95
Dee valley, X. 115
Deer, The Book of, XII. 513
Deeside, XII. 31
Defence for Mylke Maydes, A, III. 486
De Flores, in Middleton's *The Changeling*, VI. 76, 77, 80; XII. 222
Defoe, Daniel (1661?–1731), I. 257; II. 82; III. 363; IV. 93, 108; VI. 51, 56; VII. 167; VIII. 141; IX. 1 ff. (main entry), 80, 110, 394, 415 ff., 465, 476, 546, 569, 570; X. 1, 2, 5, 14, 18, 20, 26, 46, 386, 412; XII. 175, 201, 231, 250, 522; XIII. 314, 427; XIV. 197, 213, 461
Appeal to Honour and Justice, IX. 14 ff.
Atalantis Major (attr. to Defoe), IX. 13
Augusta Triumphans, IX. 23
Captain Singleton, IX. 22
Colonel Jacque, IX. 22
Complete English Gentleman, IX. 24, 398, 404
Complete English Tradesman, IX. 24
Consolidator, The, IX. 12, 19
Dissenters in England Vindicated, IX. 547
Due Preparations, IX. 22
Dyet of Poland, The, IX. 12
Enquiry into the occasional Conformity, X. 374
Essay on...Apparitions, IX. 24
Essay upon Projects, IX. 7, 397, 404
Experiment, The, IX. 12
Family Instructor, The, IX. 16, 19
Farther Adventures of Robinson Crusoe, IX. 19
Fortunate Mistress. See *Roxana*
Four Years Voyages of Capt. George Roberts, IX. 23
Friendly Demon, IX. 21
General History of Trade, IX. 15
Giving Alms no Charity, IX. 11
Great Law of Subordination Considered, IX. 23
History of...Mr Duncan Campbell, IX. 21
History of Peter the Great, IX. 22
History of the Union, IX. 13
History of the Wars of Charles XII, IX. 16
Hymn to the Pillory, IX. 9
Impartial History of Peter Alexowitz, IX. 22
Journal of the Plague Year, IX. 22
Jure Divino, IX. 12
Legion's Address, IX. 8
Letter to Mr Howe, X. 374
Manufacturer, The, IX. 14

Defoe, Daniel
Memoirs of a Cavalier, IX. 22
Memoirs of Captain George Carleton, IX. 23
Memoirs of the Church of Scotland, IX. 17
Mercator, IX. 14, 15
Minutes of Mesnager, IX. 17
Moll Flanders, IX. 22; X. 48
Mrs Veal, IX. 19
New Test, IX. 9
New Voyage round the World, IX. 23
Of Royall Educacion, IX. 406
Original Power of the Collective Body, IX. 8
Periodicals with which he was connected, IX. 432
Plan of the English Commerce, IX. 24
Political History of the Devil, IX. 24
Reasons against the Succession of the House of Hanover, IX. 14
Religious Courtship, IX. 22
Review, The, IX. 1, 4, 5, 10, 11, 13, 14, 34, 432
Robinson Crusoe, IX. 1, 11, 17, 19, 20, 21, 25, 106, 141, 142; X. 84; XI. 323, 366, 373, 477; XII. 251; XIII. 201, 265; XIV. 255, 438
Roxana, IX. 22 ff.
Secret History of the October Club, IX. 19
Secret History of the White Staff, IX. 15, 16
Serious Reflections during the Life... of Robinson Crusoe, IX. 19
Shortest Way with the Dissenters. IX. 7 ff., 19; X. 374
System of Magic, IX. 24
Tour thro' the Whole Island of Great Britain, IX. 21, 23
True-Born Englishman, IX. 8
True Relation of the Apparition, IX. 12
Defoe, Daniel, the younger, IX. 24
Defoe, Hannah, IX. 21
Defoe, Sophia, IX. 24
Degare, Sir, I. 311, 471
Degge, Sir Simon (1612–1704), VIII. 468
Degrevant, Sir, I. 289, 471
Deguileville, Guillaume, II. 170, 200, 201, 503; *Pilgrimage of the Soul*, IV. 353
De Heretico Comburendo, II. 67, 422
Deianeira, in *Confessio Amantis*, II. 148
d'Eichthal, G., XIV. 477
Deimling, Hermann, ed. of *Chester Plays*, II. 426
Deirdre's Lament, XIV. 304
Deism, XI. 286, 287
Dekker, Thomas (1570?–1641?), III. 114, 371, 485; IV. 115, 323, 351 ff., 363, 393, 434, 526 ff., 532, 534; V. 117, 184, 251, 254, 311, 312, 319, 323, 327, 332, 334, 345, 371; VI. 4, 13, 18, 29–57 (main entry), 64, 66, 68, 69, 95 ff., 142, 145, 146, 165, 168 ff., 184, 190, 195, 218, 226 ff., 231, 250, 345, 424 ff., 427, 443, and see Add.; VII. 389, 395; VIII. 162; IX. 32, 51, 262
Belman of London, The, IV. 354, 517
Canaan's Calamitie, IV. 324

Dekker, Thomas
Civil Wars in France, The, vi. 55
Dead Tearme, The, vi. 57
Dekker his Dreame, vi. 51, 57
Fowre Birds of Noahs Arke, vi. 57
Friar Rush, vi. 53
Gul's Hornbooke, iii. 82; iv. 356; vii. 379; ix. 263
Honest Whore, The, vi. 53, 54, 62, 95, 173
If It Be Not Good, the Divel is in it, vi. 53; viii. 123
Knight's Conjuring, A, iv. 354
Lady Jane, vi. 168
Lanthorne and Candle-light, iv. 354
Match mee in London, vi. 53, 98
Newes from Hell, iv. 352, 353; vii. 381
North-Ward Hoe, vi. 54, 170 ff.
Old Fortunatus, vi. 52
Page of Plymouth, vi. 12, 54, 96
Patient Grissill, vi. 54, 97, 100, 231
Phaeton, vi. 51, 54
Robert the Second, vi. 13, 54
Rod for Runawayes, A, vi. 56
Satiro-Mastix, vi. 4, 42, 53, 171, 173
Seven Deadly Sinnes of London, The, iv. 352, 510, 516; viii. 10
Shoemaker's Holiday, The, iii. 371; v. 255, 357, 373; vi. 52
Spanish Moor's Tragedy, The, vi. 55
Strange Horse Race, A, iv. 356
Sun's Darling, The, v. 125
Troilus and Cressida, vi. 51
West-Ward Hoe, vi. 54, 170 ff., 212
Whore of Babylon, The, vi. 53, 91, 150
Wonder of A Kingdom, The, vi. 54, 215
Wonderfull Yeare, The, iv. 351; vi. 56
Worke for Armorours, vi. 56
Wyat, The Famous History of Sir Thomas, vi. 54, 169, 173
Delacour, lady, in Miss Edgeworth's *Belinda,* xi. 297
Delacroix, Eugène, v. 302
Delamere, Lord, ii. 414
Delane, John Thaddeus (1817 1879), xiv. 172, 180 ff., 533
Delany, Mrs Mary Granville (1700–1788), xi. 343, 347, 354, 365, 473
Delany, Patrick (1685?–1768), ix. 97, 459, 464, 466, 467
Delap, John (1725–1812), xi. 457; *Royal Suppliants,* xi. 274
De La Quintinye, viii. 449
De La Ramée, Louise. *See* Ouida
de la Rochejaquelin, xii. 377
Delectable Demaundes, iii. 489
Delft, ii. 327
Delgan, in Layamon, i. 236
Delight, in *The Playe of Playes and Pastimes,* vi. 392
Delight, in *The Tears of the Muses,* iii. 241
De l'Isle, Alain, *Anti-Claudianus,* viii. 59
De Lisle, Ambrose Lisle March Phillipps (1809–1878), xii. 276, 454
Delitiae Poetarum Scotorum, ix. 550, 554 ff.
Delius, Nicolaus, v. 257, 278, 279, 305

Dell, William (d. 1664), vii. 316; ix. 386, 570, 571
Della Cruscan poets, xi. 40, 158, 172, 176 (main entry), 178, 180; xii. 124
Della Porretta family, in Richardson's *Sir Charles Grandison,* x. 11
Della Porta, G. B., *L'Astrologo,* vi. 322, 479; *La Cintia,* vi. 305; *La Fantesca,* vi. 305; *Trappolaria,* vi. 322, 477
Delolme, Jean-Louis, x. 500; *The Constitution of England,* x. 296
Deloney, Thomas (1543?–1607?), ii. 415; iii. 340, 343, 359 ff., 367 ff., 533; iv. 390, 536
The Gentle Craft, iii. 368, containing the following tales: *Crispine and Crispinus,* iii. 368; *Jack of Newbury,* iii. 368; *Master Peachey and his men,* iii. 369; *Richard Casteler,* iii. 369; *Simon Eyre,* iii. 368, 369, 371; *Sir Hugh,* iii. 368; *Thomas of Reading,* iii. 368, 370, *also see* Add.; v. 373
Deloraine, in Scott's *Lay of the Last Minstrel,* xii. 46
Delphic Oracle, in *Saturnalia,* vi. 319
Delphium (*i.e.* Pont-à-Mousson), in *Euphormio,* ix. 256
Deluge, the, xiv. 192
Delves, in Norton's *Ordinall,* ii. 213
Demands, Budget of, iii. 489
Demaundes joyous, iii. 95, 489
Dembley, John Malham, xiii. 557
De Méré, chevalier (afterwards marquis), viii. 376
Demetrias, St, i. 74
Demetrius, in *Confessio Amantis,* ii. 147
Demetrius, in *The Poetaster,* vi. 18, 42, 44
De Mille, James (1836–1880), xiv. 360, 581
Democritus, viii. 338
Democritus, riddles of, iii. 489
Demogorgon, in Shelley's *Prometheus Unbound,* xii. 67
Demonio, in Calderon's *El Magico Prodigioso,* xiii. 144
Demonology, vii. 367 ff., 503 ff.
De Morgan, Augustus (1806–1871), iv. 263; xii. 370, 521; xiv. 10, 262, 263, 472, 474, 556
Demosthenes, iii. 420, 429; iv. 1, 436; vii. 130, 131, 313, 316; ix. 229, 528; xi. 13; xii. 329, 332, 481, 485, 486, 489, 493, 495; *De Falsa Legatione,* xii. 330
Dempster, George (1732–1818), x. 191, 477
Dempster, Thomas (1579?–1625), iv. 253; vii. 315, 486; xii. 522
Dempster, in George Eliot's *Janet's Repentance,* xiii. 387
Denania, x. 237
Denbigh, earl of. *See* Feilding, William
Dence, Jael, in Reade's *Put Yourself in his Place,* xiii. 425
Denham, Henry (*fl.* 1591), iv. 400, 546
Denham, Sir John, father of the poet (1559–1639), vii. 59

Denham, Sir John (1615–1669), IV. 156;
VII. 58 ff., 63, 67, 69, 70, 409, 431, 465;
VIII. 3, 91, 247, 371, 410; IX. 67
   Aeneid, trans. of second book, VII. 59
   Cooper's Hill, VII. 38, 59, 60; IX. 69,
   179; X. 111
   Destruction of Troy, The, VII. 59, 61
   *Elegy on the Death of Henry, Lord
   Hastings*, VII. 61
   Essay on Translation, VII. 264
   Horace (Corneille's), begun by Mrs
   Philips, finished by Sir John Denham,
   VIII. 180
   Instructions to a Painter, VIII. 81, 408
   Of Justice, VII. 61
   Of Old Age, VII. 61
   Of Prudence, VII. 61
   On Mr Abraham Cowley's Death, VII. 61
   Passion of Dido for Aeneas, The, VII. 61
   Poems, VII. 61
   Second Western Wonder, VII. 350
   Sophy, The, VII. 59, 61
   Version of the Psalms of David, A, VII. 61
   Western Wonder, VII. 348
Deniehy, Henry (1828–1865), XIV. 362, 585
Denino, Fife, XI. 243
Denis, St, II. 102
Denison, Gedge Anthony (1805–1896),
XIV. 591
Denison, John Evelyn, 1st viscount Os-
sington (1800–1873), XII. 307
Denman, admiral Joseph, XIV. 512
Denman, Thomas Denman, lord, 'Parlia-
ment and the Courts,' XII. 153
Denmark, V. 171, 200, 222, 307; VII. 197;
VIII. 267; XII. 351; XIV. 293
Denmark, king of, in *Faire Em*, V. 252
Dennis, John (1657–1734), V. 189; VI. 28;
VII. 265; VIII. 4, 143, 428, 433, 436, 438;
IX. 73, 78, 122, 140, 142 (main entry),
143, 168, 435, 442, 448, 456, 473 ff.,
512; XI. 250
   *Advancement and Reformation of Modern
   Poetry*, IX. 142, 143
   A Plot and No Plot, VIII. 194
   Essay on…Shakespeare, IX. 142
   Essay on the Operas, IX. 142
   Grounds of Criticism in Poetry, IX. 143
   Impartial Critic, The, VIII. 375
   Reflections on Pope's Essay on Criticism,
   VIII. 61
   *Reflections upon…An Essay upon
   Criticism*, IX. 77
   Rinaldo and Armida, VIII. 194
   *Three Letters on the Genius and Writings
   of Shakespeare*, VIII. 193
   Usefulness of the Stage, VIII. 167
Dennis, John (1873), IX. Add.; XI. 423
Dennis, Ned, in *Barnaby Rudge*, XIII. 321
Denny, Sir Anthony (1501–1549), VII. 329,
330
Dennys, John (d. 1609), *Secrets of Angling*,
IV. 374, 541; VII. 464
Dent, John Charles (1841–1888), XIV. 583;
   Last Forty Years, The, XIV. 358; *Story of the
   Upper Canadian Rebellion, The*, XIV. 358

Denward, Mrs E., XIV. 390
Denys, in *The Cloister and the Hearth*,
XIII. 429
De Oculo Morali, II. 365
Deor, Complaint of, I. 4, 19 ff., 36, 373,
423, 428; II. 397; V. 26
De Palacio Garcia, IV. 455
Depazzi, in *The Traytor*, VI. 199
Depden, Suffolk, X. 294
De Phillide et Flora, I. 460
Deptford, V. 142; VIII. 260
De Quincey, Thomas (1785–1859), X. 476,
483; XI. 246, 344, 409, 417, 423; XII.
159, 160, 164, 174, 178, 203 ff., 219,
223, 224 ff. (main entry), 249, 430, 433,
437, 441, 444 (main entry), 490, *also
see* Add.; XIII. 148, 158; XIV. 184, 203,
313, 462, 532
   Autobiography, XII. 204
   Confessions of an Opium-Eater, XI. 147
   Confessions of an English Opium Eater,
   XII. 160, 194, 215, 224
   Miscellanea, XII. 206
   On Murder as one of the Fine Arts, XII.
   175, 225
   Our Ladies of Sorrow, XII. 226
   Suspiria de Profundis, XIII. 109
De Raaf, V. 53
Derar, in Ockley's *History of the Saracens*,
X. 281
Derby, X. 28; XI. 426, 431; XIV. 28, 437
Derby Ale-house, IX. 261
Derby, countess of. *See* Stanley, Alice
Derby, earl of, in *Edward III*, V. 246
Derby, earls of. *See* Stanley
Derbyshire, VII. 289; VIII. 106; IX. 277;
X. 2, 131, 386; XII. 230, 507, 511; XIII.
390
De Refuge, E., IV. 526
Derham, William (1657–1735), IX. 506,
529; X. 512; *Physico-Theology*, X. 346
Derham, William (1846), XIV. 563
Dering, Edward (1540?–1576), IV. 236,
492; VII. 316
Dering or Deering, Sir Edward (1598–
1644), VII. 440
Dermody, Thomas (1775–1802), XIV. 568
Dermot and the Earl, II. 502
Deronda, Daniel, George Eliot's, XIII. 400
De Ros, William L. L. Fitz-G., lord, XII.
509
Derosne, C. B., XIII. 546
Derozio, Henry Louis Vivian, XIV. 575;
   The Fakeer of Jungheera, XIV. 336
Derrick, Samuel (1724–1769), X. 442; XI.
448
Derry, IV. 311; VII. 285, 301
Derry, deanery of, IX. 281
Derwent river, XI. 95
'De Sawdust, Thomas' (De Quincey), XII.
225
Descartes, René, VII. 266, 284, 292, 302,
303, 394; VIII. 279, 285, 286, 290, 329,
334, 338, 340, 347, 348, 455, 472; IX.
61, 229, 282, 285, 287, 298, 314; X.
322, 348; XIV. 8, 268

Descartes, René
Dioptrique, VII. 285
Discours de la Méthode, VII. 285
Meditationes de prima philosophia, VII. 285, 286
Objectiones, VII. 285
Traité des passions de l'âme, VIII. 372
Deschamps, Eustache, II. 159, 467
Deschamps, J., IX. 435, 436
Deschapelles, V. 173
Desdemona, in Othello, IV. 78; V. 202, 203; VI. 95; VIII. 164
Desire, in prince Arthur's marriage pageant, VI. 332
Desire, in The Bowge of Courte, III. 73
Desire, in Tom Tyler, V. 117
Des Maizeaux, Pierre (1673?–1745), VIII. 471, 481; IX. 509
Desmarets de Saint Sorlin, J., VII. 270
Desmond, earl of. See Fitzthomas, Maurice
Despair, in Piers the Plowman, II. 28
Despair, cave of, in The Faerie Queene, III. 237
Despair, giant, in Bunyan's Pilgrim's Progress, VII. 173
Despauterius, Johannes, III. 429
Despenser or Spencer, Henry le (d. 1406), bishop of Norwich, II. 56
Desportes, Philippe, III. 251, 257, 258, 260, 261, 262, 263, 264, 523, also see Add.; IV. 24, 196, 223, 377, 443; IX. 167; Diane, III. 258, 261
Despréaux, Boileau, IX. 482. See, also, Boileau
De Stefani, A., XIII. Add. 2
Destiny, in Tom Tyler, V. 117
Destouches, Philippe-Néricault, X. 68, 78; Philosophe marié, X. 79
D'Estrades, count, VIII. 263
De Tabley, lord. See Warren, John Byrne Leicester
Detection of Damnable Drifts, VII. 373
Detraction, in Confessio Amantis, II. 147
Detraction, in The Faerie Queene, II. 234
Deuceace, Thackeray's, XIII. 277, 279 ff.
Deusdedit (d. 663/4), I. 82
Deuteromelia, III. 84; IV. 536
Deutschbein, M., Englische Sagengeschichte, I. 293
Deventer, III. 13
De Vere, Sir Aubrey (1788–1846), XI. 409; XII. 416
De Vere, Aubrey Thomas (1814–1902), XII. 441, 456; XIII. 188, 501
Devereux, lady Jane, of Merivale, IV. 170
Devereux, Penelope (lady Rich), VI. 189
Devereux, Robert, 2nd earl of Essex (1566–1601), III. 212, 254, 508; IV. 103, 114, 132, 133, 135, 142, 163, 164, 170, 200, 214, 215, 239, 276, 282, 376, 466; V. 346, 361, 371; VI. 30, 37, 101, 166, 248, 339, 344, 385; VII. 194, 343, 447, 454; XII. 440; XIV. 308
Devereux, Robert, 3rd earl of Essex (1591–1646), VII. 383, 447; VIII. 71

Devereux, Walter, 1st earl of Essex (d. 1576), III. 254, 508, also see Add.; IV. 466; V. 346
Devereux, Walter (brother of Robert, earl of Essex), IV. 376
de Vigny, Alfred, XII. 412
Devil, the, II. 366, 409
Devil, The, seen at St Albans, VII. 507
Devil, in Mirour de l'Omme, II. 140
Devil o'er Stirling, The, IX. 376
Devils, The Parliament of, II. 325, 501
Devine, Molly, Charlotte Eccles's, XIV. 325
Devizes. See Richard of
Devon booksellers and printers, XI. 468
Devonian system, the, XIV. 294
Devonshire, IV. 157, 190, 235, 314; V. 255; VI. 188, 237; VII. 1, 6, 9, 17, 386; IX. 162, 538; X. 21, 385, 490; XI. 34, 39; XII. 132. 345, 346, 514, 519; XIII. 276, 355, 360, 363, 364, 368; XIV. 84, 292
Devonshire, duchesses of. See Cavendish, Georgiana; Cavendish, Margaret
Devonshire, dukes of. See Cavendish, Spencer Compton; Cavendish, William
Devonshire, earls of. See Blount, Charles; Cavendish, William
Devotion, in Ane Pleasant Satyre, III. 125
Devotion, in Mirour de l'Omme, II. 142
De Waal, Daphne, XIV. Add. 4
Dewart, E. H., XIV. 582
Dewes, Giles (d. 1535), III. 550
D'Ewes, Sir Simonds (1602–1650), VI. 486; VII. 440, 441, 449; Autobiography, VII. 223, 224
De Wet, Christiaan Rudolf, XIV. Add. 6
De Witt, Dutch traveller, VI. 252, 260, 261
Dewsbury, William (1621–1688), VIII. 110, 415
Dey, Lal Behari, XIV. 575, 576
Deyverdun, George (fl. 1768–1783), X. 311, 507, 508
Dialogue between James II and his Italian queen, VIII. 93
Dialogue between the devil and George II, IX. 371
Dialogus duarum sororum, III. 81
Dialogus linguae et ventris, II. 321
Diana, II. 179; IV. 122, 196; VI. 163
Diana, in Colin Blowbol's Testament, III. 86
Diana, in Frier Bacon, V. 340
Diana, in The Flower and the Leaf, II. 219
Diana, in Reason and Sensuality, II. 202
Diana, George Meredith's, XIII. 444
Diaper, William, Eclogues, IX. 126
Diaries and personal memoirs in Jacobean times, VII. 449
Dibben, Thomas (d. 1741), IX. 482
Dibdin, Charles (1745–1814), VIII. 423; X. 89, 425, 426, 443; XI. 281, 448, 453, 457; XIV. 224
Dibdin, James C., Annals of the Edinburgh Stage, X. 192, 444; XIII. 514
Dibdin, Thomas Frognall (1776–1847), XII. 350, 362, 520, 521
Aedes Althorpianae, XII. 366
Bibliographical Decameron, The, XII. 367

Dibdin, Thomas Frognall
  Bibliographical Tour, A, XII. 367
  Bibliomania, XII. 365, 366
  Bibliophobia, XII. 367
  Bibliotheca Spenceriana, XII. 366
  Introduction to the Greek and Latin Classics, XII. 366, 367
  Library Companion, The, XII. 367
  Reminiscences of a Literary Life, I. 216; XII. 367
Dibdin, Thomas John (1771–1841), XI. 447; XIII. 514, 516
Dibelius, W., XIII. 543; *Englische Romankunst*, XIII. 341
Diccon, in *Gammer Gurtons Nedle*, VI. 297
Dice Play, IX. 51
Diceto. *See* Ralph of
Dicey, Albert Venn, XIV. 536
Dicey, Edward, XIV. 192
Dick, Ernst, XIII. 570
Dick, in Mrs Trimmer's *Robins*, XI. 379
Dick, Mr, in *David Copperfield*, XIII. 327
Dick Amlet, in Vanbrugh's *Confederacy*, VIII. 162
Dick o' the Cow, II. 415
Dicke Droom, in *The Glasse of Governement*, V. 113, 114
Dicke of Devonshire, VI. 432; VII. 453
Dickens, Charles (1812–1870), II. 177; VI. 24, 28, 359; VII. 137; VIII. 20; X. 37, 64; XI. 287, 385, 478; XII. 25, 219 ff., 250 ff., 431; XIII. 57, 178, 263, 265, 267, 275, 294, 301, 303 ff. (main entry), 344, 351, 376, 377, 386, 388, 420, 422, 423, 427, 442, 447, 458, 459, 461, 470, 495, 514, 516, 518, 523, 530 ff., 573, *also see* Add. 3; XIV. 148, 163, 170, 187, 189, 190, 236, 326, 444, 445
  All the Year Round, XII. 441
  American Notes, XIII. 322, 323; XIV. 348
  Barnaby Rudge, X. 255; XIII. 318, 320, 325, 332, 457
  Battle of Life, The, XIII. 323
  Bleak House, XIII. 328, 332
  'Boots at the Holly Tree Inn,' XIII. 335
  Child's History of England, A, XIII. 320, 329
  Chimes, The, XIII. 323, 324
  Christmas Books, XIII. 323, 326
  Christmas Carol, A, XIII. 323, 324
  Christmas stories, XIII. 305
  Cricket on the Hearth, The, XIII. 323, 324
  David Copperfield, XIII. 305, 322, 326 ff., 331, 333, 337, 391
  Doctor Marigold's Prescriptions, XIII. 335
  Dombey and Son, XIII. 317, 324, 325
  Edwin Drood, The mystery of, XIII. 310, 334, 335
  George Silverman's Explanation, XIII. 323, 334
  'Ghost in Master B's room, The,' XIII. 335
  Great Expectations, XIII. 314, 328, 330, 333, 421
  Hard Times, XIII. 310, 313, 328 ff., 332, 336, 337, 375, 378
  Haunted House, The, XIII. 335

Dickens, Charles
  Haunted Man, The, XIII. 323, 324, 326
  Holiday Romance, A, XIII. 334
  Hunted Down, XIII. 334
  'Island of Silver-store, The,' XIII. 335
  Letters of Charles Dickens to Wilkie Collins, XIII. 438
  Little Dorrit, XIII. 317, 330, 331
  Martin Chuzzlewit, XIII. 322, 324, 325
  Master Humphrey's Clock, XIII. 308, 318, 321
  Message from the Sea, A (with Wilkie Collins), XIII. 335
  Mrs Lirriper, XIII. 335
  Mudfog Papers, The, XIII. 308
  Mugby Junction, XIII. 335
  Nicholas Nickleby, XIII. 314, 315, 317, 325
  No Thoroughfare (with Wilkie Collins), XIII. 335
  Old Curiosity Shop, The, XIII. 318, 319, 325
  Oliver Twist, X. 49; XIII. 315 ff., 325, 334
  Our Mutual Friend, XIII. 314, 319, 334 ff.
  'Our Parish,' XIII. 309, 313
  'Parliamentary Sketch,' XIII. 309
  Perils of Certain English Prisoners, The, XIII. 335
  Pickwick Papers, The, X. 45; XII. 119; XIII. 305, 307, 308, 310 ff., 318, 319, 322, 323, 325, 333, 377, 418; XIV. 218, 234, 255
  Pictures from Italy, XIII. 314, 324
  Seven Poor Travellers, The, XIII. 335
  Sketches by Boz, XII. 221; XIII. 305, 307 ff., 319
  Sketches of Young Couples, XIII. 308
  Sketches of Young Gentlemen, XIII. 308 313
  Somebody's Luggage, XIII. 335
  Tale of Two Cities, A, XIII. 268, 313, 320, 332, 333, 337
  Tom Tiddler's Ground, XIII. 335
  Uncommercial Traveller, The, XII. 119; XIII. 307, 332, 335
  Works (Rochester ed.), XIII. 456
  Wreck of the Golden Mary, The, XIII. 335
Dickens, Charles, Forster's *Life* of, XIII. 305
Dickens, Mary, XIII. 532
Dickenson, John (*fl.* 1594), III. 350, 367, 536; IV. 117, 469; *Shepheardes Complaint*, IV. 119
Dickins, Bruce, I. Add.
Dickinson, Francis Henry, XIV. 488
Dickinson, Henry, VIII. 42
Dickinson, William (1746–1823), XIV. 216
Dickson, David (1583–1663), IX. 543
Dickson, Robert, XII. 521
Dickson, William Purdie (1823–1901), XII. 371, 521
Dictionaries, English-Latin, III. 444
Dictionary, The New English, IV. 46
Dictionary of National Biography, IX. 236, 346, 347; X. 269; XII. 307, 309; XIV. 111, 143
Dictys Cretensis, I. 170, 467; II. 172
Dicuil (*fl.* 825), I. 434

Didactic Literature, Old French, II. 507
Diderot, Denis, I. 209; V. 292; VI. 82;
  IX. 301; X. 68, 78, 79, 81, 264; XI. 292,
  295, 296; XIII. 9, 468
  De la Poésie Dramatique, X. 79
  Éloge de Richardson, X. 17, 413
  Fils Naturel, Le, X. 79
  Paradoxe sur le Comédien, XI. 448
  Père de Famille, Le, X. 79; XI. 275
Dido, IX. 45, 60, 257, 258; XIII. 123
Dido, in *The Legend of Good Women*, II. 264
Dido, in *The Shepheards Calendar*, III. 224
Dido, queen of Carthage, IV. 18; V. 74,
  102; VIII. 65
Dido, tragedy on, in Vergilian hexa-
  meters, VI. 300
Dido, V. 70
Didot, printing press of, IV. 267
Didot Percival, in the Graal legend, I. 271
'Didymus Mountain' (*i.e.* Thomas Hill),
  IV. 375
Diego, in Arbuthnot's *History of John
  Bull*, IX. 135
Diego di Miranda, Don, in *Don Quixote*,
  IX. 269
Dieppe, IV. 142; XIII. 381
Dies Irae, IX. 178; XII. 9; XIII. 170
Dietary of ghostly health, The, II. 327
Dietrich, Franz, I. 49, 123
Dietrich von Bern, I. 36
Dieu save Dame Emme, in *Piers the Plow-
  man*, II. 5
Diffidence, in Bunyan's *Pilgrim's Pro-
  gress*, VII. 173
Digby, Everard (*fl.* 1590), IV. 274 ff., 507;
  VII. 278
  Arte natandi, De, IV. 275
  *Dissuasive from taking away the lyvings
  and goods of the Church*, IV. 275
  Duplici methodo, De, IV. 275
  *Theoria analytica, viam ad monarchiam
  scientiarum demonstrans*, IV. 275
Digby, George, 2nd earl of Bristol (1612–
  1677), VII. 440; *Elvira*, VIII. 130, 417
Digby, John, 1st earl of Bristol (1580–
  1653), VII. 440
Digby, Sir Kenelm (1603–1665), IV. 432;
  VII. 223, 238, 281, 302, 449, 470; VIII.
  64, 76, 323, 354, 359, 407; XIV. 281;
  *Journal of a Voyage into the Mediter-
  ranean*, VII. 222; *Observations on Religio
  Medici*, VII. 235; *Private Memoirs of*,
  VII. 222
Digby, Kenelm Henry (1800–1880), XII.
  448
Digby, Venetia, lady (born Stanley) (1600
  –1633), VII. 222
Digby plays, V. 19, 44, 390
Digby's Farewell, VIII. 96
Digges, Sir Dudley (1583–1639), IV. 310,
  510; VII. 441, 456; *The Compleat Am-
  bassador*, V. 477; VII. 191, 437
Digges, Dudley, the younger (1613–1643),
  VII. 456, 457
Digges, Leonard (1588–1635), IV. 436;
  VIII. 129

Diggon Davie, in *The Shepheards Calender*,
  III. 224
Dighton, Robert (1752?–1814), XIV. 225
Diligence, in *Ane Pleasant Satyre*, III.
  125, 126, 127, 128
Diligence, in *The Assembly of Ladies*, II.
  217
Dilke, Charles Wentworth (1789–1864),
  IX. 84; XI. 390; XII. 407
Dilke, Sir Charles Wentworth (1843–
  1911), XIV. 184, 200, 551; *Greater
  Britain*, XIV. 98, 255; *Problems of
  Greater Britain*, XIV. 255
Dillenius, John James (1687–1747), XIV.
  286, 560
Dillingham, John (*fl.* 1649), VII. 360;
  The Moderate Intelligencer, VII. 349;
  The Parliament Scout, VII. 349
Dillon, John Blake (1816–1866), XIV.
  317
Dillon, Peter (1785?–1847), XIV. 551
Dillon, Wentworth, 4th earl of Roscom-
  mon (1633?–1685), VII. 109; VIII. 219 ff.,
  409, 444, 446; IX. 70, 181, 473, 476;
  X. 183, 465; *Ars Poetica*, VIII. 221;
  Essay on Translated Verse, VIII. 220,
  221, 395
Dilly, Charles (1739–1807), X. 479; XI. 326,
  327
Dilly, Edward (1732–1779), X. 203, 481;
  XI. 325 ff.
Dilnot, Frank, XIV. 533
Dilworth, W. H., IX. 447, 466
Dimnet, Ernest, XIII. 557
Dingelstedt, Franz, V. 306
Dingley, Francis, of Munston, III. 197
Dingley, Rebecca, IX. 93, 95, 99, 126;
  XIV. 197
Dinmont, Dandie, in Scott's *Guy Man-
  nering*, XII. 17, 25
Dinsdale, Frederick T., IX. Add.
Dio Cassius, VI. 154
Dio Chrysostomus, XII. 495
Diocletian, I. 309
Diocletian, in *The Prophetesse*, VI. 139
Diodati, Charles (1608?–1638), VII. 100.
  131; X. 122
Diodati, Giovanni, VII. 481, 482
Diodati, villa, XII. 60
Diodorus Siculus, III. 67; VII. 488; XIV.
  579; *Bibliothecae Historicae*, XII. 49
Diogenes, in D'Avenant's *First Day's
  Entertainment*, VIII. 117
Diogenes, in *The Palice of Honour*, II.
  260
Diogenes Laertius, V. 125
Diogenes Laertius, in *The City Witt*, VI.
  225
Diomed, VIII. 76
Diomed, in *Confessio Amantis*, II. 148
Diomede, in *The Testament of Cresseid*,
  II. 248
'Dion, Halicarnasseus,' VII. 65
Dionysia, in *Alls Lost by Lust*, VI. 72
Dionysius, IV. 436
Dionysius Longinus, XII. 494

Dionysius the Areopagite, I. 204; III. 6, 214; IV. 270; IX. 314
Dionysius of Halicarnassus, VI. 182
Dionysius, in *Damon and Pithias*, v. 118
Dionysius, Pseudo-, III. 6, 9, 216
Dionysius the Tyrant, The History of, III. 122, 141
Dionysius's Geography, IX. 393
Diotima (Plato's), III. 216
Directioun, in Douglas's *Aeneid*, II. 264
Director, The, IX. 433
Directorium Sacerdotum, II. 315
Disciplina Clericalis, I. 365; II. 150
Discipline, The First Book of, III. 146. *See, also, under* Knox, John
Discobolus, XIII. 452
Discordia, in Arbuthnot's *History of John Bull*, IX. 134
Discourse of Poesy, A, VIII. 240
Discovery of 29 Sects, A, VII. 386
Discretion, in *Ane Pleasant Satyre*, III. 125
Discretion, in *Piers the Plowman*, II. 19
Discretion, in *The Example of Virtue*, II. 227, 230
Discretion, in *The Palice of Honour*, II. 261
Disdain, in *The Faerie Queene*, III. 230
Disdain, in *The Passetyme of Pleasure*, II. 234
Disney, John, XIV. 593
Disobedience, in *Mirour de l'Omme*, II. 140
Dispatch, in Thomson's *Castle of Indolence*, x. 106
Disputational learning, 1600-1660, VII. 484
Disraeli, Benjamin, earl of Beaconsfield (1804-1881), IX. 243; XIII. 20, 258, 340, 345 ff. (main entry), 400, 423, 545 ff.; XIV. 115, 124, 127, 129, 130, 164, 183, 195, 196, 198, 488, 508
   Alroy, XIII. 347, 349
   Coalition, XIII. 353
   Coningsby, XII. 155; XIII. 288, 346 ff., 352, 360, 373
   Contarini Fleming, XIII. 346, 352
   Count Alarcos, XIII. 353
   Endymion, XIII. 348 ff.
   Henrietta Temple, XIII. 346 ff., 350, 352
   Infernal Marriage, The, XIII. 351
   Ixion in Heaven, XIII. 351
   Letters of Runnymede, XIII. 347, 348
   Lothair, XIII. 348 ff.
   Popanilla, XIII. 351
   Revolutionary Epick, The, XIII. 352
   Rise of Iskander, The, XIII. 347
   Runnymede Letters, The, XIV. 181
   Spirit of Whiggism, The, XIII. 347
   Sybil, XIII. 347, 348, 350, 352, 373
   Tancred, XIII. 345, 346, 348 ff., 352
   Venetia, XIII. 346, 347, 352
   Vindication of the English Constitution, XIII. 347
   Vivian Grey, XIII. 346, 349, 351, 352, 436
   Whigs and Whiggism, XIII. 348
   Young Duke, The, XIII. 347, 350

Disraeli, Isaac (1766-1848), III. 78; XI. 466; XII. 366, 367, 521
   Amenities of Literature, XII. 364
   Calamities of Authors, XII. 364
   Curiosities of Literature, XII. 353, 364
   Literary Miscellanies, XII. 370
   Quarrels of Authors, XII. 364
Diss, Norfolk, II. 258; III. 67, 70, 72, 93
Dissait, in *Ane Pleasant Satyre*, III. 124
Dissertation sur la poésie anglaise, v. 287
'Dissidence of Dissent,' the, XIII. 101
Dissimulation, in *Kynge Johan*, v. 66
Distaff, Jenny, in *The Tatler*, IX. 39, 40, 53
Distaff-lane, in *The Masque of Christmas*, VI. 359
Distracted Emperor, The, VI. 459
Ditchley, near Woodstock, VIII. 206
Diu Krône, by Heinrich von dem Türlin, I. 269
Diurnall of Remarkable Occurents, The, III. 149, 502
Diurnalls, VII. 346, 385
Dives and Pauper, II. 321, 323
Dives Pragmaticus, v. 355
Divine Correctioun, in *Ane Pleasant Satyre*, III. 126, 128
Divine Poems, XI. 370
Divinity, lady (in an anti-Martinist play), III. 393
Divyāvadāna, XII. 489
Dixie, Sir Woolstone (1525-1594), v. 131
Dixon, Henry Hall, 'The Druid' (1822-1870), XIV. 543
Dixon, Richard Watson (1833-1900), XIII. 119, 184, 194, 203, 501; XIV. 487
   Fallen Rain, XIII. 197
   Feathers of the Willow, The, XIII. 197
   Last Poems, XIII. 196
   Love's Consolation, XIII. 197
   Mano, XIII. 196, 197
   Ode on Advancing Age, XIII. 198
   Poems, XIII. 197
   To Shadow, XIII. 198
Dixon, Robert (d. 1688), VII. 507; IX. 499
Dixon, William Hepworth (1821-1879), XII. 451; XIV. 193, 253, 501, 551, 570
Dixon, William Macneil, XIII. 476, 488, 497, 570; *Edinburgh Book of Scottish Verse*, XI. 443
Dixon, W. W., XIV. 533
Dobbin, major William, in Thackeray's *Vanity Fair*, XIII. 287, 289, 293
Dobell, Bertram (1837-1914), VI. 5; VII. 42; XII. 400 ff.; XIII. 108, 489, 501
Dobell, Sydney Thompson (1824-1874), XIII. 156 ff., 411, 501, 557, 558
   Balder, XII. 114; XIII. 158 ff.
   England in Time of War, XIII. 159
   Keith of Ravelston, XIII. 159
   Nuptial Song, A, XIII. 159
   Roman, The, XIII. 159
   Tommy's Dead, XIII. 159
Do-best, in *Piers the Plowman*, II. 2 ff., 18 ff., 24, 26, 28

Do-better, in *Piers the Plowman*, II. 2 ff., 18 ff., 24, 26, 28

Dobree, Peter Paul (1782–1825), XII. 325, 327, 328, 482, 491; *Adversaria*, XII. 328; *Lexicon rhetoricum Cantabrigiense*, XII. 328; *Notes on Inscriptions*, XII. 328

Dobson, Austin (1840–1923), IX. 73; X. 3, 12, 261, 413, 418, 483, *also see* Add.; XI. 374, 458, 468, 469, 475; XII. 444, 446; XIII. 211, 504; XIV. 540; *Horace Walpole*, X. 245

Dobson, William (*fl.* 1734), IX. 482

Doctor, in *Ane Pleasant Satyre*, III. 128

Doctor Syntax in Paris, XIV. 219

Doctrinal of Death, The, II. 323

Doctrine, tower of, in *The Passetyme of Pleasure*, II. 225, 231

Dodd, A., IX. 79

Dodd, William (1729–1777), X. 470

Dodd, in Reade's *Hard Cash*, XIII. 428

Doddridge, Philip (1702–1751), IX. 563; X. 371, 381 ff., 521; *Rise and Progress of Religion in the Soul*, X. 383

Doderidge, Sir John (1555–1628), VIII. 468, 470

Dodger, the, in *Oliver Twist*, XIII. 316

Dodgson, Charles Lutwidge (*pseud.* 'Lewis Carroll,' 1832–1898), XI. 477, 478; XIII. 501; XIV. 163, 206, 472

   Alice in Wonderland, VII. 30; XI. 387; XIII. 166

   Hunting of the Snark, The, XIII. 167

   Jabberwocky, XIII. 167

   Rhyme? and Reason? XIII. 167

   Sylvie and Bruno, XI. 387; XIII. 167

   Walrus and the Carpenter, The, XIII. 167

Dodington, George Bubb, lord Melcombe (1691–1762), IX. 86, 188, 253, 254, 497; X. 94, 103; *Diary*, IX. 254

Dodoens, Rembert, IV. 542; *A Niewe Herball*, III. 551; IV. 374, 408; *Pemptades*, IV. 374

Dodona, site of, XII. 329

Dodsley, James (1724–1797), XI. 142, 324

Dodsley, Robert (1703–1764), V. 41, 54; IX. 177, 188, 189, 190–191 (main entry), 475, 484; X. 123, 124, 132, 135, 138, 144, 167, 170, 177, 245, 271, 273, 439, 445, 456; XI. 318, 323, 324, 327, 332, 334, 468, 490

   Collection of Poems, VIII. 44; IX. 190, 191; X. 274, 454, 496; XI. 324

   Compendium of Voyages, X. 41

   Muse in Livery, IX. 190

   Select Collection of Old Plays, VIII. 129; IX. 190; XI. 324

   The Toyshop, XI. 323

Dodsworth, Roger (1585–1654), IX. 342, 343, 348, 350, 532, 533, 539; XII. 349

Dodwell, Edward (1767–1832), XII. 496; *Classical and Topographical Tour through Greece*, XII. 338

Dodwell, Henry, the elder (1641–1711), VIII. 306, 307, 459; IX. 329, 330, 505, 506, 515, 527, 534; X. 308, 356, 516, 521; *De Cyclis*, IX. 330

Dodwell, Henry, the younger (d. 1784), IX. 288; *Christianity not founded on argument*, IX. 295, 506, 507

Dodwell, Miss, IX. 511

Doe, Charles, VII. 430

Doeg, in *The Second Part of Absalom and Achitophel*, VIII. 41, 42, 192

Doesborch or Desborowe, John of, II. 329, 330; III. 82; IV. 69; (printed by), *Of the newelandes and of ye people founde by the messengers of the Kynge of Portyngale named Emanuel*, II. 330; IV. 70, 71

Dogberry, in *Much Ado about Nothing*, IV. 360; V. 191, 362; VI. 46, 217; XI. 266; XIII. 64

Doggrel, Sir Iliad [Burnet, Thomas], IX. 258, 448

Dol Common, in *The Alchemist*, V. 377; VI. 22

Dolben, Digby Mackworth (1848–1867), XII. 271, 276, 456; XIII. 502

Dolben, John (1625–1686), VIII. 302

Dolby, George, XIII. 532

Dolce, Lodovico, III. 359; V. 63, 72, 76

   Didone, V. 74 ff.

   Giocasta, V. 71

   Phoenissae, IV. 4

   Troiane, V. 69

Dole, Nathan Haskell, XIII. 497

Dolet, Etienne, IV. 322, 517

Do-little Lane, in *The Masque of Christmas*, VI. 358

Doll, in *Henry IV*, V. 187

Dolléans, Edouard, XIV. 478

Dolling, Robert William Radclyffe (1851–1902), XIV. 502

Döllinger, Johann J. I., XIV. 117

Dolman, John (*fl.* 1551), IV. 5, 435

Dolman, Miss, X. 273, 496

Dombey, Paul, Dickens's, XIII. 325

Domesday, Fifteen Signs before, I. 356, 458

Domesday Book, I. 390; VIII. 313; XII. 509, 511

Domestic drama, English, VI. 97, 133

Domestic tragedies, English, V. 376

Domett, Alfred (1811–1887), XIII. 502; XIV. 585

   'Centuries ago,' XIII. 187

   Christmas Hymn, A, XIII. 187

   Flotsam and Jetsam, XIV. 368

   Ranolf and Amohia, XIII. 186; XIV. 368

Dominic, St, I. 200, 339

Dominica, XIV. 214

Dominicans, I. 200, 355; II. 370; III. 68, 70; VI. 257; VIII. 59; X. 282

Dominicans, in Cambridge and Oxford, II. 349

Dominicans, in Paris, II. 349, 350

Dominichi, Lodovico, III. 93

Dominis, Antonio de, VII. 308

Dominus, in *Saturnalia*, VI. 319

Domitia, in *The Roman Actor*, VI. 155, 159

Domitian, I. 226; III. 433

Domitian, in *The Roman Actor*, VI. 153, 155, 159

Domitilla, in *The Royall Master*, **VI.** 205

Don Armado, in *Love's Labour's Lost*, **VIII.** 127

Don Diego, in Jonson's *The Alchemist*, **VIII.** 127

Don Gayferos, **I.** 293

Don Juan, in Shadwell's *Libertine*, **VIII.** 174

Don Quixote, **I.** 293; **VIII.** 67, 68, 70

Dôn, the children of, **I.** 252

Donald, in Holcroft's *Deserted Daughter*, **XI.** 277

Donaldson, Alexander, **XI.** 315, 342

Donaldson, Augustus Blair, **XIII.** 504

Donaldson, David, **II.** 118

Donaldson, James (*fl.* 1713), **IX.** 559

Donaldson, Sir James, **XIV.** 538, 597

Donaldson, John William (1811–1861), **XII.** 482
 Classical Scholarship and Classical Learning, **XII.** 331
 New Cratylus, The, **XII.** 330
 Theatre of the Greeks, The, **XII.** 330
 Varronianus, **XII.** 330

Donati, Eduardo, **III.** 296

Donatists, the, **XII.** 260

Donatus, grammars of, **I.** 114, 118; **II.** 359

Doncaster, **II.** 45, 88, 321; **XI.** 168; **XII.** 516; **XIII.** 351; **XIV.** 225

Doncaster, viscount. *See* Hay, James

'Done oracio,' **v.** 160

Doni, **IV.** 443

Donne, John (1573–1631), **III.** 173, 426; **IV.** 55, 145, 163, 169, 187, 196–223 (main entry), 224, 226, 239 ff., 329, 390, 434, 488 ff., 492, 495; **V.** 338; **VI.** 2, 9 ff., 15, 72, 177, 185, 187; **VII.** 3, 10, 17, 19, 26, 38, 46, 49, 62, 64, 69, 81, 82, 85, 86, 130, 148, 157, 163, 166, 180, 250, 252, 258, 463, 488; **VIII.** 228, 229, 238, 292, 293, 365, 366; **IX.** 157, 446; **X.** 226; **XII.** 259; **XIII.** 191, 219, 448; **XIV.** 460, 491
 Aire and Angels, **IV.** 210
 Anatomy of the World, The, **IV.** 204
 Anniversaries, **IV.** 212 ff., 216, 217
 Annunciation and Passion, **IV.** 217
 Apparition, The, **IV.** 210
 'At Court,' **IV.** 200
 Autumnal, **IV.** 209
 Bait, The, **VII.** 8
 ΒΙΑΘΑΝΑΤΟΣ, **IV.** 202, 208, 219
 Blossom, The, **IV.** 211
 Break of Day, The, **IV.** 212
 'By our first strange and fatal interview,' **IV.** 212
 Calme, The, **IV.** 200, 215
 Canonization, The, **IV.** 212
 Chain, The, **IV.** 210, 215
 (?) 'Come Fates,' **IV.** 209
 'Dear Love, continue nice,' **IV.** 209
 Death be not proud, **IV.** 216
 Death I recant, **IV.** 216
 Death's Duel, **IV.** 204
 Devotions, **IV.** 204, 219

Donne, John
 Dialogue, **IV.** 209
 Divine Poems, **IV.** 204, 205; **VII.** 27, 31
 Dream, The, **IV.** 210, 212
 Ecstacy, The, **IV.** 212
 Eighty Sermons, **IV.** 241
 Elegie on Prince Henry, **IV.** 204
 Elegies, **IV.** 203, 205, 208 ff., 213
 Epigrams, **IV.** 205
 Epistles to Wotton, **IV.** 215
 Epithalamiums, **IV.** 203, 205
 Essays in Divinity, **IV.** 219
 Expiration, The, **IV.** 212
 'For Godsake hold your tongue,' **IV.** 212
 Funerall, The, **IV.** 211
 Funerall Elegies, **IV.** 202, 205, 213, 215
 'Go catch a falling star,' **IV.** 210; **VII.** 23
 Holy Sonnets, **IV.** 217
 Ignatius his Conclave, **IV.** 203, 218
 'I love to talk with some old lover's ghost,' **VII.** 23
 Indifferent, The, **IV.** 210
 'Kind pity checks my spleen,' **IV.** 197
 La Corona, **IV.** 217
 Lamentations of Jeremy, The, **IV.** 205, 217
 Letters to countess of Bedford, **IV.** 216
 Letters to Severall Personages, **IV.** 205, 215
 Litany, The, **IV.** 217; **VII.** 15
 Love's War, **IV.** 209
 'Now thou hast loved me one whole day,' **VII.** 23
 Paradoxes, **IV.** 203, 208, 218
 Perfume, The, **IV.** 210
 Picture, The, **IV.** 210
 Primrose, The, **IV.** 211
 Problems, **IV.** 203, 218
 Progress of the Soule, The, **IV.** 203, 205, 214
 Pseudo-Martyr, **IV.** 203, 208, 217 ff.
 Satyres, **IV.** 203, 205, 213
 'Send home my long stray'd eyes to me,' **IV.** 210
 Sermons, **IV.** 204
 Songs and Sonets, **IV.** 205, 208, 209; **VII.** 2
 'Soul's joy,' **IV.** 209
 Storm, The, **IV.** 200, 215
 Sun-rising, The, **IV.** 212
 To Christ, **IV.** 217
 To God, my God, **IV.** 217
 To God the Father, **IV.** 217
 'To make the doubt clear,' **IV.** 209
 To Sir Nicholas Smith, **IV.** 206
 Twickenham Garden, **IV.** 211
 Upon Mr Thomas Coryat's Crudities, **IV.** 204
 Valediction: forbidding Mourning, **IV.** 212
 Valediction: of Weeping, **IV.** 211
 Woman's Constancy, **IV.** 210

Donne, John (1604–1662), **IV.** 240

Donne, William Bodham (1807–1882), **XII.** 475; **XIII.** 142; *Essays on the Drama*, **XII.** 305

Donusa, in *The Renegado*, VI. 155 ff.
Doolittle, Thomas (1632?–1707), X. 386;
  Sufferings of Christ, IV. 388
Doomsday, I. 227, 458
Doomsday (a broadside), IV. 414
Doomsday poems, I. 444
Doon, river, XI. 235
Doones, the, in Blackmore's *Lorna Doone*,
  XIII. 434
Dora, in *David Copperfield*, XIII. 327,
  331
Doran, Cecily, Gissing's, XIII. 461
Doran, John (1807–1878), XI. 447, 474;
  XIV. 518
  A Lady of the last Century, X. 261, 262
  Knights and their Days, XIV. 139
  *Mann and Manners at the Court of
  Florence*, X. 249
  Their Majesties' Servants, XIV. 139
Dorastus, in *Pandosto*, III. 356
Dorax, in Dryden's *Don Sebastian*, VIII. 31
Dorchester, XII. 326; Roman amphi-
  theatre at, VI. 252
Dorchester, viscount. *See* Carleton, Sir
  Dudley
Dorigen, in *The Franklin's Tale*, II. 184
Dorilant, Sir John, in Whitehead's *School
  for Lovers*, X. 86
Dorimant, in Etherege's *Man of Mode*,
  VIII. 138, 214
Dorislaus of Holland, IV. 159
Dorlandus, Petrus, *Elckerlijk*, II. 329
Dormer, Robert, 1st earl of Carnarvon
  (d. 1643), IV. 157; VI. 143
Dormer's News Letter, IX. 432
Dornton, in Holcroft's *Road to Ruin*, XI.
  277
Dorothea, I. 74, 75
Dorothea, in *James IV*, V. 137, 138
Dorothea, in Massinger's *The Virgin Mar-
  tir*, VI. 54, 150, 154, 165; XII. 68
Dorothea, in *Middlemarch*, XIII. 392, 398
Dorrington, Edward (? pseudonym), XI.
  489
Dorrits, the, Dickens's, XIII. 320, 331
D'Orsay, Alfred Guillaume Gabriel, count
  (1801–1852), XIV. 115
Dorset, II. 414; VII. 74; IX. 146; X. 20, 25;
  XI. 99; XII. 346, 511, 513, 520; XIII.
  320; XIV. 292
Dorset dialect, XII. 413
Dorset, Catherine Ann (1750?–1817?), XI.
  476, 478; *Lion's Masquerade*, XI. 386;
  Peacock at Home, XI. 386
Dorset, countess of, IX. 148
Dorset, earls of. *See* Sackville, Charles,
  Richard, Thomas
Dort, IV. 402, 403
Dort, synod of, VII. 152, 322, 437
D'Orville, XII. 484
Dory, John, II. 414
Dostoëvsky, F. M., *The Brothers Kara-
  mazov*, XIII. 462
Dotheboys hall, in *Nicholas Nickleby*, XIII.
  317
Douady, Jules, XII. 343

Douay, III. 426; IV. 127, 274, 402; VII.
  302, 303; XIV. 53
Douay commentary, VII. 481
Double Falsehood, V. 444
Doubledick, Richard, in Dickens's *Seven
  Poor Travellers*, XIII. 335
Douce, Francis (1757–1834), II. 122, 329
Douglas, in Mrs Oliphant's *Kirsteen*, XIII.
  431
Douglas, captain (1667), VIII. 381
Douglas, Catherine, duchess of Queens-
  berry (d. 1777), IX. 162 ff.
Douglas, Charles, 3rd duke of Queens-
  berry (1698–1778), IX. 163, 164; X. 102;
  XI. 317
Douglas, Charles Mackinnon, XIV. 478
Douglas, Francis (1710?–1790?), IX. 557,
  563; X. 477, 478, 479
Douglas, Gawin or Gavin (1475?–1522),
  II. 91, 92, 94, 96 ff., 126, 239, 244,
  249 ff., 258–265 (main entry), 275,
  476 ff.; III. 115, 116, 117, 119, 120,
  138, 185, 200, 278; X. 223, 239; XI.
  203, 204, 431
  Aeneid, trans. of, II. 240, 259, 261 ff.;
  IV. 397
  Aurae Orationes, II. 259
  Conscience, II. 259, 262
  King Hart, II. 228, 259, 262
  Palice of Honour, The, II. 126, 259, 260,
  262, 266, 268; III. 117, 119; IV. 397,
  412; VII. 174; IX. 359
  Vergil, IX. 359, 562
Douglas, George, *pseud. See* Brown,
  George Douglas
Douglas, Sir George Brisbane Scott, II.
  396; XII. 453; *Book of Scottish Poetry,
  The*, XI. 443
Douglas, Sir James (1286?–1330), II. 114
Douglas, James, XIII. 510
Douglas, James, 4th duke of Hamilton
  (1658–1712), IX. 424
Douglas, Dr James (1675–1742), XII. 363
Douglas, James of, in *Bruce*, II. 101, 105
Douglas, John (1721–1807), X. 292, 293,
  499; *Criterion of Miracles*, X. 346, 512
Douglas, lady Juliana, in Susan Ferrier's
  Marriage, XII. 245, 246
Douglas, M. A., XIV. 599
Douglas, William, 8th earl of Douglas
  (1425?–1452), II. 113
Douglas, William (*fl.* 1660), IX. 543
Douglas, William Scott (1815–1883), XI.
  438, 440
Douglas ballad, the, II. 398
Douglas cause, X. 191
Douglas family, II. 113, 114, 115; III. 118
Douglas Tragedy, I. 300; II. 410
Douglas-Albany quarrels, the, II. 259
Douglasdale, II. 105
Douglass, Arthur, XIV. Add. 6
Douse, Francis, XII. 376
Dove, Sir Benjamin and lady, in Cumber-
  land's *Brothers*, XI. 264, 279
Dove, Dr Daniel, in Southey's *Doctor*, XI.
  168

Dove, Jane Frances, xiv. 599
Dove cottage, xi. 102, 103, 409
Dover, iii. 3; iv. 418; vii. 183; viii. 202, 263; ix. 240, 268; x. 118, 201, 244, 395
Dow, Alexander (d. 1779), xiv. 576; *Sethona*, xiv. 334; *Zingis*, xiv. 334
'Doway,' university of, v. 113
Dowden, Edward (1843–1913), xi. 404, 406, 409, 412, 413, 417, 420, 422, 423; xii. 399, 401 ff., 415, 423; xiii. 65, 464, 465, 476, 480, 487, 495, 553; xiv. 211, 487, 518, 527; *Life of Shelley*, xiv. 147; *Shakespeare...his Mind and Art*, xiv. 147
Dowel, John, vii. 470
Do-well, in *Piers the Plowman*, ii. 2 ff., 15, 18 ff., 24, 26, 28
Dowland, John (1563?–1626?), iv. 114, 463, 464; xiv. 307; *A Pilgrim's Solace*, iv. 113
Dowland, Robert (17th cent.), iv. 113, 464
Dowler, Mr, in *The Pickwick Papers*, xiii. 314
Dowling, Richard, xiv. 568; *Mystery of Killard, The*, xiv. 327; *On Babies and Ladders*, xiv. 327
Down, county, xii. 361; xiii. 404
Down, Kent, xiv. 298
Down hall, Essex, ix. 152, 153
'Down Survey,' the, of forfeited lands, viii. 343
Downefall of Dagon, The, vii. 382
Downefall of temporizing poets, The, vii. 386
Downes, Andrew (1549?–1628), iii. 425; vii. 312, 488; *De Caede Eratosthenis*, vii. 316; *De Pace*, vii. 316
Downes, John (*fl.* 1662–1710), *Roscius Anglicanus*, viii. 189, 192, 423
Downey, Edmund, xiv. 569
Downing, Emanuel (*fl.* 1650), vii. 353
Downing, Sir George (1684?–1749), viii. 253
Downman, Hugh (1740–1809), xi. 451
Dowsabell, in Drayton's *Eglogs*, iv. 173
Dowsing, William (1596?–1679?), vii. 34
Dowson, Ernest (1867–1900), xiii. 212, 220, 502; *I have been faithful to thee, Cynara*, xiii. 219
Dowson, John (1820–1881), xii. 516; xiv. 337
Dowson, M. E. See Palmer, William Scott
Doyle, Sir Francis Hastings Charles (1810–1888), xiii. 45, 502; xiv. 597; *Private of the Buffs, A*, xiii. 186; *Red Thread of Honour, The*, xiii. 186
Doyle, James E. (1822–1892), xiv. 502
Doyle, John Andrew (1844–1907), xiv. 98, 487
Doyle, Martin, xiv. 312
Doyle, Richard (1824–1883), xi. 480, 487; xiii. 294, 499; xiv. 238, 548, 549
D'Oyly, Christopher, x. 405, 410
Dracontius, i. 76
Drage, William (1637?–1669), vii. 507
Draghi, John Baptist (17th cent.), viii. 394

Drake, Sir Francis (1540?–1596), iii. 52, 327; iv. 1, 68, 72, 73, 78, 85 ff., 92, 93, 96, 102, 103, 261, 299, 454, 510; v. 345, 361; vii. 248; x. 164, 464; xiii. 364
Drake, Sir Francis (the younger), *Sir Francis Drake Reviv'd*, iv. 96, 455
Drake, Francis (1696–1771), *York*, ix. 353, 532
Drake, James (1667–1707), viii. 91, 410, 433
Drake, Nathan (1766–1836), *Essays illustrative of the Rambler*, x. 172, 461, 476, 483
Drake, The, vi. 53
Drakenberg, the, xiv. 372
Drama and the stage in the age of Johnson, the, x. 67 ff., 425 ff.
Drames v. 192
Drane, Augusta Theodosia (1823–1894), xiv. 601
Drant, Thomas (d. 1578?), iii. 201; iv. 23, 437, 492, 518; v. 156
Draper, Mrs Eliza (1744–1778), x. 47
Draper, Sir William (1721–1787), x. 403, 407, 526
Drapier, M. B. (Swift's pseudonym), ix. 115
Drawcansir, in *The Rehearsal*, viii. 27
Drawcansir, Sir Alexander (Fielding's pseudonym), x. 34
Drayton, Michael (1563–1631), i. 170; iii. 183, 220, 247, 256, 258, 260, 263 ff., 268, 270, 286, 305, 523, 526; iv. 87, 95, 117, 118, 121, 136, 138, 153, 158, 168–195 (main entry), 211, 248, 266, 351, 357, 401, 434, 455, 485 ff., 530; v. 148, 226, 228, 236, 311, 312, 319, 323, 332, 338, 371, 474; vi. 2, 61, 113, 250, 312; vii. 50, 52, 56, 58, 250, 264, 387, 465; viii. 226, 228, 237, 239
Agincourt, Ballad of, iv. 170, 188, 192
Agincourt, The Battaile of, iv. 192
Amours, iv. 178
'An evill spirit,' iv. 179
Baron's Wars, The, iii. 198, 305; iv. 174, 181, 182, 191, 192
Cromwell, The Legend of Great, iii. 198; iv. 176, 177, 188
David and Goliah, iv. 194
Eclogues, iii. 220; iv. 118, 172, 173
Elegies upon sundry occasions, iv. 192, 194
Endimion and Phoebe, iv. 173, 175, 176, 180, 181, 183, 195
England's Heroicall Epistles, iii. 198; iv. 169, 175, 182 ff., 206; vii. 49
Epistle to George Sandys, iv. 184
Harmonie of the Church, The, iv. 170, 171, 173, 357
Heavenly Harmonie of Spirituall Songs, A, iv. 171
'How many paltry,' iv. 179
Hymn to his Ladies Birth-Place, iv. 174
Idea, the Shepheard's Garland, iii. 256, 258, 260; iv. 118, 170 ff., 184, 193

Drayton, Michael
  Ideas Mirrour, III. 263; IV. 177, 178, 180
  'Into these loves,' IV. 179
  Man in the Moone, The, IV. 181, 185
  'Many there be excelling,' IV. 179
  Matilda, III. 198; IV. 176, 177, 182
  Miseries of Queene Margarite, The, IV. 193
  Moone-Calfe, The, IV. 185, 194
  Mortimeriados, III. 305; IV. 175, 176, 181, 182
  Moses, his Birth and Miracles, IV. 185, 194
  Moyses in a Map of his Miracles, IV. 185, 194
  Muses Elizium, The, IV. 193, 194
  Noah's Floud, IV. 194, 195
  Nymphidia, I. 289; IV. 193
  Odes, IV. 174, 185 ff., 193
  Of his Ladies not Coming to London, IV. 194
  Of Poets and Poesy, Epistle to Henry Reynolds, III. 201; IV. 138, 194; VII. 273
  Owle, The, IV. 184, 185
  Paen Triumphall, IV. 184
  Piers Gaveston, III. 198; IV. 176, 177, 182
  Poems, Lyric and Pastoral, IV. 118, 168, 172
  Polyolbion, II. 209; III. 183; IV. 136, 174, 177, 183, 188 ff., 401
  Quest of Cynthia, The, IV. 193
  Remedy for Love, His, III. 264
  Robert, Duke of Normandy, III. 198; IV. 175 ff., 182
  Shepheards Sirena, The, IV. 193
  'Since there's no help,' IV. 179
  To his Coy Love, IV. 187
  To His Rivall, IV. 186
  To the Majestie of King James, IV. 184
  To the New Yeere, IV. 186
  To the Virginian Voyage, IV. 187
  'Whilst thus my pen,' IV. 179
  See, also, under Middleton, Rowland
Drayton Beauchamp, III. 406
Dread, in *Piers the Plowman*, II. 8
'Dread Maria's Universal Fall,' IX. 148
Dream of the Cabal, VIII. 81
Dream of the Rood (? Cynewulf), I. 42, 51 ff., 56, 57, 63, 133, 430
Dream of the Rood, Ruthwell Cross, I. 12; II. 88
Drede, in *The Bowge of Courte*, III. 73
Drelincourt, Charles (1644–1722), IX. 12
Drennan, William (1754–1820), XIV. 311, 568; *Erin*, XIV. 310; *Letters of Orellana*, XIV. 310; *Wake of William Orr, The*, XIV. 310
Dresden, VI. 165; IX. 515; XIII. 388
Drift, Adrian, IX. 149, 151, 153, 217, 482, *also see* Add.
Dring, Thomas, VII. 123
Drinkwater, John, XIII. 493, 495
Driver, Samuel Rolles (1846–1914), XII. 466, 501; *Introduction to the Literature of the Old Testament*, XII. 341
Droeshout, E. P., V. 89

Drogheda, VII. 196, 351, 353, *also see* Add.
Drogheda, lady (d. c. 1681), wife of Wycherley, W., VIII. 143
Drogheda, St Peter's church, VII. 354
Dromios, in *The Comedy of Errors*, V. 178
Dromodotus, in *Pedantius*, VI. 306
Dromore, deanery of, IX. 280
Dromore, Ireland, VIII. 290; XII. 354, 361
'Drone Hall,' Oxford, IX. 414
Drosomell (Herrick's), VII. 12
Droyn, Jehan, III. 59
Druce, George Claridge, XIV. 560, 562
Drugger, Abel, in *The Alchemist*, VI. 22; X. 265; XI. 257
Druidism, IX. 352, 354
Druids, I. 13
Drummond, Henry (1851–1897), XII. 466
Drummond, J., XIII. 467
Drummond, John, 1st earl Melfort (1649–1714), VIII. 263
Drummond, Sir John (d. 1610), IV. 150
Drummond, Margaret (1472?–1501), II. 253, 281
Drummond, Peter Robert (1802–1879), XIII. 507
Drummond, William, of Hawthornden (1585–1649), III. 267, 269, 523, *also see* Add.; IV. 130, 138, 139, 150 ff. (main entry), 157, 159, 166, 189, 196, 197, 201, 205, 209, 214, 413, 434, 480; V. 343; VI. 1, 2, 5, 11, 36, 38, 39, 44, 47, 58, 112, 221, 353; VII. 30, 273, 274, 466; VIII. 227, 322; IX. 69; X. 484
  Cypress Grove, The, IV. 153
  Flowers of Sion, IV. 153, 154
  Forth Feasting, IV. 152
  Hymn of the Fairest Fair, IV. 153
  Madrigals and Epigrams, VII. 14
  Tears on the Death of Moeliades, IV. 151, 152
Drummond, William Hamilton (1778–1865), XIV. 568, 573
Drummond, William Henry (1854–1907), XIV. 343, 354 ff., 360, 582
  Canadian Country Doctor, XIV. 355
  Great Fight, The, XIV. 355, 356
  Habitant, The, XIV. 354, 356
  Johnnie Courteau, XIV. 356
  Ole Doctor Fiset, XIV. 355
  Philorum's Canoe, XIV. 356
  Vieux Temps, Le, XIV. 355
  Voyageur, The, XIV. 356
  Wreck of the Julie Plante, The, XIV. 355
Drumsoy, IX. 370
Drunkard's Character, The, VII. 384
Drury, Elizabeth (d. 1610), IV. 202, 214, 216
Drury, Joseph (1750–1834), XIV. 386
Drury, Sir Robert (*fl.* 1574?–1613), IV. 202
Drury, Robert (b. 1687), XIV. 551; *Journal*, IX. 23
Dryburgh abbey, I. 333
Dryden, Elizabeth, IX. 91
Dryden, Erasmus, VIII. 2
Dryden, Sir Erasmus Henry (1669–1710), IX. 91

Dryden, Honor, daughter of Sir John Dryden, VIII. 4

Dryden, John (1631–1700), I. 283; II. 165, 168, 186, 195, 219, 220; III. 157, 165, 312; IV. 2, 4, 25, 131, 140, 168, 177, 183, 208, 214; V. 174, 206, 209, 222, 347; VI. 7, 9, 11, 25, 28, 34, 57, 109, 111, 112, 122, 125, 126, 133, 240, 323, 479; VII. 7, 12, 61, 68, 72, 73, 76, 87 ff., 92, 93, 105, 107, 109, 126, 138, 176, 183, 184, 244, 259, 262, 264, 268, 270; VIII. 1–57 (main entry), 62, 75, 79, 89, 90, 92, 94, 121, 130, 136, 139, 143, 146, 150, 158, 166, 168, 174, 178, 179, 181, 185, 193, 201, 202, 204, 205, 209, 212, 214, 215, 217, 219 220, 222, 227, 229, 231 ff., 292, 293, 302, 369, 372 ff., 389, 391 ff., 410, 411, 418, 427, 428, 434, 437, 441, 442, 447, also see Add.; IX. 67 ff., 73, 77, 119, 122, 141, 146, 147, 157, 173 ff., 177, 180, 184, 185, 187 ff., 199, 237, 264, 266, 267, 270, 271, 348, 362, 444, 473, 482; X. 27, 67, 120, 126, 145, 153, 156, 158, 167, 169, 185, 202, 218, 219, 221, 226, 232, 398, 432, 433, 484; XI. 27, 40, 170, 171, 174, 201, 206, 316, 318, 320, 466; XII. 41, 88, 108, 136, 177, 207, 221, 224, 253, 376, 494; XIII. 86, 96, 122, 233, 237 ff., 253, 312, 552; XIV. 113, 396, 436, 448, 501

Absalom and Achitophel, VIII. 31, 35 ff. (main entry), 40, 41, 77, 142, 192, 235; XI. 36

Account of the Ensuing Poem, in a letter to Sir Robert Howard, An, VIII. 9

Aeneis, VIII. 50, 239

Albion and Albanius, VIII. 30, 135, 375

Alexander's Feast, VIII. 44, 53, 234

All for Love, VIII. 28, 33, 235, 375, 386; IX. 140; XI. 171

Amboyna, VIII. 7, 27

Amphitryon, VIII. 17, 134

Annus Mirabilis, VII. 71; VIII. 8 ff., 34, 38, 238; IX. 169; X. 124

Apology for Heroick Poetry, VIII. 374

Assignation, or Love in a Nunnery, The, VIII. 17, 140

Astraea Redux, VIII. 6; XIV. 444

Aureng-Zebe, VIII. 16, 21, 22, 27, 235

Author's Apology for Heroick Poetry and Poetic Licence, The, VIII. 27

Boccaccio, reproductions of, VIII. 51

Britannia Rediviva, VIII. 44, 49

Character of a Good Parson, VIII. 52

Charleton, To my Honoured Friend Dr, VIII. 8, 362

Chaucer, reproductions of, VIII. 51

Cleomenes, the Spartan hero, VIII. 31, 53, 190

Congreve, on his Comedy Called The Double Dealer, To my dear Friend, Mr, VIII. 55

Conquest of Granada, The, VIII. 22, 25 ff., 53, 235

Dedication of Examen Poeticum, VIII. 375

Dedication of the Aeneis, VIII. 239

Dryden, John
Defence of an Essay of Dramatick Poesie, A, VIII. 16, 24

Defence of the Epilogue, A, VIII. 17, 25, 370

Discourse Concerning the Original and Progress of Satire, A, VIII. 19, 26, 36, 39, 40, 44, 49, 373, 374

Don Sebastian, VIII. 31, 32, 164; XIII. 523

Duke of Guise, The (with Lee), VIII. 16, 30, 186

Epigrams, lines by 'J. Dryden of Trin. C.' in, VIII. 4

Epilogue to the Second Part of the Conquest of Granada, VIII. 25

Essay of Dramatick Poesie, An, II. 163; VI. 136; VII. 275; XI. 171; XIV. 460

Essay of Heroick Plays, VIII. 18, 22 ff., 26

Evening's Love, An, VIII. 16, 17, 53, 127, 131, 134, 367

Examen Poeticum, VIII. 50, 57

Fables, Ancient and Modern, VII. 48, 53, 57; VIII. 32, 51, 433; X. 241; XI. 171; XII. 46; XIII. 238

Granville, on his excellent Tragedy, called 'Heroick Love,' To Mr, VIII. 55

Heroick Stanzas, VIII. 5 ff.

Hind and the Panther, The, VIII. 43, 45 ff., 235

His Sacred Majesty, To, VIII. 7

History of the League, Maimbourg's, translation of, VIII. 34

Iliad, VIII. 51

Indian Emperor, The, VIII. 21, 22, 24, 53

Indian Queen, The, VIII. 21, 123, 235

Killigrew, To the Pious Memory of the Accomplisht Young Lady, Mrs Anne, VIII. 32, 45, 53, 57, 234

Lachrymae Musarum, contribution to, VIII. 2

Letter to Sir George Etherege, VIII. 49

Limberham, or the Kind Keeper, VIII. 17

Love Triumphant, VIII. 20

Lucian, life of, VIII. 402

Mac Flecknoe, VIII. 36, 40, 41, 235; IX. 79, 179

Mall, The, or the Modish Lovers, VIII. 399

Marriage-à-la-Mode, VIII. 17, 20, 140

Medal, The, VIII. 35, 39, 40, 188

Miscellanies, VII. 86; VIII. 44, 49, 50, 231, 375; IX. 148, 455; X. 223

Mistaken Husband, The, VIII. 399, 401, 422

My Lord Chancellor, To, VIII. 7

Œdipus, King of Thebes (with Lee), VIII. 30, 186

Palamon and Arcite, X. 120

Parallel of Poetry and Painting, A, VIII. 20, 29, 49

Plutarch, preface to a translation of, VIII. 44

Poem upon the Death of His Late Highness, Oliver, Lord Protector of England, Scotland and Ireland, A, VIII. 5

Preface concerning the Grounds of Criticism in Tragedy, VIII. 29

Dryden, John
  Preface to the Fables, VIII. 52, 56, 57, 235, 390
  Prologue, addressed to Oxford, VIII. 3, 4
  Prologue to Secret Love, VIII. 24
  Prologue to the Duchess [of York], VIII. 34
  Prosodia, VIII. 50
  Religio Laici, IV. 197; VIII. 15, 41 ff., 46, 235
  Rival Ladies, The, VII. 48; VIII. 4, 17, 19, 123, 131, 137, 370; XIV. 460
  St John's Eve, VIII. 54
  Satire on the Dutch, VIII. 7
  Secret Love, or the Maiden Queen, VIII. 20, 426
  Secular Masque, VIII. 31
  Sir Geoffrey Kneller, To, VIII. 50
  Sir Martin Mar-all, VIII. 17, 134, 420
  Song for St Cecilia's Day, VIII. 53
  Southern, on his Comedy Called 'The Wives' Excuse,' To Mr, VIII. 55
  Spanish Fryar, The, VIII. 20, 33, 49
  State of Innocence and Fall of Man, The, VIII. 27, 422; IX. 58
  Sylvae, VIII. 44
  Te Deum, translation of, VIII. 54
  Tempest, The (with D'Avenant), VIII. 28, 120, 398, 418
  Threnodia Augustalis, VIII. 44
  Translations of: *Juvenal*, VIII. 49, 77; *Latin Hymns*, VIII. 397; *Lucretius*, VIII. 396; *Ovid*, VIII. 50, 51, 396, 397; *Persius*, VIII. 2, 49, 77; *Tacitus*, VIII. 402; *Theocritus*, VIII. 397; *Vergil*, VIII. 50, 397
  Troilus and Cressida, VIII. 29; XI. 319
  Tyrannick Love, VIII. 21, 22, 235
  Veni Creator Spiritus, paraphrase of, VIII. 54
  Verses to Her Royal Highness the Duchess (of York), VIII. 8
  Vindication of the Duke of Guise, VIII. 30
  Wild Gallant, The, VIII. 16, 17, 131
  Works, XII. 16
Dryden, John, junior (1668–1701), VIII. 400, 402
Dryden, Sir John, VIII. 4
Drydeniana, VIII. 404 ff.
Drystan, son of Tallwch (Tristram), I. 273
Drythelm, vision of, I. 82, 86
Drywood, Mr, of Trinity, VI. 397
Du Bartas, William de Salluste, IX. 269; *Semaines* (trans. as *Divine Weekes and Workes*), IV. 23, 131, 331, 443
Du Baudrier, Sieur, IX. 455
Du Bellay, Joachim, III. 250, 251, 258, 263; IV. 24, 264, 443; *Les Antiquités de Rome*, III. 250
Dublin, IV. 142, 161, 414, 434; VI. 197, 200, 203, 205, 206; VII. 58, 148, 197, 355; VIII. 122, 220; IX. 79, 84, 91, 93, 96 ff., 118, 126, 166, 327, 330, 406, 413, 452 ff.; X. 58, 257, 258, 379, 408; XI. 1. 283, 288, 340, 342, 373; XII. 285, 351, 361; XIII. 240, 258; XIV. 96, 104, 173,

Dublin
  261, 269, 311, 315, 318a, 319, 321, 323, 348, 397, 417
  Dublin society. *See* Royal Dublin society
  Historical society, XIV. 317
  Mountrath court, X. 199
  Parliament square, X. 198
  Phoenix park, XIV. 317
  Record office, XII. 360, 361
  Reindeer tavern, X. 199
  St Patrick's cathedral, IX. 93, 96, 99, 100, 119, 132
  Smock (or Smoke) Alley theatre, VIII. 170; X. 426 ff.; XI. 455
  Theatre royal, VIII. 180; X. 425 ff.
  Trinity college, III. 426; IV. 276, 433; VII. 148; VIII. 146, 170, 332; IX. 91, 92, 166, 280, 282, 362; X. 58, 197, 198, 293, 356, 358; XI. 1, 2; XII. 159, 338, 342, 360, 362, 494; XIV. 211, 263, 309, 313, 318, 571, *also see* Add. 3
Dublin, archbishopric of, XII. 272
Dublin, books printed and published in, XI. 470
Dublin Penny Journal, The, XIV. 312, 315, 318a
Dublin printers, IV. 547, 548
Dublin Review, The, XII. 260, 426, 460, 461, 463
Dublin Translations into Greek and Latin Verse, XIV. 211
Dublin University Magazine, The, XIII. 407, 414, 415; XIV. 313, 319, 326
Dublin University Review, The, XIV. 211, 538
Dubricius, archbishop of the "City of Legions," I. 259
Ducarel, Andrew Coltee (1713–1785), IV. 422; IX. 532
Ducci, L., IV. 526
Du Chaillu, Paul B. (1835–1903), XIV. 551
Duchal, James (1697–1761), X. 521
Ducis, Jean François, V. 294, 298, 299, 301, 306 ff.
Duck, Sir Arthur (1580–1648), VIII. 317, 468
Duck, Stephen (1705–1756), IX. 187, 448, 485
Du Deffand, madame, X. 248, 250, 495
Dudley, earl of. *See* Ward, John William
Dudley, Edmund (1462?–1510), IV. 297, 510
Dudley, lord Guilford (d. 1554), IV. 169, 182
Dudley, Sir Henry Bate (1745–1824), XIV. 188
Dudley, John, 1st duke of Northumberland (1502?–1553), VII. 325, 326
Dudley, Louisa, in Cumberland's *West Indian*, XI. 264, 265
Dudley, Robert, earl of Leicester (1532?–1588), III. 207, 241, 421, 422, 424; IV. 1, 8, 10, 20, 116, 172, 274, 384, 390, 401, 406, 410; V. 341, 345, 346, 365; VI. 246, 247, 302, 336, 381, 393; VII. 191, 306

Dudleys, the, in Cumberland's *West Indian*, XI. 264, 265
Duelling, VII. 204
Duessa, in *The Faerie Queene*, III. 231, 234
Duff, James Grant (1789–1858), XIV. 490, 576; *A History of the Mahrattas*, XIV. 337
Duff, Sir Mountstuart Elphinstone Grant, XII. 147; XIII. 497
Dufferin, lady. *See* Blackwood, Helen Selina
Dufferin, marquis of. *See* Blackwood, Frederick Temple
Duffet, Thomas (*fl.* 1678), VIII. 422
Duffy, Sir Charles Gavan (1816–1903), XIII. 471; XIV. 317 ff., 370, 568, 572
    Innishowen, XIV. 318
    Irish Chief, The, XIV. 318
    Irish Library, XIV. 325
    Lay Sermon, XIV. 318
    Patriot's Bride, The, XIV. 318
Dufresnoy, Charles-Alphonse, VIII. 49, 402; IX. 256, 444, 538
Dugdale, Sir William (1605–1686), VII. 438; VIII. 318, 469; IX. 342 ff., 348, 355, 356, 533, 539, 540
    Antiquities of Warwickshire, IX. 341, 342, 345, 352
    Baronage of England, IX. 344
    History of Imbanking, IV. 308, 510; IX. 343
    History of St Paul's Cathedral, IX. 343, 354
    Life, Diary and Correspondence, IX. 343
    Monasticon Anglicanum, IX. 342, 343, 350; XII. 346, 349
    Origines Juridicales, VIII. 320, 464; IX. 344
    Short view of the late troubles, IX. 344
Duglas river, battle of, I. 259
Du Guérins, the, XIII. 98, 99
Du Halde, Jean Baptiste, X. 206, 465
Dukas, Jules, IV. 257
Duke, Richard (1658–1711), VIII. 408, 409, 446; IX. 174, 176, 485
Duke and the Emperor, The Meeting of the, II. 308
Duke of York's company, the, VI. 262
Duke Rowland and Sir Ohiel of Spayne, I. 470
Dukes, Ashley, XIII. 514
Dulcimer, in *The Fawne*, VI. 48
Dulcinea, in *Don Quixote*, X. 51
Dulcinea del Toboso, in *Don Quixote*, VIII. 70
'Dulness's Laureate Son,' in Pope's *Dunciad*, IX. 88
Dulwich, VI. 249, 278
Dumas, Alexandre, *père*, V. 302; XI. 307, 458; XII. 212, 381, 525; XIII. 257, 263
Du Maurier, George Louis Palmella Busson (1834–1896), XIII. 562; XIV. 235, 239, 548
    History of the Jack Sprats, The, XIII. 433
    Martian, The, XIII. 433
    Peter Ibbetson, XIII. 433
    Trilby, XIII. 433

'Dumb Philosopher,' the, IX. 21
Dumb Wyf, The, II. 280
Dumbarton, X. 36
Dumbartonshire, X. 36
Dumbiedykes, laird of, in *The Heart of Midlothian*, VIII. 355
Dumbleton, John (*fl.* 1340), *Summa*, II. 363
Dumfries, IX. 565; XI. 225, 235, 237, 470
Dumfries Journal, The, XI. 235
Dumfriesshire, XI. 222, 242, 444, 445; XII. 350; XIII. 2 ff., 10
Dumfriesshire, The Poets of, IX. 568
Dumont, Étienne, XI. 59, 60, 70, 397, 398
Du Moulin, Peter, VII. 309, 418, 420; *Regii Sanguinis Clamor*, VII. 105
Dun Monidh, XIV. 304
Dunalbius, in *Argenis*, IV. 295
Dunbar, Elizabeth, countess of Moray (d. 1591), II. 113
Dunbar, William (1460?–1520?), I. 292; II. 91, 93, 121, 122, 126, 154, 192, 221, 239, 244, 249, 250 ff., 259, 261, 265, 266, 269, 275, 276, 278, 280, 331, 401, 475, 507; III. 115 ff., 119, 121, 122, 131, 133 ff., 159, 179, 486; IV. 322, 517, 527; VII. 351; IX. 359; XI. 203, 204; XII. 95, 517
    Beauty and the Prisoner (Sen that I am a presoneir), II. 253
    Black Lady, II. 255
    Blitheness, II. 256
    Complaint to the King, II. 257
    Dance of the Sevin Deidlie Synnis, II. 228, 255, 256
    Dreme, The, III. 116
    Epitaph on Donald Owre, The, II. 255; III. 133
    Flyting of Dunbar and Kennedie, The, II. 90, 99, 250, 256, 266; III. 72, 490
    Freiris of Berwick, The, II. 253, 279; VIII. 226
    General Satire, II. 255
    Golden Targe, The, II. 228, 231, 252, 253, 260; III. 116; VII. 174
    Good Counsel, II. 256
    How Dunbar wes desyrd to be ane freir, II. 251
    Interlude of the Droichis Part of the Play, The, II. 253, 255, 275; III. 122
    Joustis of the Tailȝeour and the Sowtar, II. 255; III. 121, 135
    Kynd Kittok, Ballad of, II. 255, 275
    Lament for the Makaris, II. 109, 116, 245, 256, 257, 266, 268
    London thou art the flower of cities all, II. 252, 331
    Petition of the Grey Horse, III. 120
    Satire on Edinburgh, II. 255
    Testament of Mr Andro Kennedy, II. 256, 278, 501; III. 85, 483, 484
    Thrissil and the Rois, The, II. 253; III. 116, 120
    Tidings from the Session, II. 255
    Tretis of the Tua Mariit Wemen and the Wedo, II. 192, 254
    Vision, II. 256

Dunbar, William, friend of Burns, XI. 222, 223
Dunblane, II. 275; VIII. 298
Duncan, in Boece, III. 156
Duncan I, II. 89
Duncan, Andrew (1744–1828), XI. 442
Duncan, David, XIV. 481
Duncan, Geilis, VII. 372
Duncan (Holinshed's), V. 241
Duncan, William, XIV. 533
Duncan Gray, II. 274
Dunckley, Henry (1823–1896), Crown and Cabinet, XIV. 189, 504
Duncombe, John (1729–1786), IX. 477
Duncombe, William (1690–1769), IX. 477; Brutus, X. 82, 439
Duncombe, in Mrs Gaskell's Mr Harrison's Confessions, XIII. 372
Duncon, John (fl. 1648), VII. 155 ff.; Life of Lettice Falkland, VII. 151
Duncumb, John (1765–1839), XII. 509
Dundas, III. 69
Dundas, Henry, 1st viscount Melville, XI. 16, 31, 35; XIV. 179
Dundee, III. 122, 142; XI. 399; XII. 350; XIII. 51
Dundee, University college, XIV. 432
Dundee, viscount. See Graham, John, of Claverhouse
Dundee Advertiser, The, XIV. 531, 534
Dundee Book, The, III, 141
Dundonald, earl of. See Cochrane, Thomas
Dundreary, lord, in Our American Cousin, VIII. 176
Dunfermline, II. 245, 250
Dunk, George Montague, 2nd earl of Halifax (1716–1771), X. 243, 245, 249, 251, 495
Dunkeld, II. 259; IV. 277
Dunkin, William (1709?–1765), IX. 466
Dunkirk, IX. 135, 440, 455, 461; XIV. 387
Dunkirk, battle of, VII. 24, 452
Dunlop, Andrew, XIV. 533
Dunlop, Mrs Frances Anne Wallace (1730–1815), XI. 222, 223, 438
Dunlop, John Colin (d. 1842), XIV. 487
Dunlop, Robert, XIV. 510
Dunmow flitch, the, II. 20
Dunn, Henry, XIV. 605
Dunn, William, XIV. 512
Dunnere, in The Battle of Maldon, I. 145
Dunois of Orleans, V. 83
Dunraven, earl of. See Quin, Edwin Wyndham
Duns Furens, VI. 307
Duns Scotus, John, Doctor subtilis (1265?–1308?), I. 200, 210 ff., 453; II. 350, 355; III. 4, 19, 48, 50, 416; IV. 269, 272; VII. 505
Dunsinane, in Orygynale Cronykil, II. 132
Dunstable, V. 7, 38
Dunstable, annals of, I. 178
Dunstan, St (924–988), I. 113, 114, 118, 127, 131, 150, 151, 153, 243, 446; II. 76; XIV. 76; Memorials of, XIV. 74

Dunstan, St, in The Devil and his Dame, V. 329
Dunstaple, IX. 535
Dunster, Somerset, III. 188
Dunton, John (1659–1733), IV. 388; VIII. 99; IX. 4, 41, 267; XI. 320, 329, 334, 340, 468; Athenian Gazette, IX. 5; Athenian Mercury, IX. 5, 34, 41, 92; Life and Errors, IX. 5; XI. 327, 330
Dupatys Lettres sur l'Italie, XII. 395
Dupely, in Burgoyne's Maid of the Oaks, XI. 265
Du Plessis, J., XIV. Add. 6
Dupont de Nemours, Pierre Samuel, X. 336
Du Pontavice de Heussey, R., XIII. 543
Duport, James (1606–1679), IV. 427; VII. 317, 488
Duport, John (d. 1617), VII. 316
Duport, Paul, V. 302
Duppa, Bryan (1588–1662), bishop of Winchester, VI. 7
Duppa, Richard (1770–1831), X. 455, 463
Durand, David (1680–1763), IX. 235, 495
Durand, Sir H. Mortimer, XIII. 505; XIV. 493
Durand, W. Y., V. 64
Durand, Durandus, William (d. 1296), Speculum Juris or Speculum Judiciale, II. 364
Durandus, bishop of Meaux, commentary of, II. 363
Durant, Gilles, IV. 24
Durastanti, Signora Margarita, IX. 468
Durazzo, in The Guardian, VI. 161
Dürer, Albert, VI. 333
D'Urfé, Honoré, Astrée, VI. 123, 138, 239
D'Urfey, Thomas (1653–1723), II. 414; VI. 33; VIII. 96, 166 ff., 174 ff., 408, 411, 428; IX. 264, 475, 499
    Campaigners, The, VIII. 167
    Famous History of the Rise and Fall of Massaniello, The, VIII. 175
    Modern Prophets, The, VIII. 175
    New Reformation, The, VIII. 167
    Pills to Purge Melancholy, VIII. 232
    Scotch Wedding, IX. 363
    Sea Voyage, The, VIII. 120
    Siege of Memphis, The, VIII. 175
    Trimmer, The, VIII. 97
Durham, III. 49; IV. 416, 418, 421; VII. 84; VIII. 282, 295; IX. 249, 303, 387, 392, 393; X. 127; XI. 244; XII. 10, 327, 340, 348, 354, 508, 510 ff., 515; XIII. 70, 427
Durham, Benedictine priory at, II. 349
Durham, earl of. See Lambton, John George
Durham, James (1622–1658), IX. 543
Durham. See Simeon of
Durham cathedral, XII. 507
Durham university, VII. Add.; XIV. 411, 431
Durham, Book of (or Lindisfarne Gospels), I. 14
Durham Field, II. 415
Durham, Poem on the city of, I. 147

Durham Ritual, runes in, I. 12
Durie. See Dury, John
Durlaven, prebend of, IX. 93
Dursley, lord, IX. 148
Dury, Giles (*fl.* 1649), VII. 363
Dury, John (1596–1680), IV. 549; IX. 194; The Reformed School (1650), VII. 479; IX. 389, 568
Duse, Eleanora, V. 307
'Dusky Night rides down the sky,' X. 22
Düsseldorf, V. 305
Duszeperez, II. 116
Dutch, the, IX. 134; in the East Indies, VI. 183
Dutch, Howell's satire against the, VII. 200
Dutch, Low, XIII. 112
Dutch Annotations on the Bible, VII. 322
Dutch artists, XIV. 212
Dutch church, the, XIV. 380
Dutch drama, V. 109, 284, 285, 307
Dutch India company, the, IV. 99
Dutch language and literature, IX. 331, 385; X. 19, 291; XIV. 457 ff.
Dutch paper, XI. 377
Dutch people, VIII. 7, 27, 140, 202, 247, 272, 342, 381, 382, 384
Dutch printing presses, VII. 308, 344
Dutch scholars, VII. 263, 307
Dutch towns, English actors in, V. 283
Dutch trade in the far east, V. 345
Dutch wars, VII. 183, 184, 234, 306, 434; VIII. 10, 81, 218, 249, 252, 254, 329
'Dutch sublime, the,' XI. 126
Dutchman, the, in A Woman will have her Will, V. 329
Dutchman, the, in The Weakest Goeth to the Wall, V. 316
Du Toit, S. J., XIV. Add. 6
Dutt, Gorrind Chandra, XIV. 342, 576
Dutt, Michael Madhu Sadan, XIV. 576; The Captive Ladie, XIV. 342
Dutt, Romesh Chunder, XIV. 576; Lays of Ancient India, XIV. 341
Dutt, Sasi Chandra, XIV. 342, 576
Dutt, Torulata, XIV. 576; Ancient Ballads and Legends of Hindustan, XIV. 342; Sheaf Gleaned in French Fields, A, XIV. 342
Dutton, John, VI. 249
Dutton, Sir Thomas (step-father of Sir Thomas Browne), VII. 232, 233
Duty, in Horestes, V. 64, 65
Du Vair, Guillaume, Moral Philosophy of the Stoics, IX. 276, 499
Duval, Dennis, Thackeray's, XIII. 300
Dux Morand, V. 390
Dwerga, in Darley's Becket, XII. 114
Dyaloge betwene ij Beggers, A, III. 492
Dyalogue du fol et du sage, V. 93
Dyboski, R., Tennyson's Sprache und Stil, XIII. 29
Dyccon of Bedlam, VI. 296
Dyce, Alexander (1798–1869), V. 129, 247, 278 ff.; VI. 58, 138, 169; IX. 145; X. 452, 454; XII. 353, 408, 491; XIII. 175, 497

Dyer, Sir Edward (d. 1607), III. 217, 303, 507; IV. 113, 114, 116, 117, 163, 164, 466; VII. 271; XI. 247; 'My mind to me a kingdom is,' IV. 126; The Prayse of Nothing, VIII. 213
Dyer, George (1755–1841), XII. 183, 186, 187, 196, 198, also see Add. 2
Dyer, Sir James (1512–1582), Law Reports, VIII. 316, 466
Dyer, John (1700?–1758), VIII. 230; IX. 5, 169; X. 138, 144 ff. (main entry), 156, 452, 454
    Country Walk, The, X. 145
    Fleece, The, X. 145
    Grongar Hill, IX. 191; X. 97, 136, 137, 145, 146
    Ruins of Rome, The, X. 145
Dymock, Cressy, IV. 511
Dymock, Edward, IV. 445; VI. 490
Dymok, Roger (*fl.* 1390), II. 441
Dysdayne, in The Bowge of Courte, III. 74
Dysert castle, IX. 280
Dyson, Jeremiah (1722–1776), X. 452
Dyspare, in Magnyfycence, III. 77

'E. B.' (probably Edmund Bolton), IV. 118
E. C., III. 256
E. I. O., III. 283
E. K. See Kirke, Edward
E. S. (? Edward Sharpham), Discoverie of the Knights of the Poste, IV. 350, 354
Eachard, John (1636?–1697), VII. 156, 301, 471; IX. 418
Eadberg, I. 148
Eadfrith, I. 148
Eadgils, Beowulf and Widsith, I. 24, 25, 35
Eadmer (d. 1124?), I. 162 ff., 168, 172, 449
Eadric, I. 126
Eadwine, in Widsith, I. 35
Eagle, the, Henry of Lancaster in Mum, Sothsegger, II. 36
Eagle, The, St John's college magazine, IV. 275; VI. 3; VIII. 243; XII. 487
Eagles, John (1783–1855), XII. 425
Eagles, Thomas (1746–1812), X. 485
Eaha, in Finnsburh, I. 31
Eahfrid, I. 73
Ealhhild, in Widsith, I. 34, 35
Ealing, X. 35
Eames, John (d. 1744), X. 384
Eames, W., XI. 470
Eanmund, in Beowulf, I. 24, 26
Eanred's ring, I. 11
Earl Brand, II. 410, 411
Earle, John (1601–1665), bishop of Salisbury, III. 114; IV. 521; VI. 113; VII. 156, 218, 329, 366, 379; VIII. 245, 407; Microcosmographie, IV. 260, 341, 342, 395, 522; V. 368, 477; VII. 151; VIII. 63, 64
Earle, John (1824–1903), I. 104, 141, 418; XII. 504; XIV. 611; Philology of the English Tongue, XIII. 248, 512
Early English dialect, IX. 361
Early English Text society, II. 41, 166, 199, 500; XI. 368; XII. 344, 355, 504

Earth upon Earth, II. 502
Earthquake council, the, II. 64, 443
Earwaker, John Parsons (1847–1895), XII. 509
Easden, John, IV. 464
East, Thomas (1540?–1608?), IV. 400, 546
East Anglia, XIV. 78
East Grinstead, IX. 150
East India bill, XI. 6
East India company, the, IV. 98; VIII. 342; XI. 6, 16, 17; XIII. 275; XIV. 97, 248, 332
East Indies, VI. 183; VIII. 23; XIV. 241, 250, 434, 457
East Molesey, III. 379, 380
East Ruston, Norfolk, XII. 323
East Stour, X. 20, 23
Eastbrook, IX. 146
Eastbury Park, X. 94, 103
Easter controversy, I. 73, 81, 82
Easter liturgical drama and plays, V. 11, 36 ff.
Eastern church, XII. 478
Easthealon, I. 126
Eastlake, Sir Charles Lock (1793–1865), XIV. 238
Eastlake, Elizabeth, lady, born Rigby (1809–1893), XIII. 414, 558; XIV. 523
Eastland company, the, IV. 310
Eastwell, IX. 168, 169
Eastwood, IV. 91
Easy, Sir Charles, in *The Careless Husband*, VIII. 176
Easy, Mr, in Marryat's *Mr Midshipman Easy*, XII. 250
Easy club, IX. 369
Eatanswill, in *The Pickwick Papers*, XIII. 304
Eatanswill journalism, XIV. 170
Eaton, John Richard Turner, XII. 334
'Ebbaac, G.,' XI. 140
Ebionite heresy, I. 224
Eblis, in Beckford's *Vathek*, XI. 290, 291; XIII. 357
Ebrington, X. 113
Ebsworth, Joseph Woodfall, IX. 361, 364; *Roxburghe Ballads*, IX. 378
Eccho, in *The Glasse of Governement*, V. 113, 114
Ecclefechan, XIII. 2, 9, 20
Eccles, Charlotte O'Conor (1860?–1911), XIV. Add. 3
    Aliens of the West, XIV. 325
    Matrimonial Lottery, A, XIV. 325
    Rejuvenation of Miss Semaphore, The, XIV. 325
    Tom Connolly's Daughter, XIV. 325
Eccles division of Lancashire, XII. 337
Ecclesdown castle, in Arbuthnot's *History of John Bull*, IX. 135
Ecclesiastes, II. 242
Ecclesiastical learning (1600–1660), VII. 484, 485
Ecclesiastick, The, XIV. 70
Ecclesiologist, The, XIV. 70
Eccleston, Thomas de. *See* Thomas de
Ecgfrith, I. 10

Ecglaf, I. 145
Ecgtheow, Beowulf's father, I. 22
Echard, Laurence (1670?–1730), IX. 237, 238, 492; *History of England*, IX. 235, 494
Échecs amoureux, II. 202
Echo, in *Narcissus*, VI. 316
Echo, The, XIV. 195
Eckel, John C., XIII. 531
Eckermann, Johann Peter, XII. 379
Eckhart, *Meister* (1260?–1329?), IX. 315
Eclectic Review, The, XIII. 61
École de Chartes, XIV. 53
Economist, The, XIV. 28, 141, 199
Edda, The, I. 8, 21, 62; X. 202, 228, 490
Eddius Stephanus (*fl.* 669), I. 85, 434
Eden, garden of, III. 231, 244; IV. 60, 61; VII. 370
Eden, Richard (1521?–1576), IV. 79, 80, 101, 107, 455
    Arte of Navigation, The, IV. 71, 443
    Compendium, IV. 104
    History of Travayle, etc., The, IV. 75
    Trans. of Peter Martyr's *The Decades of the Newe World*, IV. 70, 71, 75, 441
    Treatyse of the Newe India, A, IV. 70, 71
Edern, son of Nuð, I. 255
Edgar, Sir James (1841–1899), XIV. 357, 582
Edgar, Sir John (*fl.* 1720), IX. 439, 442, 473, 475
Edgar, king of the English (944–975), I. 110, 113, 114, 121, 123, 137 ff., 305; II. 76; IV. 68; V. 36; VIII. 310; X. 111
Edgar, Matilda, lady (1844–1910), XIV. 583; *Colonial Governor in Maryland, A*, XIV. 359; *Life of Brock*, XIV. 359; *Ten Years of Peace and War*, XIV. 359
Edgar, in *King Lear*, III. 448
Edgcumbe, mount, X. 115
Edgcumbe, R. P., XIV. 537
Edge-hill, X. 112, 113, 271, 272
Edgehill, battle of, IV. 195; VIII. 361
Edgeman, Clarendon's secretary, VII. 188
Edgeworth, F. A., XI. 460
Edgeworth, Honora, born Sneyd (d. 1780), XIV. 393
Edgeworth, Jane, born Lovell, XIV. 392
Edgeworth, Maria (1767–1849), XI. 286, 296 ff. (main entry); 304, 381, 459, 475; XII. 2, 241, 245, 447; XIII. 376, 377, 425; XIV. 392, 598, 599, 605
    Absentee, The, X. 66; XI. 297
    Amie Inconnue, La, XI. 299
    Belinda, XI. 285, 297, 299
    Castle Rackrent, XI. 297
    Frank, XI. 382
    Harry and Lucy, XI. 382
    Helen, XI. 148, 297
    Letters for Literary Ladies, XIV. 395
    Moral Tales, XI. 296, 382
    Ormond, XI. 297
    Parent's Assistant, The, XI. 382; XIV. 393, 394
    Practical Education (with R. L. Edgeworth), XIV. 393
    Simple Susan, XI. 299, 382

Edgeworth, Richard Lovell (1744–1817),
XI. 296, 460; XIV. 601, 605
  Harry and Lucy, XIV. 393
  Memoirs, XIV. 392
  Practical Education (with M. Edge-
    worth), XIV. 393
  Professional Education, XIV. 394
  Rational Primer, A, XIV. 394
Edgeworths, the, XIV. 391, 601
Edgeworthstown, X. 197; XIV. 391
Edgware, X. 212, 214
Edgworth, Roger (d. 1560), III. 51
Edial, near Lichfield, X. 160, 161
Edinburgh, II. 92, 109, 126, 128, 284, 370;
  III. 120, 182, 426; IV. 150, 151, 215,
  267, 409, 412 ff., 547; VI. 5, 47, 369;
  VII. 197, 452, 455; IX. 130, 214, 290,
  359, 366, 367, 369, 371, 379, 380, 537;
  X. 40, 42, 55, 87, 94, 182, 190 ff., 200,
  201, 230, 281, 283, 290, 296, 322, 324,
  336; XI. 75, 149, 220 ff., 233 ff., 238,
  315, 327, 338, 341, 342; XII. 2, 5, 11, 18,
  19, 23, 143, 155, 156, 158, 159, 321,
  349, 370; XIII. 3, 4, 5, 9, 10, 362, 372;
  XIV. 139, 159, 176, 199, 204, 257, 263,
  267, 274, 294, 373, 374, 406
  Advocates' library, III. 137; XII. 26,
    358, 370 ff., 372
  Apollo press, XI. 325
  Bibliographical society, XI. 469, 470
  Botanic garden, XIV. 286
  Bruntsfield-links, IX. 366
  Calton hill, III. 123
  Canongate, IX. 366; XII. 2
  Castle, III. 122, 148
  College of Justice, III. 150
  Corporation buildings, XI. 435
  Cowgate, XII. 2
  George street, XII. 149
  High school, XII. 3, 4; XIV. 404
  Holyrood house, VIII. 394, 395
  Holyrood palace, XII. 29
  Infirmary, XIII. 213
  Leith Walk, XIII. 6
  New college, XII. 371; XIV. 47
  Periodical Press, the, VII. 502; XI. 469
  Portrait Gallery, XI. 435
  Printers and booksellers, XI. 469
  Register house, XII. 359
  Royal society, XIV. 288; *Transactions*,
    XI. 76
  St Andrew's church, XI. 233
  St Giles, II. 259
  Signet library, XII. 358, 371, 521; XIV.
    101
  Theatre Royal, X. 479
  Tolbooth, XII. 17, 18
  University, IV. 150, 434; VIII. 298; IX.
    550; X. 93, 287; XI. 222, 244; XII. 332,
    335, 350, 359, 372, 484; XIII. 2, 3, 19;
    XIV. 6, 7, 209, 210
  University library, XI. 435
Edinburgh Annual Register, The, XII. 13,
  373
Edinburgh Courant, The, IX. 432; X. 479;
  XIV. 203

Edinburgh Encyclopaedia, XIII. 4
Edinburgh Magazine, The, XI. 243, 439
Edinburgh Magazine and Review, X. 258
Edinburgh Monthly Magazine, The, XII.
  425; XIV. 373
Edinburgh Review, The (1755–1756), IX.
  561; X. 173, 474; XII. 426
Edinburgh Review, The (1802–   ), X.
  232, 239; XI. 442; XII. 32, 33, 92, 141 ff.
  (main entry), 151 ff., 155, 156, 158, 162,
  163, 288, 293, 310, 325, 426; XIII. 5, 8,
  29, 35, 38, 78, 241, 245, 359, 374, 467;
  XIV. 5, 7, 8, 54, 59 ff., 71, 97, 138, 194,
  395, 403, 405, 407, 409 ff., 416, 596,
  605, 609
Edinburgh University Magazine, The, XIV.
  210, 538
Edith, in *Dombey and Son*, XIII. 325
Edith, in *The Bloody Brother*, VI. 129,
  138
Edith, in *Widow Edith*, III. 88, 89
Edkins, Joshua, XIV. 572
Edmond, John Philip (1850–1906), XII.
  521
Edmondes, Sir Clement (1564?–1622), IV.
  435
Edmondes, Sir Thomas (1563?–1639), VII.
  436; X. 498
Edmonds, Charles, XI. 392
Edmonton, V. 252; XII. 118, 201 ff.
Edmund, in *King Lear*, V. 204, 213, 262
Edmund Ironside (981?–1016), I. 127, 140,
  337
Edmund Ironside, V. 399
Edmund, king of the East Angles (841–
  870), VIII. 310
Edmund of Abingdon (d. 1240), I. 200
Edmund, St (1170?–1240), I. 121; V. 10
Edmund, St, in *The Example of Virtue*,
  II. 227
Edmund, St, in *The Golden Legend*, II. 335
Edmund (922?–946), son of Edward the
  Elder, I. 137
Edmundson, Henry (d. 1659), VII. 486
Ednam, Roxburghshire, X. 93
Edom o' Gordon, X. 233
Edomites, in Cowley's *Davideis*, VII. 67
Edstone, near Henley-in-Arden, X. 109,
  112, 271
Education, books on, IX. 568 ff.
Education, early books of, II. 499
Education, English and Scottish, II.
  341 ff., 487 ff.
Education act (1870), XIV. 415, 427;
  (1902–3), XIV. 433
Education department, XIV. 420, 421, 433
Education society of the northern coun-
  ties, X. 385
Edward I, king of England, I. 350, 351,
  370; II. 103, 130, 132; III. 104, 132;
  IX. 535; X. 129; XIV. 75, 81, 101
Edward I, Elegy on, I. 370
Edward II, I. 342, 355, 356, 370; II. 81,
  352, 421, 502; III. 421; IV. 181; IX.
  222, 535; X. 287
Edward II, Evil Times of, I. 370

Edward III, I. 213, 284, 292, 338, 344, 353, 357 ff.; II. 22, 37, 102, 117, 156, 157, 296, 311, 356, 358, 421; III. 440; IV. 181; V. 244; VI. 330; VII. 206; VIII. 313; IX. 535

Edward III, V. 146, 237, 238, 243, 245, 398, 441, 443

Edward III, in Barbour's *Bruce*, II. 106

Edward the Third, The Raigne of King, IV. 394

Edward IV, II. 211, 287, 298, 317, 338, 482; III. 196; IV. 137, 182; V. 28; VI. 279, 280, 301; VII. 327; VIII. 314; IX. 535

Edward V, VIII. 314

Edward VI, II. 503; III. 30, 31, 33, 34, 36, 50, 51, 80, 81, 94, 107, 110, 143, 162, 181, 195, 198, 287, 338, 400, 403, 419, 427, 428, 430, 477; IV. 229, 230, 232, 234, 300, 314, 379, 380, 396; V. 56, 59, 90, 104, 108, 109; VI. 297; VII. 208, 325 ff., 330, 331, 336, 337; IX. 197, 210; XII. 355; XIV. 111

Edward VII, king of Great Britain, XII. 321

Edward (ballad), II. 412

Edward, prince, in *Henry VI*, V. 186

Edward, prince of Wales (1453–1471), II. 210, 297

Edward, son of Edgar, I. 138, 139

Edward aetheling, I. 140

Edward the Confessor (St Edward), I. 111, 140, 149, 180, 337, 355, 390, 449; V. 31; VIII. 310; XIV. 72

Edward the Confessor, in *The Example of Virtue*, II. 227

Edward the Elder, I. 137; VIII. 310

Edwardes, Sir Herbert Benjamin, XIV. 495

Edwardian commissioners, IV. 427

Edwards, Amelia Blandford (1831–1892), XIII. 562; XIV. 552

Edwards, Edward (1812–1886), XII. 521; *Lives of the Founders of the British Museum*, XII. 368; *Memoirs of Libraries*, XII. 368

Edwards, Eliseus James, XIV. Add. 7

Edwards, Henry Sutherland, XIV. 238

Edwards, John (1637–1716), VIII. 471, 473

Edwards, Jonathan (1629–1712), IX. 281

Edwards, Richard (1523?–1566), V. 120, 126, 396, 402; VI. 283 ff.
   Damon and Pithias, V. 63, 64, 70, 77, 118 ff., 123; VI. 284, 286, 299, 300
   In going to my naked bed, III. 189
   Palamon and Arcyte, V. 70, 118, 256; VI. 284, 286, 299, 300, 471
   Paradyse of Daynty Devises, The, III. 98, 189, 523

Edwards, Thomas (*fl.* 1595), *Cephalus and Procris*, IV. 469

Edwards, Thomas (1599–1647), *Gangraena*, VII. 386, 514

Edwards, Thomas (1699–1757), V. 273; IX. 475; *Canons of Criticism*, IX. 144; *Gangraena*, IX. 307

Edwards, Thomas (*fl.* 1810), X. 310, 507

Edwin, John (1749–1790), XI. 257, 453

Edwin, monk, I. 390

Edwin and Paulinus story, in Milton's *History of England*, VII. 128

Edwin of Northumbria (585?–633), I. 81; IV. 67

Edwy, Dunstan and, II. 76

Egan, Pierce (1772–1849), XIII. 418; XIV. 222 ff., 230, 233, 543
   Anecdotes, XIV. 226
   Book of Sports, XIV. 231
   Boxiana, XIV. 231
   Finish to the Adventures of Tom, Jerry, and Logic, The, XIV. 226
   Life in London, XIII. 265; XIV. 222 ff., 229, 238
   Life of an Actor, The, XIV. 226
   Pierce Egan's Life in London and Sporting Guide, XIV. 231

Egbert, bishop of Lindisfarne, I. 86

Egbert or Ecgberht of York (d. 766), I. 5, 80, 83, 84, 87

Eger, Sir, I. 291, 467

Egerton, lady Alice, VII. 113

Egerton, Hugh Edward, XIV. 563

Egerton, John, 1st earl of Bridgewater (1579–1649), VII. 113

Egerton, John, bookseller, XI. 336

Egerton, Sir Thomas, baron Ellesmere and viscount Brackley (1540?–1617), IV. 138, 161, 199, 200, 214, 215, 221, 265; VII. 112

Egerton, Thomas, IV. 200

Egerton, T. and J., *Theatrical Remembrancer, The* (1787), XI. 448

Egerton Papers, V. 477

Egeus, in *A Midsummer-Night's Dream*, V. 172

Egham, VII. 59

Egidia, step-sister of Robert II, II. 117

Egidius Romanus (d. 1316), II. 363

Egil Skallagrimsson, I. 9, 62; X. 224

Egilssaga, XII. 484

Egisthus, in Thomson's *Agamemnon*, X. 108

Egistus, in *Horestes*, V. 65

Eglamor, XIII. 59

Eglamour of Artois, Sir, I. 316, 471; II. 182

Eglantine, Archibald, in Thackeray's *The Ravenswing*, XIII. 281

Egypt, II. 79, 87; IV. 89; VI. 301; X. 503; XII. 198, 317, 320, 339, 340, 351, 478; XIV. 246, 247, 252

Egypt, Frederick Tennyson's ode on, XIII. 45

Egypt, khedive of, XIV. 195

Egypt exploration fund, XII. 339, 340

Egyptologists, XII. 342

Egyptology, VII. 318

Ehangwen, Arthur's hall, I. 254

Eichler, A., XIII. 502

Eight Letters, VIII. 277

Eighty-eight, VIII. 96

Eikon Basilike. See Gauden, John

Eilhart von Oberge, I. 273

Einaudi, L., XIII. Add. 2

Einenkel, Eugen, I. 118

Einhart's *Life of Charles the Great*, I. 90
Ekkehard of St Gall, I. 32, 33; V. 37
Elaine, Tennyson's, XIII. 37
Elbing, in Alfred's *Orosius*, I. 94
Elbodugus. *See* Elfoð
Elckerlijk, the Dutch, V. 53
Eld, in *Confessio Amantis*, II. 148
Eld, George, IV. 394
Elder, John (*fl.* 1555), III. 194
Elderton, William (d. 1592), III. 201; IV. 169, 390, 535; V. 102; VI. 218; *Doctor Stories stumblinge into Englonde*, IV. 380
Eldon, earl of. *See* Scott, John
Eleanor, in Thomson's *Edward and Eleonora*, X. 108
Eleanor, duchess of Augustine, queen of Henry II, I. 264
Eleanor, lady, in Mrs Inchbald's *Every one has his Fault*, XI. 279
Eleanor of Castile, queen of Edward I, VIII. 125
Eleanor of Provence, queen of Henry III, I. 194, 361
Electra (Herrick's), VII. 6
Elegant Extracts, XI. 472
Elena, in Taylor's *Philip van Artevelde*, XII. 113
Elford, Staffordshire, XII. 277
Elflēdes Boc, I. 110. *See, also*, Aethelflaed
Elfoð, or Elbodugus, bishop of Bangor (d. 809), I. 70, 246
Elgin, II. 100
Elginbrod, David and Margaret, in George Macdonald's novel, XIII. 432
Elia. *See* Lamb, Charles
Elias of Jerusalem, I. 106
Elicea, in *Celestina*, V. 99
Elidure, king, in *No-Body, and Some-Body*, VI. 92
Elidure the Just, IV. 190
Elie de Beaumont, J.-B.-J., X. 61
Eliensis, Historia, II. 397
Elijah, I. 67, 74
Elijah, in Cowley's *The Muse*, VII. 66
Elinor, queen, in *Robert, Earle of Huntington*, V. 324
Eliot, Francis Perceval (1756?-1818), XIV. 513
Eliot, George (Mary Ann Cross, born Evans, 1819-1880), XI. 146; XII. 154, 292, 446; XIII. 108, 175, 292, 341, 345, 373, 379, 381 ff. (main entry), 422, 431, 442, 445, 446, 551 ff., 570, *also see* Add. 3; XIV. 199
   Adam Bede, XIII. 382, 383, 386, 388 ff.
   Address to Working-Men, XIII. 396
   Agatha, XIII. 401
   Amos Barton, XIII. 386 ff.
   Armgart, XIII. 401
   'Brother and Sister,' XIII. 382
   Brother Jacob, XIII. 401
   Daniel Deronda, XIII. 384, 394 ff.
   Evangelical Teaching of Dr Cumming, The, XIII. 385
   Felix Holt, the Radical, XIII. 396, 397
   How Lisa loved the King, XIII. 400

Eliot, George
   Impressions of Theophrastus Such, The, XIII. 382, 386, 401
   Janet's Repentance, XIII. 386 ff.
   Legend of Jubal, The, XIII. 401
   Lifted Veil, The, XIII. 401
   'Looking Backward,' XIII. 382
   Middlemarch, XIII. 382, 398 ff.
   Mill on the Floss, The, XIII. 391, 392, 394
   Minor Prophet, The, XIII. 401
   Mr Gilfil's Love Story, XIII. 386 ff.
   Poems, XIII. 382, 401
   Romola, XIII. 393 ff., 398
   Scenes of Clerical Life, XIII. 386 ff.
   Silas Marner, XIII. 393, 401
   Spanish Gypsy, The, XIII. 396, 397, 400
   Tales from Clerical Life, XIII. 386
   Translations by, XIII. 383, 385
   Wise, Witty, and Tender Sayings of George Eliot, XIII. 388
   Works, XIII. 382
   Life of. See Cross, J. W.
Eliot, Sir John (1592-1632), VII. 440; X. 287
Elipandus of Toledo, I. 85
Elisabeth of Schönau, St, I. 229
Elisha, I. 74
Eliza, in Barnfield's *Cynthia*, IV. 120
Eliza, in Wycherley's *Country Wife*, VIII. 145
Elizabeth, countess of Kent. *See* Grey, Elizabeth
Elizabeth, Epitaph on the lady, VII. 40
Elizabeth, princess (1635-1650), daughter of Charles I, IX. 403
Elizabeth, princess (1596-1662), daughter of James I, afterwards queen of Bohemia, IV. 143, 145, 154, 203; VI. 112, 250, 318, 353; VII. 46, 437, 439; the company of, VI. 261, 262
Elizabeth, queen of England, I. 99, 319, 381; II. 359; III. 1, 34, 35, 45, 54, 81, 96, 97, 114, 145, 148, 172, 181, 198, 201, 207, 212, 215, 219, 224, 226, 243, 245 ff., 252, 254, 264, 267, 290, 311, 314, 322, 326, 327, 331, 332, 337, 351, 374, 375, 377, 399 ff., 405, 406, 412, 418, 420 ff., 426, 432, 433, 437, 449, 454; IV. 1, 3, 6, 9, 16, 23, 51 ff., 57, 60, 64, 84, 87, 94, 95, 98, 104, 110, 111, 113, 120, 124, 126, 127, 132, 135, 142, 144, 150, 160, 163, 165, 172, 173, 176, 184, 193, 195, 208, 214, 232, 234, 298, 299, 301, 302, 305 ff., 312, 320, 329, 333, 351, 360, 380, 384, 391, 401, 405, 442; V. 29 ff., 35, 56, 60, 65, 66, 68, 77, 78, 102, 104, 109, 117, 118, 124, 152, 170, 247, 253, 256, 262, 309, 311, 328, 336 ff., 345, 347, 348, 354, 360, 361, 363, 366, 371, 376, 377, 480 ff.; VI. 33, 53, 91, 110, 141, 175, 212, 217, 241 ff., 246, 251, 264, 270, 272, 278, 285, 286, 291, 292, 297 ff., 301, 305, 309, 316, 320, 321, 326, 327, 335, 336, 365, 374, 380, 396, 400, 401; VII. 4, 28, 77, 157, 166, 190, 191, 196,

Elizabeth, queen of England
203, 221, 304 ff., 309, 314, 325, 326,
331, 333, 337, 338, 343, 366, 369, 386,
432; VIII. 44, 115, 350, 351, 356, 371;
IX. 222, 271, 306, 534; X. 174, 287, 498,
499, 504; XI. 106, 350, 368; XII. 354,
355, 512, 514; XIII. 366; XIV. 52, 55,
84, 86, 93, 100, 101, 396; trans. of
Boethius, II. 186
Elizabeth (1465–1503), queen of Henry
VII, II. 391; III. 17
Elizabeth Brownrigge, XIII. 278
Elizabeth de Burgh. *See* Burgh, Elizabeth
de; Clare, Elizabeth de
Elizabethan age, VII. 26, 150, 440, 449;
X. 142; XI. 248, 369; XII. 80, 93, 168,
169, 358; XIII. 255, 364, 423; XIV. 443 ff.
Elizabethan church settlement, VII. 208
Elizabethan criticism, III. 289 ff., 526 ff.
Elizabethan divines, VII. 306
Elizabethan drama, IX. 56; X. 1, 5, 68,
69, 73, 78, 86, 92; XI. 258; XII. 68, 69,
112, 186; XIII. 257, 259
Elizabethan English, X. 180, 236
Elizabethan grammar schools, VII. 317
Elizabethan literature, II. 200, 209, 267,
387, 429; VII. 1, 7 ff., 17, 20, 23 ff., 48,
73, 93, 135, 148, 149, 155, 188, 256,
261, 263, 264, 270, 275, 323, 387; VIII.
25, 28, 125 ff., 130, 152, 179, 180, 184,
187, 195, 222, 308, 321, 387; IX. 265,
266; X. 184, 218, 221, 238; XII. 107, 113,
116, 253, 262, 364; XIII. 233, 238, 241,
269; XIV. 171, 460
Elizabethan lyrists, I. 362
Elizabethan moralities, V. 393
Elizabethan poets, X. 130; XI. 182, 183;
XII. 47, 58, 79, 81; XIII. 130, 244, 245
Elizabethan prose fiction, III. 339 ff.,
533 ff., *also see* Add.
Elizabethan public, XI. 262
Elizabethan sonnet, the, III. 247 ff., 522 ff.;
XIII. 117
Elizabethan wars, VII. 447
Ellangowan, XIII. 234
Ellangowan, laird of. *See* Bertram, God-
frey
Ellen, in *Child Waters*, II. 413
Ellen, in Scott's *Lady of the Lake*, XII. 12
Ellena, in Mrs Radcliffe's *Italian*, XI. 302
Ellenberger, D. Frederic, XIV. Add. 7
Ellenborough, earl of. *See* Law, Edward
Elleray, lake Windermere, XII. 158
Ellesmere, lord. *See* Egerton, Sir Thomas
Ellicott, Charles John (1819–1905), IV. 46;
XII. 340, 500
Elliot, Anne, in Jane Austen's *Persuasion*,
XII. 240, 242
Elliot, the Hon. Arthur Ralph Douglas, XII.
426
Elliot, Charles, XI. 327, 342
Elliot, Edward Elliot, lord, X. 306
Elliot, Sir Gilbert (1722–1777), *My Apron
Dearie*, IX. 373
Elliot, Sir Henry Miers (1808–1853), *His-
tory of India*, XIV. 337, 576
Elliot, Hugh S. R., XIV. 477

Elliot, Jane (1727–1805), XI. 231, *Ewe
'I've heard them Lilting at the* 232;
Milking,' IX. 373
Elliot, Miss, in Jane Austen's *Persuasion*,
XII. 240, 243
Elliot, Sir Walter, in Jane Austen's *Per-
suasion*, XII. 240
Elliot, Sir Walter (1803–1887), XII. 509
Elliott, Charlotte (1789–1871), XII. 416
Elliott, Ebenezer (1781–1849), XII. 135,
416; XIII. 156, 418; XIV. 327; *Battle
Song*, XII. 136
Elliott, Mary (Mrs Belson, *fl.* 1810–1820),
XI. 382, 478; *Aunt Mary's Tales*, XI.
383; *Rambles of a Butterfly*, XI. 383;
Tales for Boys, XI. 383
Ellis, Alexander John (1814–1890), XII.
504; XIII. 248; XIV. 611; *Early English
Pronunciation*, XIV. 441
Ellis, Annie Raine, X. 260
Ellis, Clement (1630–1700), IX. 395, 569;
The Gentile Sinner, IX. 397
Ellis, Edmund, *Dia Poemata* (1655), VII. 412
Ellis, Edwin J., XI. 431, 433, 434
Ellis, F. S., XII. 403, 405
Ellis, George (1753–1815), VII. 73, 86;
X. 234, 487, 491; XI. 35, 36, 39, 53, 391,
392; XII. 144, 149 ff., 357; *Early English
Poets*, XII. 146; *Specimens of Early
English Romances in Metre*, XI. 172;
XII. 368
Ellis, Sir Henry (1777–1869), XII. 508,
509; *Introduction to Domesday Book*,
XII. 346; *Original Letters, illustrative of
English History*, XII. 346
Ellis, Hercules, XIV. 572, 573
Ellis, James (1763?–1830), XII. 376
Ellis, John (1643?–1738), IX. 495
Ellis, Robert (1820–1885), XII. 496
Ellis, Robert Leslie (1817–1859), IV. 280
Ellis, Robinson (1834–1913), XII. 483;
XIII. 175, 502; *Appendix Vergiliana*,
XII. 337; *Catullus* (trans.), XII. 337
Ellis, Thomas, in *The merry jests of the
widow Edith*, II. 327
Ellis, Thomas, "sailer," IV. 456
Ellis, Thomas Flower (1796–1861), XIV.
493
Ellis, William (1800–1881), XIV. 414, 415,
601
Ellisland, Dumfriesshire, XI. 222
Ellison, Henry, XIII. 502
Ellison, O., XIII. 532
Elliston, Robert William (1774–1831),
XII. 189
Ellistone, John (*fl.* 1651), IX. 515, 517
Ellwood, Thomas (1639–1713), VII. 107,
118, 120, 121; VIII. 104 ff., 110, 414,
415; IX. 406; *A Collection of Poems on
Various Subjects*, VIII. 113; *The History
of the Life of Thomas Ellwood, written by
his own hand*, VIII. 105
Elmham, Thomas (d. 1440?), II. 496; IX.
535
Elmsley, Peter (1736–1802), XI. 327
Elmsley, Peter (1773–1825), XII. 327 ff.,
333, 483

Elmy, Sarah. *See* Crabbe, Mrs
Eloisa, IX. 71
Elphin (*i.e.* Sir P. Sidney), in Drayton's *Idea*, IV. 172
Elphin, Roscommon, X. 196, 197, 199
Elphinstone, Mountstuart (1779–1859), XIV. 487, 552, 576; *The History of India*, XIV. 337
Elphinstone, William (1431–1514), II. 251, 369
Elrington, Charles Richard (1787–1850), XIV. 572
Elrington, Thomas (1688–1732), IX. 457
Elsinore, V. 159
Elstob, Elizabeth (1683–1756), IX. 402, 533; *Grammar*, IX. 355; *Homily on the Birthday of St Gregory*, IX. 355
Elstob, William (1673–1715), IX. 355
Elstow, Beds., VII. 167
Elsynge, Henry (1598–1654), X. 491
Eltham, VI. 283
Elton, Charles Isaac (1839–1900), XII. 401, 403, 521; XIV. 199
Elton, Mary Augusta, XII. 521
Elton, Mr, in Jane Austen's *Emma*, XII. 234, 243
Elton, Mrs, in Jane Austen's *Emma*, XII. 239, 240, 243
Elton, Oliver, I. 425; IV. 168, 178, 179, 180, 183, 186, 188, 195; XII. 230, 433, 524; XIII. 477, 495, 570, 572, *also see* Add. 1, 3; XIV. 497; *Survey of English Literature*, XI. 20, 434, 439
Elton, Richard (*fl.* 1650), IV. 456
Eltraine, IV. 363
Elwin, Whitwell (1816–1900), IX. 84; X. 422, *also see* Add.; XI. 404; XII. 153, 429
Elwina, in Hannah More's *Percy*, XI. 274
Elwood, Anne K., XI. 473, 463 ff.
Ely, II. 342, 347, 350, 352, 353, 358; IV. 190, 224, 238, 409, 422; VIII. 288, 301; IX. 330, 335, 339, 343, 356, 532; XII. 305, 325, 507; XIII. 366; monastery of, I. 16, 114, 140; II. 397
Ely, Mr, in George Eliot's *Amos Barton*, XIII. 387
Ely. *See* Thomas of
Elyot, Sir Thomas (1490?–1546), III. 21 ff. (main entry), 107, 302, 341, 423, 433, 445, 467, 486; IV. 437, 439, 495; VI. 492; VII. 304
   Bankette of Science, The, III. 23
   Castel of Helth, The, III. 23, 107, 445
   Dictionary of Syr T. Eliot, Knyght (*Bibliothecae Eliotae*), III. 23; VII. 315
   Doctrine of Princes, made by the noble oratour Isocrates, The, III. 23
   Education or Bringinge up of Children, translated out of Plutarche, The, III. 23
   Governour, The Boke named the, III. 21 ff., 105, 302, 341, 433
   Holy Saynt Ciprian, A swete and devout sermon of, III. 23
   Image of Governance, compiled of the actes and sentences notable of the moste

Elyot, Sir Thomas
   noble Emperour Alexander Severus, The, III. 23
   Of the Knowledge which maketh a wise man, IV. 5
   Rules of a Christian lyfe made by Picus, The, III. 23
Elysian fields, XI. 107, 352
Elysium, Dekker's, IV. 354
Elze, Karl, V. 305
Elzevir press, Amsterdam, VII. 286
Elzevir texts, VII. 315
Elzevirianum, the, X. 245
Emancipation act, XIV. 54
Emarè, I. 310, 311, 316, 467
Emaricdulfe (E. C.'s), III. 256, 523
Emblem books, VII. 405, 479
Emdale, county Down, XIII. 404
Emelye, in *The Knightes Tale*, XIII. 123
Emerson, Oliver Farrar, XIV. 611
Emerson, Ralph Waldo, XI. 153, 171, 409, 439; XII. 440, 441; XIII. 10, 15, 465, 466, 469, 471
Emery, Thomas, XIV. 591
Emilia, in *Othello*, V. 202
Emilia, in *The Two Noble Kinsmen*, V. 256
Emilie, in *The Knight's Tale*, II. 243; V. 256
Emily, in *Palamon and Arcyte*, VI. 299
Emily, in Mrs Cowley's *Runaway*, XI. 274
Emily, in Mrs Radcliffe's *Mysteries of Udolpho*, XI. 302, 303
Emily, in Richardson's *Sir Charles Grandison*, X. 10
Emily, in Wordsworth's *White Doe of Rylstone*, XI. 106, 107
Emily, lady, in Burgoyne's *Heiress*, XI. 275
Emily, little, in *David Copperfield*, XIII. 327
Emin pasha, XIV. 192
Emlyn, in *The boke of Mayd Emlyn*, III. 88
Emlyn, Thomas (1663–1741), X. 386
   Humble Enquiry, X. 379
Emma, in Jane Austen's novel, XII. 239, 243
Emmanuel, in *The Weakest goeth to the Wall*, V. 316
Emmaus, V. 39
Emmeline, in Dryden's *King Arthur*, VIII. 31
Empire, The, XIV. 364
Empiric, The, VI. 28
Emulo, in *Patient Grissill*, VI. 40
Encyclopaedia Biblica, XII. Add.
Encyclopaedia Britannica, XI. 76, 235; XII. 296, 370, 375; XIV. 5, 13, 59, 61, 63, 98, 144
Encyclopaedia Metropolitana, XI. 133, 415; XII. 474; XIV. 26, 428
Encyclopédie, L', I. 207; V. 292
'Endeavour,' ship, XIV. 289
Endimion (Lyly's), V. 341
Endor, witch of, VII. 370
Endowed Schools acts, XIV. 422

Endowed Schools commission, XII. 336;
    XIV. 421, 422, 429, 430
Endymion, in *The Faithfull Shepheardesse*,
    VI. 368
Endymion, in Keats's poem, XII. 57, 81, 82
Énéas, Roman d', I. 285
Eneydes, Le livre des, II. 316
Enfans sans souci, V. 22, 25
Enfield, XII. 79, 182, 186, 200, 201
Enfield chase, V. 253
Enfield, William (1741–1797), X. 385;
    XIV. 606; *The Speaker*, XIV. 399
Engagement, The, VIII. 275
Engel, Carl (1818–1882), XII. 521
Engelbrecht, Johann, IX. 519
England, church of, IV. 204, 305; V. 365;
    VI. 3, 150; VII. 142 ff., 208, 214, 217,
    223, 310, 321, 340; VIII. 43, 46, 273,
    286, 292, 293 ff.; IX. 210; X. 287, 351,
    352, 359, 362, 364, 366, 370, 375, 377 ff.,
    381; XI. 1, 167; XII. 254, 259 ff., 266,
    267, 274 ff., 295; XIII. 103, 348, 453;
    XIV. 76, 383, 402, 411
England, The Political History of, XII. 322
England's Helicon, III. 178; IV. 52, 109,
    113, 116 ff., 121, 122, 125, 159, 222,
    467, 487; V. 148; VII. 2
England's Joy, VI. 263
England's Miserie, VII. 385
England's Parnassus, V. 129, 134, 148,
    162; XII. 113
Englefield, Sir Henry C. (1752–1822), XII.
    509
English association, the, XIII. 377
English canon law, XIV. 80
English dialect society, XII. 344
English, earliest documents in, III. 440
English grammar, XIV. 396 ff., 440 ff.
English, history and literature, Old, XII.
    344
English language, I. 379 ff., 480; XIV.
    434 ff.
English language, Middle, I. 481
English language, Old, I. 480
'English Men of Letters' series, XIV. 144
English Annotations of the Bible, VII. 322
English Courtier and the Countrey Gentle-
    man, The, III. 489; V. 349, 351, 478
English Historical Review, The, X. 295,
    409; XIV. 100, 118
English Miscellany, An, IV. 119
English Poets, XI. 325
English Post, The, XI. 333
English Review, X. 310
English Rogue, The (1665), VII. 516
English Spy, The, XIV. 238
Englishman, The, IX. 220, 441
Englishman, the, in *The Fyrste Boke of*
    the Introduction of Knowledge, III. 105
Englishman's Magazine, The, XII. 437
Enid, I. 280
Enitharmon, Blake's, XI. 194 ff.
Ennius, IV. 17, 264; VIII. 58
Ennui, in Reynolds's *Dramatist*, XI. 281
Enoch, in Byron's *Cain*, XII. 48
Enoch, Book of, I. 133

Enquirer, The (1797), XI. 394
Ensor, George (1769–1843), XIV. 605
Ent, Sir George (1604–1689), VIII. 356,
    363, 476; XIV. 281
Entepfuhl, in Carlyle's *Sartor Resartus*,
    XIII. 9
Entick, John (1703?–1773), X. 522; *Latin*
    and English Dictionary, X. 388; *Spelling*
    Dictionary, X. 388
Entries (legal) (1546), VIII. 466
Envy, in *Confessio Amantis*, II. 147, 148
Envy, in *Mucedorus*, V. 254
Envy, in *Piers the Plowman*, II. 12
Envy, in *The Passetyme of Pleasure*, II.
    229, 234
Eoganesius, Janus Julius, IX. 292
Eormenric, in *Beowulf* and *Widsith*, I. 26,
    34 ff.
Epaminondas, XII. 313
Epeircte, in *Argenis*, IV. 259
Ephraim, XIII. 149
Epicharmus, III. 433
Epicoene. See Jonson, *Silent Woman, The*
Epictetus, I. 286; II. 308; IV. 436, 523;
    VI. 34, 50; VII. 489; IX. 54, 300; XI.
    356 ff., 473; XII. 335, 487; XIII. 90;
    Enchiridion, IX. 246; XI. 357
Epicurus, VIII. 288, 289; XII. 340
Epigrams and satires, IV. 518
Epinasse, Francis, XIV. 519
Epiphany, festival of, II. 378
Epistolae Cantuarienses, XIV. 74
Epistolae Obscurorum Virorum, III. 91,
    106, 107, 398, 496; VII. 370
Eppie Morrie, II. 411
Epsom, VIII. 136, 199; IX. 130, 268; X. 260
Epternach, I. 83
Epworth, X. 364
Equatoria, XIV. 192
Erasmus, Desiderius (1466?–1536), I. 363;
    II. 67, 325, 330, 367, 369, 370; III. 1 ff.,
    7, 8, 11 ff., 18, 26 ff., 32, 40 ff., 49, 52,
    59, 67, 80, 93, 96, 104, 113, 155, 346,
    347, 363, 365, 429, 433, 466 ff., 487,
    496, *also see* Add.; IV. 225, 227, 228,
    322, 358, 414, 420, 422, 428, 430, 443,
    444, 491, 492, 530; VI. 9; VII. 261, 304,
    310, 315, 331, 366; VIII. 23; IX. 418,
    529; XI. 367; XII. 324, 332, 468, 477,
    485; XIV. 79, 86
    Adagia, III. 4, 20, 347; VIII. 59, 407
    Apophthegmata, III. 93, 347
    Colloquia, III. 1, 4, 20, 81, 104, 346, 347,
        429; IV. 347; VI. 87; VII. 370; IX. 273 ff.;
        XIII. 428
    Compendium vitae, XIII. 428
    Constructione, De, III. 20, 21
    Convivium Fabulorum, III. 93
    Copia, III. 4, 12, 20, 21
    Ecclesiastes, sive concionator Evangelicus,
        IV. 224
    Enchiridion Militis Christiani, III. 4,
        20, 27
    Encomium Moriae, III. 4, 18, 19, 96;
        V. 9, 13; VII. 376; VIII. 36, 59, 407
    Institutio Principis Christiani, III. 4

Erasmus, Desiderius
Jerome and Chrysostom, editions of and commentaries on, III. 4
Laudibus Britanniae, De, III. 67
Novum Instrumentum, III. 4, 12
Paraphrase of the New Testament, v. 104
Paraphrases, III. 4
Erastianism, VII. 296; IX. 193; X. 355, 370, 372; XII. 256
Erce, "the mother of the Earth," I. 40
Erceldoune, Thomas of. *See* Thomas de
Erckmann-Chatrian, XIV. 322
Erdeswicke, Sampson (d. 1603), III. 532; IX. 533
'Erebus,' ship, XIV. 296
Erec (Geraint), Sir, I. 284
Eremyt and the Outlawe, The, II. 503
Erewhon, Butler's, XIII. 453
Erichto, in *The Wonder of Women*, VI. 49
Erick, Abigail, IX. 91
Erigena, John. *See* Scotus
Erin, port, Isle of Man, XIV. 297
Erkenwald, I. 333, 334
Erl of Tolous and the Emperes of Almayn, I. 471
Erlinton, II. 411
Ermyn, in *Beves*, I. 305
Ernley or Arley Regis, Worcester, I. 234
Ernulf (1040–1124), I. 449; *Textus Roffensis*, IX. 535
Ernulphus, in Sterne's *Tristram Shandy*, X. 53, 55
Eromena, VII. 74
Erondelle, Peter, IV. 456
Errand, Tom, in Farquhar's *Constant Couple*, VIII. 169
Error, in *Time's Complaint*, VI. 320
'Ersch,' or 'Yrisch' speech, II. 90, 99
Erse poetry, X. 487
Erskine, Andrew, X. 191, 477
Erskine, David Steuart, 11th earl of Buchan (1742–1829), XI. 220; XII. 149
Erskine, Ebenezer (1680–1754), IX. 548
Erskine, Francis Robert St Claire, earl of Rosslyn (1853–1890), XIII. 502
Erskine, Henry (1746–1817), XI. 220; XII. 149
Erskine, J., XIV. Add. 3
Erskine, Ralph (1685–1752), IX. 548
Erskine, Thomas, 1st lord Erskine (1750–1823), XI. 139; XII. 149; XIV. 509, 513; *Defence of the Whigs*, XIV. 121
Erskine, Thomas, of Linlathen (1788–1870), IX. 328, 521; XII. 283, 466; *Brazen Serpent, The*, XII. 289; *Letters*, XII. 284; *Unconditional Freeness of the Gospel, The*, XII. 284
Erskine, William, lord Kinneder (1769–1822), XII. 13, 375
Erythraeus, *Eudemia*, IV. 260
Esau, VI. 93; XIII. 208
Esau, in *Jacob and Esau*, v. 111, 112
Eschenbach. *See* Wolfram von
Eschenburg, Johann Joachim, v. 298, 304

Escott, Thomas Hay Sweet, XIII. 564, 567; XIV. 185, 531, 533; *Masters of English Journalism*, XIV. 180, 187
Esdaile, Arundell, *A chronological list of George Meredith's publications*, XIII. 440, 568
Esher, III. 337
Esmond, colonel, in *The Virginians*, XIII. 298
Esmond, Henry, Thackeray's, XIII. 292, 293, 297, 300, 407
Esmond, lady Maria, in *The Virginians*, XIII. 298
Español Gerardo, El, VI. 123
Espinasse, Francis, IX. 236; XIV. Add. 2
Espriella, Don Manuel Alvarez (i.e. Southey), XI. 421
Espronceda, XII. 393
Esquemeling, John, IV. 456
Essay, the, IV. 523 ff.
Essay concerning the Origin of Sciences, IX. 137
Essay on Tragedy (1749), X. 161
Essay to revive the antient education of Gentlewomen, IX. 403
Essays and Reviews, XII. 285, 294 ff., 466; XIII. 452
Essays on a liberal education, XIV. 425
Essex, II. 208; IV. 127; VII. 37, 46, 58, 89, 454; IX. 152, 153, 537, 539; X. 386, 393; XII. 305, 513, 514; XIV. 74, 221
Essex, countess of. *See* Howard, Frances
Essex, earls of. *See* Cromwell, Thomas; Devereux, Robert; Devereux, Walter
Essex-Head club, X. 187, 471
Estcourt, Richard (1668–1712), VIII. 158, 177
Este, house of, III. 305
Este, Isabella de, v. 69
Este, Italy, XII. 63
Este, Leonora de, XII. 50
Este, Michael, IV. 113, 464
Estella, in *Great Expectations*, XIII. 330, 334
Estesian 'proofs,' XI. 163
Esther, v. 106
Estienne, Charles, VI. 484
Estienne, Henri, III. 157, 162, 424; IV. 8, 403, 408, 444; VII. 479
Estienne, Robert, III. 162
Estlin, John Prior (1747–1817), XI. 416
Estmere, King, II. 410, 411, 414
Esto Perpetua club, XI. 34, 35
Estrifs, v. 2, 27, 31
Estrild, in *Locrine*, v. 239, 240
État des hommes, II. 139
Eternity, in *The Passetyme of Pleasure*, II. 226
Etesia (Vaughan's), VII. 40
Ethelbald. *See* Aethilwald
Ethelbert, king of Kent, VIII. 309, 310
Ethelburga, St (d. 676?), I. 82
Etheldreda, St (630?–679), I. 82; II. 210
Ethelred. *See* Aethelred
Ethelwold. *See* Aethelwold
Ethelwulf's poem on ? Crayke, I. 86, 434

Etherege, Sir George (1635?–1691), VIII.
136 ff., 142 ff., 155, 214, 401, 418, 423,
424, 445; IX. 474; X. 67
Comical Revenge or Love in a Tub, The,
VIII. 18, 136, 137, 139, 143
Letter books, VIII. 137, 138
*Man of Mode, The, or Sir Fopling
Flutter,* VIII. 136
She Would if She Could, VIII. 136, 138
Ethiopians, IX. 138
Ethiopic learning, VII. 319
Etiquette, book on table, III. 19
Eton college, II. 305, 321, 355, 357, 359,
489; III. 183, 315, 418, 420, 426 ff., 433,
434; IV. 164, 165, 275, 406, 431; V. 102,
104, 105; VI. 246; VII. 53, 152, 192, 312,
326 ff., 331, 334, 341, 492; VIII. 279,
281; IX. 392, 405, 408 ff., 573; X. 20,
113, 114, 116, 117, 242, 247, 272; XI.
173, 341, 346; XII. 58, 323, 324; XIII.
24, 45, 129; XIV. 56, 121, 207, 225, 251,
386, 387, 390, 413, 422
Eton Greek grammar, III. 429
Eton, printing press, IV. 400, 411
Etonian, The, XIV. 539
Ettrick, XI. 239
Ettrick Banks, IX. 374
Ettrick shepherd, the. *See* Hogg, James
Etty, William (1787–1849), XIV. 203
Etymologicum Magnum, XII. 328
Eubulus, in *Damon and Pithias,* V. 118
Eubulus, in F. Davison's eclogue, IV. 124
Eubulus, in *The Anatomy of Wit,* III. 345
Eubulus, in *The Picture,* VI. 161
Eucharist, Aelfric on the, I. 117, 127, 128
Eucharist, Cranmer on the, III. 33, 34,
404
Eucharist, Lanfranc on the, I. 154
Eucharist, the, X. 354, 360; XII. 299
Eucherius, bishop of Lyons, VII. 405
Euclid, I. 153; II. 362; III. 420; VII. 266,
284, 287, 320; VIII. 360; IX. 305, 410
Euclid, first English translation, III. 425,
551; IV. 436
Euclio, in Pope's *Epistles,* IX. 82
Euganean hills, XII. 63; XIV. 293
Eugenia, in *The Duke of Millaine,* VI. 155
Eugenia, St, I. 74
Eugenius, in Sterne's *Tristram Shandy,*
X. 47, 50; XI. 174
Eugonus, in *Misogonus,* V. 110, 111
Eulalia, queen, in *The Queen and Concu-
bine,* VI. 231
Eulalia, St, I. 74
Eulenspiegel, III. 79, 81, 82, 94, 490; IV.
356, 360, 448, 533
Eulogium, Latin compendium, II. 301
Eumolpus, IX. 266
Eunapius Sardianus, IV. 436
Eunomia, in *The Masque of the Middle
Temple,* VI. 355
Eupelas, in *Misogonus,* V. 110
Euphorion, in Goethe's *Faust,* XII. 34
Euphormio (John Barclay's), IV. 255
Euphrasia, in *Philaster,* VI. 120, 126
Euphrates, the, IV. 90

Euphuism, IV. 145, 146, 194, 328; V. 214,
378; VI. 142, 163, 189, 387, 392. *See,
also, under* Lyly
Euripides, III. 161, 420, 429, 430; IV. 348,
436; V. 5; VI. 296; VII. 334; VIII. 164,
194; IX. 477, 524, 527; XII. 68, 325, 330 ff.,
475, 480, 483, 488, 489, 491, 493 ff.
Alcestis, XII. 329; XIII. 81
Bacchae, XII. 318, 327, 338
Hecuba, XII. 324, 326
Heraclidae, XI. 274; XII. 327
Hippolytus, XII. 329
Iphigenia, XII. 329
Medea, X. 124; XII. 101, 324, 327
Orestes, XII. 324
Phoenissae, IV. 4; V. 71; XII. 324
European literature, X. 14, 16, 17
European studies, X. 176
European Magazine, X. 192, 193, 471,
473, 479, 483
Euryalus and Lucrece, II. 329
Eurydice, I. 295, 311; X. 114
Eurydice, in *King Orfeo,* II. 414
Eurydice, in a Shetland ballad, II. 417
Eurymachus, in *Ulysses Redux,* VI. 303
Eusden, Laurence (1688–1730), IX. 181,
188, 448, 485
Eusebius, I. 66, 75; II. 293; XII. 484, 503
Eusebius (Hwaetberct), I. 60, 78, 79
Eusebius of Emesa, III. 416
Eustace, count, I. 111
Eustace, legend of St, I. 292, 315
Eustace, lord, in Mrs Griffith's *School for
Rakes,* XI. 263
Eustace the Monk, II. 507, 508
Eustathius, IX. 75
Eustochium, St, I. 74
Eutheo, in *The Third Blast of Retreat from
Plays and Theatres,* V. 313
Eutropius, I. 81; IV. 436
Evadne, in *The Jealous Lovers,* VI. 325
Evadne, in *The Maides Tragedy,* VI. 120,
126, 127
Evadne, in Sheil's play, XIII. 259
Evander, II. 231
Evans, Anne (1820–1870), XIII. 180, 198,
210, 502; *Pevensey and Hurstmonceaux,*
XIII. 177; *Roses and Rosemary,* XIII. 177
Evans, Arise (b. 1607), VII. 509
Evans, Sir Arthur (b. 1851), XII. 316, 339,
also see Add. 4
Evans, Arthur William, XIII. 471
Evans, Caleb, X. 387
Evans, Elizabeth, XIII. 389
Evans, Evan (1731–1789), X. 487
Evans, George Essex (1863–1909), XIV.
585; *Australian Symphony,* XIV. 369;
Repentance of Magdalene Despar, The,
XIV. 369
Evans, Gwenogvryn, I. 252
Evans, Henry, VI. 258, 289 ff.
Evans, Hugh, X. 387
Evans, Sir Hugh, in *The Merry Wives of
Windsor,* V. 189; XIV. 307
Evans, Isaac, XIII. 382
Evans, John (1680?–1730), IX. 212

Evans, John (1767–1827), XI. 486
Evans, Sir John (1823–1908), XII. 509;
XIII. 198; *Ancient Bronze Implements*,
XII. 347; *Ancient Stone Implements*, XII.
347; *Coins of the Ancient Britons*, XII.
347
Evans, Lewys, *How to Wyve well*, III. 486
Evans, Margaret, XIV. 595
Evans, Marian or Mary Ann. *See* Eliot,
George
Evans, Mary, XI. 118
Evans, Maurice S., XIV. Add. 7
Evans, Robert Wilson (1789–1866), *Trea-
tise of Versification*, XIII. 244, 512
Evans, Sebastian (1830–1909), I. 258, 260,
271; XIII. 194, 198, 502; *Brother Fabian's
Manuscripts*, XIII. 199; *High History of
the Holy Graal, The*, XIII. 199; *Shadows*,
XIII. 199
Evans, Thomas, VI. 276
Evans, Thomas (1742–1784), IX. 482;
XI. 327
Evans, Thomas Saunders (1816–1889),
XII. 483
Evans, William (d. 1718), X. 387
Evanthe, in *A Wife for a Month*, VI. 122,
132
Eve, I. 134; IV. 214; IX. 28, 60
Eve, in Dryden's *The State of Innocence*,
VIII. 28
Eve, in *Paradise Lost*, VII. 101; XII. 85
Eve, in the *Coventry play*, II. 425
Eve, in *The Cytezen and Uplondyshman*,
III. 63, 64
Eve, in *The Golden Legend*, II. 335
Eve, in the mystery plays, V. 56, 390, 391
Eveleigh, John (1748–1814), XII. 284
Eveleigh, William, XIV. Add. 7
Evelina, in Mason's *Caractacus*, XI. 273
Evelyn, George, brother of John, VIII. 244
Evelyn, John (1620–1706), IV. 426, 456;
VII. 54, 99, 234, 270, 394, 482, 486, 496,
518; VIII. 10, 163, 209, 241 ff. (main
entry), 258, 259, 264, 308, 354, 355, 359,
365, 369, 371, 378, 448 ff., 477; IX. 32,
276, 331, 387, 396; XIV. 281
Diary, VIII. 134, 265, 301; IX. 389, 574
*Fumifugium, or The inconvenience of
the Air and Smoke of London dissipated*,
VIII. 247
Gardening, VIII. 378
Golden Book of St John Chrysostom, The,
translation of, VIII. 247
Kalendarium Hortense, VIII. 378
Liberty and Servitude, translated from
an essay by François de la Mothe Le
Vayer, VIII. 246
Life of Margaret Godolphin, VIII. 250,
251
Sylva, VIII. 248, 355
Tyrannus, or the Mode, VIII. 248
Evelyn, lady, VIII. 242
Evelyn, Mrs John, born Browne, VIII. 245,
246
Evelyn, Richard, eldest child of John
Evelyn, VIII. 246

Evelyn, Richard, father of John, VIII. 244
Evelyns, the, IX. 243
Evening News, The, XIV. 195
Evening Standard, The, XIV. 188, 189
Evening Star, The, XIV. 190
Everard, John (1575?–1650?), VII. 488
Everett, George, IV. 456
Everett, James (1784–1872), XII. 420
Everie Woman in her Humor, VI. 27, 459
Eversfield, Sir Thomas, IV. 157
Eversfield, Tymothy, IV. 157
Eversley, Hampshire, XIII. 355, 365, 369
Every-man, II. 328; V. 17, 53, 54, 392
Evesham, II. 67; IV. 174, 190; IX. 535;
XIV. 185
Evesham, battle of, I. 336, 338
Evesham, monastery of, I. 89
Evesham, vale of, X. 111
Evesham, Vision of the Monk of, II. 318,
486, 503
Evesham or Worcester *Chronicle*, I. 109,
111
Evesham. *See* Walter of
'Ewaipanoma race,' the, IV. 78
Ewald, Georg Heinrich August von, XII.
321
Ewart, Nanty, in Scott's *Redgauntlet*, XII.
21
Ewen, John (1741–1821), *O weel may the
Boatie Row*, IX. 374
Ewing, Alexander (1814–1873), XII. 466
Ewing, Juliana Horatia (1841–1885), XI.
387, 478; XIV. 163
Examen Miscellaneum (1702), VIII. 444
Examen Poeticum Duplex, IX. 434
Examiner, The, IX. 95, 131, 151, 217, 218,
220, 440, 455, 446, 461, 465, 470, 491;
XI. 128; XII. 157, 171, 172, 193, 194,
432, 434, 436; XIII. 258, *also see* Add. 1;
XIV. 177, 197, 198, 324
Excalibur, XIV. 307
Excalibur, in *Morte Arthure*, II. 120
Excellencie of a Free State, The, VII. 359
Exceptiones ad Caesandum Brevia, VIII. 465
Exchange, The, VII. 449
Exchange Ware, VI. 481
Exchequer, Dialogue of the, IV. 511
Excise bill, IX. 224
Exclusion bill, the, VIII. 36, 90; IX. 225
Exempla, collections of, III. 92, 93, 489;
IV. 343
Exeter, IV. 235, 350, 408, 422; V. 55; VI.
241; VII. 245, 246, 309; VIII. 360; IX.
164, 538; X. 379, 380, 384; XIII. 276
Exeter, duke of. *See* Holland, John
Exeter, earl of, IX. 147
Exeter academy, X. 384
Exeter Book, The, I. 12, 34, 39, 48, 52, 53,
60 ff., 151, 374, 428
Exeter meetings, X. 373
'Exodus, Desert of the,' the, XII. 342
Exoniensis, Liber, IV. 422
Expedients for Publique Peace, VII. 386
'Extravagants,' the, II. 364
Eynsham, abbey of, I. 125, 127, 133
Eynsham, Aelfric's letters, I. 114, 125, 126

Eynsham, synod of, I. 129, 130
Eyrbiggia Saga, The, XII. 375
Eyre, Sir James, X. 406
Eyre, Jane, Charlotte Brontë's, XIII. 408
Eyre, Simon, in *The Shomakers Holiday*,
VI. 52, 172
Eyton, Robert William (1815–1881), XII.
509
Eyton, Shropshire, IV. 292
Eyzat, Edward, IX. 560
Ezechias, v. 104
Ezekiel, I. 92; IV. 238; v. 48; x. 130
Ezra, fourth book of, XII. 341

Fabell, Peter, in *The Merry Devill*, v. 252,
253
Faber, Frederick William (1814–1863),
XII. 259, 275, 456, 460; XIII. 167, 502;
Cherwell Water Lily, The, XIII. 171;
Pilgrims of the Night, The, XIII. 172;
Sorrowful World, The, XIII. 172
Fables, XI. 479
Fables bestiaires, VIII. 59
Fabliaux, I. 158, 365; II. 279, 280; III. 91,
93, 487, 489; VII. 380
Fabricius, II. 106
Fabula Atellana, Old Italian (Campanian),
v. 24
Fabyan, Robert (d. 1513), *Chronicles*, I.
477; II. 101, 302, 322, 485, 496; VII. 203
Fabyl, The Merry Pranks of, v. 253
Fabyl's Ghoste, v. 253
Face, in *The Alchemist*, VI. 22
Facetiae, III. 92, 93, 95, 489
*Facetie et motti arguti di alcuni eccellent-
issimi ingegni et nobilissimi signori*, III.
93
Faery, king of, in *Gyre Carling*, II. 275, 276
Fag, in Sheridan's *Rivals*, XI. 266, 267
Fagan, Louis Alexander, XIV. 540
Faggus, Tom, in *Lorna Doone*, XIII. 434
Fagin, in *Oliver Twist*, XIII. 316, 317, 319
Fagius, Paul (1504–1549), III. 34, 53
Faiel, Eudes de, XI. 274
Fainall, in Congreve's *Way of the World*,
VIII. 153, 154
Fainall, Mrs (Congreve's), VIII. 155
Fair Annie, II. 410
Fair Flower of Northumberland, The, II. 411
Fair Janet, II. 412
Fair Margaret and Sweet William, II. 412
Fair Quiet (Marvell's), VII. 181
Fairbairn, John, XIV. 378
Fairbridge, Charles Aiken, XIV. Add. 4
Fairbridge, Kingsley, XIV. Add. 4
Fairbrother, William Henry, XIV. 473
Faire Em, v. 136, 161, 237, 238, 251, 252,
419, 441, 443
Faire Maide of Bristow, The, VI. 96
Fairfax, Edward (d. 1635), IV. 23, 448;
VII. 83; VIII. 234
Discourse of Witch-craft, A, VII. 374, 506
Fairfax Correspondence, The, VII. 194
Godfrey of Bulloigne, VII. 57, 374; IX. 418
Memorials of the Civil War, VII. 194
Tasso, translation of, VII. 374; VIII. 227

Fairfax, Jane, in Jane Austen's *Emma*,
XII. 240
Fairfax, Mary (b. 1638), VII. 180
Fairfax, Thomas, lord (1612–1671), VII.
178, 190, 225, 449, 512, 513
Fairfax, William, VII. 83
Fairfax Correspondence, the, VII. 439
Fairhaven, IV. 93
Fairholt, Frederick William (1814–1866),
XII. 509
Fairless, Michael, *pseud. See* Barber,
Margaret Fairless
Fairy Queen, II. 182
Fairy Queen, in Spenser, II. 234
Fairy tales, XI. 479
Faith, in *Piers the Plowman*, II. 27
Faith, in *Portuus of Noblines*, etc., II.
284
Faith of one God Who is only the Father,
x. 378
Faithful Friends, The, VI. 132, 140
Faithorne, William (1616–1691), VII. 487
Falconbridge the bastard, in *Edward IV*.
VI. 90
Falconbridge, in *The Merchant of Venice*,
v. 359
Falconer, C. M., XIV. 522
Falconer, Edmund. *See* O'Rourke, Ed-
mund
Falconer, Lanoe, *pseud. See* Hawker,
Mary
Falconer, Thomas (1738–1792), *Strabo*,
XIV. 409
Falconer, William (1732–1769), x. 154
(main entry), 155, 398, 453, 454, 525;
The Shipwreck, x. 154
Falkiner, Caesar Litton (1863–1908), VII.
209, 436; XI. 410; XIV. 97, 487
Falkirk, battle of, II. 108
Falkland, in Godwin's *Caleb Williams*,
XI. 46, 293
Falkland, lady. *See* Cary, Lettice
Falkland, viscount. *See* Cary, Sir Henry;
Cary, Sir Lucius
Falkland islands, x. 404, 462, 474
Fall, The, v. 391
Fallaw, Lance, XIV. Add. 4
False, in *Piers the Plowman*, II. 7, 8, 32
False Bachelor, the tale of, in *Confessio
Amantis*, II. 148
False Semblant, in *Confessio Amantis*, II.
148
Falsehood of Man (Bi manne lease), I. 62
Falset, in *Ane Pleasant Satyre*, III. 124
Falstaff, Sir John (Shakespeare's), III. 371;
IV. 78; v. 187, 189, 194, 239, 269, 315,
316, 321, 358, 367; VI. 15, 23, 249;
VII. 204; XII. 196, 280, 349; XIII. 39,
64, 72
Falstaff, Sir John, Original Letters, etc., of,
XII. 438
Falstaff, The Bouncing Knight, VIII. 116
Fame, in Drayton's *Robert of Normandy*,
IV. 177
Fame, in *Hudibras*, VIII. 70
Fame, in *The Masque of Queens*, VI. 349

Fame, in *The Passetyme of Pleasure*, II. 225, 226

Family Library, The, XII. 318; XIV. 67

'Family of Love' books, IV. 402

Famous Battel of the Catts, The, VII. 409

Famous Flower of Serving Men, The, II. 411

Fancy, in *Magnyfycence*, III. 77

Fancy, in *The Floating Island*, VI. 325

Fancy, The, XIV. 231

Fane, Charles Fane, 2nd viscount, X. 249

Fane, Sir Francis (d. 1689?), VIII. 204, 422

Fane, Mildmay, 2nd earl of Westmorland (d. 1665), VII. 5, 407

Fane, Violet, *pseud. See* Currie, Mary Montgomerie, lady

'Fannikin' (Fanny Burney), X. 260

Fanny, in Fielding's *Joseph Andrews*, X. 26

Fanny, in Parnell's *Elegy*, IX. 167

Fanshawe, lady Anne (born Harrison), (1625–1680), VIII. 270, 359; *Memoirs*, VIII. 270, 452

Fanshawe, Catherine Maria (1765–1834), XII. 416

Fanshawe, Sir Henry (1569?–1616), IV. 265

Fanshawe, Sir Richard (1608–1666), VIII. 130, 452; *La Fida Pastora*, Latin translation of Fletcher's *Faithfull Shepheardesse*, VIII. 271; version of Luis de Camoëns' *Lusiads*, VIII. 271; translation of Guarini's *Pastor Fido*, VI. 490; VII. 61, 264; VIII. 271, 441

Fantosme, Jordan, *Chronicle of the Scottish Wars*, I. 446; II. 420, 508

Faques, Richard, ballads of Flodden printed by, II. 327; *The booke of the pylgrymage of man (Le Pelerinage de l'homme)*, II. 327

Faraday, Michael (1791–1867), XIV. 259 ff., 267 ff., 270, 280, 556, 557

Farces, V. 22, 91, 92, 97, 98, 115

Farces, A Collection of (1809), XI. 456

Fareham, XIII. 276

Farel, William, III. 411

Faret, N., *L'Art de plaire à la Cour*, IV. 345, 526

Fargus, Frederick John (*pseud.* Hugh Conway, 1847–1885), XIII. 562

Faria y Sousa, M. de, IX. 501; *The Portuguese Asia*, IX. 278

Faricius, I. 72

Farindon, Antony (1598–1658), VII. 152

Farish, William (1759–1837), XIV. 385

Farjeon, Benjamin Leopold (1838–1903), XIV. 370, 585

Farley, F. E., XII. Add. 1

Farley's *Bristol Journal*, XI. 133, 134

Farman, priest of Harewood, Leeds, I. 132

Farmer, John (*fl.* 1591–1601), IV. 113, 464

Farmer, Priscilla, XII. 436

Farmer, Richard (1735–1797), XII. 365, 493

Farnaby, Giles (*fl.* 1598), IV. 113, 464; VII. 2

Farnaby, Thomas (1575?–1647), VII. 307, 335, 486, 488

Farnham, IX. 91

Farnham castle, Surrey, IV. 156

Farnworth, Richard (d. 1666), VII. 507

Faro, Portugal, IV. 56

Faroe version of *The Maid Freed from the Gallows*, II. 405

Faron, Jean, II. 312

Farquhar, George (1678–1707), VIII. 146, 168 ff., 178, 423, 427, 429, 430; X. 67, 72, 202, 211, 216; XII. 443

Adventures of Covent Garden, The, VIII. 166, 170

Beaux' Stratagem, The, VIII. 171, 172, 173; XI. 322

Constant Couple, The, VIII. 169, 170, 175

Inconstant, The, VI. 135; VIII. 120

Love and a Bottle, VIII. 169, 170

Recruiting Officer, The, VIII. 171

Sir Harry Wildair, VIII. 169

Stage-Coach, The (with P. A. Motteux), VIII. 171

Twin Rivals, The, XI. 322

Farr, Dr Samuel (1741–1795), X. 209

Farra, Alessandro, VII. 264

Farrar, Frederic William (1831–1903), XII. 466; XIV. 425, 426, 606

Farrell, John (1851–1904), XIV. 369, 585

Farren, Robert, XII. 357

Farrer, John, *Virgo Triumphans* (1650), IV. 462

Fastidious, British bishop, I. 65

Fastidious Brisk, in Jonson's *Every Man Out of his Humour*, IV. 207; VI. 40, 44

Fastnachtsspiele, III. 58, 81

Fastolf, Sir John (1378?–1459), II. 68, 308, 309; V. 187

Fates of Men (Bi manna wyrdum), I. 61, 428

'Father of Candor, The,' X. 399

Father's Blessing Penn'd for the Instruction of his Children, XI. 370

Father's Instruction, A, I. 62, 219, 363, 428

Fathers, Lives of the, II. 127, 317, 323

Fathers, the, II. 129; III. 11, 92, 145, 212, 409, 410, 416; VII. 305, 312, 313, 316, 318, 321, 482, 483; VIII. 112, 294, 296, 302; IX. 211; XII. 269, 277, 298, 355, 454

Fathers of the Holy Catholic Church, XII. 259

Fathom, count, in Smollett's novel, X. 39

Fatum Vortigerni, VI. 483

Faucit, Helena, afterwards lady Martin (1817–1898), XIII. 59, 69, 261; XIV. 112

Fauconbridge, Sir Richard, in *Looke About You*, V. 321

Faulkland, in Sheridan's *Rivals*, XI. 267

Faulkner, George (1699?–1775), IX. 123; X. 257; XI. 342

Fauntelte (childishness), in *Piers the Plowman*, II. 25

Fauntleroy, Henry (1785–1824), XIII. 418

Faust, XIII. 153, 274

Faust, E. K. R., *Richard Brome*, VI, 225

Faust, in Goethe's drama, XII. 34, 47

Faust legend, the, VII. 369

Faustulus (Mantuan's), III. 224

132

Faustus, in (?) Ralegh's *Dialogue*, IV. 109
Faustus, in *The Cytezen and Uplondyshman*, III. 63
Fauvel, Henri, XIII. 465
Favel, in *Piers the Plowman*, II. 7, 8
Faversham, Kent, V. 240; IX. 536; XII. 347
Favine, André, IV. 543
'Favonius' (Richard West), X. 118, 121
Favour, in *The Bowge of Courte*, III. 73
Favourite, The, VI. 28
Fawcett, Henry (1833–1884), XIV. 472, 509, 513, 606
Fawcett, Millicent Garrett, XIV. 606
Fawconbridge, in *The Troublesome Raigne of King John*, V. 83
Fawkes, Francis (1720–1777), X. 183, 454, 469; XI. 172, 426, 431
Fawnia, in *Pandosto*, III. 356, 357
Fawsley, III. 380, 386
Fay, Eliza, XIV. 576; *Original Letters from Calcutta*, XIV. 335
Fear, in *Mirour de l'Omme*, II. 140
Featherston, of Ardagh, X. 197, 214
Featley, Daniel (1582–1645), IV. 382, 495; VII. 484, 502; *Britanicus Vapulans*, VII. 351; *Dipper Dipt, or the Anabaptist Duck't and Plung'd over Head and Ears in a Disputation, The*, VII. 145; *Mercurius Urbanus*, VII. 351
Featley, John (1605?–1666), VII. 308
Fécamp, monks of, I. 202
Fedalma, in George Eliot's *The Spanish Gypsy*, XIII. 398
Fedele, in *Fedele and Fortunio*, V. 315
Feenix, cousin, in *Dombey and Son*, XIII. 325
Fehr, Bernhard, XIII. 570
'Feilding, Beau,' in *The Tatler*, IX. 34
Feilding, Mary, IX. 243
Feilding, Susan, countess of Denbigh, VII. 35
Feilding, William, 3rd earl of Denbigh, IX. 243
Felice, in *Guy of Warwick*, I. 304 ff.
Felismena, in Montemayor's *Diana*, VIII. 126
Felix, anti-pope, IV. 322
Felix, Don, in Mrs Centlivre's *The Wonder*, X. 72
Felix, in Montemayor's *Diana*, VIII. 126
Felix, St (d. 647?), I. 74, 75
Felix and Philiomena, The History of, VIII. 126
Felix of Croyland, *Life of St Guthlac*, I. 58, 85, 131, 434
Felix of Urgel, I. 85
Fell, John (1625–1686?), VII. 457, 488; IX. 265, 329, 345, 348, 527; XI. 341
Fell Smith, Miss C., VIII. 270
Fellmar, lord, in Fielding's *Tom Jones*, X. 89
Fellowes, Robert (1771–1847), XI. 312; XII. 466
Fellows, Sir Charles (1799–1860), XII. 339, 496
Fellowship, in *Every-man*, V. 53

Felltham, Owen (1602–1668), *Resolves*, IV. 248, 348, 524, 525
Felpham, Sussex, XI. 195, 197
Felsted, VII. 454; VIII. 269, 359
'Female dream,' the, in Blake's poems, XI. 194
Fencer, the, in *Pan's Anniversarie*, VI. 355, 361
Fénelon, François de Salignac de la Mothe, IV. 260; VII. 176; VIII. 303; IX. 307, 520, 521; X. 114, 134, 420, 424, 491; *Aventures de Télémaque*, XII. 190
Fenian Sagas, XIV. 304
Fenians, XIV. 313, 318, 321, 322
Fenn, Eleanor, lady (1743–1813), XI. 479, 480; *Cobwebs to Catch Flies*, XI. 379
Fennell, Charles Augustus Maude, XIII. 537
Fennor, William, IV. 518; *The Compter's Commonwealth*, IV. 350, 530
Fens, the, IV. 190, 308, 509; XII. 417
Fenton, Elijah (1683–1730), VII. 410, 414; VIII. 446; IX. 76, 181, 183, 184, 484, 485; XI. 246; *Mariamne*, X. 83, 430
Fenton, Sir Geoffrey (1539?–1608), IV. 441, 445; VI. 390, 492; *Forme of Christian pollicie gathered out of French*, VI. 377, 386; *Tragicall Discourses*, III. 343, 536; IV. 2, 6, 7; VI. 377
Fenton, Mr, in Brooke's *Fool of Quality*, IX. 327
Fenton, Richard (1746–1821), XII. 509
Fenton, Roger (1565–1615), IV. 313, 510; VII. 316
Fenwick, John, XII. 188
Fenwick, Mrs, XI. 486
Ferars, in *A Challenge for Beauty*, VI. 103
Ferdia, XIII. 188
Ferdinand, in *The Doubtfull Heir*, VI. 205
Ferdinand, in *The Dutchesse of Malfy*, VI. 182
Ferdinand, in *The Tempest*, V. 201, 206 VIII. 9; XII. 54
Ferdinand, Don, in *Don Quixote*, IX. 269
Ferdinand I, grand duke of Tuscany, IV. 163; VI. 175
Ferdinand II, emperor, IV. 259; VII. 453
Ferentes, in *Loves Sacrifice*, VI. 192
Fergus, in *Gorboduc*, V. 67
Fergus's Gaist, Laying of Lord, II. 277
Ferguson, Adam (1723–1816), IX. 561; X. 285, 501, 512; XI. 450; *Essay on the History of Civil Society*, X. 296, 319; *History of the Roman Republic*, X. 296, 319, 320
Ferguson, John, *Bibliotheca Chemica*, XII. 371, 519; *Some Aspects of Bibliography*, XII. 371, 519; *Witchcraft Literature of Scotland*, XII. 371, 519
Ferguson, J. W., XIV. 238
Ferguson, Mary Catherine, lady, born Guinness (1823–1905), XII. 360; *Sir Samuel Ferguson*, XIV. 319; *Story of Ireland*, XIV. 319
Ferguson, Robert, 'the Plotter' (d. 1714), VIII. 41

Ferguson, Sir Samuel (1810–1886), XII.
516; XIV. 305, 319 ff., 568
At the Polo Ground, XIV. 320
Conary, XIV. 320
Congal, XIV. 320
Curse of the Joyces, The, XIV. 320
Deirdre, XIV. 320
Forging of the Anchor, The, XIV. 319
In Carey's Footsteps, XIV. 320
Lays of the Western Gael, XIV. 320
Ogham Inscriptions, XII. 360
Return of Claneboy, The, XIV. 319
Tain Quest, The, XIV. 320
Thomas Davis, XIV. 319
Welshmen of Tirawley, The, XIV. 320
Fergusson, James (1621–1667), IX. 543
Fergusson, James (1808–1886), XII. 510
Cave Temples of India, XII. 353
Illustrated Hand-book of Architecture,
XII. 353
Rock-cut Temples of India, XII. 353
Tree and Serpent Worship, XII. 353
Fergusson, Robert (1750–1774), I. 290;
II. 267; IX. 378 ff., 562, 566; X. 226;
XI. 204 ff., 209, 211, 217, 221, 228
Auld Reekie, IX. 380
Bill of Fare, IX. 380
Death of Scots Music, IX. 378
Elegy on John Hogg, IX. 378
Farmer's Ingle, The, IX. 379, 380; XI.
206
Gowdspink, The, IX. 379
Hallow Fair, IX. 379; XI. 215
Leith Races, IX. 379; XI. 215, 216
Planestanes and Causeway, IX. 380
To the Bee, IX. 379
Ferishta, Mohamed Kasim, *Muhammedan
Power in India*, XIV. 337
Ferishtah, Browning's, XIII. 84
Fermor, Arabella, IX. 70
Fermor, Henrietta Louisa, countess of
Pomfret (d. 1761), IX. 248; X. 274, 496
Fernandez, Jerónimo, IV. 444
Fernando, in *Loves Sacrifice*, VI. 192, 194
Ferndean, Charlotte Brontë's, XIII. 408
Ferne, Sir John (d. 1610), IV. 376, 543
Ferrabosco, Alphonso (*fl.* 1544–1587), IV.
113, 464; V. 125; VI. 348
Ferrar, Nicholas (1592–1637), IV. 406;
VII. 27 ff., 32, 46, 153 ff., 162, 402, 424,
427, 482; XII. 488
Ferrara, III. 5, 7, 167; V. 62, 69, 114; VI.
365; VII. 100; XII. 50
Ferrara, duke of, in *The Imposture*, VI. 205
Ferrarius. *See under* Montanus
Ferrars, Edward, in Jane Austen's *Sense
and Sensibility*, XII. 237, 239, 241
Ferrers, George (1500?–1579), III. 193,
195, 494
Ferret, in Smollett's *Sir Launcelot Greaves*,
X. 41
Ferrex, in *Gorboduc*, V. 66, 67
Ferrex and Porrex, V. 396
Ferriar, John (1761–1815), IV. 252; VIII.
442; X. 422; *Bibliomania*, XII. 366; *Il-
lustrations of Sterne*, XII. 366

Ferrier, James Frederick (1808–1864),
XII. 160, 425, 487; XIV. 40 ff., 472
Institutes of Metaphysic, The, XIV. 40, 41
Lectures on Greek Philosophy, XIV. 41
'Philosophy of Consciousness, The,'
XIV. 40
Scottish Philosophy, XIV. 7
Ferrier, James Walter, XIV. 210
Ferrier, Susan Edmonstone (1782–1854),
XII. 246, 449; XIII. 431, 432
Destiny, XII. 245
Inheritance, The, XII. 245
Marriage, XII. 245
Ferris, Richard (*fl.* 1600), *The Most dan-
gerous and memorable Adventure*, IV. 361
Ferumbras, Sir, I. 288, 291, 293, 302, 303,
465, 471
Feste, in *Twelfth Night*, V. 190, 193; VII. 3
Festing, Gabrielle, XIII. 503
Festiniog, vale of, X. 115
Festive songs of the 16th and 17th cen-
turies, V. 477
Festus, Bailey's, XIII. 153
Festus, in Browning's *Paracelsus*, XIII. 57
Fet Asaver, VIII. 465
Fethe, Fethy or Futhy, Sir John, Scots
poet, II. 282; III. 131
Fetherstone, Henry, IV. 398, 403
Feuerbach, Ludwig, *Essence of Chris-
tianity*, XIII. 385, 553
Feuillerat, Albert, V. 341, 478, *and see*
Add. 2; VI. 270; VII. 454
Fever, in *Piers the Plowman*, II. 22
Feverel, Sir Austin, Meredith's, XIII. 445
Feverel, Richard, Meredith's, XIII. 443,
444
Few may fend for falsett, II. 280
Feylde, Thomas, *The Controversy between
a Lover and a Jay*, II. 224, 326
'Fiall,' in *The Fair Maid Of the West*, VI.
101
Fichte, Johann Gottlieb, XI. 136; XIII. 7,
13; XIV. 9, 41, 467, 478
Ficino, Marsilio, III. 8, 214 ff., 221
Fickle, madame (D'Urfey's), VIII. 175
Fiddes, Richard (1671–1725), *Body of
Divinity*, XI. 322
Fidelia, in *The Faerie Queene*, VI. 335
Fidelia, in Wycherley's *Country Wife*, VIII.
145
Fidelity, in *The Passetyme of Pleasure*,
II. 229
Fidge, George, *The English Gusman* (1652),
VII. 516
'Fidget' (Elizabeth Montagu), X. 262
Fidus, in *Euphues and his England*, III. 345
Field, Barron (1786–1846), VI. 104; XII.
182, 199; XIV. 586; *First Fruits of
Australian Poetry*, XII. 194; XIV. 362;
Kangaroo, The, XII. 195
Field, Elizabeth. *See* Lamb, Mrs Elizabeth
Field, Frederick (1801–1885), XII. 341, 501
Field or Feilde, John (d. 1588), III. 377,
378, 385, 390, 403, 548; VI. 220, 224;
Admonition to Parliament, VI. 393
Godly Exhortation, VI. 393, 493

Field, Kate, XII. 441; XIII. 514, 543
Field, Michael, *pseud.* (Katharine Harris Bradley and Edith Emma Cooper), XIII. 502; *Callirrhoe*, XIII. 181
Field, Mrs, Charles Lamb's grandmother, XII. 182
Field, Nathaniel (1587–1633), IV. 360; V. 370; VI. 28, 33, 116, 128, 137, 138, 140, 145, 146, 165, 211, 212, 220–225 (main entry), 232, 274, 402, 403, 443, 455, 491; VIII. 195; *Amends for Ladies*, VI. 223; *Woman is a Weathercocke, A*, VI. 221
Field, Richard (1561–1616), *Of the Church*, VII. 323, 484; VIII. 276, 277
Field, Richard (*fl.* 1579–1624), IV. 394, 400, 401
Field, The, XIV. 201
Field, Theophilus (1574–1636), bishop of Hereford, VI. 220, 402
Field, William (1768–1851), XII. 490
Field of the Cloth of Gold, II. 228, 338; III. 57, 175, 317; VI. 284, 334
Fielde, J., IV. 447
Fielding, Charlotte (d. 1744), X. 22, 23, 27, 28
Fielding, Edmund, X. 20
Fielding, Henry (1707–1754), IV. 246, 255; VI. 24, 28; VIII. 162, 168; IX. 243, 248, 254, 471; X. 16, 20 ff. (main entry), 36, 37, 39, 41 ff., 50, 56, 71, 77, 78, 88, 211, 216, 317, 413 ff., 438, 440, *also see* Add.; XI. 264, 288, 296, 331; XII. 2, 168, 177, 231, 242, 251; XIII. 285, 305, 307, 310, 352, 386, 388, 398; XIV. 223, 552
Amelia, X. 21, 23, 33, 34; XI. 262, 265, 279, 324
'Apology for the Clergy,' X. 24
Author's Farce, The, X. 21, 22; XI. 329
Charity, essay on, X. 24
Coffee-House Politician, The, X. 21
Covent Garden Tragedy, X. 22, 83
Don Quixote in England, X. 22
Enquiry into the causes of the late Increase of Robbers, X. 33
'Essay on Conversation,' X. 23
Examples of the Interposition of Providence, in the Detection . . . of Murder, X. 34
Good-Natured Man, The, X. 23
Historical Register, The, X. 23, 84
Intriguing Chambermaid, The, X. 22
Jonathan Wild, X. 27, 30, 39; XIII. 279, 280
Joseph Andrews, IX. 405, 407; X. 6, 20, 24 ff., 30, 44; XII. 235; XIII. 295; XIV. 213
Journey from this World to the Next, X. 27
Love in Several Masques, X. 21
Miscellanies, X. 21, 23, 26 ff.
Miser, The, X. 22
Mock Doctor, The, X. 22
Pasquin, X. 23, 24, 84
Pleasures of the Town, X. 21
Proposals for erecting a country workhouse, X. 29, 34

Fielding, Henry
  Proposals for making an effectual provision for the poor, X. 34
  Provoked Husband, The, X. 92
  Temple Beau, The, X. 21
  Tom Jones, IX. 405; X. 9, 15, 20, 22, 26, 28 ff., 39, 48, 89, 92, 272, 508; XI. 260, 448; XIII. 295; XIV. 255
  Tom Thumb, X. 22, 26, 73, 83
  Tragedy of Tragedies, X. 22, 83
  Voyage to Lisbon, X. 35, 252
  Wedding Day, The, X. 23
Fielding, Sarah (1710–1768), XI. 479, *also see* Add.; *David Simple*, X. 20, 28, 415; *Governess or Little Female Academy, The*, XI. 376, 380; XIV. 600
Fielding, William, X. 28
Fields, James T., XIII. 543, 565
Fiennes, Madame de, VIII. 248
Fiennes, Nathaniel (1608–1669), VII. 450
Fient a crum of thee she faws, IX. 360
Fierabras, I. 284
Fiesole, XIII. 73
Fife, II. 89, 131, 371; IX. 364, 367, 552; XI. 242, 243; XII. 513
Fifeshire, XIII. 3
Fifteen Tokens, The (*L'Art de bien mourir*), II. 329
Figaro, XIV. 235
Figaro in London, XIV. 235, 236
Figg, James (d. 1734), IX. 191; XIV. 229, 231
Figgis, John Neville, XIV. 484
Figures, in Cowley's *The Muse*, VII. 65
Fikenhild, in *Horn*, I. 304
Filidh (Filé), XIV. 302
Fillingham, T., X. 492
Filmer, Edward (*fl.* 1707), VIII. 433
Filmer, Sir Robert (d. 1653), VII. 301, 420, 471, 507; VIII. 341; *An Advertisement to the Jury-men of England*, VII. 395; *Originall of Government*, VII. 300; *Patriarcha*, VII. 300
Filon, Augustin, XIII. 514
Finch, Anne, countess of Winchester (d. 1720), IX. 483, 484; X. 145; XII. 124
  Fanscombe Barn, IX. 169
  Lines to Prior, IX. 169
  Nocturnal Reverie, IX. 168
  Sigh, The, IX. 169
  Spleen, The, IX. 169
  To Mr F now Earl of W, IX. 169
  To Mr Jervas, IX. 169
  To Mr Pope, IX. 169
  To the Nightingale, IX. 169
Finch, Daniel, 2nd earl of Nottingham (1647–1730), IX. 9, 95, 135
Finch, Heneage, 1st earl of Aylesford (1647?–1719), VIII. 410
Finch, Heneage, 4th earl of Winchilsea, IX. 168
Finch, Sir Henry (1558–1625), VIII. 468
Finch, Sir John (1584–1660), VIII. 110
Finch-Hatton Correspondence, VII. 196
Finchley, XIII. 52
Findern, Derbyshire, X. 386

Findlay, John Ritchie (1824–1898), XII.
445
Findlay, Joseph John, XIV. 601
Fine Arts Quarterly, XIV. 539
Fingal, X. 227, 229, 231, 232, 487
Finglass, IX. 166
Finical, Father, in Crowne's *English Frier*,
VIII. 189
Finland, II. 405
Finlason, Thomas, IV. 547
Finlay, George (1799–1875), XII. 475
  Greece under the Romans, XII. 314
  History of Greece, XII. 314, 315
  *History of the Byzantine and Greek Em-
  pires*, XII. 314
  History of the Greek Revolution, XII. 314
Finlayson, James (1840–1906), XII. 521
Finn, in *Beowulf, Finnsburh* and *Widsith*,
  I. 23, 31, 34
Finn, Irish tales of, X. 231
Finn, Phineas, Trollope's, XIII. 423
Finnsburh, I. 30, 47, 423, *also see* Add.;
  X. 223, 224
Fiordespina, in *Orlando Furioso*, III. 231
Fiorinda of Urbino, in *The Great Duke of
Florence*, VI. 156
Fiormonda, in *Loves Sacrifice*, VI. 192
Firdusi, I. 293
Fire of London, the great, VII. 289
Firebrace, lady, X. 464
Firenzuola, Agnolo, III. 252
Firmin, Giles (1614–1697), VII. 424; X.
  359; *A Brief Vindication of Mr Stephen
  Marshal*, VII. 145
Firmin, Philip, in Thackeray's *Adventures
  of Philip*, XIII. 299, 300
Firmin, Thomas (1632–1697), X. 377
Firouzkah, princess, in Beckford's *Epi-
  sodes*, XI. 291
Firth, Charles Harding, VII. 214, 218, 219,
  432, 451; VIII. 352; IX. 202, 204, 208;
  XIV. 88, 493, 594
Fischer, Lisbeth, Balzac's, XIII. 287
Fischer, Thomas A., XIII. 465, 466, 471
Fish, Simon (d. 1531), III. 473; *Sum of
  Scripture, The*, III. 39; *Supplication for
  the beggars*, III. 26, 101, 105; IV. 314,
  510; VII. 432
Fisher, George William, *Annals of Shrews-
  bury School*, XIV. 413, 598
Fisher, Herbert Albert Laurens, XIV. 494
Fisher, Jasper (*fl.* 1639), VI. 472
Fisher, John (1459–1535), bishop of
  Rochester, III. 7, 12 ff., 19, 27, 36, 53,
  332, 468, 473; IV. 224 ff., 231, 232, 492,
  495, *also see* Add.; IX. 197, 531; XII. 488
  Assertio septem Sacramentorum, a de-
  fence of Henry VIII's, III. 15
  Confutatio Assertionis Lutheranae, III.
  15
  *De Eucharistia contra Johannem Oeco-
  lampadium libri quinque*, III. 15
  Funeral sermon on Henry VII, II. 325
  Mourning Remembrance, II. 325
  Penitential Psalms, Sermons on the, II.
  325; IV. 226

Fisher, John
  *Sacri Sacerdotii Defensio contra Lu-
  therum*, III. 15
Fisher, John (1569–1641), VIII. 300
Fisher, John, of Warwick (*fl.* 1500), IV.
  309, 510
Fisher, Joseph Robert, XIV. 536
Fisher, Payne (1616–1693), VII. Add.;
  XI. 317
Fisher, Robert, III. 3, 7
Fisher, Samuel (1605–1665), VIII. 111, 416
Fishing with an angle, II. 323
Fishwick, Henry (1835–1914), XII. 519
Fitch, Sir Joshua Girling (1824–1903),
  XIII. 48; XIV. 601, 606
Fitch, Ralph (*fl.* 1583–1606), XIV. 332, 576
Fitch, Walter Hood, XIV. 561
Fitela, in *Beowulf*, I. 23, 26
Fitton, Anne, VII. 196
Fitton, Mary (*fl.* 1600), V. 229, 231; VII.
  196
Fitz-Alan, house of, II. 103
Fitzball, Edward (1792–1873), XIII. 257,
  264, 518
Fitz-Boodle, George Savage, *pseud.* of
  W. M. Thackeray, XIII. 281
Fitzdottrel, 'duke of Brownlands' and
  Mrs Fitzdottrel, in *The Divell is an
  Asse*, VI. 24
Fitzgeffry, Charles (1575?–1637), IV. 168,
  360, 475; VII. 406
Fitzgerald, Edward (1809–1883), XI. 147,
  418, 439; XII. 135, 199, 305, 413, 438;
  XIII. 31, 35, 47, 142 ff. (main entry),
  172, 253, 277, 497 (main entry), 530;
  XIV. 146, 519
  Agamemnon, XIII. 145
  *Bird's-eye View of Farid-Uddin Attar's
  Bird-Parliament*, XIII. 145
  Euphranor, XIII. 143, 146
  Meadows in Spring, The, XIII. 143
  Mighty Magician, The, XIII. 144
  Oedipus at Athens, XIII. 144
  Oedipus at Thebes, XIII. 144
  Painter of his own Dishonour, The, XIII.
  144
  Polonius, XIII. 143
  Readings in Crabbe, XIII. 143
  Rubáiyát of Omar Khayyám, XIII. 145,
  146, 174
  Salámán and Absál of Jámí, XIII. 145
  Six Dramas of Calderon, XIII. 143
  Such Stuff as Dreams are Made of, XIII.
  144
Fitzgerald, lord Edward (1763–1798), XII.
  412
Fitz-Gerald, lady Elizabeth (1528?–1589)
  III. 176
Fitzgerald, George Francis (1851–1901),
  XIV. 269, 556
Fitzgerald, Gerald, 9th earl of Kildare
  (1487–1534), III. 176
Fitzgerald, Percy H., XIII. 514, 519, 532,
  543
FitzGerald, Shafto Justin Adair, XIII. 543
Fitz-hamon, Robert (d. 1107), I. 256

Fitzherbert, Sir Anthony (1470–1538), IV. 309, 369, 510; VIII. 466; *Abridgment of the Year Books*, VIII. 315

Fitzherbert, John of Norbury, IV. 307, 364, 371, 510, 541; *Book of Husbandry*, IV. 300, 369, 370, 510; *Book of Surveying* IV. 369, 370

Fitz-James, Richard (d. 1522), bishop of London, III. 9

Fitzmaurice, Edmund George Petty, 1st lord, XIV. 510

Fitzmaurice Kelly, James, VIII. 126, 129

Fitz-Neale or -Nigel, Richard, bishop of London (d. 1198), I. 173, 449; IV. 510; *Dialogus de Scaccario*, I. 174

Fitzpatrick, Sir Percy, XIV. Add. 7

Fitzpatrick, Richard (1747–1813), XI. 35; *Lyars*, XI. 36

Fitzpatrick, T., XI. 450

Fitz-Patrick, William John (1830–1895), XII. 379, 451; XIV. 568, 569

FitzRalph, Richard (d. 1360), archbishop of Armagh, II. 42, 44, 52, 53, 74, 308, 355; *Defensio Curatorum, De Pauperie Salvatoris*, II. 53

Fitzroy, Augustus Henry, 3rd duke of Grafton (1735–1811), X. 133, 402, 404 ff., 523, 526, 527

Fitzsimons, Frederick William, XIV. Add. 7

Fitz-Stephen, William (d. 1190?), I. 449; II. 505; V. 7, 38

Fitzthomas, Maurice, 1st earl of Desmond (d. 1356), X. 20

Fitztraver, in Scott's *Lay of the Last Minstrel*, XII. 9

Fitzwarine, Fulk, II. 399, 428, 503, 507

Fitzwater, in *Robert, Earle of Huntington*, V. 318, 324

Fitzwater, lady, III. 357

Fitzwater, Matilda, IV. 182, 183

Fitzwilliam, John (d. 1699), VIII. 272

Fitzwilliam, William, viscount Milton (1839–1877), XIV. 553

Fitzwilliam, William Wentworth, 2nd earl Fitzwilliam (1748–1833), XI. 4, 388

Five Joys of the Virgin, I. 231, 458

Five Plays in One, VI. 87, 128

Five Starches, the, in *The World tost at Tennis*, VI. 75

Flacius Illyricus, XIII. 172

Flagellant, The, XI. 155; XIV. 387

Flamboroughs, the Miss, in *The Vicar of Wakefield*, X. 210

Flamineo, in *The White Divel*, VI. 175

Flaminius, in *Believe as you List*, VI. 148

Flaminius, in *Laelia*, VI. 305

Flamsteed, John (1646–1719), VIII. 477; IX. 470

Flanders, II. 56; VI. 3; X. 51, 200; XII. 43

Flandria (Flanders), in *Colkelbie's sow*, II. 127

Flannislie, in *Colkelbie's sow*, II. 126

Flapsy, in Mrs Trimmer's *Robins*, XI. 379

Flatman, Thomas (1637–1688), VII. 88, 241, 251, 412; VIII. 412, 444

Flatterie, in *Ane Pleasant Satyre*, III. 124, 125, 126, 128, 129

Flattery, A Discourse against, IX. 524

Flattery, in *Piers the Plowman*, II. 28

Flaubert, Gustave, XI. 293; XIII. 456; *Salammbô*, XIII. 461; *Trois contes*, IX. 39

Flavel, John (1630?–1691), X. 387

Flavia, in Law's *Serious Call*, IX. 323

Flavia, in *The Fancies*, VI. 194

Flavia, in *The Spectator*, IX. 57

Flavia (Waller's), VII. 55

Flaxman, John (1755–1826), XI. 181; XII. 172

Fleance, son of Banquo, II. 104

Fleay, Frederick Gard (1831–1909), III. 206; V. 146, 316, 318, 332; VI. 4, 5, 9, 17, 23, 83 ff., 89, 90, 92, 93, 98, 100, 102, 103, 204, 216, 224, 228, 232, 233, 235, 240, 274, 287, 288, 345, 348, 358, 459

Flecker, James Elroy (d. 1915), XIII. 502

Flecknoe, Richard (d. 1678?), VII. 183, 412; VIII. 40, 422; *Short Discourse of the English Stage*, VII. 238, 251, 272, 441

Fled Bricrend (the feast of Bricriu), I. 327

Fleet, publisher, XI. 375

Fleet prison, the, IV. 78

Fleetwood, in Meredith's *The Amazing Marriage*, XIII. 445

Fleetwood, Charles (d. 1692), VIII. 121; XI. 449

Fleetwood, E., VII. 514

Fleetwood, George (1605–1667), VII. 450

Fleetwood, William (1535?–1594), VI. 382, 393

Fleming or Flemming, Abraham (1552?–1607), IV. 435, 437, 439, 442

Fleming, Caleb (1698–1779), X. 521

Fleming, Contarini, Disraeli's, XIII. 346, 348, 361

Fleming, Francis, XIV. Add. 7

Fleming, John (*fl.* 1726), X. 385

Fleming, Marjorie (1803–1811), XI. 476 XIV. 228, 229, 543

Fleming, Mary, Scott's, XII. 27

Fleming, Rhoda, George Meredith's, XIII. 447

Fleming, Richard (d. 1431), II. 358

'Fleming,' *Be Merry Brethren*, III. 131

Fleming, the, in *The Fyrste Boke of the Introduction of Knowledge*, III. 105

Flemings, VII. 306

Flemish clothmakers, II. 311

Flemish towns, trade in, V. 355

Flemming or Fleming, Robert (d. 1483), dean of Lincoln, III. 5; IV. 428

Flesh of Man, in *Mirour de l'Omme*, II. 140

Fleta (c. 1290), VIII. 313, 465

Fletcher, Andrew, of Saltoun (1655–1716), IX. 492; X. 449

  Account of a Conversation, IX. 215

  Discorso delle cose di Spagna, IX. 215

  Discourse of…Militias, IX. 214

  Political Works, IX. 214

  Speech upon the State of the Nation, IX. 215

  Two Discourses, IX. 215

Fletcher, Charles Robert Leslie, XIII. 465
Fletcher, Francis, IV. 87, 456
Fletcher, Giles, the elder (1549?–1611),
  III. 198, 256, 264, 265; *Licia*, III. 265,
  523; *Richard III*, III. 198
Fletcher, Giles, the younger (1588?–1623),
  IV. 150, 164 ff. (main entry), 456, 481;
  VI. 111
  Christs Victorie, IV. 164
  Death of Eliza, Canto upon the, IV. 164,
  165
  Description of Encolpius, A, IV. 164
  Prince Henry's Death, IV. 164
Fletcher, John (1579–1625), IV. 115; V.
  148, 181, 195, 217, 218, 256 ff.; 347, 356,
  362, 364, 371; VI. 2, 26, 27, 36, 65, 69,
  89, 107–136 (main entry), 142, 144,
  145, 151, 152, 157, 177, 182, 184, 185,
  195, 199, 205, 206, 208, 211, 223, 231,
  234, 235, 239, 240, 248, 272, 340, 353,
  363, 366 ff., 371, 372, 427, 435 ff., 490;
  VII. 3, 39, 272, 275; VIII. 12, 13, 29,
  31, 116, 119, 127, 128, 132, 133, 141,
  150, 162, 184, 192, 202, 219, 226, 425;
  IX. 140, 145; X. 91, 145; XII. 89, 186,
  444; XIII. 144, 218, 260, 289; *Thierry
  and Theodoret*, XII. 190. *See, also*, Beau-
  mont and Fletcher
Fletcher, John William (1729–1785), X.
  365 ff., 516; *Scriptures Scales*, X. 367;
  Zelotus and Honestus, X. 367
Fletcher, Phineas (1582–1650), IV. 150,
  164 ff. (main entry), 481; VI. 111, 321;
  VII. 46; XII. 79; XIII. 218
  Brittain's Ida, IV. 165
  Elisa, IV. 166
  Locusts or Apollyonists, The, IV. 166, 167
  Piscatorie Eclogues, IV. 165
  Purple Island, The, IV. 164, 166
  Sicelides, IV. 165
Fletcher, Richard (father of John), VI.
  110
Fletcher, Sir Robert, IX. 192, 488
Fletcher, R. H., *The Arthurian Material
  in the Chronicles*, I. 257
Fletcher, William Younger, XII. 519
Fletching church, X. 312
Fleury, religious revival of, I. 113. *See,
  also*, Abbo of
Fleury's Ecclesiastical history, XII. 460
Fleury-sur-Loire, V. 37
Flexney, bookseller, X. 191
Flinders, Matthew (1774–1814), XIV. 289
Flint, Robert (1838–1910), XIV. 472
Flint cottage, Box hill, XIII. 440
Flintwinch, in *Little Dorrit*, XIII. 331
Flodden, battle of, II. 40, 41, 109, 251,
  327, 369; III. 70, 197; XII. 10, 11; XIV.
  185
Flodden Field, II. 415
Flood, Henry (1732–1791), XIV. 311
Flood, the, III. 130, 318
Flora, in Beaumont's masque, VI. 356
Flora, in Owen's *Epigrammata*, IV. 265
Flora, in *The Flower and the Leaf*, II. 219
Flora, in *The Penates*, VI. 341

Flora, in *The Vision of the Twelve God-
  desses*, VI. 338
Florabell (Herrick's), VII. 12
Florac, in *The Newcomes*, XIII. 295, 297
Floras dames, The glyttering showes of, III.
  190
Florence, II. 350; III. 5, 6, 8, 167; IV. 69,
  163; V. 61, 69, 115, 247, 350; VI. 144;
  VII. 99, 100, 284; X. 41, 119, 122, 249,
  303; XII. 204, 324, 327, 401; XIII. 46,
  54, 70, 72, 73, 77, 79, 103, 393 ff.
  Laurentian library, IV. 429
  San Marco, XIII. 394
Florence of Rome, I. 467
Florence of Worcester (d. 1118), I. 90, 91,
  160 ff., 451; IV. 68
Florence wine, IX. 412
Florent, tale of, in Gower, II. 183
Florentine, in *The Seven Sages*, I. 309
Florentine academy, XI. 176
Florentine nobleman, in Congreve's *In-
  cognita*, VIII. 146
Florentine renascence, IX. 306
Flores, Juan de, *Historia de Aurelio y de
  Ysabela*, VI. 123, 138; VIII. 128
Flores and Blancheflour, I. 286, 303, 308,
  309, 465, 468
Flores Historiarum, I. 449
Florestan, king, in Disraeli's *Endymion*,
  XIII. 350
Florida, IV. 70, 81
Floridan peat, X. 392
Florimel, in Dryden's *Secret Love*, VIII. 20
'Florimel,' in *The Tatler*, IX. 34
Florinda, in *Count Julian*, XII. 211
Florio, John (1553?–1625), IV. 442; VI.
  221; VIII. 387; *A Worlde of Wordes*,
  IV. 15, 395; XIV. 448; *Montaigne*, IV. 8,
  15, 248, 395, 447, 523; IX. 265, 276, 277
Floripas, in *Sir Ferumbras*, I. 302, 303
Florizel, in *The Winter's Tale*, V. 217
Florus, Lucius Annaeus, IV. 436
Florus of Lyons, I. 81
Floud, Rachel (d. 1640), VII. 250
Flower, Benjamin (1755–1829), XIV. 533
Flower, Eliza (1803–1846), XIII. 53
Flower, 'Maister,' V. 77
Flower, Sir William Henry (1831–1899),
  XIV. 295, 560
Flower and the Leaf, The, II. 162, 164, 166,
  167, 215, 217 ff., 221, 223, 429
Flowerdales, the, in *The London Prodigall*,
  V. 254
Flowerdew, mistress, in *The Muses Look-
  ing-Glasse*, VI. 234
Flowers of the Forest, The, IX. 373; XI. 232
Fludd, Robert (1574–1637), IV. 278, 508;
  VII. 378; IX. 386
Fluellen, in *Henry V*, V. 189, 195; XIV.
  307
Flügel, Ewald, XIII. 470, 471
Flute, in *A Midsummer-Night's Dream*,
  VI. 285
Flutter, Sir Fopling, in Etherege's *Man
  of Mode*, VIII. 138
Fly, in *The New Inne*, VI. 25

Flying Island, in *Gulliver's Travels*, IX. 104

Flying Post, IX. 5, 15, 432; XI. 333; XIV. 230

Flyting between Thomas Smith and William Gray, the, III. 490

Flytings, IV. 517

Foe, James, father of Defoe, Daniel, IX. 6

Foersom, P., V. 307

Fogg, Peter Walkden, XI. 250; XIII. 240

Foggo, A., XIII. 546

Fog's Weekly Journal, IX. 433

Foigny, Gabriel de, *Journey of Jacques Sadeur*, IX. 106

Foix, count of, in Froissart, II. 338

Foker, Henry, in *Pendennis*, XIII. 291, 292

Folio, Tom, in *The Tatler*, IX. 46

Foliot, Gilbert (d. 1187), I. 173, 449

Folk-drama and early pageantry, V. 24, 385

Folk-Lore Journal, The, XII. 518

Folk-lore Society, XII. 506

Follett, Sir William Webb (1798–1845), XIV. 509

Folly, in *Ane Pleasant Satyre*, III. 124, 129

Folly, in *Magnyfycence*, III. 77

Folly, in *The World and the Child*, II. 233; V. 54

Fonblanque, Albany, XIII. 558; XIV. 186, 198, 533

Fonblanque, E. B. de, XIV. 533

Fondlewife, in Congreve's *Old Bachelor*, VIII. 147, 149

Fonseca, Jeronymo Osorio da, IV. 444

Fontainebleau, V. 284

Fontainebleau, library at, IV. 429

Fontenelle, Bernard le Bovyer de, VIII. 261; IX. 477, 572; X. 464; *Dialogues of the Dead*, IX. 143; *Les Anciens et les Modernes*, IX. 390

Fonthill abbey, XI. 289; XII. 345, 508

Foolish Virgins, The, V. 11

Fools, feast of, V. 8

Foot, Jessé (1744–1826), X. 438

Foote, G. W., XIII. 489

Foote, Samuel (1720–1777), X. 82, 83, 87, 317, 430, 441; XI. 257, 260, 262, 448, 451, 453, 454; XIII. 514
  The Cozeners, XI. 278
  Maid of Bath, X. 88
  Minor, The, X. 88; XI. 451
  Piety in Pattens, X. 214

Fopling Flutters, X. 90

Foppington, lord, in Sheridan's *A Trip to Scarborough*, XI. 269

Foppington, lord, in Vanbrugh's *The Relapse*, VIII. 76, 160, 161, 164, 165, 170; X. 90; XI. 257, 269, 283

Forbes, Alexander Penrose (1817–1875), XII. 456

Forbes, Archibald (1838–1900), XIV. 173, 190

Forbes, Edward (1815–1854), XII. 339, 498; XIV. 210, 296, 560

Forbes, James (1749–1819), *Oriental Memoirs*, XIV. 334

Forbes, James David (1809–1868) XIV. 552

Forbes, John (1593–1648), IX. 544

Forbes, Patrick (1564–1635), IX. 544

Forbes, Robert (1708–1775), IX. 563, 564; *Journals*, X. 356

Forbes, Robert, in Pennecuick's *Presbyterian Pope*, IX. 370

Forbes, Sir William (1739–1806), X. 453, 480, 512; XIV. 601

Forbes, William Henry (1851–1914), XII. 483

Forçade, Eugène, XIII. 558

Forcellini, Egidio, XII. 335

Forcet, or Forsett, Edward, VI. 306, 481

Ford, in *The Merry Wives of Windsor*, V. 206

Ford, Charles (*fl.* 1726), IX. 103

Ford, E., *Fair Play in the Lottery* (1660), VII. 516

Ford, Emanuel (*fl.* 1607), *Parismus*, III. 359, 536; VI. 305; *Parismenos*, III. 359, 536

Ford, John (*fl.* 1639), IV. 353, 527; VI. 69, 96, 144, 182, 188–209 (main entry), 226, 424, 425, 447 ff.; VII. 3; XII. 415; XIII. 426
  Beauty in a Trance, VI. 195
  Bristowe Merchant, The, VI. 195
  Broken Heart, The, V. 347; VI. 186, 191; XII. 190
  Elegy on death of Charles Blount, earl of Devonshire, VI. 189
  Elegy on Mountjoy's death, V. 347
  Fairy Knight, The, VI. 54, 195
  Fame's Memorial, VI. 189, 191
  Fancies, Chart and Noble, The, VI. 193
  Honor Triumphant, VI. 189
  Ill Beginning has a Good End, An, VI. 195
  Ladies Triall, The, VI. 194
  Line of Life, A, VI. 189
  London Merchant, The, VI. 195
  Lover's Melancholy, The, VI. 190; VII. 36
  Loves Sacrifice, VI. 192
  Masque of Melancholy, VI. 190
  Monarches Meeting, The, VI. 189
  Perkin Warbeck, VI. 193
  Royal Combat, The, VI. 195
  Sun's Darling, The: A Moral Masque, V. 125; VI. 54, 190
  Tis Pitty Shees a Whore, VI. 192
  See, also, under Rowley, W. and Webster

Ford, joint lessee of Drury Lane theatre, X. 265

Ford, mistress, in *The Merry Wives of Windsor*, V. 169, 189

Ford, Richard (1796–1858), XIV. 251, 552; *Handbook for travellers in Spain*, XIV. 250

Ford, Thomas (d. 1648), IV. 113, 115, 464

Ford Lectures, XIV. 81

Forde, Thomas (*fl.* 1660), VII. 439, 457, 514, 517; VIII. 481; *Lusus Fortunae*, VIII. 377; *Times Anatomised*, VII. 384; *Virtus Rediviva*, VII. 444

Fordhook, Fielding's house, x. 35
Fordoun, Kincardineshire, ii. 128
Fordun, John (d. 1384?), ii. 128, 129, 132, 280, 451; *Scotichronicon*, ix. 535
Fordyce, William, xii. 510
Foreign Quarterly Review, The, xiii. 5
Foreign Review, The, xiii. 5
Foresight, in Congreve's *Love for Love*, viii. 151
Foresight, in *King Hart*, ii. 262
Foresight, Mrs, in Congreve's *Love for Love*, viii. 152
Forest, in *Fortune by Land and Sea*, v. 361
Forest of Reason, in *Reason and Sensuality*, ii. 202
Forfarshire, ix. 372; xiv. 436
Forgues, F. D., xiii. 549, 551
'Forland' (Caxton's egg-story), ii. 316
Form of Living, The, or *Mending of Life* (school of Rolle), ii. 46, 47
Forman, Harry Buxton, xii. 399 ff., 403 ff.; xiii. 480, 481, 491, 570; xiv. 527
Forman, Simon (1552–1611), v. 204; vi. 23, 460; vii. 369; viii. 357
Forme of Cury, ii. 71, 500
Formey, J. H. S., x. 482
Formosus, in *The Bugbears*, v. 115
Forneron, H., *Histoire de Philippe II*, x. 291
Forres, ii. 100
Forrest, David William, xiv. 517
Forrest, Edwin, v. 308
Forrest, Old, in *Fortune by Land and Sea*, vi. 104
Forrest, Thomas (*fl.* 1580), iv. 437
Forrest, William (*fl.* 1581), iv. 476
Forrester, Alfred Henry ('Alfred Crowquill'), xiv. 201, 238
Forrester, Thomas (1635?–1706), ix. 546
Forsett, Edward (d. 1630?). *See* Forcet
Forshall, Frederick Hale, xiv. 598
Forshall, Josiah (1795–1863), ii. 45, 73, 431; xii. 517
Forster, John (1812–1876), x. 195, 201, 202, 483; xii. 206, 211, 230, 303, 439, 441; xiii. 57, 58, 69, 471, 484, 485, 513, 530 ff.; xiv. 190, 198, 502, 598
  Life of Charles Dickens, xiii. 305; xiv. 114
  Life of Oliver Goldsmith, xiv. 113
  Life of Swift, xiv. 114
  Life of Walter Savage Landor, xiv. 114
  Lives of the statesmen of the Commonwealth, xiv. 114
  On English Freedom under Plantagenets and Tudors, xiv. 114
Förster, Max, i. 117; iii. 277
Forster, William Edward (1818–1886), xiv. 427, 505, 509
Forster collection, x. 263
Forsyth, Joseph (1763–1815), xiv. 552
Forsyth, J. M., xiv. 467
Forsyth, William (1812–1899), xiv. 518
Forsyth, William (1818–1879), xiv. 533
Fortescue, George Knottesford (1847–1912), xii. 521

Fortescue, Sir John (1394?–1476?), ii. 286, 296 ff., 307, 336, 481, 482; viii. 315, 318, 465, 466, 469
  De Laudibus Legum Angliae, ii. 297; iv. 297, 511; viii. 314
  De Natura Legis Naturae, ii. 296
  Declaration, etc., ii. 298
  Monarchia (The Difference between an Absolute and a Limited Monarchy), ii. 297
  Understanding and Faith, ii. 299
Fortescue, Sir John (1531?–1607), vi. 290
Fortescue, Lucy. *See* Lyttelton, Lucy
Fortescue, Thomas, *Foreste or Collection of Histories*, trans. from French, iii. 536; iv. 446; viii. 126
Fortescue, William (1687–1749), ix. 251
Forth, firth of, ii. 88, 89, 100, 131; ix. 552; xii. 11; xiii. 6
Fortias-Santarelli, xiv. 490
Fortitude, in *The Passetyme of Pleasure*, ii. 229
Fortnightly Review, The, xii. 296; xiii. 425, 440, 467
'Fortoun buik, Ane lytill,' iv. 414
Fortrey, Samuel (1622–1681), viii. 367, 477
Fortune, in *Ara Fortunae*, vi. 319
Fortune, in *Ira seu Tumulus Fortunae*, vi 320
Fortune, in Drayton's *Robert of Normandy*, iv. 177
Fortune, in *Locrine*, v. 240
Fortune, in *Reason and Sensuality*, ii. 203
Fortune, in *The Bowge of Courte*, iii. 73
Fortune, in *The Example of Virtue*, ii. 227, 228, 234
Fortune, in *The Kingis Quair*, ii. 241, 242
Fortune, in *The Passetyme of Pleasure*, ii. 228, 231, 234, 235
Fortune, in *Piers the Plowman*, ii. 25, 26 28
Fortune, lady, in *Old Fortunatus*, vi. 52
Fortune, Sir Edward, in *Jacke Drums Entertainment*, vi. 41
Fortunia (play), vi. 486
Forty-one, viii. 96
Forum, the (debating society), xi. 239
Fosbroke, Thomas Dudley (1770–1842), xii. 510
Foscari, in Byron's *The Two Foscari*, xii. 49
Foscari, in *The Gratefull Servant*, vi. 203
Fosco, count, in Wilkie Collins's *Woman in White*, xiii. 438
Foscolo, Ugo, xii. 384, 525; *Lettere di Jacopo Ortis*, xi. 288
Foskett, Bernard, x. 387
Foster, Elizabeth, Milton's grand-daughter (d. 1754), vii. 107; x. 461
Foster, Ernest, xiv. 531
Foster, George, vii. 509
Foster, Gregory, i. 143
Foster, James (1697–1753), x. 381, 521
Foster, John (1731–1774), xi. 250

Foster, John (1770–1843), XII. 286, 466, 472; XIV. 518; *On the Aversion of Men of Taste to Evangelical Religion*, XII. 281

Foster, Sir Michael (1836–1907), XIV. 295, 560

Foster, Myles Birket (1825–1899), XIV. 201

Foster, Samuel (d. 1652), VII. 488

Foster, W., XIV. 580

Fotherby, Martin (1549?–1619), *Atheomastix*, VII. 277, 471

Fotherby, Robert (*fl.* 1615), IV. 93

Fotheringay, Miss, in *Pendennis*, XIII. 276, 291

Fotheringham, Alma, Gissing's, XIII. 460

Fotheringham, James, XIII. 484

Fouché, Leo, XIV. Add. 7

Foulis, Andrew (1712–1775), XI. 342, 470

Foulis, Robert (1707–1776), XI. 342, 470

Foulis, R. and A., XII. 324, 530

Foulis press, IX. 262, 562, 567; X. 132

Fountain, Lucy, in Reade's *Love me Little, Love me Long*, XIII. 426

Fountainhall, lord. See Lauder, Sir John

Fouqué, Friedrich Karl Heinrich de la Motte, XIII. 4, 192, 465

Four Elements, A New Interlude and a Merry of the nature of the, IV. 70

Four Sirens, the, in *Filostrato e Panfila*, v. 62

Four Sons of Aymon, I. 292. *See under* Caxton

Foure Ages of England, The, VII. 408

Fourier, baron de, XIV. 267

Fowell, Frank, XIV. 536

Fowler, Sir Henry Hartley, viscount Wolverhampton (1830–1911), XIV. 511

Fowler, Thomas (1832–1904), XIV. 472

Fowler, William (*fl.* 1603), *The Triumphs of Petrarch*, III. 137

Fowler, William (1761–1832), XII. 510

Fowler, William Warde (1847–1921), XII. Add. 3; XIV. 521

Fowles, William, IV. 437

Fox, Caroline (1819–1871), XIV. 502

Fox, Charles James (1749–1806), X. 306; XI. 1, 2, 19, 34, 35, 51, 52 ff. (main entry), 143, 146, 389, 396, 405; XII. 151, 326, 439, 495; XIII. 24; XIV. 98, 119 ff., 132, 184, 214, 502

Fox, Edward Long, XI. 414

Fox, Elizabeth, countess of Ilchester, XI. 174

Fox, George (1624–1691), VII. 169, 509; VIII. 101, 110, 413, 414; XI. 167; XII. 198, 476; *Journal*, VII. 352; VIII. 103 ff.; IX. 307, 523; *The Great Mystery*, VIII. 111

Fox, Henry, 1st lord Holland (1705–1774), X. 388, 389

Fox, Henry Richard Vassall, 3rd lord Holland (1773–1840), XI. 174; XIV. 503

Fox, Joseph, XIV. 606

Fox, capt. Luke (1586–1635), IV. 107, 456; *North West Fox; or Fox from the North-West Passage*, IV. 106

Fox, Stephen, 1st earl of Ilchester, XI. 174

Fox, William Johnson (1786–1864), XII. 428, 466; XIII. 53, 54, 57; XIV. 132, 137, 509, 591, 601

Foxcroft, A. B., XIV. 584

Foxcroft, H. C., *Life of Gilbert Burnet*, IX. 195, 198, 202 ff., 208; *Supplement to Burnet's History*, IX. 201, 204, 205

Foxe, John (1516–1587), I. 124; II. 60, 294; v. 247; VI. 374; *Actes and Monuments (Book of Martyrs)*, III. 26, 331 ff., 447, 528; IV. 389, 397, 400, 403, 433; VII. 322; *Book of Martyrs, The*, XI. 326, 369; XIV. 79; *Christus Triumphans*, v. 394

Foxe or Fox, John, of Woodbridge (*fl.* 1577), IV. 84

Foxe or Fox, Richard (1448?–1528), III. 468

Foxwell, Herbert Somerton, XIV. 4

Foy, VI. 101

Fracastor, Girolamo, IX. 60

Fracastorius, IV. 261

Fragmenta Aulica, VIII. 470

Fragmenta Regalia, XII. 376

Frail, Mrs, in Congreve's *Love for Love*, VIII. 152

Framlingham, II. 305

Frampton, in Mrs Griffith's *School for Rakes*, XI. 263

Frampton, John (*fl.* 1577–1596), IV. 446, 530

Frampul, lord and lady, in *The New Inne* VI. 25

France, II. 340; v. 25 ff., 34, 38, 43, 44, 49, 55, 58, 91, 121, 123, 137, 140, 222, 262, 284 ff., 288, 291, 299, 303, 306, 308, 334, 341, 344, 355, 359; VI. 5, 90, 175, 270, 271, 365; VII. 21, 22, 54, 61 ff., 180, 191, 197, 200, 205, 214, 221, 234, 282, 283, 285, 286, 301, 306 ff., 338, 381, 437; VIII. 11, 142, 206, 245, 256, 263, 265, 267, 296, 314, 330, 342, 364, 380, 384, 385; IX. 6 ff., 11, 13, 37, 81, 89, 95, 118, 130, 132, 142, 216, 218, 224 ff., 228, 229, 231, 232, 237, 256, 257, 265, 280, 332, 365, 390, 395, 396, 401, 406; X. 16, 17, 41, 47, 49, 63, 78, 79, 115, 119, 159, 182, 200, 219 ff., 261, 264, 274, 282, 283, 302, 306, 322, 323, 335, 336, 353, 388; XI. 1, 7, 22 ff., 25, 26, 30, 39, 42, 44, 47, 50, 71, 73, 97, 98, 118, 136, 189, 344, 374, 380, 382; XII. 26, 27, 30, 31, 43, 59, 174, 254, 276, 282, 343, 367; XIII. 20, 88, 119, 132, 211, 238, 357, 372, 428, 437, 444, 445; XIV. 42, 53, 57, 60, 110, 122, 151, 178, 179, 182, 183, 188, 192, 215, 292 ff., 322, 324, 382, 383, 388, 392, 399, 404, 419, 437

France, Hazlitt in, XII. 432

France, Martin de, *Le Champion des Dames*, VIII. 59

France, trials for sorcery in, VI. 183

France and Byron, XII. 392, 394 ff.

France and Shelley, XII. 403

Frances, Madame, in *The Tatler*, IX. 50

Francesca, I. 363

Francesco, in *Never too late*, III. 360

Francesco, grand duke of Florence, VI. 174, 175

Francillon, Robert E., XIII. 567; XIV. 528

Francis I, king of France, III. 46, 158, 160, 163, 224, 437; X. 105

Francis, John (1811–1882), XIV. 200, 534; *History of the Athenaeum*, XIV. 174

Francis, Philip (1708?–1773), X. 389, 408, 455, 523; *Letter from the Cocoa-Tree*, X. 390

Francis, Sir Philip (1740–1818), X. 400, 401, 405, 408 ff., 522, 526, 527; XI. 17; XIV. 513

Francis, St, I. 200, 201, 339; III. 159; X. 367

Franciscans, the (Minorites, Grey Friars), I. 200 ff., 209; II. 66, 71, 251, 255, 349, 350; III. 57, 92, 123, 159, 162; IV. 419; V. 13; VII. 303, 337; VIII. 59; IX. 538

Franciscans in Cambridge, I. 200; II. 349, 350

Franciscans in Oxford, I. 200 ff., 452 ff.; II. 349, 350

Franciscans in St Andrews, II. 370

Francisco, in *The Duke of Millaine*, VI. 155, 159

Francisco, in *The Renegado*, VI. 157

Francisco, in *The White Divel*, VI. 176

Francison, A., XIII. 471

Franck, Richard (1624?–1708), XII. 376

Franck, Sebastien, IX. 315

Francklin, Richard (1624?–1708), IX. 220, 221

Francklin, Thomas (1721–1784), X. 41, 128, 420, 431; *Orestes*, X. 86, 439

Franckton, John, IV. 414

Franco-Prussian war, XIV. 173, 182, 190, 192, 328

Francorum, Gesta Regum, I. 26. *See, also,* Gregory of Tours

Franeker university, in Friesland, VII. 308

Frank, in *The Witch of Edmonton*, VI. 190

Frank, Elizabeth, XII. 505

Frank, Mark (1613–1664), VII. 147, 424

Frankenstein, in Mary Shelley's novel, XII. 248

Frankford, Mrs, in *A Woman Kilde with Kindnesse*, VI. 84, 98

Frankfort-on-the-Main, III. 144, 434; IV. 366, 403, 545, 548; *also see* Add.; VII. 304, 308; XI. 331

Frankish law, VIII. 311

Frankland, Sir Edward (1825–1899), XIV. 272, 277, 557

Frankland, Richard (1630–1698), IX. 392; X. 386

Franklin, in *Arden of Feversham*, V. 240

Franklin, Benjamin, XII. 165; XIV. 394

Franklin, Sir John (1786–1847), XIV. 245, 552, 583

Franks, in *Beowulf*, etc., I. 25, 26, 32, 34

Franks, Sir Augustus Wollaston (1826–1897), XII. 347, 510

Franks casket, I. 12, 426

'Frantics,' in *The Lords' Masque*, VI. 353

Fraser, Alexander Campbell (1819–1914), IX. 280; XIV. 473
  Berkeley, XIV. 47
  Berkeley and Spiritual Realism, XIV. 47
  Biographia Philosophica, XIV. 48
  Essays in Philosophy, XIV. 47
  Locke, XIV. 47
  Philosophy of Theism, The, XIV. 48

Fraser, James (1818–1885), XIV. 606

Fraser, Peter, XIV. 180

Fraser, Simon, 12th lord Lovat (1667?–1747), IX. 563, 564

Fraser's Magazine, XII. 159, 163, 427, 431, 441; XIII. 10, 95, 278 ff., 347, 356, 360, 362, 465; XIV. 20, 86, 152, 161, 316

Fraunce, Abraham (*fl.* 1587–1633), III. 425, 432, 551; IV. 436, 476; VIII. 238
  Aminta, VI. 365, 490
  Arcadian Rhetorike, The, III. 432
  Countess of Pembrokes Emanuell, The, IV. 131
  Countess of Pembrokes Yvychurch, The, IV. 131
  Nativity, The, IV. 131
  Victoria, VI. 304, 472

Fraunhofer, Joseph von, XIV. 266

Fraus Pia, VI. 483

Frazer, Hugh, XIV. 536

Frazer, James (1818–1885), bishop of Manchester, XIII. 553

Frazer, Sir James George, XI. 85

Frazer, Robert Watson, XIV. 574

Frazer, William (1817–1879), XIV. 602

Fréchette, Louis, XIV. 356

Frederica, in Jane Austen's *Lady Susan*, XII. 233

Frederick, in *A Wife for a Month*, VI. 122, 132

Frederick, in Mrs Gaskell's *North and South*, XIII. 378

Frederick, in *The Weakest goeth to the Wall*, V. 316

Frederick II, emperor, I. 199; VII. 102, 159

Frederick V, elector Palatine and king of Bohemia, IV. 259; VI. 148, 149, 250, 321, 353

Frederick, Don, in *The Chances*, VI. 135

Frederick, duke, in *As You Like It*, V. 192

Frederick, lord, in *Nicholas Nickleby*, XIII. 317

Frederick, Louis, prince of Wales (1707–1751), IX. 230, 251; X. 94, 95, 108, 110; XIV. 287

Frederick, Sir, in *The Returne from Pernassus*, VI. 313

Frederick, William III, king of Prussia, XIV. 416

Frederick the Great, XII. 410; XIII. 18, 19; XIV. 63, 382, 416

Frederick of Jennen, II. 329

Freedom, in *She Would if She Could*, VIII 138

Freedom's Farewell, IX. 376

Freeholder, The, IX. 437

Freelove, lady, in Colman's *Jealous Wife*, X. 89, 90

Freeman, in *Discoverie of the Knights of the Poste*, IV. 350

Freeman, in Wycherley's *Country Wife*, VIII. 145

Freeman, Anthony, in *The Spectator*, IX. 57

Freeman, Edward Augustus (1823–1892), I. 163, 171, 197, 199; II. 399; VII. 330; X. 313; XII. 261, 271, 321, 379, 475; XIV. 62, 67, 69 ff. (main entry), 76, 85, 86, 99, 101, 198, 487
   Greek People and the Greek Kingdom, The, XIV. 71
   Historical Essays, XII. 308, 316
   Historical Geography, XIV. 72
   History and Conquests of the Saracens, XIV. 71
   History of Architecture, XIV. 71
   History of Federal Government, XII. 315; XIV. 71
   History of the Norman Conquest, XII. 316; XIV. 71 ff.
   History of Sicily, XII. 316
   History of Wells Cathedral, XII. 348
   Old English History for Children, XIV. 72
   Poems, legendary and historical (with G. W. Cox), XII. 314; XIV. 70
   Reign of William Rufus, The, XIV. 73

Freeman, Thomas (*fl.* 1614), IV. 520

Freeman's Journal, The, XIV. 318

Freemantle, H. E. S., XIV. Add. 7

Freeport, Sir Andrew, in *The Spectator*, IX. 51, 52

Freher, Dionysius (1649–1728), IX. 308, 520

Freiligrath, Ferdinand, V. 303

Freind, Robert (1667–1751), IX. 151, 153, 217, 250

Freiris of Berwick, IX. 367

Freke, Harriot, in Miss Edgeworth's *Belinda*, XI. 297

Freke, William (1662–1744), X. 377

French, Samuel, XIII. 516

French, the, X. 40, 255, 264, 282, 294; XI. 28; XII. 326; XIII. 282, 283, 339, 446; XIV. 173, 195, 213, 223, 225, 230, 247, 328

French academy, V. 293, 294; VIII. 369, 371; X. 173; XI. 354; XIV. 264

French actresses, VI. 404; VIII. 118

French artists, XIV. 214

French characters in English plays, VIII. 144

French constituent assembly, XI. 71

French dancers, XI. 282

French directory, XI. 26

French drama, X. 78, 81, 86, 211; XI. 281, 354; XIII. 265, 267, 270, 272

French economists, XIV. 381

French education, IX. 399; X. 283: XIV. 391, 423, 428

French *émigrés*, X. 66, 261

French empire, XI. 103

French fleet, X. 291

French historians, IX. 227; XII. 271; XIV. 102

French institutions, X. 42

French interest in Shakespeare, V. 209, 287–296

French invasion panic, the, XIV. 137

French July revolution, XIII. 357

French king, the, in *The Duke of Millaine*, VI. 158, 163

French lady, in *Godfrey of Bulloigne*, VI. 89

French language and literature: IX. 4, 26, 30, 214, 233, 267, 276, 331, 385, 390, 393, 395, 402 ff., 410, 412, 413; X. 17, 60, 69, 71, 90, 114, 120, 123, 135, 173, 174, 202 ff., 241, 250, 257, 259, 281, 283 ff., 288 ff., 296, 302, 303, 305, 313, 316, 317, 319, 323; XI. 58, 59, 181, 224, 289, 291, 292, 295 ff., 327, 330, 332, 334, 347, 353 ff., 359, 382; XII. 3, 154, 208, 247, 254, 308, 328; XIII. 99, 124, 129, 162, 199, 208, 213, 219, 259, 263, 346; XIV. 62, 107, 185, 224, 306, 327, 333, 342, 358, 360, 385, 387, 388, 391, 406, 408, 434, 438, 442, 455, 457, 458; (French, Old): no more spoken in England, II. 70; influence on our medieval poetry, (carols), II. 376, (songs), 377, 384 ff., 388 ff.; in legal works, VIII. 313 ff., 319; writers of, II. 507 ff.; (Renascence): influence of, on Chapman, VI. 33, 172; on Hobbes, VII. 266, 268, 269; and translation, VII. 263; (17th century): influence of, VIII. 124, 186 ff., 194, 214, 270, 321, 322, 332, 371 ff.; on Dryden, VIII. 23, 56; on satire, VIII. 59; on Temple, VIII. 381, 383, 385; *see, also*, Hamilton, Anthony. *See, also*, French poets and poetry; French stage, etc.

French encyclopedists, XIII. 19; XIV. 402

French *fabliaux*, XI. 175

French fiction, XIII. 283, 442, 456

French novelists, X. 18

French octave, the, or ballad royal, XI. 217

French law, XII. 354

French mathematicians, XIV. 258

French *mélodrame*, XIII. 263, 264

French music, in *Albion and Albanius*, VIII. 30

French mysticism, VII. 155

French national assembly, XI. 12, 21 ff., 26; XII. 144

French national convention, IX. 386; XI. 47

French opera, IX. 163; XIII. 256

French oratory, XII. 268

French periodicals, VII. 360

French *philosophes*, X. 296

French pietism, XII. 262

French poets and poetry, IX. 67; X. 79, 217, 219; XI. 209; XII. 4, 354; XIII. 129, 140, 210 ff., 252
French prosody, VIII. 239
French romances, V. 314; VI. 239, 240; VII. 74, 391
French romantic school, X. 181; XIII. 9
French sonnet writers, V. 173, 230
French translations, VI. 124; VII. 263; VIII. 123, 126 ff.
French troubadours, IX. 365
French press, V. 286, 295
French prints, XIV. 215
French publicists, XI. 42
French queen, in *The Conspiracie and Tragedie of Charles Duke of Byron*, VI. 30
French 'Reign of Terror,' XIV. 459
French revolution, II. 81; V. 197, 294; IX. 213, 233; X. 43, 59, 251, 318; XI. 4, 6, 14, 16, 19, 21, 22, 25 ff., 39, 44, 47, 79, 97, 106, 117, 118, 138, 155, 190, 194, 225, 236, 430, 433, *also see* Add.; XII. 39, 107, 149, 164, 249, 279, 310, 429; XIII. 2, 10, 11, 19, 257, 258, 300, 345, 420; XIV. 50, 66, 187, 214, 215, 382
French society, IX. 243
French stage, the:
  Classical, V. 1, 61, 63, 76, 91
  Medieval, V. 36, 39 ff., 46, 52
  Influence on English drama, VIII. 13 ff., 28, 29, 31, 131 ff., 157, 162, 179 ff., 187; X. 108
French theatres, XI. 265
French theology, XII. 254
French wines, V. 358
French-Canadians, XIV. 348, 354
Frenchman, in *A Woman will have her Will*, V. 329
Frend, William (1757–1841), XII. 279, 466, 467; XIV. 591, 593
Frere, Sir Bartle (1815–1884), XI. 392
Frere, John Hookham (1769–1846), XI. 39, 40, 392; XII. 52, 394; XIII. 175, 236, 238, 241, 246, 502; XIV. 206, 387; *Brunanburh*, X. 487
Frere and the Boye, The, II. 501, 502
Fréron, Élie Catherine, X. 264
Frescobaldi, in *Cromwell*, V. 247
Freund, Wilhelm, XII. 335
Freyr (Old Norse alphabet), I. 10
Friar, The, and the Boy, XI. 334
Friar Rush, II. 507; III. 94, 488
Friars, poems against, II. 443
Friars Minor. *See* Franciscans
Fribourg, XIV. 404
Fricker, Edith. *See* Southey, Mrs
Fricker, Sara. *See* Coleridge, Mrs
Frideswide, in *The Golden Legend*, II. 335
Friedrich, J., X. 454
Friend, Sir John (d. 1696), VIII. 163
Friends, society of, VIII. 112, and *ante*; XIV. 271
Friendship's Offering, XIV. 149
Frigidianus, bishop, I. 105
Frische Haff, the, I. 94

Frisco, in *A Woman will have her Will*, V. 330
Friscobaldo, Orlando, in *The Honest Whore*, VI. 53
Friscus, in Marston's *Scourge of Villanie*, IV. 332
Frisians, XIV. 68
Frisians, the, in *Beowulf*, I. 24 ff., 31
Frisius, Gemma, IV. 73, 74
'Frissis, Duk of,' in Wyntoun's *Chronicle*, II. 131
Frith, John (1503–1533), III. 26, 31, 40, 41, 140, 473; IV. 40; *Disputation of Purgatory*, III. 40; *The Revelation of Anti-Christ*, III. 39; *The Supper of the Lord*, III. 40
Friuli, IX. 150
Frizer, Ingram, V. 142
Frobel, John, of Basel, III. 41
Froben, J., II. 322; IV. 403
Frobisher, Martin (1535?–1594), IV. 73, 74, 76, 85, 88, 456; VII. 305
Froda, in *Beowulf*, I. 24, 25
Froebel, Friedrich, IX. 389; XIV. 394, 600, 608
Frog, Nicholas, in Arbuthnot's *History of John Bull*, IX. 134, 135
Frogges of Egypt, IV. 530
Frohman, Daniel, XIII. 514
Froissart, Jean, I. 213, 358; II. 159; V. 244; IX. 236; X. 133, 135; XIII. 428; *Chronicles*, II. 228, 322, 336, 338, 340; V. 246; XII. 146
Frollicke, Sir Frederick, in Etherege's *She Would if She Could*, VIII. 138
Frollo, I. 236
Fronia, in *The Misfortunes of Arthur*, V. 78
Frontinus, II. 366
Froschover, C., II. 322; III. 44
Frost, Thomas, XIII. 543; XIV. 534
Frost, Walter, *A Briefe Relation*, VII. 354
Frost, The Great, IV. 532
Frost's Lives of Eminent Christians, XIII. 455
Froth, Abraham, in *The Spectator*, IX. 57
Froth, lady, in Congreve's *Double-Dealer*, VIII. 149, 375; XI. 266
Froth, lord, in Congreve's *Double-Dealer*, VIII. 149, 156
Fróði (Frotho IV), I. 25
Frotho I, I. 28
Froude, James Anthony (1818–1894), IV. 45, 96; VII. 178; XII. 179, 255, 292, 319, 430, 445, 456, 460, *also see* Add. 1, 2; XIII. 17, 18, 358, 424, 467, 469, 471, 547; XIV. 83 ff., 96, 152, 488, 552
Council of Trent, The, XIV. 86
England's Forgotten Worthies, XIV. 84
English in Ireland, The, XIV. 86, 105
English Seamen in the Sixteenth Century, XIV. 86
History of England, XIII. 369; XIV. 84 ff.
Life and Letters of Erasmus, XIV. 86
Life of Carlyle, XIV. 86
Nemesis of Faith, The, XIV. 84
'Scientific Method Applied to History, The,' XIV. 85

Froude, James Anthony
    Short Studies, XIV. 85, 86
Froude, Richard Hurrell (1803–1836),
    XII. 257 ff., 454 ff., 461; *Remains*, XII.
    258, 259
Froumond, I. 101
Frugal, Luke, in *The City Madam*, VI. 160
Fry, Elizabeth (1780–1845), VIII. 114
Fry, Francis (1803–1886), XII. 521
Fry, John (1609–1657), X. 377
Fryer, John (d. 1733), XIV. 576; *New Ac-
    count of East India and Persia*, XIV. 333
Fryer Bacon, The Famous Historie of, I.
    210
Fuess, Claude Moore, *Lord Byron as a
    Satirist in Verse*, XII. 55
Fueter, E., XIV. 484; *Geschichte der neueren
    Historiographie*, XIV. 107
Fugitive tracts in verse, 1403–1600, V. 478
Fulbecke, William (1560–1603?), III. 551;
    VIII. 468
Fulke, William (1538–1589), III. 446, 473;
    IV. 508; *Confutation of the Rhemish
    Testament*, IV. 389
Fuller, XII. 434
Fuller, Nicholas (1557?–1626), VII. 317,
    482
Fuller, Robert H., XIV. Add. 7
Fuller, Thomas (1608–1661), II. 190, 353;
    III. 50, 324, 328, 332, 426, 463, 473;
    IV. 12, 14, 245, 370, 420; VII. 158, 232,
    244–249 (main entry), 253, 256 ff., 462;
    XIV. 460
    Abel Redivivus, VII. 248
    Andronicus, VII. 248
    Appeal of Injured Innocence, VII. 246
    Church History, VII. 207, 246 ff.; VIII. 15
    Davids Heinous Sin, VII. 244
    Good Thoughts in Bad Times, VII. 245,
    247
    *History of the University of Cambridge,
    The*, VI. 307; VII. 248
    Holy and Profane State, The, VII. 245,
    247, 248
    Holy War, The, VII. 245, 247, 248
    'Pisgah Sights,' VII. 248
    Worthies of England, The, IV. 308, 511;
    VII. 246 ff.
Fuller, Thomas, father of Thomas Fuller,
    VII. 244
Fuller, Sir Thos. E., XIV. Add. 7
Fullerton, lady Georgiana Charlotte (1812
    –1885), XIII. 562
Fulman, William (1632–1688), IX. 533
Fulmers, the, in Cumberland's *West In-
    dian*, XI. 264
Fulston St Peter's, Wilts., VII. 29
Fulwell, Ulpian (*fl.* 1586), *Like will to
    Like*, V. 57, 393; VI. 284
Fun, XIV. 196, 239
Fungoso, in *Every Man out of His Humour*,
    VI. 40
Furetière, Antoine, IX. 256; *Le roman
    Bourgeois*, X. 26
Furlong, Thomas (1794–1827), XIV. 312,
    568

Furly, Benjamin (1636–1714), VIII. 414
Furneaux, Henry (1829–1900), XII. 483
Furness, Horace Howard, V. 308; VI. 305
Furnivall, Frederick James (1825–1910), I.
    ix, 344; II. 166, 216, 424 ff.; VI. 375; IX.
    361; X. 233; XII. 504; XIII. 484; XIV. 408,
    506; *An English Miscellany* presented
    to, II. 504
Fursey, the Irish hermit, vision of, in
    Bede, I. 82, 86
'Fusbos,' *pseud.* See Plunkett, Henry
    Grattan
Fuscara (Cleiveland's), VII. 93
Fuscus, in *The Scourge of Folly*, IV. 334
Fuseli, Henry (1741–1825), XIV. 214
Futhy. See Fethe
Fy, let us all to the Bridal, X. 233
Fyfe, Thomas Alexander, XIII. 543
Fyffe, Charles Alan (1845–1892), XIV. 488
Fyfield elm, the, XIII. 93
Fyn, in Dunbar's *Interlude*, II. 255
Fyshe, Simon. See Fish
Fyve Bestis, Talis of the, II. 279, 280

G. Al., V. 72
G. S. B., *A Study of the Prologue and Epi-
    logue in English Literature*, VIII. 34
Gaberlunzie Man, The, III. 130; IX. 560;
    XI. 218
Gaboriau, Émile, XIII. 437
Gabriel, in Cowley's *Davideis*, VII. 66, 67
Gabriel, in *The Example of Virtue*, II. 227
Gabriel, the angel, I. 115; II. 382
Gabrielson, Arvid, XIII. 512
Gace, William (*fl.* 1580), IV. 446
Gadbury, John (1627–1704), VII 509
Gaddesden. See John of
Gadshill place, XIII. 332
Gaelic language and literature, I. 464;
    IX. 377, 559; X. 225, 229 ff., 487; XII.
    24; XIV. 302 ff., 357, 457, 458
Gaelic league, the, XIV. 305
Gage, Sir Henry (1597–1645), VII. 454
Gage, Thomas (d. 1656), *A New Survey
    of the West Indies*, IV. 97, 456
Gager, William (*fl.* 1580–1619), V. 82; VI.
    318, 324, 378, 399, 409, 472, 491
    Dido, VI. 303
    Meleager, VI. 302
    Oedipus, VI. 303
    Rivales, V. 128; VI. 302, 303, 398
    Ulysses Redux, VI. 303, 327, 398
Gaguin, Robert, III. 71
Gahagan, major Goliah O'Grady, *pseud.*
    of W. M. Thackeray, XIII. 279
Gailhard, Jean, *The Compleat Gentleman*,
    IX. 397, 569
Gaillard, Michel, IV. 527
Gaimar, Geoffrey (d. 1140), *Estorie des
    Engles*, etc., I. 104, 170, 236, 264, 446;
    II. 420, 508
Gainsborough, Thomas (1727–1788), X.
    267
Gainsford, captain Francis, VII. 345
Gainsford, Thomas, VI. 493; *Perkin War-
    beck*, VI. 193

Gair, J., ix. 371

Gairdner, James (1828–1912), ii. 67; xii. 356; xiv. 485, 489
Divine Right of Kings, The, xiv. 83
Historical Element in Shakespeare's Falstaff, The, xiv. 83
History of the English Church, vol. iv, xiv. 83
Life of Richard III, xiv. 82
Lollardy and the Reformation, xiv. 83
Studies in English History (with J. Spedding), xiv. 82, 83

Gaisford, Thomas (1779–1855), xii. 327, 328, 333, 483, 484, 491

Gaius, xii. 492

Galafridus de Vino Salvo. *See* Geoffrey de Vinsauf

Galahad, in Arthurian legend, i. 271

Galahad, Sir, Tennyson's, xiii. 29

Galán escarmentado, El, viii. 16

Galaor, vii. 75

Galatea, iii. 224

Galathea, in Lyly's *Galathea*, v. 126

Gale, Roger (1672–1744), ix. 355, 358, 533, 534; xii. 350

Gale, Samuel (1682–1754), ix. 358, 533

Gale, Theophilus (1628–1678), vii. 471, *also see* Add.; x. 385; *Court of the Gentiles*, vii. 303

Gale, Thomas (1507–1587), iv. 444

Gale, Thomas (1635?–1702), ix. 355, 534

Galen, Claudius, i. 192, 193; ii. 365; iii. 5, 6, 20, 21, 23, 427, 433; iv. 444; viii. 350; xii. 521

Galeron of Galloway, in *Awntyrs of Arthure*, i. 312; ii. 122, 123

Gali, Francisco de, *Discourse of the East and West Indies*, iv. 78

Galicia, xiv. 294

Galignani's Messenger, xii. 383

Galileo Galilei, iv. 278, 290; vii. 100, 283, 292; viii. 276, 282, 338, 350, 352, 358; xiv. 27; *Dialogue*, vii. 284

Galiot, in *Golagros and Gawane*, ii. 124

Gall, Richard (1776–1801), *Farewell to Ayrshire*, xi. 234; *Now Bank and Brae*, xi. 234; *Poems and Songs*, xi. 234, 443

Gallant, A Treatise of a, iii. 98, 491

Gallant Grahams, The, ix. 373

Galley late come into England from Terra Nova, iii. 87, 482

Gallia Christiana, x. 282

Gallican liberties, viii. 308

Gallienus Redivivus, xiv. 65

Gallio, in Hall's *Virgidemiarum*, iv. 331

Gallipoli, xiv. 367

Galloway, ii. 99, 101, 104; vii. 79; xi. 446

Galloway, lady, x. 64

'Galloway poet,' the. *See* Nicholson, William

Gallus, iii. 224

Gallus, Evaldus, *Pueriles Confabulatiunculae*, xi. 367

Gally, Henry (1696–1769), xi. 250

Galt, John (1779–1839), x. 445; xii. 30, 384, 385, 394, 449; xiii. 377; xiv. 188
Annals of the Parish, The, xi. 64; xii. 251
The Ayrshire Legatees, xii. 251
The Entail, xii. 251
The Last of the Lairds, xii. 251

Galton, Arthur Howard, xiii. 488

Galton, Sir Francis (1822–1911), xiv. 473, 560

Galvano, Antony, *Discoveries of the World*, iv. 83, 444, 457

Galway, Queen's college, xiv. 417

Gama, Vasco da, iv. 68, 82, 86

Gamba, count Pietro, xii. 35, 36, 38, 384

Gamba family, the, xii. 36, 37

Gambado, Geoffrey. *See* Bunbury, Henry William

Gamble, John (d. 1687), vii. 83

Gamble, William, xiv. 532

Gambol, in *The Masque of Christmas*, vi. 358, 359

Game, The Master of, ii. 286

Game of Cardes, Comedie or Morrall devised on, vi. 286

Gamelyn, Tale of, i. 289, 298, 299, 367, 468; ii. 162, 164, 178, 194 ff., 211, 215, 216, 467; iii. 279, 358; v. 193, 220; xiii. 252

Gammer Gurton's Garland, xi. 375

Gammer Gurton's Needle, ii. 233; v. 111; vi. 296, 297, 478

Gamp, Sarah, in *Martin Chuzzlewit*, xiii. 304, 323

Gandersheim, v. 6, 7

Gandy, Henry (1649–1734), x. 355

Ganymede, ii. 175

Ganymede (Barnfield's), iii. 264; iv. 120, 126

Gaping Wide-mouthed Waddling Frog, xi. 386

Garbett, James (1802–1879), xiii. 171

Garçon et l'Aveugle, Le, v. 25

Garden, Francis (1810–1884), xii. 454

Garden, George (1649–1733), ix. 519, 520

Garden, James (1647–1726), ix. 520

Garden of Delight, in *Reason and Sensuality*, ii. 202

Gardening, writers on, iv. 542

Gardiner, Edmund, *The Triall of Tabacco*, iv. 349, 531

Gardiner, col. James (1688–1745), ix. 563

Gardiner, R., *England's Grievance Discovered*, vii. 507

Gardiner, Samuel Rawson (1829–1902), iv. 42; vi. 148, 149; vii. 190; ix. 193; xiii. 480; xiv. 99, 489, 500
Cromwell's Place in History, xiv. 88
History of England, xiv. 87
Letters and Documents illustrating the relations between England and Germany, xiv. 87
Parliamentary Debates in 1610, xiv. 87
Thirty Years' War, The, xiv. 88

Gardiner, Stephen (1483?–1555), bishop of Winchester, III. 33, 81, 194, 418 ff., 444, 474; V. 365; VI. 91, 296, 397, 475; *Contra Turneri vulpem*, III. 81; *Explication and Assertion of the true Catholic Faith*, III. 33

Gardiner and Mullinger, *Introduction to the Study of English History*, XII. 356

Gardner, Alan Gardner, 1st lord (1742–1809), XIV. 245

Gardyne, Alexander (1585?–1634?), IX. 555

Gareth, in Malory, I. 295

Garfit, Arthur, XIV. 591

Gargantua (Rabelais), II. 256, 258; IV. 8

Gargantua his Prophecie, IV. 9

Gargantua's mare, VIII. 67

Gargery, Joe, in *Great Expectations*, XIII. 334

Garibaldi, Giuseppe, XIII. 132

Garland, John, *Organum*, XIV. 308

Garlandia, Joannes de (*fl.* 1230), I. 193, 194, 453; III. 84

Garnesche, Christopher. *See under* Skelton

Garnett, Edward, XIV. 527, 601

Garnett, Henry (1555–1606), IV. 127; VIII. 85, 86

Garnett, Richard (1835–1906), IV. 111; XI. 412, 434, 462, 463; XII. 159, 248, 399 ff., 412, 435, 444, 521; XIII. 194, 464, 467, 471, 476, 481, 499, 503; XIV. 509, 518, 601; *Twilight of the Gods, The*, XIV. 144

Garnett, Robert S., XIII. 530

Garnier, Robert, V. 63, 163; VI. 366; VIII. 13, 133; *Marc-Antoine*, V. 334; *Cornélie*, V. 157, 334; *Porcie*, V. 157

Garnier de Pont-Sainte-Maxence, *Vie de St Thomas Becket*, II. 420, 508

Garonne, river, XIV. 302

Garraway, Anne, VII. 232

Garret (a London character), IV. 360

Garrett, Edmund, XIV. 534

Garrett, F. E., XIV. Add. 7

Garrick, David (1717–1779), V. 291, 298; VI. 28, 262, 323; VIII. 184, 191, 196; X. 36, 39, 40, 71, 72, 82, 83, 85 ff., 90, 91, 128, 161, 172, 204, 211, 212, 214, 215, 260, 261, 263 ff. (main entry), 268, 395, 405, 426, 428, 429, 432 ff., 437 ff., 441, 445, 460, 461, 471, 483, 493; XI. 257 ff.; 264, 265, 271, 282, 284, 360 ff., 448 ff., 453, 454; XII. 180, 200

Bon Ton, X. 88

Cymon, XI. 282

Gamesters, X. 86

Irish Widow, X. 88

Lethe, X. 85

Lying Valet, X. 88

Miss in her Teens, X. 88

Garrick, Eva Marie Violetti, X. 268

Garrick and Colman, *The Clandestine Marriage*, X. 211

Garrick collection (British Museum), V. 35

Garrick plays, XII. 436

'Garrison, The,' in Smollett's *Peregrine Pickle*, X. 38

Garter, Order of the, I. 328; II. 38; IX. 355

Garth, Caleb, in *Middlemarch*, XIII. 382

Garth, Sir Samuel (1661–1719), VIII. 410, 411; IX. 75, 151, 175, 177 ff. (main entry), 485; X. 156; XI. 246; *Claremont*, IX. 179; *Dispensary, The*, IX. 179, 333

Gartha, in D'Avenant's *Gondibert*, VII. 71

Garulf, in *Finnsburh*, I. 31

Gascoigne, George (1525?–1577), III. 201–210 (main entry), 248, 249, 281, 282, 284, 285, 296 ff., 302, 303, 312, 447, 448, 517 ff., 526, *also see* Add.; IV. 52, 73, 329, 441; V. 70 ff., 120, 181, 344, 386, 394, 402 ff.; VII. 271; XI. 248; XIII. 253

Adventures of Master F. J., The, III. 205, 206

Certayne notes of Instruction in English, III. 206, 207, 281, 296

Complaint of Phylomene, The, III. 207

Councell given to Master Bartholmew Withipoll, III. 203, 205, 206

Dan Bartholmew of Bathe, III. 203, 205, 210, 484

Delicate Diet, for daintie mouthd Droonkardes, A, III. 207

Droome of Doomes daie, The, III. 207, 208

Dulce Bellum inexpertis, III. 202, 206

Ferdinando Jeronimi, VI. 192

Fetters, The fruite of, III. 206

Glasse of Government, The, III. 207; V. 113, 114

Gloze upon this text, Dominus iis opus habet, A, III. 207, 208

Grief of Joye, The, III. 207

Hemetes the heremyte, The Tale of, III. 202, 205, 207, 208

Hollande, Voyage into, III. 203, 206

Hundreth sundrie Flowers, A, III. 205; IV. 399

Jocasta, III. 203, 206; IV. 4; V. 70 ff., 76, 77, 396, 399

Posies, IV. 399

Princelye Pleasures, The, III. 210

Spoyle of Antwerp, The, III. 208; IV. 324

Steele Glas, The, III. 202, 205, 207, 209; VIII. 223

Supposes, III. 203, 204, 206; V. 114, 115, 220; VIII. 126

Weedes, III. 202

Gascoigne, Sir John (father of George Gascoigne), III. 202

Gascoigne, Thomas (1403–1458), chancellor of Oxford university, II. 66, 157, 294, 496; IV. 419, 428

Gascony, II. 293

Gascoyne-Cecil, Robert A. T., 3rd marquis of Salisbury (1830–1903), XII. 155, 430; XIV. 134, 196, 198, 511

Gashford, in *Barnaby Rudge*, XIII. 320

Gaskell, Elizabeth Cleghorn (1810–1865), XIII. 326, 345, 371 ff. (main entry), 386, 408, 431, 458, 549 ff., 555, 558

Cousin Phillis, XIII. 371, 380, 403, 406

Cranford, XIII. 371, 376 ff., 381, 403, 430

Gaskell, Elizabeth Cleghorn
  Life of Charlotte Brontë, XIII. 379, 403,
    414
  Lizzie Leigh, XIII. 371, 373
  Manchester Marriage, The, XIII. 379
  Mary Barton, XIII. 362, 371 ff., 381, 403
  Moorland Cottage, The, XIII. 377
  Mr Harrison's Confessions, XIII. 371,
    376, 377
  My Lady Ludlow, XIII. 379
  North and South, XIII. 375, 378, 381
  Round the Sofa, XIII. 372, 379
  Ruth, XIII. 371, 372, 377 ff., 381, 403
  Sketches among the Poor, XIII. 372
  Sylvia's Lovers, XIII. 378 ff., 403
  Wives and Daughters, XIII. 372, 377,
    378, 380, 381
Gaskell, William, XIII. 372
Gasquet, cardinal Francis Aidan, XIV. 484
Gassendi, Pierre, VII. 284, 286
Gataker, Thomas (1574–1654), VII. 308,
    315 ff., 320, 321, 488, 490; *Annotations
    on the Bible*, VII. 322; *Cinnus*, VII. 318;
    Marcus Antoninus, VII. 316
Gate House, the, in *The Martin Marpre-
    late Controversy*, III. 387
Gath, VII. 67
Gatherer, J., IX. 550
Gatty, Margaret (1807–1873), XI. 248, 479
Gatty, mistress (Etherege's), VIII. 138
Gatty laboratory, XIV. 297
Gau, John (1493?–1553?), *Richt Vay*, II.
    285, 479
Gaubius, Hieronymus David, X. 200
Gauchos, the, XIV. 250
Gauden, John (1605–1662), bishop of
    Worcester, III. 407; VII. 160 ff., 425;
    VIII. 269; *Anti-Baal-Berith*, VII. 161;
    Eikon Basilike, VII. 140, 161, 162; VIII.
    67; X. 355, 517
Gaudifer, in *Golagros and Gawane*, II. 124
Gaufridus, Arturus, I. 257
Gaul, XIV. 110
Gaul, *joculatores* in, II. 386
Gaul, women of, I. 151
Gaule, John (*fl.* 1646–1660), VII. 507, 509;
    Πΰς-μαντια, *The Mag-astromancer*, VII.
    394
Gaulish scholars, XIV. 302, 303
Gaulmin, Gilbert, IV. 249, 259
Gauls, the, IV. 13
Gaultier, abbé, IX. 151, 152
Gaunt, Griffith, Charles Reade's, XIII. 426
Gaunt, John of, duke of Lancaster (1340–
    1399). *See* John
Gaunt house, in Thackeray's *Vanity Fair*,
    XIII. 287
Gauss, Karl Friedrich, XIV. 258, 268
Gaussen, Alice, *Percy: Prelate and Poet*,
    X. 206
Gaussen, François S. R. L., XII. 283
Gaussin, Mlle, X. 118
Gautar, the, in Old Norse literature, I. 26
Gautier, archbishop of Sens, I. 190
Gautier, Théophile, XIII. 129, 307; XIV.
    349; *La Chimère*, XIII. 208

Gautier de Doulens, I. 328; II. 450
Gaveston, in *Edward II*, V. 154
Gaw, A., VIII. 131
Gawain, Gawayne (Walgainus), I. 243,
    260, 261, 269, 270, 295, 297, 309,
    311 ff., 336, 468; II. 100; III. 68; VII. 75.
    See, also, *Gawayne and the Grene Knight*
Gawain, Sir, in *Awntyrs of Arthure*, II. 116,
    121, 122
Gawain, Sir, in *Golagros and Gawane*, II.
    123, 124, 450
Gawain, Sir, in *Morte Arthure*, II. 119, 120
Gawain, Wedding of, I. 295, 312, 471
Gawaine, The Marriage of Sir, II. 414
Gawane, Anteris of, II. 116, 121
Gawayn, Syr, XIV. 307
Gawayne, Sir, and the Grene Knight, I. 281,
    284, 285, 287, 296, 297, 312, 320, 325 ff.,
    330 ff., 333, 334, 378, 462, 468, 471, 472;
    II. 133, 272, 308, 379; VII. 75; XIV. 307
Gawdy, Philip (*fl.* 1601), VI. 291
Gawdyfer at Gaddris, Alexander story of,
    II. 112
Gawin, in *The Misfortunes of Arthur*, V. 78
Gay, Florence, XIV. 584
Gay, John (1685–1732), IX. 78, 98, 103,
    106, 137, 139, 152, 160 ff. (main entry),
    169, 220, 247, 249, 442, 446, 447, 452,
    468, 472, 480, 483; X. 80, 84, 102, 202,
    429, *also see* Add.; XI. 88, 173, 248, 479;
    XII. 122; XIII. 239, 265
  Beggar's Opera, IX. 163; X. 71, 83, 428;
    XI. 218, 260
  Birth of the Squire, IX. 164
  Black-eyed Susan, IX. 161
  Eclogues, XI. 36
  Fables, IX. 162
  Fan, The, IX. 161
  Funeral, The, IX. 164
  Ladies' Petition, IX. 164
  Mr Pope's Welcome from Greece, IX. 75,
    164
  Polly, IX. 163
  Rural Sports, IX. 160
  Shepherd's Week, IX. 131, 161, 162, 164,
    165; XI. 144
  Tea-Table, The, IX. 164
  Three Hours after Marriage, VIII. 168;
    IX. 72, 132; XI. 322
  Toilette, The, IX. 164
  Tragical Comical Farce, IX. 160
  *Trivia, or The Art of Walking the Streets
    of London*, IX. 161, 164; XI. 322
  'Twas when the Seas were roaring, IX. 161
  What D'ye-Call-it, IX. 161; X. 83
  Wife of Bath, IX. 161; XI. 322
  Wine, IX. 160
Gay, John (1699–1745), *Dissertation*, X.
    342; *Gazetteer, The*, X. 400, 525
Gay, Joseph, XI. 330
Gay, Thomas, IX. 160
Gay, William (d. 1695), IX. 160
Gay, William (1865–1897), XIV. 369, 586
Gay Lussac, XIV. 557
Gay Goshawk, The, II. 411
Gayley, Charles Mills, V. 134 ff., 418; VI. Add.

Gaynour, queen (Guinevere), in *Awntyrs of Arthure*, II. 122
Gay's Chair, IX. 164
Gayton, Edmund (1608-1666), VII. 516
Gayville, lord, in Burgoyne's *Heiress*, XI. 275
Gaza, Theodorus, grammar of, III. 14
Gazeau, J., XIII. 471
Gazet, in *The Renegado*, VI. 161
Gazette, The, IX. 2, 4
Gazette, The (Manchester), XIV. 169
Gazetteer, The, XIV. 186
Gazettes, VII. 345
Geat, in *Deor*, I. 36
Geatas, the, in *Beowulf*, I. 24 ff.
Geddes, Alexander (1737-1802), XII. 467
  Charming Highlandman, IX. 372
  Iliad, IX. 372
  Lewie Gordon, IX. 372
  Linton, IX. 372
  Wee Wifukie, IX. 372
Geddes, John (1735-1799), XI. 223
Geddes, William (1600?-1694), IX. 546
Geddes, Sir William Duguid (1828-1900), XII. 335, 484
Gedell-Glaiss, son of Sir Newill, in *Orygynale Cronykil*, II. 130
Gedike, Friedrich, XIV. 382
Gee, J., VIII. 453
Geesh (Abyssinia), XIV. 246
Geffe, or Goffe, N., *The Perfect Use of Silk-wormes*, IV. 487, 542
Geikie, Sir Archibald, XIV. 291, 559, 561
Geikie, Walter (1795-1837), II. 270
Geiler von Kaisersberg, John, III. 14, 59, 482, 490
'Geist,' Matthew Arnold's dachshund, XIII. 96
Gelasimus, Herod's fool in *Archipropheta*, VI. 295
Gell, Sir William (1777-1836), XII. 497; *Pompeiana*, XII. 338
Gellert, Christian Fürchtegott, *Das Leben der schwedischen Gräfen von G.*, X. 18
Gelli, Giovanni Battista, IV. 444
Gellia, in Owen's *Epigrammata*, IV. 265
Gellibrand, Henry (1597-1636), IV. 456
Gellius, Aulus, IV. 6, 249, 348
Gelon, Sicilian ruler, XII. 316
General Advertiser, The, X. 466
General assembly, the (1650), VII. 254
General assembly of the Church of Scotland, IX. 129
Generous, in *The Late Lancashire Witches*, VI. 105
Generydes, I. 291, 468
Genest, John (1764-1839), VIII. 123, 124, 168, 188; XI. 447, 456; *Some Account of the English Stage*, X. 85, 161, 443
Geneva, III. 45, 53, 144, 145, 399, 400, 402, 403; IV. 163, 276, 303, 402, 403, 429; V. 113; VI. 374; VII. 100, 304, 306, 308; VIII. 245, 291; X. 296; XI. 59; XIII. 383
Geneva, lake of, XII. 44
Geneviève, St, IX. 68

Gengiscan the Great, X. 110
Genius, priest of Nature, in *Roman de la Rose*, II. 150
Genius, priest of Venus, in *Confessio Amantis*, II. 146, 150
Genius of the Wood, the, in *Arcades*, VII. 113
Genlis, comtesse de, XI. 491; XIII. 273; XIV. 606; *Adèle et Théodore*, XI. 382; XIV. 388; *Tales of the Castle*, XI. 382
Genoa, II. 79, 118, 157, 305; IV. 68; VII. 99; IX. 245; X. 41, 469
Genoa, villa Saluzzo, XII. 37
Genovino, in D'Urfey's *Famous History of Massaniello*, VIII. 175
Gent, Thomas (1693-1778), XI. 341, 469
Gentile Christians, IX. 291
Gentiles, the, XII. 209
Gentili, Alberico (1552-1608), VI. 399; VII. 309; VIII. 466; *De Jure Belli*, III. 423, 424; VIII. 316; *De Legationibus*, III. 423
Gentillet, Innocent, *Discours sur les moyens de bien gouverner et maintenir de bonne paix un royaume*, IV. 8, 444
'Gentle river,' X. 233
Gentleman, Francis (1728-1784), X. 443
Gentleman, Tobias (*fl.* 1614), IV. 511
Gentleman's Calling, The, IX. 397, 570
Gentleman's Journal, IX. 270; X. 163
Gentleman's Magazine, The, IX. 191; X. 144, 159, 161 ff., 168, 171, 173, 175, 181, 183, 193, 460, 461, 463, 464, 467, 471 ff., 479, 480; XI. 323, 324, 339, 355; XII. 140, 181, 193, 345, 347, 365, 428; XIV. 230, 594
Gentleman's Magazine Library, XII. 506, 519
Gentûs, the, XI. 17
Gentylnes and Nobylyte, V. 409
Gentz, Friedrich von, IX. 233; X. 306
Geoffrey de Vinsauf (*fl.* 1200), *Art of Poetry*, I. 193, 453
Geoffrey of Monmouth (1100?-1154), I. 68, 71, 158, 159, 168 ff., 175, 235, 237, 245 ff., 250, 252, 257 ff., 264, 266 ff., 284, 336, 338, 350, 351, 450, 451, 461; II. 118; III. 234, 237, 314; IV. 67, 422; V. 67, 68, 78, 239; VI. 92; X. 231; XIV. 307
Geoffrey of Waterford, II. 508
Geoffrey the cripple, in *Tale of Beryn*, I. 298
Geoffrey the grammarian or Starkey (*fl.* 1440), *Promptorium Parvulorum*, II. 483, 496; III. 555
Geoffrey the Norman, bishop of St Albans, V. 7
Geological Magazine, The, XIV. 289, 566
Geological society of London, XII. 347; XIV. 287
Geometry, in *The Passetyme of Pleasure*, II. 225
George I, king of Great Britain (elector of Hanover), IV. 251; VII. 299; IX. 132, 231, 235, 237, 238, 243, 249, 308, 309, 330, 407, 408; X. 283; XIV. 229

George II, king of Great Britain, IX. 87, 104, 230, 243, 249, 250, 252 ff., 381, 407, 408, 410, 413; x. 44, 295, 388; XIV. 57, 381

George III, king of Great Britain, v. 208; IX. 230, 252, 253; x. 66, 136, 184, 206, 363, 389 ff., 400, 404, 406, 463, 469, 477; XI. 5, 11, 13, 37, 52, 166, 261; XII. 36, 53, 475; XIV. 60, 90, 213, 215, 244, 328, 386, 389

George IV, king of Great Britain, IX. 213; XI. 49, 54; XII. 36, 70; XIII. 295, 342; XIV. 114, 201, 222, 229, 432

George, duke of Saxe-Meiningen, v. 306

George, prince, in the mummers' play, v. 33

George, prince, of Denmark (1653–1708), IX. 33, 130

George, St, VII. 167; XI. 373

George, St, in early drama, II. 309, 406; v. 32 ff., 49

George, St, in *Richard Coeur de Lion*, I. 308

George inn, the, in the *Paston Letters*, II. 309

George of Gorbals, in *The Bon Gaultier Ballads*, XIII. 161

George tavern at Edmonton, v. 252

Georgia, IX. 324, 325

Georgian drama, XI. 257 ff., 272, 447, *also see* Add.

Georgian era, IX. 192; x. 1, 142; XI. 284, 372, 373, 377

Georgian poets, XII. 106

Georgian public, XI. 259, 267, 268, 270

Georgian theatre, XI. 269, 273

Geraint (Sir Erec), I. 274, 284

Gerald of Wales. *See* Giraldus Cambrensis

Geraldine. *See* Fitz-Gerald, lady Elizabeth

Geraldine, in Coleridge's *Christabel*, XII. 88

Geraldine, in Heywood's *History of Women*, VI. 102

Geraldine, in *The English Traveller*, VI. 102

Geraldine, in *The Unfortunate Traveller*, III. 363

Geraldine (Surrey's), IV. 182

Geraldines of Wales, the, I. 94

Gerard, in *The Cloister and the Hearth*, XIII. 428, 429

Gerard, John (1545–1612), *Herball or generall historie of Plantes*, III. 551; IV. 374, 542

Gerard, John (1564–1637), VII. 444

Gerard of Cremona, II. 365

Gerbel, v. 308

Gerbelius, Nicholas, IV. 250

Gerbert of Aurillac, I. 209

Gerbier, Sir Balthazar (1591?–1667), VII. 353

Gerbier, Charles, VII. 514

Geree, John (1601?–1649), VII. 509, 517

Gereint or Geraint, son of Erbin, in *The Black Book*, I. 250, 253, 255

Gerhoh of Reichersberg, VI. 374

Germ, The, XIII. 111, 112, 114, 120, 138; XIV. 139

Germain, George Sackville, 1st viscount Sackville (1716–1785), x. 526

German ballads, XII. 5

German criticism, XIV. 140

German doctor in *Hymenaeus*, VI. 304

German drama, XI. 41, 281; XII. 372; XIII. 265, 272

German education, XIV. 382, 391, 423

German flute, x. 198

German historians, IX. 227; XII. 271; XIII. 18; XIV. 102

German history, XIV. 92, 99

German interest in Shakespeare, v. 167, 283, 284, 285, 289, 298

German language and literature, IX. 314, 331, 400; x. 18, 60, 79, 80, 217, 291, 296; XI. 177, 300, 355, 356, 414; XII. 4, 113, 154, 157, 221, 247, 254, 288, 302, 308, 340; XIII. 3 ff., 10, 12, 53, 227, 244, 247, 259, 263, 323, 383; XIV. 306, 318 *a, b*, 391, 406, 434, 457 ff.

German philosophy, XII. 270; XIV. 9, 13, 40, 41

German politics, x. 388

German reformation, XIV. 108

German reforming princes, the, VII. 103

German romanticism, XIII. 7 ff., 192, 259, 261

German stage, Massinger and, VI. 165

German stage (medieval), v. 36, 39, 41, 44, 48

German stage (modern), v. 346; VI. 49, 374

German theology, XII. 254, 318

German universities, XIII. 2, 9; XIV. 382, 410 ff.

Germanic kingdoms, the, XIV. 68

Germanic origins in Britain, XIV. 69, 70, 79

Germanist historical school, XIV. 51, 68, 69, 75

Germanus, St, of Auxerre, I. 70, 81

Germany, v. 25, 33, 43, 55, 101, 171, 222, 284, 286, 294 ff., 298, 299, 303, 306, 359; VI. 35; VII. 201, 283, 306, 309, 314, 345, 378; VIII. 182, 265, 330; IX. 6, 22, 70, 89, 106, 222, 315, 401, 406; x. 18, 19, 41, 63, 78, 79, 148, 200, 234, 353; XI. 102, 121, 136, 284, 303; XII. 34, 174, 263, 280, 282, 315, 343, 365, 367; XIII. 3, 20, 22, 156, 277, 281, 441, 455, 457; XIV. 8, 42, 53, 184, 293, 294, 382, 383

Germany and Byron, XII. 392 ff.

Germany and De Quincey, XII. 445

Germany and Shelley, XII. 402

Gernutus, x. 234

Gerrard, in *The Triumph of Love*, VI. 120

Gerrold, W., XIV. 536

Gerson, Jean, VIII. 59

Gerstenberg, H. W. von, v. 297, 298

Gert Beyers, XIV. 377

Gertrude, in *Hamlet*, v. 169

Gervase of Canterbury (*fl.* 1188), I. 173, 175, 449; II. 34

Gervase (Gervasius) of Tilbury (*fl.* 1211), *Otia Imperialia*, I. 173, 176, 192, 449, 453; VII. 504

Gervasius, I. 75

Gervinus, Georg Gottfried, V. 305

Gesner, Conrad, IV. 444

Gessner, Salomon, XI. 181; *Death of Abel*, XI. 182; XII. 48

Gesta Grayorum, V. 78

Gesta Romanorum, I. 135, 365, 367, 477; II. 85, 151, 207, 299, 300, 301, 314, 338, 482; III. 92, 489, 490, 494; V. 49; VI. 138, 139; XI. 366, 372

Geta, in *Confessio Amantis*, II. 148

Get Up and Bar the Door, II. 414

Geulincx, Arnold, VIII. 347

Geystes of Skoggan, The, IV. 327

Ghent, II. 338; V. 37; VIII. 160; XII. 365; XIII. 61

Ghent, church of Saint-Baron, XIII. 112

Ghibellines, XIII. 59, 60

Ghismonda (Boccaccio's), V. 72, 73

Ghose, J. C., XIV. 580

Ghost, the, in *Hamlet*, VI. 248

Ghost of King Charles II, The, VIII. 93

Ghulam Hussein Khan, *Siyar-ul-Muta'akh-khirin*, XIV. 335

'Giant Walker, The,' XIV. 320

Gibb, Elias John Wilkinson (1857–1901), XII. 503; *History of Ottoman Poetry*, XII. 342

Gibbet, in Farquhar's *Beaux' Stratagem*, VIII. 171

Gibbon, Edward (1666–1736), IX. 308

Gibbon, Edward, father of the historian, X. 299, 301, 305

Gibbon, Edward (1737–1794), I. 165, 244; VII. 220, 248; IX. 323, 381, 436, 574; X. 216, 240, 248, 280, 288 ff., 294, 297 ff. (main entry), 319, 320, 335, 390, 489, 506 ff., 527, *also see* Add.; XI. 260, 327, 400; XII. 300, 305, 318, 319, 322, 324, 477; XIII. 461; XIV. 461, 504

Address (on *Scriptores Rerum Angl.*), X. 312

Antiquities of the House of Brunswick, X. 311

Critical Enquiries concerning the Title of Charles VIII, X. 305

Decline and Fall of the Roman Empire, III. 332; X. 281, 298, 300, 304, 306 ff., 312 ff., 317, 318; XI. 71, 326

Essai sur l'Étude de la Littérature, X. 302

Introduction à l'Histoire…des Suisses, X. 304, 305

Letters (1814), X. 299

Mémoire Justificatif, X. 306

Memoirs, IX. 308, 313, 326, 414; X. 279, 289, 292, 297 ff., 302 ff., 306, 307, 310 ff., 316, 317

Miscellaneous Works, X. 304 ff., 308, 310, 312

Nomina Gentesque Antiquae Italiae, X. 305

Observations on the…VIth Book of the Aeneid, X. 305

Outlines of the History of the World— Ninth Century to Fifteenth, X. 305

Gibbon, Edward

  Private Letters, X. 299, 301, 306, 311

  Remarks on Blackstone's Commentaries, X. 305

  Vindication of some Passages, X. 308, 315

Gibbon, Hester, IX. 308, 514

Gibbon, Perceval, XIV. Add. 4

Gibbon Commemoration, Proceedings, X. 299

Gibbons, Grinling (1648–1720), VIII. 250

Gibbons, Orlando (1583–1625), IV. 113, 464

Gibbs, J. W. M., XIV. 477, 506

Gibicho, in *Waltharius*, I. 32

Gibraltar, XIV. 101

Gibson, Charles Dana, XIII. 540

Gibson, Edmund (1669–1748), bishop of London, IV. 422; VIII. 469; IX. 351, 353, 355, 512, 534, 539; X. 223, 226, 484

Gibson, John (d. 1852), XIII. 74

Gibson, J. Y., XIV. Add. 7

Gibson, Leon, *Tantara*, III. 191

Gibson, Mr, in Mrs Gaskell's *Wives and Daughters*, XIII. 381

Gichtel, Johann Georg, IX. 515, 523

Gide, André, XIV. 528

Gideon, IV. 43

Gideon, in *Confessio Amantis*, II. 151

Gife Langour makis men licht, III. 131

Giffard, lady Martha, VIII. 382; IX. 92, 98, 467; *Letters*, VIII. 380; *Life of Sir William Temple*, VIII. 379, 482, 483

Giffard, Stanley Lees (1788–1858), XIV. 534

Gifford, Edwin Hamilton (1820–1905), XII. 484

Gifford, George (d. 1620), VII. 371, 372, 390, 394, 395, 506; *A Dialogue of Witches and Witchcraft*, V. 478; VII. 371; *Discourse of the subtile Practises of Devilles*, IV. 325, 534, 535; VII. 371

Gifford, Humfrey (*fl.* 1580), III. 114, 188; VIII. 231; *For Souldiers*, III. 188; *Posie of Gilloflowers*, III. 188

Gifford, John (1758–1818), XI. 392

Gifford, William (1756–1826), VI. 1, 339, 341, 346, 359, 361; XI. 37, 39, 166, 177, 392, 393; XII. 142, 150 ff., 170, 175, 193, 429, 430, 432, 443, 526; XIV. 138; *The Baviad*, XI. 40; XII. 41; *The Maeviad*, XI. 40; XII. 41

Gifford lectures, XII. 333; XIV. 45, 48

Gifica (Gibicho), in *Widsith*, I. 34

Gifts of Men (Bi monna craeftum), I. 61, 428

Gil Brenton, II. 411

Gilbert, in *The Sparagus Garden*, VI. 227

Gilbert, Henry March, XII. 519

Gilbert, Sir Humphrey (1539?–1583), III. 114, 341, 438; IV. 67, 74, 76, 85, 86, 88; *Discourse of a Discoverie for a new passage to Cataia*, IV. 73, 456; *Queene Elizabethes Achademy*, III. 341, 438, 551; IV. 355

Gilbert, Sir John (1817–1897), XI. 483; XII. 448; XIV. 201, 238

Gilbert, Sir John Thomas (1829–1898), XII. 515; XIV. 489, 568
Celtic Records and Historic Literature of Ireland, XII. 361
Facsimiles of the National Manuscripts of Ireland, XII. 361
Historic and Municipal Documents of Ireland, XII. 361
History of Dublin, The, XIV. 328
History of the Irish Confederation, The, VII. 212; XIV. 96
History of the Viceroys of Ireland, The, XIV. 96
Gilbert, Mrs. *See* Taylor, Ann
Gilbert, William (1540–1603), IV. 278, 286, 508; VIII. 350; *De Magnete, magneticisque corporibus*, III. 425; IV. 277
Gilbert, William (1760?–1825?), XII. 416
Gilbert, William (1804–1890), XIII. 562
Gilbert, Sir William Schwenck (1836–1911), XIII. 162, 513, 518; XIV. 206, 544
Bab Ballads, The, XIII. 274
Broken Hearts, XIII. 273
Engaged, XIII. 274
Grand Duke, The, XIII. 274
Gretchen, XIII. 274
Palace of Truth, The, XIII. 273
Pygmalion and Galatea, XIII. 273, 274
Sweethearts, XIII. 274
Trial by Jury, XIII. 274
Wicked World, The, XIII. 273
Gilbert de la Porrée, I. 184, 185
Gilbert of Sempringham (1083?–1189), I. 229, 364
Gilbert the Englishman (*fl.* 1250), I. 453
Gilbertine order, I. 344
Gilby, Anthony (d. 1585), III. 45
Gilby, Goddard (*fl.* 1561), IV. 436
Gilchrist, Alexander (1828–1861), XI. 434; XIV. 525
Gilchrist, Mrs Anne (1828–1885), XII. 433, 437
Gilchrist, John, *Collection of Scottish Ballads*, IX. 373
Gilchrist, J. D. F., XIV. Add. 7
Gilchrist, Octavius Graham (1779–1823), IX. 451
Gildas (516?–570?), I. 5, 65 ff., 70, 71, 81, 247, 262, 350, 435, 461; III. 314
Gildemeister, Otto, V. 303
Gildon, Charles (1665–1724), VIII. 423, 428, 444, 445; IX. 86, 141, 142, 289, 475, 479, 504; X. 146; XI. 250; *A Comparison between the Two Stages*, IX. 141; *Life... of Mr D— De F—*, IX. 141; *Lives of the English Dramatic Poets*, IX. 141, 479
Gilds, English, V. 389
Giles, Jacob, VIII. 373, 428
Giles, Miss, X. 409
Giles, Nathaniel (d. 1634), V. 125; VI. 221, 257, 258, 283, 287 ff.
Giles, Peter (Aegidius), III. 18
Giles, Thomas (*fl.* 1608), VI. 344, 348
Gilfillan, George (1813–1878), XI. 390, 393, 402, 409, 417, 419, 423, 424, 437 ff.,

Gilfillan, George 442, 443; XII. 372, 379, 403, 407, 410, 412, 418, 431, 433, 437, 441, 445, 452, 472; XIII. 471, 477, 484, 499, 501, 509, 530; XIV. 481, 525, 555
Gilfillan, Robert (1798–1850), XI. 443; *O Why Left I my Hame*, XI. 243
Gilkes, Arthur H., XIV. 606
Gill, Abraham, IX. 12
Gill, Alexander, the elder (1565–1635), VII. 97, 98; *Logonomia Anglica*, VII. 332
Gill, Alexander, the younger (1597–1642), VII. 98
Gill, Sir David, XIV. Add. 7
Gill, Dr John (1697–1771), X. 387
Gill, John (1818–1910), XIV. 606
Gill, William Archer, XIII. 504
Gilla Coemgin, I. 70
Gillamor, in *The Misfortunes of Arthur*, V. 78
Gillespie, George (1613–1648), IX. 544
Gillian, in *Richard Casteler*, III. 369
Gillies, John (1712–1796), X. 518
Gillies, Robert Pearse (1788–1858), XII. 379, 445; XIV. 502
Gilliland, Thomas (*fl.* 1804–1816), X. 443
Gillingham, Kent, IV. 99; X. 25
Gilliver, Lawton, IX. 79; XI. 323
Gillman, James, XI. 121, 129, 417
Gillmans, the, of Highgate, XI. 417
Gillmore, Parker, XIV. Add. 7
Gillray, James (1757–1815), VIII. 160; XI. 392; XIV. 214, 216, 223, 225, 235, 540
Gillus. *See* Gildas
Gillyflower, Matthew, XI. 332
Gil Morrice (Percy's *Reliques*), X. 137
Gilpin, Bernard (1517–1583), IV. 225, 234, 492
Gilpin, William (1724–1804), XIV. 217, 543, 544; *Observations on the River Wye*, XIV. 221; *Picturesque Remarks*, XIV. 221; *Remarks on Forest Scenery*, XIV. 221
Gilpin, William Sawrey (1762–1843), XIV. 221
Gilpin Horner, border legend, XII. 7, 8
Gilpin's Rig (1783?), XI. 402
Gilston, XII. 182
Ginevra, in Rogers's *Italy*, XII. 98
'Gingerbread, Giles,' XI. 377
Ginsburg, Christian David (1831–1914), XII. 501; *Facsimiles of MSS. of the Hebrew Bible*, XII. 341
Gioliti's publishing house, V. 71
Giordano, Paolo, duke of Bracciano, VI. 173
Giovanna of Naples, XII. 212
Giovanni, in *The White Divel*, VI. 175, 177
Giovanni, in *Tis Pitty Shees a Whore*, VI. 195
Giovanni, prince, in *The Great Duke of Florence*, VI. 156, 158
Giovio, Paolo, IV. 132, 444
Giraffi, Alessandro, VII. 446
Giraldo, Baptista, IV. 444
Giraldus, X. 293

Giraldus Cambrensis (1146?-1220?), I. 160, 171, 173, 176, 177, 188 ff., 194 ff., 202, 243, 292, 449, 451, 453; II. 76; III. 314, 319; IV. 67; XII. 5, 10; *Topographia Hibernica*, II. 342, 483, 488

Girard, father, XIV. 404

Girard, Guillaume, *Life of the Duke of Espernon*, IX. 276, 499

Girardin, Émile de, XIII. 273

Girls' Public Day School company, XIV. 430

Girondists, the, XI. 157

Gisborne, Thomas (1758-1846), XII. 472

Gisippus, v. 103

Gismond of Salerne, v. 72, 73, 75 ff., 399

Gissing, George Robert (1857-1903), XIII. 455 ff., 533, 543, 573
  Born in Exile, XIII. 455, 458, 459
  By the Ionian Sea, XIII. 456, 461
  Charles Dickens: A Critical Study, XIII. 456
  Crown of Life, The, XIII. 456, 460
  Demos, XIII. 455, 458
  Denzil Quarrier, XIII. 455
  Dickens in Memory, XIII. 456
  Emancipated, The, XIII. 455, 460
  Eve's Ransom, XIII. 456, 458, 460
  Forster's Life of Dickens (abridgment), XIII. 456
  House of Cobwebs, XIII. 456, 458
  Human Odds and Ends, XIII. 456, 458
  In the Year of Jubilee, XIII. 455, 458
  Isabel Clarendon, XIII. 455, 457, 460
  Letters from George Gissing to Edward Clodd, XIII. 457
  Life's Morning, A, XIII. 455, 460
  'Mount of Refuge, The,' XIII. 461
  Nether World, The, XIII. 455, 458
  New Grubb Street, XIII. 455, 458 ff.
  Odd Women, The, XIII. 455, 458 ff.
  Our Friend the Charlatan, XIII. 456, 460
  Paying Guest, The, XIII. 456
  Private Papers of Henry Ryecroft, The, XIII. 456, 462
  Sleeping Fires, XIII. 455
  Thyrza, XIII. 455, 458, 459
  Town Traveller, The, XIII. 456, 459
  Unclassed, The, XIII. 455
  Veranilda, XIII. 456, 461
  Whirlpool, The, XIII. 456, 460
  Will Warburton, XIII. 456, 459
  Workers in the Dawn, XIII. 455

Given, John L., XIV. 531

Gladstone, John Hall, XIV. 557

Gladstone, Mary, XIV. 484

Gladstone, William Ewart (1809-1898), X. 358, 361; XI. 4; XII. 152, 155, 255, 312, 426, 484; XIII. 23, 24, 31, 38, 477; XIV. 119, 128, 131, 132, 134 ff. (main entry), 195, 198, 199, 509, 513
  Bulgarian Horrors, XIV. 136
  Homeric Synchronism, XII. 334
  Juventus Mundi, XII. 334
  Lessons in Massacre, XIV. 136
  Letters to the Earl of Aberdeen, XIV. 136

Gladstone, William Ewart
  State in its Relations with the Church, The, XIV. 135
  Studies on Homer, XII. 334
  Vatican Decrees, The, XIV. 136
  Vaticanism, XIV. 136

Glamorganshire, XII. 512

Glanvill, Joseph (1636-1680), VII. 471, 507, 517, *also see* Add.; VIII. 292, 454, 456; IX. 436
  Antifanatick Theologie, and Free Philosophy, VII. 303
  Lux Orientalis, VIII. 291
  Philosophical Considerations touching Witches and Witchcraft, VII. 395
  Plus Ultra, VIII. 291
  Sadducismus Triumphatus, VIII. 291
  Scepsis Scientifica, VII. 302
  Vanity of Dogmatizing, The, VII. 302, 393

Glanville, Ernest, XIV. Add. 7

Glanville, Ranulf de (d. 1190), I. 173, 181, 195, 449; VIII. 311, 312, 465

Glanville, Sir Reginald, in Lytton's *Pelham*, XII. 417

Glapthorne, Henry (*fl.* 1639), VI. 240, 456; VII. 88
  Albertus Wallenstein, VI. 240
  Argalus and Parthenia, III. 355; VI. 240
  Ladies Privilege, The, VI. 240
  The Paraside, a Revenge for Honour, VI. 35

Glas, John (1695-1773), IX. 548

Glas Keraint, the Welsh, II. 412

Glascock, William Nugent (1787?-1847), XII. 251, 449

'Glascurion,' in Chaucer's *House of Fame*, II. 412

Glasgerion, II. 412

Glasgow, VIII. 298; IX. 133, 193; X. 132, 188, 191, 335, 348; XI. 237, 244, 341, 373; XII. 17, 29, 350, 358, 370, 419, 513, 515; XIII. 161, 194; XIV. 279, 286, 410

Glasgow, Andersonian institution, XIV. 407

Glasgow, Mechanics' institution, XIV. 407, 408

Glasgow, university of, II. 245, 369, 371; III. 151, 426; IV. 276; IX. 290, 301; X. 36; XII. 143, 157, 158, 165, 330, 332, 371, 409, 521; XIV. 7, 43, 45, 267

Glasgow Courier, The, XI. 237

Glasgow Herald, The, XIV. 531

Glasgow press, XI. 470; XII. 520

Glasgow Sentinel, The, XI. 236

Glasgow Theatrical Register, The, XI. 452

Glasgow University Magazine, The, XIV 209, 538

Glasscock, Thomas, X. 386

Glastonbury, I. 150, 164, 198, 243, 262, 272, 313; IV. 417; IX. 535; X. 20

Glastonia, abbey of, in *Life of Gildas*, I. 262

Glaucilla, in *Sicelides*, VI. 323

Glaucus, in Keats's *Endymion*, XII. 82

Gleanings from an Old Portfolio, XI. 348

Gleig, George Robert (1796–1888), XII. 303, 449, *also see* Add.

Glen, William (1789–1826), XI. 443; XII. 416; *Wae's me for Prince Charlie*, XI. 243

Glencairn, earls of. *See* Cunningham, Alexander; Cunningham, James

Glencoe, massacre of, IX. 564; XIV. 65

Glendower, Owen, in *Henry IV*, V. 187; XIV. 307

Glenesk, lord. *See* Borthwick, Sir Algernon

Glenfallen, lord and lady, in Le Fanu's story, XIII. 415, 416

'Glenkroden,' river, XI. 287

Glenriddell MSS. (Burns), XI. 435, 438

Glewlwyd Gavaelvawr or Glewlwyd of the Mighty Grasp, one of Arthur's porters, I. 251

Gliddon, George Robins (1809–1857), XII. 500

Glisson, Francis (1597–1677), VIII. 359, 363, 473, 477; XIV. 281

Globe, Le, V. 302

Globe, The, XIV. 185, 194, 316, 530, 533

Globe and Blackfriars company, XIII. 256

Glogau, siege of, VII. 22

'Glomery, Master of' (*Magister Glomerial*), II. 346, 347, 356

Gloriana, in *The Faerie Queene*, III. 234, 236, 246; V. 183

Glories of Ireland, The, XIV. 307

Glorious Tipto, Sir, in *The New Inne*, VI. 25

Glossaries, IV. 424

Glossin, in Scott's *Guy Mannering*, XII. 21

Gloster, earl of, in *Looke about You*, V. 320, 323

Gloster, earl of, in Thomson's *Edward and Eleonora*, X. 109

Gloucester, II. 349; VIII. 245; IX. 296, 341, 393, 531; XI. 484; XII. 329, 340, 510; XIV. 389

Gloucester, duke of, in *Henry VI*, V. 186

Gloucester, dukes of. *See* Henry (1639–1660); Humphrey (1391–1447); Thomas (1355–1397); William (1689–1700)

Gloucester, earl of, in *King Lear*, III. 355; V. 204, 262

Gloucester, earl of. *See* Robert (d. 1147)

Gloucester, or South English Legendary. See Legendary

Gloucester academy, X. 386

Gloucester Chronicle. See Robert of Gloucester

Gloucester Journal, The, XIV. 169

Gloucestershire, III. 39; V. 187; VII. 312; X. 111; XII. 346

Glover, Arnold, X. 44; XI. 150; XII. 167, 431

Glover, James Mackey, XIII. 514

Glover, Jean (1758–1801), IX. 374

Glover, Julia (1779–1850), VIII. 186

Glover, Richard (1712–1785), IX. 183; X. 148, 434, 455; XI. 402

Admiral Hosier's Ghost, X. 148, 233

Atheniad, The, X. 148

Glover, Richard
Boadicea, XI. 258
Leonidas, X. 148; XI. 323
Medea, XI. 179

Glover, Robert (1544–1588), III. 528

Glover, Stephen (d. 1869), XII. 501, 507

Glover, William, X. 195, 482, 483

Gloys, James, chaplain to Margaret Paston, II. 306

Glutton, in *Piers the Plowman*, II. 12, 16, 23

Gluttony, in *Confessio Amantis*, II. 147, 149

Gluttony, in *The Passetyme of Pleasure*, II. 236

Gnaphaeus, William, *Acolastus*, III. 363; V. 101, 109, 110, 112, 113, 410, 412

Gnomaticus, in *The Glasse of Governement*, V. 113

Gnomic Verses, O.E., I. 218, 428, 432

'Go from my Window,' IX. 362

Goad, Caroline, X. Add.

Gobble, Mrs, in Smollett's *Sir Launcelot Greaves*, X. 41

Gobbo, in *The Merchant of Venice*, V. 183

Gobelive, Godfrey, in *The Passetyme of Pleasure*, II. 225, 232, 233, 235

Gobrias, in *Argenis*, IV. 259

God Ureism of ure Lefdi, On (A Good Orison of Our Lady), I. 232, 450

Godard, in *Havelok*, I. 303

Godard, J. G., XIV. 601

Goddard, William (*fl.* 1615), IV. 520

Godden, Gertrude M., X. 29, 418

Godefroy of Le Mans, V. 38

Godfrey, in *Orlando Furioso*, III. 230

Godfrey, captain, XIV. 229, 544; *The Useful Art of Self-defence*, XIV. 230

Godfrey, Sir Edmund Berry (1621–1678), VIII. 86, 189, 257; IX. 6

Godfrey, G. W., XIII. 519

Godfrey, Walter H., VI. 269

Godfrey of Bologne, II. 313, 485

Godfrey of Bouillon, cycle of, I. 291

Godfrey of Cambrai and Winchester, I. 191, 454

Godfrey of Viterbo, II. 144, 150

Godiva, lady, I. 364; IV. 174

Godkin, Edwin Lawrence, XIV. 534

Godley, Alfred Denis, XII. 410, 421, 422

Godley, A. D., XIV. 537

Godly Queene Hester, V. 393

Godman, Frederick Du Cane, XIV. 297

Godolphin, Cornwall, VII. 86

Godolphin, Francis, 2nd earl of (1678–1766), VIII. 159

Godolphin, John (1617–1678), IV. 456; VIII. 468

Godolphin, Mrs (Margaret Blagge) (1652–1678), VIII. 250, 251, 264

Godolphin, Sidney (1610–1643), VII. 87, 218; VIII. 133, 215
Aeneid, trans., VII. 86
Chorus, VII. 86
Meditation, VII. 86
'No more unto my thoughts appear,' VII. 86

Godolphin, Sidney
  'Or love me less or love me more,' VII. 86
  Poem to Sandys, VII. 86
  Psalms, paraphrase of the, VII. 86
  "'Tis Affection but dissembled,' VII. 86
Godolphin, Sidney, 1st earl of (1645–1712), VIII. 251; IX. 12, 13, 44, 94, 95, 150, 151
Godolphin, Sir William (d. 1613), VII. 86
Godolphin, Sir William (1634?–1696), VIII. 380
Godric, in *Battle of Maldon*, I. 145
Godric, St (1065?–1170), I. 375; *Cantus Beati Godrici*, I. 220, 458
Godrich, household of, in *Havelok*, I. 303, 304
Godstow bridge, XIII. 93
Godwin, I. 111, 139
Godwin, F., *Voyaye of Domingo Gonsalez*, IX. 106
Godwin, Francis (1562–1633), VII. 444
Godwin, Mrs Mary Jane (Mrs Clairmont), XI. 294; XII. 189, 191
Godwin, Mrs Mary Wollstonecraft (1759–1797), XI. 43 ff., 189, 293, 394, 395; *also see* Add.; XII. 61, 191; XIV. 388, 600; *Vindication of the Rights of Women*, XI. 43, 44; XIV. 400
Godwin, Mary Wollstonecraft (1797–1851). *See* Shelley, Mrs
Godwin, William (1756–1836), VII. 452; XI. 24, 43 ff., 48, 98, 119, 189, 277, 292 ff. (main entry), 393, 395, 399, *also see* Add.; XII. 39, 59, 60, 64, 65, 67, 73, 93, 188, 190, 248, 401 ff.; XIII. 258, 427; XIV. 137, 237, 606
  Caleb Williams, X. 59; XI. 43, 46, 280, 292 ff.; XIII. 418, 437
  Cloudesley, XI. 292
  Enquiry concerning political justice, XIV. 400
  Fleetwood, XI. 292
  Juvenile Library, XI. 385
  Life of Chaucer, XII. 146
  Mandeville, XI. 292
  Political Justice, XI. 43, 46, 73, 276, 292, 294
  St Leon, XI. 43, 46, 285, 292, 293; XIII. 419
  See, also, Baldwin, Edwin
Godwine, earl, XIV. 72
Goertz, baron de, IX. 20
Goethe, Johann Wolfgang von, V. 209, 298 ff., 305, 465; VIII. 49; X. 52, 227, 228, 232, 422, 488; XI. 42, 135, 416; XII. 7, 38, 42, 64, 157, 168, 254, 375, 377, 379, 380, 392, 394, 397, 402, 403, 480, 526, 527; XIII. 1, 6, 7, 9, 10, 18, 21, 90, 93, 94, 105, 153, 277, 417, 442, 464, 465; XIV. 109, 113
  Faust, V. 20; XI. 131; XII. 34, 47, 48, 86; XIII. 360, 467; XIV. 138, 367
  Goetz von Berlichingen, V. 301; XII. 4
  Hermann und Dorothea, XIII. 105, 380
  Shakespeare als Dichter überhaupt, XI. 284

Goethe, Johann Wolfgang von
  Shakespeare als Theaterdichter, XI. 283
  Sprüche in Prosa, X. 52
  Werther, X. 19, 60
  Wilhelm Meister, V. 299, 300, 304; X. 49, 52; XIII. 4, 5, 346
Goffe, Thomas (1591–1629), VI. 144, 369, 473, 491; VIII. 436; *The Careless Shepherdess*, VI. 366
Gog and Magog, in Dickens's *Master Humphrey's Clock*, XIII. 319
Gog Magog, II. 275, 278
Golagros and Gawane, I. 312, 333, 334, 468; II. 112, 121, 123, 124, 126, 450
Goldberg, Isaac, XIII. 519
Goldburgh, in *Havelok*, I. 303, 304, 351
Golden Cross, the, in *The Pickwick Papers*, XIII. 310
'Golden Hind' (ship), IV. 74
Golden Legend, The, I. 55, 134, 343; II. 80, 127, 300, 314, 316, 333 ff., 482, 485; V. 15
Golden Rump, The, X. 84
Golden Treasury, The, XIII. 192
Golden Treasury series, XIII. 95, 196
Goldey (*i.e.* Lodge), IV. 180
Goldfinch, in Holcroft's *Road to Ruin*, XI. 277
Goldfinch, The, IX. 566
Goldhan, A. B., XIII. 564
Golding, Arthur (1536?–1605?), III. 302, 303, 446, 448; IV. 4 ff., 8, 19 ff., 24, 397, 435, 437 ff., 441, 442, 445, 447, 448; V. 394
  Translations:
  Caesar's *Gallic War*, IV. 4, 21, 397, 435
  Histories of Trogus Pompeius, The abridgment of the, IV. 21
  Ovid's *Metamorphoses*, IV. 19, 20, 397, 438
  Politicke, Moral and Martial Discourses, IV. 21
  Worke concerning Benefyting, The, IV. 6
Goldingham, William, VI. 473
Goldoni, Carlo, X. 19, 411
Goldring, Maude, XIII. 558
Goldsborough, Miles, VI. 307
Goldsmith, Catharine, X. 198
Goldsmith, Charles, X. 196
Goldsmith, Henry, X. 197, 199, 201, 205, 207, 209, 212
Goldsmith, Oliver (1728–1774), II. 413; IV. 40; VI. 51; VIII. 137; IX. 166, 167, 173, 220, 223, 325, 481; X. 39, 47, 68, 195 ff. (main entry), 263, 317, 318, 344, 422, 475, 480 ff., 489, 501, *also see* Add.; XI. 32, 163, 206, 207, 246, 252, 260, 262, 265, 266, 271, 376, 377, 385, 448, 466, 479, 489; XII. 43, 97, 132; XIII. 226, 244, 269, 445; XIV. 61, 169, 223, 313, 320, 439, 446, 448, 451, 552
  Adventures of a Strolling Player, X. 205
  Beauties of English Poesy, X. 210
  Bee, The, X. 205, 206, 208
  Captivity, The, X. 207, 480
  City Night-Piece, A, X. 205

Goldsmith, Oliver
 Description of an Author's Bedchamber,
  x. 205
 Deserted Village, The, x. 134, 212, 213,
  470; xi. 2, 144, 145, 361
 Double Transformation, x. 198, 208
 'Edinburgh, 1753,' x. 205
 Elegy on Mrs Mary Blaize, x. 201, 205
 English Grammar, x. 210
 *Enquiry into the Present State of Polite
  Learning*, x. 92, 203 ff., 207, 211
 Essay on the Theatre, x. 92
 Essays, x. 208, 210
 Fame Machine, The, x. 205
 Gift, The, x. 205
 Good-Natur'd Man, The, x. 91, 92, 211,
  212, 214, 465, 470; xi. 261, 263
 Haunch of Venison, The, x. 214, 215
 Hermit (The) or Edwin and Angelina,
  x. 209
 History of Animated Nature, x. 212
 History of England, x. 212, 293, 501
 *History of England in Letters from a
  Nobleman to his Son*, x. 207
 History of Mecklenburgh, x. 206
 History of Philosophy, x. 210
 Life of Bolingbroke, x. 213
 Life of Richard Nash, x. 206
 Memoirs of a Protestant, x. 203
 Memoirs of Voltaire, x. 204, 206
 New Simile, The, x. 208
 *Old House, a New Inn (She Stoops to
  Conquer)*, x. 214
 On the Death of Wolfe, x. 205
 'On the Stage,' x. 204
 Plutarch's Lives, x. 206
 Poems for Young Ladies, x. 210
 Present State of Polite Learning, The,
  xi. 323, 331
 Retaliation, x. 215
 Reverie in the Boar's Head Tavern, x. 205
 Roman History, x. 212, 213
 She Stoops to Conquer, x. 91, 197, 214,
  479; xi. 265
 Traveller, The, x. 128, 170, 201, 205,
  207, 208, 210, 213, 467, 470; xii. 42
 Vicar of Wakefield, The, x. 15, 25, 44,
  195, 200, 203, 206 ff.; xi. 2; xiii. 524
 Vida's Game of Chess, x. 480
Golgotha, v. 45
Goliardi, v. 27
Goliardic literature, ii. 256, 499
Golias, bishop, and *Goliardic Poems*, i.
 177, 189, 190, 364
Goliath, in Cowley's *Davideis*, vii. 67
Goliath, in *Cursor Mundi*, i. 343
Gollancz, Sir Israel, i. 58, 61, 428; ii. 37
'Golldyn Arber in the Arche yerd of
 Plesyer, the,' vi. 283
Gómara, Francisco Lopez de, iv. 444
Gomberville, M. Le Roy de, viii. 15;
 Polexandre, vii. 391; viii. 371
Gomersal, Robert (1602–1646?), vii. 88,
 412
Gomme, Sir Laurence, xii. 506
Goncourt, Edmond de, xiii. 457

Goncourt, Jules de, xiii. 457
Gondibert, in D'Avenant's *Gondibert*, vii.
 71
Gondomar, don S. de Acuña, marquis de,
 ambassador, v. 365, 478; vi. 58, 79,
 248; vii. 205
Goneril, in *King Lear*, v. 169
Gongora y Argote, Luis de, iv. 213; vii.
 83
Gongorism, iii. 348; iv. 213
Gonville, Edmund (d. 1351), ii. 354
Gonzalo, in *The Tempest*, v. 207
Gooch, George Peabody, xiii. 545; xiv.
 484; *English History and Historians*, xii.
 313; xiv. 117
Good, John Mason (1764–1827), x. 526
Good Counsel, ii. 472, 473
Good Hope, cape of, iv. 85, 86, 99
Good Hope, in *The Kingis Quair*, ii. 242
Good Old Cause Revived, viii. 91
Good Words, xii. 472; xiii. 366
Goodall, Walter (1706?–1766), x. 501;
 Examination of the [Casket] Letters, x.
 288
Goodcole, Henry (1586–1641), iv. 535
Goodcoll, in *Discoverie of the Knights of the
 Poste*, iv. 350
Good-deeds, in *Every-man*, v. 54
Goode, William (*fl.* 1644), *Intelligence*, vii.
 351
Goode, William (1801–1868), xii. 472
Goodere, Anne (*fl.* 1595), iv. 174 ff., 190,
 194, 211
Goodere, Frances, iv. 174
Goodere, Sir Henry, of Powlsworth, iv.
 169, 174, 204, 205, 216, 221, 265
Goodere, Sir Henry, the younger, iv. 170
Goodhope, in *Magnyfycence*, iii. 77
Goodluck, in *Ralph Roister Doister*, v. 106
Goodman, Christopher (1520?–1603), iv.
 303, 511
Goodman, Gabriel (1529?–1601), vii. 333,
 450
Goodman, Godfrey (1583–1656), iv. 431;
 vii. 450
Goodman, W., xiii. 514
Goodrich, ix. 91
Goodrich, Samuel Griswold, xi. 387, 481.
 See, also, Parley, Peter
Goodwill, in Bunyan's *Pilgrim's Progress*,
 vii. 173
Goodwin, Charles Wycliffe (1817–1878),
 xii. 294, 466
Goodwin, Philip (d. 1699), vii. 510
Goodwin, Thomas, junior (1650?–1716),
 x. 385
Goody Two Shoes, xi. 376
Googe, Barnabe (1540–1594), iii. 177,
 185, 186, 187, 219, 302, 508; iv. 110,
 121, 171, 370, 447, 538
 Cupido Conquered, ii. 228; iii. 185
 Eclogs, Epytaphes and Sonettes, iii. 185,
 186, 523
 Four bookes of Husbandry, iv. 371, 511
 Zodiacus Vitae, translation of, iii. 185
Goose, mother, xi. 375

Goranson, x. 490

Gorboduc, III. 284, 301; IV. 397; V. 66 ff., 85, 152, 155, 239, 337, 395; VII. 271; VIII. 223, 224; x. 70; XII. 190

Gordale scar, x. 101

Gordon, Ada, XII. 32

Gordon, Adam Lindsay (1833–1870), XIV. 365 ff., 371, 586

Ashtaroth, XIV. 367

Bush Ballads, XIV. 366, 367

Doubtful Dreams, XIV. 367

How we beat the Favourite, XIV. 367

Ride from the Wreck, The, XIV. 367

Sea Spray and Smoke Drift, XIV. 367

Sick Stockrider, The, XIV. 366, 367

Whisperings in Wattle-Boughs, XIV. 367

Wolf and Hound, XIV. 366, 367

Gordon, Alexander (d. 1752), IX. 553

Gordon, Alexander (1692?–1754?), IX. 355; *Itinerarium Septentrionale*, IX. 352, 534

Gordon, Catherine, of Gight, XII. 31

Gordon, Sir Cosmo, XII. 394

Gordon, lord George (1751–1793), XIII. 320; XIV. 121

Gordon, George Hamilton, 4th earl of Aberdeen (1784–1860), XIV. 134, 181, 182, 184, 420, 508

Gordon, James (1615?–1686), IX. 550

Gordon, Jane, duchess of (1749?–1812), XI. 220

Gordon, Margaret, XIII. 3

Gordon, Mrs Mary, XII. 445

Gordon, Patrick (*fl.* 1614–1650), IX. 555

Gordon, surgeon in Glasgow, x. 36

Gordon, Thomas (d. 1750), IX. 462, 471

Gordon, William (*fl.* 1726), IX. 553

Gordon riots, XI. 27. *See, also,* Gordon, lord George

Gore, Catherine Grace Frances (1799–1861), XII. 449; *Mothers and Daughters*, XII. 246; *Mrs Armytage, or Female Domination*, XII. 246

Gorges, lord, IX. 343

Gorges, Sir Arthur (d. 1625), IV. 438

Gorges, Sir Tristram, IV. 94

Gorges, William, IV. 456

Gorgious Gallery of Gallant Inventions, A, III. 190, 191, 248, 511, 523; IV. 471. *See, also,* Proctor, Thomas

Gorgo, in *The Adoniazusae*, III. 226

Gorgonius, in *The Scourge of Folly*, IV. 334

Gorhambury, IV. 279; VII. 203, 283

Goring, Charles, *Irene, or the Fair Greek*, x. 161

Goring, George, lord (1608–1657), VII. 22

Gorion, Joseph Ben, IV. 323

Görlitz, IX. 314

Gorlois, in Arthurian legend, I. 259

Gorlois, in *The Misfortunes of Arthur*, v. 77, 78

Goscelin (*fl.* 1099), II. 479

Gosnold, Bartholomew (d. 1609), IV. 94

Gospels, Early English, I. 444

Gosse, Edmund, IV. 203, 217, 241; VIII. 18; IX. 169; XI. 491; XII. 115, 173, 414, 432; XIII. 53, 211, 482, 484, 486, 494, 495, 508, 558, *also see* Add. 2; XIV. 526, 576; *Questions at Issue*, XIII. 457

Gosson, Stephen (1554–1624), III. 491; IV. 317, 323, 492, 518; v. 139, 359, 478; VI. 397, 461, 493

Apologie for the Schoole of Abuse, An, VI. 389, 392

Captain Mario, The Comedie of, v. 116; VI. 387

Catalines Conspiracy, VI. 387

Ephemerides of Phialo, The, VI. 388, 389

Playes Confuted in five Actions, v. 116; VI. 391, 392, 406

Pleasant Quippes for Upstart Gentlewomen, IV. 329; VI. 392

Pleasaunt invective against Poets, Pipers, Plaiers, Jesters and such like Caterpillers of a Commonwealth, VI. 387

Praise at Parting, VI. 387

School of Abuse, The, III. 299, 300, 526; v. 360; VI. 387 ff., 391

'Gossouin, Maistre,' II. 313

Goswell street, in *The Pickwick Papers*, XIII. 310

Gosynhyll, Edward (*fl.* 1560), III. 486; *The Prayse of all women, called Mulierum paean*, III. 90; *The Schole-house of women*, III. 84, 89, 90, 97

Götaland, I. 26, 27

Götar (Gautoi), I. 27

Gothic architecture, x. 217, 218, 238; XIV. 151, 246

Gothic art, x. 219; XI. 181

'Gothic Castle, The,' x. 245

Gothic gospels, x. 223, 225

Gothic language, XII. 326, 327, 343

Gothic nations, x. 222

'Gothic' romances, x. 233

Gothic rule in Italy, XII. 322

Gothic taste, x. 239

'Gothick' manner, the, x. 219

Goths, the, I. 21, 35; XIII. 363; XIV. 302

Gott, Samuel, VII. 421, 517

Gottfried von Strassburg, I. 268, 273, 316

Göttingen, II. 327

Gottlieb, T., IV. 419

Gottsched, J. C., v. 286, 290, 295

Gouda, II. 314

Gouge, William (1578–1653), VII. 322

Gough, Richard (1735–1809), XI. 530; x. 255; XII. 510; *Anecdotes of British Topography*, XI. 335; XII. 344, 345; 'History of the Society of Antiquaries,' XII. 345; *Sepulchral Monuments of Great Britain*, XII. 345

Goujon, French cadet, x. 203

Goulart, *Histoires Admirables*, VI. 183

Gould, G. M., XIII. 471; XIV. 166, 519

Gould, Robert (d. 1709?), VIII. 91, 404, 410

Gouldman, Francis (d. 1688?), VII. 486

Gouldsbury, Cullen, XIV. Add. 4, 7

Goupy, Joseph (d. 1763), XIV. 213

Gourgand, General, XII. 379

Gourlaw, Robert (d. 1585), IV. 414
Governance, a greyhound, in *The Passetyme of Pleasure*, II. 229
Governesses' Benevolent institution, XIV.
429
Government of Princes, the pseudo-Aristo-
telian, II. 284
Gow, Niel, XI. 233
Gowans, the, in *Little Dorrit*, XIII. 331
Go-well, in *Piers the Plowman*, II. 19
Gower, John (1325?–1408), I. 191, 204,
277, 280, 282, 332, 389; II. 133–155
(main entry), 159, 162, 164, 174, 183,
197, 210, 214, 225, 227, 228, 243, 252,
261, 262, 419, 422, 452 ff.; III. 57, 68,
70, 192, 273 ff., 281, 301, 440; V. 221;
VI. 144, 311; VIII. 232; X. 239; XII. 504;
XIII. 211, 238
  *Carmen de pacis commendacione, In
  Praise of Peace*, II. 153
  Cinkante Balades, II. 138, 154
  Confessio Amantis, I. 135, 286, 291, 347,
  352; II. 134, 142, 143, 145 ff. (main
  entry), 155, 214, 219, 230, 314; III. 57
  Cronica Tripertita, II. 137, 154
  Henry IV, English poem to, II. 153
  *Mirour de l'Omme (Speculum Hominis,
  Speculum Meditantis)*, II. 134, 137 ff.,
  147, 174; III. 192
  Vox Clamantis, II. 136 ff., 143 ff., 154
Gower, Sir Robert, of Brabourne, II. 134
Gownsman, The, XIII. 277; XIV. 207
Gowrie conspiracy, the, VI. 347; VII. 454
Gowther, Sir, I. 311, 314, 471
Grabbe, Christian, V. 303
Grabut, monsieur, VIII. 135
'Gracchus,' XIV. 513
Grace, a greyhound, in *The Passetyme of
Pleasure*, II. 229
Grace, in *The Example of Virtue*, II. 227,
228
Grace-dieu (Leicestershire), VI. 111
Grâce Dieu, house of, in de Guileville's
Pilgrimage of the Sowle, VII. 173
Gradgrinds, the, in Dickens's *Hard Times*,
XIII. 330
Gradus ad Parnassum, VIII. 216
Graeci, Poetae Minores, XII. 328
Graelent, I. 295
Graevius, John George, IX. 331, 332, 524
Graf, Urs, II. 329
Grafton, III. 337
Grafton, duke of. *See* Fitzroy, Augustus
Henry
Grafton, Richard (d. 1572), I. 170; III.
44, 316, 323, 332, 334, 337, 529; IV. 400;
Abridgemen of the Chronicles of England,
IV. 396; *A Chronicle at Large*, IV. 396;
Grammar of Oxford and Cambridge, IV.
407
Graham, colonel, of Gartmore, XI. 232
Graham, Dougal (1724–1779), IX. 564, 566
  Comical Transactions of Lothian Tam,
  IX. 373
  Full...Account of the Rebellion, IX. 373
  History of Buchhaven, IX. 373

Graham, Dougal
  Jocky and Maggie's Courtship, IX. 373
  Turnimspike, The, IX. 373
Graham, George (d. 1767), *Telemachus*,
X. 467
Graham, H. G., XIV. 535
Graham, James (1612–1650), 1st marquis
of Montrose, IX. 193, 550, 556; XII. 21
Graham, James (d. 1742), 4th marquis
and 1st duke of Montrose, IX. 215; X.
94
Graham, Sir James, VI. 47
Graham, Sir James Robert George (1792–
1861), XIV. 130, 181, 326, 510
Graham, John, of Claverhouse, viscount
Dundee (1649?–1689), IX. 264, 363, 564;
XII. 21; XIV. 65
Graham, Patrick (d. 1478), II. 369
Graham, Richard (*fl.* 1680–1720), IX. 444
Graham, R. B. Cunningham, XIII. 493
Graham, Thomas, lord Lynedoch (1748–
1843), X. 230
Graham, Thomas (1805–1869), XIV. 272,
279, 557
Graham, William (1839–1911), XIV. 473
Graham of Balgowan, X. 230
Graham's Town, XIV. 377
Grahame, James (1765–1811), XI. 443;
  Birds of Scotland, XI. 244; *Mary Queen
  of Scots*, XI. 244; *The Sabbath*, XI. 244
Grahame, Simion (1570?–1614), VII. 406;
IX. 555
Grail, Gilbert, in Gissing's *Thyrza*, XIII.
459
Grail, the Holy (St Graal), in Arthurian
romance, I. 261, 270 ff., 462, 469
Grail, the Holy, Malory on, II. 336, 337
Grail, the Holy, Map and the prose *Quest
of*, I. 190, 270 ff.
Grainger, James (1721?–1766), X. 40, 455,
also see Add.; *The Sugar Cane*, X. 204,
467
Grammar, lady, in *The Passetyme of
Pleasure*, II. 225
Grammar schools, English, II. 70, 356 ff.,
VII. 491 ff.
Gramont, marshal de, brother of P. de
Gramont, VIII. 263
Gramont, Philibert, comte de, VIII. 207,
209, 262, 266, 359; key to the *Memoirs
of the Comte de Gramont*, VIII. 261;
Mémoires de Gramont, VIII. 199, 268;
IX. 236
Grampian club, X. 193
Grampians, the, XII. 31
Gramsbergen, Matthus, V. 285
Granada, IV. 9
Granada, Luis de, IV. 444
Granard, XIV. 311
Granby, marquis of. *See* Manners, John
Grand Combatant, mounsier, French
braggadocio, in *Club Law*, VI. 309
'Grand Council,' The, X. 403
Grandcourt, in *Daniel Deronda*, XIII. 399,
400
Grande Chartreuse, VII. 338; X. 119, 127

Grandison, Sir Charles, in Richardson's novel, VIII. 308; X. 2. 10, 11, 14, 18, 31, 62; XI. 356; XII. 128; XIII. 390

Grandison, Charlotte, in Richardson's novel, X. 11

Grandison, John (1292?–1369), bishop of Exeter, V. 25, 55

Granger, James (1723–1776), XIV. 502

Grant, Sir Alexander (1826–1884), XII. 334, 484, 487; XIV. 595

Grant, Mrs Anne, of Laggan (1755–1838), XI. 443; XIV. 502
  Eighteen Hundred and Thirteen, XI. 232
  Letters from the Mountains, XI. 232
  O Where tell me Where, XI. 232
  Poems, XI. 232

Grant, Charles, baron Glenelg (1778–1866), XII. 417

Grant, or Graunt, Edward (1540?–1601), *Spicilegium*, III. 429

Grant, Mrs Elizabeth, of Carron (Mrs Murray: 1745?–1814), *Roy's wife of Aldivalloch*, XI. 232

Grant, George Monro (1835–1902), XIV. 359, 583

Grant, James (1802–1879), XIV. 531; *The Newspaper Press*, XIV. 177

Grant, James (1822–1887), XIII. 471, 562

Grant, James (1840–1885), XIV. 591

Grant, James Augustus (1827–1892), XIV. 552

Grant, Sir Robert (1779–1838), XII. 417

Grant, Robert Edmond (1793–1874), XIV. 298, 560

Grant, Roger, IX. 41

Grant Duff, James. *See* Duff, James Grant

Grant Duff, Sir Mountstuart Elphinstone (1829–1906), XIV. 494, 502, 594

Granta, The, XIV. 207, 208, 537

Grantham, IV. 23; VIII. 279

Grantham, Henry, IV. 441, 443

Grantham school, VII. 330

Grantly, archdeacon, Trollope's, XIII. 422

Granville, Augustus Bozzi, *Travels in Russia*, XII. 302

Granville, Sir Bevil (d. 1706), IX. 175

Granville, earls of. *See* Carteret, John; Leveson-Gower, Granville George

Granville, George, baron Lansdowne (1667–1735), VIII. 221, 436, 444, 445; IX. 69, 174 ff., 476, 486; X. 432, 458
  British Enchanters, The, VIII. 53, 194
  Heroick Love, VIII. 55, 194, 396
  'Love is by Fancy led about,' IX. 175
  Merchant of Venice, The, VIII. 194
  'Myra,' IX. 174, 175
  She-Gallants, The, VIII. 194
  'Thoughtful nights and restless waking,' IX. 175

Graphic, The, XIV. 196, 201, 530, 535

Grasby, Lincolnshire, XIII. 46

Grasmere, XI. 102, 103, 109; XII. 337

Grasse, admiral de, XIV. 214

Grassi, Giacomo, IV. 457

Gratian, III. 50, 416

Gratian's *Decretum*, II. 350; VIII. 312

Grattan, Henry (1746–1820), XI. 55, 56, 396; XIV. 126, 311, 510

Grattan, Henry ('Fusbos'). *See* Plunkett, Henry Grattan

Grattan, Thomas Colley (1792–1864), XIV. 552

Gratton, John (1641–1712), VIII. 106, 416

Graund Amour, in *The Passetyme of Pleasure*, II. 225, 226, 228, 229, 232, 234, 235, 238

Graunt, John (1620–1674), VIII. 473, 477; *Natural and Political Observations*, VIII. 367

Grave, The, I. 147

Grave Diggers' Colloquy, The, VIII. 116

Gravelot, H., XIV. 212

Graves, Alfred Perceval, XII. 361; XIII. 556; XIV. 573, 574

Graves, Charles (1812–1899), XII. 516; XIV. 328

Graves, Charles Edward (1839–1920), XII. Add. 3

Graves, James (1815–1886), XII. 510

Graves, Richard (1715–1804), IX. 412; X. 273, 275 ff., 497
  Columella, or the Distressed Anchoret, X. 276, 277
  Eugenius or Anecdotes of the Golden Vale, X. 277
  Euphrosyne, X. 275
  Festoon, The, X. 275
  Plexippus, X. 277
  Recollection of...Shenstone, X. 275
  Spiritual Quixote, X. 276, 277

Graves, Stanzas of the, I. 243, 249, 250

Gravesend, III. 203; IV. 362

Gray, Andrew (1633–1656), IX. 544

Gray, D., IV. 457

Gray, David (1838–1861), XIII. 194, 503

Gray, Dorothy, mother of Thomas Gray, X. 116

Gray, G. J., X. 457

Gray, James (d. 1830), XI. 408

Gray, John Hamilton, XIV. 593

Gray, Philip, father of Thomas Gray, X. 116

Gray, Rosamund, in Lamb's *Rosamund Gray*, XII. 186

Gray, Sir Thomas (d. 1369?), *Scalacronica*, II. 128, 451

Gray, Thomas, parson of Liberton, II. 110

Gray, Thomas (1716–1771), I. 275; II. 204, 410; VIII. 234; IX. 169, 173, 189 ff., 412, 481; X. 87, 93, 109, 116 ff. (main entry), 147, 149, 155, 198, 205, 220, 239, 241 ff., 251, 450, 475, 489, *also see* Add.; XI. 77, 91, 124, 140, 207, 248, 250 ff., 255; XII. 133, 177, 208; XIII. 27, 29; XIV. 109, 117, 385, 453, 507, 517
  Agrippina, X. 119, 120
  Alliance of Education and Government, X. 123
  Bard, The, X. 127 ff., 132, 136, 137, 186, 225
  De Principiis Cogitandi, X. 122

Gray, Thomas
  Descent of Odin, x. 129, 132, 221, 225,
    227
  Elegy, vi. 189; ix. 167; x. 118, 123 ff.,
    128, 132, 185, 186, 208, 273; xi. 85, 144,
    206, 248, 323; xii. 41; xiii. 44, 149, 170
  Fatal Sisters, The, x. 129, 132, 221, 225
  Hymn to Adversity, x. 121
  Hymn to Ignorance, x. 121
  Journal in the Lakes, x. 101
  Letters, x. 134
  Long Story, A, x. 126, 127, 132
  Metrum, x. 131; xi. 252
  Observations on the poems of Lydgate,
    x. 131
  Ode on the Death of a Favourite Cat, x.
    123
  Ode on a Distant Prospect of Eton College,
    ix. 409; x. 121, 122; xi. 323
  Ode on the Spring, x. 121
  Odes, x. 202
  On the pleasure arising from Vicissitude,
    x. 128, 129
  Poems (1898 ed.), x. 123
  Progress of Poesy, x. 119, 127 ff.
  Sonnet on the Death of Richard West, x.
    121
  Stanzas to Richard Bentley, x. 126
Gray, Thomas and Erasmus, iii. 7
Gray MS., ii. 478
Gray and his Friends, x. 121
Grayes-Inne, Certaine devises and Shewes
  presented to her Majestie by the Gentle-
  men of, v. 77
Gray's Inn Journal, x. 466
Grazzini, A. F., v. 413; La Spiritata, v.
  115; La Strega, v. 69
Great Baddow, iii. 57
Great Berkhampstead, xi. 78
Great Braxted, viii. 321
Great Malvern, x. 276
Great North road, the, xii. 19
Great Parham, xi. 144
Great Rissington, ix. 145
Great Tew, vii. 150 ff., 155, 305; viii. 63,
  298
Great Assizes holden in Parnassus, The,
  vii. 387
Great Silkie of Sule Skerry, The, ii. 413
Greaves, John (1602–1652), vii. 488; viii.
  360; ix. 530
Greaves, J. P., ix. 328
Greaves, Sir Launcelot, in Smollett's
  novel, x. 41
Greaves, Thomas (fl. 1604), iv. 113, 154,
  464
Grech, W. L., xiii. 543
Greece, ii. 238; iv. 3, 64; v. 24, 29, 30;
  vi. 8; vii. 99, 303; ix. 112, 138, 256;
  x. 104, 107, 128, 154, 202, 318; xi. 57,
  72; xii. 32, 38 ff., 44, 46, 56, 62, 82,
  89, 90, 93, 209, 272, 302, 304, 314 ff.,
  329 ff., 338, 339, 411, 417; xiii. 130,
  461; xiv. 8, 23, 70, 71
Greece, history of, xii. 300, 302, 307 ff.
Greece and Byron, xii. 392, 394 ff.

Greedy, in A New Way to pay Old Debts,
  vi. 161
Greek anthologists, the, xiii. 193
Greek anthology, xii. 420, also see Add.
Greek architecture, xii. 339
Greek atomic theory, xiv. 272
Greek chair at Cambridge, ix. 341
Greek chorus, xi. 265; xiii. 445
Greek church, viii. 297
Greek coins, xii. 338
Greek drama, v. 1, 5, 61, 62, 65, 71, 182,
  296, 297, 334; vi. 14, 215, 232, 294 ff.;
  x. 78, 108; xii. 68, 113, 327; xiii. 130,
  133
Greek epigram, xiii. 387
Greek heroes, xiii. 354
Greek history, xiv. 175
Greek hymns, xii. 273
Greek inscriptions, xii. 339
Greek kings, in The Four Ages, vi. 92
Greek language and literature, v. 362;
  vii. 3, 7, 9, 13, 14, 74, 80, 130, 164, 165,
  237, 282, 283, 312, 313, 315 ff., 319,
  320, 323, 329, 333, 340 ff., 348; viii.
  58, 86, 112, 229, 287, 353, 364; ix. 75,
  144, 266, 267, 270, 273, 331, 334, 336,
  337, 341, 382, 383, 385, 388, 390, 391,
  393, 396, 403, 404, 409, 410, 562; x. 202,
  335; xi. 2, 58, 90, 181, 343, 354 ff.;
  xii. 40, 60, 83, 89, 94, 208 ff., 212, 215,
  230, 278, 308, 317, 323 ff., 329, 330,
  334, 338, 340, 343; xiii. 53, 71, 81, 90,
  92, 126, 129, 165, 175, 187, 245, 249,
  353; xiv. 209, 302, 307, 327, 382, 385,
  388, 391, 405, 406, 413, 416, 426, 440,
  454, 455, 457, 458
Greek learning (1600–1660), vii. 487 ff.
Greek manuscripts, xii. 323
Greek mythology, xii. 65, 111; xiii. 271;
  xiv. 154
Greek poetry, ix. 67, 331; xii. 58, 329,
  330, 332, 333; xiii. 36, 45, 95
Greek press, Early Parisian, xii. 522
Greek printing, 15th century, xii. 523
Greek pronunciation, ix. 210
Greek revolution, xii. 314
Greek, study of, ii. 359, 367, 370, 371
Greek Testament, vii. 317, 339; ix. 336
Greek war of liberation, xii. 38, 75
Greek and Latin Measures in English
  Poetry, xiii. 244
Greeks, the, xi. 30, 273, 352, 363; xii.
  38, 45, 69, 80; xiii. 90, 205
Greeks, the, in Milton's England, vii. 129
Green, Alice S. A., xiv. 77, 490
Green, Mrs Everett, vii. 189
Green, George (1793–1841), xiv. 265 ff., 556
Green, Henry, xiii. 549
Green, John (1706?–1779), ix. 571
Green, J. A., xiii. 549
Green, John Richard (1837–1883), i. 196,
  201; vii. 168, 305; xii. 321; xiii. 465;
  xiv. 64, 74, 76 ff. (main entry), 100,
  198, 490
  Conquest of England, The, xiv. 77
  Making of England, The, xiv. 77

Green, John Richard
  Short History of the English People, A,
  XIV. 76, 77
  Studies from England and Italy, XIV.
  76
Green, Joseph Henry (1791–1863), XI,
  417; XIV. 471
Green, Mary Anne Everett, born Wood
  (1818–1895), XIV. 502; *Letters of Queen
  Henrietta Maria*, XIV. 111; *Letters of
  Royal Ladies of Great Britain*, XIV. 111;
  Lives of the Princesses of England, XIV.
  111
Green, Matthew (1696–1737), X. 137, 138,
  144, 146 (main entry), 156, 455, 480;
  The Spleen, IX. 191; X. 146
Green, rector of Kilkenny West, X. 196
Green, Robert, Ἐγκυκλοπαιδεία, IX. 411
Green, Thomas Hill (1836–1882), X. 511;
  XII. 298, 467; XIV. 38, 43 ff., 473
  *Lectures on the Principles of Political
  Obligation*, XIV. 44
  Prolegomena to Ethics, XIV. 43
  Works, XIV. 43
Green, William Charles (1832–1914), XII.
  484
Green willow, Sing all of, III. 190
Greenaway, Kate, XI. 475, 483, 485
Greene, Edward Burnaby (d. 1788), X. 485
Greene, John, *A Refutation of the Apology
  for Actors*, VI. 401
Greene, Robert (1560?–1592), III. 114,
  208, 241, 243, 305, 340, 342, 343, 350,
  351, 355 ff., 359 ff., 366, 367, 370, 371,
  395, 396, 534, 545, 546; IV. 116 ff.,
  317 ff., 323, 324, 358, 363, 469, 470,
  472, 473, 514 ff., 517, 521, 527, 528,
  530, 535; V. 63, 85, 87, 121–141 (main
  entry), 147, 166, 169, 170, 175, 185,
  206, 219, 239, 246, 251, 309, 327, 353,
  364, 370, 418 ff., 439, *and see* Add. 2;
  VI. 13, 14, 249, 287, 300, 301, 365, 494;
  VII. 395; VIII. 223; IX. 26, 51, 161; XI.
  262; XIV. 234
  ? *A most rare and excellent dreame*, IV.
  116
  Alcida, III. 357
  Alphonsus King of Arragon, V. 134 ff.;
  VIII. 125
  Arbasto, III. 357
  Battell of Alcazar, VIII. 125
  Black Booke's Messenger, The, III. 361
  'Cupid abroad was lated in the night,'
  VII. 2
  Defence of Conny-Catching, A, III. 361;
  IV. 319
  *Disputation between a He Conny-Catcher
  and a She Conny-Catcher, A*, III. 361;
  IV. 319
  Edward I, VIII. 125
  Euphues his Censure to Philautus, III.
  350, 356
  Farewell to Folly, V. 133, 252
  Francesco's Fortunes, IV. 118; VI. 396
  Frier Bacon and Frier Bongay, I. 210;
  V. 135 ff., 252, 316, 340

Greene, Robert
  George a Greene, the Pinner of Wakefield,
  V. 35, 135, 373, 418
  Greenes Mourning Garment, V. 133, 137
  Groatsworth of Wit, III. 357, 360, 545;
  IV. 320; V. 322
  Gwydonius, III. 357
  James IV, V. 135, 137, 138, 245
  Job, V. 134
  *Looking Glasse for London and England,
  A*, V. 135, 354
  Mamillia, III. 350; IV. 398; V. 133, 161
  Menaphon, III. 208, 256, 357, 545; IV.
  118; V. 80, 121, 133, 134, 140, 157
  Morando, V. 133
  Mourning Garment, III. 360
  Myrrour of Modestie, The, III. 350, 356
  Never too late, III. 356, 360
  Notable Discovery of Coosnage, A, III.
  360, 361; IV. 319; V. 132
  Orlando Furioso, V. 134 ff.; VI. 250
  Orpharion, III. 357; VII. 2
  Pandosto, III. 356; V. 133, 220
  Penelope's Web, III. 350
  Perimedes the Blacksmith, III. 356; V.
  133, 134, 136
  Philomela, III. 357; V. 133; VI. 137
  Planetomachia, III. 356, 357; V. 133
  Quip for an Upstart Courtier, A, III.
  361, 396, 545; IV. 319
  Repentance of Robert Greene, The, III.
  360; V. 133, 136
  Spanish Masquerado, III. 357; V. 133
  Vision, V. 133, 137
  Trans. of Anacreon, from *Orpharion*,
  IV. 124
  See also, *Faire Em* and *Selimus*
Greene, Thomas, actor, VI. 219
Greene, Thomas (1658–1738), bishop of
  Ely, IX. 335, 339
Greenham or Grenham, Richard (1535?–
  1594?), III. 389
Greenhill, William (1591–1671), VII. 322
Greenhill, William Alexander (1814–
  1894), VII. 235
Greenland, VII. 64; XII. 420
Greenock, IX. 374; XI. 410
Greenough, George Bellas (1778–1855),
  XIV. 287, 560, 611
'Greensleeves,' III. 130
Greenwell, Dorothy (Dora) (1821–1882),
  XIII. 177, 503
Greenwell, William (b. 1820), XII. 354,
  510; *British Barrows*, XII. 348; *The
  electrum coinage of Cyzicus*, XII. 348
Greenwey, Richard, IV. 5, 440
Greenwich, II. 158; III. 80; V. 90, 170, 219;
  VIII. 260; IX. 281
Greenwich hospital, VIII. 249
Greenwood, Frederick (1830–1909), XIV.
  189, 194, 195, 534
Greenwood, G., XIV. 561
Greenwood, James (d. 1737), IX. 474
Greenwood, John (d. 1593), III. 390
Greenwood, T., XIV. 543
Greenwood, William, *Philalethes*, IV. 251

Greevous Grones for the Poore, IV. 513

Greg, Walter Wilson, V. 253, 331; VI. 96, 274, 365

Greg, William Rathbone (1809–1881), XII. 291, 467; XIII. 359, 373, 377, 471, 548; XIV. 519
    Creed of Christendom, The, XIV. 164
    Enigmas of Life, XIV. 164
    Essays, XIII. 374
    Mistaken Aims, XIII. 374; XIV. 164
    Rocks Ahead, XIV. 164

Grego, J., XIII. 530; XIV. 540

Gregorian Gospels at Corpus Christi college, Cambridge, I. 72

Gregory VII, pope, XII. 418

Gregory IX, pope, I. 203; VII. 367; VIII. 312

Gregory XI, pope, II. 49

Gregory, David (1661–1708), IX. 378

Gregory, George (1754–1808), X. 485; 486; XIII. 241

Gregory, lady Isabella Augusta, XIII. 514

Gregory, John, M.D. (1724–1773), XI. 486; XIV. 600

Gregory, Olinthus Gilbert (1774–1841), XI. 399

Gregory, Padraic, XIV. 574

Gregory, Robert, XIV. 591

Gregory, T., VIII. 459

Gregory, Saint, XII. 266

Gregory, St, Trentals of, I. 312

Gregory, William (d. 1467), II. 302, 482

Gregory the Great, I. 53, 61, 81, 85, 91, 92, 96, 117, 224, 231, 347, 355; II. 76, 264, 365; III. 9; IV. 424; *Cura Pastoralis*, I. 91, 92; *Dialogues*, I. 75, 86, 103, 105, 436, 437, 439; VII. 391

Gregory the Great and the English boy slaves, I. 234, 351, 379, 380

Gregory Nazianzen, St, I. 74; II. 75; V. 5

Gregory of Tours, I. 26, 67, 117

Grein, C. W. M., I. ix, 48, 91, 420

Grelot, Guillaume Joseph, *Voyage to Constantinople*, IX. 268, 500

Grendel, in *Beowulf*, I. 2, 11, 22, 23, 28, 115; II. 398

Grendles mere, Wiltshire, I. 27

Grenville, George (1712–1770), X. 399, 402 ff., 408, 409, 523, 527; XI. 5, 7, 10 ff.

Grenville, George (master of Magdalene college, Cambridge), VIII. 242

Grenville, lord George (Nugent Temple) (1753–1813), VIII. 242

Grenville, Sir Richard (1541?–1591), IV. 10, 56; VII. 75

Grenville, Richard Temple, earl Temple (1711–1779), X. 402, 409, 410, 523

Grenville, William Wyndham, lord Grenville (1759–1834), XIV. 513

Grenville Correspondence, X. 400, 402

Grenville library, XII. 368

Grenville party, the, XIV. 120

Gresham, Sir Thomas (1519?–1579), III. 426; V. 354; VI. 84, 91, 300; VII. 333; IX. 530; XIV. 186

Gresham's law, XIV. 186

Greshams, the, in Trollope's novels, XIII. 422

Gresset, Jean-Baptiste-Louis, X. 137; *Sur ma convalescence*, X. 129

Greswell, William, XIV. Add. 7

Greswell, William Parr (1765–1854), XII. 522

Greta hall, XII. 188

Greta hall, Keswick, XI. 156, 168

Gretchen, XIII. 153

Grete herball, The, IV. 542

Grettir, I. 27; XIII. 125

Grettis Saga, I. 27, 28; XIII. 125

Greville, Charles Cavendish Fulke (1794–1865), XIV. 123, 124, 171, 184, 187, 503; *The Greville Memoirs*, XIV. 114, 115, 181, 182, 189; *The Policy of England to Ireland*, XIV. 115

Greville, Sir Fulke, lord Brooke (1554–1628), III. 189, 257, 267; IV. 114, 117, 132, 133, 150, 159–161 (main entry), 465, 482; V. 204, 335, 474; VI. 19; VII. 278, 337, 471, *also see* Add.; VIII. 133
    Alaham, IV. 159; V. 334
    Caelica, III. 257, 267; IV. 160, 523, 551
    Certaine learned and elegant workes, IV. 159
    Inquisition upon Fame and Honour, An, IV. 159
    Monarchy and Religion, IV. 160
    Mustapha, IV. 159; V. 334
    Of Fame and Honour, IV. 160
    Of Humane Learning, IV. 160
    Of Warres, IV. 160
    Remains, IV. 160
    Treatie of Warres, A, IV. 159
    Treatise of Humane Learning, A, IV. 159

Greville, Robert, 2nd lord Brooke (1608–1643), VII. 277 ff.; *The Nature of Truth*, VII. 278, 471; *A Discourse...of... Episcopacy*, VII. 278

Greville, Mrs, *Prayer for Indifference*, XII. 124

'Grewellers,' VIII. 98

Grew, Nehemiah (1641–1712), VIII. 477; XIV. 282, 560

Grew, Obadiah (1607–1689), X. 385

Grey, Arthur (1536–1593), baron Grey de Wilton, III. 202, 206, 207, 212, 229; IV. 51, 53; VII. 211

Grey, Charles, 2nd earl Grey (1764–1845), XI. 52; XIV. 116, 120, 124, 125, 172, 510

Grey, Douglas, XIV. 536

Grey, Elizabeth, countess of Kent (1581–1651), VIII. 60

Grey, Elizabeth, queen of Edward IV, IV. 137

Grey, Sir George (1812–1898), XIV. 487

Grey, lady Jane (1537–1554), III. 431; IV. 169, 182; VI. 54

Grey, Vivian, Disraeli's, XIII. 346, 417

Grey, William (d. 1478), bishop of Ely, II. 303, 496, 499; III. 5; IV. 427

Grey, Mrs William [Maria Georgina Grey, born Shirreff], XIV. 600, 606

Grey, Zachary (1688–1766), v. 273; VIII.
59; IX. 145, 212, 476, 494, 531
Grey collection, the (South Africa), XIV.
Add. 4
Grey Friars, church of, II. 335
Gride, Arthur, in *Nicholas Nickleby*, XIII.
322
Grierson, Constantia (1706?–1733), XI.
172, 426
Grierson, Sir George Abraham (b. 1851),
XII. Add. 4
Grieve, Mrs, in Foote's drama, x. 88
Griff house, XIII. 382
Griffin, Bartholomew (*fl.* 1596), III. 256,
264, 266; v. 224; *Fidessa*, III. 256, 266,
523; *Venus and Adonis*, III. 266
Griffin, Gerald (1803–1840), XIV. 568;
Collegians, The, XIV. 320; *Gisippus*, XIV.
320
Griffin, maker of Arthur's spear, in *Laya-
mon*, I. 265
Griffin, Mrs, VII. 360, 361
Griffin, Sir, in *John a Kent*, v. 317
Griffin, W., publisher, x. 212
Griffin, W. H. and H. C. Minchin, *The
Life of Robert Browning*, XIII. 71
Griffith, Mrs Elizabeth (1720?–1793), XI.
457; *School for Rakes*, XI. 263
Griffith, Matthew (1599?–1665), VII. 106,
141, 416
Griffith, Ralph Thomas Hotchkin (1826–
1906), XII. 502
Griffith, Roger, x. 387
Griffith and Farran, XI. 377
Griffiths, Ralph (1720–1803), IX. 563;
x. 40, 201 ff., 206, 483
Griffiths, Vavasor, x. 386
Grignan, château de, x. 248
Grillparzer, Franz, v. 303
Grim, in *Damon and Pithias*, v. 119
Grim, in *Havelok*, I. 303, 304
Grim, the collier, in *The Devil and his
Dame*, v. 329
Grimald or Grimoald, Nicholas (1519–
1562), III. 179 ff., 185, 508; IV. 5, 24,
435; v. 394; VI. 473
Archipropheta, v. 82; VI. 295, 327
Christus Redivivus, VI. 295
*Funerall song upon the deceas of Annes
his mother*, III. 180
The Garden, III. 180
The Lover asketh pardon of his dere, III.
180
Grimaldi, Joseph, XIII. 514
Grimalfi, in *Perfidus Hetruscus*, VI. 302
Grimbald of St Bertin (820?–903), abbot
of Winchester, I. 89, 92
Grime, in Holcroft's *Deserted Daughter*,
XI. 277
Grimefield, J., *The Sage Senator Delineated*,
VII. 518
Grimeston, Edward, *Admirable and Memo-
rable Histories*, III. 536; translation of
de Serres's *Inventaire Général de l'His-
toire de France*, IV. 448; VI. 33; transla-
tion of *History* of Polybius, VII. 488

Grimm, H., XIII. 470
Grimm, Jacob, I. 55, 383, 420; XII. 344
Grimm, Jacob Ludwig Carl and Wilhelm
Carl, XI. 381, 491; *German Popular
Stories*, XI. 386
Grimm, Samuel Hieronymus (1734–1794),
XIV. 214
Grimmelshausen, H. J. C. von, *Simplicis-
simus*, IV. 256
Grimoard, comte, IX. 217
Grimsby, in *Havelok*, I. 303, 351, 364
Grimshawe, Thomas Shuttleworth (1778–
1850), XI. 401, 402; XII. 472
Grimston, Sir Harbottle (1603–1685), IX.
194
Grindal, Edmund (1519?–1583), arch-
bishop of Canterbury, III. 213, 214,
374, 375, 468; IV. 493; v. 56, 482; VI.
297, 381; IX. 496
Gringoire, Pierre, XIII. 428; *Chasteau de
labour*, II. 329; III. 56
Grinsell, Thomas, VII. 250
Grischow, J. H., x. 515
Griselda (Chaucer's), v. 243
Griselda (Petrarch's), II. 184
Griseldis, in school plays, v. 103
Griseldis-Motiv, in English drama, VI. 97
Grisone, IV. 444
Gritsch, Johan, III. 489
Grizzle, Dr Syntax's mare, XIV. 218, 219
Grobian, St, IX. 32, 46
Grobiana's Nuptialls, VI. 483
Grobianism, IV. 517, 528
Grobianus, in *Das Narrenschiff*, III. 82
Grobianus, in *Grobiana's Nuptials*, III. 82
Grocer's Play, The, v. 390
Grocyn, William (1446?–1519), II. 367;
III. 3, 6, 10, 12, 13, 15, 17, 430; VII. 326
Grolier, Jean, IV. 406
Grolier club, XIII. 476
Gronovius, J. F., VII. 307; IX. 527
Groome, Francis Hindes (1851–1902),
XIV. 519; *In Gypsy Tents*, XIV. 146;
Kriegspiel, XIV. 145, 146; *Suffolk Par-
son, A*, XIV. 146
Grosart, Alexander Balloch (1827–1899),
IV. 165; v. 85; VII. 11, 29, 34, 35; XI.
407, 442, 445; XIII. 508
Grose, captain, II. 275
Grose, Francis (1731?–1791), XII. 510
Ancient Armour and Weapons, XII. 349
Antiquities of England and Wales, XII.
349
Antiquities of Ireland, XII. 349
Antiquities of Scotland, XII. 349
Dictionary of the Vulgar Tongue, XIV.
224, 540
Grose, T. H., x. 511; XIV. 473
Grosseteste, Robert (d. 1253), bishop of
Lincoln, I. 203, 204 ff., 209, 210, 342,
353; II. 42, 44, 48, 52, 345, 348, 350, 365;
IV. 269, 307, 369, 370; v. 8, 39; VI. 374;
Château d'Amour, I. 204, 343, 454;
II. 26
Grosvenor, Richard Grosvenor, 1st earl
(1731–1802), XI. 40

Grote, George (1794–1871), XI. 72, 398;
XII. 307 ff., 318, 322, 475, 476; XIV. 14,
187, 407, 473
  Essentials of Parliamentary Reform, XII.
  310
  Fragments on Ethical Subjects, XIV. 23
  History of Greece, XII. 311, 312
  Plato and the Companions of Sokrates,
  XII. 311
  *Seven Letters on the Recent Politics of
  Switzerland*, XII. 311
  *Statement of the Question of Parliamen-
  tary Reform*, XII. 310
Grote, Harriet, *Personal Life of George
  Grote*, XII. 309, 476
Grote, John (1813–1866), XII. 493; XIV.
  26, 473; *Examination of the Utilitarian
  Philosophy*, XIV. 25; *Exploratio Philo-
  sophica*, XIV. 25; *Treatise on the Moral
  Ideals*, XIV. 25
Grotius, Hugo, III. 157, 423; IV. 259, 293;
  VII. 52, 99, 281, 300, 518; VIII. 316;
  IX. 331, 525; X. 291; *Adamus Exul*, VII.
  118; *Mare Liberum*, VII. 307; VIII. 318
Groto, Luigi, V. 62; *Pentimento Amoroso*,
  VI. 317; *La Dalida*, VI. 302
Groundolf, Agnes (Gower's wife), II. 135
Grove, Sir George (1820–1900), XII. 493
Grove, Henry (1684–1738), X. 386
Grove, Matthew (*fl.* 1587), III. 508; *Epi-
  grams, songes and sonnettes*, III. 188;
  The History of Pelops and Hippodamia,
  III. 188
Grove, Sir William Robert (1811–1896),
  XIV. 556
Grove, The, IV. 209
Grover, Henry Montague (1791–1866),
  XIII. 261, 519
Groves, a Jesuit, VIII. 266
Growoll, A., *Three centuries of English
  booktrade bibliography*, XI. 339, 470, 471
Grub, George (1812–1892), XII. 513; XIV.
  490
Grub, J., XIV. 497
Grub street, VIII. 91, 174; IX. 118, 122,
  256, 258, 261, 262, 264, 265, 268, 271,
  272; X. 139, 201, 389; XI. 317, 329, 330;
  XII. 204; XIII. 163; XIV. 168
Grub-street Journal, The, IX. 80, 449; X.
  162; XI. 466; XIV. 200
Gruffydd ap Cynan, XIV. 307
Grumio, in Lacy's *Sawny the Scot*, VIII. 140
Grumio, Shakespeare's, XIV. 443
Grundtvig, S. H., II. 398, 413, 417
Grundy, Frances H., XIII. 558
Grundy, Mrs, in Morton's *Speed the Plough*,
  XI. 281
Grundy, Sydney (1848–1914), XIII. 519
Grunnius Corocotta, Testament of, III. 482
Gruter, J., IV. 261
Gryphius, Andreas, V. 285, 290, 458
Gryphius, Sebastian, III. 427
Guala, cardinal, I. 238
Gualter, Katherine, in Burton's *Anatomy*,
  IV. 246
Guardeloop, in *The Tatler*, IX. 41

Guardian, The, IX. 64, 69, 77, 161, 165,
  437 ff., 441, 446, 456, 462; XII. 454, 459;
  XIV. 67, 71, 199, 202
Guardian of Education, The, XI. 380; XIV.
  402
Guarini, in Jonson's *Volpone*, VII. 274
Guarini, Gian Battista, *Pastor Fido*, IV.
  134, 445; VI. 21, 137, 317, 365, 366, 371,
  485, 490; VIII. 271, 441
Guarino, Battista, III. 5; IV. 323
Guarna, A., *Grammaticale Bellum*, VI. 482
Guarsi, Andrew, VI. 38
Guary miracles, V. 15
Guayaquil, XIV. 242
Guazzo Stefano, *Civile Conversation*, III.
  432, 551; IV. 445
Guben, siege of, VII. 22
Gude and Godlie Ballatis, The, III. 138,
  141, 502; IX. 359, 360, 365
Gude Counsell, in *Ane Pleasant Satyre*,
  III. 124, 125, 126
Gude Wallace, II. 399
Gudgeon Credulous, Sir, in Wilson's *The
  Projectors*, VIII. 123
Gudius, X. 457
Gudrun, in Morris's *Sigurd the Volsung*,
  XIII. 126
Gudrun, in Morris's *The Lovers of Gudrun*,
  XIII. 125
Guelphs, XIII. 59
Guenevora, in *The Misfortunes of Arthur*,
  V. 78, 79
Guericke, Otto von, VIII. 364
Guernsey, XII. 328; XIII. 135
Guernsey, A. H., XIII. 471
Guest, Edwin (1800–1880), I. 333; XII.
  510; XIII. 241 ff., 247, 248, 512; *A His-
  tory of English Rhythms*, XI. 170; XIII.
  228, 232, 240, 512
Guest, lady Charlotte, *Mabinogion*, I. 247,
  252, 253, 276, 461
Guest, Stephen, in *The Mill on the Floss*,
  XIII. 392
Guevara, Antonio de, II. 340; III. 341,
  344 ff., 348, 551; IV. 9, 445, 525; *El
  Relox de Principes*, III. 341; V. 123; VI.
  377; VII. 390
Guiana, IV. 56, 57, 59, 61, 88; XIV. 249
Guiboux, Carolingian heroine, I. 303
Guicciardini, F., IV. 445
Guiccioli, count, XII. 34
Guiccioli, Theresa, countess, XII. 33 ff.,
  37, 49, 50, 383, 395
Guido, in Browning's *The Ring and the
  Book*, XIII. 66
Guido de Baysio's *Rosarium*, II. 364
Guido delle Colonne, I. 170; *Hystoria
  Troiana*, II. 104, 118, 150, 172, 201, 363
Guido Reni, XII. 67
Guiffardière, M. de, X. 65, 254
Guild, William (1586–1657), IX. 544
Guildenstern, in *Hamlet*, V. 201, 262
Guildford, III. 428
Guildford. See Nicholas of
Guildford, Sir Richard (1455?–1506), IV.
  457; *Pilgrimage of*, II. 321

Guileville, G. de, *Pilgrimage of the Sowle*, VII. 173, 430

Guilford, earls of. *See* North, Francis; North, Frederick

Guillaume de Lorris, II. 169, 219

Guillaume de Machault, II. 467

Guillaume de Palerme. See *William of Palerne*

Guillaume de Tignoville, *Les ditz moraulx des philosophes*, II. 313

Guillaume de Twicé, II. 509

Guillaume le Roy, II. 316

Guillaume le Maréchal, L'Histoire de, I. 477; II. 420

Guillemard, G., IX. 435

Guillemins, church of the, Mandeville's burial place, II. 81

Guillim, John (1565–1621), *Display of Heraldrie*, IV. 376, 543

Guilpin, Edward, IV. 332, 362, 363; *Skialetheia, or A Shadowe of Truth*, IV. 138, 331, 519, 533; VI. 461

Guilsborough, XII. 256

Guinea, IV. 72, 75, 88

Guinevere or Guenever, I. 261, 262, 266, 270, 312, 313, 327; II. 122, 176; VII. 75

Guinevere, Tennyson's, XIII. 37, 38

Guiney, Louise Imogen, XIII. 503

Guingelot, Wade's boat, I. 218

Guinicelli, IV. 196

Guinnion, castle of, I. 246

Guiomar, in *The Custome of the Countrey*, VI. 131

Guirimir, or miracle-plays, VI. 252

Guisburn, priory of, I. 181

Guiscard, in *Gismond of Salerne*, V. 75 ff.

Guiscard, marquis de, IX. 461

Guise, duke of, in *The Massacre at Paris*, V. 145

Guise, Henry, duke of, IV. 259; VI. 34

Guise, John (d. 1765), XII. 377

Guisnes, I. 356; III. 175

Guizot, François Pierre Guillaume, V. 301, 302; X. 314, 317, 507; XII. 304; *Histoire de la Civilisation*, XIV. 56, 102

Gules, Thomas, in *The Tatler*, IX. 53

Gull, Arctic, in *King Berdok*, II. 276

Gulley, John (1783–1863), XIV. 231

Gullio, in *The Returne from Parnassus*, VI. 311, 312

Gulnare, in Byron's *Corsair*, XII. 46

Gummere, Francis Barton, V. 130

Gundicarius (Gundaharius), king of the Burgundians, I. 33

Gunnar, in Morris's *Sigurd the Volsung*, XIII. 126

Gunnell, Doris, *Stendhal et l'Angleterre*, X. 181

Gunning, Elizabeth, duchess of Argyll (1734–1790), XI. 451

Gunning, Henry (1780–1854), XIV. 601

Gunnings, the, XI. 260

Gunpowder, plot, the, IV. 166, 254; VII. 45, 162; VIII. 85, 86

Gunter, Edmund (1581–1626), IV. 457; VIII. 356, 477

Guntharius, in *Waltharius* (*Waldhere*), I. 32

Gunthorpe, John (d. 1498), III. 5

Gunton, Simon (1609–1676), *History of the Church of Peterborough*, IX. 354, 534

Gurney, Edmund (1847–1888), XIII. 248, 512; XIV. 473

Gurney, Mary, XIV. 600

Gurney, William Brodie (1777–1855), VIII. 243

Gurton, Gammer, XI. 375

Gurwood, John (1790–1845), XIV. 107

Gustavus Adolphus, king of Sweden, VII. 20, 21, 231; VIII. 111; IX. 194

Gustus, in *Lingua*, VI. 315

Gutch, John (1746–1831), IX. 346, 541

Gutch, John Mathew (1776–1861), XII. 187; XIV. 534

Guthere, in *Waldhere* and *Widsith*, I. 33, 35

Guthkelch, Adolph Charles Louis, IX. Add.

Guthlac, St, in Old English, I. 51, 52, 58, 428, 430

Guthlac, St, Life of, I. 85, 86, 131. *See, also,* Felix of Croyland

Guthlaf, in *Beowulf* and *Finnsburh*, I. 31

Guthrie, Henry (1600?–1676), bishop of Dunkeld, X. 500

Guthrie, Thomas (1803–1873), XII. 472

Guthrie, William (1620–1665), IX. 546

Guthrie, William (1708–1770), IX. 553; X. 163, 501, 523; *History of England*, X. 291

Guthry, Henry (1600?–1676), VII. 455

Guy Faux, in *Friar Rush*, VI. 53

Guy of Warwick, the traditional, I. 218; III. 68; IV. 190, 191; V. 108; VIII. 68; XI. 373

Guy of Warwick, I. 282, 293, 294, 303 ff., 468; II. 199, 308, 320, 321, 323, 500; VII. 96

Guy, The Goste of, II. 320, 485

Guy and Colbronde, II. 308

Guy's Porridge Pot, XII. 439

Guye, P. A., XIV. 557

Guyon, abbé de, X. 464

Guyon, madame (1648–1717), VIII. 103; IX. 307, 314, 520, 523; XI. 90, 401, 403

Guyse, John (1680–1761), XI. 479

Guystarde and Sygysmonde, The History of, II. 325, 486

Gwalchmei = Gawain, in the Welsh Triads and in the *Mabinogion*, I. 269

Gwendolen, in *Daniel Deronda*, XIII. 392, 399, 400

Gwestad, I. 255

Gwevyl, son of Gwestad, I. 255

Gwinne or Gwynne, Matthew (1558?–1627), VI. 318, 473; *Vertumnus sive Annus Recurrens*, VI. 317

Gwyneth, Owen, in Southey's *Madoc*, XI. 162

Gwynn, John (d. 1786), X. 469, 470

Gwynn, Nell (1650–1687), VIII. 20, 93, 99, 199, 213

Gwynn, Stephen, XII. 410, 412; XIII. 477

Gwynn, son of Nuð, I. 254
Gwynne, John (*fl.* 1660), XII. 377
Gybbys, J., VII. 511
Gyles Goosecappe, Sir. See under Chapman
Gyliane, in *Rauf Coilȝear*, II. 125
Gyngalyn, in *Libeanus Desconus*, I. 312
Gyraldus, Lilius, IV. 249
Gyre Carling, II. 275

H. B., *The Craftsmans Craft*, VII. 386
H. G., IV. 7
Haak, Theodore (1605–1690), VII. 322, 481
Habbie Simson, piper of Kilbarchan, I. 290
Habbie Simson, IX. 365, 366, 374, 378, 379
Habeas Corpus act, VII. 441
Haben's (or Hyberdine's) *A Sermon in praise of thieves*, v. 480
Habert, P., *Le Temple de la Mort*, VIII. 443
Habington or Abingdon, Thomas (1560–1647), VII. 445, 479; IX. 530
Habington, William (1605–1654), IV. 522; VII. 25, 26, 38, 401
  Castara, v. 277; VI. 30; VII. 4, 45, 46, 445
  Cupio dissolvi, VII. 46
  Et exultavit Humiles, VII. 46
  History of Edward IV, begun by Thomas, and completed by William, Habington, VII. 45
  Nox nocti indicat Scientiam, VII. 46
  Queene of Arragon, The, VI. 456; VII. 46
Hack, Maria (1777–1844), XI. 479; *Fireside Stories*, XI. 384; *Harry Beaufoy*, XI. 384
Hacker, col. Francis (d. 1660), VIII. 470
Hacket, John (1592–1670), IV. 422; VII. 329, 333, 342, 477, 491; *Life of Archbishop Williams*, VII. 334; IX. 165; *Loiola*, VI. 324, 473
Hacket, Thomas (*fl.* 1550), v. 105
Hackluyt, John (*fl.* 1644), VII. 356, 494
Hackman, James (1752–1779), x. 479
'Hackney, Iscariot' (Richard Savage), XI. 330
Hackney academy, x. 385; XII. 166
Hackwood, Frederick William, XIV. 520
Haddan, Arthur West (1816–1873), XIV. 75, 499
Haddeby, in the Baltic, I. 94
Hadden, R. H., XIV. 609
Haddington, XIII. 5
Haddington, hens of, II. 276
Haddingtonshire, III. 151; IX. 214
Haddon, Walter (1516–1572), III. 423; VII. 328
Hades, in Byron's *Cain*, XII. 48
Hades, king of, in *Preiðeu Annwvn*, I. 251
Hadington, viscount. *See* Ramsay, Sir John
Hadleigh, Suffolk, VIII. 284; XII. 256, 257
Hadley, near Barnet, XIII. 276
Hadow, James (1670?–1764), IX. 548, 549
Hadow, William Henry, XIII. 514
Hadrian, abbot, I. 5, 71 ff., 77, 82
Hadrian, emperor, x. 314
Hadrian IV, pope (Nicholas Breakspear), I. 185

Haethcyn, in *Beowulf*, I. 24
Hafiz, x. 144; XIV. 318 *b*
Hagall (Old Norse alphabet), I. 10
Hagano, in *Waldhere* and *Waltharius*, I. 32, 33
Hagberg, Carl August, v. 307
Hagena, in *Waldhere* and *Widsith*, I. 33
Haggard, A. M., XIV. 515
Haggard, Sir Henry Rider, XIV. 208
Hagley park, x. 101, 102, 113, 115, 150
Hagthorpe, John (*fl.* 1625), IV. 457; VII. 406
Hague, the, IV. 430; v. 286; VII. 16, 152, 188, 434, 437; VIII. 267, 380; IX. 148, 149, 158, 199, 208, 235, 236
Hahn, Theophilus, XIV. Add. 4
Hahn-Hahn, countess, XIV. 138
Haidée, in Byron's *Don Juan*, XII. 46, 54
Haig Brown, William (1823–1907), XIV. 597, 601
Haigh, Arthur Elam (1855–1905), XII. 484
'Hail to the Knight of the post,' ballad, VIII. 95
'Hail to the Myrtle Shades,' ballad, VIII. 95
Haile, Martin, XIV. 492
Hailes, lord. *See* Dalrymple, Sir David
Haileybury, XIV. 59
Hain, Ludwig, *Repertorium Bibliographicum*, XII. 369, 520
Hake, Edward (*fl.* 1579), III. 199; *Newes out of Poules Churcheyarde*, IV. 329, 518
Hake, Thomas Gordon (1809–1895), XIII. 156, 187, 503; *Maiden Ecstasy*, XIII. 185; *Old Souls*, XIII. 185; *Palmist, The*, XIII. 185
Hakewill, George (1578–1649), VII. 323, 425, 465, 471; *An Apologie or Declaration of the Power and Providence of God*, VII. 277
Hakluyt, Richard (1552?–1616), I. 95; II. 424; III. 187, 438; IV. 9, 66, 69, 71 ff., 78 ff., 87, 91 ff., 101, 103, 191, 457, *also see* Add.; v. 338; XIV. 332
  Divers Voyages touching the Discoverie of America, IV. 81
  Miraculous Victory achieved by the English flete, IV. 84
  Notable Historie...voyages made by... French Captains unto Florida, A, IV. 81
  Principal Navigations, III. 438, 551; IV. 67, 76, 78, 79, 80, 82, 88, 94, 398
  Virginia Richly Valued, IV. 94
Hakluyt, Richard (uncle of above), IV. 85
Hakluyt society, the, IV. 81, 107; XII. 355
'Hal wes thu, folde, fira modor,' I. 3
Haldane, Elizabeth S., XIV. 472
Haldenstone, or Haldenstoun, or Haddenston, James (d. 1443), II. 368
Hale, Lancashire, II. 122
Hale, Sir Matthew (1609–1676), VII. 234, 323, 392, 476; VIII. 319 ff., 357, 466, 468; IX. 198, 240, 489; *London Liberties*, VIII. 319
Hale, Thomas, IV. 457
Hales. *See* Alexander of; Thomas de

Hales, John (d. 1571), *Discourse of the Commonweal*, IV. 300, 307, 511; V. 478
Hales, John (*fl.* 1589), III. 381, 383
Hales, John (1584–1656), IV. 431; V. 222; VII. 21, 151 ff., 157, 163, 218, 316, 425, 465; *Golden Remains*, VII. 152, 479
Hales, John Wesley (1836–1914), V. 346; X. 233; XI. 409; XII. 504; XIV. 426, 606
Hales, Stephen (1677–1761), X. 466; XIV. 283, 284, 560
Halévy, Elie, *Formation du radicalisme philosophique*, XI. 69, 397
Halfdan, I. 25
Halga, in *Beowulf*, I. 25
Halgoland, I. 94
Hali Meidenhad, I. 229, 234, 362, 458
Haliburton, Thomas Chandler (*pseud.* Sam Slick, 1796–1865), XII. 449; XIV. 343, 345 ff., 581, 583
    Attaché, The, XIV. 348
    Bubbles of Canada, The, XIV. 359
    Clockmaker, The, XIV. 348
    Historical and Statistical Account of Nova Scotia, XIV. 359
    Nature and Human Nature, XIV. 348
    Rule and Misrule of the English in America, XIV. 359
    Wise Saws, XIV. 348
Halicarnassus, mausoleum of, XII. 339
Halidon hill, battle of, I. 357
Halifax, earl of. *See* Montague, Charles
Halifax, marquis of. *See* Savile, Sir George
Halifax, Nova Scotia, XIV. 346, 347
Halifax, Yorkshire, VII. 233, 235
Halkett, George (d. 1756), IX. 371, 372; *Logie O'Buchan*, IX. 371, 372; *Occasional Poems*, IX. 371; *Wherry Whigs Awa*, IX. 371
Halkett, Sir James, VII. 450
Halkett, lady (Ann Murray) (1622–1699), VII. 450
Halkett, Samuel (1814–1871), XII. 522; *Dictionary of Anonymous...Literature*, XII. 371
Halkirk, Caithness, II. 115
Hall, Anna Maria (Mrs S. C. Hall) (1800–1881), XI. 486; XIV. 312, 568
Hall, Anthony (1679–1725), XII. 7
Hall, Arthur (*fl.* 1563–1604), IV. 23, 437; VI. 37
Hall, Arthur Vine, XIV. 374, *also see* Add. 4
Hall, Basil (1788–1844), XIII. 562; XIV. 249, 552; *Schloss Hainfeld*, XIII. 432
Hall, Edward (d. 1547), II. 339; III. 315 ff.; VI. 333 ff.; *Union of the two Noble and Illustre famelies of Lancastre and Yorke* (*Chronicle*), III. 315 ff., 320, 325, 334, 529; IV. 396; V. 58, 83, 247; VII. 432
Hall, Hubert, V. 354
Hall, John (1575–1635), V. 219
Hall, John (1627–1656), VII. 86, 87, 94, 111, 359, 412, 501, 517; VIII. 229
    Call, The, VII. 85
    Crystal, The, VII. 85
    Dithyramb, A, VII. 85
    Epicurean Ode, An, VII. 85

Hall, John
    Epilogue, The, VII. 85
    Height of Eloquence, The, VII. 85
    Horae Vacivae, VII. 84, 392, 517
    Julia Weeping, VII. 85
    Lure, The, VII. 85
    Mercurius Brittanicus, VII. 357
    Mercurius Censorius, VII. 357
    Morning Star, The, VII. 85
    Ode, 'Descend, O Lord,' VII. 85
    Ode from an undergraduate to his tutor, Pawson, VII. 85
    Ode, 'Lord, send thine hand,' VII. 85
    Of Beauty, VII. 85
    Poems, VII. 84
    Sedition Scourg'd (probably by John Hall), VII. 344
    Self, VII. 85
Hall, John, of Gray's Inn, VII. 488, 489
Hall, John Richard Clark, I. 421, Add.
Hall, Joseph (1574–1656), bishop of Exeter and Norwich, III. 173, 199, 207; IV. 129, 206, 207, 239, 329 ff., 336 ff., 341, 342, 357, 363, 376, 519, 525; V. 338; VI. 15, 38, 59; VII. 105, 124, 139, 250, 265, 383, 425, 450, 471, 481; VIII. 63
    Characters of Virtues and Vices, IV. 336, 521; VII. 280
    Decisions of Diverse Practicall Cases of Conscience, VII. 280
    Episcopacy by Divine Right Asserted, VII. 158
    King's Prophecie, The, IV. 351
    Meditations and Vowes, IV. 265, 336
    Mundus alter et idem, IV. 336
    Occasional Meditations, VIII. 270
    Quo Vadis? A Just Censure of Travell, IV. 345
    Six Decads of Epistles, VII. 391
Hall, Joseph, *Satires*, IX. 87; *Virgidemiarum*, III. 173; IV. 329, 330, 337, 511, 519; VII. 432
Hall, Robert (1764–1831), XI. 399; XII. 472
Hall, R. N., XIV. Add. 7
Hall, Samuel Carter (1800–1889), XII. 410; XIV. 519
Hall, sergeant, in *The Tatler*, IX. 41
Hall, Theophilus D., XII. 335
Hall, Thomas (1610–1665), IX. 571
Hall, William (1748–1825), XII. 417
Hall-Stevenson, John (1718–1785), X. 47
Hallam, Arthur Henry (1811–1833), XIII. 23, 24, 32, 40, 477
Hallam, Henry (1777–1859), III. 417; IV. 45, 241, 264; V. 173, 234, 276; VI. 115; VII. 175; VIII. 262, 295; X. 284, 288; XII. 144, 311, 433; XIV. 56 ff., 75, 102, 143, 490; *Constitutional History of England*, XIV. 57 ff.; *Introduction to the Literature of Europe*, XIV. 58; *View of the state of Europe during the Middle Ages*, XIV. 56, 57
Hallam, Henry Fitzmaurice (1824–1850), XIV. 494
Hallamshire, XII. 516
Halle, Adam de la (*c.* 1235–1287), V. 34

Halle, John (d. 1479), III. 107, 108, 482, 493
Halle, Joseph, *The Chyrurgens Book*, **v.** 369, 478
Hallett, Joseph (1628?–1689), x. 384
Hallett, Joseph (1656–1722), x. 379, 384
Hallett, Joseph (1691?–1744), x. 381, 521
Halley, Edmund (1656–1742), VIII. 361, 477
Halliburtons, Memorials of the, XII. 376
Halliwell, Edward, VI. 303; *Dido*, VI. 298
Halliwell, J. O. *See* Halliwell-Phillipps
Halliwell-Phillipps (Halliwell), James Orchard (1820–1889), II. 199, 204, 422, 425; v. 165, 278, 314, 315; VI. 276; XI. 475; XII. 353, 369, 522; *Dictionary of Archaic and Provincial Words*, XII. 369; *Dictionary of Old English Plays*, XII. 369
Halloran, Henry, XIV. 362, 586
Hallward, N. L., XII. 437
Hallywell, Henry, VIII. 456
Halyblude, The, III. 122
Hama, in *Beowulf* and *Widsith*, I. 26, 35
Haman, in Biblical plays, v. 101
Hamauorum, pagus, I. 34
Hambden, Mr (John Hampden the younger?), VIII. 411
Hamber, captain, XIV. 180, 196
Hamburg, III. 42, 43; IV. 310; v. 298, 299, 307; XI. 259; XII. 4; XIV. 201
Hame, Hame, Hame, IX. 377
Hamerton, Philip Gilbert (1834–1894), XII. 524
Hamilton, IX. 193, 194
Hamilton, Alexander (d. 1732?), XIV. 576; *A New Account of the East Indies*, XIV. 333
Hamilton, Alexander (1762–1824), XII. 144, 343
Hamilton, Anne, duchess of (1636–1716), IX. 193
Hamilton, Anthony (1646?–1720), VIII. 208, 210, 262; XI. 290, 291, 307, 309; *Mémoires de la Vie du Comte de Gramont*, VIII. 261, 445, 446, 451; IX. 270; x. 245
Hamilton, Archibald, printer, x. 40, 201
Hamilton, Charles, marquis of, VII. 21
Hamilton, Charles (1753?–1792), XIV. 334, 576
Hamilton, Elizabeth, sister of Anthony, married comte de Gramont, VIII. 262, 263, 266
Hamilton, Elizabeth (1758–1816), XI. 460; XIII. 431; XIV. 600; *Cottagers of Glenburnie*, XI. 232; *My Ain Fireside*, XI. 232
Hamilton, Emma, lady (1761?–1815), XIV. 213
Hamilton, Gavin, XI 213
Hamilton, Sir George (d. 1679), VIII. 261, 263
Hamilton, James, 1st earl of Abercorn (d. 1617), VIII. 261
Hamilton, James, 1st duke of Hamilton (1606–1649), IX. 193, 194, 488

Hamilton, Janet (1795–1873), XII. 417
Hamilton, John (1511?–1571), archbishop of St Andrews, II. 369; *Catechism*, III. 153, 503
Hamilton, John (*fl.* 1568–1609), *Ane Catholik and Facile Traictise*, II. 94
Hamilton, John (1761–1814), XI. 234, 440
Hamilton, J. A., XIV. 509 ff.
Hamilton, Mary, II. 414
Hamilton, Nicholas, v. 278
Hamilton, Patrick (1504?–1528), III. 138, 140, 503; *Patrikes Places*, III. 140
Hamilton, Richard (*fl.* 1688), VIII. 263
Hamilton, Richard Winter (1794–1848), XIV. 606
Hamilton, Thomas (1789–1842), XII. 449
Hamilton, Thomas, 6th earl of Haddington (1680–1735), IX. 422
Hamilton, Walter, XIII. 491
Hamilton, Sir William (1788–1856), x. 274, 514; XI. 400; XII. 158; XIV. 1, 2, 7 ff. (main entry), 16, 29, 40, 41, 47, 139, 140, 411, 412, 473, 474, 476, 477, 481, 483, 596
Discussions on Philosophy and Literature, XII. 370; XIV. 7, 9
Lectures on Logic and Metaphysics, XII. 370; XIV. 8, 9
'Logic,' XIV. 7
'Philosophy of Perception, the,' XIV. 7, 10, 12
'Philosophy of the Unconditioned, the,' XIV. 7, 11
Hamilton, William, of Bangour (1704–1754), IX. 566; *Braes of Yarrow*, IX. 371; *Ode to the battle of Gladsmuir*, IX. 371
Hamilton, William, of Gilbertfield (1665?–1751), II. 108; IX. 372, 566, 567; XI. 204, 211; *Bonnie Heck*, IX. 364, 366; *Willie was a Wanton Wag*, IX. 364
Hamilton, W. D., XIV. 486
Hamilton, William, 2nd duke of Hamilton (1616–1651), IX. 194, 488
Hamilton, William Gerard (1729–1796), XI. 5, 173; *Parliamentary Logic*, x. 181, 463
Hamilton, Sir William Rowan (1805–1865), XIV. 262, 263, 556
Hamilton papers, VII. 435; IX. 194; XI. 290
Hamilton-King, Harriet Eleanor, XIII. 503; *The Disciples*, XIII. 179
Hamlet, Shakespeare's, I. 292; IV. 336; XII. 196; XIII. 34, 39, 60, 146
Hamlet, W. H. W. Betty as, XI. 283
'Hamlet's Aunt,' XIII. 327
Hamley, Sir Edward Bruce (1824–1893) XIII. 471
Hammer, Sir Thomas, XIV. 558
Hammersmith, IX. 254; x. 3, 95
Hammerton, J. A., XIII. 533, 544, 570
Hammond, Anthony (1668–1738), IX. 188, 485
Hammond, Henry (1605–1660), IV. 228; VII. 148, 151, 157, 425; VIII. 276, 293; *Paraphrase and Annotations on the New*

Hammond, Henry
  Testament, VII. 147; *Poor Man's Tithing,
  The*, VII. 147; *Practical Catechism, A*,
  VII. 147; VIII. 277
Hammond, James (1710–1742), IX. 188,
  485
Hammond, Mary, VII. 83
Hammond, Col. Robert (1621–1654), X.
  499
Hammond, William (*fl.* 1655), VII. 88,
  412; IX. 188
Hamond, Walter (*fl.* 1643), IV. 457
Hampden, John (1594–1643), IV. 54, 55;
  VII. 219, 439; VIII. 312
Hampden, Renn Dickson (1793–1868),
  XII. 259, 286 ff., 467
*Hampden's, Mr, Speeches occasioned upon
  the Londoner's Petition for Peace* (1642),
  VII. 385
Hamper, William (1776–1831), IX. 343,
  344
Hampole. *See* Rolle, Richard
Hampole, near Doncaster, II. 45, 47, 88
Hampole's *Pricke of Conscience*, XII. 504
Hampshire, III. 46; V. 103; XI. 49; XII.
  231, 236, 346; XIII. 355, 381; XIV. 221,
  294
Hampshire militia, X. 303, 320
Hampstead, XI. 149; XII. 79, 89, 91
Hampsthwaite, XIII. 275
Hampton, Benjamin, VIII. 474
Hampton, James (1721–1778), X. 466
Hampton, Middlesex, VII. 4; XI. 362
Hampton court, III. 208; V. 102; VI. 237,
  274, 326, 337; VII. 4, 6, 42; VIII. 245
Hampton court conference, III. 34, 45
Hanan, in *Jacob and Esau*, V. 111
Hanbury, David T., XIV. 583
Handel, George Frederick (1685–1759),
  VIII. 428; IX. 326; XIII. 250; XIV. 213;
  Ariadne, X. 199; *Scipio*, XI. 88
Handefull of pleasant delites, A, III. 190,
  191, 249, 511, 512, 524; IV. 111
Handley, Clement, XIV. Add. 7
Hangman's Tree, The, II. 396
Hanky and Panky, in Butler's *Erewhon
  Revisited*, XIII. 453
Hanmer, Sir Thomas (1677–1746), V. 271,
  272, 274; IX. 145, 476; X. 167, 454, 460,
  465
Hanna, William (1808–1882), XII. 472
Hannah, in Swift's *Grand Question de-
  bated*, IX. 119
Hannah, John (1818–1888), IV. 52, 53;
  VII. 82
Hannay, D., X. 421; XII. Add.
Hannay, James (1827–1873), XI. 392, 439,
  463; XIII. 162, 466; XIV. 140, 203, 238,
  519, 583; *Satire and Satirists*, XIV. 141;
  Singleton Fontenoy, XIV. 141
Hannay, James (1842–1910), XIV. 583;
  History of Acadia, XIV. 359; *The War
  of 1812*, XIV. 359
Hannay, Patrick (d. 1629?), VII. 412
  Anne of Denmark, elegies on, VII. 79
  Happy Husband, The, IV. 521; VII. 79

Hannay, Patrick
  Philomela, VII. 79
  Sheretine and Mariana, VII. 79
Hannes, Edward (d. 1710), IX. 478
Hannibal, IV. 62; X. 510
Hannibal's passage of the Alps, XII. 496,
  497
Hanover, V. 33; VIII. 50; IX. 45, 161, 200,
  201, 251, 309; X. 311
Hanover, elector of. *See* George I
Hanover, Sophia (princess), electress of,
  V. 284; VIII. 220, 452
Hanover archives, VIII. 272; X. 295
Hanover club, IX. 165
Hanoverian period, X. 355; XIV. 88
Hanoverian protestantism, X. 352
Hanoverian queens of England, XIV. 111
Hanoverian succession, IX. 14, 192, 440;
  X. 354, 374
Hansard, Thomas Curson (1776–1833),
  XI. 49
Hansard's Analytical Parliamentary Di-
  gest, XIV. 508
Hansard's Parliamentary Debates, XIV.
  508
Hanseatic league, II. 100; IV. 310; V. 355;
  VII. 198; XIV. 72
Hanserd Knollys society, X. 520
Hanway, Jonas (1712–1786), X. 467
Hanway, Mary Ann, X. 475
Haphazard, in *Apius and Virginia*, V. 64
Harapha, in *Samson Agonistes*, VII. 122,
  137
Harbord, William (1635?–1692), VIII. 257
Harbury, X. 112, 271
Harcourt, Lewis Vernon, XIV. 506
Harcourt, Robert (1574?–1631), IV. 97,
  457
Harcourt, Simon, 1st viscount Harcourt
  (1661?–1727), IX. 162
Harcourt, Simon (1684–1720), VIII. 410
Harcourt, Sir William Vernon, XIV.
  198
Hardcastle, Ephraim, *pseud. See* Pyne,
  William Henry
Hardcastle, Mr, in *She Stoops to Conquer*,
  X. 214
Hardcastle, Miss, in *She Stoops to Conquer*,
  X. 482
Harden, W. T., XIII. 481
Hardenberg, Friedrich Ludwig von. *See*
  Novalis
Harder, H., IV. 267
Hardicanute, V. 31
Hardie, in Reade's *Hard Cash*, XIII. 428
Hardie, M., XIV. 540
Hardie, William Ross (1862–1919), XII.
  Add. 3
Hardiman, James (1790?–1855), XIV. 568;
  Irish Minstrelsy, XIV. 305, 325
Harding, Septimus, Trollope's, XIII. 422
Hardinge, George (1743–1816), X. 244,
  248, 250; XI. 390
Hardinge, Henry Charles, viscount Hard-
  inge (1857–1924), XIV. 505
Hardres court, Canterbury, XIV. 390

Hardwick, VII. 283, 289
Hardwicke, earls of. *See* Yorke, Philip
Hardy, Alexandre (c. 1570–1631), *Marianne*, VIII. 13
Hardy, Laetitia, in Mrs Cowley's *Belle's Stratagem*, XI. 275
Hardy, Thomas, I. 240; II. 414; IV. 48; XIII. Add. 2; XIV. 121
Hardy, Sir Thomas Duffus (1804–1878), XII. 516; *Descriptive catalogue of materials relating to the history of Great Britain and Ireland*, XII. 355
Hardyng, John (1378–1465?), X. 498; *Chronicle*, II. 496; III. 334; IV. 396
Hare, Augustus J. C. (1834–1903), XI. 460; XIV. 503, 519
Hare, Augustus William (1792–1834), IV. 40; XII. 467; *Guesses at Truth*, X. 218; XII. 301
Hare, Christopher, XIII. 18
Hare, David, XIV. 336
Hare, Francis (1671–1740), IX. 336, 455, 525
Hare, Julius Charles (1795–1855), XI. 491; XII. 282, 289, 308, 425, 467, 478; *Guesses at Truth*, X. 218; XII. 301; *Mission of the Comforter, The*, XII. 288; *Vindication of Niebuhr's History*, XII. 302
Hare, Thomas, IX. 216
Haredales, the, in *Barnaby Rudge*, XIII. 320
Harefield, Middlesex, VII. 113
Harewood, Leeds, *Rushworth Gospels*, written by a priest of, I. 132
Harflete, Henry (*fl.* 1653), IV. 503; VII. 509, 517
Hargraves, the, in Mrs Cowley's *Runaway*, XI. 274
Hargrove, William (1788–1862), XII. 510
Harington, Sir John (1561–1612), III. 199, 231, 252, 268, 270, 304, 305, 425, 509; IV. 24, 263, 265, 267, 328, 334, 520, 533; V. 82, 345, 478; VI. 314, 480; VII. 271
An Apologie of Poetrie, IX. 61
Ariosto, III. 199, 526; IV. 23, 248, 401, 441
Epigrams, III. 270, 523
Nugae Antiquae, IV. 55
Treatise of Playe, VI. 397
Hark, the thund'ring Cannons roar, VIII. 96
Harland, Henry (1851–1905), XIII. 563
Harlaw, II. 415; XIII. 234
Harleian *Collection of Voyages and Travels*, X. 166
Harleian library, IX. 357; X. 465, 468; XI. 336, 467; XII. 363
Harleian manuscripts, IX. 356; XII. 491, 522
Harleian Miscellany, IV. 65; VII. 455; VIII. 411; IX. 357, 534; X. 166, 468
Harleian society, XII. 355
Harley, Edward, 2nd earl of Oxford (1689–1741), IX. 79, 84, 87, 152, 153, 357, 482; X. 166, 262; XI. 347
Harley, George Davies (d. 1811?), XI. 452

Harley, Henrietta, countess of Oxford, IX. 248
Harley, lady Henrietta-Cavendish Holles, IX. 483
Harley, Margaret, duchess of Portland, X. 262
Harley, Margaret Cavendish Holles, IX. 153, 155
Harley, Mrs, in Kelly's *False Delicacy*, X. 91; XI. 263
Harley, Robert, 1st earl of Oxford (1661–1724), III. 97; IX. 5, 8, 10 ff., 20, 77, 78, 94 ff., 99, 113, 117 ff., 124, 130, 131, 151 ff., 161, 166, 167, 217, 219, 336, 357, 443, 444, 455, 461, 465; X. 280, 386; XI. 317; XIV. 168, 462, 463
Harlot, the, in a broadside, III. 87
Harlow, XI. 153
Harlowe family, in Richardson's *Clarissa*, X. 9
Harman, Thomas (*fl.* 1567), III. 85, 87, 103, 104, 320; IV. 317, 318, 320, 354; VII. 395; *A Caveat or Warening for Commen Corsetors*, III. 103, 104, 320; 343, 448, 482, 492; IV. 521; V. 480
Harmar, John (1555?–1613), VII. 316, 482
Harmer, Anthony. *See* Wharton, Henry (1664–1695)
Harmer, Florence Elizabeth, I. Add.
Harnack, Adolf, XII. 467
Haro, Don Lewis de, VII. 391
Harold I, king of the English, I. 149, 150, 278; XIII. 366; XIV. 72
Harold the Fair-haired, I. 26
Haroun, in Beckford's *Vathek*, XI. 290
Haroun, Abraschid, XII. 499
Harp of Caledonia, XI. 443
Harpagon, Molière's, XIII. 446
Harpalus, in Owen's *Epigrammata*, IV. 265
Harper, Charles George, XIV. 540
Harper, Thomas Norton (1821–1893), XIV. 474
Harpsfield, John (1516–1578), IV. 493
Harpur, Charles (1817–1868), XIV. 586
Bushrangers, The, XIV. 363
Creek of the Four Graves, The, XIV. 363
Thoughts, XIV. 363
Tower of the Dream, The, XIV. 363
Words, XIV. 363
Harrington, James (1611–1677), VII. 300, 362, 389, 421, 471, 472, 518, *also see* Add.; IX. 201, 384, 570; *Oceana*, VII. 298, 299; IX. 385; *Political Aphorisms*, VII. 299
Harrington, John, 1st baron of Exton (d. 1613), IV. 175
Harrington, John, 2nd baron of Exton (1592–1614), IV. 216
Harrington, or Harington, John (*fl.* 1550), trans. of Cicero *On Friendship*, IV. 5, 436
Harriot, in Colman's *Jealous Wife*, X. 89, 90
Harriot, Thomas (1560–1621), IV. 55, 59, 452, 508
Harris, Benjamin, VIII. 98
Harris, Edwin, XIII. 543

Harris, F., XIII. 465

Harris, Furlong Elizabeth Skipton, XII. 456

Harris, James (1709–1780), X. 512

Harris, James (*Hermes* Harris), XI. 250

Harris, James, 1st earl of Malmesbury (1746–1820), XIV. 504

Harris, James Howard, 3rd earl of Malmesbury (1807–1889), XIV. 504

Harris, John, alias Sirrahniho or Oxford Jack, VII. 494, 495; *Anti Mercurius*, VII. 357; *Mercurius Militaris*, VII. 357

Harris, John (1667?–1719), VII. 266; IX. 534

Harris, John (1756–1846), XI. 377

Harris, John, XIV. 552

Harris, Joseph (1661–1702), VIII. 401, 436; IX. 264

Harris, J. F., XIII. 572

Harris, Thomas (d. 1820), XI. 451, 452; XII. 69

Harris, Thomas Lake, XIV. 165

Harris, William (1675?–1740), X. 381, 521

Harrison, Elizabeth, X. 467

Harrison, Frederic (1831–1923), X. 299, 302, 312, 316; XIII. 471, 477, 509, 543, 548, 558, 573; XIV. 24, 469

Harrison, George, XIV. 606

Harrison, Ralph (1748–1810), XIV. 599

Harrison, Robert (d. 1585), III. 106

Harrison, Thomas (1606–1660), VII. 219; VIII. 470

Harrison, William (1534–1593), *Chronologie*, VI. 381; *Description of England and Scotland*, III. 319, 320, 321, 323, 328, 331; IV. 308, 511; V. 342, 348, 350, 352 ff., 357, 358, 360 ff., 367, 373 ff., 478; VI. 394, 462

Harrison, William (1685–1713), VIII. 158; IX. 125, 485; X. 140

Harrison, William (1802–1884), XII. 519

Harrison, Rev. William, XIII. 548

Harrovian, The, XIV. 539

Harrow school, VII. 326, 336, 492; IX. 142, 408; XII. 31, 41, 326, 329, 333; XIII. 241; XIV. 386, 390, 413, 422

Harrow-upon-the-Hill, VII. 336

Harrowby, earl of. See Ryder, Dudley

Harrowby, lady, XIV. 115

Harrowing of hell, in *Piers the Plowman*, II. 27

Harrowing of Hell, The, I. 48, 99, 251, 465; V. 2, 14, 15, 20, 27, 41, 390

Harruney, Luke, *i.e.* Henry Walker, VII. 351, 352, 499

Harry, Blind, or Henry the Minstrel (*fl.* 1460–1492), II. 108 ff.; IV. 412, 413; *Wallace*, II. 108 ff., 124, 239, 251, 280, 399, 447, 449; IV. 412; XI. 204, 237

Harsnett, Samuel (1561–1631), IV. 535

Hart, Andro (d. 1621), IV. 151, 413, 547

Hart, Charles (d. 1683), VIII. 186

Hart, John (d. 1574), III. 556; *An orthographie*, IV. 397

Hart, S. Hopgood, XIII. 564

Hart, W. H., *Index Expurgatorius Anglicanus*, V. 482

Harte, Bret, XIII. 543; XIV. 349, 368, 369; *Heathen Chinee, The*, XIV. 206

Harte, Walter (1709–1774), IV. 368; XI. 472; *Essay on Husbandry*, IV. 371

Hartington, marquis of. See Cavendish, Spencer Compton

Hartis Tale, in *Talis of the Fyve Bestis*, II. 280

Hartleborough, X. 386

Hartley, David (1705–1757), X. 345, 513; XI. 100, 137; XII. 168, 431; XIV. 5, 23, 393, 477; *Observations on Man*, X. 342, 343

Hartley, Elizabeth (1751–1824), XI. 273

Hartley, Thomas (1709?–1784), IX. 512

Hartlib, Samuel (d. 1670?), VII. 305, 310, 472; IX. 388; *Considerations...of England's reformation*, IX. 389; *Macaria*, IX. 389, 570

Hartly House, XIV. 335, 574

Hartmann, M., I. 102

Hartmann von Aue, I. 268, 280

Hartog, Philippe Joseph, XIV. 597

Hartop, Job, IV. 73

Hartshill, Warwickshire, IV. 168

Hartshorne, Charles Henry (1802–1865), XII. 369, 522

Hartson, Hall (d. 1773), X. 534

Hartwell, A. (the elder?), IV. 298

Hartwell, Abraham (the younger) (*fl.* 1600), IV. 382, 445, 446

Harun-ar-Rashid, I. 153

Harvard, VII. 29; X. 386

Harvard, Elizabethan stage at, VI. 266

Harvard, John (1607–1638), VII. 339

Harvard college library, XII. 401, 405

Harveian oration, IX. 132

Harvey, Baldwin, *Bustorum Aliquot Reliquiae*, VIII. 362

Harvey, Charles, VII. 356, 501

Harvey, Christopher (1597–1663), VII. 405; *Synagogue*, VII. 44, 406

Harvey, Clarence, in Miss Edgeworth's *Belinda*, XI. 297

Harvey, Gabriel (1545?–1630), III. 179, 190, 201, 202, 213, 214, 217, 219, 220, 229, 252, 271, 293, 294, 302, 305, 392, 393, 395, 396, 520, 526, 545, 546; IV. 8, 17, 18, 23, 54, 125, 131, 134, 322, 327, 360, 399, 514, 517, 523; V. 122, 140, 372, 394, 478; VI. 218, 288, 480, 494; VII. 316; IX. 32

A New Letter, III. 546

Advertisement to Papp-Hatchet, IV. 395, 537

Gratulationes Valdinenses, III. 201

Have with you to Saffron-Walden, IV. 326

Musarum Lachrymae, VI. 306

Pierces Supererogation, III. 252, 546; IV. 323

Trimming of Thomas Nashe, III. 546; VI. 307

Harvey, Gilbert, VI. 307

Harvey, John (d. 1592), III. 545

Harvey, John (*fl.* 1729), IX. 557

Harvey, Joseph, XI. 377
Harvey, Richard (d. 1623?), III. 393, 394, 396; IV. 322; VI. 307; *Plaine Percevall the Peace-maker of England*, III. 393, 396, 543; *A Theologicall Discourse of the Lamb of God and his enemies*, III. 396, 540
Harvey, Thomas, translator of Owen's *Latin Epigrams*, IV. 503
Harvey, William (1578–1657), IV. 278, 290, 292; VII. 314, 396, 478, 479; VIII. 276, 350, 351, 359, 361 ff., 477; IX. 391; XIV. 281, 283, 284; *Exercitatio*, VIII. 361; *Exercitationes de Generatione Animalium*, VIII. 362
Harvey, William Henry, XIV. Add. 7
Harvey-Nashe controversy, III. 395, 545; IV. 322, 332
Harward, Simon (*fl.* 1572–1614), IV. 542
Harwich, VIII. 257
Harwood, Edward (1729–1794), XII. 522
Harwood, Sir Edward (1586?–1632), IV. 457
Harwood, Isabella (*pseud.* Ross Neil, 1840?–1888), XIII. 180, 503, 519
Harwood, Philip (1809–1887), XIV. 534
Haselrigge, Sir Arthur, IX. 258
Hasely, village of, III. 380, 382
Haslewood, Joseph (1769–1833), XII. 516
Hassall, Arthur, XIV. 508
Hasted, Edward (1732–1812), XI. 426; XII. 510
Hastings, VII. 54
Hastings, battle of, I. 111, 149 ff., 157; XI. 34
Hastings, Charles, XIII. 514
Hastings, lady Elizabeth (1682–1739), IX. 38
Hastings, Francis Rawdon, 2nd earl Moira (1754–1826), XII. 103
Hastings, Henry, lord, VII. 7; VIII. 2
Hastings, Lucy, countess of Huntingdon, IV. 161, 216
Hastings, Selina, countess of Huntingdon (1707–1791), V. 365, 366
Hastings, Warren (1732–1818), X. 260, 408; XI. 6, 14, 16 ff., 20, 25, 54, 78, 167, 389, 390, 396; XII. 343, 515; XIV. 63, 98, 333, 334, 493
Hastings, William, lord (1430?–1483), III. 335; X. 291
Haswell, in Mrs Inchbald's *Such Things Are*, XI. 278
Hatch, Edwin (1835–1889), XII. 467
Hatch, F. H., XIV. Add. 7
Hatcham, XIII. 61
Hatcher, Henry (1777–1846), XII. 510
Hatcher, Orie Latham, VI. 122
Hatchett, William, *Rival Father*, X. 86
Hatchway, lieutenant, in Smollett's *Peregrine Pickle*, X. 38
Haterius, IV. 349
Hatfield, VII. 435; X. 126
Hatfield, Thomas of (d. 1381), XII. 510
Hatfield Broadoak, II. 198
Hathaway, Agnes, V. 168

Hatherton, lord. *See* Littleton, Edward John
Hathwaye, or Hathway, Richard (*fl.* 1602), V. 311, 312, 319, 328; VIII. 126; *King Arthur*, VII. 331
Hathwey or Hathaway, Anne, V. 168, 219
Hatred, in *Pathomachia*, VI. 324
Hatter, Richard (*fl.* 1649), VII. 354
Hatteraick, Dirk, in Scott's *Guy Mannering*, XII. 21
Hatto, bishop (ballad), III. 81
Hatton, Sir Christopher (1540–1591), IV. 1; V. 72; VII. 196
Hatton, Christopher, 1st viscount (1632–1706), VII. 196; IX. 344
Hatton, Correspondence of the Family of, VII. 196, 439
Hatton, Joseph (1841–1907), XII. 428; XIII. 563; XIV. 532, 549
Hatton, Warwickshire, XII. 326
Hatton house, VIII. 115
Hattuariorum, pagus, I. 34
Haughton, William (*fl.* 1598), V. 117, 311, 312, 326, 328, 474; VI. 54, 96, 97, 219, 424
 Conquest of Spayne, The, VIII. 126
 English Men For My Money, V. 328
 Grim the Collier of Croyden; or, The Devil and his Dame, V. 328; VIII. 123
 Roben Hood's penerthes, V. 35
 Woman will have her Will, A, V. 328 ff.
 See, also, under Day, Dekker and Marlowe
Haukin, John, in *The merry jests of the widow Edith*, II. 327
Haultain, Arnold, XIV. 498
Hausted, Peter (d. 1645), VI. 473, 474; *The Rival Friends*, VI. 324
Hávamál, I. 62
Havard, William (1710?–1778), XI. 257; *Regulus*, XI. 273
Havell, Ernest Binfield (b. 1861), XII. Add. 5
Havelok the Dane, Lay of, I. 218, 277, 286, 287, 288, 303, 305, 306, 309, 315, 351, 360, 364, 367, 399, 468; II. 420; III. 372; XII. 517
Haverfield, Francis John (1860–1919), XII. 507, *also see* Add. 5
Haverfordwest, X. 386
Havergal, Frances Ridley (1836–1879), XI. 479
Haversham, lord. *See* Thompson, Sir John
Haviland, John, VII. 361
Havisham, Miss, in *Great Expectations*, XIII. 334
Havre, Le, XIII. 119
Haward, Nicolas (*fl.* 1569), IV. 436
Haweis, Rev. Hugh Reginald, XIII. 483
Hawes, Stephen (d. 1523?), II. 223, 225, 231, 265, 325, 330, 428, 470, 471; III. 168, 282, 291
 Comfort of Lovers, The, II. 224
 Conversion of Swearers, The, II. 224, 226, 230, 325
 Example of Virtue, The, II. 224, 226, 228, 233

Hawes, Stephen
  Joyful Meditation to all England of the Coronation of Henry the Eighth, A, II. 224, 226, 325
  Passetyme of Pleasure, The, II. 223 ff., 228 ff., 325; VII. 174
Hawes, William (1736–1808), X. 483
Hawick, IX. 565
Hawk, Sir Mulberry, in *Nicholas Nickleby*, XIII. 317
Hawke, Sir John, *The Englishman's Right* (1680), VIII. 469
Hawke, Michael, *The Groundes of the Laws of England* (1657), VIII. 469
Hawker, Mary (*pseud.* Lanoe Falconer, 1848–1908), XIII. 563
Hawker, Robert Stephen (1803–1875), XII. 417
  'And shall Trelawney die?' XII. 134
  Morwenna poems, XII. 134
  Pater Vester Pascit illa, XII. 134
  Queen Gwennyvar's Round ('Naiad for Grecian Waters'), XII. 134
  Quest of the Sangraal, The, XII. 134
  Sea-Bird's Cry, The, XII. 134
  Silent Tower of Bottreau, The (*Bells of Bottreau*), XII. 134
  Song of the Western Men, XII. 134
Hawkesworth, John (1715?–1775), VIII. 191, 442; IX. 124, 453; X. 175, 188, 465, 466; XI. 457; XIV. 244, 552; *Account of Voyages*, XI. 327
Hawkesworth, Walter (d. 1606), VI. 474; *Labyrinthus*, VI. 305; *Leander*, VI. 305
Hawking, writers on, IV. 541
Hawkins, Alexander (*fl.* 1601), VI. 290
Hawkins, Henry (1571?–1646), *Parthenia Sacra*, VII. 88, 412
Hawkins, Sir John (1532–1595), III. 327; IV. 1, 68, 77, 85, 88; VII. 305; *A True Declaration of the Troublesome voyage of Mr John Hawkins...in the years... 1567 and 1568*, IV. 72, 458
Hawkins, Sir John (1719–1789), X. 157, 158, 161, 163, 215, 459, 466, 471, 472; XI. 333; XII. 490; *Life of Johnson*, X. 189, 190, 483
Hawkins, Laetitia M., X. 473; XI. 473
Hawkins, Sir Richard (1562?–1622), IV. 77 ff.; *Observations of Sir R... H..., in his voiage into the South Sea*, IV. 77, 78, 458
Hawkins, William (d. 1554?), IV. 72
Hawkins, capt. William, IV. 99
Hawkins, W., VIII. 460
Hawkins, son-in-law of Izaak Walton, VII. 256
Hawkshead grammar school, XI. 95
Hawkyn and Dawkyn and Tomkyn, in *The Turnament of Totenham*, I. 366
Hawley, Henry (1679?–1759), IX. 378
Haworth, Yorkshire, XIII. 404 ff.
Haworth, Miss Euphrasia Fanny, XIII. 61
Hawthorn, Jerry, in Egan's *Life in London*, XIV. 223, 227, 230
Hawthornden, IV. 151, 153; VIII. 322

Hawthorne, Nathaniel, XI. 439, 492
Hawthorne, The Testament of the, III. 483
Hawtrey, Edward Craven (1789–1862), XIV. 413
Haxey-hood contest, Lincolnshire, v. 30
Hay, Sir Gilbert (*fl.* 1456), II. 284, 479; *Buik of King Alexander*, I. 291; II. 448; *Buke of the Law of Armys, The*, or *Buke of Bataillis*, II. 284; *Buke of the Order of Knichthood, The*, II. 284
Hay, James, 1st viscount Doncaster (d. 1636), IV. 202, 203; VII. 437
Hay, John Barras, XIV. 595
Hay, Thomas, 8th earl of Kinnoul (1710–1787), X. 408; XI. 351
Hay, William, XIV. Add. 5
Hay Now the Day daws, IX. 362
Haydn, Joseph, XI. 232
Haydocke, Richard (*fl.* 1605), IV. 445
Haydon, Benjamin Robert (1786–1846), XII. 79, 81, 172, 173, 407, 433; XIV. 519; *Autobiography*, XIV. 156, 157; *Lectures on Painting and Design*, XIV. 156
Hayes, Edward, XIV. 573
Hayes, lord (*fl.* 1607), IV. 143, 144
Hayes Barton, Budleigh, IV. 51
Hayley, William (1745–1820), XI. 90, 172, 176 ff., 180, 195, 401 ff., 426, 457; *Triumph of Temper*, XI. 176
Hayman, Henry (1823–1904), XII. 484
Hayman, Robert (d. 1631?), IV. 502, 520
Haymo, I. 117
Haynie, Henry, XIV. 534
Hayward, Abraham (1801–1884), X. 473, 484; XI. 344, 392; XII. 408; XIV. 198, 491, 519; *Art of Dining, The*, XIV. 138; *Faust* (trans.), XIV. 138; *More about Junius*, X. 409; XIV. 139
Hayward, Frank Herbert, XIV. 480
Hayward, Sir John (1564?–1627), III. 318, 334, 337, 338, 529, 530; IV. 302, 511
  Henry IV, III. 338
  Lives of the Three Normans, Kings of England, III. 338
  The Beginning of the Reigne of Queene Elizabeth, III. 338
  The Life and Reigne of King Edward the Sixt, III. 338
Hayward, W., translator, VI. 482
Haywood, Mrs Eliza (1693?–1756), IX. 18, 21, *also see* Add.
Haywood, Ralph, IV. 160
Hazard-Wilding plot, in *The Gamester*, VI. 202
Hazlitt, John, brother of W. Hazlitt, XII. 166
Hazlitt, Margaret, sister of W. Hazlitt, XII. 165
Hazlitt, Mrs (formerly Mrs Bridgewater), XII. 167
Hazlitt, Sarah (born Stoddart), XII. 167, 188
Hazlitt, William (1778–1830), III. 255; IV. 132; V. 222, 234, 252; VI. 53, 278; VII. 104; IX. 70, 87, 451; X. 43, 118; XI. 99, 112, 120, 128, 151, 159, 168, 171, 284,

Hazlitt, William
288, 391, 393, 394, 409, 417, 423, 439, 447, 461; XII. 77, 79, 104, 108, 118, 160, 164 ff. (main entry), 188, 192, 199, 203, 219, 223, 379, 410, 412, 430 ff., 438, 442, 444; XIII. 148, 275 ff., 311, 429, 513, 515; XIV. 138, 170, 171, 198, 230

Cant and Hypocrisy, XII. 177
Conversations of James Northcote, XII. 173
Disagreeable People, On, XII. 174
Essay on the Principles of Human Action, XII. 168
Familiar Style, On, XII. 174
Fear of Death, On the, XII. 174
Feeling of Immortality in Youth, The, XII. 174, 176
Fight, The, XII. 174, 175
Genius and Common Sense, XII. 177
Going a Journey, On, XII. 174, 176
Lectures on the Dramatic Literature of the Age of Elizabeth, VIII. 185
Lectures on the [English] Comic Writers, VIII. 162; X. 44
Letter to William Gifford, XII. 175
Liber Amoris, XII. 167
My First Acquaintance with Poets, XII. 166, 174, 176
Past and Future, XII. 177
Patronage and Puffing, XII. 177
Persons One Would Wish to have Seen, Of, XII. 174
Reading New Books, On, XII. 174
Reading Old Books, On, XII. 174
Review of the English Stage, A, XII. 171
Sick Chamber, The, XII. 174
Spirit of the Age, The, XI. 150; XII. 170
Taste, On, XII. 174
Thought and Action, XII. 177
Wit and Humour, XII. 177
Writing and Speaking, XII. 177

Hazlitt, William, unitarian minister, father of above, XII. 165
Hazlitt, William Carew (1834–1913), XII. 433, 438, 522; *Remains of the Early Popular Poetry of England*, II. 500
Hazlitts, the, XII. 192
Head, Barclay Vincent (1844–1914), XII. 497
Head, Sir Francis Bond (1793–1875), XIV. 249, 552
Head, G. O. A., Disraeli's, XIII. 351
Head, Richard (1637?–1686?), VII. 516; IX. 500
Headda, or Hedda, I. 77
Headlam, Walter George (1866–1908), XII. 485, *also see* Add.; *A Book of Greek Verse*, XII. 333
Headley, Henry (1765–1788), X. 455
Headpiece, Sir Francis, in Vanbrugh's *Journey to London*, VIII. 162
Headrigg, Cuddie, in Scott's *Old Mortality*, XII. 25
Headrigg, Mause, in Scott's *Old Mortality*, XII. 25

Headstrong, Jonathan, VIII. 122
Healey, John (d. 1610), III. 487; IV. 395, 436, 441, 521; VII. 482, 489
Healfdene, in *Beowulf*, I. 22, 25, 31, 32
Health, in *The Pride of Life*, V. 52
Heardred, in *Beowulf*, I. 24
Hearn, Lafcadio (1850–1904), XIV. 138, 519, *also see* Add. 3
Glimpses of Unfamiliar Japan, XIV. 166
Japan: an Attempt at Interpretation, XIV. 166
Karma, XIV. 166
Two Years in the French West Indies, XIV. 165
Hearne, Thomas (1678–1735), I. 143; VIII. 241, 463; IX. 57, 167, 170, 171, 342, 349 (main entry), 391, 413, 467, 534, 536, 541; X. 220, 355, 356; *Ductor Historicus*, IX. 349; *Reliquiae Bodleianae*, IX. 349, 574
Hearniana, Bibliotheca, XII. 515
Heart, king, in *King Hart*, II. 262
Heartfree, in Congreve's *Old Bachelor*, VIII. 147
Heartfree, in Fielding's *Jonathan Wild*, X. 27
Hear-well, in *Piers the Plowman*, II. 19
Heath, Benjamin (1704–1766), V. 273; IX. 477; XII. 365; XIV. 386; *A Revisal of Shakespeare's Text*, IX. 144, 145
Heath, Charles (1785–1848), XIV. 225
Heath, Douglas Denon, IV. 282
Heath, John (*fl.* 1615), IV. 520; VII. 486
Heath, Robert (*fl.* 1650), *Clarastella*, VII. 88, 412
Heathcliff, in Emily Brontë's *Wuthering Heights*, XIII. 411, 412
Heathobeardan, the, in *Beowulf*, I. 24, 25
Heaviness, in *The Goldyn Targe*, II. 253
Heavitree, Exeter, III. 405
Heavysege, Charles (1816–1876), XIV. 350, 582; *Saul*, XIV. 357
Hebbel, Christian Friedrich, V. 304
Heber, Reginald (1783–1826), XII. 365, 417, 467; XIV. 576; *If thou wert by my side, my love*, XII. 139; *Morte d'Arthur*, XII. 138; *Narrative of a Journey*, XIV. 336
Heber, Richard (1773–1833), XII. 5, 365, 366, 377, 522
Heberden, William (1710–1801), XI. 333
'Hebraism and Hellenism,' XIII. 101
Hebraists, XII. 262, 341
Hebrew, knowledge of, in Elizabethan days, V. 362
Hebrew, study of, II. 370
Hebrew language and literature, VII. 53, 316 ff., 333, 341, 348, 353, 490; VIII. 75, 112, 281, 288, 307, 323, 364; IX. 337, 382, 385, 393, 403, 558; X. 229, 237; XI. 181, 354; XII. 341, 362; XIV. 406, 459
Hebrew poetry, II. 406
Hebrew professor at Cambridge, IX. 335
Hebrew prophets, XI. 32; XIII. 36
Hebrews, the, IV. 27 ff.
Hebrides, the, IX. 560; XI. 287; XIII. 432

Hebron, in *Absalom and Achitophel*, VIII. 37

Hecate, in *Macbeth*, VI. 76

Hecate, in *The Witch of Edmonton*, VI. 76

Hecht, G., XIII. 470

Hecht, Hans, IX. 360; *Songs from David Herd's Manuscript*, IX. 374

Heckmondwike academy, X. 385

Hector, in Dryden's *Troilus and Cressida*, VIII. 29

Hector, in *Iliad*, VIII. 50

Hector, in *The Birth of Merlin*, V. 249

Hector, Edmund (*fl.* 1732), X. 159

'Hector of Sarum' (Burnet), IX. 217

Hedderwick, J., XIII. 503

Hedelin, François, abbé d'Aubignac, VII. 368, 504

Hedon, in *Cynthia's Revels*, VI. 41, 42, 44

Hedwig, I. 229

Hedworth, Henry, X. 377

Heenan, John C., pugilist, XIV. 183

Heep, Uriah, in *David Copperfield*, XIII. 327; XIV. 437

Hegel, Georg Wilhelm Friedrich, V. 304, 305; IX. 328, 522; XI. 121, 139; XIV. 1, 9, 11, 16, 40 ff., 47, 48, 479, 481, 483; *Encyclopaedia*, XIV. 45

Hegelian philosophy, XI. 57

Héger, Constantin, XIII. 405, 406

Heichen, Paul, XIII. 532

Heidegger, Gotthard, XIV. 213

Heidegger, John James (1659?–1749), IX. 477

Heidelberg, IV. 159

Heidelberg, Mrs, in Colman's *Clandestine Marriage*, X. 90

Heimskringla, the, XIII. 127

Heine, Heinrich, XI. 307; XII. 169, 396, 397; XIII. 9, 98, 99, 108, 552

Heinse, Johann J. W., XI. 303

Heinsius, Daniel, VI. 9; VII. 261, 307

Heinsius, N., VII. 307

Helen, in *Dr Faustus*, V. 155

Helen, in Goethe's *Faust*, XII. 34

Helen, in Shelley's *Rosalind and Helen*, XII. 62

Helen, in Tennyson's *Helen's Tower*, XIII. 177

Helen of Kirkconnel, IX. 364

Helen of Troy, VII. 101

Helena, in *A Midsummer-Night's Dream*, V. 180, 272

Helena, St, finder of the Cross, I. 55, 56, 133, 134

Helfta, in Saxony, convent, I. 229

Helgakviða Hiörvarðssonar, Old Norse poem, I. 21

Helgakviða Hundingsbana II, Old Norse poem, I. 21

Helgi, son of Halfdan, I. 25

Heliand, I. 46, 47

Helias of Jerusalem, I. 136

Helias, Knight of the Swan, The History of, II. 325, 485

Helicon, VI. 310; VIII. 201

Hélie de Barron, I. 273

Helinand de Froidmont, *Vers de la Mort*, II. 140, 142

Heliodorus, III. 351; IX. 536; *Aethiopian Historie*, IV. 3, 19, 436

Hell, XI. 188

Hell, Eleven Pains of, I. 227, 458

Hellena, in *A Challenge for Beauty*, VI. 103

Hellenic studies, society for the promotion of, XII. 340

Hellenism, XII. 34, 40; XIII. 26, 36, 101, 123

Hellfire club, X. 391

Hello, Ernest, V. 208, 209, 222

Hellowes, Edward (*fl.* 1574–1600), IV. 445, 458

Helm, William Henry, XIII. 543

Helmgisl, I. 87

Helmholtz, Hermann von, XIV. 269

Heloise, IX. 477, 538

Helps, Sir Arthur (1813–1875), XIV. 98, 503, 519, 520, *also see* Add. 3
    Brevia, XIV. 164
    Friends in Council, XIV. 163, 164
    Realmah, XIV. 164
    The Spanish Conquest of the New World, XIV. 99

Helston, VII. 86

Helston school, Cornwall, XIII. 355

Helstone, Caroline, in Charlotte Brontë's *Shirley*, XIII. 408, 409

Helstonleigh, Mrs Henry Wood's, XIII. 430

Helvétius, Claude Adrien, IX. 401; XI. 70; XII. 168, 431; XIV. 8; *De l'Esprit*, XI. 63

Hemans, Felicia Dorothea (1793–1835), XI. 442; XII. 124 ff., 129, 417; XIII. 149, 175, 177; XIV. 311
    Better Land, The, XII. 127
    Casabianca, XII. 125, 127
    England's Dead, XII. 127
    They grew in beauty side by side, XII. 127

Heming, or Hemminge, or Heminge, John (d. 1630), V. 169; VI. 248, 249, 276, 358

Hemingburgh. *See* Walter of

Hemingford, Walter de (*fl.* 1300), IX. 535

Hemming (*fl.* 1096), IX. 535

Hempstead, IV. 411

Henbury, Gloucestershire, X. 111

Henchman, Humfrey (1592–1675), bishop of London, VIII. 302

Henderson, Alexander (1583?–1646), IX. 544

Henderson, Andrew (*fl.* 1734–1775), IX. 564, 565; X. 475, *also see* Add.

Henderson, Archibald, XIII. 515, 570

Henderson, John (1747–1785), XI. 402, 454

Henderson, May J. S., XIII. 570

Henderson, Thomas Finlayson, II. 413; XI. 438, 439, 445; XII. 373, 451

Hendley, William (1691?–1724), IX. 571

Hendon, IX. 155; X. 214

Hendred, Dane William, prior of Leominster, II. 327

Hendyng, Proverbs of, I. 219, 363, 477

Hengest, in *Finnsburh*, I. 31, 32. *See, also,* I. 104, 246

Hengham, Ralph de (d. 1311), VIII. 465, 469

Hengo, in Fletcher's *Bonduca*, VI. 128; VIII. 31

Henley, John (1692–1756), x. 21

Henley, Samuel (1740–1815), x. 423; XI. 289, 291, 460

Henley, W. E. (1849–1903), x. 418; XI. 161, 438, 440; XII. 167, 179, 225, 384; XIII. 194, 197, 207, 211, 214 ff. (main entry), 477, 499, 503, 523, 570; XIV. 199, 520, 535

Beau Austin (with R. L. Stevenson), XIV. 163

Bric-à-Brac, XIII. 213

Echoes, XIII. 214

Essay in *The Century Burns*, XIV. 148

Hawthorn and Lavender, XIII. 214

Hospital Verses, XIII. 213

I loved you once in Old Japan, XIII. 213

In Hospital, XIII. 214

In the year that's come and gone, XIII. 214

London Voluntaries, XIII. 214

Love, his flying feather, XIII. 214

Lyra Heroica, XIII. 195

Out of the Night that covers me, XIII. 214

Pro rege nostro, XIII. 214

Rhymes and Rhythms, XIII. 214

Song of the Sword, The, XIII. 214

Views and Reviews, XIV. 147

What is to come? XIII. 213

Henley, Walter of, IV. 541

Henley-in-Arden, x. 109, 112, 271

Henman, Charles, XII. 512

Hennell, Charles Christian (1809–1850), XII. 467; *Origin of Christianity, The*, XIII. 383

Hennell, Mrs Charles, XIII. 383

Hennell, Sara, *Thoughts in Aid of Faith*, XIII. 383

Henneman, IV. 119

Henning, Archibald S., XIV. 236

Henning, F. W. J., XIV. 540

Henri II, king of France, III. 156

Henri III, king of France, III. 437; IV. 259, 376

Henri IV (Henry of Navarre), king of France, III. 244; IV. 142, 256, 259, 312; v. 341; VIII. 370

Henrietta, duchess of Orleans (1644–1670), daughter of Charles I, VII. 245; VIII. 180, 248, 266

Henrietta, queen, in Shelley's *Charles I*, XII. 75

Henrietta Maria (1609–1669), queen of Charles I, v. 348; VI. 83, 148, 149, 197, 237, 240, 262, 324 ff., 404; VII. 13, 35, 53 61, 189, 195, 218, 439, 449; VIII. 262, 294, 358, 371; x. 499; XIV. 93

Henriot, in Lytton's *Zanoni*, XIII. 420

Henrique, Don, in *The Spanish Curate*, VI. 139

Henry I, king of England, I. 151, 154, 157, 162, 222, 256, 278, 336; II. 343; 419; III. 368; v. 320; VIII. 310; XIV. 73

Henry II, king of England, I. 156, 157, 167, 171 ff., 176, 181, 185, 188, 189, 191, 197, 198, 202, 238, 243, 258, 264, 272, 307, 337, 397, 398, 449; II. 342, 504; IV. 182; VII. 206; VIII. 311; IX. 535; x. 115, 292, 502; XIV. 72; *Gesta Regis Henrici Secundi*, I. 449

Henry II, in *Looke about you*, v. 320, 321

Henry III, king of England, I. 180, 184, 194, 233, 238, 337, 368; II. 343; VI. 33; VII. 386; x. 287; XI. 301

Henry IV, king of England, I. 322; II. 36, 70, 137, 138, 153, 154, 206, 217, 284, 287, 303, 422; III. 316, 317; v. 44, 340; VII. 189, 190

Henry V, king of England, II. 40, 206, 286, 287, 303; IV. 137, 298; v. 373; VI. 280; IX. 534, 535; x. 303

Henry VI, king of England, II. 210, 296, 297, 355, 357 ff.; III. 334; IV. 193, 243, 428; v. 9, 340; VII. 247, 248, 327; x. 291

Henry VII, king of England, II. 223, 224, 226, 228, 316, 325, 329, 338, 358, 375; III. 5, 7, 8, 13, 17, 65, 67, 70, 97, 152, 175, 316, 325; v. 29, 50; VI. 246, 280, 332; VII. 203; IX. 211; x. 283, 284; XIV. 53, 83

Henry VIII, king of England, II. 161, 224, 325, 338, 354, 358, 375, 388, 389; III. 6, 14 ff., 23, 26, 30, 31, 32, 36, 39, 41 ff., 46, 50, 57, 61, 65, 67, 69, 70, 78, 95 ff., 110, 111, 160, 166, 167, 172, 181, 182, 188, 316, 320, 328, 332, 368, 403, 418, 478; IV. 63, 66, 72, 109, 113, 196, 225 ff., 293, 299, 400, 405, 409; v. 10, 50, 54, 56 ff., 90, 91, 102, 109, 124, 247, 375; VI. 91, 241, 256, 268, 280, 333 ff.; VII. 59, 103, 124, 192, 203, 333, 337, 442; VIII. 125; IX. 197, 210, 355; x. 184, 290; XIV. 52, 59, 82, 84, 85, 329

Henry VIII, in *When you see me, etc.*, v. 333

Henry VIII, *Book of Payments*, v. 89

Henry VIII, Household Book of, VI. 283

Henry VIII, Letters and Papers of, II. 393; XIV. 232

Henry, Alexander (1739–1824), XIV. 583; *Travels and Adventures*, XIV. 358

Henry, Aurelia, VI. 22

Henry, D., XII. 428

Henry, duke of Gloucester (1639–1660), VII. 58; VII. 383; VIII. 254

Henry, Frederick, prince of Wales (1594–1612), IV. 58, 59, 68, 90, 135, 143, 151, 154, 157, 188, 216, 263, 265, 366, 429, 431; VI. 30, 31, 37, 185, 250, 316, 318, 339, 345, 348, 350, 353; VIII. 363; x. 499

Henry, James (1798–1876), *Aeneidea*, XII. 338

Henry, Robert (1718–1790), *History of England*, x. 290, 502, 505; XI. 326

Henry, William Charles, XIV. 557, 601

Henry (Benedictine monk), IV. 417

Henry de Bracton. *See* Bracton

Henry of Ghent (d. 1293), *Questiones*, II. 365

Henry of Huntingdon (1084?–1155), I.
159, 160, 162, 166 ff., 170, 172, 174,
191, 218, 257, 262, 336, 337, 450, 454,
461; II. 399
Henry of Saltrey (fl. 1150), I. 191, 454, 474
Henry of Susa (d. 1271), cardinal of Ostia,
commentary of, II. 364
Henry the Fifth, The Famous Victories of,
v. 82, 152, 187, 220, 398
Henry's (King) Mirth or Freemen's Songs,
III. 84
Henryson, Robert (1425?–1500?), II. 91,
93, 115, 204, 239, 244, 245, 248, 249,
252 ff., 263 ff., 473 ff.; III. 85, 173, 484;
IV. 413; XI. 203
   Age, II. 249
   Bludy Serk, The, II. 249
   Death, II. 249
   Hasty Credence, II. 249
   Morall Fabillis of Esope, II. 245 ff., 263;
   IX. 359
   Orpheus and Eurydice, II. 247, 260
   Prayer for the Pest, A, II. 249
   Robene and Makyne, II. 245, 249; XI. 215
   Sum Practysis of Medecyne, II. 249, 269
   Testament of Cresseid, II. 162, 164, 240,
   245, 247, 253, 264, 266
   *Uponlandis Mous and the Burges Mous,
   The,* II. 246
   Want of Wise Men, II. 249
Hensel, P., XIII. 471
Henshaw, Thomas (1618–1700), VII. 360;
VIII. 247
Henslow, John Stevens (1796–1861), XIV.
289, 290, 560
Henslowe, Francis (fl. 1593–1595), VI. 277
Henslowe, Philip (d. 1616), v. 35, 135,
136, 143, 145, 157, 158, 160, 161, 236,
251, 256, 309 ff., 316, 319, 321 ff., 327,
328, 330 ff., 382, 473; VI. 3, 4, 7, 12,
17, 32, 33, 40, 45, 51, 53, 54, 83, 97,
141, 146, 168, 178, 210, 212, 216, 247,
250, 254, 255, 258, 261, 267, 269, 271,
275, 278, 290, 395, 411, 454; VIII. 123,
125
Hentzner, Paul, v. 356, 365, 369, 379, 478;
   A Journey into England, X. 245
Heoden (Heðinn), in *Deor,* I. 37
Heodeningas, the, in *Deor,* I. 37
Heorogar, in *Beowulf,* I. 25
Heorot, Hrothgaishall, in *Beowulf,* I. 22
Heoroweard, in *Beowulf,* I. 25
Heorrenda, minstrel, in *Deor,* I. 37
Hepburn, George (fl. 1695), IX. 560
Hepburn, John (d. 1522), II. 369, 370
Hepburn, Patrick (d. 1508), 1st earl of
Bothwell, II. 251
Hephaestion, *Manual of Greek Metre,* XII.
328
Hepple, Norman, XI. 409
Her Trippa, in Rabelais's *Pantagruel,* VIII.
67
Heraclitus, IV. 31; VIII. 386; XIII. 193
Heraclitus' Dream, VII. 381
Heraclitus, riddles of, III. 489
Herald, the, in *Horestes,* V. 64

Heraldes, Debate Betwene the, IV. 296
Heraldry, writers on, IV. 543
Heraud, John Abraham (1799–1887), XII.
128, 129, 417, 428; XIII. 520
'Heraudee, Jawbrahim,' XII. 129
Herball, Grete, IV. 374
Herbals, IV. 542
Herbarium, Old English, I. 135
Herbarum, De virtutibus, II. 364
Herbert, prosodist, XIII. 241
Herbert, Arthur, earl of Torrington (1647–
1716), IX. 490
Herbert, Auberon E. W. M. (1838–1906),
XIV. 474
Herbert, Charles, lord, VI. 144
Herbert, Edward, 1st baron Herbert of
Cherbury (1583–1648), IV. 292 ff., 508;
VII. 16, 26, 29, 222, 277, 278, 283, 412,
413, 445; VIII. 352, 353, 355; IX. 288;
XIII. 32
   Appendix ad Sacerdotes, IV. 293
   Autobiography, VII. 204, 205
   De Causis Errorum, IV. 293
   De Religione Gentilium, IV. 293
   De Religione Laici, IV. 293; VIII. 42
   De Veritate, IV. 293
   Dialogue between a Tutor and his Pupil,
   IV. 293
   Life of, X. 245
   Life and Reign of King Henry the Eighth,
   VII. 201, 204, 205
Herbert, Sir Edward (1591?–1657), IV. 265
Herbert, Edward, earl of Powis (1785–
1848), XIV. 578
Herbert, George (1593–1633), I. 232; IV.
123, 203, 240, 292; VII. 15, 26 ff. (main
entry), 42, 45, 47, 153, 162, 163, 252,
401 ff., 425, 463, *also see* Add.; VIII.
229, 299; X. 360, 369; XI. 79; XIII. 169
   Aaron, VII. 30
   Antiphon, VII. 31
   Avarice, VII. 30
   Church, The, VII. 32
   Church Porch, The, VII. 32
   Collar, The, VII. 30, 32
   Dawning, The, VII. 31
   Decay, VII. 30
   Eastern Song, XIII. 139
   Heaven, VII. 30
   Home, VII. 30
   Hygiasticon, VII. 32
   Jordan, VII. 30
   Justice, VII. 30
   Man, VII. 32
   Odour, The, VII. 3
   Outlandish Proverbs, 32
   Parentalia, VII. 27
   Prayer, VII. 30
   Priest to the Temple, A, VII. 26, 155, 156
   Providence, VII. 31
   Pulley, The, VII. 30
   Quip, The, VII. 30
   Temple, The, II. 226; IV. 218; VII. 26, 27,
   29, 30, 32, 40, 44
   Throw away thy rod, VII. 32
   'Shaped' verses, VII. 30

Herbert, George Robert Charles, 13th earl of Pembroke (1850–1895), XIV. 554
Herbert, Henry, 2nd earl of Pembroke (1534?–1601), III. 188; IV. 265
Herbert, Sir Henry (1595–1673), IV. 383; VI. 102, 147, 202, 246; VIII. 118, 119
Herbert, Henry Howard Molyneux, 4th earl of Carnarvon (1831–1890), X. 259
Herbert, Lucy, VII. 45
Herbert, Mrs Magdalen, afterwards lady Danvers (b. 1565), IV. 197, 203, 210, 211, 240; VII. 27
Herbert, Mary, countess of Pembroke (1561–1621), III. 241, 254; IV. 116, 124, 132, 135, 172, 390, 434, 447; V. 63, 157, 334, 476; VI. 9; *Antonie*, IV. 133; *Dialogue between two shepheards*, IV. 124
Herbert, Matthew, VII. 37
Herbert, Sir Percy, VII. 515
Herbert, Philip, earl of Montgomery and 4th earl of Pembroke (1584–1650), V. 347; VI. 143, 144, 149; VII. 5, 29, 450, 513
Herbert, Philip, 5th earl of Pembroke (1619–1669), VII. 61
Herbert, Sidney, lord Herbert of Lea (1810–1861), XIV. 131, 510
Herbert, Thomas (*fl.* 1642), IV. 389
Herbert, Sir Thomas (1606–1682), VII. 450
Herbert, Thomas Martin (1835–1877), XIV. 474
Herbert, William, 3rd earl of Pembroke (1580–1630), IV. 123, 132, 209, 390, 431; V. 174, 225, 347; VI. 143, 149, 150; VII. 219; VIII. 377
Herbert, William (1718–1795), IX. 531; XII. 520, 522
Herbert, William (1778–1847), XIV. 298, 561
Herbert family, the, IV. 157; V. 370; VI. 141
Herbert of Bosham (*fl.* 1162–1186), I. 448
Herbert's *Typographical Antiquities*, II. 319
Herbes, A Boke of the properties of, IV. 397
Herbier, Grand, IV. 374
Herculaneum, XII. 340, 413
Hercules, VIII. 68; IX. 136, XIII. 81
Hercules, in *Confessio Amantis*, II. 148
Hercules, in *Dialogues of the Dead*, XI. 351
Hercules, in *Pleasure Reconciled*, VI. 360, 361
Hercules, in *Saturnalia*, VI. 319
Hercules, in *The Masque of Christmas*, VI. 359
Hercules, captain, in *The Champion*, X. 23
Hercules, duke, in *Parasitaster*, VI. 48
'Hercules,' ship, XII. 38
Herd, David (1732–1810), II. 409; IX. 360, 362 ff., 373, 374, 566; X. 487, 490; *Ancient and Modern Scottish Songs*, XI. 204, 218
Herd MS., XI. 229, 235
Herder, Johann Gottfried von, V. 290, 297, 298, 304; X. 232
Here awa there awa, IX. 374

Here Prophecy, I. 218, 459
Herebeald, in *Beowulf*, I. 24
Hereford, II. 61; III. 28; IV. 131, 190, 421; VI. 220; VII. 42, 444; IX. 538; XII. 286; XIV. 414
Hereford, Henry of. *See* Henry V
Hereford, Nicholas (*fl.* 1390), II. 60, 61, 63, 73
Herefordshire, II. 216; XI. 430; XII. 509; XIII. 70
Heremod, in *Beowulf*, I. 23, 26
Heresye's Testament, III. 483
Hereward the Wake (*fl.* 1070–1071), I. 111, 287, 364, 478; II. 399, 428, 507; V. 27; IX. 343
Hereward the Wake, Kingsley's, XIII. 366
Herford, Charles Harold, VI. 17; XI. 409; XII. 433, 524; XIII. 52, 56, 62, 79, 480, 484
Herford, John (*fl.* 1534), IV. 409
Hergest. See *Red Book of*
Heriot, George (1766–1844), XIV. 583; *History of Canada*, XIV. 358; *Travels through the Canadas*, XIV. 358
Heriricus, in *Waltharius*, I. 32
Herkomer, Sir Hubert von, XII. 330
Herman, Guillaume, V. 21
Herman, Henry (1832–1894), XIII. 524
Herman, Hugo, *Pia Desideria*, VII. 47
Herman of Wied, archbishop of Cologne, III. 31
Hermann, Johann Gottfried Jakob, XII. 324, 325
Hermegild, in D'Avenant's *Gondibert*, VII. 71
Hermenegild, St, I. 105
Hermes, IV. 45
Hermes, Johann Timotheus, *Geschichte der Miss Fanny Wilkes*, X. 18
Hermes, Trismegistus, VII. 488
Herminia, in *Orlando Furioso*, III. 230
Hermione, in *Horestes*, V. 65
Hermione, in *The Winter's Tale*, V. 169, 189, 206
Hermogenes, III. 420
Hermsprong, Bage's, XI. 295
Herne, Hierome, VI. 348, 349
Hernishowe, in Trevisa, II. 78
Hero, in *Much Ado about Nothing*, V. 191
Hero and Leander (Nashe's burlesque), IV. 327
Herod, III. 78; V. 17, 46, 50, 87, 151; VI. 154, 295; X. 83
Herodas, *Mimes*, XII. 340
Herodian, IV. 436
Herodias, VI. 295
Herodotus, III. 430, 433; IV. 4, 6, 436; IX. 39, 43; X. 135; XII. 328, 330, 334, 477, 479, 480, 484; XIV. 85
Heroic Virtue, in *The Masque of Queens*, VI. 349
Heroical adventures of the Knight of the Sea, IV. 359
Herolt's *Promptuarium*, III. 489
Heron, Robert (1764–1807), X. 446, 526; XI. 440, 472

Heron, The Vows of the (leus veus du hairon), II. 421

Herondas, XII. 492

Herrenhausen, IX. 249

Herrera, Antonio de, IX. 501

Herrick, Nicholas (d. 1592), VII. 4

Herrick, Robert (1591–1674), II. 393; IV. 193; VI. 1, 11, 27, 215; VII. 1, 4–16 (main entry), 22, 23, 81, 180, 398, *also see* Add.; VIII. 3, 229, 231; XI. 318, 383; XII. 223; XIII. 495
'Alas! for me, that I have lost,' VII. 11
'Among the myrtles as I walked,' VII. 7
Apparition of his Mistress calling him to Elysium, The, VII. 7
Canticles to Bacchus, VII. 9
Cherry Ripe, IV. 145; VII. 8
Christian Militant, The, VII. 10
Corinna's Going a-Maying, VII. 8, 13
Country Life: to his Brother, Mr Tho. Herrick, A, VII. 4, 9, 11, 12
Cruel Maid, The, VII. 9
Description of a Woman, The, VII. 7
Dirge of Jephthah's Daughter, VII. 15
Farewell to Sack, A, VII. 6, 7
Hesperides, VII. 1, 6 ff., 11, 13, 15, 19
His Age, VII. 9, 11
His Content in the Country, VII. 6
His Creed, VII. 15
His Departure Hence, VII. 11
His Farewell unto Poetry, VII. 5
His Ode for Ben Jonson, VII. 11
His Litany to the Holy Spirit, VII. 15
His Request to Julia, VII. 10
Hock-Cart, The, VII. 12
Mad Maid's Song, The, VII. 8
May-pole is up, The, VII. 8
Night-Piece to Julia, VII. 10, 13
Noble Numbers, VII. 7, 10, 14
Nuptial Song on Sir Clipseby Crew, A, VII. 11
Oberon's Diet, VII. 7
Ode to Endymion Porter upon his Brother's Death, An, VII. 11
Panegyric to Sir Lewis Pemberton, VII. 10
Primrose, The, VII. 7
Thanksgiving to God for his House, A, VII. 6, 15
Tinker's Song, The, VII. 8
To Anthea, VII. 13
To Daffodils, VII. 13, 14
To his Book, VII. 14
To Keep a true Lent, VII. 15
To Phyllis to love and live with him, VII. 8, 13
To Primroses filled with Morning Dew, VII. 11 ff.
To the reverend Shade of his religious Father, VII. 10
Upon Himself, VII. 14
Upon the Death of his Sparrow, VII. 9
'When a daffodil I see,' VII. 14

Herrick, Sir William (1562–1653), VII. 4, 5

Herries, John, XI. 250; XIII. 250

Herring, Thomas (1693–1757), IV. 251; X. 362, 516

Herringman, Henry, VIII. 6, 392; XI. 318, 319

Herrington, Sir Jasper, in Fanny Burney's *Wanderer,* X. 65

Herriott, Frank I., *Sir William Temple on the Origin and Nature of Government,* VIII. 384

Herrys, William, VII. 33

Herschel, Sir John Frederick William (1792–1871), XIV. 258, 288, 474, 555; *Discourse on the Study of Natural Philosophy,* XIV. 17

Herschel, Sir William (1738–1822), XIV. 258, 556

Hertford, III. 330

Hertford, earl of. *See* Seymour, Edward

Hertford, lady. *See* Somerset, Frances

Hertford, marquis of. *See* Seymour-Conway, Francis Charles

Hertfordshire, VI. 29, 196; VII. 252; IX. 532, 538; X. 120; XI. 78; XII. 180, 182, 183, 201, 509; XIV. 79

Hertogenbosch, III. 2

Hertz, Heinrich Rudolf, XIV. 269

Hervarar Saga, I. 35

Hervet, Gentian, IV. 440, 543

Hervey, Augustus John, 3rd earl of Bristol (1724–1779), IX. 252

Hervey, Carr (1691–1723), IX. 250

Hervey, James (1714–1758), IX. 506; X. 365 ff., 369
Contemplations, X. 365, 366
Meditations, X. 124, 365; XI. 325
Reflections, X. 365
Theron and Aspasia, X. 365

Hervey, John, 1st earl of Bristol (1665–1751), IX. 250, 496

Hervey, John, lord (1696–1743), IX. 85, 250 ff., 449, 497
Letters from a nobleman, IX. 86, 251
Memoirs, IX. 250 ff.
Miscellaneous Thoughts, IX. 252
Three Speeches, IX. 252

Hervey, Mary, lady (1700–1768), IX. 85, 250, 251; X. 248

Hervey, Sir Thomas (1698–1775), IX. 250, 496; XI. 394

Herveys, the, IX. 248, 251

Hervier, Paul Louis, XIII. 532

Hervor, X. 223, 224

Hesiod, I. 77; III. 429; IV. 436; IX. 220, 526, 527· XII. 331, 484, 489

Hesketh, Harriet, lady (born Cowper) (1733–1807), XI. 78, 88, 89, 91, 402, 404

Hesperus, X. 137

Hesse-Cassel, X. 466

Hester, in Mrs Inchbald's *To Marry or not to Marry,* XI. 279

Hesternit, in Mandeville, II. 84

Hesychius, IX. 330

Hetel (Heðinn), in *Kudrun,* I. 37

Hetherington, Henry (1792–1849), XIV. 534

Heðinn, I. 37

Heton, Northumberland, II. 128

Hettner, H., I. viii

Hetware (Chattuarii), in *Beowulf*, I. 25, 26

Heurodys, in *Sir Orfeo*, I. 311

Hew, Sir, of Eglintoun (c. 1376), II. 103, 116, 117, 123, 451

Hewer, William, VIII. 258

Hewes, John, IV. 170, 186, 188

Hewett, Mrs, IX. 248

Hewitt, Bob, in Gissing's *The Nether World*, XIII. 458

Hewlett, Esther, XI. 383, 486

Hewlett, Henry Gray, XIV. 517

Hewlett, Maurice (1861–1923), XIII. 572, *also see* Add. 1

Hewson, the shoemaker, in the *Mercuries*, VII. 356

Hewson, John (d. 1662), VIII. 121

Hexham, Henry (1585?–1650?), VII. 454

Hey, boys, Up we go! VIII. 96

Heydon, Sir Christopher (d. 1623), IV. 535; VII. 508, 510; *A Defense of Judiciall Astrologie*, VII. 377

Heydon, John (*fl.* 1667), VII. 378, 510

Heylyn, Peter (1600–1662), III. 478; IV. 458; VII. 246 ff., 427, 445, 447, 479, 518
  Aerius Redivivus, VII. 208
  Cosmography, VII. 207
  Cyprianus Anglicus, VII. 208
  Ecclesia Restaurata, VII. 207
  Examen Criticum, VII. 207
  Geography, VII. 207
  Mercurius Aulicus, VII. 207
  Microcosmus: a little Description of the Great World (later edition *Cosmographie*), IV. 89

Heyne, Christian Gottlob, XII. 490; XIII. 468

Heyse, Paul, V. 303

Heywood, Elizabeth (daughter of John Heywood), IV. 198

Heywood, Elizaeus (1530–1578), V. 90

Heywood, Jasper (1535–1598), III. 189, 198; IV. 440; V. 89, 395

Heywood, John (1497?–1580?), II. 269, 328; III. 124, 179, 279; IV. 198, 334, 518; V. 25, 89 ff., 97, 110, 404 ff., 409 ff., *and see* Add. 2
  Foure P. P., The, V. 92, 95, 97
  Johan the husbande Johan Tyb his wyfe and Syr Jhān the priest, V. 92, 96 ff., 105, 111
  Pardoner and the frere, The, V. 92, 96, 97, 108
  Play of Love, A, V. 92 ff.
  Proverbs, V. 105
  Wether, The, V. 92 ff., 97
  Witty and Witless, V. 92 ff., 99

Heywood, Oliver (1630–1702), XI. 486

Heywood, Samuel (1753–1828), XIV. 490

Heywood, Thomas (d. 1650?), II. 202; IV. 4, 115, 434, 438, 439, 458; V. 145, 158, 222, 224, 243, 254, 259, 263, 311, 312, 361, 370, 371, 373; VI. 80–106 (main entry), 168, 204, 219, 378, 389,

Heywood, Thomas
  409, 430 ff., 445, 487, *and see* Add. 2; VIII. 169; XI. 286; XII. 191
  Actor's Vindication, The, VI. 83, 408
  Ambrosius Merlin, Life of, VI. 88
  Apology for Actors, An, VI. 83 ff., 241, 401, 408, 461, 494
  Blind eats many a fly, The, VI. 97
  Bold Beachams, The, VI. 89
  Brazen Age, The, VI. 93
  Captives, or The Lost Recovered, The, VI. 102
  Challenge for Beautie, A, VI. 82, 103
  Christmas comes but once a year, VI. 97
  Edward IV, VI. 84, 88, 90
  England's Elizabeth, V. 342; VI. 86, 91
  English Traveller, The, V. 351; VI. 81, 84, 94, 97, 102; VIII. 172
  Fair Maid of The West, The, VI. 85, 97, 101
  Fayre Mayde of the Exchange, The, VI. 84, 86, 99
  Fortune by Land and Sea, VI. 69, 104
  Four Ages, The, VI. 92
  Foure Prentises of London, The, With the Conquest of Jerusalem, VI. 84, 88, 89
  General History of Women, The, VI. 86, 102, 103, 138
  Godfrey of Bulloigne, VI. 89
  Golden Age, The, VI. 93, 97
  Hercules, VI. 92
  Hierarchy of the Blessed Angels, VI. 86, 87
  If you know not me, You know no bodie: Or, The troubles of Queene Elizabeth, V. 342, 344, 345, 354, 365; VI. 84, 85, 91, 97, 300; VIII. 125
  Iron Age, The, VI. 84, 92, 93
  Jew of Malta, The, Heywood work in, VI. 103
  Joan and my Lady, VI. 97
  Late Lancashire Witches, The, VI. 104
  Lives of all the Poets, VI. 86
  Loves Maistresse, VI. 84, 103
  Marshal Osric, VI. 100
  Mayden-Head well lost, A, VI. 84, 103
  Nine Most Worthy Women of the World, VI. 91
  Pleasant Dialogues and Drammas, VI. 87, 88
  Porta Pietatis, VI. 88
  Rape of Lucrece, The, V. 367; VI. 19, 101
  Royall King, The, and the Loyall Subject, VI. 81, 83, 97, 100, 102, 138
  Silver Age, The, VI. 93
  Sovereign of the Seas, The, pamphlet on, VI. 84
  Troicus Britannicus, or Great Britain's Troy, VI. 86
  Wise-woman of Hogsdon, The, VI. 83, 93, 97, 99
  Woman Kilde with Kindnesse, A, V. 252; VI. 84, 92 ff., 97, 99, 101; VII. 3; X. 73

Hezekiah, English verse play on, VI. 300

Hezekiah, in *Ezechias*, VI. 298

Hiarrandi, father of Heðinn, I. 27
Hiaðningar, I. 37
Hiatt, Charles, XIII. 515
Hibernian society, XIV. 397, 398
Hibernica, VII. 211
Hichyns (Tindale, William), III. 39
Hick, in *Piers the Plowman*, II. 16
Hick Scorner, V. 54, 392
Hickathrift, XI. 373
Hickeringill, Edmund (1631–1708), IV. 458; VIII. 403
Hickes, Francis (1566–1631), IV. 438; VII. 316
Hickes, George (1642–1715), I. 31, 147, 382; VII. 43; VIII. 258, 306, 460; IX. 212, 355, 535; X. 220, 224 ff., 229, 355, 356; *Constitution of the Catholic Church*, IX. 310, 511; Icelandic grammar, X. 223; *Linguarum veterum septentrionalium thesaurus grammatico-criticus et archaeologicus*, VIII. 307; X. 223, 225, 484
Hickes, William, *Coffee-house Jests*, VII. 390, 516
Hickes, Sir William, VIII. 83
Hickford, R., X. 485
Hickman, Francis (*fl.* 1690), VIII. 394
Hickman [? Henry], X. 387
Hickman, Thomas, XIV. 230
Hickes, G. Dawes, XIV. 467, 474
Hicks, Thomas, *Dialogue between a Christian and a Quaker*, VIII. 110
Hickson, William Edward (1803–1870), XII. 430
Hicky, James Augustus (*fl.* 1780), XIV. 334
Hicky's Bengal Gazette, XIV. 334
Hidaspes, in *Cupid's Revenge*, VI. 128
Hiero (Mantuan's), III. 224
Hierocles, X. 464
Hieroleander, in *Argenis*, IV. 259
Hieron Osorius, bishop, library of, IV. 56
Hieronimo, in *The Spanish Tragedie*, V. 158, 162, 164, 240; VI. 13; VIII. 87
Hierophilus, *pseud. See* McHale, John
Higden, Betty, in *Our Mutual Friend*, XIII. 336
Higden, Henry (*fl.* 1693), VIII. 395
Higden, Ranulf (d. 1364), *Polychronicon*, II. 71, 72, 74 ff., 313, 333, 334, 444; IV. 320, 521; XII. 480
Higford, William (1581?–1657), *Institutions of a Gentleman*, IX. 396, 570
Higgins, John (*fl.* 1570–1602), III. 196, 197; V. 407
Higgins, Matthew James ('Jacob Omnium,' 1810–1868), XIV. 238, 534
'Higgins, Mr, of St Mary Axe,' XI. 43
Higgs, in Butler's *Erewhon Revisited*, XIII. 453
Higgs, Griffin or Griffith (1589–1659), *Thomas Tucker*, VI. 318, 320, 474
High Dutch, VII. 314
High Ercall, Shropshire, VII. 27
High Wycombe, VII. 53
Highland Scots, IX. 373
Highlanders, the, X. 28, 182, 230, 231

Highlands, the, IX. 215; XII. 19, 24, 26, 83, 84, 255; XIII. 106; XIV. 65, 434
'Hightest thou Urse,' I. 460
Highwaymen, Lives of the, XI. 352
Hilarion, I. 74
Hilarius or Hilary (*fl.* 1125), I. 191, 454; V. 7, 8, 11, 38; *Image of St Nicholas*, I. 191; *The Raising of Lazarus*, I. 191; V. 11
Hilda or Hild, St (614–680), abbess of Streoneshalh, Whitby, I. 42, 43, 45, 82
Hildebrandslied, the, I. 36
Hildeburh, in *Beowulf*, I. 31
Hildegard, St, of Bingen, I. 229
Hildesham, Hildersam, or Hildersham, Arthur (1563–1632), VII. 322, 482
Hildilid, or Hildelitha, St, abbess of Barking (*fl.* 700), I. 74
Hildr, daughter of Högni, I. 37
Hildreth, Richard, XI. 68, 398
Hilgay, Norfolk, IV. 165
Hill, Aaron (1685–1750), IX. 160, 187, 447, 485; X. 94, 434, 439; *Alzira*, X. 82; *Merope*, X. 82, 86; *Zara*, X. 81, 82
Hill, Abigail (d. 1734), IX. 130
Hill, Abraham (1635–1721), VIII. 296, 458
Hill, Constance, XI. 365, 460; XII. 447
Hill, David Octavius (1802–1870), XI. 437
Hill, Eleanor M., XIV. 599
Hill, Frederic (1803–1896), XIV. 591, 601
Hill, George (1810–1900), XIV. 568
Hill, George Birkbeck (1835–1903), IX. 308, 313, 326; X. 181, 184, 186, 267, 279, 289, 297, 317; XI. 13, 344; XIV. 503, 606
Hill, John (d. 1765), IX. 455
Hill, John (1716?–1775), XI. 472
Hill, Joseph, XI. 87, 402
Hill, Richard (*c.* 1500), II. 500
Hill, Richard, III. 189
Hill, Rowland (1744–1833), XII. 472
Hill, Sir Rowland (1795–1879), XIV. 606
Hill, Samuel Charles, XII. 437
Hill, Thomas ('Didymus Mountain') (*fl.* 1590), III. 484; IV. 542; *A most briefe and pleasaunt treatyse, etc.*, IV. 375; *The proffitable arte of gardening*, IV. 375
Hill, Thomas, uncle of Southey, XI. 155
Hill, Wills, 1st earl of Hillsborough (1718–1793), X. 403
Hillard, George Stillman, XIII. 73
Hillier, Alfred P., XIV. Add. 8
Hills, Henry, XI. 330
Hillsborough, earl of. *See* Hill, Wills
Hiltgund, in *Waldhere* and *Waltharius*, I. 32 ff.
Hilton, Arthur Clement (1851–1877), XIV. 537; *Heathen Pass-ee, The*, XIV. 206; *Octopus, The*, XIV. 206; *Vulture and the Husbandman, The*, XIV. 206
Hilton, John (d. 1657), IV. 464
'Hinchinbroke, lord,' in *The Tatler*, IX. 34
Hinchingbrooke, X. 133
Hincks, Edward ('1792–1866), XII. 342, 499
Hind, Arthur Mayger, XIV. 539

Hind, Henry Youle, XIV. 583
Hind, James (d. 1652), IX. 258
Hind Horn, II. 410, 411, 414
Hindley, Charles, XIV. 540, 544
Hindlip hall, near Worcester, VII. 45
Hindoos, the, XI. 17
Hindshaw, W., XIV. 592
Hindu religion, XIV. 98
Hindu romance, XI. 164
Hindustan, XI. 12
Hindustani language, XI. 242; XIII. 279
Hine, Henry George (1811–1895), XIV. 238
Hingston, Edward Perron, XIII. 515
Hinkson, Henry Albert, XIV. 573
Hinkson, Katharine Tynan, XIV. 316, 573
Hinnom, XII. 82
Hinton, James (1822–1875), XII. 467; XIV. 475
Hinton, John Howard (1791–1873), XIV. 591
Hinxman, John (*fl.* 1760), XI. 341
Hiordis, in Morris's *Sigurd the Volsung*, XIII. 126
Hiörvarŏr, brother-in-law of Hrólfr, I. 25
Hippel, X. 422
Hippocrates, II. 365; III. 427; IV. 436; VII. 488; VIII. 350, 363; XII. 521
Hippolito, in *Loves Crueltie*, VI. 199
Hippolyta, in *A Midsummer-Night's Dream*, V. 183; VI. 213, 214
Hippolyta, in *The Custome of the Countrey*, VI. 122, 131
Hippolytus, VI. 163
Hippomedon. See *Ipomedon*
Hiram's hospital, in Trollope's *The Warden*, XIII. 422
Hislop, Andrew, XI. 237
Hispanus, play, VI. 484
Hisperica Famina, I. 69, 70, 435
Histoire Littéraire de la France, XI. 172
Historia, in *Technogamia*, VI. 323
Historia Brittonum. See Nennius
Historical MSS. commission, IX. 119, 141; XIV. 89, 97
Histories and tragedies, early printed, and in MSS., V. 395 ff.
History of Henry Earl of Moreland, IX. 328
History of Savarambes, IX. 106
History of the Sixteen Wonderful Old Women, XI. 386
History of the Union (1698), X. 377
History of the Works of the Learned, X. 176
Hitchcock, Richard, translator of Sansovino, IV. 448
Hitchcock, Robert (*fl.* 1580–1591), IV. 309, 511
Hitchcock, Robert (d. 1809), X. 443
Hitchener, Elizabeth, XII. 401, 402
Hitchin, V. 103; VI. 29; XIV. 430
Hitchman, Francis, XIII. 545, 547
Hitopadesa, the, XI. 343, 502, 503
Hnaef, in *Beowulf* and *Widsith*, I. 23, 31, 32, 34

Hoadley or Hoadly, Samuel (1643–1705), VI. 482
Hoadly, Benjamin (1676–1761), IX. 20, 41, 221, 309 ff., 428, 505, 506, 511; X. 354, 355, 357, 516, 517
  Nature of the Kingdom of Christ, IX. 310, 311; X. 354
  Plain Account of the...Sacrament, X. 354
  Preservative against the...Non-Jurors, IX. 310; X. 354
  Reasonableness of Conformity, X. 374
Hoadly, Benjamin (1706–1757), X. 87, 435
Hoadly, John (1711–1776), X. 87, 433, 439
Hoare, Prince (1755–1834), X. 276; XI. 281, 457; XII. 473
Hoare, Sir Richard Colt (1758–1838), XII. 510; *Wiltshire*, XII. 346
Hoares, the, XI. 149
Hobbes, John Oliver, *pseud. See* Craigie, Pearl Mary Teresa
Hobbes, Thomas (1588–1679), IV. 292, 297; VII. 54, 70, 71, 84, 85, 217, 259, 260, 265 ff., 275, 276–298 (main entry), 409, 465, 469 ff., *also see* Add.; VIII. 462, 469, 475; IX. 75, 269, 301 ff., 351, 384, 386, 397, 571; x. 325, 332, 335; XI. 7, 32, 57, 318; XIV. 16, 24, 29, 479
  Behemoth, VII. 289, 445; IX. 385
  De Cive, VII. 286, 291
  De Corpore, VII. 287, 288, 291
  De Corpore Politico, VII. 285
  De Homine, VII. 287
  Decameron Physiologicum, VII. 289
  Dialogue between a Philosopher and a Student of the Common Laws of England, VII. 289
  Elements of Law natural and politic, VII. 284, 285, 291, 294
  Heresy, VII. 289
  Historia Ecclesiastica, VII. 289
  Homer, VII. 267, 289
  Human Nature, VII. 285
  Latin works, VII. 289, 291
  Leviathan, The, VII. 286 ff., 296, 297, 301, 371; IX. 385; x. 372
  Of Liberty and Necessity, VII. 288
  Philosophical Rudiments concerning Government and Society, VII. 286, 291
  Short Tract on First Principles, VII. 284
  Thucydides, VII. 284
  Tractatus Opticus, VII. 286
Hobbinol, in *The Shepheards Calender*, III. 224
Hobby-horse, V. 33
Hobhouse, John Cam, lord Broughton de Gyfford (1786–1869), XII. 32, 34, 382 ff., 387, 393, 395; XIV. 407, 550
Hobhouse, Leonard T., XIV. 469
Hobhouse, Thomas, X. 472
Hobie Noble, II. 415
Hoblyn, Robert (1710–1756), XII. 522
Hobs, the tanner of Tamworth, in *Edward IV*, V. 373; VI. 90, 91

Hobson (a London character), IV. 360
Hobson, Mrs Carev, XIV. Add. 8
Hobson, Paul, X. 377
Hobson, Thomas (1544?–1631), VII. 244
Hoby, Sir Edward (1560–1617), IV. 443, 446
Hoby, Sir Thomas (1530–1566), III. 290, 433, 437, 444; IV. 3; *The Courtier*, III. 437, 505, 550; IV. 3, 7, 397, 443
Hoccleve. *See* Occleve
Hocken, Thomas Morland, XIV. 587
Hockenhull, prosodist, XIII. 244
Hockley, William Browne (1792–1860), XIV. 338, 557; *Pandurang Hari*, XIV. 337; *Tales of the Zenana*, XIV. 337
Hockliffe, or Hocelyve, in Bedfordshire, II. 206
Hocktide plays, V. 30, 31
Hocus, in Arbuthnot's *History of John Bull*, IX. 134
Hoddesdon, John (*fl.* 1650), VIII. 395
Hodell, Charles W., XIII. 484
Hodge, in *Cromwell*, V. 247
Hodge, in *Horestes*, V. 64
Hodge, in *Piers the Plowman*, II. 16
Hodge, D., XIII. 471
Hodges, Anthony, VII. 489
Hodges, Richard, XIV. 441
Hodges, Sir William (1645?–1714), IV. 102, 458
Hodgetts, John, *Terra Australis incognita*, IV. 101, 458
Hodgkin, Thomas (1831–1913), XII. 476, *also see* Add.; *Italy and her Invaders*, XII. 322
Hodgkins, John, III. 382
Hodgson, Francis (1781–1852), XII. 395
Hodgson, George B., XIV. 533
Hodgson, Geraldine Emma, XIV. 591
Hodgson, John (d. 1684), XII. 16, 376
Hodgson, Shadworth Hollway (1832–1912), XIII. 248; XIV. 40, 474
  Metaphysic of Experience, The, XIV. 39
  Philosophy of Reflection, The, XIV. 39
  Theory of Practice, The, XIV. 39
  Time and Space, XIV. 39
Hodgson, William Ballantyne (1815–1880), XIV. 414, 600, 601, 606, 607
Hodnet, XII. 365
Hody, Humphrey (1659–1707), X. 354, 516
Hoefuðlausn of Egill Skallagrimsson, I. 62
Hoel, in *The Misfortunes of Arthur*, V. 78
Hoel, king of Brittany, I. 259, 260
Hoey, J. C., XIV. 510
Höffding, H., XIV. 467
Hoffmann, Ernst Theodor Wilhelm, XIII. 4, 465
Hoffmann, F., IX. 442
Hoffmanswaldau, Christian Hofman von, III. 348
Hofland, Mrs Barbara (1770–1844), XI. 480; *Clergyman's Widow*, XI. 384; *Son of a Genius*, XI. 384; *Theodore*, XI. 384
Hofmeyr, J. H., XIV. Add. 8

Hog, James (1658?–1734), IX. 520, 548, 549
Hog (Hogaeus), Latin translations of Milton, VII. 118, 414
Hogarth, David George, XIV. 551
Hogarth, George, XIII. 542
Hogarth, William (1697–1764), IX. 122, 145; X. 22, 263, 354, 396, 429, 524; XII. 177, 182, 192, 434; XIII. 458; XIV. 212 ff., 540, 541
  Beer Street, XIV. 213
  Calais Gate, XIV. 213
  England, XIV. 213
  Enraged Musician, The, XI. 282; XIV. 213
  France, XIV. 213
  Gin Lane, X. 33; XIV. 213
  Harlot's Progress, X. 24, 75; XIV. 213
  Marriage-à-la-Mode, X. 90; XII. 432
  Rake's Progress, X. 24; XIV. 213, 214
Hogben, John, XIV. 534
Hogg, Alexander, XI. 326
Hogg, Ethel M., XIV. 602
Hogg, James (1770–1835), XI. 237 ff., 437, 443, *also see* Add.; XII. 5, 95, 96, 156, 159, 160, 373, 379, 425, 444, 445, 449; XIII. 108
  Bonny Kilmeny, XI. 241
  Cam Ye by Athol, XI. 242
  Fate of Macgregor, XI. 241
  Forest Minstrel, XI. 241, 243
  Gathering of the Clans, XI. 242
  Haunted Glen, XI. 242
  Jacobite Relics, IX. 371 ff., 375 ff., 566
  Lock the Door Lauriston, XI. 242
  M'Kinnon, XI. 242
  Mador of the Moor, XI. 241
  Mountain Bard, XI. 239
  O Weel Befa', XI. 242
  Pilgrims of the Sun, XI. 241
  Queen Hynde, XI. 241
  Queen's Wake, XI. 239 ff.
  Rise Rise Lowland and Highland Man, XI. 242
  Skylark, The, XI. 242
  Spy, The, XI. 239
  When the Kye comes Hame, XI. 242
  Witch of Fife, XI. 240
Hogg, Quintin (1845–1903), XIV. 602
Hogg, Thomas Jefferson (1792–1862), XII. 60, 79, 401, 403
Hoggarty, Mrs, in Thackeray's *Great Hoggarty Diamond*, XIII. 281
Hoggins, Mary Ann, in Thackeray's Contributions to *Punch*, XIII. 279
Hogglestock, Trollope's, XIII. 424
Högni, I. 37
Hogsden. *See* Hoxton
Hogsflesh, in Lamb's *Mr H—*, XII. 189
Hohenstiel-Schwangau, prince, Browning's, XIII. 72
Hoker, John, *Piscator, or The Fisher Caught*, VI. 294
Holberg, Ludwig, X. 200
Holborn, II. 233
Holbroke, John (d. 1437), II. 347, 362

Holcot, Robert (d. 1349), III. 489
Holcroft, Thomas (1745–1809), x. 443, 480; XI. 119, 189, 270, 276 ff., 281, 295, 454, 457, 461, *also see* Add.; XII. 432
Alwyn, XI. 294
Anna St Ives, XI. 292, 294
Autobiography, XI. 294
Crisis, The, XI. 277
Deserted Daughter, The, XI. 277, 278
Duplicity, XI. 277
Hugh Trevor, XI. 294
Road to Ruin, The, XI. 277
Holden, Hubert Ashton (1822–1896), XII. 331, 485
Holdernesse, earl of. *See* D'Arcy, Robert
Holdsworth, Dr, VIII. 473
Holdsworth, Philip Joseph (1849–1902), XIV. 369, 586
Holdsworth, Richard (1590–1649), IV. 425, 426, 434
Hole, Richard (1746–1803), x. 487
Hole, Samuel Reynolds, XIV. 238, 503
Hole, William (*fl.* 1600–1630), IV. 168
Holiday, Barten, *Technogamia, or The Marriage of the Arts*, VI. 323, 474
Holiness, house of, in *The Faerie Queene*, II. 234; VI. 336
Holiness, in *Piers the Plowman*, II. 25
Holinshed, Raphael (d. 1580?), I. 170; II. 104, 339; *Chronicles of England, Scotland and Ireland*, III. 111, 156, 237, 316, 318 ff., 438, 530; IV. 7, 192, 398 ff.; v. 100, 220, 221, 239 ff., 244, 271, 371; VI. 138, 301; XIV. 308
Holkot, Robert, *Moralitates*, I. 214, 454
Holland, v. 101, 286, 288, 308; VII. 64, 180, 261, 285, 307, 360, 453, 456, 460; IX. 3, 199, 203, 213, 214, 231, 255, 300, 306, 350, 515; x. 203; XI. 19, 25, 321; XII. 165; XIII. 88, 429; XIV. 212, 423, 459
Holland, Abraham (d. 1626), VII. 502
Holland, Bernard, XIV. 509
Holland, earl of. *See* Rich, Sir Henry
Holland, Henry (d. 1604), *A Treatise against Witchcraft*, IV. 325, 534; VII. 371, 506, 511
Holland, Henry (1583–1650?), III. 324; *Basiliologia*, IV. 543
Holland, Henry Scott, XII. 453, 455, 458
Holland, Henry Wilkinson, XIV. 591
Holland, John, duke of Exeter (1352?–1400), II. 170
Holland, John (1794–1872), XII. 420
Holland, lords. *See* Fox, Henry; Fox, Henry Richard Vassall
olland, Mary Sibylla, XIII. 549
Holland, Philemon (1552–1637), III. 324, 328, 528; IV. 1, 3 ff., 15, 21, 266, 438 ff., 442, 446, 523, 527; VII. 487; IX. 267; *Plutarch*, IX. 265; Plutarch's *Moralia*, VII. 316; Xenophon's *Cyropaedia*, VII. 316
Holland, Sir Richard (*fl.* 1450–1482), *Buke H of the Howlat*, II. 100, 112, 114, 115, 120, 272, 449
Holland, lady Saba (d. 1866), XII. 427

Holland, Thomas (d. 1612), VII. 312, 317
Holland family, XIII. 372
Hollar, Wenceslaus (1607–1677), VI. 262; VII. 487
Holles, Denzil, lord (1599–1680), VII. 225, 451, 457; IX. 194
Hollingford, in Mrs Gaskell's *Wives and Daughters*, XIII. 372
Hollingshead, John, XIII. 515
Hollway, H. C. Schunke, XIV. Add. 4
Hollyband, Claudius, IV. 446
Hollybush, J., IV. 442
Holm, in Norway, I. 179
Holman, in Mrs Gaskell's *Cousin Phillis*, XIII. 372, 380
Holme, Randle (1627–1699), *Academy of Armory*, IX. 355, 535
Holmes, Arthur (1837–1875), XII. 485
Holmes, George (1662–1749), IX. 495
Holmes or Homes, Nathaniel (1599–1678), VII. 507, 515
Holmes, Oliver Wendell, XIV. 378; *The Last Leaf*, XIII. 164
Holmes, Thomas Rice Edward, XIV. 496
Holmes, William (*fl.* 1582), IV. 386
Holofernes, I. 142
Holofernes, in *Love's Labour's Lost*, v. 178; VI. 30, 336
Holroyd, A., VIII. 558
Holroyd, John Baker, 1st earl of Sheffield (1735–1821), x. 299, 301, 302, 310, 312, 508, 509
Holroyd, Maria Josepha (lady Stanley of Alderley), x. 509
Holt, Felix, George Eliot's, XIII. 342, 397
Holt, Joseph (1756–1826), XII. 516
Holt, L. H., VI. 5
Holwell, John Zephaniah (1711–1798), XIV. 577; *India Tracts*, XIV. 334; *Narrative of the… Black Hole*, XIV. 334
Holy alliance, the, XI. 108; XII. 39, 40
'Holy Club,' the, x. 364
Holy Ghost, The Emission of the, v. 17
Holy Grail, the, XII. 518
Holy island, XII. 10
Holy land, the, IV. 89
Holy Roman empire, I. 318; III. 244
Holy Rood, The, I. 445
Holy Sepulchre, the, IV. 201; XIV. 252
Holy week carols, II. 378
Holybourne, Hampshire, XIII. 381
Holyhead, IX. 99
Holyoake, George Jacob, XIV. 478, 534
Holyoke, Francis (1567–1653), *Dictionary*, VII. 315, 486
Holyoke, Thomas (1616?–1675), VII. 486
Holyrood, IV. 239; VII. 435
Holyrood press, the, XI. 470
Holywood. *See* Johannes de Sacro Bosco
Home, Daniel D., XIII. 72
Home, Henry, lord Kames (1696–1782), IX. 561, 547; x. 190, 513, 514; XI. 250; XIV. 606; *Elements of Rhetoric*, XIV. 398; *Loose Hints upon Education*, XIV 391

Home, John (1722–1808), v. 297; ix. 557, 561, 564; x. 435; xi. 450, 457; *Douglas*, ii. 410; ix. 549; x. 87, 202, 230, 369; xi. 273; xiii. 258; *Siege of Aquileia*, xi. 273

Home and Foreign Review, The, xiv. 118
Home office, the, xiv. 328
Home Rule, xiv. 136, 198
Homer, i. 77, 170; ii. 109, 110; iii. 22, 229, 230, 271, 272, 305, 420, 429, 452; iv. 21 ff., 33. 42, 43, 47, 414, 418, 429, 437, 516, 526; v. 51, 71, 138, 214; vi. 18, 31, 36, 82, 86, 93, 101, 197, 303, 347; vii. 70, 117, 138, 267, 268, 274, 289, 317, 334, 381; viii. 205, 219, 221, 372, 375, 433; ix. 44, 59, 68, 72, 74 ff., 88, 183, 256, 258, 338 ff., 366, 443, 446, 448, 474, 481, 483, 484, 527; x. 27, 128, 167, 180, 186, 220, 227, 232, 415; xi. 79, 88 ff., 355, 403, 433; xii. 99, 256, 310, 311, 422, 480, 482, 484, 485, 487 ff., 491, 492, 496, *also see* Add.; xiii. 35, 90, 92, 104, 312; xiv. 135, 164, 252, 365, 375

  Iliad, i. 293; viii. 9, 25, 50, 64; ix. 297, 372, 410; x. 231, 232, 240; xi. 88, 320, 322, 401; xii. 54, 280, 331, 334, 477; xiii. 450; xiv. 329
  Odyssey, ix. 410; xi. 321, 322; xii. 190, 333, 334, 500; xiii. 125 ff., 175, 450
Homeric hexameter, the, xiii. 127
Homerides, by 'Sir Iliad Doggrel,' ix. 258, 448
Homerton, x. 384
Homes and Haunts of Famous Authors, xiii. 456
Homicide, in *Two Lamentable Tragedies*, v. 326
Homilies (1547 and later), iii. 35; iv. 304, 511
Homilies, Middle English, i. 221, 474
Homilies, Old English (*see, also*, Aelfric, Wulfstan, etc.), i. 218, 458, 459; iv. 424
Hone, Percy F., xiv. Add. 8
Hone, William (1780–1842), xiv. 520; *Every-Day Book*, xii. 181; *Table Book*, xii. 200, 436, 437
Hone's Year-Book, xiii. 143
Honeycomb, Will, in *The Spectator*, ix. 51
Honeycombe, Polly, in Colman's drama, x. 89
Honeyman, Charles, in *The Newcomes*, xiii. 295
Honeyman, Martha, in *The Newcomes*, xiii. 297
Honiton, x. 387
Honor, in *The Masque of the Middle Temple*, vi. 355
Honoria, in Dryden's *The Rival Ladies*, viii. 4
Honoria, in *The Picture*, vi. 156, 158
Honorius I, ii. 347
Honorius of Autun, *Elucidarium* of, i. 343
Honour, in *Portuus of Noblines*, etc., ii. 284

Honour, in *The Faerie Queene*, iii. 236
Honour, lady, in *Amends for Ladies*, vi. 223
Honour, prince of, in *The Palice of Honour*, ii. 261, 262
Honourable society for the Advancement of Experimental Philosophy, ix. 389
Honyman, Andrew (d. 1676), ix. 546
Hood, Edwin Paxton, xiii. 471
Hood, Thomas (*fl.* 1582–1598), iv. 458
Hood, Thomas (1799–1845), x. 135; xi. 160; xii. 107, 108 ff. (main entry), 119 ff., 129, 131, 139, 418, 429, 449; xiii. 161, 230, 238
  Bridge of Sighs, The, xii. 109, 110; xiii. 239
  Clapham Academy, xii. 109
  Comic Annual, xiv. 235
  Death Bed, A, xii. 110
  Desert Born, The, xii. 111
  Elm Tree, The, xii. 110
  Eugene Aram, xii. 110
  Fair Ines, xii. 111
  Farewell, Life, xii. 110
  Giver of glowing light, xii. 111
  Haunted House, The, xii. 110, 111; xiii. 239
  Hero and Leander, xii. 110
  It was not in the Winter, xii. 110
  Lake and a Fairy Boat, A, xii. 111
  Lycus the Centaur, xii. 110
  Miss Kilmansegg, xii. 109, 111
  Plea of the Midsummer Fairies, The, xii. 110, 111
  Serious Poems, xii. 109
  Song of the Shirt, The, xii. 109; xiv. 238
  Spring it is cheery, xii. 111
  Stars are with the Voyager, xii. 111
  United Family, The, xii. 121
  Up the Rhine, xii. 121
  Works, xii. 109
Hood, Thomas, the younger (1835–1874), xiii. 512; xiv. 339; *The Rules of Rhyme*, xiii. 248
Hood's Magazine, xiii. 69
Hooghe, Pieter de, xiv. 212
Hook, Theodore Edward (1788–1841), xii. 103, 123, 429, 449; xiii. 307 ff.; xiv. 200; *Gervase Skinner*, xii. 251; xiii. 309; *Sayings and Doings*, xii. 251
Hook, Walter Farquhar (1798–1875), xii. 274, 457; xiv. 101, 503, 507, 591; *Lives of the Archbishops of Canterbury*, xiv. 112
Hooke, Nathaniel (d. 1763), x. 509; *Account of the...Duchess of Marlborough*, x. 319; *Observations on the Roman Senate*, x. 319; *Roman History*, x. 319
Hooke, Robert (1635–1703), viii. 250, 364; xiv. 561; *Micrographia*, viii. 356, 477; xiv. 283
Hooker, Joan, iii. 406
Hooker, John (1526?–1601), iii. 406
Hooker, Sir Joseph Dalton (1817–1911), xiv. 296, 299, 300, 550, 561

Hooker, Richard (1554–1600), II. 290; III. 319, 399–417, 459; IV. 221, 226, 235 ff., 239, 268, 303, 411, 493, 511; V. 338; VII. 125, 146, 158, 163, 236, 252, 280, 295, 463; VIII. 72, 308; X. 174, 360; XI. 28, 32; XII. 253; *Christian Letter, The*, III. 415; *Of the Laws of Ecclesiastical Polity*, III. 399–417 (main entry), 547; VII. 323; VIII. 336

Hooker, Sir William Jackson (1785–1865), XIV. 290, 561

Hookham, Edward, XI. 463

Hoole, Charles (1610–1667), V. 80; VII. 480; *New Discovery of the Old Art of teaching Schoole*, IX. 387, 569

Hoole, John (1727–1803), X. 435, 469, 473; XI. 246; *Cyrus*, X. 87, 435, 439; XI. 263; *Timanthes*, XI. 263

Hooly and Fairly, IX. 374

Hooper, John (d. 1555), bishop of Gloucester and Worcester, sermons upon *Jonah*, III. 36, 474; IV. 232, 493

Hooper, Richard, VII. 51

Hoosier writers, XIV. 349

Hope (Spes), in *Piers the Plowman*, II. 27

Hope, in prince Arthur's marriage pageant, VI. 332

Hope, Thomas (1770?–1831), XI. 461; *Anastasius*, XI. 306, 307

Hope, Sir William, IV. 369

Hope, Sir William Henry St John (1854–1919), XII. Add. 5

Hope End, Herefordshire, XIII. 70

Hopeful, in Bunyan's *Pilgrim's Progress*, VII. 173

Hope-Scott, James Robert (1812–1873), XII. 454; XIV. 505

Hopewell, the Rev. Mr, Haliburton's, XIV. 346

Hopkins, Charles (1664–1700), VIII. 437

Hopkins, Ellice, XII. 467

Hopkins, Gerard, XIII. 207, 210

Hopkins, J. Castell, XIV. 581

Hopkins, John (d. 1570), III. 46; *Psalms*, VIII. 41

Hopkins, Matthew (d. 1647), *The Discovery of Witches*, VII. 375

Hopkins, Richard (d. 1594?), IV. 444

Hopkins, Robert Thurston, XIV. 528

Hopkins, William (1793–1866), XIV. 265, 561

Hoppner, John (1758–1810), XII. 323

Hoppus, John, XIV. 591

Hopton, Ralph, lord (1598–1652), VII. 86, 245, 246, 348, 454

Horace, I. 76, 193, 221; II. 264; III. 20, 113, 173, 232, 259; IV. 2, 17, 23, 30, 124, 186, 197, 206 ff., 235, 248, 250, 329, 332, 418, 437; V. 65; VI. 221, 313, 348, 362, 406; VII. 1, 4, 12, 62, 69, 180, 181, 265, 267, 334, 370; VIII. 44, 58, 61, 85, 89, 203, 214, 215, 220, 271, 278, 408, 446; IX. 39, 46, 58, 59, 72, 85 ff., 119, 146, 158, 264, 269, 277, 336 ff., 445, 449, 455, 456, 458 ff., 462, 473, 478, 482, 484, 497, 499, 525, 526, 528,

Horace
561; X. 117, 124, 128, 197, 201, 430, 457, 464, *also see* Add.; XI. 2, 81, 82, 90, 134, 136, 403, 426; XII. 73, 318, 326, 335, 363, 419, 482, 484, 486 ff., 490, 491, 493 ff., 497, *also see* Add.; XIII. 294; XIV. 205
    Ars Poetica, VI. 6, 8; VIII. 221; IX. 70
    Beatus ille, VII. 9
    Coelum non animum, VII. 100
    Carmina, X. 130
    Epistles, XII. 337
    Integer vitae, VII. 2
    Odes, XI. 359
    Translations from, by Sir Richard Fanshawe, VIII. 271

Horace, in *The Poetaster*, VI. 18, 39, 42

Horae Subsecivae, IV. 524

Horant, in *Kudrun*, I. 37

Horatio, in Rowe's *Fair Penitent*, VIII. 196

Horatio, in *The Dukes Mistris*, VI. 200

Horatio, don, in *The Spanish Tragedie*, V. 158, 163, 240

Horatius Cocles, in *The Rape of Lucrece*, VI. 101

Horm, Danish viking, I. 287

Horman, William (d. 1535), II. 321; III. 555

Horn, cape, XIII. 16

Horn, John, II. 66

Horn, The Gest of King, I. 218, 281, 286, 287, 291 ff., 299, 303 ff., 309, 468

Horn Childe, I. 282, 291, 468

Hornby, near Lancaster, XIV. 54

Horne, Andrew (d. 1328), VIII. 465

Horne, George (1730–1792), IX. 512; X. 472; XII. 467

Horne, John. *See* Tooke, John Horne

Horne, Richard Henry or Hengist (1803–1884), XI. 410; XII. 107, 117, 418, 428, 441; XIII. 471, 483, 484, 520, 543; XIV. 365, 520, 586
    Australian Autobiography, XIV. 371
    Australian Facts and Fancies, XIV. 371
    Cosmo de' Medici, XII. 118; XIII. 262
    Death of Marlowe, The, XII. 118; XIII. 262
    Gregory VII, XIII. 262
    Judas Iscariot, XIII. 262
    Laura Dibalzo, XII. 118
    New Spirit of the Age, A, XII. 118
    Orion, XII. 118; XIV. 363

Horne, Thomas (1610–1654), VII. 480

Horne, Thomas Hartwell (1780–1862), IV. 426; XI. 472, 522

Horneck, Anthony (1641–1697), VIII. 301, 302, 460

Hornecks, Mrs and the Miss, X. 213

Horner, Francis (1778–1817), XII. 144, 426; 'The Paper credit of Great Britain,' XII. 145

Horning, L. E., XIV. 581

Horologium, Old English, I. 136

Horrocks, Jeremiah (d. 1641), VIII. 477

Horsa, I. 104

Horse, book on care of, III. 19

Horse, the, in *Mum, Sothsegger*, II. 36
Horses, writers on, IV. 540
Horsfield, Thomas Walker (d. 1837), XII. 511
Horsham, Sussex, X. 378; XII. 58
Horsham school, VII. 342
Horsley, John (1685–1732), *Britannia Romana*, IX. 355, 536
Horsley, Samuel (1733–1806), XI. 399; XII. 279, 280
Horsleydown, X. 382
Horsman, Edward (1807–1876), XIV. 133, 172, 510
Horstmann, Carl, I. 338, 340
Hort, Fenton John Anthony (1828–1892), XII. 340, 465, 467, *also see* Add.; *The Way the Truth the Life*, XII. 298
Hort, Josiah (1674?–1751), IX. 465; X. 385
Hortense, in Charlotte Brontë's *Shirley*, XIII. 409
Hortensio, in *The Bashful Lover*, VI. 155, 158
Hortensius, in Grave's *Columella*, X. 277
Horton, Bucks., VII. 98, 99, 107, 113
Hosack, John (d. 1887), XIV. 503; *Mary Queen of Scots and her Accusers*, XIV. 94
Hosein, in Ockley's *History of the Saracens*, X. 281
Hoskins, John (1566–1638), IV. 59, 209, 265
Hoskins, Sir John (1634–1705), VIII. 247
Hoskins, William (*fl.* 1591), V. 322
Hospitall of incurable fooles, The, III. 482
Hospitallers. *See* St John, knights of
Host, the, in the *Canterbury Tales*, III. 192
Hôtel de Rambouillet, VII. 391
Hotham, Charles (1615–1672?), IX. 515, 517, 518
Hotham, Durant (1617?–1691), IX. 515, 518; *The Spie*, VII. 351
Hotham, Sir John (d. 1645), VII. 351
Hothbroddus, I. 25
Hothead, in Crowne's *Sir Courtly Nice*, VIII. 189
Hotspur, II. 415; V. 256
Hotspur, in *Macbeth*, XI. 284
Hotten, John Camden (1832–1873), XII. 506; XIII. 467, 532
Hottentots, X. 160; XIV. 375
Houbraken, X. 498
Houdancourt, Mlle La Motte, VIII. 262
Houghton, X. 246
Houghton, lord. *See* Milnes, Richard Monckton
Houghton Conquest, Beds., IX. 145
Hounslow heath, VIII. 93
Hour, The, XIV. 196
Hour before Marriage, An, XI. 265
Hours, Books of, II. 315; IV. 426
House of Commons, II. 286, 303
Household books, II. 503
Household Words, XII. 221; XIII. 178, 315, 323, 326, 328, 329, 332, 335, 373, 375 ff., 379

Housewifery, writers on, IV. 543
Housman, Laurence, XI. 433
Houyhnhnms, in *Gulliver's Travels*, IX. 105
Hoveden, John (d. 1275), I. 194, 454
Hoveden, Roger of (d. 1201?), I. 160, 161, 172 ff., 178, 450; III. 314; IV. 68
How, Frederick Douglas, XIV. 599
How a man may chuse a good Wife from a bad, VI. 93, 96, 432
How a Merchande dyd hys Wyfe Betray, II. 501
How the Good Wife taught her Daughter, II. 501, 502
How the Plowman lerned his Pater Noster, II. 501
How the Wise man taught his Son, II. 501, 502
How unhappy is Phyllis in love, VIII. 96
Howard, Charles, of Effingham, admiral, 1st earl of Nottingham (1536–1624), IV. 82; VI. 249, 250
Howard, Charles, 11th duke of Norfolk (1746–1815), XIV. 186
Howard, Edward (*fl.* 1669), VIII. 217, 422; *The Usurper*, VIII. 21; *The Women's Conquest*, V. 277; version of Rochester's *British Princes*, VII. 267
Howard, Sir Edward, lord high admiral (d. 1513), III. 64
Howard, Edward Granville George (d. 1841), XII. 449
Howard, lady Elizabeth, Dryden's wife, VIII. 8
Howard, Frances, countess of Essex (and Somerset), IV. 143, 145, 202, 259; VI. 31, 344
Howard, Frederick, 5th earl of Carlisle (1748–1825), XI. 392
Howard, Henrietta, countess of Suffolk (1681–1767), IX. 82, 249, 470, 498; X. 257; *Letters*, IX. 250
Howard, Henry, earl of Surrey (1517?–1547), II. 213, 331; III. 23, 24, 168, 169, 171, 174 ff. (main entry), 201, 210, 212, 227, 247 ff., 281 ff., 285, 287, 293, 294, 298, 300, 302, 303, 363, 365, 442, 447, 509; IV. 108, 110, 116 ff., 130, 138, 182, 183, 196, 197; VII. 1; VIII. 222, 223
Aeneid, V. 155; VII. 133
Beautie, Frailtie and hurtfulnesse of, III. 176
Complaint of a dying lover, III. 176
Complaint of the absence of her lover, III. 177
Complaint that his ladie after she knew of his love kept her face alway hidden from him, III. 176
Liricks, VII. 271
Phylida was a fayer mayde, III. 178
Richmond, Elegy on the Duke of, III. 178
Spring, wherein eche thing renewes, III. 176
Vow to love faithfully howsoever he be rewarded, III. 176
Howard, Henry, 1st earl of Northampton (1540–1614), VI. 4; VII. 435

Howard, James (*fl.* 1674), VIII. 422; *All Mistaken*, VIII. 21; version of *Romeo and Juliet*, VIII. 21, 120

H[oward], J., *Panegyric on King William*, VIII. 92

Howard, John (1726?–1790), XI. 16, 278, 424, 427

Howard, lady Margaret, VII. 23

Howard, Philip, 1st earl of Arundel (1557–1595), *Fourefould Meditation, of the foure last things*, IV. 130

Howard, Sir Robert (1626–1698), VIII. 6, 8, 26, 395, 398, 419, 444
  Committee, The, VIII. 20, 121
  Foure New Plays, VIII. 23
  Great Favourite, The, VIII. 21, 24
  Indian Queen (with Dryden), VIII. 123

Howard, Thomas, 2nd duke of Norfolk (1443–1524), II. 503; III. 56, 174

Howard, Thomas, 3rd duke of Norfolk (1473–1554), III. 174

Howard, Thomas, 1st earl of Suffolk (1561–1626), IV. 427; VI. 344; VII. 338

Howard, Thomas, 2nd earl of Arundel and Surrey (1586–1646), VII. 219, 307

Howe, Frederick A., v. 250

Howe, John (1630–1705), X. 379; *Calm and Sober Enquiry*, X. 378; *Some Considerations*, X. 374

Howe, Joseph (1804–1873), XIV. 346, 357, 359, 582

Howe, Miss, in Richardson's *Clarissa*, X. 8, 17

Howe, Percival Presland, XIII. 515

Howe Johan Splynter made his testament, A mery gest, II. 327

Howell, James (1594?–1666), VII. 84, 99, 197, 359, 439, 446, 457, 458, 466, 480, 513; IX. 416
  Brief Character of the Low Countries, A, VII. 200
  Dendrologia, Dodona's Grove, or the Vocall Forest, VII. 200
  England's Teares for the present Warres, VII. 200
  Familiar letters, VII. 197 ff.; XIV. 168
  Instructions for Forreine Travell, VII. 200, 201
  Londinopolis, VII. 201
  Perfect Description of the Country of Scotland, A, VII. 200

Howell, Thomas, translator of Ovid, IV. 438

Howell, Thomas (*fl.* 1568), III. 509
  A Dreame, III. 188; XI. 217
  Arbor of Amitie, The, III. 187
  Devises, III. 188; XI. 217
  Newe Sonets and pretie Pamphlets, III. 188

Howes, Edmund (*fl.* 1607–1631), VI. 254

Howgill, Francis (1618–1669), VIII. 416

Howie, John (1735–1793), IX. 549

Howitt, Mary (1799–1888), XI. 387, 480, 491; XIII. 373; XIV. 520

Howitt, Samuel (1765?–1822), *The British Sportsman*, XIV. 232, 544

Howitt, William (1792–1879), XI. 387, 410, 440, 480; XII. 379; XIII. 549; XIV. 371, 520, 586; *A Boy's Adventures in the Wilds of Australia*, XIV. 369

Howleglass, Tyll Howleglas, II. 329; III. 82, 94, 488

Howson, Edmond W., XIV. 597

Howson, John Saul (1816–1885), XII. 472

Hoxton (Hogsden), III. 316; IV. 361, 362; X. 384; XII. 183

Hoy, Thomas (1659–1718?), VIII. 404

Hoyden, Miss, in Vanbrugh's *Relapse*, VIII. 161

Hoyden, Miss, in Vanbrugh's *Relapse* and Sheridan's *Trip to Scarborough*, XI. 269

Hoyden, Timothy, in *The Sparagus Garden*, VI. 227

Hoyle, Joshua (d. 1654), VII. 322

Hrethel, in *Beowulf*, I. 24

Hrethric, in *Beowulf*, I. 25

Hróarr (Roe), son of Halfdan, I. 25

Hroerekr (Roricus), I. 25

Hrólfr, I. 25

Hrólfr Kraki, I. 25, 27

Hrólfs Saga Kraka, I. 25, 27

Hrothgar, in *Beowulf* and *Widsith*, I. 20, 22, 23, 24, 25, 29, 32, 34; v. 26

Hrothwulf, in *Beowulf* and *Widsith*, I. 23, 25, 34

Hrotsvitha, Roswitha, Benedictine abbess of Gandersheim, v. 6, 101; VII. 503

Huarte Navarro, J. de D., *Examen de Ingenios*, IV. 445; VII. 260

Hubba, X. 237

Hubbard, Frank Gaylord, v. 85, 87

Hubbard, John, X. 384

Huber, Victor Aimé, XIV. 593

Hubert, in *King John*, v. 185

Hübner, XII. 523

Huchon, R., XI. 419, 420, 474; *Un Poète Réaliste Anglais*, XI. 142

Huchoun of the Awle Ryale (*fl.* 14th cent.) I. 284, 333; II. 100, 115 ff., 121, 123, 450, 451

Hucknall Torkard, XII. 39, 393

Huddesford, George (1749–1809), XII. 418

Huddesford, William (1732–1772), IX. 535, 541

Hudibrastic couplet, the, XI. 247

'Hudibrastics,' X. 151; XIII. 233

Hudson, Henry (d. 1611), IV. 99, 107

Hudson, Henry Norman, v. 277

Hudson, John (1622–1719), *Dionysius*, XI. 341

Hudson, Thomas (*fl.* 1610), IV. 443

Hudson, William Henry, XIII. 488, 489

Hue, François, XIV. 66

Hue de Rotelande (*c.* 1185), I. 190, 270, 285, 470; *Ipomedon*, I. 190, 270, 281, 285, 286, 291, 313, 314, 465, 468

Hue and Cry after those rambling protonotaries of the times, Mercurius Elencticus, Britanicus, Melancholicus and Aulicus, The, VII. 359, 502, 514

Hueffer, Ford H. Madox, XIII. 499, 561, 574

Hueil or Huel, king of Scotland, I. 262
Huff, Ruff and Snuff, in *Cambises*, v. 64
Hügel, baron von, XII. 275
Hugessen, Edward Hugessen Knatchbull, 1st lord Brabourne. *See* Knatchbull-Hugessen
Huggins, William (1696–1761), x. 492
Huggins, Sir William (1824–1910), XIV. 556
Hugh, in *Barnaby Rudge*, XIII. 320, 321
Hugh, Sir, II. 414
Hugh de Campden's *Boctus and Sidrac*, II. 214
Hugh of Kirkstall (*fl.* 1200), I. 450
Hugh Spencer's Feats in France, II. 414
Hughes, A. M. D., XIII. Add. 2
Hughes, Charles, VII. 201
Hughes, H. R., of Kinmel, IV. 262
Hughes, Jabez (1685?–1731), VIII. 405
Hughes, John (1677–1720), VIII. 395, 410, 411, 437; IX. 57, 71, 143 ff., 181, 183, 437, 438, 477; *Apollo and Daphne*, VIII. 194; *Calypso and Telemachus*, VIII. 194; *The Siege of Damascus*, VIII. 194; IX. 144, 184; x. 73
Hughes, J. L., XIII. 543
Hughes, Michael (*fl.* 1746), IX. 564
Hughes, Patrick, x. 197
Hughes, Thomas (*fl.* 1587), *The Misfortunes of Arthur*, v. 77 ff., 152, 239, 397
Hughes, Thomas (1822–1896), XI. 480; XIII. 355, 358, 547, 553; XIV. 408; *Tom Brown's School Days*, XIII. 370, 435; XIV. 413
Hughes, Thomas McKenny, XII. 508
Hughes, W., *Abridgment* (1660–1662), VIII. 469
Hughes, William Richard, XIII. 543
Hugo, Herman, *Pia Desideria*, VII. 405
Hugo, Thomas, XIV. 540
Hugo, Victor, I. 279; v. 222, 234, 303; x. 221; XII. 208, 395; XIII. 129, 134, 137, 283, 425, 427, 428, 495
  Art d'être Grandpère, L', XIII. 135
  Châtiments, Les, XIII. 132
  Cromwell, v. 302; XIII. 133
  Égout de Rome, L', XIII. 133
  Les Misérables, x. 49
  Notre Dame de Paris, x. 218; XIII. 419
  Roi s'amuse, Le, XIII. 267
Scott's *Quentin Durward*, XII. Add. 1
Hugo de Balsham (d. 1286), II. 346, 347, 350, 351, 353, 355
Hugo de Petra, in *The Usurper*, VIII. 21
Hugo de St Victor, I. 228, 232, 234, 355; II. 365
Hugucio, bishop of Ferrara (d. 1213), *Dictionary*, II. 363, 366
Huguenots, the, v. 286; VII. 306, 308, 322; VIII. 174, 261; IX. 236, 240; XI. 354
Hugues of Saxe-Gotha, Master, Browning's, XIII. 67
Huish, Robert (1777–1850), XI. 393
Hull, IV. 106, 310; VII. 184, 224
Hull, Eleanor, XIV. 574

Hull, Thomas (1728–1808), x. 273, 274, 447; XI. 457
Hull Packet, The, XIV. 203
Hull grammar school, VII. 179
Huloet, Richard (*fl.* 1552), III. 555
Hulsean lectures, XII. 298
Hulton, Samuel Fletcher, XIV. 541
Humanities, the study of the, II. 366, 370
Humanity, in *The Palice of Honour*, II. 261
Humanum Genus, in *The Castle of Perseverance*, v. 52
Humber, the, II. 88, 100
Humble Address of the Atheists, The, VIII. 100
Humboldt, Alexander von, XIV. 249
Hume, Abraham (1814–1884), XII. 511
Hume, or Home, Alexander (1560?–1609), *Hymns and Sacred Songs*, III. 137, 498
Hume, Alexander (*fl.* 1612), IX. 558
Hume, Alexander (1811–1859), XIII. 503
Hume, Anna (*fl.* 1644), IX. 555
Hume, David, of Godscroft (1560?–1630?), IX. 550; *History of Douglas and Angus*, IX. 555
Hume, David (1711–1776), IV. 57, 292; VII. 278, 289, 290; VIII. 328, 335, 336, 340, 472; IX. 287, 547, 561, 565; x. 41, 87, 190, 263, 280, 281, 282 ff., 288, 291 ff., 296, 297, 301, 303, 305, 307, 313, 316 ff., 321 ff. (main entry), 337, 341 ff., 347 ff., 502, 505, 507, 510; XI. 57, 70, 71, 73, 74, 137, 139, 351; XII. 300; XIV. 5, 8, 17 ff., 41, 48, 469, 470, 473, 606
  Dialogues concerning Natural Religion, x. 324, 332, 333
  Enquiry concerning Human Understanding, x. 323, 327, 328, 331, 332
  Enquiry concerning the Principles of Morals, x. 323, 332
  Essay on Miracles, x. 332; XII. 285
  Essays, x. 322 ff., 362; XIV. 398
  Four Dissertations, x. 324
  History, XI. 324, 326
  History of England, x. 40, 283 ff., 289, 290, 293, 323, 362; XIV. 50, 54
  History of Great Britain, x. 283 ff.
  Letters to Strahan, x. 290, 303
  Natural History of Religion, IX. 296; x. 332, 333
  'Of Morals,' x. 322
  'Of the Origin of Government,' x. 334
  Own Life, x. 321, 324
  Philosophical Essays, x. 323
  Political Discourses, x. 323
  Treatise of Human Nature, IX. 285; x. 282, 322 ff., 330 ff., 335, 342; XI. 63, 64; XIV. 43
Hume, David (1757–1838), x. 324
Hume, Joseph (1777–1855), XIV. 198, 407, 510
Hume, Martin Andrew Sharp, XIV. 490
Hume, Hugh, 3rd earl of Marchmont (1708–1794), x. 185
Hume, Patrick (*fl.* 1695), VII. 109

Hume, Patrick, 1st earl of Marchmont (1641–1724), III. 136, 137; IX. 364
Hume, capt. Tobias (d. 1645), IV. 113, 464
Humfrey or Humphrey, Laurence (1527?–1590), III. 421, 422, 445; IV. 429; *Optimates*, III. 445
Humil, in *The two Maids of More-clacke*, VI. 217
Humilitas, in *Psychomachia*, V. 51
Humility, in *Piers the Plowman*, II. 10
Humility, in *The Example of Virtue*, II. 227, 234
Humiltá, in *The Faerie Queene*, II. 234; VI. 335
Hummun's Turkish bath, IX. 263
Humourist, The, XIV. 223
Humours, the four, in *Hymenaei*, VI. 345
Humours, The Comedy of, V. 331
Humphrey, R., VII. 483
Humphrey, duke of Gloucester (1391–1447), II. 198, 286 ff., 318, 362, 497; IV. 182, 430; V. 367
Humphrey, Master, in Dickens's *Master Humphrey's Clock*, XIII. 318
Humphrey, squire, in Vanbrugh's *Journey to London*, VIII. 162
Humphris, E., and Sladen, D., *Adam Lindsay Gordon*, XIV. 365, 586
Huna, V. 31
Hundred Merry Tales, A, II. 327; III. 90, 93, 104, 109, 486, 487, 489; IV. 327, 340, 360
Hundred Years' war, XI. 280
Hunferth (Unferth), king's "orator," in *Beowulf*, I. 22
Hungarian language, XIV. 458
Hungary, II. 80; V. 308; VII. 79, 453
Hunger, in *Piers the Plowman*, II. 14, 22
Hungerford, XIV. 230
Hungerford, Margaret Wolfe (1855?–1897), XIV. 568
Hungerford academy, X. 386
Hunnis, John, VI. 283
Hunnis, Thomas, VI. 283
Hunnis, William (d. 1597), III. 189; IV. 121, 473, 495; V. 411; VI. 283, 286, 288, 291, *and see* Add. 2
Huns, the, I. 33, 35; XIV. 302
Hunsdon, lords. *See* Carey, George; Carey, Henry; Carey, John
Hunt, F. Knight, XIV. 532
Hunt, Henry (1773–1835), XIV. 125, 510
Hunt, James Henry Leigh (1784–1859), VI. 58, 76; VIII. 166, 167, 170; IX. 446; X. 483; XI. 326, 391, 449, 454; XII. 70, 74, 79 ff., 157, 160, 162, 171, 172, 178, 192, 194, 199, 204 ff., 219, 220 ff. (main entry), 227, 384, 395, 396, 399 ff., 403, 407, 428, 433, 437, 441 ff., *also see* Add.; XIII. 148, 258, 259, 337 ff., 328, 401, 469, 484, 513; XIV. 171, 180, 191, 198, 202
Abou ben Adhem, XII. 222
Autobiography, XIV. 197
Captain Sword and Captain Pen, XII. 223

Hunt, James Henry Leigh
Chat of the Week, The, XII. 443
Companion, The, XII. 443
Examiner, The, XII. 442, 444
Feast of the Poets, The, XII. 223
Feast of the Violets, The, XII. 223
Glove, The, XII. 223
Hero and Leander, XII. 222
Indicator, The, XII. 442, 443
Jenny kissed me, XII. 222
Journal, XII. 443
Liberal, The, XII. 36, 37, 443
Literary Examiner, The, XII. 443
Literary Pocket-Book, The, XII. 442
London Journal, XII. 443
Man, Fish and Spirit, XII. 222
Monthly Repository, The, XII. 440, 443
Old Court Suburb, The, XII. 223
Palfrey, The, XII. 223
Poetical Works, XII. 222
Reflector, The, XII. 223, 442
Story of Rimini, The, XII. 222; XIII. 237
Tatler, The, XII. 223, 443
Hunt, John (*fl.* 1805), XIV. 197
Hunt, John, D.D., *Religious Thought in England*, IX. 294
Hunt, Joseph, XIV. 201
Hunt, Mary, XIV. 490
Hunt, Thornton Leigh (1810–1873), XII. 443; XIV. 191, 196, 202
Hunt, Tufton, in Thackeray's *Adventures of Philip*, XIII. 299
Hunt, William, XIV. 83, 101, 532
Hunt, William Holman, XIII. 110 ff., 491
Hunter, Mrs Anne (1742–1821), XI. 444; *Adieu Ye Streams*, XI. 232; *My Mother bids me bind my hair*, XI. 232; *Poems*, XI. 232
Hunter, John (1728–1793), XIV. 286, 561
Hunter, Joseph (1783–1861), XII. 516; *Hallamshire*, XII. 346; *South Yorkshire*, XII. 346
Hunter, Mrs Leo, X. 277
Hunter, Sir William Wilson (1840–1900), XIII. Add. 2; XIV. 338, 490, 577
Annals of Rural Bengal, The, XIV. 339
History of British India, A, XIV. 339
Imperial Gazetteer, The, XIV. 339
Old Missionary, The, XIV. 339
Thackerays in India, The, XIV. 339
Hunterian club, XII. 358
Hunterian collection, XIV. 286
Hunterian professor, XIV. 295
Hunting, writers on, IV. 541
Hunting of the Cheviots, XI. 215
Hunting of the Hare, II. 502; III. 483
Huntingdon, XI. 80
Huntingdon. *See* Henry of
Huntingdon, countesses of. *See* Hastings, Lucy; Hastings, Selina
Huntingdon grammar school, VIII. 253
Huntingdonshire, VII. 342
Huntingford, George Isaac (1748–1832), XII. 490
Huntly, in *Perkin Warbeck*, VI. 193
Huntly, earl of (Holland's *Howlat*), II. 113

Hunton, Philip (1604?–1682), VII. Add.
Hunt's Up, The, IX. 362
Huon of Bordeaux, I. 292; II. 322, 339;
v. 220
Hupe, I. 343
Hurault, Jacques, *Politicke, Moral and
Martiall Discourses*, IV. 8, 21, 445
Hurd, Richard (1720–1808), IX. 509; X.
241, 363, 516; XI. 133, 449; *Letters on
Chivalry and Romance*, X. 240, 484
Hurdis, James (1763–1801), XI. 427
Hursley, XII. 277
Hurstmonceaux rectory, XII. 288
Hurtado, Luis, IV. 445
Hurwitz, Hyman (1770–1844), XI. 413
Hus, John (1369–1415), II. 59, 69; III. 39,
69
Husbandman, Song of the, I. 370
Husbandry, writers on, IV. 541
Husbands, J., *A Miscellany of Poems by
Several Hands*, X. 159, 467
Husband's Message, The, I. 4, 39, 424,
428; runes in, I. 12
Huskisson, William (1770–1830), XIV. 131
Hussey, Edward, XI. 174
Hussey, Thomas (1741–1803), bishop of
Waterford, XI. 6
Hutcheon, William, XIII. 348, 547
Hutcheson, Francis (1694–1746), IX. 301,
302, 506, 508, 548; X. 122, 332, 335,
337; XI. 63, 67; *Essay on the...Passions
and Affections*, IX. 301; *Inquiry into...
Ideas of Beauty and Virtue*, IX. 301;
System of Moral Philosophy, IX. 301
Hutcheson, Mrs, IX. 308
Hutcheson, W. G., XIV. 488
Hutchins, John (1698–1773), XII. 511
Hutchinson, John (1615–1664), IV. 523;
VII. 225, 226, 227
Hutchinson, Julius, VII. 226
Hutchinson, Lucy (b. 1620), VI. 402, 403;
VII. 225, 226, 451; VIII. 270
Hutchinson, Mary, XI. 103
Hutchinson or Hutchenson, Ralph (1553?
–1606), VII. 316
Hutchinson, Roger (d. 1555), IV. 493
Hutchinson, Thomas (1698–1769), XII. 490
Hutchinson, Thomas (d. 1919), editor of
Wordsworth and Lamb, XI. 405 ff.,
410, 413; XII. 399, 434 ff.
Hutchinson, William (1732–1814), XII. 511
Hutten, Leonard (1557?–1632), III. 80;
VI. 482
Hutton, Arthur Wollaston, XIV. 509
Hutton, Catherine (1756–1846), XI. 469;
XIV. 520
Hutton, Charles (1737–1823), XIV. 556
Hutton, Hon. C. W., XIV. Add. 10
Hutton, Henry (*fl.* 1619), IV. 520; V. 478
Hutton, James (1726–1797), XIV. 290 ff.,
561
Hutton, Luke (d. 1598), IV. 529, 530; *The
Blacke Dogge of Newgate*, IV. 350
Hutton, Richard Holt (1826–1897), XI.
410; XII. 461, 467; XIII. 91, 189, 394,
471, 477, 484, 488, 489, 553; XIV. 197,

Hutton, Richard Holt
198, 515, 520, 521, 534; *Aspects of Re-
ligious and Scientific Thought*, XIV. 141;
Essays, Theological and Literary, XIV.
141
Hutton, William (1723–1815), XI. 338,
340, 469; XII. 511; XIV. 521
Hutton, William Holden, XI. 420; XIV.
486, 488, 499
Huxley, Leonard, XIV. 603
Huxley, Thomas Henry (1825–1895), IV.
42, 50; VIII. 352; X. 511; XII. 297; XIV.
296, 300, 474, 606
Collected Essays, XIV. 299
Ethics and Evolution, XIV. 34
Life of Hume, XIV. 34
'On the Hypothesis that Animals are
Automata,' XIV. 34
'Physical Basis of Life, The,' XIV. 34
'Science and Morals,' XIV. 34
Huyche, William, translator of Calvin's
Common Praiers, IV. 442
Huygens, Christian, IX. 129
Hwaetberct. *See* Eusebius
Hwon holy chirche is under uote, I. 226, 458
Hyatt, Stanley Portal, XIV. Add. 8
Hyberdine, parson, IV. 319
Hyde, near Winchester, Benedictine abbey
at, IV. 417
Hyde, Anne, duchess of York (1637–1671),
VII. 220
Hyde, Douglas, XIV. 314, 573
Hyde, Edward, 1st earl of Clarendon
(1609–1674), V. 364; VI. 6, 235; VII. 16,
85, 150, 183, 184, 212 ff. (main entry),
226, 229, 296, 434, 436, 438, 439, 441,
443, 449, 453, 454; VII. Add.; VIII. 7,
8, 23, 38, 81, 206, 271, 295, 308, 323,
368, 384, 480; IX. 209, 214, 221, 226,
237, 238, 347; X. 113, 315; XI. 12, 28
*A Collection of Some of the Massacres
and Murthers committed on the Irish*, VII.
212
Against Multiplying Controversies, VII.
217
An Active and Contemplative Life, VII.
217
*Brief Survey of the dangerous and per-
nicious Errors to Church and State in
Mr Hobbes's book*, VII. 301
Concerning Education, IX. 396
*Contemplations and Reflections upon the
Psalms of David*, VII. 215, 217
Essays Divine and Moral, VII. 217, 221
History of the Rebellion, VII. 188, 202,
212, 214 ff.; VIII. 63, 389; IX. 204, 206,
208, 227, 394; X 280; XI. 341
Life (autobiography), VII. 213, 216 ff.,
221; VIII. 322; IX. 208
Miscellaneous Works, VII. 215, 217
Of Contempt of Death, VIII. 389
Of Friendship, VIII. 389
Of Human Nature, VII. 217
Of Liberty, VII. 217
Of Repentance, VII. 217; VIII. 389
Of the Want of Respect due to Age, IX. 396

Hyde, Edward
  On Education, VII. 217, 220
  On the Reverence due to Old Age, VII. 217
  Reflections upon several Christian Duties,
  VIII. 389
  *Short View of the State and Condition of
  the Kingdom of Ireland, A*, VII. 212
  State Papers, VII. 188
  Vindication, VII. 217
Hyde, Edward, 3rd earl of Clarendon
  (1661–1724), IX. 161
Hyde, Henry, 2nd earl of Clarendon (1638
  –1700), VIII. 249, 250; IX. 534
Hyde, Henry, viscount Cornbury and
  lord Hyde (1710–1753), IX. 226, 227
Hyde, Jane, lady, IX. 162
Hyde, Lawrence, 1st earl of Rochester
  (1641–1711), VII. 218; VIII. 43, 97, 268
Hyde, Thomas (1636–1703), IX. 529
Hyder Ali, XI. 17, 18
Hye Way to the Spyttel Hous, The, II. 324,
  485, 501; III. 492
Hygd, in *Beowulf*, I. 23, 24
Hygeia, in Garth's *Dispensary*, IX. 180
Hygelac, in *Beowulf*, I. 23, 24, 25, 26, 29,
  41
Hyland, Inez K. (1863–1892), XIV. 586
Hylton, or Hilton, Walter (d. 1396), II.
  482; *Ladder of Perfection* or *The Devout
  book to a temporal man*, II. 299, 300; *The
  Treatise of the Song of the Angels*, II. 327
Hymen, in *Hymenaei*, VI. 345, 346
Hymen, in *The Hue and Cry after Cupid*,
  VI. 347
Hymen, in *The Jealous Lovers*, VI. 325
Hymenaeus, VI. 304, 327, 484
Hynd, James, VII. 513
Hynde, S., *Iter Lusitanicum*, IV. 458
Hyndlulióð, Old Norse poem, I. 23
Hypatia, Kingsley's, XIII. 363
Hyperides, XII. 331, 340
Hyperion, in Keats's poem, XII. 86
Hypermnestra, II. 177
Hypochondriack, The, X. 479
Hypocrisy, in *Ane Pleasant Satyre*, III. 127
Hypocrisy, in Medwall's interlude, V. 54
Hypocrisy, in *Mirour de l'Omme*, II. 140
'Hypolito, cardinall, of Est,' in *The Famous
  Whore*, IV. 376
Hyslop, James (1798–1827), XII. 418;
  Cameronian's Dream, XI. 243
Hyspanus (Petrus), IV. 445

'I canna come every day to Woo,' XI. 235
I had a horse, IX. 374
I mak it kend, he that will spend, II. 279
'I saw a Peacock with a fiery Tail,' XI. 370
I sing of a maiden, III. 280
Iachimo, in *Cymbeline*, V. 205
Iago, in *Othello*, III. 188; V. 202, 203, 213;
  VI. 274; XII. 171
Ianthe, in *The Siege* (D'Avenant's), VIII.
  118
Ibbitson, Robert (*fl.* 1650), VII. 352, 355,
  356
Ibbotson, J., VIII. 463

Ibburranes, in *Argenis*, IV. 259
Ibrahim Mollac, in Lyttelton's *Persian
  Letters*, X. 114
Ibrahim pasha, XIV. 252
Ibsen, Henrik, X. 77; XII. 116; XIII. 273
Iceland, IV. 325; XIII. 125; XIV. 289
Icelanders, the, X. 222
Icelandic language and literature, X. 220,
  223 ff., 489 ff.; XIII. 124 ff.; XIV. 458.
  See, also, Norse and Scandinavian
Icelus, XIII. 330
Icilius, in *Appius and Virginia*, VI. 182
Ickworth, IX. 251, 252
Ida, in *James IV*, V. 138, 245
Iden, Henry, IV. 444
Ider, I. 297
Idler, The, XIV. 594
Idolatry, in *A True Inventory*, VII. 382
Idumeans, the, VII. 382
Iffley, river, XIV. 209
Igerna, in Arthurian legend, I. 259
Igerna, in *The Misfortunes of Arthur*, V.
  78
Ignatius, St, VII. 318; XII. 340; *Epistles*,
  VII. 149; VIII. 297; XII. 341, 503
Ignatius, *Epistles*, rendering by Grosse-
  teste, I. 204
Ignatius of Antioch, IX. 329
Ignorance, in Medwall's interlude, X. 54
Ignorance, in *The Nature of the Four Ele-
  ments*, V. 57
Ignorance, in *The Tears of the Muses*, III.
  241
'Ignoto,' IV. 52, 116, 117; V. 224; *The
  Nymph's Reply*, VII. 8
Ilchester, I. 205; VII. 54
Ilissus, river, XIV. 132
Ilium (*i.e.* Paris), in *Euphormio*, IV. 256
'I'll tell thee, Dick,' VIII. 96
Illtyd, St, St Iltut or Iltutus (*fl.* 520) of
  Lantwit Major, Wales, I. 66, 67, 69
Illustrated London News, The, XIV. 192,
  196, 201
*Illustrated Sporting and Dramatic News,
  The*, XIV. 201
Illustrated Times, The, XIV. 196
Illustrations of Northern Antiquities, XII.
  358
Illyrians, the, IV. 43
Ilmington, I. 126
Ilsington (Devonshire), VI. 188
Imaginative, in *Piers the Plowman*, II. 27
Imlay, Gilbert (*fl.* 1793), XI. 44, 395
Imma, in Bede, I. 10
Immalee, in Maturin's *Melmoth*, XI. 305
Immerito, in *The Returne from Pernassus*,
  VI. 314
Immerito and G. H., *Three proper and
  wittie familiar Letters*, VI. 388
Immermann, Karl, V. 305
Imogen, in *Cymbeline*, V. 169, 189, 205,
  206; XII. 87
Impartial Trimmer, The, VIII. 92
Impatient Poverty, V. 60, 393
*Imperial Dictionary of Universal Bio-
  graphy*, XIV. 326

Imperial Tragedy, The (1669), VIII. 434

Impey, Sir Elijah (1732–1809), XI. 78

In and In Medley, in *A Tale of a Tub*, VI. 26

In Diebus Dominicis, I. 227, 458

In January last, IX. 360

In May in a morning, II. 282

Inamorato and Misogamos, VII. 512

Incest, in *Confessio Amantis*, II. 149

Inchbald, Mrs Elizabeth (1753–1821), IX. 435; XI. 224, 270, 276, 281, 294–295 (main entry), 454, 456, 457, 461
    Every one has his Fault, XI. 279
    I'll tell you What, XI. 278
    Mogul Tale, The, XI. 278
    Nature and Art, X. 49, 59; XI. 294
    Simple Story, A, XI. 279, 292, 294
    Such Things Are, XI. 278
    To Marry or not to Marry, XI. 278
    Wives as they Were, XI. 279

Inchbald, Joseph (d. 1779), XI. 278

Inchcolm, Firth of Forth, II. 128, 129

'Inche of Lowchlewyn,' II. 131

Inderwick, Frederick Andrew (1836–1904), XIV. 503

Index Expurgatorius Anglicanus, VII. 432

Index librorum prohibitorum, XIV. 108

India, II. 79; IV. 92, 98, 99, 102; IX. 138; X. 294, 408, 491 (poems), 503, 504; XI. 3, 5, 6, 11, 12, 14 ff., 27, 242, 381; XII. 343, 352, 353, 361; XIII. 199; XIV. 59, 61, 64, 78, 97, 98, 130, 133, 221, 331 ff.

India office, XII. 502

Indian alphabets, XII. 352

Indian antiquities, XII. 512

Indian architecture, XII. 509, 510

Indian army, the, XIV. 253

Indian civil service, XIII. 202

Indian geography, XIV. 334

Indian languages, XIV. 457, 458

Indian law, XII. 327

Indian mutiny, the, XII. 227; XIV. 176, 339

Indian mythology, XIV. 339

Indian poetry, XIV. 340

Indian princes, in *The Masque of the Middle Temple*, VI. 355

Indian rebels, XIII. 40

Indian sage, IX. 317

Indians, in *The Moonstone*, XIII. 437

Indians, the, in Cowley's *The Passions*, VII. 64

Indicator, The, XII. 194, 436

Indolence, in Thomson's *Castle of Indolence*, X. 107

Ine, king of Wessex (d. 726), VIII. 310

Ine, laws of, I. 97, 98

Infant School society, XIV. 405

Infida, in *Never too late*, III. 357

Infidelity, in *The Faerie Queene*, III. 234

Ingannati, Gl', V. 115; VI. 305; VIII. 126

Ingeld, in *Beowulf* and *Widsith*, I. 24, 25, 34

Ingelend, Thomas (*fl.* 1560), *The Disobedient Child*, V. 109, 404; VI. 94

Ingelow, Jean (1820–1897), XI. 387, 487; XIII. 503; *Divided*, XIII. 179

Ingenioso, in *The Pilgrimage to Parnassus*, VI. 310

Ingenioso, in *The Returne from Parnassus*, VI. 311

Ingialdr, I. 25

Ingleborough, X. 101

Ingler, William (*fl.* 1643), *Certaine Informations*, VII. 350

Inglis, Sir James, abbot of Cambus Kenneth, III. 153

Inglis, Sir James, abbot of Culross (d. 1531), III. 131, 153

Inglis, Sir Robert Harry, XIV. 596

Ingoldsby, Lincolnshire, VIII. 456

Ingram and Marlowe. *See* Frizer

Ingram, David, IV. 73

Ingram, Herbert, XIV. 201

Ingram, J. Forsyth, XIV. Add. 5, 8

Ingram, John H., XIII. 484, 499, 561

Ingram, John Kells (1823–1907), XIV. 568; *Who fears to speak of Ninety-Eight?* XIV. 318

Ingram, Robert Acklon (1763–1809), XIV. 606; *Necessity of introducing divinity, The*, XIV. 385; *Remarks upon the enormous expense*, XIV. 385

Ingram, Thomas Dunbar (1826–1904), XIV. 490

Ingram, William (*fl.* 1601), IV. 517

Ingulph of Croyland, Chronicle of the pseudo, II. 497; IV. 417

Iniquity, in *Nice Wanton*, V. 110

Inis Eogain, IX. 292

Inishowen, IX. 292

Injunctions given by the Queenes Majestie, IV. 380, 381

Inkle, in Colman's *Inkle and Yarico*, XI. 279

Innes, Alexander (*fl.* 1728), IX. 548

Innes, Cosmo (1798–1874), XII. 516; *Lectures on Scotch Legal Antiquities*, XII. 359

Innes, captain Robert, VII. 361

Innes, Thomas (1662–1744), IX. 553

Innholders' play, V. 46

Innocence, in Marvell's *The Garden*, VII. 181

Innocent III, I. 193; VIII. 296; *De Contemptu Mundi*, III. 208

Innocent IV, I. 201

Innocent VIII, III. 5

Innocents, Boy bishop at the feast of the, V. 8

Innocents, murder of, in early plays, V. 50

Inns of Court, II. 305

Inns of Court Masque (1623), VII. 230

Innsbruck, V. 283

Inny river, X. 199

Inquisition, the, III. 16, 162; XI. 414

Insolence, in *Respublica*, V. 60

Institoris, H., VII. 368, 504

Institucion of a Gentleman, The, III. 552

Intellectus Agens, in *The Floating Island*, VI. 325

Intelligencer, The, IX. 458

Interludes, anonymous, of Heywood's period, v. 409
Intermedii, v. 69
Inverness, II. 100; VII. 254
Inverquharity, IX. 376
'Invisible College,' the, IX. 389
Inwit, Sir (Discretion), in Piers the Plowman, II. 19
Iolante, in The Guardian, VI. 157
Iona, I. 30, 42
Iona society, XII. 361
Ionian sea, XIII. 38
Iphigenia, VII. 371
Iphigenia, in The Bugbears, v. 115
Iphigenia, schoolboy play, v. 123
Iphis, in Confessio Amantis, II. 152
Ipreswel, or Hipswell, near Richmond, Yorkshire, II. 49
Ipsden, lord, in Reade's Christie Johnstone, XIII. 425
Ipsen, A., XIII. 532
Ipswich, II. 156; IV. 409; X. 355; XI. 140, 418; XIV. 190
Ipswich, queen Elizabeth's school, XII. 331
Ipswich, Wolsey's school at, II. 358; III. 428, 429
Ipswich Journal, The, XIII. 440
Ira, in Psychomachia, v. 51
Ira seu Tumulus Fortunae, VI. 320, 474
Irato, in The Floating Island, VI. 325
Irby, Adeline P., XIV. 553
Irby, Sir Antony, IV. 166
Ireland. See John of
Ireland, I. 71; II. 423; IV. 67; v. 137, 344, 347; VI. 197; VII. 46, 58, 78, 79, 114, 148, 149, 190, 207, 209 ff., 223, 225, 233, 253, 355, 358, 436, 442, 451, 458; VIII. 122, 169, 170, 190, 267, 342, 343; IX. 91 ff., 110, 114 ff., 121, 123, 126, 130, 132, 139, 166, 167, 171, 280, 282, 290; X. 58, 195, 200, 202, 203, 231, 256, 293; XI. 1, 3 ff., 12, 14 ff., 19, 39, 342, 343; XII. 165, 337, 344, 351, 360, 361, 433; XIII. 207, 348, 357, 364; XIV. 86, 115, 128, 133, 201, 302 ff., 343, 391, 392, 417, 434, 437
Ireland, Alexander (1810–1894), XII. 444
Ireland, Annie E. (d. 1893), XIII. 52, 467
Ireland, John (d. 1808), XI. 454; Letter to Henry Brougham, XIV. 406, 604
Ireland, Richard (fl. 1600), VII. 27
Ireland, Samuel (d. 1800), XII. 490
Ireland, William Henry (1777–1835), XI. 414, 457; XII. 364; XIV. 203
Ireland, Anglo-Irish political relations, VIII. 21
Ireland, books printed in, XI. 470
Ireland, church of, X. 358; XII. 272
Ireland, National University, XIV. Add.
Ireland, poems on, II. 502, 508
Ireland, printers in, IV. 547
Ireland, Ancient Laws of, XII. 360, 361
Ireland, English Conquest of, II. 483
Ireland, Good Newes from, IV. 389
Ireland, The Glories of, XIV. 307
Ireland's Eye, XIV. 327

Irena, a Tragedy, X. 161
Irenaeus, Aelfric's homily on, I. 118
Irenaeus (i.e. Edmund Spenser), VII. 210
Irene, Middleton's, XIII. 220
Irene, St, I. 74
Ireton, Henry (1611–1651), VII. 383, 513
Iris, in Beaumont's masque, VI. 356
Iris, in The Vision of the Twelve Goddesses, VI. 337, 338
Irish airs, XIV. 314
Irish archaeological society, XII. 361
Irish archaeology, XII. 351, 352, 360
Irish bar, the, XIV. 126
Irish booksellers, X. 11; XI. 342
Irish catholics, X. 58; XI. 7, 108
Irish channel, IX. 126
Irish church, the, XIV. 126
Irish clergy, IX. 394
Irish cronan, IX. 362
Irish dances, XIV. 328
Irish dialect, XIV. 447
Irish drama, XIII. 264; XIV. 330
Irish education, XIV. 328, 393
Irish expedition, Essex's, v. 346
Irish folk-songs, XIV. 328
Irish harpers, XIV. 311
Irish history, X. 280; XI. 15; XII. 360; XIV. 96, 105, 328
Irish land acts, XIV. 97
Irish language and literature, VII. 318; X. 196; XII. 360 ff.; XIV. 302 ff., 458
Irish literary societies, XIV. 319
Irish literary theatre, XIV. 329
Irish manners, XIII. 426
Irish music, X. 232
Irish national anthem, XIV. 321
Irish orators, XIV. 127, 128
Irish Ossianic poems, X. 232
Irish parliament, IX. 290, 291; XI. 6, 55, 344; XIV. 393
Irish people, the, XIV. 127
Irish place names, XIV. 328
Irish poets and poetry, XII. 114; XIII. 188, 190, 234; XIV. 211, 302 ff.
Irish policy, X. 403
Irish politics, XIV. 211, 311, 317
Irish potato famine, XIV. 318, 320
Irish rebellion of 1848, the, XIV. 242, 318
Irish 'revolution,' XI. 24
Irish saints, XIV. 303
Irish scenery, XIII. 283
Irish scholars, X. 231
Irish sea, XIII. 414
Irish sees, the, XII. 257
Irish State papers, VII. 436
Irish stories, XI. 297; XIII. 42, 415, 421
Irish Text society, XII. 516, 518; XIV. 305, 309
Irish trade, XI. 5, 6
Irish university system, XIV. 432
Irish Citizen, The, XIV. 326
Irish Hudibras, The, IX. 258, 502
Irish Liber Hymnorum, XII. 515
Irish Monthly, The, XIV. 329
Irish Penny Journal, The, XIV. 312, 315
Irish People, The, XIV. 321

Irish-Canadians, xiv. 345
Irishman, the stage, xi. 257
Irishmen, xiii. 283, 284, 404
'Irishmen, the Society of United,' xiv. 310, 325
Irnerius, of Bologna, ii. 349; viii. 312
Irnham, Simon, lord, xiv. 217
Ironmongers' company, vii. 250
Ironsides, Cromwell's, vii. 460
Irus, in *Ulysses Redux*, vi. 303
Irvine, Christopher (*fl.* 1638–1685), vi. 482; ix. 551
Irving, David (1778–1860), xi. 440, 445; xii. 522; *History of Scottish Poetry*, xii. 370; *Lives of Scottish Poets*, xii. 370; *Memoirs of...George Buchanan*, xii. 370
Irving, Edward (1792–1834), xii. 472; xiii. 3 ff., 467, 468
Irving, Sir Henry (1838–1905), v. 306; xi. 448; xiii. 474, 513, 514
Irving, Washington, x. 483; xii. 379, 409; *Bracebridge Hall*, xiii. 323; *The Sketch Book*, xiii. 429
Irwin, in Mrs Inchbald's *Every one has his Fault*, xi. 279
Irwin, Sidney, x. 202
Irwin, Sidney Thomas, xiii. 499; xiv. 145, 521
Irwin, Thomas C. (1823–1892), xiv. 569
Irwine, Mr, in *Adam Bede*, xiii. 390
Isaac, i. 46, 123
Isaac, Arabian physician, ii. 364, 365
Isaac, in the religious plays, ii. 424, 426, 427
Isaac, in *Jacob and Esau*, v. 111, 112
Isabel, in *The Decameron*, xii. 82
Isabel, in *Misogonus*, v. 111
Isabel of Castille, duchess of York, ii. 170
Isabel, Lady, and the Elf-Knight, ii. 410, 411
Isabella, in Emily Brontë's *Wuthering Heights*, xiii. 411
Isabella, in Keats's poem, xii. 86, 88
Isabella, in *Laelia*, vi. 305
Isabella, in *Measure for Measure*, i. 1; v. 190, 191, 245
Isabella, in Southerne's *Fatal Marriage*, viii. 191, 192
Isabella, in *The White Divel*, vi. 176, 177
Isabella, countess of Swevia, in *The Insatiate Countesse*, vi. 45, 49
Isabella, queen, in *A Challenge for Beautie*, vi. 103
Isabella, queen, in *Edward II*, v. 153
Isabella of France (1292–1358), queen of Edward II, ii. 338
Isabella of France (1389–1409), queen of Richard II, iv. 169, 181, 182
Isaiah, ii. 106; ix. 69; x. 229
Isenbarth, M., xiii. 553
Iseo, Lago di, ix. 245
Iseult, i. 272 ff., 298, 310. *See, also,* Tristram
Isidora, in Maturin's *Melmoth*, xi. 305

Isidore of Seville, i. 71, 75, 80, 224, 343, 436; ii. 86, 319, 365; iii. 109; *Etymologies* of, i. 119; ii. 86, 363
'Isis Idols,' xiv. 208
Isis river, vii. 327
Isis, The, xiv. 208, 537
Islam, ix. 184; xiii. 13; xiv. 252, 338
Island of Sorcerers, in *Gulliver's Travels*, ix. 105
Islands expedition (Azores, 1597), iv. 103, 200, 201
Isle of Birds, i. 339
Isle of Man, in *Horn*, i. 304
Isle of Wight, xii. 509
Isleworth, iv. 418
Isley, Henry, vi. 112
Isley, Ursula (wife of Beaumont), vi. 112
Islington, iii. 316, 371
Islip, John (d. 1532), iii. 69
Ismael, in *The Loyal Brother*, viii. 190
Ismail, siege of, in Byron's *Don Juan*, xii. 55
Isocrates, iii. 429; iv. 437; x. 202
Isola, Agostino, ix. 412; xiv. 385
Isola, Charles, xii. 200
Isola, Emma. *See* Moxon, Mrs Emma
Ispahan, x. 114
Israel, in Cowley's *Davideis*, vii. 67
Israel, people of, iv. 311; viii. 78; xii. 299
Israel, royal house of, in *Absalom*, vi. 296
Istakar, in Beckford's *Vathek*, xi. 289, 290
Isumbras, Sir, i. 289, 292, 315, 465, 471
Isyphena, in Amory's *Memoirs of Several Ladies*, xi. 287
It cannot rain but it pours, ix. 132
It was a' for our Rightfu' King, ix. 376
It was a lover and his lass, ii. 393
Italian art, xii. 33
Italian characters, xiii. 447
Italian epic, xi. 39
Italian historians, ii. 227
Italian history, xiv. 99
Italian humanists, xiv. 100
Italian interest in Shakespeare, v. 289, 290
Italian language and literature, v. 61, 69 ff., 75, 76, 88, 114 ff., 314, 361; vi. 64, 96, 125, 302, 310, 317, 334, 335, 366, 387; vii. 2, 3, 7, 10, 34, 155, 265, 266, 268, 269, 271, 273, 308, 318, 439; viii. 58, 126, 127, 135, 239, 352; ix. 54, 214, 384, 385, 402 ff., 412, 413; x. 159, 254, 303; xi. 181, 347, 355, 359; xii. 3, 52, 83, 137, 202, 308; xiii. 110, 118, 231; xiv. 128, 135, 385, 391, 434, 457 ff.
Italian medley-poets, xii. 51, 52
Italian *novella*, xii. 53
Italian novels attacked, vi. 378
Italian opera, xiv. 134; ix. 58, 88, 163; x. 70, 71, 83, 84; xiii. 256; xiv. 213
Italian oratory, xii. 268
Italian peasantry, xiii. 453
Italian poets and poetry, ix. 67; xi. 134; xii. 4, 33, 55, 71; xiii. 116, 118, 236
Italian renascence, xiii. 259; xiv. 108

Italian romances, v 127, 254, 319, 350, 413
Italian sonnet writers, v. 173, 230
Italian sonnets, XIII. 46, 117, 252
Italian sources and influence, v. 124, 127, 157, 181, 191, 220, 225, 314; VI. 45, 46, 94, 102, 174, 218, 304, 305, 322, 323, 345, 364, 365, 377; VIII. 14. See, also, under Boccaccio, Bandello, etc.
Italian theatre, XI. 266
Italian theology, XII. 254
Italian, the, in A Woman will have her Will, v. 329
Italianate Englishman, VI. 219
Italians, the, XIII. 306
'Italomania,' XIII. 159, 179
Italy, II. 238, 310; v. 61, 63, 101, 110, 121, 123, 132, 140, 286, 288, 301, 304, 306, 313, 350, 359; VI. 154, 158, 159, 175, 199, 203, 271; VII. 21, 100, 116, 154, 180, 201, 261, 283, 318; VIII. 206, 245, 296, 364, 365; IX. 6, 138, 142, 245, 256, 280, 300, 396; x. 19, 41 ff., 47, 104, 115, 128, 200, 221, 249, 274, 292, 304; XI. 302, 344; XII. 33 ff., 42 ff., 49, 50, 52, 54, 57, 62, 64, 67, 82, 92, 248, 338, 422; XIII. 44, 46, 59, 61, 69 ff., 73 ff., 83, 84, 132, 133, 260, 324, 372, 393, 436, 441, 449, 461; XIV. 77, 102, 108, 118, 151, 184, 217, 292 ff., 322 ff.
Italy and Byron, XII. 392, 395 ff.
Italy, Hazlitt in, XII. 432
Italy and Landor, XII. 440, 441
Italy and Shelley, XII. 402
Item, in Holcroft's Deserted Daughter, XI. 277
Ithaca, IX. 76; XII. 338
Ithamore, in The Jew of Malta, v. 326
Ithocles, in The Broken Heart, VI. 191
Itinerarium...Regis Ricardi, XIV. 74
Itis, VI. 320
Ivan the Terrible, in Milton's Moscovia, VII. 128
Ive, Paul (fl. 1602), IV. 443
Ivernian society, Journal, XII. 351, 360
Ivry, duchesse d', in The Newcomes, XIII. 295
Iwain and Gawain, I. 468
Izarde, John, VI. 287
Izoulet-Loubatières, J., XIII. 466

J. B., Heroick Education, VII. 393, 517
J. C. R., The, XIV. 537
J. D. (1597), IV. 5, 435
J. D. (1656), VIII. 47, 238, 447
J. H. (John Hoskins), 'Absence, hear thou my protestation,' IV. 209
J. K. S. See Stephen, James Kenneth
Jacinta, in Alls Lost by Lust, VI. 72
Jacinta, in The Brothers, VI. 203
Jack, in Arbuthnot's History of John Bull, IX. 135
Jack, in Damon and Pithias, v. 119
Jack, in Swift's Tale of a Tub, IX. 100
Jack, A. E., II. 34, 435
Jack, Chaffing, Disraeli's, XIII. 351

Jack, Sir T. Gresham's nephew, in If you know not me, VI. 91
Jack and Jill, XI. 303, 385
'Jack in the Box,' III. 80
Jack of Dover, IV. 532
'Jack of Lent,' III. 80
Jack of Newbery, XI. 334
Jack Napes, The Dirge of, II. 288, 424
Jack Presbyter, VII. 383
Jack Straw, v. 152, 397, 426
Jack the Giant Killer, XI. 374
Jacke Drums Entertainment, VI. 41
Jacke Jugeler, v. 107, 411
Jacke Upland, II. 39, 40, 162, 432, 434
Jacke Upland, The Rejoinder of, II. 40
Jackman (traveller), IV. 88
Jacks, Lawrence Pearsall, XIV. Add. 2
Jackson, Andrew, XI. 327
Jackson, B. D., XIV. 566
Jackson, chaplain, in Foote's drama, x. 88
Jackson, Henry (1586-1662), VII. 312, 486
Jackson, Henry, XIII. 537
Jackson, John (1686-1763), IX. 507
Jackson, John (fl. 1761-1792), x. 443; XI. 452
Jackson, John, pugilist, XIV. 223, 230, 231
Jackson, Mason, The Pictorial Press, XIV. 201, 532, 541
Jackson, Thomas (1579-1640), VII. 425
Jackson, Thomas (d. 1646), VIII. 276, 277
Jackson, Thomas (1783-1873), Life of Charles Wesley, IX. 325
Jackson, William Hatchett, XIV. 300, 563
Jacob, XIII. 208
Jacob, Edward (1710?-1788), v. 240
Jacob, Giles (1686-1744), VIII. 159; IX. 260; The Poetical Register, 1719-1720, XI. 425
Jacob, Hildebrand (1693-1739), IX. 188, 486
Jacob and Esau, v. 39, 111 ff., 411
Jacobean dramatists, x. 108
Jacobean essayists, IX. 28, 36
Jacobean poets, XII. 221; XIII. 237
Jacobi, Karl Gustav Jacob, XIV. 258, 264
Jacobinism, XI. 1, 7, 25 ff., 30, 32, 119, 138, 155, 156, 165, 380
Jacobins, x. 119; XI. 40, 98, 118, 139, 157
Jacobite literature, XI. 563 ff.
Jacobite rising, x. 251; XII. 1, 26; XIV. 95
Jacobite songs, IX. 371, 372, 375 ff.; XI. 233, 242, 243, 443; XIII. 190
Jacobites, VIII. 92, 99, 122, 194; IX. 11, 13 ff., 110, 113, 117, 201, 211, 218, 219, 223, 226, 249, 325, 407, 413; x. 28, 58, 251, 281, 300, 335, 338, 352, 360
Jacobites' Journal, The, x. 29, 417
Jacobitism, XI. 233
Jacobs, Joseph, XI. 480, 491
Jacobs, J. and Wolf, L., Bibliotheca Anglo-Judaica, XI. 428
Jacobus a Voragine. See Voragine
Jacobus de Cessolis, Liber de ludo scacchorum, II. 312
Jacomo, in The Gratefull Servant, VI. 204
Jacques de Vitry (d. 1240), II. 80, 504

Jacquier, Nicholas (*fl. c.* 1458), VII. 368, 504

Jacuppus, in *Machiavellus*, VI. 315

Jaffa, II. 79

Jaffier, in Otway's *Venice Preserv'd*, VIII. 183, 184

Jaffray, Alexander (1614–1673), IX. 551

Jaggard, Isaac, IV. 395

Jaggard, William (1567?–1623), III. 266; IV. 394, 395, 548; v. 221, 223, 224. 234

Jaggers, Mr, in *Great Expectations*, XIII. 334

Jago, Richard (1715–1781), X. 110, 271 ff., 275, 448

  Adam, X. 112

  Edge-Hill, X. 112, 113

  Goldfinches, The, X. 112

  To William Shenstone, esq., X. 112

Jahangir, court of, XIV. 333

Jahaziel, IV. 43

Jamaica, VIII. 158; X. 36, 467; XI. 37, 222; XIV. 241, 242

James I of England and VI of Scotland, II. 93; III. 34, 136, 137, 150, 160, 164, 198, 271, 378, 498, 503; IV. 53, 57, 59, 63, 64, 95, 132, 134, 135, 137, 149 ff., 154, 155, 161, 163, 165, 184, 187 ff., 203, 237, 239, 253, 254, 256, 259, 266, 276, 279, 293, 302, 304 ff., 310 ff., 334, 351, 374, 392, 403, 405, 406, 427, 428, 531; v. 56, 219, 253, 262, 333, 340, 341, 348, 349, 352, 354, 358 ff., 365, 375, 376, 478, 480 ff.; VI. 4, 5, 7, 38, 47, 86, 101, 107, 108, 147, 149, 172, 217, 220, 234, 243, 245, 250, 254, 255, 258, 262, 271, 272, 278, 283, 290, 298, 314, 316 ff., 321 ff., 327, 333, 336, 337, 342 ff., 358, 360 ff., 401, 403; VII. 4, 21, 49, 54, 158, 166, 188, 190, 191, 196, 199, 203, 205, 206, 208, 209, 219, 223, 309, 310, 312, 314, 327, 331, 337, 340, 343, 366, 390, 394, 433, 435, 436, 438, 439, 441, 450, 451, 454, 455, 458, 506, *also see* Add.; VIII. 127, 128, 130, 132, 143, 277, 316, 319, 323, 356, 363, 470; IX. 202, 222, 235, 357, 359, 360, 558, *also see* Add.; X. 84, 283, 286, 290, 295, 499 ff.; XI. 217, 235; XII. 18, 21, 376; XIII. 256; XIV. 55, 83, 84, 93, 95, 333, 396

  Ane Schort Treatise, II. 285

  Basilicon Doron, IV. 384

  Counterblast to Tobacco, A, IV. 349, 531; VI. 318

  Demonology, IV. 535; VII. 372, 373

  Essays of a Prentice in the Divine Art of Poetry, I. 291; III. 137, 271

  King's Majesties Declaration to his Subjects concerning Lawful Sports to be used, The, IV. 339

  Poetical Exercises, III. 137

  True Lawe of Free Monarchies, The, IV. 301, 304, 511

  Secret History of, XII. 16

James II, king of England, II. 77; IV. 426, 458; VII. 96, 183, 365; VIII. 10, 30, 31, 39, 46, 49, 82, 90, 92 ff., 99,
100, 113, 189, 202, 216, 221, 228, 249, 254, 256, 266, 267, 302, 304, 305, 452; IX. 4, 7, 148, 175, 199, 200, 202, 203, 207, 233, 235, 236, 253; X. 287, 295, 351, 373, 503; XI. 313, 396; XIV. 55, 64, 65, 98

  Memoirs, IX. 213, 214, 493

James I (1394–1437), king of Scotland, II. 129, 171, 239 ff., 283, 284, 368; III. 138, 154, 197; *The Kingis Quair*, II. 91, 94, 154, 171, 219, 240, 241, 243, 244, 250, 253, 267, 270, 281, 471 ff.

James II (1430–1460), king of Scotland, II. 113, 285; III. 148

James III (1451–1488), king of Scotland, II. 284

James IV (1473–1513), king of Scotland, II. 94, 251, 253, 260, 369; III. 61, 70, 135, 152, 197; X. 193

James IV and Flodden Field, The Lamentation of, III. 197

James V (1512–1542), king of Scotland, II. 270; III. 116, 123, 130, 132, 138, 149, 156, 159, 160; IV. 322; v. 59

James VI, king of Scotland. *See* James I, king of England

James (1688–1766), prince of Wales (the Old Pretender), IX. 150, 201, 211, 213, 218, 219, 222, 223, 231; X. 353

James, in *Witty and Witless*, v. 92, 93

James, C. C., XIV. 581

James, George Payne Rainsford (1799–1860), I. 287; XII. 250, 449; XIII. 307; *Richelieu*, XII. 249

James, Henry (1843–1916), XIII. 499, 553, 558, 567, 574, *also see* Add. 3; XIV. 526, 548, *also see* Add. 2

James, John (d. 1680), VIII. 257

James, John, XIV. 595

James, John, seaman, IV. 76

James, Montague Rhodes, IX. 424; XII. 516

James, Richard (1592–1638), VII. 316, 489

James, Robert (1705–1776), X. 467

James, R. A. Scott, XIV. 532

James, St, I. 118, 231; II. 12; IV. 237

James, St, shrine of, at Compostella, II. 313

James, Stephen (d. 1725), X. 386

James, Thomas (1573?–1629), IV. 431, 550; *Catalogus...T. Bodleius*, III. 552

James, Thomas (1593?–1635?), *The Strange and Dangerous Voyage of Captain Thomas James in his Intended Discovery of the North West Passage*, IV. 105 ff., 458

James, Thomas (1748–1804), IX. 408; XIV. 386

James, William (1635?–1663), VII. 486

James, William (d. 1827), XIV. 490

James the Sext, The History and Life of, III. 149

James's powder, X. 215

Jameson, Mrs Anna Brownell, born Murphy (1794–1860), XI. 487; XIV. 503, 521, 569, 583
  Characteristics of Women, XIV. 157
  Diary of an Ennuyée, The, XIV. 323
  Loves of the Poets, The, XIV. 157
  Winter Studies and Summer Rambles, XIV. 323, 358
Jameson, Robert, XIV. 323
Jameson, William (*fl.* 1689–1720), IX. 546
Jámi, *Salámán and Absál*, XIII. 145
Jamie, Don, in *The Spanish Curate*, VI. 139
Jamieson, John (1759–1838), XIV. 611; *Barbour's Bruce*, XII. 517
Jamieson, Robert (1780?–1844), XII. 358, 517; *Popular Ballads and Songs*, XII. 357
Jamnes, legend of, I. 135
Jane, in *A Chast Mayd*, VI. 75
Jane, dame, V. 33
Jane (Seymour) (1509?–1537), queen of Henry VIII, III. 175
Jane, servant of S. Pepys, VIII. 254
Janet, in George Eliot's *Janet's Repentance*, XIII. 387, 388
Janeway, James (1636?–1674), XI. 480; *Token for Children*, XI. 371
Janeway, Richard, VIII. 98
Janin, Jules, V. 302
Janina, in Albania, XII. 43
Januarius, saint, XIV. 247
Janus, XII. 139; XIII. 460
Janus, temple of, I. 95
Janusa, in Chamberlayne's *Pharonnida*, VII. 75
Japan, IV. 75, 92, 99, 100; X. 42; XIV. 138, 165, 166
Japan wares, IX. 271
Japanese language, XIV. 421, 459
Japp, Alexander Hay, XII. 444, 445; XIII. 471
Jaques, in *Alls Lost by Lust*, VI. 70
Jaques, in *As You Like It*, III. 349; V. 192, 193
Jardine, David (*fl.* 1750), X 386
Jardine, Sir William (1800–1874), X. Add.
Jarley, Mrs, in *The Old Curiosity Shop*, XIII. 319
Jarrow, I. 5, 72, 78, 79, 83, 85, 89; IV. 418
Jarvie, Baillie Nicol, in Scott's *Rob Roy*, XII. 25
Jasher, the lost book of, XII. 331
Jason, William Morris's, XIII. 123, 134
Jason, in *Confessio Amantis*, II. 151
Jason, or Joshua, in *Parlement of the Thre Ages*, I. 333
Jason, The History of, II. 313, 319
Jatāka, XII. 489
Javanese language, XIV. 459
Jawleyford, Mr, Surtees's, XIV. 234
Jay, Harriet, XIII. 500, 517
Jeaffreson, John Cordy (1831–1891), XIII. 567; XIV. 503
Jeake, Samuel (1623–1690), IX. 536; *Charters of the Cinque Ports*, XI. 322
'Jeames,' Thackeray's, XIII. 279, 284
Jean à la Barbe. *See* Jehan de Bourgoigne

Jean de Hauteville (*fl.* 1184), I. 193, 454
Jean de Meun, I. 99; II. 169; III. 90; VII. 367
Jean d'Outremeuse, *Myreur des Histors*, II. 81, 82
Jean de Vignay, II. 312
Jean de Waurin, II. 508
Jeanroy, Alfred, II. 392
Jeany where has thou been, IX. 360
Jebb, John (1736–1786), XIV. 385, 593
Jebb, John (1775–1833), bishop of Limerick, XII. 256, 457
Jebb, Sir Richard Claverhouse (1841–1905), XII. 324, 485, 486, 492; XIII. 477; XIV. 493
  Attic Orators, The, XII. 332
  Bentley, XII. 332
  Introduction to Homer, XII. 332
  Pindaric Odes, XII. 332
Jebb, Samuel (1694?–1772), I. 207
Jed valley, X. 93
Jedburgh, X. 93; XI. 444
Jefferies, Richard (1848–1887), XI. 480; XIV. 521
  Field and Hedgerow, XIV. 166
  Gamekeeper at Home, The, XIV. 166
  Hodge and his Master, XIV. 166
  Story of my Heart, The, XIV. 166
  Wood Magic, XIV. 166
Jefferson, Samuel (1809–1846), XII. 511
Jeffery, John (1647–1720), VIII. 457
Jeffes, Abel (*fl.* 1595), IV. 383; V. 158
Jeffrey, Alexander (1806–1874), XII. 511
Jeffrey, Francis, lord Jeffrey (1773–1850), IX. 127; X. 188, 413; XI. 149, 440; XII. 8 ff., 42, 92, 103, 142 ff., 152, 153, 156, 158, 161, 163, 378, 379, 384, 411, 426, 427; XIII. 8, 467; XIV. 112, 138; *Contributions to the Edinburgh Review*, XII. 146; 'Don Cevallos, and the French Usurpation in Spain,' XII. 149
Jeffrey, in *Edward IV*, VI. 91
Jeffrey or Jeffreys, Sarah, VII. 96
Jeffreys, George, 1st baron Jeffreys (1648–1689), VII. 365; VIII. 410, 411; IX. 5, 6, 240; X. 274; XIII. 434
Jeffreys, John Gwyn (1809–1885), XIV. 296, 561, 562
Jehan de Bourgoigne (John ad barbam), in the Mandeville myth, II. 80 ff.
Jehan de Bel, I. 478
Jehovah, XI. 194, 199
Jekyll, Sir Joseph (1663–1738), X. 385
Jena, XIV. 416
Jeninges, Edward (*fl.* 1593), IV. 309, 511
Jenkin Careaway, in *Jacke Jugeler*, V. 107
Jenkin, Henry Charles Fleeming (1833–1885), XIII. 248
Jenkins, Elijah. *See* Mottley, John
Jenkins, Herbert, XIV. 516
Jenkins, J., X. 386
Jenkins, Sir Leoline (1623–1685), IX. 213
Jenkins, Mrs Winifred, in Smollett's *Humphrey Clinker*, X. 43; XIII. 279
Jenkinson, Anthony (d. 1611), IV. 84, 88
Jenkinson, Ephraim, X. 202

Jenkinson, Robert Banks (1770–1828), 2nd earl of Liverpool, XI. 154; XII. 439; XIV. 407

'Jenks,' *pseud. See* Beckford, William

Jenkyns, Patheryke, or Patrick, VII. 88, 413

Jenner, Thomas, *Sea Coasts of England, The,* IV. 458

Jenner, Sir T., Speech to his Wife and Children, VIII. 97

Jennings, David (1691–1762), X. 384

Jennings, John (d. 1723), X. 384

Jennings, Mrs, in Jane Austen's *Sense and Sensibility,* XII. 236

Jennings, Theodore (*fl.* 1647), VII. 515

Jenny, Jenny, IX. 363

Jenyns, Soame (1704–1787), X. 461, 523, 525; XI. 350; *Free Enquiry into the Nature and Origin of Evil,* X. 177

Jephson, Henry, XIV. 536

Jephson, Robert (1736–1803), XI. 457; *Count of Narbonne,* XI. 274

Jephthah, II. 151

Jeppe, Carl, XIV. Add. 8

Jerdan, William (1782–1869), XI. 463; XII. 418; XIV. 177, 200, 534

Jeremiah, I. 74

Jeremy, in Congreve's *Love for Love,* VIII. 151

Jermyn, Henry, 1st earl of St Albans (d. 1684), VII. 22, 63, 70, 219

Jerningham, Edward (1727–1812), VII. 84; X. 487

Jerome, in *Witty and Witless,* V. 93

Jerome, Don, in Sheridan's *Duenna,* XI. 257

Jerome, Jerome K., XIII. 543

Jerome, St, and writings of, I. 66, 70, 75, 103, 117, 120, 189, 355; II. 293, 365; III. 4; IV. 36, 37; VII. 304; XII. 496; *Vitae Sanctorum Patrum,* II. 317, 323

Jerome, St, in *The Example of Virtue,* II. 227

Jeronimo, in *The Spanish Tragedie,* V. 160 ff.

Jeronimo, The First Part of, V. 158 ff.; VI. 23; VIII. 125

Jerrold, Wm Blanchard, XIV. 541

Jerrold, Douglas William (1803–1857), XIII. 268, 520; XIV. 193, 196, 236 ff., 544, 548

   Blackey'd Susan; or, 'All in the Downs,' XIII. 265; XIV. 237

   Catspaw, The, XIII. 269

   Men of Character, XIV. 237

   Mrs Caudle's Curtain Lectures, XIV. 237

   Punch's Complete Letter-writer, XIV. 237

   Punch's letters to his son, XIV. 237

   Prisoner of War, The, XIII. 269

   Time Works Wonders, XIII. 269

Jerrold, Walter, XIII. 530, 533, 570; XIV. 548

Jerrold, William Blanchard (1826–1884), XIII. 563; XIV. 193

Jersey, VII. 196, 214, 215, 217, 218, 316; XIII. 46

Jersey, earl of. *See* Villiers, Edward, 1st earl

Jerusalem, I. 134; II. 79, 80, 85, 114, 299, 321; III. 230; IV. 90, 323, 324; V. 49; VI. 84, 89; VIII. 23; XII. 107, 249, 260, 321, 514; XIV. 251

Jerusalem, in *The Faerie Queene,* III. 231

Jerusalem, Battle of, I. 356

Jervas, Charles (1675?–1739), IX. 169, 171, 444, 529; X. 40

Jervois, Miss, in Richardson's *Sir Charles Grandison,* X. 11, 18

Jespersen, Otto, XIV. 611

'Jessamy Bride,' the, X. 213

Jesse, Edward (1780–1867), X. Add.; XIV. 544

Jesse, John Heneage (1815–1874), XIV. 503

Jessica, in *The Merchant of Venice,* V. 183

Jessopp, Augustus (1824–1914), IX. 198, 238, 494; XIV. 490; *Arcady for better for worse,* XIV. 78

Jest-books, III. 487 ff.; IV. 531; VII. 516

Jesu Christ, The Seven Sheddings of the blood of, II. 325

Jesuit printing press, IV. 411

Jesuits, the, III. 162; IV. 100, 127, 167, 202, 218, 220, 244, 255, 256, 296, 429; V. 89, 90, 344, 345, 365, 371; VI. 150, 157, 302, 324, 377; VII. 33, 36, 47, 88, 151, 236, 305, 309, 311, 320, 335, 336, 353, 392; VIII. 85, 86, 88, 173, 175, 266, 300, 305, 449; IX. 197; X. 282, 283, 292, 300, 319, 322; XIII. 210, 366, 435; XIV. 101, 127, 253, 308, 316, 329, 382

Jesus, Orm's treatment of the name of, I. 225. See, also, *Childhood of,* and under Christ

Jesus (a Samaritan), in *Piers the Plowman,* II. 27

Jesus, in Cowley's *Davideis,* VII. 66

Jesus, in Douglas's *Aeneid,* II. 264

Jesus, in *Mirour de l'Omme,* II. 141

Jesus, in transition songs, II. 383

Jesus, in Wyclif's *Dialogus,* II. 65

   See, also, under Christ *and* Child Christ

Jesus Christ, IX. 28, 29, 312, 325, 327; X. 371, 378; XI. 185, 194, 196 ff., 326, 369; XII. 40, 65, 67, 256, 259, 273, 284, 287, 290, 295 ff.; XIII. 102; XIV. 444

Jesu's Psalter, V. 323

Jeux, V. 4, 27

Jevons, Harriet A., XIV. 475

Jevons, William Stanley (1835–1882), XIV. 475

   Principles of Science, The, XIV. 23

   Pure Logic, XIV. 23

   Substitution of Similars, The, XIV. 23

   Theory of Political Economy, The, XIV. 23

Jew, in *Machiavellus,* VI. 305

Jew, the, in Sheridan's *Duenna,* XI. 267

Jewel, John (1522–1571), bishop of Salisbury, III. 406, 548; IV. 236, 433, 493; Challenge sermon, IV. 235

Jewell for Gentrie, A, 1614, IV. 541
Jewish antiquities, IX. 393
Jewish Christians, IX. 291
Jewish church, XII. 321, 478
Jewish doctor, in *The Duke of Millaine,* VI. 159
Jewish faith, XII. 14
Jewish history, IX. 227
Jewish religion, XI. 48
Jewish writers, I. 478
Jewitt, Llewellyn Frederick William (1816–1888), X. 473; XII. 511
Jewkes, Mrs, in Richardson's *Pamela,* X. 5
Jews, the, I. 63, 133, 176; II. 24, 343, 345, 350, 362, 365; V. 44, 49, 366; VI. 86, 154; VII. 102, 147, 198, 200, 281, 300, 319; VIII. 274; IX. 297; X. 362; XII. 318, 477, 478; XIII. 349, 353, 384, 400; XIV. 2, 67, 136, 309
Jews, the Council of the (Coventry Mysteries), V. 19
Jews, queen of the, in *Gyre Carling,* II. 276
Jewsbury, Geraldine Endsor (1812–1880), XIII. 563
Jhan, Sir, the priest, in *Johan Johan,* V. 98, 99
Jingle, Alfred, in Dickens's *Pickwick Papers,* X. 41; XIII. 310, 351
Jo, in *Bleak House,* XIII. 328, 329
Joab, IV. 231
Joab, in Cowley's *Davideis,* VII. 67
Joan, in *The Devil and his Dame,* V. 329
Joan, pope, II. 131; VII. 240
Joan Go-to-'t, in *The Birth of Merlin,* V. 249, 251
Joan of Naples, VII. 248
Joan of Navarre (1370?–1437), queen of Henry IV, II. 217
Joanna, in Holcroft's *Deserted Daughter,* XI. 277
Joanna, in Middleton's *Changeling,* XII. 222
Joannes de Garlandia. *See* Garlandia
Joannides, A., XIII. 515
Job, VII. 370; XII. 64
Job, in school plays, V. 103
Jobson, Richard (*fl.* 1620–1623), IV. 458
Jocelin of Brakelond (*fl.* 1200), I. 176, 450, 451, 458; XIII. 15
Jocelyn, Rose, Meredith's, XIII. 426
Jock o' the Side, II. 415
Jockey club, X. 191
Jockie, in *Edward IV,* VI. 91
Jocky Fou and Jenny Fain, IX. 360
Jocky met with Jenny fair, IX. 360
Jocky said to Jeany, IX. 360
Joculatores. See *Jongleurs*
Jodelle, Étienne, IV. 124; *Cléopatre Captive,* V. 63
Joel, II. 106
Joffred, abbot of Crowland, II. 343
Johan Baptistes, Enterlude of, V. 391
Johan the Evangelist, V. 60, 391
Johannes de Hese's *Itinerarius,* II. 330

Johannes de Sacro Bosco (d. 1252), or John of Holywood, I. 200, 456; II. 185
Johannes Secundus, IV. 264; XII. 223
Johannesburg, XIV. 380
Johannicius, *Isagoge,* II. 364, 365
John, in *Witty and Witless,* V. 92, 93
John, in *The Wowing of Jok and Jynny,* II. 275
John, Don, in *The Chances,* VI. 123, 135
John, Don, in *The two Maids of Moreclacke,* VI. 217
John, Dr, in Charlotte Brontë's *Villette,* XIII. 409
John, king of England, I. 175, 194, 198; II. 342; IV. 182, 183; V. 318; VII. 194
John, king (Shakespeare's), V. 153, 213, 318
John, king, in *Robert, Earle of Huntington,* V. 323, 324
John, king of England, *The Troublesome Raigne of,* V. 82, 135, 147, 153, 236 ff., 344, 397, 434
John, king of France, II. 307
John II, king of Portugal, IV. 69
John III, king of Portugal, III. 162
John XXII, pope, I. 212
John XXIII, pope, II. 348
John, Passion of, by Pseudo-Melito, I. 75
John, prince, in *Looke about you,* V. 321, 323
John, prior of Hexham (*fl.* 1180), I. 161, 450
John, St, the Baptist, I. 74, 126; VI. 295
John, St, the Baptist, tragedy on, III. 141
John, St, the Baptist, in *Baptistes,* III. 161
John, St, of Beverley, I. 82
John, St, evangelist, I. 74, 198, 354; II. 79, 383; V. 37, 48
John, Sir, the priest, in *Misogonus,* V. 110
John, Sir, the priest, in *The Merry Devill,* V. 252
John Bull, XIV. 200
John Chrysostom, St. *See* Chrysostom
John come kisse me, IX. 362
John de Cella, I. 178
John de Janua. *Catholicon,* II. 363
John de Oxenedes, or Oxnead (d. 1293?), I. 450
John de Tayster or Taxster (d. 1265), I. 182, 450
John George, elector of Saxony, VII. 453
John Lemouicensis, *Pharaoh's Dream,* II. 363
John Ochiltree, IX. 360
John Uponlandis Complaint, II. 280
John of Basingstoke (d. 1252), I. 204, 207
John of Bridlington, II. 443
John of Bury (*fl.* 1460), II. 497
John of Corbie, abbot of Aethelney, I. 89, 92
John of Cornwall, II. 70, 504
John of Doesborch. *See* Doesborch
John of Doncaster, I. 357
John of Dunstable, IV. 462, 463

John of Gaddesden (d. 1361), I. 453
John of Gaunt, duke of Lancaster (1340–1399), II. 55, 60, 73, 135, 157, 158; XI. 394
John of Gaunt, in *Richard II*, IV. 78
John of Glastonbury (*fl.* 1400), IX. 535
John of Guildford, I. 238
John of Hainault, Sir, II. 338
John of Hildesheim, *Historia Trium Regum*, II. 323, 503
John of Ireland, II. 94, 97; *Opera Theologica*, II. 284; On the Passioun, II. 284
John of Leyden, IV. 528
John of Lindebergh, I. 343
John of Salisbury (d. 1180), I. 173, 176, 183 ff., 202, 214, 216, 450, 454; IV. 269; VII. 376, 505
John of Trokelowe (*fl.* 1330), I. 181, 450; IX. 535
John of Usk (*fl. c.* 1360), abbot of Chertsey, II. 54
John of Worcester, I. 162
John the Common Weill, in *Ane Pleasant Satyre*, III. 128, 129
John the Common Weill, in *The Dreme*, III. 117
John the Reeve, I. 468; II. 126, 280
Johnie Cock, II. 416
Johnnie Cope, IX. 373
Johnny Armstrong, II. 413; IX. 166
Johns, Claude Hermann Walter (1857–1920), XII. Add. 4
Johnson, in Buckingham's *Rehearsal*, IX. 147
Johnson, Memoirs of the Life and Writings of, X. 177
Johnson, Abraham, VII. 340
Johnson, Charles (1679–1748), VI. 471; X. 89, 435; *Caelia*, X. 80, 414
Johnson, Charles (*fl.* 1724–1736), IX. 500
Johnson, Charles Plumptre, XIII. 531, 534
Johnson, Esther (1681–1728) (Swift's 'Stella'), IX. 93 ff., 97 ff., 120, 124, 126, 166; X. 168; XI. 332; XIV. 197
Johnson, E. Pauline (1862–1913), XIV. 582; *A Prodigal*, XIV. 357
Johnson, James (1787–1803), *Scots Musical Museum*, IX. 360, 361, 368, 373, 376, 377, 566; XI. 225, 226, 231 ff., 435, 444; XII. 14
Johnson, James (1850), XIV. 188
Johnson, John, father of Aphra Behn, VIII. 140
Johnson, John (1662–1725), X. 516; *The Unbloody Sacrifice*, X. 360
Johnson, John, LL.D. (d. 1833), XI. 403, 404, 427
Johnson, Joseph (1738–1809), XI. 189, 327
Johnson, Joseph (1905), XIII. 564
Johnson, J. P., XIV. Add. 8
Johnson, Laurence or Laurentius Baricona of Ketteringe (*fl.* 1603), *Cometographia*, V. 110
Johnson, Lionel Pigot (1867–1902), XIII. 503, *also see* Add. 2; *Postliminium*, XI. 30

Johnson, Michael, father of Samuel Johnson, XI. 340
Johnson, Nathaniel, brother of Samuel Johnson, X. 159
Johnson, Richard (1573–1659?), IV. 532, 536; *Anglorum Lachrymae*, IV. 351; *Looke on me, London*, IV. 530; *Seven Champions*, V. 34
Johnson, Reginald Brimley, XIII. 477
Johnson, Robert (1540–1625), IV. 442, 525; VII. 340; *Essaies or Rather Imperfect Offers*, IV. 345, 524; *The Traveller's Breviat*, IV. 89, 458
Johnson, Samuel (1649–1703), rector of Corringham, IX. 507; X. 355, 464, 517; *Julian the Apostate*, X. 351; *Reflections on the History of Passive Obedience*, X. 351
Johnson, Samuel (1691–1773), X. 439; *Hurlothrumbo*, X. 463
Johnson, Samuel (1709–1784), III. 157; IV. 247, 252; V. 209, 222, 235, 267, 270, 273 ff.; VI. 7; VII. 31, 72, 89, 115, 119, 135, 176, 235; VIII. 40, 42, 47, 48, 52, 146, 151, 152, 159, 196, 197, 210, 213, 217, 218, 220, 230, 237, 322, 323, 366, 386; IX. 133, 137, 140, 143, 144, 146, 164 ff., 171 ff., 178 ff., 185, 186, 188 ff., 243, 254, 313, 325, 330, 340, 357, 380, 538, *also see* Add.; X. 36, 39, 48, 63, 64, 66, 95, 96, 120, 124, 138, 140, 145 ff., 149, 157 ff. (main entry), 198, 201, 206 ff., 210, 212 ff., 231, 252, 255, 260, 262, 263, 266 ff., 274, 285, 289, 290, 312, 315, 355, 363, 392, 397 ff., 406, 407, 438, 452, 454, 459 ff., 482, 484, 523, *also see* Add.; XI. 2, 27, 31, 32, 38, 143, 145, 146, 246, 247, 251 ff., 260, 331, 333, 334, 345, 346, 350 ff., 355, 360 ff., 364, 365, 448 ff., 472, 473, 475, 476; XII. 218, 357, 363, 490; XIII. 13, 96, 224, 226, 232, 250, 465, 468; XIV. 61, 120, 122, 144, 160, 168, 169, 209, 216, 437 ff., 448, 452, 454, 461 ff., 503, 552, 554, 607
Account of the Harleian Library, X. 166
Charles of Sweden, X. 162
Choice of Life, The, X. 178
Compleat Vindication of the Licensers of the Stage, X. 165
Considerations on the Corn Laws, X. 181
Dictionary of the English Language, VII. 307; X. 167, 169, 173 ff., 177, 184, 187, 205, 350; XI. 324; XII. 504; XIV. 396, 439, 447, 463
Dictionary (abridgement), X. 177
'Dissertation on Pope's Epitaphs,' X. 183
'Easy Writing,' X. 178
'Engaging in Politicks with H—n,' X. 181
Essay on Epitaphs, X. 164
Essay on...Small Tracts, X. 166
Falkland's Islands, X. 181
False Alarm, The, X. 181, 182
Friendship, An Ode, X. 168

Johnson, Samuel
Γνῶθι σεαυτὸν post Lexicon Anglicanum auctum et emendatum, x. 177
'Grammar of the English Tongue,' x. 176
'Hard Words,' x. 178
'History of the English Language,' x. 176
Idler, The, x. 171, 178, 179, 184
Irene, x. 86, 161, 162, 170, 181
Journey to the Western Islands of Scotland, x. 181, 194
Life of Collins, x. 125
Life of Cowley, VII. 69; VIII. 379
Life of Denham, VII. 61; x. 167
Life of Dryden, VIII. 38
Life of Gray, x. 188
Life of Hammond, x. 475
Life of Milton, VI. 302; x. 161; XI. 84
Life of Pope, x. 168, 186
Life of Prior, x. 162
Life of Savage, x. 162, 165, 166, 169, 170, 183
Life of Thomson, x. 96
Lives of the Poets, IX. 170, 438, 448, 453, 466, 477, 479, 480; x. 165, 172, 182 ff., 292; XI. 325; XII. 137; XIII. 487; XIV. 447
London, x. 136, 168, 172; XI. 323
Marmor Norfolciense, x. 165
Miscellaneous Observations on the Tragedy of Macbeth, x. 167
Patriot, The, x. 181
Plan of a Dictionary of the English Language, x. 167, 173, 174, 176
Prayers, x. 170
Prince of Abissinia. See Rasselas
Proposals (for an edition of Shakespeare), x. 167, 177, 460
Proposals (for printing the Harleian Catalogue), x. 166
Proposals (for printing the Harleian Miscellany), x. 166
Rambler, The, x. 11, 157, 160, 170 ff., 175, 178, 181, 187, 188, 192, 205; XI. 253, 356, 365
Rasselas, x. 49, 159, 172, 178, 179
Shakespeare, x. 172, 179, 180, 186; XI. 320, 352
'Sufficiency of the English Language,' x. 178
Taxation no Tyranny, x. 181, 182
To Miss Hickman, playing on the Spinnet, x. 168
Trans. of Pope's Messiah, x. 168
Urbane, nullis fesse laboribus, x. 163
Vanity of Human Wishes, The, IV. 329; IX. 191; x. 160, 167 ff., 178
Verses (on the opening of Garrick's theatre), x. 136
Vision of Theodore, the Hermit of Teneriffe, x. 170
Voyage to Abyssinia, x. 159, 176, 179, 187
Written at the request of a gentleman, x. 168

Johnson, Samuel
'Young Authour, The,' x. 167
See, also, the bibliography by Courtney, W. P., revised by Smith, D. Nichol
Johnson, Samuel (of New York), x. 463
Johnson, Samuel (of Shrewsbury), x. 463
Johnson, Thomas (d. 1644), IV. 375
Johnson, T. (fl. 1649), VII. 368
'Johnson, Will.' (viscount Bolingbroke), IX. 220
Johnson, William, Valetudinarium, VI. 474
Johnson, William (fl. 1574), actor, VI. 246
Johnson, William (fl. 1774), bookseller, XI. 325
Johnson, William (1784–1864), XI. 406
Johnson, William. See Cory, William Johnson
Johnson, William Savage, XIII. 471
Johnson's literary club, XI. 345
Johnston, Alexander Keith, XIV. 485
Johnston, Arthur (1587–1641), IX. 550, 554, 555
Johnston, Sir Harry Hamilton, XIV. 192
Johnston, James (1643?–1737), IX. 203
Johnston, Robert (1567–1639), IX. 550
Johnston's Edinburgh Magazine, XII. 430
Johnstone, Charles (1719?–1800?), XI. 461; Chrysal, x. 524
Johnstone, Christian Isobel (1781–1857), XIII. 563
Johnstone, Christie, Charles Reade's, XIII. 425
Johnstone, John (1768–1836), XII. 490; XIV. 602
Johnstone, Maggie, IX. 366
Johny's Escape from Bonny Dundee, IX. 363
Joici et Sales...ab Ottomaro Luscinio, III. 93
Joinville, John, Sieur de, IV. 30
Jolles, Sir John (fl. 1617), VII. 339
Jollie, Timothy (1659?–1714), x. 386
Jolly, colonel, in Cutter of Coleman Street, VIII. 122
Jolly, William, XIV. 609
Jolly Beggar, The, II. 414; IX. 364; XI. 218
Jolly Beggars, tune of, VIII. 96
Jolly's academy, IX. 393
Jolter, in Peregrine Pickle, IX. 410
Joly, Charles Jasper (1864–1906), XIV. 263, 556
Jonah, XIV. 282
Jonah, in Pearl and Patience, I. 323, 325
Jonathan, in Cowley's Davideis, VII. 66
Jones, D., VIII. 380
Jones, Ebenezer (1820–1860), XIII. 503
Face, The, XIII. 157
Hand, The, XIII. 157
Rain, XIII. 157
Studies of Sensation and Event, XIII. 156
Jones, Ernest Charles (1819–1869), XIII. 157, 504; Poet's Parallel, The, XIII. 156; Song of the Lower Classes, The, XIII. 156; Songs of Democracy, XIII. 156
Jones, Evan Rowland, XIV. 533

Jones, Henry (1721–1770), *The Earl of Essex*, x. 86, 435
Jones, Henry, Sir, XIII. 477, 484
Jones, Henry Arthur, XIII. 515
Jones, H. Bence, XIV. 557
Jones, Henry Festing, XIII. 450, 570 ff., *also see* Add. 1
Jones, Inigo (1573–1652), v. 125, 372, 481; VI. 6, 26, 30, 271, 326, 333, 335, 342, 348, 350, 353, 354, 361; IX. 354, 536; *Britannia Triumphans*, VII. 433
Jones, Jeremiah (1693–1724), x. 521
Jones, John, of Neyath, Brecon, VII. 515
Jones, John, servant (*fl.* 1827), XI. 423
Jones, col. John (d. 1660), VIII. 470
Jones, Oliver (*fl.* 1740), x. 196
Jones, Richard (*fl.* 1564–1602), IV. 390; v. 144
Jones, Richard (1790–1855), XIV. 475
Jones, Robert (*fl.* 1616), IV. 113, 464; *Second Book of Songs and Airs*, IV. 109
Jones, Rufus Matthew, *Studies in Mystical Religion*, IX. 306, 307
Jones, Samuel (1680?–1719), IX. 393, 394; x. 386, 387
Jones, Stephen (1763–1827), *Biographia dramatica*, XI. 453, 457
Jones, Sir Thomas (d. 1692), VIII. 90
Jones, Tom, in Fielding's novel, x. 30 ff., 89
Jones, William (1559), IV. 383
Jones, William (1593), v. 145
Jones, William (1690), x. 378
Jones, William (1726–1800), IX. 512; XII. 453
Jones, Sir William (1631–1682), VIII. 312; IX. 196
Jones, Sir William (1746–1794), XI. 427; XII. 343, 353, 502; XIV. 334, 577, 602; *Asiatic Researches*, XII. 327; *From the Persian*, XI. 180; *Ode in imitation of Alcaeus*, XI. 180
Jones, William Basil (1822–1897), XIV. 488
Jongleurs, v. 3, 26, 41
Jonson, Benjamin (1573?–1637), III. 68, 81, 114, 228, 269, 271, 288, 308, 312, 444, 458, 482; IV. 46, 55, 59, 63, 115, 130, 138, 145, 153, 158, 185, 198, 199, 206, 207, 209, 214 ff., 248, 266, 349, 390, 392, 395, 406, 434, 437, 481, 501, 517, 520, 521, 524, 529, 533; v. 125, 142 ff., 148, 158, 161, 164, 166, 167, 171, 206, 222, 224, 254, 311, 312, 314, 315, 323, 328, 330, 334, 338, 343, 344, 347, 355, 361, 368, 370 ff.; VI. 1–30 (main entry), 32, 36, 38, 44, 47, 51, 53 ff., 58, 69, 85, 95, 96, 107, 111, 116, 118, 120, 121, 129, 133, 134, 138, 144, 151, 177, 188, 196, 198, 202, 206, 210, 211, 213, 214, 219 ff., 232 ff., 237, 239, 249, 250, 267, 271, 274, 291, 313, 329 ff., 339–355 (masques), 372, 376, 413 ff., 422, 423, 427, 458, 487, 488, 489, 491, *also see* Add.; VII. 2 ff., 7, 9, 14, 16 ff., 23, 25, 26, 33, 38, 49, 77, 81, 82, 85, 176, 184, 250, 259, 261 ff., 272 ff., 283, 335, 387, 413, 466, 467, 477, 502, *also see* Add.; VIII.

Jonson, Benjamin
13, 16 ff., 25, 32, 116, 122 ff., 127, 132, 133, 137, 138, 141, 142, 145, 147, 150, 155, 157, 173, 174, 214, 227, 229, 233, 368, 443, 447; IX. 351; x. 50, 219, 220, 505; XI. 170, 248, 266; XII. 105, 125, 177, 224; XIII. 32, 108, 233, 495; XIV 444, 527
Alchemist, The, v. 365, 369; VI. 5, 22 ff., 26, 28, 222; VIII. 357, 366
Apologetical Dialogue, VI. 4
Ars Poetica (trans. of), with commentary from Aristotle, VI. 6
Bartholomew Fayre, v. 158, 365, 376; VI. 2, 4, 5, 19, 22 ff., 26, 28, 220, 224, 261, 337; VIII. 121
Case is Altered, The, v. 321; VI. 4, 5, 13, 17, 290
Catiline, VI. 5, 19, 20, 112, 221, 235; VIII. 85; XIV. 448
Celebration of Charis, A, VI. 10
Celia, To ('Drink to me only with thine eyes'), VI. 10
Challenge at Tilt, A, VI. 357
'Come, leave the loathed Stage,' VI. 25
'Come, my Celia, let us prove,' VII. 17
Conversations with William Drummond, III. 269; v. 343; VI. 7; VIII. 238, 322
Cooke Laurell, III. 482
Court Worm, VI. 9
Cynthia's Revels, IV. 337; v. 158, 359; VI. 4, 18, 25, 41, 42, 170, 171, 220, 290, 336, 337; VII. 19; VIII. 118
Discourse of Poesy, VIII. 238, 239
Divell is an Asse, The, v. 252, 358; VI. 5, 24; VIII. 123
Dreame, VI. 10
English Grammar, An, II. 152; VI. 6 ff.; VIII. 238
Epicoene, x. 429
Epigrams, VI. 5, 9
Epistle to a Friend, An, to perswade him to the Warres (Master Colby), VI. 10
Eupheme; or, the faire fame…of… Lady Venetia Digby, VI. 10
Every Man in His Humour, IV. 137; v. 219, 331, 350; VI. 2, 3, 13, 15, 16, 20, 26, 28, 39, 248; x. 432
Every Man out of His Humour, IV. 333, 358; v. 358; VI. 4, 16 ff., 40, 170, 225; VIII. 16
Execration upon Vulcan, An, VI. 6, 10
Expostulation with Inigo Jones, v. 372
Fall of Mortimer, The, VI. 7, 19
Fit of Rhyme against Rhyme, VII. 3
For the Honour of Wales, VI. 361, 371
Forest, The, VI. 5, 9; VII. 18
Fortunate Isles, The, VI. 362
Golden Age Restored, The, VI. 358
Gipsies, The, IV. 361
Henry V, A history of, VI. 6
Hesperus's song in *Cynthia's Revels*, VI. 10
Hot Anger Soon Cold, VI. 12
Hue and Cry after Cupid, The, marriage masque for lord Haddington, VI. 346, 347

Jonson, Benjamin
  'Humbler gleanings in divinity,' VI. 6
  Hymenaei, VI. 344, 345, 347
  Induction, The, IV. 333
  Irish Masque, The, VI. 357, 361, 371
  Jeronimo, Jonson's additions to, V. 311
  Love freed from Ignorance and Folly,
    VI. 350, 351
  Love Restored, VI. 351, 357, 358, 371
  Lovers Made Men, VI. 359
  Magnetic Lady, The: Or Humors Reconcil'd, IV. 333; VI. 6, 25
  *Magnificent Entertainment, The: Given
    to King James*, VI. 55
  Masque of Augures, The, VI. 345, 350;
    VII. 3
  Masque of Beauty, The, VI. 344
  Masque of Blacknesse, The, VI. 5, 341,
    344, 347
  Masque of Christmas, The, VI. 355,
    357 ff.
  Masque of Lethe, The, i.e. *Lovers made
    Men*, VI. 359
  Masque of Owls, The, VI. 361
  Masque of Queens, The, VI. 344, 345,
    347, 348, 370
  *Masque of the Metamorphos'd Gypsies,
    A*, VI. 361; VII. 10
  May Lord, The, VI. 11, 369 ff.
  Mercury Vindicated from the Alchemists,
    VI. 357; VII. 3
  Miscellanies, XI. 181
  Neptune's Triumph, VI. 361
  New Inn, The, IV. 361; VI. 6, 15, 25,
    132, 140, 370
  *Newes from the New World discovered
    in the Moone*, VI. 361
  Nymphs Passion, A, VI. 10
  Oberon the Faery Prince, VI. 340, 350,
    351; X. 429
  Ode to Himself, VI. 2
  Pan's Anniversarie, VI. 355, 361, 362
  Penates, The, VI. 341
  Penshurst, To, VI. 9; VII. 10, 20
  Philological collections, VI. 6
  Pindaric ode on the death of Sir H.
    Morison, VI. 10
  Pleasure Reconciled to Virtue, VI. 359,
    361, 363
  Poetaster, V. 187, 239; VI. 4, 18, 39 ff.,
    53, 166, 171, 172, 220, 290
  Proserpine, a poem on the rape of, VI. 6
  Prosodia, VIII. 239, 240
  'Queen and huntress' in *Cynthia's
    Revels*, VI. 10, 11
  Richard Crookback, VI. 13, 18
  Sad Shepherd, The, V. 34; VI. 7, 11, 366,
    369 ff., 491
  Satyr, The, VI. 339
  Scotland, poetical narrative of his
    journey to, VI. 6
  Sejanus, V. 371; VI. 4, 19, 20, 28, 43,
    152, 235, 248
  Shakespeare, poem to, VI. 10
  Shift, Lieutenant, epigram on, VI. 9
  Silent Woman, The (*Epicoene*), VI. 5, 22,

Jonson, Benjamin
  24, 28, 112, 153; VII. 275; VIII. 120, 357,
    401
  'Slow, slow, fresh fount, keep time with
    my salt tears,' VII. 19
  Spanish Tragedie, The, additions to, VI.
    13, 17, 18, 369, 370
  Staple of News, The, III. 81; IV. 137;
    VI. 6, 25; VII. 345
  Tale of a Tub, A, VI. 4, 6, 26, 290
  *Timber: or, Discoveries made upon men
    and matter*, IV. 25, 336, 348, 524; VI. 2,
    6 ff.; VII. 262, 272, 273, 307, 466
  Time Vindicated, VI. 362
  'To my Bookseller,' XI. 335
  Twelfth Night Masque, VI. 357
  Underwoods, VI. 6, 9, 10; VII. 18; XI.
    181
  Vision of Delight, The, VI. 359
  Volpone, III. 269; VI. 5, 21, 22, 28, 112,
    194, 221, 222, 348; VII. 261, 274
  Voluptuous Beast, Sir, epigram on, VI. 9
  Wroth, sonnet to Lady Mary, VI. 10
  See, also, under Beaumont and Fletcher,
    Chapman, Dekker and Middleton
Jonson and Porter's *Hot Anger soon Cold*,
  V. 331
Jonson's son, VI. 224
Jonsonus Virbius, VI. 7, 235, 237; VII. 3,
  261, 272, 401, 466
Jónsson, Arngrim, I. 31
Jonston, Arthur (1587–1641), *Delitiae
  Poetarum Scotorum*, IV. 261
Joppa, IV. 68
Jordan, in *Absalom and Achitophel*, VIII.
  37
Jordan, Denham ('A Son of the Marshes'),
  XIV. 166, 521
Jordan, Dorothea or Dorothy, born Bland
  (1762–1816), XI. 452, 454
Jordan, Thomas (1612?–1685), VII. 413,
  514; VIII. 422; *The Plotting Papists'
  Litany*, VIII. 97
Jordanes, I. 35
Jorrocks, Mr, Surtees's, X. 111; XIII. 311;
  XIV. 234, 239
Jortin, John (1698–1770), IX. 75; XII. 468
Joseph, I. 74; IX. 42
Joseph, in Emily Brontë's *Wuthering
  Heights*, XIII. 411
Joseph, in the mysteries, V. 42, 47
Joseph I, emperor, IX. 228
Joseph of Arimathaea, I. 133, 271, 272,
  462, 468
Joseph of Arimathea, V. 15
Joseph of Exeter (*fl.* 1190), *Flos Regum
  Arthurus* (*Antiocheis*), I. 195, 454, 467,
  468
Josephine, empress of the French, XIII. 366
Josephus, I. 224; II. 334; III. 173, 416;
  IV. 427, 437; VI. 206; IX. 273, 275, 295,
  418; XI. 326
Joshua, II. 231
Joshua, in *The Silver Age*, VI. 93
Josian, in *Beves*, I. 305, 306
Josselin, in *Edward IV*, VI. 90

Josselin, or Joscelyn, John (1529–1603)
  secretary to Matthew Parker, III. 55
Josselyn, John (*fl.* 1675), IV. 458
Joubert, André, XIII. 532
Joubert, Joseph, IX. 175; XII. 527; XIII.
  98, 99
Joule, James Prescott (1818–1889), XIV.
  261, 556
Jourdan, Philip, XIV. Add. 8
Journal Britannique, X. 173
Journal Encyclopédique, Le, V. 292
Journal littéraire, Le, V. 287
Journal of Anatomy and Physiology, The,
  XIV. 289, 566
Journal of Association, The, XIII. 358
Journal of Horticulture, The, XIV. 289
Journalism, the beginnings of English,
  VII. 494 ff.. *also see* Add.
Journalism, English, VIII. 412
Jove, in *Gismond of Salerne*, V. 75
Joviall Crew, A, V. 376
'Jovian Ferreri Piedmontese,' III. 319
Jovis et Iunonis nuptiae, VI. 484
Jovius, Paulus, III. 478; VI. 137; VII. 406
Jowett, Benjamin (1817–1893), XII. 292 ff.,
  333, 334, 442, 466, 468, 479, 482, 486;
  XIV. 503, 607; *The Epistles of St Paul*,
  XII. 293
Joy for another's grief, in *Confessio
  Amantis*, II. 147
Joyce, in Greene's *Tu Quoque*, VI. 219
Joyce, in the *Mercuries*, VII. 356
Joyce, Patrick Weston (1827–1914), XII.
  517; XIV. 569
    Ancient Irish Music, XII. 361
    Irish Music and Song, XII. 361
    Irish Names of Places, XII. 361
    Irish Peasant Songs, XII. 361
    Old Celtic Romances, XII. 361; XIV. 306,
    328
    Social History of Ancient Ireland, XII.
    361; XIV. 328
Joyce, Robert Dwyer (1836–1883), XIV.
  569; *Blacksmith of Limerick, The*, XIV.
  321; *Blanaid*, XIV. 321; *Deirdre*, XIV. 321
Joye, George (d. 1553), III. 39, 40, 43, 473
Joyner, William (1622–1706), VIII. 437
Juan, Browning's, XIII. 72
Juan, Don, in Byron's poem, XII. 46, 54, 55
Juan, G., XIV. 552
Juan Fernandez, XIV. 242, 243
Juba, in Addison's *Cato*, IX. 63, 64
Juby, Ed., V. 135
Judaea, IX. 274
Judaic law, VIII. 75
Judaism, XII. 521
Judas, XIII. 199
Judas, in *The Second Part of Absalom and
  Achitophel*, VIII. 41
Judas, in *The York Plays*, V. 46
Judas (ballad), II. 194, 408
Judas Iscariot, I. 340; VIII. 86; IX. 234;
  XIV. 306
Judd, John W., *The Coming of Evolution*,
  XIV. 298, 299, 301
Jude, St, I. 354

Judge, the, in *The Daunce and Song of
  Death*, III. 87
Judicio, in *The Returne from Parnassus*,
  IV. 139; VI. 311
Judicium Essoniorum, VIII. 465
Judith, IV. 170
Judith, I. 48, 49, 77, 110, 123, 137, 141 ff.,
  150, 230, 445
Judith, in Amory's *Memoirs of Several
  Ladies*, XI. 287
Judith, in Biblical plays, V. 101, 103
Judith, daughter of Charles the Bald, I.
  88
Judy, XIV. 239
Jugge, Richard (*fl.* 1531–1577?), IV. 384,
  400, 401
Juigné, Antoine É. L. Leclerc de, arch-
  bishop of Paris, XI. 189
Julia, in Morton's *Way to get Married*, XI.
  281
Julia, in *The Dutchesse Of Malfy*, VI. 182
Julia, in *The Poetaster*, VI. 18
Julia, in *Two Gentlemen of Verona*, V. 180;
  VI. 157; VIII. 126
Julia (Herrick's), VII. 6, 9, 17
Julian, in Aldhelm's treatise on virginity,
  I. 74
Julian, in Landor's *Count Julian*, XII. 211
Julian, coffee-house haunter, VIII. 89
Julian, emperor, IX. 507; X. 27, 318; XII.
  416, 497
Julian, Epistle to Mr, VIII. 394
Julian, J., XIII. 498
Julian house, the (*Aeneid*), III. 305
Julian of Toledo, I. 76
Juliana, lady, in Susan Ferrier's *Marriage*,
  XII. 245
Juliana, St, I. 53, 229, 459
Juliana of Norwich (1342–1442), *Revela-
  tions of Divine Love*, II. 300, 482
Julianus, in *Alls Lost by Lust*, VI. 77
Julie, XII. 60
Juliet, in *Romeo and Juliet*, V. 169, 193,
  331; VI. 265, 335; XII. 54
Julio, Don, in Mrs Cowley's *Bold Stroke
  for a Husband*, XI. 275
Julius Agricola, IX. 552
Julius Caesar, XII. Add.
Julius Caesar (Shakespeare's), II. 337
Julius Caesar, translation of, IV. 4, 21, 435
Julius Valerius, I. 135
Julleville, L. Petit de, I. ix
Jullien, A., *L'Histoire du Costume au
  Théâtre*, XI. 258
'Jumping Jenny,' the, in Scott's *Red-
  gauntlet*, XII. 21
Junge, H., XIII. 558
Jungfrau, the, XII. 47
Jung-Stilling. *See* Stilling
Junia, in Racine's *Britannicus*, X. 119
Junilius, I. 76
Juniper hall, X. 63, 261
Junius, X. 133, 182, 509; XI 34; XII. 54;
  XIV. 335, 496
Junius, *Letters* of, X. 305, 399 ff., 455,
  525 ff.; XI. 55; XIII. 52, 347; XIV. 186

Junius, Franciscus (1589–1677), VII. 118, 480; IX. 355, 536; X. 223, 225; XII. 504; Caedmon, edition of, VII. 307; *De Pictura Veterum*, VII. 307; Moeso-Gothic text of Ulfilas, VII. 307

Juno, VII. 370

Juno, in *Hymenaei*, VI. 345, 346

Juno, in *Troiane*, V. 69

Juno (Herrick's), VII. 13

Jupiter, II. 276; III. 71, 433; VI. 313; XII. 64, 80

Jupiter, in Alfred's *Boethius*, I. 101

Jupiter, in *Amphitruo*, V. 107

Jupiter, in Shelley's *Prometheus Unbound*, XII. 65, 66

Jupiter, in *The Four Ages*, VI. 92, 93

Jupiter, in *The Play of the Wether*, V. 93, 94, 95

Jupiter's satellites, VIII. 350

Jupps, Mrs, in Butler's *The Way of all Flesh*, XIII. 454

Jusserand, J. J., I. ix, 2; II. 2, 3, 24, 28 ff., 32, 34; IV. 246; V. 4, 17, 285, 289, 293; VI. 2; XIV. 518

Justamond, John Obadiah, X. 494

Justice, in Fortescue's *De Natura Legis Naturae*, II. 296

Justice, in *Pathomachia*, VI. 324

Justice, in *The Example of Virtue*, II. 227, 228

Justice, in *The Faerie Queene*, II. 234; III. 233; VII. 209

Justice, in *The Passetyme of Pleasure*, II. 229, 234

Justin, IV. 437, 438; XIV. 579; *The abridgemente of the Histories of Trogus Pompeius*, IV. 21

Justina, St, I. 74

Justinian, VIII. 312; XII. 488, 492
    Coaex, II. 364; III. 113
    Digestum, II. 364
    Pandects, II. 350
    Parvum Volumen, II. 364
    Institutes, IV. 151

Justiniano, in *West-Ward Hoe*, VI. 171 ff.

Justitia, in the *Coventry Plays*, V. 21

Juvenal, I. 68, 76; III. 68, 429; IV. 17, 206, 207, 250, 321, 329, 331 ff., 349; VII. 335, 487, 503; VIII. 58, 61, 85, 87, 88, 165; IX. 63, 87, 257, 269, 473; X. 21; XI. 40, 81, 393; XII. 487, 493; *Third Satire*, X. 169, 460

Juvencus. *See* Cyprianus

Juxon, William (1582–1663), IV. 306, 425; VI. 319; VII. 159

Jyl of Breyntford's Testament, II. 324, 485; III. 84, 85, 88, 483, 484

Kabbalah, the, XII. 501

Kaermerðin, I. 266

Kaffirs, the, XIV. 376

Kai or Kay, Sir, a knight of Arthur, I. 250, 254, 255, 260, 312, 313

Kaisersberg. *See* Geiler von

Kaled, in Byron's *Lara*, XII. 46

Kalenborowe, The Parson of, II. 329, 486

Kalendar of Shepherds, II. 233, 324, 328, 329, 485

Kalendar of the new legend of England, II. 322

Kalendrier des Bergers, III. 221, 226; IV. 353

Kalidasa, *Sakuntala*, XIV. 334; *Vikramorvasi*, XII. 502

Kalilah, in Beckford's *Episodes*, XI. 292

Kalote, in *Piers the Plowman*, II. 34

Kaltoff, mechanician, VIII. 359

Kaluza, Max, XIII. 512; XIV. 611

Kames, lord. *See* Home, Henry

Kant, Immanuel, IV. 292; VIII. 333; X. 333, 348, 511, 512; XI. 121, 136 ff.; XIV. 8, 9, 11, 12, 37, 40, 42, 43, 45, 404, 467, 469, 478, 483

Kantian philosophy, XI. 57

Kapur-di-Giri rock-inscription, XII. 352

Karlamagnus Saga, I. 283

Karlemeyne and the Duzeper, I. 226

Karolin, in *The Sad Shepherd*, VI. 370

Karroo, the, XIV. 372

Kashinath Trimback Telang, XIV. 341

Kastrill, in *The Alchemist*, VI. 22

Kate, in *Cocke Lorell's bote*, III. 84

Kate, Corinthian, in Egan's *Life in London*, XIV. 226

Katharine, in *A Woman is a Weathercocke*, VI. 222

Katharine, in *The Taming of the Shrew*, V. 181

Katharine, in *The Womans Prize*, VI. 135

Katharine, St, Life of, I. 229, 459, 460

Katharine, the, a ship, VIII. 202

Katharine Jaffray, II. 411

Katherine, in *Perkin Warbeck*, VI. 193

Katherine of Senis, The life of St, II. 327

Katrine, loch, XII. 11, 12

Kaufmann, Moritz, *Charles Kingsley*, XIII. 356, 358, 548

Kavanagh, Julia (1824–1877), XIII. 563; XIV. 569; *French Women of Letters*, XIV. 324; *Natalie*, XIV. 324; *Summer and Winter in the Two Sicilies, A*, XIV. 324

Kavanagh, Morgan Peter (d. 1874), XIV. 324

Kavanagh, Rose, XIV. 329

Kay, in *Golagros and Gawane*, II. 123

Kay, Joseph (1821–1878), XIV. 607

Kay-Shuttleworth, Sir James Phillips (1804–1877), XIV. 419, 420, 607

Kaye, Sir John William (1814–1876), XIV. 450; XIV. 491, 495, 577, 579; *A History of the Sepoy War*, XIV. 337

Keach, Benjamin (1640–1704), X. 522; *Travels of True Godliness*, XI. 334; *War with the Devil*, XI. 334

Keach in the Creel, The, II. 414

Kean, Charles John (1811?–1868), XIII. 69, 255, 514

Kean, Edmund (1787–1833), V. 302; VIII. 186, 423; IX. 190; XI. Add.; XII. 171, 421; XIII. 255, 259

Kearney, John (d. 1600?), *ABC and Catechism*, IV. 384, 386, 397, 409, 412, 414

Kearsley, George (*fl.* 1785), x. 459
Keary, Annie (1825–1879), xi. 480; xiv. 569
  Castle Daly, xiv. 324
  Doubting Heart, A, xiv. 324
  Heroes of Asgard, The, xiv. 324
  York and Lancaster Rose, A, xiv. 324
Keate, George (1729–1797), xi. 427
Keate, John (1773–1852), xiv. 387
Keating, Geoffrey (1570?–1644?), xiv. 308, 569; *Geoffrey Keating to his Letter*, xiv. 309; *The History of Ireland*, xiv. 304, 309
Keatly, Joseph (*fl.* 1704), viii. 157
Keats, George (1797–1842), xii. 84, 90
Keats, Georgiana (born Wylie), wife of Keats, George, xii. 81
Keats, John (1795–1821), i. 275; iii. 246; vii. 73, 75, 77, 109; viii. 227; x. 122; xi. 102, 117, 119, 150, 171, 182, 192, 202, 410, 440; xii. 40, 57, 58, 79 ff. (main entry), 106, 107, 113, 117, 126, 139, 157, 160, 162, 205, 221, 222, 395, 399, 400, 403, 404, 405 ff. (main entry), 433, 438, 445, *also see* Add. 2; xiii. 25 ff., 44, 101, 122, 185, 197, 198, 208, 219, 229, 230, 236, 250, 420; xiv. 311, 350, 373, 453
  Adonais, xiii. 53
  Autumn, To, xii. 72, 81, 89, 91
  Bards of Passion and of Mirth, xii. 89
  Belle Dame sans Merci, La, xi. 183; xii. 87, 88, 94; xiii. 238
  Bright star! xii. 92
  Cap and Bells, The, xii. 88
  Endymion, vi. 367; vii. 76; xii. 58, 81 ff., 88, 89; xiii. 237, 238, 240, 251
  Eve of Saint Agnes, The, xi. 131; xii. 81, 86 ff.; xiii. 114, 237, 238
  Eve of St Mark's, The, xii. 87; xiii. 237, 238, 252
  Fall of Hyperion, The, xii. 85, 86
  Fancy, xii. 89
  Fanny, Ode to, xii. 92
  Grecian Urn, Ode on a, xii. 58, 72, 90
  Homer, To, xii. 92
  Hymn to Pan, xii. 82
  Hyperion, xii. 74, 84 ff., 92, 94, 305, 477; xiii. 237, 238
  I stood tiptoe, xii. 80
  Isabella, xii. 58, 83, 88; xiii. 238
  June's sea, xii. 92
  King Lear, On sitting down to read, once again, xii. 58, 83, 91
  Lamia, iv. 252; viii. 237; xi. 132; xii. 88, 194; xiii. 135, 237, 238; xiv. 436
  Maia, Ode to, xii. 89
  Melancholy, Ode on, xii. 90
  Mermaid Tavern, Lines on the, xii. 89
  Nightingale, Ode to a, xii. 91, 92; xiv. 352
  O Sorrow, xii. 82
  Otho the Great, xii. 88
  Oxford, On, xii. 202
  Psyche, Ode to, xii. 89, 90
  Robin Hood, xii. 89

Keats, John
  Sleep, To, xii. 92
  Sleep and Poetry, xii. 80, 81, 85
  Spenser, Imitation of, xii. 79
  Stephen, xii. 88
  Teignmouth, xii. 202
  The Day is gone, I cry you mercy, xii. 92
  To..., xii. 92
  To some ladies, xii. 80
  When I have fears, xii. 91
Kebbel, Thomas Edward, xiii. 471, 509, 547; xiv. 508, 509
Keble, John (1792–1866), vii. 147; viii. 308; x. 369, 518; xii. 153, 253 ff., 264 ff. (main entry), 271, 274, 277, 380, 454 ff.; xiii. 147, 167 ff. (main entry), 504
  Christian Year, The, xii. 257, 261, 264; xiii. 167, 169 ff.
  Evening Hymn, xiii. 170
  O for a sculptor's hand, xiii. 170
  Praelections, xiii. 168
  Red o'er the forest peers the setting sun, xiii. 170
  See Lucifer like lightning fall, xiii. 170
  What went ye out to see, xiii. 170
Keble, Thomas (1793–1875), xii. 454, 457
Keeling, William (d. 1620), iv. 99
Keene, Charles Samuel (1823–1891), xiv. 239, 548
Keene, Henry George (1825–1915), xiv. 338, 339, 577, 578
Keepsake, The, xiv. 149
Keightley, Thomas (1789–1872), xii. 306, 476; xiv. 569
  Fairy Mythology, xi. 475; xii. 368
  History of Greece, xii. 302
  History of the War of Greek Independence, xii. 302
  Mythology of Ancient Greece and Italy, xii. 302
  Outlines of General History, xii. 302
Keill, John (1671–1721), viii. 474
Keith, George (1639?–1716), ix. 546
Keith, Sir George, of Cowburn, iv. 151
Keith, Robert (1681–1757), x. 467
Keith of Ewern, in Rossetti's *Sister Helen*, xiii. 115
Keith-Falconer, Ion Grant Neville (1856–1887), xii. 499
Kelke, Roger (1524–1576), vi. 297
Keller, W., v. 82
Kellett, Ernest Edward, xiv. 537
Kellner, Leon, xiv. 528, 611
Kelly, Charles Arthur, xiv. 339, 340, 578
Kelly, Cornelius (*fl.* 1740), x. 197
Kelly, Edward (1555–1595), v. 377; vii. 369; viii. 350
Kelly, Frances Maria (Fanny) (1790–1882), xii. 194
Kelly, Hugh (1739–1777), x. 90 ff., 436; xi. 451
  Clementina, x. 91
  False Delicacy, x. 91, 92, 212; xi. 263
  Man of Reason, x. 92
  School for Wives, x. 92; xi. 263

Kelly, Hugh
  Word to the Wise, x. 91
Kelly, Michael (1764?–1826), xi. 454
Kelmscott manor-house, xiii. 120
Kelmscott press, the, xii. 405; xiii. 127,
  491 ff.
Kelsall, Thomas Forbes, xii. 115, 414
Kelso, xi. 342, 444; xii. 5; xiv. 373
Kelso, A. P., xiii. 488
Kelvin, lord. *See* Thomson, Sir William
Kemble, Charles (1775–1854), v. 302;
  viii. 186, 196
Kemble, Frances Anne (Fanny) (1809–
  1893), xiii. 142, 177, 497, 504; xiv. 504
Kemble, John Mitchell (1807–1857), xiii.
  142, 177; xiv. 52, 68, 491; *Codex Diplo-
  maticus Aevi Saxonici*, xii. 344; xiv. 69;
  Horae Ferales, xii. 347; *Saxons in
  England, The*, i. 420; xii. 344; xiv. 69
Kemble, John Philip (1757–1823), viii.
  184, 196, 437, 439, 440, 442; ix. 435;
  x. 458; xi. 260, 262, 283, 428, 454, 456,
  457; xiii. 255; xiv. 319, 440; *Corio-
  lanus*, xi. 274; *The Tempest*, xi. 274
Kembles, the, xii. 119, 171
Kemerton, near Evesham, ii. 67
Kemnay, Aberdeenshire, viii. 347
Kemp, in *The Returne from Pernassus*,
  vi. 44, 312
Kemp, Flora van, in Le Fanu's story, xiii.
  416
Kemp, William (*fl.* 1600), v. 313, 316, 329;
  vi. 217, 247, 248, 273, 276, 467; *Kemp's
  nine days wonder*, iv. 361, 533
Kemp Owyne, ii. 414
Kemp's Jigge, iv. 362
Kempe, Alfred John, *Losely Manu-
  scripts*, iv. 221
*Kempe, ancresse of Lynn, The book of
  Margery*, ii. 327
Kempis, Thomas à, i. 99; ii. 300; iii. 291;
  viii. 458; ix. 519; *Imitatione Christi,
  De*, ii. 482
Ken, Anne, wife of Isaac Walton, vii. 250
Ken, Thomas (1637–1711), bishop of Bath
  and Wells, vii. 241, 250; viii. 460;
  Ichabod, viii. 306; Sermon for the
  Funeral of the Right Hon. the Lady
  Margaret Mainard, viii. 307
Kendal, v. 56; xi. 408; xiv. 203
Kendal, duchess of. *See* Schulenburg,
  countess Ehrengard
Kendal academy, x. 385, 386
Kendall, Edward Augustus (1776?–1842),
  xi. 480
Kendall, Henry Clarence (1841–1882),
  xiv. 368, 369, 586
  Leaves from an Australian Forest, xiv.
  364
  Poems and Songs, xiv. 364
  Songs from the Mountains, xiv. 364
  To a Mountain, xiv. 365
Kendall, Thomas (*fl.* 1601), vi. 290
Kendall, Timothy (*fl.* 1577), *Floweres of
  Epigrammes*, iv. 23, 434, 438, 519
Kendals, the, xiii. 515

Kenealy, Edward Vaughan Hyde (1819–
  1880), xiv. 197, 238
Kenelm, St, i. 336, 339
Kenilworth, iii. 207, 210; iv. 181; v. 30
Kennedy, Benjamin Hall (1804–1889),
  xii. 331, 332, 336, 419, 486; *Between
  Whiles*, xii. 329; *Latin Primer*, xii.
  329; *Public School Latin Grammar*, xii.
  329
Kennedy, Charles Rann (1808–1867), xii.
  329, 419, 486; xiii. 175, 504
Kennedy, Edward Shirley, xiv. 553
Kennedy, Gilbert, 2nd earl of Cassillis
  (d. 1527), iii. 154
Kennedy, Gilbert, 3rd earl of Cassillis
  (1517?–1558), iii. 158, 159
Kennedy, H. A., xiv. 236
Kennedy, James (1406?–1465), bishop of
  St Andrews, ii. 368, 369, 370
Kennedy, John (1789–1833), xii. 419
Kennedy, Patrick (1801–1873), xiv. 569
  Banks of the Boro', xiv. 315
  Bardic Stories, xiv. 315
  Evenings in the Duffrey, xiv. 315
  Fireside Stories, xiv. 315
  Legendary Fictions of the Irish Celt,
  xiv. 315
Kennedy, Quintin (1520–1564), iii. 119,
  153, 154, 503; iv. 322, 412; *The Com-
  pendius Tractive*, iii. 154; *Ressoning*,
  iii. 154
Kennedy, Rann (1772–1851), xii. 419;
  xiii. 175
Kennedy, Walter (1460?–1508?), ii. 250,
  261, 266, 268; xi. 203
  *Ane agis Manis invective against Mouth-
  thankless*, ii. 266
  Ane Ballat in praise of Our Lady, ii.
  266
  Pious Counsale, ii. 266
  The Passioun of Christ, ii. 266
  The Praise of Aige, ii. 266
Kennett, Basil (1674–1715), x. 319
Kennett, White (1660–1728), bishop of
  Peterborough, vii. 442; ix. 212, 234, 235,
  493, 536, 539, 541; x. 356, 517; *Com-
  pleat History of England*, viii. 384; ix.
  143; *Parochial Antiquities of Ambrosden,
  The*, x. 354; *Register and Chronicle*, ix.
  234
Kenney, James (1780–1849), xiii. 520;
  xiv. 569
Kenrick, John (1788–1877), xii. 511;
  Ancient Egypt, xii. 348; *Phoenicia*, xii.
  348; *Primeval History*, xii. 348
Kenrick, William (1725?–1779), v. 274;
  x. 455, 474, 479; xi. 451, 458, 472;
  Duellist, xi. 265
Kensington, vii. 360
Kent, ii. 134, 158, 311, 424; iii. 321, 344;
  iv. 190; v. 343; vi. 112; vii. 23, 24,
  28, 53, 83, 176, 341, 361; viii. 309, 310;
  ix. 24, 534, 536, 539; x. 249; xi. 426;
  xii. 347, 510, 513; xiii. 447; xiv. 128,
  221, 298
Kent, laws of, i. 98

Kent, Maid of, II. 330
Kent, William (1684–1748), IX. 162
Kent, William Charles Mark, XIII. 543
Kentish Chronicle, I. 111, 112. See, also, under *Chronicle*
Kentish petitioners, IX. 8
Kentish Sermons, Old, I. 221, 459
Kenulph, bishop of Winchester, I. 125
Kenwigses, the, in *Nicholas Nickleby*, XIII. 318
Kenyon, Sir Frederick G., XIII. 479, 480, 481, 484, 485, 502
Kenyon, John (1784–1856), XII. 419; XIII. 69, 72, 74
Keper, John (*fl.* 1580), III. 438; IV. 448
Kepler or Keppler, Johann, IV. 278, 290; VIII. 361
Keppel, Arnold Joost van, 1st earl of Albemarle (1669–1718), VIII. 202
Keppel, George Thomas, 6th earl of Albemarle (1799–1891), XIV. 500, 598
Ker, John, of Kersland (1673–1726), IX. 493; *Memoirs*, XI. 328
Ker, John, 3rd duke of Roxburgh (1740–1804), XII. 365
Ker, Robert, 1st earl of Roxburgh (1570?–1650), VI. 366
Ker, William Pater (1855–1923), I. 420, VIII. 49; XI. Add.; XIII. 239, 477, 484; XIV. 487
Keroualle, Louise Renée de, duchess of Portsmouth (1649–1734), VIII. 93, 99, 268
Kerr, John, X. 385
Kerr, J. (1887), XIII. 472
Kerr, Robert (1755–1813), XI. 440, 470
Kerr, Robert (*fl.* 1811–1824), XIV. 552
Kersal moor, Manchester, XIII. 373
Kersey, John, *Dictionarium Anglo-Britannicum*, X. 236
Kester, in Mrs Gaskell's *Sylvia's Lovers*, XIII. 380
Kestevene, I. 344
Keswick, X. 133; XI. 156, 161; XII. 84
Kethe, William (d. 1608?), III. 46
Kett, Francis (d. 1589), V. 143
Kett, Rev. George, XIV. Add. 5
Kettering, V. 110
Kettlewell, John (1653–1695), VIII. 306, 307, 460, 461; IX. 574
Kettner, Gustav, VII. 176
Kew, IV. 374
Kew, earl of, in *The Newcomes*, XIII. 295
Kew, lady, in *The Newcomes*, XIII. 296
Kew gardens, XIV. 286, 287, 289
Key, Thomas Hewitt (1799–1875), XII. 486; *Latin Dictionary*, XII. 335; *Latin Grammar*, XII. 335
Keyber, Conny, X. 411
Keymor or Keymer, John (*fl.* 1610–1620), IV. 309, 511
Keynes, Geoffrey, XI. 431
Kharosthi alphabet, the, XII. 352
Khatmanda, XIV. 165
Kiartan, in Morris's *The Lovers of Gudrun*, XIII. 125
Kibworth academy, X. 384

Kickham, Charles Joseph (1826–1882), XIV. 321, 569; *Irish Peasant Girl, The*, XIV. 322; *Knocknagow*, XIV. 322
Kidd, Dudley, XIV. Add. 8
Kidd, Thomas (1770–1850), X. 508; XII. 327, 486, 491
Kidder, Richard (1633–1703), VIII. 460
Kidderminster, VII. 145, 146
Kidderminster school, VII. 342
Kidwelly, VIII. 372
Kiel, V. 286
Kiffin, William (1616–1701), XII. 523
Kiftsgate, Gloucestershire, X. 111
Kilbarchan, I. 290; IX. 364
Kilburne, Richard (1605–1678), IX. 536
Kilburne, William, VII. 496
Kilby or Kilbye, Richard (1561?–1620), VII. 317
Kilcolman castle, III. 229, 244
Kildare, earl of. See Fitzgerald, Gerald
Kildare. See Michael of
Kildare, Satire on the people of, II. 502
Kilima-njaro, XIV. 192
Kilkenny, VII. 436; VIII. 146; XII. 510; XIV. 316
Kilkenny, Roman Catholic council of 1650, VII. 190
Kilkenny archaeological society, XII. 351
Kilkenny school, IX. 91, 280
Kilkenny West, X. 196, 207
Killaloe, bishopric of, X. 257
Killearn, Stirlingshire, III. 157
Killiecrankie, IX. 373, 376
Killigrew, Anne (1660–1685), VIII. 395, 444; IX. 168
Killigrew, Henry (1613–1700), VI. 456; VIII. 419; *Conspiracy, The*, VIII. 120; *Pallantus and Eudora*, first published as *The Conspiracy*, VIII. 120, 139
Killigrew, Thomas, the elder (1612–1683), VI. 240, 456; VIII. 118, 119, 207, 419
Cecilia and Clorinda, VIII. 119
Claracilla, VIII. 119
Parson's Wedding, The, VIII. 120, 130
Princess, The, VIII. 119
Prisoners, The, VIII. 119
Thomaso the Wanderer, VIII. 141
Killigrew, Thomas, the younger (1657–1719), VIII. 120; *Chit-Chat*, XII. 322
Killigrew, Sir William (1606–1695), VIII. 419, 434
Ormasdes, or Love and Friendship, VIII. 120
Pandora, VIII. 120
Selindra, VIII. 120
Siege of Urbin, The, VIII. 120
Killing no Murder, VII. 358
Killychrankie, XI. 218
Kilmarnock, XI. 342, 435, 438 ff.
Kilmarnock, earl of. See Boyd, William
Kilmore, VII. 318, 442
Kilner, Dorothy, XI. 480; *Adventures of a Pincushion*, XI. 378; *Jemima Placid*, XI. 379; *Memoirs of a Peg-top*, XI. 378
Kilner, Mary Jane, XI. 480
Kilpin, Ralph, XIV. Add. 8

Kilroot, IX. 92
Kilwardby, Robert (d. 1279), I. 210, 454; II. 363
Kilyð, I. 254
Kimber, Isaac (1692–1755), VIII. 459
Kimcote, near Lutterworth, X. 112
Kinbelin, in Layamon, I. 237
Kincardineshire, IX. 129
Kinch, Horace, in Dickens's *Uncommercial Traveller*, XII. 119
Kind (God), in *Piers the Plowman*, II. 19
Kind-Wit (Natural Intelligence), in *Piers the Plowman*, II. 10, 21
'Kinde-Kit of Kingstone,' IV. 361
Kindred, in *Every-man*, V. 53
King, Charles William (1818–1888), XII. 335, 497
King, Daniel (d. 1664?), IX. 536
King, Edward (1612–1637), VII. 114, 131, 415; XII. 74
King, Henry (1592–1669), VII. 81 ff., 413, 425, *also see* Add.
  Dirge, The, VII. 82
  Exequy, The, VII. 82
  Legacy, The, VII. 82
  Poems, VII. 82
  Sic Vita, VII. 82
  Silence, VII. 82
  'Tell me no more how fair she is,' VII. 82
King, John (1559?–1621), IV. 91, 92, 203, 383; VII. 250
King, John (1696–1728), IX. 527
King, J. E., XIV. 597
King, Leonard William (1869–1919), XII. Add. 4
King, Richard John (1818–1879), XII. 517; XIV. 613
King, Thomas, actor (1730–1805), XI. 257
King, Tom, prizefighter (1835–1888), XIV. 231
King, William (1650–1729), archbishop of Dublin, VIII. 347, 474; IX. 97, 127, 139, 166, 461, 507; *Origin of Evil*, X. 342
King, William (1663–1712), IX. 174, 478
  Art of Cookery, IX. 139, 176
  Dialogue showing the way to Modern Preferment, IX. 139
  Dialogues of the Dead, IX. 139
  Journey to London, IX. 139
  Miscellanies in Prose and Verse, IX. 139
  Molly of Mountown, IX. 139
  Orpheus and Eurydice, IX. 176
  Rufinus, IX. 139
  Transactioner, The, IX. 139
  Useful Miscellanies, IX. 140
  Useful Transactions in Philosophy, IX. 139
King, William (1685–1763), IX. 174; *The Toast*, IX. 139
King, W., bishop of Rochester, XI. 388
King, Zoe, XII. 116
King and the Barber, The, II. 451, 500
King and the Cobbler, The, XI. 334
King and the Miller, The, II. 451, 500
King Arthur, or the British Worthy, VIII. 30
King Darius, V. 393

King Estmere, X. 233
King James and Brown, II. 414
Kingcote, Bernard, in Gissing's *Isabel Clarendon*, XIII. 457
Kinghorn, IX. 367
Kinglake, Alexander William (1809–1891), XI. 307; XII. 199, 491, 552; *Eothen*, XIII. 346; XIV. 94, 240, 251, 252; *Invasion of the Crimea*, XIV. 94
King's Book, The, III. 36
King's Cliffe, IX. 308, 309, 326
King's College Miscellany, The (Aberdeen), XIV. 209
King's companies, the, VI. 221, 247, 256 ff., 274, 275
'King's Friends,' the, IX. 230, 231
King's Head society academy, X. 384
King's pamphlets, the British Museum, VII. 455
Kingsborough, lady, XI. 43
Kingsford, William (1819–1898), XIV. 491, 583; *History of Canada*, XIV. 358, 359
Kingsland, W. G., XIII. 483, 484
Kingsley, Charles (1819–1875), XI. 387, 481; XII. 102, 267, 290, 291, 430, 431, 460, 468; XIII. 147, 158, 160, 340, 345, 353 ff. (main entry), 378, 384, 397, 547, 548; XIV. 86, 323, 408, 552, 607
  Alexandria and her Schools, XIII. 362
  Alton Locke, XIII. 189, 358 ff.
  Ancien Régime, The, XIII. 369
  Andromeda, XIII. 245, 368
  At Last, XIII. 369
  Cheap Clothes, and Nasty, XIII. 358, 359
  Friends of Order, The, XIII. 359
  Glaucus, XIII. 363
  Hereward the Wake, XIII. 366
  Hypatia, XIII. 362 ff., 394
  Hypotheses Hypochondriacae, XIII. 356
  Lectures delivered in America, XIII. 369
  Letters and Memories, XIII. 354, 356, 358, 365, 366
  Life and Works, XIII. 368
  Limits of Exact Science as applied to History, XIII. 368
  Nun's Pool, The, XIII. 358
  Phaethon, XIII. 363
  Plays and Puritans, XIII. 356, 369
  Prose Idylls, XIII. 366, 369
  Psyche, a Rhapsody, XIII. 356
  Roman and the Teuton, The, XIII. 368
  St Maura, XIII. 368
  Saint's Tragedy, The, XIII. 356, 426
  Sands of Dee, The, XIII. 368
  Three Fishers, The, XIII. 368
  Two Years Ago, XIII. 364 ff., 399
  Village Sermons, XIII. 369
  Water-Babies, The, XIII. 369
  Westward Ho! XIII. 363, 364, 366; XIV. 84, 255
  Who causes Pestilence? XIII. 365
  Why should we fear the Romish Priests, XIII. 356
  Yeast, XIII. 359 ff., 363, 420; XIV. 84
Kingsley, George Henry (1827–1892), XIV. 552, 554

Kingsley, Henry (1830–1876), XIII. 563;
  Austin Elliot, XIII. 433; Geoffrey Ham-
  lyn, XIII. 432; XIV. 363; Ravenshoe,
  XIII. 433
Kingsley, Mary Henrietta (1862–1900),
  XIV. 240, 552; Travels in West Africa,
  XIV. 254
Kingsmill, Sir William (fl. 1661), IX. 168
Kingston, dukes of. See Pierrepont,
  Evelyn; Pierrepont, William
Kingston, Felix, IV. 400
Kingston-on-Thames, III. 379, 370, 383,
  385, also see Add.; X. 300
Kingswood school, IX. 313
Kingussie, X. 230
Kinneder, lord. See Erskine, William
Kinnoul, 8th earl of. See Hay, Thomas
Kinross, IX. 552
Kinsale prison, XII. 165
'Kinsayder' (Marston), VI. 39, 43
Kintyre, Scotland, XII. 514
Kinwelmersh or Kindlemarsh, Francis
  (d. 1580?), III. 203; IV. 4, 113, 436; V.
  70; A Vertuous Gentlewoman in the
  praise of her love, III. 189; From Virgin's
  wombe, III. 189; Ode to Concord, V. 71
Kiomi, Meredith's, XIII. 442, 446
Kipling, Rudyard, XIV. 208, 211, 372, 373,
  380
Kippis, Andrew (1725–1795), X. 384; XI.
  472; XIV. 593. See, also, Biographia
  Britannica
Kirby, Margaret (Margaret of Ainderby),
  II. 45, 47
Kirby, Thomas Frederick, XIV. 598
Kirby, William (1817–1906), XIV. 581;
  Le Chien d'Or, XIV. 360
Kirbye, George (d. 1634), IV. 113, 464
Kirchhoff, Gustav Robert, XIV. 267
Kirchmayer, Thomas (Naogeorgos), Pam-
  machius, II. 28; V. 101, 392; VI. 296,
  397, 474
Kirchner, E., XIV. 490
Kirk, John Foster, XII. 519
Kirk, Robert (1641?–1692), IX. 559
Kirk of Field, XIII. 133
Kirk Michael, X. 359
Kirkbride, XI. 470
Kirkby, T., artist, XII. 323
Kirkcaldy, X. 335, 336; XIII. 3
Kirkcaldy, Sir William, of Grange (d.
  1573), III. 503; Ane Ballat of the Captane
  of the Castell, III. 150
Kirkcudbrightshire, XI. 234
Kirke, Edward (1553–1613), III. 220, 227,
  240, 304, 526
Kirkham, Edward (fl. 1601), VI. 290, 292
Kirkham, monastery of, I. 342
Kirkham's children of the queen's revels,
  IV. 132
Kirkley, J. (1705–1754), VIII. 476
Kirkman, Francis (fl. 1674), V. 249, 251;
  VI. 69, 86, 185, 464; VIII. 116, 417;
  The Wits, VI. 266
Kirkman, James Thomas, Memoirs of
  Charles Macklin, XI. 258

Kirkpatrick, John, X. 385
Kirkpatrick, Mr, in Mrs Gaskell's Wives
  and Daughters, XIII. 381
Kirkstall. See Hugh of
Kirkstall abbey, X. 131
Kirkton, James (1620?–1699), IX. 551;
  XII. 518
Kirkwood, Sidney, in Gissing's The Nether
  World, XIII. 458
Kirsteen, Mrs Oliphant's, XIII. 431
Kit, in The Old Curiosity Shop, XIII. 319
Kitcat club, the, VIII. 160; IX. 151, 456;
  XI. 320
Kitchener, Francis Elliot, XIV. 602
Kitchin, George William (1827–1912), XII.
  354, 517; History of France, XII. 348
Kitchin, John, Jurisdictions, 1605, VIII.
  469
Kitely, in Every Man in His Humour, VI.
  16
Kitte, in Piers the Plowman, II. 34
Kitto, John (1804–1854), XII. 472
Kitton, Frederick George (1856–1903),
  XIII. 531, 532, 533, 539, 540, 543, 573;
  XIV. 549
Kittredge, George Lyman, I. ix; II. 400,
  405, 408; XIV. 611
Kiuprili, in Coleridge's Zapolya, XI. 414
Klaas Gezwint en Zijn Paert, XIV. 377
Kleist, H. von, V. 303
Klesmer, in Daniel Deronda, XIII. 401
Klinger, Friedrich Maximilian von, V. 303
Klopstock, Friedrich Gottlieb, X. 18, 232
Knack to Know a Knave, A, V. 313; VI. 217
Knapdale, Scotland, XII. 514
Knapp, Andrew, and Baldwin, William,
  The Newgate Calendar, XIV. 228, 229;
  The New Newgate Calendar, XIV. 228,
  229
Knapp, William Ireland, XIV. 516
Knapton, James, XI. 323
Knapton, J. and P., IX. 76
Knaresborough, VII. 224; XII. 421; XIII.
  275
Knatchbull, Sir Norton (1602–1685), VII.
  341
Knatchbull-Hugessen, Edward Hugessen,
  1st lord Brabourne (1829–1893), XI. 486
Knebworth, XIII. 417
Kneller, Sir Godfrey (1646–1723), VIII.
  50; IX. 483; XI. 319
Knichthood, the Buke of the Order of, II. 284
Knight, Charles (1791–1873), V. 279; XII.
  445; XIV. 93, 409, 491, 495, 534, 597,
  612; English Cyclopaedia, XII. 345;
  Penny Cyclopaedia, XII. 307; Shadows
  of the Old Booksellers, XI. 337, 466
Knight, Ellis Cornelia (1757–1837), X.
  461; XII. 450
Knight, Henrietta, lady Luxborough (d.
  1756), X. 271 ff., 277, 278, 496
Knight, Joseph, XII. 428; XIII. 490, 491,
  515; David Garrick, XI. 258, 453
Knight, Richard Payne (1750–1824), XII.
  490; XIII. 241; Progress of Civil Society,
  XI. 41

Knight, Robert. *See* Catherlough, earl of
Knight, Robert, lord Luxborough, IX. 217
Knight, Samuel (1675–1746), IX. 529
Knight, the, in the *Canterbury Tales*, III. 192
Knight, The Baffled, II. 414
Knight, William, editor of Wordsworth, XI. 406 ff., 407, 408, 410, 411, 416, 423; XIII. 487; XIV. 472; *Memorials of Coleorton*, IX. 328
Knight, William A., XIII. 507
Knight and Shepherd's Daughter, II. 413
Knight of Arts and Industry, in Thomson's *Castle of Indolence*, X. 107
Knight of Curtesy, I. 300, 468
Knight of the Red Shield, I. 294
Knight of the Sea, The, IV. 533
Knightley, in Jane Austen's *Emma*, XII. 239
Knightley, Sir Richard (1533–1615), III. 380, 381, 383
Knighton, or Cnitthon, Henry (*fl.* 1363), II. 30, 38, 59, 497
Knighton, Sir William (1776–1836), XIV. 504
Knight's Quarterly Magazine, X. 320; XIV. 60
Knock, Duncan, in Scott's *Heart of Midlothian*, XII. 19
Knolles, Richard (1550?–1610), IX. 247; *Generall Historie of the Turkes*, IV. 58, 88, 89, 458; X. 161
Knott, Edward (1582–1656), VII. 151
Knowell, in *Every Man in His Humour*, VI. 16
Knowle, X. 150
Knowledge, in *Every-man*, V. 54
Knowles, Sir Charles (d. 1777), X. 40
Knowles, Herbert (1798–1817), XII. 419
Knowles, James Sheridan (1784–1862), XIII. 267, 268, 520; XIV. 309, 310, *also see* Add. 3
Beggar's Daughter of Bethnal Green, The, XIII. 269
Caius Gracchus, XIII. 261
Hunchback, The, XIII. 269
Virginius, XIII. 261
Wife, The, XIII. 261
William Tell, XIII. 261
Knowles, Sir James Thomas (1831–1908), XIV. 534
Knowles, John (*fl.* 1646–1668), X. 377
Knowles, Mrs Mary (1733–1807), X. 472
Knox, Alexander (1757–1831), XI. 422; XII. 256, 457
Knox, Isa, born Craig, XIII. 178, 501; *The Woodruff*, XIII. 179
Knox, John (1505–1572), III. 45, 116, 122, 132, 138 ff. (main entry), 154, 155, 157, 385, 503; IV. 232; VII. 209; IX. 359; XII. 517; XIII. 13, 133, 268, 467, 469; XIV. 491, 493
Answer to a great Number of blasphemous cavillations, An, III. 145
Declaration of the True Nature and Object of Prayer, A, III. 143

Knox, John
Epistle on Justification, The, III. 143
Epistle to the Congregation of the Castle of St Andrews, An, III. 143
Exposition upon the Sixth Psalm of David, The, III. 143
Faithful Admonition to the Professors of God's Truth in England, A, III. 144
First Blast of the Trumpet against the Monstruous Regiment of Women, The, III. 144, 385; IV. 303, 512
First Book of Discipline, The, III. 146
Harborowe for Faithfull and Trewe Subjects agaynst the late blowne Blaste concerning the Government of Women, III. 145
History of the Reformation in Scotland, The, II. 285; III. 132, 141, 146, 148, 149
Narrative of the Proceedings and Troubles of the English Congregation at Frankfurt, III. 144
Ressoning, III. 154
Summary according to the Holy Scriptures of the Sacrament of the Lord's Supper, A, III. 143
Two comfortable Epistles to his afflicted Brethren in England, III. 144
Vindication of the Doctrine that the Sacrifice of the Mass is Idolatry, A, III. 143
Knox, Robert (1640?–1720), IX. 493
Knox, Vicesimus (1752–1821), VIII. 230; XI. 472; XIV. 385, 593, 600, 607; *Essays, Moral and Literary*, XIV. 383; *Letter to Lord North, A*, XIV. 334; *Liberal Education*, XIV. 384, 388, 399
Knutsford, XIII. 372
Knyveth, Sir Henry, IV. 512
Koeppel, Emil, V. 85, 238, 366; VI. 140, XIII. 480
Kögel, R., I. 21
Kok, Abraham, V. 307
Kolax, in *The Muses Looking-Glasse*, VI. 233
Kolbe, F. C., XIV. Add. 5
Kölbing, E., I. ix
Königsberg, V. 283
Koran, the, I. 153; IV. 42; VIII. 291; XII. 499
Korea, IX. 248
Körting, G. E., I. 420; IV. 257
Kosciusko, in Campbell's *Pleasures of Hope*, XII. 100
Koszue, A., XI. Add.
Koszul, A. H., XII. 401, 403
Kottabos, XIV. 211
Kottabos, Echoes from, XIV. 211
Kotzebue, August F. F. von, XI. 42, 281, 414, 455; XII. 526; XIII. 260
Kraszewski, J. I., V. 308
Krebs, H., I. 105
Kretschmar, A. von, XIII. 464
Kreyssig, Friedrich, V. 305
Kritchev, Russia, XI. 58
Kruger, S. J. P., XIV. Add. 8. 10
Ktesias, the Knidian, XIV. 579
Küchler, F., XIII. 465

Kudrun, Austrian poem, I. 37
Kuffler, Dr, VIII. 355
Kulhwch and Olwen, I. 247, 250 ff
Künzelsau, V. 48
Küster, Ludolf, IX. 335
Kyd, Benjamin, VI. 312
Kyd, Francis, V. 156
Kyd, John, V. 158
Kyd, Thomas (1558?–1594), V. 63, 81, 85, 127, 134, 138, 142–164 (main entry), 239, 240, 242, 324, 327, 334, 370, 371, 424; VI. 13, 167, 178, 316, *also see* Add.; VIII. 133
  Cornelia, VII. 122
  Hamlet, V. 157 ff., 164; VI. 178
  Householders Philosophie, The, V. 157
  Murthering of John Brewer, The, V. 157
  Pompey the Great, V. 157
  Richt Fontane of hailfull Sapience, The, III. 131
  Solimon and Perseda, V. 158, 159, 161, 162
  Spanish Tragedie, The, V. 134, 138, 142, 146, 156 ff., 239, 240; VI. 4, 45, 46, 178, 300, 316, 370; VIII. 125
  See, also, under *Jeronimo* and Jonson
Kyffin, Maurice (d. 1599), IV. 440
Kylie, Edward, I. Add.
Kyllour, friar, his play against the Papists, III. 122; *The History of Christ's Passion*, III. 141, 504
Kymry, early poetry of, I. 249
Kynaston, Sir Francis (1587–1642), II. 163, 474; VII. 34, 73, 80, 85, 87, 278, 413, 487
  'April is past, then do not shed,' VII. 81
  Cynthiades or Amorous Sonnets, VII. 81
  'Dear Cynthia, though thou bear'st the name,' VII. 81
  'Do not conceal those radiant eyes,' VII. 81
  Leoline and Sydanis, VII. 78
  'Look not upon me with those lovely eyes,' VII. 81
  Troilus, Kynaston's version of, II. 165; VII. 78, 79, 314
  'When I behold the heaven of thy face,' VII. 81
Kynaston, Herbert (1835–1910), XII. 486
Kynðylan, hall of, I. 275
Kynge, John (d. 1561?), III. 90
Kyngeston, Richard (*fl.* 1403), VI. 280
Kyrle, John (1637–1724), X. 277
Kyteler or Kettle, Alice (*fl.* 1324), II. 500

'L. E. L.' *See* Landon, Laetitia Elizabeth
Laban, II. 293
Labbé's *Concilia*, I. 190
Labeo (Hall's), IV. 332
Labouchere, Henry, XIV. 173, 190, 200, 534
Labourers, statutes of, II. 61
Labrador, IV. 66, 73
La Broue, Solomon de, *Le cavalerice François*, IV. 368
La Bruyère, Jean de, IV. 523; XIII. 447; *Caractères*, VIII. 373, 389; *Des Ouvrages de l'Esprit*, VIII. 376

La Butte, René, IX. 412
La Calprenède, G. de C. de, VII. 391; *Cassandre*, VIII. 185, 371, 434; *La Cléopâtre*, VII. 439; VIII. 15, 25, 185, 272, 371; *Pharamond*, VIII. 371; IX. 55, 268, 500
La Chaises, Father, Project for the Extirpation of Heretics, VIII. 100
La Chalotais, Louis René de, IX. 401, XIV. 382
La Chapelle, Jean de, *Les Carrosses d'Orléans*, VIII. 171
La Chaussée, Pierre Claude Nivelle de, X. 68, 79
Lachrymae Musarum, VII. 180; VIII. 395
Lackington, James (1746–1815), XI. 337, 338, 340, 468; *Confessions*, XI. 327, 472; *Memoirs*, XI. 327, 337, 338
Lacordaire, Jean Baptiste Henri, XII. 254
Lacroix, P., XII. 380
Lactantius, I. 58, 76; III. 416; VII. 505; IX. 489
Lacy, in *Frier Bacon*, V. 137
Lacy, in *The Shomaker's Holiday*, V. 255
Lacy, Alexander, IV. 390
Lacy, earl of Kent, in *The Devil and his Dame*, V. 329
Lacy, J., *The Steeleids* (1714), IX. 442
Lacy, John (d. 1681), VIII. 419
  Dumb Lady, The, VIII. 140
  Old Troop, The, VIII. 122, 140
  Sawny the Scot, VIII. 140
  Sir Hercules Buffoon, VIII. 140
Lacy, Margaret de, countess of Lincoln (*c.* 1240), IV. 370
Lacy, T. H., XIII. 516
Ladder of Perfection, The, II. 299, 300
Ladies Collegiate, the, in *The Silent Woman*, VI. 22
Ladislaus, in *The Picture*, VI. 158
Ladislaw, Will, in *Middlemarch*, XIII. 399
Lads of Wamphray, The, II. 415
Lady, the, in *Comus*, VII. 113, 137
Lady, the, in *Hudibras*, VIII. 77
Lady Jane, VI. 168
Lady of the Fountain, I. 253, 274
Lady's Magazine, The, X. 205, 206; XIII. 430
Ladysmith, South Africa, XIV. 193
Laelia, VI. 305, 327, 484
Laertes, in *Hamlet*, V. 201, 262
Laertius, Diogenes, IV. 5, 436
La Fayette, countess de, *La Princesse de Clèves*, VIII. 15, 186, 373; X. 58
Lafeu, in *All's Well that Ends Well*, V. 180
La Flèche, X. 282, 322
La Flechère, J. W. *See* Fletcher, John William
La Fontaine, Jean de, VIII. 373, 376, 427; IX. 162, 168; X. 202; XI. 38, 175, 491
Laga Eadwardi. See *Leges*
Lagado, in *Gulliver's Travels*, IX. 106
Lagden, Sir Godfrey, XIV. Add. 8
Lagrange, Joseph Louis, comte, XIV. 258
La Harpe, V. 293, 302

Lahore, IV. 90
Lai du Corn, La, I. 464
Laidlaw, William (1780–1845), XI. 238;
  XII. 5; XIII. 504; XIV. 278; *Lucy's
  Flittin,* XI. 241
Laily Worm, The, II. 414
Laing. David (1793–1878), II. 115, 126,
  276; IV. 412; XI. 444, 446; XII. 358, 372,
  517, 520
Laing, John (1809–1880), XII. 371, 522
Laing, Malcolm (1762–1818), X. 229, 232,
  487, 502; XIV. 491
Laing, Samuel, the elder (1780–1868), XIV.
  552
Lairesse, Gerard de, XIII. 84
Lake, Sir Francis (*fl.* 1556), VI. 242
Lake, J. W., XII. 383, 395, 410
Lake, Osmund, *A Probe Theologicall,* VI.
  375, 494
Lake, William Charles (1817–1897), XII.
  454
Lake poets, XI. 308
Lake school, X. 363
Lakes, the, X. 133; XI. 302; XIV. 220, 221,
  291, 292
Laleham, XII. 302; XIII. 86
Lamarck, Chevalier de, XIII. 450
Lamartine, A. M. L. de, V. 302
Lamb, lady Caroline (1785–1828), XII.
  383, 397, 450
Lamb, Charles (1775–1834), III. 255; IV.
  154, 155, 160, 252, 327, 328; V. 145,
  222, 239, 252; VI. 45, 55, 58, 61, 73,
  76, 100, 129; VII. 72, 185, 228, 236;
  VIII. 386; IX. 22, 24, 86, 277, 300; X. 78,
  216, 242, 358; XI. 40, 91, 118, 126, 200,
  201, 284, 286, 407, 410, 413, 417, 453;
  XII. 110, 114, 130, 131, 135, 164, 166,
  167, 172 ff., 176, 178, 179, 180 ff. (main
  entry), 219, 221 ff., 282, 421, 433 ff.,
  also see Add.; XIII. 9, 135, 143, 148,
  158, 188, 198, 299, 307, 429; XIV. 109,
  138, 160, 161, 169 ff., 186, 198, 313, 361,
  515, 591, 597
  Adventures of Ulysses, The, XII. 189, 190
  Album Verses, XII. 202
  Blakesmoor in H—shire, XII. 182
  *Blank Verse, by Charles Lloyd and Charles
  Lamb,* XII. 184
  Confessions of a Drunkard, XII. 193
  Convalescent, The, XII. 200
  Curious Fragments, XII. 187, 188
  Dissertation on Roast Pig, XII. 160
  Dream Children, XII. 182, 202
  Essays of Elia, IV. 250; XII. 160, 183,
  193, 196, 197, 201, 202
  Extracts from the Garrick plays, VIII. 188
  First Going to Church, XII. 191
  Genius and Character of Hogarth, The,
  XII. 193
  Gipsy's Malison, The, XII. 202
  Going or Gone, XII. 202
  Hester, XII. 194
  Hypochondriacus, XII. 187
  Imperfect Sympathies, XII. 198
  In His Own Album, XII. 202

Lamb, Charles
  In the Album of Lucy Barton, XII. 202
  John Woodvil (Pride's cure), XII. 186 ff.,
  191, 194; XIII. 276
  King and Queen of Hearts, The, XI. 385
  'Lady Blanch,' XII. 187
  Last Essays of Elia, XII. 200, 201
  Macbeth, in *Tales from Shakespear,* XII.
  189
  Mr H—, XII. 188, 189, 194
  New Year's Eve, XII. 197
  Newspapers Thirty-five years ago, XII.
  188; XIV. 184
  Old China, XII. 186
  Old Familiar Faces, The, XII. 184, 202
  *On the Artificial Comedy of the Last Cen-
  tury,* VIII. 156
  *On the Inconveniences Resulting from
  being Hanged,* XII. 193
  Othello, in *Tales from Shakespear,* XII.
  189
  Oxford in the Vacation, XII. 187
  Poems, XI. 385
  Popular Fallacies, XII. 197, 200
  Pride's Cure, XII. 186
  Prince Dorus, XI. 385; XII. 191
  Quaker's Meeting, A, XII. 198
  Recollections of Christ's Hospital, XII.
  193, 197
  Recollections of the South-Sea House,
  XII. 195
  Shakespeare, Tragedies of, XII. 193
  Specimens from the Writings of Fuller,
  XII. 193
  Specimens of English Dramatic Poets,
  XII. 193, 191
  Starkey, Captain, XII. 181
  Superannuated Man, The, XII. 200
  Table-Talk, XII. 193
  *Tale of Rosamund Gray and Old Blind
  Margaret,* XII. 185, 186, 194
  Theses quaedam theologicae, XII. 185
  Two Races of Men, The, XII. 198
  Wife's Trial, The, XI. 148
  Witch Aunt, The, XII. 191
  Witches and other Night Fears, XII. 191
  Works (1818), XII. 194
  See, also, Tremebundus
Lamb, Charles and Mary, XII. 433 ff.;
  Mrs Leicester's School, XI. 385; XII. 182,
  191; *Poetry for Children,* XI. 384; XII.
  191; *Tales from Shakespeare,* XI. 385,
  481; XII. 188 ff.
Lamb, Mrs Elizabeth (born Field), XII. 180
Lamb, Sir James. *See* Burges, Sir James
  Bland
Lamb, John, father of Charles Lamb,
  Poetical Pieces on Several Occasions, XII.
  180
Lamb, John, brother of Charles Lamb, XII.
  181 ff., 195
Lamb, Mary Ann (1764–1847), XII. 167,
  173, 181 ff. (main entry), 434 ff.; XIV.
  198; 'Highborn Helen,' XII. 182, 186,
  188; *Visit to the Cousins,* XII. 191;
  Young Mahometan, The, XII. 182, 191

Lamb, Mary Montgomerie. *See* Currie, lady
Lamb, Sarah (d. 1797), XII. 184
Lamb, William, 2nd viscount Melbourne (1779–1848), XIV. 61, 115, 124, 125, 181, 194, 419, 510
Lambarde, William (1536–1601), III. 530; VIII. 467; IX. 352
　　Archaionomia, VIII. 315
　　Archeion, VIII. 315
　　Eirenarcha, VIII. 315
　　Perambulation of Kent, IV. 84
Lambe, John (d. 1628), VII. 369, 509
Lambert, Hetty, in *The Virginians*, XIII. 298, 299
Lambert, John (1619–1683), VII. 230, 353; VIII. 121
Lambert, lady, VIII. 121
Lambert, Martin, in *The Virginians*, IV. 253
Lambert, Theo, in *The Virginians*, XIII. 298, 299
Lambeth palace, II. 55; VII. 356
Lambinus, VII. 307; XII. 326
Lambton, lady Betty, in Kelly's *False Delicacy*, XI. 263
Lambton, John George, 1st earl of Durham (1792–1840), XIV. 125, 509
Lambwell, Sir, I. 295
Lamennais, Hugues Félicité Robert de, XII. 254
Lament of Gudrun, The, X. 228
Lamentable Lory, VIII. 97
Lamentation of Souls, I. 356
Lami, E., XII. 525
Lamia, in Keats's poem, XII. 88
Lamia, in *Promos and Cassandra*, V. 120
Lamia, in *The Glasse of Government*, V. 113
Lamilia, in *A Groatsworth of Wit*, III. 357; IV. 320
Lamkin, II. 412
Lamont, John (*fl.* 1671), IX. 551
Lamont, L. M., XIII. 562
Lamont, T. R., XIII. 433
La Motte Fouqué, F. H. C. de, baron. XI. 491; XII. 411
Lamp, The, XIV. 326
Lampatho, in *What You Will*, VI. 43
Lampe, John Frederick (1703?–1751), X. 426, 427, 440
Lampman, Archibald (1861–1899), XIV. 343, 350 ff., 582
　　Alcyone, XIV. 353
　　Among the Millet, XIV. 351
　　April, April in the Hills, XIV. 352
　　Athenian Reverie, An, XIV. 351
　　Between the Rapids, XIV. 353
　　By an Autumn Stream, XIV. 353
　　City of the End of Things, The, XIV. 354
　　Comfort of the Fields, The, XIV. 352
　　Frogs, The, XIV. 353
　　Heat, XIV. 353
　　June, XIV. 353
　　Land of Pallas, The, XIV. 353
　　Lyrics of Earth, XIV. 353
　　Meadow, The, XIV. 352

Lampman, Archibald
　　Monk, The, XIV. 351
　　Morning on the Lièvre, XIV. 352
　　September, XIV. 353
　　Snow, XIV. 353
　　Solitude, XIV. 353
Lampranus, in *Perfidus Hetruscus*, VI. 302
Lanarkshire, IX. 366; XIV. 66
Lancashire, III. 215, 448; IV. 190, 232; VI. 104; VII. 342, 373; X. 358; XI. 469; XII. 337, 346, 355, 507, 514, 519; XIII. 372, 373, 376; XIV. 185, 195
Lancashire and Cheshire Record society, XII. 506
Lancashire witches, VII. 374
Lancaster, II. 325; XI. 383; XIV. 54
Lancaster, duke of, in *Richard II*, V. 185
Lancaster, house of, II. 296; V. 340; X. 254
Lancaster, Henry Hill (1829–1875), XIII. 467; XIV. 607
Lancaster, Sir James (d. 1618), IV. 85, 92, 98, 99
Lancaster, John of, duke of Bedford (1389–1435), II. 336
Lancaster, John, V. 77
Lancaster, Joseph (1778–1838), XIV. 404, 405, 591, 602, 607, 610; *Improvements in Education*, XIV. 390, 393, 401 ff.
'Lancaster,' *pseud.* of lord *de Tabley*, XIII. 204
Lancastrian court, the, VIII. 314
Lancastrian kings, IX. 222
Lancastrian system of education, XI. 133
Lancastrian writers, X. 291
Lancelot, I. 236, 261, 267, 270, 313; II. 337; III. 68; VII. 75
Lancelot, Tennyson's, XIII. 37
Lancelot, prose romance of (*Lancelot de Lake, du Lac*), I. 190, 264, 270, 271, 363, 462
Lancelot and Guinevere, II. 174
Lancelot of the Laik, I. 469; II. 91, 94
Land of Cockaygne, I. 365, 477; X. 225
Landells, Ebenezer (1808–1860), XIV. 236
Lander, Richard Lemon (1804–1834), XIV. 552
Landon, Laetitia Elizabeth, 'L. E. L.' (1802–1838), XII. 124 ff., 129, 380, 419, 450; XIII. 175, 177; *Ethel Churchill*, XII. 247
Landor, Robert Eyres (1781–1869), XII. 228 ff. (main entry), 442
　　Count Arezzi, XII. 228
　　Earl of Brecon, The, XII. 228
　　Faith's Fraud, XII. 228
　　Fawn of Sertorius, The, XII. 228 ff.
　　Ferryman, The, XII. 228
　　Fountain of Arethusa, The, XII. 229, 230
　　Impious Feast, The, XII. 229
Landor, Walter Savage (1775–1864), VII. 137; IX. 159; XI. 153, 164, 396, 410, 423; XII. 204 ff. (main entry), 223, 266 ff., 404, 407, 439 ff. (main entry); XIII. 57, 73, 129, 132, 148, 181, 187, 188, 193, 228, 230, 328, 463; XIV. 462, 598
　　Acts and Scenes, XII. 211 ff., 215

Landor, Walter Savage
  Andrea of Hungary, XII. 212
  Browning sonnet, XII. 214
  'Cenci' scenes, XII. 213
  Citation and Examination of Shakespeare, The, XII. 215, 216, 220
  Coresus and Callirrhoe, XII. 212
  Count Julian, VI. 71; XII. 209, 211, 212, 214
  Dirce, XII. 214
  Dream of Boccaccio, XII. 226
  Dry Sticks, XII. 214
  Duke de Richelieu, Sir Firebrace Cotes, etc., XII. 216
  Essex and Spenser, XII. 220
  Euthymedes, XII. 217
  Gebir, XI. 300; XII. 209 ff., 229
  Guidone and Lucia, XII. 214
  Gunlaug, XII. 214
  Hamadryad, XII. 213
  Hellenics, XII. 212, 213
  Ianthe poems, XII. 214
  Imaginary Conversations, XII. 205, 209, 211, 215, 217, 230
  Menelaus and Helen, XII. 212
  Miscellanies, XII. 205
  Neapolitan trilogy, XII. 211, 212
  Pentameron, The, XII. 215
  Pericles and Aspasia, XII. 215, 217
  Poems, XII. 205, 211, 217
  Rose Aylmer, XII. 214, 220
  Rose the Third, XII. 215
  Sensible Girl's Reply, A, XII. 215
  Works, XII. 212
Landors, the, XII. Add.
Landrecy, siege of, III. 175
Landseer, Sir Edwin (1802–1873), XIV. 545
Land's End, XIII. 204
Lane, Edward William (1801–1876), XII. 342, 499
Lane, John (*fl.* 1620), V. 478
Lane, John, XIII. 568
Lane, Theodore (1800–1828), XIV. 225, 226
Laneham, John (*fl.* 1574), VI. 246, 249
Laneham, Robert (*fl.* 1575), III. 496, 518 IV. 472; V. 30, 31, 386; VI. 466, 494
Lanercost Chronicle, II. 497
Lanferth, letter of, I. 120
Lanfranc (1005?–1089), archbishop of Canterbury, I. 128, 149, 153, 154, 222, 446
Lanfranc's *Chirurgia Parva*, II. 483; V. 478
Lang, Andrew (1844–1912), II. 398, 408, 414; XI. 374, 438 ff., 481, 491, 492; XII. 154, 362, 373, 374, 380, 430, 433. 436, 493, 522; XIII. 207, 210 ff., 467, 477, 504, 509, 530, 533, 537, 543, 566; XIV. 191, 206, 210, 491, 521, 522, 526, 538
  Ballade of his Choice of a Sepulchre, XIII. 210
  'Bibliomania in France,' XII. 371
  Books and Bookmen, XII. 371
  Colonel Burnaby, XIII. 210
  'Elzevirs,' XII. 371
  Helen of Troy, XIII. 210

Lang, Andrew
  History of Scotland, XIV. 96
  Library, The, XII. 371
  Life and Death of Jeanne D'Arc, XIV. 96
  Lockhart, Life of J. G., XII. 162
  Odyssey, The, XIII. 210
  Orange Fairy Book, XIV. 164
Lang, John, XIV. 339, 578
Lang, John Dunmore (1799–1878), XIV. 586; *Aurora Australis*, XIV. 362; *Historical Account of New South Wales*, XIV. 371
Langar, Nottingham, XIII. 449
Langbaine, Gerard, the elder (1609–1658) VII. 316, 485, 489; IX. 536
Langbaine, Gerard, the younger (1656–1692), IV. 376; VI. 69, 122, 200, 202; VIII. 131, 141, 183, 423; *Account of the English Dramatic Poets*, IX. 141, 357, 475, 479
Langcake, Thomas (*fl.* 1764–1781), IX. 318, 511, 512, 515, 516
Langdale, lord. *See* Bickersteth, Henry
Langelye, Robertus, alias Robertus Parterick, II. 35
Langer, Ernst Theodor, X. 311
Langford Magna, IX. 287
Langham, W., *The garden of health*, IV. 542
Langhorne, John (1735–1779), X. 455
Langhorne, William (1721–1772), X. 455
Langland or Langley, William (1330?–1400?), I. 292; II. 2, 34, 35, 38, 433, 435, 436; XI. 368; XIII. Add. 2. See, also, *Piers Plowman*
Langley, Francis (*fl.* 1589), VI. 259
Langley, Henry (1611–1679), X. 387
Langres, I. 34
Langrishe, Sir Hercules (1731–1811), XI. 6, 389
Langtoft. *See* Peter of
Langton, Bennet (1737–1801), X. 207, 215; XI. 333, 346, 365; XIV. 590, 594
Langton, Robert, XIII. 532
Langton, Stephen (d. 1228), archbishop of Canterbury, I. 200, 455; II. 365; V. 21, 65, 151
Language, the English, from Chaucer to Shakespeare, III. 439 ff., 555 ff.; since Shakespeare, XIV. 434 ff., 611
Languet, Hubert, III. 351; *Vindiciae contra Tyrannos*, VII. 353, 499
Languish, Lydia, in Sheridan's *Rivals*, X. 89; XI. 266
Langwith, Benjamin (1684?–1743), IX. 469, 472
Laniere, Nicholas (1588–1666), VII. 5
Lanier, Sidney, XIII. 553
La Noue, François de, IV. 8, 445
Lanquet, Thomas, III. 530
Lansdowne, baron. *See* Granville, George
Lansdowne, marquises of. *See* Petty-Fitzmaurice, Henry; Petty, William
Lanson, G., XII. 525
Lantwit, major (Wales), I. 66
Lanum, IV. 360

Lanval, I. 295
Laocoon, XI. 432
Laodamia, Wordsworth's, XI. 107
Laon, in Shelley's *Revolt of Islam*, XII. 61
Laon, monks of, I. 250
La Pérouse, J. F. G. de, XIV. 553
Lapidaries, I. 460
La Place, P. A. de, V. 290 ff., 296
Laplace, Pierre Simon, marquis de, XIV.
    258, 261; *Mécanique Céleste*, XIV. 409
Lapraik, John (1727–1807), *Jenny was
    Frail and Unkind*, XI. 234; *Poems*, XI.
    234; *When I upon thy Bosom Lean*, XI.
    234
La Primaudaye, Pierre de, IV. 8, 445
Laputans, the, in *Gulliver's Travels*, XIII.
    452
Lār, I. 146
Lara, in Byron's poem, XII. 46
Laracor, IX. 93
La Ramée, Louise de. *See* Ouida
Lardner, Dionysius (1793–1859), XIV. 556,
    613
    Cabinet Cyclopaedia, XII. 303, 376, 412;
        XIV. 59
    Critical Library, XII. 303
    Cyclopaedia, XII. 308
    Edinburgh Cabinet Library, XII. 303
Lardner, Nathaniel (1684–1768), IX. 507;
    X. 380, 381, 513; *Credibility of the Gospel
    History*, X. 346, 521
Large, Robert (*fl.* 1438), II. 311
Lariche, Benjamin, V. 302
Lark, The, IX. 373, 566; XI. 206, 232
Larkbeare, Devon, XIII. 276
Larkins, Miss, in *David Copperfield*, XIII.
    327
Larminie, W., I. 294, 465
Larmor, Sir Joseph, XIV. 269
La Roche, Sophie, *Geschichte des Fräuleins
    von Sternheim*, X. 18
La Rochefoucauld, François, duc de, IV.
    523; V. 169; VIII. 385, 386; XII. 97;
    Maximes, VIII. 373
La Rochelle, VII. 306
*Larum for London or the siedge of Antwerpe,
    A*, IV. 324; V. 146, 344
Lascelles, Anne, wife of Smollett, X. 36
Lasco, Albertus, VI. 303
Las Coveras, *Don Fenise*, VIII. 141
Lashmar, Dyce, Gissing's, XIII. 460
Laska, in Coleridge's *Zapolya*, XI. 414
Lassalle, Ferdinand, XIII. 444
Lasseran-Massencone, B. de, IX. 499
Last, Joseph, XIV. 236
Last Judgment, The, I. 428; XI. 198
'Last Sorrowful Lamentations,' XIV. 228
Last Will and Testaments, III. 483
Latey, John (1842–1902), XIV. 534
Lathacan, Laidcenn or Loding, Irish
    prince, I. 68
Latham, Robert Gordon (1812–1888), XII.
    504; XIII. 245
Latham, Simon (*fl.* 1618), *Falconry*, IV.
    374, 541
Lathbury, near Newport Pagnell, II. 61

Lathbury, Daniel Conner, XII. 455
Lathom almshouse, X. 358
Latimer, Hugh (1485?–1555), bishop of
    Worcester, II. 334; III. 27, 31, 36 ff.,
    42, 51, 81, 432, 471, 496, 532; IV. 227 ff.,
    238, 300, 324, 380, 493; VII. 236; X. 365;
    XIII. 184; *Conferences*, III. 38; *Sermon
    on the Plough*, IV. 234; *Sermons on the
    Card*, III. 36; IV. 229
Latimer, William (1460?–1545), III. 6, 12
Latin, early study of, II. 70, 283, 359, 367,
    370, 371
Latin, on the medieval stage, V. 37, 39,
    43, 46
Latin, written in Britain (to the time of
    Alfred), I. 65 ff., 433 ff.
Latin chroniclers, I. 156 ff., 448 ff.
Latin drama, V. 2, 24, 26, 37, 38, 61, 62,
    69, 70, 72, 75, 80, 82, 100 ff., 103, 108 ff.,
    117 ff., 394; VI. 14, 21, 26, 64, 293 ff.,
    300, 398; XI. 266
Latin grammar, IX. 382, 390, 562
Latin Heptateuch, XII. 487
Latin hymns, XI. 217; XII. 273; XIII. 135,
    172, 173
Latin hymns and carols, II. 375, 377, 383
Latin language and literature, VII. 3, 4,
    7, 9, 18, 78, 90, 125, 165, 201, 204, 206,
    220, 221, 230, 235, 237, 241, 261, 263,
    267, 272, 280, 282, 283, 302, 307, 308,
    313 ff., 320, 322 ff., 326, 332, 335,
    339 ff., 453; VIII. 49 ff., 58, 61, 87, 88,
    112, 271, 277, 279, 281, 282, 310, 313,
    314, 319, 332, 353, 378, 381; IX. 43,
    67, 68, 76, 253, 264, 266, 270, 292,
    329 ff., 337, 341, 382, 385, 388, 390,
    393, 396, 402 ff., 409; X. 14, 97, 133,
    137, 158, 159, 163, 178, 187, 188, 205,
    225, 257, 276, 289, 308, 335; XI. 2, 54,
    58, 83, 90, 181, 334, 343, 347, 354, 355,
    359; XII. 40, 106, 134, 208, 223, 230,
    265, 278, 308, 317, 326, 327, 330,
    335 ff., 343, 354; XIII. 23, 29, 45, 53,
    124, 164, 165, 168, 169, 175, 249; XIV.
    91, 120, 209, 249, 302, 303, 306, 308,
    309, 316, 327, 374, 382, 385, 388, 391,
    394, 405, 406, 410, 413, 424, 426, 454,
    455, 457, 460, 461
Latin poets, X. 119
Latin Prayer Book, VII. 327
Latin terms, on the stage, V. 255; VI. 93,
    162, 163, 225, 229, 354, 372
Latin verse, X. 159, 177; XII. 58, 265, 305,
    329
Latmus, in *The Faithfull Shepheardesse*,
    VI. 368
La Tour Landry, G., II. 483, 485, 508. *See,
    also*, Caxton, *Knight of the Tower*
Latria, shrine of (Day's), VI. 216
Latta, Robert, XIV. 479
Laube, Heinrich, V. 306, 346
Laud, William (1573–1645), archbishop of
    Canterbury, III. 388, 420; IV. 204, 239,
    306, 411, 424, 426, 432; V. 365; VI. 196,
    319, 326, 405; VII. 35, 98, 115, 147, 148,
    150, 152, 154, 157 ff., 162, 163, 182,

Laud, William
187, 207, 208, 216, 218, 223, 225, 334,
349, 350, 425, 427, 441, 445, 459, 498,
also see Add.; VIII. 274, 293, 301, 462;
IX. 306; *Diary*, VII. 160, 451; *Relation
...Pretended Answer to T. C.*, VIII. 300
Lauder, George (*fl.* 1677), IX. 555
Lauder, Sir John, lord Fountainhall (1646
–1722), IX. 553; XII. 376
Lauder, Sir Thomas Dick (1784–1848), XII.
450
Lauder, William (1520?–1573), II. 497;
III. 498; *Tractate concernyng the office
and dewtie of Kyngis, etc.*, III. 132
Lauder, William (d. 1771), VII. 109, 118;
IX. 557; X. 175, 468
Lauderdale, duke of. *See* Maitland, John
Lauderdale, earls of. *See* Maitland, James;
Maitland, John
Laudian movement, the, XII. 253
Laudian statutes, at Oxford, IX. 383
Laudine, in *Ywain and Gawain*, I. 312
Laughter, in *The Tears of the Muses*, III.
241
Laughton, Sir John Knox (1830–1915),
XII. 427; XIV. 491
Launce, in *The Two Gentlemen of Verona*,
V. 180, 190; XIII. 64
Launcelot, in Kingsley's *Yeast*, XIII. 360,
361
Launcelot, in *The Merchant of Venice*, V.
190
Launceston, VII. 348
Launfal (Landavall), I. 295
Launfal, Sir, I. 281, 291, 294, 295, 299,
310, 462, 471
'Launsknights,' V. 31
Laura, in *Pendennis*, XIII. 290, 291, 293,
295, 296
'Laura,' Della Cruscan poet, XI. 177
Laura (Petrarch's), III. 225, 251, 252, 254,
265, 268, 272; IV. 210
Laura, the, in Kingsley's *Hypatia*, XIII.
363
Laurence (actor), VI. 249
Laurence, friar, in *Romeo and Juliet*, V. 357
Laurence, French (1757–1809), XI. 35,
388, 391
Laurence, R. V., XIV. 484
Laurence, St, V. 49
Laurentian manuscripts, XII. 324, 327, 328
Laurie, Simon Somerville (1829–1909),
XIV. 475, 607
Laurie, William Ferguson Beatson, XIV.
574
Lausanne, II. 315; X. 298, 301, 302, 304,
311, 312
Lavater, J.-G., XI. 432
Laveleye, Emile de, XIV. 477
Lavenham, Richard (*fl.* 1380), I. 455; II. 61
Lavensforth, in Mrs Inchbald's *To Marry
or not to Marry*, XI. 279
Lavington, John (1690?–1759), X. 384
Lavinia, in Thomson's *Autumn*, X. 104
Lavoisier, Antoine Laurent, XIV. 271, 273,
278

Law, in *Piers the Plowman*, II. 10
Law, Edmund (1703–1787), VIII. 474: IX.
507; X. 131, 342
Law, Edward, 1st earl of Ellenborough
(1790–1871), XII. 401; XIV. 124, 130,
502
Law, John, of Lauriston (1671–1729), IX.
492, 559
Law, Robert (d. 1690?), IX. 551; XIII. 518
Law, Thomas Graves (1836–1904), XII.
522; XIV. 101, 491 *Collected Essays*,
XII. 371
Law, William (1686–1761), IV. 342, 522;
VI. 494; VII. 155; VIII. 433; IX. 305 ff.
(main entry), 404, 507, 510 ff., 515, 519,
520, 569; X. 354, 355; XII. 284
Absolute Unlawfulness of the Stage, The,
X. 70
Appeal to all that Doubt, IX. 318 ff., 328
Case of Reason, IX. 302, 311, 312
*Malebranche, and the Vision of All
Things in God*, IX. 313
*Practical Treatise upon Christian Per-
fection*, IX. 312, 318, 323, 325
Remarks on the Fable of the Bees, IX. 302,
311, 322 ff.
Serious Call, VI. 408; IX. 308, 309, 312,
313, 318, 321 ff., 402; X. 350, 362; XII.
282
*Some Animadversions upon Dr Trapp's
late Reply*, IX. 313, 326
Spirit of Love, IX. 314
Spirit of Prayer, IX. 319, 320, 322 ff., 326
Three Letters to the Bishop of Bangor,
IX. 310
Way to Divine Knowledge, IX. 307,
318 ff., 321
Law, William John (1787–1869), XII. 497
Lawder, Mrs (Jane Contarine), X. 481
Lawes, Henry (1596–1662), VI. 325, 326;
VII. 5, 22, 52, 113, 116, 123, 409, 413;
VIII. 117
Lawes, William (d. 1645), VII. 5
Lawford, Essex, XII. 305
Lawkerry, Neh., VII. 499
Lawless, Emily (d. 1913), XIV. 569
Grania, XIV. 324
Hurrish, XIV. 324
With Essex in Ireland, XIV. 324
With the Wild Geese, XIV. 324
Lawley, Francis, XIV. 543
Lawrence, bishop of Durham (d. 1154),
I. 191, 455
Lawrence, George Alfred (1827–1876),
XIII. 563; *Guy Livingstone*, XIII. 436
Lawrence, Sir Henry (1806–1857), XIV.
495
Lawrence, John (1753–1839), XIV. 544
Lawrence, John Laird Mair, 1st baron
Lawrence (1811–1879), XII. 316, 478
Lawrence, Leonard, *Arnalte and Lucenda*,
VII. 80, 413
Lawrence, Polly, of Bath, XI. 175
Lawrie, Sir Archibald Campbell (1837–
1914), XII. 517; *Annals of Malcolm and
William*, XII. 360; *Early Scottish*

Lawrie, Sir Archibald Campbell
  Charters, XII. 360; *Index to the Scots
  Acts*, XII. 360
La Writ, in *The Little French Lawyer*, VI.
  134
Laws, Old English, I. 130. *See, also*, the
  chapter on Alfred, I. 97 ff., 436, 437, 439
Laws, Bute MS. of, II. 284
Lawson, Edward Levy, lord Burnham,
  XIV. 191
Lawson, George (d. 1678), VII. 473
Lawson, Sir John (d. 1665), VIII. 11, 218
Lawson, William (*fl.* 1618), *A New Orchard
  and Garden*, IV. 373, 375, 542
Laxdaela saga, XIII. 125
Lay by your pleading, VIII. 96
Lay Folk's Mass Book, I. 353; II. 48
Layamon (*fl.* 1200), I. 137, 139, 170, 218,
  222, 234 ff., 264, 265, 278, 287, 288,
  292, 337, 375, 378, 393, 398, 458, 459,
  462; II. 103, 189, 420; V. 6; *Brut*, XII.
  356, 517
Layard, Sir Austen Henry (1817–1894),
  XII. 339, 497; XIV. 552; *Early Adven-
  tures in Persia, Susiana and Babylonia*,
  XIV. 253; *Popular account of Discoveries
  at Nineveh, A*, XIV. 253
Layard, George Somes, XII. 441; XIII. 536;
  XIV. 548
Lays of Helgi, X. 228
Layton, in Strype's *Ecclesiastical Me-
  morials*, I. 212
Lazarillo, in *Blurt Master-Constable* (Mid-
  dleton), VIII. 127
Lazarillo de Tormes, III. 94, 342, 364;
  VIII. 127
Lazarus, in school plays, V. 103
Lea, James, IV. 458
Leabhar Breac, the, XII. 362, 515
Leabhar na g-Ceart, the Book of Rights,
  XII. 518
Leach, Arthur Francis, VII. 336; XIV. 591;
  History of Warwick School, IV. 261
Leach, Edmund, VII. 515
Leach, Francis (*fl.* 1643), VII. 347
Lead, Jane (1623–1704), IX. 307, 513 ff.,
  523
Leadbeater, Mary, born Shackleton (1758–
  1826), XIV. 569
  Annals of Ballitore, XIV. 323
  Cottage Dialogues, XIV. 323
  Extracts and Original Anecdotes, XIV.
  323
  Leadbeater Papers, The, XIV. 323
Leader, The, XIII. 385; XIV. 199
Leader-Haughs and Yarrow, IX. 364
Leadhills, Lanarkshire, IX. 366
Leaf, Walter, XIV. 522
League, the (French), III. 398; IV. 142;
  VI. 174; VIII. 16
Leake, William Martin (1777–1860), XII.
  497; XIV. 552
  Numismata Hellenica, XII. 338
  Researches in Greece, XII. 338
  Topography of Athens, XII. 338
  Travels, XII. 338

Leakey, Caroline Woolmer (1827–1881),
  XIV. 587
Lean, Florence (born Marryat). *See*
  Marryat, Florence
Leanchops, in Wilson's *Projectors*, VIII. 123
Leander, Hero and, in Nashe's *Prayse of
  the Red Herring*, IV. 327
Leandro, in *The Spanish Curate*, VI. 134, 139
Leanthe, in Farquhar's *Love and a Bottle*,
  VIII. 169
Leapor, Mary (1722–1746), XI. 172, 427
Lear, in Shakespeare's play, XII. 47
Lear, Edward (1812–1888), XI. 386, 481;
  XIII. 167, 504; *Book of Nonsense*, XI.
  377; XIII. 163; *Jumblies*, XIII. 163; *Owl
  and the Pussy-Cat, The*, XIII. 163
Lear, Garrick as, X. 265; XI. 360
Lear or Leir, in the *Bruts* and *Chronicles*,
  I. 171, 235, 237, 336. *See, also*, Leir, Llŷr
Learning (Clergy), in *Piers the Plowman*,
  II. 20
Learning-with-Money, in *All for Money*,
  V. 57
Learning-without-Money, in *All for Money*,
  V. 57
Leask, W. Keith, XIV. 538, 594
Leasowes, X. 149, 271, 275, 276, 456
Leathley, Mrs, XI. 487
Lebanon, IV. 33
Le Blanc, abbé, V. 289, 290
Le Bossu, René, VIII. 375; *Du poème
  Épique*, VIII. 374; IX. 59
Le Brun, N., IV. 266
Lecher, in *Piers the Plowman*, II. 12
Lechery, in *Confessio Amantis*, II. 147
Lechery, in *Piers the Plowman*, II. 20
Lechery, in *The Example of Virtue*, II. 234
Lecky, William Edward Hartpole (1838–
  1903), VIII. 167, 291, 292; X. 503; XI.
  396; XII. 464; XIII. 552; XIV. 86, 89,
  96, 103 ff. (main entry), 492, 509, 510
  Declining Sense of the Miraculous, The,
  XIV. 104
  Democracy and Liberty, XIV. 106
  *History of England in the Eighteenth
  Century*, XIV. 86, 105
  History of European Morals, XIV. 104
  *History of the Spirit of Rationalism in
  Europe*, XIV. 104
  Leaders of Public Opinion in Ireland,
  XIV. 104
  Map of Life, The, XIV. 106
  Religious Tendencies of the Age, The,
  XIV. 104
  Memoir of, by his Wife, XIV. 104
Leclerk, George Louis. *See* Buffon, comte
  de
Le Clerc, Jean, or Johannes Clericus, VIII.
  472; IX. 336, 435, 495, 525; X. 177;
  Bibliothèque universelle, VIII. 330
L'Ecluse (Clusius), IV. 374
Leconte de Lisle, Charles-Marie, *L'Épée
  d'Angantyr*, X. 223; *Poèmes barbares*,
  X. 223
Lecount, Mrs, in Wilkie Collins's *No
  Name*, XIII. 437

Lediard, Thomas (1685–1743), x. 502;
    *History of the Reigns of William III and
    Mary, and Anne*, IX. 235; *Life of John
    Duke of Marlborough*, IX. 235; *Naval
    History of England*, IX. 235
Lee, Edward (1482?–1544), archbishop of
    York, III. 20, 42
Lee, Elizabeth, XIII. 565
Lee, Francis (1661–1719), IX. 307, 514,
    515
Lee, Harriet (1757–1851), XI. 306, 461
Lee, Sir Henry (1530–1610), IV. 113
Lee, Henry (*fl.* 1712), VIII. 347, 474
Lee, Miss Jane, v. 129, 135
Lee, John (1779–1859), XI. 469
Lee, John Edward (1808–1887), XII. 511;
    Imperial Profiles, XII. 346
Lee, Nathaniel (1653?–1692), VI. 49; VIII.
    16, 21, 30, 185 ff., 189, 190, 194, 235,
    395, 398, 400, 401, 437, 438; x. 67, 73
    Alexander the Great, VIII. 179
    Brutus, x. 82
    Caesar Borgia, VIII. 186
    Constantine the Great, VIII. 186
    Gloriana, VIII. 185
    Guise, Duke of (with Dryden), VIII. 16,
    30, 186
    Lucius Junius Brutus, VIII. 186, 187
    Massacre of Paris, The, VIII. 186
    Mithridates, King of Pontus, VIII. 185
    Nero, Emperour of Rome, VIII. 185
    Oedipus, King of Thebes (with Dryden),
    VIII. 30, 186
    Princesse of Cleve, The, VIII. 186
    Rival Queens, The, VIII. 185, 186, 261,
    426
    Theodosius, or the Force of Love, VIII. 186
Lee, Samuel (18th century bookseller),
    XI. 330
Lee, Samuel (1783–1852), XII. 341, 501;
    XIV. 593, 602
Lee, Sir Sidney, v. 165, 173, 225, 230,
    368; XI. 385, 447; *Elizabethan Sonnets*,
    IV. 24; *Memoir of George Smith*, XIV. 111
Lee, Sophia (1750–1824), XI. 306, 461
Lee, Sophia and Harriet, *Canterbury
    Tales*, XII. 37, 50
Lee, William (d. 1645), VII. 407
Lee, William (1869), IX. 13, 15 ff., 24, 418;
    XII. 522; XIV. 498
Lee Priory press, XII. 364, 520
Lee-Hamilton, Eugene (1845–1907), XIII.
    504
Leech, H. J., XIV. 508
Leech, John (*fl.* 1623), VII. 487
Leech, John (1817–1864), XIV. 201, 232,
    234, 236 ff., 541, 546 ff.
Leech-book, The, I. 106, 135, 136
Leeds, IX. 540; XI. 340, 341; XII. 274, 507,
    514; XIV. 112
Leeds, Yorkshire college, XIV. 432
Leeds Mercury, The, XIV. 169, 199, 529,
    533, 534
Leeds school, VII. 330
Lees, Abraham, x. 384
Leesehing, L F., XIV. 522

Leeu, Gerard, of Antwerp, II. 314, 319
    Chronicles of England, The, II. 319
    *Dialogue or communing between the wise
    king Solomon and Marcolphus*, II. 319
    History of Jason, The, II. 319
    History of Paris and Vienne, The, II.
    319
Leeward islands, x. 95
Lee-Warner, Sir William, XIV. 578
Le Fanu, Joseph Sheridan (1814–1873),
    XIII. 407; XIV. 309, 569
    *A Chapter in the History of a Tyrone
    Family*, XIII. 414
    Beatrice, XIV. 310
    House by the Churchyard, The, XIV. 310
    Legend of the Glaive, The, XIV. 310
    Phaudrig Crohoore, XIV. 310
    Purcell Papers, The, XIII. 414, 555, 556
    Room in the Dragon Volant, The, XIV.
    310
    Shamus O'Brien, XIV. 310
    Song of the Bottle, The, XIV. 310
    Uncle Silas, XIV. 310
    Watcher, The, and other Weird Stories,
    XIII. 414; XIV. 310
Le Fanu, W., XIV. 569
Lefebvre, Denys (Syned), XIV. Add. 5
Le Felure, VIII. 354
Le Fevre, in Sterne's *Tristram Shandy*,
    x. 54
Le Fèvre, Jean, III. 90
Lefèvre d'Étaples, Jacques, III. 20
Leffmann, H., XIII. 543
Lefroy, Edward Cracroft (1855–1891),
    XIII. 216, 504
Le Gallienne, Richard, XIII. 570
Legate, John (d. 1620), IV. 410
Legeay, U., XIV. 485
Legenda Aurea. See *Golden Legend* and
    Voragine
Legendaries, I. 317, 335 ff., 474. *See, also*,
    under various saints
Legendary, South English, I. 134, 335 ff.,
    340, 341
Légende de St Julien l'Hospitalier, IX. 39
Legendre, Adrien Marie, *Elements of
    Geometry and Trigonometry*, XIII. 4, 464
Leger, Augustin, *John Wesley's Last Love*,
    x. 368
Leges Edwardi Confessoris, VIII. 310, 465
Leges Henrici, VIII. 310, 311, 465
Leges Willelmi I, VIII. 310, 465
Legge, Cantrell, IV. 164, 410
Legge, George, 1st baron Dartmouth
    (1648–1691), VIII. 257
Legge, James (1815–1897), XII. 343, 500
Legge, Thomas (1535–1607), *Richardus
    Tertius*, v. 81, 82; VI. 301, 304, 327,
    475
Legge, William, 1st earl of Dartmouth
    (1672–1750), IX. 209, 216, 483
Legh, Gerard (d. 1563), *Accedens of
    Armory*, IV. 376, 543
Leghorn, x. 43; XII. 37, 38
Legion, *Smec*, in Butler's *Hudibras*, VIII.
    72

Legouis, Emile, XI. 410; XIII. 570; *The Early Life of Wordsworth*, XIII. 418

Legrand, Antoine, VII. 303, 474

Legrand, Jacques, *Le livre de bonnes meurs*, II. 315

Legrand, Joachim, IX. 197, 488; X. 160, 460

Le Grice, Charles Valentine (1773–1858), XII. 419

Le Grys, Sir Robert (d. 1635), IV. 501

Lehmann, Max, XIV. 92

Lehmann, Rudolph Chambers, XIII. 542; XIV. 537

Leibbrandt, Hendrick Carel Vos, XIV. Add. 8

Leibniz, Gottfried Wilhelm von, IV. 260, 292; VIII. 50, 300, 361; IX. 200, 290, 291, 297, 301, 400, 505; X. 220, 312; XIV. 8; *Annales imperii occidentis Brunsvicenses*, X. 311; *Nouveaux Essais*, VIII. 347; *Reflexions*, VIII. 347

Leicester, II. 67; III. 337; VII. 4, 340; IX. 91, 532; XI. 431; XII. 512

Leicester, earl of, in *Robert, Earle of Huntington*, V. 318, 324

Leicester, earls of. *See* Dudley, Robert; Sidney, Philip; Sidney, Robert

Leicester play, V. 391

Leicester's company, VI. 246, 249, 251, 383

Leicestershire, VI. 111; X. 159

Leicht, A., I. 102

Leigh, Sir Amyas, in *Westward Ho!* XIII. 364

Leigh, Augusta, XII. 34

Leigh, Edward (1602–1671), VII. 480, 484; *Advice on Travel*, VII. 314; *Critica Sacra*, VII. 319, 482, 490

Leigh, Elizabeth Medora, XII. 396

Leigh, George (*fl.* 1788), XI. 336

Leigh, Henry Sambrooke (1837–1883), XIII. 162, 505; XIV. 549

Leigh, John (1689–1726), VIII. 177

Leigh, Percival (*pseud.* Paul Prendergast, 1813–1889), XIII. 162, 505; XIV. 239, 549; *The Comic Latin Grammar*, XIV. 236

Leigh, Richard (b. 1649), VIII. 403

Leigh on Thames, IV. 91

Leighton, Alexander (1568–1649), VI. 403

Leighton, Robert (1611–1684), VIII. 298, 299, 460; IX. 193; XI. 415; XII. 283, 284

Leighton, Sir William (*fl.* 1603–1614), VII. 406

Leighton Ecclesia, prebend of, VII. 28

Leinster, VIII. 384

Leinster, Book of, XII. 362, 515

Leipzig, IV. 267; V. 284, 290; VII. 20, 21, 308; XII. 280

Leir, King, The True Chronicle History of, V. 83, 310, 399, 434; VI. 92

Leire, Danish royal residence, I. 27

Leith, siege of, III. 182

Leith, South, XI. 244

Leitrim, county, XIV. 355

Le Kain, Henri Louis, X. 264

Le Keux, John Henry, XII. 357

Lekpreuik, Robert (*fl.* 1561–1588), Scots printer, II. 126; III. 149; IV. 412; IX. 359

Leland or Leyland, John (1506?–1552), I. 131; II. 49, 399; III. 48, 54, 55, 313, 321, 328, 330, 468, 530; IV. 461; V. 103; IX. 345, 352, 534, 535, 541; *Collectanea*, III. 328; IX. 349; *Itinerary*, III. 328, 330; IV. 66, 308, 512; IX. 349; XII. 518; *Journey and Serche*, III. 329

Leland, John (1691–1766), IX. 502, 507; X. 520, 521

Leland, Thomas (1722–1785), *History of Ireland*, X. 293, 502

Lelia, in *The Captain*, VI. 122, 128

Le Long, Gautier, *La Veuve*, III. 88

Lely, Sir Peter (1618–1680), IX. 241

Lembcke, E., V. 307

Lemercier, N., v. 301

Le Moine, *Peintures Morales*, IV. 523

Lemoine, Henry (1756–1812), XI. 472

Lemon, Mark (1809–1870), XI. 387, 487; XIII. 516; XIV. 236, 238, 548, 549

Lemoyne, P., *Saint Louis*, VII. 268

'Lend me Half-a-Crown,' X. 206

Le Neve, John (1679–1741), IX. 536; *Fasti Ecclesiae Anglicanae*, XII. 355, 516

Le Neve, Peter (1661–1729), IX. 353, 358

Leng, Sir John (1828–1906), XIV. 534

Leng, Sir William Christopher (1825–1902), XIV. 534

Lennox, in Barbour's *Bruce*, II. 107

Lennox, Charles, 3rd duke of Richmond, XI. 36

Lennox, Charlotte (1720–1804), X. 467, 469; XI. 462; XIII. 561; *The Female Quixote*, X. 175, 468; *Shakespear Illustrated*, X. 175; *The Sister*, XI. 275

Lennox, earls of. *See* Stewart, Esmé; Stewart, Matthew

Lennox, lord William Pitt (1799–1881), XIII. 563; XIV. 238

Le Noir, Elizabeth Anne (1755?–1841), XII. 450

Lent, in Christmas carol, II. 379

Lenthall, William (1591–1662), VII. 190, 439, 443

Lenz, V. 298, 303

Leo IV, pope, I. 88

Leo X, pope, IV. 334; XIV. 99

Leo XII, pope, XIV. 54

Leo, emperor, II. 115

Leo Africanus (Leo, John), IV. 445

Leofric (d. 1072), 1st bishop of Exeter, I. 151; IV. 422

Leon, count Reginald de St, XI. 394

Leonard, St, V. 97

Leonardo da Vinci, XII. 187

Leoni, Michele, V. 306

Leonid shooting stars, XIV. 264

Leonides, Nicolaus, III. 6

Leonora, in Fielding's *Joseph Andrews*, X. 30

Leonora, in *The Devils Law-case*, VI. 183, 187

Leonora, in *The Gratefull Servant*, VI. 204

Leonora, in *The Parliament of Love*, VI. 154

Leonore, in *The Gamester*, VI. 202

Leontes, in *The Winter's Tale*, v. 206

Leontius, in *The Humorous Lieutenant*, VI. 122

Leopardi, count Giacomo, XII. 72, 393, 395, 396, 402, 405, 525; XIII. 489

Leopold, prince, of Coburg, XII. 232

Leosthenes, in *The Bond-Man*, VI. 155, 158

Leoven, my Lady of, VI. 291

Lepanto, XII. 38

Lepell, Mary. *See* Hervey, lady Mary

Lepidus, I. 95

Lepointe, E. L., XIII. 469

Leprohon, Rosanna Elenora (1832–1879), XIV. 581, 582; *Antoinette de Mirecourt*, XIV. 360

Lerici, XII. 37

Leroy, Loys (*dit* Regius), IV. 3, 5

Le Sage, Alain-René, VIII. 162; IX. 35 x. 17, 216; XII. 168; *Gil Blas*, X. 37, 420

Le Sage, J. M., XIV. 191

Lesbia, in *The Returne from Pernassus*, VI. 311

Lesbia (Catullus's), VII. 2, 9

Lescarbot, M., IV. 456

Lescurel, Jehannot de, XIII. 211

Leslie, Alexander, 1st earl of Leven (1580?–1661), VII. 22

Leslie, Charles (1650–1722), IX. 11, 475, 507, 564; X. 355, 356; *Rehearsal*, IX. 5; *Short and Easy Method*, IX. 289; *Snake in the Grass*, IX. 201, 520

Leslie, Charles Robert (1794–1859), XII. 380

Leslie, Forbes, XII. 511

Leslie or Lesley, John (1527–1596), bishop of Ross, II. 285, 398, 415; *De Origine, Moribus et Rebus Scotorum*, III. 154, 155, 504

Leslie, Mary E., XIV. 339, 578

Leslie, Thomas Edward Cliffe (1827?–1882), XIV. 475; *Essays in Political Economy*, XIV. 36

Lesse, Nicholas (*fl.* 1550), IV. 441

Lessing, Gotthold Ephraim, IV. 265, 267; V. 287, 288, 290, 293 ff., 300, 463; VI. 82; VIII. 172, 430; IX. 61, 450, 466; XI. 121, 449; XII. 526, 527; *Laocoon*, XI. 3; *Minna von Barnhelm*, XI. 262; *Miss Sara Sampson*, X. 76, 79

Lessingham, Mrs, XI. 451

Lessius (1564–1623), VII. 402

Lester, John Ashby, v. 63

L'Estrange, Alfred Guy, XIII. 565

L'Estrange, Hamon (1605–1660), VII. 445, 446, 447

L'Estrange, Sir Roger (1616–1704), VII. 197, 363 ff., 390, 416, 496, *also see* Add.; VIII. 68, 387, 388, 412, 445, 481; IX. 2 ff., 265, 273 ff., 415 ff., XI. 312, 313, 331, 466; XIV. 461
   Bona's *Guide to Eternity*, IX. 274
   Colloquies of Erasmus, IX. 273 ff.
   Considerations...Regulation of the Press IX. 2
   Discourse of the Fishery, IX. 3
   Fables and Storyes Moralized, IX. 4

L'Estrange, Sir Roger
   Fables of Æsop, IX. 4, 275
   Intelligencer, The, VII. 365
   Josephus, IX. 273, 275
   L'Estrange his Apology, IX. 2
   News, The, VII. 365
   No Blinde Guides, IX. 2
   Observator, The, VII. 365; IX. 3, 4
   Seneca's Morals, IX. 273, 275
   Spanish Decameron, IX. 274
   Tully's Offices, IX. 274
   Visions of Quevedo, IX. 3, 274

Le Sueur, Gordon, XIV. Add. 8

Le Tourneur, Pierre Félicien, v. 292, 293, 296, 301

Let us a' to the Bridal, IX. 379

Leti, Gregorio, X. 291

Letter concerning Libels, Warrants, etc., X. 399

Letter from a Blacksmith, XI. 216

Letter from a friend of the universities, IX. 411

Letter from Avignon, IX. 218

Letter to a schoolmaster in the country, A, XIV. 398

Letter to Henry Brougham...from an M.A. of Queen's College, Oxford, XIV. 407

Letter to...Lord John Russell, A, XIV. 416

Letter to The Public Advertiser, X. 399

Letters between the Hon. Andrew Erskine and James Boswell, Esq., X. 191

Letters from a Tutor to his Pupils, XI. 371

Letters from Corsica, XIV. 180

Letters of the Insurgent Leaders, II. 432, 434

Letters, private and domestic, in Jacobean times, VII. 438, 439

Letters...to Sir Joseph Williamson, IX. 212

Letton, John (*fl.* 1480), II. 318; VIII. 314

Leucippus, in *Cupid's Revenge*, VI. 128

Leusden, Jan, IV. 47

Levant, the, IV. 67, 80, 84, 98; VII. 201

Levant company, VII. 308

Levantine traveller, in *The Fair Maid Of The West*, VI. 102

Le Vayer, François de la Mothe, *Liberty and Servitude*, VIII. 246

Leve, Antoine De, *Testament of*, III. 483

Levellers, the, VII. 190

Leven, loch, XI. 244

Leven, vale of, X. 36

Lever, Charles James (1806–1872), XIII. 307; XIV. 255, 314, 569; *Cornelius O'Dowd*, XIV. 313; *Lord Kilgobbin*, XIV. 313

Lever, Christopher (*fl.* 1627), VII. 406

Lever or Leaver, Ralph (d. 1585), *Arte of Reason rightly termed Witcraft*, VII. 276, 474

Lever, Robert (*fl.* 1641), VII. 342

Lever or Leaver, Thomas (1521–1577), III. 419, 473; IV. 232, 233, 493

Leverrier, Urbain J. J., XIV. 264

Leveson-Gower, Granville George, 2nd earl Granville (1815–1891), XIV. 131, 510

Levett, Robert (1701?–1782), X. 187, 465, 467, 479

Levey, R. M., XIII. 515
Levi, Leone (1821–1888), XIV. 475
Levi-Lawson family, XIV. 191
Levidolche, in *The Ladies Triall*, VI. 194
Levins, Peter, III. 555
Levis, Howard L., XIV. 541
Levison, Sir Richard, VII. 438
Levitt, William, VII. 515
Levy, Amy (1861–1889), XIII. 181, 505
Levy, Joseph Moses (1812–1888), XIV. 534
Lévy-Bruhl, L., XIV. 477
Lewes, battle of, I. 368
Lewes, George Henry (1817–1878), V. 276; XIII. 391, 393, 396, 401, 513, 515, 516, 558; XIV. 171, 199, 475, 504
　Aristotle, XIV. 32
　Biographical History of Philosophy, The, XIV. 32, 113
　Comte's Philosophy of the Sciences, XIV. 32
　Foundations of a Creed, The, XIV. 33
　Life of Goethe, XIII. 385; XIV. 113
　On Actors and Acting, XIII. 257
　Problems of Life and Mind, XIV. 33
Lewine, J., XIV. 541
Lewinsky (German actor), V. 306
Lewis, Charles Lee, XIII. 552
Lewis, David (1683?–1760), IX. 188, 436, 445; *Miscellany*, X. 145; *My Winifreda*, XII. 139
Lewis, Erasmus (1670–1754), IX. 103, 456
Lewis, Sir George Cornewall (1806–1863), XII. 301, 310, 311, 426, 498
　Astronomy of the Ancients, XII. 339
　Credibility of Early Roman History, XII. 305, 339
　Essays on the administration of Great Britain, 1864, XI. 396
　'Legislation for the Working Class,' XII. 153
Lewis, John (1675–1747), II. 54; IX. 536
Lewis, Leopold David (1828–1890), XIII. 520
Lewis, Matthew Gregory ('Monk' Lewis) (1775–1818), I. 287; X. 223; XI. 160, 283, 286, 300, 303 ff., 414, 458, 462; XIII. 260, 264; *Alonzo the Brave*, XI. 304; *Monk, The*, XI. 303, 304; XIII. 418 *Tales of Wonder*, XI. 5, 373, 405
Lewis, William Thomas (1748?–1811), XI. 260
'Lewis Baboon' (Louis XIV), XIV. 212
Lewis of Bavaria, I. 212
Lewis de Bretaylles, II. 313
Lewis the Pious, I. 47
Lewkenor, Lewis, IV. 443
Lewte, in *Piers the Plowman*, II. 10, 25, 32
Lex Ecclesiae, in *The Passetyme of Pleasure*, II. 226
Lexicon rhetoricum Cantabrigiense, XII. 328
Leybourn, William (1626–1700?), IV. 459; VII. 509
Leycester, Sir Peter (1614–1678), IX. 536
Leyden, IV. 402; VII. 233, 307, 308, 310, 322; IX. 290; XIV. 282, 290

Leyden, John (1775–1811), XI. 444; XII. 5, 419; XIV. 334, 578
　Cout of Keeldar, The, XI. 242
　Lord Soulis, XI. 242
　Mermaid, The, XI. 242; XII. 133
　Ode to an Indian Gold Coin, XIV. 335, 340
　Ode to Scottish Music, XI. 242
　Scenes of Infancy, XI. 242; XII. 133
Leyden riddle, I. 61
Leyden, university, VIII. 347; X. 21, 22, 200, 390
Leyds, Willem Johannes, XIV. Add. 8
Leyland, Francis A., XIII. 557, 558
Leyser, Polycarp, XIII. 172
Lhwyd, Edward (1660–1709), IX. 412, 536
Liancourt, duc de, X. 66
Liar, in *Piers the Plowman*, II. 8
Libanius, VI. 22
Libeanus Desconus, or *Sir Libeanus*, or *Libius Disconius*, I. 282, 284, 289, 295, 312, 469
Libel of English Policy, The, II. 423, 424; IV. 67, 84
'Libell' (Otway's), VIII. 94, 95
Liber Hymnorum (Irish), XII. 362
Liber Monstrorum, I. 26
Liber Niger Domus Regis, VI. 279, 280
Liber Vagatorum, XIII. 428
Liberal, Letitia, XIV. 591
Liberal, The, XII. 36, 37, 389, 391, 392
Liberal Theology, The Growth of, XII. 464 ff.
Liberate Rolls, XII. 355, 516
Liberton, II. 110
Liberty, in *Cooper's Hill*, VII. 60
Liberty, in Thomson's poem, X. 104, 107
Liberty vindicated against slavery, VII. 388
Libido, in *Psychomachia*, V. 51
Libius Disconius, X. 233
Libraries, the foundation of, IV. 415 ff., 549 ff.
Library of Entertaining Knowledge, The, XIV. 409
Library of the Fine Arts, The, XIV. 539
Library of the Fathers, The, XII. 274, 454
Library of Useful Knowledge, The, XIV. 409
Licensing act (1662), VIII. 89, 90; XI. 312
Licensing act (1737), X. 23, 24; XI. 335
Licensing act, IX. 5
Licentiousness of the Times, The, VIII. 90
Lichfield, IV. 225, 421, 472; V. 38; VII. 278; IX. 196, 530; X. 158 ff.; XI. 340; XII. 124, 328; XIII. 449
Lichfield, Henry, IV. 464
Lichfield, John, IV. 411
Lichfield, Nicholas, IV. 442, 448
Lichfield school, VII. 330
Lichtenberg, G. C., IX. 467
Lichtounis Dreme, II. 277, 278
Liddell, Henry George (1811–1898), XII. 333, 487
Liddesdale, XII. 4, 19
Liddon, Henry Parry (1829–1890), XII. 254, 273, 454, 457, 458, 462
Lidia, in *The Great Duke of Florence*, VI. 156, 158, 163, 164

Lidius, in *The Lovers Progress*, VI. 131

Liebermann, Felix, XIV. 494

Liège, II. 80 ff.

Lien Chi Altangi, X. 206, 207

Lieven, princess, XIV. 115, 172

Life, in *Death and Life*, II. 40

Life, king of, in *The Pride of Life*, v. 2

Life (lady Anima), in *Piers the Plowman*, II. 19, 21, 22, 28

Life, in *The Playe of Playes and Pastimes*, VI. 391

Life in London (Catnach's), XIV. 227

Life in Paris, XIV. 225

Life of James the Second, IX. 213; X. 295

Liggan Waters, The, IX. 363

Light Green, The, XIV. 206

'Light Within,' the, VIII. 105, 110, 112

Lightfoot, John (1602–1675), VII. 319, 482, 490

Lightfoot, Joseph Barber (1828–1889), XII. 298, 340, 468, 501

Lighthall, William Douw, XIV. 582

Lightwood, James T., XIII. 544

Ligon, Richard, *History of Barbadoes*, XI. 280

Lilburne, John (1614?–1657), VII. 456, 458, 459, 509; VIII. 75

Lilius Giraldus, II. 160

Lilley, Alfred Leslie, XIV. 601

Lilliburlero, X. 233

Lillie, Charles (*fl.* 1725), IX. 56

Lilliput, IX. 104, 128

Lilliput, Account of the state of learning in the Empire of, IX. 132

Lilliputian Magazine, The, XI. 376

Lillo, George (1693–1739), VII. 176; X. 68, 73 ff., 92, 436

    Arden of Feversham, X. 78, 84

    Britannia and Batavia, X. 78

    Christian Hero, The, X. 77

    Elmerick, or Justice Triumphant, X. 78

    Fatal Curiosity, X. 77, 79, 80, 83, 84, 414, 429

    London Merchant, or The History of George Barnwell, IX. 163; X. 73 ff., 78 ff., 84

    Marina, X. 78

    Silvia, X. 73

Lilly, William (1602–1681), VII. 357, 369, 394, 446, 447, 501, 509; *Observations*, VII. 207, 510

Lilly, W. S., XII. 459; XIII. 492

Lily, William (1468?–1522), III. 11, 13, 14, 67, 72, 429, 468, 552; IV. 322; VII. 335; *Eton Latin Grammar*, II. 367; III. 12; *Latin Syntax*, VII. 332; IX. 384

Limber Magna, Lincolnshire, I. 343

Limborch, Philip van, VIII. 330

Limerick, X. 293; XIII. 364; XIV. 127, 311

'Limerick,' the, XIII. 163

Linacre, Thomas (1460?–1524), II. 367; III. 2, 3, 5, 6, 7, 11, 12, 13, 15, 20, 158, 468, 469, 532; IV. 428; *Grammar*, III. 158

Linche or Lynche, Richard (*fl.* 1596–1601), *Diella*, III. 256, 266, 523

Lincke, O., XIII. 465

Lincoln, II. 49, 57, 116, 307, 341, 344, 348, 358; IV. 190, 224, 228, 369, 382, 422, 428; v. 39, 48, 50, 56; VII. 280, 338; X. 387; XII. 180, 329, 330, 340, 507

Lincoln, Abraham, IV. 50

Lincoln, countess of. *See* Lacy, Margaret de

Lincoln, earl of. *See* Clinton, Henry Fiennes

Lincoln, earl of, the mad lord, VIII. 380

Lincoln castle, in *Havelok*, I. 351

Lincoln cathedral, VII. 28

Lincoln grammar school, IV. 275

Lincolnshire, v. 30, 32, 33; VI. 82; VII. 330; XIII. 23, 46; XIV. 101

Lincolnshire, Rebellion in (1470), II. 302, 482

Lincus, in *The Queenes Arcadia*, VI. 318

Lindelöf, I. 132

Lindesay or Lindsay, Robert, of Pitscottie (1500?–1565?), *The Historie and Cronicles of Scotland*, II. 285; III. 147, 148, 504

Lindisfarne, I. 5, 83, 86, 89; XII. 10

Lindisfarne Gospels, The, I. 14, 72, 132

Lindley, John (1799–1865), XIV. 290, 562

Lindsay, lady Anne. *See* Barnard, lady Anne

Lindsay, James Ludovic, earl of Crawford (1847–1914), XII. 521; XIV. 541

Lindsay, lord, in Scott's *Abbot*, XII. 27

Lindsay family, XI. 231

Lindsays of Balcarres, the, XII. 377

Lindsey, Theophilus (1723–1808), X. 380, 519

Lingard, John (1771–1851), VII. 356; XIV. 52 ff., 71, 492; *Antiquities of the Anglo-Saxon Church*, XIV. 53; *History of England*, XIV. 53 ff.; *Vindication, A*, XIV. 54

Linger, Sir John, in Swift's *Complete Collection of...Conversation*, IX. 107

Linlathen, IX. 328

Linley, Elizabeth Anne, afterwards Mrs Sheridan (1754–1792), X. 88

Linley, Thomas (1732–1795), X. 265

Linlithgow, III. 123; IX. 552

Linnaean society, XIV. 287, 566

Linnaean system, XIV. 287, 290

Linnaeus (Carl Linné), X. 135; XIV. 287

Linnell, John (1792–1882), XI. 432

Linschoten, John Huighhen van, IV. 78, 460

Linskill, Mary (1840–1891), XIII. 563

Linton, in Emily Brontë's *Wuthering Heights*, XIII. 411

Linton, A., IV. 459

Linton, Elizabeth Lynn (born Lynn) (1822–1898), XIII. 563; XIV. 198

Linton, Kent, X. 249

Linton, William James (1812–1898), XII. 424; XIII. 186, 505; *A Dream*, XIII. 187; *Epicurean*, XIII. 187

Lintot, Barnaby Bernard (1675–1736), IX. 162, 445, 446; XI. 318, 320 ff., 327, 335, 471; *Miscellaneous Poems and Translations*, IX. 70, 160; XI. 320; *Monthly Catalogue*, XI. 339

Lintot, Henry (1703–1758), XI. 323
Linwood, William (1817–1878), XII. 487
Linz, IV. 163
Lion and the Mouse, in Henryson's *Fables*, II. 246
'Lion of the fold of Judah, The,' XIV. 329
Lion, The book of the, II. 160, 161
Lionardi, Alessandro, *Dialogi della Inventione Poetica*, IX. 60
Lionel, duke of Clarence, son of Edward III (1338–1368), II. 156, 170
Lionel, Sir, II. 414
Lipscomb, George (1773–1846), XII. 511
Lipsius, Justus, IV. 248, 250, 260; VI. 9; VII. 261, 315
Lisbon, X. 35, 91, 466; XI. 155, 156
Lisbon inquisition, III. 16
Liskeard, X. 306
Lisle, William (1569?–1637), I. 123, 442; IX. 536
Lismahago, captain, in Smollett's *Humphrey Clinker*, X. 38, 43
Lismore's Book, the Dean of, X. 488
Lisobeta, in *The Decameron*, XII. 82
Lissoy, in Westmeath, X. 196, 209, 212
List of goods for Sale, VIII. 99
Lister, Joseph Lister, lord, XIII. 213
Lister, Martin (1638?–1712), IX. 139, 478
Lister, Thomas Henry (1800–1842), *Granby*, XII. 247, 450
Litany, the, III. 30 ff.; VI. 407
Litchfield, William (d. 1447), II. 497
Literary club, the, X. 91, 181, 207
Literary Garland, The, XIV. 360
Literary Gazette, The, XII. 348, 523; XIV. 177, 199
Literary Journal, The, XII. 301
Literary Magazine, X. 177, 181, 203, 463, 466
Literary Miscellany (Ollier's), XII. 74
Literature of dissent, the (1660–1760), X. Add.
Lithgow, William (1582–1645?), IX. 366, 555
Lithuanians, rebel, in *Brennoralt*, VI. 238
Little, A. G., *Grey Friars at Oxford*, I. 209, 210. *See, also*, Add. to third impression
Little, Richard, *Mercurius Academicus*, VII. 351
Little Easton, Essex, VIII. 307
Little Endians, IX. 229
Little Gidding, IV. 406, 548; VII. 32, 34, 153 ff.; XIII. 435
Little Gidding story books, VII. 154, 427
Little Horkesley, Essex, VII. 58
Little John, in legend of Robin Hood, II. 110, 402; V. 35, 108; XII. 3
Little Leighs park, Essex, VIII. 268, 269
Little Musgrave and Lady Barnard, II. 412
Little Pretty Pocket Book, XI. 376
Little Sister, in Thackeray's *Adventures of Philip*, XIII. 288, 299
Little Sodbury, III. 39
Littlebury, Isaac, VII. 451
Littledale, H., XIII. 477
Littlemore, Oxfordshire, XII. 260, 261

Littleton, Adam (1627–1694), IX. 527
Littleton, Edward John, 1st baron Hatherton (1791–1863), XIV. 323
Littleton, Sir Thomas (1402–1481), II. 497; VIII. 315; *Tenures*, VIII. 314, 317, 466
Littlewit, in *Bartholomew Fayre*, VI. 23
Litton, Edward Arthur, XII. 472
Lively, Edward (1545?–1605), VII. 317
Liverpool, XI. 338; XIII. 89, 103, 348, 372 XIV. 115, 122, 134, 414
Liverpool, earl of. *See* Jenkinson, Robert Banks
Liverpool, University college, XIV. 432
Liverpool Athenaeum, XI. 435
Liverpool Courant, The, XIV. 169
Lives of the English Saints, XIV. 83
Livia, in *Women beware Women*, VI. 78
Livia (Lyly's), III. 346
Livingston, Luther S., XII. 434
Livingstone, Christian, VII. 253
Livingstone, David (1813–1873), XIII. 553; XIV. 253, 375, 552, *also see* Add. 8
Livingstone, Guy, in Lawrence's novel, XIII. 436
Livingstone, James, 1st earl of Callander (d. 1674), IX. 556
Livingstone, John (1603–1672), IX. 546
Livingstone, Michael (*fl.* 1680), IX. 556
Livio, in *The Fancies*, VI. 193, 194
Livy, III. 131, 156, 164, 314, 337, 429, 432; IV. 1, 4, 6, 13, 15, 438; VI. 49, 182, 225; X. 119, 197; XII. 493; XIV. 91, 98, 106
Lizie Wan, II. 412
Llanbedr, XII. 440
Llandaff, IV. 421; IX. 540
Llangattock, VII. 37
Llangynwyd, X. 386, 387
Llansantffread, VII. 37, 42
Llongborth (viz. Portsmouth), I. 250
Lloyd, Charles (1735–1773), X. 399, 523, 526
Lloyd, Charles (1775–1839), XI. 413, 417; XII. 187, 419, 434, 436, 438; XIV. 184; *Blank Verse, by Charles Lloyd and Charles Lamb*, XII. 184; *Edmund Oliver*, XII. 185; *Nugae Canorae*, XII. 194
Lloyd, David (1635–1692), IX. 493·
Statesmen and Favourites of England, IV. 54
Lloyd, Edward (1745), XI. 78
Lloyd, Edward (1815–1890), XIV. 192, 193, 534
Lloyd, Lodowick (*fl.* 1573–1610), III. 189
Lloyd, Lucy C., XIV. Add. 8
Lloyd, Pierson, X. 394
Lloyd, Robert (1733–1764), X. 394, 395, 455, 524
Lloyd, Robert, XII. 181, 185, 193
Lloyd, William (1627–1717), VIII. 297; IX. 196, 329, 335, 527
Lloyd's Illustrated London Newspaper, XIV. 192
Lloyd's Weekly London Newspaper, XIV. 192, 530, 533, 534
Lloyd's Weekly Newspaper, XIV. 192, 193

Lluð and Llevelys, I. 252
Lluelyn, Martin (1616–1682), IV. 497
Llwyd, Humphrey (1527–1568), III. 531;
  IV. 436, 445
Llwyd, Morgan (1619–1659), IX. 514
Llwynllwyd, X. 386
Llŷr, I. 252, 255. *See, also,* Lear
Llywarch Hen (496?–646?), I. 248, 249,
  275, 461
Llywelyn, in Mannyng, I. 351
Llywelyn, prince of Wales, I. 180
Llywelyn ap Gruffuð (d. 1282), I. 263
Lobb, Stephen (d. 1699), X. 377, 386
Lobb, Theophilus (1678–1763), X. 385
Lobban, John Hay, XI. 473; XIII. 476
Lobeira, Vasco de, IV. 445; *Amadis of
  Gaul*, XI. 422
L'Obel, Matthias de, IV. 374
Löber, Valentine, IV. 266
Lobo, Jerome, X. 160, 179, 460
Locabara, X. 237
Local Education authorities, XIV. 433
Locher, Jacob, III. 59, 60
Lochlee, IX. 372
Lochleven castle, XII. 27
Lochlin, king of, X. 231
Lochmaben Gate, IX. 377
Lochnagar, XII. 31
Locke, Alton, Kingsley's, XIII. 156, 160
Locke, John (1632–1704), VII. 266, 300,
  301, 396; VIII. 295, 328–348 (main
  entry), 367, 372, 384, 472 ff., *also see*
  Add.; IX. 61, 146, 150, 159, 180, 181,
  233, 279, 282, 283, 286, 287, 292, 293,
  297 ff., 301, 314, 331, 388, 390, 406,
  412, 569, 574; X. 122, 296, 324 ff., 332,
  342 ff., 347 ff., 350, 378, 379, 385; XI.
  22, 57, 65, 136; XIV. 8, 17, 41, 43, 383,
  384, 391 ff., 397, 399, 405, 421, 428,
  461, 472, 473
  Commentary on the Pauline epistles,
    VIII. 332
  Common-Place Book, VIII. 344
  Conduct of the Understanding, The, VIII.
    332, 346; IX. 400
  Discourse on Miracles, VIII. 332
  Epistola de Tolerantia, VIII. 330, 331
  *Essay concerning Human Understand-
    ing,* VIII. 328, 330 ff., 336, 346, 347;
    IX. 58, 282, 285, 290, 393, 400, 401, 411;
    XIV. 16, 48
  *Examination of Father Malebranche's
    Opinion of Seeing all things in God, An,*
    VIII. 332
  *Further Considerations on Value of
    Money,* VIII. 332, 344
  Letter on Toleration, First, VIII. 344
  Letter on Toleration, Second, VIII. 331
  Letter on Toleration, Third, VIII. 331
  Letter on Toleration, fragment of a
    fourth, VIII. 332
  Letter to the Bishop of Worcester, VIII.
    331
  Letters on Toleration, X. 372
  Reasonableness of Christianity, The, VIII.
    332; IX. 289, 290

Locke, John
  *Some Considerations of the Consequences
    of the Lowering of Interest,* VIII. 332, 344
  Some Thoughts concerning Education,
    VII. 341; VIII. 332, 346; IX. 396 ff.;
    XIV. 396
  Two Treatises of Government, VIII. 331,
    341
  Vindication, A, VIII. 332
Locke, Matthew (1630?–1677), *Psyche,*
  VIII. 135
Locke, owner of Norbury Park, X. 261
Locker, John (1693–1760), IX. 529
Locker-Lampson, Frederick (1821–1895),
  XII. 121; XIII. 505, 558
  London Lyrics, XIII. 163
  My Guardian Angel, XIII. 165
  My Neighbour Rose, XIII. 165
  Our Photographs, XIII. 165
  Patchwork, XIII. 163, 164
  To My Grandmother, XIII. 164
Lockhart, Charles Stewart Montgomery
  XII. 380
Lockhart, George (1673–1731), IX. 493
Lockhart, John Gibson (1794–1854), IV.
  45; XI. 166, 305, 410, 419, 437, 439,
  440, 459, *also see* Add.; XII. 2, 7, 10,
  19, 20, 26, 28, 153, 154, 156 ff., 161 ff.,
  372, 373, 376, 377, 380, 384, 425, 429,
  430, 433, 449, *also see* Add. 2; XIII. 25,
  207, 353, 434, 477, 563; XIV. 233, 313,
  327, 491, 504
  History of Napoleon, XIV. 106
  History of the late War, XIV. 106
  Life of Scott, XIV. 106, 278
  Peter's Letters to his Kinsfolk, XII. 158
  Valerius, XIII. 419
Lockhart, John Hugh, XII. 375, 376
Lockhart, Laurence William Maxwel
  (1831–1882), XIII. 563
Lockhart, Milton, XII. 430
Lockier, Lionel, VII. 518
Lockit, in Gay's *Beggar's Opera,* IX. 163
Lockwood, in Emily Brontë's *Wuthering
  Heights,* XIII. 411
Lockwood, Edward, XIV. 598
Lockwood, Sir Frank (1846–1897), XIII. 544
Lockyer, Sir Norman, XIII. 477
Lockyer, Winifred L., XIII. 477
Locrine, V. 84 ff., 129, 146, 152, 236,
  238 ff., 398, 417, 442, 443
Loda, spirit of, X. 228, 229
Lodge, Thomas (1558?–1625), I. 298; III.
  114, 198, 249, 251, 256, 261, 262, 265,
  299, 340, 342, 350, 351, 355, 358, 363,
  367, 370, 526, 534; IV. 2, 6, 24, 25, 86,
  116 ff., 121, 122, 139, 318, 437, 440,
  444, 470, 471, 473, 516, 517, 519, 521,
  523, 528; V. 71, 85, 121–141 (main
  entry), 322, 353, 371, 420, 431; VI. 40,
  249, 250, 378, 409, 494; IX. 275
  Alarum against Usurers, An, III. 363;
    IV. 317, 512; VI. 392
  Barginet of Antimachus, VII. 2
  *Defence of Poetry, Music and Stage-
    Playes, A,* VI. 389, 391, 401

Lodge, Thomas
  Euphues Shadow, III. 350; v. 139
  'Fatall starre that at my birthday
    shined, The,' IV. 116
  Fig for Momus, A, IV. 180, 328, 329;
    v. 139; XII. 515
  Forbonius and Prisceria, III. 358; v. 139
  Honest Excuses, VI. 379
  'Like desart woods,' IV. 116
  *Looking Glasse for London and England,
    A*, v. 134, 139
  Margarite of America, III. 358; IV. 77,
    118; v. 139
  'My bonnie Lasse thine eie,' IV. 117
  Phyllis, III. 262, 523; IV. 116, 118; v. 139
  Prosopopeia, IV. 357
  *Robert, Second Duke of Normandy,
    Surnamed Robin the Divell*, v. 139
  Rosalynde, III. 355, 358; IV. 77, 118;
    v. 139, 193, 220; VI. 365, 389
  Scillaes Metamorphosis, v. 139, 140
  Seneca, IX. 265
  Tragical Complaynt of Elstred, The,
    III. 198; v. 239
  William Longbeard, III. 367; v. 139
  Wounds of Civill War, The, v. 139; VI.
    19
Lodovico, in *The White Divel*, VI. 176, 177
Lodwick, in *Edward III*, v. 244
Lodowick, in *The Gratefull Servant*, VI. 204
Loe, William (d. 1645), VII. 407
Lofft, Capel, the younger (1806–1873),
  XIII. 505
Lofsong of ure Lefdi, On, I. 232, 458
Lofsong of ure Louerde, On, I. 233, 459
Loftus, Adam (1533?–1605), archbishop of
  Armagh and Dublin, III. 426
Loftus, Smyth, *Reply to the Reasonings of
  Mr Gibbon*, X. 308, 507
Lofty, in *The Good-Natur'd Man*, X. 211,
  212
Logan, George (1678–1755), IX. 561, 562
Logan, James (1794?–1872), XII. 511;
  Clans of the Scottish Highlands, XII. 350;
  The Scottish Gael, XII. 350
Logan, John (1748–1788), IX. 557; XI.
  442, 444; *Braes of Yarrow, The*, XI. 244;
  Cuckoo, The, XI. 244; *Runnamede*, XI.
  244
Logan, Sir Robert, of Restalrig (d. 1606),
  IX. 551
Logan Water, IX. 363
Logan Water, XI. 235
Logic, in *The Passetyme of Pleasure*, II. 225
Logic, Bob, in Egan's *Life in London*,
  XIV. 223, 224, 226, 230
Logic land, in *The Pilgrimage to Par-
  nassus*, VI. 310
Logie, Margaret, II. 129
Logres, in Arthurian legend, I. 279
Lohenstein, Daniel Caspar von, III. 348
Loir, river, X. 282; XIV. 302
Lok or Lock, Henry (1553?–1608?), III.
  523; IV. 159; *Sundrie Sonets of Christian
  Passions*, III. 271
Lok, Michael (*fl.* 1615), IV. 82, 84, 459

Loliée, Frédéric, XIII. 567
Lollards, I. 364, 371; II. 40, 43, 47, 49, 53,
  57, 62, 63, 66 ff., 162, 288, 289, 290,
  292 ff., 348, 422, 441 ff.; III. 25, 26, 45;
  XIV. 83
Lollards, An Apology for the, II. 49
Lollards, poems against, II. 443, 502
Lollio, in Hall's *Virgidemiarum*, IV. 331
Lollius, in Chaucer's *Troilus and Criseyde*,
  II. 172
Lomas, Mrs S. C., VII. 189, 190, 434
Lomazzo, G. P., IV. 445
Lombard, Peter (*c.* 1100–1164), Master of
  the Sentences, I. 201, 211, 212; II. 46,
  350, 365, 366, 371; *Sentences*, I. 208;
  II. 350, 365; III. 50, 400; VII. 405
Lombards, the, v. 24, 248
Lombards, the, in *Confessio Amantis*, II.
  148
Lombardy, VIII. 245; XII. 63
Lombart, Pierre (1620?–1681), VII. 487
Londesborough, XII. 509
London, II. 302, 318, 320, 322, 496, 505,
  508; III. 3, 15, 18, 40, 63, 71, 183, 213,
  244, 267, 316, 317, 321, 330, 359 ff.,
  367 ff., 371, 379, 381 ff., 386, 393, 395,
  396, 399, 406, 427, 436, 440; IV. 3, 76,
  80 ff., 98, 106, 151, 154 ff., 161, 168,
  190, 191, 198, 202 ff., 207, 224, 233,
  243, 253, 255, 292, 293, 300, 310, 311,
  316 ff., 321, 323 ff., 327, 328, 334, 338,
  341 ff., 349, 360 ff., 378 ff., 402, 407 ff.,
  424 ff., 514 ff., 531 ff., 544 ff.; v. 30, 35,
  38, 44, 57, 68 ff., 80, 104, 110, 128,
  134, 139, 143, 166, 169 ff., 248, 253 ff.,
  290, 293, 306, 310, 312, 316, 320 ff.,
  325, 330, 342, 353, 358, 361, 366 ff.,
  371, 376, 378; VI. 4, 13, 15, 16, 23, 27,
  28, 50, 52 ff., 60, 72, 92, 104, 107, 110,
  134, 135, 141, 149, 151, 196, 201, 211,
  220, 233, 242, 243, 249 ff., 259 ff., 281,
  323, 330 ff., 345, 362, 365, 376, 378,
  381 ff., 386 ff., 397 ff., 400; VII. 6, 7, 9,
  54, 78, 88, 91, 98, 120, 151, 157, 183,
  188, 190, 200, 201, 227, 230, 283, 284,
  286, 287, 289, 305, 314, 322, 343, 346,
  348, 379, 380, 383, 437, 453; VIII. 3 ff.,
  12, 37, 53, 60, 81, 83, 89, 94, 108, 113,
  117, 118, 122, 127, 134, 160, 170, 180,
  182, 187, 190, 210, 247, 249, 250, 263,
  265, 286, 297, 301, 302, 305, 329, 330,
  333, 363, 373, 377; IX. 3, 6, 11, 24, 26,
  27, 31 ff., 36, 43, 44, 46, 51, 52, 57, 58,
  62, 64, 65, 67, 94 ff., 112, 120, 126,
  129 ff., 146, 149, 153, 160, 170, 194,
  202, 212, 213, 215, 220, 234, 240, 246,
  249, 256, 261 ff., 277, 280 ff., 290, 331,
  336, 345, 353, 354, 357, 359, 363, 369,
  394, 406, 537, 539; x. 2, 21, 23, 28, 35,
  36, 39, 42, 77, 87, 94, 120, 149, 157,
  160, 161, 169, 182, 192, 193, 200, 237,
  261, 262, 276 ff., 296, 303, 305, 307,
  311, 312, 323, 324, 344, 356, 358, 375 ff.,
  382, 385 ff., 391, 394, 404, 408, 409, 460;
  XI. 37, 44, 58, 59, 80, 81, 96, 104, 130,
  133, 148, 156, 181, 195, 263 ff., 270 ff.,

London
278, 283, 286, 315, 325, 338, 340 ff.,
346, 360, 363; xii. 18, 31, 32, 37, 38,
57, 81, 142, 150, 164, 166, 167, 169,
172, 181, 203, 232, 234, 290, 291, 310,
323, 325, 329, 341, 347, 349, 511; xiii.
5, 12, 14, 18, 20, 55, 72, 77, 84, 107,
142, 202, 216, 259, 260, 266, 295, 325,
357, 358, 373, 383, 384, 409, 423, 455,
458; xiv. 13, 23, 34, 77, 91, 100, 101,
119, 167 ff., 173, 177, 179, 186, 189,
193, 195, 199, 202 ff., 206, 213 ff., 217,
220, 225, 252, 257, 263, 279, 293, 295,
298, 311, 312, 323, 327, 332, 344, 346,
362, 369, 373, 406, 407, 410
Adelphi, the, xi. 362
Aldermanbury, vi. 278
Aldermary churchyard, xi. 373
Aldersgate, iv. 399; vii. 100
Aldgate, Chaucer's house in, ii. 157, 158
All Hallows, Lombard street, iii. 57
Angel sign, xi. 335
Antelope, sign of the, iv. 389
Antiquities, xii. 507, 513
Arcade (the New Exchange), viii. 138
Arches, court of, iv. 426
Arlington street, x. 243, 246
Artillery garden, vi. 89
Artillery row, vii. 107
Axe yard, Westminster, viii. 254
Baldwin's gardens, xiv. 404
Bankside, Southwark, vi. 111, 255, 258,
259, 261; x. 201
Barbican, vii. 103, 116
Barbican chapel, x. 381
Bartholomew fair, ix. 263
Bedford college, xiv. 429
Bedlam, vi. 172; viii. 186
Bell, the, Gracechurch street, vi. 251
Bell Savage, the, Ludgate hill, vi. 251
Berkeley square, x. 246, 248
Bible, sign, xi. 332
Billingsgate, iii. 371; iv. 361; vii. 130;
viii. 95, 372; ix. 257, 263, 272
Birkbeck college, xiv. 408
Birkbeck schools, xiv. 414, 415
Bishopsgate, vi. 251; ix. 263
Bishopsgate street, ix. 393, 471
Black Boy, sign, xi. 335
Blackfriars, vi. 251, 257, 352; viii. 118;
xi. 330
Blackfriars bridge, x. 179, 467
Black Swan, Tower street, viii. 208
Blue Coat school. See Christ's hospital
Bolt court, x. 187
Bolton row, xi. 345
Bond street, xiv. 223
Bow, vii. 339
Bow street, viii. 34, 199; xii. 128;
xiv. 188
Brainford, iv. 361
Bread street, vii. 96, 107
Bread street, the Mermaid, iv. 90, 91
Brick court, x. 212
British museum, iii. 190; iv. 117, 429;
ix. 11, 124, 234; x. 95, 131, 253, 295;

London
xi. 295; xii. 200, 339, 340, 342, 345 ff.,
356, 368, 372, 382, 521, 523; xiii. 54,
140, 455, 483, 486, 507, 531, 555, 571,
572; xiv. 51, 80, 87, 153, 226, 281, 284,
285, 295, 524, 539, 558, 560, 566, 580,
610
Broad street, Golden square, xi. 433
Bromley-St-Leonard, vii. 339
Bryanstone square, xiii. 295
Buckingham palace, viii. 358; xiv. 415
Bunhill fields, vii. 107; ix. 25
Burlington gardens, ix. 163
Burlington house, xiv. 281, 287
Calf's Head club, vii. 124
Camberwell, xiii. 51
Camden town, xiii. 305
Cannon street, vii. 334
Caversham house, iv. 143
Chancery lane, vi. 354; vii. 250; xii. 187
Channel row, ix. 146
Chapel Royal, the, v. 122
Chapel street, xii. 184
Chapter coffeehouse, xi. 325
Charing Cross, vii. 513; viii. 409; ix.
146, 260
Charles street, xi. 142
Charterhouse, the, v. 17; viii. 26, 38,
193, 292, 403; ix. 45; x. 364; xiv
222, 422
Charterhouse school, vii. 24, 33, 338,
492
Cheapside, iii. 371; v. 9, 366; vi. 330;
vii. 96, 382; xi. 332, 402
Chelsea, vii. 310; ix. 126, 132; x. 39;
xiii. 10, 440
Chelsea, college at, iii. 391; iv. 424
Chelsea physic garden, xiv. 286
Chester's inn, Strand, ii. 206
Cheyne row, xiii. 10, 21
Cheyne walk, xiii. 372
Chiswick mall, xiii. 276
Christ church, vii. 361
Christ's hospital (Blue Coat school),
iii. 327; vii. 143, 326, 337, 492; viii.
450; xi. 118; xii. 181, 183, 434
Clapham, x. 385
Clarges street, xi. 345, 359
Clerkenwell, vi. 262; x. 385, 390; xiii.
457
Cleveland row, ix. 168
Clifford's inn, iv. 157; xiii. 449
Clink liberty, Southwark, the, vi. 254
Colebrook row, xii. 198
College street, x. 300
Colonial office, xiv. 109
Conduit close, vii. 336
Cork street, ix. 133
Cornhill, ix. 6; x. 116; xi. 141, 332, 335
Counter in the Poultrey, the, vi. 51
Coutts old bank, Strand, vii. 363
Covent garden, vii. 246; viii. 34, 172,
218; ix. 160, 348; xi. 333, 336; xii
187, 194
Cripplegate, vi. 251, 253, 258
Crosbie house, vi. 84

London
Cross Keys inn, Gracechurch street, VI. 247, 251
Cross Keys, sign, XI. 320
Crown inn, Islington, X. 212
Crown Office row, XII. 181
Curtain close, VI. 253
Curtain road, Shoreditch, VI. 251, 253
Denmark house, VI. 103
Devereux court, IV. 376
Devil tavern, XI. 326
Devil tavern, Temple Bar, Apollo room in, VI. 6; VII. 3
Doctors' Commons, IX. 139; XIII. 305, 327
Dog tavern, VII. 5
Dover street, IX. 132; XI. 348
Downing street, VIII. 253; X. 36
Drury lane, VI. 262; IX. 63; XI. 327
Duck lane, XI. 325, 331
Dulwich college, XII. 336
Dulwich gallery, XIII. 52
Earl street, XIV. 226
East India house, XII. 183, 192, 198, 200
Essex street, XII. 279
Eyebright, IV. 361
Fetter lane, XII. 181
Finsbury, XIV. 326
Finsbury fields, VI. 251 ff., 255, 257
Finsbury pavement, XII. 79
Finsbury square, XI. 337
Fire, the Great, IV. 433; VIII. 9, 10, 11, 249, 253, 320
Fish lane, IX. 263
Fish-market, the Old, II. 35
Fish street hill, X. 201
Fishmongers' company, IV. 386
Fleet, the, X. 393, 395
Fleet prison, the, II. 209; III. 175, 389; V. 140, 320; VII. 197, 199; IX. 139; XIII. 322
Fleet street, II. 159; III. 371; IV. 390, 398; VI. 218; VII. 61, 120, 250; X. 206, 207, 397; XI. 323, 339; XII. 188, 205; XIV. 185
Fleet street, sign of the Sun in, III. 194
Fleet tavern, the, V. 321
Flesh-shambles, the, II. 35
Free-masons hall, XI. 402
Freemasons' tavern, XIV. 287
Fulham, X. 12; XII. 201
Fulwood rents, IX. 260
Furnival's inn, III. 15
Gatehouse prison, Westminster, VII. 24, 357; VIII. 258
Gerrard street, X. 212
Globe tavern, VII. 38
'Globe,' Paternoster row, XI. 323
Gloucester place, XIII. 70
Goldsmiths' alley, VII. 335
Goldsmiths' company, IV. 184
Goldsmiths' row, Cheapside, V. 366; VII. 4
Gore house, XIV. 322
Gough square, X. Add.
Gower street, XIV. 290, 411

London
Gracechurch street, VI. 247, 251
Gray's inn, III. 202, 315; V. 58, 70, 71, 77, 78, 114, 219, 357, 367; VI. 112, 197, 356; VII. 21; VIII. 369; IX. 211, 220
Gray's-inn-gate, IX. 274
Gray's inn gateway, XI. 332
Great Coram street, XIII. 278
Great Eastern street, VI. 251
Great George street, IX. 246
Great Portland street, XIV. 226
Great St Andrew street, XIV. 227
Green Arbour court, X. 204
Greenstreet house, East Ham, IV. 412
Gresham college, III. 426; VII. 309, 320; VIII. 61, 249, 355, 365; IX. 385, 386, 390, 530, 573; XIV. 284
Grosvenor chapel, IX. 246
Guildhall, III. 324
Gunpowder alley, VII. 24
Guy's hospital, XIII. 53
Hackney, IX. 393; XII. 184
Hammersmith, XIII. 120, 128
Hampstead, IX. 133; X. 212
Hanson street, IX. 166
Haymarket, X. 87
Heralds' college, VII. 207
Hickford's dancing-room, IX. 483
Highgate, VI. 341; XI. 121; XII. 201; XIII. 112
Highgate academy, X. 385
Hill street, X. 262; XI. 348, 350
Holborn, XI. 168; VII. 104; X. 191; XI. 329, 332; XII. 183
Holywell lane, VI. 251
Holywell, priory of, VI. 251, 253
Homer's Head, Fleet street, XI. 323
Howard house, VII. 338
Hoxton, XIII. 457
Hoxton academy, XI. 43
Hoxton square academy, X. 385
Hyde park, XIII. 20
India office, Westminster VIII. 254; XII. 305; XIV. 14
India office library, XIV. 574
Inner Temple, IV. 157; V. 68, 70, 72, 73, 77; VI. 112, 356; VII. 221; VIII. 116, 142; IX. 51; XII. 180, 181, 183
Inner Temple lane, X. 207; XII. 191, 192
Inns of Court, III. 424; IV. 208; V. 368; VI. 218; VII. 62
Islington, IX. 261, 393; X. 207, 212; XII. 184, 196, 198, 200, 201
Islington academy, X. 385, 386
Jermyn street, XIII. 294
Jermyn street museum, XIV. 292, 294
Jewin street, X. 385
Kelmscott house, XIII. 128
Kennington, manor of, VI. 330
Kensington, XII. 331, 440, 444; XIII. 294, 300
Kensington gardens, IX. 483
Kent street, IX. 269
King's Bench prison, XIV. 217
King's college, XII. 290; XIII. 355; XIV. 82, 411, 429

London
  Kingsland, VIII. 253
  Knightrider street, IV. 398
  Knightsbridge, VIII. 211
  Lambeth, IV. 422, 424; XI. 189, 432;
    XII. 507, 508; XIII. 457
  Lambeth palace, X. 223, 498
  Lambeth palace library, VIII. 463; XII.
    367; XIV. 74, 79
  Lant street, XIII. 305
  Latine coffee-house, VII. 389
  Leadenhall, III. 369; XII. 198, 200
  Leadenhall street, XII. 183
  Leathersellers' company, IV. 391
  Leicester fields, XI. 333, 364
  Limehouse, IV. 73, 99
  Lincoln's inn, III. 15; IV. 199, 203, 219,
    240; V. 273; VI. 404; VII. 46, 59, 226;
    VIII. 320, 369; X. 362; XII. 354; XIV. 251
  Lincoln's inn fields, VI. 262; VII. 104;
    VIII. 150, 153, 195
  Lindsay row, Chelsea, XIII. 372
  Little Bartholomew's Well-yard, XI. 334
  Little Britain, IV. 390; IX. 274; X. 385;
    XI. 331, 332, 335
  Little Old Bailey, X. 204, 206
  Little Queen street, XII. 183
  Lombard street, XI. 330
  London academy, X. 386
  London bridge, IV. 390, 399, 546; VI.
    330; VII. 339; VIII. 11; XI. 332, 335, 467
  London institution, XII. 323
  London library, XII. 519
  London wall, IV. 418
  Lower mews, XI. 333
  Ludgate hill, VI. 251
  Maiden lane, VI. 255
  Mall, the, IX. 256, 263
  Marshalsea, the, IV. 155, 156; XIII. 305,
    331; XIV. 194
  Marylebone gardens, IX. 369
  Mechanics' institution, XIV. 408, 415
  Mercers' company, III. 11, 12
  Mercers' school, the, VII. 332
  Merchant Taylors' school, III. 213, 428,
    435; IV. 238; V. 102, 116, 122, 156;
    VI. 196, 221, 246, 288; VII. 326, 334,
    335, 493; XIV. 422
  Mermaid tavern, VI. 1, 5, 112; VIII. 322;
    XII. 89
  Middle Temple, the, IV. 80, 141; V. 220;
    VI. 37, 188; VII. 16; VIII. 146, 464;
    X. 23; XI. 2; XIII. 277
  Miles's coffee-house in Palace-yard, VII.
    389
  Milk street, II. 307
  Mitre court buildings, XII. 187
  Monmouth court, XIV. 227
  Monmouth house, X. 39
  Moorfields, IX. 25, 260; X. 385, 386
  Moorfields academy, X. 384
  Moorgate, VI. 251
  Mulberry gardens, VIII. 9, 138
  Munimenta Gildhallae Londoniensis
    (*Liber custumarum*), II 428
  National gallery, XIV. 154, 233

London
  National Portrait gallery, XIV. 89
  New Bond street, XI. 323, 332
  New Exchange, Strand, VII. 363; VIII.
    6, 138
  Newgate (prison), II. 336; IV. 156, 381;
    V. 54; VI. 330
  Newgate, IX. 2, 9, 10, 30, 163, 263, 272;
    X. 27, 351; XIV. 178, 228
  Newington butts, VI. 58
  Newington green, IX. 393
  Old Bailey, XII. 279
  Old Kensington palace, X. Add.
  Onslow square, XIII. 294
  Palace green, XIII. 300
  Palace yard, VII. 389
  Pall Mall, X. 266; XI. 323, 332, 333
  Paper office, IX. 197
  Paris garden, VI. 220, 255, 259, 383,
    393, 402
  Park lane, XIII. 295
  Park street, VI. 256
  Parliament, houses of, XII. 508
  Parson's dock, IX. 257
  Parson's green, X. 12
  Paternoster row, II. 307; IV. 398; X.
    201, 202; XI. 323, 325, 327, 332, 339;
    XII. 205
  Paul's Cross, II. 288, 289, 302; III. 406;
    IV. 234, 235; VI. 375, 379, 386; VII.
    146, 147
  Peacock, sign, XI. 339
  Pelican, sign, XI. 335
  Pentonville, XII. 184, 186, 187, 194;
    XIV. 51
  Petre house, Aldersgate, VII. 24
  'Petty France,' or York street, VII. 104
  Pewter Platter inn, XI. 329
  Physicians, royal college of, III. 6, 107
  Pimlico, IV. 362; XII. 365
  Pinners' hall, X. 377
  Pipe office, the, VI. 257
  Poor Jewry lane, X. 381
  Pope's Head alley, Cornhill, VI. 358;
    VII. 344
  Portman square, X. 262
  Poultry, VI. 51; XI. 326, 332
  Primrose hill, XIII. 269
  Prince's Arms, sign, XI. 318
  Priory, the, Regent's park, XIII. 396
  Pudding lane, VI. 358
  Quaker's tavern, IX. 263
  Queen-hive, IV. 361
  Queen's college, XIII. 355; XIV. 429
  Ram-alley, VI. 217, 219; IX. 268
  Ranelagh, XI. 259, 352
  Ranelagh house, X. 425
  Record office, XIV. 87, 111
  Red Lion square, XIII. 119
  Red Pale, Westminster, sign of the,
    II. 312
  Regent's park, XIV. 289
  Rhenish tavern, VI. 146
  Rolls chapel, IX. 195, 198
  Ropemakers' alley, IX. 25; X. 385
  Rota club and coffee-house, VII. 362, 389

London
Royal Caledonian asylum, XIII. 107
Royal Cockpit, the, XIV. 222
Royal college of surgeons, XIV. 286, 295
Royal Exchange, III. 395; VI. 83, 100,
   300; IX. 49, 260; XI. 141, 327, 332
Royal institution, XII. 343; XIII. 369;
   XIV. 259 ff.
Rummer tavern, IX. 146
Russell street, VIII. 34; XI. 333; XII.
   194, 198
St Andrew's, Holborn, IV. 141; VI. 168
St Augustine's, X. 377
St Bartholomew's hospital, VII. 361
St Clement Danes, IV. 237; IX. 195
St Dunstan's church, XII. 191
St Dunstan's churchyard, XI. 318
St Dunstan's in the West, IV. 143, 219;
   VII. 250
St Giles's in the Fields, VI. 30
St Giles without Cripplegate, VI. 258;
   VII. 107
St Giles, Cripplegate, IX. 6
St Helen's, II. 306
St James's, XIII. 269
St James's, court of, XIV. 348
St James's coffeehouse, IX. 247, 463, 471
St James's palace, VIII. 266; IX. 78,
   249, 250, 331
St James's park, VIII. 7; XIV. 284
St James's street, XIII. 294
St John street, Clerkenwell, VI. 262
St John's, Westminster, X. 393
St Lawrence, Jewry, III. 15; VIII. 369
St Leonard's, Eastcheap, VII. 223
St Magnus, church of, XI. 467
St Margaret Pattens, X. 294
St Margaret's church, XII. 319
St Martin's, Ludgate, IV. 91
St Martin in the Fields, VIII. 250
St Martin's lane, VIII. 173
St Martin's vintry, VII. 355
St Mary's, Aldermanbury, VI. 278
St Mary's, Westminster, Chaucer's
   house at, II. 158
St Mary Overy, VI. 224
St Matthew's, Friday street, VII. 456
St Michael-le-Quern, Cheapside, VII. 232
St Mildred, Poultry, parish of, III. 183
St Olave's school, VII. 339
St Pancras, IX. 257
St Paul's cathedral, II. 208, 365, 367;
   III. 9, 11, 183; IV. 203, 204, 219, 225,
   232, 240, 265, 320, 330, 332, 356, 366,
   388, 398, 433, 546; VI. 57, 84, 251; VII. 59, 82, 345,
   458; VIII. 299, 304, 369; IX. 330, 343,
   533; X. 358; XI. 332; XII. 271 ff., 319,
   320, 477; XIII. 34, 260; XIV. 13, 403
St Paul's churchyard, III. 11; IV. 393,
   398, 403; VII. 146; X. 205; XI. 318, 325,
   331, 339, 376
St Paul's school, II. 489; III. 13, 428,
   435; V. 58, 102, 125; VI. 40, 41, 246,
   287, 288; VII. 96, 97, 326, 329, 332, 334;
   VIII. 253; IX. 573; X. 408; XIV. 422

London
St Paul's, Covent garden, VIII. 301
St Peter's, Cornhill, VIII. 301
St Saviour's church, Southwark, VI.
   111, 144
St Saviour's school, Southwark, III.
   428; VII. 339
St Stephen's, Westminster, II. 208
Salisbury court, X. 201
Salisbury court in Whitefriars, thea-
   trical company at, VIII. 118
Salisbury square, X. 12
Salter's hall, X. 377, 379, 380
Savoy, the, VII. 63; VIII. 319
Savoy chapel, VII. 245, 246; VIII. 301
Savoy hospital, VIII. 249, 377
Savoy hospital, church of the, IV
   156
'Saynt Magnus Corner,' IV. 399
Seething lane, VIII. 255
Seven Dials, XI. 469; XIV. 226, 227
Seven Stars, Strand, VII. 363
Shakespear's Head, sign, XI. 319, 320
Shoreditch, III. 316; VI. 251, 253
Sion college, IV. 418, 433
Skinner street, XII. 191
Smithfield, II. 422; VII. 304; IX. 263
Smyrna coffee-house, IX. 471
Snow hill, VII. 361
Soho square, X. 482
Somerset house, VI. 366; VII. 353; XIV
   284
Somerset place, X. 266
South Audley street, IX. 246
South Kensington museum, XIV. 284,
   285
South Molton street, XI. 432
Southampton buildings, XII. 187, 191
Southampton street, Camberwell, XIII.
   51
South-Sea house, XII. 183, 195
Southwark, IV. 361, 374; VI. 111, 144,
   247, 250, 254, 255; VII. 339; IX. 269
Spencer house, XII. 356
Spital, the, IV. 225; VII. 146
Spread Eagle, the, Bread street, Cheap-
   side, VII. 96
Staining-lane, II. 35
Stationers' hall, III. 393, 397; IV. 170,
   171, 180, 184
Stationers' register and court, III. Add.
Stepney, IV. 547
Stock exchange, XIV. 2
Stocks market, XI. 332
Stoke Newington, IX. 393
Strand, II. 206; IV. 202; V. 9, 366; VII.
   38, 362; XI. 319, 323, 325, 332; XII. 181,
   188
Stratford, VII. 339
Stratford-le-Bow school, VII. 339
Sun tavern, VII. 5
Surgeon's hall, X. 204
Swan tavern, XI. 328
Synagogue, the Great, St James's place,
   Aldgate, XI. 413
Taverns, VI. 101

London

Temple, the, III. 406; IV. 236, 237; VI. 218; VII. 83; X. 212, 358; XI. 79; XII. 183, 187, 194

Temple bar, XI. 326, 332

Temple church, VI. 38; VII. 197; VIII. 251, 304, 370; X. 215; XII. 191

Tenter alley, X. 384

Thames, the, II. 145, 233; III. 238, 380; IV. 72, 77, 177, 392, 532; VI. 252, 258; VII. 38, 59, 60, 334; VIII. 24

Thames embankment, IV. 418

Thames street, II. 156; V. 98

Thavies's inn, IV. 199

Threadneedle street, XI. 280

Three-legs, sign, XI. 332

Three Pigeons, sign, XI. 332

Tottenham Court road, XIII. 450; XIV. 229

Tottenham cross, IX. 403

Tower, the, III. 16, 17, 167, 176, 431; IV. 53, 57 ff., 103, 143, 181, 230, 425; VI. 90; VII. 203, 226, 254, 453; VIII. 36, 107, 111, 207, 253, 257, 259; IX. 175, 348, 356; X. 352; XII. 507, 509

Tower hill, VII. 224

Tower street, VIII. 208

Triple Tun tavern, VII. 5

Tully's Head, sign, XI. 323

Turk's Head coffee-house in Palace yard, VII. 362

Turk's Head inn, X. 215

Tuttle fields, III. 369

Tyburn, IV. 128, 381; VII. 2; VIII. 163; IX. 268; X. 351

University, XII. 350; XIV. 411, 412, 414, 417, 429, 430, 432

University college, XII. 297, 309, 335, 336; XIII. 53; XIV. 24, 290, 412, 426, 429

University College hospital, XIII. 107

Vauxhall gardens, XI. 352

Victoria and Albert museum, X. 263; XIII. 482, 483, 516, 530, 531; XIV. 539

Walpole house, XIII. 276

Walworth, XIII. 51

Wapping, XII. 362

Wapping academy, X. 385

Warwick lane, XI. 323

Watling street, V. 255

Well Close square, X. 384; XI. 452

Westminster, IX. 139, 146, 147, 397, 539; X. 29, 33, 351, 352, 393, 394, 397, 470; XII. 272, 275, 294, 411, 507, 513; XIV. 181

Westminster abbey, IX. 55, 153, 164, 532; X. 187, 232, 265; XI. 181; XII. 312, 319, 365, 383, 478, 508; XIII. 20, 84, 369; XIV. 222, 295

Westminster hall, IX. 160, 247; XI. 332, 467; XIV. 124

Westminster school, IX. 158, 188, 250, 333, 390, 405, 408 ff., 414, 483, 573; X. 300, 393; XI. 78, 83, 155, 157, 328, 421, 423; XII. 334; XIV. 225, 283, 386, 387, 422

London

White Horse tavern, Strand, VIII. 266

Whitefriars, VII. 349; VIII. 174; IX. 268

Whitefriars monastery, VI. 262

Whitehall, IV. 219; V. 64, 70, 253; VI. 36, 112, 237, 342, 348, 350, 351, 354, 356, 361, 404; VII. 1, 4, 5, 13, 16, 17, 20, 104, 215, 254, 264; VIII. 11, 115, 199, 206, 249, 268, 269, 358; IX. 215; X. 307

Williams library, VII. 29

Willis's rooms, XIII. 294

Will's coffee-house, VIII. 34, 159, 172, 212, 370, 376

Wimpole street, XIII. 70

Winchester house, VI. 356

Wine Office court, X. 206, 207

Wits' coffeehouse, IX. 263

Wood street, Cheapside, VII. 4

York buildings, Buckingham street, VIII. 258

York house, IV. 278

York street, XI. 336

York street, or 'Petty France,' VII. 104

Young street, XIII. 294

See, also, under Islington, Lambeth, Southwark, Westminster, etc.

London, XIV. 162

London, William (fl. 1658), VII. 480; VIII. 464; Catalogue of the most vendible Books, XI. 338, 470

London and the development of popular literature, IV. 316 ff., 514 ff.

London Chanticleer (1659), VII. 512

London Chronicle, III. 532; X. 177, 467

London Corresponding society, XIV. 121

London Cries, XI. 487

London Daily Chronicle, The, XIV. 193

London Evening Courier, The, XIV. 176

London Gazette, The, VII. 363, 364; IX. 1; XI. 333; XIV. 167

London Journal, IX. 221

London life, VI. 225, 226, 228

London Magazine, The, X. 192, 467, 474, 479; XI. 339; XII. 141, 160–161 (main entry), 171, 193, 195, 199, 200, 428; XIII. 4, 257, 465

London Magazine, The, or Gentleman's Monthly Intelligencer, XII. 428

London Magazine, The, and Monthly Chronologer, XII. 428

London merchant, a, in A Woman will have her Will, V. 329

London Missionary society, XIII. 51

London Monthly Miscellany, The, XIV. 149

London Packet, X. 474

London Post, IX. 432

London Prodigall, The, V. 236, 238, 254, 332; VI. 97

London Review, The, XII. 430, 440; XIV. 199

London Star, The, XI. 235

London theatres, XII. 508

Adelphi, XII. 171; XIII. 265, 270; XIV 224

Aquatic, XII. 171

London theatres
Astley's, XIV. 222, 224
Blackfriars, V. 256; VII. 59
Coburg, XII. 171
Cockpit, Drury lane, VIII. 115, 116, 118, 180
Covent garden, X. 89, 91, 211, 212, 214, 425 ff., 444; XI. 244, 259 ff., 264, 273, 277, 278, 283, 448, 450 ff.; XII. 69, 171; XIII. 256, 258; XIV. 227, 319
Dorset garden, VIII. 119, 182, 193; X. 70
Drury lane, VIII. 134, 148, 150, 189, 400; X. 21, 40, 70, 73, 85, 87 ff., 91, 161, 167, 209, 212, 265, 425 ff.; XI. 258 ff., 263, 264, 271, 273, 277, 283, 304, 393, 402, 449 ff., 454 ff.; XII. 35, 171, 189, 194, 386, 390, 434; XIII. 256, 265, 514, 515; XIV. 334
Drury lane Theatre Royal, Covent garden (1663), VIII. 119
Duke's, VIII. 400
East London, XII. 171
Globe, V. 218, 242
Goodman's fields, X. 21, 427, 432, 440
Haymarket, VIII. 162, 163; IX. 471; X. 21, 23, 426 ff., 444; XI. 259, 278, 279, 451, 452, 454; XII. 171; XIII. 256
King's, XII. 171
Lincoln's Inn fields, X. 426, 428, 430, 434, 436, 439, 440; XI. 258
Little theatre in the Haymarket, X. 23, 87; XI. 452
Lyceum, XII. 171; XIII. 513 ff.
Newington, V. 256
Olympic, XIV. 224
Portugal row, Lincoln's Inn fields, VI. 262; VIII. 119, 152, 399
Prince of Wales's, XIII. 271
Red Bull playhouse, VIII. 115; theatrical company at, VIII. 118
Rose, V. 316
Royalty, XI. 452
Sadler's wells, VIII. 184; XIII. 264
Salisbury court, Fleet street, VIII. 119
Surrey, XII. 171; XIII. 264, 265
Whitefriars, V. 346; VI. 220, 251
Winter, XI. 452
London Topographical society, XII. 506
London and Westminster Review, XI. 398; XII. 430
Londonderry, VIII. 122, 170; IX. 290
Long, Mrs Anne (1681?–1711), IX. 126, 456
Long, George (1800–1879), XII. 487, also see Add.; Decline of the Roman Republic, The, XII. 307, 335
Long, Kingsmill, translator of Barclay His Argenis, IV. 501
Long, loch, XI. 236
Long, Roger (1680–1770), Life of Mohammed, X. 281
Long Life, I. 228, 458
Long Meg of Westminster, in Richard Casteler, III. 369, 487
Long Megg of Lincoln, IX. 268

Long parliament, the, III. 397; IV. 299; VI. 235; VII. 6, 22, 24, 54, 206, 223, 224, 230, 285, 346, 440, 441, 456, 458; VIII. 79, 80, 323; IX. 387; XI. 311
Longcastell (Lancaster), in Wallace, II. 110
Longe, Julia G., IX. 92
Longfellow, Henry Wadsworth, I. 147; XIII. 245, 246; XIV. 365, 378; Children of the Lord's Supper, XIII. 244; Evangeline, XIII. 241, 244
Longford county, X. 195
Longing, the land of, in Piers the Plowman, II. 25
Longinus, VII. 85, 316, 489; IX. 51, 59, 188, 527; X. 144; XII. 324; On the Sublime, V. 234
Longland, John (1473–1547), bishop of Lincoln, III. 36, 38; IV. 228, 493, 494; Tres Conciones, IV. 226
Longleat, IX. 153, 443
Longleat Papers, IX. 147, 156, 443, 483. See, also, Bath, marquis of, Papers
Longman, Thomas (1699–1755), XI. 323
Longman, Thomas Norton (1771–1842), XI. 327
Longman and Rees, publishers, XII. 142
Longman's Magazine, XII. 427
Longmore, George, XIV. Add. 5
Longmuir, John (1803–1883), XII. 517
Longside, IX. 372
Long-tongue, in The Disobedient Child, V. 109
Longueville, Charles, VIII. 62
Longueville, William (1639–1721), VIII. 60, 62
Longus, IV. 438; VII. 489
Longwood, St Helena, XIII. 276
Looke about you, V. 35, 320, 328, 329, 476
Looking Glass for George Fox, IX. 307
Looking Glass for the Mind, XI. 382
Looking glasse for all proud, ambitious, covetous and corrupt Lawyers, A, VII. 388
Lope de Vega, Don Lope de Cardona, VI. 204; El Mayordomo de la Duquesa de Amalfi, VI. 180; El Peregrino en su patria, VI. 139
Lopes, Duarte, IV. 445
Lopez, in The Merchant of Venice, V. 181
Lopez, in The Spanish Curate, VI. 139
Lopez, Trollope's, XIII. 422
Lopez de Gomara, Francisco, Istoria de las Indias y conquista de Mejico, IV. 69
Lorain, P., XIII. 545
Loram, Charles Templeman, XIV. Add. 8
'Lord Fanny,' in Pope's Imitations of Horace, XI. 85, 251
Lord Governaunce, V. 58
Lord Love went maying, XIII. 133
Lord Lovel, II. 412
Lord Maxwell's Last Good Night, II. 413
Lord Randal, II. 407, 412
Lord Thomas and Fair Annet, II. 412
Lord's Prayer, XI. 368
Lord's Prayer, exposition on the, in Speculum Christiani, II. 319
Lord's Prayer, Rolle, II. 48

Lords, house of, III. 11; IV. 279; IX. 195, 251; X. 192, 246, 397; XI. 17, 29, 34, 79, 315, 328; XII. 32, 285
Loreau, Mme H., XIII. 550
Lorens, frère, I. 354
Lorenz, Theodor, XIV. 532
Lorenzo, in Keats's *Isabella*, XII. 86
Lorenzo, in *May Day*, III. 199
Lorenzo, in *The Bashful Lover*, VI. 152
Lorenzo, in *The Decameron*, XII. 82
Lorenzo, in *The Merchant of Venice*, V. 183
Lorenzo, in *The Spanish Tragedie*, V. 240
Lorenzo, in *The Traytor*, VI. 199
Loreto, litany of, IV. 129
Loretto, VII. 35, 63
Lorica, or *Cuirass*, I. 68, 69
Lorimer, of Hoxton square academy, X. 385
Lorraine, Claude, VIII. 217
Lorraine, duke of, IX. 149
Lorrington, Mrs, in Marston's *Favourite of Fortune*, XIII. 269
Lorrique, in *The Tragedy of Hoffman*, V. 327
Lorris, Guillaume de, II. 169, 219
Lort, Michael (1725–1790), X. Add.
Los, Blake's, XI. 194 ff., 199
Loseley MSS., the, V. 408
Losely, IV. 200
Loserth, J., II. 54, 69, 440
Losinga, Herbert de (1054?–1119), II. 497
Lot, F., I. 262
Lot, Parson (Charles Kingsley), XIII. 358
Loth, or Lot, in Arthurian legend, I. 259, 326
Lothair, Disraeli's, XIII. 352
Lothario, XIII. 378
Lothario, in Rowe's *Fair Penitent*, VIII. 196
Lothian, XI. 244
Lothians, the, II. 89, 90, 95, 259, 368, 371
Loti, Pierre, IX. 248
Lotos Eaters, I. 373
Lot's wife, in Bunyan's *Pilgrim's Progress*, VII. 173
Loudon, John Claudius (1783–1843), XIV. 562; *Magazine of Natural History*, XIV. 149
Loughborough, VII. 91
Loughborough, Alexander Wedderburn, lord. *See* Wedderburn, Alexander
Louis IX (St Louis), king of France, I. 336, 354; II. 284; III. 160; IV. 30
Louis XI, VI. 90; XII. 21, 26
Louis XII, V. 93
Louis XIII, IV. 254, 257, 259; VII. 205
Louis XIV, VII. 24; VIII. 14, 132, 195, 246, 248, 262, 263, 272, 276; IX. 148, 150, 151, 153, 391; X. 105; XI. 355; XIV. 110, 212
Louis XVI, X. 306, 507; XI. 28, 189, 430; XIV. 66
Louis XVII, XIII. 343
Louis XVIII, X. 261
Louis-Philippe, king of the French, XIII. 283; XIV. 60

Louisa, in Dickens's *Hard Times*, XIII. 329, 330
Louisa, princess, IX. 162
Louise de Gonzague, queen of Poland, V. 201
Lounger, The, X. 55; XI. 440, 449; XIV. 591, 600
Lounsbury, Thomas R., XIII. 477, 484; XIV. 611; *Shakespeare and Voltaire*, X. 81, 82; *The first editors of Shakespeare*, IX. 77, 78
Louth, Robert, XIV. 607
Louth grammar school, XIII. 23, 45
Louth school, Lincolnshire, VII. 330
Louvain, II. 245, 311; III. 67; IV. 402; V. 90; X. 200; XIV. 313
Louverture, Toussaint, XI. 114
Louverture, Toussaint, in Martineau's *The Hour and the Man*, XIII. 343
Lovat, lord. *See* Fraser, Simon
Lovato de' Lovati, V. 61
Love, in *Complaint upon Love to Reason*, III. 187
Love, in *Filostrato e Panfila*, V. 62
Love, in *Love Restored*, VI. 352
Love, in *Pathomachia*, VI. 324
Love, in *Piers the Plowman*, II. 10, 27, 28
Love, in *The Shepheards Calender*, III. 222
Love, in prince Arthur's marriage pageant, VI. 332
Love, Pretty parables and proverbs of, III. 190
Love, Sir Anthony, in Southerne's *Sir Anthony Love*, VIII. 191
Love, the king of, in *The Example of Virtue*, II. 227
Love Prevented, V. 330
'Lovechild, Mrs,' XI. 377, 379
Loveday, Robert (*fl.* 1655), VII. 439 IX. 57
Lovel, in Lamb's *Elia*, XII. 180
Lovel, lord, in *The New Inne*, VI. 25
Lovelace, in Richardson's *Clarissa Harlowe*, VIII. 196; X. 8, 17
Lovelace, Dudley VII. 24
Lovelace, earl of. *See* Milbanke, Ralph
Lovelace, Richard (1618–1658), VII. 4, 23 ff. (main entry), 178, 399
    Althea from Prison, To, VII. 24, 25
    Ellinda's Glove, VII. 25
    Going to the Wars, VII. 25
    Grasshopper, The, VII. 25
    Loose Saraband, A, VII. 25
    Lucasta: Epodes, Odes, Sonnets, Songs, etc., VII. 24, 25
    Lucasta going beyond the Seas, To, 25
    Lucasta Posthume Poems, VII. 24
    Lucasta Weeping, VII. 25
    Lucasta's Muff, VII. 25
    Pastoral: to Amarantha, VII. 25
    Poems, VII. 180
    Scholar, The, VII. 24
    Snail, The, VII. 25
    Soldier, The, VII. 24
    To Lucasta, XIV. 436
Lovelace, Sir William, VII. 23

Loveless, in Vanbrugh's *Relapse*, VIII. 161; XI. 268

Loveless, in Sheridan's *Trip to Scarborough*, XI. 268

Loveless, in *The Scornful Ladie*, VI. 133

Lovelich, Henry, I. 469

Lovell, Robert (1770?–1796), XI 161, 420

Lovely Lass of Inverness, IX. 377

Lover, Samuel (1797–1868), XI. 440; XIV. 313 ff., 321, 569, 573; *Gridiron, The*, XIV. 314; *Handy Andy*, XIV. 314; *Paddy's Pastoral Rhapsody*, XIV. 314

Lover, the, in *Confessio Amantis*, II. 146 ff., 152

Lover Loved, the, in Heywood's *Love*, V. 93

Lover not Loved, the, in Heywood's *Love*, V. 93

Lovere, IX. 245

Loves of the Triangles, The, XI. 41, 175

Love's Garland IV. 467

Lovett, William (1800–1877), XIV. 414, 602

Lovibond, Edward (1724–1775), X. 455

Low, Frances, XIII. 551

Low Countries, II. 311, 320, 329; V. 113, 143, 344, 361; VII. 306, 345; VIII. 267

Lowde, James (*fl.* 1694–1696), VIII. 474

Lowe, John (1750–1798), X. 456; *Mary's Dream*, XI. 234

Lowe, Peter (1550?–1612?), XII. 521

Lowe, Robert, viscount Sherbrooke (1811–1892), XIV. 133, 137, 420, 511, 512, 607

Lowe, Robert W., X. 67; XI. 447, 449, 452; XII. 522; XIV. 518

Lowe, W. E., XIII. 513

Lowell, James Russell, II. 250; X. Add.; XI. 407, 410; XII. 179, 399; XIII. 143, 371, 472; XIV. 349

Lower, Richard (1631–1691), VIII. 363, 477

Lower, Sir William (1600?–1662), VIII. 119, 438; *Horatius* (Corneille's), translated by, VIII. 133, 180; *Polyeucte* (Corneille's), translated by, VIII. 133, 180

Lowin, John (1576–1659), VI. 139, 248, 249, 276, 277

Lowman, Moses (1680–1752), X. 521

Lowndes, William (1652–1724), *An Essay for the amendment of the Silver Coins*, VIII. 344, 474, 476

Lowndes, William Thomas (d. 1843), XII. 445, 522; *The Bibliographer's Manual*, X. 410; XII. 368; *The British Librarian*, XII. 368

Lowood, in *Jane Eyre*, XIII. 404

Lowry, J. M., XIV. 573

Lowth, Robert (1710–1787), II. 406; X. 136; XII. 468; *A Short Introduction to English Grammar*, XIV. 396

Lowther, Sir James, X. 131; XI. 95

Loyal Garland, The (1686), VII. 512

Loyal Observer, The, IV. 65

Loyal Songs, IX. 566

Loyal Subject's Litany, VIII. 96

Loyalist, The, IX. 566

Loyaltie and Bewtie, History of, VI. 286, 287

Loyalty, in *Assembly of Ladies*, II. 217

Loyalty, in *Piers the Plowman*, II. 10, 25, 32

Loyalty, in *Portuus of Noblines*, II. 284

Loyola, Ignatius de, VIII. 86

Loyola, Ignatius, in *A Game at Chesse*, VI. 150

Luard, Henry Richards (1825–1891), I. 182, 204; XII. 324, 356, 491, 492

Lubbock, John, baron Avebury (1834–1913), XII. 348, 511; XIV. 476, 562

Lubbock, Percy, XIII. 484

Luby, T. Clarke (1821–1901), XIV. 321, *also see* Add. 3

Lucan, I. 76; II. 366; III. 20, 113; IV. 23, 395, 438; VII. 206, 263, 267, 268, 270, 503; VIII. 61; IX. 44, 182, 256, 337, 338, 525; XII. 67, 306, 402; *Pharsalia*, IV. 138; VI. 37, 235; VIII. 197, 440

Lucar, Cyprian (*fl.* 1590), IV. 448

Lucas, Charles (1713–1771), X. 466; XIV. 569

Lucas, Sir Charles Prestwood, XIV. 509

Lucas, Edward Verrall, X. Add.; XI. 395, 417, 459, 475, 483, 484, 488, 492; XII. 414, 422, 433 ff., 437, 438; XIV. 521, *also see* Add. 3

Lucas, S., *Life of Peter Borthwick*, XIV. 185

Lucas, Samuel (1811–1865), editor of *The Morning Star*, XIV. 196

Lucas, Samuel, editor of *The Press*, XIV. 196

Lucas, Theophilus (*fl.* 1714), IX. 500

Lucas, Thomas (d. 1740), X. 387

'Lucasia,' K. Philips's, VII. 88

Lucasta, alias Lucy Sacheverell, VII. 24, 25

Lucca, XII. 62

Luce, Morton, XIII. 477

Luce, in *The London Prodigall*, V. 254, 255; VI. 97

Lucentio, in *The Taming of the Shrew*, V. 181

Luces, the two, in *The Wise-woman of Hogsdon*, VI. 99

Luces de Gast, I. 273

Lucia, in Addison's *Cato*, IX. 63

Lucian, III. 15, 20, 22; IV. 438, 516, 527; V. 221; VI. 18, 21, 87; VII. 131, 263, 274, 316, 318, 489; IX. 106, 159, 257, 266, 267, 500, 528; X. 474; XI. 332; XIII. 351; *Dialogues*, VIII. 36; *Menippus*, IV. 354; *Timon*, VI. 137

Lucianic reverie, X. 205

Lucifer, II. 30; III. 17, 76; IV. 166, 167; IX. 327

Lucifer, in Bailey's *Festus*, XIII. 153

Lucifer, in Byron's *Cain*, XII. 48

Lucifer, in Byron's *Vision of Judgment*, XII. 53

Lucifer, in FitzGerald's *The Mighty Magician*, XIII. 144

Lucifer, in religious plays, V. 15, 57

Lucifer, in *The Black Book*, VI. 60

Lucifer, in *The foure P.P.*, V. 96

Lucilius, VIII. 58

Lucilla, in *The Anatomy of Wit*, III. 345, 346
Lucina, in *The Birth of Merlin*, v. 249
Lucina, in *Valentinian*, VI. 122
Lucinda, in *Don Quixote*, IX. 269
Lucio, in *Measure for Measure*, v. 190
Lucius, in *The Rival Friends*, VI. 325
Lucius, king, III. 332
Lucius Iberius, in *Morte Arthure*, I. 313; II. 115, 118
'Lucius' (Junius), x. 403, 410
Luckin, M. W., XIV. Add. 8
Luckless, in Fielding's *Pleasures of the Town*, x. 21
Lucky Spence's Last Advice, IX. 366
Lucrece, in *Confessio Amantis*, II. 152
Lucrece, in *Gismond of Salerne*, v. 73, 75
Lucrece, The Play of, v. 100, 410
Lucretia, XII. 68
Lucretius, IV. 347; VII. 268, 451, 486; VIII. 61, 277, 288, 449; IX. 55, 526; XII. 67, 326, 335, 488, 492, 495; XIII. 25, 40, 45, 145; XIV. 276, 374
Lucullus, IX. 270
Lucy, in Charlotte Brontë's *Villette*, XIII. 410
Lucy, in Congreve's *Old Bachelor*, VIII. 147, 152
Lucy, in Meredith's *Richard Feverel*, XIII. 444, 446
Lucy, in Sheridan's *Rivals*, x. 89; XI. 266
Lucy, in Wordsworth's poems, XI. 113
Lucy, Sir Henry W., XIV. 534
Lucy, St, I. 74, 356
Lucy, William (1594–1677), VII. 474
Ludi or 'disgysynges,' VI. 294
Ludlow, Edmund (1617?–1692), VII. 451; *Diary*, VII. 225
Ludlow, John Malcolm, XIII. 355; XIV. 408
Ludlow castle, VI. 363; VII. 113; VIII. 60
Ludlow school, VII. 330
Ludolphus, J., *History of Aethiopia*, IX. 268
Ludovicus Vives, VI. 225
Ludus Accidiae, v. 52
Ludus Coventriae. See *Coventry Plays*
Ludwig, Lavaterus, *Of Ghostes and Spirits*, III. 495
Ludwig, Otto, v. 304
Ludwig the Pious, Life of, by Thegan, I. 90
Luft, Hans, III. 472
Lufton, lord, Trollope's, XIII. 422
Lugwardine, Antony, in Robert Landor's *Fountain of Arethusa*, XII. 230
Luick, K., II. 32, 436
'Luitprandus,' x. 204
Luke, St, I. 74; II. 15
Luke, Sir Samuel (d. 1670), VII. 167; VIII. 60, 63, 64, 66
Luke is losse, My (poems signed), III. 189
Lukin, Henry, *Practice of Godliness*, XI. 334
Lul, letter from, I. 79
Lulli, J.-B. de, musician to Charles I, and Quinault, P., *Cadmus and Hermione*, VIII. 134; *Les Fêtes de l'Amour et de Bacchus*, VIII. 134

Lully, or Lulle, Raymond, VII. 277
Lumby, Joseph Rawson (1831–1895), I. 146; II. 284; XII. 487
Lumen, in *Lingua*, VI. 315
Lumfanane, in Wyntoun's *Cronykil*, II. 132
Lumley, Eliza, afterwards Sterne, x. 47
Lumley, Richard, 2nd earl of Scarborough (d. 1721), x. 256
Lumond, sea of, in Layamon, I. 236
Lumpkin, Tony, in Goldsmith's *She Stoops to Conquer*, x. 206, 214
Luna, in Hawes's *A Joyful Meditation*, etc., II. 226
'Lunatics,' in *The Lords' Masque*, VI. 353
Lund, Thomas William Moy, XIII. 488
Lunenburg, duke of, in *The Tragedy of Hoffman*, v. 327
Luntowski, A., XIII. 465, 476
Lupset, Thomas (1498?–1530), III. 20, 105, 474
Lupton, Donald (d. 1676), VI. 494; *London and Country Carbonadoed*, IV. 351, 522
Lupton, Roger (d. 1540), VII. 329, 330
Lupton, Thomas (*fl.* 1583), *All for Money*, v. 57, 393
Lurewell, lady, in Farquhar's *The Constant Couple*, VIII. 176, 178
Luria, Browning's, XIII. 67
Lushington, Edmund Law (1811–1893), XII. 487; XIII. 24; *On the Study of Greek*, XII. 330
Lushington, Sir Franklin, XIV. 494
Lusitania, in *The Masque of Blacknesse*, VI. 342
Lutel Soth Sermun, I. 226, 458
Luther, Martin, II. 69; III. 7, 53, 69, 127, 139, 151, 363, 365, 472, 492; IV. 215, 224, 301, 380, 445, 446, *also see* Add.; v. 58, 103; VII. 103; VIII. 291, 321 ff.; XII. 273, 281; XIII. 13, 20, 388, 428; XIV. 99; *Table Talk, or Colloquies* (*Colloquia Mensalia*), VII. 391; VIII. 321, 322
Lutheran drama, VI. 374
Lutheranism, III. 31, 37, 140, 142
Lutherans, VII. 124, 378
Luton, IX. 169
Lutonsky, Paula, XIII. 489
Lutterworth, II. 65, 66; x. 112
Luttrell, Henry (1765?–1851), XII. 419; XIV. 115
Luttrell, Narcissus (1657–1732), *Brief Historical Relation of State Affairs*, VIII. 241, 451
Lutwidge, in Miss Edgeworth's *Belinda*, XI. 297
Luvah, in Blake's *Vala*, XI. 195
Luvaris Lament, The, II. 282
Lux Mundi, XII. 299
Luxborough, earl of. See Catherlough, R.K.
Luxborough, lady. See Knight, Henrietta
Luxborough, lord. See Knight, Robert
Luxuria, in *The Castle of Perseverance*, v. 52
Luxury, in *The Cradle of Security*, v. 57
Luynes, C., duc de, VII. 205

Lyall, Sir Alfred Comyn (1835–1911),
XIII. 194, 477, 505; XIV. 93, 493, 500,
578
  Asiatic Studies, XIV. 98, 340
  Badminton, XIII. 203
  British Dominion in India, The, XIV. 340
  Land of Regrets, The, XIII. 203; XIV. 340
  Old Pindaree, The, XIII. 202
  Retrospection, XIII. 203
  *Rise and Expansion of the British
    Dominion in India*, XIV. 98
  Siva, XIV. 340
  Theology in Extremis, XIII. 202
  Verses written in India, XIII. 202; XIV.
    340
Lyall, Sir Charles James (1845–1920), XII.
  Add. 4
Lyberte, in *Magnyfycence*, III. 77
Lycanthropy, belief in, I. 316
Lyce, an elderly Lady, To, X. 168
Lycia, XII. 339
Lycidas (Herrick's), VII. 12
Lycogenes, in *Argenis*, IV. 258, 259
Lycophron, IX. 527
Lycosthenes, Conrad, *Prodigiorum ac
  Ostentorum Chronicon*, III. 111
Lycurgus, X. 59
Lydd, V. 34
Lydgate, John (1370?–1450?), I. 285;
  II. 104, 159, 161, 163, 164, 166, 175,
  197–205 (main entry), 206 ff., 214,
  218 ff., 224 ff., 231, 237, 239, 245, 246,
  252, 253, 258, 261, 266, 332, 467, 468,
  470; III. 68, 70, 168, 192 ff., 198, 199,
  227, 277, 282, 292, 301, 411 ff., 441 ff.;
  IV. 441; X. 239; XIII. 211
  Aesop, II. 199, 204
  Albon and Amphabel, II. 199
  Assembly of Gods, The, II. 199, 203
  Balade of the Goos, A, II. 308
  Ballade of the Midsummer Rose, II. 204
  Bochas, John, Tragedies of, II. 202
  Churl and the Bird, The, II. 199, 204,
    312; IV. 409
  Complaint of the Black Knight, The,
    II. 162, 164, 166, 204
  Court of Sapience, The, II. 199, 231
  Danse Macabre, II. 199; V. 12
  De Duobus Mercatoribus, II. 199
  December and July, II. 199
  Edmund and Fremund, II. 199, 203
  Falls of Princes, The, II. 199, 200, 202,
    204, 321; III. 192, 194, 195
  Flower of Courtesy, The, II. 199
  Horse, the Sheep and the Goose, The,
    II. 199, 204, 312
  Jak Hare, II. 505
  Life of our Lady, II. 199, 203, 314
  London Lickpenny, II. 200, 201, 204,
    206, 470, 505
  Lyfe and Passion of Saint Alban, IV. 409
  Minor Poems, II. 199
  Miracles of St Edmund, II. 199
  Nightingale Poems, II. 199, 204
  Pilgrimage of the Life of Man, The, II.
    199, 200

Lydgate, John
  Prioress and her Three Sisters, The, II.
    204
  Reason and Sensuality, II. 199, 202
  St Austin, II. 199
  St Giles, II. 199
  St Margaret, II. 199, 203
  Saints' Loves, II. 203
  Secrets of the Philosophers, The, II. 199,
    208
  Serpent of Dissension, The, V. 66
  Stans Puer ad mensam, II. 313
  Temple of Glass, The, II. 199, 202, 225,
    230, 231, 235, 308, 312
  Testament, II. 199, 204
  Thank God of all, II. 204
  Thebes, Story of, II. 164, 199 ff.
  Troy Book, II. 199, 202; V. 221
Lydgate, in *Middlemarch*, XIII. 399
Lydia, in Gissing's *Thyrza*, XIII. 459
Lydia, in Jago's *Edge-Hill*, X. 113
Lydia, in *Pedantius*, VI. 306
Lye, Edward (1694–1767), IX. 536; X. 225;
  XII. 344, 504
Lyell, Sir Charles (1797–1875), XIV. 292,
  562
  Antiquity of Man, The, XIV. 293
  Elements of Geology, The, XIV. 293
  Principles of Geology, The, XIV. 293, 299
  Second Visit to the United States, A,
    XIV. 293
  Travels in North America, XIV. 293
Lyle, Eustace, in Disraeli's *Coningsby*,
  XIII. 350
Lykewakes, I. 124
Lyly, John (1554?–1606), III. 241, 300,
  340, 341, 344 ff., 349, 350, 354 ff., 358,
  364, 365, 370, 392, 395, 397, 534, 544;
  V. 120, 121–141 (main entry), 142, 149,
  177, 414 ff.; VI. 13, 18, 215, 288, 336,
  387; VII. 154; VIII. 127; XI. 262; XIV.
  460
  Alexander and Campaspe, IV. 115; V.
    125, 126; VI. 287
  'Cupid and my Campaspe played at
    cards for kisses,' IV. 115; V. 125
  Endimion, V. 122, 124, 341
  Euphues, II. 340; III. 344 ff., 365, 366;
    IV. 344, 523; V. 114, 122, 127, 193, 338;
    VI. 388, 389
  Euphues and his Ephoebus, III. 346
  Galathea, IV. 77; VI. 365
  Love's Metamorphosis, V. 122; VI. 287,
    365
  Midas, IV. 115; V. 122, 124, 345, 369
  Mother Bombie, IV. 394; V. 122; VI. 14,
    99
  Pappe with a Hatchet, III. 394, 395, 397,
    543
  Sapho and Phao, V. 122, 124, 341; VI.
    287
  'Sing to Apollo,' IV. 115
Lyme Regis, VIII. 30; X. 20, 387; XII. 241
Lymington, X. 306
Lymne, XII. 347
Lynam, Robert (1796–1845), X. 459

Lynch, Hannah, XIII. 570
Lynch, Thomas Toke (1818–1871), XIII. 167, 174, 505
Lyndhurst, lord. *See* Copley, John Singleton
Lyndon, lady, in Thackeray's *Barry Lyndon*, XIII. 282
Lyndsay, Sir David (1490–1555), II. 91, 94, 249, 250, 265, 279; III. 115–130 (main entry), 135, 138, 142, 153, 156, 159, 498; IV. 322, 412 ff., 527; V. 392, 394; IX. 359; XI. 203, 204, 215; XII. 10, 350, 508, 517
  Answer, An, III. 121
  Deploratioun of the Death of Queen Magdalene, The, III. 130
  Description of Pedder Coffeis, Ane, III. 121
  Dialog betwix Experience and Ane Courteour, III. 130, 133
  Dreme, The, III. 116, 138
  Epistle to the Kingis Grace, III. 116
  Exhortation to the King, An (epilogue to *The Dreme*), III. 118
  Exclamatioun to the Redar, II. 283
  Historie of the Squyer Meldrum, The, I. 291; II. 245; III. 130
  John the Commonweill, II. 280
  Justing betwix James Watson and Johne Barbour, The, III. 121, 135
  Kitteis Confessioun, III. 121
  Pleasant Satyre of the Thrie Estaitis, Ane, III. 122 ff.; V. 59; IX. 365
  Publict Confessioun of the Kingis auld Hound callit Baysche, Ane, III. 121
  Supplicatioun againis Syde Taillis, Ane, III. 121
  Testament and Complaynt of our Soverane Lordis Papyngo, The, II. 266; III. 118, 119, 131, 484
  Tragedie of the Cardinal, The, III. 130
Lyndwood, William (1375?–1446), II. 62, 498; VIII. 466
Lyne, Charles E., XIV. 587
Lynedoch, lord. *See* Graham, Thomas
Lynn, Norfolk, II. 287; IX. 2; X. 244, 460
Lynn, Elizabeth. *See* Linton, Elizabeth Lynn
Lynne, Walter (*fl.* 1550), III. 81
Lynton, in *Lorna Doone*, XIII. 434
Lynton, Thomas de, VI. 280
Lyon, John (1514?–1592), VII. 336
Lyon, John, 9th earl of Strathmore (1737–1776), X. 131
Lyonesse, I. 279
Lyons, II. 316, 323
Lyra, II. 365
Lyra Apostolica, XII. 257, 454, 456, 457; XIII. 171
Lyra Heroica, XIII. 195
Lyrical Ballads, X. 234
Lyrick, the poet, in Farquhar's *Love and a Bottle*, VIII. 170
Lyrics, Harleian (B.M. 2253), I. 360 ff., 370, 378
Lysias, VII. 316; IX. 528

Lysons, Daniel (1762–1834), XII. 511; *Magna Britannia*, XII. 345; *Environs of London*, XII. 345
Lysons, Samuel (1763–1819), XII. 511; *Reliquiae Britannico-Romanae*, XII. 345
'Lyster, Lynn,' XIV. Add. 5
Lyte, Henry (1529?–1607), III. 551; *A Niewe herball*, IV. 374, 542
Lyte, Henry Francis (1793–1847), XII. 419
Lyttelton, Charles (1714–1768), X. 247, 251
Lyttelton, George, 1st baron Lyttelton (1709–1773), IX. 220, 229, 230, 313; X. 29, 34, 36, 39, 94, 95, 100, 102 ff., 110, 113 ff. (main entry), 262, 263, 292, 448, 450, 456, 502; XI. 347, 349, 474
  Dialogues of the Dead, IX. 159, 160; X. 20, 114, 115; XI. 351
  History of Henry II, IX. 160; X. 114, 292, 311; XI. 345
  Monody, X. 113, 114
  Observations on the Conversion of St Paul, X. 114
  Persian Letters, X. 114
  Progress of Love, X. 114
Lyttelton, George William, 4th baron (1817–1876), XII. 484
Lyttelton, Lucy, born Fortescue, wife of Lyttelton, George, 1st baron, X. 113
Lyttelton, Sir Thomas (1647?–1710), X. 113
Lytteltons, the, X. 273
Lytton, Edward George Earle Lytton Bulwer-Lytton, 1st baron (1803–1873), XI. 304, 387; XII. 131, 414, 428, 429, 432; XIII. 307, 340, 386, 391, 392, 417 ff. (main entry), 427, 431, 432, 434, 516, 520, 563, 564; XIV. 174, 196, 238, 510
  Asmodeus at Large, XIII. 420
  Caxtons, The, XIII. 420
  Coming Race, The, XIII. 417, 420
  Devereux, XIII. 419
  Disowned, The, XIII. 418
  Eugene Aram, XIII. 418, 419
  Falkland, XIII. 417
  Glenallan, XIII. 419
  Godolphin, XIII. 419
  Harold, XIII. 419
  Haunted and the Haunters, The, XIII. 420
  Ishmael and other Poems, XIII. 417
  Kenelm Chillingly, XIII. 417, 420
  Lady of Lyons, The, XIII. 419
  Last Days of Pompeii, The, XIII. 419
  Last of the Barons, The, XIII. 419
  Lucretia, XIII. 418, 420
  Money, XI. 82; XIII. 419
  Mortimer, XIII. 417
  My Novel, XIII. 420
  New Timon, The, XIV. 129
  Parisians, The, XIII. 417, 421
  Paul Clifford, XIII. 418, 419
  Pausanias the Spartan, XIII. 419
  Pelham, X. 39; XIII. 417 ff., 421, 436
  Pilgrims of the Rhine, The, XIII. 417

Lytton, Edward George Earle Lytton
  Bulwer-Lytton
  Richelieu, XIII. 419
  Rienzi, XIII. 419
  Sea-Captain, The, XIII. 279
  Strange Story, A, XIII. 420
  What will he do with it? XIII. 420
  Zanoni, XIII. 419
  Zicci, XIII. 419
Lytton, Edward Robert Bulwer, 1st earl
  of Lytton (Owen Meredith) (1831–
  1891), XIII. 194, 199, 204, 505
  After Paradise, XIII. 200
  Astarte, XIII. 200
  Chronicles and Characters, XIII. 200
  Fables in Song, XIII. 200
  Fata Morgana, XIII. 200
  Glenaveril, XIII. 200
  King Poppy, XIII. 200
  Love Letter, A, XIII. 200
  Lucile, XIII. 200
  Marah, XIII. 200
  Selenites, XIII. 200
  Wanderer, The, XIII. 200
Lytton, Bulwer, lady, XII. 441
Lytton, Victor Alexander George Robert,
  2nd earl of Lytton, XIII. 564

M.P., *pseud.*, XI. 379, 480
Maasdorp, A. F. S., XIV. Add. 8
Mab, in *The Satyr*, VI. 340
Mab, queen, in *Romeo and Juliet*, VII. 8;
  XIV. 307
Mabbe, James (1572–1642?), IV. 395, 441,
  443, 447
Mabbott, Gilbert, VII. 351; *Mercurius
  Britannicus*, VII. 357; *The Moderate*, VII.
  357
Mabel, daughter of Robert Fitz-hamon,
  I. 256
Mabillon, Jean, IV. 419; XIV. 53
Mabinogion, I. 249, 252, 253, 255, 269,
  271, 276, 461. See, also, Lady C. Guest
Macalister, R. A. S., XII. 351, 352, 360
Macartney, George, 1st earl Macartney
  (1737–1806), XI. 350
Macaulay, Mrs Catharine, born Sawbridge
  (1731–1791), X. 502; XI. 390; XIV. 600
Macaulay, George Campbell (1852–1915),
  X. 449; XII. 504
Macaulay, Thomas Babington, 1st baron
  Macaulay (1800–1859), IV. 45, 480;
  VII. 129, 177, 218, 220; VIII. 107, 159,
  167, 242, 273; IX. 31, 127, 182, 240, 263;
  X. 66, 153, 242, 243, 298, 315, 320, 476,
  480, 483; XI. 167, 286, 410, 423; XII.
  129, 141, 152, 153, 155, 163, 178, 221,
  262, 319, 396, 420, 426, 444, 447, 477,
  480; XIII. 8, 43, 147 ff. (main entry),
  189, 230, 238, 320, 328, 487, 505; XIV.
  55, 58, 59 ff. (main entry), 71, 77, 88,
  89, 115, 125, 159, 170, 180, 336, 337,
  365, 462, 493, 504, 506, 509, 510
  Battle of the Lake Regillus, The, XIII. 149
  Epitaph on a Jacobite, XIII. 148, 239
  Essays, XII. 326; XIV. 5, 61 ff.

Macaulay, Thomas Babington
  Essays: Gladstone on Church and State,
  XIII. 24
  History (essay), XIV. 59
  History of England, XIII. 11; XIV. 60 ff.,
  84
  Last Buccaneer, The, XIII. 178, 239
  Lays of Ancient Rome, XII. 30; XIII. 148,
  149, 152, 153, 239; XIV. 61
  Miscellaneous Writings, XIV. 59
  Prophecy of Capys, The, XIII. 149
  Virginia, XII. 261
  *Westminster Reviewer's Defence of Mill,
  The*, XIV. 59
Macaulay, Zachary (1768–1838), XI. 259,
  475; XIV. 60
Macbean, Alexander (d. 1784), X. 470
Macbean, Lachlan, XIV. 541, *also see*
  Add. 2
Macbeth, in Boece, III. 156
Macbeth, in Wyntoun, II. 132
Macbeth, Garrick as, XI. 284
Macbeth, lady, in Shakespeare's play, XII.
  68, 171; XIV. 157
Macbeth, Shakespeare's, II. 89; VIII. 120;
  XIII. 67
Macbeth, W. H. W. Betty as, XI. 283
MacCabe, W. Gordon, XIII. 477
Maccallum, Mungo William, XIII. 477
McCalmont, Hugh. *See* Cairns, 1st earl
MacCarthy, Denis Florence (1817–1882),
  XIV. 569; *Pillar Towers of Ireland, The*,
  XIV. 318; *Shelley's Early Life*, XIV. 318;
  Waiting for the May, XIV. 318
MacCarthy, Desmond, XIII. 572
McCarthy, Justin Huntley (1830–1912),
  XIV. 493, 511, 528, 532, 569
McCaul, John, XII. 511
MacCaura clan, XIV. 318
Macclesfield, earl of. *See* Parker, Thomas
McClintock, Sir Francis Leopold (1819–
  1907), XIV. 245, 553
MacColl, Evan (1808–1898), XIV. 582;
  Poems and Songs, XIV. 357
MacColl, Malcolm (1831–1907), XIV. 513
Maccoll, Norman (1843–1904), XIV. 534
McCombie, Thomas, XIV. 587
McCormick, Charles (1755?–1807), XI. 390
McCormick, Joseph (1733–1799), IX. 492;
  X. 503; *State Papers and Letters*, X. 295
McCosh, James (1811–1894), XIV. 467,
  476
MacCowl, Finn, X. 231
McᶜCoy, Sir Frederick (1823–1899), XIV.
  563
McCracken, Henry Noble, II. 468, 470
McCrie, Thomas (1772–1835), XIV. 493,
  507; *Life of Andrew Melville, The*, XIV.
  101; *Life of John Knox, The*, XIV. 101
McCrindle, John Watson, XIV. 338, 339,
  579
MacCullagh, James (1809–1847), XIV. 261,
  556
MacCullagh Torrens. *See* Torrens
MacCulloch, John Ramsay (1789–1864),
  XII. 522; XIV. 3, 476, 513

MacCunn, John, XIII. 21, 472
M'Cutcheon, the name, II. 117
MacDermott, Martin, XIV. 573
MacDonagh, M., XIV. 541
Macdonald, Flora (1722–1790), IX. 563
Macdonald, George (1824–1905), XI. 387,
481; XII. Add. 5; XIII. 189 ff., 431, 505,
564
    Lilith, XIII. 183, 432
    Phantastes, XIII. 183, 192, 432
    Portent, The, XIII. 183, 192
    Robert Falconer, XIII. 432
MacDonald, Ronald, XIII. 564
Macdonald, William, XII. 435
Macdonell, James (1842–1879), XIV. 534
McDow, in Susan Ferrier's *Destiny*, XII.
245
Macduff, in Wyntoun, II. 132
Macedon, XII. 309
Macedonia, IV. 59
Macer (herbalist), II. 364; IV. 542
Macfarlan, James (1832–1862), XIII. 505
Macfarlane, Alexander, XIV. 263
Macfarlane, Charles (d. 1858), XIII. 564;
XIV. 487, 494, 612
Macfie, Ronald F., XIV. 538
M'Gibbon, Edinburgh musician, IX. 371,
379
McGie, Thomas D'Arcy (1825–1868), XIV.
318, 322, 357, 569, 582
    Celts, The, XIV. 318
    Home Thoughts, XIV. 318
    I left two loves, XIV. 318
    My Irish Wife, XIV. 318
    Sea-divided Gaels, The, XIV. 318
McGill university, Montreal, XIV. 355
Macgillivray, Evan James, XIV. 536
MacGregor, James Comyn, XIV. Add. 7
Macgregor, John (1825–1892), XIV. 552,
553
Macgregor, Malcolm (William Mason), X.
398, 525
McHale, John (1791–1881), XIV. 328, 329,
569
Machar (Mauricius), St, II. 127
Machiavelli, in *Romola*, XIII. 394
Machiavelli, Niccolò, III. 245, 315, 432;
IV. 342, 347, 446; VI. 167; VIII. 123;
IX. 225; XI. 32
    Arte of Warre, IV. 4, 7, 8
    Florentine Historie, IV. 7, 8, 398
    Prince, The, IV. 7, 8, 297
    Relazioni, III. 432
Machin, Lewis (*fl.* 1608), VI. 100; *Dumbe
Knight, The*, IV. 377, 539
Machlinia, William de (*fl.* 1482–1490),
VIII. 314
    Books printed by, II. 318 ff.: *Monk of
Evesham*, II. 318; IV. 353; *Speculum
Christiani*, II. 319; *Treatise of the Pesti-
lence*, II. 319
Machyn or Machin, Henry (1498?–1563?),
III. 478; V. 70; VI. 461; X. 492
Macilente, in *Every Man out of His
Humour*, VI. 17
MacIlwaine, William, XIV. 573

MacIntyre, Hector, in *The Antiquary*, X.
231
MacIvor, Fergus, in *Waverley*, XII. 26
MacIvor, Flora, in *Waverley*, XII. 22
Mackail, John William, XI. 416; XII. 407;
XIII. 493, 495
Mackaile, Matthew (*fl.* 1657–1696), IX. 559
Mackarness, Matilda Anne, born Planché
(1826–1881), XI. 489
Mackay, Angus M., XIII. 558
Mackay, Charles (1814–1889), XII. 380;
XIII. 505; XIV. 199; *Cholera Chant*, XIII.
189; *O Ye Tears!* XIII. 188
Mackay, Sir Donald, 1st baron Reay
(1591–1649), VII. 231
Mackay, Robert William (1803–1882), XII.
468
Mackay, Thomas, XIV. 506
Mackaye, Saunders, in Kingsley's *Alton
Locke*, XIII. 361, 362
Mackechnie, James, XIII. 569
Mackelvie, William (1800–1863), XI. 442
Mackenzie, Sir Alexander (1755–1820),
XIV. 583; *Voyages from Montreal*, XIV.
358
Mackenzie, George, 1st earl of Cromarty
(1630–1714), IX. 215, 492, 551, 561
Mackenzie, Sir George (1636–1691), IX.
493, 551, 561; XIV. 491; *Aretina, or the
Serious Romance*, VII. 391; VIII. 372
Mackenzie, George (1669–1725), IX. 553
Mackenzie, Henry (1745–1831), X. 46,
55 ff., 424, 436, 451, *also see* Add.;
XI. 440, 442, 449, 457; XII. 245; XIII.
326; XIV. 600
    Julia de Roubigné, X. 57, 58
    Man of Feeling, X. 15, 55 ff.; XI. 206
    Man of the World, X. 57
    Prince of Tunis, X. 55
Mackenzie, Sir James Dixon, XII. 511;
The Castles of England, XII. 349
Mackenzie, John, XIV. Add. 8
Mackenzie, Mrs, in *The Newcomes*, XIII
296, 297, 299
Mackenzie, Robert James, XIV. 601
Mackenzie, Rosey, in *The Newcomes*, XIII
296, 299
Mackenzie, William Mackay, XIV. 522
McKerrow, Ronald Brunlees, IV. 171; XI.
466
Mackery End, XII. 183, 194
Mackinder, Halford John, XIV. 596
Mackintosh, Sir James (1765–1832), VII.
203; XI. 75, 76, 396, 399; XII. 187, 303,
310; XIII. 418; XIV. 58, 110, 184, 186,
494
    *Dissertation on the Progress of Ethical
Philosophy*, XIV. 5, 59
    History of England, XIV. 59
    *History of the Revolution in England in
1688*, XIV. 59
    Memoirs, XI. 53
Mackintosh, Robert James, XI. 53
Macklin, Charles (1697?–1797), X. 85, 445;
XI. 258, 260, 262, 447, 449, 450, 454;
XIV. 569; *Love à-la-mode*, XI. 257

Macknight, Thomas, XIII. 547; XIV. 508; *Life of Bolingbroke*, IX. 217, 226, 227, 230

Mackshane, in Smollett's *Roderick Random*, X. 37

Mackworth, Sir Humphry (1657–1727), IX. 11, 420

Macky, John (d. 1726), VIII. 219; IX. 494; *Journey through England*, XI. 332

McLachlan, Alexander (1818–1896), XIV. 357, 582

Maclaren, Charles (1782–1866), XIV. 535

Maclaren, Elizabeth T., XIV. 517

Maclaurin, Colin (1698–1746), XIV. 257, 556

Maclean, Neil N., XIV. 594

M'Lean, T., XIV. 540

Macleane, Arthur John (1812–1858), XII. 487

Maclehose, Mrs Agnes ('Clarinda,' 1759–1841), XI. 222, 436, 437; *Talk not of Love*, XI. 232; *To a Blackbird*, XI. 232

McLennan, John Ferguson (1827–1881), XIV. 476; *Primitive Marriage*, XII. 348

M'Lennan, Murdoch, *Race of Sheriffmuir*, IX. 373

McLennan, William (1856–1904), XIV. 581 *In Old France and New*, XIV. 360 *Songs of Old Canada*, XIV. 360 *Span o' Life, The*, XIV. 360 *Spanish John*, XIV. 360

Macleod, Fiona. *See* Sharp, William

Macleod, Henry Dunning (1821–1902), XIV. 476

Macleod, Mary, *The Shakespeare Story Book*, XI. 385

Macleod, Norman (1812–1872), XI. 481; XII. 472

Maclis (a beast), III. 315

Maclise, Daniel (1806–1870), XII. 410, 428; XIII. 474

MacMechan, Archibald, XIII. 465, 466

Macmillan, Daniel (1813–1857), XIII. 553

Macmillan, Hugh (1833–1903), XII. 472

Macmillan's Magazine, XIII. 98; XIV 324

MacMorough, II. 301

MacMurchy, Archibald, XIV. 581

Macnab, Henry Grey (1761–1823), XIV. 607, 608

Macnally, Leonard (1752–1820), XI. 281, 458

MacNeil, Hector (1746–1818), XI. 444 *Come Under my Plaidie*, XI. 234 *Dinna think Bonnie Lassie*, XI. 234 *Donald and Flora*, XI. 234 *Harp, The*, XI. 234 *Mary of Castle Cary*, XI. 234 *My Boy Tammy*, XI. 234 *Scotland's Scaith*, XI. 234 *Waes of War*, XI. 234

Macnicol, Donald (1735–1802), X. 475

Macnish, Robert (1802–1837), XII. 450

Macpherson, David (1746–1816), XII. 517

Macpherson, Geraldine, XIV. 521, 569

Macpherson, James (1736–1796), I. 275; IX. 185, 564; X. 55, 130, 222, 227 ff.,

Macpherson, James
 230 ff. (main entry), 234, 237, 320, 487 ff., 503, 510; XI. 229
 Berrathon, X. 227
 Carric-thura, X. 228
 Cath-Loda, X. 130
 Death of Oscar, The, X. 230
 Fingal, X. 137, 225, 231
 Fragments of Ancient Poetry, X. 230
 Highlander, The, X. 230, 238
 History of Great Britain, X. 232, 295
 Hunter, The, X. 237
 Iliad (translation), X. 232
 Introduction to the History of Great Britain and Ireland, X. 295
 Original Papers, X. 295
 Ossian, XII. 40; XIII. 52, 101, 226
 Temora, X. 231
 See, also, under Ossian

Macray, William Dunn, VI. 309

Macready, William Charles (1793–1873), V. 302; XI. 447; XII. 171; XIII. 58, 59, 61, 68, 69, 255, 261; XIV. 319

Macro-plays, the, V. 391, 392

Macrobius, II. 366; X. 205, 481

Mac Roig, Fergus, XIV. 307

Macropedius, George, V. 412; *Asotus*, V. 101; *Rebelles*, V. 101, 110, 113

MacSpadden, Joseph Walker, XIII. 544

McWard, Robert (1633?–1687), IX. 546

Madagascar, IV. 101, 102; IX. 23

Madan, Falconer, XII. 469; XII. 462

Madan, Martin (1726–1790), XI. 81

Madden, D. D., XIV. 510

Madden, Sir Frederic (1801–1873), I. 269, 322, 326, 328; II. 45, 73, 431; XII. 356, 517

Madden, Richard Robert (1798–1886), XIII. 544; XIV. 532, 567, 569, 573

Madden, Samuel (1686–1765), X. 468

Madden, Virginia (Gissing's), XIII. 460

Maddison, Sir Ralph (1571?–1655?), VII. 515

Maddox, Isaac (1697–1759), IX. 212, 494

Maddox, Thomas (1666–1727), IX. 537; *Formulare Anglicanum*, IX. 355; *History of the Exchequer*, IX. 355

Madeira, XIV. 244, 293

Madeley, X. 365

Madeley, Eve (Gissing's), XIII. 459

Madeline, in Keats's *Eve of Saint Agnes*, XI. 131; XII. 86 ff.

Madeline, in *Nicholas Nickleby*, XIII. 318

Mademoiselle, in Vanbrugh's *Provok'd Wife*, VIII. 162

Madge, in *Misogonus*, V. 111

Madido, in *The Pilgrimage to Parnassus*, VI. 310

'Madonella' (Mary Astell), IX. 404

Madras, XIV. 336

'Madras' system of education, XIV. 403, 404

Madrid, VI. 203; VII. 215; VIII. 130, 141, 271

Maecenas, VII. 164

'Maecenas of Hill street,' XI. 350

Maeldun, the voyage of, XIV. 306
Maeldune. See *Maldon, The Battle of*
Maeterlinck, Maurice, XI. 384
Maevius, IV. 331
Maffei, Scipione, V. 289
'Maga.' See *Blackwood's Edinburgh Magazine*
Magazine of Zoology and Botany, XIV. 565
Magdeburg, siege of, VII. 22
Magellan, Ferdinand, IV. 69, 75, 78, 86, 92
Magellan, straits of, III. 358; IV. 77, 99
Maggie, in Burns's *Auld Farmer's Salutation*, XI. 214
Maggie, in Mrs Gaskell's *The Moorland Cottage*, XIII. 377
Maggie Lauder, IX. 364, 365
Maggie's Tocher, IX. 360
Magi, the, XII. 275
Magic, illustrations of, III. 495
Magicians, The Twa, II. 409
Maginn, William (1793–1842), XII. 123, 157 ff., 425, 428; XIII. 162, 163, 189, 292; XIV. 177, 236, 313 ff., 570; *Daniel O'Rourke*, XIV. 314; *Irishman and the Lady, The*, XIV. 313; *St Patrick*, XIV. 313
Magister Fabre, *praelector linguae Gallicanae*, IX. 412
Magistrates, A Mirror for. See *Mirror*
Maglocunus, king of Anglesey, I. 67
Magna Britannia et Hibernia, IX. 353, 537
Magna Carta, I. 151, 154, 174; VIII. 317, 465; X. 464; XIV. 75
Magna Charta, On the King's Breaking his Confirmation of, I. 376
'Magna Lilliputia,' X. 163, 464, 465
Magnano, in Butler's *Hudibras*, VIII. 68
Magnin, Charles, V. 302
Magnus, L., XIII. 486
Magnus de la Gardie, VIII. 20
Magnússon, Eiríkr, XIII. 125, 127, 492
Magomastix, H., VII. 507
Maguire, Trollope's, XIII. 422
Magyar versions of ballads, II. 405
Mahābhārata, XII. 503
Mahaffy, Sir John Pentland (1839–1919), V. 71; XII. 440, 485, 489, *also see* Add. 3
Mahan, Alfred Thayer, XIV. 486
Mahomet, IV. 214, 215; VIII. 291; IX. 54; X. 281, 503; XI. 18; XIII. 13
Mahon, viscount. *See* Stanhope, 5th earl
Mahony, Francis Sylvester (*pseud.* Father Prout, 1804–1866), XII. 123, 138, 428; XIII. 162; XIV. 185, 194, 549, 570; *Bells of Shandon, The*, XIV. 316; *Reliques of Father Prout*, XIV. 316; *Sabine Farmer's Serenade, The*, XIV. 316
Mahoun, in *Gyre Carling*, II. 276
'Mahownde,' V. 49
Mahrattas, the, XI. 17
Maia, in Keats's *Ode to Maia*, XII. 90
Maia, in *The Penates*, VI. 341
Maid Freed from the Gallows, The, II. 396, 405, 410
Maiden, Joseph Henry, XIV. 558
Maidens' tower, in *The Elegy on the Duke of Richmond*, III. 178

Maidment, James (1795?–1879), XII. 358, 517
Maidment's *Court of Session Garland*, X. 478
Maidstone, XII. 165
Maidwell, Laurence, *The Loving Enemies* (1680), VIII. 422
Maidwell, Lewis (*fl.* 1700), IX. 386, 387 397, 398, 411, 413, 570
Maigron, L., XII. 380
Maimbourg, L., VIII. 402, 456; *History of the League*, VIII. 34, 44
Main, Alexander, *Wise, Witty, and Tender Sayings of George Eliot*, XIII. 388, 551
Mainard, lady Margaret, VIII. 307
Maine, Sir Henry James Sumner (1822–1888), VIII. 312; XIV. 194, 198, 494, 502; *Ancient Law*, XII. 348; XIV. 36, 78; *Early History of Institutions, The*, XIV. 78; *Village Communities*, XII. 348; XIV. 78
Maintenon, Madame de, X. 135
Mainwaring, Edward, XI. 250
Mainwaring, Roger (1590–1653), VII. 160, 425, 433
Mainz, II. 310
Mais, Stuart Petre Brodie, XIII. 573
Maisey, Lady, II. 412
Maison Tellier, VI. 63
Maistre, Joseph de, XII. 254
Maitland, Edward (1824–1897), XIII. 564
Maitland, Frederic William (1850–1906), I. 363; VIII. 313; XIV. 79, 481, 485, 494 'Anglican Settlement and the Scottish Reformation,' XIV. 81
'Anglo-French Law Language, The,' XIV. 80
Bracton and Azo, XIV. 80
Bracton's Notebook, XIV. 80
Constitutional History of England, The, XIV. 81
Domesday Book and Beyond, I. 446; XIV. 80
English Law and the Renaissance, XIV. 81
Ford Lectures, XIV. 81
History of the English Law (with Sir F. Pollock), XIV. 80
Materials for English Legal History, The, XIV. 80
Roman Canon Law in the Church of England, XIV. 80
Year Books of Edward II, XIV. 81
Maitland, James, 8th earl of Lauderdale (1759–1839), XI. 29, 389; XII. 426, 427
Maitland, Sir John, 1st baron Maitland of Thirlstane (1545?–1595), III. 149, 150, 504
Works attributed to: *Aganis Sklanderous Tungis*, III. 150; *Ane Admonition to my Lord Regent's Grace*, III. 150; *Ane Schort Invectyve*, III. 150
Maitland, John, 2nd earl and 1st duke of Lauderdale (1616–1682), VII. 219, 435; VIII. 17, 250, 307; IX. 193, 194, 202
Maitland, Sir Richard, lord Lethington (1496–1586), III. 132 ff., 164, 499; IX. 365

Maitland, Sir Richard
  Advyce to lesum Merynes, III. 134
  Agains Discord among the Lordis, III. 133
  Agains the Division of the Lordis, III. 133
  Agains the Theives of Liddis-daill, III. 133
  Assemblie of the Congregation, Of the, III. 133
  Ballat of the Greatness of the World, III. 133
  Chronicle and History of the House and Surname of Seaton, A, III. 133
  Folye of Ane auld man maryand ane Young Woman, III. 133
  Gude Counseillis, III. 134
  Lament for the Disorders of the Cuntrie, III. 133
  Miseries of the Tyme, III. 133
  Na Kyndes without Siller, III. 134
  On the New Year, III. 133
  Quhair in the Blytheness that has been, III. 133
  Satire of the Aige, The, III. 133
  Satire of the Toun Ladies, The, III. 133
  Solace of Aige, III. 134
  Union among the Lordis, On, III. 133
Maitland, Samuel Roffey (1792–1866), XII. 367, 453, 522; XIV. 79, 495; *The Dark Ages*, X. 288
Maitland, Thomas, III. 165
Maitland, William (1528?–1573), III. 133; XII. 27
Maitland, William (1693?–1757), IX. 537
Maitland club, XII. 358, 359
Maitland MSS., II. 478; III. 132
Maittaire, Michael (1668–1747), IX. 529, 538
Major or Mair, John (1469–1550), II. 109, 244, 251, 260, 369, 371, 488; III. 151, 152, 155, 157, 319, 504; *Art of Making Puddings, The* (in *Pantagruel*), III. 151; *Commentary on the Four Books of the Sentences*, III. 151; *Historia Majoris Britanniae*, III. 151, 155
Mak, in *Secunda Pastorum*, V. 19, 47
Makculloch MS., II. 478
Makers of Canada series, XIV. 359
Makin, Mrs Bathsua (*fl.* 1673), IX. 403, 569
Makluire, John (*fl.* 1630), IX. 558
Maknab, in *Bruce*, II. 105
Makower, S. V., XIV. 208, 528
Makyne (Malkin), in *Robene and Makyne*, II. 249
Malabari, Bahramji, XIV. 341, 578; *The Indian Muse*, XIV. 342
Malacca, IV. 85
Malaprop, Mrs, in Sheridan's *Rivals*, X. 90, 91; XI. 266, 267, 277; XIV. 122, 387
Malay archipelage, XIV. 250
Malay language, XIV. 457, 459
Malbecco, in *The Devil and his Dame*, V. 329
Malbecco, in *The Faerie Queene*, V. 329
Malbie, N., IV. 540
Malchus, St, I. 74, 75, 191

Malcolm, in *Macbeth*, V. 213
Malcolm, in Wyntoun, II. 132
Malcolm, James Peller (1767–1815), XII. 507, 511
Malcolm, Sir John (1769–1833), XIV. 248, 491, 495, 553, 573, 578; *Central India*, XIV. 335; *History of Persia*, XIV. 335; *Political History of India*, XIV. 335
Malcolm of Scotland (Malcolm III), I. 140
Malden, John, X. 387
Malden, Surrey, II. 353; VII. 373
Maldon, The Battle of, I. 48, 109, 125, 137, 143, 144, 150, 278, 443
Malebranche, Nicolas, VIII. 347, 474, 476; IX. 282, 287, 521; *Recherche de la Vérité*, VIII. 348, 373; IX. 314
Malecasta, in *The Faerie Queene*, III. 231
Maleforts, the, in *The Unnaturall Combat*, VI. 153, 159
Malelas, Joannes, IX. 330, 524
Malespini, *Ducento Novelle*, VI. 202
Malet, Sir Alexander (1800–1886), XIV. 598
Malet, Harold Esdaile, XIV. 544
'Malet, Lucas,' XIII. 547
Malfato, in *The Ladies Triall*, VI. 194
Malfi, duchess of, in Webster's drama, XII. 68
Malgo, IV. 67
Malherbe, François de, VII. 2; VIII. 376
Malim, William (1553–1594), *Consuetudinary*, V. 102
Malines, V. 89, 90
Malkin, Benjamin Heath (1769–1842), *A Father's Memoir of his Child*, XI. 181, 182, 434
Malkin and Jankin, in *Lutel Soth Sermun*, I. 226
Mall, in *The Two Angry Women*, V. 330
Mallard, in Gissing's *The Emancipated*, XIII. 460
Malleson, George Bruce (1825–1898), XIV. 338, 495, 511, 578, 579; *History of the French in India*, XIV. 339
Mallet or Malloch, David (1705?–1765), IX. 181, 185–6 (main entry), 227, 295, 443, 449, 486, 504, *also see* Add.; X. 94, 107, 109, 301, 433, 437, 447, 449
  Amyntor and Theodora, IX. 186
  Birks of Endermay, IX. 186
  Edwin and Emma, IX. 186
  Elvira, X. 191, 477
  Excursion, The, IX. 186
  William and Margaret, IX. 182, 185, 186
Mallet, Sir Louis (1823–1890), XIV. 509, 512
Mallet, Paul Henri (1730–1807), X. 489; *Introduction à l'histoire du Dannemarc*, X. 225, 490; *Mythology of the Celtes*, X. 202; *Northern Antiquities*, XII. 368
Mallett, Mrs, VIII. 207
Malleus Maleficarum, III. 112
Malloch, David. *See* Mallet
Malmesbury, VII. 268, 282; VIII. 246
Malmesbury, earls of. *See* Harris, James; Harris, James Howard
Malmesbury, monk of (chronicler), II. 301

Malmesbury, William of. *See* William
Malmesbury abbey, I. 78, 159
Malone, Edmund (1741–1812), V. 143,
    146, 275 ff.; VI. 1, 249; VIII. 4, 56, 424;
    IX. 477; X. 181, 194, 201, 462, 463, 465,
    473, 478, 480, 485, 494; XI. 390; XII.
    365; *Life of Dryden*, VIII. 3
Malory, Sir Thomas (*fl.* 1470), I. 243, 245,
    268, 269, 273, 294, 295, 299; II. 315,
    334 ff., 340; III. 339; IV. 227; VII. 75,
    127; XIII. 119, 128, 199; *Morte d'Arthur*,
    II. 230, 314, 315, 332, 334 ff., 340, 486;
    IV. 397; V. 78; XIII. 35
Malpighi, Marcello, VIII. 362; XIV. 282
Malta, XI. 121, 393
Maltby, Edward (1770–1859), XII. 327,
    487, 491
Maltby, William (1763–1854), XII. 408
Malthus, Daniel (father of T. R. Malthus),
    XI. 73
Malthus, Thomas Robert (1766–1834), X.
    276; XI. 73 ff., 394, 399; XII. 431;
    Essay on the Principle of Population,
    XI. 74, 75; XIV. 298; *Inquiry into the
    Nature and Progress of Rent*, XI. 75;
    XIV. 3; *Principles of Political Economy*,
    XI. 75
Malvern, IV. 190; X. 134
'Malvern, John,' III. 325
Malvern, school of Benedictine monastery
    at, II. 2
Malvern hills, II. 2, 4, 5, 15; XIII. 49
Malvina, X. 227, 229
Malvolio, in *Twelfth Night*, IV. 78; V. 193,
    194; VII. 101
Maly Stewart, IX. 376
Malynes or Malines, Gerard (*fl.* 1586–1641),
    IV. 297, 309, 313, 512; VIII. 469
Mambres, legend of, I. 135
Mambrun, Pierre, *De Poemate Epico*, VII.
    270
Mammon, Sir Epicure, in *The Alchemist*,
    V. 356, 377; VI. 22, 23
Mammon, house of, in *The Faerie Queene*,
    III. 233, 237
Man, in *Mirour de l'Omme*, II. 140, 141,
    144
Man, isle of, IV. 190; X. 193; XII. 509, 512,
    519; XIV. 297
Man in Black, in Goldsmith's *Citizen of the
    World*, X. 198, 206
Man in the Moon, The (1609), III. 487
Man in the Moon, The (1660), VII. 360
Man of Law (Chaucer's), IV. 207
Man of no Honour, The, VIII. 92
'Man of Ross' (John Kyrle), X. 277
Man of the Hill, in Fielding's *Tom Jones*,
    X. 30
Mananan's mantle, XIV. 320
Manawyÿan, Son of Llÿr, I. 252, 255
Manchester, III. 428; V. 251; VIII. 62;
    IX. 325, 386; X. 510, 516; XII. 337, 366;
    XIII. 351, 373, 374; XIV. 23, 152, 169,
    179, 195, 204, 259, 275
    Academy, X. 385, 386; XIV. 386
    Baron's hall, IV. 433

Manchester
    Chetham library, IV. 432; XII. 369, 514,
        522
    College of Arts and Science, XIV. 386
    Cross street unitarian chapel, XIII. 372
    John Rylands library, XII. 365, 523
    Literary and Philosophical society, XIV.
        386
    Moss Side library, XII. 445
    Newton's lane, III. 392
    Owens college, XII. 333; XIII. 455; XIV.
        290, 432
    Plymouth grove, XIII. 372
    Victoria university, XII. 369; XIV. 432
Manchester, duke of. *See* Montagu,
    Charles
Manchester, earl of. *See* Montagu, Edward
Manchester, Isabella, duchess of, XI. 174
Manchester Examiner and Times, The,
    XIV. 189
Manchester Guardian, The, XIII. 373; XIV.
    91, 203, 531, 535
Mancini, VII. 61
Mancinus, Dominicus, III. 57, 187
Mandeville, Bernard (1670?–1733), IV.
    299; IX. 309, 507, 512, 571; *Essay on
    Charity*, IX. 407; *Fable of the Bees*, IX.
    302, 311, 323, 474, 507, 510, 512, 548;
    Grumbling Hive, The, IX. 302, 311
Mandeville, Sir John, XIII. 124
Mandeville, Travels of Sir John, I. 307;
    II. 70 ff., 78 ff., 231, 286, 298, 321, 323,
    338, 429, 445, 446; IV. 68, 414
Manette, Lucie, in *A Tale of Two Cities*,
    XIII. 333
Manfred, in Byron's drama, XII. 45, 47
Mangan, James Clarence (1803–1849),
    XIV. 305, 318*a*, 318*b*, 570
Mangin, Edward (1772–1852), *Essay on
    Light Reading*, X. 195, 411, 483
*Maniere de langage que l'enseignera bien a
    droit parler et escrire doulz françois*, II.
    421
*Manifest detection of the most vyle and de-
    testable use of dice play, A*, III. 98
Manila, IV. 100; XIV. 242, 243
Manilius, III. 113; IX. 338, 525, 526
Manilla, X. 403
Maning, Frederick Edward (1812–1883),
    XIV. 587
Manipulus curatorum, II. 325
Manitius, I. 83
Mankynd, V. 52, 392
Manley, Mrs Mary de la Rivière (1663–
    1724), VIII. 438; IX. 462, *also see* Add.;
    XIV. 197; *New Atalantis*, IX. 18; *Royal
    Mischief, The*, VIII. 195
Manley, Thomas (1628–1690), *Temporis
    Angustiae*, VII. 392, 517
Manlius, M., IV. 13
Manly, John M., V. Add. 2
Manly, in Wycherley's *Country Wife*, VIII.
    143, 145, 165
Mann, Sir Horace (1701–1786), IX. 246;
    X. 245, 247, 249 ff., 253, 256, 495; XI.
    259, 260; XIV. 607

Mann, Dr R. J., XIII. 478; XIV. Add. 6, 8

Mannering, Julia, in Scott's *Guy Mannering*, XII. 22

Manners, Catherine (d. 1711), wife of 2nd duke of Rutland, VIII. 272

Manners, Charles, 4th duke of Rutland (1754–1787), XI. 143

Manners, John, marquis of Granby (1721–1770), X. 197, 403, 407

Manners, lord Robert (1758–1782), XI. 145

Manners, Roger, 5th earl of Rutland (1576–1612), V. 222

Manning, Anne (1807–1879), XII. 450; *Mary Powell*, XIII. 434

Manning, Henry Edward (1808–1892), cardinal, XII. 275, 276, 458, *also see* Add.; XIV. 513

Manning, Mr, VIII. 411

Manning, Owen (1721–1801), XII. 344, 504, 511

Manning, Thomas (1772–1840), XII. 181, 187 ff.

Manning, William (1630?–1711), X. 378

Manning, William Oke (1809–1878), XIV. 594

Manningham, John (d. 1622), *Diary*, IV. 262; VI. 461; VII. 221, 451

Mannington, G., *Sorrowful Sonet made at Cambridge Castle*, III. 191

Manningtree, Essex, XII. 305

Mannyng, Robert, of Brunne (*fl.* 1288–1338), I. 204, 335, 340, 341, 344–352 (main entry), 358, 399, 475; II. 133, 139, 150, 378, 420; III. 275; IX. 535; *Chronicle of England*, I. 350 ff.; III. 289; *Handlyng Synne*, I. 341, 344 ff., 350, 352; II. 139, 143, 378; *Medytacyuns of þe soper of oure lorde Jhesu*, etc., I. 352

Manorbier castle, Wales, I. 194

Mansbridge, Albert, *University Tutorial Classes*, XIV. 409, 591

Mansel, Henry Longueville (1820–1871), XII. 289, 469; XIV. 29, 197, 474, 476 *Letters, Lectures and Reviews*, XIV. 13 *Limits of Religious Thought, The*, XIV. 13 *Metaphysics*, XIV. 13 *Philosophy of the Conditioned*, XIV. 13 *Phrontisterion*, XIV. 13 *Prolegomena Logica*, XIV. 13

Mansell of Ottery, in *The Ship of Fools*, III. 60

Mansfeld, count E. von, VII. 453

Mansfield, Charles Blackford (1819–1855), XIV. 558

Mansfield, earl of. *See* Murray, William

Mansfield, Sir James (1733–1821), XI. 58

Mansfield park, in Jane Austen's novel, XII. 241

Mansfield Woodhouse, X. 257

Mansion, Colard, II. 311

Manso, Giovanni Baptista, marquis of Villa, VII. 99

Mansoul, in *The Holy War*, VII. 177

Mant, Alicia Catherine, XI. 488

Mant, Richard (1776–1848), X. 238, 240, 473, 492, 493; XII. 420

Mantalinis, the, in *Nicholas Nickleby*, XIII. 318

Mantoux, Paul, XIV. 591

Mantua, V. 369

Mantua, duchess of, in *The Humorous Courtier*, VI. 205

Mantua, duke of, in *The Imposture*, VI. 205

Mantuan or Mantuanus (Johannes Baptista Spagnuoli), III. 62 ff., 185, 187, 219, 221, 223 ff., *also see* Add.; IV. 121, 169, 171, 446; VI. 364; *De Consuetudine Divitum erga Poetas*, III. 224; *Religio*, III. 223, 224

Mantzius, Karl, XI. 447

Manuale ad usum Sarum, IV. 427

Manuel, king of Granada, in Congreve's *Mourning Bride*, VIII. 152

Manuel, Niclas, *Krankheit der Messe*, III. 80

Manufacturer, The, IX. 14, 433

Manutius, VII. 315

Manutius, in *The Bugbears*, V. 115

Manwayring, Sir Henry, *The Sea-man's Dictionary*, IV. 107, 459

Manwood, Elegy on, V. 148

Manwood, John (d. 1610), IV. 541; VIII 467

Manzoni, Alessandro, *I promessi Sposi*, XII. 254

Maoris, the, XIV. 368

Map or Mapes, Walter (*fl.* 1200), I. 157, 160, 173, 176, 177, 188 ff., 264, 270, 271, 272, 367, 450, 455; III. 485; VII. 380; *De Nugis Curialium*, I. 177, 189, 264, 450, 455; VII. 370, 505; *Lancelot du Lac*, I. 190, 264, 270; *Quest of the Holy Grail*, I. 190, 270, 271, 272

Mapheus Vegius, 13th book of *Aeneid*, II. 262, 263

Mapledurham, IX. 443, 448

Maplet, John (d. 1592), IV. 543

Mappa Mundi, IV. 421

'Maps' (John Nicholson), XI. 338

Mar, countess of, IX. 248

Maraffi, B., IV. 446

Marathas, the, XIV. 337, 338, 341

Marathon, I. 95

Marbeck, Roger (1536–1605), VI. 286

Marble hill, IX. 250

Marbod of Rheims, I. 232

Marburg, III. 43

Marcelia, in *The Duke of Millaine*, VI. 154, 158, 159

Marcella, in *Gorboduc*, V. 67

Marcelline, G., IV. 540

Marcellinus, Ammianus, IV. 4, 438

Marcellinus Comes, I. 81

Marcello, in *The White Divel*, VI. 175, 176

'Marcellus allowance,' XIII. 219

March, earl of, letter to Henry IV of England, II. 284, 503

March, John (1612–1657), VII. 515

Marchant, John, *History of the Present Rebellion*, 1746, IX. 564; *Puerilia*, 1751, XI. 372

Marchioness, the, in *The Old Curiosity Shop*, XIII. 320

Marchmont, earls of. *See* Hume, Hugh; Hume, Patrick

Marchmont, Miss, in Kelly's *False Delicacy*, XI. 263

Marcia, in Addison's *Cato*, IX. 64

Marcia (*i.e.* Venice), in *Euphormio*, IV. 256

Marcius, in Addison's *Cato*, IX. 63

Marcks, Erich, V. 339

Marco Polo, II. 184; IV. 68, 446

Marcolf, I. 63

Marcolphus, II. 319

Marconi, G., XIV. 453

Marcus, in Owen's *Epigrammata*, IV. 265

Marcus, *The Vision of Tundale*, XIV. 306

Marcus Aurelius, III. 199, 346; IV. 435; VII. 487; VIII. 277; XII. 487

Marcus Aurelius, The Golden Book of, II. 340

Marcus Germinus, V. 70; VI. 299

Mardonius, in *A King and no King*, VI. 127

Mardontius, in Digby's *Memoirs*, VII. 222

Mare of Collington, The, IX. 366

Marfisa, in *Orlando Furioso*, III. 231, 236

Margam, chronicle of the abbey of, I. 256

Margaret, in *Faust*, V. 20

Margaret, in *Henry VI*, V. 186

Margaret, in *James IV*, V. 138

Margaret, in Mrs Gaskell's *North and South*, XIII. 378

Margaret, in Mrs Oliphant's *Kirsteen*, XIII. 431

Margaret, in *Much Ado about Nothing*, V. 191

Margaret, in *Richard III*, V. 186

Margaret, in *The Cloister and the Hearth*, XIII. 429

Margaret (d. 1093), daughter of Edward Aetheling, I. 140

Margaret, duchess of Burgundy (1446–1503), II. 307, 309, 311, 312

Margaret (Tudor), princess, queen of Scots (1489–1541), II. 252, 253, 281; III. 98; VI. 333

Margaret, queen, the 'riding against,' at Coventry, V. 10

Margaret, St, Life of, I. 229, 459; II. 321

Margaret Beaufort (lady Margaret). *See* Beaufort

Margaret of Anjou, queen of England (1430–1482), II. 199, 209, 210, 303, 358, 500

Margaret of Fressingfield, in *Frier Bacon*, V. 137

Margaret of Valois, queen of Navarre, IV. 6, 169, 182, 259; *Heptameron*, VI. 99, 199, 202

Margate, XIII. 112

Marguerite, in Godwin's *St Leon*, XI. 293

Marguerite, in *Pearl*, I. 321

Marguerite d'Angoulême, III. 1

Maria, in Lillo's *George Barnwell*, X. 75, 79

Maria, in Sheridan's *School for Scandal*, XI. 270, 271

Maria, in *Twelfth Night*, IV. 78; V. 194

Maria Grey Training college, XIV. 430

Mariamne, VI. 154

Marian, in *John a Kent and John a Cumber*, V. 317

Marian, in *The Sad Shepherd*, VI. 370

Marian, maid, V. 32, 35, 318

Marian persecution, IV. 429

Marian system of dating, VI. 255

Mariana (Tennyson's), V. 190; XIII. 29

Mariana, in *Perimedes the Blacksmith*, III. 356, 357

Mariana, Juan de, VI. 494; *Contra los Juegos Publicos*, VII. 377; *De Rege et Regis Institutione*, VII. 377; *History of Spain*, IX. 278, 501

Marianus, Scotus (1028–1082?), I. 161

Marie, in Kingsley's *Two Years Ago*, XIII. 365

Marie de France, I. 238, 239, 270, 274, 281, 294, 295, 300, 462, 469; II. 183, 420; XIII. 140; *Lai le Freine*, I. 281, 300, 465; II. 410; *Lanval*, I. 274; *Le Chèvrefeuille*, I. 274

Marie-Antoinette, queen of France, X. 251; XI. 24, 157

Maries, the three, at the tomb, V. 39

Marillier, Harry Currie, XIV. 539

Marina, in *Britannia's Pastorals*, IV. 157

Marine Biological association, XIV. 297

Marinell, in *The Faerie Queene*, III. 240

Marino, Giambattista, IV. 213; VII. 34, 83; *Adone*, VII. 268; VIII. 374; *Strage degli Innocenti*, IV. 36

Marino Faliero, in Byron's drama, XII. 49

Marion (type name of French shepherdess), V. 34, 35

Marionnettes, V. 27

Marivaux, Pierre C. de C. de, X. 68, 89, *also see* Add.; *Jeu de l'Amour*, X. 79; *Marianne*, X. 3, 26; *Paysan Parvenu*, X. 26

Mark (March) ab Meirchion, king of Cornwall, I. 273, 274, 310; II. 337

Market Bosworth, X. 159

Markham, Sir Clements Robert, XIV. 486, 553, 554

Markham, Gervase (1568?–1637), IV. 308, 364 ff., 537 ff.; V. 351, 478; VI. 456; XIV. 232

Cavelarice, or the English Horseman, IV. 365 ff.

Cheap and Good Husbandry, IV. 372

Complete Farriar, The, IV. 368

Country Contentments, IV. 372, 373

Country Housewifes Garden, IV. 375

Country-mans Recreation, IV. 375

Devoreux, or vertues tears, IV. 376, 377

Discource of Horsemanshippe, A, IV. 365

Dumbe Knight, The, IV. 377

English Arcadia, The, IV. 377

English Husbandman, IV. 375

English Huswife, IV. 373

Famous Whore, The, IV. 376

Markham, Gervase
  Gentlemans Academie, IV. 375
  Grinvile, Knight, The Most Honourable Tragedie of Sir Richard, IV. 376
  Herod and Antipater, IV. 377
  How to chuse, ride...both hunting horses and running horses, IV. 365
  How to trayne and teach horses to amble, IV. 365
  Inrichment of the Weald of Kent, The, IV. 373
  Maister-peece, IV. 367
  Marie Magdalens lamentations, IV. 376
  Markhams Faithfull Farrier, IV. 368
  Markhams Farewell to Husbandry, IV. 373
  Markhams Method: or Epitome, IV. 367
  Poem of poems, IV. 376
  Rodomonths Infernall, IV. 377, 443
  Teares of the Beloved, IV. 376
  Thyrsis and Daphne, IV. 365
  Way to get Wealth, A, IV. 369, 372, 373
  Whole Art of Angling, The, IV. 373
Markland, Jeremiah (1693–1776), IX. 341, 527; XII. 483
Markolf legend, III. 81, 94
Marlay, Richard, XI. 365
Marlborough, duchesses of. *See* Churchill, Henrietta; Churchill, Sarah
Marlborough, dukes of. *See* Churchill, John; Spencer, George
Marlborough college, XII. 332; XIII. 118; XIV. 414
Marlowe, Christopher (1564–1593), III. 241, 300, 517; IV. 23, 55, 88, 117, 248, 330, 395, 438, 517, 519; V. 81, 85, 87, 103, 134, 140, 142–164 (main entry), 177, 179, 182, 183, 188, 215, 224, 239, 240, 242, 244, 309, 324, 327, 333, 347, 366, 370, 371, 373, 377, 420 ff., *and see* Add. 2; VI. 13, 14, 45, 167, 234, 272, 295, 300, 301, 335; VII. 7 ff., 16, 49, 110, 133, 273; VIII. 223, 226; XII. 418; XIII. 153, *also see* Add. 2
  Dido Queene of Carthage, V. 140, 145, 146; VI. 287, 288
  Dr Faustus, IV. 321; V. 134, 143 ff., 147, 154, 163, 252, 253, 333, 353, 377; VI. 250; VIII. 88
  Edward II, V. 145, 152 ff., 163, 185, 186, 246; XIV. 443
  Hero and Leander, IV. 180, 222, 395; V. 147, 148; VI. 112; VIII. 227
  'I walked along a stream,' V. 148
  Jew of Malta, The, V. 145, 155, 156, 326; VI. 249
  Lucan, V. 147
  Lusts Dominion, V. 146; VI. 55, 183; VIII. 125, 195
  Massacre at Paris, The, V. 145, 344; VI. 33
  Ovid's Elegies, IV. 19, 328; V. 143, 147; VII. 432
  Passionate Shepherd to his Love, The, V. 148; VII. 8, 17, 251
  Tamburlaine the Great, III. 178; V. 82, 84, 134 ff., 142 ff., 147, 150, 154, 162, 163, 316; VI. 29, 250; VIII. 126
Marlow-on-Thames, XII. 61, 62
Marly, IX. 153
Marmaduke, in Wordsworth's *Borderers*, XI. 99
Marmion, lord, in Scott's poem, XII. 10 ff.
Marmion, Shakerley (1603–1639), VI. 456; VII. 113, 413; VIII. 227, 419; *Antiquary, The*, VI. 239; *Cupid and Psyche*, VI. 239; VII. 77, 78
Marmontel, Jean-François, X. 264; XI. 296, 492; *Contes Moraux*, X. 57; *Les Incas*, XI. 280; *Moral Tales*, XI. 385
Marneffe, Valérie, Balzac's, XIII. 286, 287
Marney, Sir Henry, II. 325
Marnock, Robert (1800–1889), XIV. 289
'Marocco' (horse), IV. 366, 531, 540
Marot, Clément, III. 46, 65, 219, 221, 222, 224, 226, 249, 250; IV. 24; X. 105
  Complaincte d'un Pastoureau Chrestien, III. 219
  Eglogue au Roi, III. 219, 222, 224
  Elegie sur Mme Louise de Savoye, III. 219, 224
  Epigrammes, III. 249
  Visions de Petrarque, Les, III. 251
Marphoreus, III. 394, 395
Marplot, in Centlivre's *Busy-Body*, X. 72
Marprelate, Martin, III. 213, 374 ff., 412, 537 ff., *also see* Add.; V. 140, 322; VI. 296, 384, 391, 393, 396, 478; VII. 144, 161, 517; X. 367
  Admonition to Parliament, An, III. 378, 403, 404
  Admonition to the People of England, An. *See under* Cooper, Thomas
  Advertisement touching the Controversies of the Church of England. *See under* Cooper, Thomas
  Almond for a Parrat, An, III. 397, 544
  Answere to a certaine libel supplicatorie, An. *See under* Sutcliffe, Matthew
  Answere unto a certaine calumnious letter, An. *See under* Sutcliffe, Matthew
  Anti-Martinus, III. 393
  Appelation of John Penri, Th'. *See under* Penry, John
  Character of a Puritan, III. 389
  Commission sente to the Pope, III. 376, 388
  Countercuffe given to Martin Junior, A, III. 394
  Defence of the Government established in the Church of England, A. *See under* Bridges, John
  Demonstration of Discipline, A. *See under* Udall, John
  Dialogue concerning the strife of our Church, A. *See under* Udall, John
  Dialogue wherein is plainly laide open the tyrannicall dealing of L. Bishopps against Gods children, A, III. 381, 382, 397
  Diotrephes, or, The State of the Church of Englande. *See under* Udall John

Marprelate, Martin
  Epistle, The, III. 379, 384, 385, 389, 391, 392
  Epitome, The, III. 381, 385 ff.
  Exhortation, An. See under Penry, John
  Friendly Admonition to Martin Marprelate, A. See under Wright, Leonard
  Hay any worke for Cooper, III. 381, 387, 390, 397
  Lives of the Saints, The, III. 394
  M. Some laid open in his coulers, III. 381, 383
  Mar-Martine, III. 388, 393
  Marre Mar-Martin, III. 393
  Martin Junior, The just censure and reproofe of, III. 382, 387, 388, 393, 394
  Martin Senior, or The just censure and reproofe, III. 388
  Martins Months Minde, III. 394, 396, 397, 544
  Minerall Conclusions, The, III. 381, 386
  More worke for the Cooper, III. 382
  Myrrour for Martinists, A. See under T. T.
  Owles Almanack, The, III. 394
  Papp-Hatchet, Advertisement to. See under Harvey, Gabriel
  Pappe with a Hatchet. See under Lyly, John
  Petition directed to her most excellent Majestie, A, III. 391, 392
  Plaine Percevall the Peace-maker of England. See under Harvey, Richard
  Protestation, The, III. 382, 383, 387 ff., 393, 394, 397
  Returne of Pasquill, The, III. 394, 395
  Sermon preached at Paules crosse, A. See under Bancroft, Richard
  Supplication to the Parliament, A. See under Penry, John
  Theologicall Discourse of the Lamb of God, A. See under Harvey, Richard
  Theses Martinianae, or Martin Junior, III. 382, 387 ff., 394, 396
  Treatise, containing the Aequity of an humble supplication, A. See under Penry, John
  Whip for an Ape, III. 393
Marprelate controversy, IV. 230, 321, 322, 332, 379, 382, 412, 547
Marprelate tracts, VII. 432
Marquis, Thomas G., XIV. 581
Marriage, The Fifteen Joys of, II. 325, 326
Marriage, The pain and sorrow of evil, II. 326, 502; III. 486
Marriage Feast, parable of, in *Cleanness*, I. 323
Marriage of Witte, The, V. 393
Married, The complaint of the too late, II. 326; III. 486
Married, The complaint of the too soon, II. 326; III. 486
Marriot, Richard (*fl.* 1653), XI. 318
Marriott, Charles (1811–1858), XII. 261, 274, 454, 458
Marriott, John Arthur Ransome, XIII. 548

'Marrow men,' IX. 549
Marryat, Florence (1838–1899), XII. 451; XIII. 564
Marryat, Frederick (1792–1848), XI. 387, 480, 481; XII. 451, *also see* Add.; XIII. 307, 322, 329; XIV. 141
  Jacob Faithful, XII. 250
  Japhet in search of a Father, XII. 250
  Masterman Ready, XII. 251
  Mr Midshipman Easy, XII. 251
  Peter Simple, XII. 250
  Settlers in Canada, XII. 251
Marryat, Zephaniah, X. 384
Mars, VIII. 76
Mars, temple of (Chaucer's), II. 179
Mars' hill, IV. 29, 270
Marsden, John Howard (1803–1891), XII. 497
Marseilles, V. 49; VI. 378, 383; VIII. 245
Marsh, Adam (Adam de Marisco) (*fl.* 1257?), I. 205, 206, 455; II. 350
Marsh, Anne. *See* Caldwell, Mrs Anne
Marsh, George Perkins, IV. 37, 450
Marsh, Herbert (1757–1839), XII. 280, 468; XIV. 403, 592
Marsh, Narcissus (1638–1713), IX. 330
Marsh or Marshe, Thomas, III. 194 ff.; IV. 384, 398
Marshall, the, in *The Royall King and the Loyall Subject*, VI. 100
Marshall, Anne, VIII. 261
Marshall, Arthur Milnes (1852–1893), XIV. 562; *Practical Zoology*, XIV. 300
Marshall, Emma (1830–1899), XIII. 564
Marshall, Sir John Hubert (b. 1876), XII. Add. 5
Marshall, Roger, IV. 423
Marshall, Stephen (1594?–1655), VII. 145, 147, 416, 425
Marshall, William (d. 1219), 1st earl of Pembroke and Striguil, regent of England, II. 420
Marsham, Sir John (1602–1685), IX. 196, 529
Marshman, John Clark (1794–1877), XIV. 338, 339, 495, 579
Marsiglio of Padua, I. 212
Marston, John (1575?–1634), III. 173, 191, 199, 207; IV. 6, 115, 185, 207, 266, 331 ff., 363, 434, 533; V. 81, 311, 322, 327, 371; VI. 2, 4, 17, 18, 28, 29–57 (main entry), 59, 154, 166, 170 ff., 182, 186, 239, 290, 422, 423, 459, *and see* Add.; VII. 383; VIII. 87
  Antonio and Mellida, VI. 15, 41, 45, 170
  Antonio's Revenge, VI. 45, 167, 178
  Certaine Satyres, IV. 331
  Dutch Courtezan, The, VI. 46, 184
  Eastward Hoe. See under Chapman
  Entertainment for a visit of the countess of Derby to her son-in-law, lord Huntingdon, An, VI. 49
  Histrio-Mastix (revision of), V. 321
  Insatiate Countesse, The, V. 362; VI. 49
  Latin pageant for the visit of king Christian of Denmark to England, a, VI. 49
  Love's Martyr, VI. 43

Marston, John
  Malcontent, The, V. 259; VI. 15, 39, 43,
    46, 48, 169, 178
  *Metamorphosis of Pygmalion's Image,
    The*, IV. 331, 332; VI. 38
  Mountebank's Masque, VI. 50
  Parasitaster, or The Fawne, VI. 48, 171
  Reactio, III. 199
  Revenge, or the Match in Newgate, The,
    VI. 47
  Scourge of Villanie, The, IV. 332, 333,
    517, 519; VI. 38 ff.
  What You Will, VI. 43
  *Wonder of Women, Or the Tragedie of
    Sophonisba, The*, VI. 49
Marston, John Westland (1819–1890),
    XIII. 152, 267 ff., 515, 516, 521, 541
  Favourite of Fortune, The, XIII. 269
  Life for Life, XIII. 263
  Life's Ransom, A, XIII. 263
  Marie de Méranie, XIII. 263
  Patrician's Daughter, The, XIII. 262
  Strathmore, XIII. 263
Marston, Philip Bourke (1850–1887), XIII.
    109, 140, 215, 489, 506
Marston moor, XII. 13
Marston moor, battle of, VI. 197; VII. 198,
    227, 229; VIII. 130
Marsyas, XIII. 90
Marteilhe, Jean, *Memoirs*, X. 203
Marten, Anthony (d. 1597), IV. 459
Marten, Henry (1602–1680), and his mis-
    tresses, in the *Mercuries*, VII. 356, 359,
    513
Martha, in Le Fanu's story, XIII. 416
Martial, I. 191; III. 429; IV. 23, 124, 206,
    242, 250, 262, 266, 334, 438; VI. 221;
    VII. 13, 131; IX. 55, 264, 499; XI. 174;
    XII. 489; *Epigrammata*, VII. 20; *To
    Bassus, on the Country-House of Faus-
    tinus*, VII. 20
Martianus Capella's *de Nuptiis Philologiae
    et Mercurii*, II. 231, 359, 363
Martin, in Kingsley's *Hereward the Wake*,
    XIII. 366
Martin, in Swift's *Tale of a Tub*, IX. 100
Martin, the (father Petre), in *The Hind
    and the Panther*, VIII. 48, 189
Martin, Arthur Patchett (1851–1902),
    XIV. 368, 511, 584, 587
Martin, Benjamin (1704–1782), *Biogra-
    phica Philosophica*, VIII. 458, 463
Martin, Frederick (1830–1883), XII. 415
Martin, George, XIV. 582
Martin, Humfrey (*fl.* 1575), V. 30
Martin, James, of Dunkeld (*fl.* 1577), IV.
    277
Martin, lady. *See* Faucit, Helena
Martin, Richard (1570–1618), IV. 161,
    162
Martin, Robert, in Jane Austen's *Emma*,
    XII. 240
Martin, St, I. 74, 118
Martin, Samuel, X. 396
Martin, T., translator of Prior's *Alma* into
    Latin, IX. 482

Martin, Sir Theodore (1816–1909), XIII.
    161, 499, 515; XIV. 504
  Helena Faucit (Lady Martin), XIV. 112
  Life of Lord Lyndhurst, XIV. 111
  Life of the Prince Consort, XIV. 111
  Memoir of W. E. Aytoun, XIV. 111
Martin, William (1801–1867), XI. 481
Martin de Franc, III. 90
Martin's office, IX. 132
Martineau, Harriet (1802–1876), XI. 387,
    481; XII. 380, 433, 445; XIII. 397, 553,
    554, 558; XIV. 190, 429, 476, 495, 607
  *A History of England during the Thirty
    Years' Peace*, XIV. 93
  Autobiographical Memoir, XIII. 343
  Crofton Boys, XIII. 343
  Deerbrook, XIII. 343, 399
  Feats on the Fiord, XIII. 343
  Hour and the Man, The, XIII. 343
  Illustrations of Political Economy, XIII.
    343
  Illustrations of Taxation, XIII. 343
  Peasant and the Prince, The, XIII. 343
  Playfellow, The, XIII. 343
  Settlers at Home, The, XIII. 343
  Trans. of Comte's *Positive Philosophy*,
    XIV. 24
Martineau, James (1805–1900), VIII. 287;
    XII. 465, 468; XIV. 26, 477, 607; *Seat
    of Authority in Religion, The*, XIV. 27;
    Study of Religion, A, XII. 298; XIV. 27;
    Types of Ethical Theory, XII. 298; XIV.
    27
Martineau, John, XIV. 510
Martinique, XIV. 165
Martinius, monk, I. 105
Martinius, P., III. 552
Martinus, in *Loiola*, VI. 324
'Martinus Scriblerus' (George Crabbe),
    XI. 142
Martyn, Henry (1781–1812), XI. 381
Martyn, Joseph (*fl.* 1619), IV. 520
Martyn, J., one of the chief contributors
    to *The Grub Street Journal* (1730–1737),
    XI. 466
Martyr, Peter (Anglerius), IV. 69, 70-1, 74,
    75, 80-2, 441, 455, 459
Martyr, Peter (Vermigli), III. 33-4, 35,
    419
Martyria, V. 38
Martyrology, Bede's, I. 80
Martyrology, The, West Saxon, I. 105,
    106, 436, 438
Marullo, in *The Bond-Man*, VI. 154, 155
Marullus, in *Julius Caesar*, V. 197
Marvell, Andrew, the elder (1586?–1641),
    VII. 178
Marvell, Andrew, the younger (1621–
    1678), IV. 214, 222; VI. 235; VII. 7, 102,
    105 ff., 166, 178–185 (main entry),
    430 ff.; VIII. 3, 40, 82, 89, 90, 91, 94,
    213, 214, 408, 409, 410, 411, 412; IX.
    416; XII. 202
  Advice to a Painter, VIII. 81
  Black List of Government Pensioners,
    X. 213

Marvell, Andrew, the younger
Britannia and Raleigh, VIII. 81
Controversial Essays, VII. 179
Coronet, The, VII. 181
Dialogue between the Resolved Soul and Created Pleasure, VII. 182
Dialogue between the Soul and the Body, VII. 181
Dialogue between two Horses, VIII. 93
Farther Instructions to a Painter, VIII. 81
Fleckno, an English Priest at Rome, VIII. 40
Garden, The, VII. 181; VIII. 99
Greek poems, VII. 179
His Majesty's Most Gracious Speech to Both Houses of Parliament, VIII. 98
Historical Poem, An, VII. 183; VIII. 81
Horatian Ode upon Cromwell's Return from Ireland, VII. 180
Last Instructions to a Painter, VII. 183; VIII. 81
Latin poems, VII. 179, 181, 183
News-letters, VII. 179, 184
Poem on the Statue in Stocks-market, VIII. 93
Poems, VII. 179, 183, 184
Rehearsal Transpros'd, The, VII. 178, 184, 185
Satires, VII. 179, 182, 183
'Where the remote Bermudas ride,' IV. 187; VII. 182
Marvin, F. S., XIII. 487
Marwood, in Lessing's Miss Sara Sampson, x. 76
Marwood, Mrs, in Congreve's Way of the World, VIII. 154, 155
Mary, in Monsieur Thomas, VI. 123
Mary, the Blessed Virgin, I. 64, 74, 115, 146, 147, 220, 248, 297, 321, 342, 343, 353, 356; II. 114, 264, 375, 376, 380 ff., 426, 507; III. 12, 59; IV. 217; V. 2, 17, 18, 40 ff., 49, 50, 53, 56, 59; VII. 33, 37, 63; XII. 291; XIV. 304
Mary, princess of Orange (1631–1660), VIII. 206
Mary I (1516–1558), queen of England, III. 1, 6, 50, 51, 53, 81, 96, 107, 145, 179, 181, 183, 194 ff., 213, 316, 332, 335, 386, 403, 420, 421, 424, 427, 432; IV. 71, 127, 198, 225, 234, 379, 380, 382, 384; V. 56, 59, 60, 90, 104, 107, 356, 365; VII. 304, 306, 325, 326, 331, 337; VIII. 267; IX. 210, 235; XIV. 55
Mary II (1662–1694), queen of England, VIII. 49, 306, 307, 380; IX. 169, 200, 208, 233; x. 502
Mary II, Memoirs of Queen, VIII. 272, 452
Mary (1542–1587), queen of Scots, II. 414; III. 1, 122, 144, 146 ff., 153 ff., 163, 164, 234, 326, 327; IV. 136, 253, 303, 396; v. 77, 341, 344, 345; x. 288, 289, 465, 498, 500, 501, 504, 505, 510; XI. 443; XII. 21, 27, 350, 416, 508, 513; XIII. 130, 133; XIV. 55, 85, 94, 161
Mary de' Medici, VII. 222
Mary de St Paul, II. 355

Mary de Valentia, II. 355
Mary of Egypt, St, Life of, I. 131
Mary of France, queen of Louis XII (1496–1533), IV. 182
Mary of Lorraine, III. 121, 123, 144
Mary of Modena (1658–1718), queen of James II, IX. 168
Mary of Nemmegen, II. 329
Mary Ambree, VIII. 231, 232; XIII. 234
Mary Magdalen, The Lamentation of, II. 162, 164
Mary Magdalene, in Christus Redivivus, VI. 295
Mary Magdalene, St, I. 341
Mary Magdalene plays, v. 19, 42, 44, 49
Maryland, XII. 350; XIV. 359
Marys, 'the four,' XII. 27
Marzials, Sir Frank T., x. Add.; XI. 291, 459; XIII. 485, 530, 532, 544
Mascall, Leonard (d. 1589), IV. 368 ff., 540 ff.
Book of Fishing, A, IV. 370
Government of Cattell, The, IV. 370
Husbandlye ordering...Poultrie, The, IV. 370
Of the arte and manner how to plant... trees, IV. 370
Masefield, John, IX. Add.; XII. 406; XIV. 551
Maseres, Francis (1731–1824), VII. 456
Masham, Abigail, lady Masham (d. 1734), IX. 124
Masham, Damaris, lady Masham (1658–1708), VIII. 330
Masham, Sir Francis, 3rd baronet, VIII. 330
Masham, Samuel, 2nd baron Masham (1712–1776), IX. 130
Maskell, William, III. 48
Maskwell, in Congreve's Double-Dealer, VIII. 148, 149
Mason, Arthur James, XIV. 486
Mason, Edward Tuckerman, XIV. 528
Mason, Francis (1566?–1621), VII. 309; Vindex Ecclesiae Anglicanae, VII. 329, 485
Mason, George, IV. 464
Mason, James, Anatomy of Sorcery, VII. 506
Mason, John (1645?–1694), VII. 407
Mason, John (1706–1763), XI. 251 ff., 255
Mason, John Monck (1726–1809), v. 277
Mason, Peter Hamnett (1827–1912), XII. 341, 501
Mason, Stuart, XIV. 528
Mason, William, A handfull of Essaies (1621), IV. 524
Mason, William (1724–1797), VII. 164; IX. 574; x. 120, 122, 123, 126 ff. (main entry), 137, 244, 248 ff., 398, 450, 495, 525; XI. 145, 458; XIV. 507
Caractacus, x. 136; XI. 273
Elfrida, x. 136; XI. 265
Isis, x. 136, 492
Life of Gray, x. 190
Musaeus, a Monody on...Pope, x. 136

Mason, William Shaw (1774–1853), x. 483

Masque of Cupid, in *The Faerie Queene*, vi. 335

Masquerado, in *Love Restored*, vi. 351, 352

Masques, vi. 487 ff.

Massachusetts, xii. 165

Massachusetts' Bay company, iv. 311

Massaniello, in D'Urfey's *Fall of Massaniello*, viii. 175

Masseck, C. J., xiv. 521

Massey, Sir Edward (1619?–1674?), vii. 356

Massey, Gerald (1828–1907), xiii. 189, 506

Massey, William Nathaniel (1809–1881), xiv. 495; *A History of England during the reign of George III*, xiv. 90

Massie, Joseph (d. 1784), x. 523

Massillon, Jean Baptiste, viii. 303

Massinger, Arthur, father of P. Massinger, vi. 141

Massinger, Miss (d. 1762), vi. 144

Massinger, Philip (1583–1640), iv. 6, 115; v. 195, 258, 344, 347, 366, 368, 370; vi. 61, 111, 114 ff., 118, 121, 124, 128 ff., 134, 136, 137–140, 141–165 (main entry), 196, 211, 427, 442 ff., 458; vii. 387; viii. 132; x. 429; xii. 68, 415; xiii. 144, 260, 289, *also see* Add. 2; xiv. 88

Bashful Lover, The, vi. 152, 155

Believe as you List, vi. 146, 147

Bond-Man, The, vi. 143, 149, 155, 157, 161, 164; viii. 121

City Madam, The, v. 357; vi. 152, 160

Duke of Millaine, The, vi. 142, 153 ff., 159, 161, 162

Emperour of the East, The, vi. 165

Fatall Dowry, The, vi. 146, 158, 165, 223; viii. 129, 195, 441; xiii. 259

Great Duke of Florence, The, vi. 154, 156, 165

Guardian, The, vi. 157, 165; viii. 142

King and the Subject, The, vi. 147

Lover's Progress, The, v. 257

Maid of Honour, The, iv. 299; vi. 149, 152, 155, 156, 162

New Way to Pay Old Debts, A, vi. 143, 151, 152, 160, 165

Parliament of Love, The, vi. 152, 154, 155, 184

Picture, The, vi. 156, 164

Renegado, The, vi. 150, 154, 155; viii. 129

Roman Actor, The, vi. 152 ff., 161, 164

Unnaturall Combat, The, vi. 142, 153, 160

Very Woman, A, vi. 116, 132, 140, 146, 156, 157; viii. 129

Virgin Martir, The, vi. 54, 142, 146, 150, 154

See, also, under Beaumont and Fletcher and Middleton

Masson, Arthur, *Collection of English Prose and Verse*, xi. 206

Masson, Charles, 'Memoir on the Topes,' xii. 352

Masson, David (1822–1907), vii. 95, 117; x. 122, 481; xi. 410, 466; xii. 206, 380, 403, 407, 444, 445; xiii. 245, 472; xiv. 95, 467, 504; *Life of Milton*, xi. 312; xiv. 112, 113; *Recent British Philosophy*, xiv. 1

Masson, Emile, xiii. 464, 470

Masson, Flora, xiii. 558

Massorah, the, xii. 341, 501

Master, John, of Sinclair, xii. 377

Master of Game, The, ii. 286, 479

Masterman, Charles Frederick Gurney, xiii. 478

Masters, Mrs Mary (d. 1759?), x. 468

Masters, Robert (1713–1798), ix. 477, 531; x. 255, 505

Masterson, George, vii. 495

Matamoros, Alfonso Garcia, v. 214

Matelant, Richard de, ancestor of Sir Richard Maitland, iii. 132

Matey, in Meredith's *Lord Ormont and his Aminta*, xiii. 444

Math, son of *Mathonwy*, i. 252

Matheo, in *The Honest Whore*, vi. 53

Matheolus, iii. 90

Mather, Cotton (1663–1728), vii. 507

Mather, Increase (1639–1723), vii. 507

Mathers, Edward P., xiv. Add. 8

Mathesis, xii. 114

Mathew, Mrs, xi. 181, 184

Mathews, Charles James (1803–1878), xiii. 521

Mathias, in *The Picture*, vi. 156, 158

Mathias, Thomas James (1754?–1835), x. 450 ff., 486, 489; xi. 177, 427; *The Pursuits of Literature*, xii. 364

Matilda, in Law's *Serious Call*, ix. 402

Matilda, in *Robert, Earle of Huntington*, v. 318, 319, 322 ff., 326

Matilda, in *The Bashful Lover*, vi. 152, 155

Matilda, in Walpole's *Castle of Otranto*, x. 61

Matilda (1080–1118), queen of Henry I, i. 151, 157

Matthew, in *Every Man in His Humour*, vi. 4

Matthew, Gospel of pseudo-, v. 49

Matthew, Patrick, xiv. 298, 562

Matthew, St, i. 54

Matthew, St, Gospel of, ii. 14, 76, 431

Matthew, Thomas. *See* Rogers, John

Matthew, Tobias (1546–1628), iv. 421; vii. 334

Matthew, Sir Toby or Tobie (1577–1655), iv. 441, 489; vi. 3; vii. 194

Matthew of Westminster, i. 179

Matthews, Charles James, xiii. Add. 2

Matthews, J. Brander, xiii. 515

Matthews, John William, xi. 410

Matthews, Josiah Wright, xiv. Add. 8

Matthews, Miss, in Fielding's *Amelia*, x. 33, 54

Matthieu, *Histoire de France*, vi. 33

Matty, Miss, in Mrs Gaskell's *Cranford*, XIII. 377

Maturin, Charles Robert (1782–1824), XI. 300, 304, 462; XIII. 257, 259 ff., 521
  Albigenses, The, XI. 305
  Bertram: or, The Castle of St Aldobrond, XI. 176, 304; XIII. 259, 260
  Fatal Vengeance or The Family of Montorio, XI. 304
  Fredolfo, XIII. 259, 260
  Manuel, XIII. 259, 260
  Melmoth the Wanderer, XI. 304, 305; XIII. 418 ff.
  Milesian Chief, XI. 304
  Wild Irish Boy, XI. 304
  Women, or Pour et Contre, XI. 304; XII. 146

Maty, Matthew (1718–1776), *Journal Britannique*, X. 173; *Memoirs of Lord Chesterfield*, X. 259, 494

Maty, Paul Henry (1745–1787), X. 302

Matz, Bertram Waldrom, XIII. 514, 532, 533

Mätzner, Eduard, I. ix; XIV. 611

Mauchline, XI. 213, 216, 219, 220

Maucroix, F. de, IX. 196

Maud, empress, I. 166

Maude, Cyril, XIII. 515

Maudlin, in *The Compleat Angler*, VII. 251, 252

Maudlin, the witch of Paplewick, in *The Sad Shepherd*, VI. 11

Maugham, Reginald Charles Fulke, XIV. Add. 8

Maulette, Genevefve Petau, IV. 376

Maundeville, J., rector of Burnham Thorpe, II. 301

Maunsell, Andrew (d. 1595), *Catalogue of English Printed Bookes*, IV. 404, 548

Maupassant, Guy de, XII. 244; XIII. 454, 457

Maurer, Georg Ludwig von, XIV. 78

Mauretania, IV. 259

Maurice, Charles Edmund, II. 38

Maurice, Sir Frederick, XIV. 602

Maurice, Frederick Denison (1805–1872), IX. 328; XI. 136; XII. 283, 288, 289 ff. (main entry), 295, 296, 465 ff., 471; XIII. 344, 345, 355, 357, 358, 368, 370, 378, 547; XIV. 82, 136, 408, 429, 477, 592, 596, 600, 602, 607
  Moral and Metaphysical Philosophy, XIV. 26
  Prophets and Kings, XII. 284
  Religions of the World, XII. 289
  Theological Essays, XII. 284, 290

Maurice, Thomas (1754–1824), XI. 428

Maurice of Nassau. *See* Orange

Mauritania, in *The Masque of Blacknesse*, VI. 342

Mavor, Wm Fordyce (1758–1837), XI. 488; XIV. 553

Mavrocordatos, prince Alexander, XII. 38

Maw, game of, VI. 98

Max Müller, F. *See* Müller, F. Max

Maxen Wledig, Dream of, I. 252

Maxentius, VII. 371, 395

Maxima, abbess, I. 75

Maximilian I, duke of Bavaria, VII. 200

Maximilian I, emperor, I. 53; III. 61, 112; VI. 333

Maximilla, martyr, V. 15

Maximin, in *Tyrannick Love*, VIII. 22

Maximus, in *Valentinian*, VI. 129

Maximus Tyrius, VII. 404

Maxse, Frederick Augustus (1833–1900), XIV. 608

Maxton, 'the new poete,' V. 311

Maxwell, Sir H., XIV. 501

Maxwell, James (1720–1800), XI. 440

Maxwell, James Clerk. *See* Clerk-Maxwell

Maxwell, John (1590?–1647), IX. 544

Maxwell, William Hamilton (1792–1850), XIII. 564; XIV. 570; *Stories of Waterloo*, XIV. 313; *Wild Sports of the West of Ireland*, XIV. 313

May, Sir Humphrey (1573–1630), IX. 250

May, John (*fl.* 1613), IV. 309, 512

'May, Phil,' XIV. 549

May, Thomas (1595–1650), IV. 438, 501; VI. 28, 144, 457; VII. 315, 446, 517
  Antigone, the Theban Princess, VI. 235
  Cleopatra, VI. 235
  Heir, The, VI. 235
  Historical Discourses, VII. 207
  History of the Parliament of England, VII. 206, 226
  Julia Agrippina, VI. 235
  Julius Caesar, VII. 206
  Lucan, VII. 359
  Mirrour of Minds, The (Barclay), IV. 254
  Old Couple, The, VI. 235
  Pharsalia (trans.), VI. 235

May, Sir Thomas Erskine (1815–1886), XIV. 495; *Constitutional History of England*, XIV. 58; *Rules, Orders and Proceedings of the House of Commons*, XIV. 58

May-game, V. 34, 35

May poems, II. 374, 392, 393

Mayberrys, the, in *North-Ward Hoe*, VI. 172

Mayd Emlyn, The Boke of, III. 88, 486; IV. 340; VII. 382

Maydes Metamorphosis, The, VI. 365, 490

Maydman, Henry, IV. 102, 459

Mayer, John (1583–1664), VII. 481

Mayer, Samuel Ralph Townshend, XIII. 483

Mayerne, Sir Théodore Turquet de (1573–1655), VIII. 477; XIV. 283; *Notes*, VIII. 363

Mayfield, XII. 103

Mayhew, Anthony Lawson, XIV. 611

Mayhew, Henry (1812–1887), XIV. 236, 544, 548

Mayhew, Horace (1816–1872), XIV. 236

Mayiola, or Mayok, in *King Berdok*, II. 276

Maynard, Constance L., XIV. 600

Maynard, Edward (1654–1740), IX. 533

Maynard, Sir John (1602–1690), VIII. 466;
  X. 373
Mayne, Jasper (1604–1672), VI. 240, 457;
  Amorous Warre, The, VI. 237; *City
  Match, The*, V. 367; VI. 237; *Lucian*
  (trans.), VI. 237
Mayne, John (1759–1836), XI. 444; XII.
  420; *Halloween*, XI. 216, 235; *Logan
  Water*, XI. 235; *Siller Gun, The*, XI. 235
Maynial, Guillaume, II. 315
Maynooth, XIV. 315, 329
Maynwaring, Arthur (1668–1712), IX. 437
Mayo, Charles (1792–1846), XIV. 608
Mayo, Charles Herbert, XII. 520
Mayor, John Eyton Bickersteth (1825–
  1910), IX. 354; X. 356; XII. 326, 357,
  481, 487, 488, 515, 523; *First Greek
  Reader*, XII. 336; *Juvenal*, XII. 336
Mayor, Joseph Bickersteth (1828–1910),
  XII. 403, 523; XIII. 512; *Chapters on
  English Metre*, XIII. 248, 512; *Handbook
  of Modern English Metre*, XIII. 248, 512
Mayow, John (1640–1679), VIII. 354, 363,
  478; XIV. 283
Mazarin, cardinal, IV. 434; VII. 189
Mazarin blue, XI. 364
Maze Pond school, X. 382
Mazzini, in George Meredith's *Vittoria*,
  XIII. 445, 447
Mazzini, Giuseppe, XIII. 15, 132, 349, 465,
  472, 492
Mazzoni, Giacomo, VII. 265
Mead, Matthew (1630?–1699), VII. 316
Mead, Robert (1616–1653), VI. 475
Mead, W. E., *Outlines of the History of the
  Legend of Merlin*, I. 268
Meade, Jacob (*fl.* 1613), VI. 261, 275
Meadows, Joseph Kenny (1790–1874), XIV.
  201, 236
Meagher, Thomas Francis (1823–1867),
  XIV. 570
Meagles family, in *Little Dorrit*, XIII. 331
Meander, in *Tamburlaine*, V. 151
Mease, Peter, VI. 475
Meath, county, XII. 351; XIV. 246
Mecca, XIV. 252
Mechanics' institutions, XIV. 407 ff.
Mechanics' Magazine, The, XIV. 408, 409
Medalle, Mme (Lydia Smollett), X. 47, 422
Medb, queen, XIV. 307
Mede or Mead, Joseph (1586–1638), IV.
  433; VII. 318, 345, 482, 490; VIII. 458;
  Works, VIII. 286
Medea, VI. 163
Medea, in *Confessio Amantis*, II. 151
Medea, in Euripides's drama, XII. 68
Medea, in Morris's *Jason*, XIII. 123, 134
Medea, in Sandys's translation of Ovid's
  Metamorphoses, VII. 51
Medhurst, Walter Henry (1796–1857), XII.
  342, 500
Media, XII. 477
Medici, Cosmo de', XII. 418
Medici, Lorenzino de', III. 5; VI. 199; VIII.
  358; XIV. 108
Medici, Marie de', VI. 175

Medici, Piero and Giovanni de', III. 5
Medici, the, VI. 175; VIII. 358; X. 303;
  XIV. 99
Medicine, books on, II. 365
Medicus, in *A Dialogue...against the fever
  Pestilence*, III. 108
Medina (Arabia), XIV. 252
Medina, Pedro de, IV. 446
Mediocrity, in *The Muses Looking-Glasse*,
  VI. 233
Mediolano, Johannes de, IV. 446
Mediterranean sea, II. 75; IV. 68, 69, 92;
  VI. 203; XII. 32, 257
Medley, in Etherege's *Man of Mode*, VIII.
  138
Medley, The, IX. 437, 461
Medmenham abbey, X. 391, 394, 524
Medows, Sir Philip, the elder (1676–1718),
  IV. 459
Medraut, or Modred, or Mordred, I. 248
Medusa, in *Fedele and Fortunio*, V. 315
Medwall, Henry (*fl.* 1486), II. 328; V. 410;
  Nature, V. 54, 392
Medway, in *The Faerie Queene*, III. 238
Medway, river, IV. 190; VII. 183; VIII. 11,
  252
Medwin, Thomas (1788–1869), XII. 50, 54,
  384, 385, 396, 403, 407; *Journal of the
  Conversations of Lord Byron*, XII. 36
Meed, lady, in *Piers the Plowman*, II.
  2 ff., 7 ff., 32
Meehan, Charles Patrick (1812–1890), XIV.
  570, 573
Meeke, Mrs Mary (? 1816), XI. 488
Meekly, Mr, in Brooke's *Fool of Quality*,
  IX. 327
Meeting of Gallants at an Ordinarie, The,
  V. 367, 479
Megaera, in *Gismond of Salerne*, V. 75, 76
Megaera, in *Thyestes*, V. 75, 76
Mégha Dūta, trans. of the, XII. 503
Mehemet Ali, pasha of Egypt, XIV. 252
Meighen, John, VII. 337
Meiklejohn, John Maller Dow, XIV. 601
Meilan, Mark Anthony (*fl.* 1812), XI. 491
Meilyr, story of, in *Giraldus Cambrensis*,
  I. 171
Meinecke, XIV. 484
Meiningen, V. 306
Meissner, V. 347
Meistersingers, the, V. 25
Mela, Pomponius, III. 420
Melancholico, in *The Floating Island*, VI.
  326
Melanchthon, Philip, III. 36, 50, 113, 127,
  143, 151, 290, 419, 421, 430; IV. 380,
  446; VI. 374; *Inita Doctrinae physicae*,
  III. 113
Melanchthoniana, VII. 391
Melantha, in *Marriage-à-la-Mode*, VIII. 17
Melantho, in *Ulysses Redux*, VI. 303
Melantius, in *The Maides Tragedy*, VI.
  126 ff.
Melayne, Sege of, I. 469
Melbancke, Brian (*fl.* 1583), *Philotimus*,
  III. 349, 536

Melbourne, International exhibition, XIV. 369

Melbourne, viscount. *See* Lamb, William

Melchior, in *William of Palerne*, I. 316

Melchisedech, in *The Palice of Honour*, II. 260

Melchizedek, I. 74; v. 48

Melcombe, lord. *See* Dodington, George Bubb

'Meldrum, Squire,' VII. 254

Meleager, XII. 485

Meleander, in *Argenis*, IV. 258, 259

Melebea, in *Calisto and Melebea*, v. 100

Mélesville (A. H. J. Duveyrier), *Sullivan*, XIII. 271

Melford, Jerry, in Smollett's *Humphrey Clinker*, x. 43

Melford, Lydia, in Smollett's *Humphrey Clinker*, x. 43

Melfort, earl. *See* Drummond, John

Melibaeus, in school plays, v. 103

Meliboeus (Vergil's), III. 224

Meliboeus, in Barnabe Googe's *Eclogues*, III. 186

Meliboeus, in ? Ralegh's *Dialogue*, IV. 109

Melicertus, in *Menaphon*, III. 357

Melior et Idoine, I. 460

Meliora Speramus, Day's 'Islands,' VI. 216

Melisea (Yong's), IV. 122

Melissa, in *Misogonus*, v. 110

Melizius, in *The Passetyme of Pleasure*, II. 225, 228, 231, 233, 234

Mellidus, in *Jacke Drums Entertainment*, VI. 41

Mellisant, in *Frier Bacon*, v. 137

Mellyagraunce, of Malory, I. 262

Melmoth, Maturin's, XI. 305

Melmotte, Trollope's, XIII. 422

Melnotte, Claud, in Lytton's *The Lady of Lyons*, XIII. 419

Melros state papers, VII. 435

Melrose, chronicle of, I. 174, 449

Melrose abbey, XII. 9, 46

Melusine, I. 470; II. 483

Melvill, Henry (1798–1871), XII. 472

Melvill, James, *Diary*, IV. 276

Melville, Andrew (1545–1622), III. 426; IV. 276, 304; IX. 556; *Anti-Tami-Cami-Categoria*, VII. 27

Melville, Elizabeth. *See* Culross, lady

Melville, George John Whyte. *See* Whyte-Melville

Melville, Helen, XIII. Add. 2

Melville, Sir James (1535–1617), of Halhill, *Memoirs*, III. 148, 505

Melville or Melvill, James (1556–1614), II. 370, 488; *Diary*, III. 148, 505

Melville, Lewis, x. 422, *also see* Add.; XI. 290, 291, 393, 459; XIII. 525, 530, 564, *also see* Add. 2

Melville, Sir Robert (1527–1621), XII. 27

Melville, viscount. *See* Dundas, Henry

Melwas, king of Somerset, I. 262

Melyonek, John, VI. 282

Memling, Hans, XIII. 112

Memnon, in *The Mad Lover*, VI. 122, 130, 152

Mémoires Littéraires de la Grande Bretagne, x. 291, 292, 311

Memoirs, Personal, in Jacobean times, VII. 449

Memoirs of a Parish Clerk, IX. 137

Memoirs of Martinus Scriblerus, IX. 103, 131, 136, 137, 139, 308, 447, 463, 469, 470

Memoirs of the Society of Grub-street, x. 162

Memorial of suche Princes as since the tyme of King Richard the Seconde have been unfortunate in the Realme of England, A, III. 194

Memorials of Coleorton, IX. 328

Memorie of the Somervilles, XII. 16

Ménage, Gilles, VIII. 321

Menai straits, x. 115

Menander, v. 5; VIII. 155; IX. 336, 525; XII. Add.

Mencke, Johann Burchard, v. 286

Mendacium (=Satan), in Wyclif's *Dialogus*, II. 65

Mendax, in *A Dialogue...against the fever Pestilence*, III. 109

Mendelssohn, Sidney, XIV. 588, *also see* Add. 4, 7, 9

Mendez, Moses (d. 1758), XI. 172, 428

Mendoza, in *The Court Secret*, VI. 206

Mendoza, Antonio de, *Fiestas de Aranjuez*, VIII. 130; *Querer por solo querer*, VIII. 130

Mendoza, Bernardino de, IV. 446

Mendoza, Daniel (1764–1836), XIV. 229, 231

Mendoza, Diego Hurtado de, III. 341; IV. 446

Mendozo, in *The Malcontent*, VI. 46

Menenius, in *Coriolanus*, v. 198

Menger, A., *The Right to the Whole Produce of Labour*, XIV. 4

Mennes or Mennis or Minnes, Sir John (1599–1671), VIII. 260; *Musarum Deliciae*, VII. 512; VIII. 231, 408

Menologium, I. 145, 445

Mensa philosophica, III. 95, 489

Mentone, XIV. 78

Mentz (Mainz), VII. 231

Meopham, Simon, archbishop of Canterbury (d. 1333), I. 353

Mephistopheles, XII. 50, 54

Mephistopheles, in *Faust*, v. 20, 187; XIII. 105

Mercator (Defoe's), IX. 14, 15, 432

Merchant, in *Ane Pleasant Satyre*, III. 128

Merchant Adventurers, IV. 71, 310; VII. 305, 308

Merchant Taylors' company, VI. 168

Mercia, I. 50, 125; II. 210

Mercia, laws of, I. 98; VIII. 310, 311

Mercian annals (or *Chronicle of Aethelflaed*), I. 109, 110. *See, also, under* Aethelflaed, the lady of Mercia

Mercier, Sébastien, v. 292, 298

Merck, x. 488

Mercure Galant, Le, IX. 270; x. 163

Mercuriale, Girolamo, III. 436

Mercuries, VII. 385
Mercurius Academicus, VII. 348
Mercurius Aulicus, VII. 351, 361
Mercurius Bifrons (1681), VIII. 412
Mercurius Britannicus, VII. 344; IX. 433
Mercurius Civicus to Mercurius Rusticus, A Letter from, VII. 502
Mercurius Democritus, VII. 356
Mercurius Diabolicus or Hell's Intelligencer, VII. 381
Mercurius Elencticus, VII. 355
'*Mercurius Gallobelgicus*,' VII. 344
Mercurius Latinus, IX. 434
Mercurius Librarius, XI. 339
Mercurius Melancholicus or Newes from Westminster, VII. 352, 381
Mercurius Politicus, IX. 21, 432
Mercurius Rusticans, VI. 484
'*Mercurius Spur*,' X. 471
Mercurius Teutonicus, IX. 518
Mercurius Trismegistus, III. 416
Mercury, II. 276
Mercury, in *Amphitruo*, V. 107
Mercury, in Carew's *Coelum Britannicum*, VII. 19
Mercury, in *Dialogues of the Dead*, XI. 351, 352
Mercury, in *Mercury Vindicated*, VI. 357, 358
Mercury, in *Pleasure Reconciled*, VI. 360
Mercury, in Shelley's *Prometheus Unbound*, XII. 65
Mercury, in *The Penates*, VI. 341, 351
Mercutio, in *Romeo and Juliet*, III. 268; V.182, 268; VII. 8
Mercy, in Anglo-Norman plays, V. 21
Mercy, in *Piers the Plowman*, II. 13
Mercy, in *The Example of Virtue*, II. 227, 228
Mercy, in *The Passetyme of Pleasure*, II. 228
Mercy, house of, in *The Faerie Queene*, VII. 173
Mercy, oil of, legend of, V. 15
Merdle household, the, in *Little Dorrit*, XIII. 331
Meredith, George (1828–1909), V. 127; VIII. 154; XI. 447; XII. 24; XIII. 413, 426, 440 ff. (main entry), 451, 458, 489, 568 ff.
  Adventures of Harry Richmond, The, XIII. 441
  Amazing Marriage, The, XIII. 441
  Attila, XIV. 249
  Ballad of Fair Ladies in Revolt, A, XIII. 444, 448
  Ballads and Poems of Tragic Life, XIII. 442
  Beauchamp's Career, XIII. 441, 446
  Case of General Ople and Lady Camper, The, XIII. 441, 445
  Celt and Saxon, XIII. 441
  Day of the Daughter of Hades, The, XIII. 448
  Diana of the Crossways, XIII. 441, 443, 446; XIV. 309

Meredith, George
  Dirge in Woods, XIII. 444
  Earth and a Wedded Woman, XIII. 443
  Earth and Man, XIII. 443, 448
  Egoist, The, XIII. 441, 445
  Emilia in England, XIII. 441
  Empty Purse, The, XIII. 442
  Essay on Comedy, An, XIII. 445, 515
  Evan Harrington, XIII. 441
  Faith on Trial, A, XIII. 440, 448
  Farina, XIII. 441
  Gentleman of Fifty and the Damsel of Nineteen, The, XIII. 441
  House on the Beach, The, XIII. 441
  Hymn to Colour, XIII. 448
  Lark Ascending, The, XIII. 448
  Last Poems, XIII. 442
  Lord Ormont and his Aminta, XIII. 441
  Love in a Valley, XIII. 440, 448
  Lucifer in Starlight, XIII. 448
  '*Maxims for Men*,' XIII. 447
  Meditations under Stars, XIII. 444
  Modern Love, XIII. 440, 441, 444, 448
  Nuptials of Attila, The, XIII. 448
  Ode to the Spirit of Earth in Autumn, XIII. 444
  Odes in Contribution to the Song of French History, XIII. 442, 445, 447
  On the Idea of Comedy, XIII. 441
  One of Our Conquerors, XIII. 441, 446, 448
  Ordeal of Richard Feverel, The, XIII. 441, 446, 454, 460
  Phaéthón, XIII. 448
  Phoebus with Admetus, XIII. 449
  '*Pilgrim's Scrip, The*,' XIII. 447
  Poems (1851), XIII. 447
  Poems and Lyrics of the Joy of Earth, XIII. 442
  Reading of Earth, A, XIII. 442
  Reading of Life, A, XIII. 442
  Rhoda Fleming, XIII. 441, 447
  Sage Enamoured and the Honest Lady, XIII. 444
  Sandra Belloni, XIII. 441
  Shaving of Shagpat, The, XIII. 441
  Tale of Chloe, The, XIII. 441
  Test of Manhood, The, XIII. 443
  Thrush in February, The, XIII. 443, 448
  Tragic Comedians, The, XIII. 441
  Vittoria, XIII. 441, 447
  Woods of Westermain, The, XI. 85; XIII. 443, 448
Meredith, Mary, born Vulliamy, XIII. 440
Meredith, Mary Ellen, born Peacock, XIII. 440
Meredith, Owen. *See* Lytton, earl of
Meredith, R., *Mr Steele Detected*, IX. 440
Meredith, Sir Rowland, in Richardson's *Sir Charles Grandison*, X. 11
Meredith, W. M., XIII. 569
Meres, Francis (1565–1647), III. 305, 359, 526; IV. 444, 526; *Palladis Tamia*, IV. 18, 139, 168, 183, 376, 394; V. 82, 166, 170, 172 ff., 181, 184, 187 ff., 194, 195 215, 219 ff., 223, 312, 323, 331; VI. 3, 30, 39, 302, 387

Meres, Sir J., IX. 440
*Meriasek, Saint, Bishop and Confessor,
The Life of*, V. 16, 391
*Merie Tales of the Mad Men of Gotam,
The*, III. 95, 488
Merione, in *The Queen of Corinth*, VI. 131
Merionethshire, X. 115
Meritt, Paul (d. 1895), XIII. 521
Merivale, Charles (1808–1893), XII. 313,
406, 476, 477
    Autobiography, XII. 307
    Conversion of the Northern Nations, The,
    XII. 306
    Conversion of the Roman Empire, The,
    XII. 306
    Fall of the Roman Republic, The, XII. 305
    General History of Rome, XII. 306
    *History of the Romans under the Empire,
    The*, XII. 305
Merivale, Herman (1806–1874), XII. 305;
XIV. 495; 'Lyall's Travels in North
America,' XII. 153
Merivale, Herman Charles (1839–1906),
XIII. 506, 521, 530, 544; *Thaisa's Dirge*,
XIII. 194
Merivale, John Herman (1779–1844), XII.
420
Merlette, Germaine-Marie, XIII. 485
Merlin (the prose), I. 269
Merlin, in legend and romance, I. 235,
259, 263, 266, 268, 269, 271, 461, 462,
469; III. 106, 234
Merlin, in *The Rolliad*, XI. 34
Merlin, Ambrose, VII. 207
Merlin, prophecies of, I. 169, 170, 193,
258, 356; IV. 363
Merlin, The Birth of, II. 325
Merlin, The Birth of (16th century ver-
sion), V. 249 ff.
Merlin de St Gelais, V. 62
Mermedonians, I. 53
Merrick, James (1720–1769), X. 456;
    Cameleon, IX. 191
Merrilies, Meg, in Scott's *Guy Mannering*,
XII. 18, 25, 29
Merriman, Henry Seton, *pseud. See*
Scott, Hugh Stowell
Merry, J., of Pembroke College, X. 472
Merry, Robert (1755–1798), XI. 172, 176,
177, 428
Merry, Thomas (*fl.* 1594), V. 325
Merry, William Walter (1835–1918), XII.
Add. 3
Merry Beggars, The, XI. 218
Merry Conceits of Bottom the Weaver, VIII.
116
Merry Devill of Edmonton, The, V. 237,
238, 251 ff., 332, 442, 443
Merry Drollery, VII. 512
*Merry Jeste of a Shrewde and Curste Wyfe
lapped in Morelles skin, The*, III. 84, 91,
487
Merry Muses, The, IX. 360, 363, 567; XI.
229
Merry Riddles, The Booke of, III. 95, 488
Merryweather, John (*fl.* 1644), VII. 235

Mersenne, Marin, VII. 284 ff.
Merton. *See* Walter de
Mery demandes, III. 489
Mery Jests of the Widow Edith. See Smith,
Walter
Mery Tales and Quicke Answers, III. 93,
94, 487; IV. 334, 343, 523
Merygreeke, Matthewe, in *R. Roister
Doister*, V. 106
Meryon, Charles Lewis (1783–1877), XIV.
506
Merz, John Theodore, XIV. 467
Mesmer, Friedrich Anton, XI. 293
Mesnager, Nicolas, IX. 151
Mesnevi of Mevlána, The, XII. 504
Meso-Gothic language, VIII. 307
Mesolonghi, XII. 38, 314
Mesopotamia, IV. 90
Messahala, II. 185
Messena, in *Sicelides*, VI. 323
Messiah, the, in Cowley's *Davideis*, VII. 67
Messina, V. 191; VII. 199
Mess-Katalog (of Frankfurt-a.-M.), IV. 403
Meston, William (1688?–1745), IX. 471,
500, 567
Metamorphosis Anglorum, VII. 391
Metamorphosis of Tobacco, The, IV. 349,
530
Metastasio, Pietro, X. 161; XI. 263, 359
Metcalfe, Charles Theophilus, 1st lord
Metcalfe (1785–1846), XIV. 491
Meteor, The, XIV. 223
Meteren, E. van, X. 291
Meteyard, Eliza (1816–1879), XIV. 504
Metham, John, II. 498; *Amoryus and
Cleopes*, II. 502
Methold, William (d. 1653), XIV. 579; *Re-
lations of the Kingdome of Golconda*,
XIV. 333
Metre, Bede's *tracts on*, I. 80
Metrical romances, I. 277 ff., 464 ff.
Metz, III. 163; V. 101
Metz, siege of, in *Morte Arthure*, II. 119
Meung, Jean de, I. 99; II. 169; III. 90;
VII. 367
Mewe, William, VI. 475
Mexia, Pedro, IV. 446; *Silva de varia lec-
ción*, VIII. 126
Mexican language, XIV. 457
Mexico, VIII. 23; XI. 72, 162
Meyer, Paul, II. 420
Meyer-Franck, Helene, XIII. 485
Meynell, Alice, XIII. 475, 476, 503, 507;
XIV. 524
Meynell, Hugo, XIV. 233
Meynell, Wilfrid, XII. 461; XIII. 510
Meyrick, Sir Samuel Rush (1783–1848),
XII. 511
Mezeray, François Eudes de, *History of
France*, IX. 150, 153
Mézières, Alfred, V. 302
Miall, L. C., *The Early Naturalists*, XIV.
283
Micah, II. 293
Micawber, Mr, in *David Copperfield*, VI.
22; XIII. 327

Michael, in Byron's *Vision of Judgment*,
  XII. 53
Michael, in *The Example of Virtue*, II. 227
Michael, in Wordsworth's poem, XI. 113
Michael, James Lionel (1824–1865), XIV.
  364, 365, 587; *John Cumberland*, XIV.
  363
Michael, St, I. 134, 227, 339
Michael of Kildare, II. 425
Michaelis, Johann David, *Introduction to
  the New Testament*, XII. 280
Michaelis, Sebastian (*fl.* 1613), VI. 183
Michal, in Browning's *Paracelsus*, XIII. 57
Michal, in Cowley's *Davideis*, VII. 66, 67
Michel, Francisque, V. 302; *Critical In-
  quiry into the Scottish Language, with the
  view of illustrating the Rise and Progress
  of Civilisation in Scotland* (1882), II.
  95, 96
Michel, Guillaume, *Lasne Dore*, IV. 3
Michel Angelo, X. 266
Michell, John (1724–1793), XIV. 257
Michell, Sir Lewis, XIV. Add. 9
Mickle, William Julius (1735–1788), X.
  456, 470; XIII. 226; *Cumnor Hall*, IX.
  374
Mickleham, X. 261
Mickleton, X. 271
Microcosm, The, XI. 392; XIV. 387
Microcosm of London, The (Ackermann's),
  XIV. 222
Micro-cynicon, Sixe Snarling Satyres, IV
  519; VI. 59
Micrologia, III. 95
Midas, III. 64; IV. 10, 327
Midas, in *Loves Maistresse*, VI. 103
Middelburg, VI. 398
Middle-Age, in *The Parlement of the Thre
  Ages*, II. 37
Middle Ages, the, I. 99, 153, 161, 187, 278,
  294, 299, 300, 306, 363, 366, 371; II. 43,
  51, 52, 61, 76, 120, 169, 172, 181, 183,
  197, 210, 231, 239, 240, 245, 301, 334,
  335, 339, 350, 359, 366, 423, 506; III. 31,
  83, 89, 94, 100, 106, 108, 114, 138, 155,
  200, 218, 418; IV. 70, 110, 269, 319, 353;
  V. 5, 9, 16, 21, 38, 41 ff., 50, 51, 53,
  55, 56, 152, 369; VI. 328, 372, 373;
  VII. 102, 367, 376 ff., 384, 391; VIII.
  319, 351; X. 217 ff., 287, 288, 355, 484 ff.;
  XI. 273, 372
Middle Ages, the literary influence of the,
  X. 217 ff., 484 ff.
Middle English, X. 225; XIV. 435 ff., 442,
  444 ff.
Middle English verse, XIII. 241, 242, 249
Middle Temple revels, VIII. 244
Middleburg, IV. 64, 402
Middlesex, III. 330; VI. 259, 292, 385;
  VII. 4, 77, 113; VIII. 37, 39, 166; X. 29,
  360, 385, 391, 399, 404; XI. 8, 183
Middlesex, earl of. *See* Cranfield, Lionel
Middleton, Christopher (1560?–1628), IV.
  487
Middleton, Clara (George Meredith's), XIII.
  446

Middleton, Conyers (1683–1750), IX. 295,
  497, 505, 525, 527; X. 123, 262, 308,
  509; XI. 347; *Free Inquiry into the
  Miraculous Powers*, IX. 296, 340; *Life
  of Cicero*, IX. 253, 340; X. 319; *Miscel
  laneous Works*, X. 319
Middleton, David (d. 1615), IV. 92, 99
Middleton, John Henry (1846–1896), XII.
  498
Middleton, Richard, XIII. 219, 220, 506,
  564, *also see* Add. 3
Middleton, Thomas (1570?–1627), IV. 515,
  519; V. 184, 252, 254, 255, 311, 319,
  362, 371; VI. 6, 26, 28, 55, 57, 58–60
  (main entry), 95, 115, 138, 145, 151,
  154, 168, 196, 211, 218, 219, 250, 329,
  426 ff.; VIII. 124, 127, 162; XIII. 495
  Any Thing for a Quiet Life, VI. 78
  Black Book, The, V. 252; VI. 60
  Blurt Master-Constable, VI. 15, 61
  Caesar's Fall, VI. 61, 168
  Changeling, The, VI. 67, 68, 76, 79, 80;
    VIII. 121; XII. 222
  Chast Mayd in Cheapeside, A, VI. 65, 74
  Chester Tragedy, The, VI. 61
  Defiance to Envy, VI. 59
  Devereux, lord, dedication to, VI. 59
  Faire Quarrell, A, VI. 61, 67, 68, 73,
    75
  Famelie of Love, The, V. 365; VI. 62, 67
  Father Hubberd's Tales, VI. 59
  Game at Chesse, A, V. 344, 365; VI. 58,
    68, 79, 80, 147, 150, 248; VII. 433
  Inner-Temple Masque, The, VI. 70, 75
  Mad World, My Masters, A, V. 125;
    VIII. 142
  Mayor of Quinborough, The, V. 187, 250,
    251; VI. 60, 61, 70
  Micro-cynicon, Sixe Snarling Satyres, IV.
    519; VI. 59
  More Dissemblers besides Women, VI. 78
  Old Law, The, VI. 15, 61, 67, 68, 145
  Phoenix, The, VI. 63
  Roaring Girle, The, VI. 54, 62, 65
  Spanish Gipsie, The (with W. Rowley),
    VI. 68, 77; VIII. 129
  Two Harpies, The, VI. 61, 168
  Widdow, The, VI. 26, 65, 140
  Wisdom of Solomon Paraphrased, The,
    VI. 59
  Witch, The, VI. 75, 76; XII. 190
  Women beware Women, VI. 68, 78, 176,
    180, 192
  World tost at Tennis, The, VI. 62, 68, 75
  Your five Gallants, VI. 63, 68
  See, also, under Beaumont and Fletcher,
    Dekker, Jonson *and* W. Rowley
Middleton and William Rowley's *A Faire
  Quarrell*, V. 349
Midgley, Robert (1653–1733), IX. 500
Midianites, IV. 43
Mido, Isaac's 'boy,' in *Jacob and Esau*,
  V. 112
Miège, Guy (1644–1718?), *The New State
  of England*, IX. 353, 537; *Present State
  of Great Britain*, XI. 333

Mielot, Jean, secretary of Philippe le Bon, II. 313

Miggs, in *Barnaby Rudge*, XIII. 321

Mignault, Claude, VII. 406

Migne, *Patrologia*, I. 186, 202, 250

Mignet, François A. M., XIV. 56, 57, 61

Milan, V. 207, 306; VI. 17; VII. 47; XII. 220

Milan, Ambrosian library, IV. 429

Milbanke, Anne Isabella. See Byron, lady

Milbanke, Ralph (earl of Lovelace), *Astarte*, XII. 396

Milbourne, Luke (1649–1720), VIII. 54, 404; *Aeneid*, VIII. 51

Mildmay, friend of John Byrom, IX. 325

Mildmay, Sir Walter (1520?–1589), VII. 340

Mildred, in *Eastward Hoe*, VI. 48

Mildred, Browning's, XIII. 65, 67

Mileham, Dorothy, VII. 233

Miles, keeper of Turk's head coffee-house, VII. 362

Miles, Alfred Henry, XIII. 497

Miles, Henry Downes, *Pugilistica*, XIV. 231, 541

Miles, William Augustus (1753?–1817), XIV. 513

Milford, Humphrey Sumner, XIII. 489

Milford Haven, VII. 353

Militia Bill, X. 466

Mill, James (1773–1836), X. 342, 513; XI. 60, 61, 398; XII. 152, 301, 309, 430; XIV. 2, 4 ff., 13, 14, 23, 119, 187, 336, 403, 407, 477, 495, 580, 608
  Analysis of the Phenomena of the Human Mind, XIV. 5
  Fragment on Mackintosh, A, XIV. 5, 59
  Government (essay), XIV. 59
  History of India, XIV. 97, 98, 337
  Political Economy, XIV. 4

Mill, John (1645–1707), IX. 330, 508, 524

Mill, John Stuart (1806–1873), XI. 61, 70, 136, 398, 410, 417; XII. 275, 285, 289, 430, 438; XIII. 11, 15, 54, 385, 465, 478; XIV. 2, 5, 8, 13 ff. (main entry), 35 ff., 43, 59, 103, 133, 187, 432, 469, 474, 477, 486, 608
  Auguste Comte and Positivism, XIV. 22
  Autobiography, XI. 64; XIV. 14, 22, 425
  Considerations on Representative Government, XIV. 20
  Dissertations and Discussions, XIV. 1
  Essays on some Unsettled Questions of Political Economy, XIV. 20
  Examination of Sir William Hamilton's Philosophy, XIV. 19
  Inaugural Address (St Andrews), XIV. 424, 425
  On Liberty, XIV. 20, 21
  On the Subjection of Women, XIV. 20
  Political Economy, XIII. 397
  Principles of Political Economy, XIV. 21, 153
  System of Logic, XIV. 16, 17, 21, 23
  Thoughts on Parliamentary Reform, XIV. 20
  Three Essays on Religion, XIV. 22
  Utilitarianism, XI. 64; XIV. 20

Mill, William Hodge (1792–1853), XII. 341

Millais, Sir John Everett (1829–1896), XI. 489; XIII. 110, 474; XIV. 363

Millamant, in Congreve's *The Way of the World*, VII. 20; VIII. 155, 156

Millamant, Mrs, in Congreve's *The Way of the World*, VIII. 148, 154

Millar, Andrew (1707–1768), X. Add.; XI. 315, 317, 323, 324, 326

Millar, John (1735–1801), IX. 553

Millar, John Hepburn, IX. Add.; XIII. 497, 561; XIV. 532; *Scottish Prose of the 17th and 18th centuries*, XI. 445

Millayn, The Duke of, and the Marques of Mantua, V. 116

Millefont, in Congreve's *Double-Dealer*, VIII. 148 ff., 156

Millenary petition, III. 34

Miller, lady Anna (1741–1781), X. 277, 456

Miller, Hugh (1802–1856), XII. 380; XIV. 160, 203, 515, 522; *My Schools and Schoolmasters*, XIV. 159; *Old Red Sandstone, The*, XIV. 159

Miller, James (1706–1744), X. 440; *Mahomet*, X. 81, 433, 439

Miller, Philip (1691–1771), IX. 182

Miller, Sanderson, X. 271, 272

Miller, T., *The O.E. Version of Bede's Ecclesiastical History*, I. 44, 96, 437

Miller, Thomas (1807–1874), XIII. 506

Miller, William (1810–1872), XIII. 506

Miller of Abingdon, The Jest of the, II. 326, 499

Miller's Daughter of Manchester, The, V. 252

Milles, bookbinder, IV. 406

Milles, Jeremiah (1714–1784), X. 255, 485, 486, 505

Milles, Thomas (d. 1627), IV. 309, 512, 543; *Catalogue of Honor* (1610), III. 528

Millicent, in *The Merry Devill*, V. 252

Milligan, William (1821–1893), XII. 469

Milliken, Richard Alfred (1767–1815), XIV. 570

Millington, Edward (*fl.* 1690), XI. 336, 340

Millington, Thomas (*fl.* 1594), IV. 393

Millington, William (d. 1466?), II. 288, 303

Millwood, in Lillo's *George Barnwell*, X. 75, 76

Milly, in Dickens's *The Haunted Man*, XIII. 324

Milly, in George Eliot's *Amos Barton*, XIII. 388

Milman, Henry Hart (1791–1868), X. 314, 317, 506, 508; XII. 211, 317 ff., 322, 384, 477; XIII. 257, 261, 521; XIV. 103, 493
  Annals of St Paul's, XII. 319
  Anne Boleyn, XIII. 260
  Belshazzar, XIII. 260
  Fall of Jerusalem, The, XIII. 260
  Fazio, XIII. 260
  History of Christianity, The, XII. 318
  History of Latin Christianity, The, XII. 317
  History of the Jews, The, XII. 318
  Martyr of Antioch, The, XIII. 260

Milne, William (1785–1822), XII. 342, 500

Milner, Dr, of Peckham, X. 201

Milner, Isaac (1750–1820), XII. 281, 472

Milner, John (1628–1702), VIII. 474

Milner, John (1752–1826), XIV. 53 ff., 514

Milner, Joseph (1744–1797), *Gibbon's Account of Christianity considered*, X. 309, 507; *History of the Church of Christ*, XII. 281, 472; XIV. 79

Milnes, Richard Monckton, 1st lord Houghton (1809–1885), X. 478; XI. 462; XIII. 184, 467, 506; XIV. 505, 606; *Brookside, The*, XIII. 185; 'Political State of Prussia, The,' XII. 153, 405, 406, 441; *Strangers Yet*, XIII. 185

Milo, island of, VII. 222

Milsand, Joseph, XIII. 71, 72, 75

Miltiades, XII. 363

Milton, Anne, Milton's eldest daughter, VII. 107

Milton, Anne, Milton's sister, VII. 96, 108

Milton, Christopher (1615–1693), VII. 96, 99, 108

Milton, Deborah (d. 1727), youngest step-daughter of Milton, VII. 107, 108

Milton, John (1608–1674), I. 43, 164, 370; II. 184, 195, 217, 220; III. 165, 168, 178, 212, 224, 295, 438; IV. 23, 45 ff., 64, 128, 136, 165, 167, 168, 186, 195, 201 ff., 238, 355, 359; V. 5, 92, 150, 151, 154, 156, 213, 214, 217, 350, 394; VI. 36, 348, 356, 489, 491; VII. 36, 75, 76, 88, 91, 95–141 (main entry), 162 ff., 166, 171, 178, 185, 240, 244, 259, 269, 276, 300, 307, 309, 314 ff., 332, 393, 413–423, 434, 466, 474, *also see* Add.; VIII. 51, 98, 106, 219, 221, 222, 229 ff., 237 ff., 279, 351, 368, 384, 394, 410, 447; IX. 1, 2, 28, 42, 64, 69, 73, 148, 167, 182, 201, 233, 265, 267, 382, 390, 410, 435, 437, 449, 473, 486, 505, 508, 525, 557, 569; X. 1, 96 ff., 101, 102, 105 ff., 109, 110, 113, 120, 127, 134, 143, 145, 148, 149, 155, 224, 232, 235, 239, 240, 304, 378, 383, 432, 462, 475, 476, 492; XI. 13, 28, 77, 84, 90, 124, 133, 140, 157, 159, 171, 179, 181, 182, 188, 193, 201, 206, 207, 224, 247, 250, 252, 254, 255, 290, 380, 394, 401 ff., 409, 415, 427, 432 ff., 466, *also see* Add.; XII. 85, 86, 94, 106, 133, 136, 137, 145, 168, 169, 177, 208, 210, 303, 407, 441; XIII. 26, 27, 29, 35, 36, 50, 66, 92, 130, 170, 173, 191, 230, 232, 237, 238, 242, 250, 253, 448; XIV. 62, 88, 112, 133, 306, 397, 440, 446, 448, 453, 460

Ad Joannem Rousium, VII. 122, 132, 135

Ad Patrem, VII. 131

Animadversions upon the Remonstrant's defence, VII. 127, 139, 141

Apology...Smectymnuus, An, VIII. 127, 139

Arcades, VII. 111 ff., 141; VIII. 230

Milton, John
Areopagitica, VII. 124, 127, 129, 130, 139, 359; IX. 307; X. 372, 446; XI. 311, 312; XII. 504; XIII. 49; XIV. 439

At a Vacation Exercise, VII. 110, 123

Brief Notes upon a late Sermon...by Matthew Griffith, VII. 141

Cambridge list of poems, VII. 117, 121, 141

Colasterion, VII. 140

Comus, V. 92, 239; VI. 126, 329, 337, 349, 359 ff., 363, 366 ff.; VII. 98, 100, 111 ff., 116, 123, 127, 128, 133, 137, 138, 141; VIII. 117, 226, 230; X. 238, 429, 461, 465, 466; XII. 68; XIII. 38, 177

Cromwell sonnet, VII. 115, 123, 141

Dagonalia, VII. 121

De Doctrina Christiana, VII. 129, 141

Defensio Pro Populo Anglicano, III. 165; VII. 105, 131, 140; VIII. 312

Defensio Secunda, VII. 105, 131, 140

Doctrine and Discipline of Divorce, The, VII. 139, 140

Eikonoklastes, VII. 105, 127, 140, 141

Epitaph on the Marchioness of Winchester, An, VII. 111

Epitaphium Damonis, VII. 100, 131; X. 122

Fairfax sonnet, VII. 115, 123, 141

First poems, VII. 109

Greek works, VII. 132

History of Britain, IX. 233

History of England, VII. 124, 128, 141, 206

History of Moscovia, VII. 124, 128, 141, 206

Hobson poems, VII. 111

Il Penseroso, IV. 251; VII. 98, 114, 133, 137; VIII. 230; X. 97, 238; XIII. 44

In quintum Novembris, Anno aetatis 17, VII. 131

Italian poems, VII. 115

Judgement of Martin Bucer Concerning Divorce, The, VII. 140

L'Allegro, IV. 251; VI. 215; VII. 12, 98, 111, 114, 133; VIII. 230; X. 97; XII. 89; XIII. 44

Latin poems, VII. 117

Latin works, VII. 127, 129, 130, 131, 132, 135, 140, 141, 221

Lawes, sonnet to, VII. 115

Lawrence, sonnet to, VII. 108, 115, 121, 141

Letter to a Friend, A, VII. 106, 140

Likeliest Means to Remove Hirelings, VII. 140, 321

Lycidas, IV. 121, 171; VII. 97, 98, 112 ff., 123, 131, 135, 137, 141; X. 114, 185, 186; XII. 74

Mansus, VII. 131

Methought I saw, XII. 91

Monck, a letter to, VII. 106

Nativity Ode, XII. 90

Nightingale sonnet, VII. 141

Observations upon the Articles of Peace with the Irish Rebels, VII. 140

Milton, John
  Of Education, VII. 100, 123, 124, 127,
    139, 265; IX. 384, 389
  Of Prelatical Episcopacy, VII. 139
  *Of Reformation touching Church-Disci-
    pline in England*, VII. 100, 125, 127,
    139, 246; VIII. 78
  *Of True Religion etc. against the growth
    of Popery*, VII. 141
  On the Death of a fair Infant, VII. 109,
    123
  On the late Massacher in Piemont, VII.
    115, 141
  On the Morning of Christ's Nativity, VII.
    110, 111, 132, 133
  On the new forcers of Conscience, VII.
    115
  *On the Religious Memory of Mrs Cathe-
    rine Thomson*, VII. 115
  Paradise Lost, III. 178, 246, 295; VII.
    103, 107, 108, 112, 116 ff. (main entry),
    125, 127, 133, 136, 141, 180; VIII. 27,
    28, 79, 105, 226, 230, 238, 352, 422;
    IX. 59 ff., 140, 182, 269, 338 ff.; X. 112,
    185, 266, 468; XI. 197, 212, 251, 315,
    319, 327, 332; XII. 48, 84, 102, 476, 518;
    XIII. 30, 33, 238; XIV. 113
  Paradise Regained, VII. 107, 120, 121,
    123, 136; VIII. 105; XII. 98
  Passion, The, VII. 110
  Poems, VII. 104, 116
  Poems (1645), XI. 318
  Poems etc., upon Several Occasions,
    2nd ed., VII. 123; X. 238
  Psalm-paraphrases, VII. 109
  *Ready and Easy Way to Establish a Free
    Commonwealth, The*, VII. 106, 140
  *Reason of Church-Government urg'd
    against Prelaty, The*, VII. 139
  Reflections on the Civil War in England,
    VII. 206
  Samson Agonistes, v. 335; VII. 107, 111,
    120 ff., 132, 133, 135, 136, 265; VIII.
    154, 231, 238; XII. 68; XIII. 95
  Second Defence, XI. 312
  Skinner, Cyriak, sonnet to, VII. 115,
    121, 123, 141
  Smectymnuus, VII. 92, 96, 127, 139, 141
  Sonnet IX, VII. 103
  Sonnet on his blindness, VII. 115, 141
  Sonnets, VII. 112, 115
  Tenure of Kings and Magistrates, The,
    VII. 140
  Tetrachordon, VII. 140
  Tetrachordon Sonnets, VII. 115
  *Treatise of Civil Power in Ecclesiastical
    Causes*, VIII. 344
  Vane, sonnet to, VII. 123, 141
  Wife, poem to his dead, VII. 116
Milton, John, the elder (1563?–1647), VII.
  96, 98
Milton, Keynes, X. 351
Milton, Mary (d. 1652), VII. 102, 104, 107
Milton, viscount. *See* Fitzwilliam, William
Miltoun, Francis, XIII. 544
Milus, St, I. 106

Milward, Richard (1609–1680), VII. 392;
  VIII. 321, 322, 324
Mime, in *The Muses Looking-Glasse*, VI.
  233
Mimus, v. 24 ff.
Minadoi, G. T., IV. 446
Minalcas, in *Codrus and Minalcas*, III. 64
Minced-Pie, in *The Masque of Christmas*,
  VI. 358
Minchin, Anne (d. 1711), IX. 166
Minchin, Thomas, IX. 166
Mind, XIV. 23, 24
Mind of Man (Bi manna mode), I. 62
Mind, Will and Understanding, v. 52
Mindelheim, IX. 174
Minerva, II. 231; IX. 60; XIII. 151
Minerva, in *Ira seu Tumulus Fortunae*
  VI. 321
Minerva, in *The Kingis Quair*, II. 242
Minerva, in *The Passetyme of Pleasure*,
  II. 225, 235
Minim, Dick, in Johnson's *Idler*, X. 178
Minns, Ellis Hovell, XII. Add. 5
Minorite convent, XIII. 282
Minos, III. 343, 433; X. 27
Minos, in *Locrine*, v. 240
Minot, Laurence (1300?–1352?), I. 290,
  335, 352, 356, 476; II. 398, 422; III. 274;
  X. 490
Minsheu, John (*fl.* 1617), VII. 480; *Ductor
  in linguas*, IV. 392
Minshull, captain, XIV. 214
Minshull, Elizabeth (3rd wife of John
  Milton, d. 1727), VII. 107
'Minstrel Burn,' IX. 364
Minstrels, II. 506; v. 3, 24, 26, 91, 385
Minto, IX. 373
Minto, William (1845–1893), VI. 30; XI.
  410, 440; XII. 373, 380, 445; XIII. 508,
  551; XIV. 146, 209, 522, 528
Minturno, Antonio Sebastiano, III. 301;
  IX. 59
'Mira' (Sarah Elmy), XI. 140, 141
Mirabeau, Honoré Gabriel de Riquetti,
  count, X. 503, 505; XI. 59; XIII. 12,
  469
Mirabel, in Disraeli's *Henrietta Temple*,
  XIII. 350
Mirabel, in *The Wild-Goose Chase*, VI. 123,
  135
Mirabell, in Congreve's *The Way of the
  World*, VII. 154 ff., 158
*Mirabilis Annus, or the Year of Prodigies
  and Wonders*, VIII. 10
Miracle of Saint Thomas, VI. 283
Miracle-plays, v. 36, 388 ff., *and see* Add.
Miracle-plays, sermons against, II. 502
Miracles of Our Lady, The, II. 323
Miraclis pleyinge, Tretise of, v. 25; VI. 374
Mirah, in *Daniel Deronda*, XIII. 400
Miranda, in Law's *Serious Call*, IX. 323
Miranda, in *The Knight of Malta*, VI. 130
Miranda, in *The Tempest*, v. 169, 172, 194,
  207; VII. 71; VIII. 9, 28; XII. 54
Mirandola, Giovanni Pico della, III. 8,
  214; VII. 264, 376

Mirk, John (*fl.* 1403?), II. 317; *Liber Festivalis*, II. 317, 498; *Instructions for Parish Priests*, II. 427

Mirobolant, Alcide, in *Pendennis*, XIII. 292

Mirror, The, X. 55; XIV. 592

Mirror for Magistrates, A, II. 202; III. 182, 183, 192 ff., 207, 228, 282, 296, 298, 300, 495, 514 ff.; IV. 134, 176; V. 83, 152; VII. 271; XII. 516

Contributors to, and editors of (under whose names also refer): Baldwin, William; Blenerhasset, Thomas; Ferrers, George; Higgins, John; Niccols, Richard; and Sackville, Thomas

Lives and Tragedies contained therein: Albanact; Alfred; Alurede; Arthur; Blacksmith, the; Bladud; Buckingham; Burdet, Sir Nicholas; Cade; Cadwallader; Caligula; Cambridge; Caracalla; Carassus; Chirinnus; Clarence; Claudius; Clifford; Collingbourne; Cordila; Curthose, Robert; Ebbe, Lady; Edric; Edward II; Edward IV; Edward V; Egelrede; Eleanor, duchess; Elstride; Emerianus; England's Eliza (queen Elizabeth); Forrex; Fulgentius; Galba; Geta; Glendower, Owen; Gloucester; Godwin; Guiderius; Hamo; Harold; Hastings; Helena; Henry, duke of Buckingham; Henry VI; Humber; Humphrey, duke of Gloucester; Iago; Irenglas; Ironside, Edmund; James I, of Scotland; James IV; John; Julius Caesar; Kimarus; Locrinus; Londricus; Madan; Malin; Mempricius; Morgan; Morindus; Mortimer; Mowbray; Nennius; Nero; Northumberland; Otho; Pendragon, Uther; Pinnar; Porrex; Richard I; Richard II; Richard III; Rudacke; Sabrine; Salisbury; Severus; Shore's Wife; Sigebert; Somerset; Stater; Suffolk; Tiberius; Tresilian; Varianus; Vitellius; Vortiger; Werwick; Wolsey, cardinal; Woodville; Worcester and York, III. 192–197

Mirror of Justices, The, VIII. 313, 317; XIV. 80

Mirror of St Edmund, The (Rolle), II. 47

Mirror of the Church, The, II. 324

Mirror of the periods of man's life, The, II. 502

Mirror of the World, The, II. 313

Mirrors, III. 198, 341

Mirrour of Worldly Fame, The, IV. 524

Mirza, in Lyttelton's *Persian Letters*, X. 114

Mirza Abdullah, XIV. 252

Misaubin, John, X. 22

Miscellanea Aulica, VIII. 379, 480; IX. 496

Miscellanies (Pope and Swift), IX. 78, 85, 131

Miscellany of Popular Scottish Poems (1841), XI. 444

Miser, the, in *The Daunce and Song of Death*, III. 87

Misericordia, in the *Coventry Plays*, V. 21

Misogonus, V. 110, 112, 113, 117, 119, 411

Misrule, in *The Masque of Christmas*, VI. 358, 359

Misrule, lord of, V. 8

Misselden, Edward (*fl.* 1608–1654), IV. 297, 512

Missolonghi, IV. 89

Mist, Nathaniel, IX. 16, 17; *Weekly Journal*, IX. 19, 21, 448

Mister, Mary, XI. 488; *The Adventures of a Doll*, XI. 383

Misyn, Richard (d. 1462?), II. 438

Mitcham, IV. 202

Mitchel, John (1815–1875), XIV. 570; *History of Ireland*, XIV. 326; *Jail Journal*, XIV. 325, 326; *Life of Hugh O'Neill*, XIV. 325

Mitchell, Sir Arthur (1826–1909), XII. 511

Mitchell, C., XIV. 532

Mitchell, Joseph (1684–1738), X. 434

Mitchell, Thomas (1783–1845), XII. 488; XIII. 175, 506

Mitford, Algernon Bertram Freeman, baron Redesdale (1837–1916), XIII. 495

Mitford, Bertram, XIV. Add. 9

Mitford, John (1781–1859), III. 298; X. 119, 451, 454, 458, 481; XI. 401; XII. 396, 420

Mitford, John (*pseud.* Alfred Burton, 1782–1831), XIV. 221, 544; *The Adventures of Johnny Newcome*, XIV. 220; *The Poems of a British Sailor*, XIV. 220

Mitford, John Freeman, 1st baron Redesdale (1748–1830), X. 510

Mitford, John Thomas Freeman, earl of Redesdale (1805–1886), XIII. 241, 245, 512

Mitford, Mary Russell (1787–1855), XI. 410, 458, 459, 461, 465; XII. 239, 242, 433, 453; XIII. 258, 377, 564; XIV. 200
Atherton, XIII. 429
Belford Regis, XIII. 430
Our Village, XIII. 429, 430
Recollections of a Literary Life, XIII. 429
Rienzi, XIII. 430

Mitford, William (1744–1827), XI. 251 ff., 255; XII. 302, 313; *History of Greece*, X. 320, 510; XII. 310

Mithridates, VII. 317

Mivart, St George (1827–1900), XII. 469

Moab, king of, in Cowley's *Davideis*, VII. 67

Moabite stone, the, XII. 501

Moallakat, laws of, XII. 502

Moberly, George (1803–1885), XII. 454, 457; XIII. 504

Moccum moccabitur, game of, V. 93

Mock Testaments, VII. 513

Mocket, Richard, (?) *God and the King*, IV. 382

Modder, river, XIV. 372

Model [army], the New, VII. 434

Moderate Intelligencer, The, VII. 355

Moderation, in *Piers the Plowman*, II. 20

Modern Theatre, The (1809), XI. 456

Modish, lady Betty, in Cibber's *Careless Husband*, VIII. 176

Modish, Mrs, in *Dialogues of the Dead*, XI. 352

Modus Componendi Brevia, VIII. 465

Modus Tenendi Parliamentum, XII. 355

Moe, J., XI. 491

Moetjen's *Recueil de pièces curieuses et nouvelles*, XI. 374

Moffat (Bannatyne MS.), II. 274

Moffat (Scotland), X. 230

Moffat, James, XIII. 570

Moffat, Sir John (attributed to), *Beware, I red you now*, III. 131; *The Wyf of Auchtirmuchty*, III. 132

Moffat, Robert, XIV. Add. 9

Moffett or Moffat, Thomas (1553–1604), IV. 519, 543; *Insectorum sive minimorum animalium theatrum*, IV. 374; *Silkewormes*, IV. 374

Mogridge, George (1787–1854), XI. 482

Mogul, the great, IV. 90, 91, 99; VII. 437; X. 110

Mogul empire, the, XIV. 332

Mogul government, XI. 16

Mohacz, battle of, VII. 79

Mohammadans (*Hudibras*), VIII. 65

Mohammed. *See* Mahomet

Mohammedan law, a, II. 292

Mohammedan learning, I. 153

Mohammedan religion, X. 313, 314

Mohammedanism, XI. 18, 194; XII. 191; XIII. 202, 362

Mohammedans, X. 377; XI. 17

Mohawks, the, XI. 261

Mohl, Mme, XIII. 381

'Mohock Magazine, the,' XII. 160, 161

Mohocks, the, IX. 126, 160

Mohun, Charles, 5th lord Mohun (1675?–1712), IX. 424

Mohun, Michael (1620?–1684), VIII. 186

Moir, David Macbeth (1798–1851), XII. 380, 450, 451; XIII. 431; *The Curate of Suverdiso*, XII. 252; *The Life of Mansie Wauch*, XII. 251

Moira, earl. *See* Hastings, Francis Rawdon

Molesey, III. 381

Molesworth, Robert, 1st viscount Molesworth (1656–1723), IX. 457, 463, 494

Molesworth, Sir William (1810–1855), XIV. 196

Molesworth, William Nassau (1816–1890), XIV. 495; *The History of England from 1830*, XIV. 93

Moleynes, lord (*Paston Letters*), II. 304

Molière, J. B. Poquelin de, I. 371; V. 189, 293; VI. 160, 214; VII. 366; VIII. 14, 134, 137 ff., 157, 159, 162, 165, 373, 374, 376, 428; IX. 29, 30; X. 88, 202, 417; XI. 322; XIII. 442, 445

Don Garcie de Navarre, XII. 211

Fourberies de Scapin, VIII. 181, 182

L'Avare, VIII. 174; X. 22; XI. 277

Le Bourgeois Gentilhomme, VIII. 140, 169

L'École des Femmes, VIII. 144

Molière, J. B. P. de

L'École des Maris, VIII. 139, 144, 183

L'Étourdi, VIII. 17, 133, 398; X. 72

Le mariage forcé, IX. 41; XI. 265

Le Médecin Malgré Lui, X. 22, 427

Le Misanthrope, VIII. 145; X. 226; XI. 269; XIII. 446

Les Fâcheux, VIII. 174

Les Précieuses Ridicules, VIII. 131, 174

Le Sicilien, ou l'Amour Peintre, VIII. 188

Monsieur de Pourceaugnac, VIII. 140, 431

Tartuffe, VIII. 189; X. 425

Molina, Tirso de, VIII. 130; *El Castigo del Pensèque*, VI. 204; VIII. 129

Molineaux, pugilist, XIV. 231

Molineux, Sir Richard, III. 265

Molinists, the, XIII. 435

Molitoris, U., *Dialogus de Pythonicis Mulieribus*, VII. 370, 505

Moll Cutpurse, in *The Roaring Girle*, VI. 54, 66, 223

Molle, H., VI. 480

Mollineux, Mary (born Southworth) (d. 1695), *Fruits of Retirement*, VIII. 114, 416; *Meditations in Trouble*, VIII. 114

Molloy, Charles (1646–1690), IV. 459

Molloy, Charles (d. 1767), XIV. 570

Molloy, Gerald, *The Irish Difficulty*, XIV. 447

Molloy, Joseph Fitzgerald, XIII. 515

Molly, in Mrs Gaskell's *Wives and Daughters*, XIII. 377, 378, 381

Moloch, XII. 36

Molteno, Sir Charles, XIV. Add. 9

Molteno, Percy Alport, XIV. Add. 9

Moluccas, the, IV. 99

Molyneux, William (1656–1698), VIII. 332, 339, 474; IX. 180, 181, 283; XIV. 570

Molza, III. 178

Momerie, Alfred Williams (1848–1900), XII. 469

Momford, lord, in *The Blind Beggar of Bednal Green*, V. 361

Mommsen, Theodor, I. 65, 66, 68, 70; XII. 306, 322; XIII. 469

Momure, in *Huon of Bordeaux*, II. 339

Momus, in *Wisdom of Solomon Paraphrased*, VI. 59

'Monarcho, fantastical,' VIII. 127

Monarchy or no Monarchy in England, VII. 207

Monardes, Nicolas, IV. 446

Monboddo, lord. *See* Burnett, James

Monçada, in Maturin's *Melmoth*, XIII. 420

Monck, George, 1st duke of Albemarle (1608–1670), VII. 140, 219, 229, 230, 360, 361, 364; VIII. 118, 121, 254

Monck, James Bury (1784–1856), XIV. 514

Monck, Mrs, VII. 362

Monck, William Henry Stanley, XIV. 474

Monckton, Mary, countess of Cork and Orrery (1746–1840), XI. 364

Moncrieff, William Thomas (1794–1857), XIII. 270, 418, 516, 521; XIV. 224;

Moncrieff, William Thomas
   *Cataract of the Ganges; or, The Rajah's
   Daughter*, XIII. 265; *Dandy Family, The*,
   XIII. 265; *Tom and Jerry*, XIII. 265
Moneta, in Keats's *The Fall of Hyperion*,
   XII. 86
Money, in *Worke for Armorours*, VI. 56
Money-without-Learning, in *All for Money*,
   V. 57
Monica, St, VII. 247, 248
Monier-Williams, Sir Monier (1819–1899),
   XII. 343, 503
Monimia, in Otway's *Orphan*, VIII. 183,
   184
Monitor, The, IX. 432; X. 388 ff., 522
Monk, James Henry (1784–1856), XII.
   327 ff., 488, 491; XIV. 595; *Life of
   Bentley*, XII. 329
Monkhouse, Mrs, in Amory's *Memoirs of
   Several Ladies*, XI. 287
Monkhouse, William Cosmo (1840–1901),
   XII. 444; XIII. 207, 506
Monks, in *Oliver Twist*, XIII. 317, 325
Monkshaven, in Mrs Gaskell's *Sylvia's
   Lovers*, XIII. 380
Monmouth. *See* Geoffrey of
Monmouth, duchess of, IX. 161
Monmouth, duke of. *See* Scott, James
Monmouth, earl of. *See* Carey, Robert
Monmouth, lord, in Disraeli's *Coningsby*,
   XIII. 288, 349
Monmouth, Humphrey (*fl.* 1523), III. 40
Monmouth, Robert Carey, 1st earl of
   (1560?–1639), V. 479; XII. 376
Monmouthshire, XI. 430
Monnet, Jean, XI. 258
Monod, Adolphe, XII. 283; XIV. 490
Monod, Gabriel, XIV. 490
Monro, Alexander (d. 1715?), IX. 547
Monro, Charles Henry (1835–1908), XII.
   488
Monro, David Binning (1836–1905), XII.
   488, 492; *Grammar of the Homeric dia-
   lect*, XII. 334
Monro, Edward (1815–1866), XII. 472
Monro, H. A. J., XII. 482
Monro, Robert (d. 1633), *Expedition with
   the worthy Scots Regiment called M'Keyes
   Regiment*, VII. 231, 451
Monro, Robert (d. 1680?), VII. 452
Monro, Thomas (1764–1815), X. 472
Monsey, R., *Scarronides*, IX. 257, 500
Monson, Sir Thomas (1564–1641), IV. 143
Monson, Sir William (1569–1643), VII.
   446; *Naval Tracts*, IV. 103, 104
Mont Blanc, XIV. 236
Mont Cenis, IX. 245; X. 115
Mont St Michel, II. 112
Montagu, Andrew, XIV. 185
Montagu, Anne Wortley, IX. 244
Montagu, Basil (1770–1851), XIV. 514
Montagu, Charles, earl of Halifax, IX. 44,
   45, 86, 150, 244; *The Hind and the
   Panther Transvers'd*, IX. 147
Montagu, Charles, 1st duke of Manchester
   (1660?–1722), VIII. 274; IX. 149, 150

Montagu, Edward, 2nd earl of Manchester
   (1602–1671), IV. 425; VII. 351, 434
Montagu, Edward, 1st earl of Sandwich
   (1625–1672), VIII. 202, 249, 253, 254;
   IX. 244; X. 262; XI. 348
Montagu, Edward (d. 1775), X. 262; XI.
   347, 348, 350
Montagu, Edward Wortley (d. 1761), IX.
   244, 246, 248
Montagu, Edward Wortley (1713–1776),
   IX. 248; XIV. 553
Montagu, Mrs Elizabeth (1720–1800), V.
   293; VII. 176; IX. 246; X. 261, 264, 268,
   494; XI. 272, 328, 343, 346 ff. (main
   entry), 358, 360, 361, 364, 365, 474;
   Dialogues of the Dead, XI. 351, 352;
   Essay on Shakespeare, X. 262; XI. 352 ff.
Montagu, George. *See* Dunk
Montagu or Mountague, James (1568?–
   1618), VII. 316; VIII. 293
Montagu, John (1655?–1728), IV. 239
Montagu, John, 4th earl of Sandwich
   (1718–1792), X. 397, 401
Montagu, lady Mary Wortley (1689–1762),
   IX. 71, 191, 243 ff. (main entry), 250,
   251, 402 ff., 449, 497, 574; X. 273, 274;
   XI. 348; XIII. 467
   'Basset-table, The,' IX. 247
   Constantinople Letters, IX. 246 ff.
   Court Poems by a Lady of Quality, IX. 247
   'Drawing Room, The,' IX. 247
   Letters and Works, IX. 248
   'On a maxim of La Rochefoucauld,'
   IX. 249
   'Toilet, The,' IX. 247
   Town Eclogues, IX. 247, 248
   Translation of the *Enchiridion* of
   Epictetus, IX. 246, 248
   Turkish Letters, IX. 244
Montagu, Matthew, X. 261
Montagu, Ralph, 1st duke of Montagu
   (1638?–1709), VIII. 156
Montagu or Mountague, Richard (1577–
   1641), VII. 312, 426, 459, 483, 484, 485
   A New Gag for an old Goose, VII. 158
   *Analecta Exercitationum Ecclesiasti-
   carum*, VII. 311
   Appello Caesarem, VII. 158, 433
   Immediate Address unto God alone, VII.
   158
Montagu, Walter (1603?–1677), VII. 517
Montague, in *Romeo and Juliet*, V. 182
Montague, Mrs Basil, XIII. 469
Montague, Charles Edward, XIV. 533
Montague, Francis Charles, XIV. 493, 536
Montague, Sir James (1666–1723), IX. 147
Montaigne, Michel Eyquem seigneur de,
   III. 160, 438, 453; IV. 10, 15, 16, 246,
   248, 254, 343, 344, 347, 395, 447, 523;
   V. 207; VI. 21, 377; VII. 199, 366, 379,
   389; VIII. 28, 52, 56, 58, 374, 376 ff.,
   385 ff., 389, 390, *also see* Add.; IX. 47,
   159, 233, 237, 265, 399; X. 50; XII. 168,
   174, 175; XIII. 467; XIV. 160, 421, 428;
   Essays, IX. 276, 277, 499
Montalembert, Charles Forbes de, XII. 276

Montalto, in the *Dunciad*, v. 271

Montalvan, J. P. de, VII. 83

Montalvo, García Ordoñez de, IV. 447; XI. 422

Montano, Reginaldo Gonzalez, IV. 447

Montanus (Lodge's), IV. 122

Montanus, Joannes Ferrarius, Latin treatise on Commonweal, VI. 377, 493

Montausier, duchess of (Julia de Rambouillet), VIII. 142

Monte. *See* Robert de

Monte Cassino, I. 214

Monteagle, lord. *See* Parker, William

Montégut, Émile, v. 302; IX. 71, 72; XIII. 551, 558

Monteith, Robert (*fl.* 1621–1660), IX. 550

Montemayor, George, III. 341; IV. 447; *Diana*, III. 186, 219, 351, 352; IV. 9, 117; v. 220; VI. 365

Montesquieu, Charles Louis de Secondat, baron de la Brède et de, IV. 295; v. 288; VIII. 292; x. 114, 135, 206, 334; XI. 163; XIII. 467; *Considérations*, x. 304; *Esprit des Lois*, x. 123, 296

Montfort, in Disraeli's *Endymion*, XIII. 349

Montfort, Simon de, I. 180, 204, 205, 338, 339, 368; XIV. 100

Montgomerie, Alexander (1556?–1610?), III. 134, 135, 188, 499, *also see* Add.; IV. 322, 517; IX. 359, 365; XI. 203
  Ane Answer to ane Helandmains Invective, III. 136
  Bankis of Helicon, The, III. 136; XI. 217
  Cherrie and the Slae, The, III. 133, 136; IX. 366, 367; XI. 217
  Flyting betwixt Polwart and Montgomerie, The, III. 136, 137, 491
  Night is near Gone, The, III. 137

Montgomery, VII. 27

Montgomery, countess of, *Urania*, VI. 200

Montgomery, H. R., XII. 412; XIV. 572

Montgomery, James (1771–1854), XII. 420; XIV. 203; *Go to dark Gethsemane*, XII. 135; *Songs of praise the angels sang*, XII. 135

Montgomery, Jemima (1807–1893), afterwards baroness Tautphoeus, XIII. 565

Montgomery, Robert (1807–1855), XII. 420; *Satan*, XII. 129; *The Omnipresence of the Deity*, XII. 129

Monthly Catalogue, The, XI. 339

Monthly Chronicle, The, XI. 374

Monthly Magazine, The, XII. 428

Monthly Magazine of Politics, Literature, The, and the Belles-Lettres, XII. 428

Monthly Magazine: or, British Register of Literature, Sciences, The, and the Belles-Lettres, XII. 428

Monthly Repository, The, XII. 428; XIII. 53 ff.

Monthly Repository of Theology and General Literature, The, XII. 428

Monthly Review, The, IX. 472; x. 40, 171, 176, 201 ff., 474, 483; XI. 142, 339, 353, 418 ff.; XII. 428

Monthly Review, The (or Literary Journal), XII. 428

Monticelso, in *The White Divel*, VI. 176

Montluc, Blaise de, *Commentaries*, IX. 276

Montoni, in Mrs Radcliffe's *Mysteries of Udolpho*, XI. 303

Montpellier, II. 364; III. 419; VII. 217, 233; VIII. 330, 389

Montpensier, Mlle de, IV. 523

Montreal, XIV. 357, 358
  Bishop's college, XIV. 355
  Shakespeare club, XIV. 355

Montreville, in *The Unnatural Combat*, VI. 159

Montrose, duke of. *See* Graham, James, 1st duke

Montrose, marquis of. *See* Graham, James, 1st marquis

Monumenta Germaniae Historica, XIV. 53

Monypenny, William Flavelle (1886–1912), XIV. 504; *The Life of Benjamin Disraeli, Earl of Beaconsfield*, XIII. 345, 346, 547

Moodie, Donald, XIV. Add. 9

Moodie, Duncan C. F., XIV. Add. 5, 9

Moodie, Susanna (1803–1885), XIV. 360, 581, 583; *Life in the Clearing*, XIV. 358; *Roughing it in the Bush*, XIV. 358

Moody, John (1727?–1812), XI. 257, 261

Moody, John, in Vanbrugh's *A Journey to London*, VIII. 162

Moor, James (1712–1779), IX. 562

Moor, John (*fl.* 1688), x. 387

Moor park, IX. 91 ff., 126

Moore, Arthur (1666?–1730), IX. 14

Moore, Arthur William (1853–1909), XII. 512

Moore, Dugald (1805–1841), XII. 420

Moore, Edward (1712–1757), x. 81, 92, 423, 437; XI. 324; *Foundling, The*, x. 80; *Gamester, The*, x. 80, 81; *Gil Blas*, x. 80

Moore, Edward, XIV. 596

Moore, Henry (1751–1844), x. 518

Moore, H. Kingsmill, XIV. 592

Moore, James (1702–1734), IX. 86

Moore, John (1646–1714), IX. 330, 335, 356

Moore, John (*fl.* 1721), x. 387

Moore, John (1729–1802), XI. 207, 462; XIII. 467; *Zeluco*, x. 38

Moore, Sir John (1761–1809), XIII. 467; XIV. 107, 294

Moore, John Howard, XIV. 553

Moore, J. Sheridan, XIV. 363, 587

Moore, Louis, in Charlotte Brontë's *Shirley*, XIII. 408

Moore, Peter (1753–1828), XIII. 276

Moore, Robert, in Charlotte Brontë's *Shirley*, XIII. 408, 409

Moore, Thomas (1779–1852), XI. 396, 456; XII. 34, 42, 44, 74, 95, 102 ff. (main entry), 110, 115, 120, 122, 126, 129, 130, 136, 138, 150, 163, 223, 303, 383 ff., 410, 444; XIII. 25, 154, 161, 166, 230, 234, 306; XIV. 180, 186, 198, 310, 314, 318a, 322, 365, 504

Moore, Thomas
  At the mid hour of night, XII. 105; XIII.
  235
  Corruption, XII. 104
  Epicurean, The, XII. 104
  Eveleen's Bower, XIII. 235
  Fables for the Holy Alliance, XII. 40
  Fudge Family, The, XII. 104, 105
  I saw from the beach, XII. 105
  Intolerance, XII. 104
  Irish Melodies, XII. 41, 102, 105; XIV.
  311, 316, 329
  Lalla Rookh, XII. 102, 105
  Last Rose of Summer, The, XII. 105
  Life of Lord Byron, XII. 53, 103
  Life of Lord Edward Fitzgerald, XIV. 107
  Life of Sheridan, XIV. 107
  Loves of the Angels, The, XII. 48, 102
  Minstrel Boy, The, XII. 105
  National Airs, XII. 105
  Oft in the stilly night, XII. 105
  '*Paradise and the Peri*,' XII. 105
  '*Phelim Connor*' letters, XII. 104
  Poems, XII. 103, 104
  Poetical works of the late Thomas Little,
  XII. 103
  Tell me the witching tale again, XIV. 311
  Two-penny Post Bag, The, XII. 105
Moore, Zachary, XI. 174
Moore Smith, G. C. *See* Smith, G. C.
  Moore
Moorish wars in Spain, XI. 280
Moors, the, XIII. 258
Mopsa, in Sidney's *Arcadia*, III. 353
Mopus, in Wilson's *The Cheats*, VIII. 122
Moral Ode. See *Poema Morale*
Moralities, V. 36, 391 ff.
Moralities, Latin, V. 58
Moran, Patrick Francis (1830–1911), XIV.
  570
Morand, duke, in a religious play, V. 40,
  43
Morant, Philip (1700–1770), IX. 537
Moravian school, Neuwied, XIII. 440
Moravians, the, IX. 324; X. 60, 350, 364
Moray, II. 115
Moray, earl of. *See* Stewart, James
Moray, Sir Robert (d. 1673), IX. 193
Morayshire, XIII. 431
Morcelli, Stefano Antonio, XII. 326
Mordaunt, Charles, 3rd earl of Peter-
  borough (1685–1735), VIII. 411; IX. 23,
  249, 250
Mordent, in Holcroft's *Deserted Daughter*,
  XI. 277
Mordred or Modred, in Arthurian legend,
  I. 235, 248, 260 ff., 266
Mordred, in *Morte Arthure*, I. 313; II. 118,
  120
Mordred, in Malory's *Morte d'Arthur*, V. 78
Mordred, in *The Misfortunes of Arthur*,
  V. 78, 79
More, Anne (afterwards Anne Donne),
  IV. 200
More, Cresacre (1572–1649), V. 247; XII.
  516

More, Edward (1537?–1620), *The Defence
  of Women*, III. 90, 486
More, Elizabeth (afterwards Rastell), IV.
  198
More, George, IV. 535
More, Sir George (of Losely), IV. 200, 201,
  221
More, Hannah (1745–1833), X. 250, 251,
  267 ff. (main entry), 494; XI. 260, 300,
  350, 359 ff. (main entry), 365, 458, 474;
  XII. 124, 445; XIV. 60, 390, 600, 608
  Bas Bleu, or Conversation, XI. 346, 348,
  362
  Bishop Bonner's Ghost, XI. 363
  Bleeding Rock, The, XI. 361
  Cheap Repository Tracts, XII. 281
  Fatal Falsehood, The, XI. 274, 362
  Inflexible Captive, The, XI. 273
  Memoirs, X. 184
  Percy, XI. 272, 273, 362
  Preface to Tragedies, XI. 259
  Repository Tracts, XI. 362
  Sacred Dramas, XI. 379
  Search after Happiness, The, XI. 360
  Sensibility, X. 268; XI. 362
  Sir Eldred of the Bower, X. 213; XI. 361
  *Thoughts on the importance of the Manners
  of the Great*, XI. 362
  Village Politics, XI. 362
More, Henry (1614–1687), VII. 84, 90,
  279, 302, 407, 507, 510; VIII. 110, 273,
  278 ff., 283, 290, 291, 347, 453 ff., 474;
  IX. 184, 518; XI. 57
  Antidote against Atheism, VIII. 285, 287
  Conjectura Cabbalistica, VIII. 285
  Divine Dialogues, VIII. 286
  Enchiridion Ethicum, VIII. 282
  Enchiridion Metaphysicum, VIII. 286
  Enthusiasmus Triumphatus, VIII. 285;
  IX. 326
  Grand Mystery of Godliness, VIII. 285
  Immortality of the Soul, The, VIII. 280,
  285
  Mystery of Iniquity, VIII. 286
  Philosophicall Poems, VIII. 282, 283
  Song of the Soul, VIII. 282, 283, 285
More, John (d. 1592), V. 133
More, P. Elmer, XI. 420; *The Shelburne
  Essays*, XII. 433
More, Richard (d. 1643), VII. 482
More, Sarah, X. 268
More, Sir Thomas (1478–1535), II. 62, 327;
  III. 2, 6, 7, 12, 13, 15–21 (main entry),
  26, 40, 43, 47, 49, 52, 80, 187, 314, 332,
  334, 363, 365, 469, 532; IV. 198, 228,
  261, 320, 512; V. 57; VII. 158, 278, 304,
  366, 392, 474; VIII. 125; IX. 160, 197,
  489, 534; X. 184; XI. 422, 427; XIV. 494
  Apology, The, III. 17
  Dialogue, The, II. 60; III. 17, 26
  *Mery geste of a Sergeaunt and Frere,
  The*, II. 326
  Frith, A Letter against, III. 17
  *Luciani...compluria opuscula...ab Eras-
  mo Roterodamo et Thoma Moro...traducta*,
  III. 16

More, Sir Thomas
  Picus, Life of John, III. 17
  Progymnasmata, III. 13, 16
  Rueful Lamentation, A, III. 17
  Salem and Bizance, The Debellacyon of,
    III. 17
  Supper of the Lord, An Answere to the,
    III. 17
  Supplication of Souls, The, III. 17, 26
  Tindale's Answere, A Confutation of,
    III. 17
  Utopia, III. 16 ff., 109, 332, 334; IV. 67,
    300; V. 90; VII. 298, 299; XIII. 452
  Works, IV. 397
More, Sir Thomas, V. 237, 238, 246 ff.,
  332, 399, 442, 444
More, Sir William, VI. 289
Morea, the, VII. 75
Morecroft, in The Scornful Ladie, VI. 133
Morell, John Daniel (1816–1891), XIV. 478
Morell, Thomas (1703–1784), Thesaurus,
  XII. 327
Moréri, Louis, Grand Dictionnaire his-
  torique, V. 286; IX. 211, 492
Moreto, A., No puede ser guardar una
  mujer (No holding a Woman), VIII. 131,
  189
Moreton Pinckney, X. 271
Morfill, William Richard (1834–1909), XIV.
  495
Morgam, chronicle of the abbey of, I. 256
Morgan, in Smollett's Roderick Random,
  X. 37
Morgan, earl of London, in The Devil and
  his Dame, V. 329
Morgan, Henry, IV. 76
Morgan, Henry James, XIV. 581
Morgan, J., Phoenix Britannicus, X. 166
Morgan, James, in Pendennis, XIII. 291
Morgan, McNamara, III. 355
Morgan, N., The Perfection of Horseman-
  ship, IV. 540
Morgan, lady Sydney (born Owenson)
  (1783–1859), XII. 451; XIV. 570
  Book without a Name, The, XIV. 322
  France, XIV. 322
  Italy, XIV. 322
  Kate Kearney, XIV. 323
  St Clair, XIV. 322
  Wild Irish Girl, The, XIV. 322
Morgan, Sylvanus (1620–1693), IX. 537
Morgan, Thomas (d. 1743), IX. 288, 508;
  X. 521; Moral Philosopher, The, IX.
  294
Morgan, Thomas, F.S.A., XII. 512;
  Romano-British Mosaic Pavements, XII.
  347
Morgan, Sir Thomas (d. 1679?), VII. 452
Morgan, Sir Thomas Charles (1783–1843),
  XIV. 322
Morgan le Fay, I. 265, 327
Morgans, the, XI. 121
Morhof, Daniel Georg, V. 286
Morice, Sir William (1602–1676), VII. 364
Morier, James Justinian (1780?–1849),
  XII. 451

Morier, Sir Robert Burnett David (1826–
  1893), XIV. 504
Morin, Lewis, X. 164, 464
Moriomachia, VII. 390
Morison, James Augustus Cotter (1832–
  1888), XIII. 467; XIV. 62, 493, 504;
  Gibbon, X. 300, 304, 305, 314, 509; XIV.
  504
Morison, Jeanie, XIII. 485
Morison, Robert (1620–1683), VIII. 478;
  XIV. 282, 562
Morisot, Claude, Alitophili Veritatis La-
  chrymae, IV. 257
Morland, Catherine, in Jane Austen's
  Northanger Abbey, XI. 299, 300; XII.
  235, 236
Morland, George (1763–1804), VIII. 66
Morland, Sir Samuel (1625–1695), VIII. 478
Morley. See Daniel of
Morley, George (1597–1684), bishop of
  Winchester, IV. 422; VII. 151, 250, 426,
  518; VIII. 294, 295, 460
Morley, Henry (1822–1894), I. viii, 47,
  218; II. 28, 35; XI. 392, 407, 418; XII.
  427, 504; XIII. 472, 515; XIV. 198, 504
Morley, John, viscount Morley of Black-
  burn, IX. 153; XI. 390, 406; XII. 396;
  XIII. 495; XIV. 123, 195, 493, 509, 592;
  Life of Gladstone, XIV. 135; Life of
  Richard Cobden, XIV. 179
Morley, Thomas (1557–1604?), IV. 113,
  121, 464, 465, 487
Mormon, Book of, IV. 47
Mornay, Philippe de, IV. 447; Work con-
  cerning the trewnesse of the Christian
  Religion, Sidney's trans., IV. 21
Morning Advertiser, The, XIV. 177, 189
Morning Chronicle, The, X. 467; XII. 171,
  183, 187, 323, 432, 490; XIV. 170, 171,
  177, 178, 184 ff., 189, 190
Morning Herald, The, XI. 34, 391; XIV.
  188, 189
Morning Post, The, XII. 187, 188, 434;
  XIII. 347, 440; XIV. 177, 179, 183 ff.,
  529, 533
Morning Star, The, XIV. 173, 188, 190
Morocco, V. 183
Morocco, Notes and Observations on the
  Empress of, VIII. 3
Morose, in Jonson's The Silent Woman,
  VI. 22, 227; X. 50
Morpeth, XIII. 129
Morpeth, Ontario, XIV. 350
Morpeth school, VII. 330
Morrice, D., XIV. 598
Morris, Charles (1745–1838), XII. 420
Morris, Dinah, in Adam Bede, XIII. 383,
  390, 391
Morris, Jane (born Burden), XIII. 119
Morris, John Brande (1812–1880), XII. 454
Morris, Sir Lewis (1833–1907), XIII. 194,
  201 ff., 221, 506
  Epic of Hades, An, XIII. 201
  Gwen, XIII. 202
  Gycia, XIII. 202
  Ode of Life, The, XIII. 202

Morris, Sir Lewis
  Songs of Two Worlds, XIII. 201
  Songs Unsung, XIII. 202
Morris, Marshall, Faulkner and Co., XIII.
  119
Morris, Miss May, XIII. 493
Morris, Richard (1833–1894), I. 115, 218;
  II. 166; XII. 504; XIV. 611; Specimens
  of Early English, XII. 344
Morris, William (1834–1896), I. 420; VIII.
  227; XII. 275; XIII. 112, 118 ff. (main
  entry), 134, 137, 139, 147, 178, 193,
  205, 251, 442, 448, 451, 458, 491 ff. (main
  entry); XIV. 537
  Aeneids of Virgil, The (translation),
    XIII. 125, 126
  Bellerophon at Argos, XIII. 125
  Bellerophon in Lycia, XIII. 125
  Beowulf (translation), XIII. 127
  Cupid and Psyche, The Story of, XIII.
    124
  Defence of Guenevere, The, X. 217, 220;
    XIII. 121, 122, 124, 125, 129
  Doom of King Acrisius, The, XIII. 124
  Dream of John Ball, A, XIII. 127
  Earthly Paradise, The, XIII. 120, 123,
    125, 128, 252
  Hollow Land, The, XIII. 121
  House of the Wolfings, The, XIII. 127
  'I know a little garden close,' XIII. 125
  King Arthur's Tomb, XIII. 121
  Land East of the Sun and West of the
    Moon, The, XIII. 124, 125
  Life and Death of Jason, The, XIII. 122,
    124, 125, 252
  Lindenborg Pool, XIII. 121
  Love is Enough, XIII. 125, 126, 135, 252
  Lovers of Gudrun, The, XIII. 125
  News from Nowhere, XIII. 127
  Odyssey (translation), XIII. 125 ff.
  'Outlanders, whence come ye last?'
    XIII. 140
  Poems by the Way, XIII. 127
  Rapunzel, XIII. 121
  Roots of the Mountains, The, XIII. 127
  Sailing of the Sword, The, XIII. 121
  Sigurd the Volsung and the Fall of the
    Niblungs, The Story of, XIII. 126, 127,
    252
  Sir Peter Harpdon's End, X. 217; XIII.
    121
  Song of the Gillyflower, The, XIII. 121
  Story of the Glittering Plain, The, XIII.
    127
  Story of the Unknown Church, The,
    XIII. 120
  Sundering Flood, The, XIII. 128
  Two Red Roses across the Moon, XIII. 121
  Water of the Wondrous Isles, The, XIII.
    128
  Well at the World's End, The, XIII. 128
  Welland River, XIII. 121
  Wood beyond the World, The, XIII. 128
Morris dancers, V. 32
Morrison, Robert (1782–1834), XII. 342,
  500

Mors, in A Dialogue...against the fever
  Pestilence, III. 109
Mors, Roderyck, The Complaint of, VII. 514
Morsbach, L., II. 152
Morse or Mosse, M., IV. 512, 518
Morte Arthure (English rime and allitera-
  tive versions), I. 235, 270, 281, 284, 290,
  313, 333, 470; II. 116, 118, 119, 122, 123,
  230, 314, 315, 332, 334 ff., 340, 486;
  III. 233, 237; IV. 6, 397; V. 78; X. 218,
  228; XIII. 35; also see Malory
Mortgage, in The Staple of Newes, VI. 25
Mortimer, Mrs Favell Lee (1802–1878),
  XI. 481
Mortimer, Roger de, 8th baron Wigmore
  and 1st earl of March (1287?–1330),
  IV. 181, 182
Mortlake, IV. 73
Morton, Charles (1627–1698), IX. 6, 393,
  394; X. 386
Morton, earl, in John a Kent, etc., V.
  317
Morton, Henry, in Scott's Old Mortality,
  XII. 27
Morton, John (1420?–1500), archbishop
  of Canterbury (bishop of Ely), III. 15,
  66, 334, 335; V. 54
Morton, John Maddison (1811–1891), XIII.
  521; Box and Cox, XIII. 270
Morton, Thomas (1564–1659), bishop of
  Durham, IV. 202, 203, 206; VII. 323,
  426, 515
Morton, Thomas (1764?–1838), XI. 270,
  276, 458; XIII. 270
  Columbus, XI. 280
  Cure for the Heartache, XI. 281
  School of Reform, XI. 281
  Speed the Plough, XI. 281
  Way to get Married, XI. 280, 281
Morus or Moir, Alexander, VII. 105, 125,
  130, 131
Morven, X. 222
Morwenstow, XII. 134
Morwent, Charles (d. 1675), VIII. 84
Moryson, Fynes (1566–1617?), IV. 459;
  VI. 466; VII. 446; History of Ireland,
  VII. 211; Itinerary, VII. 201, 211
Mosaic code, the, XI. 194
Mosbie, in Arden of Feversham, V. 242
Moscheles, Felix, XIII. 562
Moschus, III. 218, 222, 265; VII. 83, 489;
  IX. 526; X. 454; XI. 426; XII. 495
Moseley, Henry Nottidge (1844–1891),
  XIV. 297, 562
Moseley, Humphrey (d. 1661), VI. 114;
  VII. 116, 458; XI. 318, 319
Mosellanus, Figurae, III. 429
Moses, I. 134, 226; IV. 61, 170; VII. 296;
  IX. 526; X. 130; XII. 299
Moses, in The Three Laws, V. 58
Moses, Belle, XIII. 501
Mosheim, J. L. von, VIII. 453
Moslems, XII. 45; XIV. 182, 252
Moss, Joseph William (1803–1862), XII.
  523
Mossgiel, XI. 220, 224, 440

Mossop, Henry (1729?–1774?), XI. 450, 454
Most wonderful wonder that ever appeared, IX. 132
Mothe Le Vayer, Sieur F. de la, VIII. 449
Mother Goose's Melody, XI. 375, 376, 488
Mother Goose's Tales, XI. 376
Mother Redcap, V. 319
Mother Shipton, XI. 334
Motherwell, William (1797–1835), II. 409; XI. 437, 443, 444; XII. 6
   Harp of Renfrewshire, XI. 237
   Jeanie Morrison, XI. 237
   Minstrelsy Ancient and Modern, XI. 237
   Poems Narrative and Lyrical, XI. 237
Mottershead, Edward (*fl.* 1660), VII. 361
Motteux, Peter Anthony (1660–1718), VII. 256; VIII. 171, 385, 438; IX. 256, 260, 263, 270 ff. (main entry); X. 163; *Gentleman's Journal*, IX. 270; *Rabelais*, IX. 270
Mottley, John (1692–1750), IX. 500
Motto, in Drayton's *Idea*, IV. 172
Mottram, William, XIII. 552
Mouldy, in *Henry IV*, V. 360
Moulton, James Hope (1863–1917), XII. Add. 4
Moulton, Louise C., XIII. 496
Moulton, Richard Green, XIV. 528
Moulton, William Fiddian (1835–1898), XII. 501
Moultrie, John (1799–1874), XII. 420
Mounier, Jean Joseph, XII. 144
Mountcastle, Clara H., XIV. 582
Mountferrat, in *The Knight of Malta*, VI. 130
Mountfort, Harriet, in Mrs Griffith's *School for Rakes*, XI. 263
Mountfort, Mrs (Susanna Verbruggen) (1667?–1703), VIII. 191
Mountfort, William (*c.* 1664–1692), VI. 7; VIII. 189
Mounth, the, in Wyntoun, II. 132
Mountjoy, lord. *See* Blount, William
Mouse, the clown, in *Mucedorus*, V. 253
Mowbray, John, 3rd duke of Norfolk (1415–1461), II. 304, 305, 503
Mowbray, John de, VIII. 313
Mowcher, Miss, in *David Copperfield*, XIII. 336
Moxon, Edward (1801–1858), XII. 200, 201, 222, 421, 435; XIII. 61
Moxon, Mrs Emma (born Isola), XII. 200 ff., 435
Moxon, Joseph (1627–1700), IV. 459
Moyle, John (d. 1714), V. 459
Moyle, Walter (1672–1721), IX. 267
Moyra, XIV. 320
Moysie, David (*fl.* 1582–1603), VII. 455; *Memoirs of the Affairs of Scotland*, III. 149, 505
Mozart, IV. 162
Mozley, Anne (1809–1891), XII. 459, 461
Mozley, James Bowling (1813–1878), XII. 256, 261, 273, 454, 456, 459, 464; XIII. 466

Mozley, Thomas (1806–1893), XII. 453, 459, 460; XIV. 596, 599; *Reminiscences*, XII. 273
Mr Bailey, Grocer, in Gissing's *New Grub Street*, XIII. 460
'Mr F.'s aunt,' in *Little Dorrit*, XIII. 331
'Mtesa, king of Uganda, XIV. 254
Mucedorus, V. 135, 237, 238, 251, 253, 442, 443
Mucius, consul, I. 95
Muddiman, Henry, VII. 349, 362 ff., 495; IX. 2
   Current Intelligence, The, VII. 364
   Gazette, London, VII. 365
   Mercurius Publicus, VII. 362
   Parliamentary Intelligencer, The, afterwards *The Kingdom's Intelligencer*, VII. 362
Muddiman, H. and Thomas Henshaw, *Nouvelles Ordinaires de Londres*, VII. 360
Mudford, William (1782–1848), X. 476; XI. 457; XIV. 188
Mudge, Zachariah (1694–1769), X. 467
Muggins, Dick, X. 199
Muggleton, Ludowicke, X. 377
Muir, William (1799–1860), XII. 498
Muir, Sir William (1819–1905), XIV. 339, 505, 579; *The Life of Mahomet*, XIV. 338
Muir, W. M., XI. 432, 433
Muir Mackenzie, Georgina Mary, XIV. 553
Muirland Willie, IX. 360
Mulberie trees and...silkeworms, IV. 543
Mulcaster, Richard (1530?–1611), III. 311, 435, 436, 444, 446, 552, 556; IV. 238; V. 102, 123; VI. 221; VII. 332, 492; XIV. 608; *Elementarie*, III. 311, 435; *Positions*, III. 311, 435
Mulciber, in *Thersites*, V. 108
Mule sans Frein, La, I. 296
Mulgrave, John Sheffield, earl of. *See* Buckingham and Normanby, duke of
Mulholland, Rosa, XIV. 329
Müller, Friedrich Max (1823–1900), XII. 314, 502, 503; XIII. 354, 368, 469, 470, 548; XIV. 478; *Lectures on the Science of Language*, XII. 343
Müller, Johann, of Königsberg, *Ephemerides*, IV. 74, 82
Müller, Karl Ottfried, XII. 300, 483, 498; *History of Greek Literature*, XII. 331; *The Doric Race*, XII. 301, 312
Mulligan, the (Thackeray's), XIII. 283
Mullinger, James Bass (1834–1918), II. 347, 367; VI. 3; VII. 316, 320; XIV. 489, 594
Mullisheg of Fesse, king, in *The Fair Maid of the West*, VI. 101
Mulock, Dinah Maria (Mrs Craik) (1826–1887), XI. 488; XIII. 178, 506, 565; *John Halifax, Gentleman*, XIII. 435
Mulso, Hester. *See* Chapone, Mrs Hester
Mum, Sothsegger (i.e. Hush, Truthteller) (*Richard the Redeless*), II. 3, 36, 432, 434
Mumby, Frank Arthur, XI. 466
Mumford, in *King Leir*, V. 84

Mumming, in *The Masque of Christmas*, VI. 358, 359

Mun, Thomas (1571–1641), IV. 512; *Discourse of Trade to the East Indies*, IV. 310; *England's Treasure by Foreign Trade*, IV. 310

Munby, Arthur Joseph, XIII. 189, 506

Munchausen, Baron, XI. 492; XIII. 279

Munchausen romance, V. 95

Münchner Brut, I. 236

Munday, Anthony (1553–1633), III. 68, 302, 341, 349, 359, *also see* Add.; IV. 117 ff., 390, 439, 445, 447, 448, 471, 487, 525, 532, 533, 536; V. 236, 310–322 (main entry), 328, 329, 331 ff., 344, 370, 371, 474; VI. 4, 17, 41, 61, 329, 365, 391. 395, 459

'A Caveat to the Reader,' V. 313

Amadis de Gaule (trans. of), V. 314

Ballad against Plays, A, IV. 323

Banquet of Dainty Conceits, A, IV. 119

'Beauty sat bathing by a spring,' IV. 119

English Romayne Life, The, V. 313

'Fair nymphes sit ye here by me,' IV. 119

Fedele and Fortunio, V. 314 ff., 474; VI. 304

Funeral of Richard Cœur de Lion, The, V. 319

John a Kent and John a Cumber, V. 311, 315 ff., 320; VI. 347

Metropolis Coronata, V. 35

Palladino of England, V. 314, 323

Palmerin of England (trans. of), V. 314

Primaleon (trans. of), IV. 119

Robert, Earle of Huntington, V. 35, 310, 318 ff., 325, 326; VI. 236

Set at Tennis, The, V. 319

Third Blast of Retreat from Plays and Theatres, The (? by Munday), V. 313

View of Sundry Examples, A, V. 315

Woodman's Walk, The, IV. 119

Zelauto, III. 349, 536

See also, under Chettle and Middleton and *Third Blast*

Munden, Joseph Shepherd (1758–1832), XI. 454; XII. 436

Mundus, in *Confessio Amantis*, II. 151

Mundy, John (d. 1630), IV. 113, 465

Munich, V. 306

Munich, Fugger collection at, IV. 429

Munro, Hugh Andrew Johnstone (1819–1885), X. 125; XII. 327, 337, 488; *Criticisms and Elucidations of Catullus*, XII. 335; *Translations into Latin and Greek Verse*, XII. 335

Munro, W. A., XIII. 544

Munro. *See also* Monro

Munster, Ireland, III. 229, 244; IV. 433; VII. 209, 211, 438; IX. 136; XIV. 314

Münster, in *The Unfortunate Traveller*, III. 363

Münster, bishop of (C. Bernhard von Galen), VIII. 381

Münster, Sebastian, III. 109; *Cosmographia*, III. 141; IV. 70

Muralt, Béat de, V. 287

Muratori, Ludovico Antonio, X. 220, 311, 312

Murchison, Sir Roderick Impey (1792–1871), XIV. 291, 293, 294, 562

Murcia, in *The Doubtfull Heir*, VI. 205

Murderous Mychaell, V. 117, 325

Murdoch, Patrick (d. 1774), X. 105, 446, 447

Murdoch, W. M., XIII. 495

Murdstone and Grinby, in *David Copperfield*, XIII. 327

Mure, William (1799–1860), *Critical History of the Literature of Ancient Greece*, XII. 339

Mure, Sir William, of Rowallan (1594–1657), IX. 542, 556

Murger, Henri, *Scènes de la Vie de Bohème*, XIII. 433

Murillo, Bartolomeo Esteban, XIII. 52

Murimuth, Adam (1275?–1347), II. 498

Murner, III. 59

Murning Maiden, The, II. 281

Murphy, Anna. *See* Jameson, Mrs Anna

Murphy, Arthur (1727–1805), IX. 435; X. 20, 89, 163, 189, 264, 389, 390, 393, 413, 437, 439, 441, 459, 466, 472, 474, 522; XI. 453; XIV. 570

All in the Wrong, X. 88

Grecian Daughter, X. 88

Know your own Mind, XI. 269

No One's Enemy but his Own, X. 86

Orphan of China, X. 86

School for Guardians, X. 88

Upholsterer, The, X. 88

Way to keep him, X. 88

Zenobia, X. 88

Murphy, Denis Brownell (d. 1842), XIV. 323

'Murphy,' *pseud. See* Maturin, Charles Robert

Murray, Alexander Stuart (1841–1904), XII. 498

Murray, Sir David, of Gorthy (1567–1629), IV. 487; IX. 556; *Bibliography: its Scope and Methods*, XII. 363, 370, 520; *David Laing*, XII. 350, 358, 517, 520; *R. and A. Foulis*, XII. 324, 520

Murray, David Christie (1847–1907), XIII. 544, 565

Murray, Mrs Elizabeth. *See* Grant, Mrs Elizabeth

Murray, E. C. Grenville, XIV. 194

Murray, George, XIV. 582

Murray, lord George (1700?–1760), IX. 565

Murray, Grace, X. 368

Murray, Henry, XIV. 534

Murray, Sir James Augustus Henry (1837–1915), XII. 505; XIV. 454, 611; *Dialect of the Southern counties of Scotland*, II. 96, 99

Murray, John, 3rd duke of Atholl (1729–1774), X. 274

Murray, Sir John, of Broughton (1718–1777), IX. 564

Murray, John (1745–1793), XI. 327

Murray, John (1778–1843), XI. 327, 423, 468; XIV. 613

Murray, John (1808–1892), XII. 34, 47, 52, 149 ff., 154, 155, 161, 387, 396, 430; XIII. 346, 353; XIV. 613; *Memoir of*, XII. 150

Murray, Sir John (1841–1914), XIV. 297, 562

Murray, Sir John Archibald, lord Murray (1779–1859), XII. 144

Murray, Lindley (1745–1826), XII. 505; XIII. 240; XIV. 608; *English Grammar*, XIV. 397

Murray, Patrick James, XIV. 567

Murray, Sir Robert (d. 1673), VII. 435

Murray, R. F., XIV. 209, 538; *The Scarlet Gown*, XIV. 210

Murray, Thomas (1792–1872), XI. 446

Murray, William, 1st earl of Mansfield (1705–1793), X. 285, 375, 399, 404, 405, 470, 527

Murrell, John (*fl.* 1630), IV. 543

Murry, John Middleton, XIII. 573

Musa, in Ouida's *In Maremma*, XIII. 436

Musa Cantabrigiensis, VII. 180

Musae Etonenses, XIV. 56

Musaeus, IV. 438; VII. 489; X. 454; XI. 426; XIII. 465

Musaeus (*i.e.* John Daniel), IV. 180

Musarum Anglicanarum Analecta, IX. 434

Musarum Deliciae, VII. 413

Musäus, Johann Karl August, XII. 4, 465; *Grandison der Zweite*, X. 19

Muscovy voyages, IV. 67, 71, 75, 80, 84, 92, 93

Muses Farwel to Popery and Slavery, The (1689), VIII. 410

Muses Merriment, The (1656), VII. 512

Museum, The, XI. 324

Museum Criticum, XII. 329

Museum Minervae, VII. 78

Musgrave, Samuel (1732–1780), X. 270; XII. 483

Musgrave, Tom, in Jane Austen's *The Watsons*, XII. 234

Musgrave, Sir William, VIII. 263

Musgrove, Louisa, in Jane Austen's *Persuasion*, XII. 241

Musgrove, Mr and Mrs Charles, in Jane Austen's *Persuasion*, XII. 240

Music, in *The Passetyme of Pleasure*, II. 225, 229, 230

Music, Elizabethan, V. 372

Music of the 17th century, the, VIII. 424

Music, Old English popular, VIII. 411

Musical Miscellany, the, IX. 567

Musical Repository, IX. 567; XI. 444

Musicians of London, corporation of the, V. 28

Musidora, in Thomson's *Summer*, X. 104

Musidorus, in Sidney's *Arcadia*, III. 352

Musidorus (a poem in memory of James Thomson), X. 450

Musonius, in *Club Law*, VI. 308, 309

Musophilus (Daniel's), IV. 135

Mussatus (*see* Albertino), V. 62

Musselburgh, IX. 370

Musset, Alfred de, V. 302; XII. 392; XIII. 272; *Carmosine*, XIII. 401

Mustapha, in *Solymannidae*, VI. 301

Mustapha, Haji. *See* Raymond

Mutability, in *The Faerie Queene*, II. 234; III. 238

Mutimers, the, in Gissing's *Demos*, XIII. 459

Muto, in Marston's *Scourge of Villanie*, IV. 332

Muzzle for Cerberus, A, VII. 502

My Hart is quhyt, III. 132

My Jocky blyth, IX. 360

My Laddie, IX. 375

'My Uncle Toby,' X. 206

My Winifreda, IX. 188

Mycene, in *Horestes*, V. 64, 65

Mychell, John (*fl.* 1556), IV. 409

Myddleton, William (1556?–1621), V. 92

Mydlerd, a mirror called (*i.e.* the World), in *Piers the Plowman*, II. 25

Myers, E., XIV. 522

Myers, Frederic (1811–1851), XII. 466, 469

Myers, Frederic William Henry (1843–1901), XI. 110, 410; XII. 404; XIII. 43, 207, 478, 491, 506, 553; XIV. 473; *St Paul*, XIII. 209

Myll, G. (1492), II. 285

Myllar, Androw (*fl.* 1503–1508), VI. 412; IX. 359; *and see* Chepman and Myllar

Mylne, Robert (1643–1747), IX. 559

Mynshul, Geffray (1594?–1668), VII. 387; *Essayes and Characters of a Prison and Prisoners*, III. 99; IV. 345, 350, 522, 530; VII. 388

Myra (Fulke Greville's), III. 267

Myrania (Greene's), III. 357

Myrgingas, the, in *Widsith*, I. 34, 35

Myrrha, in Byron's *Sardanapalus*, XII. 49

Myrrour for Martinists, A, III. 397

Myschefe, in *Magnyfycence*, III. 77

Mysore war, the, XIV. 338

Mysteries, V. 388 ff., *and see* Chester plays, Coventry plays, etc.

Mystery plays, Non-cycle, V. 391

Mysticism in English literature, VII. Add.

Mytton, John (1796–1834), XIV. 233

'N—, Miss,' X. 274

N. G. *See* Grimald, Nicholas

Nabbes, Thomas (*fl.* 1638), VI. 28, 240, 457; XIII., *also see* Add. 2
    Bride, The, VI. 236
    Covent Garden, VI. 236
    Hannibal and Scipio, VI. 236
    Microcosmus, VI. 236
    Totenham-Court, VI. 236

Naboth, II. 297

Naboth's vineyard, X. 150

Naden, Constance Caroline Woodhill (1858–1889), XIII. 181, 506

Nairn, II. 100

Nairne, Caroline Oliphant, baroness (1766–1845), XI. 232, 233, 444
    Auld Hoose, The, XI. 233
    Caller Herrin, XI. 233

Nairne, Caroline Oliphant
  Charlie is My Darling, XI. 233
  Here's to them that are Gane, XI. 233
  He's O'er the Hills, XI. 233
  Hundred Pipers, XI. 233
  Hunting Tower, XI. 233
  John Tod, XI. 233
  Laird of Cockpen, The, XI. 233; XIV. 377
  Land of the Leal, XI. 233
  Lass of Gowrie, XI. 233
  Rowan Tree, The, XI. 233
  Wha'll be King but Charlie, XI. 233
  Will he no come back again? IX. 377; XI. 233
Nala, the tale of, XII. 490, 503
Nalson, John (1638?–1686), VII. 434
'Namby-Pamby' Philips. *See* Philips, Ambrose
Nancarrow, Totty, in Gissing's *Thyrza*, XIII. 459
Nancy, IX. 149
Nancy, in *Oliver Twist*, XIII. 316
Nannini, Remigio, IV. 447
Nanny O, IX. 363
Nano, in *James IV*, V. 138
Nantes, edict of, V. 286; VIII. 385; IX. 270; X. 203; XIV. 117
Nantwich, VII. 107
Naomi, IV. 43
Naphtali, IX. 547
Napier, Arthur Sampson, I. 53, 55, 125, 129, 133
Napier, Sir Charles (1786–1860), XIV. 107, 496
Napier or Neper, John, laird of Merchiston (1550–1617), III. 426; IV. 290, 508; VIII. 350, 478
Napier, Macvey (1776–1847), XII. 147, 153, 162, 426, 427; XIV. 5
Napier, Mark (1798–1879), XIV. 495
Napier, Sir William Francis Patrick (1785–1860), XI. 167; XIV. 495, 496
  Conquest of Scinde, The, XIV. 107
  History of Sir Charles Napier's Administration of Scinde, XIV. 107
  History of the War in the Peninsula, XIV. 107
  Life of Sir Charles Napier, XIV. 107
Naples, II. 276; IV. 163, 249; V. 207; VI. 305; VII. 99, 131; VIII. 141, 188, 364; X. 254; XII. 36, 63; XIII. 435; XIV. 247, 293
Naples, in *The Anatomy of Wit*, III. 345
Napleton, John, XIV. 596
Napoleon I, emperor of the French, IV. 310; X. 27, 227; XI. 27, 54, 103, 108, 115, 117; XII. 38, 39, 61, 164, 166, 178, 192, 237, 300, 343, 378, 379, 395, 429, 431, 432, 438, 470; XIII. 13, 255, 276, 366, 435, 445, 447; XIV. 106, 148, 179, 188, 213, 223, 327; *Code Napoléon*, XI. 26
Napoleon III, emperor of the French, XIII. 73, 74, 81, 132, 133; XIV. 171, 182, 185
Napoleonic war, XIV. 89, **176**
Napoleonisms, XIII. 405

Narborough, Sir John (1640–1688), IV. 459; VII. 364
Narcissa, in Colman's *Inkle and Yarico*, XI. 279, 280
'Narcissa' (Mrs Oldfield), in Pope's *Epistles*, IX. 81
Narcissus, II. 151
Narcissus, in Racine's *Britannicus*, X. 119
Narcissus, Confessor, I. 74
Narcissus, school play, V. 123; VI. 286, 287
Narcissus, university play, VI. 316, 484
Nares, Robert (1753–1829), X. Add.; XI. 250; XII. 505
Naseby, battle of, VII. 35; XIII. 143
Naseby, the ship, VIII. 7, 254
Nash, Richard (1674–1762), X. 481
Nash, Thomas Arthur, XIV. 507
Nashe, Thomas (1567–1601), II. 415; III. 114, 176, 183, 208, 256, 259, 293, 305, 359, 362 ff., 367, 370, 371, 392, 395 ff., 526, 535, 543 ff.; IV. 8, 17, 18, 21, 115, 133, 134, 142, 317, 321 ff., 332, 333, 343, 345, 363, 514, 515, 516, 517, 523, 534; V. 80 ff., 129, 130, 134, 137, 138, 144 ff., 148, 157 ff., 315, 322, 371, 420, 421; VI. 218, 250, 288, 300, 310 ff., 384, 385, 409; IX. 32, 51, 262; XIV. 234
  Anatomie of Absurditie, The, III. 362; IV. 318, 325; V. 140; VI. 394, 396, 494
  Apologie of Pierce Pennylesse, IV. 322
  Christs Teares over Jerusalem, III. 362, 546; IV. 323, 324, 357
  Haue with you to Saffron Walden, III. 546; V. 314; VI. 306, 480
  Isle of Dogs, III. 362; V. 140; VI. 212
  Lenten Stuff, III. 363; IV. 319, 327, 328
  Pierce Penilesse, his Supplication to the Divell, III. 259, 362, 545; IV. 321, 322, 328, 352; VI. 60, 310, 311, 396, 461, 495
  Strange Newes, III. 546; VI. 306, 480
  Summer's Last Will and Testament, V. 140; VI. 287
  Terminus et non terminus, VI. 307, 310
  Terrors of the Night, III. 363; IV. 325; VII. 371, 395, 506
  'To the Gentlemen Students,' V. 121
  Unfortunate Traveller, or the life of Jack Wilton, The, III. 176, 363 ff.; V. 141
  See, also, under Marlowe
Nasmith, James (1740–1808), IX. 540
'Naso Scarronomimus,' IX. 259, 502
Nassau, count of, and the parrot, in Temple's *Memoirs*, VIII. 383
Nasse, Erwin, XIV. 78
Nassyngton, William (*fl.* 1375?), II. 46, 47, 439
Nathan, Isaac (1791?–1864), XII. 384
Nathan, Manfred, XIV. Add. 9
Nathaniel, Sir, in *Love's Labour's Lost*, V. 178
Nation (Dublin), XIV. 317 ff., 321, 325, 327
Nation (New York), XIV. 318
Nation, The (London), XIV. 199
National Observer, The, XIV. 199
National Reformer, The, XIII. 107, 108

National Review, The, XIV. 141
National society for promoting the Education of the Poor, XIV. 403, 404, 419
National Standard, The, XIII. 277
National Union for improving the education of women, XIV. 430
Nativity, carols of the, II. 373, 376, 378
Nativity plays, v. 389
Natland, near Kendal, x. 386
Natura naturata, in *The Nature of the Four Elements,* v. 57
Natural history, writers on, IV. 542, 543
Natural Intelligence (Kind-Wit), in *Piers the Plowman,* II. 21
Nature, in Cowley's *The Muse,* VII. 65
Nature, in *The Example of Virtue,* II. 227
Nature, in *Horestes,* v. 65
Nature, in *Mercury Vindicated,* VI. 358
Nature, in *Piers the Plowman,* II. 26
Nature, in *Reason and Sensuality,* II. 202
Nature of the Four Elements, The, III. 96, 105, 445
Naudens, Gabriel, VIII. 449
Naumachia or Hollands Sea-fight, IV. 487
Naunton, Sir Robert (1563–1635), IV. 51; VII. 27, 452; XII. 376; *Fragmenta Regalia,* v. 345, 479; VII. 221
Nausicaa, v. 172
Navarre, v. 101
Navarrenus, Francis Mildapettus. *pseud. See* Temple, Sir William (1555–1627)
Navern (Strathnaver), II. 276
Navestock, Essex, XIV. 74
Navigation, The Art of, IV. 399
Navy List (1689), IV. 459
Navy Records society, IV. 103; XII. 355
Nayler, James (1617?–1660), VIII. 109, 416
Nazareth, VIII. 78
Neal, Daniel (1678–1743), IX. 476, 494; x. 518; *History of New England,* IX. 212; *History of the Puritans,* VII. 356; IX. 212
Neal, Samuel (1826–1901), XIV. Add. 3
Neal, W. G., XIV. Add. 7
Neale, John Mason (1818–1866), XI. 488; XII. 277, 353, 459; XIII. 167, 171, 506
Art thou weary, art thou languid, XIII.173
Jerusalem the Golden, XIII. 172, 173
The day is past and over, XIII. 173
Theodora Phranza, XII. 273
Neale, Sir Paul, VIII. 61, 62
Neale, Thomas (*fl.* 1643), VI. 475
Neander, in Dryden's *Essay of Heroick Plays,* VIII. 24, 370
Neander, in *The Rival Friends,* VI. 325
Neander, J. A. W., XII. 464
Neapolitan government, the, XIV. 136
Nearchus, prince of Argos, in *The Broken Heart,* VI. 191
Neate, Bill, prizefighter, XIV. 230
Neave, Richard, VII. 513
Neaves, Charles Neaves, lord (1800–1876), XII. 425; XIII. 507; XIV. 210
Nebo, VII. 67
Nebuchadnezzar, VII. 370
Necessary Doctrine and Erudition of a Christian man, III. 36

Nechtan, king of the Picts, I. 82
Neckam, Alexander (1157–1217), I. 193, 227, 238, 239, 367, 455; II. 144; *De Naturis Rerum,* I. 193, 227, 239
Neckar river, XIII. 372
Necker, Jacques, XI. 28; XIII. 467
Necker, Suzanne, x. 264, 302, 307
Nectabanus, II. 75
Nectabanus, in *Confessio Amantis,* II. 149
Necton, Humphrey (d. 1303), II. 350
Nedham, Marchamont (1620–1678), VII. 353, 355, 362, 363, 495, 496, 513; IX. 1
Interest will not lie, VII. 360
Mercurius Britanicus, VII. 351, 358, 360
Mercurius Poeticus, VII. 360
Mercurius Politicus, VII. 140, 358, 359, 361
Mercurius Pragmaticus, VII. 358, 360
The Observator, VII. 360
The Publick Adviser, VII. 360, 361
The Publick Intelligencer, VII. 360, 361
Need, in *Piers the Plowman,* II. 28
Needy Knife-Grinder, The, XI. 40, 41
Neele, Henry (1798–1828), *The Romance of History,* XIV. 59
Neil, Robert Alexander (1852–1901), XII. 489
Neil, Ross, *pseud. See* Harwood, Isabella
Neilson, George (b. 1858), II. 104, 117, 118, 120, 122; XII. 512
Neither Loved nor Loving, in Heywood's *Love,* v. 93
Neither Lover nor Loved, in Heywood's *Love,* v. 93
Neither-Money-nor-Learning, in *All for Money,* v. 57
Nell, in *Henry IV,* v. 187
Nell, Little (Dickens's), XIII. 319, 325
Nelson, Abraham, VII. 513
Nelson, Horatio, viscount Nelson (1758–1805), XIII. 435, 467; XIV. 201, 213
Nelson, James (1710–1794), XIV. 608
Nelson, Robert (1665–1715), VIII. 301, 305, 459, 460, 463; IX. 514; x. 356; *Companion for the Festivals and Fasts,* VIII. 308
Nelson, Thomas (*fl.* 1580), IV. 390
Nemnivus, I. 70
Nennius or Nynniaw (*fl.* 796), *Historia Brittonum,* I. 31, 65, 66, 68, 70, 71, 81, 169, 245 ff., 250, 257, 258, 268, 336, 435, 461
Neoplatonism, VII. 264, 273, 278, 367 370; IX. 287, 306
Neot, St, XIV. 83
Neot, St, Lives of, I. 90, 131
Nepos Cornelius, IX. 198
Neptune, VII. 370
Neptune, in *Troiane,* v. 69
Neptune, planet, XIV. 264
Neptune to England, IV. 96
Nereus, in Horace's *Carmina,* x. 130
Nero, I. 226; IV. 30; VII. 371, 443; IX. 274 x. 119, 317
Nero, in *Octavia,* VI. 301
Nero, The Tragedy of, VI. 235, 459

Nessus, in *Confessio Amantis*, II. 148
Nest, daughter of Rhys ap Tewdwr, I. 194, 256
Nestor, x. 51
Nether Stowey, Somersetshire, XI. 99, 120, 126, 416; XII. 166, 203
Netherbury, VII. 244
Netherlands, the, II. 310; III. 244, 441; v. 89, 139, 344; VI. 29, 42, 123; VII. 198, 453; VIII. 265; x. 291; XIV. 72. *See, also,* Low Countries
Netherlands, United Provinces of the, XII. 316
Nethersole, Sir Francis (1587–1659), VII. 27, 28
Netley abbey, x. 132
Nettlebed academy, x. 385
Nettleship, Archibald Lewis (1846–1892), XII. 467; XIV. 473
Nettleship, Henry (1839–1893), XII. 469, 489; XIV. 505, 594; *Contributions to Latin Lexicography*, XII. 337; *Essays*, XII. 337
Nettleship, John T., XIII. 485
Neuberg, A., XIII. 466
Neuberg, J., XIII. 466
Neue Erweiterungen der Erkenntnis und des Vergnügens, v. 295
Neugise, in *Robin Conscience*, III. 97
Neuha, in Byron's *The Island*, XII. 46
Neuhof, Switzerland, XIV. 383, 390
Neuwied, Germany, XIII. 440
Neverout Tom, in Swift's *Complete Collection of...Conversation*, IX. 106, 107
Nevile, Henry (1620–1694), VII. 514
Nevill, in *A Woman is a Weathercocke*, VI. 221
Nevill or Neville, George (1433?–1476), II. 211
Neville, lady Mary, daughter of the 4th earl of Dorset, IV. 265
Neville, Richard Griffin, 3rd lord Braybrooke (1783–1858), VIII. 243, 263
Neville, Thomas (d. 1615), IV. 264, 427
Neville, William (*fl.* 1518), *The Castle of Pleasure*, II. 327
Neville's Cross, battle of, I. 357
Nevinson, Henry W., XIII. 472, 570
Nevizanus, Johannes, *Silva nuptialis*, VIII. 59
Nevyle, Alexander (1544–1614), IV. 440; v. 80, 395
Nevynson, Stephen (d. 1581?), III. 202
New Conger, the, XI. 325
New Custom, v. 60, 393
New Edinburgh Review, The, XIII. 4
New England, IX. 281; x. 386
New England colonies, IV. 95; VII. 339
New Englanders, XIV. 345, 346
New English Art club, the, XIV. 208
New English Dictionary, XII. 293
New Fair, the, a game in *Piers the Plowman*, II. 16
New Forest, IV. 190
New Hebrides, the, IV. 101
New Holland, XIV. 241

New Institution for the Formation of Character, XIV. 404, 405
New Irish Library, The, XIV. 319
New Lanark, XIV. 404, 405
New lands found by the messengers of the King of Portugal named Emanuel, Of the, II. 330, 486
New Monthly Magazine, The, XII. 161, 200, 429, 431; XIII. 279; XIV. 230, 319
New Monthly Magazine and Humorist, The, XII. 429
New Monthly Magazine and Literary Journal, The, XII. 429
New Monthly Magazine and Universal Register, The, XII. 429
New Notbroune Mayd, II. 328; III. 491
New Presbyterian Ballad, A (1681), VIII. 97
New Quarterly Magazine, XI. 463
New Review, x. 302
New river, the, XII. 182, 198
New Scots Spy, IX. 562
New South Wales, XII. 194; XIV. 362
New Spalding club, XII. 359
New Sporting Magazine, The, XIV. 233
New Sydenham society, XII. 355
New Times, The, XII. 198
New Tunbridge Wells, IX. 261
New World, the, IV. 311
New Year's letter, II. 389
New York, XIII. 10; XIV. 318, 325, 326, 358
New York, the Bowery, XIV. 285
New York Herald, The, XIV. 192
New Zealand, XIII. 186, 364, 449; XIV. 368, 434
New Zealander, IX. 263
Newark, VII. 91
Newark, William, VI. 281, 282
Newark castle, XII. 7
Newbery, Elizabeth, XI. 377
Newbery, Francis (d. 1780), x. 207, 209, 210, 215, 482; XI. 377, 468
Newbery, Francis (1743–1818), XI. 377
Newbery, John (1713–1767), x. 41, 205, 207 ff., 476, 484; XI. 367, 374 ff., 468, 476, 490
Newbery, Ralph (*fl.* 1590), IV. 82, 398
Newbold Revell, II. 315, 335
Newburgh. *See* William of
Newbury, III. 368; VII. 55, 74
Newcastle, duchess of. *See* Cavendish, Margaret
Newcastle, dukes of. *See* Cavendish, William; Clinton, H. P. F. Pelham-Holles
Newcastle under Lyme, IV. 162
Newcastle-upon-Tyne, III. 383; IV. 310; v. 46, 391; VII. 435, 450; IX. 532, 563; x. 470; XI. 338, 341, 445, 469, 470; XII. 346, 508; XIII. 372
Newcastle Chronicle, The, XIV. 529, 533
Newcastle commission, XIV. 420 ff.
Newcastle Courant, The, XIV. 169
Newcastle Express, The, XIV. 193
Newce, Thomas, IV. 440

Newcome, Barnes (Thackeray's), v. 213; XIII. 296, 297

Newcome, Sir Brian (Thackeray's), XIII. 295, 297

Newcome, Clive (Thackeray's), XIII. 295, 296, 299, 300

Newcome, colonel (Thackeray's), XIII. 292, 296, 297

Newcome, Ethel (Thackeray's), XII. 130; XIII. 296, 297, 299

Newcome, Henry (1627–1695), x. 385

Newcome, Hobson (Thackeray's), XIII. 295, 297

Newcome family (Thackeray's), XIII. 295

Newcomen, Matthew (1610?–1669), VII. 416

Newcomen, Thomas (1663–1729), VIII. 478; XIV. 258

Newcourt, Richard (d. 1716), *Repertorium Ecclesiasticum*, IX. 354, 537

Newdigate prize poem, XII. 138; XIII. 87; XIV. 149

Newdigate-Newdegate, lady, XIII. 552; *Gossip from a Muniment Room*, VII. 196

Newes come from Hell, III. 492

Newes from Rome, IV. 534

New-fanglers, Address in verse to, III. 98

Newfoundland, IV. 70; XIV. 289

Newgate Calendar, The, XIV. 228, 229, 544, 545

Newgate chronicle, XIII. 418

Newhaven, Scotland, XI. 233

Newhaven, in Reade's *Christie Johnstone*, XIII. 425

Newhouse, Captain, *The whole Art of Navigation*, IV. 459

Newington Green academy, x. 385, 386

Newlands, John Alexander Reina, XIV. 558

Newlin, Thomas (1688–1743), VIII. 461

Newman, Francis William (1805–1897), XII. 461, 469; XIII. 175, 507; XIV. 593

Newman, John Henry (1801–1890), cardinal, IV. 45; x. 358, 369; XI. 81; XII. 178, 253 ff., 264, 265, 266 ff. (main entry), 272 ff., 276, 285, 287, 292, 299, 430, 453 ff., 459 ff., 468, *also see* Add.; XIII. 87, 148, 167, 507; XIV. 83, 118, 141, 417, 431, 462, 478, 507, 594
Apologia pro vita sua, XII. 266 ff., XIII. 369
Callista, XII. 277
Development of Christian Doctrine, An Essay on the, XII. 269
Dream of Gerontius, The, XII. 257, 268; XIII. 170, 171
Grammar of Assent, A, XII. 269; XIV. 26
Idea of a University, The, XIV. 418, 425
'Lead, kindly Light,' XII. 269
Lectures on the Prophetical Office of the Church, XII. 269
Loss and Gain, XII. 277
Pillar of Cloud, The ('Lead, kindly Light'), XIII. 170, 171, 176
'Praise to the Holiest,' XII. 269

Newman, John Henry
Scope and Nature of University Education, The, XII. 269
Sermons for Mixed Congregations, XII. 268
Thoughts on the Ministerial Commission, XII. 258
Tract XC, XII. 260, 294
Verses on various occasions, XIII. 170

Newman, Thomas (*fl.* 1578–1593), IV. 142

Newman, William, XIV. 236

Newmarket, VI. 480; VIII. 208; x. 492

Newnes, Sir George, XIV. 534

Newport, Isle of Wight, VII. 177, 206, 447, 449

Newport, Mon. and Glos., II. 74

Newport, Rhode island, IX. 281

Newport, Sir Richard, VII. 27

Newport Pagnell, II. 61; VII. 167, 169

News, The, XIV. 197

News from Hell, or the Relation of a Vision, VII. 381

News of the World, The, XIV. 192

Newsletters, VII. 436 ff.

Newspaper society, the, XIV. 176

Newspapers: *Courant, or Weekly Newes from Foreign Parts*, IV. 394; *A Currant of Newes*, IV. 394; *Swedish Intelligencer*, IV. 398

Newspapers, classified lists of, XIV. 529 ff.

News-sheets, IV. 535

Newstead abbey, XII. 379

Newstead fort, Melrose, XII. 509

Newstead priory, XII. 31, 39

Newton, Alfred, x. 269; XIV. 298

Newton, Sir Charles Thomas (1816–1894), XII. 340, 498; *Essays in Art and Archaeology*, XII. 339

Newton, Sir Isaac (1642–1727), VII. 314, 396; VIII. 332, 350, 352, 359 ff., 364, 478; IX. 115, 229, 283, 295, 298, 308, 476, 519, 524, 528; x. 134, 319, 373, 379, 384, 446, 447; XI. 194, 473; XIV. 261, 270, 555; *Letters to Bentley*, x. 466; *Optics*, IX. 297; x. 342; XIV. 283; *Principia*, VIII. 361; IX. 331, 335; XIV. 257

Newton, John (1725–1807), x. 365, 521; XI. 80, 81, 83, 259, 401 ff.

Newton, Richard (1676–1753), IX. 569, 571, 574

Newton, Thomas (1542?–1607), IV. 5, 435, 436, 440, 446, 504; v. 90, 395; *Dyce-play and prophane Gaming*, VI. 395, 495

Newton, Thomas (1704–1782), bishop of Bristol, VII. 109

Newton, Wilts., VIII. 83

Newton St Bridget (on Usk), Wales, VII. 37, 38

Newtonian school of mathematics, IX. 412, 413

New-Year's-Gift, in *The Masque of Christmas*, VI. 358

Niblung kings, the, in Morris's *Sigurd the Volsung*, XIII. 126

Nicaea, council of, XII. 278, 321

Nicaragua, xiv. 242
Niccolini, G., xii. 397
Niccols, Richard (1584–1616), editor of
  A Mirror for Magistrates (q.v.), iii. 193,
  197, 198; *Induction*, iii. 197
Nice, vii. 99; x. 41, 42; xiii. 74
Nice Wanton, v. 110, 393, 412
Nichol, John (1833–1894), xi. 439, 440;
  xii. 397, 505; xiii. 472, 507; *Hannibal*,
  xiii. 194
Nichol, John Pringle (1804–1859), xiv. 555
Nicholas I, tsar of Russia, xiv. 294
Nicholas V, pope, ii. 113, 114, 369; xiv.
  100
Nicholas, A. N., vii. 449
Nicholas, Sir Edward (1593–1669), vii.
  188, 363, 435, 436, 440
Nicholas, St, ii. 127, 318; v. 8, 37, 38
Nicholas, Sir, in *The Weakest goeth to the
  Wall*, v. 316
Nicholas, Thomas (*fl.* 1560–1596), iv. 444,
  448, 460
Nicholas, Thomas (1820–1879), xii. 512
Nicholas of Cusa, iii. 416
Nicholas of Guildford (*fl.* 1250), i. 238
Nicholas de Lyra (1340), ii. 62; *Postilla*,
  v. 42
Nicholas of Tusculum, ii. 343–344
Nicholaus, *Antidotarium* of, ii. 365
Nicholl, John (*fl.* 1607), iv. 460
Nicholls, Norton (1742?–1809), x. 133,
  134
Nichols, John (1745–1826), ix. 140, 439,
  441, 442, 453, 478, 487, 532; x. 184,
  358, 454, 476, 486, 515, *also see* Add.;
  xii. 428, 512
  Bibliotheca Topographica, xii. 345
  History and Antiquities of Leicester,
  viii. 462; xii. 345
  *Illustrations of the Literary History of
  the Eighteenth Century*, xii. 345
  Literary Anecdotes, x. 180, 244, 248,
  473, 480, 483; xi. 321, 327, 332, 335,
  337, 459, 467; xii. 345
  Literary Illustrations, x. 250
  Progresses of Elizabeth, v. 82, 256, 482
  Progresses of King James I, v. 482; vi.
  271
Nichols, John Bowyer (1779–1863), xii.
  345, 512; xiv. 541
Nichols, John Gough (1806–1873), xii.
  345, 512
Nicholson, George (1847–1908), xiv. 562
Nicholson, John ('Maps,' 1730–1796), xi.
  338
Nicholson, Joseph Shield, xiii. 545
Nicholson, Reynold Alleyne, xiv. 537
Nicholson, William (1782?–1849), xi. 444;
  xii. 421; *Brownie of Blednock*, xi. 243
'Nick Frog' (Holland), xiv. 212
'Nickie Ben,' xi. 212
Nickleby, Kate (Dickens's), xiii. 317
Nickleby, Mrs (Dickens's), xiii. 314, 317
Nickleby, Nicholas (Dickens's), xiii. 317
Nickleby, Ralph (Dickens's), xiii. 317, 322
Nicklebys, the (Dickens's), xiii. 318

Nicodemus, *The Gospel of*, i. 133; ii. 325,
  326, 383; iv. 422; v. 15, 390
Nicolai, v. 295
Nicolas, Sir Nicholas Harris (1799–1848),
  ii. 166; x. 491; xi. 437; xii. 303, 430;
  xiv. 52
Nicoll, John (1590–1667 or 1668), vii. 452;
  ix. 552
Nicoll, Robert (1814–1837), xi. 444; xiii.
  507
Nicoll, Sir William Robertson, xi. 419;
  xii. 407, 418, 423, 424; xiii. 478, 481,
  485, 537, 555 ff., 570; xiv. 528, 534
Nicolls, Mary Ellen, xiii. 440
Nicolls, Thomas (*fl.* 1550), iv. 3, 4, 440
Nicolson, William (1655–1727), *Historical
  Libraries*, ix. 356, 537
Nicopompus, in *Argenis*, iv. 258, 259
Nicuesa, iv. 68, 70
Nidd river, Yorks., vii. 180; xiii. 275
Niebuhr, Barthold Georg, xii. 280, 287,
  305 ff., 310, 321, 474, 477, 478; xiv.
  61, 119; *Griechische Heroengeschichten*,
  xii. 310; *History of Rome*, xii. 288,
  301 ff.
Nield, Jonathan, xiii. 568
Nierembergius, Johan Euseb., vii. 405
Nietzsche, Friedrich Wilhelm, xiii. 21
Nieuport, battle of (1600), vii. 454
Nieuwentyt, Bernhard, *The Religious
  Philosopher*, x. 346
Niflheim, i. 63
Nigel, in Scott's *Fortunes of Nigel*, xii. 19
Niger, in *The Masque of Blacknesse*, vi.
  342, 343
Niger, Ralph (*fl.* 1170), i. 450
Night, in *The Faerie Queene*, iii. 234
Night, in *The Vision of the Twelve God-
  desses*, vi. 337
Nightingale, in Fielding's *Tom Jones*, x. 32
Nightingale, Florence, xiii. 103, 365, 378;
  xiv. 182
Nightingale, ship, x. 203
Nigra, C., ii. 417
Nikolaer, P., xiv. 490
Nile, river, x. 160; xiv. 191
Nimeguen, x. 222
Nimrod, x. 110
Nimrod, in Alfred's *Boethius*, i. 101
Nimrod, *pseud.* *See* Apperley, Charles
  James
Nine Nobles, ii. 280
Nineteenth Century, The, xiii. 465; xiv.
  172, 190, 534
Nineveh, xii. 339, 413, 497, 499; xiv. 192
Ninewells, Berwickshire, x. 323
Ninian, St, ii. 103, 104, 127, 128
Ninus ('who built Nineveh'), ii. 103
'Nipclose, Sir Nicholas,' *The Theatres*,
  xi. 282
Niphles, the, in *Club Law*, vi. 307 ff.
Nipper, Susan, in *Dombey and Son*, xiii.
  325
Nisard, D., xii. 397
Nisbet, Alexander (1657–1725), ix. 355,
  537

Nisbet, John, VIII. 355
Nisbet, Murdoch, II. 285, 479; III. 45
Nithhad, in *Deor*, I. 36
Nithsdale, XI. 243
Nithsdale Minstrel, XI. 444
Nivernais, duc de, X. 250
Nix, Richard (1447?-1535), bishop of Norwich, III. 42, 68
Nixon, Anthony (*fl.* 1602), IV. 460; *The Black Year*, VI. 46
Nixon, John, XIV. Add. 9
Nizolius, Marius, III. 424
Noah, II. 20, 79, 86, 427; VI. 84
Noah, in religious plays, III. 91, 318; V. 19, 44, 45, 47, 48, 124, 391
Noah's Ark (play), V. 391
Nob, VII. 67
Noble, John, XIV. 532, *also see* Add. 4, 5, 9
Noblenesse of the Asse, The, IV. 517
No-Body, and Some-Body: With the true Chronicle Historie of Elydure, VI. 92, 182, 432
Nobs, Dr Dove's horse, XI. 168
Nodier, Charles, V. 301; XII. 397
Noel, Baptist Wriothesley (1798-1873), XII. 472
Noel, Sir Edward, 1st baron Noel of Ridlington (1582-1643), IV. 265
Noel, Eric, XIII. 204
Noel, Henry (d. 1597), V. 72
Noel, Roden Berkeley Wriothesley (1834-1894), XII. 397; XIII. 194, 478, 485, 507
Boy, The, XIII. 203
Little Child's Monument, A, XIII. 183, 204
Livingstone in Africa, XIII. 204
Thalatta, XIII. 204
Vision of the Desert, A, XIII. 204
Water Nymph, The, XIII. 204
Noggs, Newman, in *Nicholas Nickleby*, XIII. 318
Nokes, James (d. 1692?), VIII. 177
Nolan, E., XIV. 209
Nollekens, Joseph (1737-1823), X. 473; XIV. 226
Nonconformist, The, XIV. 28
Nonconformist's Memorial, The, X. 519
Nonjurors, the, IV. 422
Noorden, C. Van, XIII. 534
Nora, in Thackeray's *Barry Lyndon*, XIII. 282
Norbury, Derbyshire, IV. 369
Norbury park, X. 260
Norcyn, David, II. 424
Nordeling, IV. 246
Norden, John (*fl.* 1600), IV. 495
Norden, John (1548-1625), III. 313, 330, 331, 531; VI. 463; *Speculum Britanniae*, III. 330; *The Surveyors Dialogue*, III. 331; IV. 512
Nördlingen, battle of, VII. 231
Nore, the, XI. 39
Norfolk, II. 134, 287, 304, 305; III. 95; VI. 290; VII. 21, 233, 241, 321; IX. 2, 241, 277, 353, 532; XI. 43, 47; XII. 153, 323, 346, 508, 520; XIV. 221, 290

Norfolk, dukes of. *See* Howard, Charles; Howard, Thomas; Mowbray, John
Norfolk Drollery, VII. 512
Norfolk gent his will and Testament..., The, IV. 393
Norgate, Kate, I. 446; XIV. 490
Norham castle, in Scott's *Marmion* XII. 10
Norland, lord, in Mrs Inchbald's *Every one has his Fault*, XI. 279
Norman, Robert (*fl.* 1590), IV. 460, 508
Norman carols, II. 376
Norman conquest, II. 396, 419; V. 1 ff., 6, 9, 11, 26, 39, 40, 251; VIII. 310, 384; IX. 355; XII. 261, 322; XIV. 52, 70, 72, 73, 101
Norman era, XI. 367
Norman *fabliaux*, IV. 353
Norman kings of England, XIV. 72
Norman law, VIII. 310, 311
Norman literature, I. 149 ff., 446
Norman-French language, XIV. 434
Normandy, V. 3, 4; VII. 451; IX. 532; XII. 508; XIV. 72
Normans, the, XII. 26, 316; XIV. 76
Normans in England, I. 136, 149, 151, 156; II. 421, 428; V. 3, 5, 26, 27
Norris, Edwin (1795-1872), XII. 352, 512
Norris, John (1657-1711), VII. 407; VIII. 347, 474; IX. 287; *An Essay towards the Theory of the Ideal or Intelligible World*, VIII. 348
Norris, John Pilkington, XII. 457
Norris, Mrs, in Jane Austen's *Mansfield Park*, XII. 239, 243
Norse language and literature, X. 129, 132, 451, 484, 489; XIV. 51, 434, *also see* Icelandic
North, Christopher, *pseud. See* Wilson, John
North, Sir Dudley (1641-1691), VIII. 475; IX. 238, 240, 494; *Discourses upon Trade*, VIII. 342
North, Dudley (1748-1829), XI. 141, 146
North, Francis, 4th earl of Guildford (1761-1817), IX. 198, 235, 238 ff., 494
North, Frederick, 2nd earl of Guildford (1732-1792), X. 306, 403, 404, 464; XI. 6, 10, 142; XII. 475; XIV. 214, 385, 607
North, George (*fl.* 1580), III. 553; IV. 444, 447
North, John (1645-1683), IX. 240, 494
North, Montagu, IX. 234
North, Roger (1653-1734), VII. 364; IX. 235, 238 ff., 494
Autobiography, IX. 238, 241
Discourse of Fish and Fish Ponds, IX. 241
Examen, IX. 233, 234, 238, 242
Life of Dr John North, IX. 238 ff.; XI. 329
Life of Francis North, Lord Guilford, IX. 198, 235, 238 ff.
Life of Sir Dudley North, IX. 238 ff.
Lives of the Norths, XI. 331

North, Roger
  *Reflections upon...Le Clerc's life of Mr
  John Locke*, IX. 234
North, Sir Thomas (1535?–1601?), III.
  320, 341, 345, 348, 424, 448, 551; IV.
  439, 443, 445, 523; V. 100, 123, 196,
  197, 199, 338; VI. 377, 495; *Dial of
  Princes, The* (trans. of *El Relox de
  Principes*), II. 340; III. 341, 345, 348;
  IV. 9; *Plutarch*, IV. 1, 3 ff., 7, 9 ff., 15;
  IX. 265
North and Gray, lord, IX. 239
North American Indians, XI. 5, 16, 31
North American Review, The, XIII. 91
North Berwick law, II. 275
North British Review, The, XI. 463; XII.
  429, 456; XIII. 363; XIV. 118, 357
North Briton, The, X. 251, 390 ff., 522;
  XI. 33
North End, X. 12; XI. 356, 365
North Foreland, battle of, VIII. 11
North Petherton park, Somerset, II. 158
North Sea, the, I. 32
North Star, The, XIV. 193
North Walsham, Norfolk, XII. 323
North-West company, XIV. 358
Northallerton, II. 45
Northampton, II. 345; III. 380, 381, 548;
  X. 382, 384
Northampton, earls of. *See* Compton,
  Charles; Howard, Henry
*Northampton, The copy of a letter written
  from*, VII. 349
Northampton Mercury, The, XIV. 169
Northamptonshire, VIII. 5, 288; IX. 6, 532;
  X. 271, 365, 377, 505; XII. 507, 508
Northbrooke, John (*fl.* 1568–1579), V. 479;
  VI. 272, 378, 395; *A Treatise wherein
  Dicing, Dauncing...are reproved...*, VI.
  386 ff., 461, 495
Northcote, James (1746–1831), IX. 162,
  169; X. 473, 483; XI. 88, 472; XII. 172,
  432
Northcote, James Spencer (1821–1907),
  XII. 512
Northcote, Sir Stafford (1818–1887), XIV.
  491
Northern Echo, The, XIV. 193, 195
Northern Lass, The, IX. 363
Northleigh, John (1657–1705), VIII. 395
Northumberland, IV. 190; X. 490; XI. 469;
  XII. 507, 511; XIV. 100
Northumberland Household Book, X. 490
Northumberland, countess of. *See* Sey-
  mour, Elizabeth
Northumberland, dukes of. *See* Dudley,
  John; Percy, Sir Hugh
Northumberland, earls of. *See* Percy,
  Henry
Northumbria, I. 5, 14, 50, 62, 84, 89, 161,
  305
Northumbria, dialect of, I. 132
Northumbrian coast, XII. 10
Northumbrian dialect, XIV. 434
Norton, near Daventry, III. 381
Norton, B., III. 528

Norton, Caroline Elizabeth Sarah (born
  Sheridan, afterwards lady Stirling-
  Maxwell) (1808–1877), XIII. 507; XIV.
  309; *The Lady of La Garaye*, XIII. 177
Norton, Charles Eliot, XIII. 143, 467, 469,
  470, 472, 551, 553; XIV. 152; *Letters*,
  XIII. 371, 386, 400
Norton, Fletcher (1716–1789), X. 525
Norton, John (d. 1612), IV. 400, 409, 411,
  413
Norton, Robert (d. 1635), IV. 460
Norton, Thomas (*fl.* 1477), *Ordinall of
  Alchemy*, II. 211 ff.
Norton, Thomas (1532–1584), III. 46,
  552; IV. 442; V. 66 ff., 75 ff.; VII. 306.
  See, also, *Gorboduc*
Norval, in Home's *Douglas*, X. 87
Norway, VI. 200; X. 222
Norwegian language, XIV. 458
Norwich, II. 57, 304, 305, 307; III. 167,
  183, 367; IV. 361, 408, 409; V. 34, 46,
  48, 132, 391; VI. 400; VII. 233, 239, 258,
  280, 329, 330, 412, 450; X. 385; XI. 179,
  428; XII. 87
Norwich, Horsham St Faith, IV. 127
Norwich, St Peter Mancroft church, VII.
  234
Norwood, Richard (1590?–1675), IV. 460
Nostradamus, prognostication of, IV. 384
Nostradamus, in *The Bugbears*, V. 115
Notable, Miss, in Swift's *Complete Col-
  lection of...Conversation*, IX. 106, 107
Notary, Julian (*fl.* 1496–1520), II. 326, 327
*Notbrowne mayd upon the passyon of
  Cryste, The newe*, II. 328; III. 491
Notch, in *The Masque of Augures*, VI. 331
*Notes and Memorandums of the six days
  preceding the Death of a late Right
  Reverend*, IX. 132
Notes and Queries, IX. 92, 377, 387; XII.
  354, 370, 426, 428; XIII. 464
Notker of St Gall, I. 81, 99
'Notre Dame des Rochers,' X. 248
Nott, John (1751–1865), III. 170
Nottingham, II. 309; IV. 409; V. 35; VII.
  226, 357, 439; X. 387; XI. 431; XIII.
  449
Nottingham, earls of. *See* Finch, Daniel;
  Howard, Charles
Nottingham castle, IV. 181
Nottinghamshire, II. 299; IV. 365; IX. 540;
  XII. 497
Nottola, VI. 484
Nouronihar, in Beckford's *Vathek*, XI. 290,
  291
Nouveau Dictionnaire historique, Le, V. 292
Nova Britannia, IV. 511
Nova Scotia, IV. 92; VII. 224; VIII. 187;
  XIV. 346, 347, 357
Nova Scotian, The, XIV. 346
Nova Solyma, IV. 260; VII. 129, 315, 421,
  466, 476; IX. 385, 570
Novae Narrationes (1515, 1561), VIII. 465
Noval, theologian, X. 377
Novalis (Friedrich Ludwig von Harden-
  berg), XIII. 7, 9, 108, 192, 432, 468

Novella, VII. 345
Novelle, Italian, v. 127
Novello, Vincent (1781–1861), XII. 201
Novels, historical, II. 506
Novelty Fashion, Sir, in Cibber's *Love's Last Shift*, VIII. 160, 170, 176
Noverre, Jean George, *Lettres sur les Arts*, XI. 258
Now the fight's done, VIII. 96
Now ye Tories that glory, VIII. 96
Nowell, in *Every Man in His Humour*, VI. 248
Nowell, Alexander (1507?–1602), III. 552; *Catechism*, VII. 332
Noyes, Alfred, XII. 373; XIII. 493
Ntsikana's Hymn, XIV. 377
Nuce, Thomas (d. 1617), v. 395
Nugatores, v. 2
Nugent, Robert, earl Nugent (1702–1788), VII. Add.; x. 214, 456, 482
Numismatic society, XII. 347
Nun Appleton, Yorks., VII. 180, 182, 183
Nun in her Smock, XI. 328
Nuneham, IX. 162
Nuremberg Chronicon, IV. 427
Nürnberg, IV. 260; v. 25, 284; VII. 176
Nursery rhymes, XI. 475, 481
Nurture, in *The Passetyme of Pleasure*, II. 229
Nussey, Ellen, XIII. 403 ff., 408
Nut Brown Maid, The, II. 249, 320, 328, 407, 413, 429, 501; III. 280, 283, 491, 496; IV. 383; IX. 154
Nuđ, father of Gwynn, I. 255
Nutt, Alfred Trübner (1856–1910), I. 253, 271, 272; XII. 518
Nuttall, R., IV. 437
Nye, Nathaniel (*fl.* 1648), IV. 460
Nye, Philip (1596?–1672), VIII. 63, 66
Nye, Stephen (1648?–1719), x. 377
Nym, in *Henry IV*, v. 187
Nymegen, peace of, VIII. 382
Nyren, John (1764–1837), XIV. 545

O., S. G. *See* Osborne, lord Sidney Godolphin
O. P. rioters, XIV. 440
'O for a bowl of fat Canary,' v. 125
O Lusty May with Flora quene, II. 283
O Willy was so blythe a Lad, IX. 364
'Oak and Brier' measure, III. 286
Oakeley, Frederick (1802–1880), XII. 259, 453, 460, 461
Oakham grammar school, VII. 317, 340
Oakly, Charles, in Colman's *Jealous Wife*, x. 89, 90
Oakly, Mr, in Colman's *Jealous Wife*, x. 89, 90
Oakly, Mrs, in Colman's *Jealous Wife*, x. 89
Oakum, in Smollett's *Roderick Random*, x. 37
Oaten, Edward Farley, XIV. 574
Oates, in Essex, VIII. 330 ff.
Oates, Titus (1649–1705), VIII. 38, 82, 95, 188, 266, 286; IX. 3, 265, 267, 493

Oates, *The Melancholy Complaint of Dr Titus*, VIII. 94
Obadiah, in Sterne's *Tristram Shandy*, x. 50
Obadiah, the prophet, VII. 382
Oberammergau, v. 18
Oberon, II. 338
Oberon, in *A Midsummer Night's Dream*, v. 183
Oberon, in *James IV*, v. 137
Oberon, in *Nimphidia*, IV. 193
Oblivion, act of, VII. 106
O'Brien, Charlotte Grace (1845–1909), XIV. 570
O'Brien, William (d. 1815), XI. 458; XIII. 245; *The Duel*, XI. 265
Observantines of the Franciscan Order, the, II. 251
Observator, The (L'Estrange's), VIII. 412; IX. 3, 4
Observator, The (Tutchin's), IX. 5
Observator Observed, The (1681), VIII. 412
Observer, The, XIV. 201, 228, 235
O'Callaghan, John Cornelius (1805–1883), XIV. 570
Occasional Conformity act, x. 373, 374
Occleve or Hoccleve, Thomas (1368?–1450?), II. 94, 142, 154, 159, 160, 164, 205 ff., 239, 253, 258, 266, 469; III. 168, 277, 280, 292, 311; IV. 158
 Ars Sciendi Mori, II. 207
 Complaint and *Dialogue*, II. 206, 207
 Complaint of the Virgin, II. 208
 De Regimine Principum, II. 206
 Emperor Jereslaus's Wife, The, II. 207
 Jonathas, II. 207
 Letter of Cupid, The, II. 162, 164, 208
 Male Règle, II. 206, 207, 505
 Mother of God, The, II. 208
 Sir John Oldcastle, II. 208
Occultism, VII. 508 ff.
Occurrences, An abstract of some speciall forreign, VII. 345
Oceaniae, in *The Masque of Blacknesse*, VI. 342
Oceanus, in *The Masque of Blacknesse*, VI. 342, 343
Ochiltree, Edie, in Scott's *Antiquary*, XII. 25, 350
Ochino, Bernardino (1487–1564), IV. 447; v. 104
Ockham, William of (d. 1349?), I. 200, 212, 455; II. 42, 52, 350, 355; III. 9; IV. 269, 272, 273; *Defensor*, II. 308; *Summa*, II. 363
Ockley, Simon (1678–1720), *Conquest of Syria* (*History of the Saracens*), x. 280, 281, 503
Ocland, Christopher (d. 1590), *Anglorum Praelia*, III. 428, 552
O'Clery, M., XIV. 570
O'Clery family, XIV. 309
O'Connell, Daniel (1775–1847), XIII. 353; XIV. 126 ff., 318, 325, 328, 329, 417, 510
O'Connor, T. P., XIII. 546, 547; XIV. 573
Octavia, in *The Civil Wars*, IV. 137

Octavian, I. 290, 470
Octavianus, III. 224
Octavio, marquis of Siena, in *The Fancies*, VI. 193
O'Curry, Eugene (1796–1862), XII. 518; XIV. 570; *Manners and Customs of the Irish*, XII. 360; *Manuscript Materials for Ancient Irish History*, XII. 360
O'Cutter, captain, in Colman's *Jealous Wife*, x. 90
Odcombe, IV. 89, 90
Odell, Jonathan, XIII. 240, 512
O'Dennis, II. 301
Odgers, Walter Blake, XIV. 536
'Odikle,' x. 130
Odin, I. 8; x. 222; XIII. 13, 126
Odo, St, I. 153
Odo of Cheriton (d. 1247), I. 366, 478
Odofredus, II. 363
O'Doherty, in *Noctes Ambrosianae*, XII. 160
O'Doherty, Sir Morgan, Maginn's, XIV. 313
O'Donnell, John Francis (1837–1874), XIV. 570; *Agents and Evictions*, XIV. 326; *Spinning Song, A*, XIV. 326
O'Donoghue, David James (1866–1917), XIV. 314, 567, 570
O'Donovan, Edmund (1844–1883?), XIV. 570
O'Donovan, John (1809–1861), XII. 518; XIV. 570; *Grammar of the Irish Language*, XII. 360
Odoric of Pordenone (1330), II. 80, 81, 86, 87
O'Dowds (Thackeray's), XIII. 286
O'Dymsy, in Barbour's *Bruce*, II. 106
Odyssey, the, I. 293; III. 293
Oecolampadius, Joannes, III. 413
Oedipus, v. 76; IX. 60
Oelsner, Hermann, XIII. 497
Oenone, in *The Arayggnement of Paris*, v. 131
Oenophilus, in *Misogonus*, v. 110
O'er the Moor amang the Heather, IX. 374
O'er the Water to Charlie, IX. 376
Of a' the Airts, XI. 234
Offa, in *The Battle of Maldon*, I. 145; legend of, I. 218
Offa, in *Beowulf* and *Widsith*, I. 26, 34
Offa, laws of, I. 98
Offa of Mercia (d. 796), VIII. 310; XIV. 68
Offarum, Vitae Duorum, I. 34
Offering, in *The Masque of Christmas*, VI. 358
Officia Pastorum, v. 391
Officina Arbuteana, x. 245
O'Flaherty, in Cumberland's *West Indian*, XI. 257, 266
Og, in *The Second Part of Absalom and Achitophel*, VIII. 41, 42
Ogden, Rollo, XIV. 534
Ogham Inscriptions, XII. 516
Ogilby, John (1600–1676), VI. 197; VII. 487; IX. 68, 75
Ogilvie, James (*fl.* 1735), IX. 550
Ogilvy, captain, IX. 376

Ogilvy, David, lord Ogilvy (1725–1803), IX. 563
Ogir the Dane, II. 82
Ogle, Sir John (1569–1640), VII. 453
Ogleby, lord, in Colman's *Clandestine Marriage*, x. 90
Oglethorpe, Fanny, IX. 219
O'Grady, Standish Hayes (1846–1915), VII. 211; XII. Add. 5; XIV. 211, 305, also see Add. 3
O'Hagan, John (1822–1890), XIV. 570
O'Halloran, Sylvester (1728–1807), *Introduction to the...history and antiquities of Ireland*, x. 500, 503
O'Hanlon, John (1821–1905), XIV. 570
O'Hara, Kane (1714?–1782), x. 440; XIV. 570
Ohone, ohone, Fortune, my foe, VIII. 96
Ohthere (*fl.* 880), I. 94
Ohthere, in *Beowulf*, etc., I. 24, 25
O'Hussey, XIV. 318*b*
Oiseuse, dame, XIII. 210
Ojeda, IV. 68
O'Keeffe, Adelaide (1776–1855?), XI. 383, 483, 488
O'Keeffe, John (1747–1833), XI. 224, 257, 454, 458
Okehampton, x. 114
Okely, Francis (1719?–1794), IX. 328, 513, 518, 519
Okes, John, VII. 347
Olaf, I. 287
Olcon, in Drayton's *Eglogs*, IV. 173, 176
Olcott, Charles S., XIII. 553
Old English, x. 184, 223
Old English Ballads, x. 233
Old English charters, XII. 356
Old English Chronicle, IX. 355; XII. 349
Old English gospels, x. 223
Old English grammar, IX. 402
Old English history, XIV. 75
Old English language, XII. 326, 355
Old English literature, IV. 424; XIV. 52, 69, 440, 444, 449, 450, 453, 454
Old English poetry, x. 224; XIII. 151, 241, 242
Old English studies, IX. 355
Old lady, Scott's, II. 409, 414
Old Man's Lament, The, IX. 377
Old Smuggler, in Farquhar's *Constant Couple*, VIII. 175
Old Testament revision company, XII. 341
Old Tom of Bedlam, x. 233
Old Wives' Tale, I. 294
Oldbuck, Jonathan, in Scott's *Antiquary*, x. 231; XII. 25, 350
'Oldcastle, Humphry' (viscount Bolingbroke), IX. 221, 222
Oldcastle, Sir John (lord Cobham) (d. 1417), II. 47, 68, 208, 287; v. 187
Oldcastle, Sir John, IV. 394; v. 236, 319, 331 ff.
Oldcraft, Credulous, in *Wit At Severall Weapons*, v. 364
Olde, John (*fl.* 1545–1555), IV. 443
Olde Tenures (1525), VIII. 465

Oldenburg, Henry (1615?–1677), VIII. 247, 478

Oldfield, Anne (1683–1730), VIII. 176; x. 21

Oldfield, Joshua (1656–1729), x. 385

Oldfield, Laurel Cecil Francis, XIV. 536

Oldham, John (1653–1683), VIII. 82 ff. (main entry), 99, 100, 373, 395, 409, 412, *also see* Add.; IX. 473; x. 169
  Careless Good Fellow, The, VIII. 88
  Character of an Ugly Old Priest, The, VIII. 87
  Dithyrambic, a Drunkard's Speech in a Masque, VIII. 84
  Dream, The, VIII. 84
  Garnet's Ghost, VIII. 85
  Lamentation for Adonis, The, VIII. 86
  Loyola's Will, VIII. 85
  Passion of Byblis, The, VIII. 88
  Poems and Translations, VIII. 86, 89
  Prologue, VIII. 85
  St Ignatius his Image, VIII. 85
  Satyr address'd to a Friend that is about to leave the University, A, VIII. 88
  Satyr against Vertue, VIII. 84
  Satyr concerning Poetry, A, VIII. 88
  Satyr upon a Woman, A, VIII. 85
  Satyrs upon the Jesuits, VIII. 85
  Sunday-Thought in Sickness, A, VIII. 88
  Thirteenth Satyr of Juvenal, The, VIII. 88
  To the Memory of Mr Charles Morwent, VIII. 84
  Upon a Printer, VIII. 82
  Upon the Works of Ben Jonson, VIII. 84

Oldisworth, William (1680–1734), IX. 183, 425

Oldmixon, John (1673–1742), VII. 444; VIII. 438; IX. 235, 237–238 (main entry), 437, 476, 494; x. 279
  British Empire in America, IX. 237
  Clarendon and Whitelocke compared, VII. 229
  Critical History of England, IX. 204, 237, 238
  Essay on Criticism, IX. 237
  History, VIII. 168
  History of...the Royal House of Stuart, IX. 238
  Memoirs of the Press, IX. 238
  Secret History of Europe, IX. 237

Oldrent, in *A Joviall Crew*, VI. 230

Oldwater (Oudewater), in Holland, VIII. 291

Oldys, William (1696–1761), VI. 51, 248; VIII. 137; IX. 534, 537, 538; *British Librarian*, IX. 357; *Dissertation on Pamphlets*, x. 166

Olearius, Adam, IV. 455

O'Leary, Arthur (1729–1802), XIV. 570

O'Leary, Ellen (1831–1889), XIV. 321, 571

O'Leary, John (1830–1907), XIV. 321, 571

Oley, Barnabas (1602–1686), VII. 27, 29, 156, 403; *Life of George Herbert*, VII. 154

Olif and Landres, I. 283

Olinda, in *Sicelides*, VI. 323

Oliphant, Dr Charles, IX. 560

Oliphant, Laurence (1829–1888), XIV. 164, 199, 522, 553
  Altiora Peto, XIV. 165
  Autobiography of a Joint-Stock Company, XIV. 165
  Episodes in a Life of Adventure, XIV. 165
  Piccadilly, XIV. 165
  Russian Shores of the Black Sea, The, XIV. 165
  Sympneumata, XIV. 165

Oliphant, Margaret Oliphant (1828–1897), XI. 456; XII. 380, 425; XIII. 557, 558, 565; XIV. 496, 521, 522
  Autobiography, XIII. 431
  Beleaguered City, A, XIII. 431
  Chronicles of Carlingford, XIII. 430
  Cuckoo in the Nest, The, XIII. 431
  Kirsteen, XIII. 431
  Literary History of England, XI. 307
  Little Pilgrim in the Unseen, A, XIII. 431
  Margaret Maitland, XIII. 431
  Miss Marjoribanks, XIII. 430
  Salem Chapel, XIII. 430, 431
  Whiteladies, XIII. 431

Oliver, in *The London Prodigall*, V. 255

Oliver, D. E., XIII. 515

Oliver, Fielding's tutor, x. 20

Oliver, John Robert, XII. 512

Oliver, Pasfield, IX. 23

Oliver, uncle, in *The School for Scandal*, V. 254

Olives, mount of, V. 45

Olivia, in Mrs Cowley's *Bold Stroke for a Husband*, XI. 275

Olivia, in *Twelfth Night*, V. 194; VI. 305

Olivier, abbé, *Life and adventures of Signior Rozelli*, IX. 18

Olivier or Oliver, in *Sir Ferumbras* (Fierabras), I. 284, 302

Ollard, S. L., XII. 463; XIV. 592

Ollendorf series, XI. 373

Ollier, Charles (1788–1859), *Literary Miscellany*, XII. 74

Ollier, Edmund (1827–1886), XII. 436, 442

Ollier brothers, publishers, XII. 194

Ollyffe, John (1647–1717), x. 374

Olney, XI. 80, 81, 404

Olney Hymns, XI. 80, 402

Olofactus, in *Lingua*, VI. 315

Olot, in Spain, XIV. 293

Olwen, daughter of Yspaḍaden Pen Kawr, I. 254

Olwen. See *Kulhwch and O.*

Olympus, VI. 329; x. 237; XII. 90

Olyver of Castylle and the fayre Helayne, The History of, II. 324, 325

Omar Khayyám, x. 144; XIII. 145, 146

Omnia-probate, in *Piers the Plowman*, II. 21

Omnium, duke of, Trollope's, XIII. 422

'Omnium, Jacob,' *pseud.* See Higgins, Matthew J.

Omond, Thomas Stewart, XII. 524; XIII. 249, 488, 512

Once a Week, XII. 398; XIII. 428, 440

O'Neil, Henry (1817–1881), XII. 512

O'Neill, Eliza, lady Becher (1791–1872),
   VIII. 184; XII. 171; XIII. 259; XIV. 319
O'Neill, Hugh, earl of Tyrone (1540?–
   1616), III. 244; XIV. 325
Onela, in *Beowulf*, I. 24, 26
Ongar, XII. 505
Ongentheow, in *Beowulf* and *Widsith*,
   I. 24 ff., 34
Onions, Charles Talbut, XIV. 611
Onslow, Arthur (1691–1768), IX. 209;
   X. 94, 244
Onslow, George, 1st earl of Onslow (1731–
   1814), X. 401
Ontario, XIV. 350
Onwhyn, Thomas (d. 1886), XII. 448
Oothoon, in Blake's *Visions of the
   Daughters of Albion*, XI. 190
Opalinsky, L., *Polonia Defensa contra
   Joan: Barclaium*, etc., IV. 254
Opdycke, J. B., XIV. 532
Ophelia, in *Hamlet*, V. 180, 200 ff.; VII. 8;
   VIII. 164
Opie, Amelia (1769–1853), XI. 344, 462;
   XII. 447
Opie, John (1761–1807), XI. 37, 360
Opinion, in *Time's Complaint*, VI. 320
Oporinus, IV. 380
Oppian, VII. 240
Oppression, in *Respublica*, V. 60
Oracle, The, XIV. 179
Oracle of Avignon, The, IX. 564
Orange, Frederick Henry, prince of, VII.
   437
Orange, house of, VIII. 10
Orange, Mary, princess of, IX. 199
Orange, Maurice of Nassau, prince of,
   VII. 454
Orange, river, XIV. 372
Orange Free State, XIV. 375
Oranges and lemons, game of, V. 30
Orbilius, Pupillus, VIII. 159
Orbón, J. G., XIII. 466
Orc, Blake's, XI. 190, 194
Orchard, The, IV. 542
Ord, John Walker (1811–1853), XIII. 507
Ord, Mrs, XI. 346, 365
Ordella, in Fletcher's *Thierry and Theo-
   doret*, VI. 122, 129; XII. 190
Order, in *Hymenaei*, VI. 346
*Order of the Hospitalls of K. Henry the
   VIIIth and K. Edward the VIth, The*,
   1557, VIII. 451
Ordericus Vitalis (1075–1143?), I. 162,
   163, 170, 451
Orders, the enclosed, XIV. 305
Orders and Fraternities, III. 484
*Orders appointed…for setting roges and idle
   persons to worke*, VI. 495
Orders of Callettes, or Drabbys, The XX,
   III. 87, 484
Orders of Fooles, The XX, III. 87, 484
Orders of Fooles, Twenty-five, III. 484
Orders of Knaves, The XXV, III. 87, 484;
   IV. 521
Ordlaf, in *Finnsburh*, I. 31
Ordovician rocks, XIV. 292

O'Reilly, John Boyle (1844–1890), XIV.
   571, 573; *Amber Whale, The*, XIV. 322;
   Songs from the Southern Seas, XIV. 322
Oresme, N., IV. 512
Orestes, X. 108, 249
Orestes, in Kingsley's *Hypatia*, XIII. 363
Orestes and Pylades, I. 314
Orfeo, King, II. 414
Orfeo, Sir, I. 281, 288, 294, 295, 299, 300,
   310, 311, 471
Orford, countess of. *See* Walpole, Mar-
   garet
Orford, earls of. *See* Walpole, George;
   Walpole, Horatio; Walpole, Sir Robert
Orgalus, in *Misogonus*, V. 110
Orgilio, in Johnson's *London*, X. 169
Orgilus, in *The Broken Heart*, VI. 191
Orgoglio, in *The Faerie Queene*, II. 234
Oriana, in *Amadis of Gaul*, VII. 75
Oriana, in Farquhar's *The Inconstant*,
   VIII. 169
Oriana, in *The Knight of Malta*, VI. 130
Oriana, in *The Satyr*, VI. 340
Oriana, in *The Wild-Goose Chase*, VI. 123
Oriental scholars, XII. 341 ff., 499 ff.
Oriental scholarship, 1600–1660, VII. 490
Orientius, XII. 337
Origen, III. 10; VII. 238, 505; VIII. 277;
   Hexapla, XII. 341, 501
Original Weekly Journal, The, IX. 433
Origo Mundi, V. 15
Orinda, the Matchless. *See* Philips,
   Katherine
Orinoco, river, XIV. 249
Orissa, XIV. 333
Orkborne, Dr, in Burney's *Camilla*, X. 65
Orkney, II. 115; IX. 552, 560
Orkney islands, XIV. 434
Orlando, III. 305
Orlando (Ariosto's), III. 230
Orleans, XI. 97
Orm or Ormin (*fl.* 1200?), I. 224, 225, 375,
   376; II. 189; V. 6; *Ormulum*, I. 222 ff.,
   340, 375, 386 ff., 394, 398, 399, 458,
   460; III. 440; IV. 37
Orme, Robert (1728–1801), X. 503; XIV.
   97, 496, 579; *Historical Fragments of
   the Mogul Empire*, XIV. 334; *History of
   the Military Transactions…in Indostan*,
   X. 293; XIV. 333
Orme, William (1787–1830), XII. 523
Ormerod, George (1785–1873), XII. 512
Ormerod, Oliver (1580?–1626), IV. 521
Ormond, duke of, in *The Tatler*, IX. 34
Ormonde, duke of. *See* Butler, James
Ormonde, earl of, in *Secreta Secretorum*,
   II. 301
Ormont, lord (George Meredith's), XIII. 445
Ornsby, Robert (1820–1889), XII. 454,
   460; XIV. 505
O'Rorke, J., XIII. 515
Orosius, Paulus, I. 66, 76, 81, 93 ff., 239,
   436, 438, 440
O'Rourke, Edmund (Edmund Falconer,
   1814–1879), XIV. 571
Orpheus, X. 114

Orpheus and Eurydice, I. 294, 311; II. 417
Orpheus and Eurydice, in Alfred's *Boethius*, I. 100
Orphic hymns, *Carmina*, III. 409, 416
Orr, Alexandra, XIII. 485
Orrery, earls of. *See* Boyle, Charles; Boyle, John; Boyle, Roger
Orsabrin, in *The Goblins*, VI. 239
Orseolo, in *The Humorous Courtier*, VI. 205
Orsin, in *Hudibras*, VIII. 76
Orsini, the, VI. 175
Orsini, Virginio, VI. 175
Orsino, in *Twelfth Night*, VI. 305; VII. 84
Ortelius, Abraham, IV. 73, 74
Orton, Job (1717–1783), X. 521
Osaka, IV. 100
Osbaldistone, Francis, in Scott's *Rob Roy*, XII. 17, 18, 26
Osbern (*fl.* 1090), monk of Canterbury, I. 153
Osbern of Gloucester (*fl.* 1148), II. 498
Osbert de Clare (*fl.* 1136), I. 449
Osborne, Charles E., XIV. 502
Osborne, Dorothy (lady Temple) (1627–1695), VI. 452; VIII. 371, 372, 380, 483; *Letters*, VIII. 15, 279
Osborne, Francis (1593–1659), VII. 446, 459; VIII. 379, 481; XI. 481; *A Miscellany of Sundry Essayes Paradoxes and Problematical Discourses, Letters and Characters*, VIII. 377; *Advice to a Son*, VII. 193; VIII. 377; IX. 397, 569
Osborne, George, in Thackeray's *Vanity Fair*, X. 34; XIII. 287, 289
Osborne, lady, XII. 285
Osborne, lord, in Jane Austen's *The Watsons*, XII. 234
Osborne, Mr, in Thackeray's *Vanity Fair*, XIII. 287, 288
Osborne, lord Sidney Godolphin (S. G. O.) (1808–1889), XIV. 181, 182
Osborne, Thomas (d. 1767), IX. 357; X. 166; XI. 332, 337
Osbornes, the (Thackeray's), XIII. 286
Osbourne, Lloyd, XIV. 526
Oscar, X. 231
Oseas, in *A Looking Glasse for London*, V. 354
O'Shaughnessy, Arthur William Edgar (1844–1881), XIII. 140, 147, 496 (main entry)
    Bisclavaret, XIII. 141
    Chaitivel, XIII. 141
    Disease of the Soul, The, XIII. 141
    Epic of Women, An, XIII. 141
    Fair Maid and the Sun, The, XIII. 141
    Fountain of Tears, The, XIII. 141
    Lays of France, XIII. 141
    Love's Eternity, XIII. 141
    Music and Moonlight, XIII. 141
    'We are the music-makers,' XIII. 141
O'Shaughnessy, Eleanor W., XIII. 496
O'Shaunessy, in Egan's *Life in London*, XIV. 223
O'Shea, John Augustus (1839–1905), XIV. 571

Osiander, Andreas, III. 32
Oslaf (Ordlaf?), in *Beowulf*, I. 31
Osler, W., IV. 245
Osney, abbey of, and annals of, I. 178, 182, 257
Ospak, in Morris's *The Lovers of Gudrun*, XIII. 125
Osric, in *Hamlet*, VI. 170
Ossian, IX. 560; X. 55, 130, 137, 182, 222, 227 ff., 232, 234, 471, 472, 487 ff.; XI. 179, 181, 184, 187, 188, 206, 245; XII. 12, 40; XIII. 52, 151, 225 ff. *See, also, under* Macpherson
Ossianic poems, the, I. 275
Ossianic society, XII. 361; XIV. 305
Ossory, XI. 344; XIV. 246
Ossory, earl of. *See* Butler, Thomas
Ossory, lady. *See* Upper Ossory, countess of
Osteler, Thomasin, VI. 276
Ostend, fall of, VI. 170; VII. 454
Ostler, William (*fl.* 1601–1623), VI. 181, 276
O'Sullivan, Denis, XIV. 573
O'Sullivan-Beare, Philip (1590?–1660), XIV. Add. 3
Oswald, in Wordsworth's *Borderers*, XI. 99
Oswald, James (1715–1769), *An Appeal to Common Sense*, X. 348, 513, 514
Oswald, musician, X. 128
Oswald, St, king of Northumbria (605?–642), I. 82, 106, 120, 121, 148
Oswald, St, archbishop of York (d. 992), I. 113
Oswald, *Scots Airs*, IX. 361
Oswestry academy, X. 386
Oswin, Sir, in Mrs Inchbald's *To Marry or not to Marry*, XI. 279
Oswy, Oswin, king of Northumbria (612?–670), I. 12, 380
Otfried, Old High German poet, I. 118, 288
Othello (Shakespeare's), IV. 78; VIII. 164, 170; X. 73; XII. 171; XIV. 443
Othere, IV. 74
Otho, in Gray's *Agrippina*, X. 119
Otho, in *The Tragedy of Hoffman*, V. 327
Otho IV, I. 192
Otho, *Constitutions* of, II. 364
Otho de Granson, II. 187
O'Trigger, Sir Lucius, in Sheridan's *Rivals*, X. 90
Óttarr, I. 26
Ottawa, XIV. 351, 357
Otter, William (1768–1840), XI. 399; XIV. 247
Otterbourne, Thomas (*fl.* 1400), II. 498; IX. 535
Otterburn, II. 398, 408, 415
Ottery academy, X. 384
Ottery St Mary, III. 57; XII. 191; XIII. 276
Otto the Great, V. 6
Ottobon, *Constitutions* of, II. 364
Ottryngham, John, II. 366
Otuel, Sir, I. 302, 470
Otway, Caesar (1780–1842), XIV. 312, 315, 317, 571

Otway, Thomas (1652–1685), v. 292;
  VIII. 17, 21, 181 ff. (main entry), 189,
  191, 197, 409, 412, 438, 445; x. 67,
  73, 86, 87; XII. 49
  Alcibiades, VIII. 181, 182, 184
  *Atheist, The, or The Second Part of the
    Souldier's Fortune*, VIII. 184
  *Beginning of a Pastoral on the Death of
    his late Majesty, The*, VIII. 44
  Cheats of Scapin, The, VIII. 182
  Don Carlos, VIII. 182
  Friendship in Fashion, VIII. 182
  History and Fall of Caius Marius, The,
    VIII. 182
  Orphan, The, VI. 219; VIII. 184; x. 74
  Poet's Complaint to his Muse, The, VIII.
    94, 185
  Souldier's Fortune, The, VIII. 183
  Titus and Berenice, VIII. 181, 182
  Venice Preserv'd, or a Plot Discover'd,
    VIII. 94, 183 ff.
  Windsor Castle, VIII. 44, 185
Otway society, the, VIII. 184
Oua, I. 87
Oudenarde, IX. 205
Oughtred, William (1575–1660), IV. 460
Ouida (Louise de la Ramée) (1839–1908),
  XIII. 562
  Bimbi, XIII. 437
  Dog of Flanders, A, XIII. 437
  In Maremma, XIII. 436
  Two Little Wooden Shoes, XIII. 436
  Under Two Flags, XIII. 436
Oulton, Walley Chamberlain (1770?–
  1820?), x. 443; XI. 449
Oulton, Yorkshire, IX. 330
Oundle grammar school, VII. 331; VIII. 2
Ouse, river, Yorkshire, VII. 180
Ouseley, Sir Gore (1770–1844), XII. 342,
  502
Ouseley, Sir William (1767–1842), XII.
  342, 502
Ousely valley, the, XIII. 428
Outlaw's Song of Traillebaston, II. 503
Outram, George (1805–1856), XII. 421
Outram, Sir James (1803–1863), XIV. 496
Overbury, Sir Thomas (1581–1613), III.
  84, 95, 114, 487; IV. 103, 143, 338 ff.,
  345, 360, 521, 525; v. 479; VII. 384,
  389, 437, 451, 453, 454; VIII. 63, 357;
  XIV. 83; *A Perfect Wife*, IV. 265, 338,
  414; *Characters*, IV. 102, 327, 338, 340;
  VI. 401, 495
Overdo, in *Bartholomew Fayre*, VI. 23
Overreach, Sir Giles, in Massinger's *A New
  Way to Pay Old Debts*, v. 352; VI. 160;
  XII. 171
Overton, John (1763–1838), XII. 472
Overton, John Henry (1835–1903), XIV.
  496; *English Church in the Eighteenth
  Century, The* (with C. J. Abbey), XIV.
  101; *William Law, Non-juror and
  Mystic*, IX. 309, 313, 324 ff.; XIV. 101
Ovey, John, VIII. 105, 106
Ovid, I. 76, 197, 221; II. 144, 150, 151,
  176, 188, 259, 262, 316, 358, 360, 366;

Ovid
  III. 20, 86, 113, 181, 183, 187, 259, 347;
  IV. 16, 17, 19 ff., 24, 250, 349, 438, 469;
  v. 220, 221; VI. 18, 82, 87, 198, 300;
  VII. 51, 270, 370, 503; VIII. 44, 51, 88,
  372, 433, 444; IX. 46, 256, 258, 500, 502;
  x. 197, 218, 415; XI. 2, 425; XII. 337,
  489, 490, 492; XIV. 171
  Ad Macrum, v. 143
  Ars Amandi, IV. 320; VI. 213
  Metamorphoses, II. 486; IV. 19, 20, 318,
  414; VI. 207, 299, 313, 316; VII. 50;
  IX. 68, 160, 434, 435, 446, 478, 485, 559
  Salmacis and Hermaphroditus, IV. 20
  Tristia, III. 183; IV. 20
Ovid, in *The Palice of Honour*, II. 260
Ovid, in *The Poetaster*, VI. 44
Ovidius Exulans, IX. 259
Oviedo, John Gonsales de, IV. 70, 101;
  *Sumario de la natural y general Hystoria
  de las Indias* (*History of the West Indies*),
  III. 453; IV. 69
Owayn, Sir, visit to Purgatory of, I. 339
Owein, in *Geraint*, I. 274
Owen, Hugh (d. 1618), IV. 262
Owen, James (1654–1706), IX. 571; x. 386
Owen, John (1580–1651), VII. 315, 324
Owen, John (1563(?4)–1612), IV. 242, 243,
  261 ff., 502 ff.; VIII. 111, 344, 345, 475;
  x. 377; *Epigrammata*, IV. 262
Owen, Sir Richard (1804–1892), XIV. 295,
  299, 561 ff.
Owen, Robert (1771–1858), XIV. 403 ff.,
  478, 514, 602, 608
Owen, Robert Dale (1801–1877), XIV. 478,
  505, 592, 602, 608
Owen, Sir Roger (1573–1617), IV. 265
Owen, Thomas, of Plas dû, IV. 262
Owen's Weekly Chronicle, XIV. 201
Owenson, Sydney. *See* Morgan, lady
Owl and the Nightingale, The, I. 219, 222,
  223, 238 ff., 291, 361, 458, 460; II. 217;
  VII. 112
Owles Almanacke, The, IV. 534
Owun, one of the scribes of the *Rushworth
  Gospels*, I. 132
Oxenedes. *See* John de
Oxenford, clerk of, in *The Canterbury
  Tales*, VII. 156
Oxenford, John (1812–1877), XIII. 263,
  521; XIV. 236
Oxenham, John, in *Westward Ho!* XIII.
  364
Oxenstierna, count, x. 223
Oxenstjerna, chancellor of Sweden, VII.
  230, 231
Oxford, I. 89, 152, 180, 183 ff., 202, 222,
  233, 337, 382; II. 49, 50, 52, 55, 57,
  58, 60, 65 ff., 69, 74, 102, 130, 185, 198,
  204, 208, 224, 288, 294, 303, 305, 307,
  308, 317, 331, 340 ff., 487, 488; III. 5 ff.,
  9 ff., 13, 15, 19, 20, 28, 29, 33, 34, 39,
  46, 48, 50, 51, 53, 67, 82, 94, 113, 167,
  179, 185, 200, 321, 333, 344, 358,
  418 ff., 427, 430, 436; IV. 9, 19, 51, 89,
  120, 131, 136, 142, 190, 198, 200, 224,

Oxford

225, 228, 242 ff., 274, 297, 381, 398, 406 ff., 416, 427 ff., 432 ff., 548; v. 103, 109, 115, 118, 121, 132, 255, 256, 363 ff., 368; vi. 5, 29, 150, 198, 218, 285, 288, 293, 298, 312, 366, 387, 389, 397 ff., 404; vii. 35, 52, 87, 89, 97, 98, 101, 103, 104, 148, 151, 152, 157, 179, 190, 196, 200, 206, 207, 229, 246, 280, 288, 302, 303, 305, 308, 312, 316 ff., 319, 321, 336, 340, 345, 348, 357, 365, 412, 450, 454, 477, 517; viii. 4, 105, 108, 116, 118, 136, 189, 286, 304, 305, 330 ff., 363 ff., 370, 400; ix. 88, 92, 130, 170, 177, 182, 184, 188, 282, 290, 313, 324, 329, 330, 331, 334, 341, 342, 344 ff., 349, 355, 382, 383, 386, 387, 394, 395, 406, 410 ff., 533, 536, 538, 540, 541, 573, 574; x. 112, 114, 136, 159, 187, 198, 205, 238, 241, 268, 270, 294, 301, 309, 335, 356, 357, 362 ff., 378, 492; xi. 35, 40, 61, 62, 109, 118, 119, 158, 335, 357; xii. 59, 115, 138, 143, 157, 158, 187, 192, 256, 259 ff., 271, 273, 274, 277, 278, 285, 286, 288, 293 ff., 299, 304, 317, 318, 320, 327, 328, 333, 339 ff., 365; xiii. 23, 88, 89, 92, 93, 95, 96, 100, 102 ff., 120, 165 ff., 186, 196, 202, 203, 205, 209, 210, 228, 240, 280, 297, 317, 346, 350, 427, 435; xiv. 7, 24, 43, 45, 56, 69 ff., 73, 74, 76, 81, 86, 88, 90, 98, 99, 129, 149, 152, 154 ff., 191, 193, 205 ff., 215, 225, 263, 264, 295, 321, 383 ff., 409, 410, 414, 416, 417, 430 ff.

All Souls college, ii. 358; iii. 328, 423, 424; iv. 428; vii. 160, 162, 358; viii. 241, 348; ix. 294; x. 139, 275

Ashmolean museum, ix. 352; xiv. 285

Ashmolean society, xiv. 566

Ashmole's 'elaboratory,' ix. 413

Balliol college, ii. 44, 49, 50, 355; iv. 103, 427; viii. 244; ix. 539; x. 335; xi. 155; xii. 259, 260, 298, 333, 334; xiii. 87, 103, 129, 480, 483; xiv. 45

Bodleian library, iii. 201; iv. 56, 244, 248, 265, 430, 432, 433, 548; vii. 43, 64, 309; ix. 330, 342, 345, 349, 353, 357, 443, 530; x. 167, 191, 193, 281; xii. 334, 369, 503, 523; xiv. 96, 247

Botanic garden, xiv. 286

Brasenose college, iv. 428; vi. 38, 83, 295; vii. 42

Broadgates hall (Pembroke college), iii. 327, 424; vi. 111; vii. 143, 233

Canterbury hall, ii. 354, 355

Cardinal college (Christ Church), ii. 358; iii. 32

Christ Church, iii. 326, 327, 425, 434; iv. 81, 244, 250, 265; v. 70, 128; vi. 237, 286, 295, 299, 302, 303, 316 ff., 320, 323, 325, 326, 398; vii. 82, 341, 444, 457; viii. 181, 328, 329, 344; ix. 139, 147, 182, 256, 258, 264, 329, 332, 337, 345, 382, 391; x. 113, 117, 351 ff., 364; xi. 155, 322; xii. 327, 328, 333,

Oxford

339, 341, 354, 517; xiii. 93; xiv. 283. See, also, Cardinal college

Christ Church library, iii. 48

Christ Church meadows, xii. 158

Clarendon laboratory, xiv. 270

Clarendon press, xi. 341; xii. 328, 337

Corpus Christi college, iii. 19, 406, 415; iv. 235, 408, 422, 428; v. 103; vi. 303, 398, 399; vii. 16, 201, 310; viii. 125, 277; x. 139

Divinity school, iii. 320

'Drone Hall,' ix. 414

Durham (Trinity) college, i. 215; ii. 349, 362

Exeter college, ii. 73, 355; iv. 157, 278; vi. 188; vii. 86, 307, 309; viii. 291; xii. 260, 333, 334; xiii. 118

Folly bridge (Grand Pont), i. 209

Ford lectures, xiv. 81

Gloucester hall, ii. 349, 354; vii. 24

Hertford college, ix. 411, 571

Indian institute, xii. 343

Isis, vi. 93, 326, 327

Jesus college, vii. 37, 198; viii. 331, also see Add.

Jewry, i. 202

Law school, xiv. 416

Lincoln college, ii. 358; vii. 245, 317; x. 364, 365, 378; xii. 333; xiv. 109

Magdalen college, ii. 355, 358; iii. 327, 333, 420, 422, 425, 430; iv. 154, 429; vi. 294; viii. 277, 461; ix. 43, 381, 411, 412, 414; x. 300, 472; xii. 158, 260, 278, 327, 460

Magdalen college school, iii. 428, 432

Magdalen hall (now Hertford college), iv. 132; vi. 282; xii. 343

Marian foundations at, iii. 420

Merton college, i. 213, 332; ii. 163, 346, 353 ff., 363; iii. 426; iv. 427; vi. 294, 295, 300, 318; vii. 328, 329, 335; viii. 63; ix. 381, 411, 573; x. 241; xii. 234

Modern history school at, xiv. 416

Morisonian herbarium, xiv. 562

Natural Science school at, xiv. 416

New college, ii. 354, 356, 357; iii. 5, 187, 421; iv. 161, 163, 407, 408, 427; vi. 294; vii. 233, 326, 329; x. 109, 139, 270

Oriel college, ii. 288, 355; iii. 56, 325 422; iv. 427; xii. 107, 255 ff., 271, 274, 284 ff., 290, 292, 295, 334, 337, 458, 459, 464; xiii. 87, 103; xiv. 196, 418

Peckwater quadrangle, xi. 322

Pembroke college, ix. 412; x. 149, 158, 159, 268, 271, 276, 463, 472; xii. 520

Queen's college, ii. 73, 74, 326, 355, 363; iv. 161, 428; vi. 303; viii. 142; ix. 170, 483; xi. 58

Radcliffe observatory, xiv. 385

Romanes lecture, xiv. 34

Ruskin college, xiv. 409

St Alban hall, vi. 141

St Ebbe's, i. 202

St Edmund's hall, viii. 83; ix. 397

Oxford
St Edward's church, I. 202
St Frideswide, I. 191, 193; IV. 428
St Frideswide, cloister school of, II. 34
St John's college, III. 420 ff.; IV. 428;
VI. 196, 316, 317, 318, 320, 326, *and
see* Add. 2; VII. 62, 334; XIV. 384
St Mary hall, VII. 49; IX. 139
St Mary's church, II. 348; IV. 430; XII.
257, 259, 266, 268
St Mary's college, III. 3
Sheldonian press, IX. 330
Sheldonian theatre, XI. 341
Short's coffee-house in Cat Street, VII.
364
Trinity college, III. 420 ff., V. 114, 138;
VII. 58, 150, 454; X. 238; XII. 133, 265
Union, the, XIII. 119
University college, II. 355; IV. 292; VIII.
353; IX. 129; X. 112
University press, IV. 410, 411; X. 223,
225; XI. 341, 469; XIII. 98. *See, also,*
Clarendon press
Wadham college, VIII. 206, 215, 277,
364; IX. 386, 393; X. 478; XII. 330, 334
Worcester college, II. 354; VII. 342,
347, 435, 438; X. 460
Oxford, countess of. *See* Harley
Oxford, earl of, in *Death of Robert*, V. 324
Oxford, earl of, company of, V. 316
Oxford, earls of. *See* Harley, Edward;
Harley, Robert; Vere, Aubrey de; Vere,
Edward de; Vere, John de
Oxford, Franciscans of, I. 183 ff., 200 ff.,
452 ff.; II. 349, 350; III. 48; IV. 419
Oxford, The Parliament dissolved at, VIII. 94
Oxford, The University of (Ackermann's),
XIV. 222
Oxford and Cambridge Magazine, The,
XIII. 112, 120, 121, 297, 358; XIV. 537
Oxford and Cambridge Miscellany Poems,
IX. 485
Oxford and Cambridge Monthly Miscellany.
See *Student, The*
Oxford college magazines, XIV. 539
*Oxford Critic and University Magazine,
The*, XIV. 209, 537
Oxford English Dictionary, The, XIV. 438,
454, 455
Oxford Essays, XII. 294
Oxford Gazette, IX. 1
Oxford historical society, XII. 355
Oxford historical society's *Collectanea*,
IX. 413
Oxford liberals, the, XII. 290, 292
Oxford Magazine, The, XIV. 208, 537
Oxford Magazine, Echoes from the, XIV. 208
Oxford movement, the, XII. 253 ff.,
453 ff., *also see* Add.; XIV. 82
Oxford printers, IV. 547
Oxford Professorships:
Camden professorship of history, IX.
329; XII. 317, 328
Professorship of Chinese, XII. 343
Professorship of comparative philology,
XII. 343

Oxford Professorships:
Professorship of ecclesiastical history,
XII. 321
Professorship of Latin, XII. 337
Professorship of poetry, XII. 260, 265
Professorship of Sanskrit, XII. 343
Rawlinson professorship of Anglo-
Saxon, XII. 344; XIV. 385
Regius professorship of Greek, XII. 328
Savilian professorships, VII. 288; IX. 386
Slade professorship of fine art, XIV. 152,
154, 155
Vinerian professorship of law, XI. 61
Oxford Sausage, The, X. 238
Oxford Spectator, The, XIV. 209, 537
Oxfordshire, VII. 96, 101, 150, 233; IX.
256, 258, 353; X. 385
'Oxonian Latin,' XIV. 410
Oxus, river, XIII. 92
Oxyrhynchus Logia, XII. 502
Ozell, John (d. 1743), IX. 418, 527; XI. 322
Ozoro, Esther, princess, XIV. 246

Pacata Hibernia, VII. 211, 436, 448
Pace, Richard (1482?-1590), III. 7, 49
Pacific ocean, the, IV. 68, 78, 86, 87; XIV.
241, 242, 244, 245, 358, 385
Pack, Major Richardson (1682-1728),
VIII. 428
Packington, Warwickshire, X. 113
Packington's Pound, VIII. 96
Pacolet, in *The Tatler*, IX. 35
Pacquet, A, of Advice from Rome, VIII. 412;
IX. 4
Padua, I. 213; III. 5, 7, 49, 423, 426, 431;
V. 62; VI. 24, 176; VII. 233; VIII. 354,
361; X. 200; XII. 63; XIII. 61
Page, Anne, in *The Merry Wives of Wind-
sor*, V. 189
Page, Gertrude, XIV. Add. 9
Page, John, II. 505
Page, William, XIII. 74
Page of Plymouth, V. 325
Paget, Francis Edward (1806-1882), XII.
277, 458, 461
Paget, Henry, son of 1st baron Paget, III.
183
Paget, John (1811-1898), *The New
'Examen,'* XIV. 65, 493
Paget, Nathan (1615-1679), VII. 107
Paget, Thomas, 3rd baron Paget (d. 1590),
III. 183
Paget, William, 1st baron Paget (1505-
1563), III. 183
Pagitt, Ephraim (1575?-1647), *Heresio-
graphy*, IX. 307
Pagnon, J., X. 485
Pagula, William de (d. 1350?), *Pupilla
Oculi*, II. 498
Pailthorpe, F. W., XIII. 540
Pain, Barry, XIV. 537
Paine, Thomas (*fl.* 1642-1650), VII. 352
Paine, Thomas (1737-1809), X. 59, 308
508; XI. 46 ff., 189, 395, 400; XII. 279,
471; XIV. 121, 608
Age of Reason, The, XI. 48

Paine, Thomas
  Common-Sense, XI. 47
  Crisis, The, XI. 47
  Rights of Man, The, XI. 47, 48, 276;
    XIV. 401
Painter, William (1540?–1594), *Palace of
  Pleasure, The*, III. 343, 490, 536; IV.
  6, 7, 442, 447; V. 72, 73, 220, 221, 244;
  VI. 46, 49, 123, 137 ff., 150, 180, 182;
  Rhoemo and Julietta, IV. 7
Paisley, IX. 566, 568; XI. 236, 237, 439,
  440, 442 ff., *also see* Add.
Paisley, Black Book of, II. 128
Paisley Advertiser, The, XI. 237
Paita, XIV. 243
Pakington, Dorothy, lady (d. 1679), VII. 427
Palace Beautiful, in Bunyan's *Pilgrim's
  Progress*, VII. 173
Palaeographical society, XII. 356
Palaestrio, in *Miles Gloriosus*, V. 106
Palamon, in *The Knight's Tale*, II. 243
  XIII. 123
Palamon, in *The Two Noble Kinsmen*,
  V. 256
Palamon and Arcite story, V. 256
Palamon and Arsett, V. 256
Palamon and Palaemon, I. 279, 286
Palaprat, VIII. 139
Pale, the English, in Ireland, II. 301, 303;
  XIV. 308
Paleario, Aonio, IV. 447
Palemon, in Thomson's *Autumn*, X. 104
Palermo, XIV. 73
Palermo, Michael Scot at, I. 199
Palestine, II. 79, 80, 123; IV. 68, *also see*
  Add.; XII. 320, 417, 478; XIV. 251, 253
Paley, Frederick Apthorp (1815–1888),
  XII. 331, 489
Paley, William (1743–1805), X. 344, 513;
  XI. 67, 73, 74; XII. 154, 279, 280, 419
  Horae Paulinae, X. 346, 347
  Natural Theology, X. 346, 347
  *Principles of Moral and Political Philo-
    sophy*, X. 346
  View of the Evidences of Christianity,
    X. 346, 347
Palgrave, Sir Francis (1788–1861), XIV.
  52, 68, 71, 72, 496
  *Essay on the Original Authority of the
    King's Council*, XIV. 67
  History of England, XIV. 67
  History of Normandy and of England,
    XIV. 67
  History of the Anglo-Saxons, XIV. 67
  *Rise and Progress of the English Com-
    monwealth*, XIV. 67
  *Truth and Fictions of the Middle Ages:
    the Merchant and the Friar*, XIV. 67
Palgrave, Francis Turner (1824–1897),
  VII. 180; XII. 115, 132, 372, 406; XIII.
  189, 192, 489, 507; *Golden Treasury,
  The*, XIII. 192; *Visions of England*, XIII.
  193
Palgrave, William Gifford (1826–1888),
  XIV. 553; *A year's journey through
  Central and Eastern Arabia*, XIV. 253

Palingenius, Marcellus, IV. 250, 447;
  Zodiacus Vitae, III. 185
Palinode, in *The Shepheards Calender*,
  III. 226
Pall Mall Gazette, in *Pendennis*, XIII. 292
Pall Mall Gazette, The, XIV. 189, 194, 195,
  530, 534
Palladian architecture, X. 110
Palladis Palatium, IV. 526
Palladius of Rome, IV. 371
Palladius on Husbondrie, II. 363, 502
Pallas, VII. 100; VIII. 76; IX. 115
Pallas, in *The Passetyme of Pleasure*, II.
  226, 231
Pallas, Ireland, X. 195
Pallas, lady, in *The Garlande of Laurell*,
  III. 70
'Pallas the favourite of Agrippina,' IX. 225
Pallasmore, Ireland, X. 195
Palliser, Plantagenet (Trollope's), XIII. 423
Pallmall, Mr, in Jerrold's *Prisoner of War*,
  XIII. 269
Palmer, Arthur (1841–1897), XII. 338, 490,
  494
Palmer, Edward Henry (1840–1882), XII.
  342, 499
Palmer, Edwin, XII. 337
Palmer, Frank, XIV. 536
Palmer, George (1648), VII. 514
Palmer, George Herbert (of Harvard),
  VII. 29, 30
Palmer, Henry Spencer (1838–1893), XII.
  514
Palmer, Herbert (1601–1647), VII. 426
Palmer, John (1742–1798), XI. 452, 454
Palmer, John (1742–1818), XIV. 168
Palmer, John (*fl.* 1826), XII. 341
Palmer, J. F., XIV. 561
Palmer, Mary (1716–1794), XI. 472
Palmer, Miss, niece of Sir Joshua Rey-
  nolds, XII. 132
Palmer, Roger, earl of Castlemaine (1634–
  1705), IV. 460
Palmer, Sir Roundell, 1st earl of Selborne
  (1812–1895), XII. 261; XIII. 507; XIV.
  124, 511
Palmer, Samuel (d. 1724), X. 386, 475;
  Vindication, X. 374
Palmer, Samuel (d. 1732), IX. 538, 571,
  572
Palmer, William (1803–1885), XII. 258, 461
Palmer, William (1811–1879), XII. 453,
  461
Palmer, William Scott (Dowson, M. E.),
  XIV. 515
Palmerin d'Olivia, IV. 9, 447
Palmerin cycles, III. 359
Palmerin of England, XI. 422; XIII. 35
Palmers, the, in Jane Austen's *Sense and
  Sensibility*, XII. 236
Palmerston, viscount. *See* Temple, Henry
  John
Palotta, cardinal, VII. 35
Palsgrave, John (d. 1554), III. 469; V. 109;
  Esclaircissement de la Langue Francoyse,
  III. 56, 555

Palsgrave's company, the, VI. 250
Paltock, Robert (1697–1767), X. 424
Pamela, in Richardson's novel, V. 245;
    X. 2, 4, 14, 15, 24
Pamela, in Sidney's *Arcadia*, III. 352, 354
Pamela's Conduct in High Life, X. 6
Pammelia, Musicks Miscellanie, IV. 536
Pampa, the, XIV. 249
Pamphilus, in *Arcadia*, VI. 192
Pamphilus, in *The Jealous Lovers*, VI. 325
Pamphleteer, The, XI. 398; XIV. 121, 125,
    512 ff.
Pamplona, VIII. 126
Pan, II. 226; VI. 368; VII. 370
Pan, in *The Penates*, VI. 341, 351
Panama, XIV. 243
Panape, in Drayton's *Eglogs*, IV. 173, 174
Pancake bell, the, in *The Shoemakers
    Holiday*, V. 357
Panchy, doctor, in Crowne's *City Poli-
    tiques*, VIII. 188
Pancks, in *Little Dorrit*, XIII. 331
Pandarus, II. 173, 175
Pandolphus, in *Perfidus Hetruscus*, VI. 302
Pandora, in Drayton's *Idea*, IV. 172
Pandora, in *The Rival Friends*, VI. 325
Pandulfus, cardinal, V. 65, 151
Pangloss, in Colman's *Heir at Law*, XI. 280
Panizzi, Sir Anthony (1797–1879), XII. 368
Pannartz, printer, II. 310
Panta river, or Blackwater, I. 41, 144
Pantagruel, II. 258; IX. 264, 267, 271
Pantagrueline Prognostication, IV. 534
Panther, The, I. 428
Pantisocracy, XI. 118, 119
Pantomimes, etc., X. 440
Pantomimus, V. 24
Panton, George A., II. 118, 450
Panurge, IX. 271, 272
Panurge, in *Pantagruel*, VIII. 66
Paoli, Pascal (1725–1807), X. 190, 477, 479
Paolo and Francesca, I. 270, 363
Papal Falsehood, in *The Faerie Queene*,
    III. 234
Papal States, XII. 36
Paper office, the, VIII. 158
Papilia, in Pope's *Characters of Women*,
    IX. 82
Papillon, F. W., *Memoirs of Thomas Pa-
    pillon*, IX. 240
Papillon, Thomas (1623–1702), IX. 240
Papineau, Louis Joseph (1786–1871), XIV.
    348
Parable of the Three Jackdaws, VIII. 99
Paracelsus (T. B. von Hohenheim, 1493–
    1541), III. 113; IV. 278; VII. 235, 378,
    396, 510; VIII. 354; IX. 315; XIII. 55 ff.
Paracelsus (Browning's), XIII. 55 ff.
Paradin, Claude, *The Heroicall Devices of*
    (1591), VII. 405
Paradise, II. 277
Paradyse of Daynty Devises, The, III. 179,
    512; IV. 113, 121
Parcae, the, in Alfred's *Boethius*, I. 100
Parcy Reed, I. 300
Pardoe, Julia S. H. (1806–1862), XIII. 565

Pardoner, in *Ane Pleasant Satyre*, III. 124,
    127
Pardoner (Chaucer's), VI. 160
Pardoner and Tapster, The, II. 162, 164,
    179
*Pardonneur, d'un triacleur et d'une ta-
    vernière, Farce nouvelle d'un*, V. 98
Paré, Ambrose, VII. 368, 505
Parganas, the, XIII. 276
Parian Chronicle, The, XII. 490
Paris, I. 152, 183 ff., 200; II. 71, 92, 96,
    125, 126, 198, 245, 251, 310, 315, 320,
    329, 341 ff., 350, 356, 360, 367, 370, 371,
    395; III. 2 ff., 44, 97, 151, 153, 155, 157,
    158, 167, 175, 208, 214, 418, 440; IV. 78,
    81, 82, 127, 255, 256, 270, 293, 366,
    368, 396, 402, 426, 429; V. 21, 25, 61,
    101, 293, 301 ff.; VI. 146, 238, 269, 271,
    390; VII. 22, 35, 45, 99, 183, 193, 205,
    215, 268, 284 ff., 288, 296, 308, 312,
    438, 484; VIII. 111, 133, 136, 137, 198,
    245, 246, 265, 282, 354, 371, 374, 379,
    385; IX. 139, 149 ff., 213, 318; X. 38,
    91, 118, 119, 213, 248, 250, 284, 303,
    304, 307, 323, 324, 335, 395; XI. 1, 59,
    60, 353, 354; XII. 103, 198, 365; XIII.
    5, 58, 71, 82, 142, 277, 283, 381, 421;
    XIV. 66, 173, 183, 185, 190, 196, 217,
    225, 235, 316, 328, 329, 342, 392
    Abbey of St Victor, I. 183; library, III.
        151
    Academy of, XI. 274
    Bastille, the, VIII. 160; X. 38, 251; XI.
        97, 189
    Bibliothèque Nationale, VII. 360
    British embassy, XIII. 278
    Cathedral school of Notre Dame, I. 183,
        200
    Cemetery of the Innocents, III. 87
    Collège Montaigu, II. 370; III. 2
    Collège de Navarre, IV. 276
    Collège Royal, III. 158
    Hill and church of Ste Geneviève, I.
        183, 184
    Hôtel de Carnavalet, X. 248
    Ile de la Cité, I. 183, 185
    Louvre, the, VII. 70; VIII. 9; XII. 166
    Opéra-Comique, XI. 258
    Palais Royal, VIII. 266
    Passy, XIII. 433
    Place Maubert, III. 7
    Quartier Latin, I. 185
    Rue St Jacques, XI. 331
    Rue Vaugirard, VIII. 134
    Scottish college, X. 295
    Sorbonne, the, I. 215; II. 251; III. 151
    Théâtre de la Foire, XI. 258
    Théâtre Français, V. 302
    University of, IV. 276; VIII. 59
Paris, in *The Araygnement of Paris*, V.
    131
Paris, in *The Roman Actor*, VI. 153, 155,
    157, 159, 163
Paris, count, in *Romeo and Juliet*, V. 182
Paris, English scholars of, I. 152, 177,
    183 ff., 233, 452 ff.

Paris, Gaston, I. 269, 283, 286, 290, 326; II. 398, 399, 417, 419

Paris, influence of, I. 149, 222

Paris, Matthew (d. 1259), I. 153, 160, 174, 178 ff., 179, 182, 183, 204, 214, 364, 450; II. 342, 488; III. 314; IV. 424; V. 38; XII. 515; *Historia Minor*, XII. 356, 517

Paris, Mrs, of Cambridge, XII. 200

Paris, peace of, X. 391; XI. 7

Paris, the judgment of, VI. 207

Paris, the judgment of, in *Reason and Sensuality*, II. 202

Paris and Vienne, II. 314, 315, 319, 332, 486

Parisian Greek press, XII. 522

Parisian salons, XI. 346, 351, 354, 364

Parisian scenery, XI. 258

Parisian stage, X. 79

Parisian typography, XII. 522

Park, Mungo (1771–1806), XIII. 467; XIV. 553

Park, Thomas (1759–1834), X. 452, 490

Parke, Gilbert, IX. 216

Parker, Charles Stuart, XIV. 505, 510, 606

Parker, Eric, XIV. 597

Parker, Gilbert, *Manifest Detection of Dice-Play*, III. 491; IV. 318

Parker, Henry (d. 1470), *Dives and Pauper*, II. 321, 323

Parker, Henry, 8th lord Morley (1476–1556), IV. 447

Parker, Henry (1604–1652), III. 114; IV. 310, 512

Parker, Henry Meredith (1796?–1868), XIV. 579; *Bole Ponjis*, XIV. 337; *The Draught of Immortality*, XIV. 336

Parker, Irene, *Dissenting Academies in England*, XIV. 51

Parker, John (*fl.* 1387), II. 61

Parker, John Henry (1806–1884), XII. 498

Parker, Martin (d. 1656?), II. 416; VII. 497, 499
   Ballads, IV. 363
   Mercurius Melancholicus, VII. 356
   Robin Conscience, III. 491
   When the King shall Enjoy his Own Again, VII. 352

Parker, Matthew (1504–1575), archbishop of Canterbury, I. 89, 90; III. 45, 46, 55, 470, 531; IV. 55, 397, 406, 423, 424, 426, 432, 545; V. 362, 482; VI. 397, 475; VII. 331; IX. 355, 357, 496; XIV. 486; *De Antiquitate Britannicae ecclesiae*, IV. 405

Parker, Sir Peter (1785–1814), XII. 389

Parker, Richard (1572–1629), IX. 538

Parker, Samuel (1640–1688), VII. 179, 184, 185, 303, 474; VIII. 98, 460; *Discourse of Ecclesiastical Polity*, VIII. 305, 475

Parker, Thomas, 1st earl of Macclesfield (1666?–1732), IX. 14, 16

Parker, William, 4th baron Monteagle (1575–1622), VII. 45

Parker society, VII. 306; XII. 355

Parkes, Bessie Rayner, XIV. 600

Parkes, Sir Henry (1815–1896), XIV. 364, 587; *Murmurs of the stream*, XIV. 362

Parkes, Joseph, *Memoirs of Sir Philip Francis*, X. 400, 401; XIV. 495

Parkes, William (*fl.* 1612), V. 479

Parkin, Charles (1689–1765), IX. 532

Parkin, Sir George Robert, XIV. 602

Parkinson, Anthony (1667–1728), IX. 538

Parkinson, John (1567–1650), IV. 542; XIII. 223; *Paradisi in sole Paradisus terrestris*, IV. 375; *Theatrum botanicum*, IV. 375

Parkyns, Sir William (1649?–1696), VIII. 163

Parlament of Byrdes, The, II. 501

Parlement of the Thre Ages, I. 333, 334; II. 37, 432, 434

Parley, Peter, *pseud.*, used by several writers, XI. 387, 481, 482

Parliament, the Good, II. 54

Parliament, use of English in, II. 70, 446

Parliament of Devils, The, II. 325, 502

Parliamentary Debates, XI. 49

Parliaments Letanie, The, VII. 383

Parma, XIII. 60

Parma, duke of, in *The Humorous Courtier*, VI. 205

Parmegiano, Il, X. 130

Parmeno, in *Celestina*, V. 99

Parmentier, F. J. A., XIII. 544

Parnaso Italiano, XIII. 224

Parnassus, III. 260; VI. 36, 310, 388; VII. 59; VIII. 372; IX. 102, 257; XIII. 210

Parnassus Biceps (1656), VII. 512

Parnassus trilogy, VI. 309 ff., 314, 315, 320, 327, 484; *The Pilgrimage*, VI. 310; *The Returne*, III. 270; IV. 139, 410, 533; V. 171, 221, 364; VI. 2, 39, 44, 309 ff., 322; *The Returne, Part II* (*Scourge of Simony*), VI. 313

Parnell, Charles Stewart (1846–1891), IX. 166; XIV. 183

Parnell, Henry Brooke, 1st lord Congleton (1776–1842), XIV. 513

Parnell, James (1637?–1656), VIII. 101, 416

Parnell, Thomas (1679–1718), VII. 198; IX. 75, 78, 131, 137, 166 ff. (main entry), 171, 444, 481, *also see* Add.; X. 482
   Elegy to an old Beauty, IX. 167
   Flies, The, IX. 167
   Hermit, The, IX. 167
   Homer's Battle of the Frogs and Mice, IX. 168
   Hymn to Contentment, IX. 167
   'Life, Writings and Learnings of Homer,' IX. 167, 168
   Nightpiece on Death, IX. 167
   Poem on Queen Anne's Peace, IX. 166
   Poems on Several Occasions, IX. 77, 167

Parolles, in *All's Well that Ends Well*, V. 180; VI. 103

Parr, Samuel (1747–1825), IX. 526; X. 479; XI. 394; XII. 325 ff., 363, 490, 523; XIV. 602; *Memoirs*, XII. 325

Parrot or Perrot, Henry (*fl.* 1600–1626), III. 114; IV. 519, 522
Parrot, the, in *Speke, Parrot,* III. 76
Parry, John (d. 1782), x. 130
Parry, William (d. 1585), v. 345; in *If you know not me,* VI. 91
Parry, William (*fl.* 1823–1825), XII. 384, 397
Parry, Sir William Edward (1790–1855), XIV. 245, 553
Parsimonia, in *Psychomachia,* v. 60
Parson Hyberdyne's Sermon in praise of Thieves, III. 492
'Parson Lot' (Charles Kingsley), XII. 291
Parson of Kalenborowe, The (Der Pfarrer von Kalenberg), III. 82, 94, 488, 490
Parsons, in *Westward Ho!* XIII. 364
Parsons, Philip (1594–1653), VI. 475
Parsons or Persons, Robert (1546–1610), IV. 127, 306, 411, 495, 512; *Christian Directory,* IV. 237; *Christian Exercise,* IV. 410; *Conference about the Next Succession,* attributed to, VII. 352
Parsons, Robert (1647–1714), VIII. 213, 446
Parsons, Samuel (*fl.* 1732–1735), x. 384
Partenay, Romans of, I. 470
Parterick, Robertus, *alias* Robertus Langelye, II. 35
Parthenia, VI. 317, 485
Parthenopaeus, I. 286
Parthenopex de Blois, I. 286
Parthia, XII. 478
Particular Baptist fund, x. 387
Partington, Charles Frederick (d. 1857?), *The British Cyclopaedia,* XIV. 174
Partition treaty, IX. 112, 215
Partonope, I. 286, 470
Partridge, in Fielding's *Tom Jones,* IX. 405; x. 31, 39
Partridge, John (*fl.* 1566–1573), IV. 449
Partridge, John (1644–1715), IX. 94, 454, 461
Partridge, The, I. 428
Parzival, I. 269, 271, 280, 462. See, also, Wolfram von Eschenbach
Pascal, Blaise, III. 416; VII. 152; XII. 272; XIV. 483; *Lettres Provinciales,* VIII. 372; *The Mysterie of Semitism,* a translation of Pascal's *Lettres Provinciales,* VIII. 372; *Pensées,* VIII. 270, 373
Paschale, Lodovico, III. 262, 359
Paschasius Radbertus, I. 124
Pascoe, Charles Eyre, XIII. 544
Pascolato, M. P., XIII. 466
Pasiphaë, VI. 163
Pasor, Matthias (1599–1658), VII. 309
Pasqualigo, Luigi, *Il Fedele,* VI. 304, 472
Pasquier, *Les Recherches de la France,* VI. 35
Pasquill, III. 394, 395, 544
Pasquill, Pasquine of England, III. 394. *See, also, under* Marprelate
Pasquils Jests, IV. 532
Pasquils Palmodia, IV. 534

Pasquin, x. Add.
'Pasquin Pillar,' a, IV. 123
Passarowitz, peace of, IX. 244
Passe, C. de, IV. 542
Passerat, Jean, IV. 264; *Nihil,* VIII. 213
Passio Domini, v. 15, 16
Passion, Confrérie de la, v. 22
Passion of Christ, The. See Christ
Passion of the Fox, The, III. 482, 483
Passion of our Lord, The, I. 225, 226, 458
Passionate Morrice, The, IV. 526
Passionate Pilgrim, The, III. 266; IV. 119, 395
Passions of Martyrs, I. 75
Pastime of People, The, II. 328
Paston, Agnes, II. 305, 306
Paston, Anne, II. 308
Paston, Clement, II. 305
Paston, Edmund, II. 306
Paston, Elizabeth, II. 306
'Paston, George' (*i.e.* Emily Morse Symonds), XI. 429, 443, 457, 468; XII. 431, 451; XIV. 519, 520, 541; *Lady Mary Wortley Montagu,* IX. 244
Paston, John (1421–1466), II. 304 ff.
Paston, Sir John (1442–1479), II. 304 ff.
Paston, J., XIV. 541
Paston, Margaret, II. 304 ff.
Paston, Walter, II. 308
Paston, William (1378–1444), II. 304, 308, 359
Paston family, the, II. 304
Paston Letters, The, II. 286, 303, 429; v. 35; VII. 196; XIV. 82
Pastor Fidus, VI. 317, 485
Pastorals, VI. 487 ff.
Patenostre à l'Userier, La, III. 90, 487
Patent Rolls, the, VI. 280; XII. 355, 516
Pater, Walter Horatio (1839–1894), VII. 260, *also see* Add.; XI. 410, 417; XII. 271, 277, 438; XIII. 491; XIV. 462, 522, 523
Appreciations, XIV. 158
Child in the House, The, XIV. 159
Imaginary Portraits, XIV. 158
Marius the Epicurean, XIV. 158
Plato and Platonism, XIV. 158
Studies in the History of the Renaissance, IX. 39; XIV. 158
Winckelmann, XIV. 158
Paterculus, Gaius Velleius, XII. 337
Patericke, Simon (d. 1613), IV. 8, 444
Paternoster, I. 220, 375, 376, 458
Paternoster, in *The Exeter Book,* I. 428
Paternoster, Kentish versions of the, I. 355
Pater Noster play, v. 51, 52
'Paternoster Row numbers,' XI. 325
Paterson, Alexander, XIV. 532
Paterson, Alice, XIV. 601
Paterson, Daniel (1739–1825), XIII. 223
Paterson, James (1805–1876), XI. 441; XIV. 536
Paterson, Ninian (*fl.* 1688), IX. 556; *Epigrammaton libri octo,* IV. 267
Paterson, Samuel (1728–1803), XI. 336; XII. 363, 523
Paterson, William (1755–1810), XIV. 553

Pathelin, Maître, II. 96; v. 19, 92, 101
Pathomachia or The Battell of Affections,
VI. 323, 485
Patience, I. 320 ff., 333, 334, 472
Patience, in *Piers the Plowman,* II. 26 ff.
Patience, in *Tom Tyler,* v. 117
Patientia, in *Psychomachia,* v. 51
Patin, Guy, VII. 235
Patmore, Coventry Kersey Dighton (1823–
1896), XII. 275, 421; XIII. 110, 189 ff.,
208, 507; XIV. 238
    Angel in the House, The, XIII. 190, 191,
218, 247
    Odes, XIII. 218
    Unknown Eros, The, XIII. 190, 191
    Victories of Love, The, XIII. 190, 191
Patmore, Peter George (1786–1855), XII.
433; XIV. 523
Paton, George (1721–1807), x. 490
Paton, Waller Hugh (1828–1895), XI. 437
Paton, William Roger (1856–1921), XII.
Add. 4
Patras, gulf of, XII. 38
Patrician, The, IX. 442
Patricius (Howell's), VII. 458
Patrick, St (373–463), I. 65, 68, 70, 339,
435; XII. 519; *Colloquy of St Patrick
with Oisin, The,* XIV. 303
Patrick, Simon (1626–1707), VIII. 288,
292, 298, 301, 456, 457, 461
Patrick, Swift's servant, IX. 126
Patrick, Sir William Francis, XIV. 495,
496
Patrizzi, Francesco, III. 434, 438; v. 234
Patrum, Vitae Sanctorum, II. 323. *See,
also,* Fathers
Patten, Robert (*fl.* 1717), IX. 565
Patten, William (*fl.* 1548–1580), III. 531
Patterne, Sir Willoughby (George Mere-
dith's), XIII. 444 ff.
Pattison, Mark (1813–1884), VII. 101, 109,
114, 123, 127, 238, 310, 324; VIII. 352;
XII. 254, 255, 292, 334, 460, 466, 469,
also see Add. 1; XIV. 113, 432, 505, 594,
596, 602
    Essays, XIV. 109
    Essays and Reviews, IX. 280
    Isaac Casaubon, XII. 333; XIV. 109
    Memoirs, XIV. 109
    Milton, XIV. 109
    Scaliger, XII. 333
    Suggestions on academical organisation,
XIV. 431
    'The Tendencies of Religious Thought,'
XII. 295
Paues, Anna C., II. 59, 65
Paul, in Udall's *Diotrephes,* III. 378
Paul, father. *See* Sarpi
Paul, Lanfranc's kinsman, I. 153
Paul, Hamilton (1773–1854), XI. 436
Paul, Harry Gilbert, *John Dennis,* IX. 142
Paul, Herbert Woodfield, XIII. 478, 488,
503, 558, 568; XIV. 484, 487, 488, 493,
525; *Life of Froude,* XIII. 358
Paul, W. J., XIV. 573
Paul IV, III 401

Paul, St, I. 72, 74, 115, 227; II. 129, 201,
227, 231, 234; III. 6, 10, 127, 415; IV.
224, 270; v. 50, 59; VI. 102; VII. 168;
VIII. 291; IX. 28; XII. 285, 293, 477
Paul, St, tractate on the *Epistles* of, II. 365
Paul, St, Revelation or *Vision of,* I. 75, 86,
118, 227, 459, 460
Paulet, Sir Amyas (d. 1538), IV. 278
Pauli, Reinhold, I. 91, 102
Paulina, in Charlotte Brontë's *Villette,*
XIII. 409
Paulina, in *Confessio Amantis,* II. 151
Paulina, in Markham's *Famous Whore,*
IV. 376
Paulina, in *The Renegado,* VI. 155
Paulina, in *The Winter's Tale,* III. 356;
v. 206
Pauline (Browning's), XIII. 53, 57
Pauline epistles, the, XII. 298
Paulinus, I. 75, 81
Paulinus of Périgueux, I. 76
Paulus Diaconus, I. 35; II. 364; VII. 503
Paulus Quaestor, I. 76
Pauper, in *Ane Pleasant Satyre,* III. 124,
126, 127, 128
Pausanias, III. 328; XII. 491
Pavia, IV. 429
Pavier, Thomas (*fl.* 1600–1608), IV. 394
Pavillard, Calvinist minister, x. 301
Pavillon, Nicholas, bishop of Aleth, VIII.
308
Pavy, duke of, in *Loves Sacrifice,* VI. 192
Pavy, Salathiel, VI. 9, 291
'Pavyllyon un [on] the Plas Parlos, the,'
VI. 283
Pawson (tutor of John Hall), VII. 85
Pax, in the *Coventry Plays,* v. 21
Payn, James (1830–1898), XII. 426, 445,
451; XIII. 438, 565
Payne, Edward John (1844–1904), XI.
388; XIV. 496; *A History of the New
World called America,* XIV. 98
Payne, G. A., XIII. 551
Payne, Henry, brother of Thos. Payne
(1719–1779), XI. 333
Payne, John (d. 1787), x. 385, 469
Payne, Joseph (1808–1876), XIV. 608
Payne, Joseph Frank (1840–1910), XIV.
563
Payne, Roger (1739–1797), XI. 468
Payne, Thomas (*fl. c.* 1700), x. 385
Payne, Thomas (1719–1799), XI. 333 ff.,
337, 468
Paynell, Thomas (*fl.* 1528–1568), III. 341;
IV. 4, 439, 443, 445, 446, 447, 448
Pazzarello, in *The Young Admirall,* VI. 204
Peace, in Anglo-Norman plays, v. 21
Peace, in *The Castle of Perseverance,* v. 52
Peace, in *The Example of Virtue,* II. 228
Peace, in *The Passetyme of Pleasure,* II. 228
Peace, in *Piers the Plowman,* II. 10
Peace, Temple of, in *The Vision of the
Twelve Goddesses,* VI. 337
Peacham, Henry (1576?–1643?), III. 114,
432; IV. 355, 520, 526, 533; v. 479;
Compleat Gentleman, The, IV. 328, 543;

Peacham, Henry
VII. 263; IX. 396, 570; *Garden of Elo-
quence*, III. 432, 553; *Minerva Britannia*,
VII. 406, 479, *also see* Add.
Peacham, Henry (the elder), IV. 355, 525
Peachum, in Gay's *Beggar's Opera*, IX. 163
Peacock, George (1791–1858), VIII. 361
XIV. 258, 555, 595
Peacock, Nathaniel, in Smollett's *History
of an Atom*, X. 42
Peacock, Thomas Love (1785–1866), I.
275; IV. 137; IX. 183; XI. 285, 286,
307 ff. (main entry), 462, 489, *also see*
Add.; XII. 60, 63, 255, 401, 404, 405,
412; XIII. 440, 442
Crotchet Castle, XI. 308
Four Ages of Poetry, The, XII. 74
Gryll Grange, XI. 285, 307, 308, 310
Headlong Hall, XI. 183, 308
Maid Marian, XI. 308
Melincourt, XI. 308, 309
Misfortunes of Elphin, The, I. 252; XI.
308, 309
Nightmare Abbey, XI. 308, 310
Peak, Godwin, in Gissing's *Born in Exile*,
XIII. 459
Peak, the, Derbyshire, III. 322; X. 131
Peake, R., III. 553
Peaks, passes and glaciers, XIV. 254
Pearce, E. H., XIV. 597
Pearce, Zachary (1690–1774), IX. 527;
X. 470
Pearch, George (*fl.* 1770–1775), IX. 190;
X. 138, 465
Pearl, I. 148, 296, 320 ff., 326, 329, 332,
333, 378, 472; II. 18, 133
Pearson, Charles Henry (1830–1894), II.
35; XI. 456; XIV. 496
Pearson, John (1613–1686), VII. 152, 481;
VIII. 461; X. 357; *Exposition of the
Creed*, VII. 323, 485; VIII. 297, 300; IX.
329; *Vindiciae Epistolarum S. Ignatii*,
IX. 329
Pearson, Karl, VII. 367; XIV. 470, 556, 560
Peasants' revolt, I. 371; II. 47, 53, 63,
136, 143, 144; III. 18
Peasenhall, X. 378
Peblis to the Play, II. 244, 250, 270, 274,
471, 473; III. 130; XI. 215
Pebody, Charles, XIV. 532
Peck, Francis (1692–1743), IX. 538
Peckard, G. P., VII. 154
Pecke, Samuel (*fl.* 1641–1655), VII. 347,
348, 497
*A Continuation of Certain Speciall and
Remarkable Passages*, VII. 347
Diurnall Occurrences, VII. 347
Mercurius Candidus, VII. 347
Perfect Diurnall, A, VII. 347, 354, 360
Pecke, Thomas (*fl.* 1655–1664), III. 470;
IV. 503; VII. 355, 360, 361
Peckham, X. 201, 203
Peckham, John, archbishop of Canterbury
(d. 1292), I. 210, 455
Peckover, Clem, in Gissing's *The Nether
World*, XIII. 458

Pecksniff, Mercy, in *Martin Chuzzlewit*,
XIII. 322
Pecksniffs, the, in *Martin Chuzzlewit*, XIII.
323
Pecksy, in Mrs Trimmer's *Robins*, XI. 379
Pecock, Reginald (1395?–1460?), bishop
of Chichester, I. 286 ff., 296, 299, 301,
307, 471, 473, 480; IV. 226; XII. 134
Abbreviatio R. Pecock, II. 288
Book of Faith, The, II. 293
Donet, The, II. 294
Filling of the Four Tables, The, II. 291
Poor Men's Mirror, The, II. 294
*Repressor of overmuch blaming of the
clergy*, II. 288, 289, 293, 294, 296; XII.
480
Pecunia, in *The Staple of Newes*, VI. 25
Pedante, in *Fedele and Fortunio*, V. 315
Pedantius, IV. 326; VI. 306, 327, 480
Pedantius, in Ascham's *Scholemaster*,
III. 434
Peden, Alexander (1626?–1686), IX. 549
Pedersen, Christiern, II. 285
Pedlar, in Wordsworth's *Excursion*, XI.
106
Pedringano, in *The Spanish Tragedie*,
V. 163
Pedro, Don, king of Spain, in *The King
and the Subject*, VI. 147
Peebles, II. 277
Peebles, Peter, in Scott's *Redgauntlet*, XII.
25
Peeke or Pike, Richard (*fl.* 1620–1626),
VII. 453
Peel, Arthur W., XIV. 505
Peel, George, XIV. 505
Peel, Sir Robert (1788–1850), XI. 154,
415; XII. 154; XIII. 16, 24, 347, 348,
350, 353; XIV. 115, 127, 128 ff. (main
entry), 134, 181, 186, 227, 412, 505, 510,
571
Peele, George (1558?–1597?), III. 300;
IV. 113 ff., 117, 121, 471, 473, 532;
V. 85, 121–141 (main entry), 147, 182,
239, 255, 322, 327, 370, 416 ff., *also see*
Add.; VI. 13, 249, 300, 303, 366; VII.
111; VIII. 223
Arraignment of Paris, The, IV. 118;
V. 128, 129; VI. 287, 337, 363, 365
Battell of Alcazar, The, V. 129, 239
Complaint of Oenone, XI. 179
Discursus Astraeae, V. 131
Edward I, V. 35, 129, 152, 153
'His golden locks time hath to silver
turned,' IV. 113
Hunting of Cupid, The, IV. 118; V. 129
King David and Fair Bethsabe, V. 129,
131
Merrie Conceited Jests of George Peele,
IV. 360; V. 132, 255
Old Wives Tale, The, V. 129 ff.; VII. 113
Turkish Mahomet, The, V. 129; X. 161
'Whenas the rye did reach to the chin,'
V. 131
See, also, under *Sir Clyomon*
Peelites, XIV. 130, 187, 190, 198

Peers, Richard (1645–1690), IX. 345, 346

Peerson, Martin (1590?–1651?), IV. 465

Peet, W. Hubert, XI. 466; XIV. 531

Peg, in Arbuthnot's *History of John Bull*, IX. 135

Pegasus, XI. 166; XII. 101, 104

Pegge, Samuel (1704–1796), *Life of Grosseteste*, I. 204, 454

Peile, John (1838–1910), XII. 490

Peile, Thomas Williamson (1806–1882), XII. 490

Peirce, James (1674?–1726), X. 379

Peiresc, Nicolas Claude Fabri de, IV. 253, 257

Pekin, XIV. 248

Pelagius (*fl.* 400–418), I. 65

Pèlerinage de l'homme, Le, II. 327

Pèlerinaiges por aler en Iherusalem (*c.* 1231), II. 80

Pelham, Henry (1695?–1754), IX. 230, 243, 250; X. 388

Pelham, Henry (lord Lytton's), XIII. 417, 418

Pelham, Henry Francis (1846–1907), XII. 477; *History of the Roman Empire*, XII. 317; *Outlines of Roman History*, XII. 317

Pelham-Holles, Thomas, 1st duke of Newcastle (1693–1768), IV. 369; IX. 166; X. 35, 256, 388, 390

Pell, John (1611–1685), VII. 314

Pellegrini, M., *Fonti dell' Ingegno*, VII. 269

Pellew, George (1793–1866), XIV. 506

Pellico, Silvio, XII. 390

Pember, Robert (d. 1560), III. 432

Pemberton, Henry (1694–1771), VIII. 230; XI. 250

Pemberton, T. Edgar, XIII. 515, 544

Pembroke, countess of. *See* Herbert, Mary

Pembroke, earl of, in *John a Kent*, etc., V. 317

Pembroke, earls of. *See* Herbert, George Robert Charles; Herbert, Henry; Herbert, Philip; Herbert, William

Pembroke family, the, VI. 6, 143

Pembrokeshire, XII. 509

Penaunce, in *The Faerie Queene*, VI. 336

Pencrich, Richard, II. 70, 504

Pendarves, Mrs. *See* Delany, Mrs

Pendennis, Arthur (Thackeray's), XIII. 276, 290, 291, 293, 295, 297, 299

Pendennis, Helen (Thackeray's), XIII. 290, 291

Pendennis, major (Thackeray's), XIII. 291

Pendleton, John, XIV. 532

Pendragon, IX. 502

Penelope. *See* Rich, Penelope

Penelope, in *Confessio Amantis*, II. 152

Penelope, in *Gismond of Salerne*, V. 73

Penelope, in *Orchestra*, IV. 162

Penelope, in *Ulysses Redux*, VI. 303

Penelope to Ulysses, letter of, III. 181

Pengry, Moses, *Cooper's Hill latina redditum* (1676), VII. 487

Peniarth library, Welsh MS. in, I. 252

Penington, Isaac (1616–1679), VIII. 105, 106, 108, 109, 415, 416

Penington, Mary, wife of Isaac Penington, VIII. 109, 416

Peninsular war, the, XIV. 107, 122, 250, 459

Penitence, in *The Example of Virtue*, II. 227

Penitent Traytor, The, VII. 386

Penitentials, I. 87

Penlez, Bosavern, X. 33

Penn or Pen, Sir William (1621–1670), VIII. 107, 218

Penn, William (1644–1718), VIII. 105, 107, 111 ff., 268, 413, 414, 456; IX. 9, 406, 546; X. 377; XIV. 65, 509

  Address to Protestants, VIII. 108

  Christian Quaker, The, VIII. 111

  Innocency with her Open Face, VIII. 111

  More Fruits of Solitude, VIII. 113

  No Cross No Crown, VIII. 107

  Sandy Foundation Shaken, The, VIII. 107, 111

  Some Fruits of Solitude, VIII. 107, 112

Pennant, Thomas (1726–1798), X. 270; XII. Add. 5; XIV. 246, 553; *British Zoology*, X. 269; *Tour in Scotland*, X. 182

Penne, George, XIV. 65

Pennecuick, Dr Alexander (1652–1722), *Description of Tweeddale*, IX. 370

Pennecuick, Alexander (d. 1730), IX. 370, 567

  Britannia Triumphans, IX. 370

  Elegy on Robert Forbes, IX. 370

  Flowers from Parnassus, IX. 370

  Merry Wives of Musselburgh, IX. 370

  Presbyterian Pope, IX. 370

  Rome's Legacy, IX. 370

  Streams from Helicon, IX. 370

  Truth's Travels, XI. 217

Pennell, Henry Cholmondeley (1837–1915), XIV. 545

Pennenden heath, XIV. 128

Pennethorne, John (1808–1888), XII. 340

Penniless Parliament of Threadbare Poets, The, IV. 345

Penniman, Josiah Harmar, VI. 4, 17, 23

Pennington, Montagu (1762–1849), *Memoirs of the Life of Mrs Elizabeth Carter*, X. 473; XI. 356, 473

Pennington, Sarah, lady, XIV. 600

Penniworth of Wit, II. 501

Pennsylvania, IV. 95; VIII. 107; XI. 47; XIV. 263, 350

Pennsylvania Magazine, XI. 47

Penny Cyclopaedia, The, XII. 487; XIV. 259, 409

'Penny Godlinesses,' XI. 334

Penny Illustrated Paper, The, XIV. 534

Penny Magazine, The, XIV. 409

'Penny Merriments,' XI. 334

Pennyboy, in *The Staple of Newes*, VI. 25

Penrith, H. 116; XI. 95, 414, 486; XII. 188

Penroodocke, Maister, V. 77

Penrose, Francis Cranmer (1817–1903), XII. 498; *Principles of Athenian Architecture*, XII. 340

Penry, John (1559–1593), III. 377 ff., 385, 390, 397
  Aequity of an humble supplication, The, III. 377, 378, 538
  An Exhortation, III. 378, *also see* Add.
  A Supplication to the Parliament, III. 381
  Defence of that which hath been written, III. Add.
  Th'Appelation of John Penri, III. 381, 383
Penshurst, III. 351; VII. 54, 55; X. 500
Penthea, in *The Broken Heart,* VI. 191
Penthesilea, in *The Masque of Queens,* VI. 349
Penton, Stephen (1639–1706), IX. 405, 570; *Guardian's Instruction,* IX. 397; *New Instructions,* IX. 397
People, in *Res publica,* v. 60
People's Friend, The, XIII. 359
'People's Poet Laureate, The,' XIII. 150
Pepeling (Calais), III. 328
Pepwell, Henry (d. 1540), books printed by, II. 327
Pepys, John, father of Samuel, VIII. 253
Pepys, Sir Lucas (1742–1830), XI. 365
Pepys, Mrs, VIII. 256, 260
Pepys, Paulina, Samuel's sister, VIII. 259
Pepys, Samuel (1633–1703), II. 207; III. 97; IV. 460; v. 222; VI. 262; VII. 141, 214, 228, 362, 364; VIII. 22, 81, 107, 120, 124, 131, 136, 199, 200, 206, 215, 216, 218, 241 ff., 252 ff. (main entry), 262, 263, 301, 302, 320, 350, 355, 356, 358, 369, 385, 398, 399, 422, 424, 450; IX. 129, 244, 274, 275; XI. 319, 334; XIV. 283; *Diary,* VII. 184; VIII. 15; *Memoires of the Navy,* VIII. 258, 259
Pepys, Sir William Weller (1758–1825), XI. 363, 365, 473
Pepys Cockerell family, descendants of Samuel Pepys, VIII. 260
Pera, IX. 245
Peraldus, William, I. 355
Perceval, Arthur Philip (1799–1853), XII. 258, 453, 461
Perceval le Gallois, I. 271, 462, 471
Percies, the, in *Henry IV,* v. 187
Percius and Anthomiris (Perseus and Andromeda), v. 102
Percival, Sir John, IX. Add.
Percival, Thomas (1740–1804), XI. 489
Percy, in Hannah More's play, XI. 274
Percy, lady Elizabeth, afterwards duchess of Somerset (1667–1722), VIII. 380
Percy, Sir Henry, 1st earl of Northumberland (1342–1408), II. 55
Percy, Sir Henry, 6th earl of Northumberland (1502?–1537), III. 336, 337, 427; IV. 2
Percy, Sir Henry, 9th earl of Northumberland (1564–1632), VII. 435
Percy, Sir Hugh, 1st duke of Northumberland, of the third creation (1715–1786), X. 457

Percy, Thomas (1729–1811), bishop of Dromore, II. 494; X. 155, 170, 195, 201, 204, 215, 220, 273, 470, 480, 489, 496, *also see* Add.; XI. 333, 449
  Complaint of Harold, X. 224
  Dying Ode of Ragnar Lodbrog, X. 223
  Five pieces of Runic Poetry, X. 222, 223, 225, 229; XIV. 51
  Funeral Song of Hacon, X. 224
  Incantation of Hervor, X. 223, 224, 229
  Ransome of Egill, X. 224
  Reliques of Ancient Poetry, II. 408, 410, 413, 494; IX. 188; X. 137, 202, 217, 225, 226, 232 ff.; XI. 360; XII. 4, 6, 133, 354; XIII. 225, 226
Percy, Thomas (1768–1808), X. 472, 489
Percy, William (1575–1648), III. 256, 264, 266; *Sonnets to the fairest Coelia,* III. 256, 266, 523
Percy anecdotes, the, XI. 472
Percy ballad, II. 398
Percy Folio MS., II. 40, 401, 408, 410, 414, 416, 428
Percy Memoir, X. 209
Percy papers, II. 409
Percy society, II. 199, 502; XII. 353, 355, 368, 369
Percyvelle, Sir (Perceval, Percevall, Percival), I. 267, 269, 271, 272, 284, 289, 294, 462. See, also, *Parzival*
Perdita, in *The Winter's Tale,* v. 34, 206, 217; XII. 87
Peredur, son of Evrawc, I. 253, 271
Peregrin (Howell's), VII. 458
Peregrinatio Religionis ergo, III. 12
'Peregrine of Odcombe,' X. 200
Perenna (Herrick's), VII. 6
Peres the Ploughmans Crede, II. 38, 39, 432, 434
Perfect, lady, in *Amends for Ladies,* VI. 223
Perfect Occurrences, VII. 354
Perfidious Britain, IX. 375
Perfidus Hetruscus, VI. 302, 486
Periander, VI. 474
Periander, tyrant of Corinth, VI. 321
Pericles, III. 313
Pericles of Tyre, I. 135
Perin, VII. 316
Perin, Ales, in Stow's *Chronicle,* III. 314
Perindus, in *Sicelides,* VI. 323
Perkin, Sir William Henry, XIV. 558
Perkins, Jane G., XIII. 507
Perkins, John (d. 1545), *Profitable Book,* VIII. 315, 467
Perkins, Peter, *The Seaman's Tutor,* IV. 460
Perkins, Richard (*fl.* 1612), VI. 401
Perkins, William (1558–1602), IV. 235, 433, 494; VII. 373, 394, 395, 474; VIII. 277
  Armilla aurea, and translation *A Golden Chaine,* VII. 280
  Art of Prophesying, IV. 226, 491
  Discovery of the damned Art of Witchcraft, IV. 535; VII. 372, 506
  Whole Treatise of the Cases of Conscience, VII. 280

Perkins folio of Shakespeare, v. 278
Perkyn, John (*fl.* 1574), vi. 246
Perl mewn adfyd, iv. 411
Perlin, Étienne, iii. 478
Permo-Triassic strata, xiv. 292
Perne, Andrew (1519?–1589), iv. 141, 423, 432
Pernel Proudheart, in *Piers the Plowman*, ii. 12, 16
Pernet qui va au vin, Farce de, v. 98
Pérouse, J. F. G. de la (1741–1788), xiv. 553
Perowne, Thomas Thomason, xiv. 486
Perrault, Charles, viii. 163; ix. 390, 572; x. 220; xi. 380, 477, 485, 492; *Histoires ou Contes du Tems Passé*, xi. 374, 375; *Le Siècle de Louis le Grand*, ix. 391; *Parallèle des Anciens et des Modernes*, ix. 391
Perrin, Pierre, viii. 135; *Ariadne* (with Grabut), viii. 134
Perronet, Vincent (1693–1785), viii. 347, 475
Perrot, Thomas (*fl.* 1720–1733), x. 386
Perry, James (1756–1821), xii. 323; xiv. 170, 178, 184, 186, 187
Perry, John Tavenor, xii. 512
Perseus, xiii. 354
Perseus, in *Confessio Amantis*, ii. 147, 148
Perseus, in *The Masque of Queens*, vi. 349
Perseverance, in *The Example of Virtue*, ii. 228
Perseverance, in *The Passetyme of Pleasure*, ii. 225, 228
Perseveraunce, in *Magnyfycence*, iii. 77
Persia, ii. 71; iv. 84; vi. 238; x. 281, 503; xii. 342, 477; xiii. 55; xiv. 248
Persian language and literature, vii. 319; xii. 327, 342, 362; xiii. 145; xiv. 332, 334, 457, 458
Persians, in *The Royall Slave*, vi. 326
Persius, i. 76; iii. 20, 173; iv. 17, 206, 207, 264, 329, 345; vii. 311, 335; viii. 58, 61, 85; ix. 264, 269; xi. 393; xii. 222, 337, 482, 487, 489
Pertelote, in *Phyllyp Sparowe*, iii. 71
Perth, ix. 565 ff.; xi. 470
Perth, the Charterhouse, xiii. 115
Perth, duke and duchess of, ix. 563
Perthshire, x. 348; xiv. 436
Pertinax Surly, in *The Alchemist*, vi. 22
Pertz, Georg Heinrich, xiv. 92
Peru, iv. 86, 99; ix. 391
Perugia, chapter of, i. 212
Perugini, Mrs Kate, xiii. Add. 3
Peruvian speech, xiv. 457
Peshall, Sir John (1718–1778), ix. 346, 541
Pestalozzi, Johann Heinrich, ix. 389; xiv. 383, 390, 393, 404, 600, 602, 608
Pestilence, Treatise of the, ii. 319
Pet (seafarer), iv. 88
Peter, Gregory's deacon, i. 105
Peter, in Mrs Gaskell's *Cranford*, xiii. 378
Peter, in Swift's *Tale of a Tub*, ix. 100
Peter, Revelation of, i. 86

Peter, St, i. 118; ii. 275; iii. 400; iv. 264; v. 37, 50
Peter, St, shrine of, ii. 87
Peter, St, in *Lycidas*, vii. 114, 137
Peter, St, in *Piers the Plowman*, ii. 27
Peter, the wild boy (1712–1785), ix. 132
Peter de Alvernia, ii. 363
Peter de Bella Pertica (d. 1308), ii. 363
Peter of Blois (*fl.* 1160–1204), i. 173, 176, 187, 188, 450, 455
Peter de la Celle, i. 186
Peter Hispanus, *Summa*, ii. 363
Peter of Langtoft (d. 1307?), *Chronicle* of, i. 344, 350 ff., 358, 478; ii. 420; ix. 535
Peter of Peckham, ii. 507
Peter Pratefast, ii. 232
Peter de Riga, ii. 144
Peter the writer, i. 202
Peterborough, ix. 349, 534, 535; xii. 166, 329; xiv. 100, 101
Peterborough. *See* Benedict of
Peterborough, abbey of, i. 49, 398; iii. 95, 428; iv. 417, 418
Peterborough, earl of. *See* Mordaunt, Charles
Peterborough Chronicle, i. 109, 111 ff., 138, 386, 387, 397
Peterkin, Alexander (1780–1846), xi. 441
Peterloo affair, the, xii. 69; xiii. 14
Peters, Hugh (1598–1660), iv. 458; vii. 353, 355, 513; viii. 21, 319, 470; ix. 258
Peterson, Robert (*fl.* 1576–1606), iv. 442; *Il Galateo* (trans. of), iii. 341, 438, 550
Peterson, Sir William (1856–1921), xii. Add. 3
Petgoose, Dr, in Jerrold's *The Catspaw*, xiii. 269
Petit de Julleville, ii. 419
Petit-Dutaillis, C., *Studies and Notes supplementary to Stubb's Constitutional History*, xiv. 75, 499
Petition of Right, vii. 440
Petition to the King's most Excellent Majestie, A, vii. 388
Petowe, Henry (*fl.* 1598–1612), iv. 438
Petrarch, i. 216; ii. 184, 188; iii. 23, 62, 65, 68, 167 ff., 174, 176, 186, 188, 215, 218, 222, 226, 249 ff., 255, 257, 262, 263, 265, 268 ff., 272; iv. 124, 196, 197, 210, 213, 261, 322, 429, 447; v. 173, 230; vi. 364, 378; vii. 1, 2, 4, 7, 17, 18, 23; ix. 555; x. 158; xii. 217, 396, 410
De Remediis utriusque Fortunae, ii. 367
Epistles, ii. 366
Passa la nave mia colma d' obblio, iii. 171
Philologia, v. 101
Sonnets to Laura, iii. 251
Trionfi, xii. 76
Una candida cerva, iii. 167
Petrarch, in Jonson's *Volpone*, vii. 274
Petrarchian rime form, xii. 91, 81
Petre, father (the Martin) in Dryden's *Fables*, viii. 48, 189
Petre, lord, ix. 70
Petre, M. D., xii. 470
Petrie, A., xiv. Add. 4

Petrie, George (1789–1866), XII. 512, 518;
    XIV. 317, 571
    Ancient Music of Ireland, XIV. 328
    Antiquities of Tara, XII. 351
    Ecclesiastical Architecture of Ireland,
    XII. 351
    Essay on Tara Hill, XIV. 312
    Irish Military Architecture, XII. 351
    Origin and uses of the Round Towers,
    XIV. 312
    Round Towers of Ireland, XII. 351
Petrie, Henry (1768–1842), XII. 355, 356,
    516, 518
Petrie, William Matthew Flinders, XII. 339
Petrograd, XI. 59; XII. 55; XIII. 55
Petronel Flush, Sir, in *Eastward Hoe*, VI.
    48
Petronius, II. 178; IV. 256; VI. 32; VII. 164,
    261, 503; IX. 255, 264, 266, 499
Petronius, in Cowper's *Progress of Error*,
    XI. 82
Petruchio, in *The Taming of the Shrew*,
    V. 181; X. 90
Petruchio, in *The Womans Prize*, VI. 135
Petrus Alphonsus, I. 479
Petrus Carmelianus, *The epitaph of the
    King of Scotland*, II. 330
Petrus Comestor, I. 154, 192, 226, 343
Petryonylla, The Life of St, II. 321, 486
Pettie, George (1548–1589), III. 343, 348,
    432, 446, 447, 536; IV. 445; *The Petite
    Pallace of Pettie his Pleasure*, III. 343,
    348; V. 123
Pettigrew, Thomas Joseph (1791–1865),
    XII. 523; *Life of Lord Nelson*, XII. 367
Pettitt, Henry (1848–1893), XIII. 267
Pettman, Rev. Charles, XIV. Add. 9
Pettus, Sir John (1613–1690), *Lovedays
    Letters Domestic and Forreine*, VII. 390
Petty, Sir William (1623–1687), VIII. 342,
    473, 475, 478; *Political Arithmetic*, VIII.
    343; *The Advice of W. P.*, IX. 389, 569;
    Treatise of Taxes, VIII. 343, 367
Petty, Sir William, 1st marquis of Lans-
    downe (1737–1805), XI. 59, 142; XIV. 214
Petty-Fitzmaurice, Sir Henry, 3rd mar-
    quis of Lansdowne (1780–1863), XII.
    103; XIII. 87
Petulant, in Congreve's *Way of the World*,
    VIII. 153
Petyt, William (1636–1707), IX. 196, 356,
    538; *Jus Parliamentarium*, IX. 357
Peutinger Table, I. 71
Pevensey, III. 95
Peyton, Kate, in Reade's *Griffith Gaunt*,
    XIII. 426
Peyton, Thomas (1595–1626), *The Glasse of
    Time*, VII. 406
Pfaffe Amis, III. 81
Pfannkuche, A., XIII. 464
Pfarrer von Kalenberg, Der, III. 82, 94, 490
Pfeiffer, Emily Jane (1827–1890), XIII.
    179, 180, 508; XIV. 600
Phaedra, V. 74, 78; VI. 163
Phaedra, in Euripides' *Hippolytus*, VIII.
    164

Phaedrus, III. 216; IX. 525, 561; X. 457
Phaedrus, *Fables*, XI. 479
Phaer, Thomas (1510?–1560), II. 213; III.
    295, 302, 303, 448; IV. 17 ff.; *Of the
    Nature of Writts*, IV. 19; *Vergil*, IV. 19,
    440
Phaëthon, in Sandys's *Ovid*, VII. 51
Phaëton, VI. 342
Phalaris, IX. 332 ff., 338, 391, 527, 572;
    XII. 324; *Epistles*, VIII. 385; IX. 93, 102,
    115, 329, 524, 525
'Phalaris' (Junius), X. 409
Phalaris controversy, X. 352
Phantasma Radulphi, I. 332
Phant'sie, in *The Vision of Delight*, VI.
    359
Pharamond, in Morris's *Love is Enough*,
    XIII. 125
Pharamond, in *The Spectator*, IX. 55
Pharaoh, VII. 370
Pharaoh, I. 428
Pharaoh, Sermon on the five wiles of, in
    The Golden Legend, II. 335
Pharetra, II. 366
Pharicles, in *Mamillia*, III. 350
Pharonnida (Chamberlayne's), VII. 75
Pharsalia, battle of, V. 171
Phelps, Samuel (1804–1878), VIII. 184,
    XIII. 69
Phelps, William (1776–1856), XII. 512
Phelps, W. L., XIII. 485
Phemis, in *The Masque of the Middle
    Temple*, VI. 355
Phenix, The, X. 166
Philadelphia, XI. 47, 49
Philadelphian society (1697–1703), IX.
    308, 514, 515
Philador, in Greene's *Mourning Garment*
    III. 360
Philalethes (Henry Portsmouth), VII. 414
Philalethes (Robert Fellowes), XII. 466;
    Eirenaeus Philoponos, VII. 509
Philalethes, in Collier's *Essays*, IX. 211
Philammon, in Kingsley's *Hypatia*, XIII.
    363
Philanagnostes Criticus, IX. 511
'Philander,' VII. 413
Philanglus (Howell's), VII. 458
Philanthropist, The, XII. 193
Philarete (Wither's), IV. 155
Philastrogus, *Lillies A pe Whipt* (1652), VII.
    509
Philatus, in *The Glasse of Governement*, V.
    113
Philautus, in Lyly's *Euphues*, IV. 523
Philautus, in Riche's *Don Simonides*, III.
    349
Philautus, in *The Anatomy of Wit* and
    Euphues and his England, III. 345
Phileleutherus Anglicanus, X. 400
'Phileleutherus Lipsiensis,' IX. 336, 337,
    525
Philemon, IX. 336, 525
Philemon and Baucis, VII. 252
Philenius, in *Club Law*, VI. 308, 309
Philibert, Vision of, II. 502

Philibert de Vienne, *The Philosopher of the Court*, III. 553; IV. 447

Philine, in Goethe's *Wilhelm Meister*, XIII. 346

Philip, in Mrs Gaskell's *Sylvia's Lovers*, XIII. 379

Philip, Alexander John, XIII. 544

Philip II, king of France, I. 307, 308

Philip II, king of Spain, X. 291, 505; III. 24, 196, 401, 431; IV. 71; V. 344; VI. 91; VII. 326; VIII. 125

Philip II, in Otway's *Don Carlos*, VIII. 182

Philip III (the Bold), king of France, I. 354

Philip III, king of Spain, X. 505

Philip V, king of Spain, IX. 228

Philip VI (of Valois), king of France, I. 357

Philip, James (*fl.* 1617), IX. 565

Philip or Phillip, John (*fl.* 1566), *The Plaie of Pacient Grissell*, V. 116, 117, 407

Philip, Rev. John, XIV. Add. 9

Philip of Macedon, III. 24

Philip of Spain, VIII. 125

Philippa of Hainault (1314?–1369), queen of England, I. 358

Philippe de Thaon, *Bestiary*, II. 419; *Li Cumpoz*, II. 420

Philippe le Bon, II. 313

Philipps, Fabian (1601?–1690), VII. 513

Philippus (Horace, *Epist.*), IX. 39

Philips, Ambrose (1675?–1749), VIII. 373; IX. 78, 86, 161, 165–166 (main entry), 181, 182, 190, 446, 481; XI. 144; XIII. 191
Andromaque, adapted by, VIII. 181
Collection of Old Ballads, IX. 166, 182
Distressed Mother, The, VIII. 181, 372; IX. 166, 183; X. 22, 69, 83, 86
Epistle to the Earl of Dorset, IX. 165
Pastorals, IX. 69, 77, 165

Philips, Claudy, musician, X. 464

Philips, James, VII. 88

Philips, John (1676–1709), IX. 181, 182, 486, 487; X. 109 ff.; 'Bacchanalian song,' IX. 182; *Cyder*, IX. 182; X. 96; *The Splendid Shilling*, IX. 169, 182, 256; X. 111, 147

Philips, John (*fl.* 1716), IX. 565

Philips, Katherine (b. Fowler, 'the Matchless Orinda') (1631–1664), IV. 260, 267; VII. 39, 413; VIII. 380; IX. 168, 473; XII. 124
'As men that are with visions graced,' VII. 88
'Come, my Lucasia, let us see,' VII. 88
'I did not love until this time,' VII. 88
'I have examined and do find,' VII. 88
Trans. of *Horatius* (Corneille's), VIII. 133
Trans. of *Pompée*, VIII. 180

Philips, Miles (*fl.* 1568–1582), IV. 73

Philisides, III. 352

Philistine war, in Cowley's *Davideis*, VII. 67

Philistines, the, IV. 31; XIII. 88, 91, 99, 101

Philistines, the, in *Samson Agonistes*, VII. 136

Philistus, IV. 122

Phillida, in *Galathea*, V. 126

Phillida flouts me, VIII. 96

Phillip, William, IV. 460

Phillippes, Henry, IV. 460

Phillips, Augustine (d. 1605), V. 219; VI. 248, 276

Phillips, Charles (1787–1859), XIV. 505

Phillips, Edward (1630–1696?), VII. 15, 96, 107, 117, 118, 120, 141, 265, 267; XI. 394

Phillips, John, nephew of Milton (1631–1706), VII. 96; IX. 264, 265, 267 ff., 272, 500; XI. 394
Don Quixote, IX. 268 ff., 275
Maronides, IX. 258
Present State of Europe, IX. 267
Trans. of *Pharamond and Almahide*, VIII. 371
Translations, IX. 268

Phillips, John (*fl.* 1841), XIV. 236

Phillips, Le Roy, XIII. 574

Phillips, Lionel, XIV. Add. 9

Phillips, Mrs Lionel, XIV. Add. 9

Phillips, Samuel (1814–1854), XIII. 565

Phillips, Stephen (1866–1915), XIII. 508, 522

Phillips, Sir T., IV. 512

Phillips, Watts (1825–1874), XIII. 522; XIV. 238
Camilla's Husband, XIII. 268
Dead Heart, The, XIII. 268
Lost in London, XIII. 268
Woman in Mauve, The, XIII. 268

Phillips of Bankside, mother, VI. 99

Phillis, in Mrs Gaskell's *Cousin Phillis*, XIII. 380

Phillis, in Steele's *Conscious Lovers*, IX. 64

Phillis, in *The Fayre Mayde of the Exchange*, VI. 100

Phillpotts, Henry (1778–1869), bishop of Exeter, XIV. 492, 514

Philo, VII. 264

Philobiblon society, the, XI. 416

Philobiblon Soc. Miscellanies, XII. 406

Philobone, in *The Court of Love*, II. 220, 221

Philoclea, in Sidney's *Arcadia*, III. 352

Philocles, in Dryden's *Secret Love*, VIII. 20

Philocosmia, in *De Eodem et Diverso*, I. 153

Philocosmus, in Daniel's *Musophilus*, IV. 88

Philodemus, XII. 340

Philogenet of Cambridge, in *The Court of Love*, II. 167, 218, 220, 221

Philogonus, in *Misogonus*, V. 110, 111

'Philo-Junius,' X. 404

Philological Museum, The, XII. 308

Philological society, XII. 344

Philomathes, VI. 320, 474

Philomathes, in *Fucus Histriomastix*, VI. 324

Philomedé, in Pope's *Characters of Women*, IX. 82

Philomela, VI. 319, 320, 474

Philomela, in *Confessio Amantis*, II. 151

Philomela, in Orosius, I. 95

Philomela, in *Progne*, VI. 300

Philomelus, in Thomson's *Castle of Indolence*, x. 107

Philomusus, in *The Glasse of Governement*, v. 113

Philomusus, in *The Pilgrimage to Parnassus*, vi. 310

Philomusus, in *The Returne from Pernassus*, vi. 311, 312

Philonices, in *Time's Complaint*, vi. 320

Philosarchus, in *The Glasse of Governement*, v. 113

Philosophia, in *De Eodem et Diverso*, i. 153

Philosophical or 'Invisible' college, viii. 364

Philosophical Transactions. See Royal society

Philosophy, land of, in *The Pilgrimage to Parnassus*, vi. 310

Philosophy, the beginnings of English, iv. 268 ff., 504 ff.

Philostratus, iv. 25; vi. 9; viii. 229; ix. 504

Philotas, in Daniel's *Philotas*, iv. 133, 135

Philotimus, in Collier's *Essays*, ix. 211

Philotimus, in *The Glasse of Governement*, v. 113

Philotus, iii. 122; v. 394; ix. 556

Philoxenus, in *Believe as you List*, vi. 148

Philpot, Thomas (*fl.* 1630–1660), vii. 361

Philpot, William Benjamin (1823–1889), xiii. 508

Phipps, Edmund (1808–1857), xii. 452; xiii. 554

Phiston, William (*fl.* 1571–1609), iv. 447

'Phiz,' *pseud.* See Browne, Hablot Knight

Phobetor, xiii. 330

Phoebades, or Virginian priests of the Sun, in Chapman's masque, vi. 355

Phoebe, in *As You Like It*, vi. 304

Phoebe, in *The Faerie Queene*, iii. 233

Phoebe, in *The Faithfull Shepheardesse*, vi. 368

Phoebe, in *Rosalynde*, iii. 358

Phoebus, iv. 122

Phoebus, Mr, in Disraeli's *Lothair*, xiii. 349

Phoenicia, xii. 316, 317, 478

Phoenix, i. 42, 52, 58, 59, 428, 430

Phoenix, the, in *Phyllyp Sparowe*, iii. 71

Phoenix Britannicus, x. 166

Phoenix Nest, The, iii. 523; iv. 109, 113, 116, 118, 159, 467

Photiades, Constantin, xiii. 570

Photius (codex Galeanus), xii. 325, 328, 491

Phraxanor, in Wells's *Joseph and his Brethren*, xii. 117

Phreas, John (d. 1465), ii. 499

Phronesis (Theology) in Wyclif's *Trialogus*, ii. 65

'Phylida was a fayer mayde,' iv. 119

Phyllida, iv. 122

Phyllis, xii. 133

Phyllis, in *Confessio Amantis*, ii. 151

Phyllis, in Owen's *Epigrammata*, iv. 265

Physicians, college of, viii. 361

Physicians, tracts from, iii. 493; vii. 511

Physiologus, Old English, i. 59, 60, 430. See, also, *Bestiaries*

Physiologus of Thetbaldus, i. 227. *See, also*, i. 60, 239

Picardy, ii. 251

Picart, Bernard, xiv. 212

Piccadilly, duke of, in Goldsmith's *Citizen of the World*, x. 206

Piccolomini, Allesandro, *Allesandro*, vi. 32

Pichot, Amédée, xi. 410; xii. 385, 397, 525

Picke, Samuel, *Festum Voluptatis*, 1639, vii. 413

'Pickel, colonel,' in *The Tatler*, ix. 34

Picken, Andrew (1788–1833), xiii. 565

Pickering, a Jesuit, viii. 266

Pickering, Edward (*fl.* 1662), viii. 358

Pickering, Sir Gilbert (1613–1668), viii. 2, 5

Pickering, Henry, grandfather of Dryden, viii. 2

Pickering or Pikering or Pickeryng, John, *Horestes*, v. 63 ff., 77, 396; vi 284

Pickering, William (*fl.* 1556–1571), iv. 390, 399, 546

Pickerings, the (Dryden's relatives), vii. 105

Pickersgill, Joshua, *The Three Brothers*, xii. 50

Pickle, Gamaliel, in Smollett's *Peregrine Pickle*, x. 38

Pickle, Mrs, in Smollett's *Peregrine Pickle*, x. 38

Pickle, Peregrine, x. 38

Picks, R., iii. 191

Pickwick, Samuel (Dickens's), ii. 177; xiii. 311, 322, 324

Picton, James Allanson (1832–1910), xii. 466; xiv. 478

Pictorial Times, The, xiv. 201

Pictorius, G., vii. 509

Picts, ii. 276

Picturesque Sketches of Rustic Scenery, xiv. 222

Piedmont, vii. 306; x. 119; xiii. 88

Pierce, G. A., xiii. 544

Pierce, Robert (1622–1710), viii. 358

Pierce, Thomas, vii. 474

Pierce Plowman. See *Peres* and *Piers*

Piero, in *Antonio and Mellida*, vi. 45

Pierre, in Otway's *Venice Preserv'd*, viii. 183

Pierre d'Ailly, *Imago Mundi*, i. 209

Pierre de la Seppade of Marseilles, version of *Paris and Vienne*, ii. 315

Pierrepont, Evelyn, 1st duke of Kingston (1665?–1726), ix. 243, 244

Pierrepont, William, 4th earl of Kingston, viii. 83

Piers, in *The Shepheards Calender*, iii. 225, 226

Piers of Fullham, ii. 501

Piers the Usurer, tale of, i. 341, 346

Piers Plowman, Vision of, I. 281, 291, 334, 348, 349, 352, 357, 360, 369, 371, 378; II. 1–42 (main entry), 72, 77, 192, 215, 233, 295, 351, 399, 422, 428, 432, 433, 435, 436; III. 181, 273, 274, 302, 303, 325, 448; IV. 37, 382, 414, 521; V. 4, 6, 13, 22, 35, 51; X. 120, 233; XII. 344, 354
Pigafetta, Antonio, IV. 69, 80
Pigeon, the, in Dryden's *Fables,* VIII. 48
Pigott, Mostyn T., XIV. 537
Pigott, Richard (1828?–1889), XIV. 183
Pigwiggen, in *Nimphidia,* IV. 193
Pike, G. Holden, XIV. 533
Pilate, I. 272; VII. 169
Pilate, in the religious plays, V. 16, 17, 19, 42, 44 ff.
Pilgrim Fathers, the, IV. 311, *also see* Add.; VII. 308
Pilgrimage of Grace, the, XIII. 366
Pilgrimage of the Soul, The, II. 314. *See, also,* II. 327, *and under* Lydgate *and* Deguileville
Pilgrims' Sea-voyage, The, II. 503
Pilkington, Francis (1560?–1625?), IV. 113
Pilkington, Gilbert (*fl.* 1350), I. 366
Pilkington, Letitia (1712–1750), XIV. 571
Pilkington, Mrs Mary (1766–1839), XI. 384, 482, 492
  Biography for Boys, XI. 385
  Biography for Girls, XI. 385
  Marvellous Adventures, XI. 385
  Moral Tales (trans.), XI. 385
Pilkington, Matthew (*fl.* 1729–1733), IX. 464, 466
Pillans, James (1778–1864), XIV. 404, 608
Pills to Purge Melancholy, II. 414
Pilon, Frederick (1750–1788), XI. 451
Pilot, The, XIV. 202
Pimlyco, or, Runne Red-cap, III. 482; IV. 362, 517, 532
Pinart, IV. 406
Pinch, Tom, in *Martin Chuzzlewit,* XIII. 323
Pindar, III. 259; IV. 30; VII. 64, 65; IX. 189, 487; X. 114, 127, 128, 458, 493; XII. 330, 482, 485, 489, *also see* Add.
  Nemean ode, VII. 64
  Olympian odes, VII. 64, 65
  Paeans, XII. 340
  Partheneia, XII. 340
Pindar, Sir Paul (1565?–1650), IV. 513
Pindar, Peter, *pseud. See* Wolcot, John
Pindaric odes, VIII. 44, 55, 84 ff., 94, 170, 233; XII. 128
'Pindarics,' XI. 248; XIII. 191, 198, 218, 227, 239
Pindarus, in Dryden's *Troilus and Cressida,* VIII. 29
Pine, John (1690–1756), XIV. 212
Pine, William, XI. 341
Pinero, Sir Arthur Wing, XIII. 514
Pinkerton, John (1758–1826), II. 113, 116, 269, 283; X. 312, 460, 490, 503, *also see* Add.; XII. 518; XIV. 553; *Walpoliana,* X. 246, 496
Pinkerton, Miss, XI. 379

Pinkie, battle of, II. 109; III. 147, 152
Pinkney, Miles (1599–1674), VII. 34, 35, 400
Pinner academy, X. 385
Pinwell, George John (1842–1875), XI. 489
Pinzon, Vincenzo, IV. 70
Piot, Lazarus, IV. 438
Piozzi, Gabriel, X. 187
Piozzi, Hester Lynch (Mrs Thrale) (1741–1821), VII. 176; X. 63, 65, 66, 158, 168, 170, 181, 186, 187, 267, 463, 471 ff., 484; XI. 350, 354, 364, 365; *Anecdotes of the late Samuel Johnson,* X. 189, 190
Pip, in *Great Expectations,* XIII. 333, 334, 339
Pipe, Hannah E., XIV. 600
Piper o' Dundee, The, IX. 378
Piper of Hamelin, The, III. 81
Pipes, Tom, in Smollett's *Peregrine Pickle,* X. 38
Pipkin, in *How a man may chuse,* etc., VI. 93
Pippa, Browning's, XIII. 59, 62, 81
Piraeicus, VIII. 66
Pirkheimer, Wilibald, III. 1, 22
Pisa, III. 49; V. 306; VII. 316; XII. 37, 70, 72, 75, 398
Pisa, palazzo Lanfranchi, XII. 36
Pisan, Christine de, VIII. 59
Pisano, in *The Traytor,* VI. 199
Piscator of Strassburg, IV. 276
Pistill of Susane. See Swete Susane
Pistol, Ancient, IV. 78; VI. 194; VIII. 127; XIV. 125; in *The Merry Wives of Windsor,* V. 187, 195, 203, 361
Pistorius, Hermann Andreas, X. 513
Pitcairn, Robert (1793–1855), XII. 517; XIV. 545
Pitcairne, Archibald (1652–1713), VIII. 409; IX. 559; *De Juramento illicito,* VIII. 97
Pithias, in *Damon and Pithias,* V. 119
Pits, John (1560–1616), IX. 538
Pitseus, John (1560–1616), V. 89, 406
Pitt, Christopher (1699–1748), IX. 486; X. 493; *The Art of Preaching,* X. 363; trans. of *The Æneid,* IX. 188; trans. of Vida's *Art of Poetry,* IX. 188, 189
Pitt, Humphrey, of Shifnal, X. 233
Pitt, Thomas (1653–1726), IX. 409, *also see* Add.
Pitt, Thomas, 1st lord Camelford (1737–1793), X. 250
Pitt, William, 1st earl of Chatham (1708–1778), VIII. 295; IX. 250, 409, 561; X. 102, 164, 190, 250, 256, 263, 272, 273, 388, 390 ff., 398, 399, 402, 403, 406, 408 ff., 476, 523, 526, 527; XI. 11, 12, 16, 51, 165, 351, *also see* Add.; XIII. 467; XIV. 63, 602
Pitt, William, the younger (1759–1806), VIII. 296; XI. 25, 29, 31, 33 ff., 39, 51, 52 ff. (main entry), 74, 118, 157, 392, 396; XII. 260; XIII. 467; XIV. 61, 91, 97, 119, 121, 122, 124, 128, 194, 214
Pitt-Rivers, Augustus Henry Lane F. St (1827–1900), XII. 512

Pittis, Wm (1674–1724), VIII. 405; IX. 15
Pitts, publisher, XIV. 227, 228
Pity, in *The Castle of Perseverance*, V. 52
Pity, in *The Court of Love*, II. 220
Pius II, II. 369; IV. 334
Pius IV, VIII. 296
Pius V, III. 401; IV. 302
Pius IX, XIV. 417
Pix, Mary, born Griffith (1666–1720?),
    VIII. 439
Pixérécourt, René C. Guilbert de, XIII. 264
Place, Francis (1771–1854), XIV. 408, 478,
    602, 608
Placebo, in *Ane Pleasant Satyre*, III. 124,
    126
Placidas, or *St Eustace*, V. 104
Placids, the, in Mrs Inchbald's *Every one
    has his Fault*, XI. 279
Plagiary, Sir Fretful, in Sheridan's *Critic*,
    XI. 272
Plague, the (1582), VI. 376, 383
Plague, the (1665), VII. 289, 512; VIII. 9,
    253
Plain Man's Pathway to Heaven, The,
    VII. 168; XI. 369
Plan for a Prize Novel, A, XIII. 344
Planché, James Robinson (1796–1880),
    XII. 512; XIII. 270, 271, 273, 522;
    History of British Costume, XII. 348
Planché, Matilda Anne. *See* Mackarness
Planet, in *Jacke Drums Entertainment*,
    VI. 44
Plano Carpini, *Historia Mongolorum* of,
    II. 80
Plantagenet era, XI. 367
Plantagenets, the, IX. 222
Plantin, Christopher, III. 427; IV. 402, 403;
    IX. 167
Planudean anthology, the, VII. 14
Plarr, Victor Gustavus, XIII. 502
Plas Gwynant, Wales, XIV. 84
Plassey, XIV. 338
Plat or Platt, Sir Hugh (1552?–1611?),
    IV. 370, 513, 541 ff.
    Divers new sorts of soyle, etc., IV. 371
    Floraes Paradise, IV. 375
    Jewell House of Art and Nature, IV. 371
    *New and admirable arte of setting corne,
        The*, IV. 371
Plate fleet, the, IV. 200
Plato and Platonism, I. 99, 187, 213; II.
    231; III. 3, 6, 173, 187, 214 ff., 219, 221,
    222, 225, 234, 243, 245, 263, 299, 416,
    420, 433, 434; IV. 73, 250, 270, 271,
    285, 430, 439, 526; V. 209; VI. 21; VII. 7,
    154, 277 ff., 302, 304; VIII. 24, 132, 273,
    274, 276 ff., 282, 285, 287, 289, 291,
    334, 348; IX. 46, 282, 300; XI. 70, 100;
    XII. 60, 67, 93, 284, 293, 475, 479, 480,
    482, 484 ff., 489, 491, 492, 494, 495;
    also see Add.; XIII. 99; XIV. 23
    Axiochus, V. 5
    Euthydemus, XII. 327
    Gorgias, XII. 327, 330
    Phaedo, XII. 333, 335
    Phaedrus, III. 234; XII. 330

Plato
    Republic, The, III. 18, 214; X. 134; XII.
        333
    Symposium, III. 214 ff.; XII. 62, 73
    Theaetetus, XII. 329
    Timaeus, III. 214; XII. 333
Platonic love, V. 379
Platonists, III. 9, 258
Platt, E. A., XIV. 598
Plattes, Gabriel (*fl.* 1638–1640), VII. 509
Plautus, III. 24, 53, 92; IV. 245; V. 101,
    105 ff.; VI. 14 ff., 21, 22, 24, 26, 28, 303,
    304, 306, 320; VIII. 17, 164, 165, 247;
    IX. 338, 526; X. 417; XI. 265; XII. 490,
    492, 494
    Amphitruo, V. 107
    Aulularia, VI. 297; VIII. 123; XI. 277
    Menaechmi, IV. 4, 439; V. 102, 177, 220;
        VI. 300
    Miles Gloriosus, V. 102, 105, 162; VIII.
        127; XII. 338
    Mostellaria, VI. 102
    Rudens, VI. 102
Playe of Playes and Pastimes, The, VI. 391
Players Petition to Parliament, The, VI.
    407, 495
Playfair, John (1748–1819), XII. 144, 427;
    XIV. 292, 406, 409, 561, 563; *Illustra-
    tions of the Huttonian Theory of the
    Earth*, XIV. 291
Playford, John (1623–1686?), VII. 402;
    Choice Ayres, IX. 364; *Introduction to
    the Skill of Musicke*, IV. 144
Pleasance, queen, in *King Hart*, II. 262
Pleasand Ballatis, III. 142
*Pleasant Battle between two Lap-dogs of
    the Utopian Court, A*, VIII. 99
Pleasure, in Carew's *Coelum Britannicum*,
    VII. 19
Plegmund (d. 914), I. 92
Plegwin, Bede's letter to, I. 80
Pléiade, The, III. 227, 250, 258, 265; IV.
    197; VII. 1; XIII. 211
Pleshy, Essex, XII. 510
Pleyel, Ignaz Joseph, XI. 226
Pliant, Dame, in *The Alchemist*, VI. 22
Pliny, the elder, I. 76, 80, 81, 191; II. 79,
    80, 363; III. 5, 20, 71, 109, 347, 420
    IV. 1, 14, 15, 249, 439; VI. 9; VII. 261,
    316; VIII. 66, 77; IX. 38, 534; XII. 336,
    402, 487; *Epistolae*, IX. 349; *Natural
    History*, III. 347; V. 123, 126
Pliny, the younger, IV. 264, 439
Plomer, Henry R., XI. 466, 467, 469
Plot, Robert (1640–1696), IX. 413, 538;
    Natural History of Oxfordshire, IX. 352;
    Natural History of Staffordshire, IX. 352
Plotinus, VIII. 273, 277, 278, 282, 287 ff.;
    IX. 315, 323
Plouffe, Gédéon, XIV. 355
Plough Monday, V. 32
Ploughman's Tale, The, II. 36, 39, 162,
    164, 215, 432, 434
Plow boys' performances, V. 32
Plowden, Edmund (1518–1585), *Law Re-
    ports*, VIII. 316, 467

Pluck, in *Nicholas Nickleby*, XIII. 317
Plume, captain, in Farquhar's *Recruiting Officer*, VIII. 171
Plume, Thomas (1630–1704), VII. 342
Plumers, the, XII. 182
Plumian professorship of astronomy, Cambridge, VII. 342; IX. 412, 413
Plummer, Charles, I. 79, 81, 83, 85, 93, 104, 112
Plummer, John (*fl.* 1444), VI. 281
Plumporridge, in *The Inner-Temple Masque*, VI. 70, 75
Plumpton Correspondence, II. 483, 500
Plunket, David, XIV. 126
Plunket, William Conyngham, 1st baron Plunket (1764–1854), XIV. 128, 510; *Life, Letters and Speeches*, XIV. 126
Plunkett, Henry Grattan ('Fusbos'), XIV. 236
Plutarch, III. 68, 92, 313, 346, 347, 429, 433; IV. 1, 3, 5, 10, 12, 15, 16, 23, 24, 342, 344, 439, 442, 527; V. 197, 221; VI. 19, 138, 406; VII. 392, 404; VIII. 31, 401; IX. 28, 265, 267, 337, 500; XI. 330, 351, 352; XII. 332, 335, 485, 487, 490, 497; XIV. 579
De Educatione Puerorum, III. 346
Life of Agis, VIII. 191
Lives, X. 206, 481
Moralia, IV. 6, 14, 249, 523; VII. 316
Pluto, I. 295; IV. 349
Pluto, in *The Devil and his Dame*, V. 329
Pluto, in *Friar Rush*, VI. 53
Pluto, in *The Merchant's Tale*, II. 184
Pluto, in *Troiane*, V. 69
Plutus, in *Love Restored*, VI. 351, 352, 355
Plutus, in *The Masque of the Middle Temple*, VI. 355
Plyant, lady, in Congreve's *Double-Dealer*, VIII. 148
Plyant, Sir Paul, in Congreve's *Double-Dealer*, VIII. 148, 149, 156
Plymouth, IV. 78, 200, 311, 350; VII. 449; VIII. 122; XI. 468; XIV. 122, 297
Plymouth, the Hoe, VI. 101
Plymouth Sound, X. 115
Plynlimmon, I. 250
Pneustis (Unbelief), in Wyclif's *Trialogus*, II. 65
Pocock, Isaac (1782–1835), XIII. 270, 522
Magpie or the Maid? The, XIII. 265
Miller and his Men, The, XIII. 264, 265
Montrose; or, The Children of the Mist, XIII. 265
Rob Roy Macgregor; or, Auld Lang Syne, XIII. 265
Robber's Wife, The, XIII. 265
Robinson Crusoe, XIII. 265
Twenty Years Ago, XIII. 265
Pocock, Nicholas (1814–1897), IX. 196
Pococke, Edward, the elder (1604–1691), IX. 183, 529
Pococke, Edward, the younger (1648–1727), VII. 308, 319; IX. 529
Pococke, Richard (1704–1765), XIV. 246, 553

Podestà, the, in Crowne's *City Politiques*, VIII. 188
Podmore, Frank, XIV. 473, 478, 602
Poe, Edgar Allan, XIII. 121, 141, 438, 505; XIV. 318 *b*, 365; *Murders in the Rue Morgue, The*, XIII. 437
Poema Morale, I. 220, 227, 338, 376, 459, 460; X. 225
Poems on Affairs of State, VIII. 91, 410, 411, 445, 447
Poenitentia, in *The Castle of Perseverance*, V. 52
Poeta, in *Technogamia*, VI. 323
Poetical Amusements at a Villa near Bath, X. 278
Poetical Calendar (Fawkes and Woty's), X. 183
Poetical Magazine, The, XIV. 217, 218
Poetical Register, The, XI. 413
Poetry, land of, in *The Pilgrimage to Parnassus*, VI. 310
Poet's laureate, II. 506
Poggio, in *The Palice of Honour*, II. 260
Poggio Bracciolini, G. F., III. 93, 489; IV. 322
Poictiers, II. 336
Poins, in *Henry IV*, V. 189
Poiret, Pierre, IX. 307, 519 ff.
Poisson, Siméon Denis, XIV. 261
Poland, V. 308; VI. 303; VII. 200; XIV. 172
Poland, The Last Will and Testament of Anthony K. of, VIII. 93
Polar seas, the, XII. 248
Pole, in Meredith's *Sandra Belloni*, XIII. 445
Pole, David (d. 1568), IV. 428
Pole, Reginald (1500–1558), cardinal, archbishop of Canterbury, III. 7, 105, 420, 474; IV. 428
Pole, Thomas (1753–1829), XIV. 592
Pole, William de la, 1st duke of Suffolk (1396–1450), II. 288, 304, 424; IV. 182
Pole, William (1814–1890), XIV. 503
Polemia, in Arbuthnot's *History of John Bull*, IX. 134
Polemo-Middinia, X. 223
Polesworth. *See* Powlsworth
Poliarchus, in *Argemis*, IV. 258 ff.
Policy, in *The Passetyme of Pleasure*, II. 226
Polidori, G., XIII. 490, 496
Polidori, John William, XII. 247, 397
Polimanteia, V. 368, 369, 479
Polisarda, in *Palmerin of England*, VII. 75
Polish language, XIV. 458
Politian, VII. 315; X. 159
Political and social aspects of the later Elizabethan and earlier Stewart period, V. 476 ff.
Political Eclogues, XI. 34, 36, 40
Political Miscellanies, XI. 35
Political pamphlets, IV. 535
Political Register, X. 525
Political Science Quarterly, The, XIV. 80
Political Songs of England, I. 370
Political treatises and pamphlets in Jacobean times, VII. 455

Politick Would Be, Sir, in *Volpone*, VI. 21

Politicke perswasion, the Vice, in *Pacient Grissell*, V. 117

Politics, in *Confessio Amantis*, II. 149

Politics and economics, early writings on, IV. 295 ff., 509 ff.

Politics for the People, XIII. 358

Poliziano, Angelo, III. 5, 6, 20; IV. 69

Polla, in *Ignoramus*, VI. 322

Pollard, Alfred William, IV. 394; V. 18, 20, 92, *and see* Add. 3; VII. 11; XI. 467

Pollen, John Hungerford (1820–1902), XII. 462; *A Narrative of Five Years at St Saviour's, Leeds*, XII. 275

Pollexfen, Sir Hargrave, in Richardson's *Sir Charles Grandison*, X. 11

Pollitt, Charles, XIV. 532

Pollock, Sir Frederick, VIII. 313; XIV. 80, 470, 494

Pollock, Sir F. and Maitland, F. W., *History of English Law*, I. 174, 181

Pollock, Walter Herries, XI. 448; XII. 447

Pollok, Robert (1798–1827), XI. 444; XII. 421; *The Course of Time*, XI. 244; XII. 129

Polly, in Dickens's *Mugby Junction*, XIII. 335

Polly, in Gay's *Beggar's Opera*, IX. 163; XI. 260

Polly, in *The Little Pretty Pocket Book*, XI. 376

'Polonaland,' V. 111

Polonia, prince (Thackeray's), XIII. 288

Polonius, in *Hamlet*, II. 384; III. 349; IV. 120; V. 172, 200 ff., 272, 278; VI. 161, 200; VIII. 221, 377

Polter, R., IV. 460

Polwarth, IX. 364

Polwhele, Richard (1760–1838), X. 490; XII. 376

Polyander (Howell's), VII. 458

Polybius, III. 432; IV. 259, 439; VII. 311, 488; IX. 528; X. 466; XII. 493

Polycarp, XII. 340

Polydore, in Otway's *Orphan*, VIII. 183

Polynesian languages, XIV. 459

Polyphilus, in *The Rambler*, X. 172

Pomfret, countess of. *See* Fermor, Henrietta Louisa

Pomfret, John (1667–1702), VIII. 444; IX. 167, 169, 170, 482; X. 183; *Choice, The*, IX. 170; *Poems on Several Occasions*, IX. 169

Pompeii, XII. 417, 497

Pompey, IV. 196

Pompey, in *Measure for Measure*, V. 190

Pompey the Little. See Coventry, Francis

Pompey's Ghost, XI. 234

Pompilia, in Browning's *The Ring and the Book*, XIII. 50, 66, 79

Pomponius Laetus, III. 13

Pomponius Mela, IV. 439

Ponder, Nathanael, VII. 178

Ponet, John (1514?–1556), bishop of Winchester, III. 473; IV. 447; V. 104

Ponsonby, William (1546?–1603), IV. 395, 397, 398

Ponsonby de Tomkyns, Mrs (Du Maurier's), XIII. 433

Pont-à-Mousson, IV. 253, 256

Pont-neuf, II. 395

Ponthus, The History of King, II. 325

Pontia, in Owen's *Epigrammata*, IV. 265

Pontifex, in Butler's *The Way of all Flesh*, XIII. 454

Pontine marshes, in Thackeray's *Ravenswing*, XIII. 281

Pontis, L. de, IX. 499

Ponto family, in Thackeray's *Book of Snobs*, XIII. 285

Pontoux, Claude de, IV. 24; *L'Idée*, IV. 178

Pontresina, XIII. 380

Pontus de Tyard, III. 258, 263; *Les Erreurs Amoureuses*, III. 258

Pool, John, *County Astrology* (1650), VII. 509

Poole, Austin Lane, X. Add.

Poole, John (1786?–1872), XIII. 522; *Lodgings for Single Gentlemen*, XIII. 270; *Paul Pry*, XIII. 270; *'Twixt the Cup and Lip*, XIII. 270

Poole, Joshua (*fl.* 1632–1646), VIII. 238; XI. 249; *The English Parnassus*, VII. 466; VIII. 238, 447

Poole, Matthew (1624–1679), VII. 323, 477; *Synopsis Criticorum Bibliorum*, VII. 322, 481

Poole, Reginald Lane, I. 420; XIV. 485, 500

Poole, Reginald Stuart (1832–1895), XII. 498

Poole, Stanley Lane, XI. 459; XIV. 252

Poole, Thomas (1765–1837), XI. 121, 405

Poor law, Elizabethan, V. 374, 375

Poor Man's Pittance, A, III. 198

Poor priests (Wyclif's), II. 56, 57, 59, 63, 66

Poor Tom. *See* Abraham man

Poore, Richard, bishop of Salisbury (d. 1237), I. 230

Pop upon Pope, A, IX. 85

Pope (actor) (d. 1604), IV. 360; VI. 248, 276

Pope, Alexander (1688–1744), III. 78, 200, 452; IV. 21, 208, 280, 335; V. 209, 249, 268 ff., 274, 296; VI. 113; VII. 12, 20, 73, 269; VIII. 39, 50, 51, 62, 77, 89, 143, 160, 177, 193 ff., 203, 229, 234, 235, 237, 284, 292, 370, 386, 427; IX. 17, 45, 66 ff. (main entry), 103, 123, 127, 129, 131, 133, 137, 138, 141 ff., 160, 161, 163 ff., 171, 174, 175, 177, 179 ff., 184, 185, 187 ff., 220, 228, 230, 247, 248, 250 ff., 258, 260, 340, 357, 369, 437, 442 ff., 452, 462, 466, 468 ff., 472, 474 ff., 480, 481, 483, 484, 497, 498, 509, *also see* Add.; X. 77, 80, 95, 102, 110, 113, 115, 119 ff., 126, 128, 138, 141, 145, 153, 169, 172, 174, 180, 184, 202, 208, 218, 219, 221, 227, 232, 238 ff., 242, 273, 277, 297, 299, 301, 319, 398, 447, 448, 457, 458, 461, 465 ff., 475, 493, *also see* Add.; XI. 36, 77, 79, 82, 86, 91, 142, 150, 175, 178, 201, 206 ff., 216,

Pope, Alexander
247, 254 ff., 320 ff., 330, 335, 356, 402,
410, 466, 467, 473; XII. 36, 40, 100, 145,
169, 177, 218, 363, 384, 397, 419, 438,
444; XIII. 27, 29, 43, 51, 70, 71, 239,
253, 512; XIV. 62, 108, 144, 200, 212,
249, 396, 399, 435, 436, 439, 447
Alcander Prince of Rhodes, IX. 68
Art of Sinking in Poetry (Bathos). See
Martinus Scriblerus below
Augustus, To, XII. 42
Correspondence, XI. 328
Dialogues, IX. 87, 88
Dunciad, The, IV. 332; V. 270, 276; VII.
89; VIII. 40, 41; IX. 32, 77 ff., 82, 85, 88,
89, 131, 143, 144, 165, 188, 237, 251,
340, 409; X. 121, 163, 202; XI. 140, 212,
320, 328; XII. 41, 42
*Elegy to the Memory of an Unfortunate
Lady*, IX. 70
Eloisa to Abelard, IX. 70, 71; X. 218
Epistle to a Young Lady, IX. 71
Epistle to Dr Arbuthnot, IX. 78, 86, 88,
133, 147, 171, 251; XII. 42, 73
Epistle to Mr Jervas, IX. 71
Epistle to Robert Earl of Oxford, IX. 74, 77
Epistles, IX. 81, 82, 86, 87
Essay on Criticism, VII. 69; IX. 70, 73,
77, 89
Essay on Man, IX. 73, 81 ff., 85, 89,
169, 295, 296; X. 185; XI. 140
Ethic Epistles, IX. 89
Fragment of a Satire, IX. 78
Full and True Account...Edmund Curll,
IX. 78
Homer, V. 269; VIII. 158; IX. 72, 74 ff.,
164, 167, 171; XI. 89, 90, 246, 320 ff.
Imitations of Horace, VII. 69; IX. 85 ff.,
251
Letter to a Noble Lord, IX. 86, 251
Letter to H. Cromwell, XI. 250
*Martinus Scriblerus...or the Art of
Sinking in Poetry (Bathos)*, IX. 78, 171,
251, 271
Messiah, IX. 69; X. 159, 168
Moral Essays, IX. 81, 82
Narrative of Dr Robert Norris, IX. 77
Ode for Music on Saint Cecilia's Day,
IX. 72
Ode on Solitude, IX. 68
Of False Taste, IX. 81
Of Taste, IX. 81
Of the Characters of Women, IX. 82
Of the Knowledge and Characters of Men,
IX. 81
Of the Use of Riches, IX. 81
*One Thousand Seven Hundred and
Thirty-Eight*, X. 168
Ovid's *Metamorphoses*, translation of,
IX. 68
Pastorals, IX. 68, 69, 78
Prologue to the Satires, IX. 86
Rape of the Lock, The, IX. 70, 73, 241;
X. 167; XIII. 263
Satires, VII. 89; IX. 86, 87
Selecta Poemata Italorum, IX. 76; X. 159

Pope, Alexander
Shakespeare, edited by, IX. 77; XI. 320
'Sober advice from Horace,' IX. 86
Song by a Person of Quality, XII. 101
Statius's *Thebais*, translation of, IX. 68
Temple of Fame, X. 219
Windsor Forest, IX. 69
Works (1717), IX. 74
Works in Prose, IX. 84
1740, IX. 88
Pope, Sir Thomas (1507?–1559), III. 51,
420, 424; X. 492
Pope, Walter (d. 1714), IX. 500; *The
Catholic Ballad*, VIII. 97, 411
Popery, X. 301
Popes, The History of the, X. 499
Popham, Sir John (1531?–1607), VI. 188
Popish Courant, The (1678–1683), VIII. 412
Popish Plot, A Narrative of the, VIII. 97
'Poplicola,' X. 403
Poppaea, in Gray's *Agrippina*, X. 119
Popple, William (d. 1708), Locke's *Epis-
tola de Tolerantia* trans. by, VIII. 331,
471
Porcher, Edwin A., XII. 339, 498
Porcupine, Peter, XI. 49
Porcupine, The, XI. 49
Pordage, in Oldham's *Thirteenth Satyr of
Juvenal*, VIII. 89
Pordage, John (1607–1681), VII. 303, 474;
IX. 307, 519
Pordage, Samuel (1633–1691?), VIII. 91,
403, 409; *Azaria and Hushai*, VIII. 92;
The Medal Revers'd, VIII. 92
Porlock, in *Lorna Doone*, XIII. 434
Pornic, XIII. 77
Porphyro, in Keats's *Eve of St Agnes*, XII.
86, 87; XIII. 114
Porphyry, II. 363; VIII. 288
Porphyry, Commentary on, by William of
Ockham, I. 212
Porrex, in *Gorboduc*, V. 67
Porritt, Edward, XIV. 532
Porrus (Porus), I. 307
Porson, Richard (1759–1808), IV. 263;
IX. 526; XII. 323 ff. (main entry), 329 ff.,
363, 481 ff., 486, 488, 490 ff.
Adversaria, XII. 329
Aristophanica, XII. 328
Letters to Mr Archdeacon Travis, X. 309,
317, 508; XII. 323
Miscellaneous Works, XII. 324
'Porson' type, XII. 324, 329
Porsoniana, XII. 408
Port, Sir John (d. 1557), VII. 331
Port Glasgow, XIII. 107
Port Royal, III. 424
Porte, the, IX. 244
Porten, Catharine, X. 300
Porteous mob, the, XII. 18
Porter, Anna Maria (1780–1832), XI. 305,
463
Porter, Charlotte, XIII. 479
Porter, Elizabeth, X. 160
Porter, Endymion (1587–1649), VI. 235;
VII. 5, 12

Porter, Henry (*fl.* 1596–1599), v. 311, 312, 331, 475; vi. 12, 219; *The two angry Women of Abington*, v. 330

Porter, James (1753–1798), xi. 395

Porter, Jane (1776–1850), xi. 305, 464; *Scottish Chiefs*, xi. 306; *Thaddeus of Warsaw*, xi. 306

Porter, John, xiv. 541

Porter, Joseph, x. 385

Porter, P., *Tachmas, Prince of Persia*, viii. 190

Porter, Sir Robert Ker (1777–1842), xiv. 553

Porter and Jonson's *Hot Anger Soon Cold*, v. 331; vi. 12

Porteus, Beilby (1731–1808), x. 517

Portfolio of a Man of the World, ix. 191

Portia, in *The Merchant of Venice*, v. 169, 183, 197, 262, 379

Portiforiums, iii. 19

Portjafe, ii. 277

Portland, vii. 61

Portland, duchess of. *See* Harley, Margaret

Portland, earls of. *See* Bentinck, William

Porto Bello, x. 36; xiv. 201

Portraits, French, iv. 522, 523

Portsmouth, xii. 243; xiv. 225

Portsmouth, duchess of. *See* Keroualle, Louise Renée de

Portsmouth academy, in O'Keeffe's *Wild Oats*, xi. 281

Portsmouth's Picture, On the duchess of, viii. 94

Portugal, ii. 276; vi. 169; viii. 271; x. 408, 500; xi. 72, 155; xii. 32, 488; xiv. 294

Portugal, prince of, in *The Spanish Tragedie*, v. 240

Portugal History, The (1677), viii. 451

Portuguese, the, xii. 13

Portuguese king, in *Believe as You List*, vi. 147

Portuguese language, xi. 355; xiv. 457, 458

Portuguese navy, the, xiv. 187

Portuguese songs, ii. 405

Portuguese writers, viii. 126

Portuus of Noblines, ii. 284

Pory, John (1570?–1635), iv. 445

Positive Atall, Sir, in Shadwell's *Sullen Lovers*, viii. 21

Possum, Peter, *pseud. See* Rowe, Richard

Post and Pair, in *The Masque of Christmas*, vi. 358

Post Boy, The, ix. 5; xi. 333

Poste, Edward (1823–1902), xii. 492

Postgate, John Percival, xii. 483

Posthast, in *Histrio-Mastix*, v. 322; vi. 43, 86

Posthumus, in *Cymbeline*, v. 206

Postman, The, xi. 333

Pote, Joseph (1703?–1787), xi. 341

Potez, H., xii. 525

Potion, in Smollett's *Roderick Random*, x. 36

Potiphar, xii. 117

Potpan, in *Romeo and Juliet*, v. 182

Potter, John (1674?–1747), ix. 527

Potter, Robert (1721–1804), x. 475, 476 xiii. 145

Potter's bar, xii. 186

Potts, R. A., xii. 400

Potts, Thomas (*fl.* 1612), iv. 535; vi. 104; vii. 374, 506; *Discoverie of Witches*, vi. 105

Poulton, Edward Bagnall, xiv. 560

Pounce, Peter, in Fielding's *Joseph Andrews*, x. 25

Pound, Ezra, xiii. Add. 2

Poundtext, Peter, in Scott's *Old Mortality*, xii. 27

Pourceaugnac, M. de (Molière's), vi. 160

Poussin, Nicholas, x. 106; xii. 173; xiii. 52

Pouts, captain, in *A Woman is a Weathercocke*, vi. 222

Poutsma, H., xiv. 611

Poverte, in *Magnyfycence*, iii. 77, 78

Poverty, in *Worke for Armorours*, vi. 56

Povey, Charles (1652?–1743), ix. 462; x. 411

Powell, Baden (1796–1860), xii. 295, 466, 469; xiv. 479

Powell, David (1552?–1598), i. 262; iii. 531

Powell, Frederick York (1850–1904), i. 369; ii. 39; xiv. 497

Powell, George (1658?–1714), xii. 177

Powell, Humphrey (*fl.* 1548–1556), iv. 414; *The Wyll of the Devyll*, iii. 86, 87

Powell, Mary, 1st wife of John Milton, vii. 101, 122

Powell, Mrs, actress (d. 1831), viii. 186

Powell, Stephen, xi. 342

Powell, Thomas (1572?–1635?), iv. 526; v. 479; vii. 39

Powell, William (*fl.* 1562–1563), iv. 384

Powell family, vii. 103

Power, in *Cooper's Hill*, vii. 60

Power, Cecil, *pseud. See* Allen, Grant

Power, John, xii. 523

Power, Lionel, xiv. 308

Power, Marguerite. *See* Blessington, countess of

Powers Key, in *The Bowge of Courte*, iii. 73

Powis, 1st baron, vii. 45

Powis, earl. *See* Herbert, Edward

Powis, lord, in *John a Kent*, v. 317

Powis castle, x. 115

Powlsworth (now Polesworth), iv. 169, 174, 186

Powys, prince of, i. 196

Poynter, Sir Edward John, xiii. 433

Poyntz, Sydnam (*fl.* 1645–1650), vii. 453

Poyser, Mrs, in *Adam Bede*, ix. 323

Poysers, the, in *Adam Bede*, xiii. 390, 392

Praagh, L. V., xiv. Add. 9

Practice of Piety, The, vii. 168

Praed, Winthrop Mackworth (1802–1839), x. 152; xi. 160; xii. 107, 108, 111–112 (main entry), 119 ff., 129, 130, 138, 421 xiii. 149, 161, 164, 230, 238, 253; xiv. 205, 206, 539

Arminius, xii. 111

Praed, Winthrop Mackworth
  Gog, XII. 111
  Goodnight to the Season, XII. 122
  I enter thy garden of Roses, XII. 122
  Josephine, XII. 111
  Letter from Teignmouth, XII. 122
  Letter of Advice, XII. 122; XIII. 239
  Molly Mog, XII. 122
  Red Fisherman, The, XII. 111, 112; XIII. 239
  Tales, III. 111
  Time's Song, XII. 111, 112
  Twenty Eight and Twenty Nine, XII. 122
  Vicar, The, XII. 122
Prague, XII. 206; XIII. 162, 163
Praise, in *Mirour de l'Omme*, II. 142
Praise of Women, A, II. 162
Prat, in *The pardoner and the frere*, V. 97
Prat, D., IX. 511
Pratt, Ambrose, XIV. 535
Pratt, Charles, 1st earl Camden (1714–1794), X. 263
Pratt, Josiah (1768–1844), XII. 471
Pratt, Samuel Jackson (1749–1814), X. 265; XI. 395, 429
Praxapostolos, I. 77
Praxaspes, in *Cambises*, V. 65
Praxinoe, in *The Adoniazusae*, III. 226
Prayer, in *The Example of Virtue*, II. 227
Prayer, A, in *The Exeter Book*, I. 428
Prayer, Book of Common, III. 25, 28, 29, 31, 34, 445, 465, 475, 476; X. 362
Prayer Book, American, Scots and Irish, III. 34
Prayer-Book of 1552, VII. 325
Prayer to Our Lady, A, I. 232, 458
Prayer to the Virgin, A, I. 232, 458
Prayse of All Women, The, III. 90, 486
Preceptor, The, X. 170, 468
Preiddeu Annwvn, or *The Harrowings of Hell*, I. 251
Premierfait, Laurent du, III. 192
Prendergast, John Patrick (1808–1893), XIV. 497, 571; *History of the Cromwellian Settlement, The*, XIV. 96; *Ireland from the Restoration to the Revolution*, XIV. 96
Prendergast, Paul, *pseud*. See Leigh, Percival
Prentys, Richard (*fl.* 1403–1412), VI. 280
Pre-Raphaelite school of painting, XII. 154
Pre-Raphaelites, the, XIII. 8, 27, 110, 111, 113 ff., 121, 122, 139, 155, 156, 189, 196, 197, 207, 208, 211, 216, 218, 223; XIV. 139, 151, 363
Presbyterian histories, X. 519
Presbyterians, X. 522
Presbyterians, Satire against the, VII. 85
Prescott, William Hickling, X. 504; XII. 380, 524
Present State of Europe, IX. 267
Present State of the Republic of Letters, X. 176
Present State of the War, IX. 44
Press, The, XIII. 347, 353, 449; XIV. 181, 196, 198
Presse full of Pamphlets, A, 1642, VII. 502

Prester John, II. 79, 86, 87; IV. 70; X. 160
Prester John, The Letter of, II. 80
Preston, XI. 409
Preston, battle of, X. 358
Preston, John (1587–1628), IV. 433
Preston, Thomas (1537–1598), V. 396
  'A geleflower gentle,' VI. 285
  'A Lamentation from Rome,' VI. 285
  Cambises, V. 63 ff.; VI. 284, 285, 298
  Syr Clyomon and Clamydes, V. 129; VI. 284
Preston, *pseud*. of lord de Tabley, XIII. 205
Prestonpans, IX. 373
Prestwich, Edmund, *Hippolitus and Poems* (1651), VII. 413
Preti, Girolamo, VII. 87
Prevention of Cruelty to Animals Act, XIV. 445
Prévost, abbé, V. 289; XI. 465
Prévost, Antoine-François, X. 16; *L'Histoire de M. Cleveland*, X. 118; *Manon Lescaut*, X. 58, 118
Prevost, Sir George (1804–1893), XII. 454, 457, 463
Priam, in *Dido*, V. 145
Priamus, Sir, in *Morte Arthure*, II. 119
Priapus, VII. 360
Price, Bonamy, XIV. 596
Price, C., XIII. 504
Price, Fanny, in Jane Austen's *Mansfield Park*, XII. 235, 238, 239, 243
Price, John (1600–1676?), VII. 316, 489
Price, Laurence (*fl.* 1625–1680?), VII. 509
Price, Miss, maid of honour, VIII. 208
Price, Rees, X. 387
Price, Richard (1723–1791), X. 344, 345, 380, 513; XI. 20, 21, 71; XIV. 608
  Additional Observations, X. 344
  Appeal to the Public, X. 344
  Discourse on the Love of our Country, X. 344
  General Introduction, X. 344
  Observations on Reversionary Payments, X. 344
  Observations on the Nature of Civil Liberty, X. 344
  Review of the Principal Questions in Morals, X. 344
Price, Richard (1790–1833), X. 492
Price, Sir Uvedale (1747–1829), XI. 472
Price, William, in Jane Austen's *Mansfield Park*, XII. 239
Prichard, Iltudus Thomas, XIV. 579; *The Chronicles of Budgepore*, XIV. 340
Prichard, James Cowles (1786–1848), XIV. 563
Pride, in *Confessio Amantis*, II. 147, 148
Pride, in *The Example of Virtue*, II. 227, 234
Pride, in *The Faerie Queene*, II. 236; III. 230, 234
Pride, in *Mirour de l'Omme*, II. 140
Pride, in *The Passetyme of Pleasure*, II. 231
Pride, in *Pathomachia*, VI. 324
Pride, in *Piers the Plowman*, II. 27, 28

Pride, colonel Thomas (d. 1658), XIV. 313
Pride, the swineherd in the *Mercuries*, VII. 356
Pride and Lowliness, A Debate between, III. 361
Pride of Life, The, V. 2, 52, 57, 391, 392
Prideaux, Edmund B. R., XIV. 592
Prideaux, Humphrey (1648–1724), IX. 495; X. 503; *LVIII Articles*, IX. 414
Prideaux, John (1578–1650), VII. 307
Prideaux, William Francis, XI. 416, 417, 488; XIII. 497; XIV. 526
Priest (translator), IV. 374
Priestis of Peblis, Thrie, II. 279
Priestley, Joseph (1733–1804), IX. 302; X. 346, 380, 384, 385, 513, 514; XI. 63, 64, 70, 390, 393, 399; XII. 165, 174, 183, 279; XIV. 23, 51, 258, 272 ff., 284, 385, 394, 398, 399, 402, 556, 558, 602, 608
    Disquisitions relating to Matter and Spirit, X. 345
    Doctrine of Philosophical Necessity, X. 345
    Essay on the first principles of government, XIV. 400
    Examination, An, X. 345, 348
    Free Discussion, X. 345
    History...of Electricity, X. 345
    History of the Corruptions of Christianity, X. 309, 507
    Miscellaneous Observations, XIV. 386, 395
    Rudiments of English Grammar, XIV. 396
Priestley, Timothy (1734–1814), X. 385
Prillisk, county Tyrone, XIV. 314
Prima Pastorum, V. 17
Primaudaye, Peter de la, *French Academy*, III. 356, 437, 552
Primer or Office of the Blessed Virgin Mary, The, VIII. 54
Primerose, the Hon. Miss, X. 479
Primers, III. 28, 30, 31; IV. 384, 386, 495
    Bishop Hilsey's, III. 30
    Henry VIII's, III. 30
    Marshall's, III. 30
Primitive Christianity Revived, VIII. 111
Primrose, Archibald Philip, 5th earl of Rosebery, X. Add.; XI. 390, 396, 438, 441; XIV. 507; *Chatham*, IX. 253
Primrose, David, VII. 308
Primrose, Dr, in *The Vicar of Wakefield*, X. 206, 209
Primrose, George, in *The Vicar of Wakefield*, X. 200, 201, 209
Primrose, James, VII. 511
Primrose, Moses, in *The Vicar of Wakefield*, X. 209
Primrose, Mrs, in *The Vicar of Wakefield*, X. 209
Primrose, Olivia, in *The Vicar of Wakefield*, X. 209
Primrose, Sophia, in *The Vicar of Wakefield*, X. 209
Prince (of Wales)'s company, the, VI. 261

Prince, John Critchley (1808–1866), XIII. 508
Pring, Martin (1580–1626?), IV. 94
Pringle, Thomas (1789–1834), XII. 421; XIV. 373 ff., *also see* Add. 5, 9
    Afar in the Desert, XIV. 374
    Bechuana Boy, The, XIV. 375
    Captive of Camalu, The, XIV. 377
    Ghona Widow's Lullaby, The, XIV. 376
    Koranna, The, XIV. 377
    Lion and Giraffe, The, XIV. 375
    Lion Hunt, The, XIV. 375
    Narrative of a Residence in South Africa, XIV. 373
    Songs of the Emigrants, XIV. 374
Pringle-Pattison, Andrew Seth, XIII. 465; XIV. 469
Prinsep, James (1799–1840), XII. 512; *Benares illustrated*, XII. 352; *Essays on Indian Antiquities*, XII. 352, 353
Printers (1557–1625), IV. 546 ff.
Printing, Introduction of, into England, II. 310 ff., 483 ff.
Prior, Arthur, kinsman of Matthew Prior, IX. 146
Prior, George, father of Matthew Prior, IX. 146
Prior, Sir James (1790?–1869), X. 199 ff., 480, 483; XI. 390; *Life of Malone*, X. 159, 473
Prior, Matthew (1664–1721), III. 184; VIII. 48, 217, 218, 232, 444, 445; IX. 96, 141, 146 ff. (main entry), 162, 163, 165, 168, 169, 176, 182, 216, 217, 270, 461, 482, *also see* Add.; X. 96, 139, 202, 205, 214, 216, 369, *also see* Add.; XI. 88, 173, 174, 247, 248, 317, 327, 328; XII. 120, 223; XIII. 164; XIV. 205, 206, 211
    Account of Examination before the Committee of Council, IX. 149
    Advice to the Painter, IX. 148, 155
    Alma: or the Progress of the Mind, IX. 152, 154
    Answer to the Report of the Committee of Secrecy, IX. 149
    Better Answer to Cloe Jealous, IX. 156
    Carmen Seculare, IX. 149, 155
    Cloe Hunting, IX. 156, 159
    Dialogues of the Dead, IX. 153, 159, 160
    Down-Hall, IX. 152, 155
    English Ballad on the Taking of Namur, IX. 148, 155
    English Padlock, IX. 155
    Epistle to Fleetwood Shephard, IX. 148
    Epistle to Lord ——, IX. 155
    Erle Robert's Mice, IX. 151
    Essay upon Learning, IX. 158, 159
    Essay upon Opinion, IX. 159
    Essays, IX. 153
    Fable from Phaedrus, IX. 151
    First and Second Hymns of Calliomachus, IX. 157
    Georgics, The, IX. 157
    Hans Carvel, IX. 155
    Henry and Emma, IX. 153, 157
    Hind and the Panther Transvers'd to the

Prior, Matthew
  Story of the Country Mouse and the City
    Mouse (with Montagu), VIII. 48, 404,
    410, 411; IX. 147, 159
  History of His Own Time, IX. 147, 217
  Hymn to the Sun, IX. 148
  Jinny the Just, IX. 156, 159
  Journal at the Court of France, IX. 149
  Journey to Copt-Hall, IX. 156
  Letter to... Miss Margaret-Cavendish-
    Holles-Harley, IX. 153, 156
  Letter to Monsieur Boileau Despréaux,
    IX. 155
  'Noble lovely little Peggy,' XI. 347
  Nut-brown Maid, The, IX. 152
  Ode, An, IX. 147
  Ode...to the Memory of...Colonel George
    Villiers, IX. 150
  Ode Humbly Subscrib'd to the Queen, IX.
    151
  Ode presented to the King, IX. 148
  Ode presented to the Queen, IX. 157
  Orange, IX. 148
  Picture of Seneca, IX. 147
  Prelude to a Tale from Boccace, IX. 157
  Satire on the Modern Translators, IX. 147
  'Saunt'ring Jack and Idle Joan,' IX. 156
  Secretary, The, IX. 148, 155
  Seeing the Duke of Ormond's Picture,
    IX. 155
  Session of the Poets, IX. 147, 155
  Solomon on the Vanity of the World,
    IX. 143, 152, 154, 157
  To a Child of Quality, IX. 156
  To Cloe Weeping, IX. 156
  To the Bishop of Rochester, IX. 148
  To the Countess of Exeter, IX. 147, 149
  To the King, IX. 148
  Translation of an Epitaph upon Glan-
    ville, Bishop of Rochester, IX. 158
  Two Riddles, IX. 151
  Written in...Mezeray's History of France,
    IX. 150, 156
Prior, Melton, XIV. 534
Prior, Samuel, IX. 146
Prior park, Bath, X. 29
Priscian, I. 114, 118, 185, 210; II. 360,
  363, 366
Priscus, I. 20
Prison tracts, IV. 529; VII. 515
Prisoner, the, in The Daunce and Song of
  Death, III. 87
Pritchard, Andrew (1804–1882), XIV. 298,
  563
Pritchard, Hannah (1711–1768), XI. 261
Prithevi Raj, king of Delhi, XIV. 342
Private Wealth, in Kynge Johan, V. 65
Privy Malice, in The Passetyme of Pleasure,
  II. 226, 234
Priwen or Pridwen, Arthur's ship, I. 248,
  251
Proast, Jonas, VIII. 475
Probationary Odes, X. 239; XI. 34, 36, 40
Probert, William (1790–1870), XIV. 201
'Probus,' XIV. 514
Probyn, John Webb, XIV. 513

Processus Talentorum, V. 19
Proclus, VIII. 289
Procne, III. 343
Procopius, I. 26
Procrustes, VIII. 165
Procter, Adelaide Anne (1825–1864), XIII.
  508, 542; The Message, XIII. 178
Procter, Bryan Waller (pseud. Barry
  Cornwall) (1787–1874), XI. Add.; XII.
  115, 129–130 (main entry), 201, 407,
  421, 433, 437, 438; XIII. 178, 469, 515;
  XIV. 200; Sit down, sad soul, XII. 130;
  Song for Twilight, XII. 130
Proctor, Ellen A., XIII. 496
Proctor, John, III. 531
Proctor, Robert George Collier (1868–
  1903), XII. 523; Bibliographical Essays,
  XII. 369; Index of Early Printed Books,
  XII. 369; The Printing of Greek in the
  Fifteenth Century, XII. 369
Proctor, Thomas (fl. 1578–1584), III. 190;
  Pretie Pamphlets or Proctor's Precepts,
  III. 190
Prodigal Son, story of the, III. 360
Prodigal Son, The, V. 108, 412
Prodigal Son, the Dutch Latin comedies
  of, IV. 320
Prodigal Son plays, V. 101, 109 ff., 410, 412
Prodromos, Theodore (Hilarion), IV. 249;
  V. 5
Prognostications, IV. 534
Progress of Man, The, XI. 41
Prologues and epilogues, collections of,
  X. 441
Prometheus, II. 79
Prometheus, in Mercury Vindicated, VI. 358
Prometheus, in Shelley's poem, XII. 64 ff.
Prometheus, in The Lords' Masque, VI. 353
Promptorium Parvulorum. See Geoffrey
  the Grammarian
Promptorium Parvulorum sive Clericorum,
  XII. 519
Propertius, XII. 489, 490
Proserpine, VI. 313; XII. 339; XIII. 183
Proserpine, in The Merchant's Tale, II. 184
Prosody of Old and Middle English
  before Chaucer, I. 372 ff., 480
Prosody from Chaucer to Spenser, III. 273
  ff., 525
Prosody of the 17th century, VIII. 222 ff.,
  447 ff.
Prosody of the 18th century, XI. 446
Prosody of the 19th century, XIII. 225 ff.,
  511 ff.
Prosper, I. 75, 76
Prospero, in The Rambler, X. 172
Prospero, in The Tempest, V. 206, 207, 214;
  VII. 71; VIII. 9; XII. 220
Pross, Miss, in A Tale of Two Cities, XIII. 332
Protagon (i.e. Henri IV), in Euphormio,
  IV. 256
Protasius, I. 75
Protesilaus, I. 279, 470
Protesilaus, in Wordsworth's Laodamia,
  XI. 107
Protestant drama, VI. 374

Protestant Post Boy, IX. 13, 432
Protestantism, VII. 304 ff.
Proteus, in *The Two Gentlemen of Verona*,
  III. 268; VI. 157; VIII. 126
Prothero, Sir George Walter, XII. 429, 520;
  XIV. 92, 497
Prothero, Rowland Edmund, V. 352; X.
  299, 509; XII. 385, 386, 388, 397, 429,
  470, 478
Proud Beauty, in *Robin Conscience*, III. 97
Proude Wyves Paternoster, The, III. 90, 97,
  487
Proudies, the (Trollope's), XIII. 422, 424
Prout, father. *See* Mahony, Francis Syl-
  vester
Prout, Samuel (1783–1852), *Sketches in
  Flanders and Germany*, XIV. 149
Prout, William (1785–1850), XIV. 558
Provençal legends, I. 115
Provençal poetry, X. 219; XIII. 211
Provençal version of Boethius, I. 99
Provence, V. 11, 49; X. 221
Proverbs, Old English, I. 363. *See, also,
  Hendyng* and *Alfred*
Prowse, William Jeffery ('Nicholas,'
  1836–1870), XIII. 163, 508; *The City
  of Prague*, XIII. 162
Prudentia, in *The Tatler*, IX. 34
Prudentius, I. 75, 76; *Psychomachia*, I. 75;
  V. 51, 59
Prudentius, in *The Floating Island*, VI. 325
Prue, in Congreve's *Love for Love*, VIII.
  150, 152, 161
Prusias, king of Bithynia, in *Believe as
  you List*, VI. 148
Prussia, X. 466; XIII. 19; XIV. 382, 383,
  416, 419
Prussian army, the, XIII. 282
Prussian order of merit, XIII. 20
Prussian protestantism, XII. 260
Prussian *Realgymnasium*, XIV. 424
Pryme, George (1781–1868), XIV. 602
Prynne, William (1600–1669), IV. 306, 513,
  518; VI. 204, 326, 387, 391, 401, 403,
  406, 409, 495, 496; VII. 160, 197, 208,
  352, 441, 446, 459, 498, 515; VIII. 67,
  319, 469; IX. 348
  *Animadversions on the Fourth Part of
  Coke's Institutes*, VIII. 320
  Histrio-Mastix, V. 343, 372; VI. 40, 262,
  391, 392, 403 ff.; VII. 145, 207, 313, 433
  *Mr William Prynne, his defence of Stage-
  Playes or a Retraction of his former book*,
  VI. 408
  *The Republican and others Spurious good
  Old Cause briefly and truly anatomised*,
  VII. 383
Pryor, Mrs, in Charlotte Brontë's *Shirley*,
  XIII. 409
Pryor, William, VII. 515
'Psalmanazar, George' (1679?–1763), IX.
  498
Psalms, II. 14, 46, 318, 359, 502. *See, also,
  under* Bible
Psalms, Old English versions, I. 106, 147,
  437, 438, 444; *Northern Psalter*, I. 341

Psalters, II. 318, 365
  Early English, I. 444
  Hampole's, II. 46, 47
  Old French, II. 420, 508
Psellus, in Lyly's *Euphues*, IV. 523
Pseudo-Kallisthenes, I. 135
Pseudo-Melito, I. 75
Psyche, XIII. 206; XIV. 311
Psyche, in Keats's *Ode to Psyche*, XII. 90
Psyche, in *Lingua*, VI. 314, 315
Psyche, in *Loves Maistresse*, VI. 103
Psyche et Filii ejus, VI. 486
Ptolemy and the Ptolemaic system, I. 213;
  II. 362, 366; III. 153, 156, 425; VIII. 282,
  283, 350, 352; XIV. 579
Public Advertiser, The, X. 305, 400 ff., 479,
  525; XI. 402
Public Ledger, X. 205, 208
Public Register, The, XI. 324
Public School Latin Primer, The, XIV. 413
Public Schools, principal (prior to 1650),
  VII. 492
Public Schools act (1868), XIV. 422
Public Schools commission, XIV. 421
Publick Oppression, in *Ane Pleasant
  Satyre*, III. 127, 128
Publius Cornelius, in *The Play of Lucrece*,
  V. 100
Publius Syrus, IX. 525; X. 471
Puca, the Irish, XIV. 307
Pucell, La Bel, in *The Passetyme of
  Pleasure*, II. 225, 226, 229, 232, 234
Puck, in *A Midsummer Night's Dream*,
  V. 160, 183; XIV. 307
Puck-Hairy, in *Love Restored*, VI. 370
Puck-Hairy, in *The Sad Shepherd*, VI.
  371
Puckle, James (1667?–1724), IX. 479
Pudicitia, in *Psychomachia*, V. 51
Pueriles Confabulalunculae, VII. 315
Puff, in Sheridan's *Critic*, XI. 272
Pug, in *The Divell is an Asse*, VI. 24
Pugh, E. W., XIII. 544
Pughe, William Owen (1759–1835), XII.
  518
Pugin, Augustus Charles (1762–1832),
  XII. 508; XIV. 222
Pugliano, Giovanni Pietro, IV. 149
Pui, the (a fourteenth century association),
  II. 428
Pulcheria, in *The Emperor of the East*, VI.
  163
Pulci, Luigi, XII. 51, 52, 56; *Morgante
  Maggiore*, XII. 35
Pullen, Robert (d. 1147?), I. 185, 456;
  Sententiarum Libri Octo, II. 342
Pulling, F. S., XIV. 511
Pulpit, the English, from Fisher to Donne,
  IV. 224 ff., 490 ff.
Pulteney, David, IX. 220
Pulteney, Miss, IX. 165
Pulteney, William, earl of Bath (1684–
  1764), IX. 88, 162, 219, 220, 223, 224,
  250 ff., 433, 491; X. 452; XI. 174, 248,
  350, 352, 358; XIII. 239; *Seasonable
  Hints*, X. 389, 522

Pulton, Andrew (1654–1710), VIII. 305, 462

Pulton, Ferdinando (1536–1618), VIII. 46

Punch, X. 162; XIII. 162, 279, 282, 284, 294; XIV. 196, 235 ff., 548, 549

Punch and Judy, II. 385

Punch in London, XIV. 236

Punchinello, XIV. 236

Pundler, The, in *Lichtounis Dreme*, II. 278

Punic war, the second, XII. 303

Punic wars, the, IV. 62, 64

Puntarvolo, in Jonson's *Every Man out of his Humour*, X. 50

Punter, Mr, of St John's, Cambridge, VI. 397

Purcell, E. S., XII. 454, 458; *Life of Ambrose de Lisle*, XII. 276

Purcell, Francis, XIII. 555

Purcell, Henry (1658?–1695), VIII. 30, 395, 397, 428, 437; IX. 148; X. 433; *Dido and Aeneas*, VIII. 135; *Lilliburlero*, VIII. 96

Purcell, John, XIII. 142

Purchas, Samuel (1575?–1626), IV. 79, 85, 90 ff., 101, 103, 107, 460; XIV. 332, 333 *Hakluytus Posthumus, or Purchas his Pilgrimes*, IV. 91, 92, 99, 398, 408 *Purchas his Pilgrim; Microcosmus or the Historie of Man*, IV. 91 *Purchas his Pilgrimage*, IV. 91 *Relation of a Voyage to Guiana...Performed by Robert Harcourt, The*, IV. 97

Purfoote, Thomas, IV. 22, 384, 437

Purgatorio, The, X. 361

Purgatory of St Patrick, I. 191, 474

Puritan, The, IV. 360

Puritane Or The Widdow of Watling-streete, The, IV. 360; V. 236, 238, 254, 255, 442, 444; VI. 62

Puritane set forth in his lively Colours, A, VII. 384

Puritanism, VII. 158, 305, 370

Purley, XI. 400

Purnell, Thomas (1834–1889), XII. 435

Purser, Louis Claude, XII. 338

Pursuits of Literature, The, XII. 364

Purvey, John (1353?–1428?), II. 61; *Regimen Ecclesiae*, II. 61; translation of the Bible, II. 61, 62, 285, 442; III. 45; IV. 38

Purvis, David L., XIV. 553

Puschkin, XII. 395

Pusey, Edward Bouverie (1800–1882), XII. 253, 254, 261 ff. (main entry), 271 ff., 454, 457, 458, 462, *also see* Add.; XIII. 168 *Commentary on the Minor Prophets*, XII. 341 *Entire Absolution of the Penitent: A Sermon*, XII. 263 *Lectures on the Prophet Daniel*, XII. 341 *Spiritual Letters*, XII. 264 *Thoughts on the Benefits of the System of Fasting*, XII. 258

Puseyite, a, XIV. 198

Puteanus, VII. 113

Putney, IX. 290, 308, 324 ff.; X. 299

Puttenham, George (d. 1590) or Richard (1520?–1601?), *Arte of English Poesie*, III. 180, 207, 269, 295, 302 ff., 450, 526; IV. 21, 23, 24, 52, 113, 114, 123; VII. 263, 271; XI. 248

Puysieu, de, IV. 257

Pwyll, prince of Dyved, I. 252

Pye, Henry James (1745–1813), XII. 133 *Aelfored*, XII. 128, 422 *Commentary illustrating the Poetics of Aristotle*, XII. 128 *Comments on the commentators of Shakespeare*, XII. 128 *Summary of the duties of a J.P.*, XII. 128

Pyeboard, George, in *The Puritan*, IV. 360; V. 255

Pyke, in *Nicholas Nickleby*, XIII. 317

Pylades, I. 314; X. 249

Pym, in Browning's *Strafford*, XIII. 59, 67

Pym, Horace N., XIV. 502

Pym, John (1584–1643), V. 345; VII. 147, 441; IX. 258; XIV. 91

Pyne, William Henry (*pseud.* Ephraim Hardcastle, 1769–1843), XIV. 545; *Royal Residences*, XIV. 222; *Wine and Walnuts*, XIV. 222

Pynson, Richard (d. 1530), II. 161, 210, 319 ff., 326, 329 ff.; III. 56, 57, 59, *also see* Add.; IV. 400

Pyramus, in *A Midsummer Night's Dream*, V. 285; VI. 207, 316

Pyramus and Thisbe, in Sandys's *Ovid*, VII. 50

Pyrenees, the, XIII. 369; XIV. 251

Pyrenees, peace of the, IX. 226, 228

Pyrford, IV. 202

Pyrgopolinices, V. 105

Pyrocles, in Sidney's *Arcadia*, III. 352

Pyrrhus, II. 106

Pyrrye, C., *The prayse and disprayse of women*, III. 486

Pythagoras, VIII. 278, 282; IX. 515, 527

Pythagoras, in Sandys's translation of Ovid's *Metamorphoses*, VII. 5

Pythagorean doctrines, X. 103

Pythagorean numbers, VIII. 67

Pythagorism, VII. 376

'Q,' *pseud. See* Jerrold, Douglas William

'Quack Maurus' (Sir Rich. Blackmore), in Dryden's *Secular Masque*, VIII. 32

Quadragesms, VIII. 313

Quadratus, in *What You Will*, VI. 43

Quadrio, Francisco, V. 289

Quadripartitus, VIII. 310, 465

Quadrivium, the, II. 229, 230, 359, 362, 366; VII. 320

Quaker *Journals*, VIII. 103

Quaker literature, XII. 53

Quakers. *See* Society of Friends

Qualmsick, in *Pompey the Little*, IX. 408

'Quantification of the Predicate, the,' XIV. 9

Quare of Ielusy, The, II. 91

Quaritch, Bernard (1819–1899), XII. 523; *General Catalogue*, XII. 368

Quarles, Francis (1592–1644), IV. 434; VII. 30, 45 ff. (main entry), 83, 153, 169, 176, 403, 513; VIII. Add.
Argalus and Parthenia, III. 355
Divine Fancies, VII. 46
Emblems, VII. 47; XIII. 52
Enchiridion, IV. 162
False World, thou ly'st, VII. 47
Feast for Wormes, A, VII. 46
World's a Theater, The, VII. 47

Quarll, Philip, XI. 373, 489

Quarterly Journal of Education, The, XIV. 409

Quarterly Journal of Microscopical Science, XIV. 289, 566

Quarterly Review, The, X. 270; XI. 40, 157, 162, 166, 393; XII. 141, 142, 149 ff. (main entry), 162, 163, 193, 194, 199, 288, 302, 364, 429; XIII. 230, 415, 467; XIV. 55, 82, 107, 115, 118, 141, 233, 314, 322, 403, 598, 600, 608

Quarterly reviewer (Keats's), VII. 75

Quater Brailes, the, III. 190

Quatre derniers choses, II. 312, 313

Quatrefoil of Love, The, II. 441

Quattuor novissimis, De, II. 313

Quebec, XIV. 360

Queen, The, XIV. 201

Queen Eleanor's Confession, II. 144

Queen of Portugal, ship, X. 35

'Queen of the Blues,' XI. 346

Queene, The, or the Excellency of her sex, VI. 449

Queene Elizabethe's Academy, XI. 368

Queen's company, the, V. 136; VI. 245 ff., 249, 262, 277

Queen's Crawley, in Thackeray's *Vanity Fair*, XIII. 286

Queen's university, Ireland, XIV. 417

Queensberry, duchess of. *See* Douglas, Catherine

Queensberry, duke of. *See* Douglas, Charles

Queensland, XIV. 368, 369

'Quene of Evene,' XIV. 462, 463

Quentin Durward, II. 96

Querelle des femmes, VIII. 59

Querenghi, Antonio, IV. 259

Querolus, VI. 26

Quesnay, François, *Maximes générales*, X. 336; *Tableau économique*, X. 336

Questions concerning Liberty, Necessity, and Chance, The, VII. 288

Quevedo, IX. 277; *Visions*, IX. 3, 274, 418

Quha hes gud malt, and makis ill drynk, II. 279

Quhen Flora had ourfret the firth, II. 283

Quhy sowld nocht Allane honorit be? II. 279

Quia amore langueo, II. 426; III. 283

Quick, John (1748–1831), XI. 262

Quick, Robert Herbert (1831–1891), XIV. 602, 608

Quickly, Dame, XII. 438

Quickset, Sir Harry, in *The Tatler*, IX. 46, 50

Quicksilver, Francis, in *Eastward Hoe*, VI. 172

Quiggin, Edmund Crosby, XIV. 306, 307; 'Irish Influence on English Literature,' XIV. 307

Quignon, cardinal, III. 31

Quiller-Couch, Sir Arthur Thomas, XIII. 486, 497; XIV. 526

Quiller-Couch, Lillian Mary, IX. 574

Quillinan, Edward (1791–1851), XII. 422

Quilp, Daniel, in *The Old Curiosity Shop*, XIII. 319

Quilter, Harry, XIII. 568, 572, *also see* Add.

Quin, Edwin R. W. Wyndham, 3rd earl of Dunraven (1812–1871), XII. 509; XIV. 328, 568

Quin, James (1693–1766), X. 95, 96, 114, 264; XI. 258, 284, 454

Quinault, P., VIII. 17, 134

Quiney, Judith. *See* Shakespeare, Judith

Quiney, Thomas (*fl.* 1616), V. 219

Quinlan, M. A., XIII. 515

Quinte Essence, Book of, II. 427

Quintessence, queen, in Rabelais, IX. 106

Quintilian, II. 366; III. 23, 290, 294, 420, 434; IV. 348; VI. 9; VII. 261, 272; VIII. 58; XII. 220, 326, 487, *also see* Add.; XIV. 453

Quintus, in Owen's *Epigrammata*, IV. 265

Quintus Calaber, XIII. 478

Quintus Fabius, V. 123

Quintus Smyrnaeus, XII. 331

Quinze joyes de mariage, Les. *See* Sale, Antoine de la

Quiros, Pedro Fernandez de, IV. 101

Quisquilius, in *The Rambler*, X. 172

Quixote, Don, X. 41, 51, 52; XIV. 218

'Quixote in petticoats,' IX. 30

Quiz (*pseud.*), XIV. 545

Quod-bonum-est-tenete, in *Piers the Plowman*, II. 21

R. B. (? Richard Bower), *Apius and Virginia*, V. 63 ff., 396; VI. 284, 285

R. B. E., XIII. 466

R. C., *The Times Whistle*, IV. 333, 516, 520

R. C., *Mercurius Civicus*, VII. 349, 350; *The Weekly Intelligencer of the Commonwealth*, VII. 350; *The Kingdomes Weekly Intelligencer*, VII. 349, 353, 354

R. L. *See* Linche

'R. S., of the Inner Temple, Gentleman,' IV. 116, 467

R. S., *Foure-fould Meditation*, IV. 130

R. T., *The Opinion of Witchcraft Vindicated*, VII. 395, 507

R. W. See under *Tancred and Gismund*

R. W. *See* Wilson, Robert

R. W. (1643), VII. 385

Rab (Dr John Brown's), XIV. 160

Rabanus of Mainz (Rabanus Maurus), I. 81; IV. 418

Rabbards, Ralph, II. 211

Rabbett, VII. 316

Rabelais, François, II. 94, 103, 257; III. 94, 151, 328, 453, 485; IV. 14, 246, 248, 321, 326, 533; VII. 256; VIII. 67 ff., 72, 77, 166, 372, 407; IX. 106, 263, 264, 270 ff.; X. 34, 50, 53; XI. 288; XII. 123, 168; *Gargantua*, IV. 8, 414; VIII. 59; IX. 267; *Pantagruel*, IV. 8, 353, 527; VIII. 59, 66, 385

Rabshakeh, in *Ezechias*, VI. 298

Raby, earl, in Hannah More's *Percy*, XI. 274

Raby, J. T., *Bi-centenary of the Birth of Johnson*, X. 161, 180

Racedown, Dorsetshire, XI. 99

Rachael, in Dickens's *Hard Times*, XIII. 329

Rachel, Elisa, XIII. 410

Racine, Jean, V. 202, 292, 293; VIII. 14, 27, 31, 133, 134, 376, 422, 435, 483; X. 86, 444; XII. 47, 381
Achilles, VIII. 181
Andromaque, VIII. 187, 373; IX. 166, 183; X. 69
Athalie, VIII. 165
Bajazet, X. 221
Bérénice, VIII. 181, 182
Britannicus, X. 118 ff.
Iphigénie, X. 69, 221
Mithridate, VIII. 22
Phaedra and Hippolitus, VIII. 181
Phèdre, IX. 103

Racine, Louis, V. 289

Radcliff, Ralph (1519?–1559), V. 103

Radcliffe, Alexander (*fl.* 1669–1696), IV. 18; VIII. 403; IX. 272, 500; *Ovid Travestie*, IX. 259; *The Ramble*, IX. 259, 263

Radcliffe, Ann (1764–1822), I. 279; XI. 286, 300 ff. (main entry), 304, 306, 464; XII. 58, 249; XIII. 420
Castles of Athlin and Dunbayne, XI. 301
Gaston de Blondeville, XI. 301
Hazel Tree, The, XI. 301
Italian, The, XI. 302, 303
Letters, XI. 301
Mysteries of Udolpho, XI. 300, 302, 303; XII. 235; XIII. 264
Poems, XI. 301
River Dove, The, XI. 301
Romance of the Forest, XI. 302
St Albans Abbey, XI. 301
Sicilian Romance, XI. 301

Radcliffe, Elizabeth, daughter of the 3rd earl of Sussex, VI. 347

'Radcliffe, Dr John,' in *The Tatler*, IX. 34

Radcliffe, Nicholas (*fl.* 1368–1396), II. 442

Radcliffe, Richard, XIV. 595

Radford, D., XIII. 498

Radigund, in *The Faerie Queene*, III. 231, 236

Radirobanes, in *Argenis*, IV. 258, 259

Radley school, XIV. 414

Radnors, the, in Meredith's *One of Our Conquerors*, XIII. 443 ff., 448

Radway, X. 272

Radwinter, Essex, III. 321; V. 357

Rae J., *Life of Adam Smith*, X. 335

Rae, Peter (1671–1748), IX. 565

Rae, W. Fraser, XI. 266, 454, 456

Rae press at Kirkbride and Dumfries (1711–1720), XI. 470

Raeburn, Sir Henry (1756–1823), XI. 442

Raffaelle Sanzio. *See* Raphael

Raffles, Sir Thomas Stamford (1781–1826), XIV. 288, 563

Rafflesia, XIV. 288

Ragau, in *Jacob and Esau*, V. 112

Raglan, lord. *See* Somerset, lord Fitzroy James Henry

Ragley, near Alcester, VIII. 280; X. 271

Ragman Roll, II. 499, 501

Ragnar Lodbrok, X. 221, 222, 224, 227

Ragnell, in *Wedding of Sir Gawain*, I. 312

Rahab, in Blake's *Four Zoas*, XI. 196, 197

Rahere, V. 26

Raikes, Elizabeth, XIV. 599

Raikes, Jack (George Meredith's), XIII. 447

Raikes, Robert (1735–1811), XIV. 389

Raikes, Thomas (1777–1848), XIV. 505

Rainbow, the, in George Eliot's *Silas Marner*, XIII. 393

Raine, James (1791–1858), XII. 354, 512

Raine, John, XII. 354, 512

Rainham, Essex, X. 393

Rainolde, Richard, *Foundation of Rhetorike*, III. 432, 553

Rainolds or Reynolds, John (1549–1607), IV. 235, 236, 494; VI. 303, 319, 324, 472; VII. 309, 310, 317, 484, 489; *De Idolatria ecclesiae Romanae*, IV. 408; *Th'Overthrow of Stage-Playes*, VI. 398, 399, 496

Rainolds, William (1544?–1594), VII. 309, 485

Rainsford, lady Anne. *See* Goodere

Rainsford, Sir Henry, IV. 174

Rait, Robert Sangster, IX. Add.

Rajputana, XIV. 335

Ralegh, Sir Carew (1550?–1625?), IV. 55

Ralegh, Carew (1605–1666), VII. 447

Ralegh, Sir Walter (1552?–1618), III. 189, 212, 229, 233, 234, 272, 303; IV. 45, 51–65 (main entry), 67, 75, 78, 81, 85, 86, 88, 94, 103, 114, 117, 160, 164, 299, 450 ff.; V. 224, 338, 347; VI. 5; VII. 75, 190, 222, 271, 305, 306, 366, 440, 454; IX. 351, 537; X. 303; XII. 427
Arts of Empire, The, IV. 55
Breviary of the History of England, under William I (attributed to), IV. 55
Cabinet Council, The, IV. 55, 64
Cynthia, IV. 53
Discourse on War in General, IV. 65
Discovery of the large...Empire of Guiana, IV. 56
History of the World, The, IV. 54, 58 ff.; VII. 433; IX. 146, 357
Lie, The, IV. 54, 124
Like Hermit Poor, IV. 54, 65
Observations concerning the Royal Navy and Sea Service, IV. 58, 65
Pilgrimage, The, IV. 54
Prerogative of Parliaments, The, IV. 64
Relation of the Cadiz Action, A, IV. 57

Ralegh, Sir Walter
  Remains of Sir Walter Ralegh, The, IV. 65
  *Report...of the Fight about the Isles of
    the Açores this last summer*, IV. 56
  'Shepherd, what's love I pray thee tell,'
    IV. 109, 124
  Steel Glass, In commendation of the, IV.
    52
  To-day a man, To-morrow none, IV. 65
  Trade and Commerce, IV. 65
  *Vision upon this conceit of the Faery
    Queene*, III. 272
  War with Spain, A, IV. 65
Raleigh, Sir Walter (1861–1922), X. 418,
  421; XI. 410, 433, 436, *also see* Add.;
  XII. 399, 405, 447; XIII. 491, 558; XIV.
  526, 594; *Johnson on Shakespeare*, X.
  181; *Six Essays on Johnson*, X. 184
Ralph, earl of Norwich, I. 141
Ralph, James (1705?–1762), X. 23; XI.
  467; *The case of Authors by Profession*,
  X. 204
Ralph, Julian, XIV. 532
Ralph, in *Rauf Coilȝear*, II. 125 ff.
Ralph of Coggeshall (*fl.* 1207), I. 175, 449
Ralph of Diceto (d. 1202?), I. 159, 160,
  173, 175, 188, 449
Ralpho, the squire, in *Hudibras*, VIII. 67,
  70 ff., 76
Ram, William, *Rams little Dodeon*, IV. 374,
  542
Ramah, in *Davideis*, VII. 66
Rámáyan of Válmiki, The, XII. 502
Rāmāyana, the, XII. 343, 502
Rambler, The, XIV. 118
Rambouillet, Hôtel de, VII. 391
Rambouillet, Mme de, IV. 338; IX. 37
Rameses II, XII. 487
Ramillies, IX. 151
Rampain, Zechariah, VII. 223
Ramsay, A., XIV. 613
Ramsay, Allan (1686–1758), I. 290; II. 95,
  267, 269; IX. 361 ff., 366 ff. (main
  entry), 379, 438, 567; X. 110; XI. 144,
  205, 209, 211, 212, 215 ff., 221, 228, 231,
  338
  Evergreen, The, II. 479; IX. 369, 567;
    X. 226; XI. 204, 217
  Gentle Shepherd, The, IX. 161, 368; XI.
    224, 237
  Last Speech of a Wretched Miser, IX. 366,
    367
  Lochaber no more, IX. 368
  Lucky Simpson's Last Advice, IX. 367
  Monk and the Miller's Wife, The, IX. 367
  My Peggy is a young thing, IX. 368
  Scribblers lashed, IX. 369
  Tea-Table Miscellany, IX. 360, 364, 368,
    369, 371, 567; X. 233; XI. 206, 218
  Vision, The, IX. 367; XI. 217
Ramsay, Andrew (1574–1659), IX. 556
Ramsay, Andrew Michael (1686–1743),
  Vie de Turenne, IX. 213
Ramsay, James Andrew Brown, marquis
  of Dalhousie (1812–1860), XIV. 575
Ramsay, John, scribe, II. 109, 110, 449

Ramsay, Sir John, viscount Haddington
  (1580?–1626), VI. 346
Ramsay, Robert (*fl.* 1630), VII. 5
Ramsay or Ramesey, William (*fl.* 1645–
  1676), VII. 509
Ramsay, William (1806–1865), XII. 492
Ramsden, J., XIII. 558
Ramsey, Edward Bannerman (1793–
  1872), XIV. 505
Ramsey, dame Mary, VII. 338
Ramsey school, Hunts., VII. 342
Ramus, Petrus, III. 416, 424; VII. 141,
  276, 277; *Dialectica*, IV. 275, 276
Ramusio, Giovanni Battista (Ramutius),
  IV. 69, 101, 442
Rand, Benjamin, IX. Add.
Rand, Theodore H., XIV. 582
Randal, in Lillo's *Fatal Curiosity*, X. 78
Randal, Lord, I. 300
Randall, Jack, pugilist, XIV. 227
Randall (Randolph), Thomas (1605–
  1635), IV. 517, 520
Randolf, earl of Chester, rimes of, II. 399;
  V. 320
Randolf's Hall, in *Awntyrs of Arthure*,
  II. 122
Randolph, Robert, brother of Thomas
  Randolph (1605–1635), VI. 476
Randolph, Sir Thomas, 1st earl of Moray
  (d. 1332), in *Bruce*, II. 105
Randolph, Thomas (1523–1590), III. 187
Randolph, Thomas (1605–1635), VI. 28,
  212, 475, 476; VII. 4, 38, 317, 489
  Amyntas or the Impossible Dowry, VI.
    234, 366, 371
  Aristippus, or, The Joviall Philosopher,
    VI. 232, 233, 325, 372
  Conceited Pedler, The, VI. 232, 325
  Eglogue to Mr Johnson, An, VI. 232
  Jealous Lovers, The, VI. 232, 325
  Muses Looking-Glasse, The, VI. 233,
    234, 371
Randolph, Thomas (1701–1783), X. 307,
  507; XIV. 593
Random, Roderick, in Smollett's novel,
  X. 37, 204
Rands, William Brighty (1823–1882), XI.
  489; XIV. 164, 523
  Chaucer's England, XIV. 163
  'Great, wide, beautiful, wonderful
    world,' XIV. 163
  Henry Holbeach, XIV. 163
  Lilliput Lectures, XIV. 163
  Lilliput Legends, XIV. 163
  Lilliput Levee, XIV. 163
  Lilliput Revels, XIV. 163
  Tangled Talk, XIV. 163
Ranger, in Hoadly's *Suspicious Husband*,
  X. 87
Ranke, Frederick Heinrich, VII. 176
Ranke, Leopold von, IX. 207, 208, 213;
  XIV. 100; *History of England*, IX. 206;
  X. 295, 503; *History of the Popes*, XIV. 63
Rankins, William (*fl.* 1587–1601), IV. 323,
  516, 518, 519; V. 312; *Mirrour of
  Monsters*, VI. 395, 496

Ransome, Arthur, XIV. 528
Ransome, Cyril, XIII. 466
Ranulf de Glanville. *See* Glanville
Ranulph, earl of Chester. *See* Randolf
Raoul le Fevre, *Recuyell of the Histories of Troy*, II. 230, 311 ff.
Raper, Robert William, XIV. 208
Raphael, in Kingsley's *Hypatia*, XIII. 363
Raphael (Milton's), VII. 101
Raphael Sanzio, IX. 59; X. 130; XII. 172; XIII. 111; XIV. 99
Rapids, the, in Morton's *Cure for the Heartache*, XI. 281
Rapin, René de (1621–1687), VIII. 374, 375, 449; *Réflexions sur la poétique d'Aristote*, VIII. 374
Rapin de Thoyras, Paul de (1661–1725), VII. 268; IX. 140, 495; X. 279; *Histoire d'Angleterre*, IX. 235, 236; X. 280
Rare Triumphs of Love and Fortune, V. 117, 162, 413
Rare Willie drowned in Yarrow, IX. 371
Rashdall, Hastings, XIV. 469, 480; *Universities of Europe*, I. 202
Rashleigh, in Scott's *Rob Roy*, XII. 21, 26
Rask, Rasmus Christian, *Anglo-Saxon Grammar*, XII. 344
Rasor, in Vanbrugh's *Provok'd Wife*, VIII. 162
Raspe, Rudolf Eric (1737–1794), X. 424; *Baron Munchausen*, XI. 492
Rastall, William (1601), VI. 290
Rastell, Elizabeth, sister of Sir T. More, wife of John Rastell, lawyer and printer, IV. 198; V. 90
Rastell, Elizabeth (afterwards wife of John Heywood), IV. 198; V. 90
Rastell, John (d. 1536), II. 327; IV. 70, 198, 354, 546; V. 57, 99, 100, 103, 253; VIII. 467; *Interlude of the Nature of the Four Elements*, V. 57
Rastell, William (1508?–1565), III. 40; V. 90, 92, 95; VIII. 467
Ratcliffe, IV. 238
Rate, David, II. 449
Rathbone, Hannah Mary (1798–1878), XIII. 565; *Diary of Lady Willoughby*, XIII. 434
Rathery, J. B., XII. 525
Rathmell academy, X. 386
Rathmill, Yorkshire, IX. 393
Rathmore, D. R. P., lord, XIV. 510
Ratis Raving, II. 449, 498
Ratisbon, III. 155; VIII. 137
Ratramnus, I. 75, 117, 120, 124
Ratsey, Gamaliel, The Life and Death of, IV. 530
'Rattlesnake,' ship, XIV. 296
Rattlin, Jack, in Smollett's *Roderick Random*, X. 37
Rattray, Sylvester (*fl.* 1650–1666), XII. 521
Rauf Coilȝear, I. 291, 470; II. 112, 125, 280, 451, 501
Raunce, John, VII. 509
Rausch, Danish tale of, III. 94
Ravaillac, in *Friar Rush*, VI. 53

Ravaillac, Francis, IV. 363
Ravenna, II. 364; XII. 34, 35, 48 ff., 324
Ravenscroft, Edward (*fl.* 1671–1697), VIII. 168, 420
    Careless Lovers, The, VIII. 140
    Italian Husband, The, VIII. 194
    King Edward and Alfreda, VIII. 194
    London Cuckolds, VIII. 140
    Mamamouchi, or the Citizen Turned Gentleman, VIII. 140
    Titus Andronicus, Ravenscroft's adaptation of, VIII. 120, 140
Ravenscroft, Thomas (1592?–1635?), IV. 113, 465
Ravenswood, in Scott's *Bride of Lammermoor*, XII. 23
Ravis, Christian (1613–1677), VII. 309, 491
Ravis, Thomas (1560?–1609), VII. 316
Rawley, William (1588?–1667), IV. 278, 284
Rawlidge, Richard, VI. 496; *A Monster lately found out and discovered or the Scourging of Tipplers*, VII. 400, 403
Rawlins, John (*fl.* 1622), VII. 449
Rawlins, Thomas (1620?–1670), VI. 458; *The Rebellion*, VIII. 129, 440
Rawlins, T. J., XIV. 542
Rawlinson, George (1812–1902), XII. 316, 334, 477, 478, 499; *The History of Herodotus*, XII. 317
Rawlinson, Sir Henry Creswicke (1810–1895), XII. 316, 317, 342, 477, 499
Rawlinson, Richard (1690–1755), IX. 342, 353, 355, 530, 531, 533, 535, 537, 538; X. 355; *Natural History of Surrey*, IX. 351
Rawnsley, Hardwicke Drummond, XIII. 479, 558
Rawnsley, Willingham Franklin, XIII. 478
Raworth, widow, VII. 361
Ray, James (*fl.* 1745), IX. 563, 565
Ray, John (1627–1705), VII. 479; VIII. 478, 479; IX. 412; XIV. 282, 563, 565; *The Wisdom of God*, X. 346, 514
Rayleigh, lord. *See* Strutt, John William
Raymond, IV. 98
Raymond (Haji Mustapha), XIV. 335, 579
Raymund of Pennaforte, I. 355
Raymundus, in *Kynge Johan*, V. 66
Rayne, in Aberdeenshire, II. 103
Rayner, Edward, X. 387
Rayner, J., of the Inner Temple (1658), IV. 511
Rayner, John, X. 387
Reach, Angus Bethune (1821–1856), XIV. 545
Read, Charles Anderson, XIV. 573
Read, Meredith, *Historic Studies*, X. 301
Reade, A. L., *Johnsonian Gleanings*, X. 157; *The Reades of Blackwood Hill*, X. 157
Reade, Charles (1814–1884), XIII. 267, 268, 425 ff., 432, 458, 459, 516, 522, 565, 566
    Autobiography of a Thief, The, XIII. 427
    Christie Johnstone, XIII. 425

Reade, Charles
  Cloister and the Hearth, The, XIII. 426,
    428; XIV. 255
  Drink, XIII. 425
  Foul Play, XIII. 425, 427
  Gold, XIII. 425
  Good Fight, A, XIII. 428
  Griffith Gaunt, XIII. 425, 426
  Hard Cash, XIII. 426, 427
  Hero and a Martyr, A, XIII. 427
  It is never too late to mend, XIII. 425, 427
  Jack of all Trades, XIII. 427
  Love me Little, Love me Long, XIII. 426
  Masks and Faces, XIII. 425
  Peg Woffington, XIII. 425
  Put Yourself in his Place, XIII. 425, 427
  Terrible Temptation, A, XIII. 426, 427
  Wandering Heir, The, XIII. 426
  Woman Hater, A, XIII. 427
Reade, John, XIV. 582
Reade, William Winwood (1838–1875),
  XIV. 479, 553; *African Sketch-Book*,
  XIV. 254
Reader, The, XIV. 200
Reading, II. 342; V. 116; IX. 563; XI. 376;
  XIII. 427, 430
Reading, John (1588–1667), VII. 514
Real Life in London, XIV. 225, 545
Real Presence, doctrine of the, I. 154
Real Presence and the Rule of Faith, A
  Poem on the, VIII. 47
Reardon, in Gissing's *New Grub Street*,
  XIII. 460
Reason, in *Complaint upon Love to Reason*,
  III. 187
Reason, in *The Goldyn Targe*, II. 253
Reason, in *Hymenaei*, VI. 346
Reason, in *Mirour de l'Omme*, II. 140, 141
Reason, in *Nature*, V. 54
Reason, in *Piers the Plowman*, II. 10, 26,
  27
Reasons humbly offered by the Company…
  of Upholders, IX. 132
Rebecca, in *Jacob and Esau*, V. 112
'Rebel, A' (Defoe's), IX. 19
Recarede, king, I. 105
Recklessness, in *Piers the Plowman*, II.
  25, 26
Reclus de Moiliens, the *Charité* of, II. 140;
  the *Miserere* of, II. 140
Record, The, XII. 258
Record commission, XII. 357; XIV. 52, 67
Record office, XIV. 67, 82
Recorde, Robert (1510?–1558), III. 107,
  425, 493, 494; IV. 460; *The Castel of*
  Knowledge, III. 425, 553
Recorder, the, in *The Returne from Per-*
  nassus, VI. 313, 314
Recreation, in *The Playe of Playes and*
  Pastimes, VI. 392
Rectitudines Singularum Personarum, VIII.
  310, 465
Recueil des Historiens des Gaules, X. 282
Reculver, XII. 347
Red Barn murder, the, XIV. 228
Red Book of Hergest, I. 249, 252, 263, 461

Red Cross Knight, in *The Faerie Queene*,
  II. 234; III. 232; VII. 173
Red Horse, vale of, X. 112
Red house, Bexley Heath, XIII. 119
Red Indians, the, XIV. 459
Red Lion, the, in George Eliot's *Janet's*
  Repentance, XIII. 387
Red Riding Hood, XI. 375
Red sea, IV. 30
Redcap, in *Looke about you*, V. 321
Redding, Cyrus (1785–1870), XI. 289, 459
  XII. 410; XIV. 534
Rede, Sir Robert (d. 1519), II. 360
Rede, William (d. 1385), IV. 427
Rede lecture, XIV. 81
Redesdale, lord. *See* Mitford, John Free-
  man
Redford, John (*fl.* 1535), V. 57, 392
Redhouse, Sir James William (1811–
  1892), XII. 342, 504
Redi, Francesco, XII. 443
Redman, William, bishop of Norwich (d.
  1602), III. 432
Redmond, in *Britannia's Pastorals*, IV. 157
Redresse, in *Magnyfycence*, III. 77
Reed, Arthur William, V. Add. 2
Reed, Isaac (1742–1807), V. 275, 277; VI.
  296; VIII. 423; IX. 497; X. 442; XI. 453
Reed, Joseph (1723–1787), X. 40, 440
Reede, in *Arden of Feversham*, V. 241
Rees, A., XIV. 599
Rees, Thomas Mardy, XIII. 503
Rees's *Cambro-British Saints*, I. 262
Reeve, Anne (Restoration actress), VIII. 9
Reeve, Clara (1729–1807), X. 47, 424; XI. 464
  Champion of Virtue, X. 61; XI. 300
  Charoba, X. 300
  Old English Baron, X. 61 ff.; XI. 300
  Progress of Romance, XI. 300
Reeve, Henry (1813–1895), XII. 153, 426,
  427; XIV. 114, 171, 503
Reeve, John (1608–1658), X. 377
Reeve, L., XIV. 560
Reeve, Richard (1642–1693), IX. 345
Reeves, Mr, in Pepys's *Diary*, VIII. 350
Reeves, William (1815–1892), XII. 518;
  XIV. 328, 571; *Ecclesiastical Antiquities*
  of Down and Connor, XII. 361
Refined Courtier, III. 438
Reflector, The, XII. 192, 193, 434, 437, 442
Reform act, XI. 50
Reform bill, XI. 58; XIII. 24, 262, 342, 347,
  348, 357, 384, 397; XIV. 57, 125, 129,
  414, 427
Reformation, in *Respublica*, V. 60
Reformation, Scottish, and the stage, VI.
  374
Reformation and Renascence in Scotland,
  III. 138 ff., 500 ff.
Reformation literature in England, III.
  25 ff., 471 ff., *also see* Add.
Regales Aphorismi (1650), VIII. 470
Regan, in *King Lear*, V. 169
Regan, Morice (*fl.* 1171), *History of Ire-*
  land, VII. 211, 448
Regeln für Schauspieler, XI. 284

Regensburg, XIV. 306
Reggio, X. 119, 224
'Regina' (K. Philips's), VII. 88
Reginald of St Augustine's, Canterbury,
     I. 191, 456
Reginella, in *The Goblins*, VI. 239
Regiomontanus. *See* Müller
Registrum Omnium Brevium (1531), VIII.
     467
Regnard, Jean-François, *Le Retour Im-
     prévu*, X. 22, 417
Regnault, Elias, XIII. 465
Regnault, François, IV. 402, 421
Regrets, in *The Court of Love*, II. 221
Regula placitandi (1691), VIII. 469
Regulus, XI. 273
Regulus, in Alfred's *Boethius* and *Orosius*,
     I. 95, 100
Rehearsal, The (Leslie's), IX. 5
Reid, John (1808–1841?), XII. 523
Reid, Stuart Johnson, XIV. 509
Reid, Thomas (1710–1796), IV. 294; X.
     345, 347 ff., 512, 514; XI. 76, 400; XIV.
     9, 10, 37, 49, 393, 474
     Essays on the Active Powers of Man,
     X. 348
     Essays on the Intellectual Powers of Man,
     X. 348
     Inquiry into the Human Mind, X. 348
     Works, XIV. 7, 11
Reid, T. D. (d. 1624), IV. 550
Reid, Sir Thomas Wemyss (1842–1905),
     XIII. 506, 558, 560; XIV. 199, 505, 509,
     534; *Charlotte Brontë*, XIII. 379
Reidpath MS., II. 475
Reitz, Francis W., XIV. Add. 8, 9; *Afri-
     caanse Gedigte*, XIV. 373; *Ver in de
     Wildernis*, XIV. 375
Relation...of the isle of England (an
     Italian's), II. 500
*Relation of the Ten grand, infamous Tray-
     tors, A*, VII. 388
Relations, VII. 344 ff., 348
Religion, in Carew's *Coelum Britannicum*,
     VII. 19
Religious Tract society, X. 203; XI. 362
Reliquiae Antiquae, Wright and Halliwell,
     I. 362, 365
Remarks on the Academic, IX. 414
Rembrandt van Ryn, XI. 12; XII. 172, 173
*Remedies against Discontentment...from
     the writings of auncient philosophers*, IV.
     343, 524
Remedy of Love, The, II. 162
Remembrance, dame, in *The Dreme*, III.
     117, 118
Remembrancia, VI. 381, 491
Remonstrant clergy, VIII. 330
Remus, Uncle, XIV. 314
Renan, Ernest, I. 253, 274; XIII. 99 ff.,
     458; XIV. 502; 'The Poetry of the Celtic
     Races,' XIII. 100
Renard, G., XII. 525
Renascence, Englishmen and the Classical,
     III. 1 ff., 466 ff.
Renauard the fox, I. 366

Renaud de Beaujeu, I. 284
Renfrewshire, IX. 364, 370, 559; X. 500;
     XI. 237
Renfrewshire, Harp of, XI. 443
Rengifo, Spanish critic, VII. 265
Rennell, James (1742–1830), XIV. 334, 579
Rennie, John (1761–1821), XIV. 381
Renouard, A. A., IV. 263
Renouf, Sir Peter le Page (1822–1897),
     XII. 500
Renton, Richard, XIII. 485, 544; XIV. 502
Renuchio, in *Gismond of Salerne*, V. 75, 76
'Repentance,' ship, IV. 77
Repentance, in *The Faerie Queene*, III. 239
Repentance, in *Piers the Plowman*, II. 12,
     23
Repington, Philip (d. 1424), II. 442
Reply of Friar Daw Topias, II. 40, 432, 435
Reports of cases, VIII. 319
Repository of Arts, Literature, etc., XIV. 216
Repository Tracts, XI. 362
Representative, The, XIII. 353
Reproch, in *The Faerie Queene*, III. 239
Repton school, VII. 331, 493
Requests, master of, III. 16
Reresby, Sir John (1634–1689), VIII.
     264 ff., 451; *Memoirs*, VIII. 264, 265;
     Travels, VIII. 265
Resch, Wolfgang, dialogues, III. 81
'Resolution,' ship, XI. 145
Respublica, IV. 513; V. 59, 124, 392
Restless, Tom, in Johnson's *Idler*, X. 178
Restoration, the, IV. 107 140, 228, 315,
     421, 425
Restoration comedy, VI. 214
Restoration pamphlets, XI. 470
Resurrection, V. 39
Retines, Robert de. *See* Robert the
     Englishman
*Retinues of the Great People, A Song
     against the*, I. 370
Retrospective Review, The, XII. 346, 430
'Retters,' Rethel or Retiers, near Reims,
     II. 156
Returne from Pernassus, The. See Par-
     nassus trilogy
*Return of the Knight of the Post from
     Hell..., The*, IV. 352
Retz, cardinal de, VII. 436
Reuchlin, Johann, III. 113; VII. 264; *De
     arte cabbalistica*, IV. 275; *De verbe miri-
     fico*, VII. 370; *Henno*, V. 101
Reunert, Theodore, XIV. Add. 9
Revels, Documents relating to the Office
     of the, V. 478
Revels, Master of the, VIII. 423
Revels Accounts, V. 122
Revenge, goddess of, in *Locrine*, V. 239
Revenge, in *Jeronimo*, V. 160
'Revenge,' the, lord Sandwich's battle-
     ship, VIII. 202
'Revenge,' the, Sir Richard Grenville's
     ship, IV. 56, 376
Reverdies, V. 34
Revesby in Lincolnshire, V. 32, 33
Revett, Nicholas (1720–1804), XII. 499

Review, The (Defoe's), IX. 1, 4, 5, 10, 11, 13, 14, 34, 432

Reviews and magazines in the early years of the 19th century, XII. 425 ff.

Revue des deux Mondes, La, IX. 71; XIII. 71, 75

Rex Fabarum, VI. 294

Rex Humanitas, in *Ane Pleasant Satyre*, III. 124

Reyher, A., *Les Masques Anglais*, VI. 334, 335, 487

Reynard the Fox, I. 366, 479; II. 245, 313, 314, 332, 486; III. 494; XI. 334

Reynolds, chancellor, X. 382

Reynolds (clerk to Essex), VII. 343

Reynolds, Edward (1599–1676), VII. 329

Reynolds, Edward, of Nottingham, X. 387

Reynolds, Frederick (1764–1841), XI. 428, 458; XIII. 522; *The Dramatist*, XI. 281

Reynolds, G. F., VI. 265, 266, 270

Reynolds, George William McArthur (1814–1879), XIII. 566; XIV. 545; *Pickwick Abroad*, XIII. 319

Reynolds, Henry (*fl.* 1627–1632), III. 305; IV. 138, 169; VI. 490; *Mythomystes*, VII. 264, 273, 466

Reynolds, John (1621–1650), IV. 526; *God's Revenge against Murder*, VI. 199

Reynolds, John (1667–1727), X. 386

Reynolds, John Hamilton (1796–1852), XII. 70, 82, 89, 418, 422

Reynolds, Sir Joshua (1723–1792), X. 85, 157, 181, 207, 213, 215, 262, 263, 265 ff. (main entry), 268, 348, 461, 462, 470, 472, 473, 483, 494, *also see* Add.; XI. 32, 143, 326, 350, 353, 360, 364, 472; XII. 132, 166, 172; *Discourses*, X. 265 ff.; XI. 200, 432

Reynolds, Myra, IX. 168

Reynolds's Weekly Newspaper, XIV. 192

Reysby, Nicholas, II. 480

Rhadamanth, in *Locrine*, V. 240

Rhadamanthus, XII. 136

Rhampsinitus's Treasure Chamber (Herodotus), IX. 39

Rhé, isle of, IV. 293; VII. 5

Rheged, Urien's lordship of, I. 249

Rheims, VI. 311; X. 119

Rheims, council of, I. 185

Rheims, English college at, IV. 274

Rhenanus, Beatus, III. 41

Rhetoric, in *The Passetyme of Pleasure*, II. 225, 231

Rhetorique, land of, in *The Pilgrimage to Parnassus*, VI. 310

Rhind, Alexander Henry (1833–1863), XII. 512; *Thebes, its Tombs and their Tenants*, XII. 351

Rhind lectures in archaeology, XII. 351

Rhine, the, V. 6; VII. 20; XI. 302; XII. 33, 418; XIII. 443; XIV. 221

Rhineland, the, XIV. 294

Rhinwallon and his sons, XII. 514

Rhodalind, in D'Avenant's *Gondibert*, VII. 71

Rhode, in *Solymannidae*, VI. 301

Rhode island (America), IX. 281, 282

Rhodes, island of (Mediterranean), II. 111; VIII. 117; XII. 339

Rhodes (prompter at Blackfriars), VI. 262

Rhodes, Cecil, XIV. Add. 8, 9

Rhodes, Hugh (*fl.* 1550–1555), *Boke of Nurture*, III. 341; XI. 368

Rhodes, John (*fl.* 1660), VIII. 118, 121

Rhodes, William Barnes (1772–1826), XIII. 523

Rhodes, W. E., XIV. 75

Rhonabwy, Dream of, I. 253

Rhone, the, II. 123

Rhuddlan, X. 115

Rhuys, life of Gildas by a monk of, I. 65

Rhyme of Sir Launcelot Bogle, The, in *The Bon Gaultier Ballads*, XIII. 161

Rhys, Ernest, XII. 399, 401; XIII. 485

Rhys, Sir John, I. 250 ff., 254, 255, 273, 463

Rhys ap Tewdwr, I. 256

Riah, in *Our Mutual Friend*, XIII. 336

Ribemont, in *Edward the Black Prince*, XI. 450

Ricardo, in *The Coxcombe*, VI. 120, 133

Ricardo, David (1772–1823), X. 335; XI. 75, 399; XIV. 2 ff., 21, 22, 186, 407, 479; *Principles of Political Economy and Taxation*, XIV. 2

Riccaltoun, Robert (1691–1769), *Winter*, X. 94

Riccoboni, Louis or Lewis, V. 289; X. 442

Rice, James (1843–1882), XIII. 560

Rich, Anthony (1804–1891), XII. 412

Rich, Barnabe (1540?–1620?), III. 536; IV. 4, 18, 436, 460, 526, 527, 528, 531, 535, 540; V. 220, 358, 479; IX. 556

   Apolonius and Silla, VI. 305

   Dialogue, between Mercury and an English Souldier, etc., V. 360

   Don Simonides, III. 349

   Farewell to the Military Profession, V. 316

   Honesty of this Age, The, IV. 317, 526; V. 349, 358, 360

   New Description of Ireland, VI. 173

Rich, Charles, 4th earl of Warwick, VIII. 268

Rich, St Edmund, of Abingdon or Pontigny (1170?–1240), I. 205, 339, 343, 456

Rich, Sir Henry, earl of Holland (1590–1649), VII. 224

Rich, Jeremiah (d. 1660?), VIII. 243

Rich, John (1682?–1761), IX. 163; X. 39, 70, 71, 85, 211; XI. 258, 282; XIII. 264; XIV. 213

Rich, Mary, countess of Warwick (1625–1678), VIII. 453

   Autobiography, VIII. 268, 269

   Diary, VIII. 269

   Occasional Meditations, VIII. 269

   Rules for a Holy Life, VIII. 269

Rich, Penelope, lady Rich (1562?–1607), III. 254; VII. 54

Rich, Richard (*fl.* 1609–1610), IV. 460

Rich, Sir Robert, 1st earl of Warwick, III. 254

Rich, Sir Robert, 2nd earl of Warwick (1587–1658), VII. 454; VIII. 269

Rich Cabnit furnished with a Varietie of exquisite Discriptions, The, VI. 401

Rich Closet of Physical Secrets, A (1652), VII. 512

Richard, in *Richard Casteler*, III. 369

Richard I, in *Histoire de la Guerre Sainte*, II. 420

Richard I, king of England, I. 174 ff., 199, 337; III. 325; VI. 97; IX. 535

Richard I, History of King, I. 175

Richard II, A Poem on the Deposition of, ed. T. Wright, II. 35

Richard II, king of England, I. 322; II. 3, 35 ff., 55, 71, 134, 137, 144, 145, 153, 154, 157, 158, 170, 346; III. 195, 196, 337; IV. 137, 169, 182; V. 44; VI. 280, 330; VII. 211; IX. 222, 233, 535; X. 284, 287

Richard II, pre-Shakespearean, V. 83

Richard III, king of England, III. 196, 282, 314, 334, 335; VII. 443; VIII. 123; X. 85, 131, 291, 505

Richard III, in Shakespeare's play, XII. 171

Richard III, Garrick as, XI. 257

Richard III, History of, III. 17, 334, 335, 531

Richard III, W. H. W. Betty as, XI. 283

Richard (Fitznigel), bishop of London, *Dialogus de Scaccario*, IV. 309

Richard, prior of Hexham (*fl.* 1138–1154), I. 161, 450; *Acts of King Stephen and the Battle of the Standard*, I. 161, 163, 167, 168, 449

Richard, Sir, in Robin Hood legends, II. 416

Richard, 3rd duke of York (1411–1460), II. 302

Richard Coeur de Lion, I. 287, 307 ff., 317, 318, 399, 470; II. 308, 325

Richard Coeur de Lion, in *Looke about you*, V. 320

Richard Coeur de Lion, in *Robert, Earle of Huntington*, V. 318, 319

Richard Duke of Yorke, The True Tragedie of, V. 135, 153, 184, 220, 237, 238, 260, 398, 433

Richard of Almaigne, X. 233

Richard of Armagh. *See* FitzRalph

Richard of Bury (1281–1345), I. 183, 213, 214, 456; II. 362; *Philobiblon*, IV. 411, 414, 415

Richard of Cirencester (d. 1401?), IX. 540; XII. 488

Richard de Conyngton (d. 1330), I. 453

Richard of Cornwall, brother of Henry III, I. 368

Richard of Devizes (*fl.* 1189–1192), I. 159, 163, 173, 176, 449; II. 342, 488

Richard of Dover, I. 188

Richard L'Evêque, I. 184

Richard of Middleton (d. 1308), VII. 505

Richard of St Victor (d. 1173?); *Benjamin*, II. 327, 498

Richard the Englishman (Richard of Wendover, d. 1252), II. 365

Richard the Redeless, II. 3, 36, 432 ff.

Richard the Third, The True Tragedy of, IV. 393; V. 153, 185, 398

Richardes, Thomas, V. 110

Richards, John Morgan, XIII. 562

Richards, Nathaniel (d. 1652), VII. 413; *Messallina*, VI. 266, 268, 458

Richardson, of Stratford, V. 168

Richardson, Sir Benjamin (1828–1896), IX. 138

Richardson, David Lester (1801–1865), XIV. 579; *Literary Chit-Chat*, XIV. 337; *Literary Leaves*, XIV. 337; *Literary Recreations*, XIV. 337

Richardson, Fanny, in Le Fanu's story, XIII. 415, 416

Richardson, Frederika, XIII. 555, 558

Richardson, John (1796–1852), XIV. 581, 583; *Canadian Brothers, The*, XIV. 360; *Wacousta*, XIV. 359; *War of 1812, The*, XIV. 359

Richardson, Jonathan (1665–1745), IX. 70, 443, 448; XII. 172

Richardson, Joseph (1755–1803), XI. 35, 36, 391

Richardson, Mary (d. of Samuel R.), X. 12, 61

Richardson, Robert (1850–1901), XIV. 369, 587

Richardson, Samuel (*fl.* 1643–1658), X. 520

Richardson, Samuel (1689–1761), I. 319; VI. 82; IX. 144, 248, 475; X. 1 ff. (main entry), 30, 31, 43, 46 ff., 58, 61, 63, 64, 171, 201, 411 ff., 458, *also see* Add.; XI. 327, 358, 365, 468, 474; XII. 168, 231 ff.; XIII. 340, 421

Clarissa Harlowe, VIII. 196; IX. 245; X. 2, 7 ff., 15 ff., 29, 48, 57, 252, 273; XI. 265, 277, 356

Collection of the Moral and Instructive Sentiments, X. 11

Meditations collected from the Sacred Books, X. 12

Pamela, VI. 99; IX. 400; X. 3 ff., 14 ff., 17 ff., 24 ff., 48, 79, 84, 89, 273; XI. 325; XII. 235

Sir Charles Grandison, X. 9, 10, 15 ff., 252, 273; XII. 238

Richardson, Thomas (? 1584), III. 191

Richardson, Thomas (1828–1831), XIII. 516

Richardson, Sir Thomas (1569–1635), VIII. 319

Richborough, XII. 347

Richelieu, Armand-Jean Duplessis duc de, cardinal, IV. 258, 260; VII. 446; VIII. 371, 383; IX. 228

Riches, in *Piers the Plowman*, II. 20

Richey, Alexander George (1830–1883), XIV. 497

Richmond, IX. 251; X. 95, 102, 395; XI. 259, 364; XIII. 281

Richmond, duke of. *See* Lennox, Charles

Richmond, Legh (1772–1827), XII. 472; *The Dairyman's Daughter*, XII. 281

Richmond, Yorkshire, II. 49

Richmond churchyard, XII. 419

Richmond Examiner, The, XIV. 326

Richmond forest, VI. 239

Richmond gardens, XIV. 286

Richmond hill, X. 101, 104

Richmondshire, XII. 514

Richter, Helene, XIII. 553; XIV. 528

Richter, Jean Paul Friedrich, X. 422; XII. 445; XIII. 4, 7 ff., 447, 465, 468

Rickets, J., *Byrsa Basilica*, VI. 300, 476

Rickett, A. Compton, XIII. 493

Rickman, John, XI. 167, 169; XII. 188, 433

Ridd, John, in *Lorna Doone*, XIII. 434

Riddell, James (1823–1866), XII. 492

Riddell, Robert (d. 1794), IX. 368

Riddell MS., II. 474

Riddles, Old English, I. 49, 51, 60, 61, 428, 430; runes in, I. 12; Latin, I. 78

Riddles, books of, III. 488

Rideal, Charles F., XIII. 544

Rider, John (1562–1632), III. 555; VII. 486

Riderhood, in *Our Mutual Friend*, XIII. 336

Ridgeley, Thomas (1667?–1734), X. 384

'Ridings,' V. 34

Ridley, Annie E., XIV. 599

Ridley, Glocester, X. 136

Ridley, Nicholas (1500?–1555), bishop of London, III. 38, 179, 213, 419, 432, 473; IV. 232, 234

Ridolfi conspiracy, III. 401

Ridpath, George (d. 1726), IX. 15, 550; *The Flying Post*, IX. 5, 434

Ridpath, George (1717?–1772), IX. 554

Rievaulx. *See* Ailred of

Rievaulx abbey, IV. 421

Rigaud, in *Little Dorrit*, XIII. 317, 331

Rigby, in Disraeli's *Coningsby*, XII. 155; XIII. 349, 350

Rigby, Elizabeth. *See* Eastlake, lady

Rigg, James Harrison, XIII. 548

Right of Succession, Poem on the, VIII. 92

Righteousness, in Anglo-Norman plays, V. 21

Riguelme, Don Francisco, XII. 439

Rigveda, the, XII. 343, 503

Riley, Thomas, VI. 476

Riming Poem, I. 62, 374, 428

Rimini, Francesca, XII. 395

Rimmer, A., XIII. 544

Rinaldo (Tasso's), VIII. 25

Ring of the Roy Robert, II. 280

Ringsfield, Suffolk, VII. 33

Rintoul, Robert Stephen (1787–1858), XIV. 198, 534

Rio, A. F., XII. 440

Riot act, XIV. 387

Rip van Winkle, XIII. 266

Ripert-Monclar, count Amédée de, XIII. 55

Ripley, George (d. 1490?), II. 469; *The Compound of Alchemy or the Twelve Gates*, and *Medulla Alchemiae*, II. 211ff.; *Vision*, II. 212; *Scroll*, II. 212

Risdon, Tristram (1580?–1640), *Survey of Devon*, IX. 353, 538

Rishanger, William (1250?–1312?), I. 181, 450

Ristori, Adelaide, V. 307; XIII. 514, 515

Ritchie, lady Anne Isabella (born Thackeray), XI. 491; XII. 447; XIII. 478, 485, 502, 529, 530, 549, 551, 558; XIV. 524, 605; *A Discourse on Modern Sibyls*, XIII. 377, 379

Ritchie, David George (1853–1903), XIV. 479

Ritchie, Leitch (1800?–1865), XII. 421, 451; XIV. Add. 5; *Schinderhannes*, XI. 304

Ritchie, William (1781–1831), XIV. 535

Ritson, Joseph (1752–1803), I. 361; II. 205, 391; V. 277; VII. 443; IX. 567; X. 234, 239, 490, 492; XII. 516, 523

Bibliographia Poetica, II. 198; XII. 363

Collection of all the Songs etc. on Robin Hood, XII. 364

Engleish Romanceës, X. 233

Northern Chorister, XI. 231

Observations on Warton's *History of English Poetry*, XII. 363

Select Collection of English Songs, XII. 364

Ritwise, John (? 1532), III. 13; V. 102

Rivers, Alice, VII. 16

Rivers, earl of. *See* Woodville, Anthony

Rivers, Sir John, lord mayor of London, VII. 16

Rivers, Sir John (Charlotte Brontë's), XIII. 409

Rivière, Pierre, III. 59

Rivière des Prairies, XIV. 355

Rivington, Charles (1688–1742), XI. 323

Rivington, Charles (1754–1831), XI. 327

Rivington, Francis (1745–1822), XI. 327

Rivington, Septimus, XIV. 598

Rivingtons, publishers, XI. 468

Rizzio, David, XIII. 133

Roach, Richard (1662–1730), IX. 307, 515, 575

Rob Roy (Robert Macgregor), in Scott's novel, XII. 18, 26

Robberds, J. W., XII. 380, 429

Robbers and Shefters, A ballett, III. 492

Robene (Robin), in *Robene and Makyne*, II. 249

Robert, duke, in *Thomas of Reading*, III. 368

Robert, earl of Gloucester (d. 1147), I. 156, 166, 168, 169, 256, 258; V. 320

Robert, earl of Huntington, in *Looke about you*, V. 320

Robert, prior of Winchester, I. 176

Robert II, king of Scotland, II. 102, 103, 117

Robert III, king of Scotland, II. 280, 369

Robert of Artois, II. 421

Robert of Avesbury (*fl.* 1350), II. 498; IX. 535

Robert of Cicylye, Kynge, V. 13, 49, 50

Robert of Cricklade (1157–1170), I. 191, 456

Robert of Gloucester (*fl.* 1260–1300), I. 336; II. 133; III. 440; IX. 535; *Chronicle*, I. 152, 170, 298, 335 ff., 347, 350, 377, 476; II. 194, 211; III. 279

Robert de Gretham (*fl.* 13th cent.), II. 508

Robert of Jumièges, archbishop of Canterbury (*fl.* 1037–1052), I. 111

Robert of Melun (d. 1167), I. 184, 456

Robert de Monte (1110?–1186), or Robert of Torigni, I. 168, 170, 172, 175, 256, 450

Robert of Sicily, I. 286, 465, 470

Robert the Bruce. *See* Bruce

Robert the Devil, I. 471; II. 501

Robert the Englishman, or Robert de Retines (*fl.* 1141–1143), I. 153

Robert the Robber, in *Piers the Plowman*, II. 12, 33

Roberto, in Greene's *Groatsworth of Wit*, III. 360

Roberts, Alexander, *A treatise of Witchcraft*, IV. 535; VII. 506

Roberts, C. T., XIV. Add. 9

Roberts, Daniel, *The Memoir of John Roberts*, VIII. 106, 416

Roberts, David (1757–1819), *The Military Adventures of Johnny Newcome*, XIV. 220, 545

Roberts, James (*fl.* 1564–1606), IV. 384, 394

Roberts, James, publisher, IX. 247; XI. 323

Roberts, Lewes or Lewis (1596–1640), IV. 513

Roberts, Robert Davies, XIV. 595

Roberts, William (1767–1849), XI. 475; XIV. 600

Robertson, Charles, XIV. 608

Robertson, Eben William (1815–1874), XII. 512

Robertson, Eric S., XI. 410

Robertson, Frederick William (1816–1853), XI. 411; XII. 290 ff., 469; XIII. 475; 'On the Glory of the Virgin Mother,' XII. 291

Robertson, George Croom (1842–1892), VII. 288; XII. 309, 476; XIV. 24, 473, 479

Robertson, James, X. 95

Robertson, James Logie, XII. 373, 409; XIII. 546

Robertson, John G., IX.

Robertson, John Mackinnon, VI. Add.; XIII. 472, 489

Robertson, Joseph (1810–1866), XII. 513, 518; XIV. 497; *Illustrations of the Topography of Aberdeen and Banff*, XII. 359

Robertson, T. (*fl.* 1520–1561), *Inventory of the Riches of the Cathedral of Sarum*, IV. 422

Robertson, Thomas William (1829–1871), XIII. 271 ff., 523

Caste, XIII. 272

David Garrick, XIII. 271

M.P., XIII. 272

Robertson, Thomas William
Ours, XIII. 272
Play, XIII. 272
School, XIII. 272
Society, XIII. 271, 272

Robertson, William (d. 1686?), VII. 490

Robertson, William (1721–1793), X. 132, 281, 285, 287 ff. (main entry), 294, 297, 303, 307, 313, 315, 316, 324, 504, 505; XI. 76, 400; XII. 142, 300, 426; XIV. 102
Disquisition concerning the Knowledge which the Ancients had of India, X. 288
History of America, X. 288, 289
History of Charles V, X. 287 ff.; XI. 326
History of Scotland, X. 287 ff.; XIV. 50

Robertson, William Archibald Scott (1836–1897), XII. 513

Robespierre, Maximilien Marie Isidore, XI. 413; XIII. 12, 420

Robethon, Jean, IX. 236

Robethon, John (d. 1722), X. 295

Robin, in de la Halle's plays, V. 34

Robin, in Mrs Trimmer's *Robins*, XI. 379

Robin Conscience, The Booke in Meeter of, III. 81, 97, 491; IX. 51

Robin Good-fellow, IV. 353, 532, 533; V. 320

Robin Goodfellow, in *Love Restored*, VI. 351, 352, 357, 358, 370, 371

Robin Goodfellow, in *The Devil and his Dame*, V. 329

Robin Goodfellow, in *The Sad Shepherd*, VI. 11

Robin Hood, I. 218, 300, 369, 371; II. 110, 194, 309, 323, 399, 402, 411, 416, 417, 428, 502, 507; III. 68, 358; IV. 529; V. 32, 34, 35, 108, 317 ff., 324 ff.; VI. 238, 365; X. 490; XII. 3, 516

Robin Hood, IX. 166

Robin Hood, in *Looke about you*, V. 320

Robin Hood, in *Robert, Earle of Huntington*, V. 319, 323

Robin Hood, in *The Sad Shepherd*, VI. 11, 369 ff.

Robin Hood, True Tale of, II. 416. See, also, *Robyn*

Robin Hood and his Crew of Soldiers, V. 35

Robin Hood and Little John, The Pastoral Comedy of, V. 318

Robin Hood and the Monk, II. 402, 408, 416

Robin Hood and the Potter, II. 408

Robin Hood's Death, II. 416

Robin's Courtship, IX. 364

Robins, Robert, *Whip for the Marshal's Court, A*, IV. 530

Robinson, Agnes Mary Francis, XIII. 481, 484

Robinson, Benjamin (1666–1724), X. 386

Robinson, Clement (*fl.* 1566–1584), III. 190, 191, 249, 524

Robinson, Elizabeth. *See* Montagu, Mrs Elizabeth

Robinson, Emma, XIII. 566

Robinson, George (1737–1801), XI. 327

Robinson, Henry (1605?–1664?), IV. 310, 513; X. 372

Robinson, Henry Crabb (1775–1867), XI. 122, 133, 192, 197 ff., 411, 417, 423, 434; XII. 167, 201, 433, 441; XIV. 173, 178, 505; *Diary*, XIV. 113

Robinson, J., *The Birth of a Day* (1654), VII. 517

Robinson, James (*fl.* 1600), VI. 289, 290

Robinson, John, *Endoxa*, VII. 239

Robinson, John (1650–1723), bishop of London, IX. 249

Robinson, Sir John Richard, XIV. 532, 535, *also see* Add. 9

Robinson, Matthew, X. 262

Robinson, Matthew (1628–1694), XII. 488

Robinson, Mrs, widow of Rich. Burbage, VI. 276

Robinson, Nicholas (d. 1585), VI. 298

Robinson, Philip Stewart (1847–1902), XIV. 580; *In my Indian Garden*, XIV. 341

Robinson, Richard (*fl.* 1576–1600), 'Eupolemia,' IV. 391, 461, 545; *Harmony of King Davids Harp*, IV. 391

Robinson, Robert (1735–1790), X. 522

Robinson, Thomas, *New Citharen Lessons*, IV. 465

Robinson, Thomas (D.D.), IX. 527

Robinson, Mrs William, X. 261

Robinson des enfants, Le, XIII. 201

Rob's Jok cam to woo our Jenny, IX. 361

Robson, Mary, XI. 482

Roby, Henry John (1830–1915), XII. 492; XIV. 609

   Elementary Latin Grammar, XII. 336

   Essays on the Law of Cicero's Private Orations, XII. 337

   Introduction to Justinian's Digest, XII. 337

   Latin Grammar from Plautus to Suetonius, XII. 336

   Roman Private Law, XII. 337

Robyn and Gandelyn, II. 408

Robyn Hode, The Gest of, II. 329, 402, 408, 416, 428

Robynson, Ralph (*fl.* 1551), VII. 298

Roca, Don Juan, in FitzGerald's *Painter of his own Dishonour*, XIII. 144

Rochdale, XII. 31, 519; XIV. 93

Roche, J., XIII. 465

Roche, James (1770–1853), XIV. 571

Roche, Regina Maria (1764?–1845), XI. 464; *Children of the Abbey*, XI. 299

Rochefort, XIV. 201

Rochefort, expedition to, X. 466

Rochefoucauld, XII. 432

Rochelle, III. 381, 382

Rochester, III. 95; IV. 421; VII. 82; VIII. 5; IX. 145, 538, 540; X. 352, 362; XIII. 335; XIV. 238

Rochester, in *Jane Eyre*, XIII. 407, 408

Rochester, bishop of, in *The merry jests of the widow Edith*, II. 327

Rochester, earls of. *See* Hyde, Lawrence; Wilmot, Henry; Wilmot, John

Rochow, F. E. von, XIV. 382

Rocke, Life of St, in *The Golden Legend*, II. 333

Rockingham, marquis of. *See* Watson-Wentworth, Charles

Rockingham ministry, the, X. 399

'Rod. Staf.,' V. 72

Rodamant, in *St Patrick for Ireland*, VI. 206

Roderick, Visigothic king, XII. 211

Roderigo, in *Othello*, V. 203

Rodes, Sir John, VII. Add.

Rodger, Alexander (1784–1846), XIII. 508

Rodger, M., XIV. 525

Rodney, George Brydges, 1st baron Rodney (1719–1792), XIV. 214, 245

Rodomont, III. 305

Roe, Sir John, IV. 206, 209, 216

Roe, Richard B., XIII. 240, 512

Roe, Sir Thomas (1581?–1644), IV. 90, 216; VII. 434, 437; X. 412; XIV. 332, 333, 580

Roe Head, XIII. 405

Roebuck, in Farquhar's *Love and a Bottle*, VIII. 70

Roebuck, John Arthur (1801–1879), XIV. 419

Roet, Sir Payn, II. 157

Roet or Rouet, Katharine (Swynford), II. 157

Roet or Rouet, Philippa, wife of Chaucer, II. 157

Roger, in *A Dialogue...against the fever Pestilence*, III. 109

Roger, in *The English Traveller*, VI. 94

Roger, count of Sicily, XII. 316

Roger, Mons., dancing-master, X. 440

Roger of Hoveden or Howden (d. 1201?), I. 160, 161, 172 ff., 178, 450; III. 314; IV. 68

Roger of Wendover (d. 1236), I. 159, 178, 179, 451; *Flores Historiarum*, I. 178, 179, 451; II. 318

Rogero, IV. 24

Rogero, the new, a tune, III. 190

Rogers, Arthur George Liddon, XIV. 497

Rogers, A. W., XIV. Add. 9

Rogers, Benjamin Bickley (1828–1919), XII. Add. 3

Rogers, Charles (1825–1890), X. 193, 478; XI. 441, 444; XII. 515

Rogers, Frederic, lord Blachford (1811–1889), *Letters*, XII. 277, 454

Rogers, F., *The Seven Deadly Sins in Literature*, IV. 321, 516

Rogers, Henry (1806–1877), XII. 427, 472, 473; 'The Religious Movement in Germany,' XII. 153

Rogers, James Edwin Thorold (1823–1890), XIV. 479, 497, 508, 509; *History of Agriculture and Prices, A*, XIV. 68; *Protests of the Lords*, XIV. 78

Rogers, John (1500?–1555), III. 44, 474; IV. 446

Rogers, John (1627–1665?), VII. 515; VIII. 319

Rogers, Mrs, X. 121, 126

Rogers, Samuel (1763–1855), IX. 170;
XI. 148, 149, 291; XII. 36, 95 ff. (main
entry), 101, 102, 124, 133, 139, 148,
150, 381, 382, 384, 408, 491; XIII. 230;
XIV. 139, 403, 438
  'Campagna of Rome, The,' XII. 98
  Italy, XII. 96, 98
  Jacqueline, XII. 96
  Pleasures of Memory, The, XII. 41, 96,
  97, 100
  Table Talk, Porsoniana, XII. 325
Rogers, solicitor, X. 117
Rogers, Thomas (d. 1616), IV. 441, 495
Rogers, William (1819–1896), XIV. 609
Rogers, Woodes (d. 1732), XIV. 242, 553
Rogges, a Ballette, III. 492
Rogue pamphlets, IV. 529
Rogue pamphlets and burlesques, VII. 515
Rohan, house of, VIII. 35
Rohault, Jacques, *Traité de physique*, IX.
297
Rohilcand, XIV. 334
Rohilla Afghans, XIV. 334
Roi d'Angleterre et le Jongleur d'Ely, Le,
V. 25
Rojas, Fernando de, *Celestina*, IV. 9, 447;
V. 99, 100, 409; VIII. 125
Rokayle or Rokesle, Stacy de, II. 35
Roland, in *Rauf Coilʒear*, II. 126
Roland, tales and *Song* of, I. 281, 283,
291, 302, 470
Roland and Vernagu, I. 302, 465, 470
Rolfe, shoemaker, in the *Mercuries*, VII.
356
Rolland, John (*fl.* 1560), III. 499; *The
Court of Venus*, III. 131; *The Sevin
Sages*, III. 131
Rolle, Edward, X. 136
Rolle, Henry (1589?–1656), *Abridgment
des plusiers Cases et Resolutions del
Commun Ley*, VIII. 320, 469
Rolle, John (1750–1842), XI. 34
Rolle, Richard, of Hampole (1290?-1349),
I. 364, 399; II. 43 ff., 49, 51, 58, 59, 62,
89, 91, 189, 299, 424, 425, 437 ff.; III. 31,
274, 275
  Works by, or attributed to, Rolle:
  Canticles, on the, II. 48
  Ego dormio et cor meum vigilat, II. 47,
  48
  E.I.O. poem, II. 439
  Lord's Prayer and Commandments, II. 48
  Mending of Life (or the *Form of Living*),
  II. 46, 47
  Mirror of St Edmund, The, II. 47
  Pricke of Conscience, II. 48
  Psalter (Rolle's versions and commen-
  taries), II. 46, 47
Rolleston, George (1829–1881), XII. 513;
XIV. 563; *Forms of Animal Life*, XIV. 300
Rolleston, Thomas William, XII. 401;
XIV. 310, 330, 573
Rolliad, The, X. 239; XI. 34 ff., 39, 40, 42,
53, 391; XII. 120; XIII. 161
Rollington, Ralph, XIV. 532
Rollo, in *The Bloody Brother*, VI. 129, 138

Rollo, Norman duke, in *The Rolliad*, XI.
34
Rollock, Robert (1555?–1599), III. 553
Rolls series, the, XII. 336, 356; XIV. 74, 82
Rolt, Richard (1725?–1770), X. 468
Romagna, the, XII. 36
Romaine, William (1714–1795), X. 365;
XII. 473
Roman alphabet in England, I. 426
Roman antiquities, IX. 352, 355, 538 ff.,
552; XI. 286; XII. 346, 347, 350, 476, 510
Roman Breviary, I. 53; XII. 420
Roman Britain, XII. 507
Roman Caesars, in *The Roman Actor*, VI.
153
Roman catholic doctrine, XII. 261, 270
Roman catholicism, IX. 245; X. 42; XI.
167, 295; XIII. 44, 260, 366; XIV. 53, 55
Roman catholics, IX. 3, 4, 100, 101, 110;
XII. 259, 260, 267, 271, 273, 275, 276;
XIV. 212, 249, 314, 317, 329, 417
Roman catholics attacked, in *Loiola*, VI.
324
Roman conquest of Britain, XIV. 71
Roman empire, VIII. 286, 309, 378
Roman history, X. 319, 320
Roman history and life, Jonson's treat-
ment of, VI. 19, 20
Roman jubilee of 1600, V. 161
Roman law, VIII. 309, 310, 312 ff., 317;
X. 314; XI. 16; XII. 335; XIV. 80
Roman mythology, XIII. 271
Roman poets, IX. 68
Roman republic, the, IX. 561; X. 501
Roman ritual, in *Hymenaei*, VI. 345
Roman soldiers, in *Christus Redivivus*, VI.
295
Roman stage, VI. 373, 376, 390, 399
Roman studies, society for the promotion
of, XII. 340
Roman tragedy, IX. 64; XI 273
Roman wall, the, XII. 346, 508
Roman de Renart, Le, VIII. 59
Roman de la Rose. See *Rose*
Romance qualities in English verse, VIII.
223
Romances, I. 277 ff., 465 ff.; II. 194, 506
Romanello, III. 167
Romanes, George John (1848–1894), XIV.
479, 563
Romanes lecture, XIV. 34
Romanno, IX. 370
Romans, the, X. 232; XI. 273, 352, 362;
XII. 249, 316
Romans, the, in *Believe as you List*, VI. 148
Romans, the, in *The Roman Actor*, VI. 152
Romany novels, XIV. 145, 146
Rombus, in *The May Lady*, VI. 336
Rome, I. 64, 71, 79, 149, 185, 196; II. 50,
55, 61, 66, 67, 71, 74, 75, 77, 79, 84,
119, 131, 238, 287, 288, 310, 345, 350;
III. 5, 29, 32, 99, 154, 316, 329, 340,
365, 376, 400, 401; IV. 3, 127, 243, 254,
257, 264, 323, 424, 428, 429; V. 8, 16,
38, 58, 198, 312; VI. 8, 18 ff., 147 ff.,
174, 311; VII. 10, 35, 99, 100, 180, 183,

Rome
206, 276, 297; VIII. 23, 221, 267, 291,
310, 388; IX. 73, 112, 159, 256, 274;
X. 41, 104, 107, 169, 202, 231, 304, 313,
318, 319; XI. 273; XII. 50, 63, 67, 76,
92, 257, 273, 302, 340, 401; XIII. 72, 74,
77, 79, 104, 393, 435; XIV. 100, 108, 230
Capitol, the, IV. 13; X. 298, 304
English college, III. 422; IV. 127; V. 313
Temple of Jupiter, X. 304
Vatican library, IV. 429
Rome (state), XIV. 61, 68 ff., 79, 110, 175;
history of, XII. 280, 301 ff., 322
Rome, church of, IV. 166, 262, 348, 352;
V. 2, 10, 36, 40, 139, 209, 344, 366;
VI. 3, 149, 150, 197, 324, 387; VII. 10,
142 ff., 208, 212, 217, 222, 223, 297,
304, 309 ff., 327, 378; VIII. 45 ff., 82,
86, 93, 111, 275, 294, 297, 302, 305,
306, 309, 310, 345; IX. 147, 195, 197;
X. 293, 301, 373; XII. 259, 261, 262, 264,
269, 274, 276, 292, 299, 331; XIII. 178,
348, 361; XIV. 26, 54, 55, 110
Rome, court of, in *Mirour de l'Omme*, II.
141
Rome, St Paul at, XII. 477
Rome, street cries of, VI. 101
Rome and Keats, XII. 407
*Rome for Canterbury or a true relation of
the Birth and Life of William Laud*, VII.
145
Romei of Ferrara, count Annibale, III.
437, 438; IV. 448; *Discorsi*, III. 438
Romelio, in *The Devils Law-case*, VI. 183
Romeo, in *Romeo and Juliet*, IV. 79; VII. 8;
XII. 54
Romeo, W. H. W. Betty as, XI. 283
Romeus et Iulietta, VI. 486
Romford, Essex, VII. 46
Romford, Facey (Surtees's), XIV. 234
Romfrey, lord (George Meredith's), XIII.
446
Romillon, VI. 183
Romilly, John, 1st lord Romilly (1802–
1874), XII. 356
Romilly, Sir Samuel (1757–1818), XI. 59;
XIII. 418; XIV. 403, 479, 505, 511, 604
Romney, George (1734–1802), XI. 427
Romney, earl of. *See* Sidney, Henry
Romney, Kent, V. 90
Romola (George Eliot's), XIII. 383, 392,
395, 396
Romont, in *The Fatall Dowry*, VI. 223
Ronaldshay, II. 115
Roncesvalles, II. 112
Rondiel, in *Turnament of Totenham*, I. 366
Ronksley, William, XI. 482; *The Child's
Week's Work*, XI. 371
Ronsard, Pierre de, III. 136, 250 ff., 257,
259, 262 ff., 266, 269, 296, 524; IV. 24,
196, 197, 210, 472; VI. 334; VIII. 385
Abrégé de l'art Poétique Français, III. 296
Amours, III. 259
Odes, III. 259
Sonnets, III. 259
Sonnets pour Hélène, III. 259

Röntgen rays, XIV. 270
Rood, legend of, I. 133, 341, 342. See, also,
Dream of the Rood and Cross
Rood-Tree, Holy, V. 15, 389
Rookery, the, in *David Copperfield*, XIII.
327
Rooper, Thomas Godolphin (1847–1903),
XIV. 609
Roper, Abel (1665–1726), IX. 461; XI. 471;
Post Boy, IX. 5, 434
Roper, Mary, daughter of viscount Bal-
tinglas, VII. 245
Roper, William (1496–1578), III. 470;
V. 247; IX. 534
Roper, William John Duff, XIV. 597
Ros, Sir Richard, *La Belle Dame Sans
Merci*, II. 161, 162, 164, 215, 216
Rosa, Salvator, X. 100, 106
Rosabella, in *Ignoramus*, VI. 322
Rosabelle, in Scott's *Lay of the Last
Minstrel*, XII. 9
Rosalind, in *As You Like It*, I. 298; V. 169,
192, 193; VI. 123, 304
Rosalind, in Shelley's *Rosalind and Helen*,
XII. 62
Rosalind (Spenser's), III. 214, 215, 217,
222, 224, 243
Rosaline, in *Love's Labour's Lost*, V. 178
Rosamond, in *The Civil Wars*, IV. 137
Rosamond's Pond, IX. 36
Rosamund, Fair, in *Looke about you*, V.
320
Rosamund, the Fair (d. 1176?), IV. 182;
VII. 206
Roscellinus, I. 212
Roscius, VI. 250
Roscius, the English, XI. 282
Roscius, the young, XI. 452, 453. *See,
also*, Betty, W. H. W.
Roscoe, Edward Stanley, XIV. 509
Roscoe, Elizabeth M., XIV. 521
Roscoe, Sir Henry E., XIV. 597
Roscoe, Robert, son of W. Roscoe, XI. 385
Roscoe, William (1753–1831), IX. 451;
XI. 482; XIV. 505, 514
Butterfly's Ball, The, XI. 377, 385, 386,
476
Life of Leo X, XIV. 108
Life of Lorenzo de' Medici, XIV. 108
Memoirs of Benvenuto Cellini, XIV. 108
Roscoe, William Caldwell (1823–1859),
XI. 420; XII. 408; XIII. 189, 508, 559
Roscommon, X. 196
Roscommon, earl of. *See* Dillon, Went-
worth
Rose (George Meredith's), XIII. 446
Rose, poem by Hilarius, 191
Rose, F. Horace, Add. 9
Rose, George (1744–1818), XIV. 506
Rose, G. M., XIV. 581
Rose, Henry John (1800–1873), XIV. 593
Rose, Hugh James (1795–1838), XII. 254,
256, 272, 453, 454, 462
Rose, John Holland, XI. 396; XIII. 465
Rose, the Red, in *The Example of Virtue*,
II. 227

Rose, Romaunt of the, or *Roman de la,* I. 280, 291, 321, 330; II. 150, 201, 202, 219, 222, 228, 230, 240, 244, 261, 280, 463; III. 170; V. 22; VIII. 59

Rose, Samuel (1767–1804), X. 480

Rose, the White, in *The Example of Virtue,* II. 227

Rose, William Stewart (1775–1843), XII. 422, *also see* Add.

Rose the Red and White Lily, II. 411

Rose-alley ambuscade, VIII. 35

Rosebury, earl of. *See* Primrose, Archibald Philip

Roseilli, in *Loves Sacrifice,* VI. 192

Rosemund, in *Confessio Amantis,* II. 151

Rosencrantz, in *Hamlet,* V. 201, 261

Roses, wars of the, I. 301; II. 228, 335, 358; III. 166, 211; IV. 137; VI. 90; VII. 194; XI. 280

Rosetta stone, XII. 491

Rosiall, in *The Court of Love,* II. 220, 221

Rosicrucianism, VII. 378

Rosicrucians, the, IV. 278

Rosier, James (1575–1635), IV. 461

Rosières, R., XII. 535

Rosimunda, in *The Bugbears,* V. 115

Rosin, Will, in *The Tatler,* IX. 41

Rosinante, in *Don Quixote,* VIII. 67; IX. 268

Rosiphelee, in *Confessio Amantis,* II. 151, 219

Roslyn, Guy, XIII. 552

Ross, Alexander (1591–1654), VII. 238, 239, 407, 466, 474, 511, 512; VIII. 408

Ross, Alexander (1699–1784), IX. 374, 567
   Bridal O't, The, IX. 372
   Helenore, or the Fortunate Shepherdess, II. 110; IX. 372
   Rock and the Wee Pickle Tow, The, IX. 372
   Wooed and Married and a', IX. 372

Ross, Sir James Clark (1800–1862), XIV. 245, 296, 553, 563

Ross, John. *See* Rous

Ross, John, printer, IV. 413

Ross, Sir John (1777–1856), XIV. 245, 554

Ross, J. H., XIV. 586

Ross, Robert E., XIII. 524; XIV. 527, 528

Rossaline, in *Antonio and Mellida,* VI. 48

Rossall school, XIV. 414

Rosset, François de, VI. 33, 174, 176

Rosseter, Philip (1575?–1623), IV. 113, 142, 143, 465

Rossetti, Christina Georgina (1830–1894), IX. 178; X. 369; XI. 482; XII. 119, 276, 277; XIII. 111, 137, 138 ff. (main entry), 147, 148, 175, 178, 181, 252, 496 (main entry)
   Ballad of Boding, A, XIII. 140
   Birthday, A, XIII. 139
   Brandons Both, XIII. 140
   Christmas Carol, A, XIII. 140
   Dream Land, XIII. 138
   End, An, XIII. 138
   German-French Campaign, The, XIII. 140
   Goblin Market, XIII. 138, 139

Rossetti, Christina Georgina
   Later Life, XIII. 138
   Martyr's Song, XIII. 139
   Maude Clare, XIII. 140
   Monna Innominata, XIII. 138
   New Poems, XIII. 138
   Oh roses for the flush of youth, XIII. 138
   Old and New Year Ditties, XIII. 140
   '*Passing away,*' XIII. 140
   Pause of Thought, A, XIII. 138
   Prince's Progress, The, XIII. 138
   Sleep at Sea, XII. 128
   Testimony, A, XIII. 138

Rossetti, Dante Gabriel (1828–1882), X. 220; XI. 305, 416, 431; XII. 87, 92, 119, 154, 275; XIII. 52, 54, 72, 110 ff. (main entry), 119, 120, 122, 129, 132, 133, 137, 140, 147, 166, 185, 187, 205, 207, 219, 221, 223, 252, 440, 442, 448, 474, 490 ff. (main entry), 496, *also see* Add. 2; XIV. 462
   Ave, XIII. 112
   Ballads and Sonnets, XIII. 112
   Blessed Damozel, The, XIII. 111 ff., 116, 138
   Bride's Prelude, The, XIII. 114
   Burden of Nineveh, The, XIII. 112, 138
   Card-Dealer, The, XIII. 115
   Dante and his Circle, XIII. 112
   Dante at Verona, XIII. 118
   Early Italian Poets, The, XIII. 112
   Eden Bower, XIII. 115
   Hand and Soul, XIII. 111
   House of Life, The, XIII. 112, 117
   Jenny, XIII. 116
   King's Tragedy, The, II. 472; XIII. 112, 114
   Last Confession, The, XIII. 116
   Love's Nocturn, XIII. 116
   My Sister's Sleep, XIII. 111, 113, 138
   Pax Vobis (World's Worth), XIII. 112
   Poems (1870), XIII. 112, 211
   Rose Mary, XIII. 112, 115
   Sister Helen, XIII. 115
   Song of the Bower, The, XIII. 117
   Staff and Scrip, The, XIII. 112, 116
   Stream's Secret, The, XIII. 116
   Troy Town, XIII. 115
   White Ship, The, XIII. 112, 114, 116
   Wood-spurge, XIII. 179
   World's Worth, XIII. 112

Rossetti, Elizabeth Eleanor (born Siddal), XIII. 112

Rossetti, Maria Francesca, XIII. 118

Rossetti, William Michael (1829–1919), XI. 406, 412, 431, 433, 441; XII. 381, 384, 397, 399 ff., 404, 405, 407, 409, 410, 418; XIII. 72, 110, 138, 490, 491, 495, 496, 499, 561, *also see* Add. 2

Rossi, V. 307

Rosslyn, earls of. *See* Erskine, Francis; Wedderburn, Alexander

Ross-shire, XIV. 294

Rostand, Edmond, *Chantecler,* VIII. 47

Rostgaard, Frederik, *Deliciae Quorundam Poetarum Danorum,* IV. 267

Roswall and Lilian, I. 291, 470
Roswitha. *See* Hrotsvitha
Rot amongst the Bishops, VII. 145
Rota, The Censure of the, VII. 389
Rota club, VII. 362, 389
Rotha, river, XIII. 94
Rotheram, Thomas (1423–1500), IV. 432
Rotherham, Caleb (1694–1752), X. 386
Rotherham school, III. 428; v. 80
Rotherhithe, VII. 308, 318
Rothes, lady, wife of Benet Langton, XI. 365
Rothesay, duke of. *See* Stewart, David
Rothwell, X. 371
Rothwell, John, bookseller, XI. 338
Rotrou, Jean de, VIII. 13
Rotterdam, VII. 308; VIII. 282; IX. 246
Rotterdam, in *The Unfortunate Traveller*, III. 363
Rotuli de oblatis et finibus, XII. 355
Rotuli Normanniae, XII. 355
Rouen, II. 335, 352, 505; IV. 142, 402, 427; VII. 22, 308; IX. 256, 270; XIV. 73
Rouen academy, XI. 274
Rougham, IX. 241
Rougon-Macquart family, Zola's, XIII. 457
'Round Robin,' III. 80
Round Table, the, I. 235, 251, 255, 260, 264, 266, 267, 286, 327, 336; II. 116, 122, 123; XII. 354
Roundway Down, battle of, VII. 350
Rous or Ross, John (1411?–1491), II. 498; *Historia Regum Angliae*, v. 31; IX. 349, 534
Rous, John (1584–1644), *Diary* of, VII. 224, 225, 453
Rous or Rouse, John, Bodley's librarian (1574–1652), IV. 251; VII. 132, 135, 453
Rouse, William Henry Denham, XIII. 486; XIV. 598
Rousseau, Jean-Jacques, IV. 260; v. 292; VIII. 141; IX. 399, 401; X. 18, 57 ff., 134, 155, 190, 323, 324, 458; XI. 19, 27, 32, 71, 73, 79, 87, 93, 292, 295, 296, 305, 382; XII. 44, 76, 164, 168, 177, 178, 397, 525; XIII. 13, 341, 417; XIV. 248, 405
Discourse, X. 57, 59
Émile, X. 59, 135; XIV. 382, 391 ff., 395, 421
La Nouvelle Héloïse, X. 17, 19, 60; XIV. 382
Le contrat social, XI. 139
Letter to Philopolis, X. 57
Rêveries, X. 60
Routh, Edward John (1831–1907), XIV. 265, 556
Routh, Martin Joseph (1755–1854), IX. 209; XII. 260, 327, 462; *Reliquiae Sacrae*, XII. 278, 327
Rover, in O'Keeffe's *Wild Oats*, XI. 281
Rovers, The, XI. 41
Row, Charles Adolphus, XIV. 417, 596
Row, John (1568–1646), IX. 550; XII. 515
Row, John (1598?–1672?), IX. 558
Rowallane, the House of, IX. 556

Rowbotham, John Frederick, XIV. 598
Rowcroft, Charles, XIV. 369, 587
Rowe, Nicholas (1674–1718), v. 166, 222, 267 ff., 271; VI. 3, 248; VIII. 193, 195 ff., 440, 445; IX. 75, 144, 476; X. 69, 82, 86, *also see* Add.
Ambitious Stepmother, The, VIII. 195
Biter, The, VIII. 196
Fair Penitent, The, VI. 165; VIII. 195, 197; X. 68, 73
Lucan, trans. of, VIII. 197
Lutrin, trans. of Boileau's, VIII. 197
Rowley, Satyr on Old, VIII. 97
Royal Convert, The, VIII. 196
Shakespeare, XI. 319, 320
Tamerlane, VIII. 195
Tragedy of Jane Shore, The, VI. 90; VIII. 196; X. 68, 74
Tragedy of Lady Jane Grey, The, VIII. 181, 196; XI. 322
Ulysses, VIII. 196
Rowe, Richard, *pseud.* Peter Possum (1828–1879), XIV. 362, 587
Rowe, Thomas (1657–1705), X. 385
Rowland (*i.e.* Michael Drayton), IV. 172, 173, 175
Rowland, David (*fl.* 1569–1586), trans. of *Lazarillo de Tormes*, III. 536; IV. 9, 446; VIII. 127
Rowland, William, VII. 509
Rowlands, *alias* Verstegen, Richard (*fl.* 1565–1620), VII. 353; *Restitution of Decayed Intelligence*, III. 81
Rowlands, Samuel (1570?–1630?), III. 114, 482; IV. 323, 334, 357 ff., 363, 516, 517, 519, 526, 529, 530; v. 371, 479; VII. 395, 407; IX. 32, 51; XII. 376
Betraying of Christ, The, IV. 357
God save the King, IV. 351
Greenes Ghost haunting Coniecatchers, IV. 358
Letting of Humours Blood in the Head-Vaine, The, IV. 333, 357, 360
Looke to it for Ile Stabbe ye, IV. 358
Melancholy Knight, The, IV. 359
Terrible Battell betweene the two consumers of the whole world, A, IV. 358
Tis merrie when Gossips meete, IV. 341, 357
Tis mery when Knaves mete, IV. 517
Rowlandson, Thomas (1756–1827), X. 479; XIV. 215 ff., 221 ff., 225, 232, 235, 540, 541, 543
Rowley, in Sheridan's *School for Scandal*, XI. 271
Rowley, Alexander, VII. 490
'Rowley, Old,' VIII. 207
Rowley, Samuel (d. 1633?), v. 312, 475, 476; VI. 215
Bristow Tragedy, The, VI. 96
Joshua, v. 333
Noble Souldier, The, VI. 215
When you see me, You know me, v. 333, 334, 344, 362
Rowley, Thomas (*pseud., see* Chatterton), X. 236; XI. 390

Rowley, William (1585?-1642?), IV. 532, 533; V. 236, 249 ff., 333, 349, 366, 370; VI. 58-80 (main entry), 104, 116, 132, 138 ff., 145, 184, 185, 190, 424, 427, 445, 455; VIII. 132
Alls Lost by Lust, VI. 59, 68, 71; VIII. 129
Birth of Merlin, The. See *Birth*
Match at Midnight, A, VI. 68
New Wonder, A Woman never vext, A, VI. 68, 70, 72
Search for Money, A; or, the Lamentable Complaint for the Loss of the Wandering Knight, Monsieur L'Argent, VI. 59
Shoo-maker a Gentleman, A, III. 371; VI. 68, 70
Witch of Edmonton, The, VI. 58, 69, 76, 96, 190
Rowley, William and J. Fletcher, *The Maid in the Mill*, VIII. 128, 129
Rowley, William and T. Middleton, *The Spanish Gipsie*, VIII. 129
Rowley poems, the, X. 234, 236, 237, 241, 485, 486, 492
Rowlis Cursing, Sir John, II. 269, 280
Rowntree, John Wilhelm, XIV. 592
Rowton heath, battle of, VII. 6, 39
Roxana, in Lee's *Rival Queens*, VIII. 261
Roxburgh, duke of. *See* Ker, John
Roxburgh, earl of. *See* Ker, Robert
Roxburghe Ballads, VIII. 411; IX. 361, 378; XII. 368
Roxburghe club, II. 503; XII. 357, 365, 393
Roxburghshire, X. 93; XII. 511
Roxolana, in D'Avenant's *Siege of Rhodes*, VIII. 261
Roy, J. A., XIV. 571
Roy, Ram Mohan, XIV. 336, 341, 580
Roy, Richmond (Meredith's), XIII. 441
Roy, William (*fl.* 1527-1531), III. 40, 80, 473; translation of *Dialogus inter patrem christianum et filium contumacem*, III. 80; *Rede me and be not wrothe*, III. 80, 105, 481
Royal academy, X. 265, 266; XI. 181; XIII. 449
Royal Archaeological institute, XII. 349
Royal Asiatic society, XII. 352
Royal Botanic society, XIV. 288
Royal Dublin society, XIV. 288
Royal Historical and Archaeological association of Ireland, XII. 351
Royal Horticultural society, XIV. 287
Royal Irish academy, XII. 351, 352
Royal Lancasterian institute, XIV. 403
Royal society, VII. 222, 234, 270, 302, 303, 305, 478; VIII. 8, 61, 62, 247, 248, 277, 291, 329, 354 ff., 358, 359, 361, 364 ff., 368, 369; IX. 27, 32, 130, 213, 352, 358, 387, 389, 412, 413, 573; X. 466; XI. 334; XII. 319; XIV. 266, 280, 283, 284, 286, 287, 460, 461; *Philosophical Transactions*, IX. 139, 358, 538; *Proceedings*, XIV. 264
Royal society of Antiquaries of Ireland, XII. 352

Royal society of Painters in Water Colours, XIV. 221
Roydon, Matthew (*fl.* 1580-1622), IV. 471
Roydon, Owen, III. 190; IV. 471
Rubens, Peter Paul, V. 331; XI. 12; XIV. Add. 3
Rubini, Giovanni Battista, X. 199
Rudd, Anthony (1549?-1615), IV. 199
Rudd, Mrs, X. 190
Rudd, Thomas (1584?-1656), IV. 456
Ruddiman, Thomas (1674-1757), IX. 493, 561, 562, 566; X. 193, 498; XI. 342, 470; XII. 350, 508
Ruddiman, Walter, printer, IX. 567
Ruddiman's Magazine, XI. 234, 235
Ruddiman's Weekly, IX. 562
Rudge, Barnaby (Dickens's), XIII. 317, 320
Rudolf II, emperor, in *Euphormio*, IV. 256
Rudyerd or Ruddier, Sir Benjamin (1572-1658), *Le Prince d'Amour*, IV. 209; VII. 512
Rueda, Lope de, *Comedia de los Engaños*, VIII. 126
Rufa, in Pope's *Characters of Women*, IX. 82
Ruff, in *Cambises*, V. 64
Ruffhead, Owen (1723-1769), IX. 447; X. 390, 522
Ruffians Rant, The, XI. 232
Ruffio (Hall's), IV. 330
Rufina, St, I. 74
Rufinus, I. 66, 75, 117
Rugbeian, The, XIV. 539
Rugby school, VII. 326, 336, 493; IX. 408; XII. 288, 302, 304, 328, 474; XIII. 86, 87, 102, 103, 370; XIV. 386, 413, 414, 422
Rugge, Thomas (d. 1672), *Diurnall*, the, VIII. 241
Ruggieri (Boccaccio's), VI. 304
Ruggiero, in *Orlando Furioso*, III. 231, 236
Ruggle, George (1575-1622), *Ignoramus*, IV. 410, 518; VI. 314, 322, 323, 327, 476
Ruhnken, David, XII. 325
Ruin, The, I. 1, 4, 39, 423, 428
Rule, Britannia, IX. 186
Rule, Gilbert (1629?-1701), IX. 547
Rümelin, Gustav, V. 209, 305
Rumford, in *Club Law*, VI. 309
Rumford, count von. *See* Thompson, Sir Benjamin
Rump: or an exact collection of the choycest Poems and Songs relating to the Late Times, VII. 1, 385, 512
Rump parliament, VI. 408; VII. 161, 355 ff., 360 ff., 383; VIII. 74, 75, 79
Runcie, John, XIV. Add. 5
Runciman, James (1852-1891), XIV. 535
Runes, I. 7, 424. *See, also,* Add. to third impression
Runic monuments, XII. 513
Runic ode, X. 224
Runic Poem, I. 62
Runic poems, X. 489
Runnymede, VII. 60

Rupert, prince (1619–1682), VII. 178, 227, 383, 438, 512, 513; VIII. 202, 358, 359; XIV. 459

'Rupert of debate,' the, XIV. 129

Rusconi, Carlo, V. 306

Rushe, Anthony (1537–1577), V. 102

Rushton, Northants., VIII. 46

Rushworth, John (1612?–1690), I. 132; VII. 351, 355 ff., 434, 435, 440; IX. 193; *Collections of Private Passages of State*, VII. 187, 350; *London Poet, The*, VII. 187, 350; *Perfect Diurnall of the Armies*, VII. 355

Rushworth, Mr, in Jane Austen's *Mansfield Park*, XII. 239, 241

Rushworth Gospels, I. 132

Ruskin, John (1819–1900), I. 217; IV. 45; VII. 25, 126; IX. 321; XI. 28, 386, 387, 482, 485, 491, *also see* Add.; XII. 173, 177, 178, 372, 438, *also see* Add. 1; XIII. 8, 110, 120, 128, 451, 458; XIV. 139, 148 ff. (main entry), 157, 158, 408, 416, 462, 515, 523, 524, *also see* Add. 3
  Academy Notes, XIV. 151
  Aratra Pentelici, XIV. 155
  Arrows of the Chace, XIV. 154
  Art of England, The, XIV. 156
  Cestus of Aglaia, The, XIV. 154
  Crown of Wild Olive, The, XIV. 154, 415, 416
  Elements of English Prosody, XIII. 248, 512
  Enquiries on the causes of the Colour of the Water of the Rhine, XIV. 150
  Ethics of the Dust, The, XIV. 154
  Facts and Considerations on the Strata of Mont Blanc, XIV. 150
  Fors Clavigera, XIV. 148, 154, 155
  Joy for Ever, A, XIV. 152
  Lectures in Landscape, XIV. 155
  Lectures on Architecture and Painting, XIV. 152
  Lectures on Art, XIV. 155
  Modern Painters, XIV. 138, 148 ff., 155, 157
  Mornings in Florence, XIV. 155
  Munera Pulveris, XIV. 138, 152
  Note on the Peforration of a Leaden Pipe by Rats, XIV. 150
  Notes on the Construction of Sheepfolds, XIV. 151
  On the Old Road, XII. Add.; XIV. 149
  Pleasures of England, The, XIV. 156
  Poetry of Architecture, The, XIV. 149, 150
  Political Economy of Art, The, XIV. 152, 153
  Praeterita, XIV. 148, 150, 156, 157
  Pre-Raphaelitism, XIV. 151
  Queen of the Air, The, XIV. 154
  Relation between Michael Angelo and Tintoret, The, XIV. 155
  St Mark's Rest, XIV. 155
  Salsette and Elephanta, XIV. 149
  Sesame and Lilies, XIV. 154
  Seven Lamps of Architecture, The, XIV. 150, 151, 153

Ruskin, John
  Stones of Venice, The, XIV. 150, 151, 415
  Time and Tide, XIV. 154
  Two Paths, The, XIV. 152
  Unto this Last, XIV. 148, 152 ff.

Ruskin, John, and Scott's MSS., XII. 372

Ruskin college, XIV. 409

Rusport, lady, in Cumberland's *West Indian*, XI. 264

Russel, Alexander (1814–1876), XIV. 203, 204, 535

Russell, Alexander (1715?–1768), X. 466

Russell, Arthur, of Killowen, XIV. 329

Russell, Charles, 1st baron Russell (1832–1900), XIV. 329

Russell, Sir Edward R., XIII. 515; XIV. 535

Russell, E. S., XIII. 573

Russell, Francis, 5th duke of Bedford (1765–1805), X. 246; XI. 29, 30, 389

Russell, George, XIV. Add. 9

Russell, George William Erskine, *Collections and Recollections*, XIV. 296, 537; *Matthew Arnold*, XIII. 87, 88, 488; *Sydney Smith*, XIV. 203

Russell, John, 1st earl of Bedford (1486?–1555), III. 167

Russell, John, 4th duke of Bedford (1710–1771), X. 29, 404

Russell, lord John, 1st earl Russell (1792–1878), XI. 396; XII. 319, 412; XIII. 350; XIV. 107, 116, 121, 126, 198, 417, 502, 506, 511, 604; 'Earls Grey and Spencer,' XII. 153; *Life of William Lord Russell*, IX. 199

Russell, Lucy, countess of Bedford (d. 1627), IV. 15, 175, 176, 197, 202, 203, 205, 211, 216, 265; VI. 9, 337

Russell, Matthew (1834–1912), XIV. 329, 571

Russell, R., contributor to *The Grub Street Journal*, XI. 466

Russell, Rachel, lady (1636–1723), VIII. 272, 452; *Letters*, VIII. 272, 452; IX. 201; X. 500

Russell, Robert, XIV. Add. 9

Russell, Robert C., XIV. 373

Russell, Thomas (1762–1788), X. 456

Russell, William, lord Russell (1639–1683), VIII. 272, 452; IX. 199, 203, 239, 490; X. 351, 500

Russell, William (1741–1793), X. 504; *History of Modern Europe*, X. 294

Russell, William Clark (1844–1911), XIII. 566

Russell, Sir William Howard, XIV. 173, 178, 182, 190, 535

Russell, Wriothesley, 2nd duke of Bedford (1680–1711), VIII. 272

Russell, house of, XI. 30

Russell's Farewell, VIII. 96

Russet, in Colman's *Jealous Wife*, X. 89

Russia, V. 308; X. 466; XI. 58, 72, 358; XII. 46, 55; XIII. 55; XIV. 132, 137, 173, 294

Russia and Landor, XII. 440
Russian language, XIV. 434, 457, 458
Russo-Turkish war, XIV. 179
Rust, George (d. 1676), VIII. 290, 456
Rusticus, in *Horestes*, v. 64
Rusticus ad Academicos, VIII. 111
Ruth, IV. 43; x. 104
Ruth, in Biblical comedies, v. 101
Ruth, in Crabbe's *Tales of the Hall*, XIII. 380
Rutherford, Mark (William Hale White)
    (d. 1914), XI. 412; XIII. 438–439, 567;
    Autobiography, XIII. 431; *The Revolu-
    tion in Tanner's Lane*, XIII. 438
Rutherford, Samuel (1600–1661), VII.
    483; IX. 544, 545
Rutherford, William Gunion (1853–1907),
    XII. 492; *The New Phrynichus*, XII. 334
Rutherforth, Thomas (1712–1771), VIII.
    473
Ruthven, x. 230
Ruthven, William, 1st earl of Gowrie
    (1541?–1584), XIV. 486
Ruthwell Cross, the, Dumfriesshire, I. 12,
    56, 57, 425; II. 88
Rutland, VII. 340; IX. 541
Rutland, duchess of. *See* Manners, Cathe-
    rine
Rutland, duke of. *See* Manners, Charles
Rutland, earl of. *See* Manners, Roger
Rutt, John Towill, XIV. 608
Rutter, Joseph (*fl.* 1635), VIII. 13; *Shep-
    herd's Holiday, The*, VI. 366, 491; ver-
    sion of the *Cid* by, VIII. 180
Ruysbroek, Johannes, IX. 314, 318
Ruyter, admiral de, VIII. 11
Ryan, Richard (1796–1849), XIV. 571
Rycaut, Sir Paul (1628–1700), IX. 247, 495
Rydal mount, XI. 109, 409
Ryder, Dudley, 1st earl of Harrowby
    (1762–1847), XIV. 115, 510
Rye, Sussex, VI. 110
Rye, Walter, XII. 520
Rye house plot, VIII. 44, 90; IX. 199, 202,
    239, 364
Ryland, John Collett (1723–1792), x. 522
Ryland, Jonathan Edwards (1798–1866),
    XIV. 518
Ryland, William Wynne (1732–1783),
    XIV. 216
Rylands, Mrs John, XII. 365
Ryle, John Charles (1816–1900), XII. 471,
    473
Ryley, J. Horton, XIV. 576
Rymenhild, princess, in *Horn*, I. 304, 306
Rymer, Thomas (1641–1713), v. 222; VI.
    21, 129, 441; VII. 268; VIII. 164, 167,
    194, 213, 374 ff., 410, 433, 441; IX. 122,
    473; x. 219, 220; XI. 286
    Edgar, or the English Monarch, VIII.
    195, 441; IX. 140
    Foedera, VIII. 195; IX. 141, 356, 495;
    x. 280; XII. 355, 516
    *Reflections on Aristotle's Treatise of
    Poesie*, IX. 140
    Short View of Tragedy, A, VII. 275;
    VIII. 163, 195, 221, 375; IX. 140

Rymer, Thomas
    Tragedies of the Last Age, The, VIII. 195,
    375
    Tragedies of the Last Age considered.
    IX. 140
Ryswick, peace of, VIII. 90; IX. 149, 205,
    214
Ryves, Bruno (1596–1677), *Mercurius
    Rusticus*, VII. 351

S., J. K. *See* Stephen, James Kenneth
S., Mr, VI. 296, 297
S. B., VII. 250
S. G. O. *See* Osborne, lord Sidney Go-
    dolphin
S. R., *The Noble Souldier*, v. 333
S. S., *pseud.*, XI. 378, 430
'Sa Singularité' (duchess of Queensberry),
    IX. 162
Saadi, x. 144
Sabellian heresy, I. 224
Sabellianism, x. 377
Sabie, Francis (*fl.* 1587–1596), IV. 471, 472
Sabina, in Kingsley's *Two Years Ago*, XIII.
    365
Sabine, Joseph (1770–1837), XIV. 287, 288,
    563
Sabine women, VI. 392
'Sabinus,' in Pope's *Epistles*, IX. 81
Sablé, Mme de, XIII. 552
Sabren, in *Locrine*, v. 239
Sabrina, in Geoffrey of Monmouth, I. 171
Sabrinae Corolla, XII. 329
Sacharissa (Dorothy, countess of Sunder-
    land), VIII. 267, 380. *See, also,* Sunder-
    land
Sacharissa (Waller's), VII. 54 ff.
Sacheverell, Henry (1674?–1724), IX. 11,
    13, 95, 130, 139, 234, 394, 473, 478,
    490, 571; x. 353, 374, 390; XIV. 212
Sachs, Hans, *Goodly disputation*, III. 80
Sachs, Julius von, XIV. 283
Sack-full of News, The, III. 95, 488
Sackville, Charles, 6th earl of Dorset
    (lord Buckhurst) (1638–1706), VII. 180;
    VIII. 49, 91, 133, 136, 198 ff., 203 ff.,
    212, 214 ff., 410, 411, 444, 445; IX. 146,
    148, 169, 278; x. 226; *To all you Ladies
    now at Land*, VIII. 217; *To Mr Edward
    Howard*, VIII. 217; version of *Pompée*,
    VIII. 180
Sackville, Sir Edward, 4th earl of Dorset
    (1591–1652), VII. 222, 235
Sackville, lord George. *See* Germain,
    George Sackville
Sackville, Richard, 5th earl of Dorset
    (1622–1677), VIII. 13
Sackville, Thomas, 1st earl of Dorset and
    lord Buckhurst (1536–1608), II. 220;
    III. 192, 193, 197, 199 ff., 228, 283, 285,
    287, 517; IV. 145, 193, 265; v. 66, 67, 69,
    78, 227; VIII. 222; *Induction*, II. 228;
    III. 192, 193, 200, 201, 228. See, also,
    Gorboduc
Sacrament, songs based on the, II. 387
Sacred Books of the East, XII. 343

Sacrifice of Abraham, The, v. 390, 391
Sacro Monte, at Varallo-Sesia, XIII. 450
Sad Circumspeccyon, in *Magnyfycence*,
  III. 77
Sadducees, VII. 303, 370
Sadler, John (d. 1595?), IV. 440
Sadler, John (1615–1674), VI. 477; VII. 509
Sadler, Sir M. E., XIV. 592, 596
Sadler, Sir Ralph (1507–1587), XII. 376;
  Life, Letters and State Papers, XII. 16
Sadler, Thomas (1822–1891), XIV. 505
Sadlier, Mary Ann, XIV. 581
Sadoleto, Jacopo, bishop of Carpentras,
  III. 420
Saeferth (Sigeferth?), in *Widsith*, I. 34
Saemund, X. 487
Saenger, S., XIV. 478
Saewulf of Malmesbury, IV. 68
Saffron Walden, III. 213; v. 372
Saffron Walden academy, X. 385
Saga library, XIII. 127
Sage, John, bishop (1652–1711), IV. 151;
  IX. 547, 561
Sagittarius, bishop of Embrun, I. 67
Sahara, the, XIV. 167
St Albani, Chronica Monasterii, I. 449, 451
St Albans, I. 153, 159, 174, 178, 179, 181,
  182, 193, 214; II. 80, 81, 302, 317, 318;
  IV. 409, 426; v. 7, 38; VI. 196; XI. 80;
  XII. 182
St Albans, library at, III. 48
St Albans, duke of. *See* Beauclerk, Charles
St Albans, earl of. *See* Jermyn, Henry
St Albans, The Book of, II. 318, 323, 420;
  IV. 364, 370, 375, 543
St Albans' grammar school, VI. 197; VII.
  330
St Aldegonde, in Disraeli's *Lothair*, XIII.
  350
St Andrews, II. 126, 129, 250, 259, 273,
  285, 367, 368 ff.; III. 122, 140, 142, 149,
  151, 157, 424, 426; VII. 448; IX. 129,
  359, 378, 542, 545, 566; X. 295; XI. 243;
  XII. 359; XIV. 40, 209, 210, 297, 424, 432
  St Leonard's college, II. 369, 370
  St Mary's college, II. 369, 370
  St Salvator's college, II. 369; X. 291
  United college, XII. 259
St Andrews College Echoes, The, XIV. 209
St Andrews University Magazine, The,
  XIV. 538
St Angelo, X. 314
St Anne, v. 48, 56
St Asaph, II. 288; IX. 196, 329, 350, 541;
  XI. 364, 399
St Barbe, in Disraeli's *Endymion*, XIII. 351
St Bartholomew, massacre of, III. 402;
  IV. 276; v. 341; VII. 191, 304; VIII. 87;
  XIV. 54, 118
St Bertin's monastery in Flanders, I. 89
St Brice's day, massacre of, v. 31
St Catharine's convent, mount Sinai, XII.
  341
Saint Chaumont, marchioness de, sister
  of Gramont, VIII. 263
St David's, I. 89, 194, 196; VIII. 305; IX. 540

St David's, see of, XII. 308
St Domingo, v. 361
Saynt Dyryk, v. 97
St Edmund's. *See* Bury St Edmunds
St Edmundsbury. *See* Bury St Edmunds
Saint-Évremond, Charles de Marguetel de
  Saint-Denis de (1613?–1703), VI. 273;
  VIII. 30, 135, 174, 199, 212, 376, 377,
  402, 424, 445, 481; IX. 499
St Gall or St Gallen, v. 36, 37; Bede's
  Death Song at, I. 61
St-Gelais, Mellin de, v. 62
St Gelais, Octavien, bishop of Angoulême,
  III. 153, 502
St George, guild of, XIV. 153 ff.
St Germain, court of, VIII. 267; X. 295
Saint-German, Christopher (1460?–1540),
  Doctor and Student, VIII. 315, 467
St Gluvias, Cornwall, X. 193
St Helena, XIII. 276
St Hubert's abbey in the Ardennes, I. 82
St Ives, VII. 54
St James's Chronicle, X. 479; XI. 402
St James's Gazette, IX. 445; XIV. 189, 195
St Jean de Luz, XIII. 456
St John, Charles George William (1809–
  1856), XIV. 545
St John, Henrietta, IX. 217
St John, Henry, 1st viscount Bolingbroke
  (1678–1751), v. 288; VIII. 410, 411;
  IX. 14, 15, 81, 83, 85, 89, 95 ff., 112, 124,
  131, 150 ff., 161, 166, 185, 192, 207,
  216 ff. (main entry), 252, 288, 433, 434,
  444, 445, 467, 472, 478, 483, 487, 504,
  509, 547; X. 272, 279, 301, 386, 482,
  521; XI. 2 ff., 9, 12, 26; XII. 426; XIII.
  346, 419
  Case of Dunkirk consider'd, IX. 224
  Craftsman Extraordinary, IX. 221
  Dissertation upon Parties, IX. 224, 225
  Final Answer, A, IX. 223
  First Vision of Camelick, IX. 221
  Idea of a Patriot King, IX. 230, 231
  Letter on the Spirit of Patriotism, IX. 229,
  230
  Letter on the True Use of Retirement,
  IX. 228, 233
  Letter to Sir William Wyndham, IX. 218,
  219, 223
  Letters and Correspondence, IX. 216
  Letters on the Study...of History, IX.
  226 ff.
  Occasional Writer, The, IX. 223, 491
  *Of the State of Parties at the Accession
  of George I*, IX. 231
  Philosophical Works, IX. 295
  Plan of a General History of Europe,
  IX. 228
  Reflections on Exile, IX. 218
  Remarks upon the History of England,
  IX. 221, 223
  *Some Reflections on the Present State of
  the Nation*, IX. 231
St John, Henry. *See* Oldcastle, Humphry
St John, knights of (Hospitallers), I. 189;
  II. 111; III. 13; VII. 333

St John, Percy Bolingbroke (1821–1889), XI. 387, 489

St John's day, VIII. 54

St Kilda, X. 102

St Leonards, lord. See Sugden, Edward Burtenshaw

St Lo, George (1682?–1729), IV. 102, 461

Saint-Martin, Louis Claude de (1743–1803), IX. 328, 521

St Mary Charlcombe, X. 22

St Michael's mount, IV. 200

St Michael's mount, in Arthurian legend, I. 256, 260

St Michel, Elizabeth, wife of Samuel Pepys, VIII. 253

'Saynt Modwin,' V. 97

'Saynt Myghell,' in The Four P.P., V. 97

St Neot, X. 510

St Ogg's, in The Mill on the Floss, XIII. 392

St Omer, IX. 213; college at, III. 422; IV. 402; VII. 45; VIII. 266

St Osyth, VII. 373

St Patrick's Purgatory. See Staunton, W.

St Petersburg. See Petrograd

St Pierre, Eustace de, in Colman's Siege of Paris, XI. 257

Saint-Pierre, Jacques Henri Bernardin de, Paul et Virginie, XI. 280

St Pierre, Martinique, XIV. 165

St Prassede, church of, XIII. 69

St Praxed's, the bishop of (Browning's), XIII. 63

Saint-Preux, in Rousseau's La Nouvelle Héloïse, X. 17; XII. 60

Saint-Réal, Abbé de, Don Carlos, VIII. 182, 439; La Conjuration des Espagnols contre la république de Venise en 1618, VIII. 183

St Scholastica's day, II. 345, 346

St Serf, in Wyntoun, II. 131

St Serf's priory, Lochleven, II. 129

St Serfe, Sir Thomas, Taruzo's Wiles, or the Coffee House, VIII. 131, 189, 422

Saint-Simon, Louis de Rouvroy, duc de, IX. 250; X. 66; XIII. 22, 442, 447; Memoirs, III. 147

St Stephen, Life of, in The Golden Legend, II. 314

St Stephen and Herod, II. 408

'Saint Sunday,' V. 97

St Thomas, play on, V. 56

Saint Thomas de l'Enfer, rue de, in Sartor Resartus, XIII. 6

St Ursula, Guiscard and Sigismund, The Life of, II. 486

Sainte-Beuve, Charles Augustin, III. 147; IX. 61; X. 255, 317; XI. 87, 404; XII. 211, 524, 525; XIII. 99

Sainte Maria Virgine, I. 220

Ste Marie, near Pornic, XIII. 77

Saints, Legends of the, I. 298; III. 92

Saints, Lives of the, I. 120 ff., 128, 151, 229, 286, 298; III. 19. See, also, under Barbour, Bokenam, Lydgate

Saintsbury, George, II. 233; V. 20, 21; VIII. 8, 30, 42, 54; IX. 158; X. 413, 418, 421, also see Add.; XI. 183, 393, 419, 423, 429, 434, 443, 446, 459, 463, 492, also see Add.; XII. 376, 381, 410, 412, 413, 418, 421, 425, 426, 433, 441, 444 ff., 449, 453, 524, also see Add.; XIII. 27, 472, 478, 485, 488, 495, 498, 509, 530, 544, 553, 559, 567, 568, 570, also see Add. 3; XIV. 493, 509, 516, 524, 528, 570; History of Criticism, XI. 353; History of English Prosody, A, I. 289, 338, 350; II. 424; IX. 157; XIII. 32, 512

Sakuntala, XII. 502, 503

Sala, George Augustus Henry (1828–1896), XII. 435; XIII. 532, 541; XIV. 191, 192, 535

Saladin, I. 307; II. 87; VII. 159

Salamenes, in Byron's Sardanapalus, XII. 49

Salamis, XIII. 135

Salanio, in The Merchant of Venice, IV. 79

Saldar, countess de (Meredith's), XIII. 441

Sale, Antoine de la, Les Quinze Joyes de Mariage, III. 89, 90, 485; IV. 8, 526; VIII. 59

Sale, George (1697?–1736), IX. 529

Sale of Authors, The, X. 131

Salem, grand jury of, XI. 12

Salernitano, Masuccio, VI. 102

Salerno, Salernum, Salerne, III. 109; V. 76; VI. 304

Salesbury or Salisbury, William (1520?–1600?), A Dictionary of Englishe and Welshe, III. 461, 555

Salisbury, IV. 190, 228, 274, 409, 421; VI. 141; VII. 29, 244, 245, 277, 333; VIII. 245, 319, 360; IX. 200, 221, 287, 294, 538; X. 22, 207, 209, 346, 470; XI. 424; XII. 192; XIII. 424

Salisbury. See John of

Salisbury, countess of (Drayton's), IV. 182

Salisbury, countess of, in Edward IV, V. 244, 245

Salisbury, earl of. See Cecil, Sir Robert

Salisbury, marquis of. See Gascoyne-Cecil, Robert A. T.

Salisbury breviary, IV. 427

Salisbury cathedral inventory, V. 37

Salisbury plain, V. 251; IX. 269

Salisbury Postman, The, XIV. 169

Salisbury theatre, XI. 451

Salle, Eusèbe de, XII. 385

Sallust, I. 76; II. 366; III. 20, 164, 290, 291, 416, 429, 431; IV. 439; VI. 86; VII. 131; IX. 340, 528; XII. 306, 476; Catiline, IV. 4; Jugurtha, IV. 4

Sally in our Alley, II. 272

Salmacis and Hermaphroditus, in Sandys's trans. of Ovid, VII. 50

Salmasius or Saumaise, Claude de, III. 157; VII. 125, 131, 307, 422; Defensio Regia, VII. 104; Plinianae Exercitationes, VII. 316

Salmon, David, XIV. 592, 602

Salmon, George (1819–1904), XIV. 263, 556

Salmon, Nathaniel (1675–1742), IX. 355, 538

Sal-Nitro, de, VIII. 354

Salomon and Marcolf, I. 218

Salomon and Saturn, Dialogue of, I. 11, 62, 76, 432

Salonius, bishop of Gap, I. 67

Salt, Henry (1780–1827), XIV. 247

Salt, Henry Stephens, XII. 445; XIII. 478, 489, 570

Salt, Samuel (d. 1792), XII. 180, 181, 183, 189, 191

Salter, Samuel (d. 1778), VIII. 457

Salter, Thomas (*fl.* 1580), IV. 518

Salterne, George, *Tomumbeius*, VI. 301, 477

Saltire, lord, in Henry Kingsley's *Ravenshoe*, XIII. 433

Saltmarsh, John (d. 1647), VII. 246, 352, 426, 494, 499

Saltonstall, Wye (*fl.* 1630–1640), III. 114, 487; IV. 461, 521, 522; VII. 485; *Picturae loquentes or Pictures drawn forth in characters*, IV. 341

Saltrey. *See* Henry of

Salutati, Coluccio, V. 61

Salutation and Conception, The, V. 21

Salutation tavern, in Arbuthnot's *History of John Bull*, IX. 135

Salvian, *De Gubernatione Dei*, VI. 390

Salvin, Osbert (1835–1898), XIV. 297, 563

Salvini, Tommaso, V. 307; XIII. 515

Salzmann, Auguste, XII. 339

Salzmann, C. G., XI. 395

Samarah, XI. 289

Samaria, woman of, III. 88

Samaritan, in *Piers the Plowman*, II. 24, 27

Samaritan language, VII. 319

Samber, Robert, XI. 374, 492

Sambourne, Edwin Linley (1844–1910), XIV. 239

Sampson, dominie, in Scott's *Guy Mannering*, XII. 25

Sampson, Elizabeth. *See* Inchbald, Mrs

Sampson, George, XII. 405; XIV. 528

Sampson, John, XI. 184, 431 ff.

Sampson, Thomas (1517?–1589), III. 45

Sampson, William (1590?–1636?), *The true tragedy of Herod and Antipater*, IV. 377, 539; VI. 456

Sampson Legend, Sir, in *Love for Love*, VIII. 151, 164

Samson, I. 74; VIII. 164

Samson, abbot, of Bury (1135–1211), I. 176; II. 342; XIII. 15, 16

Samson, in *Samson Agonistes*, VII. 121, 122, 136

Samson de Nanteuil, II. 508

Samuel, II. 106; XII. 321

Samuel, son of Beulan, I. 70

San Domingo, XI. 114

San Francisco, VIII. 112

San Juan de Ulloa, IV. 73

Sanazzaro or Sannazaro or Sannazarius, Jacopo, III. 219, 262, 300, 351, 352, *also see* Add.; IV. 261, IX. 69; *Arcadia*, III. 219, 351; VI. 364

Sanazzaro, in *The Great Duke of Florence*, VI. 156

Sancho, in *The Spanish Gipsie*, VI. 77

Sancho Panza, in *Don Quixote*, VIII. 70; X. 41, 51

Sancroft, William (1617–1693), archbishop of Canterbury, IV. 55, 426; VII. 159; VIII. 99, 298, 461, 463; X. 355; *Fur Praedestinatus*, VIII. 306

Sand, George (Mme Dudevant), XIII. 71, 272, 283

Sandars, Nicholas, *De Origine ac Progressu Schismatis Anglicani*, IX. 196, 198

Sandells, of Stratford, V. 168

Sanders, Lloyd C., XI. 456; XIV. 510

Sanderson, John (d. 1602), *Institutionum Dialecticarum libri quatuor*, IV. 274, 508

Sanderson, Robert (1587–1663), IX. 513; VII. 149, 150, 157, 252, 426, 463, 474; VIII. 293; *De juramenti promissorii obligatione*, VII. 280; *De obligatione conscientiae*, VIII. 280

Sanderson, Robert (1660–1741), IX. 495; X. 280

Sanderson, Sir T. H., XIV. 509

Sanderson, William, seaman, III. 327

Sanderson, Sir William (*c.* 1586–1676), VII. 447, 454, 518

Sandford, Sir Francis (1824–1893), XIII. 88

Sandford, Harry, in *Sandford and Merton*, XI. 382

Sandford or Sanford, James (*fl.* 1567), IV. 436; VI. 377; VII. 517

Sandham, Elizabeth, XI. 383, 489

Sandle bridge, Cheshire, XIII. 372

Sandon, Essex, II. 208

Sandoval, Prudencio de, *History of Charles V*, IX. 278, 501

Sandown castle, VII. 227

Sandwich, earls of. *See* Montagu, Edward; Montagu, John

Sandwich islands, XIV. 245

Sandys, Edwin (1516?–1588), archbishop of York, III. 189; IV. 235, 299, 494, 513; VII. 49

Sandys, Sir Edwin (1561–1629), III. 406; IV. 235; *Europae Speculum*, III. 548

Sandys, George (1578–1644), IV. 439, 461; VI. 102; VII. 16, 49 ff. (main entry), 56 ff., 409; VIII. 229; IX. 67
  Aeneid, trans. of 1st book, VII. 52
  Christ's Passion, VII. 52
  Ovid, VII. 53, 67
  Paraphrase of songs in Old and New Testaments, VII. 52
  Paraphrase upon the Psalms of David, VII. 52, 67
  Paraphrases, VII. 86
  Paraphrases of Job, Ecclesiastes, Lamentations of Jeremiah, etc., VII. 52
  Relation of a Journey, IV. 89, 401
  Song of Solomon, VII. 52

Sandys, Sir John Edwin (1844–1921), XII. 482, 485, 489; *Classical Scholarship*, 206

Sangster, Charles (1822–1893), XIV. 350, 357, 582
Sannie Beyers, XIV. 377
Sanny Briggs, IX. 365
Sansfoy, in *The Faerie Queene*, III. 234
Sanskrit language and literature, XII. 318, 327, 343, 352, 362; XIV. 97, 416
Sanskrit scholars, XIV. 334, 335, 337
Sansovino, F., IV. 448
Santa Maria Maggiore, XIII. 69
Santander, VII. 53
Santon Downham, Suffolk, VII. 224
Santorio, VI. 175
Santos, Brazil, Jesuit college (library) at, III. 359
Sapience, in *Ane Pleasant Satyre*, III. 125
Sapience, in *The Example of Virtue*, II. 228
Sapience, in *The Palice of Honour*, II. 260
Sapience (Wisdom), in *The Passetyme of Pleasure*, II. 228
Sapientia Salomonis, play, VI. 486
Sapless, Miss, in Morton's *Way to get Married*, XI. 281
Sappho, IV. 30; XI. 232, 426; XII. 329
'Sappho,' in Pope's *Imitations of Horace*, IX. 85, 251
Saracen, princess, in *The Golden Legend*, II. 334
Saracenic wars, VII. 367
Saracens, in romance, I. 282, 293, 302, 304 ff., 317
Saracens, the, II. 350, 366; IV. 68; X. 281; XI. 25
Saravia, Adrian (1531–1613), III. 409; VII. 309, 317
Sarcastic, Mr, in Peacock's novel, XI. 309
Sardanapalus, in Byron's drama, XII. 49
Sardego, in *The City Witt*, VI. 225, 229
Sardinia, IV. 259
Sardinian legation, X. 301
Sardou, Victorien, XIII. 266, 272, 525
Sargent, E., XII. 409
Sargent, John Young (1829–1915), XII. 493
Sarmiento, IV. 78
Sarpedon, IX. 70, 74
Sarpi, Paolo (father Paul), IV. 448; VII. 190, 308; X. 164, 460, 464; *History of the Council of Trent*, IX. 197
Sarrazin, Gabriel, V. 161; XIII. 485, 491, 495
Sarsnet, Mrs, in Holcroft's *Deserted Daughter*, XI. 277
Sarto, Andrea del, X. 119
Sarum, dean of. *See* Bridges, John
Sarum Missal, II. 315; III. *also see* Add.; IV. 421, 427
Sarum Ordinale, II. 315
Sarum play, V. 37
Sarum Use, the, II. 377; IV. 427
Sassanian or New Persian Empire, the, XII. 478
Satan, IV. 167; VII. 370, 373, 375, 397, 503, 509; XI. 106, 193, 196, 197, 199, 305; XIV. 306

Satan, in Dryden's *The State of Innocence*, VIII. 28
Satan, in *Genesis B*, I. 46, 47
Satan, in *Mary Magdalene*, V. 20
Satan, in Milton's *Paradise Lost*, I. 47; VII. 118, 119, 136; IX. 60, 339; XII. 48, 85, 398
Satan, in *The Devill is an Asse*, VI. 24
Satan, Old English, I. 428
Satire, in *The Muses Looking-Glasse*, VI. 233
Satire, political and ecclesiastical, VIII 408 ff.
Satire against Satirists, The, VI. 88
Satyre against Separatists, A, VII. 408
Satire Ménippée, III. 388, 398; IV. 449
Satires, Satyres, IV. 518, 519
Satires on political characters (Civil War), VII. 512
Saturday papers, in *The Spectator*, IX. 59
Saturday Review, The, XII. 306, 471, 475; XIV. 71, 76, 85, 110, 146, 180, 194, 198, 199, 531, 533 ff.
Saturn, II. 276
Saturn, in Alfred's *Boethius*, I. 100
Saturn, in Keats's *Hyperion*, XII. 85
Saturn, in *The Four Ages*, VI. 92, 93
Saturn, in *The Testament of Cresseid*, II. 248
Saturnalia, V. 8; VI. 319, 474; X. 226
Saturn's rings, VIII. 350
Saul, II. 10, 151; VII. 67, 296, 395
Saul, in Cowley's *Davideis*, VII. 66
Saumur (in Anjou), VIII. 265
Sauncepere, lady, in *The Bowge of Courte*, III. 73
Saunders, Charles, *Tamerlane the Great* (1681), VIII. 401
Saunders, Sir Edmund (d. 1683), VIII. 469
Saunders, Sir Edward (d. 1576), III. 189
Saunders, Julius, X. 385
Saunders, Montagu, XIII. 537
Saunders, 'Silenus,' IX. 240
Saurin, Bernard-Joseph, *Béverlei*, X. 68, 81
Savage, Eliza Mary Ann, XIII. 454
Savage, Henry (1604?–1672), IX. 539
Savage, John (1673–1747), IX. 499
Savage, Marmion W. (1803–1872), XIV. 323, 571; *Bachelor of the Albany, The*, XIV. 324; *Falcon Family, The*, XIV. 324; *Reuben Medlicott*, XIV. 324
Savage, Richard (d. 1743), IX. 449, 486, *also see* Add.; X. 95, 165, 274, 454, 460, 464, 465; XI. 246; XII. 424
Author to be Let, The, XI. 330
Bastard, The, IX. 186, 187
Volunteer Laureat, IX. 187
Wanderer, The, IX. 186
Savage, Samuel Morton (1721–1791), X. 384
Savage family, Warwickshire, XII. 441
Savannah, X. 368
Savery, Thomas (1650?–1715), IV. 461; XIV. 258

Savigny, Friedrich Karl von, XIV. 79;
  *Geschichte des römischen Rechts im Mit-
  telalter*, XIV. 80
Savile, in *The Scornful Ladie*, VI. 133
Savile, Sir George, marquis of Halifax
  (1633–1695), VIII. 268, 370, 387 ff., 481,
  also see Add.; IX. 190, 201, 490
  A Lady's Gift: Advice to a Daughter,
  VIII. 388; XI. 371
  Anatomy of an Equivalent, VIII. 388
  Character of a Trimmer, The, VIII. 387,
  388
  Character of King Charles the Second,
  VIII. 387, 388
  Letter to a Dissenter, VIII. 387; IX. 4, 418
  Miscellanies, VIII. 387
Savile, Sir Henry (1549–1622), I. 213;
  III. 421, 424 ff., 428; IV. 4, 265, 411, 440;
  VII. 205, 312, 314, 316, 328, 329, 443,
  483, 485, 487; VIII. 360
Savile, Henry (1642–1687), VIII. 200, 210,
  212, 452
Savile family, VII. 87
Savilian professor of astronomy, IX. 386
Savilian professorships at Oxford, VII. 288
Saville or Savile, captain Henry, IV. 461
Saviolo, Vincentio (*fl.* 1595), III. 553; V.
  479
Savonarola, Girolamo, III. 8, 17; VII. 376;
  XII. 440, 477
Savonarola, in *Romola*, XIII. 394, 395
Savonarola, Don Jeremy, *pseud. See*
  Mahony, Francis Sylvester, XIV. 316
Savory, Hester, XII. 194
Savoy, XIII. 74
Savoy, Charles Emmanuel, duke of, VII.
  306
Savoy, house of, III. 402
Savoy alps, the, XIII. 83
Savoy and Shelley, XII. 403
Savoy conference, III. 34; VIII. 7, 273,
  285, 294; IX. 383
Saw ye my Father, IX. 374
Sawbridge, John (1732?–1795), X. 503
Sawle, Rose, lady Graves, XII. 441
Sawles Warde, I. 227, 228, 355, 459
Sawney will ne'er be my love again, VIII. 96
Sawtrey, William (d. 1401), II. 422
Sawyer, Bob, in *Pickwick Papers*, X. 41
Sawyer, Edmund (d. 1759), X. 504
Sawyer, Elizabeth (d. 1621), VI. 190
Sawyer, mother, in *The Witch of Edmon-
  ton*, VI. 54
Saxe Coburg, house of, XII. 232
Saxo Grammaticus, I. 8, 9, 25, 27, 28,
  34, 37; V. 159, 221
Saxon, Old, paraphrase of Bible, I. 46
Saxon drummer, in *The Rolliad*, XI. 34
Saxon language, XIII. 29
Saxon poems, X. 237
Saxons, the, XII. 26; XIV. 68, 76
Saxony, VII. 231, 453
Saxony, Eastphalian, V. 6
Say, Samuel (1676–1743), XI. 250
Say, Sir William, III. 3
Sayce, Archibald Henry, XIV. 533

Sayer, James (1748–1823), *A Nightmare*,
  XIV. 214; 'Elijah's Mantle,' XIV. 214
Sayers, Frank (1763–1817), XI. 160, 161,
  172, 177 ff., 428; XIII. 227, 512
  Cyclops, XI. 179
  Dramatic Sketches, XI. 179
  Moina, XI. 179
  Starno, XI. 179
  To Night, XI. 179
Sayers, Tom (1826–1865), XIV. 183, 231
Sayes court, Deptford, VIII. 245, 246, 354,
  365
Sayings of the Fathers, XII. 341
Sayle, Charles Edward, XII. 518
Say-well, in *Piers the Plowman*, II. 19
Scaccario, Dialogus de. See Fitz-Neale
Scales, lord. *See* Woodville, Antony
Scaliger, Julius Caesar and Joseph Justus,
  III. 301, 305, 424, 426; IV. 22, 255,
  259 ff., 322, 500, 519; VI. 9, 37, 225;
  VII. 261, 263, 268, 272, 307, 310, 320,
  477; VIII. 321; IX. 170; XIV. 109
Scaliger, Julius Caesar, *Poetices libri
  septem*, IX. 60
Scaliger, Joseph Justus, *Censura Euphor-
  mionis*, IV. 260
'Scallogrim,' X. 224
Scamperdale, lord (Surtees's), XIV. 234
Scandal, in Congreve's *Love for Love*,
  VIII. 152
Scandaroon, VII. 449
Scandinavia, V. 283, 307; XIII. 123; XIV.
  293
Scandinavian gods, the, XII. 271
Scandinavian legend, X. 221, 490. *See,
  also*, Norse *and* Icelandic
Scandinavian poetry, X. 132, 228, 487
Scandinavian studies, X. 222, 484
Scarborough, II. 424
Scarborough, Sir Charles (1616–1694), VII.
  320
Scarborough, earl of. *See* Lumley, Richard
Scardassale, Tomasso, XII. 55
Scarron, Paul, VIII. 67, 69, 183, 407; IX.
  256, 257, 259, 500, 502; X. 482
  City Romance, VIII. 170
  Don Japhet d'Arménie, VIII. 372
  Les trois Dorothées, VIII. 372
  Nouvelles tragi-comiques, VIII. 372
  Roman Comique, VIII. 372; X. 26
  Typhon, IX. 268
  Virgile Travesti, VIII. 65; IX. 256, 257
Scarth, Harry Mengden (1814–1890), XII.
  513
Scattercash, lord, XIV. 232
Sceldwea, in *Beowulf*, I. 28
Scenici, V. 24
Schaarschmidt, C., *Joh. Saresberiensis*, I.
  184
Scharf, Sir George (1820–1895), X. 254
Schaub, lady, X. 126
Schaub, Sir Luke (d. 1758), X. 126
Schaw, Quintyne, II. 268; *Advyce to a
  Courtier*, II. 266
Schedoni, in Mrs Radcliffe's *Italian*, XI.
  302, 304

Scheidt, Caspar, III. 82

Schelling, Felix E., v. 129; VI. 4, 7, 8, 11, 17, 23, 90, 305, 363; XIII. 515

Schelling, Friedrich Wilhelm Joseph von (1775–1854), IX. 328, 522; XI. 137; XIV. 9, 11, 16; *System des transzendentalen Idealismus*, XI. 136

'Schembertlaufen,' v. 25

Scheppig, Richard, XIV. 481

Schepss, Georg, I. 101

Scherer, Edmond, VII. 138; XIII. *also see* Add. 3

Schevill, Rudolph, VIII. 125, 126, 128

Schiavonetti, Luigi (1765–1810), X. 453

Schick, John, II. 237

Schiedam, II. 327

Schildburg, witticisms on, III. 95

Schilders, Richard, III. Add.; IV. 402

Schiller, Johann Christoph Friedrich von, v. 300, 303, 465; VIII. 182, 439; X. 504; XI. 42, 138, 414; XII. 4, 7, 90, 168, 254, 436, 526; XIII. 4, 22, 277, 465, 468
  Das Ideal und das Leben, XI. 130
  Das Reich der Schatten, XI. 130
  Der Pilgrim, VII. 177
  Die Räuber, XI. 303, 414
  Die Sehnsucht, VII. 177
  Horen, v. 299
  Robbers, The, XIII. 418
  Wallenstein, XIII. 260

Schipper, Jakob, I. 96

Schism, the Great, I. 371

Schism act, IX. 394; X. 373, 374

Schisme, A Treatise of, IV. 381

Schlegel, August Wilhelm and Johann Elias, v. 209, 222, 290, 299, 300, 303, 304, 307

Schlegel, August Wilhelm von, XI. 135, 448; XII. 169, 527; XIII. 3, 4, 8

Schlegel, Caroline, v. 299

Schlegel, Friedrich, v. 304; IX. 328; XII. 343

Schlegel, Johann Heinrich, X. 448

Schlegel, Karl Wilhelm Friedrich von, IX. 522

Schleich, II. 320

Schleiermacher, Friedrich Daniel Ernst, *A Critical Essay on the Gospel of St Luke*, XII. 280, 288, 289, 308, 470

Schlettstadt, III. 13

Schlosser, F. C., IX. 226; X. 302

Schmidt, Alexander, v. 305; XIII. 466

Schmidt, Erich, X. 18

Schmidt, K., XIII. 465

Schmitz, Leonhard, XII. 478

Schofield, W. H., Pref. X, I. 61

Scholars and scholarship, 1600–1660, VII. 476 ff.

Scholastica, I. 74

Scholefield, James (1789–1853), XII. 329, 473, 482, 491

Schole-howse of Women, The, III. 486; IV. 318, 340, 523

Schomberg, Frederick Hermann, duke of (1615–1690), VIII. 202

Schomburgh, Sir Robert (1804–1865), IV. 57

School plays, v. 410

Schoole of Slovenrie, The (trans. of Dedekind's *Grobianus*), III. 82; IV. 528

Schooling, John Holt, XIV. 549

Schoolmen, VII. 482, 483

Schools, public, to the time of Colet, 341 ff., 487 ff.

Schopenhauer, Arthur, IX. 522; XIII. 457

Schort Memoriale of the Scottis corniklis for addicioun, The, II. 285, 479

Schott, Peter, of Strassburg, III. 14

Schreiner, Olive, XIV. Add. 9

Schröder, F. L., v. 298, 299, 307

Schröer, Arnold, I. 114; VI. 155

Schück, Henrik, v. 308

Schulenburg, Countess Ehrengard Melusina von der, duchess of Kendal (1667–1743), IX. 115

Schulpforte, IV. 260

Schulze-Gävernitz, G. von, XIII. 545

Schwellenberg, Mrs, X. 260

Schwenckfeld, Caspar von, IX. 315

Schwenter, Daniel, v. 285

Sciarrha, in *The Traytor*, VI. 199

Science, in Tudor moralities, v. 57

Scientific periodicals, XIV. 565, 566

Scilly isles, VII. 214; X. 466

Scintilla, or a light broken into darke warehouses, IV. 407, 545

Scioppius, Gaspar, IV. 260; VII. 311

Scipio, I. 95; IV. 62

Scipio, C. (*pseud.*), XII. 427

Scipio Africanus, v. 123

Sclater, William Lutley, XIV. Add. 9

Scobell, Henry (d. 1660), VIII. 469; *Severall Proceedings in Parliament*, VII. 354

Scoble, John, XIV. Add. 9

Scogan, Henry (1361?–1407), II. 159, 161, 162, 164, 187, 498

Scogan, John (*fl.* 1480?), II. 498; III. 92, 94. See, also, *Skoggan, Geystes of Scogin's Jests*, XI. 334

Scolimorrhodia (*i.e.* England), in *Euphormio*, IV. 256

Scoloker, Anthony (*fl.* 1548), IV. 448

Scoop, the, I. 3, 58; v. 26, 27

Scoresby, William (1789–1857), XIV. 554

Scornfu' Nansie, IX. 360

'Scorpion, The' (J. G. Lockhart), XII. 154, 158

Scot, John (*fl.* 1552–1571), IV. 412

Scot, Michael (1175?–1234?), I. 153, 199, 456

Scot, Reginald (1538?–1599), III. 495; v. 479; VII. 366, 370, 371, 374, 395, 396, 506; VIII. 357; *Discoverie of Witchcraft*, III. 112 ff.; IV. 326, 530, 534; *Perfite platforme of a hoppe-garden, A*, IV. 542

Scot, Robert, XI. 331

Scot, Thomas (*fl.* 1605), IV. 520

Scot or Scott, Thomas (d. 1660), VII. 361; VIII. 470

Scot of Scotstarvet, Sir John (1585–1670), IV. 261; IX. 550

Scot the Minotaur, in the *Mercuries*, VII. 356

Scota, Pharaoh's daughter, in *The Orygynale Cronykil*, II. 130

Scotch Drink, II. 278

Scotch jig, IX. 362

Scotch Presbyterian Eloquence, IX. 548

Scotch Wooing of Willy and Nanny, IX. 363

Scotia, dame, in *The Complaynt of Scotland*, III. 153

Scotichronicon, II. 128, 451

Scotish Feilde, I. 292; II. 40, 432, 435

Scotists, theological school of, I. 211

Scotland, v. 35, 171, 262; VI. 5, 169, 238, 361, 371; VII. 206 ff., 253 ff., 358, 435, 438; VIII. 47, 111, 356; IX. 4, 11 ff., 19, 130, 192, 194, 202, 203, 214, 215, 259, 301, 352, 359, 361 ff., 519; X. 42, 43, 55, 131, 132, 154, 182, 192, 226, 227, 231, 281, 282, 291, 321, 324; XI. 209, 211, 217, 232, 235, 240, 241, 315; XII. 1, 6, 12, 18, 30, 129, 142, 143, 156, 161, 167, 251, 337, 344, 349 ff., 357 ff.; 370; XIII. 2, 115; XIV. 94, 95, 103, 159, 185, 204, 209, 255, 291, 327, 357, 374, 434, 437

    Church of, IV. 305; XI. 244; XII. 478

    Court of exchequer, XII. 350

    Free church, XII. 296

Scots, VII. 200, 214, 231, 308, 363, 458

Scots, lowland, XII. 24

Scots, The Tragedie of the King of, VI. 286

Scots Acts, The, XII. 357

Scots (Middle) anthologies, II. 267 ff., 478 ff.

Scots dialect, XIII. 233

'Scots Gentleman in the Swedish Service,' *i.e.* Defoe, IX. 19

Scots Magazine, IX. 562; X. 191, 192, 477, 479; XI. 232, 242, 243

Scots Minstrelsie, IX. 567; XI. 444

Scots Nightingale, IX. 372

Scots novels, XIII. 431

Scots Observer, The, XIV. 199

Scots papers, the (1646), VII. 347

Scots Spy, IX. 562

Scotsman, The, XIV. 176, 192, 203, 204, 531 ff., 535

Scotsmen, X. 148, 281, 282, 285, 289, 393, 396; XIV. 243, 345, 368

Scott, Alexander (1525?–1584?), II. 269, 281; III. 132, 134, 135, 136, 499, *also see* Add.; IX. 361, 365; XI. 203

    Derisioun and Scorne of Wantoun Wemen, III. 135

    Justing and Debait, The, III. 135; XI. 215

    Lament of the Master of Erskine, III. 134, 135

    Lo Quhat it is to Lufe, III. 135

    New Yeir Gift to Queen Mary, III. 134, 135

    Of May, III. 134

    Oppressit Hairt Indure, III. 135

    Up Helsum Hairt, III. 135

    When his Wife Left Him, IX. 360

Scott, Alexander John (1805–1866), XII. 466

Scott, Charles W. H., 4th duke of Buccleuch (1772–1819), XI. 239

Scott, Clement, XIII. 515, 525; XIV. 192, 535

Scott, D. C., XIV. 350

Scott, Henry, 3rd duke of Buccleuch (1746–1812), X. 335

Scott, Hew (1791–1872), *Fasti Ecclesiae Scoticanae*, XII. 359, 518

Scott, Hugh Stowell (*pseud.* Henry Seton Merriman, 1862–1903), XIII. 566

Scott, H. Spencer, XIV. 537

Scott, James, duke of Monmouth (1649–1685), VII. 364; VIII. 30, 36, 37, 90, 92, 99; IX. 6, 159, 160, 214; XIII. 434

Scott, James, of Heckmondwike academy, X. 385

Scott, James (1733–1814), X. 401, 525

Scott, James R. A., XIII. 485

Scott, John (*fl.* 1654–1696), VIII. 257

Scott, John (1730–1783), X. 474

Scott, John (1783–1821), XII. 161, 163

Scott, John, 1st earl of Eldon (1751–1838), XI. 158; XII. 62; XIV. 406, 509

Scott, Martha, X. 393

Scott, Michael (1175?–1234?), XI. 131

Scott, Michael (1789–1835), XII. 451; *Tom Cringle's Log*, XIV. 255

Scott, Robert (1811–1887), XII. 333, 487

Scott, Robert Falcon (1868–1912), XIV. 554; *Journal of Last Expedition*, XIV. 246

Scott, Sir Robert Forsyth, IV. 275; *Admissions to the College of St John*, X. 393

Scott, Temple, XIII. 491, 555

Scott, Thomas (1580?–1626), IV. 452

Scott, Thomas (*fl.* 1695), VIII. 441

Scott, Thomas (1747–1821), IX. 313; XII. 281, 461, 473

Scott, Walter (1614?–1694), IX. 552

Scott, Sir Walter (1771–1832), I. 199, 279, 283, 287; II. 87, 107, 186, 250, 409 ff., 414; III. 148, 366; IV. 45; VI. 58, 132, 226; VII. 231; VIII. 4, 5, 20, 42, 44, 54, 167, 261, 441, 451; IX. 12, 150, 154, 453; X. 26, 27, 41, 50, 55, 56, 58, 62, 93, 133, 137, 158, 190, 217, 232, 234, 236, 238 ff., 424, 451, 476, 489 ff.; XI. 27, 109, 117, 131, 145, 149, 150, 154, 158, 162, 170, 219, 220, 231, 236, 240, 241, 285, 286, 295 ff., 300 ff., 304, 305, 307, 309, 382, 405, 410, 416, 423, 441, 442, 444, 459, 464, 465; XII. 1 ff. (main entry), 34, 45, 46, 51, 57, 62, 95, 101, 102, 112, 120, 122, 125, 126, 128, 131, 133, 138, 144, 147, 150, 155, 157, 161 ff., 168, 170, 205, 212, 213, 223, 230, 237, 241, 245, 249 ff., 254, 255, 266, 300, 303, 357, 358, 367, 370, 372 ff. (main entry), 384, 385, 394, 397, 412, 422, 429, 430, 447, 451, 513, 517, *also see* Add.; XIII. 9, 15, 25, 63, 137, 160, 171, 226, 228, 230, 259, 263, 292, 295, 303, 306, 307, 312, 320, 338, 340, 379, 434, 457, 469; XIV. 50,

Scott, Sir Walter
94, 96, 156, 170, 223, 228, 278, 334, 341,
346, 373, 375, 399, 450, 491
Abbot, The, XII. 26, 29
Albert Graeme, XII. 7, 9
Allan a Dale, XII. 14
Anne of Geierstein, XIV. 106
Antiquary, The, XII. 29, 151, 350; XIII.
265
Apology for Tales of Terror, XII. 5
Black Dwarf, The, XII. 156
Bonnie Dundee, XII. 14; XIII. 234, 235
Border Antiquities, XII. 16
Bridal of Triermain, The, XII. 13
Bride of Lammermoor, The, XII. 22
Brignal Banks, XII. 14
County Guy, XII. 14
Donald Caird, XII. 14
Doom of Devorgoil, The, XII. 13
Eve of St John, The, XII. 7
Fortunes of Nigel, The, VIII. 174; XII.
18, 372
Gray Brother, The, XII. 7
Guy Mannering, XII. 18, 21, 151; XIV.
255
Hail to the Chief, XII. 12
Halidon Hill, XII. 13
Harold the Dauntless, XII. 13
Heart of Midlothian, The, XII. 17, 18;
XIII. 380
Ivanhoe, X. 63, 220, 227; XII. 26, 378,
379; XIV. 107
Kenilworth, XII. 372
Kinmont Willie, II. 415, 417; XII. 6
Lady of the Lake, The, XII. 11, 12, 377
Lay of the Last Minstrel, XI. 127, 131;
XIII. 7 ff., 14, 146, 381; XIII. 233
Legend of Montrose, The, XII. 29, 372
Life of (Lockhart's), XIV. 106
Life of Dryden, VIII. 124
Life of Napoleon, XII. 16, 372, 378, 379;
XIV. 106
Lord of the Isles, II. 108; XII. 13
Love Wakes and Weeps, XII. 14
Macduff's Cross, XII. 13
Macgregor's Gathering, XII. 14
Marmion, XII. 9 ff., 42, 149, 365, 372
Minstrelsy of the Scottish Border, IX.
373, 375; XI. 242; XII. 6, 7, 364, 372,
378, 380
Old Mortality, XII. 18, 21, 22, 27; XIII.
265
One Volume More, XII. 364
Otterbourne, XII. 6
Peveril of the Peak, XIII. 265
Pibroch of Donald Dhu, The, XII. 14
Poetical Works, XII. 364
Prefatory Memoir to Sterne, XII. 366
Proud Maisie, XII. 14; XIII. 234
Quentin Durward, X. 44; XII. 26; XIII.
419
Rebecca's Hymn, XII. 14
Redgauntlet, XII. 18, 21, 26, 29
Rest, Warrior, Rest, XII. 12, 14
Rob Roy, XII. 17, 29
Rokeby, XII. 12, 13, 105

Scott, Sir Walter
Sun upon the Weirdlaw Hill ,The, XII. 14
Swift's Works, XII. 372
Tales of a Grandfather, XII. 16
Tales of my Landlord, XII. 151, 380
Talisman, The, X. 227
Tragedy of Auchindrane, The, XII. 13
Vision of Don Roderick, The, XII. 13
Waken Lords and Ladies Gay, XII. 14
Wandering Willie's Tale, XII. 22, 29
Waverley, VII. 86, 88; XI. 301; XII. 26,
151, 372; XIII. 239
Waverley novels, XI. 293; XII. 251; XIV.
163
Weary Lot, A, XII. 14
When Israel of the Lord Beloved, XII. 14
Woodstock, XII. 372; XIII. 265
Young Lochinvar, XII. 14; XIII. 234, 235
Works edited by, XII. 16
Scott, Sir W., Sheriff Court at Selkirk,
XII. Add.
Scott, Wm (1813–1872), XII. 454; XIV. 198
Scott, Wm Bell (1811–1890), XII. 384, 399,
405, 450; XIII. 110, 156, 186, 187, 508;
Sphinx, The, XIII. 187
Scott of Amwell, VIII. 230
Scottish antiquities, XII. 25, 351
Scottish ballads, XII. 125, 358
Scottish bar, X. 191; XII. 143; XIV. 7, 112
Scottish book-clubs, XII. 355, 357, 359
Scottish booktrade, XI. 342
Scottish Calvinism, XIII. 18
Scottish campaigns of 1639 and 1640, VII.
22, 24, 194
Scottish-Canadians, XIV. 345
Scottish Chaucerians, I. 297; II. 239 ff., 471
ff.
Scottish church, X. 356
Scottish dialect, IX. 361; X. 174; XI. 204,
238; XII. 125; XIV. 209, 447, 457
Scottish dialect, in *The Sad Shepherd*, VI.
371
Scottish divines, XII. 284
Scottish drama, X. 87
Scottish education, XIV. 405 ff.
Scottish historians, XIV. 94 ff.
Scottish Historical Review, The, XII. 358
Scottish history, X. 295; XIV. 101
Scottish humour, XIV. 209
Scottish king, in *Eastward Hoe*, VI. 30
Scottish language, the, II. 88 ff., 446; VII.
455
Scottish literature, the earliest, II. 100 ff.,
447 ff.
Scottish literature from 1603–1786, IX.
Add.
Scottish Minstrel, The, XI. 233
Scottish moors, XIII. 10
Scottish music, X. 232
Scottish novels, XII. 25 ff., 30
Scottish parliament, IV. 306; X. 36
Scottish Pasquils, VIII. 411
Scottish peasants, XI. 206; XII. 414; XIII.
2, 16
Scottish people, VIII. 69, 121, 298, 299
Scottish philosophers, X. 345, 347

Scottish philosophy, XIV. 6 ff., 41, 48, 209
Scottish poems, XIV. 377
Scottish poetry, X. 226, 233; XII. 14, 45, 358
Scottish popular music, IX. 361 ff.
Scottish popular poetry, IX. 359 ff., 565 ff.
Scottish press, IV. 412, 547
Scottish prose literature, IX. 215
Scottish pulpit, XIV. 119
Scottish Registers, The, XIV. 95
Scottish school of rhetoric, XIV. 398, 399, 428
Scottish schools commission, XIV. 421
Scottish State Papers in Jacobean times, VII. 435
Scottish Text society, XII. 344, 359
Scottish theology, XII. 296
Scottish universities, II. 487, 489; X. 182; XIII. 2; XIV. 410, 411, 424
Scottish university periodicals, XIV. 239
Scottish verse, XI. 203 ff.
Scottish writers, X. 285, 290 ff.
Scotts of Eskdale, the, XII. 9
Scotus or Erigena, Joannes (*fl.* 850), I. 154, 434; III. 214; IV. 269 ff.; *De Divisione Naturae,* IV. 270; trans. of pseudo-Dionysian writings, IV. 270
Scougal, Henry (1650–1678), IX. 547
Scourge, The, XIV. 221, 223
Scourge of Simony, The. See Parnassus trilogy
Scrag, Sir Gosling, in Smollett's *Peregrine Pickle,* X. 39
Scrape, Ezekiel, VIII. 122
Scratch, lord, in Reynolds's *Dramatist,* XI. 281
Scribes, I. 17
Scriblerus, XIII. 452
Scriblerus, Martinus. See *Memoirs of Martinus Scriblerus*
Scriblerus club, IX. 103, 131, 166, 167, 281
'Scriblerus Secundus' (Henry Fielding), X. 21
Scriptores Rerum Anglicanarum, X. 312
Scriptoria, I. 18, 153, 426
Scriptural chronology, IX. 227
Scripture, in *Piers the Plowman,* II. 20, 21, 25
Scripture paraphrases (metrical), XI. 244
Scriven, Yorks., VII. 224
Scrivener, Frederick Henry Ambrose (1813–1891), XII. 340, 501
Scrocca, in *Sicelides,* VI. 323
Scroggs, The Lord Chief Justice, his Speech in the King's Bench, VIII. 90
Scroop, Adrian (1601–1660), VIII. 470
Scroop, Sir Car or Carr (1649–1680), VIII. 213
Scroope-Grosvenor suit, II. 156, 158
Scrope, George Julius Poulett (1797–1876), XIV. 292, 563
Scrope, Richard le (1350?–1405), II. 422, 423
Scrope, William (1772–1852), XIV. 545
Scroupe, Jane, in *Phyllyp Sparowe,* III. 71

'Scrub,' X. 201
Scruple, in Wilson's *Cheats,* VIII. 122
Scruton, William, XIII. 559
Scudamore, James, *Homer à la Mode,* IX. 258, 500
Scudéry, Georges de, IX. 500; *Ibrahim,* VIII. 22, 193
Scudéry, Madeleine de, IV. 327; VI. 239; VII. 222, 391; VIII. 132, 186, 434
    Almahide, VIII. 22, 371; IX. 268
    Clélie, IV. 523; VIII. 22, 371, 372
    Ibrahim, ou L'illustre Bassa, VIII. 20, 193, 371
    Le Grand Cyrus, IV. 523; VIII. 15, 20, 22, 119, 194, 371; X. 14
Scudmore, in *A Woman is a Weathercocke,* VI. 221
Scully, William Charles, XIV. 589, *also see* Add. 5, 10
Scyld, in *Beowulf,* I. 2, 22, 25, 28
Scylla, III. 343
Scylla, in Keats's *Endymion,* XII. 82
Scythia, II. 130
Sea and travel, the literature of the, IV. 66 ff., 453 ff.
Seafarer, I. 1, 2, 38, 42, 54, 275, 423, 428
Seafaringe Men, in Hope of Good Fortune, In Prais of, IV. 97
Seagrim, Molly, in Fielding's *Tom Jones* X. 31
Seagull, capt., in *Eastward Hoe,* VI. 47, 48, 355
Seaman, Lazarus (d. 1675), XI. 336
Seaman, Owen, XIII. 500; XIV. 548
Search, Edward. *See* Tucker, Abraham
'Searle, J.,' XII. 416
Searle, Laurence, IV. 141
Sebastian, in *The Tempest,* V. 194, 206
Sebastian story, the, VI. 149
Seccombe, Thomas (1866–1924), XI. 448; XIII. 573; XIV. 537
Sechnall, Hymn of St, I. 65
Secker, Thomas (1693–1768), X. 386, 517; XI. 355 ff.; *Lectures on the Church Catechism,* X. 362; *Memoirs,* IX. 393, 394, 574
Second and Third Blast of retrait from plaies and theatres, A, VI. 390, 392, 496. See, also, *Third Blast, The*
Second collection of tracts proving...the only true God, X. 378
Second Maiden's Tragedy, The, VI. 178
Second Merchant's Tale, The. See *Beryn, The Tale of*
Secreta Secretorum, II. 149, 301, 483
Secularist, The, XIII. 108
Secunda, St, I. 74
Secunda Pastorum, V. 15, 18, 19
Secundus, Johannes, VII. 83, 489
Security, bill of, IX. 215
Sedaine, Michel-Jean, X. 79; *Le philosophe sans le savoir,* X. 68; XI. 265
Sedan, XIII. 445
Sedbergh school, III. 427; VII. 329, 330, 493
Seddon, John (1725–1770), X. 385

Sedgefield, Durham, XI. 244
Sedgwick, Adam (1785–1873), XIV. 289, 291, 292, 294, 295, 563, 593, 595; XIV. 300
Sedgwick, Joseph (*fl.* 1653), IX. 571
Sedgwick, William (1610?–1669?), VII. 509
Sedition, in *Kynge Johan*, V. 65
Sedley, Amelia, in *Vanity Fair*, XIII. 286 ff., 290, 296
Sedley, Catharine, countess of Dorchester (1657–1717), VIII. 216
Sedley, Sir Charles (1639?–1701), VII. 180; VIII. 133, 136, 142, 143, 198 ff., 215, 217, 420, 423, 444, 446; IX. 169, 174
  Antony and Cleopatra, VIII. 139, 216
  Beauty the Conqueror, VIII. 139
  Bellamira, or the Mistress, VIII. 139
  Grumbler, The, VIII. 139
  Happy Pair, The, VIII. 216
  Mulberry Garden, VIII. 134, 137, 139, 143, 216
  'Not Celia that I juster am,' VIII. 216
  'Phyllis is my only Joy,' VIII. 216
  Tyrant King of Crete, VIII. 139, 216
  Vergil's *Eclogues*, VIII. 216
Sedley, Jos, in *Vanity Fair*, XIII. 286
Sedley family, in *Vanity Fair*, XIII. 286, 288
Sedulius, copy at Antwerp, I. 72, 76
Seebohm, Frederic (1833–1912), XII. 513; XIV. 78, 497; *English Village Community, The*, XII. 348; XIV. 79; *Oxford Reformers of 1498, The*, XIV. 79; *Tribal System of Wales, The*, XII. 348
Seeley, Sir John Robert (1834–1895), XII. 469, 493; XIV. 90 ff., 197, 426, 479, 497, 594, 606, 609
  Ecce Homo, XII. 154, 297; XIV. 91
  Essays on a liberal education, XIV. 432
  Expansion of England, The, XIV. 61 ff.
  Growth of British Policy, The, XIV. 93
  Lectures and Essays, XIV. 91
  Life and Times of Stein, The, XIV. 92
  Natural Religion, XIII. 452
Seeley, Robert Benton (1789–1886), XII. 473
See-well, in *Piers the Plowman*, II. 19
Segar, Sir William (d. 1633), IV. 543; *Honor Military and Civill*, IV. 401
Segismundo, in Calderon's *La Vida es Sueño*, XIII. 144, 145
Seine, river, XIV. 185, 221
Selborne, X. 270, 271
Selbourne, earl of. *See* Palmer, Sir Roundell
Selden, Camille, XIII. 559
Selden, John (1584–1654), III. 97; IV. 49, 55, 190, 299, 425, 432, 434, 461; V. 371, 479; VI. 6, 376; VII. 148, 315, 318 ff., 442, 475, 484, 485, 496; VIII. 62, 309, 469; IX. 355; XIV. 309
  De Dis Syris, VII. 281, 318
  De jure naturali et gentium juxta disciplinam Hebraeorum, VII. 281
  Fleta, edition of, VIII. 318, 465
  Fortescue's *De Laudibus*, edition of, VIII. 318

Selden, John
  Historia Placitorum Coronae, VIII. 320
  History of the Common Law of England, VIII. 320
  History of Tithes, VII. 281; VIII. 322
  Jani Anglorum Facies Altera, VIII. 318
  Mare Clausum, VII. 281, 307; VIII. 318
  Marmora Arundeliana, VII. 316, 489
  Table-Talk, VII. 392; VIII. 60, 321 ff.; X. 472
  Titles of Honour, IV. 408, 513
  Works, VIII. 322
Selden society, XII. 355; XIV. 80, 81
'Select Society,' the, X. 281, 288, 290
Selena, in Drayton's *Eglogs*, IV. 173, 175, 176
Selim, in Lyttelton's *Persian Letters*, X. 114
Selimus, V. 85 ff., 134, 238, 398, 418
Sélincourt, Ernest de, XI. 408, *also see* Add.; XII. 405 ff.
Selio and Olimpio (*Caelo and Olympo?*), VI. 93
Selkirk, Alexander (1676–1721), IX. 19; XIV. 243, 554
Selkirkshire, XII. 5
Sell, Henry, XIV. 532
Sell's *Dictionary of the World's Press*, XIV. 174
Sellar, William Young (1825–1890), XII. 493; *Roman Poets of the Republic*, XII. 337
Seller, John (*fl.* 1700), IV. 461
Selling. *See* Tilly, William
'Selma,' X. 130, 227, 229
Selvaggia, XIII. 118
Selwyn, George Augustus (1719–1791), X. 88, 494; XIII. 364
Selwyn, Thomas Kynaston, XIV. 597
Selwyn, William, XIV. 589, 595, *also see* Add. 5
Selymus, in *Solymannidae*, VI. 301
Semans sacred safetye..., *The*, IV. 399
Semitic peoples, XII. 296
Semitic religions, VII. 318
Semly academy, X. 387
Sempill, Francis (1616?–1682), *The Banishment of Povertie*, IX. 365
Sempill, Sir James (1566–1625), IX. 545
Sempill, Robert (1530?–1595), II. 280; III. 122, 132, 149, 150, 505; IV. 412
  Ballat on Margret Fleming, II. 280
  Defence of Crissell Sandelandis, II. 280
  Life of the Tulchene Bischope of St Andrews, III. 132
  Legend of a Lymaris Lyfe, III. 150
  Sege of the Castel of Edinburgh, III. 150
Sempill, Robert (1595?–1665?), IX. 364, 365, 372; *Life...of Habbie Simson*, IX. 365; XI. 211
Sempills of Beltrees, the, IX. 556
Semple, John, IX. 543
Sempringham, I. 344. *See, also*, Gilbert of
Sempronio, in *Celestina*, V. 99
Sempronius, in Addison's *Cato*, IX. 64
Semur, XIII. 431

Sénancour, Étienne Pivert de, XIII. 93, 94; *Obermann*, XI. 288

Sencer, in *The Wise-woman Of Hogsdon*, VI. 83

Sendall, Walter J., XIV. 537

Seneca, L. Annaeus, I. 76, 99, 100, 213, 355; II. 363, 366; III. 173, 189, 198, 430; IV. 2, 4 ff., 23, 333, 348, 349, 439, 440, 523, 525; V. 61 ff., 66, 70 ff., 76, 78 ff., 84, 88, 118, 149, 152, 157, 158, 162, 163, 238 ff., 248, 288, 324, 334, 394 ff.; VI. 9, 20, 296, 299 ff., 311, 319, 327, 366; VII. 261, 272, 304, 390; VIII. 13, 133, 188, 378, 447; IX. 28, 41, 55, 57, 233, 265, 418; XII. 49
   Agamemnon, V. 75, 78, 79; VI. 178
   Consolatio ad Helviam, IX. 218
   Hecuba, VI. 295
   Hercules Furens, IV. 249; V. 75, 78
   Hercules Oetaeus, V. 75, 78
   Medea, V. 75, 78; VI. 295
   Morals, IX. 273, 275
   Octavia, V. 61, 63, 75, 79; VI. 301
   Oedipus, V. 75, 78, 80, 85; VI. 295
   Phaedra, V. 75
   Tenne Tragedies, V. 80, 162, *and see* Add. 2
   Thebais, V. 68, 78, 80
   Thyestes, III. 198; V. 75, 76, 78, 79; VI. 46, 178, 301
   Troas (=*Troades*), V. 80; VI. 295

Seneca, in Gray's *Agrippina*, X. 119

Senior, Nassau William (1790–1864), XIV. 480, 506
   Conversations, XIV. 116
   Correspondence and Conversations of A. de Tocqueville, XIV. 116
   'European and American State Confederacies,' XII. 153
   Journals kept in France and Italy, XIV. 116
   Journals...relating to Ireland, XIV. 116

Senlac, XIV. 72

Sennacherib, IV. 30; XII. 499

Sense, in *Complaint upon Love to Reason*, III. 187

Sense of the House, The, VII. 385

Sensual Appetite, in *The Nature of the Four Elements*, V. 57

Sensualitie, in *Ane Pleasant Satyre*, III. 124 ff.

Sensuality, in *Nature*, V. 54

Sensuality, in *The Example of Virtue*, II. 227

Sententiae Pueriles, XI. 367

Sentry, captain, in *The Spectator*, IX. 51

Sephestia, in *Menaphon*, III. 356, 357

Septem contra Christum, XII. 294

Septennial act, IX. 224

Septuagint. See under Bible

Serafina, in FitzGerald's *The Painter of his own Dishonour*, XIII. 144

Serafino dell' Aquila, III. 187, 253

Serbia, XIV. 191

'Serena,' X. 299

Seres, William (d. 1579?), IV. 384, 386, 397

Sergeant, Emily Frances Adeline (1851–1904), XIII. 566

Sergeant, John (1622–1707), VIII. 475; *Solid Philosophy*, VIII. 346

Sergius I, II. 347

Serlio, Sebastian, III. 553

Serre, de la, VII. 391

Serres, Jean de, IV. 448; VI. 33, 138

Serres, Olivier de, IV. 312

Sertorius, in Robert Landor's *Fawn of Sertorius*, XII. 230

Servatius, Michael, prior, III. 3

Servetus, Michael, III. 400

Serving-man's Comfort, The, V. 351, 353, 374

Servius, IV. 264

Servus, in *Saturnalia*, VI. 319

Sesostris, X. 301

Set at Maw, The, VI. 98

Seth, I. 134; II. 20

Seth, James, XIV. 467

Seth's wife, VII. 255

Seton, George, 5th baron Seton (1530?–1585), XII. 27

Seton, George, 5th earl of Winton (d. 1749), IX. 247

Seton, Henry, in Scott's *Abbot*, XII. 27

Seton, Mary, in Scott's *Abbot*, XII. 27

Setoun, Christopher, in *Bruce*, II. 105

Setter, the pimp, in Congreve's *Old Bachelor*, VIII. 147

Settle, Elkanah (1648–1724), VIII. 4, 21, 271, 409, 441
   Absalom Senior, VIII. 26, 41, 92
   Cambyses, VIII. 192
   City Rambler, The, XI. 322
   Empress of Morocco, The, VIII. 192, 193, 401, 403
   Female Prelate, The, VIII. 193
   Ibrahim, VIII. 193
   Love and Revenge, VIII. 193

Seven Champions of Christendom, V. 32, 34; X. 220

Seven Dayes of the Weeke, The, VI. 319, 320, 474

Seven deadly sins, V. 42, 52, 313

Seven Deadly Sins, in Lydgate, II. 201. *See, also,* Dunbar *and* Vices

Seven Deadly Sins, in *The Faerie Queene*, III. 237; VI. 335

Seven Sages of Rome, Romance of the, I. 286, 308, 309, 470; II. 150, 177, 308; IV. 361

Seven Sins (Byrhtferth's), I. 131

Severall Proceedings, VII. 353

Severn, Joseph (1793–1879), XII. 92, 407

Severn, river, IV. 190; X. 112

Severn, river, Layamon and, I. 234, 265

Severus, Alexander, VI. 299

Sévigné, Madame de, II. 395; IX. 245; X. 248, 273; XIII. 376

Seville, III. 422; IV. 69, 71

Seward, Albert Charles, XI. 426; XIV. 559

Seward, Anna (1747–1809), X. 479, 491, *also see* Add.; XI. 459; XII. 124, 376, 422

Seward, Thomas (1708–1790), X. 136

Seward, William (1747–1799), x. 473

Sewell, Anna (1820–1878), xi. 489

Sewell, Eleanor L., xiii. 566

Sewell, Elizabeth Missing (1815–1906), xii. 462; xiii. 566; xiv. 600

Sewell, G. A., ix. 436

Sewell, John, xi. 335

Sewell, William (1804–1874), xii. 462; xiv. 596, 598, 609

Sexburga, ii. 210

Sexby, Edward (d. 1658), vii. 460

Sexton, Alexander Humboldt, xiv. 592

Sextus Placidus, English version of *Medicina de quadrupedibus*, i. 136

Seymour, Edward, 1st earl of Hertford and duke of Somerset (1506?–1552), iii. 26, 152, 175, 418, 419, 431; vii. 325, 326

Seymour, Elizabeth, countess of Northumberland, x. 209, 470, 482

Seymour, Laura, xiii. 425

Seymour, Robert (1800?–1836), xiii. 311; xiv. 232, 235

Seymour, Thomas, baron Seymour of Sudeley (1508?–1549), iv. 230, 231

Seymour, William, 2nd duke of Somerset (1588–1660), ix. 202

Seymour-Conway, Francis, earl and 1st marquis of Hertford (1719–1794), x. 118, 249, 274, 495

Seymour-Conway, Francis Charles, 3rd marquis of Hertford (1777–1842), xiv. 115

Seynt Albons, Bellum apud, ii. 302

Seyssel, Claude de, iv. 3

Seyton, Catherine, in Scott's *Abbot*, xii. 22, 27

Sforza, in *The Duke of Millaine*, vi. 155, 158, 159, 163

Shackleton, Elizabeth, xiv. 323

Shackleton, Mary. *See* Leadbeater, Mary

Shackleton, Richard (1728–1792), xi. 1, 2; xiv. 323

Shadow, in *Henry IV*, v. 360

Shadow of Night, The, vi. 30

Shadwell, Charles (d. 1726), *Fair Quaker of Deal*, viii. 168

Shadwell, Lionel Lancelot, xiv. 602

Shadwell, Thomas (1642?–1692), v. 291; vii. 183; viii. 6, 21, 28, 40, 41, 49, 91, 92, 133, 168, 173, 193, 214, 215, 398, 401, 403, 404, 409, 410, 430, 441; ix. 79

  Bury Fair, viii. 174

  Epsom Wells, viii. 174

  Humorists, The, iv. 333

  Libertine, The, viii. 174

  Medal of John Bayes, The, viii. 2, 3, 5, 40, 92

  Miser, The, viii. 134, 174

  Scowrers, The, ix. 362

  Squire of Alsatia, The, viii. 174

  Sullen Lovers, viii. 134, 173, 174

  Tempest, The, viii. 120, 398

  Timon of Athens, adaptation of, viii. 120, 174

  Tory Poets, The, viii. 40

  True Widow, A, viii. 40, 401

Snaen, Margaret Josephine, xiv. 600

Shaftesbury, vii. 74; x. 20

Shaftesbury, earl of. *See* Cooper, Anthony Ashley

Shaftesbury academy, x. 387

Shaftesbury's Farewell, viii. 92

Shafton, Sir Piercie, ii. 218

Shah, B. B., xiv. 575

Shairp, John Campbell (1819–1885), xi. 411, 417, 441; xii. 259, 381, 457, 466; xiii. 473, 504; xiv. 525

Shakebag, in *Arden of Feversham*, v. 200, 240

Shakerley, Jeremy (*fl.* 1651), vii. 509

Shakespeare, Hamnet, v. 169, 175, 219

Shakespeare, John, v. 167, 172, 219

Shakespeare, Judith, v. 169, 172, 175, 219

Shakespeare, Richard, v. 167

Shakespeare, Susanna, v. 168, 219

Shakespeare, William (1564–1616), i. 1, 7, 152, 274, 276, 296, 298, 316; ii. 104, 173, 176, 266, 391, 412, 415; iii. 24, 54, 62, 107, 156, 188, 198, 200, 212, 244, 247, 252, 253, 259, 260, 263 ff., 268, 271, 283, 284, 300, 302, 305, 320, 323, 327, 335, 351, 356, 362, 371, 374, 385, 455, 460, 465, *also see* Add.; iv. 3, 6, 7, 10, 43 ff., 49, 50, 55, 77 ff., 88, 115, 117, 129, 132, 137, 168, 183, 193, 195 ff., 199, 243, 248, 266, 300, 349, 390, 392 ff., 472, 473, 544, 545, *also see* Add.; v. 56, 63, 83, 91, 100, 119, 120, 126 ff., 131, 135 ff., 145 ff., 153, 155 ff., 165–308 (main entry), 309 ff., 314, 315, 319, 322, 323, 324, 326, 327, 328, 330 ff., 336, 346 ff., 370 ff., 380; vi. 1 ff., 13, 20, 28 ff., 39, 42, 43, 51, 52, 55, 57, 62, 69, 70, 77, 85, 95 ff., 106, 108 ff., 113, 118, 119, 123, 125 ff., 139, 140, 143, 151 ff., 157, 165, 167, 180, 185, 188, 193, 195, 196, 206, 211, 218, 256, 276, 278, 290, 291, 311 ff., 316, 330, 336, 359, 365, 370, 373, 381, 394, 399, 405, 409, 437; vii. 3, 7, 8, 16, 73, 95, 101, 111, 112, 116, 133 ff., 140, 146, 153, 161, 163, 164, 176, 221, 259, 272, 275, 366, 387, *also see* Add.; viii. 13, 17, 27 ff., 119 ff., 125, 127 ff., 150, 155, 157, 163, 164, 176, 181, 185, 191, 196, 197, 202, 205, 214, 219, 221 ff., 230, 231, 233, 237, 377, 411; ix. 42, 77, 80, 118, 140, 142, 144, 145, 188, 296, 351, 362, 363, 396, 447 ff., 474 ff., 479, 509; x. 1, 13, 27, 31, 50, 68, 69, 82, 85 ff., 120, 127, 143, 145, 146, 148, 167, 177, 179, 180, 184, 186, 202, 227, 234, 236, 445, 452, 454, 460, 462, 469, 474, 490, 505; xi. 10, 13, 133 ff., 181 ff., 206, 255, 260, 282, 284, 290, 291, 319, 320, 322, 327, 354, 414 ff., 447, 450, 451, 453, 457, 472, 474, *also see* Add.; xii. 23, 24, 30, 40, 49, 68, 70, 83, 88, 91, 93, 98, 106, 108, 111, 120, 168, 169, 171, 177, 186, 189 ff., 196, 211, 218, 243, 268, 280, 331, 347, 369, 394, 396, 398, 404, 407, 409, 422, 432, 434, 440, 476, 490, 524; xiii. 13,

Shakespeare, William
  39, 43, 63, 64, 82, 101, 117, 129, 136,
  144, 198, 210, 230, 231, 233, 242, 244,
  253, 257, 261, 303, 304, 312, 317, 382,
  390, 407, 411, 495, *also see* Add. 2
  xiv. 106, 142, 147, 157, 307, 308, 339,
  358, 434, 435, 442, 446 ff.
  Bibliography, v. 397, 426 ff.
  Boydell's edition, xiv. 215
  Folios:
  First Folio, iv. 394, 395; vi. 6, 248
  Perkins Folio, the, xii. 368
  Second Folio, iv. 394
  Plays and poems:
  All's Well that Ends Well, v. 174, 177,
  180, 181, 190, 212, 220, 265; vi. 103
  Antony and Cleopatra, v. 177, 196, 198–
  199 (main entry), 204, 217, 221, 291;
  viii. 28, 216; x. 433
  As You Like It, i. 298; iii. 349, 385;
  iv. 79; v. 126, 127, 139, 171, 177, 183,
  188, 191 ff. (main entry), 220, 300, 318,
  369; vi. 28, 213, 305, 365, 367; viii.
  224; xiv. 443
  Comedy of Errors, The, iv. 4, 79; v. 174,
  175, 177, 179, 180, 183, 188, 191, 215,
  219, 220, 283, 320; vi. 14, 215
  Coriolanus, v. 196 ff. (main entry), 202,
  221, 265, 266, 278, 374; viii. 443; xi. 274
  Cymbeline, v. 138, 189, 195, 203 ff.
  (main entry), 215, 221, 265, 290, 298;
  vi. 110, 121, 200, 236; viii. 226, 428;
  x. 433
  Hamlet, i. 16; iii. 179, 349, 456; iv.
  44, 336, 394; v. 76, 79, 81, 145, 157 ff.,
  169, 177, 179, 193, 198 ff. (main entry)
  202, 203, 210, 214, 216, 221, 248, 260 ff.,
  265, 267, 273, 274, 278, 283, 288, 290,
  294, 295, 298 ff., 304, 307, 327, 333,
  340, 349, 356; vi. 34, 45, 46, 49, 121,
  155, 162, 170, 177, 178, 186, 190, 200,
  209, 217, 220, 248, 266, 268, 272 ff.,
  302, 312, 325, *also see* Add.; viii. 116
  121, 152, 224; ix. 268; x. 77, 81, 83,
  141; xi. 135, 258; xii. 170; xiii. 66, 67;
  xiv. 447
  Henry IV, iv. 393; v. 161, 174, 184,
  187, 189, 194, 220, 260 ff., 264, 298, 300,
  356; vi. 49; viii. 116, 120
  Henry V, ii. 77; iii. 349; iv. 188, 192,
  393; v. 152, 189, 194, 195, 220, 243,
  249, 260, 261, 263, 300, 346; vi. 2, 222,
  253; ix. 187; x. 121
  Henry VI, v. 129, 147, 153, 175, 184 ff.
  (main entry), 220, 221, 237, 248, 260,
  263, 275, 280, 290, 300; vi. 247; vii.
  110; viii. 188
  Henry VIII, v. 195, 221, 261, 333, 344,
  346; vi. 116, 128, 137, 231
  Julius Caesar, v. 196–197 (main entry),
  199, 221, 265, 268, 284, 287, 288, 290,
  294, 296, 300; vi. 19, 49, 127; ix. 142;
  x. 81; xi. 353, 413
  King John, v. 147, 161, 174, 184, 185
  (main entry), 220, 294, 300, 356; viii.
  426

Shakespeare, William
  Plays and poems:
  King Lear, iii. 102, 355, 448, 517; iv.
  394, 534; v. 179, 196, 199, 203, 204
  (main entry), 214, 221, 260 ff., 266, 272,
  273, 279, 283, 294, 295, 298, 306, 310,
  333; vi. 153, 158, 186, 190, 200, 209,
  248; vii. 128; viii. 120, 443; x. 81, 91,
  429; xi. 258, 283, 450; xii. 94, 170
  Lover's Complaint, A, v. 223, 224, 233
  Love's Labour's Lost, iv. 119, 366, 394,
  434; v. 126, 174, 175, 177 ff. (main
  entry), 182, 215, 220, 224, 233, 260,
  264, 315, 356; vi. 214, 335; viii. 126, 425
  *Love's Labour's Won. See All's Well that
  Ends Well*
  Lucrece, xi. 181
  Macbeth, iv. 206; v. 169, 179, 199, 201,
  203 (main entry), 213, 221, 241, 265,
  268, 288, 290, 294, 298, 300, 315, 333;
  vi. 49, 76, 98, 158, 192, 217, 315, 318,
  349; x. 77, 81, 141, 460; xi. 261, 282,
  283, 352, 450; xii. 94; xiii. 30
  Measure for Measure, v. 119, 188, 190–
  191 (main entry), 212, 220, 245, 265,
  298, 397; vi. 99, 110, 236; viii. 120;
  xiv. 443
  Merchant of Venice, The, iv. 79, 394;
  v. 174, 175, 181, 183 (main entry), 216,
  220, 260, 278, 283, 298, 300, 301; vi.
  300; viii. 194; xiv. 441, 449
  Merry Wives of Windsor, The, iii. 181;
  v. 169, 187, 189 (main entry), 220, 252,
  260, 263, 284, 291, 298, 308, 348, 369;
  vi. 95; viii. 116, 436
  Midsummer Night's Dream, A, iii. 349;
  iv. 394, 533; v. 174, 181 ff. (main entry),
  188, 192, 203, 216, 220, 260, 265, 272,
  277, 283, 285, 298, 300, 317; vi. 207,
  213, 285, 367; viii. 120; x. 432, 433;
  xiii. 30
  Much Ado about Nothing, iv. 393; v.
  126, 127, 191 (main entry), 192, 207,
  220, 260, 284, 285, 298, 358; viii. 224;
  xiii. 262; xiv. 440
  Othello, iii. 188; v. 177, 199, 202–203
  (main entry), 204, 206, 221, 260, 261,
  264, 266, 277, 284, 288, 290, 294, 295,
  298, 301, 302, 304; vi. 186, 192, 248;
  viii. 120, 375; x. 73, 81; xi. 352; xii.
  170; xiii. 30, 67, 412
  Passionate Pilgrim, The, v. 148, 221,
  223, 224, 233
  Pericles, ii. 152; iii. 456; v. 178, 188
  (main entry), 190, 221, 236, 237, 260;
  vi. 2, 110; x. 78, 436
  Phoenix and the Turtle, The, v. 221, 224,
  233
  Poems, v. 221, 260, 275
  Rape of Lucrece, The, iii. 198; iv. 394;
  v. 166, 170, 219, 221, 223, 227 (main
  entry), 228, 233, 259; vi. 312
  Richard II, iv. 78, 393; v. 145, 153, 174,
  175, 184 (main entry), 185, 220, 260,
  262, 298, 300, 324, 326, 346, 371, 374;
  vi. 36, 49; viii. 443

Shakespeare, William
Plays and poems:
Richard III, III. 88, 458; IV. 393; V. 79,
174, 175, 184 ff. (main entry), 213, 220,
260, 261, 269, 271, 279, 281, 290, 291,
295, 297, 300; VI. 46, 129, 248, 301;
VII. 265; VIII. 123, 426; XII. 150
Roman plays, V. 100, 196, 197, 199,
221; VI. 182
Romeo and Juliet, II. 391; III. 268, 271,
359; IV. 79, 393, 434; V. 77, 174, 175,
181, 182 (main entry), 185, 216, 221,
242, 244, 260 ff., 265, 268, 269, 279,
283, 294, 296, 298, 299, 301, 322, 374;
VI. 93, 221 ff., 248, 300, 311, 335; VIII.
120, 151, 182; X. 432; XI. 133, 260
Sonnets, IV. 392, 394, 407; V. 166, 170,
172, 174, 176, 219, 221, 223 ff., 228–
233 (main entry); VI. 30; XI. 181; XIII.
450; XIV. 304
Sonnets to Sundry Notes of Music, IV.
119; V. 224
Taming of the Shrew, The, III. 454; V.
115, 147, 181 (main entry), 220, 283,
285; VI. 97, 138; VIII. 126, 140; X. 433;
XIV. 443. See, also, under *Taming of a
Shrew*
Tempest, The, III. 178; IV. 21, 78, 79;
V. 172, 178, 188, 192, 203 ff., 206–207
(main entry), 215, 220, 285, 298, 299,
300; VI. 23, 24, 110, 239; VIII. 9, 120,
126, 135, 224, 226, 430; X. 433; XI. 274;
XII. 191, 516
Timon of Athens, V. 196 (main entry),
198, 221, 265, 291, 308; VIII. 120, 174;
XI. 265
Titus Andronicus, IV. 393; V. 75, 139,
147, 152, 163, 164, 174, 175, 177, 178–
179 (main entry), 182, 184, 185, 188,
191, 194, 195, 204, 218, 221, 260, 283,
322; VI. 23; VIII. 140, 420
Troilus and Cressida, IV. 298; V. 195–
196 (main entry), 221, 260, 261, 263,
264; VI. 30, 44, 207; VIII. 29; XI. 319
Twelfth Night, IV. 78; V. 138, 191, 192,
193–194 (main entry), 220, 300; VI.
204, 305; VII. 84; VIII. 126
Two Gentlemen of Verona, III. 268; V.
126, 174, 177, 180 (main entry), 182,
220; VIII. 126
Two Noble Kinsmen, The, VIII. 120
Venetian Comedy, The, i.e. *The Merchant of Venice*, V. 175
Venus and Adonis, IV. 128, 165, 180,
195, 222, 328, 394, 413; V. 166, 169,
170, 219, 221, 223, 225 ff. (main entry),
233, 259; VI. 86, 198, 311, 312; XI. 181
Winter's Tale, The, III. 356; V. 138,
189, 194, 204 ff. (main entry), 215, 217,
220, 374; VI. 23, 24, 110, 236, 350; VIII.
226; X. 85, 429, 433; XI. 414
Songs by:
'Full fathom five,' XII. 191
'Hark, hark, the lark,' V. 126
'In me thou see'st,' XII. 92
'On a day (alack the day!),' IV. 119

Shakespeare, 'Chandos' portrait of, VIII.
50
Shakespeare and Fletcher, *History of
Cardenio, The*, VIII. 127
Shakespeare and the continent, V. 85, 209,
287 ff., 305, 306, 456 ff.
Shakespeare festival at Stratford, X. 192
Shakespeare society, V. 247; XII. 355, 368,
369, 504
Shakespearean scholars, XII. 344
Shaking of the Sheets, The, III. 87, 484
Shallow, Justice (Shakespeare's), V. 187,
189, 350
Shallow Mannerly, Sir, in Crowne's *The
Country Wit*, VIII. 188
Shalott, Lady of (Tennyson's), XIII. 37
Shame, in *The Faerie Queene*, III. 239
Shan van Vocht, The, XIV. 311
Shandon, captain, in Thackeray's *Pen-
dennis*, IV. 252; XII. 159; XIII. 292;
XIV. 177, 194
Shandy, Tristram, in Sterne's novel, XIV.
345
Shandy, Walter, in Sterne's novel, X. 50
Shandy family, in Sterne's novel, X. 49
Shankes, John (d. 1636), VI. 276, 277
Sharp, Amy, XIII. 498
Sharp, Becky (Thackeray's), V. 213; XIII.
276, 286 ff., 290, 296
Sharp, Elizabeth Amelia, XIII. 476
Sharp, Granville (1735–1813), XII. 473
Sharp, James (1613–1679), archbishop of
St Andrews, VIII. 91; XII. 22
Sharp, John (1645–1714), archbishop of
York, IX. 394
Sharp, John (*fl.* 1756), X. 131
Sharp, Robert Farquharson, XIII. 515
Sharp, William ('Fiona Macleod,' 1855–
1905), XII. 373, 404, 407; XIII. 216, 485,
491, 498, 504, 508, 559, *also see* Add. 3
Sharpe, Charles Kirkpatrick (1781?–
1851), II. 409; XI. 444; XII. 150, 430, 518
Sharpe, Gregory (1713–1771), IX. 529
Sharpe, Lewis (*fl.* 1640), VI. 458
Sharpe, Roger (*fl.* 1610), IV. 520
Sharpe, William, engraver, XII. 323
Sharper, in Congreve's *Old Bachelor*, VIII.
147
Sharpham, Edward (*fl.* 1607), IV. 350,
529; VI. 458; *Cupid's Whirligig*, VI. 218;
The Fleire, VI. 218
Sharpham park, X. 20
Shaw, Cuthbert (1739–1771), X. 471
Shaw, Stebbing (1762–1802), XI. 513
Shaw, William (1749–1831), X. 471, 472,
489; XIV. 592, 609
Shaw, William A., XIV. 484, 487, 489, 499,
501
Shawcross, J., XI. 415; XII. 527
Shawe, Isabella. *See* Thackeray, Isabella
Shaylor, J., *The Fascination of Books*, XI.
378
Sheafe, Streatfield, and Evans, X. 375
Sheale, Richard, II. 415
Sheane, Hubert, XIV. Add. 7
Sheares, William, VI. 38

Sheath and Knife, II. 412
Sheavyn, Miss Phoebe, V. 370, 371
Sheba, queen of, X. 160
Shebbeare, John (1709–1788), X. 40, 41, 523, 525; *Letters to the people of England*, X. 389
Shebden hall, Upper, near Halifax, Yorks., VII. 233
Sheehan, John (1812–1882), XIV. 571
Sheen, VIII. 386; IX. 70
Sheeres, Sir Henry (d. 1710), VIII. 402; IX. 267, 528
Sheffield, VII. 353; X. 386; XI. 340, 469; XII. 136; XIII. 156
Sheffield, earl of. *See* Holroyd, John Baker
Sheffield, John, 3rd earl of Mulgrave, afterwards 1st duke of Buckingham and Normanby (1648–1721), VIII. 50, 202, 204, 211, 219 ff., 396, 443, 444, 481; IX. 70, 152, *also see* Add.
    Essay on Poetry, VIII. 205, 219, 375, 409, 446
    Essay on Satire, VIII. 35, 212, 219
    Ode on Love, VIII. 219
    Temple of Death, VIII. 219
    Vision, The, VIII. 219
Sheffield Daily Telegraph, The, XIV. 531, 532, 534
Sheffield Iris, The, XIV. 203
Sheffield place, Sussex, X. 312
Sheffield university, XIV. 432
Sheil, Richard Lalor (1791–1851), XIII. 257 ff., 261, 523; XIV. 127, 135, 316, 326, 511, 571
    Adelaide; or The Emigrants, XIII. 258
    Apostate, The, XIII. 258; XIV. 319
    Bellamira; or, The Fall of Tunis, XIII. 258, 259
    Evadne; or, The Statue, XIII. 259; XIV. 319
    Huguenot, The, XIII. 259
    Montoni, XIII. 259
    Sketches of the Irish Bar, XIV. 319
Shelburne, earl of. *See* Petty, William
Sheldon, Gilbert (1598–1677), archbishop of Canterbury, VII. 117, 150, 151, 153, 426; VIII. 3, 298, 302, 305
Sheldon, Ralph (1623–1684), IX. 348
Shelford, Robert, *Discourses*, VII. 33, 153, 426
Shelley, lady Jane, XII. 404
Shelley, Mrs (Harriet Westbrook), XII. 59, 62
Shelley, Mrs (Mary Wollstonecraft Godwin), XII. 35, 37, 59, 61, 62, 64, 71, 76, 399 ff., 403, 404, 451, 452
    Frankenstein, XII. 247, 248
    Last Man, The, XII. 248
    Lodore, XII. 248
    Valperga, XII. 248
Shelley, Percy Bysshe (1792–1822), I. 370; IV. 153; VII. 76, 77, 109; VIII. 237; XI. 44, 46, 102, 112, 117, 150, 158, 308, 405, 410, 414, 416, 422, 463; XII. 33 ff., 37, 39, 44, 56, 57 ff. (main entry), 79, 89, 91, 92, 94, 106, 107, 112, 113, 115, 119, 120, 126, 136, 138, 139, 157, 162,

Shelley, Percy Bysshe
    174, 179, 180, 199, 205, 219, 2z2, 247, 248, 392 ff., 397, 399 ff. (main entry), 405, 407, 445, 521, 527, *also see* Add.; XIII. 23 ff., 27, 44, 52, 56, 57, 69, 108, 109, 129, 130, 137, 138, 184, 204, 230, 239, 250, 442, 481, 489; XIV. 198, 363, 373, 453
    Adonais, IV. 152; VII. 114; XII. 71, 73 ff., 78, 87, 93; XIII. 236
    Alastor, XI. 202; XII. 58, 59, 70, 71; XIII. 236, 237
    Apollo, Hymn of, XII. 72
    Arethusa, XII. 72
    Aziola, XII. 75
    Castlereagh Administration, Lines written during the, XII. 40
    Cenci, The, XII. 61, 68 ff., 213
    Certain Letters of Percy Bysshe Shelley, XIII. 75
    Charles I, XII. 75
    Christianity, On, XII. 60
    Cloud, The, XII. 71, 72, 75
    Cosimo and Fiordispina, XII. 71
    Daemon of the World, The, XII. 59
    Defence of Poetry, The, XII. 74, 75, 78
    Edward Williams, Lines to, XII. 75
    Epipsychidion, IX. 169; XII. 73, 74
    Euganean Hills, Lines written among the, XII. 63
    Future State, On a, XII. 60
    Hellas, XII. 75
    Intellectual Beauty, Hymn to, XII. 59, 60
    Julian and Maddalo, XII. 34, 62, 63
    Laon and Cythna, XII. 61
    Liberty, To, XII. 72
    Life, On, XII. 60
    Lord Chancellor, To the, XII. 62
    Love, On, XII. 60
    Maria Gisborne, Letter to, XII. 62, 73
    Masque of Anarchy, The, XII. 69
    Medusa, XII. 58
    Mercury, Hymn to, XII. 71
    Metaphysics, On, XII. 60
    Mont Blanc, XII. 60
    Morals, On, XII. 60
    Naples, To, XII. 72
    Napoleon's death, Lines on, XII. 75
    Orpheus, XII. 71
    Pan, Hymn of, XII. 72
    Peter Bell the Third, XII. 70
    Prince Athanase, XII. 61
    Prometheus Unbound, XI. 202; XII. 58, 65 ff., 70
    Queen Mab, XI. 180; XII. 59, 60; XIII. 53, 227, 236, 237
    Revolt of Islam, The, III. 246; XI. 202; XII. 59, 61; XIII. 130, 236
    Rosalind and Helen, XII. 62
    St Irvyne, XI. 299; XII. 59
    Sensitive Plant, The, XII. 70, 71
    Skylark, To a, XII. 70, 72, 77
    Stanzas written in dejection, near Naples, XII. 63
    Swellfoot the Tyrant, XII. 70
    Tasso, XII. 64

Shelley, Percy Bysshe
Translation of Plato's *Symposium*, XII. 73
Triumph of Life, The, XII. 58, 76
Vision of the Sea, A, XII. 71
West Wind, Ode to the, VII. 181; XII. 72; XIV. 351
When the lamp is shattered, XII. 75
William Shelley, To, XII. 62
Witch of Atlas, The, XII. 71
Zastrozzi, XI. 299; XII. 59
Shelley society, XII. 400 ff.
Shelton, Thomas (1601–1650?), *Tachygraphy*, VIII. 243
Shelton, Thomas (*fl.* 1612–1620), IV. 395, 443; IX. 269; *Don Quixote*, VIII. 127, 128; IX. 278
Shenstone, William (1714–1763), III. 184; IX. 217, 412, 574; X. 112, 113, 135 ff., 149 ff. (main entry), 153, 156, 271 ff., 369, 456, 496, 497; XI. 206, 248, 251, 252, 255; XII. 132; XIII. 227, 232, 239
Dying Kid, The, X. 151
Economy, X. 150
Elegies, X. 151
'Here in cool grot,' X. 151
Jemmy Dawson, X. 151
Judgment of Hercules, X. 150
Levites, X. 151
Love and Honour, X. 150
Miscellaneous Poems, X. 151
Moral Pieces, X. 150
Ode to Memory, X. 151
'Odes, Songs, Ballads, etc.,' X. 151
Pastoral, X. 151
Progress of Taste, The, X. 150
Ruined Abbey, The, X. 150
Rural Elegance, X. 274
Schoolmistress, The, IX. 191, 405; X. 105, 136, 151; XI. 247, 323
Song of Valentine's Day, X. 151
Shepheard, Henry, XIII. 559
Shepherd, Luke (*fl.* 1548), *John Bon and Mast Parson*, III. 81, 481
Shepherd, Miss, in *David Copperfield*, XIII. 327
Shepherd, Richard Herne (1842–1895), VII. 251; XI. 412, 414, 417, 433; XII. 35, 399, 401, 412, 431, 435; XIII. 464, 493, 503, 532, 541, 542
Shepherd of Hermas, I. 75
'Shepherd Tony,' III. 302; IV. 117 ff. *See, also*, Munday, Anthony
Shepherds, Play of the, v. 19. See, also, under *Secunda Pastorum* and *Officia Pastorum*
Shepherds of the Scottish border, II. 396
Shepherdson, William, XIV. 532
Sheppard, Sir Fleetwood (1634–1698), VIII. 215, 410, 411, 433, 444, 447; IX. 473; *King James's Declaration*, VIII. 94
Sheppard, Jack (1702–1724), IX. 23
Sheppard, John (1785–1879), XIV. 518
Sheppard, John George, XIV. 609

Sheppard, Samuel (*fl.* 1646–1652), VII. 274, 347, 350, 351, 356 ff., 413, 466, 497, 498
Mercurius Dogmaticus, VII. 357
Mercurius Mastix, VII. 357
Mercurius Pragmaticus, VII. 356, 357, 360
Mercurius Pragmaticus Reviv'd, VII. 357
Mercurius Scommaticus, VII. 357
Phreneticus, VII. 357
Royall Diurnall, The, VII. 357
Socratic Session, The, VII. 274, 466
Weepers, The, VII. 357, 359
Sheppard, William (d. 1675?), VIII. 469
Shepperton church, in George Eliot's *Amos Barton*, XIII. 387
Sherborne, III. 167
Sherborne school, VII. 330
Sherbrooke, viscount. *See* Lowe, Robert
Sherburne, Sir Edward (1618–1702), VII. 87, 413; VIII. 447; 'Chloris! on thine eyes I gaze,' VII. 87; 'Love once love ever,' VII. 87; *The Vow*, VII. 87
Sheridan, Alice, XIV. 309
Sheridan, Caroline E. S. *See* Norton, Caroline E. S.
Sheridan, Mrs Frances (1724–1766), X. 438; XIV. 309; *Journey to Bath*, XI. 454
Sheridan, Helen Selina, countess of Dufferin (1807–1867), XIII. 177, 499
Sheridan, Richard Brinsley (1751–1816), IV. 361; V. 127, 254; VIII. 137, 139, 153; X. 88, 90, 92, 263, 265, 438; XI. 51, 54 ff., 251, 261, 262, 265, 266 ff. (main entry), 282, 396, 414, 452, 454, 457; XII. 49, 390, 411, 412, 443; XIII. 269; XIV. 107, 120, 121, 186, 214, 309, 498
Critic, The, VIII. 26, 402; X. 83, 87; XI. 271, 272
Duenna, The, X. 71; XI. 267, 269
'Here's to the maiden,' VI. 238
Ode to Scandal, XI. 271
Pizarro, XII. 526
Rivals, The, X. 89; XI. 266, 267, 269
St Patrick's Day, XI. 267
School for Scandal, The, X. 91; XI. 268 ff., 273, 275, 276
Trip to Scarborough, A, XI. 268
Sheridan, Thomas (1719–1788), IX. 453, 464, 467; XI. 250, 255; XIV. 309, 400, 609; *British Education*, XIV. 391, 397 ff.
Sheridan, Tom (1775–1817), XIV. 309
Sheriff, Laurence (d. 1567), VII. 336
Sheriff Hales academy, X. 386
Sheriffmuir, IX. 373
Sherlock, Thomas (1678–1761), IX. 293, 503, 508; X. 360, 517; *Letter...on...the late Earthquake*, X. 358; *Remarks*, X. 357; *Trial of the Witnesses of the Resurrection*, IX. 294; X. 358
Sherlock, William (1641?–1707), VIII. 347, 461, 462, 475; X. 358; *Defence of Dr Sherlock's notion of a Trinity in Unity*, X. 378; *Practical Discourse concerning a Future Judgment*, VIII. 304; *Vindication of the Trinity*, X. 378, 379

Sherman, John (d. 1671), *Commonplaces*, VIII. 278, 279; *A Greek in the Temple*, VIII. 278

Sherman, Stuart Pratt, VI. 190 ff., 194

Sherrard, William, XIV. 286

Sherry or Shirrye, Richard (*fl.* 1550), IV. 442; *Treatise of Schemes and Tropes*, III. 432, 553

Sherwen, John (1749–1826), X. 486

Sherwood, Mrs Mary Martha (1775–1851), XI. 369, 380, 479, 482; XIV. 335, 580
  Fairchild Family, XI. 381
  Henry Milner, XI. 381
  Infant's Progress, XI. 381
  Little Henry and his Bearer, XI. 381; XIV. 336
  Susan Grey, XI. 381

Sherwood forest, IV. 190; V. 318; VI. 11, 365

Shetland, II. 413, 414, 417; IX. 552

Shetland dance, V. 32

Shetland islands, XIV. 434

Sheva, in Cumberland's *Jew*, XI. 282

Shewell, head of Coventry academy, X. 385

Shields, Alexander (1660?–1700), IX. 547

Shiels, Robert (d. 1753), *Lives of the Poets*, X. 184

Shifnal, IX. 256; X. 233

Shilleto, Richard (1809–1876), XII. 312, 330, 493

Shiloh, oracle of, in Cowley's *Davideis*, VII. 67

Shimei, in Dryden's *Absalom*, VIII. 39

Ship money fleet, the, IV. 107

Ship of Fools, The, prose version, II. 324, 325

Shipley, Sir Arthur Everett, XII. 508

Shipley, Orley, *Dryden as a Hymnodist*, VIII. 54

Shippen, William, XII. 174

Shipton-Moyne, near Tetbury, Gloucestershire, VIII. 82

Shipton-under-Wychwood, II. 35

Shipwrights' play, the, V. 391

Shirley, *pseud. See* Skelton, Sir John

Shirley (Charlotte Brontë's), XIII. 409

Shirley, Henry (d. 1627), VIII. 442; *The Martyr'd Souldier*, VI. 458

Shirley, James (1596–1666), V. 344, 366; VI. 27, 132, 135, 140, 188–209 (main entry), 211, 234, 421, 449 ff., *also see* Add.; VII. 3, 489; VIII. 124; IX. 318; XII. 190; XIII., *also see* Add. 2
  Arcadia, III. 355; VI. 205
  Ball, The, V. 350; VI. 32, 202
  Beauties, The, VI. 204
  Bird in a Cage, The, VI. 204
  Brothers, The, VI. 203
  Cardinall, The, VI. 200, 209; VIII. 121
  Changes : or, Love in a Maze, VI. 201
  Constant Maid, The, VI. 197, 203
  Contention for Honour and Riches, A, VI. 206
  Contention of Ajax and Ulysses for the Armor of Achilles, The, VI. 198, 207
  Coronation, The, VI. 132, 140, 204, 205

Shirley, James
  Court Secret, The, VI. 197, 206
  Cupid and Death, VI. 207
  Doubtfull Heir, The, VI. 197, 205
  Dukes Mistris, The, VI. 200
  Echo, or the Infortunate Lovers, VI. 198
  Example, The, VI. 202, 208
  Gamester, The, V. 352; VI. 202; X. 86, 433
  Gentleman of Venice, The, VI. 197, 200, 205, 206
  'Glories of our blood and state, the,' VI. 198
  Grateful Servant, The, VI. 144, 203
  Hide Parke, VI. 202
  Honoria and Mammon, VI. 206
  Humorous Courtier, The, VI. 205, 208
  Imposture, The, VI. 205
  Lady of Pleasure, The, VI. 202
  Latin grammars, VI. 198
  Love Tricks, VI. 201
  Loves Crueltie, VI. 199, 208
  Maides Revenge, The, VI. 199
  Narcissus, or The Self-lover, VI. 198
  Opportunitie, The, VI. 204, 208; VIII. 129
  Polititian, The, VI. 197, 200
  Rosania, or Love's Victory, VI. 205
  Royall Master, The, VI. 197, 205, 208; XIII. 401
  St Patrick for Ireland, VI. 197, 206
  Sisters, The, VI. 206
  Traytor, The, VI. 199, 200, 208; XIII. 259
  Triumph of Beauty, The, VI. 207
  Triumph of Peace, The, VI. 197, 207, 363
  Wedding, The, VI. 201, 208
  Wittie Faire One, The, VI. 201
  Young Admirall, The, VI. 204, 208; VIII. 129

Shirley, John (1366?–1456), II. 161, 166, 170

Shirley, John, *Lord Jeffrey's Life*, XI. 330

Shirley, William (*fl.* 1739–1780), *Edward the Black Prince*, XI. 449

Shirreff, Emily Anne Eliza (1814–1897), XIV. 430, 600, 609

Shirrye, Richard. *See* Sherry

Shirwood, William (*fl.* 1260), I. 456

Shore, Jane (d. 1527?), IV. 182

Shore, Jane, in *Edward IV*, VI. 90, 91

Shore, Jane, in *The History of K. Richard III*, III. 335

Shore, Jane, The tragedy of, VIII. 196

Shore, John, 1st baron Teignmouth (1751–1834), XIV. 602

Shore, Louisa (1824–1895), XIII. 509

Shore, master, in chronicle play, VI. 98

Shore, mistress, in Praed's *Red Fisherman*, XII. 112

Shore, William Teignmouth, XIII. 544

Short, Ames, X. 387

Short, John, X. 385

Short, Peter, printer, IV. 546

Short parliament, the, VII. 54, 224, 285

Short Treatise against Stage-Plays, A, VI. 403, 497

Shorter, Clement King, XIII. 464, 503, 555, 556, 559, 569; XIV. 516

Shorter catechism, the, XIV. 405

Short-hand, X. 469

Shorthouse, Joseph Henry (1834–1903), XI. 411; XIII. 566, *also see* Add. 3; *John Inglesant*, XII. 277; XIII. 434, 435

Shortreed, Robert, XII. 4

Shotover Papers, The, XIV. 207

Shower, John (1657–1715), X. 385

Shrapnel, doctor (George Meredith's), XIII. 446

Shrewsbury, II. 2; III. 182; IV. 408; V. 39, 171, 391; VI. 252; VII. 326, 337; VIII. 171

Shrewsbury, duchess of, IX. 125

Shrewsbury, duke of. *See* Talbot, Charles

Shrewsbury, earls of. *See* Talbot, George; Talbot, Sir John

Shrewsbury, lady, in Gramont's *Memoirs*, VIII. 264

Shrewsbury academy, X. 386

Shrewsbury Chronicle, The, XII. 174

Shrewsbury school, III. 424, 425, 428, 429; IV. 159; V. 103; VII. 336, 493; IX. 165, 408; XII. 328, 329, 331, 333, 335, 336, 339; XIII. 449; XIV. 386, 413, 422

Shrimp, in *John a Kent*, V. 317

Shropshire, IV. 120; VI. 37; VII. 27, 78, 330, 337; VIII. 142, 274; XI. 120; XII. 166, 346, 509, 520; XIII. 142; XIV. 233

Shuckburgh, Evelyn Shirley (1843–1906), XII. 493

Shute, bishop of Durham, XIV. 492

Shuter, Edward (1728?–1776), X. 212

Shutte, R. N., XIV. 514

Shuttlewood, John (1632–1689), X. 387

Shylock, in Shakespeare's *Merchant of Venice*, V. 145, 181, 183, 366; VI. 69; XII. 171

Shylock, Macklin as, X. 85; XI. 257

Sibbald, James (1745–1803), XI. 446

Sibbald, Sir Robert (1641–1712), IX. 552; X. 193

Sibbes, Richard (1577–1635), VII. 426

Siberch, John (*fl.* 1521–1522), IV. 409, 547

Sible Hedingham, II. 208

Sibly, Ebenezer (d. 1800), VII. 511

Sibthorp, Richard Waldo (1792–1879), XII. 454

Sic Perrell in Paramouris lyis, II. 280

Sichaeus, in *Didone*, V. 76

Sichel, Edith, XIV. 515

Sichel, Walter, IX. 231; X. 422; *Bolingbroke and his Times*, IX. 98, 132, 217, 218, 220, 232; *Life of Sheridan*, XI. 272, 456

Sicily, IV. 258, 259; V. 206; VI. 156; VII. 75, 99; IX. 280; XII. 316, 475; XIV. 73, 292, 293

Sicily, Athenian expedition to, IV. 62

Siculus, Diodorus, IV. 408, 436

Sidanen, in *John a Kent and John a Cumber*, V. 317, 475

Siddal, Elizabeth Eleanor. *See* Rossetti, Elizabeth Eleanor

Siddons, Mrs Sarah (1755–1831), VIII. 184, 191, 196; X. 88; XI. 260, 261, 454, 461; XII. 171, 409

Sidgwick, Frank, II. 408

Sidgwick, Henry (1838–1900), XII. 469; XIV. 36 ff., 425, 426, 473, 480, 602, 606; *Methods of Ethics, The*, XI. 66; XIV. 37, 38

Sidley, Sir William, IV. 265

Sidmonton, IX. 168

Sidmouth, XIII. 70

Sidmouth, viscount. *See* Addington, Henry

Sidney, in Kelly's *False Delicacy*, XI. 263

Sidney, Algernon (1622–1683), II. 163; VIII. 267, 452; IX. 240; X. 290

Sidney, Dorothy. *See* Spencer, Dorothy

Sidney, Sir Henry (1529–1586), III. 429; IV. 72, 391

Sidney, Henry, earl of Romney (1641–1704), VIII. 167, 251, 268; IX. 495; *Diary* of, VIII. 267, 453

Sidney, lord Henry, in Disraeli's *Coningsby*, XIII. 350

Sidney, lady Mary, IV. 7

Sidney, Sir Philip (1554–1586), III. 175, 188 ff., 199, 212, 219, 220, 227, 236, 240 ff., 247, 253 ff., 257, 259, 261, 264, 265, 267, 285, 299 ff., 312, 340, 342, 349, 351 ff., 357, 364, 425, 429, 432, 437, 446, 524, 527, 535, 553, *also see* Add.; IV. 10, 18, 81, 108, 113, 116 ff., 121, 124, 125, 145, 149, 150, 152, 158 ff., 172, 179, 196, 210, 264 ff., 275, 391, 434, 447; V. 66, 173, 222, 226, 341, 347, 349; VI. 2, 14, 113, 196, 272, 302, 364 ff., 392, 497; VII. 25, 26, 114, 140, 154, 259, 306, 337, *also see* Add.; IX. 35, 69; X. 174, 222; XII. 493; XIV. 460

Apologie for Poetrie (Defence of Poesie), II. 154, 415; III. 199, 219, 255, 259, 299; V. 63, 70, 117, 130, 337; VI. 15, 267, 303, 388; VII. 261, 263, 271

Arcadia, III. 188, 265, 351, 353, 354, 358; IV. 265, 398, 401, 414; V. 254, 338; VI. 137, 180, 191, 192, 205, 212, 213; VII. 263, 265; X. 221; XI. 179

Astrophel and Stella, III. 253, 254, 256, 265; IV. 117, 133, 142, 177, 222

De Mornay, trans. of, IV. 21

Excellent sonnet of a nymph, An, IV. 118

May Lady, or The Lady of the May, The, IV. 117; VI. 336, 369

Sonnets, IV. 392

Sidney, Philip, 3rd earl of Leicester (lord Lisle) (1619–1698), II. 163; VIII. 51, 267

Sidney, Robert, 2nd earl of Leicester (1595–1677), VII. 54

Sidney, Sir Robert, IV. 154

Sidney, Thomasine, VII. 86

Sidney or Sydney, house of, VII. 54; IX. 496

Sidney Letters (Sydney Papers), VII. 436, VIII. 267, 453; X. 500

Sidonia, in Disraeli's *Coningsby*, XIII. 346, 349, 351, 360

Sidonius Apollinaris, I. 76; XIV. 303

Sidrophel, in *Hudibras*, VIII. 61, 72, 73

Siege of London, The, VI. 90

Siegen, Ludwig von, VIII. 359
Siena, VIII. 126
Sievers, Eduard, ix, I. 46, 55, 60, 101, 372
Sigebert, II. 341
Sigeferth, in *Finnsburh*, I. 31
Sigemund, in *Beowulf*, I. 23, 26
Sigeric, I. 121
Sigeric, archbishop of Canterbury, I. 116
Sigerson, George [Eironach], XIV. 303, 573
Sigewulf, I. 121
Sigferth or Sigweard, I. 126, 127
Sigmund, in Morris's *Sigurd the Volsung*, XIII. 126
Signs of Death, I. 227, 458
Signy, in Morris's *Sigurd the Volsung*, XIII. 126
Sigrdrifumál, I. 62
Sigrim the wolf, I. 366
Sigurd, in Morris's *Sigurd the Volsung*, XIII. 126
Sikes, Bill, in *Oliver Twist*, XIII. 316
Sikes, George, VII. 447
Sikes, Thomas, XII. 256
Silburn, Percy Arthur Baxter, XIV. Add. 10
Silchester, XII. 513
Silence, in *Henry IV*, v. 189, 194
Silenus, III. 389
Silexedra, in *Euphues and his England*, III. 345, 350
Silia, in Pope's *Characters of Women*, IX. 82
Silius Italicus, IV. 249, 414; IX. 44, 182
Sillery, IV. 259
Silurian system, XIV. 292, 294
Silva, Juan de, IV. 448
Silvanus, VI. 304, 486
Silver, Henry, XIV. 238, 239
Silvester, pope, V. 16
Silvestre, J. B., *Universal Palaeography*, XII. 356, 517
Silvestre, P., VIII. 481
Silvia, in Congreve's *Old Bachelor*, VIII. 147
Silvia, in Farquhar's *Recruiting Officer*, VIII. 169, 171
Silvius, in *As You Like It*, VI. 304
Simancas, XIV. 85
Simancas, archives of, X. 289
Simcox, Edith, XIV. 480
Simcox, George Augustus (1841–1905), XII. 493; XIII. 207, 509
Simcox, William Henry (1843–1889), XII. 493
Simeon, Charles (1759–1836), XII. 281, 473
Simeon, Sir John (1756–1824), IV. 209
Simeon, Joseph (1594–1671), VI. 477
Simeon of Durham (*fl.* 1130), I. 90, 148, 160 ff., 174, 449
Simeon Stylites, St, XIV. 305
Simeon Stylites (Tennyson's), XIII. 29
Simiane, Madame de, X. 248
Simmias of Rhodes, IV. 123
Simmons, Bartholomew (1804–1850), *Flight to Cyprus, The*, XIV. 327; *Napoleon's last look*, XIV. 327
Simmons, Nevill (*fl.* 1692), XI. 340

Simmons, Samuel (*fl.* 1667), VII. 116, 117; XI. 315
Simnel, Lambert (*fl.* 1487–1525), VII. 203
Simon, abbot of St Albans, I. 178
Simon, H., XIV. 478
Simon, Richard, *Histoire Critique du Vieux Testament*, VIII. 42
Simon Magus, VII. 370
Simon de Meopham. *See* Meopham
Simon de Montfort. *See* Montfort
Simon of Swynsett, V. 66
Simon of Tournay, I. 456
Simon and Jude, SS., I. 354
Simond, L., XII. 525
Simonides, IX. 54
Simon's Town, XIV. 254
Simony, in *Negromansir*, III. 77
Simony, in *Piers the Plowman*, II. 7, 8
Simple, Sir Gervase, in *Changes*, VI. 202
Simplicity, in *The World tost at Tennis*, VI. 75
Simpson, Harold, XIII. 515
Simpson, Sir James Young (1811–1870), XII. 513; *Archaeological Essays*, XII. 350
Simpson, John Palgrave (1807–1887), XIII. 521; *A Scrap of Paper*, XIII. 525
Simpson, Joseph, X. 464
Simpson, Mrs Mary Charlotte Muir, XIV. 506
Simpson, Richard (1820–1876), V. 247, 248, 344; XIV. 118, 506
Simpson, Selwyn George, XIII. 499
Simpson, Thomas (1710–1761), XIV. 257
Simrock, Karl, V. 305
Simson, Archibald. *See* Symson
Simson, Habbie, IX. 364, 365
Simson, Patrick (1556–1618), IX. 550
Sin, in *Mirour de l'Omme*, II. 140, 141
Sinai, mount, II. 13, 79; VII. 170; XII. 341, 478
Sinclair, Catherine (1800–1864), XI. 482; *Holiday House*, XI. 386
Sinclair, George (d. 1696), IX. 560
Sinclair, James (d. 1762), X. 323
Sinclair, John (1683–1750), IX. 565
Sinclair, Sir John (1754–1835), X. 488; XIV. 514
Sinclair, May, XIII. 555 ff., 573, *also see* Add. 1
Sinclair, William, bishop of Dunkeld (d. 1337), II. 110
Sinfiotli, in Morris's *Sigurd the Volsung*, XIII. 126
Sing, Cheyte, XI. 20
Singer, Samuel Weller (1783–1858), V. 277; VI. 95; VII. 74, 77; IX. 67
Singleton, Hugh (*fl.* 1579), IV. 398
Singleton, Mrs Mary Montgomerie (afterwards lady Currie, *pseud.* Violet Fane, 1843–1905), XIII. 180, 504
Singleton, Thomas, IX. 392
Sinker, Robert (1838–1913), XII. 370, 523
Sinners Beware, I. 226, 227, 458
Sinon, in *The Palice of Honour*, II. 260, 261
Sion college, London, IV. 418
Sion nunnery, Chudleigh, IV. 418

Sir Bevis, IV. 529
Sir Clyomon...and Sir Clamydes, V. 414, 417
Sir Edmundbury Godfrey's Ghost, VIII. 92
Sir Eglamore, VIII. 96
Sir Gawayne, XII. 517
Sir Patrick Spens, X. 233
Sir Tristrem, XII. 7. *See also* Tristram, Sir
Siriz, Dame, V. 25, 55
Sisamnes, in *Cambises*, V. 65
Sisley, Clement, IV. 141
Sisley, Thomas, IV. 141
Sivagi, Maratha chieftain, XIV. 338
Siward, abbot of Abingdon, I. 110
Six Articles, the, IV. 299
Six Yeomen of the West, The, III. 371
Sixille, or Six Hills, priory of, near Market Rasen, I. 344
Sixtus IV, pope, II. 348
Sixtus V, pope, IV. 429; VI. 174, 175
Sixtus V, in *The White Divel*, VI. 176
Skaldskaparmál, I. 27
Skeat, Walter William (1835–1912), I. ix, 298; II. 1 ff., 5, 8, 13, 22, 23, 26, 28, 30, 34 ff., 36, 38 ff., 166, 194, 216, 236, 241; VI. 339; XII. 505; XIII. 249; XIV. 611; *Etymological Dictionary of the English Language*, XII. 344
Skelton, John (1460?–1529), II. 154, 210, 221, 223, 250, 257, 258, 316, 321, 328, 330, 331; III. 27, 52, 60 ff., 67–79 (main entry), 184, 185, 279, 302, 480, 481, 486, *also see* Add.; IV. 322, 361, 517, 521; V. 319; VIII. 65
Against the Scottes, III. 70
Against venomous tongues, III. 72
Apollo that Whirrlyd up his chare, III. 72
Bowge of Court, The, II. 323; III. 62, 73, 74, 78, 109; VII. 174
Colyn Clout, III. 69, 74 ff., 78
De bono ordine, III. 77
Edward the Forth, Of the death of, III. 70
Enterlude of Godly Queene Hester, III. 77
Eulogium pro suorum temporum conditione, III. 70
Garlande of Laurell, The, III. 67, 69, 70, 77
Garnesche, poems against, III. 68, 72, 73
Hymns on the battle of the Spurs, conquest of Terouenne, and victory of Flodden, III. 70
In Bedel, III. 72
Lawde and Prayse made for our Sovereigne Lord the Kyng, A, III. 70
Magnyfycence, III. 62, 77, 78; V. 54, 57, 60, 392
Mannes Lyfe the Peregrynacioun, Of, III. 67
Merie Tales of Master Skelton, III. 93, 94, 487; IV. 327
Nacyoun of Folys, III. 61
Negromansir, III. 77, 80
New Gramer in Englysshe compylyd, The, III. 67
Northumberlande, Upon the doulourus dethe of the Erle of, III. 70

Skelton, John
Phyllyp Sparowe, III. 68, 71 ff., 75
Prince Arturis Creacyoun, III. 70
Replycacion agaynst certayne yong scolers abjured of late, III. 69
Robin Hood, a pageant of, III. 68
Speculum principis, III. 67
Speke, Parrot, III. 67, 75, 76
Three Fooles, The Boke of, III. 61
Tunnyng of Elynour Rummyng, The, III. 73, 88; IV. 362
Ware the Hauke, III. 72
Why come ye nat to courte, III. 76, 77
Skelton, Sir John (*pseud.* Shirley, 1831–1897), XIII. 559; XIV. 506, 525; *John Dryden, In Defence*, VIII. 45; *Nugae Criticae*, XIV. 161; *Table Talk of Shirley, The*, XIV. 161
Skelton, John Henry, *My Book, or, The Anatomy of Conduct*, XIII. 278
Skelton, Matthew, X. 362
Skelton, Philip (1707–1787), IX. 465; XIV. 571
Skene or Skeyne, Gilbert (1522?–1599), III. 108, 494
Skene, James (1775–1864), XII. 26, 381
Skene, William Forbes (1809–1892), XII. 518; XIV. 497; *Celtic Scotland*, XIV. 95; *Four Ancient Books of Wales*, I. 247, 249
Skewton, Mrs, in *Dombey and Son*, XIII. 325
Skiddaw, XII. 188
Skimpole, Harold, in Dickens's *Bleak House*, IX. 81; XII. 205; XIII. 328
Skink, in *Looke about you*, V. 320
Skinner, Cyriack, VII. 108
Skinner, David, VII. 141
Skinner, John (1721–1807), IX. 567; XI. 226
Ewie wi' the Crookit Horn, IX. 372
Old Age, IX. 372
Tullochgorum, IX. 372
Tune your Fiddle, IX. 372
Skinner, Vincent, IV. 447
Skinnerswell, V. 44
Skiöldr and *Skiöldunga Saga*, I. 25, 27, 32
Skipsey, Joseph (1832–1903), XIII. 509
Skipton school, VII. 330
Skirving, Adam (1719–1803), IX. 373
Skoggan, IV. 360
Skoggan, The Geystes of, III. 91, 93, 94, 104, 487, 488
Skoloker, Anthony, III. 80
Skot, John (or Scott, or Scot) (*fl.* 1530), II. 328
Skrine, Huntley, XIV. 602
'Skroddler' (William Mason), X. 136
Skye, XII. 13; XIII. 209
Slade, Matthew (1569–1628?), VII. 308
Slade professor of fine art at Oxford, XIV. 152, 154, 155
Sladen, Douglas Brooke Wheelton, XIV. 584, 586
Slander, in *The Faerie Queene*, II. 234
Slang, Jack, X. 199
Slater, Francis Carey, XIV. Add. 5

Slater, John Herbert, XIII. 532
Slater, Samuel (d. 1704), X. 522
Slaughden quay, XI. 141
Slearys, the, in Dickens's *Hard Times*, XIII. 329
Sleeman, Sir William Henry (1788–1856), XIV. 338, 554
Sleidanus, Johannes, IV. 448
Sleigh, Dr, X. 201
Slender, in *The Merry Wives of Windsor*, III. 181; v. 189, 194
Slick, Sam, *pseud. See* Haliburton, Thomas Chandler
Slingsby, Sir Henry (1602–1658), VII. 453; XII. 376; *Civil War Memoirs*, XII. 16; *Diary*, VII. 224
Slingsby, Jonathan Freke, *pseud. See* Waller, John Francis
Slipslop, Mrs, in Fielding's *Joseph Andrews*, X. 25; XI. 266
Sloane, Sir Hans (1660–1753), IX. 139, 443; XIV. 285, 563, 566
Slop, Dr, in *Tristram Shandy*, X. 50
Slope, Obadiah (Trollope's), XIII. 422
Sloperton, XII. 103
Sloss, Duncan J., XI. 188
Sloth, in *Confessio Amantis*, II. 147
Sloth, in Dunbar's *Sevin Deidlie Synnis*, II. 255
Sloth, in *Piers the Plowman*, II. 12, 16, 23, 28, 33
Slough of Despond, in Bunyan's *Pilgrim's Progress*, VII. 178
Slowboy, Tilly, in Dickens's *The Cricket on the Hearth*, XIII. 324
Sludge, Mr (Browning's), XIII. 63, 72, 73
Sluys, battle of, I. 357, 359
Sly, in *The Malcontent*, VI. 170
Slye (actor), VI. 248, 276
Smaland, I. 94
Small, John (1828–1886), XII. 517
Small, Roscoe Addison, VI. 3, 4, 17
Small *v.* Attwood, XIV. 124
Smalridge, George (1663–1719), IX. 153; X. 352, 353, 517
Smaragdus, I. 117
Smart, Christopher (1722–1771), X. 60, 123, 138, 153–154 (main entry), 156, 177, 457; *Hannah*, X. 207; *Song to David*, X. 153, 154
Smart, lady, in Swift's *Complete Collection of...Conversation*, IX. 106
Smart, Thomas Burnett, XIII. 486, 488
Smeaton, Oliphant, XIII. 466
Smectymnuus, VIII. 72
Smedley, Francis Edward (1818–1864), XIV. 216, 545; *Frank Fairleigh*, XIV. 234; *Harry Coverdale's Courtship*, XIV. 234; *Lewis Arundel*, XIV. 234
Smedley, Jonathan (*fl.* 1689–1729), IX. 448
Smedley, Menella Bute, XIII. 177, 509
Smeeton, George (*fl.* 1800–1828), XIV. 231
Smelfungus, in Sterne's *Sentimental Journey*, X. 42
Smellie, William (1740–1795), XI. 440, 470; *Philosophy of Natural History*, XI. 327

Smelt, Jacob, in *The Weakest goeth to the Wall*, v. 316
Smelt, Leonard (1719?–1800), XI. 365
Smetham, James (1821–1889), XIV. 525
Smethwick, John (*fl.* 1623), IV. 394, 395
Smiglesius, Martin, X. 198
Smike, in *Nicholas Nickleby*, XIII. 318, 320, 321
Smiles, Samuel (1812–1904), XII. 430, 450; XIV. 506, 613
Smirdis, in *Cambises*, v. 65
Smith, in Buckingham's *Rehearsal*, IX. 147
Smith, Adam (1723–1790), IV. 312; VIII. 343; X. 158, 173, 285, 321, 324, 334, 335 ff. (main entry), 511, 512; XI. 76, 400; XII. 142, 426, 427; XIV. 2, 3, 21, 22, 153, 387; *Theory of Moral Sentiments*, X. 335, 337; *Wealth of Nations, The*, VIII. 367; X. 335 ff., 340; XI. 71; XIV. 381, 400, 401
Smith, Albert, XIV. 545
Smith, Albert Richard (1816–1860), XIV. 236, 546
Smith, Alexander (1830–1867), XI. 437; XIII. 156 ff., 509; XIV. 525
　Barbara, XIII. 159
　City Poems, XIII. 158
　Dreamthorp, XIII. 158; XIV. 160
　Edwin of Deira, XIII. 158
　Life Drama, A, XII. 114; XIII. 158 ff.
　On the Writing of Essays, XIV. 160
　Summer in Skye, A, XIII. 158; XIV. 160
Smith, Alfred Charles (b. 1822), XII. 513
Smith, Arthur Lionel, *Frederick William Maitland*, XIV. 79, 494
Smith, Blanche. *See* Clough
Smith, Charles, XIV. 555
Smith, Charles Eastlake, XIV. 523
Smith, Charles Roach (1807–1890), XII. 513; 'Antiquarian Notes' (*Gentleman's Mag.*), XII. 346; *Retrospections*, XII. 347
Smith, Charlotte (1749–1806), XI. 465; XIII. 239; *The Old Manor House*, XI. 299
Smith, Edmund (or 'Rag') (1672–1710), IX. 181 ff., 487; *Phaedra and Hippolitus*, VIII. 181; IX. 183
Smith, Edward, VII. 444
Smith, Edward, XIV. 558
Smith, Miss Egerton, XIII. 83
Smith, Francis (*fl.* 1661), VIII. 10
Smith, Gamaliel (*see* Bentham, Jeremy), XI. 398
Smith, George (*c.* 1643), VII. 498; *Scotish Dove*, VII. 350
Smith, George, editor of Bede (1693–1756), X. 498
Smith, George (1824–1901), XIV. 194, 534
Smith, George (1840–1876), XII. 499; XIV. 192; *Chaldaean Genesis*, XII. 342
Smith, George Charles Moore, IV. 350; VI. 295, 297, 307, 308, 324, 458; XIII. 559
Smith, George Gregory, III. 304; XI. Add.
Smith, Goldwin (1823–1910), XII. 447; XIII. 350; XIV. 90 ff., 343, 344, 497, 596
　Empire, The, XIV. 90

Smith, Goldwin
  Irish History and Irish Character, XIV.
  90
  Lectures on Modern History, XIV. 90
  *On the Foundations of the American
  Colonies*, XIV. 90
  Three English Statesmen, XIV. 91
Smith, Harriet, in Jane Austen's *Emma*,
  XII. 240
Smith, Harry B., XIII. 542
Smith, Henry (1550?–1591), IV. 237, 494;
  VII. 427
Smith, Henry John Stephen (1826–1883),
  XIV. 262, 264, 556
Smith, Horatio ('Horace') (1779–1849),
  XII. 422; *Rejected Addresses*, XI. 151;
  XII. 120; XIV. 238
Smith, James, Massinger's patron, VI. 144
Smith, James (1605–1667), VII. 413, 512;
  VIII. 232, 408; *Musarum Deliciae*, VII.
  512
Smith, James (1775–1839), XII. 422; *Re-
  jected Addresses*, XI. 151; XII. 120; XIV.
  200, 238
Smith, James, of Hawthorn, Virginia,
  Junius Unveiled, X. 305
Smith, James Cruickshank, XIII. 559
Smith, Sir James Edward (1759–1828),
  XIV. 287, 564
Smith, James Elimalet (1801–1857), XII.
  473; XIV. 535
Smith, John (d. 1612), III. 422
Smith, captain John (1580–1631), IV. 104,
  311, 461, 513; *General History of Vir-
  ginia*, IV. 95, 401; *Map and description
  of Virginia*, IV. 411; *Sea Grammar*,
  IV. 95, 105
Smith, John (1618–1652), VIII. 288 ff., 301,
  456, 457; *Select Discourses*, VIII. 288
Smith, John, *The Mysterie of Rhetorique
  Unvail'd* (1657), VII. 466
Smith, John (*fl.* 1673–1680), X. 377; *De-
  signed End to the Socinian Controversy*,
  X. 379
Smith, John (1747–1807), XII. 518
Smith, John (*fl.* 1819), VIII. 242, 243
Smith, John, M.D., XIII. 487
Smith, John Christopher (1712–1795), X.
  426, 432, 433
Smith, John Pye (1774–1851), XII. 469
Smith, John Russell (1810–1894), XII.
  523
Smith, John Thomas (1766–1833), X. 473;
  XI. 434; XII. 513; *A Book for a Rainy
  Day*, XIV. 226, 546
Smith, Joseph, XII. 523
Smith, Joseph T., XIV. 563
Smith, Logan Pearsall, XIV. 611
Smith, Lucy Toulmin (1838–1911), XII.
  518
Smith, Miles (d. 1624), VII. 317, 482
Smith, Miss M. Steele, Pref. ix.
Smith, Mr, in Burney's *Evelina*, X. 65
Smith, Mrs, in Jane Austen's *Persuasion*,
  XII. 240
Smith, Nowell C., XI. 408

Smith, Ralph, XI. 332
Smith, Reginald Bosworth (1839–1908),
  XII. 316, 478
Smith, Reginald J., XII. 426
Smith, Richard, IV. 399
Smith, Robert, *Strange Lamentable and
  Tragical Histories*, IV. 449
Smith, Robert Archibald (1780–1829), XI.
  233, 236, 444, 445
Smith, Robert Harvey, XIV. 538
Smith, Sir Robert Murdoch (1835–1900),
  XII. 339, 498
Smith, Robert Payne (1819–1895), XII.
  341, 503
Smith, Samuel, XI. 334
Smith, Sydney (1771–1845), XI. 343, 461,
  483; XII. 143, 144, 146, 281, 426, 427,
  also see Add. 2; XIV. 139, 203, 394, 403,
  405, 409, 410, 506
Smith, Thomas (1638–1710), IX. 349, 530
Smith, Sir Thomas (1513–1577), III. 331,
  418, 419, 423, 425, 432, 433, 553, 556;
  IV. 70, 513; VII. 191; VIII. 467; IX. 496;
  *Discourse on the Commonwealth of
  England*, III. 331, 531; IV. 297
Smith, Sir Thomas (1558?–1625), IV. 461
Smith, Sir Thomas (d. 1644), VII. 454
Smith, Thomas, university librarian,
  Cambridge, IV. 228
Smith, Walter (*fl.* 1525), *The merry jests
  of the widow Edith*, II. 327, 486; III. 88,
  89, 487
Smith, Walter Chalmers (1824–1908), XIII.
  509
Smith, Wentworth (*fl.* 1601–1623), V. 312,
  319, 371; VI. 89, 100, 168; *The Hector
  of Germanie*, V. 331. See, also, *Lady
  Jane*
Smith, William (*fl.* 1596), III. 256, 264,
  266; IV. 117; *Chloris*, III. 256, 266, 524;
  IV. 121, 472
Smith, William (Rouge Dragon) (1550?–
  1618), III. 324
Smith, William (1756–1835), XI. 157, 421
Smith, William (1769–1839), XIV. 291, 564
Smith, Sir William (1813–1893), XII. 429,
  478, 493
  Dictionary of Christian Antiquities, XII.
  335
  Dictionary of Christian Biography, XII.
  317, 335
  *Dictionary of Greek and Roman An-
  tiquities*, XII. 335
  *Dictionary of Greek and Roman Bio-
  graphy*, XII. 317, 335
  *Dictionary of Greek and Roman Geo-
  graphy*, XII. 317, 335
  Dictionary of the Bible, XII. 317, 335
  Latin Dictionary, XII. 335
Smith, William, *History of Canada*, XIV.
  358, 583
Smith, William Anderson, XIV. 535
Smith, William Henry (1808–1872), XII.
  469, 470; XIV. 480
Smith, William James, *Grenville Papers*,
  X. 410

Smith, William Robertson (1846–1894), XII. 342, 470; *Old Testament in the Jewish Church, The,* XII. 296; *Prophets of Israel, The,* XII. 296

Smith and Dame, II. 501

Smith and Elder, publishers, X. 204; XIII. 415

Smith-Hill house, X. 196

Smollett, Elizabeth (d. 1763), X. 41

Smollett, Sir James (1648–1731), X. 36

Smollett, Lydia, X. 47

Smollett, Tobias George (1721–1771), VI. 24, 28; VIII. 162; IX. 236, 245; X. 20, 21, 29, 35 ff. (main entry), 50, 56, 65, 204, 205, 395, 397, 418 ff., 431, 504, 522, *also see* Add.; XI. 264, 330; XII. 2, 30, 231, 245, 246, 250, 251; XIII. 305, 308, 309, 314; XIV. 215, 223, 225, 554

Advice, X. 36

Briton, The, X. 390

Burlesque Ode on the Loss of a Grandmother, X. 36

Don Quixote (trans.), X. 40

Ferdinand Count Fathom, X. 39, 40

'Habbakuk Hilding, Justice and Chapman,' X. 34, 39

History of an Atom, X. 40, 42

History of England, X. 40, 202, 293, 502; XI. 449; XIV. 50

Humphrey Clinker, X. 36, 39, 42, 43; XIII. 279; XIV. 255

Letters from France and Italy, IX. 247

Memoirs of a Lady of Quality, X. 39

Ode to Independence, X. 43

Peregrine Pickle, IX. 245, 405, 409, 410; X. 34, 37 ff., 43; XI. 449

Present State of the Nations, X. 41

Regicide, The, X. 36, 37, 39

Reprisal, The, X. 40; XI. 449

Reproof, The, X. 36

Roderick Random, IX. 245; X. 34, 36 ff., 43, 45, 48; XI. 262, 449

Sir Launcelot Greaves, X. 40, 41

Tears of Scotland, X. 36

Travels through France and Italy, X. 42, 43; XIV. 213

Universal History, X. 41

Smug, in *The Merry Devill,* V. 252

Smug of Lemnos, in *Mercury Vindicated,* VI. 357

Smyrna, XIV. 251

Smyth, Nicolas, IV. 436

Smyth, Richard, *A Confutation of the true and Catholic Doctrine,* III. 33

Smyth, William (1765–1849), XIV. 109, 498; *Lectures on the French Revolution,* XIV. 110

Smythe, A. J., XIII. 515

Smythe, George A. F. P. S., 7th viscount Strangford (1818–1857), XIV. 196; *Historic Doubts,* IX. 224, 231

Smythe, James Moore, IX. 449

Smythe, Sir John, IV. 461

Smythe, Robert, XIV. 597

Smythe exhibition, X. 198

Snap, Miss Laetitia, in Fielding's *Jonathan Wild,* X. 28

Snape, Andrew (1675–1742), IX. 510

'Snark' (Lewis Carroll's), XIII. 167

'Snawdoun' (=Stirling), III. 120

Sneakup, Pyannet, in *The City Witt,* VI. 229

Sneer, in Sheridan's *Critic,* XI. 272

Sneerwell, lady, in Sheridan's *School for Scandal,* XI. 270

Snell, F. J., XIII. 560

Snelling, Thomas, VI. 477

Sneyd, Honora. *See* Edgeworth, Honora

Snitterfield, X. 112

Snob, Mr, *pseud.* of W. M. Thackeray, XIII. 278, 284, 285

Snob, The, XIII. 277; XIV. 207

Snodgrass, Augustus, in *The Pickwick Papers,* XIII. 313

Snowden, Jane, in Gissing's *The Nether World,* XIII. 458

Snowdon, X. 115

Snuff, in *Cambises,* V. 64

Soames, Sir William, trans. of *Art Poétique,* VIII. 373; X. 169

Soane, George (1790–1860), XI. 491

'Soaping Club,' X. 191

Sober, Mr, in Johnson's *Idler,* X. 178

Sobieski, John III, king of Poland, VIII. 94

Sobry, Mlle A., XIII. 545

Social [and political] aspects of the later Elizabethan and earlier Stewart period, V. 476 ff.

Social satire in Middle English, I. 360 ff.

Social tracts of Elizabethan England, IV. 515

Socialism, XII. 290

Society for Promoting Christian Knowledge, IX. 407, 573

Society for the Diffusion of Useful Knowledge, XII. 307

Society for the Encouragement of Learning, XI. 325

Society for the Suppression of Vice, XI. 380

Society islands, XIV. 244

Society of Antiquaries of London, XII. 345, 347, 506, 510

Society of Antiquaries of Scotland, IX. 372; XII. 349

Society of Friends, VII. 169; IX. 307; X. 519

Society of Friends, the early, VIII. 412

Socinian heresies, the, VII. 21

Socinianism, X. 373, 377 ff.; XII. 287

Socinians, VIII. 275, 291

Socinus, VII. 150

Socrates, II. 313; III. 216, 420; V. 93; IX. 524, 529; XII. 309, 313, 442, 475

Sodom and Gomorrah, in *Cleanness,* I. 323

'Sodom of Italy,' in *The Unfortunate Traveller,* III. 364

Sodomy, in *The Three Laws,* V. 58

Sodor and Man, bishopric of, X. 359

Sohrab, in Arnold's poem, XIII. 92

Soirées de Médan, XIII. 456

Sol, in Welsh tradition, I. 255

Solace, in *Ane Pleasant Satyre,* III. 124, 126

Solander, Daniel Charles (1736–1782), XIV. 289

Solebay, battle of, VII. 56; VIII. 11, 24

Solempne, Anthony de, IV. 409

Solihull, X. 112

Solinus, Julius, I. 76, 81; IV. 448

Solitary, in Wordsworth's *Excursion*, XI. 106

Solitary Plot, Sir, in *The Example*, VI. 202

Solleysel, IV. 369

Solomon, in *New Atlantis*, VII. 299, 303

Solomon, in *The Palice of Honour*, II. 260

Solomon, king, I. 62, 63, 134, 205, 349; II. 21, 129, 207, 319, 370; IX. 337; XI. 235, 290

Solomon, The Wisdom of (15th century tract), II. 284

Solomon and Marcolphus, Dialogue or communing between the wise king, II. 319, 486

Solomon's house, in *New Atlantis*, IX. 388

Solomon's Song, II. 395

Solomons, Ikey, junior, *pseud.* of W. M. Thackeray, XIII. 279

Solorzano, A. del Castillo, IX. 418

Solway Moss, battle of, III. 147

Solyman II, sultan, in *Solymannidae*, VI. 301

Solyman the magnificent, in D'Avenant's *Siege of Rhodes*, VIII. 117

Solymannidae, VI. 301, 486

Some, Robert (1542–1609), III. 390, *also see* Add.

Some wiser than Some, VII. 386

Somer and Wynter, Debate and Stryfe Betweene, II. 501

'Somer is comen with love to toune,' II. 501

Somers, Sir George (1554–1610), IV. 78; V. 220

Somers, John, lord Somers (1651–1716), VIII. 445; IX. 8, 94, 101, 112, 113, 150; X. 295, 373

Somers' Tracts, VII. 456; VIII. 10, 411; IX. 217, 435, 539; X. 499; XII. 16, 376

Somersby, Lincolnshire, XII. 39; XIII. 23

Somerset, IV. 190; X. 393; XI. 99, 101, 155; XII. 509, 512

Somerset, lord Charles, XIV. 373

Somerset, dukes of. *See* Seymour, Edward; Seymour, William

Somerset, earl of. *See* Carr, Robert

Somerset, Edward (1557), *The Pore estate to be holden for best*, III. 179

Somerset, Edward, 4th earl of Worcester (1553–1628), IV. 143, 203, 259

Somerset, Edward, 2nd marquis of Worcester (1601–1667), VII. 392; VIII. 479; *Century of Inventions*, VIII. 359

Somerset, Elizabeth, duchess of. *See* Percy, lady Elizabeth

Somerset, lord Fitzroy James Henry, 1st baron (1788–1855), XIV. 94, 173

Somerset, Frances, duchess of (lady Hertford, d. 1754), X. 94, 271 ff.

Somerset, Frances (Devereux), duchess of (d. 1674), IV. 421

Somerset, Henry, 1st marquis of Worcester, VIII. 470, 471

Somerset, Henry Charles, 6th duke of Beaufort (1766–1835), XIV. 232

Somervile, William (1675–1742), X. 109 ff., 271, 273, 449, 497
  Chace, The, X. 109 ff.; XIV. 232
  Epistle to Mr Thomson, X. 110
  Hobbinol, X. 111
  Occasional Poems, X. 109
  Rural Sports, X. 111

Somerville, Elizabeth, XI. 489

Somerville, James (1632–1690), *Memorie of the Somervilles*, XII. 376

Somerville, Mary (1780–1872), XIV. 556

Somerville, Thomas (1741–1830), XIV. 498

Somme des Vices et des Virtus, or *Li Livres roiaux des Vices et des Vertus*, or *Somme le Roi*, I. 354

Sommer or Somer, Sir Henry (*fl.* 1407–1413), II. 208

Sommers, Will, in *When you see me, etc.*, V. 333

Somner, William (1598–1669), VII. 481; IX. 539; *Canterbury*, IX. 353; *Dictionarium*, IX. 355

Somnus, in *Lingua*, VI. 315

Somnus, in *The Vision of the Twelve Goddesses*, VI. 337

'Son of the Marshes, A.' *See* Jordan, Denham

Sonare, III. 249

Song to the Virgin, A, I. 232, 458

Song-Books and Miscellanies, IV. 109 ff., 462 ff.

Song writers, IV. 468

Songer, Ralph, IV. 432

Songes and Sonnettes. See under *Tottel's Miscellany*

Songs of Divers Noblemen and Gentlemen, IV. 142

'Songs of Selma,' X. 130

Sonnenthal, V. 306

Soothness, in *Piers the Plowman*, II. 8

Soowthern. *See* Southern

Sophia, in Cumberland's *Brothers*, XI. 264

Sophia, Charlotte, queen of Prussia, IX. 290

Sophia, Dorothea, X. 499

Sophia, electress of Hanover, IX. 200, 290, 490; XIV. 111

Sophister, The, VI. 481

Sophistici Elenchi, I. 206

Sophocles, III. 430, 433; IV. 4; V. 289, 295 ff.; VI. 295, 298; VII. 489; VIII. 30, 149; IX. 477; XII. 68, 328, 332, 333, 338, 340, 403, 480, 482, 483, 485 ff., 491, 494, 495; XIII. 90, 257, 497
  Ajax, Latin version of, VI. 300
  Electra, V. 75
  Oedipus, V. 295; IX. 142; XI. 283; XII. 327, 329; XIII. 145
  Oedipus Coloneus, XII. 327
  Philoctetes, X. 79

Sophonisba, in *The Wonder of Women*, VI. 49

Sophonisba, or Hannibal's Overthrow, VIII. 185

Sophora tree, XIV. 286

Sophron, XII. 329

Sopwell nunnery, near St Albans, II. 318

Sorastanus, duke of Tuscany, in *Perfidus Hetruscus*, VI. 302

Sorbière, Samuel de, XI. 331

Sorby, Henry Clifton (1826–1908), XIV. 293, 564

Sorcery, in *Confessio Amantis*, II. 149

Sordido, in *Every Man out of his Humour*, IV. 358; V. 354; VI. 40

Sorel, Charles, *Remarques sur le Berger extravagant*, IV. 260, 523; *Le Berger Extravagant*, VIII. 372

Sorley, Charles Hamilton (1895–1915), XIII. 509, *also see* Add. 2

Sorrel, Hetty, in *Adam Bede*, XIII. 390, 391

Sorrow, in Sackville's *Induction*, III. 200

Sorrow for another's joy, in *Confessio Amantis*, II. 147

Sorrowes Joy, IV. 165

Sosia, Amphitryon's servant, V. 107

Sotheby, Samuel (1771–1842), XI. 336

Sotheby, William (1757–1833), XII. 128, 422

Sotherton, in Jane Austen's *Mansfield Park*, XII. 241

Soties, V. 22, 91

Soto, in *The Spanish Gipsie*, VI. 77

Soto, Andrew de, IV. 94

Soudan, the, XIV. 191

Souhaits des hommes, et les souhaiz et beautés des dames, Les, III. 89

Soul, the, in *Mirour de l'Omme*, II. 140

Soul and Body Addresses, I. 61, 129, 227, 428, 458, 459

Souldiers Catechism, The, VII. 382

Soulsby, Lucy Helen Muriel, XIV. 599

Sound, the, VIII. 254

Sourton down, VII. 348

Souter, Alexander, XII. 488

Souter, Johnie, in Burns's *Tam o' Shanter*, XI. 219

South, Esquire, in Arbuthnot's *History of John Bull*, IX. 134, 135

South, Robert (1634–1716), VII. 246, 247; VIII. 303, 370, 461, 462; IX. 32, 147, 387; *Animadversions upon Dr Sherlock's Vindication*, VIII. 304; X. 378; *Sermons*, VIII. 304

South Africa, XIV. 372 ff., 457

South African Magazine, The, XIV. 588

South African Philosophical society, XIV. Add. 4

South Cadbury, Somerset, X. 393

South Eastern railway, XIII. 334

South English Legendary, The, XIV. 306

South Sea, the, XIV. 242, 243

South Sea Bubble, IX. 21, 105, 162, 220; XIV. 212

South Sea company, X. 272, 299

South Sea islands, X. 228

Southampton, IV. 190; X. 132; XII. 232, 519; XIII. 276

Southampton, Arthur at, in Wace's *Brut*, I. 237

Southampton, earl of. *See* Wriothesley, Henry

Southampton, Minot's poem on the battle of, I. 357, 359

Southcott, Joanna (1750–1814), XI. 163; XIII. 153

Southdean, X. 93

Southern, Henry (1799–1853), XII. 430

Southern or Soowthern, John (*fl.* 1584), IV. 24, 25; *Pandora*, IV. 472

Southerne or Southern, Thomas (1660–1746), VIII. 181, 195, 400, 401, 442
  Disappointment, The, VIII. 189, 191
  Fatal Marriage, The, VIII. 191, 192
  Fate of Capua, The, VIII. 191
  Isabella, X. 118, 433
  Loyal Brother, The, VIII. 34, 190
  Maids Last Prayer, The, VIII. 191
  Money the Mistress, VIII. 191
  Oroonoko, or the Royal Slave, VIII. 191, 192; X. 118
  Sir Anthony Love, VIII. 191
  Spartan Dame, The, VIII. 190, 191; XI. 317
  Wives' Excuse, The, VIII. 55, 191, 396
  Works, VIII. 190

Southesk, earl of (d. 1905), XIV. 584

Southey, Mrs Caroline Anne (born Bowles, 1786–1854), XI. 156, 421, 422; XII. 124, 127, 401, 414; *The Mariner's Hymn*, XII. 128

Southey, Charles Cuthbert, XI. 422; XII. 219

Southey, Mrs Edith (born Fricker), XI. 155, 156

Southey, Herbert, XI. 156

Southey, Isabel, XI. 156

Southey, Sir Richard, XIV. Add. 11

Southey, Robert (1794–1843), III. 78, 536; IV. 89, 252, 267; VIII. 244; IX. 170, 178; X. 217, 221, 364, 367, 368, 485, 486, 518; XI. 40, 118, 119, 122, 124, 126, 149, 153 ff. (main entry), 172, 173, 176 ff., 201, 202, 250, 254, 294, 309, 341, 393, 401, 411, 413, 415 ff., 420, 468, 490, *also see* Add.; XII. 42, 59, 95, 96, 98, 101, 107, 111, 113, 120, 122, 124, 133, 135, 136, 138, 150, 154, 158, 164, 167, 179, 182, 186, 205, 208, 210, 214 ff., 219, 268, 303, 364, 401, 415, 424, 429, 441, 527; XIII. 52, 157, 225 ff., 230, 233, 239, 244 ff., 306; XIV. 184, 312, 387, 403, 462, 506, 592, 601
  All for Love, XI. 166
  Amadis, XI. 162
  Ballads, XI. 159, 160
  Battle of Blenheim, XI. 160
  Bishop Hatto, XI. 160
  Book of the Church, The, XI. 167; XIV. 55
  Botany Bay Eclogues, XI. 159
  Chronicle of the Cid, XI. 162
  Colloquies, XI. 167; XII. 215, 230

Southey, Robert
  'Come, for ye know me!' XI. 161
  Commonplace Books, XI. 163
  Cross Roads, The, XI. 160
  Curse of Kehama, The, XI. 162, 164;
    XIII. 232
  Doctor, The, XI. 163, 168, 169
  Essays Moral and Political, XI. 167
  Expedition of Orsua, XI. 163
  Fall of Robespierre, XI. 161
  History of Brazil, XI. 162
  History of Portugal, XI. 162
  History of the Peninsular War, XI. 167;
    XIV. 107
  Holly-Tree, XI. 159
  Inchcape Rock, XI. 160
  Joan of Arc, XI. 158, 159, 161, 413
  Lay of the Laureate, XI. 166
  Letters, XI. 156, 159, 170
  Letters from Spain and Portugal, XI.
    161, 163
  Letters of Espriella, XI. 162
  Life of John Wesley, IX. 328; XI. 167
  Life of Nelson, XI. 162 ff., 167
  Lives of the Admirals, XI. 167
  Madoc, XI. 159, 161, 162, 173
  Metrical Tales, XI. 161
  Minor Poems, XI. 161
  My days among the Dead are passed,
    XI. 159
  Ode to Horror, XI. 158
  Old Woman of Berkeley, The, XI. 160;
    XII. 111, 123
  Oliver Newman, XI. 166
  Omniana, XI. 162, 163; XIII. 164
  Palmerin, XI. 162
  Poet's Pilgrimage to Waterloo, XI. 166
  Queen Orraca, XI. 160
  Roderick, XI. 159, 166
  Sappho, XI. 158
  Specimens of Later English Poetry, XII.
    132
  Story of the Three Bears, XI. 168
  Tale of Paraguay, XI. 166
  Thalaba, XI. 160, 161, 164, 180; XII. 145;
    XIII. 227, 232, 236
  Vindiciae Ecclesiae Anglicanae, XI. 167
  Vision of Judgment, A, XI. 166; XII. 36,
    53, 54, 199; XIII. 240, 244
  Wat Tyler, XI. 157 ff., 161
  Well of St Keyne, XI. 160
Southland, T., *Love à la Mode* (1663), VIII.
  422
Southover, VIII. 244
Southward, John, XIV. 536
Southwark, II. 233
Southwark, priory of St Mary Overes,
  II. 135
Southwark, St Saviour's church, II. 135,
  137
Southwell, III. 428, 478
Southwell, Robert (1561?–1595), III. 177;
  IV. 127 ff., 139, 140, 218, 237, 477, 495,
  496
  Burning Babe, The, IV. 130
  Maeoniae, IV. 130

Southwell, Robert
  New Heaven, New Warre, IV. 130
  New Prince, New Pompe, IV. 130
  Saint Peters Complaint, IV. 128 ff.
Southwell, Sir Robert (d. 1599), III. 183
Southwell, Sir Robert (1635–1702), IX. 92;
  X. 500
Southwell's *Notes and Illustrations on the
  Bible*, XI. 326
'Southwerke,' in *Colin Blowbol's Testa-
  ment*, III. 86
Sovereign of the Seas, The, VI. 84
Sowden, Mr, IX. 246
Sowdone of Babylone, I. 471
Spa, IV. 202
Spademan, John, X. 385
Spagnoletto school, IX. 252
Spain, I. 153; II. 310, 340; V. 99, 123, 132,
  304, 306, 337, 341, 347, 356, 359, 365;
  VI. 79, 103, 147, 150, 248, 364, 396;
  VII. 53, 180, 191, 194, 197, 198, 200,
  215, 219, 222, 274, 306, 367, 455; VIII.
  65, 271, 329; IX. 6, 7, 23, 221, 231, 256,
  265, 268, 277; X. 182, 306, 391, 404;
  XI. 27, 72, 280; XII. 32, 42, 149, 488;
  XIII. 2, 40, 107, 258, 396; XIV. 102 ff.,
  122, 180, 241, 250, 251, 293
Spain and Byron, XII. 393
Spalatro, VII. 309
Spalding, John (*fl.* 1650), *History of Scot-
  land*, IX. 550; XII. 359
Spalding, Robert (*fl.* 1592–1607), VII. 317
Spalding, William (1809–1859), V. 258;
  XIV. 480, 525
Spalding club, XII. 359
Spalding school, IX. 330
Spaniards, the, VII. 64, 210; X. 288; XIV.
  125, 242, 245, 250
Spanish affairs, IX. 215; X. 291
Spanish ambassador at the English court,
  VI. 148
Spanish American colonies, XIV. 122
Spanish armada, the, VII. 282; XIV. 84, 97
'Spanish Armada, The,' in Sheridan's
  Critic, XI. 272
Spanish bull-fight, XII. 43
Spanish coast, the, XIV. 73
Spanish drama and English, V. 1, 303
Spanish fleets, VII. 446
Spanish influences, VII. 165, 260; VIII. 14,
  17, 23, 124 ff., 424, 425
Spanish language and literature, VII. 142,
  265; VIII. 162, 308, 311, 353, 354; IX. 4,
  277, 403, 413; X. 40, 72, 233; XI. 359;
  XII. 13, 157, 272, 308; XIII. 143, 144;
  XIV. 251, 385, 434, 457 ff.
Spanish Main, the, XIV. 241
Spanish mysticism, VII. 155
Spanish navy, the, XIV. 187, 201
Spanish plays, VI. 124
Spanish politics, VIII. 384
Spanish prince, the, in *Mucedorus*, V. 253
Spanish romances, V. 254; VI. 239, 365
Spanish sources, VI. 123, 132, 136, 204,
  205, 208; VIII. 144
Spanish succession, the, IX. 11, 228, 231

Spanish succession, war of the, XIV. 89
Spanish (Peninsular) war, the, XI. 103
Spanish wines, V. 358
Spanus, in Robert Landor's *Fawn of Sertorius*, XII. 230
Spare your good, III. 491
Sparling, H. Halliday, XIV. 573
Sparrow, John (1615–1665?), IX. 515, 517
Sparrowe, Thomas (*fl.* 1629–1633), VI. 478
Sparsit, Mrs, in Dickens's *Hard Times*, XIII. 330
Sparta, youths of, III. 22
Speaker, The, XIV. 199, 534
Spectacle de la Nature, XI. 382
Spectacle of Lovers, II. 326
Spectacula, Roman, VI. 373
Spectacula theatralia, in Rome, V. 38
Spectakle of Luf or *Delectatioun of Wemen*, II. 284, 479
Spectator (Mr Addison's), XIII. 445
Spectator, The, V. 286, 290; VIII. 378; IX. 18, 32, 33, 35, 41, 48 ff. (main entry), 69, 144, 165, 171, 181, 220, 412, 436, 438, 439, 441, 444, 448, 455, 474, 492; X. 26, 56, 69, 90, 171, 172; XI. 146, 280, 317; XII. 140, 193, 223, 231; XIII. 284; XIV. 213, 441, 442, 444, 446, 461
Spectator, The (founded 1828), XIV. 141, 172, 194, 198, 199, 530, 534
Spectator, The (1862), XIII. 440
Speculum Christiani, II. 319, 426, 503
Speculum Ecclesiae, I. 206
Speculum Stultorum, II. 144
Spedding, James (1808–1881), IV. 280; V. 248; VII. 203; XI. 463; XIV. 24, 142, 246, 479; XIV. 506; *Evenings with a Reviewer*, XIV. 63; *Life and Letters of Bacon*, XIV. 63; *Studies in English History* (with J. Gairdner), XIV. 82, 83
Speech of a Fife Laird, IX. 366
Speeches, in Jacobean times, VII. 439 ff.
Speed, John (1552?–1629?), III. 313, 323, 325, 335, 336, 532; IV. 159, 461; VII. 203, 442; IX. 352; *Historie of Great Britaine*, III. 325; IV. 58
Speed, Miss, X. 126
Speed, Samuel (1631–1682), *Prison Pietie*, VII. 45
Speght, Thomas (*fl.* 1598), II. 162, 217; III. 449; X. 236
Speke, John Hanning (1827–1864), XIV. 554; *Journal of the discovery of the source of the Nile*, XIV. 253
Spelman, Sir Henry (1564?–1641), III. 323; VII. 442; VIII. 318, 469; IX. 344, 355, 539, 540; *Glossarium Archaiologicum*, IX. 356
Spelman, Sir John (1594–1643), IX. 534
Spence, Catherine Helen, XIV. 587; *Clara Morison*, XIV. 369
Spence, F., VIII. 481
Spence, Joseph (1699–1768), VIII. 370; IX. 67, 68, 73, 77, 131, 141, 188, 448, 451, 485; X. 119, 244; XI. 323, 467; *Anecdotes*, VIII. 322; X. 174; *Essay on Pope's Odyssey*, IX. 77

Spencer, in *The Fair Maid of the West*, VI. 101
Spencer, Dorothy (born Sidney), countess of Sunderland (1617–1684), VII. 54; VIII. 251, 267, 268, 453
Spencer, Edm. (translator), IV. 439
Spencer, Gabriel (d. 1598), VI. 3
Spencer, George, 5th duke of Marlborough (1766–1840), XII. 365
Spencer, George John, 2nd earl Spencer (1758–1834), XII. 365, 366
Spencer, Henry, 1st earl of Sunderland (1620–1643), VII. 55
Spencer, Henry le. *See* Despenser, Henry le
Spencer, Herbert (1820–1903), IX. 401; XII. 275; XIII. 385; XIV. 28 ff., 33, 38, 43, 199, 393, 478, 480, 609
    Autobiography, XIV. 28
    Classification of the Sciences, The, XIV. 28
    Data of Ethics, The, XIV. 30, 35
    Descriptive Sociology, XIV. 28
    'Development Hypothesis, The,' XIV. 28
    Education, XIV. 28, 395, 396, 421
    Factors of Organic Evolution, XIV. 28
    First Principles, XIV. 28
    'Genesis of Science, The,' XIV. 28
    Man versus The State, The, XIV. 28
    Principles of Biology, XIV. 28
    Principles of Ethics, XIV. 28
    Principles of Psychology, XIV. 28, 30
    Principles of Sociology, XIV. 28, 30
    'Programme of a System of Synthetic Philosophy,' XIV. 28
    'Progress: its law and cause,' XIV. 28
    'Proper Sphere of Government, The,' XIV. 28
    Social Statics, XIV. 28, 31
    Study of Sociology, The, XIV. 28
Spencer, Sir John (*fl.* 1595), III. 213
Spencer or Spenser, John (1559–1614), VII. 316
Spencer, John (1630–1693), VII. 490
Spencer, John Charles, viscount Althorp and 3rd earl Spencer (1782–1845), XIV. 115, 125, 180
Spencer, Sir Robert (*fl.* 1603), VI. 339, 340
Spencer, Robert, 2nd earl of Sunderland (1640–1702), VIII. 268; IX. 183, 213, 442, 483
Spencer, William, VII. 483
Spencer, William Robert (1769–1834), VII. 84; XII. 131, 422
Spencer family, of Althorp, III. 213
Spens, Sir Patrick, I. 300; II. 395, 413
Spense, *Bellum grammaticale*, IX. 551
Spenser, Edmund (1552?–1599), I. 170; II. 163, 165, 184, 213, 220, 233 ff., 332, 337; III. 66, 168, 185, 188, 199, 200, 211–246 (main entry), 247, 250 ff., 254, 256 ff., 264, 271, 272, 273, 283 ff., 293, 294, 302, 303, 305, 320, 327, 409, 425, 435, 448, 455, 519 ff., 524, 527, *also see* Add.; IV. 17, 25, 47, 77, 88, 109, 117, 121, 124, 125, 131, 135, 138, 139, 149,

Spenser, Edmund
150, 158, 165, 167, 173, 180, 183, 208,
211, 248, 266, 330, 360, 390, 434, 513,
516, 525; v. 18, 156, 171, 183, 225 ff.,
234, 327, 368; vi. 2, 11, 103, 113, 196,
311, 312, 329, 336, 366, 388; vii. 2, 10,
26, 46, 49, 62, 70, 73, 76, 110, 135, 176,
210, 272, 274; viii. 40, 48, 51, 88, 219,
222, 228, 230, 233, 239, 284, 384; ix.
68, 69, 143, 158, 165, 184, 188, 189,
338, 396, 477, 479, 483; x. 105 ff., 132,
174, 184, 221, 224, 227, 238, 239, 337;
xi. 157, 179, 182, 206, 247, 252, 255,
425; xii. 3, 86, 93, 168, 177, 208, 221,
272, 392, 440, 455; xiii. 38, 233, 235,
238, 512; xiv. 113, 307, 487
Amoretti, iii. 215, 243, 256, 257
Astrophel, iii. 240; iv. 118
Colin Clout's Come Home Again, iii.
183, 213, 214, 242, 243; iv. 53, 134
Complaints, iii. 241, 250; v. 85 ff., 136
Discourse of Civil Life, vii. 211, 448
Dreames, iii. 229
Dying Pelican, The, iii. 229
Epithalamion, iii. 228, 243; vii. 209;
xii. 79
Faerie Queene, The, i. 284; ii. 228, 233,
234; iii. 199, 213, 218, 228 ff. (main
entry), 242 ff., 271, 286, 409, 448; iv. 53,
54, 67, 76, 120, 222, 321, 398; v. 83, 87,
239, 338; vi. 330, 335, 365; vii. 173,
209, 253, 449; viii. 65, 279; x. 235, 240,
241, 492; xii. 44, 61, 79, 87; xiv. 308
Hymnes in honour of Love and Beautie,
iii. 215 ff., 221, 243
Mutabilitie, vii. 209
Nine Comedies, iii. 229
Prosopopoia or Mother Hubberd's Tale,
iii. 241, 246, 286; viii. 36, 226
Prothalamion, iii. 228, 243
Ruines of Time, The, iii. 250; v. 85
Ruins of Rome, The, iii. 250; v. 86, 238
Shepheards Calender, The, ii. 213; iii.
66, 214, 218 ff. (main entry), 225, 226,
228, 230, 238, 242 ff., 284, 286, 300,
302 ff., 442, 448; iv. 118, 171, 196, 398;
v. 157, 225, 338; vi. 305, 364, 365; vii.
13; ix. 161
Tears of the Muses, The, iii. 241, 396;
vii. 112
Veue of the Present State of Ireland, vii.
209 ff., 448
Visions of Bellay, The, iii. 250, 251
Visions of Petrarch, The, iii. 250
Spenser society, the, iv. 156
Spenserian stanza, x. 155; xi. 241, 247,
250; xii. 11, 44, 74, 100, 138; xiii.
229, 234 ff.; xiv. 311
Spenserians, iv. 149 ff., 223
Speranza, in *The Faerie Queene*, vi. 335
Spes (Hope), in *Piers the Plowman*, ii.
27
Spezia, bay of, xii. 37, 75, 76
Sphere, The, xiv. 201
Spice islands, the, iv. 67, 72, 73, 76, 98
Spickernell, Thomas (*fl.* 1594), iv. 362

Spielmann, Marion Harry, xiii. 530, 555,
559; xiv. 236, 532, 549; *The History
of Punch*, xiv. 236, 532, 549
Spigott, in *Times Complaint*, vi. 320
Spilman or Spelman, Thomas, iv. 124
Spinagros, Sir, in *Golagros and Gawane*,
ii. 123
Spingarn, Joel Elias, vi. 9; ix. 60, 61
Spinola, v. 361
Spinoza, Baruch (or Benedict), ix. 291,
298; xi. 100; xii. 60, 402; xiii. 18, 98,
439; xiv. 8, 41, 47, 469, 477; *Ethics*,
xiii. 383; *Tractatus Theologico-Politicus*,
xiii. 383
Spira, Vindelin de, iv. 421
Spirit of Men, The, i. 428
Spiritual Sangis, iii. 142
Spiritualitie, in *Ane Pleasant Satyre*, iii
125, 126, 127, 128
Spithead, xiv. 243
Splügen pass, the, xiii. 83
Sponge (Mr Surtees's), xiv. 234
Sport, in *The Tears of the Muses*, iii. 241
Sporting Magazine, The, xiv. 232
Sporting periodicals, xiv. 547
Sportive Wit (1656), vii. 512
'Sporus,' in Pope's *Epistle*, ix. 251, 252
Spottiswoode, John (1565–1637), iii. 165;
*History of the Church and State of
Scotland*, vii. 208, 448; xii. 359
Spottiswoode society, xii. 358, 359
Spoyle of Antwerp, The, v. 344
Spragge, Sir Edward (d. 1673), viii. 202
Spraggon, Jack (Surtees's), xiv. 234
Sprat, Thomas (1635–1713), vii. 257, 264;
viii. 5, 25, 26, 91, 365, 369, 378, 394,
402, 410; ix. 32, 148, 158, 495; *History
of the Royal Society*, viii. 379, 480;
ix. 387, 412, 573; xiv. 460; *Life of
Cowley*, x. 184; *True Account of that
Horrid Conspiracy*, ix. 239
Spratt, Albert William (1842–1920), xii.
Add. 3
Spratt, Thomas Abel Brimage (1811–
1888), xii. 339, 498
Sprenger, Jacob, vii. 368, 375, 377, 394,
505
Sprigg, Joshua (1618–1684), vii. 450
Spring, Tom, xiv. 231
Springer, the, in Emily Brontë's *Wuthering
Heights*, xiii. 411
Springett, Mrs (born Mary Proude, after-
wards wife of Isaac Penington), viii.
109
Springlove, in *A Joviall Crew*, vi. 230
Springly, Tom, in *The Tatler*, ix. 36
Sprott, Thomas (*fl.* 1270?), ix. 535
Spur, Mercurius, x. 471
Spurcock, Sir Launcelot, in *The London
Prodigall*, v. 255
Spurgeon, Charles Haddon (1834–1892),
xii. 473
Spurs, battle of, iii. 70
Spurstow, William (1605?–1666), vii. 416
Spy, The (Hogg's), xi. 239
'Square-Cap' (Cleiveland's), vii. 97

Squeerses, the, in *Nicholas Nickleby*, XIII. 319, 321, 325

Squeezum, justice, in Fielding's *Coffee-House Politician*, X. 21, 29

Squire of Low Degree, I. 288, 315, 471

'Squirrel,' the (ship), IV. 74

Staal Delaunay, Madame de, X. 135

Stabat Mater, II. 383

Stables, William Gordon (1840-1910), XIII. 566

Stacions of Rome, The, II. 503

Staël, Madame de, V. 301; XII. 282; XIII. 468; *De l'Allemagne*, XIII. 3, 4

Stael, Peter, IX. 412

Stafford, East Gate street, VII. 250

Stafford, Edward, 3rd duke of Buckingham (1478-1521), II. 358

Stafford, Sir Edward, ambassador (d. 1605), IV. 79

Stafford, George, III. 27, 37

Stafford, Henry, 2nd duke of Buckingham (1454?-1483), III. 193

Stafford, Henry, 1st lord Stafford (1501-1563), III. 194

Stafford, John, archbishop of Canterbury (d. 1453), II. 288

Stafford, the Hon. John, *The Spartan Dame* (1719), VIII. 442

Stafford, Thomas, lieutenant, VII. 211

Stafford, W., *A Briefe Conceipt of English Policy*, V. 355, 363, 479

Stafford family, the, III. 188; IV. 132

Staffordshire, VIII. 146; IX. 533, 538; XI. 374; XII. 509, 513; XIII. 390

Staffordshire Advertiser, The, XIV. 529, 532

Stage-Players Complaint, The, VI. 406, 497

Stage-Playes, A Short Treatise against, VI. 497

Stage-Playes, An Ordinance...for The Utter Suppression and abolishing of, VI. 495

Stagyrite, the. *See* Aristotle

Stählin, K., V. 341

Staines, in Greene's *Tu Quoque*, VI. 219

Stair, earls of. *See* Dalrymple, Sir John

Stair, viscount. *See* Dalrymple, James

Stallard, Dr, IV. 382

Stallybrass, J. S., I. 420, 424

Stamboul, XIV. 247

Stamford, II. 345; IX. 308

Stamford News, The, XIV. 202

Stamp act, XI. 5, 7, 10

Stanbridge, John (1463-1510), II. 498

Standard, colonel, in Farquhar's *The Constant Couple*, VIII. 170

Standard, The, XIV. 180, 188, 189, 196

Standish, Arthur (*fl.* 1611), IV. 541

Stanford (Lincoln, Rutland and Northamptonshire), IX. 538

Stanford, Sir Charles Villiers (1852-1924), X. 130; XIII. 474

Stanford, Sir Wm (1509-1558), VIII. 467

Stanhope, Arthur Charles (d. 1770), X. 494; XIV. 391

Stanhope, Charles, 3rd earl Stanhope (1753-1816), XI. 390

Stanhope, Sir Edward (1546?-1608), IV. 427

Stanhope, Eugenia, X. 258, 494

Stanhope, lady Hester Lucy (1776-1839), IX. 244; XIV. 506

Stanhope, James, 1st earl of Stanhope (1673-1721), IX. 17, 483, 486

Stanhope, Leicester Fitzgerald Charles, 5th earl of Harrington (1784-1862), XII. 384

Stanhope, Philip, X. 257, 258, 494

Stanhope, Philip Dormer, 4th earl of Chesterfield (1694-1773), IV. 103; VIII. 388; IX. 152, 190, 246, 250, 252, 254, 485; X. 164, 167, 173, 176, 188, 207, 255 ff. (main entry), 369, 460, 463, 475, 477, 494, *also see* Add.; XI. 82, 173, 248, 260, 323; XIII. 321; XIV. 605

Letters, VIII. 389; IX. 133, 471, 498; XI. 278, 371

Letters to his Godson, X. 257 ff.

Letters to his Son, X. 255, 257, 258; XIV. 390, 391

Letters to A. C. Stanhope, XIV. 391

'The Duty, Utility and Means of Pleasing,' X. 258

Stanhope, Philip, 5th earl of Chesterfield (1755-1815), X. 257; XIV. 391

Stanhope, Philip Henry, 5th earl Stanhope (1805-1875), IX. 498; XI. 396; XIV. 498

History of England, XIV. 89

History of the War of the Succession in Spain, XIV. 89

Life of the Younger Pitt, XIV. 90

Miscellanies, XIV. 89

Reign of Queen Anne, The, XIV. 90

Stanley, Alice, countess dowager of Derby, lady Strange (born Spencer), VII. 112, 113

Stanley, Arthur Penrhyn (1815-1881), IV. 35; XII. 153, 264, 283, 288, 295, 319, 320-321 (main entry), 464, 467, 468, 470, 474, 477, 478, *also see* Add.; XIII. 96, 473, 541; XIV. 506, 601

Epistles of St Paul to the Corinthians, XII. 292

Lectures on the Church of Scotland, XII. 321

Lectures on the Jewish Church, XII. 294; XIII. 98

Life of Arnold, XII. 320; XIII. 370; XIV. 413

Memorials of Canterbury, XII. 321

Memorials of Westminster Abbey, XII. 321

Oxford lectures, XII. 321

Sinai and Palestine, XII. 321

Stanley, Edward, 3rd earl of Derby (1508-1572), VII. 83

Stanley, Edward G. G. S., 14th earl of Derby (1799-1869), XII. 334; XIII. 175, 509; XIV. 74, 90, 125, 129, 182, 197

Iliad (trans.), XIV. 130

Stanley, Edward H. S., 15th earl of Derby (1826–1893), XIV. 509
Stanley, Ferdinando, lord Strange, 5th earl of Derby (d. 1594), VI. 247, 249
Stanley, Henry, 4th earl of Derby (1531–1593), III. 382; XII. 518
Stanley, Sir Henry Morton (1841–1904), XIV. 192, 554
Stanley, Maria Josepha, lady (d. 1863), x. 299, 302
Stanley, Owen, XIV. 296, 564
Stanley, Thomas (1625–1678), IV. 125; VI. 197; VII. 4, 85, 87, 88, 94, 413, 475, 489; XII. 324, 328
   Basia, To, VII. 83
   Blush, The, VII. 84
   Celia, To, VII. 84
   'Chide, chide no more,' VII. 84
   Clarissa, To, VII. 84
   Cupido Cruci Affixus, VII. 83
   History of Philosophy. VII. 83, 281
   Kiss, The, VII. 84
   Pervigilium, VII. 83
   'Tell me no more,' VII. 83
   Venus Vigils, trans. of, VII. 489
Stanley, Venetia, IX. 351
Stanley, William, 9th earl of Derby (1656–1702), x. 358
Stanley family, the, II. 40
Stanley of Alderley, Henrietta Maria, lady (d. 1895), XIV. 430
Stanley's remedy, or the way to reform wandring beggars, etc., IV. 513
Stanley's catalogue of Parker MSS. at Corpus, IV. 426
Stanmore, Gordon Arthur Hamilton, lord (1829–1912), XIV. 508, 510
Stannard, Henrietta E. V. (*pseud.* John Strange Winter, 1856–1911), XIII. 566
Stans Puer ad Mensam, II. 502
Stansby, William, IV. 400
Stanyhurst, Richard (1547–1618), II. 265; III. 295, 307, 318, 319, 448, 527; x. 293; *Description of Ireland*, III. 319; XIV. 308; trans. of *Vergil*, IV. 17 ff., 23, 399, 440
Stapfer, Paul, x. 422
Stapleton, Augustus Granville (1800–1880), XIV. 506, 508
Stapleton, Thomas (1535–1598), III. 415, 470
Stapylton, Sir Robert (d. 1669), VII. 487, 489; VIII. 421; *Hero and Leander*, VIII. 123; *The Slighted Maid*, VIII. 123; *The Stepmother*, VIII. 123
Star, The, XIV. 194
Star, The (1888), XIV. 195
Star Chamber, the, III. 76, 375, 378; IV. 279, 379, 380 ff., 386, 387, 411; v. 371, 372; VI. 290, 404; VII. 343, 345, 346, 441, 456; VIII. 315; x. 287; XI. 311, 312
Starcatherus, I. 25
Starkey, John (*fl.* 1671), VII. 120; XI. 339
Starkey, Thomas (*fl.* 1499?–1538), III. 478, 496; *Dialogue between Cardinal Pole and Thomas Lupset*, IV. 300, 573
Starkie, Thomas, XIV. 536

Starlight, captain, XIV. 370
State of Grace, the carvel of the, in *The Palice of Honour*, II. 261
State papers and other public documents in Jacobean times, VII. 433
State papers of the Earl of Clarendon, x. 294
State papers for 1616, VI. 402
State Poems (1697), VIII. 410
Stately, lord, in Crowne's *The English Frier*, VIII. 188
Statham, E. Reginald, XIV. Add. 10
Statham, Nicholas (*fl.* 1467), VIII. 314, 466
Statilia, in *The Bond-Man*, VI. 155
Stationers' company, III. 96, 375, 378, 445; IV. 59, 63, 378 ff., 431; v. 260, 371; x. 12; XI. 312, 313, 467
Stationers' registers, III. 79, 81, 396; IV. 9, 544 ff.; XI. 314; XII. 357, 368, 515
Statius, I. 170; II. 150, 366; IV. 250; VII. 487; IX. 44, 527; XII. 306; *Silvae*, IX. 341; *Thebais*, IV. 253; IX. 68, 446
Statuta Ecclesiae Scoticanae, XII. 359
Statutes of the Realm (1235–1713), VIII. 466
Staubach, the, XII. 47
Staunton, Howard (1810–1874), v. 279
Staunton, W., *St Patrick's Purgatory*, IV. 353, 527
Stavordale, lord, XIV. 503
Stead, J. J., XIII. 559
Stead, William Thomas (1849–1912), XIV. 193, 195, 535
Stearne, John, *A Confirmation and Discovery of Witch-Craft*, VII. 376, 507
Stebbing, William, XIV. 496
Stedman, Edmund Clarence, XIII. 485, 491
Steele, Anne (1717–1778), x. 522
Steele, Joshua (1700–1791), XI. 250, 251 (main entry), 256; XIII. 240
Steele, Sir Richard (1672–1729), VI. 82; VII. 244; VIII. 145, 175, 390; IX. 5, 26 ff. (main entry), 75, 94, 109, 114, 118, 124, 142, 144, 161, 165, 171, 172, 248, 271, 436, 438 ff., 446, 456, 462, 569; x. 26, 67 ff., 80, 92, 205, *also see* Add.; XI. 261, 280, 320; XII. 177; XIII. 312, 429; XIV. 169, 197, 441, 446, 448, 461
   Apology for Himself and his Writings, IX. 29
   Christian Hero, The, IX. 28, 30, 33, 42
   Conscious Lovers, The, IX. 57, 64
   Drummer, The, IX. 43
   Fishpool, The, IX. 439
   Funeral, or Grief-à-la-mode, IX. 30
   Lover, The, IX. 437, 439, 441
   Lying Lover, The, VIII. 131; IX. 30; XI. 322
   Miscellanies, VIII. 158
   Miscellany, IX. 169
   Old Whig, The, IX. 439, 442
   Plebeian, The, IX. 439, 442
   Reader, The, IX. 439, 442
   Spinster, The, IX. 439
   Tea-Table, The, IX. 442
   Tender Husband, The, IX. 30, 33; x. 70

Steele, Sir Richard
    Town Talk, The, IX. 439, 442
    See, also, *Spectator, The*, and *Tatler, The*
Steele sisters, the, in Jane Austen's *Sense
    and Sensibility*, XII. 237, 240, 243
Steere, W., IX. 435
Steerforth, James, in *David Copperfield*,
    XIII. 327
Steevens, George (1736–1800), III. 252;
    v. 275 ff.; IX. 477; X. 263, 462, 471, 490,
    also see Add.; XI. 333; XII. 365; *Shake-
    speare*, XI. 320
Steevens, George Warrington (1869–
    1900), XIV. 193, 208, 535
Steill, David, dean, II. 280; III. 132
    Attributed to: *The Ring of the Roy
    Robert*, II. 132; *Absent*, II. 132; *The
    Lantern of Lufe*, II. 132
Stein, III. 2
Stein, Sir Aurel (b. 1862), XII. Add. 5
Stella (lady Rich), alluded to in *Fame's
    Memorial* and *The Broken Heart*, v.
    347; VI. 191, 196
Stella (Sidney's), III. 254; IV. 196; VI. 113
Stella (Swift's). *See* Johnson, Esther
Stella (Waller's), VII. 54
Stella, To, x. 168
Stelliana (Venetia Stanley), in Digby's
    Memoirs, VII. 222
Stelvio pass, in George Meredith's novel,
    XIII. 447
Stendhal (Marie Henri Beyle), v. 301;
    XIII. 447; XIV. 138
Stengesius, G., VII. 368, 505
Stenhouse, William (1773?–1827), IX. 361;
    XI. 444, 446
Stennett, Joseph (1663–1713), x. 387, 522
Stephano, in *Damon and Pithias*, v. 118
Stephano, in *The Tempest*, v. 206
Stephen, in Dickens's *Hard Times*, XIII.
    329
Stephen, king of England, I. 111, 161, 166,
    168, 171, 172, 364, 369; II. 350; XIV. 72
Stephen, Caroline Emelia, XII. 427
Stephen, Sir James (1789–1859), x. 300;
    XII. 153, 282, 427, 471; XIII. 471;
    XIV. 507; *Essays in Ecclesiastical Bio-
    graphy*, XIV. 109, 120; *Lectures on the
    History of France*, XIV. 109, 110
Stephen, Sir James Fitzjames (1829–
    1894), XIV. 194, 198, 481, 498, 507;
    Liberty, Equality, Fraternity, XIV. 21;
    The Story of Nuncomar, XIV. 110
Stephen, James Kenneth (1859–1892),
    XIII. 162, 509; XIV. 205 ff., 337, 537;
    Lapsus Calami, XIII. 166; XIV. 206, 208
Stephen, Sir Leslie (1832–1904), VIII. 245;
    IX. 253; X. 409, 411, 413, 422, 445, *also
    see* Add.; XI. 394, 395, 397, 411, 417,
    419, 423, 439; XII. 131, 381, 404, 426,
    431, 433, 441, 445, 464, 468, 486, 524;
    XIII. 97, 100, 180, 360, 407, 473, 478,
    485, 488, 510, 553, 559, 567; XIV. 56,
    65, 81, 103, 111, 143–144 (main entry),
    467, 470, 472, 481, 486, 488, 493, 494,
    498, 509, 515, 524 ff., 561, 595

Stephen, Sir Leslie
    Agnostic's Apology, An, XIV. 144
    English Utilitarians, The, XIV. 35, 144
    *Essays on Free Thinking and Plain
    Speaking*, XIV. 143
    *History of English Thought in the 18th
    century*, IX. 310, 321, 324; X. 296; XIV.
    35, 144
    Hours in a Library, XII. 148; XIII. 379;
    XIV. 143
    Johnson, XIV. 144
    Life of Sir James Fitzjames Stephen,
    XIV. 110
    Playground of Europe, The, XIV. 143,
    248, 254
    Science of Ethics, The, XIV. 35
    Sketches from Cambridge, XIV. 143
    Studies of a Biographer, XIV. 144
Stephen de Haselfield, II. 351
Stephens, Alexander (1757–1821), x. 524
Stephens, Catherine, countess of Essex,
    XII. 171
Stephens, Frederick George, XIII. 110, 491
Stephens, French family of, printers and
    scholars, VII. 307, 477
Stephens, George (1813–1895), I. 425; XII.
    513
Stephens, James Brunton (1835–1902),
    XIV. 369, 587; *Convict Once*, XIV. 368;
    To a Black Gin, XIV. 368; *Universally
    Respected*, XIV. 368
Stephens, Jeremiah (1591–1665), IX. 539
Stephens, John (*fl.* 1615), III. 487; VI.
    497; VII. 379; *Satyrical essayes, cha-
    racters and others*, IV. 340 ff., 345, 518,
    521, 524
Stephens, John (d. 1726), IX. 277, 343,
    501, 539; *Pablo de Segovia*, IX. 278;
    Spanish Libertines, IX. 278
Stephens, Robert (1665–1732), IX. 529
Stephens, Thomas, VII. 487
Stephens, Thomas (1549?–1619), XIV. 322
Stephens, William Richard Wood (1839–
    1902), XII. 457; XIV. 488, 507; *History
    of the English Church*, vol. II, XIV. 101;
    Life and Letters of E. A. Freeman, XIV.
    67, 71
Stephens, Winifred, XIII. 566
Stephenson, B. C. and Scott, Clement,
    Diplomacy, XIII. 525
Stephenson, George (1781–1848), XIV. 381
Stepmothers Tragedy, The, v. 325
Stepney, George (1663–1707), VIII. 410,
    411, 447; IX. 174, 176, 487; XIV. 180
Sterling, John (1806–1844), XI. 441; XII.
    288, 425, 467; XIII. 18, 24, 473, 552;
    XIV. 180
Sterling, Joseph, x. 491
Sterne, Laurence (1713–1768), IV. 248,
    264; IX. 127, 128; X. 15, 39, 43, 46 ff.
    (main entry), 56 ff., 352, 369, 421, *also
    see* Add.; XI. 174, 289, 296, 347, 429;
    XII. 56, 124, 177, 250; XIII. 7, 319, 326,
    420, 421, 428; XIV. 142, 146, 217, 223,
    554; *Sentimental Journey*, x. 42, 47;
    XIV. 240, 246; *Tristram Shandy*, IV.

Sterne, Laurence
  252; IX. 136, 137; X. 44, 47 ff., 252;
  XI. 206, 260, 341; XIII. 295; XIV. 216
Sternhold, Thomas (d. 1549), III. 46;
  Psalms, VIII. 41
Stesichorus, XII. 329
Stettin, duke of, VI. 291, 292
Steuart, Archibald Francis, X. 295
Steuart, Sir James (1712–1780), Inquiry
  into the Principles of Political Economy,
  X. 337, 338, 514
Stevens, B., XIV. 584; The Golden Treasury
  of Australian Verse, XIV. 365
Stevens, George Alexander (1710–1784),
  XI. 472
Stevens, John (d. 1726), IX. 533
Stevens, William Bagshaw (1756–1800),
  X. 491
Stevenson, Elizabeth. See Gaskell, Eliza-
  beth Cleghorn
Stevenson, Francis Seymour, I. 204
Stevenson, John (1798–1827?), XIII. 378
Stevenson, Sir John Andrew (1760?–
  1833), XII. 410, 411
Stevenson, John Hall (1718–1785), X. 47;
  XI. 172 ff., 428; XII. 120
  Crazy Tales, XI. 174, 175
  Fables for Grown Gentlemen, XI. 174
  Makarony Tales, XI. 174
  Pastoral Cordial, XI. 174
  Pastoral Puke, XI. 174
Stevenson, Joseph (1806–1895), XII. 356;
  XIV. 499
Stevenson, Matthew (fl. 1654–1685), Nor-
  folk Drollery (1673), VII. 512
Stevenson, Mrs Margaret Isabella, XIV. 526
Stevenson, Robert Alan Mowbray (1847–
  1900), XIV. 525, also see Add. 3
Stevenson, Robert Louis (1850–1894), I.
  367; VI. 230; VIII. 112; XI. 387, 441;
  XII. 30, 168, 176, 178, 179, 381, 433;
  XIII. 214, 441, 509, 523; XIV. 161 ff.,
  211, 462, 525, 526, 538, 554
  A Child's Garden of Verses, XIII. 215
  Across the Plains, XIV. 162
  Amateur Emigrant, The, XIV. 162
  Beach of Falesa, The, XIV. 162
  Beau Austin (with W. E. Henley), XIV.
  163
  Black Arrow, The, XIV. 162, 443
  Catriona, XIV. 162
  Christmas Sermon, A, XIV. 162
  'College Magazine, A,' XIV. 210
  Familiar Studies, XIV. 162
  In the South Seas, XIV. 162
  Inland Voyage, An, XIV. 162, 240
  Kidnapped, XIV. 162
  Markheim, XIV. 162
  Master of Ballantrae, The, XIV. 162
  Memories and Portraits, XIV. 162, 210
  New Arabian Nights, The, XIV. 162
  'Old Scotch Gardener, An,' XIV. 210
  Ordered South, XIV. 161
  Pavilion on the Links, The, XIV. 162
  St Ives, XIV. 163
  Silverado Squatters, The, XIV. 162

Stevenson, Robert Louis
  Thrawn Janet, XIV. 162
  Travels with a Donkey, XIV. 162
  Treasure Island, XIV. 162, 255
  Virginibus Puerisque, XIV. 162
  Weir of Hermiston, XIV. 163
Stevenson, William (fl. 1546–1560), VI.
  296, 297, 478
Stevenson, William (1772–1829), XIII. 372
Stevenson, William Henry, I. 90
Steventon, Hampshire, XII. 231
Steward, Augustine, IV. 141
Steward, Richard (1593?–1651), VII. 147,
  160, 426, 428
Stewards, manor house, near Romford,
  VII. 46
Stewart, in Blind Harry's Wallace, II. 112
Stewart, Alexander (1493?–1513), II. 369
Stewart, Arabella, IV. 265
Stewart, David, duke of Rothsay (1378?–
  1402), III. 120
Stewart, Dugald (1753–1828), IX. 301; XI.
  75, 76, 221, 222, 400; XII. 4, 427; XIV. 16
  Elements of the Philosophy of the Human
  Mind, XI. 76
  Life of Adam Smith, X. 335, 504, 511,
  512, 514
  Life of Robertson, X. 289
  Outlines of Moral Philosophy, XI. 76
  Philosophical Essays, XI. 76
  Philosophy of the Active and Moral
  Powers, XI. 76
  Progress of...Philosophy, XI. 76
Stewart, Esmé, 1st duke of Lennox
  (1542?–1583), X. 288
Stewart, Henry, earl of Darnley (1545–
  1567), III. 131, 164; XIII. 133
Stewart, Henry B. M. C. (1725–1807),
  cardinal of York, II. 77
Stewart, Hugh Fraser, XII. 488
Stewart, lord James, earl of Mar and
  Moray (1531?–1570), III. 159
Stewart, Sir James (d. 1713), IX. 546, 547
Stewart, James, XIV. Add. 10
Stewart, John, duke of Albany (1481–
  1536), III. 70
Stewart, Matthew, 4th or 12th earl of
  Lennox (1516–1571), III. 164
Stewart, prince James Francis Edward,
  the Old Pretender, VIII. 44
Stewart, Robert, viscount Castlereagh
  (1769–1822), XII. 69, 392; XIV. 121,
  122, 508
Stewart, royal family of, IV. 104, 274, 304,
  307, 311, 312, 315; VIII. 2, 6, 8, 38, 258,
  261, 301, 303, 309, 312, 321, 349 ff.,
  358, 361; X. 351, 352, 355, 500
Stewart, T. B. Phillips (1864–1892), XIV.
  357, 582
Stewart of Baldines, Ane Abbregement of
  Roland Furious, III. 137
Stewart cause, the, XIV. 96
Stewart dramatists, VIII. 366; XII. 198
Stewart period, X. 40, 286, 355, 397
  XIV. 86, 114, 281, 284
Stewart princesses, XIV. 111

Stewarte, III. 131; *Flyting betwix the Sowtar and the Tailyour*, III. 131; *For to declare the hie Magnificence of Ladies*, III. 131

Stewarte, W. or Stewarte of Lorne?, *This Hinder Nycht*, III. 131; IV. 322

Stewarton, Ayrshire, II. 126

Steyne, lord (Thackeray's), XIII. 286 ff., 291

Stiefel, A. L., VI. 32, 124, 140, 204, 205, 208

Stiggins (Dickens's), VI. 28

Still, John, bishop of Bath and Wells (d. 1608), VI. 296

Stilling, Johann Heinrich (Jung-Stilling), VII. 177; IX. 328

Stillingfleet, Benjamin (1702–1771), X. 135; XI. 344, 345

Stillingfleet, Edward (1635–1699), bishop of Worcester, VIII. 46 ff., 292, 298, 302, 332, 346, 370, 402, 462, 471, 475; IX. 195, 196, 199, 330, 335; X. 373, 377; XI. 416; XII. 259

Irenicum, VIII. 300

Origines Britannicae, VIII. 300

Origines Sacrae, VIII. 300

Vindication of the Doctrine of the Trinity, VIII. 46, 331

Stillingfleet, James, IX. 313, 330

Stinstra, John, X. 19

Stipes, in *The Rival Friends*, VI. 324

Stirling, III. 120, 122; IV. 163; VII. 455; IX. 552; XI. 373, 440, 469

Stirling, Amelia Hutchison, XIV. 481

Stirling, earl of. *See* Alexander, Sir William

Stirling, James Hutchison (1820–1909), XIII. 478; XIV. 474, 481; *Secret of Hegel, The*, XIV. 42; *Sir W. Hamilton: being the Philosophy of Perception*, XIV. 7; *Text book to Kant*, XIV. 42

Stirling-Maxwell, lady. *See* Norton, Caroline E. S.

Stirry, Thos., VII. Add.

Stobaeus, Johannes, III. 416; XII. 328, 484

Stock, Thomas (*fl.* 1780), XIV. 389

Stockbridge, IX. 456

Stockdale, John (1749?–1814), X. 463; XIV. 121

Stockdale, Percival (1736–1811), X. 446, 463, 473; XIV. 609; *Memoirs*, X. 183

Stockenstrom, Sir Andries, XIV. Add. 10

Stocker, Thomas (*fl.* 1569–1592), *Diodorus Siculus*, IV. 4, 436, 439

Stockholm, V. 283

Stockport, XI. 375

Stockton, III. 95; XI. 486

Stockwell, in Cumberland's *West Indian*, XI. 264

Stockwood, John (d. 1610), VI. 386, 497

Stodart-Walker, A., XIV. 595

Stoddard, Richard Henry, XIII. 532

Stoddart, Anna M., XIV. 516, 600

Stoddart, Sir John (1773–1856), XIV. 178, 179

Stoddart, Sarah. *See* Hazlitt, Sarah

Stoddart, Thomas Tod (1810–1880), XIII. 509

Stoics, the, VII. 376; IX. 55, 63

Stoicus Vapulans, VI. 486

Stoke Newington, VIII. 199; IX. 6, 21, 24

Stoke Newington academy, X. 386

Stoke Pogis, X. 121, 123, 126

Stokes, Sir George Gabriel (1819–1903), XIV. 265 ff., 557

Stokes, Margaret McNair (1832–1900), XII. 518; XIV. Add. 3; *Early Christian Architecture in Ireland*, XIV. 328

Stokes, Whitley (1830–1909), V. 16; XII. 518; XIV. 305, *also see* Add. 3; *Thesaurus Palaeo-Hibernicus*, XII. 361

Stokes, William (1804–1878), *The Life of George Petrie*, XIV. 312, 328, *also see* Add. 3

Stoll, Elmer Edgar, VI. 169

Stone, Edmund (d. 1768), VIII. 476

Stone, William Johnson, XIII. 246, 247, 511

Stonehenge, III. 106, 322; VII. 443; IX. 354, 532, 536, 540; XI. 192

Stonehewer, Richard (1728?–1809), X. 133

Stonor park, IV. 412

Stonyhurst, XIV. 249

Stopes, Mrs Charlotte Carmichael, VI. 286

Storer, James Sargant (1771–1853), XI. 404

Storer, Thomas (1571–1604), IX. 472

Stork, Charles Wharton, VI. 170

Storm of wind, the great (15 January 1362), II. 12

Storr, Francis, XIV. 602

Storr, Vernon Faithfull, *Development of English Theology*, XIII. 384

Story, Robert Herbert (1835–1907), XII. 423; XIV. 507

Story, William Wetmore, XIII. 74

Story of the St Alb-n's Ghost, IX. 130

Stothard, Thomas (1755–1834), XI. 377; XII. 408

Stoughton, Dr, VIII. 281

Stoughton, John (1807–1897), XII. 464, 473

Stourbridge, X. 159

Stourbridge and Bromsgrove academy, X. 387

Stout, George Frederick, XIV. 469

Stow, IX. 235

Stow, David (1793–1864), XIV. 602

Stow, George William, XIV. Add. 10

Stow, John (1525?–1605), II. 162, 164, 217; III. 111, 314, 318, 321, 323 ff., 332, 335, 532, 553; IV. 389; V. 83, 371; VI. 254, 282, 463; VII. 203; IX. 352; XII. 349

Annals, I. 336; III. 438; IV. 381

Brief Chronicle, IV. 389

Chronicles of England, III. 314 ff., 324; V. 242

Summarie of Englyshe Chronicles, III. 324

Survey of the Cities of London and Westminster, III. 330; IV. 389; V. 321, 479; IX. 353; XII. 354

Stowe, X. 101 ff., 126

Stowe, Harriet Beecher, XI. 492; XII. 393, 398; *Uncle Tom's Cabin*, XIII. 427

Stowe, John (scribe of *Jack Napes*), II. 424
Stowe, William Henry (1825–1855), XIV. 535
Stowey. *See* Nether Stowey
Strabo, III. 109, 420; VII. 311
Strachan, John, XII. 519; *Thesaurus Palaeo-Hibernicus*, XII. 361
Strachan, Lionel Richard Mortimer, XIII. 499
Strachey, J. St Leo, XII. 426
Strada, *Prolusiones*, VI. 190
Stradling, Sir John (1563–1637), VII. 407, 487; *Epigrammata*, IV. 360
Strafford, earls of. *See* Wentworth, Thomas
Strafford's Letters and Despatches, The Earl of, VII. 194, 435
Strahan, George (1744–1824), X. 462, 472
Strahan, James Andrew, XIV. 536
Strahan, William (1715–1785), X. 294, 511; XI. 326
Strange, in *A Woman is a Weathercocke*, VI. 222
Strange, Ferdinando. *See* Stanley, Ferdinando
Strange, lady. *See* Stanley, Alice
Strange Metamorphosis of Man, A, IV. 522
Strange Predictions, VII. 394
Strangeness, in *The Passetyme of Pleasure*, II. 234
Strange's men, lord, V. 161; VI. 254, 255
Strangford, 7th viscount. *See* Smythe, George A. F. P. S.
Strap, in Smollett's *Roderick Random*, X. 37 ff.
Straparola, Gian Francesco, IV. 6
Strassburg, II. 329; III. 80, 333, 431, 434; VII. 304; IX. 412
Strassburg. *See* Gottfried von
Stratford, John de, archbishop of Canterbury (d. 1348), II. 352
Stratford-atte-Bowe, VIII. 313
Stratford de Redcliffe, viscount. *See* Canning, Stratford
Stratford-on-Avon, IV. 394; V. 165 ff., 171, 222, 374; VI. 141, 247; VII. 278; X. 112, 192, 271, 385; XI. 451; XII. 369
Stratford-on-Avon, New Place, V. 166, 170, 219; VI. 278
Strathclyde, II. 88, 99
Strathmore, earl of. *See* Lyon, John
Stratonice, in *The Tatler*, IX. 38
Straunge Newes out of Affrick, VI. 388
Straus, Ralph, XI. 468
Strauss, David Friedrich, XII. 467; XIII. 469, 553; *Life of Jesus*, XII. 292; XIII. 383
Straw, Jack, I. 369
Straw, Sir John, in Barnabe Googe's *Eclogues*, III. 186
Strawberry hill, VII. 204; X. 244, 245, 495, 496; XI. 341, 363
Strawberry hill press, X. 127, 244, 245, 253, 254, 496; XI. 469
Streamer, court jester, in *Beware the Cat*, III. 494

Strean, Annesley, X. 195, 483
Streater, John (*fl.* 1650–1670), VII. 358; *A Politick Commentary on the life of Caius July Caesar*, VII. 358; *Observations, Historical Political and Philosophical*, VII. 358; *Secret Reasons of State*, VII. 358
Streatfeild, Richard Alexander, XIII. 571, 572, *also see* Add. 1
Streatfield, Miss, X. 65
Streatham, X. 186, 189; XI. 364
Streatham Letters, XI. 365
Street, George Edmund (1824–1881), XIII. 119
Street, George Slythe, XII. 398
Street, Peter, a carpenter, VI. 258
Street, Sir Thomas (1626–1696), VII. 365
Street ballads, IV. 535
Strength, in *The Pride of Life*, V. 52
Strensham, in Worcestershire, VIII. 60
Streoneshalh. *See* Whitby
Strickland, Agnes (1796–1874), XI. 482; XIV. 507; *Lives of the Queens of England*, XIV. 111; *Lives of the Queens of Scotland*, XIV. 111; *The Moss House*, XI. 384
Strickland, Elizabeth (1794–1875), XIV. 111, 507
Strickland, Hugh Edwin (1811–1853), XIV. 563
Strickland, Mr (*fl.* 1572), III. 402
Stritch, A. R., XIV. 573
Strode, Ralph (*fl.* 1350–1400), I. 332, 333; II. 54, 135, 443
Strode, William (1599?–1645), VII. 160, 426; *The Floating Island*, VI. 325, 327, 478
Strong, Chevalier, in *Pendennis*, XIII. 291
Strong, Dr, in *David Copperfield*, XIII. 327
Strong, Isobel, XIV. 526
Strong, James, *Joanereidos* (1645), VII. 513
Strong, Sandford Arthur (1863–1904), XII. 499
Strowd, Tom, in *The Blind Beggar*, V. 373
Strozza, Ercole, III. 253
Struldbrugs, in *Gulliver's Travels*, IX. 105
Strumbo, in *Locrine*, V. 239
Struther, William (*fl.* 1633), IX. 545
Struthers, John (1776–1853), XII. 423
Strutt, John William, 1st baron Rayleigh, XIV. 269
Strutt, Joseph (1749–1802), XII. 376, 412, 519; XIV. 499, 546; *Sports and Pastimes*, XIV. 230
'Strutt, Lord,' in Arbuthnot's *History of John Bull*, IX. 134
'Strutt, The Lord' (Charles of Spain), XIV. 212
Struwelpeter, the English, XI. 491
Strype, John (1643–1737), V. 482; IX. 209–210 (main entry), 212, 354, 496, 539
Annals of the Reformation, IX. 210
Ecclesiastical Memorials, IX. 210
Life of Edmund Grindal, IX. 210
Life of John Aylmer, IX. 210
Life of John Whitgift, IX. 210
Life of Matthew Parker, IX. 210

Strype, John
  Life of Sir John Cheke, IX. 210
  Life of Sir Thomas Smith, IX. 210
  Memorials of Thomas Cranmer, IX. 210
Stuart, lord Bernard (1623?-1646), VII. 6
Stuart, Daniel (1766-1846), XI. 405, 416;
  XIV. 179, 183, 184, 187, 194
Stuart, Elena, XIII. 553
Stuart, Gilbert (1742-1786), X. 502, 505
Stuart, James (1713-1788), XII. 499
Stuart, James (1775-1849), XIV. 188
Stuart, James (1843-1913), XIV. 432, 602,
  also see Add. 10
Stuart, James, of Dunearn, XI. 236
Stuart, John, 3rd earl of Bute (1713-
  1792), VI. 7; IX. 245, 497, 498; X. 41,
  131, 390 ff., 394, 396, 399, 401, 523;
  XI. 174, 348; XIV. 213
Stuart, John (1813-1877), XII. 513; *The
  Book of Deer*, XII. 350; *The Sculptured
  Stones of Scotland*, XII. 350
Stuart, J. A. Erskine, XIII. 559
Stuart, lady Louisa, IX. 246; XI. 348, 349
Stuart, Peter (*fl.* 1788-1805), XIV. 179, 184
Stuart, Robert (1812-1848), XII. 513;
  Caledonia Romana, XII. 350
Stuart-Wortley, John, 2nd baron Wharn-
  cliffe (1801-1855), IX. 248
Stub, Edmund (*fl.* 1611-1631), VI. 478
Stubber, in *Blurt Master-Constable*, V. 362
Stubbs, Charles William, XIII. 548, *also
  see* Add. 2
Stubbs, Stubbes or Stubbe, Henry, the
  younger (1632-1676), VII. 317, 475, 489,
  also see Add.; *The Plus Ultra reduced
  to a Non Plus*, VIII. 291
Stubbs, John (1543?-1591), V. 341
Stubbs, John William, *History of the Uni-
  versity of Dublin*, X. 198
Stubbs or Stubbes, Philip (*fl.* 1583-1591),
  VI. 387, 393 ff., 401, 409, 462, 497; *The
  Anatomy of Abuses*, III. 362; V. 352,
  357, 359, 371, 479; VI. 376, 386, 393, 394
Stubbs, Robert, in Thackeray's *The Fatal
  Boots*, XIII. 280, 282
Stubbs, William (1825-1901), bishop of
  Oxford, I. 157, 160, 161, 172, 173, 175;
  VIII. 306; XII. 271, 273; XIV. 57, 69,
  74 ff. (main entry), 101, 143, 499
  Appendices to the *Report of the Com-
  mission on Ecclesiastical Courts*, XIV. 75
  Constitutional History of England, The,
  XIV. 75
  Councils and Ecclesiastical Documents,
  XIV. 75
  Registrum Sacrum Anglicanum, XIV. 74
  Rolls series, edited by, XIV. 74
  Select Charters, XIV. 75
Stubs, John, VIII. 414
Student, The (1751), X. 175, 466
Student, The (Edinburgh), XIV. 209, 210
Studioso, in *The Returne from Pernassus*,
  V. 360; VI. 311, 312
Studioso, in *Time's Complaint*, VI. 320
Studiosus, in *The Pilgrimage to Parnassus*,
  VI. 310

Studious Desire, in *The Nature of the Four
  Elements*, V. 57
Studley, John (1545?-1590?), IV. 440; V.
  395
Study, Wit's wife, in *Piers the Plowman*,
  II. 19, 20
Study to be Quiet, VII. 515
Stukeley, Captaine Thomas, V. 399
Stukeley, William (1687-1765), IX. 352,
  358, 540; *Itinerarium Curiosum*, IX. 352;
  Stonehenge, IX. 354
Stukely, Thomas (1525?-1578), VII. 75
Stumps, Bill (Dickens's), XIV. 444
Stupido, in *The Pilgrimage to Parnassus*,
  VI. 310
Sturgion, John (*fl.* 1657), X. 520
Sturm, John, III. 429, 430, 432, 434, 554
Sturm und Drang, V. 297 ff., 463 ff.
Sturmy, Samuel, IV. 462
Sturt, Henry, XIV. 469
Sturt, John (1658-1730), VII. 402
Stuttgart, VII. 309
Stymmelius, Christopher, V. 101, 413
Styria, XIII. 432
Styx, river, XI. 352
Suard, Jean Baptiste Antoine, X. 422;
  XI. 354
Subiaco, printing press at, II. 310
Subscription controversy, X. 377
Subtle, in *The Alchemist*, V. 369; VI. 22
Successio, IX. 68
Suckdry, in Wilson's *Projectors*, VIII. 123
Suckling, Alfred Inigo (1796-1856), XII.
  513
Suckling, Sir John (1609-1642), III. 172;
  IV. 168, 187; V. 222; VI. 11, 212, 239,
  458; VII. 2, 4, 7, 15, 20 ff. (main entry),
  25, 57, 273, 399, 466; X. 115; XI. 318
  A Session of the Poets, VII. 16, 22, 153,
  263, 274
  Aglaura, VI. 238; VII. 22; VIII. 226
  An Account of Religion by Reason, VII.
  21, 22
  Ballad of a Wedding, VII. 23
  Brennoralt, or The Discontented Colonell,
  VI. 238; VII. 22
  Fragmenta Aurea, VII. 22
  Goblins, The, VI. 238, 239; VII. 22
  Letter to Mr Henry Jermyn, VII. 21
  'O, for some honest lover's ghost,' VII.
  23
  'O, that I were all soul, that I might
  prove,' VII. 21
  'Out upon it! I have loved,' VII. 23
  The Sad One, VII. 22
  ''Tis now since I sat down before that
  foolish fort, a heart,' VII. 21
  'Why so pale and wan, fond lover?'
  VI. 238; VII. 23
Suckling, Sir John, father of the poet, VII. 21
Sudbury, Simon of, archbishop of Canter-
  bury (d. 1381), II. 55, 56
Sudbury, Suffolk, VII. 223; IX. 217
Suddard, S. J. Mary (1888-1909), VI. Add.;
  IX. Add.; XI. 411; XII. 404, 407; XIII.
  491, 566; XIV. 528

Suddene (Isle of Man), in *Horn*, I. 304
Sue, Eugène, *Mystères de Paris*, XIII. 427
Sue, Marie J. E., XIII. 559
Suetonius, III. 10; IV. 4, 14, 15, 342, 417, 440; VI. 154; VII. 370, 392, 503; VIII. 378; XII. 206
Suez canal, XIV. 195
Sufferance, in *Piers the Plowman*, II. 20
Suffolk, II. 134, 156, 197, 214, 224; III. 337; VII. 33, 223; X. 294; XI. 140; XII. 198, 256, 331, 508, 513, 520; XIII. 142; XIV. 221
Suffolk, countess of. *See* Howard, Henrietta
Suffolk, dukes of. *See* Brandon, Charles; Pole, William de la
Suffolk, earl of. *See* Howard, Thomas
Sugden, Edward Burtenshaw, baron St Leonards (1781–1875), XIV. 501, 514
Suidas, IX. 336; XII. 328, 484, 490, 491, 494
Sulby academy, X. 387
Suliotes, XII. 39
Sulky, in Holcroft's *Road to Ruin*, XI. 277
Sullivan, Alexander Martin (1830–1884), XIV. 571
Sullivan, Sir Edward (1822–1885), XIV. 538
Sullivan, Timothy Daniel (1827–1914), XIV. 571
   God Save Ireland, XIV. 321
   Madness of King Conchobar, The, XIV. 321
   Michael Dwyer, XIV. 321
   Siege of Dunboy, The, XIV. 321
   Soldier's Wake, A, XIV. 321
   Song from the Backwoods, XIV. 321
   Story of Blanaid, The, XIV. 321
Sullivan, William Francis (1756–1830), XI. 490
Sully, Maximilien de Béthune, duc de, IV. 312; IX. 231; *Mémoires*, X. 135, 467
Sulpicius Severus, I. 75
Sulpitius, III. 13, 20
Sumatra, XI. 278
'Sumer is i-cumen in,' I. 360; II. 393; IV. 462, 463; V. 29
Summa Ostiensis, II. 364
Summer, in folk-plays, V. 31
Summerly, Felix, *pseud. See* Cole, Sir Henry
Summers, Life and Death of Will, III. 488
Summerson, Esther, in *Bleak House*, XIII. 328
Sumner, Charles Richard (1790–1874), VII. 129, 141
Sumner, John Bird (1780–1862), XII. 473
Sumner, Robert Carey (1729–1771), XIV. 386
Sun, The, XIV. 194
Sun rises Bright in France, IX. 377
Sunatorrek, I. 9
Sunchildism, in Butler's *Erewhon Revisited*, XIII. 453
Sunday newspapers, XIV. 192, 201
'Sunday observance, letter sent from heaven on,' I. 134

Sunday schools, XIII. 51; XIV. 382, 389
Sunday Schools' Union, XIV. 339
Sunderland, countess of. *See* Spencer, Dorothy
Sunderland, earls of. *See* Spencer, Henry; Spencer, Robert
Sundridge, Kent, VI. 112
Sunninghill, near Windsor, VII. 16
'Sunshine,' the (ship), IV. 76
Superbia, in *Psychomachia*, V. 51
Superstition, in *A True Inventory*, VII. 382
Supplantation, in *Confessio Amantis*, II. 148
Supporters of the Bill of Rights, The, X. 401
Surat, IV. 90, 99
Surface, Charles, in Sheridan's *School for Scandal*, V. 254; X. 90; XI. 269 ff.
Surface, Joseph, in Sheridan's *School for Scandal*, VIII. 148; X. 75; XI. 270, 271
Surflet, Richard, IV. 538, 541
Surinam, VIII. 140
Surly, in Crowne's *Sir Courtly Nice*, VIII. 189
Surmy's *Mariner's Magazine*, IX. 106
Surrey, II. 353; III. 385; IV. 156, 190; VI. 247, 282; VII. 277; VIII. 242, 244; IX. 531, 539; XI. 183; XII. 507, 508, 511; XIII. 275; XIV. 294
'Surrey, Another Freeholder of,' X. 401
Surrey, countess of, in *The Garden of Laurell*, III. 70
Surrey, earls of. *See* Howard, Henry; Howard, Thomas
Surrey archaeological collections, XII. 507
Surtees, Robert (1779–1834), IX. 377; XII. 6, 513; *History of Durham*, XII. 354
Surtees, Robert Smith (1803–1864), XIV. 216, 546, 547
   Ask Mamma, XIV. 234
   Handley Cross, X. 111; XIV. 234
   Hawbuck Grange, XIV. 234
   Jorrocks' Jaunts, XIV. 234
   Mr Facey Romford's Hounds, XIV. 234
   Mr Sponge's Sporting Tour, XIV. 234
Surtees society, XII. 354
Susan, in Meredith's *Earth and a Wedded Woman*, XIII. 443
Susan, in *The Witch of Edmonton*, VI. 54
Susanna, in Biblical comedies, V. 101
Susanna, in *Ralph Roister Doister*, V. 106
Susanna, The Story of, II. 120, 121
Susanna and the elders, III. 350
Susannah, in Sterne's *Tristram Shandy*, X. 50
Susenbrotus, VI. 486
Susenbrotus, *Epitome Troporum*, III. 429
Suso, Heinrich, IX. 314
Suspirius, in *The Rambler*, X. 172
Sussex, IV. 190; V. 135; VI. 110; VII. 22, 232; VIII. 244, 298; X. 312, 378; XII. 507, 511, 523; XIV. 221, 294
Sussex, duke of. *See* Augustus Frederick
Sussex, lord, in Glover's *Boadicea*, XI. 258
Sussex archaeological collections, XII. 507
Susy Pye, in *Young Beichan*, II. 411

Sutcliffe, Matthew (1550?–1629), III. 538;
IV. 491; VII. 309, 310, 484; *An Answere
to a certaine libel supplicatorie*, III. 391;
*An Answere unto a certaine calumnious
letter*, III. 390, 391
Sutherland, Alexander (1852–1902), XIV.
584, 587; *Victoria and its Metropolis*,
XIV. 371
Sutherlandshire, VII. 231
Sutton, Christopher (1565?–1629), IV. 496
Sutton, Henry Septimus (1825–1901), XIII.
509
Sutton, Ned, IX. 191
Sutton, Oliver, bishop of Lincoln (d. 1299),
II. 348
Sutton, Thomas (1532–1611), VII. 332, 338
Sutton, Thomas (1585–1623), VI. 224, 402
Sutton, Yorkshire, X. 47
Sutton Vallamore, Kent, VII. 361
Svears, the, I. 25
Svend Aagesen, I. 34
Swabia, V. 305
Swadlin, Thomas (1600–1670), VII. 509
Swain, Charles (1801–1874), XII. 423
Swainson, Charles Anthony (1820–1887),
XII. 478
Swainson, William (1789–1855), XII. 523
Swalle, Abel, XI. 319
Swallow, Hereward's mare, in *Deeds of
Hereward*, I. 364
Swallow, in *Time's Complaint*, VI. 320
Swallow, tale of, in Henryson's *Fables*,
II. 246
Swan, the, in *Mum, Sothsegger*, II. 36
Swan, John, M.D., X. 467
Swan, privateer, XIV. 242
Swarthmore MSS., VIII. 412
Swavesey, Cambridgeshire, X. 280
Sweden, V. 307, 308; VII. 200, 345; VIII.
137, 267; X. 193, 500
Swedenborg, Emanuel, XI. 432; *Memorable
Relations*, XI. 188
Swedenborgianism, XI. 181; XIII. 46, 47
Swedes, the, in *Beowulf*, I. 24, 25
Swedish government, the, XIV. 287
Swedish language, XIV. 458
Sweet, Henry (1845–1912), XII. 505; XIII.
248; XIV. 611; *New English Grammar*,
XIV. 444
Sweet Trinity, II. 414
Sweet William's Ghost, II. 414
'Sweete violets (Loves paradice) that
spred,' IV. 117
Swete Susane, Epistill of, II. 112, 116, 120,
121, 272, 450; III. 278
Sweyn, king of England and Denmark
(d. 1014), I. 127
Sweynheym, printer, II. 310
Swift, Deane (1707–1783), IX. 124, 467
Swift, Godwin, IX. 91, 92
Swift, Jonathan, the elder, IX. 91
Swift, Jonathan, dean of St Patrick's
(1667?–1745), III. 82, 417; IV. 45, 49,
251; VII. 167, 176; VIII. 146, 158, 160,
232, 234, 292, 302, 305, 380 ff., 386;
IX. 17, 23, 25, 34, 35, 45, 46, 67, 75;

Swift, Jonathan
78 ff., 84, 85, 87, 91 ff. (main entry),
129 ff., 133, 136, 139, 144, 151, 152,
157, 158, 160, 163 ff., 172, 184, 186,
202, 208, 209, 217, 220, 250, 326, 327,
340, 390, 401 ff., 440 ff., 445 ff.,
452 ff., 469, 470, 472, 481, 569, 572,
also see Add.; X. 14, 20, 27, 140, 185,
198, 202, 214, 316, *also see* Add.; XI.
16, 18, 27, 30, 81, 173, 187, 247, 261,
286, 314, 320, 330, 332, 343, 449, 466;
XII. 20, 55, 56, 120, 164, 168, 175, 177,
376, 444; XIII. 295, 312, 453; XIV. 168,
197, 212, 215, 309, 313, 398, 448, 451,
455, 461, 518, 572
*Advantages proposed by repealing the
Sacramental Test*, IX. 110
Answer to The Story of the injured lady,
IX. 116
*Argument against abolishing Christi-
anity*, IX. 108
Battle of the Books, IX. 93, 100, 102, 333,
392
Baucis and Philemon, IX. 94, 119
Beasts Confession to the Priest, IX. 122
Cadenus and Vanessa, IX. 97, 98, 120;
XIII. 254
Character of Mrs Johnson, IX. 99
Complete collection of...Conversation, IX.
99, 106
Conduct of the Allies, IX. 95, 115, 131
Dennis's Invitation to Steele, IX. 121
Description of a City Shower, IX. 119, 161
Description of the Morning, IX. 119, 161
Directions to Servants, IX. 99, 107
*Discourse on the Dissensions in Athens
and Rome*, IX. 94, 112
Drapier's Letters, IX. 98, 115, 457, 459,
463 ff.
Epistle to Mr Gay, IX. 121
Essay on Modern Education, IX. 398
*Examination of certain Abuses in
Dublin*, IX. 117
Fable of Midias, IX. 121
Grand Question debated, IX. 119
Gulliver's Travels, IX. 98, 103 ff., 132,
137, 458, 464, 466, 471; X. 43, 84; XI.
373; XIII. 452; XIV. 169, 255, 444
Hints towards an Essay on Conversation,
IX. 106
Humours of the Age, IX. 465
Importance of the Guardian considered,
IX. 114
*Inquiry into the behaviour of the Queen's
last Ministry*, IX. 113
Journal of a Modern Lady, The, IX. 121;
XIII. 426
Journal to Stella, IX. 42, 95, 124 ff., 130,
236, 438
Lady's Dressing Room, IX. 121
Last Judgment, IX. 121
Legion Club, IX. 99, 121
Letter concerning the Sacramental Test,
IX. 110
Letter of Advice to a young Poet, IX. 118
Letter to a very young Lady, IX. 118

Swift, Jonathan
  Letter to a Young Gentleman, IX. 111
  Letter to Mr Harding the printer, IX. 115
  '*Letter to the Athenian Society,*' IX. 92
  Letter to the Lord High Treasurer, A,
    XIV. 396
  Letter to the October Club, IX. 96
  Letter to the shopkeepers...concerning the
    brass half-pence, IX. 115
  Letter to the whole people of Ireland, IX.
    116
  May the Cook-maid's Letter, IX. 107
  Memoirs relating to...the Queen's Minis-
    try, IX. 113
  Modest Proposal, IX. 99, 117
  Mr C-ns's Discourse on Free Thinking,
    put into plain English, IX. 111
  On Mrs Biddy Floyd, IX. 119
  On Poetry, IX. 99, 122
  On the Death of Dr Swift, IX. 123
  On the Education of Ladies, IX. 398, 401,
    402
  On the present miserable state of Ireland,
    IX. 117
  Petition of Mrs Frances Harris, IX. 94,
    107
  Polite Conversation, VIII. 176
  Predictions for the ensuing year...Isaac
    Bickerstaff, IX. 94, 454, 461
  Preface to the B—p of S-r-m's Intro-
    duction, IX. 110
  Progress of Beauty, IX. 121
  Progress of Marriage, IX. 121
  Project for the advancement of Religion,
    IX. 109
  Proposal for correcting...the English
    Tongue, IX. 118; XIV. 462
  Proposal for the universal use of Irish
    manufacture, IX. 98, 114
  Public Spirit of the Whigs, IX. 114, 440
  Reasons...for repealing the Sacramental
    Test, IX. 110
  Sentiments of a Church of England Man,
    IX. 108, 109
  Serious and useful Scheme, IX. 117
  Sermons, IX. 112
  Short character of Thomas Earl of
    Wharton, IX. 113
  Short view of the state of Ireland, IX. 116
  Some advice...to the members of the
    October Club, IX. 113
  Some free thoughts upon the present state
    of affairs, IX. 113
  Some Observations upon...the Report...
    relating to Wood's halfpence, IX. 116
  Some Remarks on the Barrier Treaty,
    IX. 95, 113
  Story of an injured lady, IX. 116
  Strephon and Chloe, IX. 121
  Swearers Bank, The, IX. 116
  Tale of a Tub, A, III. 398; IX. 94, 100,
    101, 135, 308, 382, 392, 396; X. 353;
    XIII. 9
  Traulus, IX. 121
  Virtues of Sid Hamet the Magician's
    Rod, IX. 95, 121

Swift, Jonathan
  W-ds-r Prophecy, The, IX. 96, 121
  Works, XII. 16, 372
  See, also, Wagstaff, Simon
Swift, Thomas, IX. 91
Swift, W., XII. 440
Swinburne, Algernon Charles (1837–1909),
  IV. 186, 209; V. 154; VI. 8, 9, 62, 71,
  77, 79, 173, 367; VII. 1, 144, 262, *also*
  see Add.; X. 152; XI. 411, 412, 420, 434,
  441; XII. 117, 130, 154, 208, 209, 218,
  219, 268, 275, 398, 400, 404, 407, 424,
  438, 441, 442, *also see* Add.; XIII. 82,
  90, 105, 116, 117, 129 ff. (main entry),
  138, 147, 191, 193, 207, 209, 214, 219 ff.,
  245, 252, 426, 432, 438, 440, 442, 448,
  478, 488, 490, 491, 493 ff. (main entry),
  506, 512, 544, 559, *also see* Add. 2, 3;
  XIV. 206, 365, 367, 453, 462
  Adieux à Marie Stuart, XIII. 135
  Anactoria, XIII. 131
  Artemis, hymn to, XIII. 130
  Astrophel, XIII. 135, 137
  Atalanta in Calydon, XIII. 130, 131, 133,
    205; XIV. 442, 444
  Athens, an ode, XIII. 135
  Ave atque Vale, XIII. 133
  Birthday Ode, XIII. 134
  Bothwell, XIII. 133, 135
  By the North Sea, XIII. 134
  Century of Roundels, A, XIII. 135, 137
  Channel Passage, A, XIII. 136
  Chastelard, XIII. 130, 133, 135
  Christmas Carol, A, XIII. 132
  Dark Month, A, XIII. 135
  Dirae, XIII. 133
  Dolores, XIII. 131, 132, 141, 253
  Erechtheus, VII. 122; XIII. 133, 136
  Essays and Studies, XIII. 136
  Faustine, XIII. 131, 132
  Forsaken Garden, A, XIII. 133
  Heptalogia, XIII. 134
  Hertha, XIII. 132
  Ilicet, XIII. 131, 132
  Itylus, XIII. 132
  Jacobite's Lament, The, XIII. 136
  Laus Veneris, XIII. 131, 132, 141, 146,
    253
  Leper, The, XIII. 131, 141
  Litany, A, XIII. 132
  Locrine, XIII. 135
  Marino Faliero, XIII. 134, 135
  Mary Stuart, XIII. 133, 135
  Masque of Queen Bersabe, The, X. 217;
    XIII. 132
  Match, A, XIII. 132
  Midsummer Holiday, A, XIII. 135
  Miscellanies, XIII. 136
  Poems and Ballads, XIII. 27, 130 ff., 136,
    137, 141, 211
  Proserpine, III. 184
  Queen Mother and Rosamund, The, XIII.
    129
  Quia Multum Amavit, XIII. 132
  Rosamund Queen of the Lombards, XIII.
    136

Swinburne, Algernon Charles
  Sisters, The, XIII. 136
  *Song for the Centenary of Walter Savage
    Landor*, XIII. 134
  Song of Italy, A, XIII. 132
  Songs before Sunrise, XIII. 132
  Songs of the Springtides, XIII. 134
  Studies in Song, XIII. 134
  Study of Shakespeare, A, XIII. 136
  Super Flumina Babylonis, XIII. 132
  'Three damsels in the queen's chamber,'
    XIII. 140
  Tristram of Lyonesse, I. 273; XIII. 134,
    135, 137, 253
  Triumph of Time, The, XIII. 131, 132, 253
Swinburne, Henry (1560?–1623), VIII. 467
Swinburne, Sir John, XIII. 129
Swineshead, Richard (*fl.* 1350), II. 498
Swinhoe, Gilbert, *Unhappy Fair Irene*,
  X. 161
Swinnerton, Frank, XIII. 573; XIV. 527
Swinnerton, Sir John, VI. 220
Swiss confederation, the, XIV. 71, 73
Swiss education, XIV. 419, 423
Swiss Family Robinson, The, XI. 492
Swiss liberty, X. 303
Swithun, St (d. 862), I. 116, 120, 121, 131
Switzerland, II. 310; VII. 306; X. 134, 200,
  201, 205, 366; XII. 33 ff., 41, 44, 59, 60,
  247, 311, 315, 420; XIII. 88, 96; XIV.
  151, 294
Switzerland and Byron, XII. 395
Switzerland and Shelley, XII. 403
Swiveller, Dick, in *The Old Curiosity
  Shop*, XIII. 320
Swoboda, V. 97
Swynderby, William (the hermit preacher
  of Lincoln), II. 61
Sybant, A., V. 285
Sybilla, in *The Lords' Masque*, VI. 354
Sybilla, in *The Vision of the Twelve God-
  desses*, VI. 338, 339
Sydenham, XII. 102
Sydenham, Thomas (1624–1689), VIII.
  363, 472, 479; X. 164, 465, 467; XII. 355
Sydenham society, XII. 355
Sydney. *See* Sidney
Sydney, Australia, XII. 330; XIV. 361 ff.
Sydney Gazette, The, XIV. 362
Sydney Mail, The, XIV. 370
Sydney Papers. *See* Sidney
Syke, Henry, IX. 335
Sykes, Frank W., XIV. Add. 10
Sykes, Sir Mark Masterman (1771–1823),
  XII. 365
Sylla's ghost, in Ben Jonson's *Catiline*,
  VIII. 85
Sylli, in *The Maid of Honour*, VI. 152, 153
Sylvanus (Mantuan's), III. 225
Sylvester, James Joseph (1814–1897),
  XIV. 262, 263, 557; *The Laws of Verse*,
  XIII. 248
Sylvester, Joshua (1563–1618), IV. 23,
  124, 131, 185, 331, 434, 443, 475, 531;
  VI. 9; VII. 407; trans. of *Du Bartas*, VII.
  118

Sylvester, St, I. 74, 75
Sylvia, in Drayton's *Eglogs*, IV. 173
Sylvius, Aeneas, III. 62, 65, 179; *Tractatus
  de curialium miseriis*, III. 65
Sylvius, lady, VIII. 251
Sym and his Brudir, II. 273; XI. 215
Sym Sadle-gander, II. 232
Syme, David, XIV. 535
Symes, John Elliotson, V. 353
Symmachus, IX. 330
Symmes (Marprelate printer), III. 382
Symmons, Edward, VII. 513
Symon, 'the Anker of London Wall'
  (*fl.* 1512–1529), IV. 496
Symon, James David, XIV. 532, 538
Symonds, John Addington (1840–1893),
  V. 149; VI. 13; XI. 411; XII. 404; XIII.
  207, 500, 504, 507, 509; XIV. 108, 527
  Blank Verse, XIII. 248
  Le jeune homme caressant sa Chimère,
    XIII. 208
  Renaissance in Italy, The, XIII. 208;
    XIV. 157
  *Shakespeare's Predecessors in the English
    Drama*, XIV. 158
Symonds, William (1566–1616?), IV. 513
Symons, Arthur, XI. 412, 415, 423, 434;
  XII. 132, 404, 406, 415, 442, 445, *also
  see* Add.; XIII. 485, 493, 496, 499, 500,
  502, 503, 508, 557, 570, *also see* Add. 2;
  XIV. 518, 521, 523, 527, 528
Symphosius, 5th cent. Latin poet, I. 60, 76
Symposium, The, XIV. 208
Symson, Archibald (1564?–1628), VII. 485;
  IX. 545
Synge, Edward, bishop of Elphin, X. 199
Synge, John Millington (1871–1909), XIV.
  571
  Aran Islands, The, XIV. 330
  Deirdre of the Sorrows, XIV. 330
  In Kerry, XIV. 330
  In Wicklow, West Kerry and Connemara,
    XIV. 330
  Playboy of the Western World, The, XIV.
    329, 330
  Riders to the Sea, The, XIV. 330
  Tinker's Wedding, The, XIV. 330
  Well of the Saints, The, XIV. 330
Synge, M. B., XIV. 551
Syntax, Dr (William Combe's), XIV. 217 ff.,
  221
Syon monastery, Isleworth, IV. 418
Syphax, in Addison's *Cato*, IX. 63
Syracusans, in *The Bond-Man*, VI. 161, 163
Syracuse, V. 118, 119; VI. 155, 225; VII.
  199; X. 135; XIII. 81
Syria, X. 503; XIV. 246, 252
Syriac language and literature, VII. 318,
  319; VIII. 364; IX. 393; XII. 341, 342

T. C., *Morall Discourses and Essayes*, VII.
  386
T. D. (? Deloney), *Canaan's Calamitie*, VI.
  51
T. F., *Newes from the North*, VI. 387, 495
T. T., *pseud.* of W. M. Thackeray, XIII. 278

T. T. *See* Thorpe, Thomas

T. T., *A Myrror for Martinists*, III. 397

Ta Fhairshon, in *The Bon Gaultier Ballads*, XIII. 161

Taal. *See* Cape-Dutch

Tabachetti, artist, XIII. 450

Tabarin, IX. 257

Tabernaemontanus, *Eicones plantarum*, IV. 375

Tablet, The, XIV. 326

Tacitus, Cornelius, I. 143, 187, 188; III. 20, 329, 338, 426, 429; IV. 30, 342, 345, 421, 440; V. 33; VI. 225, 235; VII. 131, 263, 370, 487, 503; IX. 254, 274; X. 120, 197; XI. 2, 426; XII. 306, 475, 483, 493, *also see* Add.; XIV. 59, 98; *Agricola*, IV. 4; XI. 165; *Annals*, III. 426; IV. 5; *Description of Germany*, IV. 5; *Histories*, IV. 4

Tactus, in *Lingua*, VI. 314, 315

Tadpole, in Disraeli's *Sybil*, XIII. 349

Taffy, in Du Maurier's *Trilby*, XIII. 433

Taillefer, V. 26

Tailor, Robert (*fl.* 1614), *The Hogge hath lost his Pearle*, VI. 219, 220, 459; VIII. 182

Taine, Hippolyte Adolphe, I. viii; II. 190; IV. 247; VIII. 19, 33; XIII. 456, 473, 544; *Histoire de la Littérature Anglaise*, X. 316, 483

Tait, A. (*c.* 1796), XI. 441

Tait, Archibald Campbell (1811–1882), XII. 260

Tait, Peter Guthrie (1831–1901), XIV. 263, 267, 555, 557

Tait's Edinburgh Magazine, XII. 430

Talbot, Catherine (1721–1770), X. 171; XI. 352, 356 ff., 473, 475

Talbot, Charles, duke of Shrewsbury (1660–1718), IX. 87, 151, 216

Talbot, Sir Charles, baron (1685–1737), X. 94, 95

Talbot, George, 6th earl of Shrewsbury (1528?–1590), III. 188

Talbot, George (*c.* 1635), VII. 45

Talbot, Sir John, 1st earl of Shrewsbury (1338?–1453), II. 303

Talbot, William Talbot, 1st earl, XI. 29

Talbott, James, IX. 571

Tales, An Alphabet of, II. 503

Tales in Middle English, I. 360

Talfourd, Sir Thomas Noon (1795–1854), IX. 475; XII. 201, 211, 432, 434, 435, 438; XIII. 483, 516, 523; XIV. 323; *Ion*, XII. 113; XIII. 58

Talgol, the butcher, in *Hudibras*, VIII. 68

Taliesin (*fl.* 550), I. 248, 249, 255, 268, 462

Taliesin, The Book of, I. 247, 251, 252

Talkative, in Bunyan's *Pilgrim's Progress*, VII. 173

Tallents, Francis (1619–1708), X. 386

Talleyrand-Périgord, Charles Maurice de, prince of Benevento, XIV. 115

Tallis, Thomas (1510?–1585), IV. 384

Tallwch (father of Tristram), I. 273

Tallyho, Bob, in *Real Life in London*, XIV. 227

Talma, François Joseph, V. 294, 307; XII. 198

Talmud, the, VIII. 291

Tam, in *Lichtounis Dreme*, II. 278

Tam Lin, II. 413

Tam o' Shanter, XI. 219

Tamerlane, VII. 164

Tamil language, XII. 362

Taming of a Shrew, The (ballad), III. 91, 487

Taming of a Shrew, The (anon. play), IV. 394; V. 115, 118, 147, 162, 181, 403, 438; VI. 170; VIII. 126

Tamlane, I. 295, 300

Tamworth, IV. 169

Tamworth manifesto, the, XII. 154

Tamyra, countess of Montsorry, in *Bussy d'Ambois*, VI. 33

Tancred, in *Gismond of Salerne*, V. 75, 76

Tancred (Disraeli's), XIII. 348

Tancred and Gismund, V. 87, 138, 397, 399

Tandler, Tobias, VII. 396, 505, 511

Tanfield, Elizabeth, VII. 150

Tanganyika, lake, XIV. 192

Tangent, in Morton's *Way to get Married*, XI. 281

Tangier, VIII. 202, 219, 257

Tannahill, Robert (1774–1810), XI. 237, 445

    Bonnie Wood of Craigielea, XI. 236
    Braes o' Balquither, XI. 236
    Gloomy Winter's noo Awa', XI. 236
    Jessie the Flower of Dunblane, XI. 236
    Lass of Arrinteenie, XI. 236
    Loudon's bonnie Woods and Braes, XI. 236
    Poems and Songs, XI. 236
    Rob Roryson's Bonnet, XI. 236

Tanner, John (*fl.* 1744), IX. 350

Tanner, Thomas (1674–1735), IX. 342, 350 (main entry), 351, 353, 354, 540, 541; *Bibliotheca Britannico-Hibernica*, IX. 350, 356; *Notitia Monastica*, IX. 350, 356, 358

Tantalus, in Orosius, I. 95

Tantalus, in *Thyestes*, V. 76, 78

Taoist classics, XII. 343

Taper, in Disraeli's *Sybil*, XIII. 349

Tapley, Mark, in *Martin Chuzzlewit*, XIII. 323

Tappertit, Sim, in *Barnaby Rudge*, XIII. 321

Tara hill, Ireland, XII. 512; XIV. 127

Tarant, prince of, in *A Very Woman*, VI. 156

Tarlton, Richard (d. 1588), III. 92, 201, 384, 387; IV. 353, 360, 527, 531, 533, 535; V. 313, 329; VI. 217, 232, 273, 397, 467; VII. 383; *Jigge of a horse loade of Fooles*, VI. 391; *The Seven Deadly Sins*, VI. 249

Tarn Wadling, near Hesket, in Cumberland, II. 116, 122

Tarpeia, VIII. 5

Tarquin, in *The Rape of Lucrece*, VI. 101

Tarquin and Tullia, VIII. 92

Tarrarantantara, etc., VI. 307

Tarrent, Dorset, I. 230

Tars, King of, I. 471

Tartaglia, N., IV. 448

Tartars, the, XI. 17

Tartarus, VI. 329; XII. 217

Tartary, II. 80; V. 144; XIV. 248

Tartufe (Molière's), XIII. 446

Tasker, William (1740–1800), XI. 429

Tasmania, XIV. 325

Tasso, Torquato, III. 230, 257, 261, 262,
432; IV. 23, 131, 448, 543; VI. 366, 371;
VII. 70, 74, 78, 83, 263, 265, 268; VIII.
25, 194, 219; IX. 185, 338; X. 234, 241;
XI. 157; XII. 50, 64, 423, 442
  Aminta, III. 261; IV. 131; VI. 137, 317,
318, 365, 490; VII. 264
  Gerusalemme Liberata, III. 230; VI. 98
  Jerusalem Delivered, X. 127, 435
  Padre di Famiglia, V. 157

Tassoni, Alessandro, *Secchia Rapita*, IX.
70

Taste Vin, in *Le Testament de Taste Vin*,
III. 85

Tate, Nahum (1652–1715), VIII. 196, 394,
401, 410, 411, 443
  Brutus of Alba, XI. 319
  *Cuckold's Haven, or An Alderman No
Conjuror*, VI. 47, 48
  Island Princesse, The, VIII. 120
  King Lear, adaptation of, VIII. 41, 120;
XI. 258
  Psalms, VIII. 41

Tatham, Frederick, XIII. 197

Tatham, John (*fl.* 1632–1664), VIII. 421
  Distracted State, The, VIII. 121
  Love Crowns the End, VIII. 121
  Rump, The, VIII. 121, 122, 142
  Scotch Figgaries, The, VIII. 121

Tatler, The, VIII. 140, 158, 175, 390; IX.
18, 32, 33 ff. (main entry), 63, 94, 109,
118, 119, 125, 144, 161, 165, 404, 412,
437 ff., 441, 485, 569; XI. 317, 373; XII.
140, 193; XIII. 318; XIV. 461, 462

Tatler in Cambridge, The, XIV. 208, 537

Tatlock, J. S. P., II. 174, 464

Tattle, in Congreve's *Love for Love*, VIII.
152, 156

Tatton, R. G., XIV. 609

Tattycoram, in *Little Dorrit*, XIII. 331

Tatwin (d. 734), I. 78, 435

Taubman, Matthew (d. 1690?), VIII. 97,
410

Tauler, Johann, IX. 314, 315, 519

Taunton, IV. 132

Taunton academy, X. 386

Taunton commission (Endowed schools),
XIV. 421, 422, 429, 430

Tautphoeus, baroness von. *See* Montgomery, Jemima

Taverner, Richard (1505?–1575), IV. 444

Tavernier, Jean Baptiste, XIV. 333;
  Voyages in the East, IX. 268

Tavie, Welshman, in *Club Law*, VI. 308,
309

Tavistock, IV. 157, 194, 409

Tawny-coat, in *If you know not me*, VI. 92

*Taxarum omnium beneficiorum Angliae,
Liber*, II. 364

Taxes, Song against the King's, II. 421

Tay, firth of, IX. 552

Tay, river, X. 274

Tayis Bank, II. 281

Taylor, Abraham (*fl.* 1727–1740), X. 384

Taylor, Alfred E., XIII. 567

Taylor, Mrs Ann, of Ongar (1757–1830),
XI. 384, 482

Taylor, Ann, afterwards Mrs Gilbert
(1782–1866), XI. 384, 483; *My Mother*,
XI. 383

Taylor, Ann and Jane, XI. 483; *Hymns for
Infant Minds*, XI. 383; *Original Poems*,
XI. 383; *Rhymes for the Nursery*, XI. 383

Taylor, Charles (1840–1908), XII. 341, 501

Taylor, E. J., IX. 519

Taylor, Francis (*fl.* 1654), VII. 322, 490

Taylor, Helen, XIV. 486

Taylor, Henry (1711–1785), *Thoughts on...
the Grand Apostacy*, X. 309, 507

Taylor, Sir Henry (1800–1886), XI. 411;
XII. 107, 112–113 (main entry), 211,
423; XIII. 467; XIV. 507
  Edwin the Fair, XII. 112, 113
  Isaac Comnenus, XII. 112
  Minor Poems, XII. 113
  Philip van Artevelde, XII. 112, 113;
XIII. 177, 194
  'Quoth tongue of neither maid nor
wife,' XII. 113
  St Clement's Eve, XII. 112

Taylor, Isaac (1759–1829), XI. 384, 483

Taylor, Isaac (1787–1865), XII. 470; XIV
481, 609

Taylor, Isaac (1829–1901), XII. 505

Taylor, James W., XII. 513

Taylor, Jane (1783–1824), XI. 384, 483;
Twinkle, Twinkle, Little Star, XI. 383

Taylor, Jefferys (1792–1853), XI. 384, 483

Taylor, Jeremy (1613–1667), VII. 130, 144,
146, 148, 150, 162 ff. (main entry), 213,
426, 427, 475; VIII. 250, 293, 294, 297,
303, 368 ff., 377, 386, 456; IX. 62; X.
360, 364, 366; XI. 2; XII. 169, 176, 193,
253, 277, 283; XIV. 460
  Ductor Dubitantium, VII. 163, **280**
  Golden Grove, The, VII. 163
  Great Exemplar, The, VII. 165
  Holy Dying, VII. 163 ff.
  Holy Living, VII. 163, 165
  Liberty of Prophesying, The, VII. 165;
VIII. 344; X. 372
  Marriage Ring, The, VII. 163
  *Sacred order and offices of Episcopacy,
The*, VII. 165
  'The House of Feasting,' IV. 247
  Worthy Communicant, The, VII. 163, 165

Taylor, John, the 'water-poet' (1580–
1653), III. 288; IV. 361, 517, 518, 520,
532, 533, 534, 545, 546; V. 144, 148;
VI. 261; VII. 387, 494, 498, 499, 514, 515
  All the Workes of J. T., IV. 392
  John Taylor's Wit and Mirth, IV. 360

Taylor, John
   Kicksey Winsey, or A Lerry Come-Twang, A, IV. 392
   Pennyles Pilgrimage, The, IV. 392
Taylor, John, LL.D. (1694–1761), X. 385, 409, 463; *Defence of the Common rights of Christians*, X. 380; *Scripture doctrine of Original Sin*, X. 380
Taylor, John (1704–1766), IX. 341, 528
Taylor, John (1757–1832), X. 480
Taylor, John (1781–1864), X. 527; XII. 195, 203
Taylor, John Edward (1791–1844), XIV. 535
Taylor, Joseph (1586?–1653?), VI. 248, 276, 277
Taylor, Joseph, XI. 483
Taylor, Mary, XIII. 404, 405
Taylor, Nathaniel, X. 385
Taylor, Philip Meadows (1808–1876), XIII. 566; XIV. 580
   Confessions of a Thug, XIII. 432; XIV. 338
   Ralph Darnell, XIV. 338
   Seeta, XIV. 338
   Tara, XIV. 338
   Tippoo Sultan, XIV. 338
Taylor, Robert (1784–1844), XIV. 482
Taylor, Robert, bookseller (c. 1763), XI. 315
Taylor, S. A., XIV. 541
Taylor, Thomas (c. 1704), VIII. 476
Taylor, Thomas (1758–1835), XIV. 482
Taylor, Tom (1817–1880), XII. 407; XIII. 264, 268, 516, 522, 524; XIV. 196, 238, 519, 548
   Anne Boleyn, XIII. 267
   Arkwright's Wife, XIII. 267
   Fool's Revenge, The, XIII. 267
   Jeanne Darc, XIII. 267
   Lady Clancarty, XIII. 267
   Plot and Passion, XIII. 267
   Still Waters Run Deep, XIII. 267
   Ticket-of-Leave Man, The, XIII. 267
   'Twixt Axe and Crown, XIII. 267
Taylor, William, of Norwich (1765–1836), X. 484; XI. 179, 423, 428; XII. 4, 97, 380, 429; XIII. 169, 244, 468
Taylor, William, publisher (d. 1724), IX. 19; XI. 323
Taylor, William Cooke (1809–1849), XIV. 571
Taylor, quack oculist, in Foote's drama, X. 88
Taylor family, the, XI. 384, 483
Tayster. *See* John de
Tea, X. 467
Teachum, Mrs, in Sarah Fielding's *Governess*, XI. 380
'Teachwell, Mrs,' XI. 379
Teazle, lady, in Sheridan's *School for Scandal*, X. 90; XI. 269 ff.; XII. 171
Teazle, Sir Peter, in Sheridan's *School for Scandal*, XI. 269, 270
Techmessa, in *The Jealous Lovers*, VI. 325
Techne, in *The Queenes Arcadia*, VI. 317

Teddington, VII. 42; XIV. 283
Tediousness, in Tudor moralities, V. 57
Tedman, Mr, in Fanny Burney's *Wanderer*, X. 65
Tedworth, the drummer of, IX. 436
Tees, river, XIII. 136, 149
Tegner, XII. 395
Teignmouth, lord, XIV. 577
Teixeira, Antony, IX. 501
Telegonus, in *Confessio Amantis*, II. 149
Telemachus, V. 108; X. 134
Telesius, III. 416
Telfer, Jamie, of the Fair Dodhead, XII. 3
Tellus, in *Endimion*, V. 341
Telugu language, XII. 362
Temperance, the house of, in *The Faerie Queene*, VI. 335
Temperley, Harold William Vazielle, XIV. 508
Tempesti, VI. 174, 176
Templars, the, I. 189
Temple, the, in the Cross legend, I. 134
Temple, the (Palestine), V. 15, 49
Temple, Dorothy, lady, IX. 92, 93; X. 410. *See* Osborne, Dorothy
Temple, earl. *See* Grenville, Richard Temple
Temple, Frederick (1821–1902), archbishop of Canterbury, XIV. 602, 609, 610; 'The Education of the World,' XII. 295
Temple, Henry John, 3rd viscount Palmerston (1784–1865), XIII. 422; XIV. 124, 129, 132, 171, 172, 182, 184, 185, 187, 420, 505, 508; *Civis Romanus* speech, XIV. 126
Temple, Sir Richard (1634–1697), VIII. 476
Temple, Sir Richard, viscount Cobham (1669?–1749), VIII. 428; IX. 445; X. 103
Temple, Sir William (1555–1627), IV. 274 ff., 509; VII. 343; *Admonitio*, IV. 276
Temple, Sir William (1628–1699), VII. 266 ff.; VIII. 267, 268, 342, 379–386 (main entry), 482; IX. 47, 91 ff., 102, 103, 170, 332 ff., 390, 454 ff., 524, 572; X. 221, 224, 238, 484; XIV. 51, 63
   An Essay upon the Advancement of Trade in Ireland, VIII. 384
   An Essay upon the present State and Settlement of Ireland, VIII. 384
   An Introduction to the History of England, VIII. 384
   Essay on Ancient and Modern Learning, VIII. 385; IX. 391, 392
   Essay upon the Original and Nature of Government, VIII. 384
   Letters, VIII. 380, 381
   Memoirs, VIII. 380 ff.
   Miscellanea, VIII. 384
   Observations upon the United Provinces of the Netherlands, VIII. 383
   Of Heroic Virtue, X. 222
   Of Poetry, X. 222
   Survey of the Constitution and Interests of the Empire...., A, VIII. 384
   Upon Conversation, VIII. 386

Temple, Sir William
  Upon Health and Long Life, VIII. 385,
  386
  Upon Poetry, V. 286; VIII. 385, 386
  Upon Popular Discontents, VIII. 386
  Upon the Cure of the Gout, VIII. 385,
  386
  *Upon the different conditions of life and
  fortune*, VIII. 386
  *Upon the Gardens of Epicurus or Of
  Gardening*, VIII. 385, 386
Temple, William Johnson (1739–1796),
  X. 193, 478
'Temple of the Muses,' XI. 337
Temple revels, Middle, VIII. 244
Temple's Gallicisms, VIII. 383
Templum Chrystallinum, II. 225
Temporalitie, in *Ane Pleasant Satyre*, III.
  126, 127, 128
Temptation, in *Mirour de l'Omme*, II. 140
Ten Brink, Bernhard, I. viii, 102, 143, 420;
  II. 28; III. 75; V. 20, 39
Tençons, V. 27
Teneriffe, IX. 180
Tenison, Thomas (1636–1715), archbishop
  of Canterbury, VIII. 250, 305, 307,
  431, 462; IX. 195; X. 353; *Baconiana*,
  VIII. 402; *The Creed of Mr Hobbes Ex-
  amined*, VII. 301, 475
Tennant, William (1784–1848), XI. 445
  Anster Fair, XI. 243
  Cardinal Bethune, XI. 243
  Dingin doon O The Cathedral, XI. 243
  John Baliol, XI. 243
  Tangier's Giant, XI. 243
  Thane of Fife, XI. 243
Tennent, Sir James Emerson (1804–1869),
  XIV. 197, 554
Tenniel, Sir John (1820–1914), XI. 477,
  491; XII. 411; XIV. 235, 239, 549
Tennyson, Alfred, 1st lord Tennyson
  (1809–1892), I. 247, 266, 269, 284, 373;
  II. 176, 182, 400; IV. 47, 112; VII. 137;
  IX. 73; X. 143, 152, 220; XI. 77, 111,
  158, 159, 409; XII. 39, 63, 106, 113, 118,
  126, 139, 154, 219, 271, 438, 483; XIII.
  23 ff. (main entry), 69, 71, 72, 85, 120,
  131, 140, 143, 147, 148, 152, 153, 155,
  157 ff., 176, 179, 184, 188, 192, 194,
  195, 200, 214, 216, 219, 221, 228, 230,
  231, 240, 241, 243, 244, 246, 250 ff., 277,
  297, 421, 442, 463, 473 ff. (main entry),
  also see Add. 3; XIV. 15, 148, 238, 255,
  306, 321, 349, 378 ff., 443, 456, 493,
  515, 517
  A Dream of Fair Women, VI. 338
  Akbar's Dream, and Other Poems, XIII.
  39
  Aylmer's Field, XIII. 40
  Balin and Balan, XIII. 35, 36
  Ballad of the Fleet, A, XIII. 39
  Ballads and other Poems, XIII. 39
  Becket, XIII. 39
  Brook, The, XIII. 34, 36
  'By night we linger'd on the lawn,'
  XIII. 33

Tennyson, Alfred
  'Calm is the morn without a sound,'
  XIII. 33
  Charge of the Heavy Brigade, The, XIII.
  40, 42
  Charge of the Light Brigade, The, XIII.
  186
  Claribel, XIII. 26, 27, 44
  Columbus, XIII. 40
  'Come into the garden, Maud,' XIII. 35
  Coming of Arthur, The, XIII. 35
  Crossing the Bar, XIII. 44
  Cup, The, XIV. 380
  Daisy, The, XIII. 42
  'Dark house, by which once more I
  stand,' XIII. 33
  Death of Œnone, The, XIII. 39
  Defence of Lucknow, The, XIII. 40
  Demeter, XII. 332; XIII. 41
  Demeter and other Poems, XIII. 39
  Despair, XIII. 40, 42
  Dora, XIII. 29, 39
  Dream of Fair Women, A, XIII. 25, 26
  Dying Swan, The, XIII. 26, 250
  Elaine, XIII. 35
  Enid and Nimuë, XIII. 35
  Enoch Arden, XI. 148; XIII. 38, 39, 379
  Flight, The, XIII. 42
  Four Idylls of the King, XIII. 35
  Gardener's Daughter, The, XIII. 34, 40
  Gareth and Lynette, XIII. 35, 37
  Geraint and Enid, XIII. 35
  Grandmother, The, XIII. 39, 40
  Guinevere, XIII. 35
  Harold, XIII. 39
  Helen's Tower, XIII. 177
  'Hollyhock' song, the, XIII. 244
  Holy Grail, The, XIII. 35, 37
  'I cannot see the features right,' XIII. 33
  'I have led her home,' XIII. 35
  Idylls of the King, XIII. 27, 29, 31, 35 ff.,
  41, 201, 448
  In Memoriam, VII. 42, 52; VIII. 229;
  XII. 116, 330; XIII. 10, 27, 32 ff., 37, 183;
  XIV. 380
  In the Children's Hospital, XIII. 40
  Lady of Shalott, The, XIII. 25, 26, 29;
  XIV. 442
  Last Tournament, The, XIII. 35, 37
  Locksley Hall, XIII. 30, 34, 161; XIV. 374
  Locksley Hall, Sixty Years After, XIII.
  39, 40, 42
  Lotos Eaters, The, XIII. 25 ff., 29
  Love and Duty, XIII. 30
  'Love thou thy land,' XIII. 30
  Lucretius, XIII. 39 ff.
  Mariana, XIII. 26
  Maud, XI. 151; XIII. 34, 72, 161
  Maud, and Other Poems, XIII. 34, 42
  Miller's Daughter, The, XIII. 25, 40, 190
  Morte d'Arthur, XIII. 29, 30, 35
  Nimuë (Vivien), XIII. 35
  Northern Farmer, The, XIII. 39
  'Now sleeps the crimson petal,' XII.
  31
  'O that 'twere possible,' XIII. 35

Tennyson, Alfred
  Ode on the Death of the Duke of Welling-
    ton, XIII. 34
  Œnone, XIII. 25, 26, 28, 29, 41
  'Of old sat Freedom,' XIII. 30
  'Oh yet we trust that somehow good,'
    XIII. 33
  'Old Yew, which graspest at the stones,'
    XIII. 33
  Palace of Art, The, VII. 253; XIII. 25, 26,
    28, 30
  Passing of Arthur, The, XIII. 35
  Pelleas and Ettarre, XIII. 35
  Poems (1830), XIV. 139
  Poems, Chiefly Lyrical (1830), XIII. 25
  Poems (1833), XIII. 25
  Poems, 2 vols. (1842), XII. 101; XIII. 25
  Poems, by Two Brothers, XIII. 25
  Princess, The, XIII. 30, 31, 251; XIV.
    430
  Queen Mary, XIII. 39
  Recollections of the Arabian Nights,
    XIII. 26
  Revenge, The, XIII. 39, 40, 42; XIV. 84
  Rivulet, The, XIV. 380
  Rizpah, XIII. 40
  'Sad Hesper o'er the buried sun,' XIII.
    33
  St Simeon Stylites, XIII. 41
  St Telemachus, XIII. 40, 41
  Sir John Oldcastle, XIII. 40
  Sisters, The, XIII. 42
  Spinster's Sweet-Arts, The, XIII. 40
  'Spirit haunts the year's last hours, A,'
    XIII. 26
  'Splendour falls, the,' XIII. 31
  'Sweet and low,' XIII. 31
  'Tears, idle tears,' XIII. 31, 42
  Tiresias, XIII. 40, 41, 142
  Tiresias and Other Poems, XIII. 39
  Tithonus, XIII. 29, 41
  To Virgil, XIII. 42
  'To-night the winds begin to rise,' XIII.
    33
  True and the False, The, XIII. 35
  Two Voices, The, XIII. 30, 40
  Ulysses, XIII. 29, 30, 32; XIV. 241
  'Unwatch'd, the garden bough shall
    sway,' XIII. 33
  Vastness, XIII. 30, 41
  Village Wife, The, XIII. 39, 40
  Vision of Sin, The, VIII. 237; XIII. 26,
    27, 30, 32, 253
  Voyage of Maeldune, The, XII. 361; XIII.
    42, 251; XIV. 328
  'We fell out,' XIII. 31
  'When on my bed the moonlight falls,'
    XIII. 33
  'Witch-elms that counterchange the
    floor,' XIII. 33
  'With trembling fingers did we weave,'
    XIII. 33
  Wreck, The, XIII. 42
  'You ask me, why,' XIII. 30
Tennyson, Charles. *See* Turner, Charles
  Tennyson

Tennyson, Frederick (1807–1898), XIII.
  23, 45 ff., 78, 473, 479
  Daphne, and other Poems, XIII. 46
  Days and Hours, XIII. 46
  Isles of Greece, The, XIII. 46
  Poems of the Day and Year, XIII. 46
  Psyche, XIII. 47
  River of Life, XIII. 47
Tennyson, Hallam, 2nd lord Tennyson,
  XIII. 473–474, 478, 479
'Tenth Muse,' the, XIII. 175
Tercer (America), v. 139
Terence, II. 331, 359, 360; III. 20, 24, 53,
  429, 430; IV. 4, 235, 245, 320, 414, 417,
  428, 440; V. 6, 104, 105, 116; VI. 14, 15,
  32, 297; VII. 487; VIII. 155, 247, 442;
  IX. 46, 58, 270, 274, 338, 418, 525, 526;
  X. 91, 429; XI. 266, 426; XII. 494
  Adelphi, VI. 48; X. 90; XI. 265
  Andria, V. 101, 103, 104, 115, 411; IX. 64
  Eunuchus, V. 104, 105; VI. 300; VIII. 139
  Heautontimoroumenos, V. 102, 104
  Hecyra, II. 321
  Phormio, V. 102
Terens in English, V. 103, 411
Terentia, IX. 218
Terentian, I. 120
Teresa, St, VII. 34, 35, 37, 143; XIII. 356,
  398
Tereus, in *Confessio Amantis,* II. 151
Tereus, in *Philomela,* VI. 320
Tereus, in *Progne,* VI. 299
Tereus and Procne, III. 343
Terilo, William, IV. 534; *Satire on Brazen
  Head,* I. 210
Term Catalogues, The, IV. 404; VIII. 182,
  188; XI. 339; XII. 357
Ternate, XIV. 298
Terni, cataract of, XII. 44
Terouenne, siege of, II. 338; III. 70
Terra, in *Lingua,* VI. 315
Terriss, William (1847–1897), XIII. 515
Terry, Charles Sanford, *Catalogue of publi-
  cations of Scottish Historical Societies,*
  XII. 358, 519
Terry, Edward (1590–1660), IV. 462; *Re-
  lation of a Voyage to the Easterne India,*
  XIV. 333
Terry, Ellen, XIII. 513, 515
Tertullian, III. 9, 416; VII. 34, 505, 510;
  XII. 488
Tervey, tykes of, II. 275
Tesauro, E., *Cannocchiale Aristotelico,* VII.
  269
Tessa, in *Romola,* XIII. 395
Tessaranactus (*i.e.* James I), in *Euphormio,*
  IV. 256
Test, The, X. 389, 390, 522
Test act, the, X. 374; XIII. 24
Testament, New, II. 290, 292, 300, 430;
  III. 7, 13, 27, 42 ff., 127, 233, 448;
  IV. 27, 28, 34, 47; VII. 173, 304, 316,
  317, 326
  Beza's Latin version, III. 45
  Genevan, of William Whittingham, III.
  44

Testament, New
Greek text of, VIII. 277
Irish version of, IV. 414
Luther's preface to, III. 45
Purvey's version, III. 45
Scots, of Murdoch Nisbet, III. 45
Tindale's, II. 330; III. 42, 43; VII. 432
Wycliffite, II. 285, 430; III. 45
Testament, Old, II. 230, 292, 335; III. 43 ff.,
234; IV. 27, 28, 30, 46, 49, 170; VII. 324;
VIII. 37
Tindale's, III. 44
Wycliffite, II. 430
Testament de Taste Vin, Le, III. 85, 483
Testament of the Hawthorne, The, III. 86,
483
Testaments (English, Latin and French),
III. 482 ff.
Testaments, mock, IV. 357, 521
Testimony, in Crowne's *Sir Courtly Nice*,
VIII. 189
Tetbury, Gloucestershire, VIII. 82, 83
Tetterbys, the, in Dickens's *The Haunted
Man*, XIII. 324
Teufelsdröckh (Carlyle's), XIII. 3, 6, 9
Teutonic languages, X. 223
Teutonic law, VIII. 310
Teutonic tribes, X. 313
Tewkesbury, II. 297; IX. 394
Tewkesbury academy, X. 386
Texte, Joseph, X. 16, 413, 458; XII. 407,
525, 527
Textor, J. Ravisius, V. 107 ff., 407, 410;
VI. 87; Latin *Dialogi*, V. 101; *Juvenis,
Pater, Uxor*, V. 108, 109; *Thersites*, V.
108, 109
Thackeray, Amelia (born Webb), XIII. 276
Thackeray, Anne (born Becher), XIII. 276
Thackeray, Isabella (born Shawe), XIII.
278, 280
Thackeray, Richmond, XIII. 275, 276
Thackeray, Thomas, XIII. 275
Thackeray, William, bookseller, XI. 335
Thackeray, William Makepeace (1811–
1863), I. 287; II. 176; V. 179, 212, 231;
VII. 199; IX. 40, 127, 133, 190; X. 45,
120, 154, 422; XI. 306, 307, 385, 387,
423, 476, 483; XII. 21, 24, 109, 121 ff.,
125, 128, 131, 178, 250, 252, 426, 430,
431; XIII. 142, 154, 162, 170, 177, 178,
189, 199, 275 ff. (main entry), 307, 344,
352, 386, 388, 406, 421, 422, 425, 433,
442, 457, 525 ff., 554, *also see* Add. 2;
XIV. 142, 148, 152, 171, 177, 187, 194,
205, 224, 235 ff., 539, 540, 549
Amours of Mr Deuceace, The, XIII. 279
Ballads of Policeman X, The, XIII. 294
Barbazure, XIII. 284
Barry Lyndon, The Luck of, X. 44; XIII.
281, 284, 292, 300, 414
Bedford Row Conspiracy, The, XII. 431
Book of Snobs, The, XI. 297; XIII. 281,
284
Catherine, XIII. 279, 280, 282, 418
Christmas Books, XIII. 292, 294
Comic Tales and Sketches, XIII. 281

Thackeray, William Makepeace
Denis Duval, X. 39; XIII. 300
Diary of Fitz-Jeames de la Pluche, XIV.
237
Dr Birch and his Young Friends, XIII.
294
*English Humourists of the Eighteenth
Century, The*, X. 53, 418, 484; XIII. 294
Esmond, Henry, The History of, XIII.
277, 286, 292, 293, 297, 298, 300, 407
Fatal Boots, The, XIII. 280, 282
Fêtes of July, The, XIII. 283
Fitz-Boodle, Confessions of, XIII. 281
Flore et Zéphyr, XIII. 278
Four Georges, The, XII. 431; XIII. 295
George de Barnwell, XIII. 280, 418
Great Hoggarty Diamond, The, XIII. 281,
288
Irish Sketch Book, The, XIII. 282 ff., 414
Jeames's Diary, XIII. 284, 526
Kickleburys on the Rhine, The, XIII. 294
Legend of the Rhine, A, XIII. 284, 294
Lords and Liveries, XII. 246
Lovel the Widower, XIII. 299
Major Gahagan, XIII. 279, 281
Men's Wives, XIII. 281
*Miss Tickletoby's Lectures on English
History*, XIII. 284; XIV. 237
Mr Punch's Prize Novelists, XIII. 284;
XIV. 237
Mrs Perkins's Ball, XIII. 292, 294
Newcomes, The, IV. 113; V. 213; XIII.
120, 277, 278, 295 ff., 299, 300
*Notes of a Journey from Cornhill to
Grand Cairo*, XIII. 284
Novels by Eminent Hands, XII. 246
Our Street, XIII. 292
Paris Sketch Book, The, XIII. 281, 282;
XIV. 196
Pendennis, IV. 252; X. 44; XII. 159;
XIII. 276, 290 ff., 294, 391; XIV. 440
Philip, The Adventures of, XIII. 280,
288, 299, 300
Professor, The, XIII. 310
Ravenswing, The, XIII. 281
Rebecca and Rowena, XIII. 284, 294
Rose and the Ring, XIII. 294
Roundabout Papers, X. 204; XIII. 299
Scaramouch, XIII. 351
Second Funeral of Napoleon, The, XIII.
283
Shabby Genteel Story, A, XIII. 280, 299
Snobs of England, The, XIII. 284; XIV.
237
Timbuctoo, XIII. 277; XIV. 207
Vanity Fair, V. 213; XIII. 281, 284 ff.,
292, 294; XIV. 255
Virginians, The, XIII. 297 ff.
Yellowplush Papers, The, IX. 57; XII.
431; XIII. 278, 281
Thackeray, William Makepeace, grand-
father of the novelist, XIII. 275
Thaise, in *Confessio Amantis*, II. 152
Thalaba, XIII. 357
Thalander, in *Sicelides*, VI. 323
Thalia, in *The Tears of the Muses*, III. 2

Thame, VII. 104

Thames, river, IX. 187; X. 102; XI. 362; XII. 265; XIII. 93, 120; XIV. 221

Thamesis (Thames), in *The Masque of Beauty*, VI. 344

Thanet, isle of, IX. 536

Thaon, P. de (*fl.* 1120), I. 226, 227

Tharmas, in Blake's *Vala*, XI. 195

Thaxted, Essex, IV. 91

Theagenes (Digby), in his *Memoirs*, VII. 222

Theal, G. McCall, XIV. Add. 10

Thealma and Clearchus, VII. 251

Theatre, The, IX. 144, 439, 442

Theatre, the Elizabethan, VI. 241–278, 459 ff. *See, also, under* specific names below:

Blackfriars, VI. 170, 243, 248, 255, 257 ff., 262, 270, 273, 276 ff., 289 ff., 312, 404

Cockpit, VI. 262, 272

Curtain, VI. 247, 253 ff., 378, 384 ff.

Fortune, VI. 250, 253, 255, 256, 258, 259, 261, 268, 269, 272, 292, 398

Globe, VI. 69, 247, 248, 253, 255 ff., 261, 267, 269, 270, 272, 275 ff.

Golding (now Golden) lane, VI. 258

Hope, VI. 260, 261, 264, 267, 275, 402

Newington Butts, VI. 247, 254, 255

Phoenix, VI. 262

Red Bull, VI. 262, 266, 272

Rose, Southwark, VI. 83, 247, 250, 254, 255, 257, 259, 261

Salisbury court, VI. 232, 233, 262

Swan, VI. 259 ff., 263 ff., 267, 268, 273

Theater, VI. 243, 246, 247, 249, 251 ff., 257, 378, 384 ff., 391

Theatre Royal, Drury lane, VI. 33, 261

Whitefriars, VI. 140, 262

Theatre for Worldlings, A, III. 213, 250

Theatre Regulation act, XIII. 257

Theatres, A Second and Third Blast of retrait from plaies and, VI. 390, 392, 496

Theatres, closing of the, VI. 210, 229, 234, 238

Theatres, war of the, VI. 4, 39

Theatrical histories, dictionaries and general records, X. 442 ff.

Theatrical pamphlets, Georgian era, XI. 449 ff.

Thebes, subject of the wars of, I. 279, 285, 286, 307

Thebes, The Siege of, II. 308

Thebes, Cambridge university so called by Dryden, VIII. 4

Thecla, I. 74

Thegan's *Life of Ludwig the Pious*, I. 90

Thel, in Blake's *Book of Thel*, XI. 186

Theloall, S., *Le Digest des Briefes Originals* (1579), VIII. 467

Thelwall, John (1764–1834), XI. 119; XIII. 240, 512; XIV. 610

Themech, IV. 215

Themistocles, IX. 524; XII. 363

Thenot, in *The Faithfull Shepheardesse*, VI. 368

Theobald, archbishop of Canterbury (d 1161), I. 185; II. 341

Theobald, Lewis (1688–1744), V. 270 ff.; VIII. 177; IX. 77 ff., 84, 86, 89, 143, 145, 168; X. 440; XI. 322; *Richard II*, XI. 316; *Shakespeare*, XI. 320; *Shakespeare Restored*, IX. 79, 448, 449

Theobaldus Stampensis (d. 1161), II. 341

Theocrine, in *The Unnaturall Combat*, VI. 159

Theocritus, III. 62, 218, 219, 221, 222, 224 ff., 300; IV. 121, 411, 440; VI. 364; VII. 9, 83, 87; VIII. 44; IX. 69, 372, 526; X. 492; XI. 143, 426; XII. 330, 331, 486, 489, 495; XIII. 34, 45; *The Adoniazusae*, III. 226

Theodberht, I. 26

Theodore, in Walpole's *Castle of Otranto*, X. 61

Theodore (602?–690), archbishop of Canterbury, I. 5, 71 ff., 77, 82, 87

Theodoric of Chartres, I. 185

Theodoric the great, XII. 322, 476

Theodorus Prodromus, IV. 259

Theodosius, VII. 395; XII. 476

Theodosius, in *The Emperour of the East*, VI. 158

Theodotion, IX. 330

Theodric I, I. 26

Theodric, in *Deor*, I. 36, 37

Theodric, Ostrogothic king, I. 20, 21, 34, 36, 37, 99

Theognis, XI. 392; XII. 484

Theological Falsehood, in *The Faerie Queene*, III. 234

Theological learning (1600–1660), VII. 484

Theologus, in *A Dialogue...against the fever Pestilence*, III. 109

Theology, in *Piers the Plowman*, II. 8

Theophanius, count, I. 105

Theophilus, *De Urinis*, II. 365

Theophilus, the legendary, VII. 503

Theophrastians, III. 91, 487

Theophrastus, III. 416; IV. 323, 335 ff., 339, 341 ff., 436, 521; VII. 379, 384, 386; IX. 46; *Characters*, VIII. 63; XII. 332, 485

Theophrastus Such (George Eliot's), XIII. 402

There'll Never be Peace till Samie comes Hame, IX. 377

There's nae luck aboot the Hoose, IX. 373

Therry, Sir Roger (1800–1874), XI. 392

Thersites, III. 280; V. 410

Thersites, in Dryden's *Troilus and Cressida*, VIII. 29

Thersites, in Shakespeare's *Troilus and Cressida*, VI. 44

Theseus, XIII. 354

Theseus, in Alfred's *Orosius*, I. 95

Theseus, in *A Midsummer Night's Dream*, V. 183; VI. 213, 214

Theseus, in *Palamon and Arcyte*, VI. 299

Theseus, in *The Two Noble Kinsmen*, V. 256

Thespis, V. 176

Thetbaldus, I. 227

Thetford, Norfolk, VIII. 257

Thetford, St Mary's priory, VI. 281

Thetis, in *Iliad*, VI. 347

Thierry, J. N. A., XIV. 77; *Norman Conquest*, XIV. 107

Thims, Gregory, VII. 498

Third Blast, The, VI. 378, 391, 392, 395

Third collection of Tracts, X. 378

Thirlestane keep, III. 132

Thirlwall, Connop (1797–1875), XII. 280, 288, 302, 303, 307 ff. (main entry), 318, 470, 478; XIV. 593; *History of Greece*, XII. 308; *Letters to a Friend*, XII. 309; 'On the Irony of Sophocles,' XII. 308

Thirsk, the Three Tuns, XIV. 203

Thirty years' war, VII. 50, 437, 453; XIV. 459

Thirty-Nine Articles, the, XIV. 383

'This is the Time' (refrain), VIII. 96

Thisbe, in *A Midsummer Night's Dream*, V. 285; VI. 207, 316

Thom, M., III. 189

Thom, William (1798?–1848), XI. 445

Thomalin, in *The Shepheards Calender*, III. 222

Thomas (*c.* 1170), I. 273, 310, 316

Thomas, in *Piers the Plowman*, II. 12

Thomas, Acts of, I. 75

Thomas, C. H., XIV. Add. 10

Thomas, Edward (1813–1886), XII. 352, 512, 513; *Ancient Indian Weights*, XII. 353

Thomas, Edward, XIII. 495; XIV. 516, 521, 523

Thomas, Frederick Moy, XIV. 535

Thomas, Lord Cromwell, V. 236, 238, 246, 247, 332, 442, 444

Thomas, Mrs, IX. 84

Thomas, St (apostle), I. 74, 75, 120, 232

Thomas, St, *English Song on*, I. 117

Thomas, St E. Hake, XIV. 527

Thomas, Samuel (1627–1693), X. 386

Thomas, Thomas, Cambridge printer (1553–1588), III. 427; IV. 409, 410; VII. 486, 487

Thomas, W. Moy, IX. 244, 248

Thomas, William (d. 1554), III. 554; *A Historye of Italye*, III. 105

Thomas, William (1670–1738), IX. 533, 540

Thomas, William Luson (1830–1900), XIV. 535

Thomas à Becket, Thomas of Canterbury. *See* Becket

Thomas à Kempis. *See* Kempis

Thomas Aquinas, St. *See* Aquinas

Thomas de Bungay (*fl.* 1290), I. 210, 456; II. 350

Thomas de Eccleston (*fl.* 1250), I. 203, 453

Thomas de Hales (*fl.* 1250), I. 233; *Luve Ron*, I. 233

Thomas of Accon, St, VII. 332

Thomas of Burton (*fl.* 1397), II. 498

Thomas of Ely (*fl.* 1175), I. 449

Thomas of Erceldoune (True Thomas) (*fl.* 1220?–1297?), I. 316, 356, 471; II. 100

Thomas of Woodstock, duke of Gloucester (1355–1397), II. 158

Thomas of Woodstock, V. 399

Thomas the Rimer, IV. 363

Thomas Rymer, II. 413

Thomas Saga, I. 191

Thomason, George (d. 1666), IV. 425; XI. 468, 470; collection of tracts of the times (1641–1660), VII. 346, 422, 491, 494, 499, 500, 502

Thompson, in *Cocke Lorell's bote*, III. 84

Thompson, A. Hamilton, *Military Architecture during the Middle Ages*, XII. 349

Thompson, Sir Benjamin, count von Rumford (1753–1814), XIV. 259, 556

Thompson, Benjamin (1776?–1816), XI. 260

Thompson, D'Arcy Wentworth, XIV. 610

Thompson, David (1796–1868), XIV. 359

Thompson, Edward (1738?–1786), VII. 184; X. 525

Thompson, Francis (1859–1907), XII. 404, 441; XIII. 140, 216 ff., 223, 510, *also see* Add. 2

   Absence, XIII. 219

   Hound of Heaven, The, XIII. 218

   Inconstant, The, XIII. 218

   Penelope, XIII. 219

Thompson, Henry (1797–1878), XI. 475

Thompson, Henry Yates, XIV. 195

Thompson, Sir John, 1st baron Haversham (1647–1710), IX. 12, 421, 422

Thompson, John S., XIV. 536

Thompson, John Vaughan (1779–1847), XIV. 296, 564

Thompson, Joseph, XIV. 386, 592, 597

Thompson, Nathaniel (*fl.* 1685), VIII. 98, 410, 411

Thompson, Thomas Perronet (1783–1869), XIV. 514

Thompson, William (1712?–1766?), XI. 172, 429

Thompson, William Hepworth (1810–1886), XII. 330, 331, 494; XIII. 142; XIV. 469

Thoms, William John (1803–1885), XI. 467; XII. 519; *Anecdotes and Traditions*, XII. 354

Thomson, Anstruther, XIV. 541

Thomson, Sir Charles Wyville (1830–1882), XIV. 296, 297, 564

Thomson, Clara Linklater, X. 412, 413; XIII. 553

Thomson, David (1817–1880), XII. 513

Thomson, David Croal, XIII. 541

Thomson, George (1757–1851), XI. 207, 230, 232, 435, 439, 445; XII. 373; *Irish Airs*, XI. 236; *Scottish Airs*, XI. 226, 227, 231, 236; XII. 372; *Welsh Airs*, XI. 235

Thomson, I., *Pyramus and Thisbie*, III. 191

Thomson, James (1700–1748), VI. 49; VII. 137; IX. 69, 181, 186, 254, 486; X. 73, 93 ff. (main entry), 112 ff., 147, 149, 152, 183, 230, 274, 369, 446 ff., 454, 460; XI. 86, 144, 206 ff., 216, 242,

Thomson, James
244, 314; XII. 131, 132, 136, 177, 504;
XIII. 35, 235, *also see* Add. 2
Agamemnon, x. 108
Alfred, x. 107 ff., 433, 437
Autumn, x. 94, 99 ff., 103, 104
Britannia, x. 94, 104
Castle of Indolence, The, III. 246; x. 95,
98, 100, 103, 105 ff., 114, 148, 235;
XI. 247; XII. 100
Coriolanus, x. 96, 108, 114
Edward and Eleonora, x. 108
Hymn, A, x. 103
Liberty, x. 94, 95, 104, 105, 128
*Poem sacred to the Memory of Sir Isaac
Newton*, x. 94
Return from the Fox-Chace, x. 101
Rule, Britannia, x. 109
Seasons, The, x. 93 ff., 109, 110, 112,
125, 145, 148; XI. 247, 315; XIII. 372
Sophonisba, x. 94, 108
Spring, x. 94, 96, 98 ff., 128, 273
Summer, x. 94, 96, 99 ff., 103, 104
Tancred and Sigismunda, x. 108
Winter, x. 94, 96, 99 ff.
Thomson, James, 'B.V.' (1834–1882), XI.
434; XIII. 106 ff., 147, 187, 193, 489
(main entry), 570
City of Dreadful Night, The, XIII. 106 ff.
Insomnia, XIII. 109
Sunday at Hampstead, XIII. 109
Sunday up the River, XIII. 109
To Our Ladies of Death, XIII. 109
Vane's Story, and other Poems, XIII. 109
Weddah and Om-el-Bonain, XIII. 109
Thomson, John, XII. 144
Thomson, John Arthur, XIV. 481
Thomson, J. Charles, XII. 434; XIII. 476,
493, 532
Thomson, Sir Joseph John, XIV. 269
Thomson, Richard (d. 1613), VII. 316
Thomson, Thomas (1768–1852), XII.
357 ff., 518
Thomson, Thomas Napier (1798–1869),
XI. 443
Thomson, William (*fl.* 1725), *Orpheus
Caledonius*, IX. 361, 567; x. 233
Thomson, William (1746–1817), x. 291,
505
Thomson, William (1819–1890), *An Out-
line of the Laws of Thought*, XIV. 9,
482
Thomson, Sir William, lord Kelvin (1824–
1907), XIV. 265 ff., 556, 557
Thomson, William Roger, XIII. 544; XIV.
Add. 5
Thopas, Sir (Chaucer's), IV. 359
Thopas, Sir, in Lyly's *Endimion*, VIII. 127
Thor, x. 237
Thor, children of, III. 84
Thor, myths of, I. 297
Thorbiorga, in Taylor's *Edwin the Fair*,
XII. 113
Thoreau, Henry David, XII. 166, 176
Thoresby, Ralph (1658–1725), IX. 540;
XI. 340; XII. 514, 516; *Leeds*, IX. 353, 540

Thorgerðr, daughter of Egill Skalla-
grimsson, I. 9
Thorie or Thorius, John (*fl.* 1586–1593),
IV. 253, 448
Thorius, Raphael (d. 1625), IV. 531
Thorn, A. E., XIV. 521
Thornberry, Job, in Colman's *John Bull*,
XI. 280
Thornborough, John (1551–1641), VII.
145
Thornbury, George Walter (1828–1876),
XIII. 189, 510
Thorndike, Ashley Horace, VI. 121; VIII.
181
Thorndike, Herbert (1598–1672), VIII.
462; *Epilogue to the Tragedy of the
Church of England*, VIII. 294; *The Re-
formation of the Church of England*,
VIII. 294; trans. of *Veni Creator*, VIII.
295
Thorne, J., XIV. 613
Thorne, Robert (d. 1527), IV. 87
Thorne, William (*fl.* 1397), II. 498
Thorneganus (or Byrhtferth), I. 131
Thornes, the, in Trollope's novels, XIII.
422
Thorney abbey, II. 289
Thornhill, squire, in *The Vicar of Wake-
field*, x. 209
Thornley, George, VII. 489
Thornton, in Mrs Gaskell's *North and
South*, XIII. 378, 381
Thornton, in Lytton's *Pelham*, XIII.
418
Thornton, Bonnell (1724–1768), x. 429,
455, 461; XIV. 594; *The Connoisseur*,
XI. 448
Thornton, Henry (1760–1815), XII. 281,
473
Thornton, Percy Melville, XIV. 597
Thornton, Robert de (*fl.* 1440), IV. 422
Thornton, Robert John (1768?–1837), XI.
432
Thornton, William Thomas (1813–1880),
XIV. 22, 482
Thornton-le-Dale, near Pickering, II. 44
Thornton-le-Street, II. 44
Thoroton, Robert (1623–1678), *Antiqui-
ties of Nottinghamshire*, IX. 353, 540
Thorowgood, in Lillo's *George Barnwell*,
x. 74, 75
Thorowgood, G., VII. 514
Thorpe, Benjamin (1782–1870), I. 116,
117; XI. 344, 505; XIV. 52, 69, 499;
Yule-tide Stories, XII. 368
Thorpe, Isabella, in Jane Austen's *North-
anger Abbey*, XI. 299, 300; XII. 236
Thorpe, John (1682–1750), IX. 540
Thorpe, Thomas (1570?–1635?), IV. 394,
395; V. 223 ff. (T. T.), 225
Thorpe, Thomas Edward, XIV. 557
Thorpe, William (d. 1407?), II. 69
Thorpe, Examination of William, II. 300
Thorpes, the, in Jane Austen's *Northanger
Abbey*, XII. 236
Thorstein, the, Red, I. 287

Thou, Jacques Auguste de (Thuanus), III.
    163, 326; *Historiae sui temporis*, VI. 33;
    IX. 204, 206
Though Fortune cannot favor, III. 190
Thought, in *Piers the Plowman*, II. 19
Thoyras, Rapin de, X. 502
Thracian Wonder, III. 357
Thrale, Mrs. *See* Piozzi, Hester Lynch
Thrales, the, X. 181, 182
Thrasher, justice, in Fielding's *Amelia*,
    X. 21, 29
Three Children, the, I. 74
Three Fates, the, in *Filostrato e Panfila*,
    V. 62
Three Kings' Sons, II. 483, 503
Three Mile Cross, near Reading, XIII. 430
Three Ravens, The, II. 412
Three Speeches, VII. 381
Three Systers of Mantua, The, V. 116
Thring, Edward (1821–1887), XIV. 425,
    602, 610; *Theory and Practice of Teach-
    ing*, XIV. 426
Throckmorton, Job (1545–1601), III. 380,
    381, 382, 383, 390, 391, 538, 539, 542
Throsby, John (1740–1803), IX. 540
Thrum, Sir George, in Thackeray's *The
    Ravenswing*, XIII. 281
Thrush and the Nightingale, The, I. 362,
    465; II. 500
Thrytho, in *Beowulf*, I. 23
Thuanus. *See* Thou
Thucydides, III. 429, 432; IV. 3, 4, 43,
    440; VII. 218, 283; IX. 340, 528; X. 135;
    XII. 303, 330, 333, 338, 474, 482, 483,
    485, 486, 492, 493, 495, *also see* Add.;
    XIV. 59, 85, 98
Thule, I. 26, 100, 216; II. 84
Thumb, Tom, XI. 373, 375
Thunder, Harry, in O'Keeffe's *Wild Oats*,
    XI. 281
Thunder and Lightning, in *The Rehearsal*,
    VIII. 34
'Thunderer, The' (*The Times*), XIV. 180
Thurgarton, Nottinghamshire, II. 299
Thurland, Sir Edward (1606–1683), VIII.
    83
Thurloe, John (1616–1668), VII. 188;
    Collection of the State Papers of, VII.
    187, 435, 452
Thurloe Papers, X. 294
Thurlow, Edward, 1st lord Thurlow (1731–
    1806), X. 306; XI. 78, 142, 143, 254
Thurnall, Tom, in Kingsley's *Two Years
    Ago*, XIII. 365
Thurneysen, I. 246
Thurston, king, in *Horn*, I. 287
Thurtell, John (1794–1824), XIII. 418; XIV.
    201, 228, 230
Thyer, Robert (1709–1781), VIII. 60, 62
Thylde (a seaman), IV. 68
Thynne, Francis (1545?–1608), III. 114;
    IV. 519
Thynne, lady Isabella, VII. 55
Thynne, Thomas, 3rd viscount Wey-
    mouth and 1st marquis of Bath (1734–
    1796), X. 306

Thynne, Thomas, 2nd marquis of Bath,
    XI. 148
Thynne, William (d. 1546), II. 161, 162,
    164, 169, 217, 218; III. 291, 311
Thynnes, the, IX. 168
Thyrsis, in Milton's *Arcades*, VII. 113
Thyrza, in Gissing's novel, XIII. 459, 461
Tibbe, daughter of Rondill the refe, in *The
    Turnament of Totenham*, I. 366
Tibbs, Mrs, in *A Citizen of the World*, V.
    181
Tiberius, in *Sejanus*, VI. 20
Tiberius, emperor of Rome, IX. 234; X.
    320; XII. 306
Tibet Talkapace, II. 232
Tibullus, III. 113; VIII. 215; XII. 492
Tichborne, Chidiock, IV. 129
Tichmarsh, Northants., VIII. 2
Tickell, Richard (1751–1793), X. 438;
    XI. 35, 391
Tickell, Thomas (1686–1740), IX. 165,
    170 ff., 181, 435 ff., 440, 444, 483; X.
    137, 458
    Colin and Lucy, IX. 173
    Epistle from a Lady in England, IX. 173
    Fragment of a Poem on Hunting, IX. 173
    Iliad, The, IX. 75, 171, 173
    Kensington Gardens, IX. 173
    *On Queen Caroline's rebuilding of the
        Lodgings...at Queen's College*, IX. 172
    Oxford, IX. 173
    Part of the Fourth Book of Lucan, IX.
        173
    *Poem to...the Lord Privy Seal on the
        Prospect of Peace*, IX. 171, 172
    Royal Progress, The, IX. 172
    To Mr Addison, IX. 170, 173
    To Sir Godfrey Kneller, IX. 173
    *To the Earl of Warwick on the Death of
        Mr Addison*, IX. 171
Tickler, Timothy, in *Noctes Ambrosianae*,
    XII. 160
Tieck, Dorothea, V. 303
Tieck, Johann Ludwig, V. 85, 222, 299,
    303 ff.; XIII. 4, 192, 465
Tierney, George (1761–1830), XIV. 121, 511
Tierra del Fuego, XIV. 243
Tighe, Mary (born Blackford) (1772–1810),
    XII. 423; XIV. 571; *Psyche*, XIV. 311
Tigris, river, IV. 90
Tilbury. *See* Gervase of
Tilbury, IX. 7
Tiler, Margaret, IV. 442
Tilghman, Richard, X. 409
Tillbrook, Samuel, XIII. 241, 247, 512
Tillemont, Louis S. le N. de, X. 292, 308,
    499; *Histoire des Empereurs*, X. 314;
    Mémoires Ecclésiastiques, X. 314
Tilley, Arthur Augustus, VIII. 63
Tillotson, John (1630–1694), archbishop of
    Canterbury, VII. 176; VIII. 272, 292,
    296, 297, 303, 304, 370, 389, 458, 459,
    461, 462; IX. 195, 196, 289, 293; X. 353,
    354, 359, 360, 379, 498; XII. 259; *The
    Wisdom of being religious*, VIII. 369
Tilly, count J. T. von, VII. 21

Tilly, William, of Selling or Celling (d. 1494), III. 5, 52
Tillyard, Alfred Isaac, XIV. 594
Tilney, Edmund (d. 1610), III. 536; VI. 249, 384
Tilney, Henry, in Jane Austen's *Northanger Abbey*, XII. 234, 236
Timaeus, J. J. C., X. 446
Time, in *The Passetyme of Pleasure*, II. 226
Time's Complaint, VI. 320, 474
Times, Song on the, I. 370
Times, The, XI. 155, 467; XII. 171, 273, 315; XIII. 11, 20, 69, 278, 347, 467; XIV. 118, 151, 165, 170 ff., 177 ff., 187 ff., 198, 201, 410, 536
Times of India, The, XIV. 339
Times Whistle, The. See R. C.
Timme, Thomas, IV. 448, 518
Timoclia at the sege of Thebes by Alexander, v. 102
Timoleon of Corinth, in *The Bond-Man*, VI. 163
Timon, play, VI. 487
Timon (Shakespeare's), XIII. 242
Timon's villa, in Pope's *Epistles*, IX. 81
Timor mortis conturbat me, II. 257
'Timotheus,' VIII. 55
Timothy, in *Sir Courtly Nice*, VIII. 189
Timothy Thinbeard, in *If you know not me*, VI. 84
Timperley, Charles H. (1794–1846?), XI. 467
Timur (Tamerlane), XI. 18
Tina, in George Eliot's *Mr Gilfil's Love Story*, XIII. 387
Tinchebray, battle of, I. 157
Tincker of Turney, The, IV. 362
Tindal, Matthew (1657–1733), IX. 288, 293 ff., 302, 309, 508, 512; X. 521; *Christianity as Old as the Creation*, IX. 293, 311
Tindal, Nicholas (1688–1774), *Continuation of Mr Rapin de Thoyras's History*, IX. 235, 236, 495
'Tindal, William,' X. 475
Tindale or Tyndale, William (d. 1536), I. 211; II. 330; III. 13, 26, 27, 39 ff. (main entry), 441, 462, 472; IV. 38, 39, 40 ff., 46, 380
   Articles whereof John Frith died, III. 41
   New Testament, XII. 521
   Obedience of a Christian Man, The, III. 39
   Parable of the Wicked Mammon, The, III. 39
   Practice of Prelates, The, III. 41
   Revelation of Anti-Christ, The, III. 39
   Sum of Scripture, The, III. 39
Tintagol or Tintagel, the castle of, I. 259, 273
Tintern abbey, X. 134
Tintoretto, XIII. 397
Tipperary, IX. 166; XIV. 321, 326
Tiptoft, John, earl of Worcester (1427?–1470), II. 286, 499
Tiresias, III. 173

Tiresias, in *Narcissus*, VI. 316
Tiriel, in Blake's poem, XI. 187
Tirzah, in Blake's *Four Zoas*, XI. 196, 197
Tisbury, Wiltshire, IV. 161
Titania, XI. 374
Titania, in *A Midsummer Night's Dream*, v. 183
Titania, in *Nimphidia*, IV. 193
Titania, in *The Whore of Babylon*, VI. 53
'Titanic,' ship, XIV. 195
Titans, the, in Keats's *Hyperion*, XII. 85
Titchburne, Robert, VII. 513
Titere Tu, in Wilson's *Cheats*, VIII. 122
Titian, XII. 172, 173; XIV. 171
Titinillus. *See* Tutivillus
Titmarsh, Michael Angelo, *pseud.* of W. M. Thackeray, XIII. 278, 281, 284, 294, 422
Titmarsh, Samuel, in Thackeray's *Great Hoggarty Diamond*, XIII. 281
Tito, in *Romola*, XIII. 395, 396
Titus, in school plays, v. 103
Titus, emperor of Rome, X. 303; XII. 249
Titus, Silius (1623?–1704), VII. 460; VIII. 410
Titus and Gesippus, II. 326
Titus and Vespasian, I. 333, 334, 471; v. 221
Tityrus (Vergil's), III. 223
Tiverton academy, X. 387
Tivoli, XII. 419
Tixall, IV. 184
Tixall Poetry, VII. 86
To pass the Place, III. 491
Tobacco, in *The Queenes Arcadia*, VI. 318
Tobacco, king of Trinidado, in *Lingua*, VI. 315
Tobacco in England, An Advice how to plant, IV. 531
Tobacco pamphlets, IV. 530
Tobacconist, The, VI. 28
Tobin, John (1770–1804), XI. 458; *The Honeymoon*, XI. 454
Toby, Abel's Kinsman, IX. 442, 462
Toby, uncle, in Sterne's *Tristram Shandy*, X. 25, 50 ff.
Tocqueville, Alexis C. H. Clérel de, XI. 26; XII. 475
Tod, James (1782–1835), XII. 513; XIV. 580; *Annals and Antiquities of Rajasthan*, XIV. 335; *Antiquities of Rajpootana*, XII. 352
Todd, Alpheus (1821–1884), XIV. 359, 584
Todd, Henry John (1763–1845), X. 239, 461
Todd, James Henthorn (1805–1869), XII. 360, 519; XIV. 571; *St Patrick, Apostle of Ireland*, XII. 361; *Life of St Patrick*, XIV. 328
'Todgers's,' in *Martin Chuzzlewit*, XIII. 323, 423
Todhunter, Isaac (1820–1884), XIV. 555, 565, 610
Todhunter, John (1839–1916), XII. 400, 404; XIII. 510; XIV. 211, *also see* Add. 3
Todlen Butt and Todlen Ben, IX. 360

Toft Trees, Norfolk, VI. 290
Tofte, Robert (d. 1620), III. 209, 256, 264, 266; IV. 442
  Ariostos Satyres, IV. 377, 520, 540
  Blazon of Jealousie, The, III. 209
  Laura, III. 257, 266, 524
  Pastoralls of Julietta, IV. 377
Tokens, The Fifteen, II. 329
Toland, John (1670–1722), VIII. 332, 410; IX. 17, 282, 289 ff., 294, 295, 300, 427, 508
  Amyntor, IX. 291, 297
  Christianity not mysterious, VIII. 331; IX. 289 ff.
  Letters to Serena, IX. 290, 291
  Life of Milton, IX. 291
  Nazarenus, IX. 291
  Pantheisticon, IX. 292
Toledo, XIII. 452
Toledo, scholars at, I. 153, 199; II. 365; IV. 69
Toleration act, X. 373, 376, 378, 380, 382
Toller, Thomas Northcote, XIV. 611
Tolomei, VII. 265
Tolosa, IX. 269
Tolous, Erl of, I. 471
Tolstoy, Leo, count, V. 208; XII. 250
Tom, in *King Lear*, V. 263
Tom, in Steele's *Conscious Lovers*, IX. 64
Tom, Corinthian (Egan's), XIV. 223, 224, 226, 227, 230
Tom a Lincoln, XI. 334
Tom of all Trades, V. 364
Tom of Bedlam, VI. 297
Tom Drum, in *Master Peachey and his men*, III. 369, 372
Tom Potts, II. 411
Tom Tel-Troths Message and his pens Complaint, IV. 352; V. 363
Tom Tell-Trothe's New-yeares Gift, IV. 353, 526, 527; V. 355, 479
Tom Thynne's Ghost, VIII. 92
Tom Tosspot, II. 232
Tom Tyler and his Wife, V. 117, 118, 410
Tomkin, the Tinker, in *Piers the Plowman*, II. 16
Tomkins, Thomas (d. 1656), IV. 465
Tomkis or Tomkys, Thomas (*fl.* 1604–1615), VI. 315, 479; VIII. 400; X. 433; *Albumazar*, IV. 410; VI. 314, 322, 323; VIII. 366; *Lingua*, VI. 314, 322, 323, 327
Tomkyn, in *Turnament of Totenham*, I. 366
Tomkyns or Tomkins, Thomas (1637?–1675), VII. 117, 120
Tomline, Sir George Pretyman (1750–1827), XIV. 507
Tomlins, Frederick Guest (1804–1867), XIV. 236
Tomlinson, in Lytton's *Paul Clifford*, XIII. 418
Tomlyn (Marprelate printer), III. 382
Tommy, in *The Little Pretty Pocket Book*, XI. 376
'Tommy Lucretius,' X. 122
Tommy Thumb's Pretty Song Book, XI. 375

Tompson, Charles, jun., XIV. 587; *Wild Notes*, XIV. 362
Tomson, Rosamund. *See* Watson, Rosamund Marriott
Tomy Lin, XI. 231
Tonbridge school, III. 428; VII. 330
Tone, Theobald Wolfe (1763–1798), XIV. 514, 571
Tong, William (1662–1727), X. 385
Tongue, Cornelius, XIV. 541
Tongue, Israel (1621–1680), 'Apocalyptical Expositions,' VIII. 286
Tonna, Charlotte Elizabeth, *The Maiden City*, XIV. 321
Tönnies, F., VII. 288
Tonson, Jacob (d. 1735), XI. 320
Tonson, Jacob (1656?–1736), VII. 117, 141; VIII. 44, 49, 213, 392, 394, also *see* Add.; IX. 68, 77, 162, 350; XI. 318 ff., 327, 332, 334; *Miscellany*, IX. 68, 74, 119, 165, 446; XI. 319, 320
Tonson, Jacob (d. 1767), X. 180; XI. 320, 323
Toogood, C. G., XIV. 490
Tooke, John Horne (1736–1812), X. 402, 524; XI. 400; XII. 494; *Diversions of Purley, The*, X. 401, 405; XII. 326
Tooke, Thomas (1774–1858), XIV. 482
Tooke, William (1777–1863), X. 524
Toole, John L., XIII. 515
Tooley or Toolie, Nicholas, VI. 139
Toomevara (Charlotte Eccles's), XIV. 325
Tooting, IX. 7
Toots, in *Dombey and Son*, XIII. 325
Top Book of All, XI. 375, 386, 490
Topcliffe, Richard (1532–1604), IV. 128
Topham, captain, XIV. 214
Toplady, Augustus Montagu (1740–1778), X. 365, 517; *An old Fox tarred and feathered*, X. 367; *Historic Proof*, X. 367; 'Rock of Ages,' X. 367
Topsell, Edward (d. 1638?), VIII. 479; *Historie of Fourefooted Beastes*, IV. 374; *The Historie of Serpents*, IV. 374; *Theater of Insects*, IV. 374
Torchbearers' dance, the, in *The Lords' Masque*, VI. 354
Torcy, Jean-Baptiste Colbert, marquis de, IX. 152, 216
Torfaeus, Thermodus, X. 225
Torfrida, in Kingsley's *Hereward the Wake*, XIII. 366
Tories, XIII. 14, 24
Tories Confession, VIII. 97
Tories' Triumph, VIII. 97
Torigni, Robert de. *See* Robert de Monte
Tor-lutha, X. 229
Toronto, XIV. 343, 349, 358
  Trinity college, XIV. 350
  University of, XII. 351
Torquatus (*i.e.* Ben Jonson), VI. 39
Torquemada, Antonio de, IV. 448
Torquil, in Byron's *The Island*, XII. 46
Torrens, Henry Whitelock (1806–1852), XIV. 337, 580
Torrens, Robert (1780–1864), XIV. 194, 482

Torrens, William Torrens McCullagh (1813–1894), XIV. 510, 511, 513, 571; *Life of Melbourne*, XIV. 326

Torrent of Portugal, I. 316, 472; II. 182

Torrigiano, Pietro, IV. 227

Toscar, X. 229

Tosier, captain John, IV. 462

Total Rout, A, VII. 382

Totila, king of the Goths in Italy, XIII. 461

Totnes, X. 352

Totnes, earl of. *See* Carew, Sir George

Tottel, Richard (d. 1594), II. 198; III. 166, 180, 181, 194, 248; IV. 384, 396, 546; *Tottel's Miscellany*, III. 134 ff., 166, 170, 173, 174, 179 ff., 185 ff., 248, 283, 509, 524; IV. 110, 168, 170, 387, 397, 546; VII. 1

Tottenham, XII. 417

Touchstone, in *As You Like It*, V. 190, 192, 193, 214; XIII. 64

Touchstone, in *Eastward Hoe*, VI. 48

Touchwood, lady, in Congreve's *Double-Dealer*, VIII. 148, 149

Touchwood, lord, in Congreve's *Double-Dealer*, VIII. 148

Toulmin, Joshua (1740–1815), IX. 494; X. 518, 520

Toulouse, X. 335; XIII. 88

Toulouse, Dominicans at, I. 200

Toup, Jonathan (1713–1785), XII. 494; *Emendations on Suidas*, XII. 324, 490

Tour of Dr Syntax through London, The, XIV. 219

Touraine, IX. 226

Tourguénieff, Ivan S., XIII. 195

Touris, William, *The Contemplacyon of sinners*, II. 323

Tournay, in *The Unfortunate Traveller*, III. 363

Tournay, John, VII. 33

Tournay, siege of, Laurence Minot on, I. 357, 359

Tournehem, III. 3

Tourneur, Cyril (1575?–1626), V. 327, 376; VI. 116, 128, 166–187, 444, 459, *also see* Add.; XII. 116

Atheist's Tragedie, The, VI. 137, 166, 167, 179

Funeral Poem, A (on Sir Francis Vere), VI. 166

Griefe on the Death of Prince Henry, A, VI. 166

Nobleman, The, VI. 166

Revengers Tragoedie, The, VI. 166, 167, 178, 179

Transformed Metamorphosis, The, VI. 166

Tours, VIII. 245

Tout, Thomas Frederick, XIV. 485, 497

Tovey, Duncan Crookes (1842–1912), X. 103, 451; XIII. 488, 508; XIV. 507

Towgood, Matthew (*fl.* 1710–1746), X. 385, 387

Towgood, Michaijah (1700–1792), X. 374, 384, 387; *The Dissenting Gentleman's Answer*, X. 375

Towneley MSS., IX. 565

Towneley plays, III. 91; V. 13, 15, 18, 20, 40, 47, 389, 390

Townley, in Sheridan's *Trip to Scarborough*, XI. 268

Townley, James (1714–1778), X. 432, 438; *False Concord*, X. 90; *High Life below Stairs*, X. 88

Townley Gallery, XII. 509

Townsend, Joseph (1739–1816), XI. 400; *Dissertation on the Poor Laws*, XI. 74

Townsend, Meredith White (1831–1911), XIV. 198, 535

Townshend or Townsend, Aurelian (*fl.* 1601–1643), VII. 16, 20, 413, *also see* Add.

Townshend, Charles, 2nd viscount Townshend (1674–1738), IX. 16, 17, 163, 219

Townshend, Charles (1725–1767), X. 399, 523; XI. 10, 12

Townshend, Chauncey Hare (1798–1868), XIII. 542

Townshend, Hayward (*fl.* 1601), VII. 440

Townshend, lord John, XI. 35

Towton, battle of, II. 306

Towton, battlefield of, V. 171

Towwouse, Mrs, in Fielding's *Joseph Andrews*, X. 26

Tox, Miss, in *Dombey and Son*, XIII. 325

Toynbee, Arnold (1852–1883), XIV. 592

Toynbee, Paget, XII. 415, 525

Toynbee, Mrs Paget, X. 247, 248, 250, 251, 284, 495, *also see* Add.; XI. 282

Tozer, in Mrs Oliphant's *Salem Chapel*, XIII. 431

Tozer, Henry Fanshawe (1829–1916), XII. 475, *also see* Add. 4

Trabb's boy, in *Great Expectations*, XIII. 334

Tracts, collections of, in Jacobean times, VII. 455

Tracts for the Times, XII. 256, 257, 276, 455 ff.; XIII. 358

Tracy, Antoine L. C. Destutt, comte de, XIV. 6, 8

Trade books, XI. 325

Trade catalogues, early, IV. 548

Trade and Plantations commission, IX. 406

Tradescant, John (d. 1637?), XIV. 285

Tradescant, John (1608–1662), XIV. 285, 564

Trafton, A., XIII. 559

Tragedus, in *Lingua*, VI. 315

Tragedy, in *A Warning for Faire Women*, V. 326

Tragedy, in *The Muses Looking-Glasse*, VI. 233

Tragedy, early English, V. 394

Traherne, Philip (d. 1723), VII. 404

Traherne, Thomas (1637?–1674), VII. 15, 42 ff. (main entry), 144, 153, 155, 157, 163, 403, 404, 427, *also see* Add.; XI. 384

Centuries of Meditations, VII. 43, 143

Christian Ethics, VII. 43

News, VII. 44

Poems, VII. 43

Traherne, Thomas
  Roman Forgeries, VII. 43
  Serious and patheticall Contemplation of
    the Mercies of God, A, VII. 43
  Silence, VII. 44
  Thoughts, poems on, VII. 44
  Ways of Wisdom, The, VII. 44
  Wonder, VII. 44
Traill, Catharine Parr (1802–1899), XIV.
  581; Lost in the Backwoods (The Cana-
  dian Crusoes), XIV. 360
Traill, Henry Duff (1842–1900), I. ix;
  X. 422; XI. 417; XIII. 464, 473, 478, 510,
  544, 545, 547, also see Add. 2; XIV. 511,
  527
  Age of Despair, The, XIII. 166
  Ballad of Baloonatics Craniocracs, The,
    XIII. 166
  Enfant Terrible, An, XIII. 166
  Laputa Outdone, XIII. 166
  New Fiction, The, XIV. 146
  New Lucian, The, XIV. 146
  Number Twenty, XIV. 146
  Recaptured Rhymes, XIII. 166
  Saturday Songs, XIII. 166; XIV. 146
  Social England, editor of, I. 363
Trajan, emperor of Rome, II. 76; XII. 303
Tranent Muir, IX. 373
Tranquillus, in The Tatler, IX. 39
Transit, Robert, pseud. See Cruikshank,
  Isaac Robert
Transition English, I. 217 ff., 335 ff.,
  458 ff., 474 ff.
Transition English song collections, II.
  372 ff., 490 ff.
Translators, IV. 1 ff., 435 ff.
Transome, Harold, in Felix Holt, XIII. 397
Transubstantiation, VIII. 296
Trant, Olive, IX. 219
Traperon, William, IV. 446
Trapezuntius, III. 50
Trapp, Joseph (1679–1747), IX. 181, 184,
  487, 510, 512, 519
Trappola, in The Bugbears, V. 115
Trautmann, M., I. 60, 118
Travailes of The three English Brothers,
  The, IV. 533
Traveller, The, XIV. 194
Travers, Walter (1548?–1635), III. 405,
  406, 413, 426; IV. 236
Travis, George (1741–1797), X. 310; XII.
  490; Letters to Gibbon, X. 309, 508;
  XII. 323
Treasury of South African Poetry and
  Verse, The, XIV. 377
Treatise of a Gallant, IX. 51
Trebizond, II. 79
Treble, H. R., XIV. 528
Tregarva, in Kingsley's Yeast, XIII. 360,
  361
Tregelles, Samuel Prideaux (1813–1875),
  XII. 340, 501
Trelawney, Edward John (1792–1881),
  XII. 38, 76, 398, 404, 452; XIV. 527;
  Recollections of...Shelley and Byron, XII.
  37

Trelawny, Sir Jonathan (1650–1721),
  bishop of Winchester, IX. 151; X. 352
Tremebundus or Tremulus (Charles Lamb),
  XII. 200
Tremellius, John Immanuel (1510–1580),
  III. 422
Tremor, Sir Luke, in Mrs Inchbald's Such
  Things Are, XI. 278
Trench, Miss Maria (1828?–1917), XII.
  Add. 2
Trench, Melesina (1768–1827), XII. 452
Trench, Richard Chenevix (1807–1886),
  VII. 41; XI. 407; XII. 271 ff., 452, 463;
  XIII. 24, 167, 173, 510; XIV. 611; Lord!
  many times I am aweary quite, XIII. 174;
  Sacred Latin Poetry, XIII. 172
Trench, W. F., III. 193, 194
Trent, in Fielding's Amelia, X. 33
Trent, council of, III. 30, 400; VII. 190;
  X. 460; XII. 260; XIV. 100
Trent, Mr, in The Old Curiosity Shop,
  XIII. 319
Trent, river, IV. 190
Trentals of St Gregory, I. 312
Tresham (Browning's), XIII. 67
Trevecca, X. 366
Trevelyan, George Macaulay, II. 38; XIII.
  568; The life of John Bright, XIV. 133,
  508
Trevelyan, Sir George Otto, XI. 396; XII.
  427; XIV. 60, 493, 537
Treveris, Peter (fl. 1527), IV. 374
Treves, V. 39; XIV. 303
Treves, Sir Frederick, XIII. 485
Treveth. See Trivet
Trevisa, John (1326–1412), II. 59, 70 ff.,
  85, 188, 189, 287, 295, 300, 313, 323,
  333, 444; III. 441
Trevithick, Richard (1771–1833), XIV. 258
Trevor, Sir John (1637–1717), VIII. 482
Trévoux, Mémoires de, V. 291
Trial of Treasure, The, V. 60, 393
Triamour, Sir, I. 316, 465, 471
Tribulation, in The Alchemist, VI. 22, 23
Tribulation, The Twelve profits of, II. 323
Tribune, The, XIV. 202
Trier, IV. 429
Trieste, XIV. 313
Trifler, The, XIV. 387
Trim, corporal, in Sterne's Tristram
  Shandy, X. 50, 51, 53, 55
Trim, Ireland, IX. 93
Trimmer, Mrs Sarah (1741–1810), XI. 372,
  374, 383, 476, 483; XIV. 592, 602, 610
  Comparative view of the New Plan of
    Education, A, XIV. 402, 403
  Fabulous Histories (The History of the
    Robins), XI. 378 ff.
  Familiar Introduction to the Knowledge
    of Nature, XI. 382
  Guardian of Education, XI. 380
  Oeconomy of Charity, The, XIV. 390
  Reflections upon...charity schools, XIV.
    389
Trincalo, in Albumazar, VI. 323
Trinculo, in The Tempest, V. 206

Trinidad, IV. 61
Trinitarianism, X. 379
Trinity, the, XII. 283
Trinity, the, in *The foure P.P.*, V. 97
Trinity, Pageant of the Holy, V. 9
Trinity in Unity, dogma of, III. 243
Trinket, lord, in Colman's *Jealous Wife*,
   X. 89, 90
Trinket, Mrs (Etherege's), VIII. 138
'Trip, Tommy,' XI. 377
Triple alliance of 1668, VIII. 381; IX. 228
Tripoli, XI. 72
Tripolis, in Syria, IV. 84
Trismegist, VIII. 282
Trissino, III. 290, *also see* Add.; VII. 265;
   Sofonisba, V. 62
Tristram, Sir, in Arthurian legend, I. 236,
   261, 267, 270, 272 ff., 282, 283, 290,
   297 ff., 309, 310, 313, 316, 462, 471;
   II. 100, 336, 337; III. 68
Tristram and Iseult, II. 174
Tristrem, Sir, II. 272
Trithemius, Johannes, III. 112; *Anti-
   phonus Maleficiorum*, III. 112
Trivet or Treveth, Nicholas (1258–1328?),
   I. 181, 450; II. 150; V. 61
Trivium, the, II. 229, 230, 359, 363, 366;
   VI. 310; VII. 320
Troad, the, XIV. 252
Troilus, I. 306
Troilus, in *Confessio Amantis*, II. 148
Troilus, in Dryden's *Troilus and Cressida*,
   VIII. 29
Troilus, in Henryson's *Testament of Cres-
   seid*, II. 248
Troilus and Cressida, III. 181, 190
Trojan horse, the, VIII. 73; XI. 252
Trojan war, the, IV. 136
Trokelowe, John of (*fl.* 1330), I. 181
Trollope, Sir Andrew (d. 1461), II. 303
Trollope, Anthony (1815–1882), XI. 149;
   XII. 245; XIII. 386, 421 ff. (main entry),
   427, 432, 530, 544, 566; XIV. 194, 554
   Autobiography, XIII. 421, 424
   Barchester novels, XIII. 430
   Barchester Towers, XIII. 422
   Doctor Thorne, XIII. 422
   Duke's Children, The, XIII. 423
   Framley Parsonage, XIII. 422
   Kellys and the O'Kellys, The, XIII. 421
   Last Chronicles of Barset, The, XIII. 422
   Macdermots of Ballycloran, The, XIII.
      421
   Orley Farm, XIII. 423
   Phineas Finn, XIII. 423
   Small House at Allington, The, XIII.
      422, 423
   Three Clerks, The, XIII. 421
   Vendée, La, XIII. 421
   Vicar of Bullhampton, The, XIII. 423
   Warden, The, XIII. 332, 422
   Way We Live Now, The, XIII. 423
Trollope, Frances (1780–1863), XII. 245,
   452; XIII. 322, 421; *The Vicar of
   Wrexhill*, XII. 246; *The Widow Barnaby*,
   XII. 246

Trollope, Thomas Adolphus (1810–1892),
   XII. 245; XIII. 567; XIV. 598
Trombet, Anthony, III. 50
Tropes, V. 11
'Trot, John' (viscount Bolingbroke), IX.
   221
Trot of Turriff, the, VII. 254
Trotte, Nicholas (*fl.* 1588), V. 77
Trotter, Mrs A. F., XIV. Add. 10
Trotter, John Bernard (1775–1818), XII.
   439
Trotton, Sussex, VIII. 181
Trotwood, Miss Betsey, in *David Copper-
   field*, XIII. 327
Troubadours, Provençal, V. 26
Trouvères, V. 3, 21, 26, 27
Trowbridge, Wiltshire, XI. 148, 149
Trowbridge academy, X. 387
Trowle, in *The Play of the Shepherds*, V.
   19
Troy, V. 69, 227; VIII. 23; XII. 338, 497
Troy, in *The Four Ages*, VI. 92
Troy, Gest Hystoriale of the Destruction of,
   I. 306, 333, 472; II. 118, 202, 450
Troy, legends of, I. 148, 195, 234, 258,
   279, 285, 306, 342; II. 172, 301
Troy, plains of, XIII. 353
Troy Book, I. 291, 333, 334
Troy-books, V. 196, 221
Troye, VI. 93
Troylous and Pandor, VI. 283
Trudge, in Colman's *Inkle and Yarico*,
   XI. 279
*True and impartial Narrative of the Dis-
   senters' New Plot, A*, VIII. 99
'True Blue Poet, the,' VIII. 40
*True description of the Pot-Companion
   Poet, A*, VII. 387
*True Inventory of the goods and chattels of
   Superstition, A*, VII. 382
True Loyalist, IX. 376
True Patriot, The, X. 28, 29, 417
True Presbyterian without Disguise, The
   (1680), VII. 409
True Relation, in *The Palice of Honour*,
   II. 261
Trueman, in Lillo's *George Barnwell*, X. 74,
   75
Trulla, in *Hudibras*, VIII. 68, 69
Trulliber, parson, in Fielding's *Joseph
   Andrews*, X. 20, 26
Trumbull, Thomas, in Scott's *Redgauntlet*,
   XII. 21
Trumbull, Sir William (1639–1716), IX.
   68, 74, 149
Trumpet Club, in *The Tatler*, IX. 50
Trunnion, commodore, in Smollett's *Pere-
   grine Pickle*, X. 38, 41, 43, 50
Trunnion, Grizzle, in Smollett's *Peregrine
   Pickle*, X. 38
Truscott, S. J., XIV. Add. 10
Truso, in Ohthere's voyage, I. 94
Trussell, John (d. 1642), *Touchstone of
   Tradition*, VII. 444
Truth, XIV. 190, 200
Truth, in Anglo-Norman plays, V. 21

Truth, in Carew's *Coelum Britannicum*, VII. 19

Truth, in *Horestes*, V. 64, 65

Truth, in Medwall's interlude, V. 54

Truth, in *Piers the Plowman*, II. 2 ff., 12, 13, 15

Truth, in *The Passetyme of Pleasure*, II. 229, 235

Truth, in *Two Lamentable Tragedies*, V. 326

Truth, ffaythfulnesse and Mercye, V. 102

Truth Flatters Not, VII. 381

Tryall of Chevalry, The, VI. 459

Tryan, in George Eliot's *Janet's Repentance*, XIII. 388

Tryce, John, VI. 287

Tryman, Mrs, in *The City Witt*, VI. 229

Tryon, Thomas (1634–1703), IX. 307, 515

Tschudi, Ægidius, X. 304

Tuam, XIV. 329

Tubbe, Henry, VII. Add.

Tubney academy, X. 387

Tucca, in *Satiro-Mastix*, VI. 42, 44, 272

Tucca, in *The Poetaster*, V. 315; VIII. 127

Tuck, friar, V. 35, 318

Tuck, friar, in Scott's *Ivanhoe*, XII. 18

Tucker, Abraham (1705–1774), X. 346, 514; XI. 250; XII. 431; XIII. 244; *Freewill, Foreknowledge and Fate*, X. 343; *Light of Nature pursued*, X. 343; *Man in Quest of Himself*, X. 343

Tucker, Herbert, XIV. Add. 5

Tucker, Josiah (1712–1799), XI. 73; XIV. 593

Tucker, Miss, in Jerrold's *Time Works Wonders*, XIII. 269

Tucker, R., XIV. 556

Tucker, Thomas (*fl.* 1607), VI. 319 ff.

Tuckney, Anthony (1599–1670), VIII. 274 ff., 291, 457; *Eight Letters*, VIII. 276

Tuckwell, William, XIV. 596

Tudor, Charley (Trollope's), XIII. 423

Tudor, Jasper, Duke of Bedford, The Epitaph of, II. 321

Tudor, Owen (d. 1461), IV. 182; VIII. 22

Tudor period, X. 40, 283, 284; XI. 367; XIV. 86

Tudor princesses, XIV. 111

Tudors, the, IV. 135; VIII. 132, 312, 315, 356; XIV. 75

Tuer, Andrew White (1838–1900), XI. 476; XIV. 610

Tuffley, Mary, wife of Defoe, IX. 6

Tufnell, Henry (1805–1854), XII. 301

Tufthunt, Tom, in Thackeray's *A Shabby Genteel Story*, XIII. 299

Tuftons, the, IX. 168

Tuke, Sir Brian (d. 1545), II. 161

Tuke, Sir Samuel (d. 1674), VII. 518; *Adventures of Five Hours*, VIII. 16, 130, 131, 421, 423

Tulkinghorn, Mr, in *Bleak House*, XIII. 329

Tulliver, Mr and Mrs, in *The Mill on the Floss*, XIII. 392

Tulliver, Maggie, in *The Mill on the Floss*, XIII. 382, 392, 393

Tulliver, Tom, in *The Mill on the Floss*, XIII. 382

Tulloch, John (1823–1886), XII. 286, 464; XIV. 483

Tulloch, William Weir, XIV. 516

Tullus Aufidius, in *Coriolanus*, V. 198

Tully, in *The Palice of Honour*, II. 261. *See, also*, Cicero

Tully's *Offices*, IX. 274

Tuman-bey, in *Tomumbeius*, VI. 301

Tunbridge school, XIV. 388

Tunbridge Wells, VIII. 159, 262; X. 207; XI. 347

Tundale, The Vision of, XIV. 306

Tungland, flying friar of, II. 255

Tunis, IX. 245

Tunstall, Cuthbert (1474–1559), III. 7, 40, 42

Tupper, Martin Farquhar (1810–1889), XIII. 147, 201, 510; *Crock of Gold, The*, XIII. 149; *Proverbial Philosophy*, XIII. 148 ff.

Turbervil, Henry (d. 1678), *Manual of Controversies*, VIII. 47

Turbervile, George (1540?–1610), III. 177, 186, 187, 190, 201, 204, 209, 283 ff., 510; IV. 389, 446, 541; VIII. 224, 225

Booke of faulconrie, IV. 373

Epitaphs, Epigrams, and Sonets, III. 187, 524

Green that you wish me wear, The, III. 187

Heroical Epistles of...Ovid, trans., III. 187; IV. 19, 439

Lover, The, III. 187

Noble arte of venerie or hunting, IV. 374

Pretie epigram of a scholer, III. 187

Rayling Rout of Sycophants, To the, III. 187

Tragical Tales, IV. 7, 442

Translations of Mancinus's *A Plaine Path to Perfect Vertue*, Mantuan's *Eclogues*, III. 187

'Turbulent, Mr,' X. 254

Turenne, Henri de la Tour d'Auvergne, vicomte de, VII. 452; VIII. 202

Turgenev, Ivan, *The Jew*, IX. 39

Turgesius, Norwegian conqueror of Ireland, in *Albion's England*, IV. 136

Turgis, or Clarges, Miss, wife of Giles Dury, VII. 363

Turgot (d. 1115), I. 451

Turgot, Anne-R.-J., *Réflexions*, X. 336

Turin, IV. 277; X. 323

Turk, A (Defoe), IX. 19

Turk, Milton Haight, *Legal Code of Alfred*, I. 97

Turk, the Great, V. 97

Turkestan, II. 79; IX. 248

Turkey, IV. 89, 325; VII. 200, 201; VIII. 137, 308; IX. 247, 248; XII. 42; XIV. 135, 179, 182

Turkey company, the, IV. 98; IX. 240

Turkish captain, in *A Challenge for Beautie*, VI. 103

Turkish knight, the, in the mummers' play, V. 33

Turkish language and literature, IX. 245;
  XII. 342; XIV. 458
Turkish Spy, IX. 19
Turks, in The Renegado, VI. 155
Turks, the, II. 330; VII. 442, 449, 453;
  VIII. 286; IX. 6; XII. 38, 45
Türlin, H. von dem, I. 269
Turnament of Totenham, I. 366, 480;
  II. 501
Turnbull, Arthur, XI. 416
Turnbull, William (d. 1454), II. 369
Turnebus, Adrian, III. 424; VII. 307
Turner, C. L., Original Records, X. 384
Turner, Charles Tennyson (1808–1879),
  XII. 119; XIII. 23, 45 ff., 473, 478, 479
  Buoy-Bell, The, XIII. 46
  Lattice at Sunrise, The, XIII. 46
  Letty's Globe, XIII. 46
  Ocean, The, XIII. 46
  Sonnets, Old and New, XIII. 46
Turner, Daniel (1710–1798), X. 475;
  Cautionary Stories (The Daisy, The
  Cowslip), XI. 384, 476, 483
Turner, Henry Gyles, XIV. 584
Turner, Joseph Horsfall, XIII. 557, 559
Turner, Joseph Mallord William (1775–
  1851), II. 336; XII. 173, 346, 372, 382,
  408, 409, 411; XIV. 150, 151, 154, 516,
  523, 524
Turner, Mr, and Hannah More, XI. 360
Turner, Robert (fl. 1640–1664), VII. 509
Turner, Sharon (1768–1847), XIV. 51, 67,
  499; History of England, XIV. 52; His-
  tory of the Anglo-Saxons, XII. 344
Turner, Thomas, VII. 515
Turner, W. (?), VI. 483
Turner, Whitely, XIII. 559
Turner, William, dean of Wells (d. 1568),
  III. 81, 474; IV. 542; VIII. 479
  Enlightment against Mother Messe, III.
  81
  Examination of the Mass, III. 81
  Hunting of the Fox, The, III. 81
  Hunting of the Wolf, The, III. 81
  New herball, IV. 374, 403
Turner, William (1761–1859), XIII. 372
Turnop, in John a Kent, V. 317
Turnus (Vergil's), III. 305
Turton, Thomas (1780–1864), bishop of
  Ely, XII. 325, 478, 481, 491; XIV. 593,
  599
Tuscany, II. 119
Tusculum. See Nicholas of
Tusser, Thomas (1524?–1580), III. 183 ff.,
  281, 285, 510; IV. 371, 407, 513; V. 480;
  VIII. 223, 231; XII. 416
  Conditions of Husbandrie, The, III. 184
  Five Hundreth pointes of good hus-
  bandry, III. 183; IV. 370, 375
  Hundreth good pointes of husbandrie, A,
  III. 183; IV. 370
  Hundreth good poynts of huswifery, III. 183
  Ladder to Thrift, The, III. 184
  Things Thriftie, III. 184
Tutchin, John (1661?–1707), VIII. 411;
  IX. 8; The Observator, IX. 5

Tutin, John Ramsden, XI. 406, 411
Tutivillus, the merry devil, V. 44, 47, 52,
  56
Tuvill, David, IV. 524; Essayes morall and
  theologicall, IV. 345; Essayes politicke
  and morall, IV. 345
Twa Corbies, The, II. 412
Twain, Mark, The Prince and the Pauper,
  III. 104
'Twas within a Furlong of Edinburgh
  Town, IX. 363
Tweddell, George Markham, XII. 415
Tweddell, John (1769–1799), XI. 429
Tweed, river, II. 88, 90, 100; IV. 303, 304;
  VII. 208; X. 110; XII. 11
Twelfth Day Gift, XI. 376
Twelfth Night feast, VII. 12
Twells, Leonard (d. 1740), IX. 529
Twelve Tables, the, III. 113
Twemlow, in Our Mutual Friend, XIII. 337
Twickenham, VII. 21; IX. 77, 78, 163, 246,
  250, 448; X. 360
Twineall, in Mrs Inchbald's Such Things
  Are, XI. 278
Twining, Thomas (1735–1804), XII. 494
Twiss, Horace (1787–1849), XIV. 509
Twisse, William (1578?–1646), VII. 482,
  484
Twist, Oliver (Dickens's), XIII. 316
'Twitcher, Jemmy,' X. 397
Two Noble Kinsmen, The, V. 236, 238,
  255 ff., 442, 444
Twrch Trwyth (Nennius's porcus Troit), I.
  247, 254
Twyford, in Motteux's Rabelais, IX. 272
Twyn, John, IX. 2; XI. 313
Twyne, Brian (1579?–1644), VII. 247; IX.
  346, 347, 540
Twyne, Lawrence (fl. 1576), IV. 449
Twyne, Thomas (1543–1613), III. 448;
  IV. 436, 440, 445, 447; Phisicke against
  Fortune, VI. 378, 390, 498
Twysden, Sir Roger (1597–1672), IX. 344,
  540
Twysdens, the, IX. 168
Tyb, in Johan Johan, V. 98
Tydd St Giles, X. 377
Tyerman, Luke, X. 518
Tyers, Thomas (1726–1787), IX. 438; X.
  471
Tyke, in Morton's School of Reform, XI. 281
Tyler, Josiah, XIV. Add. 10
Tyler, Miss, XI. 155
Tyler, Wat, I. 369; II. 346
Tyll Howleglas. See Howleglass
Tymme, Thomas (d. 1620), IV. 442
Tynan, Katharine. See Hinkson, Katha-
  rine Tynan
Tyndale, William. See Tindale
Tyndall, John (1820–1893), XIV. 261, 554,
  557
Tyndarus, in The Jealous Lovers, VI. 325
Tyne, river, XII. 10
Typhon, IX. 502
Typographical Antiquities, II. 319
Týr (Old Norse alphabet), I. 10

Tyre, in *King Alisaunder*, I. 307
Tyrol, XI. 27; XII. 369; XIV. 294
Tyrold, Sir Hugh, in Burney's *Camilla*, x. 65
Tyrone, county, XIV. 314
Tyrone, earl of. *See* O'Neill, Hugh
Tyros Roving Megge, IV. 519
Tyrrell, Elizabeth, lady, IV. 434
Tyrrell, George (1861–1909), XII. 461, 470; *Nova et Vetera*, XII. 299
Tyrrell, James (1642–1718), VII. 475; IX. 233, 506
Tyrrell, Robert Yelverton (1844–1914), XII. 338, 494; XIV. 211, 538, 573
Tyrrell family, II. 81
'Tyrtaeus of the United Irishmen,' XIV. 310
Tyrwhit, W., IV. 525
Tyrwhitt, Thomas (1730–1786), II. 22, 160, 163 ff., 198, 207, 215, 217; V. 277; x. 241, 485, 491; XI. 250, 251, 255, 333; XII. 494; *Essay on the Language…of Chaucer*, x. 241; *Introductory Discourse to the Canterbury Tales*, x. 241
Tysilio's *Brut*, I. 235, 263
Tyssot de Patot, S., IX. 428
Tytan, in *The Golden Age*, VI. 93
Tytler, Alexander Fraser, lord Woodhouselee (1747–1813), x. 510; XIV. 94; *Roman History*, XII. 301
Tytler, James (1747?–1805), XIV. 535; *Bonnie Brucket Lassie*, XI. 235; *I hae laid a Herring in Saut*, XI. 235
Tytler, Patrick Fraser (1791–1849), XIV. 499; *History of Scotland*, XIV. 94, 95
Tytler, William (1711–1792), II. 241; XIV. 94; *Inquiry as to the Evidence…against Mary Queen of Scots*, x. 288, 465, 505
Tyton, Francis (*fl.* 1649–1669), XI. 316

Uath Mac Denomain, giant in *Fled Bricrend*, I. 327
Ubaldini, cardinal, IV. 259
Ubbe, in *Havelok*, I. 304
Udall or Uvedale, John (1560?–1592), III. 183, 376 ff., 383 ff., 389 ff., 397, 539, 552; IV. 494; *Demonstration of Discipline, A*, III. 380, 384; *Dialogue concerning the strife of our Church, A*, III. 376; *Diotrephes*, III. 377, 378, 380, 381, 389
Udall, Nicholas (1505–1556), IV. 440, 443, 444; V. 102, 103 ff. (main entry), 111, 407; VII. 327, 328; *Ezechias*, V. 70; VI. 298, 479; *Floures for Latine Spekynge*, V. 104; *Ralph Roister Doister*, III. 448; IV. 115; V. 104 ff., 108, 111, 113, 117, 119; VI. 14
Ueberweg, F., *History of Philosophy*, I. 211
Uffenbach, Z. Conrad von, IX. 574; XII. 488
Uganda, XIV. 254
Ugolino, count (Dante's), V. 324; XII. 396
Ugolino, *Philogena*, V. 101
Ulfilas, bishop of the West Goths (b. 311?), I. 7

Ulloa, A. de, XIV. 552
Ulrici, Hermann, V. 305
Ulster, VII. 211, 212; IX. 301
Ulstermen, XIV. 310
Ulysses, III. 181, 293; IX. 60, 256, 259; XIII. 450
Ulysses, in *Confessio Amantis*, II. 149
Ulysses, in *The Four Ages*, VI. 92
Ulysses, in *Thersites*, V. 108
Ulysses, in *Troilus and Cressida*, IV. 298 v. 167, 196
Ulysses (Tennyson's), XIII. 29
Una, in *The Faerie Queene*, II. 234; III. 232, 234, 236, 237; XII. 87
Underdowne, Thomas (*fl.* 1566–1587), *Aethiopian Historie*, IV. 3, 19, 436; *Ovid*, IV. 19, 438, 439
Underhill, Cave (1634–1710?), VIII. 151
Underhill, George Frederick, IX. 164
Underhill, Thomas (*fl.* 1650–1665), XI. 316
Underwood (actor), VI. 277
Underwood (pamphleteer), VII. 356
'Unicorn,' the (ship), IV. 107
Uniformity, Act of (1662), VII. 321
Uniformity, acts of, XIV. 402
Unitarian histories, x. 519
United Irishman, The, XIV. 325
United Provinces, or Dutch republic, VIII. 384
United States of America, XI. 47 ff., 72; XIII. 88, 295; XIV. 49, 66, 72, 143, 293, 318, 321, 324, 344, 346, 434
United States of America, ballads in, II. 396
United States Catalog, XII. 520
Unity (a house), in *Piers the Plowman*, II. 27, 28
Universal Chronicle, or Weekly Gazette, x. 178, 461, 467
Universal Laughter, IX. 567
Universal Review, The, XIII. 450, *also see* Add. 1
Universal Spectator, The, IX. 433
Universal Visiter, The, x. 177, 183, 466
Universities, Act of Incorporation, III. 421
Universities, Reports on, XIV. 602, 603
Universities, schools and scholarship in the 16th century, English, III. 418 ff., 549 ff.
Universities and Public Schools to the time of Colet, II. 341 ff., 487 ff.
University dramas, V. 394; VI. 232, 293–327, 468 ff.
University Maga, The (Edinburgh), XIV. 210
University tutorial classes, XIV. 409
University wits, V. 121–141 (main entry), 181, 186, 414 ff.
Unnion and Valentine, in *The Tatler*, IX. 34
Unthrifts, Ballad against, III. 87, 474
Unwin, Mary (1724–1796), XI. 80, 81, 83, 85, 88, 90, 404
Unwin, Morley (d. 1767), XI. 80

Unwin, William Cawthorne (1745?–1786),
   XI. 91
Upcott, William (1779–1845), VIII. 242;
   XII. 507
'Upheaving of Ælfred, The,' X. 219
Upper Ossory, Anne, countess of (d. 1804),
   X. 247 ff., 255, 495
Uppingham school, VII. 340; XIV. 426
Upplönd (Norway and Sweden), I. 26
Upsala, X. 135
Upton, John (1707–1760), V. 273; IX. 479;
   Critical Observations on Shakespeare,
   IX. 145; editions of Epictetus and
   Spenser's *Faerie Queene*, IX. 145
Upton, Nicholas (1400?–1457), II. 318;
   De officio militari, IV. 376
Ural mountains, XIV. 294
Urania, XII. 74, 114
Urania, in *Cupid's Revenge*, VI. 128
Uranus, planet, XIV. 264
Urbain, Charles, IV. 500
Urban IV, V. 12
Urban V, II. 49
Urban VI, II. 56
Urban, Erich, *Owenus und die deutschen
   Epigrammatiker des XVII Jahrhun-
   derts*, IV. 267
'Urban, Sylvanus,' X. 162; XII. 428
Urbino, VI. 48, 204
Ureisun of ure Louerde, On, I. 233, 459
Urfé, Honoré d', X. 14; *Astrée*, VIII. 14
Uriah, I. 93
Urian, in Arthurian legend, I. 259
Urie, Robert, XI. 341
Urien, lord of Rheged, I. 249
Urizen (Blake's), XI. 190, 193 ff.
Urquhart, Alexander (*fl.* 1660), VII. 254
Urquhart, David (1805–1877), XIV. 137,
   512, 514
Urquhart, John (1808–1827), XII. 523
Urquhart, Sir Thomas (1611–1660), I. 69;
   II. 103; IV. 8; VII. 232, 237, 253 ff., 464;
   VIII. 59, 372, 385; IX. 271
   Ekskubalauron, VII. 255, 258
   Epigrams, VII. 255
   Gargantua, VII. 256
   Logopandecteision, VII. 255, 258
   Pantagruel, VII. 256
   Pantochronocanon, VII. 255
   Rabelais, translation of, VII. 254, 255,
   258
   Trissotetras, VII. 255
Urquhart, Sir Thomas, senior, VII. 253
Urry, John (1666–1715), II. 162; *Chaucer*,
   XI. 322
Ursa Major, constellation of, VIII. 68
Ursely, Mistress, in *The Rival Friends*, VI.
   324
Urson, John, in *The Masque of Augures*,
   VI. 362
Ursula, in Layamon, I. 237
Ursula, the pig woman, in *Bartholomew
   Fayre*, VI. 23
Urthona, in Blake's *Vala*, XI. 195
Ury, VIII. 111
'Usagers,' the, X. 356

Useful Knowledge, society for the Diffu-
   sion of, XIV. 409
Usener, H., II. 407
Ushant, IV. 79
Ushaw college, XIV. 53
Usher, House of, in *Little Dorrit*, XIII. 331
Usk, Thomas (d. 1388), *The Testament of
   Love*, I. 394; II. 159, 162, 164, 166, 469
Usk, river, VII. 37, 38
Ussher, James (1581–1656), archbishop
   of Armagh, IV. 239, 305, 433, 434, 513;
   VII. 32, 33, 46, 105, 124, 139, 148, 153,
   308, 312, 315 ff., 427, 477, 483, 485,
   489; VIII. 268; IX. 233, 530; XIV. 308,
   572; *A Body of Divinitie*, VII. 149; *An-
   nales Veteris et Novi Testamenti*, XIV.
   309; Greek works, VII. 316
Usuard, I. 81
Usuria, in Arbuthnot's *History of John
   Bull*, IX. 134
Usurped Power, in *Kynge Johan*, V. 65
Usury, tracts on, IV. 509 ff., 518
Uter Pendragon, V. 251
Uther, in Arthurian legend, I. 259, 315
Uther Pendragon, in *The Birth of Merlin*,
   V. 250
Utilitarian society (Mill's), XIV. 14
Utopia, IV. 73, 245; VII. 378; XIII. 361
Utrecht, II. 310; VI. 260; IX. 331, 335,
   336; X. 191
Utrecht, congress of, IX. 135
Utrecht, peace of, IX. 69, 171, 218, 226,
   228
Utrecht Psalter, XII. 516
Uttoxeter, XI. 340

'V,' *pseud. See* Clive, Caroline Archer
Vaal, river, XIV. 372
Vacarius, II. 34, 350
Vafprúðnismál, I. 62
Vagabond literature, III. 492
Vagatorum, Liber, III. 102, 104, 492
Vaillant, J., VIII. 466
Vain Glory, in *Mirour de l'Omme*, II. 140
Vain Glory, in *The Example of Virtue*,
   II. 227
Vala, in Blake's poems, XI. 196, 199
Valckenaer, Lodewyk Kaspar, XII. 325
Valdés, Francisco de, IV. 448
Valdes, Juan de, *A Hundred and Ten
   Divine Considerations*, VII. 155
Valence (Browning's), XIII. 64, 67
Valens, emperor of the eastern Roman
   empire, XII. 322
Valentine, in *Wit without Money*, VI. 123
Valentine, in Congreve's *Love for Love*,
   VIII. 151, 152, 158, 164, 168
Valentine and Orson, IX. 35
Valentine and Orson, translation, II. 324
Valentine and Orson, lost play, V. 319
Valentinian, emperor of Rome, XII. 322
Valerio, in *The Dukes Mistris*, VI. 200
Valerius, in *The Rape of Lucrece*, VI. 101
Valerius, Epistle of, to Rufinus, I. 177, 189
Valerius Maximus, II. 129, 150, 366
Valhalla, X. 222

Valiant Welshman, The, VI. 138, 459
Valkyries, I. 40
Valla, in *The Palice of Honour*, II. 260
Valla, Filelfo, IV. 322
Valla, Laurentius, III. 6, 20, 179, 470; IV. 3; *Elegantiae*, III. 429
Valladolid, III. 422; VI. 103
Vallance, Aymer, XIII. 491, 493
Vallans, William (*fl.* 1578–1590), III. 511
Valley of the Shadow of Death, in Bunyan's *Pilgrim's Progress*, VII. 178
Vallombrosa, VIII. 23; XIII. 352
Valpy, Abraham John, XIV. 512
Valuation of gold and silver, II. 330
Vanbrugh, Giles, father of Sir J. V., VIII. 160
Vanbrugh, Sir John (1664–1726), VIII. 133, 146, 157, 159 ff. (main entry), 171, 175, 176, 396, 423, 427, 431; X. 67, 92, 211; XI. 257; XII. 443
  Confederacy, The, translation of d'Ancourt's *Les Bourgeoises à la Mode*, VIII. 162, 168
  Journey to London, A, VIII. 162
  Pilgrim, The, VIII. 120, 396
  Provok'd Wife, The, VIII. 161, 162
  Relapse or Virtue in Danger, The, VIII. 160, 163, 164, 166
  Relapse, The, XI. 268, 455
Vancouver, George (1758–1798), XIV. 244, 245, 554
Vandals, the, XIV. 302
Vandermast (Greene's), V. 136
Van Doren, C., XI. 463
Van Dyck, Sir Anthony, VII. 55
Van Dyke, Henry D., XIII. 478
Vane, Anne (1705–1736), IX. 251
Vane, Sir Henry, the elder (1589–1655), VII. 219
Vane, Sir Henry, the younger (1613–1662), VII. 115, 219, 359, 442, 447, 513
Vane, Sir Walter, VIII. 329
Vanessa. *See* Vanhomrigh, Hester
Van Helmont, J. B., VII. 394, 396
Vanhomrigh, Hester (Swift's Vanessa), IX. 97, 98, 120, 126
Vanity Fair, XIV. 340
Van Lier, XI. 403
Van Mildert, William (1765–1836), X. 359
Van Pape Jans landendes, II. 330
Vansittart, Nicholas, 1st lord Bexley (1766–1821), XIV. 512
Van Wilder, Philip, VI. 282
Vapid, in Reynolds's *Dramatist*, XI. 281
Varallo-Sesia, XIII. 450
Varchi, Benedetto, *Lezzioni*, IX. 61
Vardens, the, in *Barnaby Rudge*, XIII. 320
Varennes, XIII. 12
Varian, Ralph (*i.e.*Duncathail), XIV. 573
Varillas, Antoine, IX. 197, 478, 488; *Histoire de l'Hérésie*, VIII. 46
Varina (Miss Jane Waring), IX. 92
Variorum Dunciad, The, IX. 132
Varnhagen von Ense, Karl August, XIII. 7
Varro, Marcus Terentius, II. 129; IV. 264, 371; VIII. 11

Varronian form of satire, VIII. 36
Vasquez, Francisco, IV. 448
Vathek, in Beckford's novel, XI. 290, 291
Vatican, the, XIII. 74
Vatican decrees, the, XIV. 118
Vaughan, Charles Edwyn, XII. 404, 524; XIII. 473, 490, 491, 493
Vaughan, Henry (1622–1695), I. 232; VII. 15, 26, 37 ff. (main entry), 45, 142, 404, *also see* Add.; XI. 185; XIII. 139, 174, 191, 195
  Amoret, poems to, VII. 38, 40
  Authoris de se Emblema, VII. 47
  Burial of an Infant, The, VII. 41
  Charnel House, VII. 38
  Childhood, VII. 41
  Christ's Nativity, VII. 41
  Corruption, VII. 30, 41
  Dawning, The, VII. 41
  Eagle, The, VII. 40
  Elizabeth, Epitaph on the little lady, VII. 39
  'I saw Eternity the other night,' VII. 41
  Mount of Olives, The, VII. 39, 41
  Olor Iscanus, VII. 38, 42
  Peace, VII. 41
  Pious Thoughts and Ejaculations, VII. 42
  Poems, with the tenth Satyre of Juvenal Englished, VII. 38
  Rainbow, The, VII. 41
  Retirement, The, VII. 42
  Retreat, The, VII. 41
  Rhapsodis, on the Globe tavern, VII. 38
  Silex Scintillans, VII. 37 ff., 47
  Thalia Rediviva, VII. 41
  They are all gone into the world of light, VII. 41
  'To his retired friend, an Invitation to Brecknock,' VII. 39
  True Christmas, The, VII. 42
  World, The, VII. 41
Vaughan, Richard (1550?–1607), IV. 265
Vaughan, Richard, 2nd earl of Carbery (1600?–1686), VIII. 60
Vaughan, Robert (1795–1868), XIV. 507
Vaughan, Robert Alfred (1823–1857), XII. 427, 470
Vaughan, Thomas (1622–1666), VIII. 455; 'Eugenius Philalethes,' VII. 37, 42, 378, 405, 511
Vaughan, Thomas (*fl.* 1772–1820), XI. 281, 458
Vaughan, Thomas (*c.* 1831), XIV. 596
Vaughan, William (1577–1641), III. 306; IV. 462
Vautor, Thomas (*fl.* 1619), IV. 465
Vautrollier, Thomas (d. 1587?), IV. 400, 413
Vaux, F. B., XI. 490
Vaux, Sir Nicholas, 1st baron Vaux of Harrowden (d. 1523), III. 57
Vaux, Thomas, 2nd baron Vaux of Harrowden (1510–1556), III. 179, 189, 508; IV. 466; *Thassault of Cupid upon the fort*, III. 179; *The aged Lover renounceth love*, III. 179; *When I look back*, III. 179

Vaux, William Sandys Wright (1818–1885), XII. 513

Vavasour, in Disraeli's *Tancred*, XIII. 350

Vavasour, Elsley, in Kingsley's *Two Years Ago*, XIII. 160, 361, 365

Veal, Edward (1632?–1708), X. 385

Veale, captain, in Fielding's *Voyage to Lisbon*, X. 35

Vedas, the, XII. 502

Vega, Lope de, VIII. 128, 130, 144; *Don Lope de Cardona*, VIII. 129; *Mayor Imposibile*, VIII. 189

Vega, Luis Gutierres de la, IV. 448

Vegetius, Flavius, II. 366; IV. 440

Veitch, John (1829–1894), XI. 446; XIV. 474, 483

Veitch, William (1640–1722), XIV. 493, 507

Veitch, William (1794–1885), XII. 494

Veitia Linage, Joseph de, *The Spanish Rule of Trade to the West Indies*, IX. 278, 501

Veldener, John, of Louvain, II. 311

Veley, Margaret (1843–1887), XIII. 510
   Japanese Fan, A, XIII. 181
   Marriage of Shadows and other Poems, A, XIII. 180
   Michaelmas Daisies, XIII. 181
   Unknown Land, The, XIII. 181

Velleius Paterculus, IV. 348

Velvet-Breeches, in *A Quip for an Upstart Courtier*, III. 361

Venables, George Stovin (1810–1888), XIII. 185, 316; XIV. 535

Venantius Fortunatus, I. 8, 76

Venedotian code of laws of Wales, I. 249

Veneering, in *Our Mutual Friend*, XIII. 336, 337

Vener, lake, I. 26

Venerie de Twety, II. 318

Venetian, in *Hymenaeus*, VI. 304

Venetian, the, in *The Fyrste Boke of the Introduction of Knowledge*, III. 105

Venetian ambassador's chaplain's account of Jonson's *Pleasure Reconciled*, VI. 360

Venezuela, XI. 72

Venice, II. 79; III. 5, 167; IV. 63, 68, 69, 90, 163, 216, 250, 256, 322, 353; V. 71; VI. 148, 157, 174; VII. 16, 100, 192, 197, 198, 200, 208, 437, 442, 449; IX. 150, 245; X. 119, 274, 496; XII. 33 ff., 49, 52, 63, 365, 396; XIII. 61, 104, 135, 397, 402; XIV. 216, 368

Venice, republic of, XI. 114

Venice, Rezzonico palace, XIII. 84

Venn, Henry (1725–1797), IX. 313; X. 365; XII. 473

Venn, John (1759–1813), XII. 281

Venn, John (1834–1923), VII. 320; XII. 471

Venn, Thomas, captain, IV. 462

Venning, Ralph (1621?–1674), VII. 316

Ventum, Harriet, XI. 490

Venus, II. 219, 261, 392, 393; III. 17; IV. 196; VII. 370; VIII. 70; IX. 153

Venus, in *Confessio Amantis*, II. 135, 146, 148, 149, 150

Venus, in *Reason and Sensuality*, II. 202

Venus, in *The Golden Targe*, II. 253

Venus, in *The Hue and Cry after Cupid*, VI. 346, 347

Venus, in *The Kingis Quair*, II. 242

Venus, in *The Masque of Christmas*, VI. 358, 359

Venus, in *The Palice of Honour*, II. 260, 261

Venus, in *The Passetyme of Pleasure*, II. 225, 229

Venus, in *The Temple of Glass*, II. 203

Venus, in *The Testament of Cresseid*, II. 248

Venus, in *Troiane*, V. 69

Venustulus, in *The Rambler*, X. 172

Verard, Antoine, books published by, II. 328, 329; III. 56

Verbruggen, John (*fl.* 1688–1707?), VIII. 191

Vercelli Book, The, I. 12, 53, 54, 56, 61, 430

Verden, IX. 231

Vere, Aubrey de, 20th earl of Oxford (1626–1703), IX. 150

Vere, Edward de, 17th earl of Oxford (1550–1604), III. 351, 508; IV. 113, 117, 466; *If women would be fair*, III. 189; 'What cunning can expresse,' IV. 116

Vere, Sir Francis (1560–1609), VI. 166; VII. 453

Vere, Sir Horace, baron Vere of Tilbury (1565–1635), VII. 453

Vere, John de, 13th earl of Oxford (1443–1513), in the *Paston Letters*, II. 305

Verelst, Harry (d. 1785), XIV. 334, 580

Verges, in *Much Ado about Nothing*, V. 191, 362

Vergil, I. 68, 71 ff., 75, 76, 192, 209, 227, 258, 330; II. 97, 175, 231, 240, 258, 259, 261 ff., 275, 308, 331, 339, 360, 486; III. 19, 20, 24, 62, 65, 113, 119, 157, 178, 200, 218, 219, 221, 223, 224, 226, 230, 234, 264, 300, 304, 305, 347, 416; IV. 16 ff., 21 ff., 121, 138, 169, 250, 252, 264, 329, 414, 440, 516, 527; VI. 197, 225; VII. 59, 68, 138, 263, 267, 268, 271, 334, 366, 503; VIII. 10, 44, 65, 69, 372, 375, 446; IX. 43 ff., 59, 69, 256, 338, 359, 372, 434, 435, 473, 486, 487, 500, 502, 561; X. 102, 114, 117, 305, 475, 493, 509; XI. 2, 426, 433; XII. 67, 76, 326, 329, 337, 422, 476, 482, 484, 486, 489, 490, 493, 495, *also see* Add.; XIII. 45, 123, 173, 175, 312, 380; XIV. 135, 303, 374

   Aeneid, I. 258, 284, 285; II. 175, 316; III. 178, 185, 304; VI. 298, 303; VII. 52, 61, 66, 86, 117, 133, 300, 451; VIII. 9, 50, 67, 70, 77; IX. 188, 257, 258; X. 231; XI. 34; XIII. 125, 126

   Bucolics, III. 62

   Eclogues, VI. 364; VIII. 216; the second, III. 264; IV. 120

   Georgics, VI. 235, 364; VIII. 50, 216; X. 96, 104, 196

   O fortunatos nimium, X. 111

Vergil, in *The Palice of Honour*, II. 260

Vergil, in *The Poetaster*, VI. 18, 42, 44
Vergil, Polydore (1470?–1555?), III. 314,
    532; VII. 203; *History*, II. 260
Verinus, Michael, IV. 267
Veritas, in the *Coventry Plays*, V. 21
Veritas, in *Time's Complaint*, VI. 320
Veritas (=Christ), in Wyclif's *Dialogus*,
    II. 65
Veritie, in *Ane Pleasant Satyre*, III. 125,
    126
Vermigli. *See* Martyr, Peter
Vernagu, I. 302
Verneuil, John (1583?–1647), VII. 309
Verney, Sir Edmund (1590–1642), VII. 194,
    195
Verney, Sir Edmund, the younger (1616–
    1649), VII. 196
Verney, Edward, VII. 194
Verney, Francis, VI. 479
Verney, Mary, VII. 194
Verney, Sir Ralph (1613–1696), VII. 195,
    196, 440
Verney, Ralph, 2nd earl Verney (1712?–
    1791), XI. 5, 6
Verney, Tom, VII. 196
*Verney Family, Letters, Papers and Me-
    moirs of the*, VII. 194, 195, 439
Vernon, Diana, in Scott's *Rob Roy*, XII.
    17, 22, 26
Vernon, Edward, admiral (1684–1757),
    X. 36; XIV. 201, 243
Vernon, lady Susan, in Jane Austen's
    Lady Susan, XII. 233
Vernon MS., I. 475
Vernon MS., poems of, III. 274
Verona, VII. 9
Verona, congress of, XII. 38
Verrall, Arthur Woolgar (1851–1912), XII.
    332, 333, 494; XIV. 208
Verres, Gaius, XI. 17
Verrier, Paul, XIII. 513
Versailles, VIII. 132; IX. 153; XI. 21, 189;
    XII. 185
Verses addressed to the Imitator of Horace,
    IX. 85, 251
Verstegen, Richard. *See* Rowlands, Richard
Vertewis of the Mess, The, II. 284
Vertot, Aubert de, X. 319
Vertue, George (1684–1756), X. 253; XIV.
    214
Vertues, the, in *The Muses Looking-
    Glasse*, VI. 233
Verulam, in *The Ruines of Time*, III. 241
Vesalius, Andreas, III. 421; VIII. 349
Vesey, Agmondesham, X. 261, 264; XI.
    344 ff.
Vesey, Mrs Elizabeth (1715–1791), X. 261,
    264; XI. 344 ff., 348, 362 ff., 473
Vesey, Sir Thomas (1668?–1730), XI. 344
Vesey-Neroni, signora (Trollope's), XIII.
    422
Vespasian, emperor, IV. 14; XIV. 309
Vespucci, Americo, III. 18
Vestiarian controversy, III. 34
Vesuvius, XIII. 460; XIV. 247
'Veteran' (Junius), X. 405

Veterano, in *The Antiquary*, VI. 239
Vetusta Monumenta, XII. 506
Vholes, Mr, in *Bleak House*, XIII. 329
Vicars, John (1580?–1652), IV. 266, 502;
    VIII. 67
Vicars, Thomas (*fl.* 1607–1641), *The Mad-
    nesse of Astrologers*, IV. 535; VII. 509
Vicary, Thomas (d. 1561), III. 107, 494
Viccars, John (1604–1660), *Against Wil-
    liam Li-Lie*, VII. 509
Vice, the, in *Horestes*, V. 64, 65
Vice, the, in *Jacke Jugeler*, V. 107
Vice, the, in *Looke about you*, V. 320
Vice, the, in stage plays, VI. 285, 297
Vice, the, Mery-reporte, in *The Play of the
    Wether*, V. 94
Vice, the, of the moralities, V. 56, 106,
    113
Vice Ambidexter, in *Cambises*, V. 64
Vicentine hills, XIV. 293
Vicenza, III. 6
Vicenza, olympic academy at, V. 62
Vices, in *Mirour de l'Omme*, II. 140 ff.
Vices, the, in *Pathomachia*, VI. 324
Vices and Virtues, I. 228, 459
Vices et des Vertus, Li Livres roiaux des,
    I. 354
Vices et des Vertus, Somme des, II. 139, 315
Viciis, Summa seu Tractatus de, I. 355
Vickers, Robert, XIV. 595
Victor, Benjamin (d. 1778), X. 442, 443;
    XI. 449
Victoria, Australia, XIV. 319
Victoria, in *Fedele and Fortunio*, V. 315
Victoria, a Latin comedy, IV. 477
Victoria, lake, XIV. 192
Victoria, queen of Great Britain, VIII.
    358; XI. 386; XII. 292, 311; XIII. 342,
    487; XIV. 111, 170
Victoria, St, I. 75
Victoria County Histories, XII. 346
Victorian age, the, X. 142; XIII. 1, 22, 23,
    85, 98, 137, 386, 451; XIV. 47, 65, 138,
    159
Victorian drama, XIV. 173
Victorian humour, XI. 281
Victorian liberals, XIII. 16
Victorian literature, XIII. 243, 244
Victorian novels, XIII. 384, 391, 408, 409,
    423, 444, 456
Victorian writers, XII. 95, 106, 177
Victory, The, VIII. 202
Vida, Marco Girolamo (*c.* 1489–1566),
    III. 290, 292; IV. 261; IX. 70; *Art of
    Poetry*, IX. 188, 189, 486
Vida's Game of Chess, X. 480
Vidocq, Eugène François, *Mémoires*, XIII.
    437
Vie de Seint Auban, XII. 515
Vienna, IV. 163; V. 283, 298, 299, 306;
    VII. 453; VIII. 330; IX. 6, 244; X. 323;
    XI. 274; XIV. 247
Vienna, congress of, XII. 39
Vietor, I. 57
*Views of Cottages and Farmhouses in
    England and Wales*, XIV. 222

Vigani, John Francis (1650?–1712), IX. 335, 412

Vígfússon, Gúdbrandr (1828–1889), XIV. 497

Vigny, Alfred de, V. 302; X. 486; XII. 398

Vigo, X. 291

Vigors, Nicholas Aylward (1785–1840), XIV. 288

Viking club, XII. 355

Viljoen, Ben J., XIV. Add. 10

Vilkina Saga, I. 32, 35

Villafranca, XIII. 73

Village, The (1783), X. 471

Village festivals, V. 24

Village Politics, XI. 362

Villanegas, Matilda de, in Lewis's *The Monk*, XI. 303

Villanus, in *Fucus Histriomastix*, VI. 324

'Villario,' in Pope's *Epistles*, IX. 81

Villemain, A. F., XII. 398

Villeroy, in Southerne's *Fatal Marriage*, VIII. 191, 192

Villiers, Barbara, countess of Castlemaine, duchess of Cleveland (1641–1709), VIII. 16, 143, 263, 264

Villiers, C. P., XIV. 513

Villiers, Edward, 1st earl of Jersey (1656–1711), IX. 149, 150

Villiers, Frederick, XIV. 535

Villiers, George, 1st duke of Buckingham (1592–1628), II. 118, 279, 282, 293; V. 288, 289, 347; VI. 149, 360; VII. 5, 17, 187, 198, 205, 219, 222, 306, 381, 434, 438, 439, 440, 451

Villiers, George, 2nd duke of Buckingham (1628–1687), VII. 63; VIII. Add.; IX. 203, 222, 476; VIII. 91, 97, 175, 208, 215, 369, 373, 376, 380, 403, 410, 411; *Advice to a Painter*, VIII. 92; *Poetical Reflections, etc., by a Person of Quality*, VIII. 39, 408; *The Rehearsal*, VII. 63; VIII. 17, 20, 21, 25, 26, 34, 48, 118, 402; IX. 147, 161; XI. 272

Villiers, George W. F., 4th earl of Clarendon (1800–1870), XIV. 131, 509

Villon, François, II. 205, 251, 257, 258, 401; XIII. 133, 211; *Ballade des Dames du temps jadis*, XIII. 118; *Le Grant et le petit Testament*, III. 85, 483

Vilvain, Robert (1575?–1663), VII. 517

Vilvorde, III. 43

Vincent, Mrs (*fl.* 1760), XI. 260

Vincent, Mrs, in Mrs Oliphant's *Salem Chapel*, XIII. 431

Vincent, Thomas (*fl.* 1627–1648), VI. 479

Vincent, Thomas (1634–1678), X. 386

Vincent, William (1739–1815), XI. 157; XII. 495; XIV. 598

Vincent de Beauvais, *Speculum* of, II. 80

Vincentio Saviolo his Practise, III. 344

Vindication of Mr Weld, A, VII. 506

Vinegar family, in *The Champion*, X. 23

Vines, Sydney Howard, XIV. 562

Vinet, Alexandre Rodolphe, XII. 283

Vinogradoff, Sir Paul, XIV. 494; *Villainage in England*, XIV. 51, 68

Vint, Mercy, in Reade's *Griffith Gaunt*, XIII. 425, 426

Vintners, The retayling, IV. 513

Viola, in *The Coxcombe*, VI. 120, 123, 133

Viola, in *Twelfth Night*, V. 126, 169, 193; VI. 126, 305; VIII. 145

Violante, in *The Gamester*, VI. 202

Violante, in *The Spanish Curate*, VI. 139

Violante, in *The Triumph of Love*, VI. 120

Violetta, in Cumberland's *Brothers*, XI. 264

Viret, P., IV. 448

Virgilius, The Lyfe of, II. 329, 486

Virgilius Restauratus, IX. 138

Virgin cult, I. 220, 223, 231, 232, 362. See, also, under Mary

Virgin Mary. See Mary, the Blessed Virgin

Virgin Mary, in *Mirour de l'Omme*, II. 141

Virgin Mary, Hymn to, in *Speculum Christiani*, II. 319

Virginia, in *Appius and Virginia*, VI. 182

Virginia, in *Confessio Amantis*, II. 152

Virginia, colony and state of, II. 396; III. 327; IV. 75, 81, 94 ff., 104, 513; V. 347; VI. 48, 355; VII. 50, 52, 70, 453; VIII. 142; X. 270; XI. 12

Virginia company, the, IV. 311; VII. 153

Virginian princes and priests, in Chapman's *Masque*, VI. 355

Virginius, in *Appius and Virginia*, VI. 182

Virginius, in Knowles's drama, XIII. 261

Virgins Complaint for the Losse of their sweethearts, The, VII. 386

Virginus, in Hall's *Virgidemiarum*, IV. 331

'Virro,' in Pope's *Epistles*, IX. 81

Virtue, in *The Example of Virtue*, II. 227

Virtues, in *Pathomachia*, VI. 324

Virtues, the seven, in *Mirour de l'Omme*, II. 141

Viry, comtesse de, X. 126

Vischer, cartographer (*fl.* 1610), *View of London*, VI. 260, 261

Vischer, Friedrich Theodor, V. 305

Visconti, Bernabo, II. 158

Vishnu Purana, The, XII. 503

Visions of Tundale, The, II. 504

'Visto,' in Pope's *Epistles*, IX. 81

Vistula, in Ohthere, I. 94

Vistula, the, in *Widsith*, I. 35

Visus, in *Lingua*, VI. 315

Vita de Do-best, in *Piers the Plowman*, II. 40

Vitalian, pope, I. 380

Vitelli, in *The Renegado*, VI. 155, 157

Vitelli, Cornelio, III. 5, 6

Vitellius, IV. 14

Vitruvius, IV. 416

Vitry, de, in *Thierry and Theodoret*, VI. 138

Vitry, Jacques de, III. 489

Vittoria, in Webster's *The White Divel*, VI. 175, 176, 185, 186; XII. 68

Vittoria (George Meredith's), XIII. 445, 446

Vives, Johannes Ludovicus (1492–1540), III. 429, 436, 470; IV. 9, 448; VII. 482, 486; *De Institutione Christianae Feminae*, VIII. 125

Vivian, I. 238

Vivian, in Lytton's *The Caxtons*, XIII. 420
Viviani, Emilia, XII. 73, 74
Vizetelly, Henry (1820–1894), XIV. 535
Vogan, Thomas Stuart Lyle, XII. 473
Vogler, Abt (Browning's), XIII. 78
Voigt, Johan Carel, XIV. Add. 10
Voiture, Vincent, VIII. 376, 385; IX. 444, 473; *Letters of Affaires, Love and Courtship*, VII. 390, 391; VIII. 372
Volksdrama, German, V. 295
Volney, XII. 403
Volpone, in Ben Jonson's play, X. 50; XII. 68
Volscians, in *Coriolanus*, V. 198
Völsunga Saga, I. 23, 35; XIII. 125, 126
Voltaire, F. M. Arouet de, II. 191; V. 209, 288 ff., 296, 301, 302, 306, 307, 459 ff.; VII. 119; VIII. 35, 159, 261, 428; IX. 49, 153, 226, 295, 529; X. 41, 68, 69, 71, 79, 83, 86 ff., 134, 135, 190, 202, 204, 210, 279, 285, 287, 288, 303, 308, 420, 431, 434, 439, 469, 481; XI. 263, 265, 290, 291, 295, 296, 307, 309, 353, 474; XII. 177, 206, 208; XIII. 9, 52, 339, 453, 468
  Almida, X. 86
  Alzira, X. 82
  Appel à toutes les Nations de l'Europe, V. 292, 293
  Brutus, V. 288; X. 82
  Candide, IV. 359; X. 49
  Écossaise, L', X. 86, 429
  Ériphyle, V. 288
  Essai sur les Mœurs, XIV. 102
  Histoire de Charles XII, X. 283
  Indiscret, L', X. 86
  Irène, V. 292
  La Henriade, XI. 79
  La Loi Naturelle, IX. 83
  Letter to the Academy, XI. 354
  Lettres Anglaises, X. 169
  Lettres philosophiques, V. 287, 288, 294
  Mahomet, V. 288; X. 81; XI. 253
  Merope, X. 82, 86
  Mort de César, V. 288 ff.
  Nanine, X. 17, 411
  Orestes, X. 86
  Sémiramis, V. 288; X. 86; XI. 352
  Tancred, XI. 352
  Zaïre, V. 288; X. 81, 82, 118; XI. 352
  Zobeide, X. 86
Volumen Britanniae, or the *Book of Britain*, I. 70 ff.
Volumnia, in *Coriolanus*, V. 198
Völundarkviða, Old Norse poem, I. 36
Volunteer movement, the, XIV. 239
Volusene, Florence (1504?–1547?), III. 470
Vondel, J. van den, VII. 423; *Lucifer*, VII. 118
Vopiscus, VI. 139
Voragine, Jacobus a (1230–1298), I. 55, 134, 343; V. 15
Vörösmarty, Michael, V. 308
Vorstius, Conrad, VII. 308
Vortigen, I. 71
Vortipor of Pembrokeshire, I. 67

Vosges, mountains, I. 33
Voss, Johann Heinrich, V. 303
Vossius, Gerardus Johannes, VII. 307
Vossius, Isaac, VII. 307, 309
Votes of Parliament, XI. 333
Vox and the Wolf, I. 366
Vox Populi, Vox Dei, III. 492
Voyage of Domingo Gonsalez, by F. Godwin, IX. 106
Voyages, burlesque and wagering, IV. 533
Vrihat-Katha, III. 494
Vril, in Lytton's *The Coming Race*, XIII. 420
Vulcan, in *The Hue and Cry after Cupid*, VI. 347
Vulcan, in *Love's Maistresse*, VI. 84
Vulcan, in *Mercury Vindicated*, VI. 357, 358
Vulcan, in *Thersites*, V. 108
Vulcan (Herrick's), VII. 13
Vulgar Errors in Practice Censured, IV. 251
Vulgate, the. *See under* Bible
Vulliamy, Mary. *See* Meredith, Mary

W. G., VIII. 9
W. H. (? William Hunnis), IV. 121
W. H. (of Shakespeare's sonnets), V. 172, 174, 225, 232
W. M., *The Man in the Moon*, IV. 337, 342, 521
W. R., IV. 2
W. R. (possibly Ralegh), III. 189
W. S., V. 238, 247, 255; VI. 62
Wace (*fl.* 1170), I. 170, 232, 234, 235 ff., 256, 263 ff., 336, 337, 343, 350, 447, 462; II. 420
Wace, Henry, XII. 317
Waddell, Peter Hately (1817–1891), XI. 437
Wadding, Luke (1588–1657), XIV. 308, 572
Waddington, Samuel, XIII. 207, 489, 510
Wade, I. 218
Wade, George (1673–1748), IX. 373
Wade, Miss, in *Little Dorrit*, XIII. 331
Wade, Thomas (1805–1875), XII. 107, 423; *Jew of Arragon, The*, XII. 119; *Mundi et Cordis...Poems and Sonnets*, XII. 119
Wade, Sir Thomas Francis (1818–1895), XII. 343, 500
Wadeson, Anthony (*fl.* 1600), *Humorous Earle of Gloster*, VIII. 126
Wadford. *See* Wodeford, William of
Wadham, Edward, *English Versification*, XIII. 247, 513
Wadington. *See* William of
Wadmore, F., XIV. 541
Wadsworth, head of Attercliffe academy, X. 386
Waes of Scotland, The, IX. 377
Wafer, Lionel (1660?–1705?), IV. 462
Wag, The, XIV. 235
Wag, Tom, in *Pendennis*, XIV. 440
Wager, Lewis (*fl.* 1566), V. 393; VI. 378, 409; *Life and Repentance of Marie Magdalene*, VI. 378, 499
'Wager,' ship, XIV. 243, 244

Wager, William (*fl.* 1566), *The longer thou livest, the more fool thou art*, v. 60, 393
Wagner, P. A., xiv. Add. 10
Wagner, Wilhelm Richard, *Lohengrin*, x. 227; *Tannhäuser*, x. 227
Wagstaff, Simon, *pseud.* of Jonathan Swift, ix. 106, 460
Wagstaff, Théophile, *pseud.* of W. M. Thackeray, xiii. 278
Wagstaffe, John (1633–1677), vii. 396; *The Question of Witchcraft debated*, vii. 395, 507
Wagstaffe, Thomas (1645–1712), x. 517; *Vindication*, x. 355; *Defence of the Vindication*, x. 355
Wagstaffe, Thomas (1692–1770), x. 355
Wagstaffe, William (1685–1725), ix. 443, 470
Wahabees, the, xiv. 253
Wainewright, Latham, xiv. 594
Wainewright, Thomas Griffiths (1794–1852), xiii. 418
Waitz, Georg, xiv. 68
Wake, Sir Isaac (1580?–1632), vi. 469
Wake, William (1657–1737), ix. 407, 509; x. 353, 354
Wakefield, v. 373; xiii. 455
Wakefield, Edward Gibbon (1796–1862), xiv. 483, 512, 514, 587, 588
Wakefield, Gilbert (1756–1801), ix. 73, 75, 443, 447, 450; x. 385; xii. 470, 495; xiv. 602; 'Diatribe,' xii. 326
Wakefield, Henry, bishop of Worcester (*fl.* 1375–1395), ii. 61
Wakefield, Mrs Priscilla (1751–1832), xi. 378, 484; xiv. 600
    Instinct Displayed, xi. 383
    Introduction to Botany, xi. 383
    Juvenile Anecdotes, xi. 383
    Leisure Hours, xi. 383
    Mental Improvement, xi. 383
Wakefield, Robert (d. 1537), iii. 53
Wakefield grammar school, ix. 330
Wakefield Plays, v. 18, 46 ff.
Wakem, Philip, in *The Mill on the Floss*, xiii. 392
Wakeman, William F., xii. 513
Waking Vision, The, viii. 92
Walbrook, Herbert Mackinnon, xiii. 515
Walcheren expedition the, xiv. 115
Walcott, Mackenzie Edward Charles (1821–1880), xii. 348, 513, 520; *History of the Cathedrals...of Scotland*, xii. 349; *Traditions and Customs of Cathedrals*, xii. 349
Waldby, John, brother of R. Waldby, ii. 443
Waldby, Robert, archbishop of York (d. 1398), ii. 443
Waldef, i.e. *Waltheof*, i. 287, 472
Waldegrave, James, 2nd earl Waldegrave (1715–1763), *Memoirs*, ix. 253, 254, 498
Waldegrave, Maria, countess, afterwards duchess of Gloucester, vii. 204
Waldegrave, Robert (1554?–1604), iii. 110, 376, 378 ff., 385, 387 ff., *also see* Add.;

Waldegrave, Robert
    iv. 363; vi. 393; *The Four Great Lyers*, iii. 110
Waldegrave, Samuel (1817–1869), xii. 473
Waldegrave, Timothy, x. 385
Walden, Thomas de (Netter) (d. 1430), ii. 443
Waldens, the, of Edmonton, xii. 201
Waldenses, the, xiv. 79
Waldershare, in Disraeli's *Endymion*, xiii. 350
Waldhere, i. 30, 32, 33, 35, 36, 41, 277, 423
Wales, v. 27, 323, 361; vi. 310, 361; vii. 37, 42, 78, 113, 143, 197, 321; viii. 60, 106; ix. 350, 352; x. 115, 182, 277, 394; xi. 12; xii. 166, 344, 349; xiii. 372; xiv. 79, 84, 215, 292, 294, 307, 434
Wales, church of, xii. 266
Wales, Joan of Kent, princess of, ii. 56
Wales, prince of, ix. 104
Wales, prince of, in *Edward III*, v. 244
Wales, The Four Ancient Books of, i. 462; xii. 518
Wales, university of, xiv. 433
Walesby, F. P., x. 478
Walewski, count, xiv. 185
Walford, Edward, xiv. 612
Walford, L. B., xiii. Add. 3
Walgainus = Gawain, in Arthurian legend, i. 269
Walhalla, i. 63
Walker, Alexander, xiv. 533
Walker, Anthony, Εὕρηκα Εὕρηκα, *The Virtuous Woman Found*, viii. 269; *A true Account of the Author of a Book called Εἰκὼν Βασιλική*, viii. 269
Walker, A. Stoddart, xiv. 516
Walker, Clement (d. 1651), vii. 450; viii. 407
Walker, Sir Edward (1612–1677), vii. 206, 447
Walker, Ferdinand, iv. 448
Walker, George, *Anglo-Tyrannus* (1650), vii. 514
Walker, Henry, vii. 351 ff. (main entry), 358, 360, 365, 494, 498 ff., 517
    Collection of passages...by one who was groom of his chamber, A, vii. 356
    Collections of Notes at the Kings Tryall, vii. 355
    Declaration called out of the Journals of both Houses of Parliament, A, vii. 355
    Heads of a Diarie, vii. 355
    History of the Life Reigne and Death of the late King Charles, vii. 353
    King's Last Farewell to the World, The, vii. 353
    Mad Designe, The, vii. 356
    Mercurius Morbicus, vii. 355
    Packets of Letters, vii. 355
    Perfect Occurrences of Every Dayes Journall, vii. 352, 353
    Prelates Pride, The, vii. 352
    Serious Observations lately made touching his Majesty, vii. 356
    Severall Proceedings, vii. 355

Walker, Henry
  Terrible outcry against the loytering exalted Prelats, A, VII. 352
  The true manner of the crowning of Charles the Second King of Scotland, VII. 356
  To your tents O Israel, VII. 352
  'Τραγήματα' Sweetmeats, VII. 355
  Tuesdaies Journall, VII. 355
  Two letters from Liverpool, VII. 354
  Wren and the Finch, The, VII. 352
Walker, captain Howard, in Thackeray's *The Ravenswing*, XIII. 281
Walker, Hugh, XI. 221, 441; XII. 453; XIII. 485, 488, 544, 559, 568, *also see* Add. 2; XIV. 528; *The Literature of the Victorian Era*, XIII. 50
Walker, Mrs Hugh, XIII. 498, 568; XIV. 528
Walker, John (1674–1747), VII. 478; VIII. 407
Walker, John (1692?–1741), IX. 528
Walker, John (1732–1807), XIII. 240
Walker, Josiah, XI. 436, 441
Walker, Obadiah (1616–1699), VIII. 305; IX. 488, 569; *Oxford Theses relating to the English Reformation*, IX. 197
Walker, Patrick (d. 1745), IX. 549
Walker, Richard (1679–1764), XIV. 286
Walker, Robert (1798–1854), XIV. 596
Walker, Sidney (1795–1846), XIII. 245
Walker, W., IX. 318
Walker, William (brother of Henry Walker), VII. 353
'Walking Morte,' the, in *A Caveat or Warening for Commen Corsetors*, III. 104
Walkington, Thomas (d. 1621), III. 91; IV. 519
Walkley, Arthur Bingham, XIII. 515
Wallace, Alfred Russel (1823–1913), XI. 75; XIV. 35, 250, 298, 299, 554, 564
Wallace, Charles Wallace, VI. 256, 257, 270 ff., 275, 278
Wallace, James (d. 1688), IX. 560
Wallace, James (*fl.* 1684–1724), IX. 554
Wallace, Robert (1697–1771), IX. 562; *Various prospects of Mankind*, XI. 74
Wallace, Sir William (1272?–1305), II. 101, 103, 105, 108 ff., 280; VI. 453; XIV. 95
Wallace, William, editor of Mackintosh's *History of the Revolution*, XIV. 59
Wallace, William (1844–1897), XIV. 483; *Hegel's Philosophy of Mind*, XIV. 45; *Lectures and Essays*, XIV. 45; *Logic of Hegel, The*, XIV. 45
Wallace, William, editor of Burns, XI. 438, 439, 442
Wallace. See Harry, Blind
Wallace Craigie, near Dundee, XII. 350
Wallas, Graham, XIV. 478, 602
Wallensis, John (*fl.* 1283), I. 456
Wallensis, Thomas (d. 1255), II. 318
Wallensis, Thomas (d. 1350?), I. 456
Waller, Alfred Rayney (1867–1922), IX. 155; X. 44; XII. 167, 431; XIII. 515; XIV. 518, 519; *The Writings of Matthew Prior*, IX. 147, 148, 153, 155, 157, 158

Waller, Edmund (1606–1687), IV. 183; VI. 437; VII. 4, 48, 49, 53 ff. (main entry), 64, 67 ff., 73, 180, 183, 268, 270, 409 ff.; VIII. 5, 18, 81, 120, 133, 227, 228, 234 ff., 267, 369, 371, 376, 381, 394, 408, 410, 411, 444, 446; IX. 67 ff., 73, 157, 158; X. 226, 432, 475; XI. 246; XII. 132; XIV. 436
  Aeneid, trans., VII. 86
  Battle of the Summer Islands, The, VII. 55, 56
  Behold the brand of beauty tossed, VII. 55, 58
  Divine Poems, VII. 55
  Go, lovely Rose! VII. 55, 58
  Instructions to a Painter, VII. 56
  Maides Tragedy, The, version of, VIII. 120
  Of the Danger His Majesty [Being Prince] Escaped in the Road at St Andere, VII. 53
  Of the Last Verses in the Book, VII. 56
  Of the Misreport of her being Painted, VII. 55
  On the Statue of King Charles I at Charing Cross, VII. 56
  Panegyric to my Lord Protector, VII. 56
  Pompée, version of, by Waller and lord Buckhurst, VIII. 180
  Puerperium, VII. 58
  Saraband, VIII. 231
  To a Very Young Lady, VII. 55
  To Amoret, VII. 58
  Upon a Late Storm, and of the Death of His Highness ensuing in the same, VII. 56; VIII. 5
Waller, John Francis (1810–1894), XIV. 572; *Kitty Neil*, XIV. 326; *Song of the Glass, The*, XIV. 326; *Spinning Wheel Song, The*, XIV. 326
Waller, lady, wife of Sir Wm Waller, VII. 350
Waller, R., *Life of Hooke*, XIV. 283
Waller, Sir William (1597?–1668), VII. 349, 350
Wallerston, VII. 453
Walley, Henry, VII. 346; *Heads of Chiefe Passages in Parliament*, VII. 350; *The Kingdomes Weekly Account of Heads*, VII. 350; *The True Informer*, VII. 350
Walley, John (*fl.* 1557), IV. 397
Wallin, head of Bristol academy, X. 387
Wallington, Nehemiah (1598–1658), *Historical Notices*, VII. 223, 454
Wallis, F., XIV. 521
Wallis, G., XIII. 545
Wallis, John (1616–1703), VII. 288, 289, 308, 475, 489; VIII. 360, 479; IX. 386, 411, 412; XIV. 281
  Arithmetica Infinitorum, VIII. 359
  Doctrine of the Blessed Trinity, X. 378
  English Grammar, XIII. 244
  Truth tried, VII. 279
Wallis, Samuel (1728–1795), XIV. 244
Walpole, George, 3rd earl of Orford (1730–1791), X. 245, 246

Walpole, Horace, 1st baron Walpole (1678–1757), IX. 223; X. 495

Walpole, Horatio (Horace), 4th earl of Orford (1717–1797), IV. 89, 293; V. 276, 292, 478; VII. 176, 204, 443; VIII. 262, 451; IX. 143, 190, 246, 248, 250 ff., 354; X. 47, 60 ff., 87, 116, 118, 119, 123, 126, 127, 135, 136, 215, 237, 242 ff. (main entry), 256, 259, 260, 262, 268, 272, 285, 316, 362, 399, 400, 425, 450, 484 ff., 505, 523, *also see* Add.; XI. 91, 145, 154, 173 ff., 258 ff., 262, 273, 282, 341, 346, 350, 351, 356, 358, 364, 365, 429, 449, 465, 469; XII. 345; XIII. 52, 321; XIV. 62, 284

Ædes Walpolianae, X. 253

Anecdotes of Painting, X. 135, 253, 254

Castle of Otranto, The, X. 60, 61, 227, 234, 254; XI. 300; XII. 3

Catalogue of the Royal and Noble Authors, X. 184, 253

Correspondence, X. 253

Description of the Villa, X. 245

Essay on Gardening, X. 250

Historic Doubts on Richard III, IX. 131, 135, 250, 254, 291, 305

Last Journals, X. 295

Letters, X. 284, 291, 292; XI. 354, 363

Letters to George Montagu, X. 247

Letters to Mann, X. 251

Memoirs, IX. 253

Miscellaneous Antiquities, X. 131

Miscellaneous Letters, X. 247

Mysterious Mother, The, X. 254, 255

Private Correspondence, X. 247

Short Notes of My Life, X. 252, 291

Works, X. 247

Walpole, Margaret, countess of Orford, wife of 2nd earl (d. 1781), X. 246

Walpole, Sir Robert, 1st earl of Orford (1676–1745), IX. 81, 87, 115, 117, 121, 163, 165, 219 ff., 229, 230, 232, 243, 251, 252, 254, 281, 426, 433; X. 71, 84, 94, 114, 116, 243, 246, 249, 252, 256, 299, 358, 389, 428; XI. 174; XIV. 63, 128, 212

Walpole, Robert, 2nd earl of Orford (d. 1751), X. 246

Walpole, Sir Spencer (1839–1907), XIV. 499, 506; *History of England*, XIV. 93

Walpole, Hon. Thomas, 2nd son of the 1st lord Walpole of Wolterton, X. 495

Walpurgis night, VII. 368

Walsh, Benjamin Dann, XIV. 595

Walsh, Edward (1805–1850), XIV. 305, 321, 572

Walsh, John Henry, *pseud.* Stonehenge (1810–1888), XIV. 547

Walsh, Shelford, XIII. 519

Walsh, William (1663–1708), VIII. 157, 402, 411, 445, 447; IX. 68, 69, 174 ff., 487; XI. 250

Antidote, The, IX. 176

'Caelia, too late you would repent,' IX. 175

Despairing Lover, The, IX 175

Walsh, William
Jealousy, IX. 175

Walsh, archbishop William John, XIV. 592

Walsh, William Shepherd, XIII. 568

Walsingham, Edward (*fl.* 1643–1659), VII. 454

Walsingham, Sir Francis (1530?–1590), IV. 80, 82, 382; V. 85, 345, 482; VI. 244, 249, 272, 383, 384, 392, 400; VII. 191

Walsingham, John (d. 1340?), I. 456; *The Reply of Friar Daw Thopas*, II. 40

Walsingham, Mrs, XI. 348

Walsingham, The Foundation of the Chapel of, II. 321, 486

Walsingham, Thomas (d. 1422?), II. 38, 499; *Historia Anglicana*, II. 47

Walter, archdeacon of Oxford, I. 168, 257

Walter, friend of Henry of Huntingdon, I. 167

Walter, Hubert (d. 1205), I. 173, 181; *Tractatus de Legibus et Consuetudinibus Regni Angliae*, VIII. 311

Walter, John (1739–1812), XIV. 177, 178

Walter, John (1776–1847), XIV. 174, 178 ff., 183

Walter, John (1818–1894), XIV. 183, 535

Walter, Richard (1716?–1785), XIV. 243, 554

Walter, Sir, in *A Chart Mayd in Cheapeside*, VI. 74

Walter, the steward, grandson of Banquo, II. 104

Walter, William (*fl.* 1520), books translated by, II. 325, 326; *The History of Titus and Gesippus*, II. 326; *The History of Guystarde and Sygysmonde*, II. 325; *The Spectacle of Lovers*, II. 326; III. 486

Walter de Bardes, IV. 309, 509

Walter de Bibelsworth (*fl.* 1270), II. 507

Walter de Merton (d. 1277), II. 351 ff., 355

Walter of Evesham (*fl.* 1320), I. 456

Walter of Hemingburgh (*fl.* 1300), I. 181, 450

Walter of Henley, II. 499; *Book of Husbandry*, IV. 307, 364, 369, 514, 541

Walters, John C., XIII. 537, 544

Waltham, IV. 238; XII. 186

Walthamstow, XIII. 118

Waltharius, I. 32, 33

Waltheof (d. 1076), II. 399

Walton (pirate), in *Fortune by Land and Sea*, VI. 104

Walton, Anne, VII. 250

Walton, Brian (1600?–1661), VII. 318, 319, 478, 481; *Polyglot Bible*, VII. 481; VIII. 294; list of contributors to *Polyglot Bible*, VII. 481

Walton, Christopher (1809–1877), IX. 309, 318, 328, 511, 513 ff.

Walton, Sir Edgar H., XIV. Add. 10

Walton, Izaak (1593–1683), III. 405, 406, 415; IV. 119, 124, 125, 163, 198, 199, 201, 236, 246, 373, 374, 422; VII. 27 ff., 76, 77, 82, 149, 156, 232, 250 ff. (main entry), 256 ff., 390, 402, 403, 463; VIII. 293, 295; IX. 277

Walton, Izaak
  Compleat Angler, The, VII. 81, 250, 251, 253; XI. 318
  Life of Donne, VII. 250
  Life of Geo. Herbert, VII. 26, 29
  Lives, VII. 250 ff.; X. 193
  Reliquiae Wottonianae, VII. 250
Walton, James, father of Izaak Walton, VII. 250
Walton, John (fl. 1410), II. 499
Wanderer, in Wordsworth's Excursion, XI. 106
Wanderer, The, I. 4, 37, 38, 275, 372, 424, 428
Wandering Jew, The, IV. 342
Wanley, Humfrey (1672–1726), I. 45, 129, 428; IX. 356, 358, 541; XI. 336, 337, 467
Wanstead, IV. 132; VI. 336
Wantage, I. 107
Wantonness, in Ane Pleasant Satyre, III. 124 ff.
Wapull, George, The Tide tarries no man, v. 60, 393; VI. 284
Warbeck, Perkin (1474–1499), VII. 203
Warburton, Bartholomew Eliott George (1810–1852), XIV. 527, 554; The Crescent and the Cross, XIV. 251
Warburton, John (1682–1759), V. 146; IX. 540
Warburton, Rowland Eyles Egerton (1804–1891), X. 119; XIII. 510
Warburton, William (1698–1779), bishop of Gloucester, v. 271 ff., 278, 296; VII. 89; VIII. 295; IX. 82, 83, 86 ff., 145, 296, 297, 327, 443, 444, 447, 449, 475, 476, 509, 510, 512; X. 167, 180, 276, 305, 396, 465, 524
  Alliance between Church and State, IX. 296; X. 375
  'Aristarchus on the Hero of the Poem,' IX. 89
  Divine Legation of Moses, IX. 296, 341
  Remarks on Hume's Natural History of Religion, IX. 296
  Shakespeare, IX. 144; XI. 320
  View of Lord Bolingbroke's Philosophy, IX. 296
Warburton's cook, VI. 36, 165, 195
Ward, Sir Adolphus William (1837–1924), v. 82, 134, 254, 368; VI. 27, 283; VIII. 124, 373; IX. 30, 326; X. 80, 350, 445; XIII. 532, 549, 551; XIV. 515; George Crabbe, XI. 140, 141, 418, 420
Ward, Artemus (pseud.), XIV. 346
Ward, Edward (1667–1731), IX. 256, 258 ff., 268, 501, 502
  Hudibras Redivivus, IX. 260, 261
  London Spy, IX. 262, 263
  Republican Procession, IX. 261
  Vulgus Britannicus, IX. 260, 261
  Wine and Wisdom, IX. 262
Ward, Harry Leigh Douglas (1825–1906), XII. 519; Catalogue of Romances, I. 191, 270
Ward, Harry Marshall (1854–1906), XIV. 564

Ward, Henry Snowden, XIII. 544
Ward, Mrs Humphry (Mary Augusta), XIII. 556, also see Add. 3; XIV. 533
Ward, James, of Nottingham, XIII. 499
Ward, Jem (1800–1885), XIV. 231
Ward, John (fl. 1613), IV. 465
Ward, John (1679?–1758), IX. 530
Ward, John William, 1st earl of Dudley (1781–1833), XIV. 126
Ward, Richard (fl. 1710), VIII. 279, 280, 456
Ward, Robert, Fucus Histriomastix, VI. 324, 327, 472, 480
Ward, Robert Plumer (1765–1846), XII. 452; XIII. 554; Tremaine, XIII. 350
Ward, Roger (fl. 1582), IV. 386, 408
Ward, Samuel, of Ratcliffe (fl. 1570), IV. 238
Ward, Samuel (1577–1640), VII. 318
Ward, Seth (1617–1689), bishop of Salisbury, VII. 288, 475, 517; VIII. 360, 364, 479; XIV. 281; Vindiciae Academiarum, IX. 386, 387, 500, 571
Ward, Thomas Humphry, XIII. 487, 488; English Poets, XIII. 100
Ward, Wilfrid Philip (1856–1916), XII. Add. 2; XIII. 501; XIV. 483, 507; Life of Newman, XII. 257, 426, 453, 456, 460, 463
Ward, William George (1812–1882), XII. 259, 271, 275, 463; XIII. 104; XIV. 483, 507, 513; Essays on the Philosophy of Theism, XIV. 26; The Ideal of a Christian Church, XII. 261, 276
Warden, Master, in Three Speeches, VII. 381
Wardlaw, Elizabeth, lady (1677–1727), XI. 231; Gilderoy, IX. 364; Hardyknute, II. 417; IX. 364; X. 226
Wardlaw, Henry (d. 1440), II. 367 ff.
Wardlaw, Walter (d. 1390), II. 128
Wardour, Isabella, in Scott's Antiquary, XII. 22
Wardour street work, XIII. 187
Ware, Christopher, the elder (1625?–1690), VII. 478, 489, 492; IX. 569
Ware, Hertfordshire, VI. 172; XII. 182
Ware, Sir James (1594–1666), VII. 481; X. 293; XII. 349; XIV. 308, also see Add. 3; History of Ireland, IV. 414
Ware, James Redding, XIV. 611
Warham, William (1450?–1532), archbishop of Canterbury, III. 9, 32, 49; VII. 326
Waring (Browning's), XIII. 186
Waring, Edward John, XII. 523
Waring, Jane (Swift's 'Varina'), IX. 92
Waring, Susan M., XIII. 559
Warinus, I. 170
Warkworth, John (d. 1500), II. 302, 482; Chronicle, IV. 423
Warne, Charles (1802–1887), XII. 513
Warner, Sir George Frederick, V. 248
Warner, George Townsend, XIV. 597
Warner, John (1736–1800), XIII. 245; Metronariston, XIII. 240, 513

Warner, John, *The Gaine of Losse* (1645), VII. 517

Warner, Mary Amelia (1804–1854), VIII. 184

Warner, Rebecca, X. 463

Warner, Richard, XII. 382

Warner, William (1558?–1609), III. 349; V. 83; *Albion's England*, III. 198, 199, 357; IV. 88, 136, 477; *Menaechmi*, IV. 4, 439; *Pan his Syrinx*, III. 350, 536

Warning for Faire Women, A, V. 81, 163, 325, 326, 398, 476; VI. 96

Warr, George Charles Winter (1845–1901), XII. 495

Warrack, Grace, II. 300, 482

Warre, Edmond, XIV. 597

Warren, Mrs Anne, XII. 452

Warren, George, *Impartial Description of Surinam* (1667), IV. 462

Warren, Hardick, VII. 509

Warren, John Byrne Leicester, 3rd lord De Tabley (1835–1895), XIII. 194, 203, 205, 206, 501; XIV. 502; *Philoctetes*, XIII. 205; *Soldier's Fortune, The*, XIII. 205

Warren, Matthew (1642–1706), X. 386

Warren, Mrs, in Holcroft's *Road to Ruin*, XI. 277

Warren, Samuel (1807–1877), XII. 452

Warren, Sir Thomas Herbert, XIII. 474, 478

Warricombe, Sidwell (Gissing's), XIII. 461

Warrington, XI. 469

Warrington, George, in *Pendennis*, XIII. 292

Warrington academy, X. 385; XIV. 51, 272, 385, 399

Warringtons, the, in *The Virginians*, XIII. 297, 298

Wars of Cyrus King of Persia, V. 398; VI. 288

Warsaw, V. 283

Warschewiczki, Stanislaus, IV. 3

Warter, John Wood (1806–1878), XI. 422; XII. 219

Warton, George, almanack maker, VII. 509

Warton, Joseph (1722–1800), IX. 443 ff., 450; X. 125, 164, 224, 238, 239, 240–241 (main entry), 473, 492, 493; *Essay on Pope*, X. 240, 466

Warton, Thomas, the elder (1688?–1745), VII. 265; X. 223, 226 ff., 492; XI. 133

Warton, Thomas, the younger (1728–1790), I. viii, 361, 377; II. 203, 205, 211, 225, 319; III. 51, 77, 157, 174, 187, 192, 193, 252; V. 71, 78, 143, 253; VI. 283, 294, 295; VII. 265; IX. 69, 73, 82, 144, 479, 574; X. 137, 184, 186, 224, 233, 238 ff. (main entry), 485, 486, 492; XI. 34, 133; XII. 133; XIV. 594, 595

History of English Poetry, X. 239; XII. 363

Pleasures of Melancholy, X. 125

Poems, X. 239

Progress of Discontent, IX. 191

Triumph of Isis, X. 136

Verses on Sir Joshua Reynolds's painted window, X. 239

Warwick, IV. 190; VIII. 291

Warwick, countesses of. *See* Rich, Mary; Rich, Penelope

Warwick, earl of, in *Henry V*, V. 262

Warwick, earls of. *See* Rich, Charles; Rich, Robert

Warwick castle, VIII. 110

Warwick school, IV. 266

Warwick's company, earl of, VI. 249

Warwickshire, II. 315; IV. 200; V. 56, 187; VII. 196; IX. 533; X. 112, 113, 271 ff., 275, 276, 278, 385; XII. 326, 441, 442; XIII. 382; XIV. 231

Warwickshire Coterie, the, X. 496

'Washer of the Ford, the,' XIV. 320

Washington, George, XI. 190

Washington, George, in *The Virginians*, XIII. 297

Waspe, in *Bartholomew Fayre*, VI. 23

Wasse, Joseph (1672–1738), IX. 340, 528

Wassel, in *The Masque of Christmas*, VI. 358

Wastell, Simon (d. 1632), VII. 83

Waster, in *Piers the Plowman*, II. 14

Wastoure. *See Wynnere*

Wat, in *Piers the Plowman*, II. 12, 16

Wat, in shepherd carols, II. 378

Waterfield, William, XIV. 339, 580

Waterford, X. 257

Waterhouse, Edward (1619–1670), VIII. 466, 469; IX. 571; *An Humble Apologie for Learning*, VII. 392, 509, 517

Waterland, Daniel (1683–1740), IX. 509; X. 354, 358, 359, 516, 517; *Advice to a Young Student*, IX. 411; *Review of the Doctrine of the Eucharist*, X. 360; *Vindication of Christ's Divinity*, X. 359

Waterloo, battle of, XII. 43, 381; XIV. 66, 227

Watermen, company of, VI. 259

Watermeyer, Egidius Benedictus (1824–1867), XIV. Add. 10; *After a Storm*, XIV. 378

Waterson, Simon, IV. 398

Waterton, Charles (1782–1865), XIV. 554; *Wanderings in South America*, XIV. 249

Watkin, William Thompson (1836–1888), XII. 514; *Roman Cheshire*, XII. 347; *Roman Lancashire*, XII. 347

Watkins, John (*fl.* 1792–1831), XI. 456

Watkins, John, of Whitby, XII. 416

Watkins, Richard, IV. 384

Watling street, I. 178

Watreman, W., translator of Boehme, IV. 442

Wats, Edmond, IV. 409

Watson, Scots poet, II. 279

Watson, Christopher (d. 1581), IV. 439

Watson, David (1710–1756), IX. 528

Watson, Emma, in Jane Austen's *The Watsons*, XII. 234

Watson, Henry, apprentice to Wynkyn de Worde, books translated by:
Church of Evil Men and Women, The, II. 324

Watson, Henry
   History of Olyver of Castylle and the
   fayre Helayne, The, II. 324
   Ship of Fools, The, II. 324; III. 59
   Valentine and Orson, II. 324
Watson, James (d. 1722), XI. 342, 470;
   Choice Collection of...Scots Poems, IX.
   366, 367, 556, 567; X. 226; XI. 204,
   217
Watson, James (1739?–1790), XIV. 216
Watson, John, XIV. 478
Watson, John (d. 1530), III. 61
Watson, John Selby (1804–1884), XII.
   491, 492; *Life of Porson*, X. 317
Watson, Joshua (1771–1855), XII. 256, 454
Watson, Richard (1612–1685), VII. 188
Watson, Richard (1737–1816), bishop of
   Llandaff, X. 508; XI. 98, 400; XII.
   279, 280; XIV. 602; *Apology for Chris-*
   tianity, X. 307, 308; *Apology for the*
   Bible, X. 308
Watson, Richard (1781–1833), XI. 483
Watson, Robert (1730?–1781), X. 505;
   History of Philip II, X. 291; *History of*
   Philip III, X. 291
Watson, Robert Addison, XIII. 488
Watson, Rosamund Marriott (born Tom-
   son) (d. 1911), XIII. 510
Watson, Seth B., XI. 415
Watson, Thomas (1513–1584), V. 394;
   VI. 490; *Absalom*, VI. 296, 480
Watson, Thomas (1557?–1592), III. 252,
   253, 256, 257, 292, 294, 524; IV. 114,
   117, 121, 171, 181, 465, 472; *Amyntas*,
   IV. 131; ΕΚΑΤΟΜΠΑΘΙΑ, or *The*
   Passionate Centurie of Love, III. 252;
   IV. 118, 123, 196; *Tears of Fancie, or*
   Love Disdained, The, III. 253
Watson, Sir William, XII. 408; XIII. 570
Watson-Wentworth, Charles, 2nd mar-
   quis of Rockingham (1730–1782), XI.
   5, 7, 52; XIV. 214
Watt, James (1736–1819), XIV. 258, 381
Watt, Lauchlan Maclean, IX. Add.; XIV.
   525
Watt, Robert (1774–1819), XI. 467; XII.
   521, 523; *Bibliotheca Britannica*, XII.
   370; *Catalogue of Medical Books*, XII.
   370
Watt, William, XI. 445; *Kate Dalrymple*,
   XI. 243; *Tinkler's Waddin*, XI. 243
Watt of Harden, XII. 3
Watteau, Antoine, VIII. 156; XIII. 52
Watton, John, II. 319, 503
Watts, Alaric Alexander (1797–1864), XII.
   423; XIII. 510; *Lyrics of the Heart*,
   XIII. 207
Watts, George Frederick, XIII. 474
Watts, Isaac (1674–1748), IX. 177 ff., 393,
   487; X. 156, 183, 274, 374, 381, 385,
   475, 521, 522; XI. 373, 383, 477, 479;
   XIII. 244
   Divine and Moral Songs, XI. 184, 372
   Divine Songs for Children, IX. 178
   Elegy on Mr Thomas Gouge, IX. 178
   Essay on Civil Power, X. 375

Watts, Isaac
   Horae Lyricae, IX. 178
   Humble attempt, X. 375
   'Hush! my dear, lie still and slumber,'
   XI. 186
   Sapphics, XI. 179
   Sluggard, The, XI. 375
   'When the fierce north wind,' IX. 179
Watts, John (1818–1887), XIV. 610
Watts, William (1590?–1649), VII. 345
Watts Dunton, Walter Theodore (1832–
   1914), IV. 35; X. 236; XI. 476; XII. 406,
   also see Add.; XIII. 137, 194, 491, 495,
   510, 544, 555; XIV. 527; *Aylwin*, XIII.
   207; XIV. 145; *Coming of Love, The*,
   XIV. 145; *Renascence of Wonder in*
   Poetry, The, XIV. 144
Waugh, Arthur, XIII. 478, 485, 486, 508,
   533, 573
Waugh, Edwin (1817–1890), XIII. 511
Waurin, *Chroniques et istoires*, I. 236
Waverley, in Surrey, monastery and an-
   nals of, I. 178, 193, 337
Waverley, Edward, in Scott's novel, XII.
   18, 22, 151
Way, Albert (1805–1874), XII. 519
Way, Arthur S., XIII. 478
Wayland, John, III. 194
Waymouth, George (*fl.* 1605), IV. 99
Waynflete, William (1395?–1486), bishop
   of Winchester, II. 355, 357, 359, 489;
   VII. 327
Waynour (Guinevere), in *Morte Arthure*,
   II. 118
Waynright, James, VII. 438
Wayte, William (1829–1898), XII. 495
Weakest goeth to the Wall, The, V. 316,
   476
Weale, John (1791–1862), XII. 523
Weale, William Henry James, XII. 523
Wealhtheow, in *Beowulf*, I. 22, 23, 24
Wealth and Health, V. 60, 393
Weare, William (d. 1823), XIV. 201, 228,
   230
Wearing of the Green, The, XIV. 311
Wearmouth, monastery of, I. 5, 71, 72, 78,
   80, 83 ff., 89; IV. 418
Weathercock, in *The London Prodigall*,
   V. 255
Weaver, John (1673–1760), X. 440; *The*
   Loves of Mars and Venus, X. 70
Webb, Alfred John (1834–1908), XIV. 572
Webb, Daniel (1719?–1798), XI. 250
Webb, John (1611–1672), IX. 540
Webb, Philip, XIII. 119
Webb, Richmond, grandfather of W. M.
   Thackeray, XIII. 276
Webb, Thomas Ebenezer (1821–1903),
   XIV. 572
Webbe, George, VII. 487
Webbe, Joseph (*fl.* 1612–1633), IV. 435
Webbe, William (*fl.* 1586–1591), III. 206,
   295, 301 ff., 527; IV. 19, 21; V. 131;
   A Discourse of English Poetrie, III. 301;
   V. 72
Webber, Byron, XIV. 541

Weber, Henry William (1783–1818), XI.
472; XII. 358, 375, 517, 519
Weber, Immanuel, *De Nigello Wirekero*,
I. 192
Weber, Wilhelm Eduard, XIV. 268
Webster, Augusta (1837–1894), XIII. 180,
511
Webster, Benjamin Nottingham (1797–
1882), XIII. 268, 515, 516, 524
Webster, James (1658?–1720), IX. 547
Webster, John (1580?–1625?), IV. 6; v.
163, 222, 311, 319, 327, 376; VI. 45, 46,
49, 55, 61, 69, 96, 166–187 (main entry),
195, 200, 401, 423, 424, 444 ff.; VII. 466;
VIII. 436; XII. 68, 116; XIII. 198, 411
  Appius and Virginia, VI. 168, 182, 445,
  also see Add.
  Cure for a Cuckold, A, VI. 69, 182, 184,
  185, 445, 447
  Devil's Law-case, The, v. 364; VI. 168,
  182 ff., 445, 447
  Dutchesse of Malfy, The, III. 355; v. 368;
  VI. 173, 175, 179 ff., 200, 445, 447, *also
  see* Add.
  Guise, The, VI. 182
  Monumental Column, A, VI. 185, 446
  Monuments of Honor, VI. 168, 185
  *Murther of the Sonne upon the Mother,
  A Late*, VI. 182, 195
  Thracian Wonder, The, VI. 69, 185, 445,
  447
  White Divel, The (*Vittoria Corombona*),
  VI. 173 ff., 177, 179 ff., 186, 445, 446;
  VIII. 443; XII. 191
Webster, John (1610–1682), VII. 496, 510,
517; IX. 384, 571; *Academiarum Ex-
amen*, VII. 392; IX. 386; *Displaying of
supposed Witchcraft, The*, VII. 396, 397,
507; IX. 62
Webster, Noah, XIV. 611
Webster, Richard, III. 197
Weckherlin, Georg Rudolph (1584–1653),
VII. 309
Wedderburn, Alexander, 1st earl of
Rosslyn (1733–1805), XII. 142, 426
Wedderburn, Alexander Dundas O., XIV.
524
Wedderburn, David (1580–1646), IX. 558
Wedderburn, James (1495?–1553), III.
141, 153
Wedderburn, John (1500?–1556), III. 141,
153
Wedderburn, Robert (1510?–1557?), III.
141, 153
Wedding of Sir Gawain. See *Gawain*
Wedgwood, Hensleigh (1803–1891), XII.
506
Wedgwood, Josiah (1730–1795), XI. 121
Wedgwood, Julia, XIII. 471
Wednesday Journal, IX. 433
Weekes, John, VII. 9
Weekly Discoverer Stripp'd Naked, The
(1681), VIII. 412
Weekly Dispatch, The, XIV. 192
Weekly Journal, IX. 433
Weekly Magazine, IX. 562

Weekly Pacquet of Advice from Rome
(Care's), IX. 4
Weekly Post, The, VII. 355
Weekly Register, The, XII. 463
Weekly Times, The, XIV. 192
Weelkes, Thomas (*fl.* 1602), IV. 113, 465
Weever, John (1576–1632), IV. 334, 517,
519; v. 253; VII. 407; IX. 350, 540
Wegener, R., VI. 266, 268
Wegg, Silas, in *Our Mutual Friend*, XIII.
336
Weier, Johann, III. 112; *De Praestigiis
Demonum et Incantationibus ac Bene-
ficiis*, III. 112
Weierstrass, Karl, XIV. 264
Weigel, Valentin, VII. 509; IX. 315
Weimar, v. 300, 306; VII. 177; XI. 259;
XII. 38, 158, 302; XIII. 277, 385
Weir, Arthur (1864–1902), XIV. 357, 582
Weir, William (1802–1858), XIV. 535
Weisse, Christian, v. 285, 297, 298
Weissel, Josefine, XIII. 489
Weland Saga, I. 12, 100, 218
Weland Saga, in *Deor*, I. 36
Welbeck Papers, IX. 99
Welby, Thomas Earle, XIII. 495
Welcum to May, II. 282
Weldon, Walter Frank Raphael (1860–
1906), XIV. 564
Wellbred, in *Every Man in His Humour*,
VI. 43
Welldon, Sir Anthony (d. 1649?), VII. 454,
518
Weller, Matilda, XIII. 107
Weller, Sam, in *The Pickwick Papers*, XIII.
314, 322, 387
Wellerisms (Dickens's), XIII. 319
Wellesley, Sir Arthur. *See* Wellington,
duke of
Wellesley, Richard Colley Wellesley, mar-
quis (1760–1842), XI. 392; XIV. 128,
511
Wellington, Arthur Wellesley, 1st duke of
(1769–1852), XI. 167; XII. 97, 154;
XIV. 115, 122, 127, 128, 136, 180, 187,
294, 411, 459, 511; *Despatches*, XIV. 107
Wellington college, XII. 333
Wells, Charles Jeremiah (1799?–1879), XII.
107, 424; XIII. 495; *Joseph and his
Brethren*, XII. 117
Wells, dean of (William Graham), IX. 96
Wells, Herbert George, XIII. 456, 573
Wells, J. T., XIII. 465
Wells, Somerset, I. 213; IV. 422
Wells, William Charles (1757–1817), XIV.
298, 564
Wellsman, W., XIV. 532
Wellwood. *See* Welwood
Welsh, Charles, XI. 376, 468, 476, 478, 479,
482, 483: *A Bookseller of the Last
Century, John Newbery*, x. 210, 482,
484; XI. 377
Welsh, Jane. *See* Carlyle, Jane Welsh
Welsh, the, XIV. 303
Welsh, the, in Jonson's *For the Honour
of Wales*, VI. 371

Welsh academy system, x. 387
Welsh bards, x, 487
Welsh character, xiv. 307
Welsh education, xiv. 433
Welsh language, xii. 308; xiv. 458
Welsh literature, xiii. 199; xiv. 304, 306, 307
Welsh mountains, x. 101
Welsh question, the, ii. 423
Welsh Tudor court, xiv. 307
Welshpool, viii. 106
Welsted, Leonard (1688–1747), ix. 78, 86, 188, 449, 487
Welton, James, xiv. 592
Welwood or Wellwood, James (1652–1727), vii. 447; viii. 440
Welwood, John, ix. 549
Welwood, William (fl. 1577–1622), iv. 462
Welwyn, x. 139
Wem, Shropshire, xii. 165, 166
Wemmick, in Great Expectations, xiii. 334
Wemys, Schir Johne of, in Wyntoun, ii. 130
Wenck, F. A. W., x. 304, 507
Wendland, i. 94
Wendoll, in A Woman Kilde with Kindnesse, vi. 83
Wendover, xi. 5
Wendover. See Roger of
Wenley, Robert Marks, xiv. 483
Wenlock, Sir John, baron Wenlock (d. 1471), ii. 303
Wentworth, captain, in Jane Austen's Persuasion, xii. 240, 242
Wentworth, Charles (1789–1864), xiv. 531
Wentworth, Sir Charles (1810–1869), xiv. 531
Wentworth, Peter (1592–1675), ix. 130
Wentworth, Thos. (1568?–1628), viii. 470
Wentworth, Sir Thomas, 1st earl of Strafford (1593–1641), iv. 311; vii. 140, 148, 187, 197, 206, 219, 223, 224, 435, 439, 441, 512; viii. 220; xiii. 58, 59; Letters and Despatches, vii. 194, 435
Wentworth, Thomas, 3rd earl of Strafford (1672–1739), ix. 151, 216
Wentworth, William Charles (1793–1872), xiv. 588; Australasia, xiv. 362; Description of New South Wales, A, xiv. 371
Werferth, i. 93, 105
Wermueller, Otto, iv. 411
Werner, Friedrich L. Z., x. 80; xiii. 468
Werther, x. 134, 227, 229
Wertherism, xiii. 417
Werwolf, the, in William of Palerne, i. 316
Wesel, ix. 235
Wesley, Charles (1707–1788), ix. 313, 324, 325; x. 364, 365, 369, 517, 518
Wesley, John (1703–1791), iv. 229; ix. 313, 324 ff., 513; x. 1, 59, 350, 363 ff., 423, 517, 518; xi. 79, 422; xii. 259, 278; xiv. 389; Journals, ix. 327, 571; x. 368, 369
Wesley, Samuel, the elder (1662–1735), ix. 393, 572; x. 374, 385, 386; Letter from a country divine, ix. 394

Wesleyans, ix. 308, 328
Wesleys, the, xi. 259
Wessels, J. W., xiv. Add. 10
Wessex, xiii. 320
Wessex, West Saxons, law of, viii. 310, 311
Wessex under Alfred, i. 88, 89
West, Sir Edward (1782–1828), xiv. 483; Essay on the Application of Capital to Land, xiv. 3
West, Gilbert (1703–1756), ix. 145, 479, 487; x. 114, 448; Abuse of Travelling, ix. 189; Education, ix. 189; The Institution of the Order of the Garter, x. 433
West, H. E., xiii. 566
West, John and West, Alice, The severall notorious and lewd cousonages of, iv. 530
West, Rebecca, xiii. Add. 3
West, Richard (fl. 1606–1619), iv. 520
West, Richard (1716–1742), ix. 189; x. 117, 118, 120 ff., 124, 132, 243, 251
West, William (fl. 1568–1594), viii. 467
West Cowes, xiii. 72
West Hythe, Kent, ii. 61
West Indian planter, xiii. 70
West Indies, iv. 92; vii. 453; viii. 191; ix. 260; x. 36, 392; xi. 264; xii. 420; xiii. 355, 369; xiv. 86, 251, 323, 434
West Saxon Gospels, i. 132, 133
Westbrook, Harriet. See Shelley, Mrs
Westbrooks, the, xii. 62
Westbury, near Bristol, xi. 159, 161
Westbury, lord. See Bethell, Richard
Westbury, William, vii. 327
Westbury-on-Trym, ii. 49, 74
Westcote, Thomas (fl. 1624–1636), Devonshire, iv. 308, 514
Westcott, Brooke Foss (1825–1901), bishop of Durham, iv. 41; xii. 298, 340, 467, 470; xiii. 496
Westeraes, Sweden, ii. 319
Western, A., xiii. 513
Western, Mrs, in Fielding's Tom Jones, x. 22
Western, squire, in Fielding's Tom Jones, viii. 161; x. 22, 89, 206; xiv. 231
Western, Sophia, in Fielding's Tom Jones, x. 28, 33, 34, 89
Western isles of Scotland, x. 231, 462, 475
Westernesse (Wirral?), in Horn, i. 304
Westgarth, William (1815–1889), xiv. 588
Australia Felix, xiv. 371
Half-a-century of Australian Progress, xiv. 371
Personal Recollections, xiv. 371
Victoria and the Australian Goldmines, xiv. 371
Victoria, late Australia Felix, xiv. 371
Westmacott, Charles Molloy (pseud. Bernard Blackmantle), xiv. 547; English Spy, The, xiv. 225; Points of Misery, xiv. 225
Westmeath, x. 196
Westminster, in Piers the Plowman, ii. 8, 32

Westminster, III. 19, 69; IV. 128, 422, 544;
v. 9, 350, 366; VI. 3, 261, 327; VII. 62,
160, 207, 333; VIII. 5, 255, 295, 301, 370.
See, also, under London
Westminster, King street, III. 244
Westminster, St Margaret's church, III. 69
Westminster abbey, II. 158, 317; VI. 6,
113; VII. 250; VIII. 21, 55, 61
Caxton's press at, II. 310 ff.
Poet's corner, IV. 195
St Benedict's chapel, II. 158
Westminster Abbey (Ackermann's), XIV.
222
Westminster assembly, IV. 382, 434; VII.
312, 319, 340; VIII. 323; x. 373
Westminster Drolleries (1671, 1672, 1674),
VII. 512; VIII. 116, 423
*Westminster and Foreign Quarterly Re-
view, The*, XII. 430
Westminster gate-house, VII. 65
Westminster Gazette, The, XIV. 195
Westminster hall, III. 61; VI. 332; VII
62, 347; VIII. 317
Westminster Magazine, x. 92
Westminster Quibbles (1672), VII. 512
Westminster Review, The, XI. 60, 61; XII.
152, 307, 310, 318, 351, 430; XIII. 384,
385, 465; XIV. 84, 158
Westminster school, III. 321, 327, 425,
427 ff.; IV. 80, 164; v. 102, 104, 105,
122; VI. 3, 232, 237, 246, 288, 325;
VII. 27, 62, 82, 317, 326, 328, 333, 334,
338, 341, 361; VIII. 2, 50, 185, 328, 344
Westminster scrutiny, XI. 53
Westmoreland (the Greyhound), in *Mum,
Sothsegger*, II. 36
Westmorland, IV. 190; VII. 440; VIII. 101;
x. 386; XI. 103, 109, 111; XIV. 221
Westmorland, earl of, in *Henry V*, v. 262
Westmorland, earl of. *See* Fane, Mildmay
Westmorland Gazette, The, XII. 445; XIV.
203
Weston, Elizabeth Jane (1582–1612), VII.
487
Weston, Jessie Laidlay, I. 270, 328, *also
see* Add.
Weston, Mrs, IX. 71
Weston, Richard, 1st earl of Portland
(1577–1635), VI. 148, 149; VII. 219
Weston, Rev. Stephen (1747–1830), XII.
490, 491
Weston, Thomas (1737–1776), XI. 257
Weston Favell, x. 365
Weston Underwood, XI. 88, 404
Westport, Wilts., VII. 282
Westropp, Hodder M. (d. 1884), XII. 514
Westward for Smelts, IV. 361, 523, 531, 532
Westwood, John Obadiah (1805–1893),
XII. 514
Westwood, Thomas (1814?–1888), XII.
201; XIII. 511; *Quest of the Sancgreall,
The*, XIII. 188; *Springlets*, XIII. 188
Wetherald, Ethelwyn, XIV. 349
Wever, R., *Lusty Juventus*, v. 59, 392
Wexford, XIV. 315
Wey, William (1407?–1476), II. 499

Weymouth, 3rd viscount. *See* Thynne
Thomas
Wha wadna fecht for Charlie, IX. 378
Whachum, in *Hudibras*, VIII. 72, 73
Whale, The, I. 428
Whalley, Peter (1722–1791), IX. 532; x.
505
Whalley, Thomas Sedgwick (1746–1828),
XI. 429
Wharfe river, VII. 180
Wharncliffe, lord. *See* Stuart-Wortley,
John
Wharton, Anne (1632?–1685), VIII. 444
Wharton, duke of, in Pope's *Epistles*,
IX. 81
Wharton, Sir George (1617–1681), VII. 501;
Mercurius Elencticus, VII. 357
Wharton, Henry (1664–1695), II. 73; VII.
483; VIII. 306, 463; IX. 489
Wharton, Philip, 4th lord Wharton (1613–
1696), VIII. 97
Wharton, Thomas, 1st marquis of Whar-
ton (1648–1715), VIII. 96; IX. 45, 94,
95, 455, 487; x. 117, 122, 123, 127, 131,
133, 135; XI. 30
Wharton, William, *A New Song of the
Times*, VIII. 97
Wharton, William James Lloyd, XIV. 551
'What bird so sings yet so dos wayl?'
v. 125
What is Love? XIV. 304
Whateley, Anne. *See* Hathwey, Anne
Whateley, Thomas (d. 1772), x. 399, 523;
XI. 389
Whately, Richard (1787–1863), XI. 415;
XII. 242, 243, 285 ff., 292, 447, 470, 471;
XIV. 116, 483, 610
Elements of Logic, XIV. 16
*Historic Doubts relative to Napoleon
Buonaparte*, XII. 285
Letters on the Church, XII. 285
Rhetoric, XIV. 428
Whatley, Stephen (*fl.* 1725–1732), IX.
495
Wheatley, Henry Benjamin, VI. 260; VIII.
Add.; XI. 396, 467, 469; XIV. 508
Wheatley, Oxon., VII. 104
Wheatstone, Sir Charles (1802–1875), XIV.
261, 557
Wheeler, George, *Journey into Greece*
(1682), IV. 462
Wheeler, Harold Felix Baker, XIV. 541
Wheeler, James Talboys (1824–1897), XIV.
338, 339, 580
Wheeler, John (*fl.* 1601–1608), IV. 310,
514
Wheeler, mistress Elizabeth, in Herrick's
Hesperides, VII. 13
Wheeler, Stephen, XII. 206, 439
Wheelock or Wheloc, Abraham (1593–
1653), I. 112; VII. 319, 320, 483, 485
Whelpdale, in Gissing's *New Grub Street*,
XIII. 455
Whetham, William Cecil Dampier, XIV.
555
Whethamstede, John (d. 1465), IX. 535

Whetstone, George (1544?–1587?), III.
189, 299, 343, 519, 536; IV. 443; V. 63,
120, 190, 220, 397, 403, 408, 409; VI. 499
  Life of Sir Nicholas Bacon, XII. 357, 515
  Mirour for Magestrates, VI. 395, 403, 499
  Promos and Cassandra, III. 299, 527;
  V. 117, 119, 120
  *Rich his Farewell to the Militarie Pro-
  fession*, III. 343
  Rock of Regard, The, III. 343
  Touchstone for the Time, VI. 395
Whewell, William (1794–1866), VIII. 351;
XIV. 207, 258, 483, 557, 565, 593, 594;
  History of the Inductive Sciences, XIV.
  17, 259, 289; *On the principles of English
  university education*, XIV. 412; *Thoughts
  on the Study of Mathematics*, XIV. 412
Whibley, Charles, XI. 396; XII. 444; XIII.
489, 499, 530, 546, 547; XIV. 537
'Which nobody can deny,' VIII. 95, 97
Whichcote or Whitchcote, Benjamin
(1609–1683), VII. 279; VIII. 273 ff., 280,
288, 290, 291, 297, 457; IX. 300;
  Aphorisms, VIII. 276, 277, 281; *Sermons*,
  VIII. 277
Whig Examiner, IX. 151, 437, 439
Whigs of Fife, The, IX. 378
Whipping of the Satyre, The (1601), IV. 517
Whirler, Jack, in Johnson's *Idler*, X. 178
Whistle Binkie, XI. 445
'Whistlecraft,' VII. 79
Whistlecraft, Mr (J. H. Frere), XII. 52
Whistler, Anthony (1714–1754), IX. 412;
X. 271 ff., 496; *The Shuttlecock*, X. 272
Whistler, James McNeill, XIII. 433, 495
Whiston, William (1667–1752), IX. 509;
X. 377
  Historical Preface, X. 379
  Josephus, IX. 295
  Primitive Christianity, X. 379
  Primitive Christianity Revived, IX. 295
Whitaker, Jeremiah (1599–1654), VII. 317
Whitaker, John (1735–1808), X. 510
  Course of Hannibal over the Alps, X. 320
  Genuine History of the Britons, X. 320
  Gibbon's History...reviewed, X. 310, 508
  History of Manchester, X. 310, 320
Whitaker, Joseph (1820–1895), XIV. 532
Whitaker, L., IV. 90
Whitaker, Thomas Dunham (1759–1821),
XII. 345, 514; *History of Richmondshire*,
XII. 346
Whitaker, William (1548–1595), III. 422;
IV. 275; VII. 309, 316
Whitbourne, Sir Richard (*fl.* 1579–1627),
IV. 462
Whitbread, Samuel (1758–1815), XIV. 120,
406, 511
Whitbread's brewery, XI. 38
Whitby, I. 42, 96; XI. 429; XII. 10; XIII.
380
Whitchurch, X. 272, 387
Whitchurch, Edward (d. 1561), III. 194,
195; IV. 396
Whitchurch, James Wadham, XIV. 610
Whitchurch, T., III. 44

Whitchurch school, VII. 330
White, Blanco. *See* White, Joseph Blanco
White, Edward (*fl.* 1594–1603), IV. 384,
393
White, Gertrude, in Black's *Macleod of
Dare*, XIII. 432
White, Gilbert (1720–1793), X. 269 ff.,
496, *also see* Add.; XIII. 429; XIV. 166;
  Natural History of Selborne, X. 269;
  Naturalist's Calendar, X. 270
White, Gleeson, XI. 476
White, Henry Kirke (1785–1806), XI. 172,
422; XII. 424; *Oft in danger, oft in woe*,
XII. 136; *The Star of Bethlehem*, XII.
136
White, James (1775–1820), XII. 438; *The
Falstaff Letters*, XII. 183, 185
White, John, *Three Letters to a Gentleman*,
X. 375
White, Joseph (1745–1814), Bampton
lectures, X. 309, 508
White, Joseph Blanco (1775–1841), XII.
471; XIII. 46
White, R. (1645–1703), VII. 402
White, Richard Grant, V. 279
White, Robert, printer, VII. 361
White, Robert (1802–1874), XI. 444
White, Sir Thomas (1492–1567), III. 420;
VII. 332, 334
White, Thomas (1550?–1624), VI. 376,
386, 499
White, Thomas (1593–1676), VII. 475;
  *Sciri, sive sceptices et scepticorum a jure
  disputationis exclusio*, VII. 302
White, Thomas (*fl.* 1700), XI. 484; *A
Little Book for Little Children*, XI. 369,
370
White, Thomas Pilkington, XII. 514
White, W. (*fl.* 1599), V. 158
White, Walter (1811–1893), XIV. 554
White, William Hale. *See* Rutherford,
Mark
White Book of Rhyðerch, The, I. 252
White Canons, II. 349
White Cock and Hen, of St Domingo, III.
106
White Harts, the, in *Mum, Sothsegger*, II.
36
White sea, the, I. 94
Whitefield, George (1714–1770), IV. 229;
X. 88, 276, 363 ff., 518, 522; XI. 79
Whitefoord, Caleb (1734–1810), X. 482
Whitefoot, John, VII. 461
Whitefriars, his eminence of, in Scott's
Fortunes of Nigel, XII. 21
Whitehall, John, VII. 476
Whitehall Evening Post, IX. 21, 433
Whitehaven, IX. 91
Whitehead, Charles (1804–1862), XII. 107
424; XIII. 418
  As yonder Lamp in my Vacated Room,
  XII. 119
  Cavalier, The, XII. 119
  Jack Ketch, XII. 119
  Richard Savage, XII. 119
  Solitary, The, XII. 118

Whitehead, George (1636?–1723), VIII. 416

Whitehead, John (1740?–1804), x. 518

Whitehead, Paul (1710–1774), x. 525; XII. 118; XIV. 547; *The Gymnasiad*, XIV. 230

Whitehead, William (1715–1785), x. 438; XI. 34; XII. 118; *Creusa, Queen of Athens*, x. 86; *Roman Father*, x. 86; *School for Lovers*, x. 86

Whitehorne, Peter (*fl.* 1550–1563), IV. 3, 7, 446, 462

Whitelocke, Bulstrode (1605–1675), VI. 408; VII. 447, 454, 460; VIII. 117
Journal of his Swedish Embassy, VII. 230
Memorials of the English Affairs, VII. 229, 230; VIII. 323
Monarchy asserted to be the best, most Ancient and legall form of Government, VII. 231
Notes upon the King's Writt, VII. 230

White's Chocolate house, IX. 33

Whiteway, Mrs, IX. 100

Whitfield, Henry, IX. 313

Whitford or Whytford, Richard (*fl.* 1495–1555?), III. 470; IV. 496

Whitford, Vernon (George Meredith's), XIII. 447

Whitgift, John (1530–1604), archbishop of Canterbury, III. 213, 375 ff., 380, 385, 390, 392, 397, 406, 413, 422, 424, 548; IV. 275, 382, 411, 494, 519, 545; V. 365, 482; VI. 384; IX. 496

Whithorn, Galloway, II. 127, 128

Whithorne, Thomas (*fl.* 1590), IV. 112, 465

Whiting, Lilian, XIII. 485

Whiting, Nathaniel, *Albino and Bellama*, VII. 80, 413

Whiting, Richard (d. 1539), III. 49

Whitley, William Thomas, x. 519

Whitlock, John (1625–1709), x. 387

Whitman, Walt, IV. 50, 246; x. 148, 368; XI. 409; XII. 404; XIII. 108, 151, 337, 489; XIV. 208

Whitney, Geoffrey (1548?–1601), VII. 479

Whitsun plays, v. 13, 34, 48

Whittaker, Edmund Taylor, XIV. 555

Whittaker, Thomas, XIV. 479; *Catalogue of Bentham's MSS.*, XI. 397

Whittaker, William Joseph, XIV. 80

Whittemore, T., XIII. Add. 2

Whitten, Wilfred, XIV. 546

Whittier, John G., VIII. 113

Whittingham, William (1524?–1579), III. 44, 45, 46

Whittington, Richard (d. 1423), II. 288

Whittington, Robert (*fl.* 1520), III. 341, 555; IV. 435, 436; Tully's *Offices*, IV. 5; *The Forme and Rule of Honest lyvinge*, IV. 5, 439; *The Remedyes against all casuall Chances*, IV. 5, 440

Whittlesea or Whittlesey or Whittlesay, William, archbishop of Canterbury (d. 1374), II. 365

Whitty, Edward Michael (1827–1860), XIV. 199

Who liveth so merry in all this land? III. 484

Whole Duty of Man, The, VII. 148, 427

Whymper, Edward (1840–1911), XIV. 255, 554

Whyte, E. A. and S., x. 480

Whyte, Samuel (1733–1811), XIV. 572

Whyte-Melville, George John (1821–1878), XIII. 434, 564; XIV. 366

Wibourne, Nathaniel, *Machiavellus*, VI. 305, 480

'Wickedshifts' (lord Brougham), XIV. 116

Wickens, William (d. 1699), x. 386

Wicket, The, III. 25

Wicket-gate, the, in Bunyan's *Pilgrim's Progress*, VII. 173

Wickfields, the, in *David Copperfield*, XIII. 327

Wickham, Edward Charles (1834–1910), XII. 495

Wickhambrook, Suffolk, XI. 140

Wickham Brook academy, x. 387

Wickins, Nathan, VII. 515

Wicklow, XIV. 329

Wicksteed, Clara Mabel, XIII. 545

Wiclif. *See* Wyclif

Wicquefort, A. de, *L'Ambassadeur et ses Fonctions*, VII. 191

Widdowes, Giles (1588?–1645), *The Lawless Kneeless Schismatical Puritan*, VII. 160, 427

Widford, Hertfordshire, XII. 182, 186

Widia (Wudga), in *Waldhere*, I. 36

Widsith, I. 1, 3, 19 ff., 31, 34, 36, 37, 424, 428, *also see* Add.; v. 26

Wieland, Christopher Martin, v. 296 ff., 301, 304, 307; VII. 177; x. 19, 422; XII. 422; *Clementina della Poretta*, x. 18

Wier, Johann, VII. 366, 371, 396; VIII. 357; *De Praestigiis demonum*, VII. 370, 506

Wife of Auchtermychty, The, IX. 361

Wife of Bath, VII. 382

Wife of Usher's Well, I. 300; II. 414

Wife's Complaint, The, I. 38, 39, 424, 428

Wiggin, Kate D., XIII. 544

Wiggington, Giles (*fl.* 1569–1592), III. 397

Wight, isle of, IV. 190; x. 252; XII. 188, 509; XIII. 129

Wight, John (*fl.* 1585), IV. 410, 411

Wight, John, editor of *Morning Post*, XIV. 188

Wight, O. W., XII. 371

Wight, Willie, of Aikwood, XII. 3

Wightman, Frances Lucy, wife of Matt. Arnold, XIII. 87

Wiglaf, in *Beowulf*, I. 1, 24, 25

Wigstons, the, III. 382, 383

Wihenoe, the Breton, I. 257

Wil Bagnal's Ghost, III. 99

Wil and Wit, I. 228, 459

Wilberforce, Henry William (1807–1873), XII. 274, 463

Wilberforce, Robert Isaac (1802–1857), XII. 454, 455, 463, 473; XIV. 507; *The Doctrine of the Incarnation*, XII. 274

Wilberforce, Samuel (1805–1873), bishop of Oxford, VIII. 250; XI. 490; XII. 473

Wilberforce, William (1759–1833), x. 262, 269; xi. 52, 259, 405; xii. 282, 473; xiv. 120, 177, 373, 403, 507, 514; *A Practical View of Christianity*, xii. 281

Wilbye, John (*fl.* 1598–1614), iv. 113, 465

Wilcock, William (*fl.* 1480), ii. 318

Wilcox, Thomas (1549?–1608), iii. 403; iv. 518

Wild, Jonathan, in Fielding's *Jonathan Wild*, x. 27, 39

Wild, Mrs Jonathan, in Fielding's *Jonathan Wild*, x. 28

Wild, Robert (1609–1679), viii. 409, 411

Wildair, Sir Harry (Farquhar's), viii. 170, 172

Wilde, George (1610–1665), vi. 326, 480; *Love's Hospitale*, vi. 326

Wilde, Jane Francisca, lady (*pseud.* 'Speranza,' 1826–1896), xiv. 318, 572

Wilde, Oscar F. O'F. W. (1856–1900), xiii. 524; xiv. 158, 211, 329, 527, 528, *also see* Add. 3; *Ballad of Reading Gaol, The*, xiv. 159; *De Profundis*, xiv. 159

Wilde, Sir William Robert Wills (1815–1876), xii. 351, 514; xiv. 572

Wilder, Theaker, x. 198

Wilderspin, Samuel (1792?–1866), xiv. 405, 610

Wilfer family, in *Our Mutual Friend*, xiii. 337

Wilford, John (*fl.* 1723–1742), *Monthly Catalogue*, xi. 339, 471

Wilfrid, St, bishop of York (634–709), i. 16, 82, 85

Wilkes, John (1727–1797), vi. 7; x. 190, 296, 390 ff. (main entry), 399, 401, 402, 404, 405, 452, 474, 522 ff., *also see* Add.; xi. 8; xii. 54; *Essay on Woman*, x. 397; *The North Briton*, vii. 200; x. 251

Wilkes, T., viii. 429

Wilkes, William, vi. 38

Wilkie, Sir David (1785–1841), xii. 177; xiv. 545

Wilkie, William (1721–1772), ix. 557

Wilkin, Simon (1790–1862), vii. 235

Wilkins, Augustus Samuel (1843–1905), xii. 337, 495

Wilkins, Sir Charles (1749?–1836), xii. 343, 503

Wilkins, David (1685–1745), viii. 322, 469; *Concilia*, ix. 350, 356, 540

Wilkins, George (*fl.* 1607), iv. 527, 532; *The Miseries of Inforst Mariage*, v. 242; vi. 69, 97; viii. 142; *The Travailes of The three English Brothers*, vi. 69, 455

Wilkins, Henry Musgrave (c. 1822–1887), xii. 495

Wilkins, John (1614–1672), vii. 466, 517; viii. 273, 277, 297, 304, 463, 476; ix. 386, 571; *Ecclesiastes or the Gift of Preaching*, viii. 369

Wilkins, William Glyde, xiii. 532, 544

Wilkins, William Henry (1860–1905), xiv. 500

Wilkinson, Charles Allix, xiv. 597

Wilkinson, J., *Select Views in Cumberland*, xi. 408

Wilkinson, James John Garth (1812–1899), xi. 433

Wilkinson, Sir John Gardner (1797–1875), xii. 317, 477, 500; xiv. 554; *Manners and Customs of the Ancient Egyptians*, xii. 342

Wilkinson, Tate (1739–1803), x. 430, 446; xi. 449, 454

Wilkinson, Thomas, a friend of Wordsworth, xi. 409

Wilkinson, William Clever, xiii. 498

Wilks, Mark (1760–1831), xiv. 580; *Historical Sketches of the South of India*, xiv. 335

Wilks, Robert (1665?–1732), viii. 170, 172, 173; x. 21

Will (Anima), in *Piers the Plowman*, ii. 27

Will, in *Damon and Pithias*, v. 119

'Will,' in Shakespeare's sonnets, v. 229

Will Stewart and John, ii. 410

'Will ye go to the coals in the morning?' ix. 373

Willem, a Fleming, i. 366

Willes or Willey, Richard (*fl.* 1558–1573), iv. 75, 456

Willet, Andrew (1562–1621), vii. 406

Willet, John, in *Barnaby Rudge*, xiii. 321

Willett, B. W., xiii. 555

William, in *Piers the Plowman*, ii. 12

William, duke of Gloucester (1689–1700), ix. 200, 236

William I (the Conqueror), king of England, i. 111, 141, 149, 150, 155, 256, 396; ii. 342; iii. 338; v. 252; viii. 310, 384; ix. 343; x. 110, 467; xii. 31; xiii. 366; xiv. 72

William II, king of England, i. 162, 189; xiv. 111

William III, king of Great Britain, viii. 49, 92, 93, 99, 122, 195, 201, 215, 220, 261, 264, 267, 268, 294, 300, 305, 306, 307, 380, 382, 452; ix. 7, 8, 92, 148, 155, 175, 180, 200, 202, 203, 208, 213, 228, 233, 235, 258, 271; x. 295, 356, 373, 389, 502; xiv. 64, 65, 212

William IV, king of Great Britain, xi. 141

William Augustus, duke of Cumberland (1721–1765), ix. 162, 563

William de Kilkenny, ii. 352

William de Mandagoto, ii. 364

William de la Mare (*fl.* 1284), i. 210, 456

William de Monte Lauduns (c. 1346), ii. 364

William de Shareshull (*fl.* 1360), ii. 37

William of Auvergne, i. 207

William of Boldensele (c. 1336), ii. 80

William of Champeaux, i. 183

William of Drogheda (d. 1245?), ii. 499

William of Durham (d. 1249), ii. 352

William of Heytesbury, *Sophismata*, ii. 363

William of Malmesbury (d. 1143?), I. 5,
72, 90, 91, 96, 97, 101, 105, 106, 155,
157, 159, 162, 164, 168, 171, 172, 218,
243, 250, 256, 257, 262, 269, 337, 450,
451, 460; II. 396, 398, 399, 412; III. 368;
XII. 355, 516
William of Newburgh (1136–1198), I. 68,
160, 161, 168, 169, 171 ff., 245, 257,
450, 451; IX. 534
William of Ockham. *See* Ockham
William of Palerne, I. 281, 286, 292, 316,
357, 378, 472
William of Ramsey (*fl.* 1219), II. 499
William of Shoreham, I. 353 ff., 476; III.
274
William of Tyre, The continuation of
(1261), II. 80
William of Wadington, *Manuel des
Pechiez*, I. 204, 344 ff., 348, 349; II. 139,
150, 420; V. 41
William of Worcester (1415–1482?), II.
308; IV. 68
William of Wychwood, II. 35
William of Wykeham. *See* Wykeham
William Rufus, in *Satiro-Mastix*, VI. 44
William the Clerk, II. 509
William the trouvère, II. 507
Williams, Alfred M., XIV. 573, 610
Williams, Anna (1706–1783), x. 187, 458,
470, 479; XI. 350; *Miscellanies*, x. 168
Williams, Caleb, in Godwin's novel, XI.
46, 293
Williams, Sir Charles Hanbury (1708–
1759), XI. 172 ff., 429; XII. 120; *Works*,
XI. 173
Williams, Daniel (1643?–1716), IX. 503;
x. 387; *Defence*, x. 387; *Gospel Truth*,
x. 377; *Peace with Truth*, x. 377
Williams, David (1738–1816), XIV. 610
Williams, Edward (*fl.* 1560), *Virgo
Triumphans; or Virginia Really and
truly valued*, IV. 96, 462
Williams, Edward Ellerker (1793–1822),
XII. 76, 383, 398
Williams, Gardner F., XIV. Add. 10
Williams, George (1814–1878), XII. 514
Williams, Helen Maria (1762–1827), XI.
177, 430; XII. 124
Williams, Isaac (1802–1865), XII. 258,
261, 265–266 (main entry), 424, 454,
455, 463; XIII. 167, 511; *Autobiography*,
XII. 266; *On reserve in communicating
religious knowledge*, XII. 260; *The
Cathedral*, XII. 266; XIII. 171
Williams, Jane, friend of Shelley, XII.
73, 75, 76
Williams, John (1582–1650), archbishop
of York, IV. 265, 266, 306, 422, 426;
VII. 62, 154, 219, 333, 491
Williams, John (1761–1818), XI. 472
Williams, John (Ab Ithel) (1811–1862),
XII. 514
Williams, J. B., XIV. 535
Williams, Mary, XIII. 544
Williams, Oliver, VII. 362, 363, 496, 501;
An Extract Accompt, VII. 361

Williams, Oliver
Occurrences from Foreign parts, VII. 361
Politicus, VII. 361
Publick Intelligencer, VII. 361
Williams, Richard D'Alton (1822–1862),
XIV. Add. 3; *The Munster War Song*,
XIV. 318
Williams, Sir Roger (1540?–1595), IV. 462
Williams, Rowland (1817–1870), XII. 295,
466, 471, 478; *Psalms and Litanies*, XII.
296
Williams, R. A., XIII. 513
Williams, Sarah or 'Sadie' (d. 1868), XIII.
180, 511
Williams, T., *The Excellency and Prae-
heminence of the Law of England* (1680),
VIII. 470
Williams, William, *Occult Physick* (1660),
VII. 510
Williams, W. S., XIII. 407, 414
Williams, Zachariah (1673?–1755), x. 468;
*Account of an Attempt to ascertain the
Longitude at Sea*, x. 176, 468
Williams murders, the, XII. 227
Williams's library, Dr, IX. 307, 511, 514,
520; x. 520
Williamson, Alexander William (1824–
1904), XIV. 272, 277, 558
Williamson, Sir Joseph (1633–1701), VII.
363, 364; IX. 212, 213, 496
Williamson, Peter (1730–1799), IX. 562
Williamson, Richard, XIV. 598
Williamson, William Crawford (1816–
1895), XIV. 290, 565
Willibald (700?–786), I. 435
Willie, in *The Shepheards Calender*, III. 222
Willie and Earl Richard's daughter, II.
411
Willie's gane to Melville Castle, IX. 374
Willie's Lyke-Wake, II. 411
Willikin, in *Ane Pleasant Satyre*, III. 127
Willing, James, XIII. 556
Willingham, lady Maria, in Mrs Gore's
Mothers and Daughters, XII. 246
Willington, James (*i.e.* Oliver Goldsmith),
x. 203
Willis, Browne (1682–1760), IX. 358, 540;
History of the Mitred Abbies, IX. 354;
Survey of the cathedrals, IX. 354
Willis, N. P., XII. 382
Willis, Richard (1664–1734), IX. 572
Willis, Robert (1800–1875), XII. 514;
Architectural History of Cambridge,
XII. 348
Willis, Thomas (1621–1675), VIII. 479;
XIV. 281
Willison, John (1680–1750), IX. 549
Willmott, Robert Aris (1809–1863), (?)*Con-
versations at Cambridge* (1836), XI. 417
Willobie his Avisa, IV. 472
Willoughby, Francis, 5th baron of Par-
ham (1613?–1666), VII. 453
Willoughby, Sir Henry (*fl.* 1616–1621),
IV. 165
Willoughby, Sir Hugh (d. 1554), I. 94;
IV. 69, 71, 72, 84, 88

Will's coffee-house, IX. 33, 122, 256, 271, 348

Wills, James (1790–1868), XIV. 312, 572

Wills, William Gorman (1828–1891), XIII. 524, 556; XIV. 572; *Charles I*, XIII. 268; *Marie Stuart*, XIII. 268

Wills, William Henry (1810–1880), XIII. 542; XIV. 236

Wills, William John (1834–1861), XIV. 364

Wills, W. R., XIV. 588

Willughby, Francis (1635–1672), VIII. 479; XIV. 565; *History of Fishes*, XIV. 282; *History of Insects*, XIV. 282; *Ornithology*, XIV. 282

Wilmington, earl. *See* Compton, Spencer

Wilmot, Hon. Alexander, XIV. 588, *also see* Add. 4, 11

Wilmot, Henry, 1st earl of Rochester (1612?–1658), VIII. 206

Wilmot, John, 2nd earl of Rochester (1647–1680), IV. 197, 214, 222, 224; VII. 180, 358; VIII. 4, 25, 28, 35, 83, 86, 91, 174, 188, 193, 199, 200 ff., 206–215 (main entry), 219, 300, 373, 379, 409 ff., 423, 444 ff., 459, 461, *also see* Add.; IX. 18, 174, 198, 445, 489; X. 169
  Commons' Petition to the King (1679), VIII. 94
  Dispute, The, VIII. 93
  Epistolary Essay, An, VIII. 209
  History of Insipids, The, VIII. 94
  Maim'd Debauchee, The, VIII. 215
  Nothing, VIII. 213
  On the Young Statesmen, VIII. 94
  Satire against Mankind, A, VIII. 214
  Session of the Poets, VIII. 136
  Valentinian, VIII. 220

Wilmot, Robert (*fl.* 1568–1608), V. 72, 73, 76

Wilmot, in Lillo's *Fatal Curiosity*, X. 77, 78

Wilson, Alexander (1766–1813), XI. 237, 445; *Watty and Meg*, XI. 236

Wilson, Alexander (d. 1852), XIII. 511

Wilson, Andrew (1831–1881), XIV. 554

Wilson, Arthur (1595–1652), IV. 64; VII. 447, 454

Wilson, Arthur, *History of King James I*, IX. 233

Wilson, Caroline (1787–1846), XII. 473

Wilson, Charles, *Memories of Congreve* (1730), VIII. 428

Wilson, Charles Robert (1863–1904), XIV. 338, 339, 580

Wilson, Sir Charles William (1836–1905), XII. 514

Wilson, Daniel (1778–1858), XII. 473

Wilson, Sir Daniel (1816–1892), XII. 514; *Archaeology and Prehistoric Annals of Scotland*, XII. 351; *Prehistoric Man*, XII. 351

Wilson, David Alec, XIII. 471

Wilson, David Mackay, XIV. Add. 11

Wilson, Fred. J. F., XIV. 536

Wilson, Henry Bristow (1803–1888), XII. 466, 471; XIV. 598; *The Communion of Saints*, XII. 284; 'The National Church,' XII. 295

Wilson, Horace Hayman (1786–1860), XII. 343, 503; XIV. 97, 337, 495, 500, 580; *Ariana Antiqua*, XII. 352, 353

Wilson, James Maurice, XIV. 426, 597, 606

Wilson, John (1627?–1696), VIII. 421
  A New Anatomie, VII. 384
  Andronicus Comnenus, VIII. 124
  Belphegor, VIII. 123
  Cheats, The, VIII. 122
  Projectors, The, VIII. 123
  Trans. of *The Praise of Folly*, III. Add.

Wilson, John (1720–1789), IX. 557

Wilson, John (1774–1855), XII. 173

Wilson, John, 'Christopher North' (1785–1854), XI. 244, 411, 437, 440, 442; XII. 156 ff., 425, 445, *also see* Add.; XIII. 25, 26, 108, 148, 187, 479; XIV. 232; *City of the Plague, The*, XII. 158; *Isle of Palms, The*, XII. 158; *Noctes Ambrosianae*, XI. 239; XII. 159, 160; XIV. 313

Wilson, John, of Kilmarnock, XI. 342

Wilson, John Dover, IV. 320; V. 114; *Martin Marprelate and Shakespeare's Fluellen*, III. Add.

Wilson, J. G., XIII. Add. 2

Wilson, John Mackay (1804–1835), XII. 452, 453; *Tales of the Borders*, XIV. 203

Wilson, John Matthias (1813–1881), XIV. 472

Wilson, Mr, in Fielding's *Joseph Andrews*, IX. 408; X. 30

Wilson, Robert, the elder (d. 1600), V. 312, 320, 370; VI. 15, 246; *The Three Ladies of London*, V. 314, 366, 393; *The Three Lords and Three Ladies of London*, V. 314; VI. 249

Wilson, Robert, the younger (1579–1610), V. 236, 312, 313, 319, 323, 331

Wilson, Robert Arthur (1820?–1875), XIV. 572

Wilson, Samuel, IV. 462

'Wilson, Rev. T.,' XI. 481

Wilson, Sir Thomas (1560?–1629), IV. 447

Wilson, Thomas (1525?–1581), III. 21, 23, 24, 290 ff., 431, 432, 446, 447, 470, 527, 554; IV. 1, 436, 438; VII. 476, 479
  Arte of Rhetorique, II. 162; III. 23, 431, 432
  Discourse uppon usurye, IV. 313, 514, 518
  The Rule of Reason, conteining the arte of logique, V. 105, 408; VII. 276
  Three Orations of Demosthenes, III. 24

Wilson, Thomas (1663–1755), bishop of Sodor and Man, IX. 572; X. 351, 358, 518; XII. 268; *Maxims*, X. 359; *Parochialia*, X. 359; *Sacra Privata*, X. 359

Wilson, Walter (1781–1847), X. 519; XII. 201

Wilson, William (1801–1860), XII. 424; XIV. 592

Wilton, III. 351; IV. 124, 132; VII. 61; XII. 192

Wilton, Ralph de, in Scott's *Marmion*, XII. 11

Wiltshire, IV. 314; VI. 281; VII. 29, 74, 282; IX. 187, 351, 531; XI. 148, 178; XII. 345, 508, 510, 513

Wiltshire, earls of. *See* Boleyn, Sir Thomas; Butler, James

Wily Beguiled (1606), V. 129; VI. 300

Wimble, Will, in *The Spectator*, IX. 53; X. 199

Wimborne, IV. 421; IX. 146

Wimpole, IX. 152, 153; XI. 347

Winch, Sir Humphrey (1555?–1625), VIII. 470

Winchcomb, John, in *Jack of Newbury*, III. 368

Winchelsea, sea fight off, II. 120

Winchester, VII. 250, 444; IX. 151, 221, 534; X. 109, 132, 139, 224, 238, 355, 492; XII. 231, 327, 348, 517; XIV. 73, 101

Winchester, annals of, I. 178

Winchester, library of, IV. 422

Winchester, monastery and school of, I. 113, 114, 116, 118, 125

Winchester, Elhanan, XII. 471

Winchester Chronicle, I. 104, 109, 112. See, also, under *Chronicle*

Winchester college, II. 355 ff., 359, 489; III. 187, 418, 427 ff.; IV. 161, 163, 242, 261, 262, 265; V. 103; VII. 233, 241, 326, 328, 329, 331, 334, 493; VIII. 181

Winchester diocese, VII. 326, 327

Winchester downs, X. 303

Winchester school, IX. 188, 300, 405, 408 ff., 573; XIV. 386, 387, 406, 422

Winchilsea, countess of. *See* Finch, Anne

Winchilsea, earl of. *See* Finch, Heneage

Wind Blaws Cauld, IX. 362

Windele, John (1801–1865), XII. 519

Windermere, lake, XII. 158

Windham, Joseph (1739–1810), X. 260, 261

Windham, William (1750–1810), X. 473; XI. 388, 389; XIV. 120, 507, 511

Windisch, Wilhelm O. E., XIV. 307

Windsor, I. 369; II. 357; IV. 191, 420; V. 116, 348; VI. 274; VII. 16, 59, 60, 98, 254, 307, 309, 327, 459; VIII. 97, 321, 358; IX. 193; X. 111, 224, 238, 260, 360; XI. 38; XII. 59

Windsor, Maidens' tower, III. 178

Windsor, Nova Scotia, XIV. 346

Windsor, St George's chapel, II. 158; VI. 288

Windsor castle, XII. 345

Windsor forest, IX. 67; XIII. 355

Wine-god, the, in Hawes's *A Joyful Meditation*, etc., II. 226

Winestead, in Holderness, VII. 178

Wing, Vincent (1619–1668), VII. 509

Wingate, David (1828–1892), XIII. 511

Wingate, Edmund (1596–1656), VIII. 465, 470

Wingfield, Anthony (1550?–1615?), VI. 306, 327, 480

Wingfield, Henry, III. 81; *Contra Expugnatores Missae* (six dialogues), III. 81

Wingfield, Lewis Strange (1842–1891), XIV. 554, 572; *Lady Grizel*, XIV. 328; *My Lords of Strogue*, XIV. 328; *Slippery Ground*, XIV. 328

Winkle, Nathaniel, in *The Pickwick Papers*, XIII. 314

Winkworth, Catherine (1827–1878), XIII. 511; XIV. 600

Winkworth, Susanna (1820–1884), XIV. 600

Winstanley, Gerrard (*fl.* 1648–1652), IX. 307

Winstanley, Lilian, XII. 405

Winstanley, William (1628?–1698), VII. 15, 25, 91, 92

Winteney, nuns of, I. 230, 458, 459

Winter, in folk-plays, V. 31

Winter, John Strange, *pseud. See* Stannard, Henrietta E. V.

Winter, R., V. 71

Winter Dreame, A, VII. 386

Winter Evening Entertainments, XI. 370

Winterslow, Wiltshire, XII. 167, 192, 432

Winterton, Ralph (1600–1636), VII. 489

Winthrop, Dolly, in George Eliot's *Silas Marner*, XIII. 393

Winthrop, John (1588–1649), VII. 353

Winton, earl of. *See* Seton, George

Winwood, Sir Ralph (1563?–1617), V. 480; VII. 438; X. 504

Winworth, lord, in Kelly's *False Delicacy*, XI. 263

Winzet, Ninian (1518–1592), III. 505; IV. 412; *Certain Tractatis for Reformation*, II. 285; III. 154

Wireker, Nigel (*fl.* 1190), I. 173, 176, 192, 455; III. 102

Wirgman, Augustus Theodore, XIV. Add. 11

Wirksworth, XIII. 389

Wirral, I. 304

Wirtenberg, Journals of two dukes of, V. 479

Wisbech, X. 377

Wisbech school, VII. 330

Wisconsin, V. 85

Wisdom, in Carew's *Coelum Britannicum*, VII. 19

Wisdom, in *The Example of Virtue*, II. 227, 228, 230

Wisdom, in *The Passetyme of Pleasure*, II. 228

Wisdom, in *Piers the Plowman*, II. 10

Wisdom, who is Christ, V. 392

Wisdome of Doctor Dodypoll, The, VI. 459

Wise, Andrew, IV. 393

Wise, Thomas J., XI. 412, 414, 419; XII. 400, 401, 406, 407, 418, 423, 424, *also see* Add.; XIII. 474, 476, 478, 481 ff., 485, 486, 493, 495, 555, 569, 570, *also see* Add. 2; XIV. 528, *also see* Add. 3

Wiseman, Nicholas Patrick Stephen (1802
–1865), XII. 259, 260, 264, 274–5 (main
entry), 352, 461, 463; XIV. 54; *Fabiola,
or the Church of the Catacombs*, XII. 275,
277; 'High Church Claims,' XII. 275
Wiseman, Sir Robert, *The Law of Laws*
(1686), VIII. 470
Wiseman of West Chester, The, V. 316
Wishart, George (1513–1546), III. 147
Wishart, George (1599–1671), bishop of
Edinburgh, IX. 550
Wishfort, lady, in Congreve's *Way of the
World*, VIII. 153
Wissembourg, battle of, XIV. 328
Wit, in *Piers the Plowman*, II. 10, 19, 20
Wit, in Tudor moralities, V. 57
Wit and Drollery (1656), VII. 512
Wit Restor'd (1658), VII. 413, 512
*Witch being overtaken, A most certain true
and strange discovery of a*, VII. 375
Witch controversy, IV. 534; V. 377; VII.
366 ff.
Witch controversy, post-classical sources,
503 ff.
Witch of Edmonton, The, IV. 535
Witchcraft, V. 482
Witchcraft, illustrations of, III. 495
Witchcraft literature of Scotland, XII.
519
Witches, VI. 104
Withals, John (*fl.* 1556), III. 555
Witham, Essex, III. 183
Witham, Henry Thomas Moire, XIV. 290,
565
Wither or Withers, George (1588–1667),
IV. 121, 150, 154 ff. (main entry), 166,
333, 434, 479, 482 ff., 518, 520, 534;
V. 371; VII. 30, 72, 112, 180, 351, 406,
466, 502; VIII. 67, 227; XII. 434, 438
*Abuses Stript and Whipt, or Satiricall
Poems*, IV. 155; VI. 401, 499; VII. 433
Faire Virtue, the Mistress of Phil'Arete,
IV. 155
Fidelia, IV. 155
Great Assises holden in Parnassus, VII.
274
Haleluiah, IV. 156
Hymnes and Songs of the Church, IV.
155, 395
Motto, IV. 155
Nuptial Poems, IV. 154
Rocking Hymn, A, IV. 156
Scholars Purgatory, The, IV. 156, 396,
546
Shepherd's Hunting, The, IV. 155
Witherow, Thomas (1824–1890), XIV. 572
Withers, Hartley, XIV. 515
Witherspoon, John (1723–1794), IX. 549
Withies, The, II. 408
Wititterlys, the, in *Nicholas Nickleby*, XIII.
317
Witness, The, XIV. 160, 203
Wits, or Sport upon Sport, The (1672), VII.
512; VIII. 116
Wits Commonwealth, IV. 348, 526
Wits Theatre of the Little World, IV. 526

Wits Treasury (1655), VII. 512
Wittenberg, III. 418; VI. 374; VIII. 29
Wittenberg, in *The Unfortunate Traveller*,
III. 363
Wittie, Robert, VII. 511
Wittol, in Congreve's *Old Bachelor*, VIII.
147
Witts Recreations, VII. 7, 401, 402, 411,
413
Witwoud, in Congreve's *Way of the World*,
VIII. 153
Wode, Thomas, III. 131
Wodeford or Wadford, William of (*fl.*
1381–1390), II. 54, 443
Woden, I. 40, 218; V. 35
Wodrow, Robert (1679–1734), VII. 452;
IX. 369, 554; *History of the Sufferings
of the Church of Scotland*, XII. 359
Wodrow society, XII. 359
Woeful Treaty, The, IX. 502
Woerth, battle of, XIV. 328
Woffington, Margaret, X. 87
Wohunge of ure Louerde, The, I. 233, 459
Wokey, Somerset, III. 57
Wolcot, John, 'Peter Pindar' (1738–
1819), VI. 102; X. 479; XI. 391, 393, 439;
XII. 7, 120
Bozzy and Piozzi, XI. 38
Instructions to a celebrated Laureat, XI.
38
Ode upon Ode, XI. 37
The Lousiad, XI. 37
Wolf, Friedrich August, XII. 28, 300;
Prolegomena ad Homerum, XII. 301
Wolf, L., XIII. 545
Wolfe, Charles (1791–1823), XII. 424;
Remains, XII. 138; *The Burial of Sir
John Moore*, XII. 122, 138; *To Mary*,
XII. 138
Wolfe, Jer., IV. 437
Wolfe, John (d. 1601), IV. 386; IX. 362
Wolfe, lieut.-gen., in *The Virginians*, XIII.
297
Wolfe, Reyner or Reginald (d. 1573), III.
318, 319; IV. 400
Wolfenbüttel, IV. 429
Wolfram, Beddoes's *Dirge* for, XII. 116
Wolfram von Eschenbach, I. 268, 269,
271, 289, 294
Wollaston, Sir John (d. 1596), VII. 354
Wollaston, William (1660–1724), IX. 294,
505, 509; *Religion of Nature Delineated*,
IX. 299
Wollaston, William Hyde (1766–1828),
XIV. 557, 558
Wollstonecraft, Mary. *See* Godwin, Mrs
Mary Wollstonecraft
Wolseley, Sir Charles (1630?–1714), VIII.
210
Wolseley, Garnet Joseph Wolseley, vis-
count (1833–1913), XIV. 507; *Life of
Marlborough*, XIV. 89
Wolseley, Robert (1649–1697), VIII. 163
Wolsey, in *Henry VIII*, V. 195
Wolsey, in *When you see me, You know
me*, V. 333

Wolsey, Thomas (1475?-1530), cardinal, II. 358; III. 7, 26, 28, 37, 41, 52, 53, 57, 69, 75, 76 ff., 80, 197, 316, 317, 368, 429; IV. 227, 314, 428; V. 58, 102; VI. 256, 298; VII. 4; VIII. 65; X. 169; XIV. 100, 487

Wolston, near Coventry, III. 382

Wolter, Charlotte, V. 306

Wolverhampton, viscount. *See* Fowler, Sir H. H.

Wolzogen, E. L. von, XIII. 561

Woman, A Song on, I. 362

Woman Loved not Loving, the, in Heywood's *Love,* V. 93

Woman of Samaria, I. 225, 226, 458

Women, controversy on, VII. 513

Women, satires on, Medieval, English and French, III. 88 ff., 485 ff.

Wonderful News from the North, VII. 375

Wonders of Creation, The, I. 428

Wonders of the East, I. 135

Wood, Adam, VII. 513

Wood, Anthony à (1632-1695), I. 199; II. 224; III. 51, 176, 199, 318, 328, 330, 419; IV. 19, 51, 198, 244, 247, 251, 427; V. 256; VI. 29, 38, 50, 196, 197, 294; VII. 15, 16, 23, 24, 38, 42, 43, 84, 160, 317, 345, 359, 363 ff., *also see* Add.; VIII. 39, 292, 301, 360; IX. 267, 341, 342, 344 ff. (main entry), 381 ff., 391, 411, 413, 530, 535, 538, 541, 573
Antiquities of the City of Oxford, IX. 346, 354
Athenae Oxonienses, IX. 345, 347, 350, 351, 353, 356
Fasti, IX. 342, 344, 345
Historia...Universitatis Oxoniensis, IX. 346 ff.; XI. 341
Life and Times (Autobiography), IX. 341, 345, 348

Wood, Butler, XIII. 554, *also see* Add. 3

Wood, Charles W., XIII. 567

Wood, Mrs Henry (1814-1887), XIII. 430, 567

Wood, John Turtle (d. *c.* 1888), XII. 514

Wood, Lucky, IX. 366

Wood, Mary Anne Everett. *See* Green, Mary Anne Everett

Wood, Robert (1717?-1771), XIV. 554

Wood, Robin à, V. 35

Wood, T. M., XIII. 562

Wood, William (1671-1730), IX. 98, 115, 123, 457, 459, 463

Woo'd and Married and a', XI. 231

Woodberry, George Edward, XII. 399, 400, 405; XIII. 495

Woodbridge, Suffolk, XI. 140; XII. 198; XIII. 142, 143

Woodcock, captain, VII. 105

Woodcock, Catherine (d. 1658), VII. 105

Woodes, Nathaniel, V. 393

Woodfall, George (1767-1844), XIV. 535

Woodfall, Henry Sampson (1739-1805), X. 400, 401, 407, 408, 525, 526; XIV. 186, 535

Woodfall, William (1746-1803), XIV. 186, 535

Woodford, Samuel (1636-1700), VII. 109; VIII. 238, 447

Woodford Bridge, Essex, X. 386

Woodhouse, Emma, in Jane Austen's *Emma,* XII. 239, 243

Woodhouse, James (1735-1820), XII. 424

Woodhouse, John (*fl.* 1676), X. 386

Woodhouse, Mr, in Jane Austen's *Emma,* XII. 240

Woodhouse, Peter (*fl.* 1605), IV. 519

Woodhouse, Robert (1773-1827), XIV. 258

Woodhouselee, lord. *See* Tytler, A. F.

Woodlarke, Robert (d. 1479), II. 358

Woodroffe, Thomas (*fl.* 1678), VIII. 269

Woods, Benjamin (d. 1596), IV. 98

Woods, Julian Edmund Tenison (1832-1889), XIV. 588; *A History of the Discovery and Exploration of Australia,* XIV. 371

Woodside, David, XIV. 470

Woodstock, II. 159; VI. 299, 323

Woodville or Wodville or Wydville, Anthony, baron Scales and 2nd earl Rivers (1442?-1483), II. 303, 499
Books translated by: *Cordyale, or the Four last things,* II. 313; *Dictes and Sayings of the Philosophers,* II. 313, 427; III. 289, 290; *Moral Proverbs of Christine de Pisan, The,* II. 313

Woodville, Elizabeth (1437?-1492), II. 358

Woodward, Account of the sickness and death of Dr, IX. 132

Woodward, George Moutard (1760?-1809), XI. 453

Woodward, Henry (1714-1777), X. 212; XI. 257

Woodward, Joan (married Edward Alleyn), VI. 250

Woodward, John (1665-1728), VIII. 479; IX. 129, 132, 467, 470; XIV. 284, 291, 565

Woodward, Josiah, IX. 523

Woodward family, the, IV. 216

Wooing of Robin and Joan, IX. 364

Wooler, Miss, XIII. 405

Wooley, Francis, IV. 202

Wooll, John, *Memoirs of Warton,* X. 164, 493

Woolman, John (1720-1772), VIII. 14; X. 520

Woolner, Thomas (1825-1892), XIII. 38, 110, 511; *My Beautiful Lady,* XIII. 111, 189; *Of my Lady in Death,* XIII. 111

Woolnoth, *The Coffee Scuffle,* VII. 516

Woolsey, Mr, in Thackeray's *The Ravenswing,* XIII. 281

Woolston, Thomas (1670-1733), IX. 288, 509; X. 358; *Discourses,* IX. 294

Woolwich, II. 158; VII. 23; XIV. 415

Wootton, IX. 243

Wootton, John (1668?-1765), IX. 162

Worcester, II. 2, 49, 57; IV. 409, 418; V. 168; VI. 241; VII. 45, 254, 255; VIII. 60; IX. 194, 196, 329, 330, 530, 540; XI. 344; XIII. 430; XIV. 100

Worcester. *See* Florence of
Worcester, annals of, I. 178
Worcester, battle of, VII. 225, 250, 254;
  VIII. 206, 246
Worcester, earls of. *See* Somerset, Edward; Tiptoft, John
Worcester, marquises of. *See* Somerset, Edward; Somerset, Henry
Worcester, or Botoner, William (1415–1482?), II. 499
Worcester copy of *Pastoral Care*, I. 93
Worcester or Evesham Chronicle, I. 109 ff.
  See, also, under *Chronicle*
Worcester's company, earl of, VI. 97, 100, 250, 254
Worcestershire, IV. 547; VI. 316; X. 113, 149; XII. 350
Word to the Wise, play, X. 465
Worde, Wynkyn de (d. 1534?), II. 224, 300, 311, 312, 315, 319, 322 ff., 329, 393, 428; III. 56, 95, 98, 482, 483, 486, 489, 491; IV. 226, 227, 369, 400, 427
Wordsworth, Anne (born Cookson), XI. 95
Wordsworth, Charles, XIV. 598
Wordsworth, Christopher (1774–1846), XII. 329; XIV. 508, 593
Wordsworth, Christopher (1807–1885), bishop of Lincoln, XI. 95, 411; XII. 340, 495; *Scholae Academicae*, IX. 411, 573, 574
Wordsworth, Dorothy (1804–1847), XI. 95, 99, 102, 103, 409 ff., 416, 442; XII. 193, 194
Wordsworth, John, brother of the poet, XI. 95, 103, 105
Wordsworth, John (1843–1911), XII. 496
Wordsworth, Mary, XI. 103
Wordsworth, William (1770–1850), I. 170, 246, 358; II. 208; III. 221, 297; IV. 45, 49, 132, 136, 195; VII. 42, 115, 137, 181, 185, *also see* Add.; IX. 69, 168, 169, 277, 450; X. 125, 133, 145, 186, 217, 234; XI. 26 ff., 31, 77, 83, 86, 93 ff. (main entry), 117, 120 ff., 126, 129, 131, 135, 149, 150, 152, 162, 198, 201, 202, 248, 309, 341, 405, 413, 416, 417, 420, 432, 442, *also see* Add.; XII. 39, 44, 57 ff., 61, 63, 77, 81, 93, 94, 100, 101, 106, 107, 110, 112 ff., 118, 119, 126, 139, 147, 158, 162, 166, 170, 174, 176, 177, 179, 181, 188, 192, 200, 201, 205, 208, 213, 214, 218, 219, 255, 266, 392, 397, 402, 403, 407, 433, 524, 527; XIII. 7, 9, 23 ff., 29, 34, 38, 43, 44, 46, 49, 50, 52, 57, 63, 69, 71, 91, 93, 94, 97, 136, 158, 168, 169, 171, 173, 186, 188, 191 ff., 195, 196, 198, 200, 219, 228, 230, 232, 236, 250, 258, 429, 431, 442; XIV. 15, 184, 187, 255, 278, 327, 346, 350, 363, 373, 399, 404
  Affliction of Margaret, XI. 110
  Apology for the French Revolution, XI. 24
  Borderers, The, XI. 98, 100; XIII. 418
  Cintra, tract on, XI. Add.
  Composed after a journey across the Hambleton hills, X. 102
Wordsworth, William
  Composed upon an Evening, XI. 108
  Convention of Cintra, XI. 27, 103
  Descriptive Sketches, XI. 97
  Ecclesiastical Sonnets, XI. 108
  Essay, X. 97
  Evening Walk, An, XI. 97
  Excursion, The, III. 178; IV. 137, 191; XI. 85, 99, 100, 102, 103, 105, 106, 113, 116; XII. 59, 79, 146, 193; XIV. 382, 395, 403
  Extempore Effusion on the Death of James Hogg, XII. 95
  Fountain, The, XI. 110
  Goody Blake, XI. 101
  Green Linnet, The, XI. 110
  Guilt or Sorrow, XI. 98
  Incidents on Salisbury Plain, XI. 98, 100
  Laodamia, XI. 107, 116; XIII. 90
  Leech-Gatherer, XI. 104
  Lucy, XI. 110, 113
  Lyrical Ballads, XI. 86, 101, 123, 150, 151; XII. 40, 42
  Michael, XI. 105, 113, 116
  Nutting, XI. 112
  Ode on Intimations of Immortality, III. 221; VII. 41; XI. 102; XII. 84; XIII. 230
  Ode to Duty, XI. 104, 105
  Peter Bell, X. 129; XI. 132; XII. 70
  Prelude, The, XI. 85, 95 ff., 100, 102, 104, 113, 116, 123; XII. 83; XIV. 351, 394, 395, 403
  Recluse, The, XI. 100 ff.
  River Duddon, XI. 108
  Ruined Cottage, The, XI. 99, 105, 109, 116
  Simon Lee, XI. 101, 114
  Skating-scene, XI. 112
  Story of Margaret, XI. 99
  There was a Boy, XI. 111
  Thorn, The, XI. 132
  Tintern Abbey, X. 102; XI. 85, 101, 113; XII. 80; XIV. 351
  Two April Mornings, XI. 110
  Venetian Republic, On the extinction of the, XII. 46
  White Doe of Rylstone, XI. 106
  Yew-trees, XI. 110
Wordsworth, William, Jnr, XI. 405
Wordsworth society, XI. 406
Wordsworths, the, XII. 445
Work for Chimney-sweepers, IV. 530
Worke for Cutlers, VI. 487
Workers' Educational association, XIV. 409
Working Men's association, XIII. 357
Working Men's college, XIV. 408, 409
Working Parson, A (Charles Kingsley), XIII. 358
Works of the Learned, IX. 83, 136
Work-well, in *Piers the Plowman*, II. 19
World, The, X. 171, 173, 253; XI. 324; XIV. 200, 231
World, the, in *Mirour de l'Omme*, II. 140

World, the (Mydlerd, a mirror called), in *Piers the Plowman*, II. 25

World and the Child, The, II. 233; V. 54, 392

World Displayed, The, XIV. 554

World in Miniature, The, XIV. 221

'World is full of care...', The,' VII. 460

Worldly Shame, in *Nice Wanton*, V. 110

Worldly Wiseman, in Bunyan's *Pilgrim's Progress*, VII. 173

Wormius, Olaus, X. 223, 238; *Literatura Runica*, X. 224

Worms, I. 33; II. 330; III. 7, 42

Worrall, John, *Bibliotheca Legum* (1736), VIII. Add.

Worseley, Ralph (*fl.* 1553), VI. 481

Worsfold, William Basil, XIII. 488

Worsley, Philip Stanhope (1835–1866), XII. 334, 482; XIII. 175, 511

Worth, Richard Nicholls (1837–1896), XII. 514

Worthies, the Nine, in *The Parlement of the Thre Ages*, II. 37

Worthington, John (1618–1671), VII. 310, 477, 478, 490; VIII. 273, 281, 285, 286, 288, 455, 457, 458

Worthy, in Vanbrugh's *Relapse*, XI. 268

Wortley, Anne, IX. 248

Wortley, lady Emmeline Stuart (1806–1855), XIII. 511

Wortley, Sir Francis (1591–1652), VII. 495, 499; *A Loyall Song*, VII. 388

Wotton, Surrey, VIII. 242, 244, 245, 354

Wotton, Sir Henry (1568–1639), III. 425, 426, 428, 554; IV. 119, 124, 163, 198 ff., 215, 216, 218, 265, 297, 484; V. 482; VI. 219, 256, 269; VII. 99, 113, 188, 191, 205, 250, 252, 308, 343, 437, 442, 463; IX. 167, 170, 187; XIV. 178

    Characters of Essex and Buckingham, VII. 192

    Courtlie Controversie of Cupid's Cautels, V. 161

    History of Venice, VII. 192

    'How happy is he born and taught,' IV. 126

    Life and Death of Essex, VII. 192

    Panegyrick of King Charles (in Latin), VII. 192, 513

    Reliquiae Wottonianae, IV. 164; VII. 192

    Some Observations by Way of Parallel, VII. 192

    State of Christendom, The, VII. 192

    Tancredo, IV. 164

    'You meaner beauties,' IV. 163

Wotton, Henry, *Essay on the Education of Children* (1672), IX. 382, 569

Wotton, John, IV. 117; *Damaetas' Jig in praise of his love*, IV. 119; 'Jolly Shepherd,' IV. 119

Wotton, Thomas, IV. 406

Wotton, William (1666–1727), IX. 93, 103, 332, 382, 465, 524, 530, 572; *Reflections*, IX. 391

Wotton-under-edge, VIII. 83

Woty, William (1731?–1791), X. 183, 469; XI. 172, 426, 431

Would Be, lady, in *Volpone*, VI. 9; VII. 274

Wowing of Jok and Jynny, The, II. 273, 274

Wrage, E., XIII. 570

Wragge, captain, in Wilkie Collins's *No Name*, XIII. 437

Wrath, in *Piers the Plowman*, II. 12, 23

Wratislaw, Albert Henry, XIV. 598

Wratislaw, Theodore, XIII. 495

Wraxall, Sir Frederick Charles Lascelles, 3rd baronet (1828–1865), XIII. 567

Wraxall, Sir Nathaniel William, 1st baronet (1751–1831), XI. 396; XIV. 508

Wrayburne, Eugene, in *Our Mutual Friend*, XIII. 336

Wreittoun, John, IV. 413

Wrekin, the, IV. 190; VIII. 171

Wren, Sir Christopher (1632–1723), IV. 427; V. 481; VIII. 250, 364; IX. 331; XIV. 281

Wren, Matthew (1629–1672), VII. 476

Wrenn, Christopher, VI. 481

Wrest, Beds., VIII. 60

Wretchedness of this World, Of the, III. 181

Wright, Abraham (1611–1690), *Five Sermons*, VII. 160, 427

Wright, Edward (1558?–1615), IV. 462

Wright, James (1643–1713), *Historia Histrionica*, VI. 408, 499; VIII. 115, 424; *History of Rutland*, IX. 353, 533, 541

Wright, John (*fl.* 1609), IV. 394

Wright, John (1805–1843?), XII. 424

Wright, John Martin Frederick, XIV. 595

Wright, Joseph, *Country Conversations* (1694), VIII. 163, 434

Wright, Leonard (*fl.* 1591), *Friendly Admonition to Martin Marprelate*, III. 397, 539

Wright, Thomas (1810–1877), I. viii, 351, 361; II. 35 ff., 39, 40, 47, 166, 420 ff., 424, 426; III. 91; XII. 347, 353, 365, 514; XIII. 366; XIV. 523, 541

    Anecdota Literaria, XII. 354

    Biographia Literaria of the Anglo-Saxon period, XII. 354

    Early English Poetry, XII. 354

    Original Letters, XII. 354

    The Glory of God's Revenge against Murther and Adultery, VIII. 194

Wright, William (1830–1889), XII. 342, 499

Wright, William, D.D., XIII. 559

Wright, William Aldis (1831–1914), I. 337; V. 280; XII. 331, 341, 493, 502; XIII. 497

Wright's Chaste Wife, The, II. 504

Wrington, Somerset, VIII. 328

Wriothesley, Charles (1508?–1562), III. 478, 532

Wriothesley, Henry, 3rd earl of Southampton (1573–1624), IV. 390; V. 169, 171, 174, 223, 225, 229, 346, 347, 370; VI. 272; VII. 447

Wrong, in *Piers the Plowman*, II. 4, 32

Wroth, lady Mary (*fl.* 1621), *Urania*, III. 355

Wroth, Sir Thomas (1584–1672), IV. 520

Wroxeter, XII. 347
Wudga, in *Widsith*, I. 35
Wulff, Peter, V. 307
Wulfgeat, Aelfric's English letter to, I. 126
Wulfmaer, I. 144
Wulfsige, I. 124, 127
Wulfstan, archbishop of York (d. 1023),
I. 5, 124, 125, 127, 128 ff., 134, 145
Wulfstan, St (1012?-1095), bishop of
Worcester, I. 164
Wulfstan, voyage of, I. 94
Wulfstan of Winchester (*fl.* 1000), I. 125,
441, 442
Wülker, R., I. ix, 50, 102, 106
Wünn, A., XIII. 546
Würzburg, VII. 20
Wyatt, Alfred John, I. Add.; XIII. 127, 492
Wyatt, Sir Francis (1575?-1644), VII. 50
Wyatt, Sir Thomas (1503?-1542), II. 213,
218, 389; III. 23, 24, 166 ff., 201, 210,
212, 227, 247 ff., 281 ff., 285, 287, 297,
298, 302, 303, 447, 511, *also see* Add.;
IV. 24, 25, 108, 110, 116, 118, 196, 197,
329; VII. 1; VIII. 222; X. 131; XIII. 253
Comparison of love to a streame, III. 172
Complaint upon Love to Reason, III. 187
Courtiers life, Of the, III. 173
Forget not yet the tried intent, III. 172
Furious goone, The, III. 187
Galley charged with forgetfulnesse, My,
III. 171
*How by a kisse he found both his life and
death*, III. 172
How oft have I, III. 169
How to use the court and him selfe therin,
III. 173
Love called Anna, Of his, III. 168
Love, Fortune, and my minde, III. 170
Love to Skorn, My, III. 171
*Lover compareth his hart to the over-
charged gonne, The*, III. 172
Lover professeth himself constant, The,
III. 173
Madame, withouten many wordes, III. 172
Meane and sure estate, Of the, III. 173
Psalm 37, III. 174
Some Fowles there be, III. 169
Though I myself be bridled of my mind,
III. 168
Unstable dream, III. 170
Was never file, III. 169
What should I say! III. 172
Whoso list to hunt, III. 167
Wiat, being in prison, to Brian, III. 173
Yet was I never of your love agreved,
III. 171
Wyche, Sir Peter (d. 1643), VIII. 369
Wycherley, William (1640?-1716), VIII.
133, 142 ff. (main entry), 165, 214, 215,
386, 421, 423, 427; IX. 68, 84, 443, 473;
X. 67, 89, 425, 433; XI. 319; XII. 443
Country Wife, The, VIII. 134, 144, 145,
168; XI. 268
Gentleman Dancing-master, The, VIII.
131, 144
Love in a Wood, VIII. 143, 144

Wycherley, William
Plain Dealer, The, VIII. 134, 143, 145,
422; XI. 269
Wychwood, XIII. 93
Wyclif, John (1320?-1384), I. 204, 211,
213, 332, 367, 371, 400; II. 41, 43 ff.,
73, 74, 77, 85, 285, 287, 299, 351, 355,
358, 439 ff.; III. 25, 39, 69, 105, 441,
442; IV. 38, 39, 46, 273, 428; V. 51; VI.
374; XII. 517
Cruciata, II. 56
De Benedicat Incarnacione, II. 53, 64, 66
De Civili Dominio, II. 49, 54
De Composicione Hominis, II. 53
De Ecclesia, II. 54
De Ente Predicamentali, II. 53
De Logica, II. 53
De Materia et Forma, II. 53
De Veritate Sacrae Scripturae, II. 56, 58,
59
Determinatio, II. 54
Dialogus, II. 65
Opus Evangelicum, II. 61, 65
Trialogus, II. 65, 66
Wyclif society, II. 49; XII. 355, 504
Wycliffe-on-Tees, II. 49
Wycliffite versions, *Old Testament*, II. 300,
335, 430, 431, 440
Wye, river, VIII. 140; IX. 258; X. 134, 277;
XII. 414
Wyer, Robert (*fl.* 1529-1556), IV. 546
Wyeth, Joseph (1663-1731), VIII. 415
Wyf of Auchtirmuchty, The, II. 273; XI. 243
Wygar, the smith, maker of Arthur's
corslet, in Layamon, I. 236, 265
Wykeham, William of (1324-1404), bishop
of Winchester, II. 355 ff., 506; VII.
326
Wykehamist, The, XIV. 539
Wykes, Thomas, of Osney (*fl.* 1258-1293),
I. 182, 451
Wyl Bucke his testament, III. 482, 483
Wyld, Henry Cecil, XIV. 611
Wylie, James Hamilton (1844-1914), XIV.
500; *History of the Reign of Henry V*,
XIV. 83
Wylie, William Howie, XIII. 473
Wylie Beguylie, VI. 300
Wylie Wife of the Hie Toun Hie, The, II.
413
Wylkin, John, IV. 435
Wylkinson, John, IV. 5
Wyll of the Devyll, The, III. 86, 484; VII.
382
Wyman, Charles William Henry, XIV. 535
Wymond, in *Rauf Coilȝear*, II. 125, 126
Wyndham, George, XIII. Add. 2
Wyndham, Henry Penruddocke (1736-
1819), IX. 254, 497
Wyndham, Henry Saxe, VIII. 515
Wyndham, Sir William, 3rd baronet (1687
-1740), IX. 252
Wynken, in Drayton's *Idea*, IV. 172
Wynn, Charles Watkin Williams (1775-
1850), XI. 154, 170; XIII. 226, 227, 232
Wynne, Arnold, XIII. 515

Wynne, John (1667–1743), VIII. 331, 476
Wynne, Luttrell, VIII. 241
Wynne, Sir Richard (d. 1649), VII. 455
Wynnere and Wastoure, I. 333, 334; II.
   35 ff., 432, 434
Wynnstay, X. 115
Wyntoun, Andrew of (1350?–1420?), II.
   103, 104, 117, 121, 122, 129–132 (main
   entry), 452; *Orygynale Cronykil*, I. 333;
   II. 91, 115, 239, 280, 452; XII. 517
Wyrd, I. 41
Wyrley, William (1565–1618), IV. 376,
   543
Wyse, Henry T., XIV. 536
Wyse, Sir Thomas (1791–1862), XIV.
   610
Wyss, J D., *The Swiss Family Robinson*,
   XI. 492
Wytfliet, IV. 101

Xanthian marbles, XII. 339
Xenophon, III. 426, 429; IV. 5, 259, 440,
   441, 543; IX. 204, 529; XI. 358; XII. 313,
   332, 339, 484, 485; *Cyropaedia*, III. 426;
   IV. 4; VII. 316
Xylander Gulielmus, IV. 249
Xystus, Betuleius, VI. 486

Yagoube, XIV. 248
Yahoos, in *Gulliver's Travels*, IX. 105
Yalden, Thomas (1670–1737), IX. 174,
   176, 188, 487; X. 183; *Hymn to Dark-
   ness*, IX. 176
Yarico, in Colman's *Inkle and Yarico*, XI.
   280
Yarington, Robert (*fl.* 1601), V. 325, 476;
   VI. 96; *Two Lamentable Tragedies*, V.
   324 ff., 332; VI. 96
Yarmouth, III. 363; IV. 327; VI. 241; VII.
   91; XII. 362
Yarranton, Andrew (1616–1684?), IV.
   462
Yarrow, II. 284; IX. 371; XI. 239, 445
Yarrow ballads, IX. 364
Yates, Edmund Hodgson (1831–1894),
   XIII. 301, 567; XIV. 200, 535
Yates, James (*fl.* 1582), IV. 472
Yates, James (1789–1871), XII. 515; XIV.
   610; *Textrinum Antiquum*, XII. 348
Yates, Mary Ann (1728–1787), X. 264
Yates, Mr, in Jane Austen's *Mansfield
   Park*, XII. 239
Yates, Richard (1706?–1796), XI. 257
Yates, William Walsh, XIII. 557, 559
Yaxley, John, VI. 307
Ydgrunites, in Butler's *Erewhon*, XIII. 452
Ye Jacobites by Name, IX. 376
Ye Mariners of England, II. 226
Year Books, VIII. 313, 314, 316, 317, 320,
   466
Year Books of Edward II, XIV. 81
Yeats, Jack Butler, XIII. 573, *and see*
   Add. 1
Yeats, William Butler, XI. 433, 434; XII.
   405; XIV. 329, 573
Yeddo, IV. 100

Yedingham, II. 45, 48
Yeldham, Walter (*pseud*. Aliph Cheem),
   XIV. 580; *Lays of Ind*, XIV. 340
Yellowplush, Charles James, *pseud*. of
   W. M. Thackeray, XIII. 278 ff., 284
Yelverton, Sir Christopher (1535?–1612),
   V. 70, 77
Yeo, H., XIV. 532
Ylmandun (Ilmington), I. 126
Yloop, M. (? Pooly), III. 189
Ynglinga Saga, I. 3, 25, 94
Ynglingatal, I. 25, 26
Yong or Young, Bartholomew (*fl.* 1577–
   1598), IV. 7, 9, 117, 121, 122, 441, 445,
   447, 472
Yonge, Charlotte Mary (1823–1901), XI.
   387, 475, 476, 484, 491; XII. 451; XIII.
   567; *Heir of Redclyffe, The*, XII. 277;
   XIII. 120, 435; *Lances of Lynwood*, XIII.
   434; *Little Duke, The*, XII. 277
Yonge, James (*fl.* 1423), II. 301
Yonge, Nicholas (d. 1619), *Musica Trans-
   alpina*, IV. 113, 114
Yonge, Philip, bishop of Norwich, XI. 143
Yonge, Walter (1581?–1649), VII. 455
'Yonge Harton' = Haughton, V. 328
Yorick, XIV. 327
Yorick, in *Hamlet*, III. 456
Yorick, in Sterne's *Tristram Shandy*, X.
   50
York, I. 59, 79, 84, 86, 111, 127, 129;
   II. 49, 72, 325, 399, 422, 423; III. 28;
   IV. 310, 408, 409; VII. 49, 197, 453;
   IX. 386, 532, 565; X. 47, 360, 362, 421,
   425, 450; XI. 312, 341, 347, 351, 366,
   373, 469; XII. 510; XIV. 9, 288
York, the Ainsty of, VII. 180
York, Anne Hyde, duchess of (1637–1671),
   VIII. 46, 402
York, cardinal of. *See* Stewart, H. B.
   M. C.
York, duke of, company of players of,
   VIII. 119, 182
York, duke of, in *Henry VI*, V. 186
York, Edward, 2nd duke of (1373?–1415),
   The Master of Game, II. 286, 479; IV.
   541
York, house of, II. 297, 298
York, James, duke of. *See* James II
York, school of, I. 5, 84, 87
York Herald, The, XIV. 203
York Manuale (1390), II. 325; (1509),
   III. 442
York Mercury, The, XIV. 169
York minster library, IV. 421
York Plays, V. 13, 15, 18, 20, 42, 45 ff., 51,
   52, 56, 389, 390, 391
York press, II. 468
York printers, IV. 547
Yorke, Philip, 1st earl of Hardwicke
   (1690–1764), IX. 209; X. 295
Yorke, Philip, 2nd earl of Hardwicke
   (1720–1790), X. 295, 502; *Miscellaneous
   State Papers*, X. 295
Yorkshire, I. 344, 357; II. 88, 396, 420;
   IV. 190; V. 242, 243; VII. 178, 180, 224,

Yorkshire
227, 233, 246, 373; VIII. 220, 271; IX.
91, 140, 330, 393; X. 47, 101, 131, 262,
385, 386; XII. 12, 246, 281, 507, 516;
XIII. 275; XIV. 185, 233, 249
Yorkshire dales, XI. 168
Yorkshire dialect, XII. 415
Yorkshire Library, the, XII. 519
Yorkshire Tragedy, A, IV. 394; V. 236, 238,
242, 243, 332, 442, 444; VI. 95; X. 73
Yorkshire United college, X. 385
Youghal, II. 303; IV. 60; VIII. 146
Youll, Henry (*fl.* 1608), IV. 465
Young, Arthur (1741–1820), XI. 400; XIV.
554, 565
    Annals of Agriculture, XI. 72, 397
    Political Arithmetic, XI. 73
    Tour in Ireland, XI. 73
    Travels in France, XI. 73
    War in North America, The, XI. 72
Young, A. B., XI. 462
Young, Bartholomew (*fl.* 1577–1598), VI.
365; *Amorous Fiammetta* (trans. from
Boccaccio), IV. 7
Young, Edward (1683–1765), V. 297;
IX. 82, 188, 190, 250, 254, 439, 449, 460,
481; X. 1, 138 ff. (main entry), 156, 183,
458, *also see* Add.; XI. 140, 250, 251;
XIII. 552
    Brothers, The, X. 140
    Busiris, X. 73, 83, 139
    Complaint (The), or *Night Thoughts.*
    See *Night Thoughts*
    Imperium Pelagi, X. 140, 141
    Job, X. 139, 142
    Last Day, The, X. 142
    Letters to Tickell, X. 139
    Night Thoughts, VIII. 380; X. 124,
    141 ff., 147; XI. 323
    Ocean, X. 140, 141
    Resignation, X. 140, 142
    Revenge, The, X. 73, 139
    Universal Passion, The, X. 139, 140, 142
Young, Elizabeth, X. 95
Young, George (1777–1848), XI. 429
Young, James (1811–1883), XII. 519
Young, John (1534?–1605), bishop of
Rochester, III. 214
Young, John (1750?–1820), X. 475; *A
Criticism on the Elegy written in a
Country Churchyard,* X. 188
Young, Patrick (1584–1652), VII. 316,
482, 483, 485, 489; IX. 530
Young, Sir Peter (1544–1628), IX. 530
Young, Richard, *A short and sure way to
Grace,* XI. 334; *The Seduced Soul re-
duced,* XI. 334
Young, Robert (*fl.* 1663), IX. 547
Young, Thomas (1587–1655), VII. 96, 98,
416
Young, Thomas (1773–1829), XIV. 259, 557
Young, William, X. 25
Young, William Thomas, XII. Add. 2
Young Beichan, II. 411
Young England' movement, IX. 231
Young Hunting, II. 412

Young Ireland party, XIV. 311, 317, 320,
321, 324, 357
Young Lochinvar, II. 411
Young Man's Calling, XI. 369
Younge, Richard (*fl.* 1637–1671), VII. 514
Younger, John (1785–1860), XII. 424
Younger, W., *A brief View, etc.,* VII. 355
Youth, in *Confessio Amantis,* II. 148
Youth, in Henryson, II. 249
Youth, in Lydgate's *Pilgrimage,* II. 201
Youth, in *Piers the Plowman,* II. 22
Youth (renamed Virtue), in *The Example
of Virtue,* II. 227, 234
Youth, in *The Parlement of the Thre Ages,*
II. 37
Youth (interlude), V. 54, 393
Ypocras, daughter of, II. 79
Ypotis, Meditations of Chylde, I. 286, 472;
II. 308
Ysopet, VIII. 59
Yspađaden Pen Kawr, I. 254
Ystorya Brenhined y Brytanyeit, I. 263
Yucatan, XIV. 241
Yule, XIV. 574
Yule, Alfred, in Gissing's *New Grub Street,*
XIII. 460
Yuletide carols, II. 379
Yuste, X. 289
Yver, Jacques, *Le Printemps d'Iver,* V.
161, 252
Ywain and Gawain, and *Sir Ywain,* I. 279,
280, 282, 284, 288, 312, 468

Zabeta, III. 207
Zacher, J., 425
Zadkiel, VII. 511
Zama, XII. 303
Zampini-Salazar, F., XIII. 485
Zanga, in Young's *The Revenge,* X. 73
Zanoni (lord Lytton's), XIII. 419
Zanzibar, IV. 85
Zara, in Congreve's *Mourning Bride,* VIII.
152
Zárate, Augustin de, IV. 448
Zarina, in Byron's *Sardanapalus,* XII. 49
Zaripha, in *The Travailes of The three
English Brothers,* VI. 69
Zeal, in *The Playe of Playes and Pastimes,*
VI. 391
Zeal-of-the-land Busy, in *Bartholomew
Fayre,* VI. 23, 28; VIII. 147
Zechariah, V. 48
Zedlitz, K. A. von, XIV. 382
Zelauto (Munday's), III. 349
Zelmane, in Sidney's *Arcadia,* III. 352
Zelotypus, VI. 487
Zend language, XII. 343
Zenocia, in *The Custome of the Countrey,*
VI. 131
Zenocrate, in *Tamburlaine,* V. 150
Zepheria, III. 256, 266, 524
Zerbst, V. 48
Zermat, U., I. 443
Zetha, in *Jacob and Esau,* V. 111
Zeuner, R., I. 444
Zeuss, J. C., I. 34, 421

Ziegler, H., I. 429

Zimmer, Heinrich, I. 65, 68, 70, 269, 464; xIV. 302; *Nennius Vindicatus*, I. 246, 464

Zimmermann, O., I. 439

Zimri (Buckingham), in Dryden's *Absalom*, vIII. 39, 41

Zinzendorf, Nicolaus Ludwig, count von, x. 350, 364

Zipangu, Iv. 86

Zittau, v. 285

Zoas, the, in Blake's *Vala*, xI. 195

Zoilus, Ix. 481

Zoilus, in *Wisdom of Solomon Paraphrased*, vI. 59

Zola, Émile, xI. 152; xII. 55; xIII. 427; *L'Assommoir*, xIII. 425, 522; *Thérèse Raquin*, xIII. 456

Zoological Journal, The, xIV. 565

Zoological Miscellany, The, xIV. 565

Zoological society of London, xIV. 287

Zoologist, The, xIV. 289, 566

Zosimus, Ix. 337

Zouch, Henry (1725?–1795), x. 252, 495

Zouche, lord. *See* Curzon, Robert

Zouche, Richard (1590–1661), vI. 481; vIII. 317, 470

Zozimus, xIV. 327

Zulkais, in Beckford's *Episodes*, xI. 292

Zupitza, J., I. ix, I. 426, 429, 432, 442, 445

Zurich, III. 44, 53; Iv. 402

Zurich letters, the, III. 415

Zutphen, battle of, III. 351

Zwingli, Huldreich (1484–1531), II. 69; III. 37, 39, 413; Iv. 448; vII. 306